Handbook of Research on Human Factors in Contemporary Workforce Development

Bryan Christiansen
PryMarke LLC, USA

Harish C. Chandan
Argosy University, USA

A volume in the Advances in Human Resources Management and Organizational Development (AHRMOD) Book Series

www.igi-global.com

Published in the United States of America by
IGI Global
Business Science Reference (an imprint of IGI Global)
701 E. Chocolate Avenue
Hershey PA, USA 17033
Tel: 717-533-8845
Fax: 717-533-8661
E-mail: cust@igi-global.com
Web site: http://www.igi-global.com

Copyright © 2017 by IGI Global. All rights reserved. No part of this publication may be reproduced, stored or distributed in any form or by any means, electronic or mechanical, including photocopying, without written permission from the publisher. Product or company names used in this set are for identification purposes only. Inclusion of the names of the products or companies does not indicate a claim of ownership by IGI Global of the trademark or registered trademark.

Library of Congress Cataloging-in-Publication Data

Names: Christiansen, Bryan, 1960- editor. | Chandan, Harish C., 1947- editor.
Title: Handbook of research on human factors in contemporary workforce
  development / Bryan Christiansen and Harish C. Chandan, editors.
Description: Hershey : Business Science Reference, [2017]
Identifiers: LCCN 2017005165| ISBN 9781522525684 (hardcover) | ISBN
  9781522525691 (ebook)
Subjects: LCSH: Personnel management. | Leadership. | Job satisfaction. | Job
  stress. | Diversity in the workplace. | International business
  enterprises--Management.
Classification: LCC HF5549 .H29766 2017 | DDC 658.3/01--dc23 LC record available at https://lccn.loc.gov/2017005165

This book is published in the IGI Global book series Advances in Human Resources Management and Organizational Development (AHRMOD) (ISSN: 2327-3372; eISSN: 2327-3380)

British Cataloguing in Publication Data
A Cataloguing in Publication record for this book is available from the British Library.

All work contributed to this book is new, previously-unpublished material. The views expressed in this book are those of the authors, but not necessarily of the publisher.

For electronic access to this publication, please contact: eresources@igi-global.com.

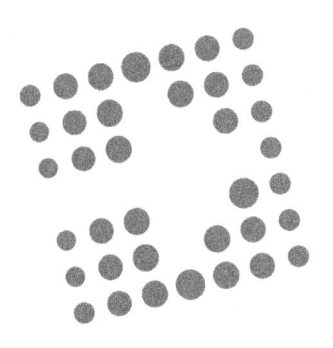

Advances in Human Resources Management and Organizational Development (AHRMOD) Book Series

Patricia Ordóñez de Pablos
Universidad de Oviedo, Spain

ISSN:2327-3372
EISSN:2327-3380

Mission

A solid foundation is essential to the development and success of any organization and can be accomplished through the effective and careful management of an organization's human capital. Research in human resources management and organizational development is necessary in providing business leaders with the tools and methodologies which will assist in the development and maintenance of their organizational structure.

The **Advances in Human Resources Management and Organizational Development (AHRMOD) Book Series** aims to publish the latest research on all aspects of human resources as well as the latest methodologies, tools, and theories regarding organizational development and sustainability. The **AHRMOD Book Series** intends to provide business professionals, managers, researchers, and students with the necessary resources to effectively develop and implement organizational strategies.

Coverage

- Personnel Retention
- Employee Relations
- Disputes Resolution
- Change Management
- Recruitment Process
- Employee Communications
- Entrepreneurialism
- Workplace Culture
- Process Improvement
- Succession Planning

IGI Global is currently accepting manuscripts for publication within this series. To submit a proposal for a volume in this series, please contact our Acquisition Editors at Acquisitions@igi-global.com or visit: http://www.igi-global.com/publish/.

The Advances in Human Resources Management and Organizational Development (AHRMOD) Book Series (ISSN 2327-3372) is published by IGI Global, 701 E. Chocolate Avenue, Hershey, PA 17033-1240, USA, www.igi-global.com. This series is composed of titles available for purchase individually; each title is edited to be contextually exclusive from any other title within the series. For pricing and ordering information please visit http://www.igi-global.com/book-series/advances-human-resources-management-organizational/73670. Postmaster: Send all address changes to above address. Copyright © 2017 IGI Global. All rights, including translation in other languages reserved by the publisher. No part of this series may be reproduced or used in any form or by any means – graphics, electronic, or mechanical, including photocopying, recording, taping, or information and retrieval systems – without written permission from the publisher, except for non commercial, educational use, including classroom teaching purposes. The views expressed in this series are those of the authors, but not necessarily of IGI Global.

Titles in this Series

For a list of additional titles in this series, please visit: www.igi-global.com/book-series

Driving Multinational Enterprises Through Effective Global Talent Management
Khaled Tamzini (University of Sousse, Tunisia) Tahar Lazhar Ayed (Umm Al-Qura University, Saudi Arabia) Aisha Wood Boulanouar (Sultan Qaboos University, Muscat, Oman) and Zakaria Boulanouar (Umm Al-Qura University, Saudi Arabia)
Business Science Reference • copyright 2017 • 272pp • H/C (ISBN: 9781522525578) • US $170.00 (our price)

Exploring the Influence of Personal Values and Cultures in the Workplace
Zlatko Nedelko (University of Maribor, Slovenia) and Maciej Brzozowski (Poznan University of Economics and Business, Poland)
Business Science Reference • copyright 2017 • 458pp • H/C (ISBN: 9781522524809) • US $205.00 (our price)

Effective Talent Management Strategies for Organizational Success
Mambo Mupepi (Grand Valley State University, USA)
Business Science Reference • copyright 2017 • 365pp • H/C (ISBN: 9781522519614) • US $210.00 (our price)

Anywhere Working and the New Era of Telecommuting
Yvette Blount (Macquarie University, Australia) and Marianne Gloet (University of Melbourne, Australia)
Business Science Reference • copyright 2017 • 295pp • H/C (ISBN: 9781522523284) • US $195.00 (our price)

Human Resources Management Solutions for Attracting and Retaining Millennial Workers
Meng-Shan Tsai (Clouder Technology Inc., Taiwan)
Business Science Reference • copyright 2017 • 269pp • H/C (ISBN: 9781522520443) • US $185.00 (our price)

Impact of Organizational Trauma on Workplace Behavior and Performance
Stanislav Háša (University of Economics, Czech Republic) and Richard Brunet-Thornton (University of Economics, Czech Republic)
Business Science Reference • copyright 2017 • 413pp • H/C (ISBN: 9781522520214) • US $190.00 (our price)

Strategic Human Capital Development and Management in Emerging Economies
Anshuman Bhattacharya (Sunbeam College for Women, India)
Business Science Reference • copyright 2017 • 321pp • H/C (ISBN: 9781522519744) • US $175.00 (our price)

IGI GLOBAL
DISSEMINATOR OF KNOWLEDGE

www.igi-global.com

701 East Chocolate Avenue, Hershey, PA 17033, USA
Tel: 717-533-8845 x100 • Fax: 717-533-8661
E-Mail: cust@igi-global.com • www.igi-global.com

Editorial Advisory Board

Mohammad Abdolshah, *Azad University, Iran*
Archie Addo, *Argosy University, USA*
Ye-Sho Chen, *Louisiana State University, USA*
Rituparna Das, *National Law University, India*
Reza Hosseini, *Deakin University, Australia*
Kijpokin Kasemsap, *Suan Sunandha Rajabhat University, Thailand*
Wiboon Kittilaksanawong, *Saitama University, Japan*
Ewa Lechman, *University of Gdansk, Poland*
Seppo Leminen, *Laurea University, Finland*
Allen McKenna, *STM Group, UK*
Jimmyn Parc, *Seoul National University, South Korea*
Agnieszka Piekarz, *Independent Researcher, Poland*
Eren Sekmez, *IBM Corporation, Czech Republic*
David Starr-Glass, *SUNY Empire State College, USA*
Gowri Vijayan, *Universiti Putra Malaysia, Malaysia*
Shefali Virkar, *University of Oxford, UK*
Sally Wallace, *Georgia State University, USA*
Norhayati Zakaria, *Universiti Utara Malaysia, Malaysia*

List of Contributors

Austin, Larry / *University of Phoenix, USA* 201
Boeltzig-Brown, Heike / *University of Massachusetts-Boston, USA* 333
Chamakiotis, Petros / *University of Sussex, UK* 283
Efeoğlu, Efe Ibrahim / *Adana Science and Technology University, Turkey* 268
Giannouli, Vaitsa / *Aristotle University of Thessaloniki, Greece* 24
Grubicka, Joanna / *Pomeranian Academy, Poland* 357
Hieker, Carola / *Richmond, The American University in London, UK* 308
Jänkälä, Raimo / *University of Lapland, Finland* 249
Kasemsap, Kijpokin / *Suan Sunandha Rajabhat University, Thailand* 1,181
Kim, Junghwan / *University of Oklahoma, USA* 132
Matuska, Ewa Maria / *Pomeranian Academy, Poland* 357
Miller, Sarah M / *University of Oklahoma, USA* 132
Mukhopadhyay, Prabir / *Indian Institute of Information Technology Design and
    Manufacturing, Jabalpur, India* 425
Muralidharan, Etayankara / *MacEwan University, Canada* 379
Naito, Yoko / *Tokai University, Japan* 403
Nomoto, Aoi / *Chiba University, Japan* 333
Ozcan, Sevgi / *Cukurova University, Turkey* 268
Pathak, Saurav / *Kansas State University, USA* 379
Patro, Chandra Sekhar / *GVP College of Engineering (Autonomous), Visakhapatnam,
    India* 110,156
Pietiläinen, Ville / *University of Lapland, Finland* 249
Rushby, Maia / *Diversity-in-Leadership, UK* 308
Rusko, Rauno / *University of Lapland, Finland* 249
Salmi, Ilkka / *University of Lapland, Finland* 249
Seino, Kai / *Toyo University, National Institute of Vocational Rehabilitation, Japan* 333
Shen, Libi / *University of Phoenix, USA* 201,226
Starr-Glass, David / *SUNY Empire State College, USA* 87
Takezawa, Tomohiro / *National Institute of Vocational Rehabilitation, Japan* 333
Tomasiak, Marta Alicja / *Thompson Reuters, UK* 283
Tran, Ben / *Alliant International University, USA* 60
Washington, Germaine D. / *Calvary University, USA* 226
You, Jieun / *Yonsei University, South Korea* 132

Table of Contents

Preface xvii

Chapter 1
The Fundamentals of Organizational Citizenship Behavior 1
    Kijpokin Kasemsap, Suan Sunandha Rajabhat University, Thailand

Chapter 2
Emotional Aspects of Leadership in the Modern Workplace 24
    Vaitsa Giannouli, Aristotle University of Thessaloniki, Greece

Chapter 3
The Art and Science in Communication: Workplace (Cross-Cultural) Communication Skills and Competencies in the Modern Workforce 60
    Ben Tran, Alliant International University, USA

Chapter 4
The Misappropriation of Organizational Power and Control: Managerial Bullying in the Workplace 87
    David Starr-Glass, SUNY Empire State College, USA

Chapter 5
Welfare Regime: A Critical Discourse 110
    Chandra Sekhar Patro, GVP College of Engineering (Autonomous), Visakhapatnam, India

Chapter 6
Organizational Learning as a Social Process: A Social Capital and Network Approach 132
    Jieun You, Yonsei University, South Korea
    Junghwan Kim, University of Oklahoma, USA
    Sarah M Miller, University of Oklahoma, USA

Chapter 7
Performance Appraisal System Effectiveness: A Conceptual Review 156
    Chandra Sekhar Patro, GVP College of Engineering (Autonomous), Visakhapatnam, India

Chapter 8
The Significance of Job Satisfaction in Modern Organizations 181
    Kijpokin Kasemsap, Suan Sunandha Rajabhat University, Thailand

Chapter 9
Communication and Job Satisfaction 201
    Libi Shen, University of Phoenix, USA
    Larry Austin, University of Phoenix, USA

Chapter 10
Emotional Intelligence and Job Stress 226
    Germaine D. Washington, Calvary University, USA
    Libi Shen, University of Phoenix, USA

Chapter 11
Experienced Stress and the Value of Rest Stops in the Transportation Field: Stress and
Transportation 249
    Ville Pietiläinen, University of Lapland, Finland
    Ilkka Salmi, University of Lapland, Finland
    Rauno Rusko, University of Lapland, Finland
    Raimo Jänkälä, University of Lapland, Finland

Chapter 12
The Relationship Between Social Problem Solving Ability and Burnout Level: A Field Study
Among Health Professionals 268
    Efe Ibrahim Efeoğlu, Adana Science and Technology University, Turkey
    Sevgi Ozcan, Cukurova University, Turkey

Chapter 13
Understanding Diversity in Virtual Work Environments: A Comparative Case Study 283
    Marta Alicja Tomasiak, Thompson Reuters, UK
    Petros Chamakiotis, University of Sussex, UK

Chapter 14
Diversity in the Workplace: How to Achieve Gender Diversity in the Workplace 308
    Carola Hieker, Richmond, The American University in London, UK
    Maia Rushby, Diversity-in-Leadership, UK

Chapter 15
The Diversity Management for Employment of the Persons With Disabilities: Evidence of
Vocational Rehabilitation in the United States and Japan 333
    Kai Seino, Toyo University, National Institute of Vocational Rehabilitation, Japan
    Aoi Nomoto, Chiba University, Japan
    Tomohiro Takezawa, National Institute of Vocational Rehabilitation, Japan
    Heike Boeltzig-Brown, University of Massachusetts-Boston, USA

Chapter 16
Employer Branding and Internet Security 357
  Ewa Maria Matuska, Pomeranian Academy, Poland
  Joanna Grubicka, Pomeranian Academy, Poland

Chapter 17
National Ethical Institutions and Social Entrepreneurship 379
  Etayankara Muralidharan, MacEwan University, Canada
  Saurav Pathak, Kansas State University, USA

Chapter 18
Factors Related to Readjustment to Daily Life: A Study of Repatriates in Japanese Multinational
Enterprises 403
  Yoko Naito, Tokai University, Japan

Chapter 19
Investigation of Ergonomic Risk Factors in Snacks Manufacturing in Central India: Ergonomics
in Unorganized Sector 425
  Prabir Mukhopadhyay, Indian Institute of Information Technology Design and
     Manufacturing, Jabalpur, India

Compilation of References 450

About the Contributors 553

Index 560

Detailed Table of Contents

Preface xvii

Chapter 1
The Fundamentals of Organizational Citizenship Behavior 1
    Kijpokin Kasemsap, Suan Sunandha Rajabhat University, Thailand

This chapter reveals the overview of Organizational Citizenship Behavior (OCB); OCB and organizational factors; OCB and Counterproductive Work Behavior (CWB); OCB and organizational identification; OCB and leadership perspectives; OCB, social exchange, and organizational silence; and OCB, abusive supervision, and work engagement. OCB encompasses the positive and constructive task that employees do, of their own volition, which supports co-workers and benefits the company. When the employees feel like the citizens of the organization, they feel that their co-workers are their fellow citizens toward enhancing the helping behaviors. Organization will benefit from encouraging employees to engage in OCB, because it can increase productivity, efficiency and job satisfaction, and reduce costs and rates of employee turnover and absenteeism in the organization. The chapter argues that promoting OCB has the potential to increase organizational performance and gain sustainable competitive advantage in the modern workforce.

Chapter 2
Emotional Aspects of Leadership in the Modern Workplace 24
    Vaitsa Giannouli, Aristotle University of Thessaloniki, Greece

Although leadership has been extensively examined in the field of industrial-organizational psychology, management and business, until now there is scarce research focusing on the different emotional aspects of the leaders and the influence that they may have on their subordinates. This review explores emotions in healthcare workplaces-hospitals through the prism of emotional intelligence, emotion regulation, emotional labor, job satisfaction, burnout, and anxiety. The above emotional aspects of employees are presented along with selected paradigms coming from the Greek and international modern healthcare management research. The chapter closes with future directions-research questions on leadership issues in the modern healthcare workplace.

Chapter 3
The Art and Science in Communication: Workplace (Cross-Cultural) Communication Skills and Competencies in the Modern Workforce 60
    Ben Tran, Alliant International University, USA

One of the challenges facing the modern workforce is the increased diversity of the workforce and similarly complex prospective customers with disparate cultural backgrounds. Language barriers, cultural nuances, and value divergence can easily cause unintended misunderstandings and how low efficiency in internal communication in a multinational environment. It leads to conflict among employees and profit loss in organizational productivity. Therefore, effective communication by people from different cultures stands out significantly in the modern workforce who want to make inroads into international markets, take advantage of multiculturalism, and avoid possible side effects. The purpose of this chapter is on communication, specifically, the art and science in communication, resulting in communication skills and competencies in the modern workforce. The chapter will cover the meaning of communication, language, and history/philosophy of communication and will conclude with factors to be sensitive about when becoming effective cross cultural managers in the modern workforce.

Chapter 4
The Misappropriation of Organizational Power and Control: Managerial Bullying in the
Workplace 87
    David Starr-Glass, SUNY Empire State College, USA

Workplace bullying has been the focus of much interest and research over the last forty years. This concern reflects the growing awareness of the organizational costs associated with all forms of bullying. Of particular importance is what has been called abusive supervision, which constitutes the most prevalent and destructive form of negative workplace conduct. This chapter understands abusive supervision to be a prototypical example of workplace bullying, rather than a narrower and more restricted expression of it. The chapter reviews workplace bullying, focuses on abusive managerial behavior, and understands such behavior as a misappropriation of legitimate organizational processes and dynamics for own personal ends. Bullying behavior violates the norms of workplace ethics, organizational justice, and the agency role of management. The chapter considers initiatives through which managerial bullying might be identified, remediated, and reduced.

Chapter 5
Welfare Regime: A Critical Discourse.. 110
    Chandra Sekhar Patro, GVP College of Engineering (Autonomous), Visakhapatnam, India

In the present competitive business environment, it is essential for the management of any organization to precisely manage the welfare services to be provided for their employees. An organization is certainly a place where employees' and employers try to get the maximum from each other. Both, there can be lot more if and when they work together as partners in an organization, and if they have compassion of understanding of each other problems, which is the basic problem in employee welfare. The extreme logic in the wake of providing welfare services is to create proficient, healthy, loyal and satisfied labour force for an organization. The aim of the chapter is to articulate the welfare services administered by the organizations to the employees and their effect on the employees' efficacy and work life. It also examines the various principles and theories of welfare along with measures to improve welfare facilities in the organizations.

Chapter 6
Organizational Learning as a Social Process: A Social Capital and Network Approach 132
    Jieun You, Yonsei University, South Korea
    Junghwan Kim, University of Oklahoma, USA
    Sarah M Miller, University of Oklahoma, USA

This chapter discusses about application of social capital and network approach to organizational learning research and practice. The shift of organizational learning perspective from a technical or system-structural perspective to a social or interpretative perspective highlights that organizational learning process is socially embedded and is based on social interaction/relationships. Social capital and network theories provides a conceptual framework to explain how organizational learning takes place as well as identifies social and network factors influencing organizational learning. Thus, the chapter provides implications for establishing a conceptual and methodological framework to describe and evaluate an organizational learning process by extensively reviewing the recent organizational learning research adopting social capital and network approach.

Chapter 7
Performance Appraisal System Effectiveness: A Conceptual Review 156
Chandra Sekhar Patro, GVP College of Engineering (Autonomous), Visakhapatnam, India

Performance appraisal system (PAS) has been noticed to be one of the most challenging activities of human resource management and is even a destructive effect on the relationship of employees and employers. It not only motivates the employee but also improves the productivity level of an organization. Performance appraisal is considered to be a key instrument and is practiced in almost all types of organizations, but with a few differences. In an effort to change the behaviors and attitudes of employees in the organizations, performance appraisal systems have incorporated the new values and desired behaviors. In this contemporary state the organizations have become more enthusiastic to augment the performance of their employees. The chapter aims at identifying the performance appraisal system undertaken in the organizations and its influence on employees' competency and efficiency. It emphasizes on the problems and consequences faced by the organizations, and also the best practices undertaken for successful execution.

Chapter 8
The Significance of Job Satisfaction in Modern Organizations.. 181
Kijpokin Kasemsap, Suan Sunandha Rajabhat University, Thailand

This chapter explains the relationship between job satisfaction and organizational constructs in modern organizations; job satisfaction, job performance, and adaptability; job satisfaction and negative organizational issues; and the importance of job satisfaction in the health care industry. Job satisfaction is an attitude that employees have about their work and job-related activities. Job satisfaction is important from the perspective of maintaining employees within the organization. High job satisfaction effectively leads to the improved organizational productivity, decreased employee turnover, and reduced job stress in modern organizations. Job satisfaction leads to a positive ambience at the workplace and is essential to ensure the higher revenues for the organization. Organizations should create the systematic management and leadership strategies to increase the high levels of job satisfaction of their employees. When employees are satisfied with their jobs, they will energetically deliver the higher levels of job performance.

Chapter 9
Communication and Job Satisfaction... 201
Libi Shen, University of Phoenix, USA
Larry Austin, University of Phoenix, USA

In a business organization, communication is imperative for employers to express their thoughts, ideas, policies, and goals to their employees. Different organizational leaders or managers have various communication styles. Effective communication between employers and employees would not only boost employees' morale and job performance, but also demonstrate employers' successful leadership. Are communication and job satisfaction related? How should employers communicate so that their employees have higher job satisfaction, better engagement, lower turnover, and stronger long-term commitment? The purpose of this chapter is to explore the relationship between communication and employees' job satisfaction. This chapter attempts to provide business executives, company leaders, and scholar-practitioners suggestions with regard to developing effective communication strategies for better company management.

Chapter 10
Emotional Intelligence and Job Stress 226
    Germaine D. Washington, Calvary University, USA
    Libi Shen, University of Phoenix, USA

Substance abuse professionals work with chemically dependent addicts and disgruntled coworkers. They experience more occupational stress and employee turnover than social workers, community support workers, and youth care workers. Three of 37 substance abuse agencies in Kansas City, Missouri have reported extremely high employee turnover rates and occupational stress. How do substance abuse professionals perceive the relationship between emotional intelligence and job stress? What are substance abuse professionals' definitions of emotional intelligence and job stress? How does emotional intelligence affect job stress in the substance abuse profession? Why do higher levels of emotional intelligence reduce people's job stress and improve their job performance? The purposes of this chapter are to explore substance abuse professionals' definitions of emotional intelligence and job stress, and their viewpoints on the relationship between emotional intelligence and job stress.

Chapter 11
Experienced Stress and the Value of Rest Stops in the Transportation Field: Stress and
Transportation 249
    Ville Pietiläinen, University of Lapland, Finland
    Ilkka Salmi, University of Lapland, Finland
    Rauno Rusko, University of Lapland, Finland
    Raimo Jänkälä, University of Lapland, Finland

Work-related stress has been a long-term research focus in the field of industrial-organizational (I-O) psychology. Transportation is marginal, but an interesting context for the study as the field contains many specific characteristics related to stress phenomena. This chapter investigates the contents of and connection between work-related stress and rest stops' value in the transportation field, specifically in a lightly settled area with long geographic distances. Professional truck drivers in Finland serve as the target group for this study. The working conditions of truck drivers are unique compared to other branches where the work is not so mobile. In addition to how the truck is equipped, the services and facilities at rest stops are important elements in wellbeing. Based on the qualitative content analysis, this study offers in-depth information concerning work-related stress as an experienced phenomenon in the transportation field. Work management and legislation are highlighted as primary results while a dangerous work environment as well as isolation and loneliness are listed as secondary research results associated with work-related stress and the value of rest stops. Recommendations for future research and practical implications are proposed.

Chapter 12
The Relationship Between Social Problem Solving Ability and Burnout Level: A Field Study
Among Health Professionals 268
    Efe Ibrahim Efeoğlu, Adana Science and Technology University, Turkey
    Sevgi Ozcan, Cukurova University, Turkey

The aim of this study is to identify the relationship between social problem solving ability and burnout level of health professionals in a southeast city of Turkey. Material and Method: Data were collected using a self-reported questionnaire with the Short Form of Social Problem Solving Inventory and Maslach Burnout Inventory. A total number of 356 health professionals participated in the study. Results: Of all the participants; 44.1% were nurses, 27.0% were doctors and 28.9% consisted of other health professionals. Functional social problem solving dimensions were negatively correlated with emotional exhaustion and depersonalization and positively correlated with personal accomplishment. Conclusion: There is a negative correlation between social problem solving ability and burnout levels of health professionals. Evaluating social problem skills may allow to identify the ones who may be at risk for burnout; and improving their social problem solving skills may protect them from burnout.

Chapter 13
Understanding Diversity in Virtual Work Environments: A Comparative Case Study 283
    Marta Alicja Tomasiak, Thompson Reuters, UK
    Petros Chamakiotis, University of Sussex, UK

This chapter presents a comparative case study which was conducted with the aim of understanding how diversity can be managed in the context of the virtual work environment. The authors argue that the unique characteristics of virtuality might influence how diversity is managed in the virtual, computer-mediated environment. In view of this, a comparative case study involving qualitative interviews with participants from two contrasting environments—a face-to-face one and a virtual one—is presented. The findings of the study show what types of diversity are found to be important in the virtual workplace and also start to unpack the relationship between some of the unique characteristics of virtuality and diversity within the context of this study. The contributions of the study are discussed and recommendations to both future researchers and also practitioners are provided.

Chapter 14
Diversity in the Workplace: How to Achieve Gender Diversity in the Workplace 308
    Carola Hieker, Richmond, The American University in London, UK
    Maia Rushby, Diversity-in-Leadership, UK

The 'diversity in the workforce' chapter looks at the current status of gender diversity in the workplace and describes initiatives that are commonly designed and implemented by organizations for their female workforce and their senior leaders in pursuit of gender parity. It is emphasized that one or two interventions in isolation will not guarantee gender parity but that a combination of interventions is necessary, depending on the size and complexity of the organization. Furthermore, it is underlined that if these interventions are perceived as attractive by senior leaders then the senior leaders should be encouraged to invest time and resources in pursuing them. It will raise their commitment to become diversity champions, which is key for sustainable change. Examples from finance and professional service firms illustrate how some of the described interventions are used to enhance diversity.

Chapter 15
The Diversity Management for Employment of the Persons With Disabilities: Evidence of
Vocational Rehabilitation in the United States and Japan 333
    Kai Seino, Toyo University, National Institute of Vocational Rehabilitation, Japan
    Aoi Nomoto, Chiba University, Japan
    Tomohiro Takezawa, National Institute of Vocational Rehabilitation, Japan
    Heike Boeltzig-Brown, University of Massachusetts-Boston, USA

The purpose of this chapter is to discuss the latest knowledge of effective diversity management—from businesses and academia—with regard to the employment of persons with disabilities. From a broad perspective, this knowledge is found in the field of industrial-organizational psychology. From a more narrow perspective, and based on evidence from a substantial study, the knowledge of vocational rehabilitation has relevance for persons with disabilities. Vocational rehabilitation is the practice of providing employment supports that will build win-win relationships between employers and persons with disabilities. This chapter reviews recent findings documenting the effective employment and management of persons with disabilities, and summarizes effective actions and workplace considerations for the employment of persons with disabilities.

Chapter 16
Employer Branding and Internet Security 357
    Ewa Maria Matuska, Pomeranian Academy, Poland
    Joanna Grubicka, Pomeranian Academy, Poland

This chapter promotes the concept of employer branding (EB) as special kind of value management being part of strategic human resources management (SHRM) and including elements of cyber security. Employees' and organization's shared values (EVPs) bring opportunity to create common sense of identity, which prevents potentially aversive behavior towards company's reputation. Chapter's background positions EB and EVP in process of SHRM, introduces the view of EB as architectural frame for core organizational values, and describes popular Internet tools of EB. The background is closed by descriptions of common Internet threats, their implications to overall organization's information security, as well as useful Internet security systems. Chapter concludes with recommendations regarding enhancing EB by better controlling company's information security. As a new research area is proposed sub-discipline of cyber security in management, with special dedication to SHRM.

Chapter 17
National Ethical Institutions and Social Entrepreneurship 379
    Etayankara Muralidharan, MacEwan University, Canada
    Saurav Pathak, Kansas State University, USA

Using insights from institutional theory, the chapter proposes understanding ethics as national institutions that deeply influence social entrepreneurship. Moreover, the chapter proposes that low behavioral ethical standards (normative ethical institutions) provide opportunities for individuals to establish social enterprises. Furthermore, it proposes that high public-sector ethical standards (regulatory ethical institutions) and values of unselfishness (cognitive ethical institutions) facilitate and motivate individuals to establish social enterprises. The chapter also explores the combined effects of public-sector ethical standards and low behavioral ethics, public-sector ethical standards and societal unselfishness, and low behavioral ethics and unselfishness, on the creation of social enterprises. The chapter contributes to cross-cultural comparative entrepreneurship by suggesting, through a multilevel framework, the effects of societal-level ethical institutions on the creation of social enterprises.

Chapter 18
Factors Related to Readjustment to Daily Life: A Study of Repatriates in Japanese Multinational Enterprises 403
Yoko Naito, Tokai University, Japan

This study explores issues arising from cross-cultural transitions, focusing on Japanese multinational enterprises (MNEs) and readjustment to daily life in general after international assignments. Employee readjustment to the home country needs to study from two perspectives: work and private life. However, most studies of repatriates focus on the work aspect, and few focus on the aspect of private life. Using structural equation modeling based on the questionnaire data, this study empirically examines nine variables that may possibly affect readjustment to daily life in general after returning to Japan. In this process, this study deals with "readjustment to daily life in general" from a viewpoint outside the organization. Based on these findings, this chapter suggests emphasizing management practices that provide assistance and support to repatriates in their readjustment to daily life in general, along with the importance of readjustment to the organization.

Chapter 19
Investigation of Ergonomic Risk Factors in Snacks Manufacturing in Central India: Ergonomics in Unorganized Sector.. 425
Prabir Mukhopadhyay, Indian Institute of Information Technology Design and Manufacturing, Jabalpur, India

Hand-made snacks (locally known as papadam) manufacturing is a popular profession in Central India employing a large number of women workers The objective of this study was to identify the ergonomic risk factors for Work related musculoskeletal disorders (WMSDs) in this sector. Direct observation, activity analysis was applied along with postural analysis methods. Pre and post exercise heart rate was measured by the 10 beats method. Lower back (30%), upper arm (30%) and shoulder were the zones where maximum post work pain and discomfort was reported in the dough cutting section. The maximum post work heart rate was at 116.3 beats per minute in the dough cutting section. High REBA score of 15/15 was observed in the grading, kneading and dough cutting sections. Similarly the RULA scores were very high at 7/7 in majority of the sections. Strain Index scores were very high at 60.8 in the dough cutting section.

Compilation of References 450

About the Contributors 553

Index 560

Preface

Workforce development is in an ongoing process that organizations and industries must conduct to stay competitive in this globalized economy of today. This publication provides the latest research in the areas of organizational learning, organizational citizenship, leadership, communication, job satisfaction, job stress, performance appraisal, diversity in virtual environment, gender diversity, employees with disabilities, ergonomics, ethics, and internet security. The target audience includes business and government executives, researchers, and undergraduate/graduate students.

This publication begins with the fundamentals of organizational citizenship behavior in chapter 1. The emotional aspects of the leadership are covered in chapter 2. Cross-cultural communication skills are discussed in chapter 3. The latest research on the managerial bullying is reported in chapter 4. Employee welfare is discussed in chapter 5. The latest findings on the social capital and network approach to organizational learning are discussed in chapter 6. The effectiveness the performance appraisal systems is discussed in chapter 7. Recent research on communication and job satisfaction is covered in chapters 8 and 9. The latest findings on the job stress and burnout are reported in chapters 10, 11, and 12. The latest research on the diversity in virtual environments, gender diversity and managing employees with disabilities are covered in chapters 13, 14, and 15. The crucial topic of the internet security is discussed in chapter 16. The social entrepreneurship and national ethical institutions is covered in chapter 17. The readjustment factors for the repatriates of the multinational enterprises are discussed in chapter 18. The last chapter discusses the research on ergonomic risk factors in the manufacturing sector in chapter 19. An understanding of these latest findings on the topics on the human factors in the contemporary workforce development will benefit the manufacturing industries and organizations for productivity enhancements and will provide insight to the government executives for policy development.

We trust this work will be of assistance to the intended audiences to spur future research in the respective areas covered.

Bryan Christiansen
PryMarke LLC, USA

Harish C. Chandan
Argosy University, USA

Chapter 1
The Fundamentals of Organizational Citizenship Behavior

Kijpokin Kasemsap
Suan Sunandha Rajabhat University, Thailand

ABSTRACT

This chapter reveals the overview of Organizational Citizenship Behavior (OCB); OCB and organizational factors; OCB and Counterproductive Work Behavior (CWB); OCB and organizational identification; OCB and leadership perspectives; OCB, social exchange, and organizational silence; and OCB, abusive supervision, and work engagement. OCB encompasses the positive and constructive task that employees do, of their own volition, which supports co-workers and benefits the company. When the employees feel like the citizens of the organization, they feel that their co-workers are their fellow citizens toward enhancing the helping behaviors. Organization will benefit from encouraging employees to engage in OCB, because it can increase productivity, efficiency and job satisfaction, and reduce costs and rates of employee turnover and absenteeism in the organization. The chapter argues that promoting OCB has the potential to increase organizational performance and gain sustainable competitive advantage in the modern workforce.

INTRODUCTION

Organizational behavior is the study of both group and individual performance and activity within an organization (Kasemsap, 2017a). Organizational citizenship behavior (OCB) is the discretionary behavior that is not directly rewarded by the organization but has been linked to the positive outcomes, such as the increased job satisfaction and the reduced turnover intention (Gilbert, Laschinger, & Leiter, 2010). OCB has significant importance in the workplace (Kasa & Hassan, 2015). OCB provides a method of managing the interdependencies among members of an organization, which increases the collective outcomes (Serim, Demirbağ, & Yozgat, 2014). Consideration of cultural differences in OCB has become

DOI: 10.4018/978-1-5225-2568-4.ch001

more important over the last few decades, as the workforce has become highly diverse and people from many different ethno-cultural backgrounds work together (Ersoy, Derous, Born, & van der Molen, 2015).

OCB ideas include a wide variety of issues (e.g., employees, acceptance, responsibilities, adherence of rules, and organizational procedures) toward developing positive attitude and job satisfaction (Ahmadi, Nami, & Barvarz, 2014). Increasing organizational competitiveness is a major goal at the managerial level (Popescu, Deaconu, & Popescu, 2015). OCB consists of behaviors to perform the job and these behaviors contribute to the overall success of the organization (Yildirim, 2015). OCB is very important to organizations because they need employees who will do more than their usual job duties (Çınar & Karcıoğlu, 2015) and will provide performance that is beyond expectations (Ng, Ke, & Raymond, 2014).

OCB continues to be recognized as a vital component to organizational effectiveness (Newton, Nowak, & Blanton, 2012). The unit-level OCB has a moderately strong relationship with unit-level performance (Whitman, van Rooy, & Viswesvaran, 2010). Individuals who think they have the power to influence the environment and the outcomes are inclined to engage in OCB (Magdalena, 2014). Personal values, group identification, and a sense of power significantly interact in predicting the change-oriented OCB of employees (Seppälä, Lipponen, Bardi, & Pirttilä-Backman, 2012). Challenge-oriented and affiliation-oriented OCBs have on organizational effectiveness through their impact on workgroup task performance (MacKenzie, Podsakoff, & Podsakoff, 2011).

This chapter focuses on the literature review through a thorough literature consolidation of OCB. The extensive literature of OCB provides a contribution to practitioners and researchers by revealing the issues and implications of OCB in order to maximize the impact of OCB in the modern workforce.

Background

Interest in OCB has grown substantially over the past 30 years (Podsakoff, Podsakoff, MacKenzie, Maynes, & Spoelma, 2014). OCB is a key factor for today's organization toward overall organization effectiveness that has become the focus in the fields of psychology and management which gain great attention in the extant organizational behavior literature (LePine, Erez, & Johnson, 2002). OCB is an important role that is related to behaviors that go beyond formal duties (Organ, Podsakoff, & MacKenzie, 2006). If employees work in their own organization as good organizational citizens, they can contribute to the organization's overall performance in competition, and change it into both organizational trust and motivation in the workplace (Ghodratollah, Matin, & Amighi, 2011).

OCB is a concept which organizations require to survive in today's challenging and competitive environment (Serim et al., 2014). Podsakoff et al. (2000) mentioned seven ways that OCB contributes to excellent organizational performance: increasing coworker or managerial productivity; releasing resources so they can be used for more productive purposes; coordinating activities across work groups; reducing the need to devote the scarce resources to the maintenance functions; strengthening the organizations' ability to attract and retain the highly qualified employees; increasing the stability of the organization's performance; and enabling the organization to adapt more effectively to the environmental changes.

Organ (1988) identified five dimensions of OCB: altruism, courtesy, sportsmanship, conscientiousness, and civic virtue. Altruism involves the helpful actions that assist other workers' performance and facilitate the favorable working relationship. Courtesy implies behaviors which aim to help co-workers and prevent problems. Conscientiousness consists of behaviors that go beyond the minimum role requirements of the organization. Sportsmanship is the willingness on the part of the employee that signifies the employee's tolerance of less-than-ideal organizational circumstances without complaining problems out of proportion. Civic virtue is characterized by behaviors that indicate the employee's organizational concerns and active interest in the life of the organization (Law, Wong, & Chen, 2005).

ISSUES AND IMPLICATIONS OF ORGANIZATIONAL CITIZENSHIP BEHAVIOR

This section describes the overview of OCB; OCB and organizational factors; OCB and counterproductive work behavior (CWB); OCB and organizational identification; OCB and leadership perspectives; OCB, social exchange, and organizational silence; and OCB, abusive supervision, and work engagement.

Overview of Organizational Citizenship Behavior

Williams and Anderson (1991) categorized the dimensions of OCB into two different types of OCB based on at whom the behaviors were directed. Organizational citizenship behavior-individuals (OCB-I) include behaviors that are aimed at other individuals in the workplace while organizational citizenship behavior-organizational (OCB-O) include behaviors directed at the organization as a whole. Altruism and courtesy are the actions aimed at other employees and relates to OCB-I. Conscientiousness, civic virtue, and sportsmanship are the behaviors intended for the benefit of the organization and can be recognized as OCB-O.

In health care organizations, both altruism and civic virtue play the most significant role (Parker & Axtell, 2001). The most important dimension of altruism is the interpersonal facilitation, which includes the cooperative and helpful actions that assist other workers' performance and facilitate the good working relationships in the workplace (van Scotter & Motowidlo, 1996). Altruism is an important feature in the nursing context (Ersoy et al., 2015). Civic virtue is characterized by behaviors that indicate the employee's deep concerns in the organization (Diefendorff, Brown, Kamin, & Lord, 2002).

The attributions regarding employees' motives for engaging in OCB are related to supervisors' emotional reactions to such behavior concerning the ratings of employee performance (Halbesleben, Bowler, Bolino, & Turnley, 2010). Lavelle et al. (2009) indicated that employees maintain the distinct beliefs about their behaviors toward the multiple targets in the workplace (e.g., the organization as a whole, their supervisor, and fellow workgroup members). OCB is associated with the self-efficacy, the internality, and length in service within the organization (Pavalache-Ilie, 2014). Self-efficacy is important when engaging in proactive behaviors, as these behaviors entail certain psychological risks for individuals (López-Domínguez, Enache, Sallan, & Simo, 2013).

Organizational Citizenship Behavior and Organizational Factors

OCB involves the essential behavior that encourages staff to voluntarily improve the organizational performance without lobbying for compensation (Tsai & Wu, 2010). Employees who are satisfied with their work develop OCB easier, based on a reciprocity relation (Vigoda-Gadot & Cohen, 2004). Employees engaged in OCB has concentrated on between-person variables, typically ignoring intra-individual influences (Spence, Ferris, Brown, & Heller, 2011). Group cohesion and collective efficacy fully mediate the direct effects of OCB toward individuals and the organization on team performance (Lin & Peng, 2010). OCB targeting individuals can improve the rated performance in the highly collectivistic teams only, whereas only organizational OCB can produce a significant improvement in the highly individualistic teams (Lai, Lam, & Lam, 2013). Innovative work behavior (IWB) and OCB positively affect organizational performance (Newton & Nowak, 2013).

There is a positive impact of human resource management (HRM) practices on OCB, through an effect on perceived job influence/discretion (Snape & Redman, 2010). The relationship between perception of organizational politics (POP) and OCB is negatively mediated by job satisfaction and positively mediated by careerism (Hsiung, Lin, & Lin, 2012). Helping behaviors can improve individuals' moods because helping others provides gratification and directs attention away from one's negative mood (Glomb, Bhave, Miner, & Wall, 2011). The favorable customer-oriented perception is associated with the increased OCB for nurses (Chang & Chang, 2010). Conscientiousness, civic virtue, and sportsmanship mediate the relationship between perceived organizational support (POS) and continuance intention, but altruism and courtesy do not (Soltani, Elkhani, & Bardsiri, 2014). Nurses' organizational support positively influences their OCB, and their organizational justice perception has a moderating effect between organizational support and OCB (Altuntas & Baykal, 2010).

Person-organization (P-O) fit perception is concerned with the perspective that individuals perceive between their own values and those of the organization (Özçelik & Fındıklı, 2014). Individuals who perceive fit with their organization are more satisfied with their jobs (Jansen & Kristof-Brown, 2006) and are more committed to their organization (Cable & Judge, 1996). P-O fit perceptions are strongly linked to organizational commitment (van Vianen, Shen, & Chuang, 2011). Employee's turnover intensions arise in case of incompatibility of P-O fit (Kristof-Brown, Zimmerman, & Johnson, 2005). P-O fit can be evaluated by three perspectives: a direct measurement of perceived fit, indirect cross-levels measurement of actual fit, and indirect individual-level measurement of actual fit (Özçelik & Fındıklı, 2014). The higher the P-O fit, the more prepared employees will be to exert more efforts of extra-role behavior (Yaniv & Farkas, 2005).

Organizational socialization is a crucial concept for both employees and employers in order to facilitate the process of employee adjustment (Özdemir & Ergun, 2015). Organizational socialization content is a significant predictor of OCB (Özdemir & Ergun, 2015). Regarding OCB perspectives, employees can learn the required knowledge, skills, and attitudes for adapting to the new job, role, and culture of the workplace through the successful organizational socialization process (Chao, O'Leary-Kelly, Wolfe, Klein, & Gardner, 1994). When an employee begins to work at an organization, the unique chance occurs toward creating a foundation through the working relationship (Cooper-Thomas, Vianen, & Anderson, 2004).

Organizations can provide the necessary tools, information, and resources for their employees' organizational responses to the changes in the environment. However, social loafing tendency means that any individual tends to expend less effort when working collectively rather than working individually (Karau & Williams, 1993). Social loafing is the phenomenon in which group membership degrades individual motivation and it occurs as the tendency of individuals in order to expend less effort while working collectively rather than working individually (Ulke & Bilgic, 2011). Social loafing has a negative reflection in OCB and makes employees individually work and expend less effort for their works (Karadal & Saygin, 2013).

Several studies in the extant OCB literature have focused on the main effects of employee dispositions and job attitudes (Bowling, Wang, & Li, 2012). OCB improves an enterprise's efficiency by enhancing the level of job satisfaction among employees (Jena & Goswami, 2013). Sportsmanship dimension of OCB is found to be a function of conservation values, work centrality, and both affective and normative commitment (Uçanok & Karabatı, 2013). There are potential benefits owing to the positive influence of workplace spirituality on OCB and affective commitment among nurses (Kazemipour, Amin, &

Pourseidi, 2012). Nurses who trust in their managers, institutions, and coworkers demonstrate the OCB of conscientiousness, civic virtue, courtesy, and altruism more frequently.

Organizational Citizenship Behavior and Counterproductive Work Behavior

Researchers have considered OCB as the positive pattern and CWB as the negative pattern of discretionary work behaviors (Reynolds, Shoss, & Jundt, 2015). CWB encompasses behaviors aimed at harming colleagues, organizational property, and the firm's profitability (Spector & Fox, 2010). Both OCB and CWB are recognized as the important components of an employee's overall job performance (Lievens, Conway, & de Corte, 2008) and are included in many organizations' performance appraisals (Rotundo & Sackett, 2002). Employees' OCB and CWB significantly affect organizational productivity (Dalal, Lam, Weiss, Welch, & Hulin, 2009).

CWB involves intentional employee acts that harm an organization's legitimate business interests (Bennett & Robinson, 2000). Engaging in CWB can lower an individual's performance evaluation as well as lead to slower promotions and even termination because such behavior violates the social expectations associated with the role of a loyal worker (Ng, Lam, & Feldman, 2016). Behaviors that individuals enact to help the organization may come with personal costs and behaviors they enact to hurt the organization may have personal gains (Reynolds et al., 2015). For example, employees who volunteer for extra tasks may feel overloaded and depleted (Bolino & Turnley, 2005), whereas employees who leave work early may enjoy more time for the social and family activities.

Bergeron (2007) indicated that time spent on OCB often involves task performance sacrifices or trade-offs on the part of individuals, which in turn result in a host of negative personal outcomes (e.g., workload and stress) while operating in the outcome-based reward systems. The higher levels of individual initiative can result in the higher levels of role overload, job stress, and work–family conflict (Bolino & Turnley, 2005). Individuals who expend the effort engaging in these behaviors when they do not have the necessary time or energy may induce further stress or personal conflict (Reynolds et al., 2015).

Organizational Citizenship Behavior and Organizational Identification

Mael and Ashforth (1992) defined organizational identification as a perceived oneness with an organization and the experience of the organization's successes and failures as one's own. Dutton and Dukerich (1991) viewed organizational identification as the shared beliefs and attitudes among employees on the enduring and distinct characteristics of the organization, which is one of the most crucial factors holding employees together and committed to the organization. Organizations with high levels of employee identification, therefore, can be expected to benefit from a more cohesive work atmosphere and greater levels of cooperation, altruism, participation and exertion of effort on behalf of the organization, including greater levels of OCB (Gonzalez & Chakraborty, 2012).

One of the key theoretical bases for understanding organizational identification is social identity theory that people utilize the groups as the sources of information about themselves and individuals may use their status or social standing in their organizations to enhance their self-worth (Cheung & Law, 2008). Organization identification is a specific kind of social identification which serves the individual's needs for belonging, safety, or self-enhancement (Kane, Magnusen, & Perrewe, 2012). An individual who identifies more strongly with an organization will have more of his or her needs satisfied and will express a greater level of job satisfaction.

Organizational support and organizational identification have positive relationships with OCB (Chen, Yu, Hsu, Lin, & Lou, 2013). Oplatka (2009) stated that positive activities (e.g., volunteering, persisting, helping, following rules, and endorsing organizational objectives) can increase employers' productivity toward organizational success. In educational settings, OCB and organizational identification affect the social and psychological environments of schools, since these perspectives involve the perceptions of oneness with the school and teachers' extra role behaviors (Demir, 2015). These teachers help students with class materials, acquire expertise in the new areas that contribute to their work, prepare special assignments for the higher or lower level students, volunteer for school committees, help the absent colleagues by assigning the learning tasks to their classes, and collaboratively work with others (Bogler & Somech, 2004).

Organizational Citizenship Behavior and Leadership Perspectives

Leadership can promote social capital, employee creativity, and innovation climate in the modern workplace (Kasemsap, 2017b). Social capital is the value that results from trust and connections that have been carefully cultivated between individuals in networks at any level (Kasemsap, 2017c). Britt et al. (2012) indicated the ratings of leadership effectiveness mediate the relationship between organizational constraints and OCB. Subordinates' trust for leaders and team citizenship behaviors are positively related at the team level (Lau & Lam, 2008). Neurotic followers are more likely than emotionally stable followers to become able to derive energy to engage in OCB through transformational leaders' inspirational motivation (e.g., giving challenging developmental assignments and increased expectations) (Guay & Choi, 2015).

By using the visionary messages, transformational leaders can reframe the big picture, promote cooperation among group members, and arouse the followers' emotions (Bass & Avolio, 1994). Given that neurotic individuals are strongly motivated to avoid social disapproval and being judged as incompetent (Bendersky & Shah, 2013), inspirational motivation can have greater influence on the neurotic followers' OCB than the emotionally stable followers' OCBs. Through engagement in OCB, neurotic followers can reduce their social anxiety. Without a transformational leader to help instill confidence, neurotics would feel anxiety from the leader's increased expectations (Guay & Choi, 2015).

Leader-member exchange (LMX) is expected to improve OCB (Chou, Jiang, Klein, & Chou, 2013). LMX positively predicts helping behavior (Podsakoff et al., 2000) and the high LMX relationships promote the subordinates' performances beyond the in-role job descriptions (Graen & Scandura, 1987). Organizational justice is the study of the concerns about fairness in the workplace (Kasemsap, 2016a). LMX, organizational justice, and job satisfaction lead to the improved OCB in the modern workforce (Kasemsap, 2013a). Organizational justice, job satisfaction, and organizational commitment are associated with OCB (Kasemsap, 2012).

Employees' exchanges with their supervisors and organizations can simultaneously influence each other in the workplace (Loi, Mao, & Ngo, 2009). Employees generally perceive an obligation to reciprocate the high-quality work relationships over time, as evidenced by studies linking LMX to positive employee behaviors (Ilies, Nahrgang, & Morgeson, 2007). Reciprocity helps explain the effect of LMX on the desired employee behaviors (Chow, Lai, & Loi, 2015). When team supervisors offer material resources, information, opportunities, and support to travel agents in a high-LMX context, the travel agents will feel obligated to behave in a way that directly benefits their supervisors. They will be obligated to not only perform the job adequately, but also go beyond the scope of the usual expectations and formal duties (Bakker, Demerouti, & Verbeke, 2004). This discretionary behavior directly benefits the supervisor because it relieves the need to closely monitor their subordinates' performances and allows them to concentrate on other strategic activities (Walz & Niehoff, 2000).

Organizational Citizenship Behavior, Social Exchange, and Organizational Silence

Social exchange theory evaluates the nature of relationships by providing the rules for evaluating the fair way of economic and social value (Serim et al., 2014). Social exchange framework is important for understanding relationship development, relationship satisfaction, and relationship stability within an organization (White & Yanamandrama, 2012). In the context of social exchange theory (Blau, 1964), organizational silence is an important organizational behavior issues that arise in lack of having the relationship equitable social change. How to break the silence culture and establish the free climate to encourage employees' voice are the big challenges faced to mangers (Beheshtifar, Borhani, & Moghadam, 2012).

When many employees in the organization prefer to conduct the organizational silence about organizational matters, silence becomes a collective behavior which is called organizational silence (Henriksen & Dayton, 2006). Organizational silence is an inefficient process which can destroy all organizational efforts and may take various forms, such as collective silence in meetings, low levels of participation in suggestion schemes, and low levels of collective voice (Nikmaram, Yamchi, Shojaii, Zahrani, & Alvani, 2012). Organizational silence causes the reduction of employee commitment (Vakola & Bouradas, 2005) and increase in the intention to leave. Morrison and Milliken (2000) indicated that organizational silence is the term used to refer to the collective-level phenomenon of doing or saying very little in response to the significant problems or issues facing an organization or industry because of negative reactions.

Employees, who have a behavior of organizational silence, possess lower tendency for OCB (Acaray & Akturan, 2015). While it is accepted that employees voluntarily participate in the organizational activities on the basis of OCB, organizational silence behavior theory indicates that employees avoid revealing their views and ideas with a conscious decision (Acaray & Akturan, 2015). Being silent may make sense if the employee fears the manager will negatively react to the upward communication of opinions and may react by destroying the employee's ability to work in the organization (Milliken, Morrison, & Hewlin, 2003). In organizations context, organizational silence obstructs the organizational development (Morrison & Milliken, 2000), gives damage to the adaption of the learning organization, and reduces the organizational communication (Tangirala & Ramanujam, 2008).

Organizational Citizenship Behavior, Abusive Supervision, and Work Engagement

Examples of abusive supervision include withholding needed information, scapegoating subordinates, humiliating them in front of others, or giving them the silent treatment (Tepper et al., 2009). A considerable body of empirical evidence has identified the destructive influences abusive supervision exerts on employee attitudes, behavior, and psychological health, such as job dissatisfaction (Tepper, 2000), reduced affective commitment (Tepper, Duffy, Hoobler, & Ensley, 2004), workplace deviance (Lian, Ferris, & Brown, 2012), poor job performance (Harris, Kacmar, & Zivnuska, 2007), dysfunctional resistance (Tepper, Duffy, & Shaw, 2001), and psychological distress (Harvey, Stoner, Hochwarter, & Kacmar, 2007).

Abusive supervision is considered as the destructive form of leadership that may seriously undermine the success of hospitality companies (Jian, Kwan, Qiu, Liu, & Yim, 2012). Since customer satisfaction is largely determined by the quality of service (Kasemsap, 2016b), the extent to which hospitality employees are motivated to engage in customer-oriented OCB directly affects the success of hospitality firms. Abusive leaders are characterized by a strong intention to exhibit enduring hostility (Tepper, 2000). Abusive leaders lead by belittling, disregarding, and ridiculing employees (Aryee, Chen, Sun, & Debrah, 2007). When led by abusive leaders, hospitality employees' motivation to conduct customer-oriented OCB can be undermined (Lyu, Zhu, Zhong, & Hu, 2016).

Because abusive supervisors usually humiliate subordinates in front of others, use aggressive eye contact, and intimidate their subordinates with threats of job loss, they deplete subordinates' resources and act as a stressor in organizations (Lyu et al., 2016). The presence of resources, such as job resources (e.g., positive feedback and social support) and personal resources (e.g., trait competitiveness and self-efficacy) would result in an accumulation of energy and thus contribute to work engagement (Karatepe & Olugbade, 2009). Work engagement is the potential result of high levels of resources (Kuhnel, Sonnentag, & Bledow, 2012).

Job involvement, organizational commitment, and OCB are positively related to organizational performance (Kasemsap, 2013b). Work engagement is related to OCB, because engaged employees invest themselves more fully and are more willing to step outside the bounds of their formally defined jobs and engage in actions that constitute OCB (Liu & Wang, 2013). It is recognized that abusive supervisor drains subordinates' resources and further depletes subordinates' work engagement (Lyu et al., 2016).

FUTURE RESEARCH DIRECTIONS

The classification of the extensive literature in the domains of OCB will provide potential opportunities for future research. Culture offers a chance to connect and share the individual's history and beliefs toward business growth and economic development (Kasemsap, 2016c). Organizational culture is the values and behaviors that contribute to the unique social and psychological environment of an organization (Kasemsap, 2016d). Businesses must recognize, respect, and reconcile cultural differences if they hope to successfully contract in the global business environments (Kasemsap, 2015). Organizational change management is a framework for managing the effect of new business processes, changes in organizational structure or cultural changes within an enterprise (Kasemsap, 2016e).

Complexity theory enables understanding the realities of the evolutionary, dynamic, and complex nature of organizations, businesses, and economics (Kasemsap, 2016f). Organizational learning is the organization-wide continuous process that enhances its collective ability to accept, make sense of, and respond to the internal and external changes (Kasemsap, 2017d). Problem solving ability develops over a long period of time and grows with experience in solving a variety of problems in many different ways (Kasemsap, 2017e). An examination of linkages among OCB, organizational culture, organizational change management, complexity theory, and problem solving in the modern workforce would seem to be viable for future research efforts.

Behavior is related to the brain and psychology. Neuroscience is the field of study encompassing the various scientific disciplines dealing with the structure, development, function, chemistry, pharmacology, and pathology of the nervous system (Kasemsap, 2017f). Social neuroscience aims to identify the biological mechanisms (e.g., psychological, neural, hormonal, cellular, and genetic mechanisms) and to specify the influences between social and neural structures and processes (Kasemsap, 2017g). Improving OCB through the development of neuroscience and social neuroscience in the modern workforce should be further studied.

CONCLUSION

This chapter provided the overview of OCB; OCB and organizational factors; OCB and CWB; OCB and organizational identification; OCB and leadership perspectives; OCB, social exchange, and organizational silence; and OCB, abusive supervision, and work engagement. OCB encompasses the positive and constructive task that employees do, of their own volition, which supports co-workers and benefits the company. Organizational citizenship beliefs encourage the employees to perform tasks that they do not have to perform, even if organization do not give them the additional rewards for doing the tasks or punish them for not performing them.

When the employees feel like the citizens of the organization, they feel that their co-workers are their fellow citizens toward enhancing the helping behaviors. Organization will benefit from encouraging employees to engage in OCB because it can increase productivity, efficiency and job satisfaction, and reduce costs and rates of employee turnover and absenteeism in the organization. Promoting OCB has the potential to increase organizational performance and gain sustainable competitive advantage in the modern workforce.

REFERENCES

Acaray, A., & Akturan, A. (2015). The relationship between organizational citizenship behaviour and organizational silence. *Procedia: Social and Behavioral Sciences*, *207*, 472–482. doi:10.1016/j.sbspro.2015.10.117

Ahmadi, S., Nami, Y., & Barvarz, R. (2014). The relationship between spirituality in the workplace and organizational citizenship behavior. *Procedia: Social and Behavioral Sciences*, *114*, 262–264. doi:10.1016/j.sbspro.2013.12.695

Altuntas, S., & Baykal, U. (2010). Relationship between nurses' organizational trust levels and their organizational citizenship behaviors. *Journal of Nursing Scholarship*, *42*(2), 186–194. doi:10.1111/j.1547-5069.2010.01347.x PMID:20618602

Aryee, S., Chen, Z. X., Sun, L., & Debrah, Y. A. (2007). Antecedents and outcomes of abusive supervision: Test of a trickle-down model. *The Journal of Applied Psychology*, *92*(1), 191–201. doi:10.1037/0021-9010.92.1.191 PMID:17227160

Bakker, A. B., Demerouti, E., & Verbeke, W. (2004). Using the job demands-resources model to predict burnout and performance. *Human Resource Management*, *43*(1), 83–104. doi:10.1002/hrm.20004

Bass, B. M., & Avolio, B. J. (1994). *Improving organizational effectiveness through transformational leadership*. Thousand Oaks, CA: Sage Publications.

Beheshtifar, M., Borhani, H., & Moghadam, M. N. (2012). Destructive role of employee silence in organizational success. *International Journal of Academic Research in Business and Social Sciences*, 2(11), 275–282.

Bendersky, C., & Shah, N. P. (2013). The downfall of extraverts and rise of neurotics: The dynamic process of status allocation in task groups. *Academy of Management Journal*, 56(2), 387–406. doi:10.5465/amj.2011.0316

Bennett, R. J., & Robinson, S. L. (2000). Development of a measure of workplace deviance. *The Journal of Applied Psychology*, 85(3), 349–360. doi:10.1037/0021-9010.85.3.349 PMID:10900810

Bergeron, D. M. (2007). The potential paradox of organizational citizenship behavior: Good citizens at what cost? *Academy of Management Review*, 32(4), 1078–1095. doi:10.5465/AMR.2007.26585791

Blau, P. M. (1964). *Exchange and power in social life*. New York: John Wiley & Sons.

Bogler, R., & Somech, A. (2004). Influence of teacher empowerment on teachers' organizational commitment, professional commitment and organizational citizenship behavior in schools. *Teaching and Teacher Education*, 20(3), 277–289. doi:10.1016/j.tate.2004.02.003

Bolino, M. C., & Turnley, W. H. (2005). The personal costs of citizenship behavior: The relationship between individual initiative and role overload, job stress, and work–family conflict. *The Journal of Applied Psychology*, 90(4), 740–748. doi:10.1037/0021-9010.90.4.740 PMID:16060790

Bowling, N. A., Wang, Q., & Li, H. Y. (2012). The moderating effect of core self-evaluations on the relationships between job attitudes and organisational citizenship behavior. *Applied Psychology*, 61(1), 97–113. doi:10.1111/j.1464-0597.2011.00458.x

Britt, T. W., McKibben, E. S., Greene-Shortridge, T. M., Odle-Dusseau, H. N., & Herleman, H. A. (2012). Self-engagement moderates the mediated relationship between organizational constraints and organizational citizenship behaviors via rated leadership. *Journal of Applied Social Psychology*, 42(8), 1830–1846. doi:10.1111/j.1559-1816.2012.00920.x

Cable, D. M., & Judge, T. A. (1996). Person-organization fit, job choice decisions, and organizational entry. *Organizational Behavior and Human Decision Processes*, 67(3), 294–311. doi:10.1006/obhd.1996.0081

Chang, C. S. (2014). Moderating effects of nurses' organizational justice between organizational support and organizational citizenship behaviors for evidence-based practice. *Worldviews on Evidence-Based Nursing*, 11(5), 332–340. doi:10.1111/wvn.12054 PMID:25132135

Chang, C. S., & Chang, H. C. (2010). Motivating nurses' organizational citizenship behaviors by customer-oriented perception for evidence-based practice. *Worldviews on Evidence-Based Nursing*, 7(4), 214–225. doi:10.1111/j.1741-6787.2010.00188.x PMID:20345521

Chao, G. T., O'Leary-Kelly, A. M., Wolfe, S., Klein, H. J., & Gardner, P. D. (1994). Organizational socialization: Its content and consequences. *The Journal of Applied Psychology*, 779(5), 730–743. doi:10.1037/0021-9010.79.5.730

Chen, S. H., Yu, H. Y., Hsu, H. Y., Lin, F. C., & Lou, J. H. (2013). Organisational support, organisational identification and organisational citizenship behaviour among male nurses. *Journal of Nursing Management*, *21*(8), 1072–1082. doi:10.1111/j.1365-2834.2012.01449.x PMID:23409728

Cheung, M. F. Y., & Law, M. C. C. (2008). Relationships of organizational justice and organizational identification: The mediating effects of perceived organizational support in Hong Kong. *Asia Pacific Business Review*, *14*(2), 213–231. doi:10.1080/13602380701430879

Chou, T., Jiang, J. J., Klein, G., & Chou, S. T. (2013). Organizational citizenship behavior of information system personnel: The influence of leader-member exchange. In M. Khosrow-Pour (Ed.), *Managing information resources and technology: Emerging applications and theories* (pp. 284–299). Hershey, PA: IGI Global. doi:10.4018/978-1-4666-3616-3.ch019

Chow, C. W. C., Lai, J. Y. M., & Loi, R. (2015). Motivation of travel agents' customer service behavior and organizational citizenship behavior: The role of leader-member exchange and internal marketing orientation. *Tourism Management*, *48*, 362–369. doi:10.1016/j.tourman.2014.12.008

Çınar, O., & Karcıoğlu, F. (2015). The relationship between cyber loafing and organizational citizenship behavior: A survey study in Erzurum/Turkey. *Procedia: Social and Behavioral Sciences*, *207*, 444–453. doi:10.1016/j.sbspro.2015.10.114

Cooper-Thomas, H. D., Vianen, A. V., & Anderson, N. (2004). Changes in person-organization fit: The impact of socialization tactics on perceived and actual P-O fit. *European Journal of Work and Organizational Psychology*, *13*(1), 52–78. doi:10.1080/13594320344000246

Dalal, R. S., Lam, H., Weiss, H. M., Welch, E. R., & Hulin, C. L. (2009). A within-person approach to work behavior and performance: Concurrent and lagged citizenship-counterproductivity associations, and dynamic relationships with affect and overall job performance. *Academy of Management Journal*, *52*(5), 1051–1066. doi:10.5465/AMJ.2009.44636148

Demir, K. (2015). Teachers' organizational citizenship behaviors and organizational identification in public and private preschools. *Procedia: Social and Behavioral Sciences*, *174*, 1176–1182. doi:10.1016/j.sbspro.2015.01.734

Diefendorff, J., Brown, D., Kamin, A., & Lord, R. (2002). Examining the roles of job involvement and work centrality in predicting organizational citizenship behaviors and job performance. *Journal of Organizational Behavior*, *23*(1), 93–108. doi:10.1002/job.123

Dutton, J. E., & Dukerich, J. M. (1991). Keeping an eye on the mirror: Image and identity in organisational adaptation. *Academy of Management Journal*, *34*(3), 517–554. doi:10.2307/256405

Ersoy, N. C., Derous, E., Born, M. P., & van der Molen, H. T. (2015). Antecedents of organizational citizenship behavior among Turkish white-collar employees in The Netherlands and Turkey. *International Journal of Intercultural Relations*, *49*, 68–79. doi:10.1016/j.ijintrel.2015.06.010

Ghodratollah, B., Matin, H. Z., & Amighi, F. (2011). The relationship between empowerment and organizational citizenship behavior of the pedagogical organization employees. *Iranian Journal of Management Studies*, *4*(2), 53–62.

Gilbert, S., Laschinger, H. K. S., & Leiter, M. (2010). The mediating effect of burnout on the relationship between structural empowerment and organizational citizenship behaviours. *Journal of Nursing Management, 18*(3), 339–348. doi:10.1111/j.1365-2834.2010.01074.x PMID:20546475

Glomb, T. M., Bhave, D. P., Miner, A. G., & Wall, M. (2011). Doing good, feeling good: Examining the role of organizational citizenship behaviors in changing mood. *Personnel Psychology, 64*(1), 191–223. doi:10.1111/j.1744-6570.2010.01206.x

Gonzalez, J. A., & Chakraborty, S. (2012). Image and similarity: An identity orientation perspective to organizational identification. *Leadership and Organization Development Journal, 33*(1), 51–65. doi:10.1108/01437731211193115

Graen, G. B., & Scandura, T. A. (1987). Toward a psychology of dyadic organizing. *Research in Organizational Behavior, 9*, 175–208.

Guay, R. P., & Choi, D. (2015). To whom does transformational leadership matter more? An examination of neurotic and introverted followers and their organizational citizenship behavior. *The Leadership Quarterly, 26*(5), 851–862. doi:10.1016/j.leaqua.2015.06.005

Halbesleben, J. R. B., Bowler, W. M., Bolino, M. C., & Turnley, W. H. (2010). Organizational concern, prosocial values, or impression management? How supervisors attribute motives to organizational citizenship behavior. *Journal of Applied Social Psychology, 40*(6), 1450–1489. doi:10.1111/j.1559-1816.2010.00625.x

Harris, K. J., Kacmar, K. M., & Zivnuska, S. (2007). An investigation of abusive supervision as a predictor of performance and the meaning of work as a moderator of the relationship. *The Leadership Quarterly, 18*(3), 252–263. doi:10.1016/j.leaqua.2007.03.007

Harvey, P., Stoner, J., Hochwarter, W., & Kacmar, C. (2007). Coping with abusive supervision: The neutralizing effects of ingratiation and positive affect on negative employee outcomes. *The Leadership Quarterly, 18*(3), 264–280. doi:10.1016/j.leaqua.2007.03.008

Henriksen, K., & Dayton, E. (2006). Organizational silence and hidden threats to patient safety. *Health Services Research, 41*(4), 1539–1554. doi:10.1111/j.1475-6773.2006.00564.x PMID:16898978

Hsiung, H. H., Lin, C. W., & Lin, C. S. (2012). Nourishing or suppressing? The contradictory influences of perception of organizational politics on organizational citizenship behaviour. *Journal of Occupational and Organizational Psychology, 85*(2), 258–276. doi:10.1111/j.2044-8325.2011.02030.x

Ilies, R., Nahrgang, J. D., & Morgeson, F. P. (2007). Leader-member exchange and citizenship behaviors: A meta-analysis. *The Journal of Applied Psychology, 92*(1), 269–277. doi:10.1037/0021-9010.92.1.269 PMID:17227168

Jansen, K. J., & Kristof-Brown, A. (2006). Toward a multidimensional theory of person-environment fit. *Journal of Managerial Issues, 18*(2), 193–212.

Jena, R. K., & Goswami, R. (2013). Exploring the relationship between organizational citizenship behavior and job satisfaction among shift workers in India. *Global Business and Organizational Excellence, 32*(6), 36–46. doi:10.1002/joe.21513

Jian, Z., Kwan, H. K., Qiu, Q., Liu, Z. Q., & Yim, F. H. K. (2012). Abusive supervision and frontline employees' service performance. *Service Industries Journal*, *32*(5), 683–698. doi:10.1080/02642069.2011.614338

Kane, R. E., Magnusen, M. J., & Perrewe, P. L. (2012). Differential effects of identification on extra-role behavior. *Career Development International*, *17*(1), 25–42. doi:10.1108/13620431211201319

Karadal, H., & Saygin, M. (2013). An investigation of the relationship between social loafing and organizational citizenship behavior. *Procedia: Social and Behavioral Sciences*, *99*, 206–215. doi:10.1016/j.sbspro.2013.10.487

Karatepe, O. M., & Olugbade, O. A. (2009). The effects of job and personal resources on hotel employees' work engagement. *International Journal of Hospitality Management*, *28*(4), 504–512. doi:10.1016/j.ijhm.2009.02.003

Karau, S. J., & Williams, K. D. (1993). Social loafing: A meta-analytic review and theoretical integration. *Journal of Personality and Social Psychology*, *65*(4), 681–706. doi:10.1037/0022-3514.65.4.681

Kasa, M., & Hassan, Z. (2015). The role of flow between burnout and organizational citizenship behavior (OCB) among hotel employees in Malaysia. *Procedia: Social and Behavioral Sciences*, *211*, 199–206. doi:10.1016/j.sbspro.2015.11.084

Kasemsap, K. (2012). Factor affecting organizational citizenship behavior of passenger car plant employees in Thailand. *Silpakorn University Journal of Social Sciences, Humanities, and Arts*, *12*(2), 129–159.

Kasemsap, K. (2013a). Innovative human resource practice: A synthesized framework and causal model of leader-member exchange, organizational justice, job satisfaction, and organizational citizenship behavior. *International Journal of e-Education, e-Business, e-. Management Learning*, *3*(1), 13–17. doi:10.7763/IJEEEE.2013.V3.185

Kasemsap, K. (2013b). Practical framework: Formation of causal model of job involvement, organizational commitment, organizational citizenship behavior, and organizational performance. *International Journal of Advances in Management, Technology & Engineering Sciences*, *2*(6-1), 22–26.

Kasemsap, K. (2015). The roles of cross-cultural perspectives in global marketing. In J. Alcántara-Pilar, S. del Barrio-García, E. Crespo-Almendros, & L. Porcu (Eds.), *Analyzing the cultural diversity of consumers in the global marketplace* (pp. 37–59). Hershey, PA: IGI Global. doi:10.4018/978-1-4666-8262-7.ch003

Kasemsap, K. (2016a). The roles of organizational justice, social justice, and organizational culture in global higher education. In N. Ololube (Ed.), *Handbook of research on organizational justice and culture in higher education institutions* (pp. 83–115). Hershey, PA: IGI Global. doi:10.4018/978-1-4666-9850-5.ch004

Kasemsap, K. (2016b). Promoting service quality and customer satisfaction in global business. In U. Panwar, R. Kumar, & N. Ray (Eds.), *Handbook of research on promotional strategies and consumer influence in the service sector* (pp. 247–276). Hershey, PA: IGI Global. doi:10.4018/978-1-5225-0143-5.ch015

Kasemsap, K. (2016c). Cultural perspectives and cultural dynamics: Advanced issues and approaches. *International Journal of Art, Culture and Design Technologies, 5*(1), 35–47. doi:10.4018/IJACDT.2016010103

Kasemsap, K. (2016d). A unified framework of organizational perspectives and knowledge management and their impact on job performance. In A. Normore, L. Long, & M. Javidi (Eds.), *Handbook of research on effective communication, leadership, and conflict resolution* (pp. 267–297). Hershey, PA: IGI Global. doi:10.4018/978-1-4666-9970-0.ch015

Kasemsap, K. (2016e). The roles of organizational change management and resistance to change in the modern business world. In A. Goksoy (Ed.), *Organizational change management strategies in modern business* (pp. 143–171). Hershey, PA: IGI Global. doi:10.4018/978-1-4666-9533-7.ch008

Kasemsap, K. (2016f). Utilizing complexity theory and complex adaptive systems in global business. In Ş. Erçetin & H. Bağcı (Eds.), *Handbook of research on chaos and complexity theory in the social sciences* (pp. 235–260). Hershey, PA: IGI Global. doi:10.4018/978-1-5225-0148-0.ch018

Kasemsap, K. (2017a). Examining the roles of job satisfaction and organizational commitment in the global workplace. In P. Ordoñez de Pablos & R. Tennyson (Eds.), *Handbook of research on human resources strategies for the new millennial workforce* (pp. 148–176). Hershey, PA: IGI Global. doi:10.4018/978-1-5225-0948-6.ch008

Kasemsap, K. (2017b). Management education and leadership styles: Current issues and approaches. In N. Baporikar (Ed.), *Innovation and shifting perspectives in management education* (pp. 166–193). Hershey, PA: IGI Global. doi:10.4018/978-1-5225-1019-2.ch008

Kasemsap, K. (2017c). The fundamentals of social capital. In G. Koç, M. Claes, & B. Christiansen (Eds.), *Cultural influences on architecture* (pp. 259–292). Hershey, PA: IGI Global. doi:10.4018/978-1-5225-1744-3.ch010

Kasemsap, K. (2017d). Organizational learning: Advanced issues and trends. In A. Bencsik (Ed.), *Knowledge management initiatives and strategies in small and medium enterprises* (pp. 42–66). Hershey, PA: IGI Global. doi:10.4018/978-1-5225-1642-2.ch003

Kasemsap, K. (2017e). Advocating problem-based learning and creative problem-solving skills in global education. In C. Zhou (Ed.), *Handbook of research on creative problem-solving skill development in higher education* (pp. 351–377). Hershey, PA: IGI Global. doi:10.4018/978-1-5225-0643-0.ch016

Kasemsap, K. (2017f). Investigating the roles of neuroscience and knowledge management in higher education. In S. Mukerji & P. Tripathi (Eds.), *Handbook of research on administration, policy, and leadership in higher education* (pp. 112–140). Hershey, PA: IGI Global. doi:10.4018/978-1-5225-0672-0.ch006

Kasemsap, K. (2017g). Mastering cognitive neuroscience and social neuroscience perspectives in the information age. In M. Dos Santos (Ed.), *Applying neuroscience to business practice* (pp. 82–113). Hershey, PA: IGI Global. doi:10.4018/978-1-5225-1028-4.ch005

Kazemipour, F., Amin, S. M., & Pourseidi, B. (2012). Relationship between workplace spirituality and organizational citizenship behavior among nurses through mediation of affective organizational commitment. *Journal of Nursing Scholarship, 44*(3), 302–310. doi:10.1111/j.1547-5069.2012.01456.x PMID:22804973

Kristof-Brown, A. L., Zimmerman, R. D., & Johnson, E. C. (2005). Consequences of individuals' fit at work: A meta-analysis of person-job, person-organization, person-group, and person-supervisor fit. *Personnel Psychology, 58*(2), 281–342. doi:10.1111/j.1744-6570.2005.00672.x

Kuhnel, J., Sonnentag, S., & Bledow, R. (2012). Resources and time pressure as day-level antecedents of work engagement. *Journal of Occupational and Organizational Psychology, 85*(1), 181–198. doi:10.1111/j.2044-8325.2011.02022.x

Lai, J. Y. M., Lam, L. W., & Lam, S. S. K. (2013). Organizational citizenship behavior in work groups: A team cultural perspective. *Journal of Organizational Behavior, 34*(7), 1039–1056.

Lau, D. C., & Lam, L. W. (2008). Effects of trusting and being trusted on team citizenship behaviours in chain stores. *Asian Journal of Social Psychology, 11*(2), 141–149. doi:10.1111/j.1467-839X.2008.00251.x

Lavelle, J. J., Brockner, J., Konovsky, M. A., Price, K. H., Henley, A. B., Taneja, A., & Vinekar, V. (2009). Commitment, procedural fairness, and organizational citizenship behavior: A multifoci analysis. *Journal of Organizational Behavior, 30*(3), 337–357. doi:10.1002/job.518

Law, S. K., Wong, C., & Chen, X. Z. (2005). The construct of organizational citizenship behavior: Should we analyze after we have conceptualized? In D. Turnipseed (Ed.), *Handbook of organizational citizenship behavior* (pp. 47–65). New York: Nova Science Publishers.

LePine, J. A., Erez, A., & Johnson, D. E. (2002). The nature and dimensionality of organizational citizenship behaviour: A critical review and meta-analysis. *The Journal of Applied Psychology, 87*(1), 52–65. doi:10.1037/0021-9010.87.1.52 PMID:11916216

Lian, H., Ferris, D. L., & Brown, D. J. (2012). Does power distance exacerbate or mitigate the effects of abusive supervision? It depends on the outcome. *The Journal of Applied Psychology, 97*(1), 107–123. doi:10.1037/a0024610 PMID:21766996

Lievens, F., Conway, J. M., & de Corte, W. (2008). The relative importance of task, citizenship and counterproductive performance to job performance ratings: Do rater source and team-based culture matter? *Journal of Occupational and Organizational Psychology, 81*(1), 11–27. doi:10.1348/096317907X182971

Lin, C. C., & Peng, T. K. (2010). From organizational citizenship behaviour to team performance: The mediation of group cohesion and collective efficacy. *Management and Organization Review, 6*(1), 55–75. doi:10.1111/j.1740-8784.2009.00172.x

Liu, X. Y., & Wang, J. (2013). Abusive supervision and organizational citizenship behaviour: Is supervisor–subordinate Guanxi a mediator? *International Journal of Human Resource Management, 24*(7), 1471–1489. doi:10.1080/09585192.2012.725082

Loi, R., Mao, Y., & Ngo, H. Y. (2009). Linking leader-member exchange and employee work outcomes: The mediating role of organizational social and economic exchange. *Management and Organization Review, 5*(3), 401–422. doi:10.1111/j.1740-8784.2009.00149.x

López-Domínguez, M., Enache, M., Sallan, J. M., & Simo, P. (2013). Transformational leadership as an antecedent of change-oriented organizational citizenship behavior. *Journal of Business Research, 66*(10), 2147–2152. doi:10.1016/j.jbusres.2013.02.041

Lyu, Y., Zhu, H., Zhong, H. J., & Hu, L. (2016). Abusive supervision and customer-oriented organizational citizenship behavior: The roles of hostile attribution bias and work engagement. *International Journal of Hospitality Management, 53*, 69–80. doi:10.1016/j.ijhm.2015.12.001

MacKenzie, S. B., Podsakoff, P. M., & Podsakoff, N. P. (2011). Challenge-oriented organizational citizenship behaviors and organizational effectiveness: Do challenge-oriented behaviors really have an impact on the organization's bottom line? *Personnel Psychology, 64*(3), 559–592. doi:10.1111/j.1744-6570.2011.01219.x

Mael, F., & Ashforth, B. (1992). Alumni and their alma maters: A partial test of the reformulated model of organizational identification. *Journal of Organizational Behavior, 13*(2), 103–123. doi:10.1002/job.4030130202

Magdalena, S. M. (2014). The effects of organizational citizenship behavior in the academic environment. *Procedia: Social and Behavioral Sciences, 127*, 738–742. doi:10.1016/j.sbspro.2014.03.346

Milliken, F. J., Morrison, E. W., & Hewlin, P. F. (2003). An exploratory study of employee silence: Issues that employees don't communicate upward and why. *Journal of Management Studies, 40*(6), 1453–1476. doi:10.1111/1467-6486.00387

Morrison, E. W., & Milliken, F. J. (2000). Organizational silence: A barrier to change and development in a pluralistic world. *Academy of Management Review, 25*(4), 706–725.

Newton, S. K., & Nowak, L. I. (2013). Attitudes and work environment factors influencing the information technology professionals' work behaviors. *International Journal of Human Capital and Information Technology Professionals, 4*(4), 46–65. doi:10.4018/ijhcitp.2013100104

Newton, S. K., Nowak, L. I., & Blanton, J. E. (2012). The relationship between the fulfillment of the IT professional's psychological contract and their organizational citizenship and innovative work behaviors. In *Human resources management: Concepts, methodologies, tools, and applications* (pp. 1085–1105). Hershey, PA: IGI Global. doi:10.4018/978-1-4666-1601-1.ch067

Ng, S. M., Ke, G. N., & Raymond, W. (2014). The mediating role of work locus of control on the relationship among emotional intelligence, organisational citizenship behaviours, and mental health among nurses. *Australian Journal of Psychology, 66*(4), 207–215. doi:10.1111/ajpy.12049

Ng, T. W. H., Lam, S. S. K., & Feldman, D. C. (2016). Organizational citizenship behavior and counterproductive work behavior: Do males and females differ? *Journal of Vocational Behavior, 93*, 11–32. doi:10.1016/j.jvb.2015.12.005

Nikmaram, S., Yamchi, G. H., Shojaii, S., Zahrani, M. A., & Alvani, S. M. (2012). Study on relationship between organizational silence and commitment in Iran. *World Applied Sciences Journal, 17*(10), 1271–1277.

Oplatka, I. (2009). Organizational citizenship behavior in teaching: The consequences for teachers, pupils, and the school. *International Journal of Educational Management, 23*(5), 375–389. doi:10.1108/09513540910970476

Organ, D. W. (1988). *Organizational citizenship behavior: The good soldier syndrome*. Lexington, MA: Lexington Books.

Organ, D. W., Podsakoff, P. M., & MacKenzie, S. B. (2006). *Organizational citizenship behavior: Its nature, antecedents, and consequences*. London, UK: Sage Publications.

Özçelik, G., & Fındıklı, M. A. (2014). The relationship between internal branding and organizational citizenship behaviour: The mediating role of person-organization fit. *Procedia: Social and Behavioral Sciences*, *150*, 1120–1128. doi:10.1016/j.sbspro.2014.09.127

Özdemir, Y., & Ergun, S. (2015). The relationship between organizational socialization and organizational citizenship behavior: The mediating role of person-environment fit. *Procedia: Social and Behavioral Sciences*, *207*, 432–443. doi:10.1016/j.sbspro.2015.10.113

Parker, S. K., & Axtell, C. M. (2001). Seeing another viewpoint: Antecedents and outcomes of employee perspective taking. *Academy of Management Journal*, *44*(6), 1085–1100. doi:10.2307/3069390

Pavalache-Ilie, M. (2014). Organizational citizenship behaviour, work satisfaction and employees' personality. *Procedia: Social and Behavioral Sciences*, *127*, 489–493. doi:10.1016/j.sbspro.2014.03.296

Podsakoff, N. P., Podsakoff, P. M., MacKenzie, S. B., Maynes, T. D., & Spoelma, T. M. (2014). Consequences of unit-level organizational citizenship behaviors: A review and recommendations for future research. *Journal of Organizational Behavior*, *35*(Suppl. 1), S87–S119. doi:10.1002/job.1911

Podsakoff, P. M., MacKenzie, S. B., Paine, J. B., & Bachrach, D. G. (2000). Organizational citizenship behaviors: A critical review of the theoretical and empirical literature and suggestions for future research. *Journal of Management*, *26*(3), 513–563. doi:10.1177/014920630002600307

Popescu, A. M., Deaconu, A., & Popescu, T., (2015). Organization's age and organizational citizenship behavior (OCB), performance criteria at SMEs level. Case study - Bucharest – Ilfov development region. *Procedia Economics and Finance*, *22*, 645–654. doi:10.1016/S2212-5671(15)00278-6

Reynolds, C. A., Shoss, M. K., & Jundt, D. K. (2015). In the eye of the beholder: A multi-stakeholder perspective of organizational citizenship and counterproductive work behaviors. *Human Resource Management Review*, *25*(1), 80–93. doi:10.1016/j.hrmr.2014.06.002

Rotundo, M., & Sackett, P. R. (2002). The relative importance of task, citizenship, and counterproductive performance to global ratings of job performance: A policy-capturing approach. *The Journal of Applied Psychology*, *87*(1), 66–80. doi:10.1037/0021-9010.87.1.66 PMID:11916217

Seppälä, T., Lipponen, J., Bardi, A., & Pirttilä-Backman, A. M. (2012). Change-oriented organizational citizenship behaviour: An interactive product of openness to change values, work unit identification, and sense of power. *Journal of Occupational and Organizational Psychology*, *85*(1), 136–155. doi:10.1111/j.2044-8325.2010.02010.x

Serim, H., Demirbağ, O., & Yozgat, U. (2014). The effects of employees' perceptions of competency models on employability outcomes and organizational citizenship behavior and the moderating role of social exchange in this effect. *Procedia: Social and Behavioral Sciences*, *150*, 1101–1110. doi:10.1016/j.sbspro.2014.09.125

Snape, E., & Redman, T. (2010). HRM practices, organizational citizenship behaviour, and performance: A multi-level analysis. *Journal of Management Studies, 47*(7), 1219–1247.

Soltani, S., Elkhani, N., & Bardsiri, V. K. (2014). The effects of perceived organizational support and organizational citizenship behaviors on continuance intention of enterprise resource planning. *International Journal of Enterprise Information Systems, 10*(2), 81–102. doi:10.4018/ijeis.2014040105

Spector, P. E., & Fox, S. (2010). Counterproductive work behavior and organisational citizenship behavior: Are they opposite forms of active behavior? *Applied Psychology, 59*(1), 21–39. doi:10.1111/j.1464-0597.2009.00414.x

Spence, J. R., Ferris, D. L., Brown, D. J., & Heller, D. (2011). Understanding daily citizenship behaviors: A social comparison perspective. *Journal of Organizational Behavior, 32*(4), 547–571. doi:10.1002/job.738

Tangirala, S., & Ramanujam, R. (2008). Employee silence on critical issues: The cross level effects procedural justice climate. *Personnel Psychology, 61*(1), 37–68. doi:10.1111/j.1744-6570.2008.00105.x

Tepper, B. J. (2000). Consequences of abusive supervision. *Academy of Management Journal, 43*(2), 178–190. doi:10.2307/1556375

Tepper, B. J., Carr, J. C., Breaux, D. M., Geider, S., Hu, C., & Hua, W. (2009). Abusive supervision, intentions to quit, and employees' workplace deviance: A power/dependence analysis. *Organizational Behavior and Human Decision Processes, 109*(2), 156–167. doi:10.1016/j.obhdp.2009.03.004

Tepper, B. J., Duffy, M. K., Hoobler, J. M., & Ensley, M. D. (2004). Moderators of the relationship between coworkers' organizational citizenship behavior and fellow employees' attitudes. *The Journal of Applied Psychology, 89*(3), 455–465. doi:10.1037/0021-9010.89.3.455 PMID:15161405

Tepper, B. J., Duffy, M. K., & Shaw, J. D. (2001). Personality moderators of the relationships between abusive supervision and subordinates' resistance. *The Journal of Applied Psychology, 86*(5), 974–983. doi:10.1037/0021-9010.86.5.974 PMID:11596813

Tsai, Y., & Wu, S. W. (2010). The relationships between organisational citizenship behaviour, job satisfaction and turnover intention. *Journal of Clinical Nursing, 19*(23/24), 3564–3574. doi:10.1111/j.1365-2702.2010.03375.x PMID:20964747

Uçanok, B., & Karabatı, S. (2013). The effects of values, work centrality, and organizational commitment on organizational citizenship behaviors: Evidence from Turkish SMEs. *Human Resource Development Quarterly, 24*(1), 89–129. doi:10.1002/hrdq.21156

Ulke, H. E., & Bilgic, R. (2011). Investigating the role of the big five on the social loafing of information technology workers. *International Journal of Selection and Assessment, 19*(3), 301–312. doi:10.1111/j.1468-2389.2011.00559.x

Vakola, M., & Bouradas, D. (2005). Antecedents and consequences of organizational silence: An empirical investigation. *Employee Relations, 27*(5), 441–458. doi:10.1108/01425450510611997

van Scotter, J. R., & Motowidlo, S. J. (1996). Interpersonal facilitation and job dedication as separate facets of contextual performance. *The Journal of Applied Psychology, 81*(5), 525–531. doi:10.1037/0021-9010.81.5.525

van Vianen, A., Shen, C., & Chuang, A. (2011). Person-organization and person-supervisor fits: Employee commitments in China context. *Journal of Organizational Behavior, 32*(6), 906–926. doi:10.1002/job.726

Vigoda-Gadot, E., & Cohen, A. (2004). *Citizenship and management in public administration: Integrating behavioral theories and managerial thinking.* London, UK: Edward Elgar Publishing.

Walz, S. M., & Niehoff, B. P. (2000). Organizational citizenship behaviors: Their relationship to organizational effectiveness. *Journal of Hospitality & Tourism Research (Washington, D.C.), 24*(3), 301–319. doi:10.1177/109634800002400301

White, L., & Yanamandrama, V. (2012). Why do some business relationships persist despite dissatisfaction? A social exchange review. *Asia Pacific Management Review, 17*(3), 301–319.

Whitman, D. S., van Rooy, D. L., & Viswesvaran, C. (2010). Satisfaction, citizenship behaviors, and performance in work units: A meta-analysis of collective construct relations. *Personnel Psychology, 63*(1), 41–81. doi:10.1111/j.1744-6570.2009.01162.x

Williams, L. J., & Anderson, S. E. (1991). Job satisfaction and organizational commitment as predictors of organizational citizenship and in-role behaviors. *Journal of Management, 17*(3), 601–617. doi:10.1177/014920639101700305

Yaniv, E., & Farkas, F. (2005). The impact of person-organization fit on the corporate brand perception of employees and of customers. *Journal of Change Management, 5*(4), 447–461. doi:10.1080/14697010500372600

Yildirim, O. (2015). The impact of organizational communication on organizational citizenship behavior: Research findings. *Procedia: Social and Behavioral Sciences, 150*, 1095–1100. doi:10.1016/j.sbspro.2014.09.124

ADDITIONAL READING

Adams, J. W., Srivastava, A., Herriot, P., & Patterson, F. (2012). Careerist orientation and organizational citizenship behavior in expatriates and non-expatriates. *Journal of Career Development, 40*(6), 469–489. doi:10.1177/0894845312472255

Alessandri, G., Vecchione, M., Tisak, J., Deiana, G., Caria, S., & Caprara, G. V. (2012). The utility of positive orientation in predicting job performance and organisational citizenship behaviors. *Applied Psychology, 61*(4), 669–698. doi:10.1111/j.1464-0597.2012.00511.x

Barbuto, J. E. Jr, & Story, J. S. P. (2011). Work motivation and organizational citizenship behaviors. *The Journal of Leadership Studies, 5*(1), 23–34. doi:10.1002/jls.20202

Bergeron, D. M., Shipp, A. J., Rosen, B., & Furst, S. A. (2013). Organizational citizenship behavior and career outcomes: The cost of being a good citizen. *Journal of Management, 39*(4), 958–984. doi:10.1177/0149206311407508

Bolino, M. C., Klotz, A. C., Turnley, W. H., & Harvey, J. (2013). Exploring the dark side of organizational citizenship behavior. *Journal of Organizational Behavior*, *34*(4), 542–559. doi:10.1002/job.1847

Bourdage, J. S., Lee, K., Lee, J., & Shin, K. (2012). Motives for organizational citizenship behavior: Personality correlates and coworker ratings of OCB. *Human Performance*, *25*(3), 179–200. doi:10.1080/08959285.2012.683904

Braun, T., Ferreira, A. I., & Sydow, J. (2013). Citizenship behavior and effectiveness in temporary organizations. *International Journal of Project Management*, *31*(6), 862–876. doi:10.1016/j.ijproman.2012.09.003

Carpenter, N. C., Berry, C. M., & Houston, L. (2014). A meta-analytic comparison of self-reported and other-reported organizational citizenship behavior. *Journal of Organizational Behavior*, *35*(4), 547–574. doi:10.1002/job.1909

Carter, L., McFadden-Wade, G., & Wells, J. T. (2016). Exploring the impact of organizational citizenship behavior on perceptions of e-filing success. *International Journal of Public Administration in the Digital Age*, *3*(1), 43–52. doi:10.4018/IJPADA.2016010103

Chou, S. Y., & Lopez-Rodriguez, E. (2013). An empirical examination of service-oriented organizational citizenship behavior: The roles of justice perceptions and manifest needs. *Managing Service Quarterly*, *23*(6), 474–494. doi:10.1108/MSQ-02-2013-0019

Cohen, A., Ben-Tura, E., & Vashdi, D. R. (2012). The relationship between social exchange variables, OCBs, and performance: What happens when you consider group characteristics? *Personnel Review*, *41*(6), 705–731. doi:10.1108/00483481211263638

Coldwell, D. A. L., & Callaghan, C. W. (2014). Specific organizational citizenship behaviours and organizational effectiveness: The development of a conceptual heuristic device. *Journal for the Theory of Social Behaviour*, *44*(3), 347–367. doi:10.1111/jtsb.12046

Du, J., Choi, J. N., & Hashem, F. (2012). Interaction between one's own and other's procedural justice perceptions and citizenship behaviors in organizational teams: The moderating role of group identification. *Group Dynamics*, *16*(4), 289–302. doi:10.1037/a0028524

Ersoy, N. C., Born, M. P., Derous, E., & van der Molen, H. (2011). Antecedents of organizational citizenship behavior among blue- and white-collar workers in Turkey. *International Journal of Intercultural Relations*, *35*(3), 356–367. doi:10.1016/j.ijintrel.2010.05.002

Evans, W. R., Goodman, J. M., & Davis, W. D. (2011). The impact of perceived corporate citizenship on organizational cynicism, OCB, and employee deviance. *Human Performance*, *24*(1), 79–97. doi:10.1080/08959285.2010.530632

Fox, S., Spector, P. E., Goh, A., Bruursema, K., & Kessler, S. R. (2012). The deviant citizen: Measuring potential positive relations between counterproductive work behaviour and organizational citizenship behaviour. *Journal of Occupational and Organizational Psychology*, *85*(1), 199–220. doi:10.1111/j.2044-8325.2011.02032.x

Ghosh, R., Reio, T. G. Jr, & Haynes, R. K. (2012). Mentoring and organizational citizenship behavior: Estimating the mediating effects of organization-based self-esteem and affective commitment. *Human Resource Development Quarterly, 23*(1), 41–63. doi:10.1002/hrdq.21121

Gillmore, P. L., Hu, X., Wei, F., Tetrick, L. E., & Zaccaro, S. J. (2013). Positive affectivity neutralizes transformational leadership's influence on creative performance and organizational citizenship behaviors. *Journal of Organizational Behavior, 34*(8), 1061–1075. doi:10.1002/job.1833

Harris, T. B., Li, N., & Kirkman, B. L. (2014). Leader-member exchange (LMX) in context: How LMX differentiation and LMX relational separation attenuate LMX's influence on OCB and turnover intention. *The Leadership Quarterly, 25*(2), 314–328. doi:10.1016/j.leaqua.2013.09.001

Ho, V. T., & Gupta, N. (2012). Testing an empathy model of guest-directed citizenship and counterproductive behaviors in the hospitality industry: Findings from three hotels. *Journal of Occupational and Organizational Psychology, 85*(3), 433–453. doi:10.1111/j.2044-8325.2011.02046.x

Jawahar, I. M. (2012). Mediating role of satisfaction with growth opportunities on the relationship between employee development opportunities and citizenship behaviors and burnout. *Journal of Applied Social Psychology, 42*(9), 2257–2284. doi:10.1111/j.1559-1816.2012.00939.x

Jensen, J. M., & Raver, J. L. (2012). When self-management and surveillance collide: Consequences for employees' organizational citizenship and counterproductive work behaviors. *Group & Organization Management, 37*(3), 308–346. doi:10.1177/1059601112445804

Jiang, J. Y., Sun, L., & Law, K. S. (2011). Job satisfaction and organization structure as moderators of the effects of empowerment on organizational citizenship behavior: A self-consistency and social exchange perspective. *International Journal of Management, 28*(3), 675–693.

Jiao, C., Richards, D. A., & Hackett, R. D. (2013). Organizational citizenship behavior and role breadth: A meta-analytic and cross-cultural analysis. *Human Resource Management, 52*(5), 697–714. doi:10.1002/hrm.21555

Kim, Y., van Dyne, L., Kamdar, D., & Johnson, R. E. (2013). Why and when do motives matter? An integrative model of motives, role cognitions, and social support as predictors of OCB. *Organizational Behavior and Human Decision Processes, 121*(2), 231–245. doi:10.1016/j.obhdp.2013.03.004

Lev, S., & Koslowsky, M. (2012). Teacher gender as a moderator of the on-the-job embeddedness-OCB relationship. *Journal of Applied Social Psychology, 42*(1), 81–99. doi:10.1111/j.1559-1816.2011.00868.x

Miao, R. T. (2011). Perceived organizational support, job satisfaction, task performance and organizational citizenship behavior in China. *Journal of Behavioral and Applied Management, 12*(2), 105–127.

Ohana, M. (2016). Voice, affective commitment and citizenship behavior in teams: The moderating role of neuroticism and intrinsic motivation. *British Journal of Management, 27*(1), 97–115. doi:10.1111/1467-8551.12146

Ozer, M., Chang, C. H., & Schaubroeck, J. M. (2014). Contextual moderators of the relationship between organizational citizenship behaviours and challenge and hindrance stress. *Journal of Occupational and Organizational Psychology, 87*(3), 557–578. doi:10.1111/joop.12063

Rayner, J., Lawton, A., & Williams, H. M. (2012). Organizational citizenship behavior and the public service ethos: Whither the organization? *Journal of Business Ethics*, *106*(2), 117–130. doi:10.1007/s10551-011-0991-x

Rubin, R. S., Dierdorff, E. C., & Bachrach, D. G. (2013). Boundaries of citizenship behavior: Curvilinearity and context in the citizenship and task performance relationship. *Personnel Psychology*, *66*(2), 377–406. doi:10.1111/peps.12018

Sharoni, G., Tziner, A., Fein, E. C., Shultz, T., Shaul, K., & Zilberman, L. (2012). Organizational citizenship behavior and turnover intentions: Do organizational culture and justice moderate their relationship? *Journal of Applied Social Psychology*, *42*(Suppl. 1), E267–E294. doi:10.1111/j.1559-1816.2012.01015.x

Shih, C. T., & Chen, S. J. (2011). The social dilemma perspective on psychological contract fulfilment and organizational citizenship behaviour. *Management and Organization Review*, *7*(1), 125–151. doi:10.1111/j.1740-8784.2010.00202.x

Sommer, K. L., & Kulkarni, M. (2012). Does constructive performance feedback improve citizenship intentions and job satisfaction? The roles of perceived opportunities for advancement, respect, and mood. *Human Resource Development Quarterly*, *23*(2), 177–201. doi:10.1002/hrdq.21132

Spence, J. R., Brown, D. J., Keeping, L. M., & Lian, H. (2014). Helpful today, but not tomorrow? Feeling grateful as a predictor of daily organizational citizenship behaviors. *Personnel Psychology*, *67*(3), 705–738.

Sun, L., Chow, I. H. S., Chiu, R. K., & Pan, W. (2013). Outcome favorability in the link between leader member exchange and organizational citizenship behavior: Procedural fairness climate matters. *The Leadership Quarterly*, *24*(1), 215–226. doi:10.1016/j.leaqua.2012.10.008

Taylor, J. (2013). Goal setting in the Australian public service: Effects on psychological empowerment and organizational citizenship behavior. *Public Administration Review*, *73*(3), 453–464. doi:10.1111/puar.12040

Turnipseed, P. H., & Turnipseed, D. L. (2013). Testing the proposed linkage between organizational citizenship behaviours and an innovative organizational climate. *Creativity and Innovation Management*, *22*(2), 209–216. doi:10.1111/caim.12027

Zhang, G., Bai, Y., Caza, A., & Wang, L. (2014). Leader integrity and organizational citizenship behavior in China. *Management and Organization Review*, *10*(2), 299–319.

Zhang, Y., & Chen, C. C. (2013). Development leadership and organizational citizenship behavior: Mediating effects of self-determination, supervisor identification, and organizational identification. *The Leadership Quarterly*, *24*(4), 534–543. doi:10.1016/j.leaqua.2013.03.007

Zheng, W., Zhang, M., & Li, H. (2012). Performance appraisal process and organizational citizenship behavior. *Journal of Managerial Psychology*, *27*(7), 732–752. doi:10.1108/02683941211259548

Zhong, J. A., Lam, W., & Chen, Z. (2011). Relationship between leader-member exchange and organizational citizenship behaviors: Examining the moderating role of empowerment. *Asia Pacific Journal of Management, 28*(3), 609–626. doi:10.1007/s10490-009-9163-2

Ziegler, R., Schlett, C., Casel, K., & Diehl, M. (2012). The role of job satisfaction, job ambivalence, and emotions at work in predicting organizational citizenship behavior. *Journal of Personnel Psychology, 11*(4), 176–190. doi:10.1027/1866-5888/a000071

KEY TERMS AND DEFINITIONS

Attitude: A predisposition or a tendency to respond positively or negatively toward a certain idea, object, person, or situation.

Behavior: A response of an individual or group to an action, environment, person, or stimulus.

Counterproductive Work Behavior: The action of employees conducting against the goals and aims of their employer.

Leader-Member Exchange Theory: The theory that describes how leaders in groups maintain their position through an array of tacit exchange agreements with their members.

Leadership: The activity of leading a group of people or an organization or the ability to do this issue.

Organizational Citizenship Behavior: The extent to which an employee's voluntary support and behavior contributes to the organization's success.

Organizational Effectiveness: The efficiency with which an association is able to meet its objectives.

Organizational Identification: The situation in which the employees and the company share the same goals and values.

Person-Organization Fit: The congruence between individuals and organizational factors.

Socialization: The process by which individuals acquire the knowledge, language, social skills, and value to conform to the norms and roles required for the integration into a group or community.

Chapter 2
Emotional Aspects of Leadership in the Modern Workplace

Vaitsa Giannouli
Aristotle University of Thessaloniki, Greece

ABSTRACT

Although leadership has been extensively examined in the field of industrial-organizational psychology, management and business, until now there is scarce research focusing on the different emotional aspects of the leaders and the influence that they may have on their subordinates. This review explores emotions in healthcare workplaces-hospitals through the prism of emotional intelligence, emotion regulation, emotional labor, job satisfaction, burnout, and anxiety. The above emotional aspects of employees are presented along with selected paradigms coming from the Greek and international modern healthcare management research. The chapter closes with future directions-research questions on leadership issues in the modern healthcare workplace.

INTRODUCTION: LEADERS AND SUBORDINATES IN MODERN ORGANIZATIONS

Leadership is considered to be a social influence process through which a leader affects thoughts, feelings, and behavior of other individuals called subordinates (Humphrey, 2002; Pirola-Merlo, Härtel, Mann, & Hirst, 2002). In the relevant scientific literature, leadership identifies mainly with the exercise of managerial or supervisory duties of the person in charge that is with the variety of behaviors used by the person in the leading position in order to influence the behavior of subordinates and to achieve the goals-objectives of the company that they have set or others have preset (Burch & Guarana, 2014; Hill & Jones, 2004; Chatzipanteli, 1998). However, it would be better to examine the concept of leadership as a behavior within the respective companies or organizations and through the prism of influence and interaction processes between two or more individuals characterized as the person exercising the influ-

DOI: 10.4018/978-1-5225-2568-4.ch002

ence (leader) and the people who receive this influence (subordinates-followers) (Chiu, Balkunid & Weinberg, 2016; Katz & Kahn, 1966; Piperopoulos, 2007).

Following this separation as in all prior studies, we can adopt the double grouping and examine individuals as belonging either to the group of the leaders or the subordinates. In recent years, a new theoretical trend has appeared in psychological research about working environments, which examines the leadership holistically and accepts that it is a complex, dynamic and mostly interactive relational process with impact and influence, not only limited to the leader, but influence that includes also the subordinates and the general social group (Avolio, 2005; House, 1996). In general, the interaction between leaders and subordinates gives emphasis on the examination of the feelings of the involved individuals and the effect they have not only on their own attitudes, cognition and behavior (Bryman, 1996), but mainly on the attitudes and behavior of other people in the workplace (Montano et al., 2016; Van Kleef, 2009; Van Kleef, Homan & Cheshin, 2012).

We must admit that emotions are not simple products of intra-individual processes (Lang, 1984; Power & Dalgleish, 1997), but also products of social processes that are not just isolated individual reactions. In fact, they should be regarded as social phenomena, since the causes of emotions are interpersonal and even culturally related with strong interpersonal consequences to other people (Parkinson, 1996; Parkinson, Fischer & Manstead, 2004). Today based on the above there is a growing interest in shaping the theory and research in workplaces through the prism of interpersonal relationships between leaders and subordinates with emphasis on the emotional dimension (Ashkanasy, Härtel & Zerbe, 2000; Garcia-Prieto, Mackie & Smith, 2007; Kupers & Weibler, 2008; Lewis, 2000).

However, the number of relevant research addressing the workplace as an 'emotional space' is still limited, while the amount of research emphasizing the unequal nature of these relations, mistakenly focuses on the one-way effect of socio-emotional capacities of leaders over their subordinates (Bono et al., 2007; George, 2000; Keller, 2003; Montano et al., 2016; Rowold, Borgmann & Bormann, 2015).

WHY ARE EMOTIONS IMPORTANT TO LEADERS?

The distinction between leaders and subordinates is clear; consequently, the argument that general positive dimensions of the emotions of the 'leaders' (e.g., developed Emotional Intelligence skills) relate (since we cannot infer that cause) to positive dimensions (e.g., emotional wellbeing, augmented performance at work) both for themselves and for their subordinates has been widely supported (Connelly & Gooty, 2015; Goleman, 1998a; Sy, Tram, & O'Hara, 2006; Wong & Law, 2002). More specifically, theories of charismatic leadership claim that leaders affect in a decisive way their followers' feelings and emotions and secondarily their performance (Braun et al., 2015; Brief & Weiss, 2002; Humphrey, Burch & Adams, 2016; Koning & VanKleef, 2015; Martin et al., 2016).

It should be noted the emotion definitions are still vague and vary considerably in the scientific literature, despite various theories that have been proposed for the feelings such as evolutionary theories, cognitive evaluation theories, and social construction theories of emotion. Generally, emotions are studied as internal phenomena that can be subject to observation and measurement by their expression through behavior. Some researchers define emotions as emotional conditions and measure these conditions with various self-report questionnaires (Niedenthal, Krauth-Gruber, & Ric, 2006). The use of self-reports of emotion suggests that emotions are or can be made conscious and that people are able to contemplate these conscious states and to quantify them in some reliable way (Barrett, 2004).

Emotions in the Workplace

Although the emotional interaction-exchange between leaders and subordinates is considered to play a crucial role in organizations (Miao, Humphrey & Quan, 2016; Pescosolido, 2002; Putnam & Mumby, 1993), until recently emotions were generally seen as dysfunctional factors that excluded the 'perfect professional' behavior, which was identified with the rational and carefully controlled emotional behavior in the workplace (Arvey, Renz, & Watson, 1998; Ashforth & Humphrey, 1995; Muchinsky, 2000). Nevertheless, emotions in the workplace greatly affect how an entire organization communicates both internally and with the outside world. The consequences of emotional states in the workplace are essential not only for individuals, but also for groups and the entire society (Weiss, 2002). Positive emotions at work help employees achieve positive outcomes, such as quicker completion of a project (Staw, Sutton, & Pelled, 1994), while negative emotions such as fear, anger, anxiety, aggression, sorrow and guilt appear to increase the predictability of deviant behavior in the workplace (Lee & Allen, 2002).

Considering leadership as an emotional process during which leaders express some feelings and attempt to stimulate some emotions to their subordinates (George, 2000; Dasborough & Ashkanasy, 2002) does not reflect the current trend in research, which shows that it is absolutely necessary not only to find the emotional aspects and the correlation between them. It also demonstrates the need to consider the nature of the relationship itself and how it interacts with the individual characteristics of both sides of the relationship. This occurs because people in the workplace do not act in a social gap simply carrying their own characteristics, but they always interact within a context of social relations and more particularly in relationships with people who are either in the upper or in the lower level of hierarchy in the workplace (having the same or different individual psychological characteristics) (Kafetsios, 2003; Riggio & Reichard, 2008; Zaccaro, 2007).

Recent research indicates there is a variation in different social-cultural contexts as far as the effect of specific emotional 'undesirable' characteristics that leaders have over their subordinates is concerned (Mccord, Joseph, & Grijalva, 2014). More specifically, in Greece some studies show evidence that 'negative' features of the leaders in the workplace, such as insecure attachment type and a greater tendency to control their personal emotions, have a positive effect on the emotions and the sensed satisfaction from work that their subordinates experience (Kafetsios, Athanasiadou, & Dimou, 2014; Kafetsios, Nezlek, & Vasiou, 2011; Kafetsios, Nezlek, & Vassilakou, 2012).

The same characteristics of the leaders seem to have a negative effect on the emotions and the satisfaction from work that their subordinates experience (Kafetsios, Athanasiadou, & Dimou, 2014; Kafetsios, Nezlek, & Vasiou, 2011; Kafetsios, Nezlek, & Vassilakou, 2012). One possible explanation for this paradox is that in countries such as Greece, where there is a widespread attitude towards leadership as something distant, leaders are deemed to be individuals who are obliged to have these 'negative' features and especially emotional repression. In this way, the perceptions of subordinates and society can shape the feelings and behaviors of their leaders (Shondrick, Dinh, & Lord, 2010).

Based on previous theoretical and empirical research, emotional aspects in the workplace can be examined as simple emotions (e.g., happiness, fear, pride) (Grandey, 2008), but also in the form of more complex emotional aspects such as emotional intelligence, emotion regulation, emotional labor, job satisfaction, burnout, and anxiety (Ashkanasy & Cooper; Bolton, 2004; Fineman, 2000).

EMOTIONAL INTELLIGENCE

Today various aspects of emotion are examined, not only individually, but also in a broader social-interactive way (Hare, 1986; Keltner & Haidt, 2001). Certainly research efforts to date place particular emphasis on the examination of the concept of Emotional Intelligence (EI) in the workplace as a general personal competence (Stein & Book, 2010) with the examination of self in the light of individual relevant to EI skills (Caruso, Mayer & Salovey, 2002), which correspond to statements such as (Goleman, 1998b; Wong & Law, 2002):

Most of the time I understand (I have a good sense) why I am possessed of some emotion
I have a good understanding of my feelings
I always understand how I really feel
I always know if I'm happy or not [awareness of emotion in self]
I can always understand how my friends feel based on their behavior
I am a good observer of the feelings of others
I am sensitive to the feelings and emotional states of other people
I have a good understanding of people's emotions [awareness of emotion in others]
I always set goals for myself and then I do my best to meet them
I always tell myself that I am a capable person
I am a person with strong incentives
I always urge myself to accomplish the best [use of emotion]
I have a good control of my emotions [emotion regulation].

Such EI-related skills can be developed and become the subject of learning (Bagshaw, 2000; Cherniss et al., 1998; Nelis et al., 2009). Increased expression of interest in the workplace for EI has arisen mainly because of the large percentage of businesses, which are now operating in the service sector, and also due to the publicity for the EI concept (Briner, 1999; Colfax, Rivera & Perez, 2010; Vakola, Tsaousis & Nikolaou, 2003), and due to the low predictive value that the classic Intelligence Quotient (IQ) has in business performance (Dulewicz & Higgs, 2000). Emotions and EI are at the heart of effective leadership (Goleman, 2001; Goleman, Boyatzis & McKee, 2001), and EI skills have positive effects on the procedures associated with the feelings-emotions of workers as well as general work-related productivity results (Ashkanasy, Härtel & Daus, 2002; Humphray, 2015; Mayer, Roberts & Barsade, 2008).

It seems that EI has a particular importance for employees; a case in point is the group of physicians working in hospital units (Arora et al., 2010). Physicians-employees with high EI tend to regulate more effectively their emotions, they can manage their interactions with other people (Wong & Law, 2002) and their patients (Weng et al., 2008), they are described as the very successful professionals by others (Dulewicz & Higgs, 2000; Weisinger, 1998), they manage more effectively private or non-private healthcare businesses (Cooper & Sawaf, 1997; Palmer, Donaldson & Stough, 2002; Prati et al., 2003; Higgs & Rowland, 2002), they achieve greater efficiency when they are the leaders of a working group (Prati et al., 2003), they can ensure greater workers' commitment, they can improve the quality of services and get greater loyalty from the customer side (Zeidner, Matthews, & Roberts, 2004), they show greater adaptability to stressful circumstances (Nikolaou & Tsaousis, 2002), they have better coping strategies for potential future problems (Bar-On & Parker, 2000; Bar-On et al., 2000), and they feel less job insecurity compared to individuals who have low EI (Jordan et al., 2002).

Specifically, findings from the Greek cultural context show that EI in the field of educational workers serves as a predictor for emotion in work and experienced job satisfaction (Kafetsios & Zampetakis, 2008). This finding is also evident in physicians (subordinates) working in hospitals, as well as in their leaders (head of clinics) (Giannouli, 2014). While for other groups of employees such as teachers working in public schools a differentiation is found for this effect depending on the age of the individuals (Kafetsios & Loumakou, 2007). Similar findings on EI from abroad for other groups of workers (e.g., food service workers) support the positive role that it plays on all aspects of behavior and on both leaders and their subordinates (Howard, 2009; Sy, Tram, & O'Hara, 2006).

EMOTION REGULATION

Emotions provide information about the relationship that an individual has with the material and social environment. The efficient management-regulation of emotions is of major importance for optimal social functioning, as this ability allows a person to express in a socially acceptable way how they feel and allows them to behave in socially acceptable ways toward others. It is of great interest that the fact that the emotion regulation or in other words the conscious (and / or unconscious sometimes) attempt to control emotions in the form of cognitive reframing (cognitive reappraisal) or expressive suppression (expressive suppression) (Gross, 1999; 2007; Gross & John, 2003) occurs in the workplace both in leaders (Glasø & Eienarsen, 2008), and subordinates.

The emotion regulation refers to the processes that people use to influence the feelings that they experience, or not experience, but also refers to the manner and to the extent that they eventually express those emotions (Niedenthal, Krauth-Gruber & Ric, 2006). In social exchanges in the workplace, emotion expression and emotion regulation have taken center stage in the management literature and are considered to be essential for the development and maintenance of interpersonal relationships (Ballinger & Rockmann, 2010; Butler et al., 2003; Gooty et al., 2015; Harker & Keltner, 2001; Lawler & Thye, 1999; Little & al., 2016; Saavedra & Van Dyne, 1999).

A research example from the physicians in the workplace has found that self-reports of their own cognitive reframing correlate positively with the satisfaction of their patients and the positive emotion of patients, and that the self-reports of physicians in their expressive suppression correlate positively with satisfaction of their patients, except when we consider as an intermediate variable the gender of the patients (Kafetsios, Anagnostopoulos, Lempesis, & Valindra, 2014). A similar finding of a positive influence of emotional regulation in leaders was found for their subordinates in healthcare settings (Giannouli, 2014).

EMOTIONAL LABOR

For the meaning of emotional labor, numerous researchers have given various definitions such as "manipulation of emotion to create a public image of emotion expression in facial expressions and body" or "as an attempt to show the exact emotions required by businesses" (Hochschild, 1979). Emotional labor has various dimensions, such as deep acting and superficial pretense (surface acting). The surface acting can be defined as the occurrence of emotions that the employee does not really feel, but which are required by the organization for which they work, but this requires the individual to suppress their own true feelings (Hochschild, 1983; Brotheridge & Grandey, 2002; Brotheridge & Lee, 2003).

However, deep acting can be defined as the adjustment of the deeper feelings of the workers so that they match the expression of emotion required by the organization. This is linked to reduced stress and increased sense of personal fulfillment (Humphrey, Ashforth, & Diefendorff, 2015). In contrast, surface acting is associated with increased stress at work, emotional exhaustion and feelings of hypocrisy (Mann, 1999), but this may be different if we consider other variables such as individual differences and organizational factors (Grandey, 2000).

Particularly for the physicians who work in hospitals, surface acting is associated with expressions of fake interest for patients or colleagues, causing a situation in which the individual becomes emotionally detached not only from the workplace, but also detached even from their own emotional state (e.g., they cannot realize the degree of depression in themselves) (Brotheridge & Grandey, 2002). Moreover, they show greater dissatisfaction with their job (Persaud, 2005). Each organization develops some emotional rules which determine in detail what are the emotions that employees should feel, as is the case with the smile for experienced employees such as waiters, commercial shop assistants, and other people in positions primarily associated with customer service (Rafaeli & Sutton, 1987; Pugh, 2001; VanDijk & Kirk-Brown, 2006).

Employees in workplaces where high rates of burnout are found seem further burdened with the need to constantly show positive emotions. Therefore, professionals and especially leaders from the field of medicine, nursing, social work, and education, where there is a strong continuous personal interaction, which requires deep and personal care, seem to demonstrate high involvement and emotional labor (Giannouli, 2014; Maslach & Schaufeli, 1993).

In this line, in hospitals as working environments for nurses, the leaders' capacity to work according to high ethical standards is found to be an important resource of protection for their employees against the negative effects of emotional labor and as a way to directly promote work engagement (Mauno et al., 2016).

JOB SATISFACTION

Job satisfaction can be defined as the "positive and negative attitudes that the individual has for their work" (Baron, 1986). Although it could be considered to be a uniform concept (Kalleberg, 1977; Spector, 1997), at the same time it could concern specific dimensions of work under consideration and is directly linked to the value system (material-economic nature and non-economic rewards) that each person possesses (Locke, 1976).

There is a distinction between emotional satisfaction from work (Thompson & Phua, 2012) and cognitive job satisfaction (Moorman, 1993). Emotional satisfaction from work involves all positive feelings the individuals have for their work in total, while cognitive job satisfaction relates to the satisfaction of individuals for particular aspects of their work, such as wages, pension arrangements, and working hours. While cognitive job satisfaction can bring emotional satisfaction from work, the two concepts in the scientific literature are treated as something different and not directly related. Although a two-way relationship (correlation) has been suggested between job satisfaction and life (Rain, Lane & Steiner, 1991), this is probably not true if we take into account that there may exist a number of other mediator-moderator variables (Rode, 2004).

Job satisfaction in physicians in the modern workplace appears to be related both with intrinsic factors (e.g., interest in the work itself, personal assessment of professional competence) and external factors such as relationships with colleagues, work conditions such as bureaucracy, and financial rewards (Bovier et al., 2009; Horowitz et al., 2003). Although satisfaction does not coincide with the incentives, one of the first motivation theories describes the reasons that can motivate a person and according to Maslow (1943) this involves a hierarchy of five needs, which were claimed to be satisfied with a particular order for all people.

Therefore, starting from the satisfaction of physiological (biological) needs, we continue to meet the safety needs (protection), social needs (sense of belonging), the esteem needs, and finally the self-actualization needs (activation of the full individual potential) (Maslow, 1943; 1970). This theory, of course, should be treated as non-verifiable, since it is not supported by experimental data and is based on an overgeneralization, while the order of fulfilling needs may not apply to all individuals or all needs may not be prioritized in the same manner.

Job satisfaction appears to have a statistically significant negative correlation with job stress (Landsbergis, 1988; Stamps & Piedmonte, 1986) especially for the group of physicians (Cooper et al., 1989), where this tendency is more prevalent than in other groups of employees (Giannouli, 2014), while organizational factors such as the burden of employment and the working conditions show similar negative correlations with job satisfaction (Vinokur-Kaplan, 1991).

Finally, although a positive correlation between job satisfaction and performance is expected, according to data from a meta-analysis, low correlations between job satisfaction and performance are found for a variety of jobs and leader-subordinate posts (Judge, Thoresen, Bono, & Patton, 2001). In a recent review, charismatic and transformational leadership behaviors are found to have the highest positive correlations with employees' job satisfaction, while non-contingent punishment and abusive supervision has been found to have low negative relationships to employees' job satisfaction (Sun et al., 2016).

BURNOUT

Burnout was first studied as a psychological syndrome in the early 1970s with studies based on workers from the health sector (Freudenberger, 1974). There are two types of approaches to describe either burnout as a situation (Brill, 1984; Maslach & Jackson, 1986; Pines & Aronson, 1988), or as a dynamic process (Cherniss, 1980a, 1980b; Edelwich & Brodsky, 1980; Etzion, 1987). The first approach defines burnout as a condition and more specifically as the emotional, mental, and physical collapse of the individual caused by the professional lifestyle and the chronic exposure to emotionally demanding and even threatening conditions (Maslach & Leiter, 2016; Winstanley & Whittington, 2002). Burnout is characterized by: a) emotional exhaustion (feeling of continuous tension and emotional alienation in interpersonal relationships), b) depersonalization (negative and crude behavior towards persons seeking and accepting professional services), and c) feeling of reduced personal achievements.

To reach the stage of burnout according to Cherniss' Process Model (1980), there are three phases: 1) the phase of "work stress" in which we have an imbalance between personal sources and availability to the required external environment, 2) the phase of "exhaustion" in which we have an emotional response to this imbalance which manifests itself in the form of different emotions (e.g., anxiety, irritability, fatigue, boredom, lack of interest, and apathy), during which the working environment is experienced as something corruptive, and 3) the "defense end" phase which presents with changes in the person's

Emotional Aspects of Leadership in the Modern Workplace

emotional attitude as stiffness in behavior and cynicism. These changes in behavior may help to reduce the physical and mental effects facilitating the aim of achieving professional survival. The Cherniss' model is characterized by positive-negative feedback loops that end with either active problem solving or burnout (Force, 2008).

According to another burnout model formulated by Edelwich and Brodsky (1980), there are the following stages: 1) the stage of idealistic enthusiasm, during which workers invest all their resources (in terms of time spent and the mental and emotional resources) at work, 2) the stage of stagnation during which the employee understands that the work does not fully meet their expectations or needs and the individual begins to distance and think of different topics such as the financial rewards, career and labor hours as major problems, 3) the phase of frustration, when the person is wondering whether it is worthwhile to conduct their duties under pressure and without the recognition by others. As a matter of fact, this stage is transitional because employees decide whether to continue working by modifying their behavior and working conditions that cause stress, or distance themselves from the job taking an indifference or alienation attitude, and 4) the phase of apathy, during which the workers invest some energy and avoid responsibilities, changing their own expectations of the job.

Generally, the effects of emotional burnout concern the individual with physical symptoms (e.g., tiredness, sleep disturbance, gastrointestinal problems, eating disorders, pain), emotional-cognitive symptoms (e.g., depression, anxiety, irritability, guilt, etc.), behavioral symptoms (e.g., substance abuse, accidents, etc.), and interpersonal relationships (conflicts with colleagues and family). The organization is affected by the aforementioned aspects of burnout as both leaders and subordinates may suffer from a voluntary withdrawal from work, multiple absences, low job satisfaction, low productivity at work and reduced efficiency (Maslach & Jackson, 1986), inability to concentrate at work (Pines, 1993; Hogan & McKnight, 2007), low creativity, and reduced ability to solve problems (Halbesleben & Buckley, 2004; Shirom, 2003).

According to a recent meta-analysis regarding nurses, job demands, job control, social support and exposure to traumatic events are determinants of burnout, as well as several organizational variables (Adriaenssens, DeGucht, & Maes, 2015). Neuroticism along with internal work locus of control are claimed to moderate the relationship between leader behavior and burnout. In a relevant well-known research, charisma is associated with lower burnout, particularly for individuals low on internal locus. The relationship between autocratic leadership and burnout is found to be positive for neurotic individuals, whereas for emotionally stable individuals this relationship weakens.

These results were found to be consistent across two independent samples: one with individual employee ratings of manager's leadership styles and the other with aggregate ratings of manager's leadership styles among employees in diverse organizations. Thus, although charismatic and autocratic leader behavior may respectively act to hinder or enhance overload and stress, the relationship between these leadership styles and burnout differs for 'followers' with different traits (De Hoog & Den Hartog, 2009). On the other hand, transformational leadership seems to have a significant positive association with personal accomplishment and is negatively related to emotional exhaustion and depersonalization in the individual. Additionally, a positive relationship exists between passive avoidance leadership and emotional exhaustion and depersonalization, while individuals with a passive avoidance leadership style exhibit higher levels of burnout (Zopiatis & Constanti, 2010).

Finally, the finding of an existing link between the perceived from the subordinates' leader empowering behaviors in the medical/nursing professions and empowerment and work engagement/ lower levels of burnout is considered to be very important for practical applications in the modern workplace (Greco, Laschinger, & Wong, 2006; Hatcher & Lashinger, 1996).

ANXIETY

Stress can be distinguished in anxiety as a personality trait which refers to the relatively stable individual differences in anxiety predisposition (e.g., the tendency to perceive one and meet psychologically demanding situations in a specific way or trait), and anxiety about a situation or incident which refers to the subjective and transient sense of tension, nervousness and anxiety in a given time (state) (Spielberger et al., 1983). Thus, a mixture of anxiety emotions, tension and stress can describe anxiety. Moreover, beyond environmental-state conditions, anxiety can be caused by disorders such as obsessive compulsive disorder or generalized anxiety disorder (Nolen-Hoeksema, 2011).

It is generally believed that as leaders ascend to powerful positions in the groups to which they belong, they tend to face ever-increasing demands. Therefore, leaders are expected to have higher stress levels than non-leaders. This is not true if leaders also experience a heightened sense of control, that is a psychological factor known to have powerful stress-buffering effects as leadership in this case is associated with reduced stress levels (Sherman et al., 2012). However, anxiety is also one of the most important factors in determining the wellbeing of leaders belonging to the physicians working in healthcare units such as hospitals (Wallace et al., 2009), but for this group of employees, it is reported in classical research that they demonstrate particularly high stress levels in comparison with other groups of workers (Caplan, 1994) affected mainly by factors such as marital status, level of salary, and the amount of work required (Chambers & Campbell, 1996).

Especially for male General Practitioners working in hospitals, increased stress is associated with lower satisfaction with their work (Cooper, Rout, & Faragher, 1989), while for nurses, somatic symptoms related to increased anxiety are prevalent (Chou, Chang, & Chung, 2016). The aforementioned are also supported by raw data for the modern Greek hospital workplaces (Giannouli, 2014). Finally, leaders' attachment style and attachment anxiety is found to be associated with more self-serving leadership motives and with poorer leadership qualities in task-oriented situations. In addition, leaders' attachment anxiety also predicts followers' poorer instrumental functioning, while leaders' attachment-related avoidance is found to be negatively associated with pro-social motives to lead, failure to act as a security provider, and with followers' poorer socio-emotional functioning and poorer long-range mental health in military settings (Davidovitz et al., 2007).

OBJECTIVES OF THE STUDY AND RESEARCH METHODS

The main objective of this study is to present the most recent information regarding the emotions in the healthcare as a workplace, and to propose a framework of emotion-related study paradigms that consider both leaders and subordinates' different emotional aspects in healthcare settings (hospitals). Therefore, a literature review was conducted in the form of a systematic review that collects and critically analyzes multiple research studies in the form of published and ahead of print articles, conference proceedings, and published and unpublished master's and doctoral theses. A 6-month literature search of electronic databases such as PubMed-Medline, PsychInfo, Embase, ISI Web of Knowledge, Scopus, and Google

Scholar was performed by the researcher to identify relevant empirical studies conducted and published between 2014 and September, 2016. This short time interval was chosen because there are no reviews so far regarding this specific period of time.

Papers were searched for those containing at least one term from each of the following key words: 'emotions', 'leaders', 'subordinates', 'healthcare', 'hospital', 'physicians', 'nurses', and/or 'workplace'. After framing the research question, 'Which are the emotional aspects of the employees in healthcare settings and how the emotional aspects of leaders influence the emotions of their subordinates?', an identification of relevant research from multiple electronic databases revealed a number of studies that were further assessed based on the number of participants, the statistical methods, and the research designs.

The inclusion criteria for the studies were seven: 1) their relevance to the research question, 2) published online, 3) published full-length in English, 4) use of quantitative data/close-ended questionnaires (not interviews) in their methods, 5) participants were healthcare professionals (leaders and/or subordinates, registered physicians and nurses) working full-time in accredited hospitals, 6) the sample size was over 100 per group of participants in order to have a small margin of statistical error and generalizable results, and 7) the papers presenting raw data, had to be peer-reviewed prior to the upload on the above digital libraries. The systematic review of existing studies was chosen as a research methodology as for this little investigated issue, the reviews can only provide the necessary information for researchers in the field of organizational psychology and management before embarking on new empirical studies regarding emotions in actual workplaces.

RESULTS AND DISCUSSION

Research so far examines the emotional aspects only of employees in healthcare workplaces as is evident in the present review (see Table 1), but there remains scant research supporting or proposing the role that the emotional aspects of leaders have on their subordinates, and vice versa, with simultaneous examination of emotional dimensions in both leaders and subordinates (Giannouli, 2014). According to the present review findings, research on emotional aspects can be grouped in six psychological constructs (as presented in Table 1) that focus mainly on emotional intelligence, burnout and job satisfaction, and less on anxiety, emotional labor, and emotion regulation.

The above emotion-related constructs in all included studies of the review were found to have positive correlations with productivity and emotional status of the employees. Thus, we can claim that healthcare provides a setting that is strongly influenced by emotions (Mark, 2005). Although a vast number of studies investigates leadership and emotions (e.g., Antonakis et al., 2009; Ashkanasy, 2003; Brotheridge & Lee, 2008; Gooty et al., 2010; Humphrey, 2008; Little, Gooty &Williams, 2016; Rajah et al., 2011), the emotional aspects of leadership at healthcare settings (hospitals) are widely neglected, while the connection-relationship of emotions in leaders and their followers is still not clear (Kent, 2006), a fact that is supported by the lack of studies simultaneously examining the emotional relationships in leaders and their subordinates.

Unfortunately, as shown in Table 1, all published research in healthcare focuses not on the emotional aspects of leaders (Gourzoulidis et al., 2015), but on the emotions of the subordinates who are in the vast majority of the reported studies represented only by nurses and not physicians. The only research that directly addresses the question of leader-subordinate emotional relationships shows that leaders' actual and perceived (by their subordinates) emotional aspect do affect in a positive way their subordinates'

Table 1. Emotional Aspects Examined in Subordinates (Within Level) and Leaders-Subordinates (Between Level) in Healthcare Workplaces-Hospitals (2014-2016)

Emotional Aspects	Studies Examining Emotional Aspects Only in Subordinates (in Alphabetical Order)	Studies Simultaneously Examining Emotional Aspects in Leaders and Subordinates at the Same Workplace
Emotional Intelligence	Al-Hamdan et al. (2016); Arora et al. (2010); Codier, Kooker & Shoultz (2008); Di Fabio & Palazzeschi (2012); Efkarpidis, Efkarpidis & Zyga (2012); Fujino et al. (2015); Güleryüz et al. (2008); Heffeman et al. (2010); Heydari, Kareshki & Armat (2016); Hong & Lee (2016); Kahraman & Hiçdurmaz (2016); Kaur, Sambasivan & Kumar (2015); Landa et al. (2008); Sharma et al. (2016); Vahidi et al. (2016); Weng et al. (2008); Weng et al. (2011); Zhu et al. (2015); Zhu et al. (2016)	Giannouli (2014) Gorgi et al. (2015)
Emotion Regulation	Kafetsios, Anagnostopoulos, Lempesis & Valindra (2014); Kovács, Kovács & Hegedűs (2010)	Giannouli (2014)
Emotional Labor	Cottingham et al., 2915; Diefendorff et al. (2011); Golfenshtein et al. (2015); Hong & Lee (2016); Liang et al. (2016); Maouno et al. (2016); Wang & Chang, 2016; Yang & Chang (2008)	Giannouli (2014)
Job Satisfaction	Akman et al. (2016); Alharbi et al. (2016); Alves & Guirardello (2016); Atefi et al. (2015); Chao et al. (2015); Chen et al. (2015); Cottingham et al. (2015); Dall'Ora et al. (2015); Goh et al. (2015); Güleryüz et al. (2008); Hayes, Douglas & Bonner (2015); Im Kim et al. (2016); Jadoo et al. (2015); Khamisa et al. (2016); Khunou & Davhana-Maselesele (2016); Laschinger & Fida (2015); Li et al. (2016); Liu et al. (2015); Lu et al. (2015); Lu et al. (2016); Ozyurt, Hayran & Sur (2006); Platis, Reklitis & Zimeras (2015); Pu et al. (2016); Purpora & Blegen (2015); Safi & Kolani (2016); Sansoni et al. (2016); Seo et al. (2016); Sojane, Klopper & Coetzee (2016); Strömgren et al. (2016); Tao et al. (2015); Top, Akdere & Tarcan (2015); Weng et al. (2011); Yang & Chang (2008)	Giannouli (2014) Safi et al. (2016)
Burnout	Abarghouei et al. (2016); Abdo et al. (2015); Akman et al. (2016); Alexandrova-Kamarova et al. (2016); Alharbi et al. (2015); Andela et al. (2015); Ang et al. (2016); Arigoni, Bovierb & Sappinoa (2010); Arli, Balkan & Erisik (2016); Biksegn et al. (2016); Bilal & Ahmed (2016); Chou, Li & Hu (2014); Dall'Ora et al. (2015); Denat et al. (2016); Erikson & Grove (2007); Estiri et al. (2016); Farziapour et al. (2016); Gabel Shemueli et al. (2016); Galleta et al. (2016); Gosseries et al. (2012); Greco, Laschinger & Wong (2006); Grisares Romero et al. (2016); Guo et al. (2016); Hanrahan et al. (2010); Hayes, Douglas & Bonner (2015); Hong & Lee (2016); Hooper et al. (2010); Jang et al. (2016); Kanai-Pak et al. (2006); Khamisa et al. (2016); Kilroy et al. (2016); Klein et al. (2010); Koivula, Paunonen & Laippala (2000); Kovács, Kovács & Hegedűs (2010); Kowalski et al. (2010); Leiter & Laschinger (2006); Li et al. 2016); Lin et al. (2016); Linqvist et al. (2015); Maruyama et al. (2016); Mcmillan et al. (2016); McMurray et al. (2000); Montgomery et al. (2015); Nantsupawat et al. (2016); Naz, Hashmi & Asif (2016); Nie et al. (2015); O' Kelly et al. (2016); Ozyurt, Hayran & Sur (2006); Pedersen et al. (2013); Permeger et al. (2012); Pisanti et al. (2016); Poghosyan et al. (2010); Prins et al. (2009); Quattrin et al. (2006); Rafferty et al. (2007); Rohland, Kruse & Rohrer (2004); Safi & Kolani (2016); Schooley et al. (2016); Seo et al. (2016); Shamali et al. (2015); Shirom, Nirel & Vinokur (2006); Sirsawy et al. (2016); Soroush, Zargham-Boroujeni & Namnabati (2016); Trbojevic-Stankovic et al. (2015); Wang, Kunaviktikul & Wichaikhum (2013); Welp, Meier & Manser (2015); Vifladt et al. (2016); Wen et al. (2016); Weng et al. (2011); Williams et al. (2007); Xie, Wang & Chen (2011); Yoon & Sok (2016)	Giannouli (2014) Safi et al. (2016)
Anxiety	Chou, Chang & Chung, 2016; Gao et al. (2012); Goh et al. (2015); Nooryan et al. (2012); Wallace et al. (2009)	Giannouli (2014)

corresponding emotional intelligence, emotion regulation, emotional labor, job satisfaction, burnout, and anxiety (Giannouli, 2014). The practical importance of these preliminary findings for healthcare management may translate into further reflection on possible personal and organizational changes that will take into account the emotional factors (Ashforth & Humphrey, 1995; Lucas, Spence Laschinger, & Wong, 2008).

Healthcare managers should (re)consider their emotional aspects and try to engage in programs that aim to augment their awareness on emotional matters and improve their emotion-related skills if they wish to influence in a positive way their subordinates. Emotions are a vital field not only for scientific research, but also a hot topic in management consulting and leadership training circles, as leaders' emotions are widely claimed to play a crucial role for leaders as well as for their subordinates in other than healthcare workplaces and sensitization-skills training programs are promoted (Freshman & Rubino, 2002; Nyberg, Bernin, & Theorell, 2005; Shirey, 2006).

Nevertheless, the process, the mechanisms, and dimensions of emotional leadership and its direct or indirect influence on subordinates' emotional status are still not neglected, and not thoroughly examined due to lack of between level research; that is, research examining emotions both in leaders and subordinates at the hospital as a workplace. Given the starring roles that managers have in such organizations, future multilevel analyses should treat the emotion-related data coming from subordinates as nested within actual emotion data coming from leaders (and not just subordinates' perceptions regarding the emotions of their leaders) (Squires et al., 2010; To, Herman & Ashkanasy, 2015).

Further investigation regarding the emotions in healthcare workplaces and how they form the relationship between leaders and subordinates is necessary as it could serve as a basis for the process that leaders should adopt to shape the emotional life of their organizations in order to establish managerial practices that can improve the psychological status of the employees and therefore their performance. These initiatives should be based on research results, which will serve as a basis for future management guidelines on healthcare administration, leadership training, and management skills.

LIMITATIONS

One of the possible limitations of this review is the heterogeneity of the included studies, which were conducted in countries with different cultural backgrounds and healthcare systems, and the fact that the demographics of the samples (types of healthcare professionals) and the examined emotional variables varied largely. This review is also restricted by its exclusion of non-English language papers. Additional limitations include the possibility of a publication bias due to the exclusion of so-called grey literature. One more possible disadvantage of the present review is the exclusion of print-only articles. Nevertheless, due to the lack of an adequate number of homogeneous studies, this attempt offers a first approach-introduction to the theme of emotions at hospitals regarding the leaders as well as the subordinates. Especially, the finding of scarce publications examining both leaders' and subordinates' emotional aspects and their interactions may be a new field for future research.

FUTURE CHALLENGES AND DIRECTIONS

Emotions play a central role in the leadership process in the workplace and this renders research on emotions necessary (George, 2000). Although today there is an augmenting body of scientific literature on emotions and leadership, and even more research on the transformational style of leadership and the role of emotions (Ashkanasy, Härtel & Zerbe, 2000; Barling et al., 2000), still emotions related to leadership and ethics are not investigated and not included in the examination of emotions (Solomon, 2004).

In tandem with a surge of interest on ethical aspects of leadership (Bollaert & Petit 2010; Brown, Treviño, & Harrison, 2005), recently researchers have highlighted the importance of examining leaders' hubristic behavior and its complex emotional connotations (Owen & Davidson, 2009). Hubris refers to emotions and cognitions relating to the exaggerated pride, over-whelming self-confidence and contempt exhibited to others (Owen, 2006). Hubristic symptoms come as a combination of persons assuming power (leaders) and undesirable personality traits (Owen & Davidson, 2009).

Leaders' hubristic behavior has been associated with less undesirable traits at individual-level (e.g., Machiavellianism, narcissism, neuroticism etc.) and the implication of those traits for followers can be significant. When executives have high hubris, it can have a negative impact on the strategic decision making process, the actual strategic choices that are made, and ultimately organizational performance (Hiller & Hambrick, 2005).

The research evidence regarding leaders' hubristic effects for followers' work outcomes and emotions is generally limited not only in the healthcare research but also in all working environments. In particular, there is lack of research on the role of group and culture-level variables in leaders' hubristic behavior towards subordinates. These concerns follow calls to examine contextual factors in leaders' hubris-related traits and behavior (Rodgers, 2011). Cultural influences in organizations are pervasive (Taras, Kirkman, & Steel, 2010). Cultures can vary on different dimensions (Hofstede, 2001) and pertinent for future analyses is power distance and independent and interdependent cultural orientations. Cultures with larger power distance (more hierarchical) and interdependence are associated with more autocratic leadership behaviors.

For example, in an analysis of influence incidents, Pasa (2000) found that in cultures with higher hierarchy distance the most frequently perceived influence behaviors were those associated with granting authority, pressurizing, and power-related. Therefore, due to less 'horizontal' and more vertical type of relationships between power/leadership figures and groups of followers, more collectivistic contexts can favor leaders' more hubristic-related behavior also influencing followers' normative perceptions of those leadership traits.

Recent research suggests that the positive effects of certain desirable leadership traits change in different cultural contexts (Mccord, Joseph, & Grijalva, 2014). In several studies conducted in Greece, it has been found that leaders' negative personality traits (insecure attachment and higher tendency to control their emotions) had a positive effect on followers' emotions at work and job satisfaction although the same leadership characteristics had a negative effect on leaders' own emotions at work and job satisfaction (Kafetsios, Athanasiadou, & Dimou, 2014; Kafetsios, Nezlek, & Vasiou, 2011; Kafetsios, Nezlek, & Vassilakou, 2012).

The results were explained by how follower groups in more collectivistic and hierarchically distant societies construe leadership roles. In such societies, implicit leadership theories construe leaders' suppression behavior as more "leadership-like", hence perceiving such behavior and emotions of leaders accordingly. Followers' perceptions can critically mediate or moderate leaders' behaviors, traits on followers' emotions, satisfaction, and performance at work (Shondrick, Dinh, & Lord, 2010). Based on the above evidence, it can be claimed that hubristic leadership traits may have differential effects on followers' work outcomes and emotions depending on the cultural context. In collectivistic and more power distant contexts, hubristic leaders' behaviors may have less of an effect on different aspects of followers' organizational experience than in more individualistic and less power distant societies.

Future challenges and directions are highly linked to the above research methodological impediments that relate to the inability to gather data simultaneously at both the individual and the organizational level, and to the problem of applying all this knowledge on the international real business world (Giannouli, 2014). Unfortunately, in addition to the inexistence of ethics-related research, cross-cultural replication studies are also still a missing part of the leadership and emotion research, while the multifaceted concept of emotional competencies and leadership's neuropsychological correlates is still an insufficiently examined topic (Gooty et al., 2010; Waldman, Balthazard, & Peterson, 2011).

REFERENCES

Abarghouei, M. R., Sorbi, M. H., Abarghouei, M., Bidaki, R., & Yazdanpoor, S. (2016). A study of job stress and burnout and related factors in the hospital personnel of Iran. *Electronic Physician*, *8*(7), 2625–2632. doi:10.19082/2625 PMID:27648189

Abdo, S. A. M., El-Sallamy, R. M., El-Sherbiny, A. A. M., & Kabbash, I. A. (2015). Burnout among physicians and nursing staff working in the emergency hospital of Tanta University, Egypt. *Eastern Mediterranean Health Journal*, *21*(12), 906. PMID:26996364

Adriaenssens, J., De Gucht, V., & Maes, S. (2015). Determinants and prevalence of burnout in emergency nurses: A systematic review of 25 years of research. *International Journal of Nursing Studies*, *52*(2), 649–661. doi:10.1016/j.ijnurstu.2014.11.004 PMID:25468279

Akman, O., Ozturk, C., Bektas, M., Ayar, D., & Armstrong, M. A. (2016). Job satisfaction and burnout among paediatric nurses. *Journal of Nursing Management*, *24*(7), 923–933. doi:10.1111/jonm.12399 PMID:27271021

Al-Hamdan, Z., Oweidat, I. A., Al-Faouri, I., & Codier, E. (2016). Correlating emotional intelligence and job performance among Jordanian hospitals' registered nurses. *Nursing Forum*. PMID:27194022

Alexandrova-Karamanova, A., Todorova, I., Montgomery, A., Panagopoulou, E., Costa, P., Baban, A., & Mijakoski, D. et al. (2016). Burnout and health behaviors in health professionals from seven European countries. *International Archives of Occupational and Environmental Health*, *89*(7), 1059–1075. doi:10.1007/s00420-016-1143-5 PMID:27251338

Alharbi, J., Wilson, R., Woods, C., & Usher, K. (2016). The factors influencing burnout and job satisfaction among critical care nurses: A study of Saudi critical care nurses. *Journal of Nursing Management*, *24*(6), 708–717. doi:10.1111/jonm.12386 PMID:27189515

Alves, D. F. S., & Guirardello, E. B. (2016). Safety climate, emotional exhaustion and job satisfaction among Brazilian paediatric professional nurses. *International Nursing Review*, *63*(3), 328–335. doi:10.1111/inr.12276 PMID:27265871

Andela, M., Truchot, D., & Van der Doef, M. (2015). Job stressors and burnout in hospitals: The mediating role of emotional dissonance. *International Journal of Stress Management*, *23*(3), 298–317. doi:10.1037/str0000013

Ang, S. Y., Dhaliwal, S. S., Ayre, T. C., Uthaman, T., Fong, K. Y., Tien, C. E., & Della, P. (2016). *Demographics and Personality Factors Associated with Burnout among Nurses in a Singapore Tertiary Hospital*. BioMed Research International.

Antonakis, J., Ashkanasy, N. M., & Dasborough, M. T. (2009). Does leadership need emotional intelligence? *The Leadership Quarterly*, *20*(2), 247–261. doi:10.1016/j.leaqua.2009.01.006

Arigoni, F., Bovierb, P. A., & Sappinoa, A. P. (2010). Trend in burnout among Swiss doctors. *Swiss Medical Weekly*, *9*, 140.

Arli, S. K., Bakan, A. B., & Erisik, E. (2016). An investigation of the relationship between nurses' views on spirituality and spiritual care and their level of burnout. *Journal of Holistic Nursing*.

Arora, S., Ashrafian, H., Davis, R., Athanasiou, T., Darzi, A., & Sevdalis, N. (2010). Emotional intelligence in medicine: A systematic review through the context of the ACGME competencies. *Medical Education*, *44*(8), 749–764. doi:10.1111/j.1365-2923.2010.03709.x PMID:20633215

Arvey, R. D., Renz, G. L., & Watson, T. W. (1998). Emotionality and job performance: Implications for personnel selection. *Research in Personnel and Human Resources Management*, *16*, 103–147.

Ashforth, B. E., & Humphrey, R. H. (1995). Emotion in the workplace: A reappraisal. *Human Relations*, *48*(2), 97–125. doi:10.1177/001872679504800201

Ashkanasy, N. M. (2003). Emotions in organizations: A multilevel perspective. *Research in Multi-level Issues*, *2*, 9–54. doi:10.1016/S1475-9144(03)02002-2

Ashkanasy, N. M., & Cooper, C. L. (Eds.). (2008). *Research companion to emotion in organizations*. Cheltenham, UK: Edward Elgar. doi:10.4337/9781848443778

Ashkanasy, N. M., Härtel, C. E., & Daus, C. S. (2002). Diversity and emotion: The new frontiers in organizational behavior research. *Journal of Management*, *28*(3), 307–338. doi:10.1177/014920630202800304

Ashkanasy, N. M., Härtel, C. E., & Zerbe, W. J. (Eds.). (2000). *Emotions in the workplace: Research, theory, and practice*. Greenwood Publishing Group.

Atefi, N., Lim Abdullah, K., Wong, L. P., & Mazlom, R. (2015). Factors influencing job satisfaction among registered nurses: A questionnaire survey in Mashhad, Iran. *Journal of Nursing Management*, *23*(4), 448–458. doi:10.1111/jonm.12151 PMID:24102706

Avolio, J. B. (2005). *Leadership development in balance: Made/Born. NJ*. Hillsdale: Erlbaum.

Bagshaw, M. (2000). Emotional intelligence–training people to be affective so they can be effective. *Industrial and Commercial Training*, *32*(2), 61–65. doi:10.1108/00197850010320699

Ballinger, G. A., & Rockmann, K. W. (2010). Chutes versus ladders: Anchoring events and a punctuated-equilibrium perspective on social exchange relationships. *Academy of Management Review, 35*(3), 373–391. doi:10.5465/AMR.2010.51141732

Barling, J., Slater, F., & Kevin Kelloway, E. (2000). Transformational leadership and emotional intelligence: An exploratory study. *Leadership and Organization Development Journal, 21*(3), 157–161. doi:10.1108/01437730010325040

Barrett, L. F. (2004). Feelings or words? Understanding the content in self-report ratings of experienced emotion. *Journal of Personality and Social Psychology, 87*(2), 266–281. doi:10.1037/0022-3514.87.2.266 PMID:15301632

Biksegn, A., Kenfe, T., Matiwos, S., & Eshetu, G. (2016). Burnout status at work among health care professionals in a tertiary hospital. *Ethiopian journal of health sciences, 26*(2), 101-108.

Bilal, A., & Ahmed, H. M. (2016). *Organizational structure as a determinant of job burnout. An exploratory study on Pakistani pediatric nurses*. Workplace Health & Safety.

Bollaert, H., & Petit, V. (2010). Beyond the dark side of executive psychology: Current research and new directions. *European Management Journal, 28*(5), 362–376. doi:10.1016/j.emj.2010.01.001

Bolton, S. C. (2004). *Emotion management in the workplace*. Basingstoke, UK: Palgrave Macmillan.

Bono, E. J., Foldes, H. J., Vinson, G., & Muros, P. J. (2007). Workplace emotions: The role of supervision and leadership. *The Journal of Applied Psychology, 92*(5), 1357–1367. doi:10.1037/0021-9010.92.5.1357 PMID:17845090

Bovier, P. A., Arigoni, F., Schneider, M., & Gallacchi, M. B. (2009). Relationships between work satisfaction, emotional exhaustion and mental health among Swiss primary care physicians. *European Journal of Public Health, 19*(6), 611–617. doi:10.1093/eurpub/ckp056 PMID:19403785

Braun, S., Aydin, N., Frey, D., & Peus, C. V. (2015). Leader narcissism predicts followers' malicious envy and counterproductive work behaviors. In Academy of Management Proceedings (vol. 2015, No. 1, pp. 16115). New York: Academy of Management.

Brief, A. P., & Weiss, H. M. (2002). Organizational behavior: Affect in the workplace. *Annual Review of Psychology, 53*(1), 279–307. doi:10.1146/annurev.psych.53.100901.135156 PMID:11752487

Brill, P. L. (1984). The need for an operational definition of burnout. *Family & Community Health, 6*(4), 12–24. doi:10.1097/00003727-198402000-00005 PMID:10264597

Briner, R. (1999). The neglect and importance of emotion at work. *European Journal of Work and Organizational Psychology, 8*(3), 323–346. doi:10.1080/135943299398212

Brotheridge, C. M., & Grandey, A. A. (2002). Emotional labor and burnout: Comparing two perspectives of people work. *Journal of Vocational Behavior, 60*(1), 17–39. doi:10.1006/jvbe.2001.1815

Brotheridge, C. M., & Lee, R. T. (2003). Development and validation of the emotional labour scale. *Journal of Occupational and Organizational Psychology, 76*(3), 365–379. doi:10.1348/096317903769647229

Brown, M. E., Treviño, L. K., & Harrison, D. A. (2005). Ethical leadership: A social learning perspective for construct development and testing. *Organizational Behavior and Human Decision Processes*, *97*(2), 117–134. doi:10.1016/j.obhdp.2005.03.002

Bryman, A. S., Stephens, M., & Campo, C. (1996). The importance of context: Qualitative research and the study of leadership. *The Leadership Quarterly*, *7*(3), 353–370. doi:10.1016/S1048-9843(96)90025-9

Burch, T. C., & Guarana, C. L. (2014). The comparative influences of transformational leadership and leader–member exchange on follower engagement. *The Journal of Leadership Studies*, *8*(3), 6–25. doi:10.1002/jls.21334

Butler, E. A., Egloff, B., Wlhelm, F. H., Smith, N. C., Erickson, E. A., & Gross, J. J. (2003). The social consequences of expressive suppression. *Emotion (Washington, D.C.)*, *3*(1), 48–67. doi:10.1037/1528-3542.3.1.48 PMID:12899316

Caruso, D. R., Mayer, J. D., & Salovey, P. (2002, April 9). Emotional intelligence and emotional leadership. *Proceedings of the Kravis-de Roulet Leadership Conference*, Claremont. McKenna.

Chambers, R., & Campbell, I. (1996). Anxiety and depression in general practitioners: Associations with type of practice, fundholding, gender and other personal characteristics. *Family Practice*, *13*(2), 170–173. doi:10.1093/fampra/13.2.170 PMID:8732330

Chao, M. C., Jou, R. C., Liao, C. C., & Kuo, C. W. (2015). Workplace stress, job satisfaction, job performance, and turnover intention of health care workers in rural Taiwan. *Asia-Pacific Journal of Public Health*, *27*(2), NP1827–NP1836. doi:10.1177/1010539513506604 PMID:24174390

Chatzipanteli, P. S. (1998). *Human resource management*. Athens: Metaixmio Publications.

Chen, S. Y., Wu, W. C., Chang, C. S., & Lin, C. T. (2015). Job rotation and internal marketing for increased job satisfaction and organisational commitment in hospital nursing staff. *Journal of Nursing Management*, *23*(3), 297–306. doi:10.1111/jonm.12126 PMID:23981132

Cherniss, C. (1980a). *Staff burnout: Job stress in the human services*. Beverly Hills, CA: Sage Publications.

Cherniss, C. (1980b). *Professional burnout in human service Organizations*. New York: Praeger.

Cherniss, C., Goleman, D., Emmerling, R., Cowan, K., & Adler, M. (1998). *Bringing emotional intelligence to the workplace*. New Brunswick, NJ: Consortium for Research on Emotional Intelligence in Organizations, Rutgers University.

Chiu, C. Y. C., Balkunid, P., & Weinberg, F. (2016). *When managers become leaders: The role of manager network centralities, social power, and followers' perception of leadership. The Leadership Quarterly*. Claremont, CA: Lawrence Erlbaum Associates Publishers.

Chou, L. P., Li, C. Y., & Hu, S. C. (2014). Job stress and burnout in hospital employees: Comparisons of different medical professions in a regional hospital in Taiwan. *BMJ Open*, *4*(2), e004185. doi:10.1136/bmjopen-2013-004185 PMID:24568961

Chou, T. L., Chang, L. I., & Chung, M. H. (2015). The mediating and moderating effects of sleep hygiene practice on anxiety and insomnia in hospital nurses. *International Journal of Nursing Practice*, *21*(Suppl. 2), 9–18. doi:10.1111/ijn.12164 PMID:26125570

Codier, E., Kooker, B. M., & Shoultz, J. (2008). Measuring the emotional intelligence of clinical staff nurses: An approach for improving the clinical care environment. *Nursing Administration Quarterly*, *32*(1), 8–14. doi:10.1097/01.NAQ.0000305942.38816.3b PMID:18160858

Colfax, R. S., Rivera, J. J., & Perez, K. T. (2010). Applying Emotional Intelligence (EQ-I) in the workplace: Vital to global business success. *Journal of International Business Research, 9*.

Connelly, S., & Gooty, J. (2015). Leading with emotion: An overview of the special issue on leadership and emotions. *The Leadership Quarterly*, *26*(4), 485–488. doi:10.1016/j.leaqua.2015.07.002

Cooper, C., Rout, U., & Faragher, B. (1989). Mental health, job satisfaction, and job stress among general practitioners. *British Medical Journal*, *298*(6670), 366–370. doi:10.1136/bmj.298.6670.366 PMID:2493939

Cooper, R. K., & Sawaf, A. (1997). *Emotional Intelligence in business*. London: Orion Business.

Cottingham, M. D., Erickson, R. J., & Diefendorff, J. M. (2015). Examining mens status shield and status bonus: How gender frames the emotional labor and job satisfaction of nurses. *Sex Roles*, *72*(7-8), 377–389. doi:10.1007/s11199-014-0419-z

DallOra, C., Griffiths, P., Ball, J., Simon, M., & Aiken, L. H. (2015). Association of 12 h shifts and nurses job satisfaction, burnout and intention to leave: Findings from a cross-sectional study of 12 European countries. *BMJ Open*, *5*(9), e008331. doi:10.1136/bmjopen-2015-008331 PMID:26359284

Dasborough, M. T., & Ashkanasy, N. M. (2002). Emotion and attribution of intentionality in leader–member relationships. *The Leadership Quarterly*, *13*(5), 615–634. doi:10.1016/S1048-9843(02)00147-9

Davidovitz, R., Mikulincer, M., Shaver, P. R., Izsak, R., & Popper, M. (2007). Leaders as attachment figures: Leaders attachment orientations predict leadership-related mental representations and followers performance and mental health. *Journal of Personality and Social Psychology*, *93*(4), 632–650. doi:10.1037/0022-3514.93.4.632 PMID:17892336

De Hoogh, A. H., & Den Hartog, D. N. (2009). Neuroticism and locus of control as moderators of the relationships of charismatic and autocratic leadership with burnout. *The Journal of Applied Psychology*, *94*(4), 1058–1067. doi:10.1037/a0016253 PMID:19594244

Denat, Y., Gokce, S., Gungor, H., Zencir, C., & Akgullu, C. (2016). Relationship of anxiety and burnout with extrasystoles in critical care nurses in Turkey. *Pakistan Journal of Medical Sciences*, *32*(1), 196. PMID:27022374

Di Fabio, A., & Palazzeschi, L. (2012). Organizational justice: Personality traits or emotional intelligence? An empirical study in an Italian hospital context. *Journal of Employment Counseling*, *49*(1), 31–42. doi:10.1002/j.2161-1920.2012.00004.x

Diefendorff, J. M., Erickson, R. J., Grandey, A. A., & Dahling, J. J. (2011). Emotional display rules as work unit norms: A multilevel analysis of emotional labor among nurses. *Journal of Occupational Health Psychology*, *16*(2), 170–186. doi:10.1037/a0021725 PMID:21244168

Edelwich, J., & Brodsky, A. (1980). *Burn-out: Stages of disillusionment in the helping professions* (Vol. 255). New York: Human Sciences Press.

Efkarpidis, A., Efkarpidis, P., & Zyga, S. (2012). A study of the emotional intelligence of employees at a district hospital of Greece. *International Journal of Caring Sciences*, *5*(1), 36–42.

Erickson, R., & Grove, W. (2007). Why emotions matter: Age, agitation, and burnout among registered nurses. *Online Journal of Issues in Nursing*, *13*(1), 1–13.

Estiri, M., Nargesian, A., Dastpish, F., & Sharifi, S. M. (2016). The impact of psychological capital on mental health among Iranian nurses: Considering the mediating role of job burnout. *SpringerPlus*, *5*(1), 1377. doi:10.1186/s40064-016-3099-z PMID:27610296

Etzion, D. (1987). *Burning out in management: A comparison of women and men in matched organizational positions*. Tel Aviv University, Faculty of Management, The Leon Recanati Graduate School of Business Administration.

Farzianpour, F., Abbasi, M., Foruoshani, A. R., & Pooyan, E. J. (2016). The relationship between Hofstede Organizational Culture and employees job burnout in hospitals of Tehran University of Medical Sciences 20142015. *Materia Socio-Medica*, *28*(1), 26. doi:10.5455/msm.2016.28.26-31 PMID:27047263

Fineman, S. (Ed.). (2000). *Emotion in organizations* (2nd ed.). London: Sage.

Force, L. M. (2008). *The influence of causal attribution on work exhaustion and turnover intention of traditional discipline engineers in the United States*. ProQuest.

Freshman, B., & Rubino, L. (2002). Emotional intelligence: A core competency for health care administrators. *The Health Care Manager*, *20*(4), 1–9. doi:10.1097/00126450-200206000-00002 PMID:12083173

Freudenberger, H. J. (1974). Staff burn-out. *The Journal of Social Issues*, *30*(1), 159–165. doi:10.1111/j.1540-4560.1974.tb00706.x

Fujino, Y., Tanaka, M., Yonemitsu, Y., & Kawamoto, R. (2015). The relationship between characteristics of nursing performance and years of experience in nurses with high emotional intelligence. *International Journal of Nursing Practice*, *21*(6), 876–881. doi:10.1111/ijn.12311 PMID:24712344

Gabel Shemueli, R., Dolan, S. L., Suárez Ceretti, A., & Nuñez del Prado, P. (2015). Burnout and engagement as mediators in the relationship between work characteristics and turnover Intentions across two Ibero-American nations. *Stress and Health*. PMID:26680339

Galletta, M., Portoghese, I., DAloja, E., Mereu, A., Contu, P., Coppola, R. C., & Campagna, M. et al. (2016). Relationship between job burnout, psychosocial factors and health care-associated infections in critical care units. *Intensive & Critical Care Nursing*, *34*, 51–58. doi:10.1016/j.iccn.2015.11.004 PMID:26961918

Gao, Y. Q., Pan, B. C., Sun, W., Wu, H., Wang, J. N., & Wang, L. (2012). Anxiety symptoms among Chinese nurses and the associated factors: A cross sectional study. *BMC Psychiatry, 12*(1), 1. doi:10.1186/1471-244X-12-141 PMID:22978466

Garcia-Prieto, P., Mackie, D. M., Tran, V., & Smith, E. R. (2007). Intergroup emotions in workgroups: Some emotional antecedents and consequences of belonging. *Research on Managing Groups and Teams, 10*, 145–184. doi:10.1016/S1534-0856(07)10007-4

George, J. M. (2000). Emotions and leadership: The role of emotional intelligence. *Human Relations, 53*(8), 1027–1055. doi:10.1177/0018726700538001

Giannouli, V. (2014). *Emotional leadership in health care units: Relationships of leaders-subordinates.* Unpublished master's thesis,. Hellenic Open University, Patras, Greece.

Glasø, L., & Einarsen, S. (2008). Emotion regulation in leader-follower relationships. *European Journal of Work and Organizational Psychology, 17*(4), 482–500. doi:10.1080/13594320801994960

Goh, Y. S., Lee, A., Chan, S. W. C., & Chan, M. F. (2015). Profiling nurses job satisfaction, acculturation, work environment, stress, cultural values and coping abilities: A cluster analysis. *International Journal of Nursing Practice, 21*(4), 443–452. doi:10.1111/ijn.12318 PMID:24754648

Goleman, D. (1995). *Emotional Intelligence: Why it can matter more than IQ.* London: Bloomsbury.

Goleman, D. (1998a). *Working with Emotional Intelligence.* London: Bloomsbury.

Goleman, D. (1998b). What makes a leader? *Harvard Business Review, 76*(6), 93–102. PMID:10187249

Goleman, D. (2001). An EI-based theory of performance. In C. Cherniss & D. Goleman (Eds.), *The Emotionally Intelligent workplace. How to select for, measure, and improve Emotional Intelligence in individuals, groups, and organizations* (pp. 27–44). San Francisco, CA: Jossey-Bass.

Goleman, D., Boyatzis, R., & McKee, A. (2001). Primal leadership: The hidden driver of great performance. *Harvard Business Review, 79*(11), 42–53.

Golfenshtein, N., & Drach-Zahavy, A. (2015). An attribution theory perspective on emotional labour in nurse–patient encounters: A nested cross-sectional study in paediatric settings. *Journal of Advanced Nursing, 71*(5), 1123–1134. doi:10.1111/jan.12612 PMID:25558788

Gooty, J., Connelly, S., Griffith, J., & Gupta, A. (2010). Leadership, affect and emotions: A state of the science review. *The Leadership Quarterly, 21*(6), 979–1004. doi:10.1016/j.leaqua.2010.10.005

Gooty, J., Thomas, J., & Connelly, S. (2015) The leader–member exchange relationship: a cross-level examination of emotions and emotion-related phenomena. In K. Niven and H. Madrid (Chairs). *Emotions and Leadership: How leader emotion influences followers. Annual Meeting of the Academy of Management*, Vancouver, Canada.

Gorgi, H. A., Ahmadi, A., Shabaninejad, H., Tahmasbi, A., Baratimarnani, A., & Mehralian, G. (2015). The impact of emotional intelligence on managers' performance: Evidence from hospitals located in Tehran. *Journal of Education and Health Promotion, 4*.

Gosseries, O., Demertzi, A., Ledoux, D., Bruno, M. A., Vanhaudenhuyse, A., Thibaut, A., & Schnakers, C. et al. (2012). Burnout in healthcare workers managing chronic patients with disorders of consciousness. *Brain Injury : [BI]*, *26*(12), 1493–1499. doi:10.3109/02699052.2012.695426 PMID:22725684

Gourzoulidis, G., Kontodimopoulos, N., Kastanioti, C., Bellali, T., Goumas, K., Voudigaris, D., & Polyzos, N. (2015). Do self-perceptions of emotional intelligence predict health-related quality of life? A case study in hospital managers in Greece. *Global Journal of Health Science*, *7*(1), 210. PMID:25560350

Grandey, A. A. (2000). Emotional regulation in the workplace: A new way to conceptualize emotional labor. *Journal of Occupational Health Psychology*, *5*(1), 95–110. doi:10.1037/1076-8998.5.1.95 PMID:10658889

Grandey, A. A. (2008). Emotions at work: A review and research agenda. In Handbook of Organizational Behavior (pp. 235-261).

Greco, P., Laschinger, H. K. S., & Wong, C. (2006). Leader empowering behaviours, staff nurse empowerment and work engagement/burnout. *Nursing Leadership*, *19*(4), 41–56. doi:10.12927/cjnl.2006.18599 PMID:17265673

Greenglass, E. R., Burke, R. J., & Fiksenbaum, L. (2001). Workload and burnout in nurses. *Journal of Community & Applied Social Psychology*, *11*(3), 211–215. doi:10.1002/casp.614

Grisales Romero, H., Muñoz, Y., Osorio, D., & Robles, E. (2016). Burnout syndrome in nursing personnel of a referral hospital in Ibague, Colombia, 2014. *Enfermería Global*, *15*(1), 244–257. doi:10.6018/eglobal.15.1.212851

Gross, J. J. (1999). Emotion regulation: Past, present, future. *Cognition and Emotion*, *13*(5), 551–573. doi:10.1080/026999399379186

Gross, J. J. (2007). Emotion regulation: Conceptual foundations. In J. J. Gross (Ed.), *Handbook of Emotion Regulation* (pp. 3–26). New York: Guilford.

Gross, J. J., & John, O. P. (2003). Individual differences in two emotion regulation processes: Implications for affect, relationships, and well being. *Journal of Personality and Social Psychology*, *85*(2), 348–362. doi:10.1037/0022-3514.85.2.348 PMID:12916575

Güleryüz, G., Güney, S., Aydın, E. M., & Aşan, Ö. (2008). The mediating effect of job satisfaction between emotional intelligence and organisational commitment of nurses: A questionnaire survey. *International Journal of Nursing Studies*, *45*(11), 1625–1635. doi:10.1016/j.ijnurstu.2008.02.004 PMID:18394625

Guo, J., Chen, J., Fu, J., Ge, X., Chen, M., & Liu, Y. (2016). Structural empowerment, job stress and burnout of nurses in China. *Applied Nursing Research*, *31*, 41–45. doi:10.1016/j.apnr.2015.12.007 PMID:27397817

Halbesleben, J. R., & Buckley, M. R. (2004). Burnout in organizational life. *Journal of Management*, *30*(6), 859–879. doi:10.1016/j.jm.2004.06.004

Hanrahan, N. P., Aiken, L. H., McClaine, L., & Hanlon, A. L. (2010). Relationship between psychiatric nurse work environments and nurse burnout in acute care general hospitals. *Issues in Mental Health Nursing*, *31*(3), 198–207. doi:10.3109/01612840903200068 PMID:20144031

Hare, R. (1986). *The social construction of emotions*. New York: Basil Blackwell.

Harker, L., & Keltner, D. (2001). Expressions of positive emotion in womens college yearbook pictures and their relationship to personality and life outcomes across adulthood. *Journal of Personality and Social Psychology, 80*(1), 112–124. doi:10.1037/0022-3514.80.1.112 PMID:11195884

Hayes, B., Douglas, C., & Bonner, A. (2015). Work environment, job satisfaction, stress and burnout among haemodialysis nurses. *Journal of Nursing Management, 23*(5), 588–598. doi:10.1111/jonm.12184 PMID:24372699

Heffernan, M., Quinn Griffin, M. T., McNulty, S. R., & Fitzpatrick, J. J. (2010). Self-compassion and emotional intelligence in nurses. *International Journal of Nursing Practice, 16*(4), 366–373. doi:10.1111/j.1440-172X.2010.01853.x PMID:20649668

Heydari, A., Kareshki, H., & Armat, M. R. (2016). Is nurses professional competence related to their personality and emotional intelligence? A cross-sectional study. *Journal of Caring Sciences, 5*(2), 121–132. doi:10.15171/jcs.2016.013 PMID:27354976

Hill, C. W. L., & Jones, G. R. (2004). *Strategic management theory: An integrated approach* (6th ed.). Boston: Houghton Mifflin Company.

Hiller, N. J., & Hambrick, D. C. (2005). Conceptualizing executive hubris: The role of (hyper-) core self-evaluations in strategic decision making. *Strategic Management Journal, 26*(4), 297–319. doi:10.1002/smj.455

Hochschild, A. R. (1979). Emotion work, feeling rules, and social structure. *American Journal of Sociology, 85*(3), 551–575. doi:10.1086/227049

Hochschild, A. R. (1983). *The managed heart: Commercialization of human feeling*. Berkeley: University of California Press.

Hogan, R. L., & McKnight, M. A. (2007). Exploring burnout among university online instructors: An initial investigation. *The Internet and Higher Education, 10*(2), 117–124. doi:10.1016/j.iheduc.2007.03.001

Hong, E., & Lee, Y. S. (2016). The mediating effect of emotional intelligence between emotional labour, job stress, burnout and nurses turnover intention. *International Journal of Nursing Practice, 22*(6), 625–632. doi:10.1111/ijn.12493 PMID:27653752

Hooper, C., Craig, J., Janvrin, D. R., Wetsel, M. A., & Reimels, E. (2010). Compassion satisfaction, burnout, and compassion fatigue among emergency nurses compared with nurses in other selected inpatient specialties. *Journal of Emergency Nursing: JEN, 36*(5), 420–427. doi:10.1016/j.jen.2009.11.027 PMID:20837210

Horowitz, C. R., Suchman, A. L., Branch, W. T., & Frankel, R. M. (2003). What do doctors find meaningful about their work? *Annals of Internal Medicine, 138*(9), 772–775. doi:10.7326/0003-4819-138-9-200305060-00028 PMID:12729445

House, R. J. (1996). Path-goal theory of leadership: Lessons, legacy and a reformulated theory. *The Leadership Quarterly, 7*(3), 323–352. doi:10.1016/S1048-9843(96)90024-7

Howard, M. C. (2009). Emotional intelligence as a predictor of job satisfaction, organizational commitment, and occupational commitment among human service workers. *Dissertation Abstracts International, 69*(12B), 7842.

Humphrey, R. (2015). The influence of leader emotional intelligence on employees' job satisfaction: a meta-analysis. *Proceedings of the International Leadership Association 17th Annual Global Conference*.

Humphrey, R. H. (2002). The many faces of emotional leadership. *The Leadership Quarterly, 13*(5), 493–504. doi:10.1016/S1048-9843(02)00140-6

Humphrey, R. H. (2008). The right way to lead with emotional labor. In R. H. Humphrey (Ed.), *Affect and emotion: New directions in management theory and research* (pp. 1–17). Charlotte, NC: Information Age Publishing.

Humphrey, R. H., Ashforth, B. E., & Diefendorff, J. M. (2015). The bright side of emotional labor. *Journal of Organizational Behavior, 36*(6), 749–769. doi:10.1002/job.2019

Humphrey, R. H., Burch, G. F., & Adams, L. L. (2016). The benefits of merging leadership research and emotions research. *Frontiers in Psychology, 7*. PMID:27458415

Im Kim, Y., Geun, H. G., Choi, S., & Lee, Y. S. (2016). The impact of organizational commitment and nursing organizational culture on job satisfaction in Korean American registered nurses. *Journal of Transcultural Nursing*.

Jadoo, S. A. A., Aljunid, S. M., Dastan, I., Tawfeeq, R. S., Mustafa, M. A., Ganasegeran, K., & AlDubai, S. A. R. (2015). Job satisfaction and turnover intention among Iraqi doctors-a descriptive cross-sectional multicentre study. *Human Resources for Health, 13*(1), 1. PMID:25588887

Jang, H. M., Park, J. Y., Choi, Y. J., Park, S. W., & Lim, H. N. (2016). Effect of general hospital nurses perception of patient safety culture and burnout on safety management activities. *Journal of Korean Academy of Nursing Administration, 22*(3), 239–250. doi:10.11111/jkana.2016.22.3.239

Judge, T. A., Thoresen, C. J., Bono, J. E., & Patton, G. K. (2001). The job satisfaction–job performance relationship: A qualitative and quantitative review. *Psychological Bulletin, 127*(3), 376–407. doi:10.1037/0033-2909.127.3.376 PMID:11393302

Kafetsios, K. (2003). Emotional Intelligence abilities: Theory and application in occupational settings. *Greek Business Academy, 2*, 16–25.

Kafetsios, K., Anagnostopoulos, F., Lempesis, E., & Valindra, A. (2014). Doctors emotion regulation and patient satisfaction: A social-functional perspective. *Health Communication, 29*(2), 205–214. doi: 10.1080/10410236.2012.738150 PMID:23537402

Kafetsios, K., Athanasiadou, M., & Dimou, N. (2014). Leaders and subordinates attachment orientations, emotion regulation capabilities and affect at work: A multilevel analysis. *The Leadership Quarterly, 25*(3), 512–527. doi:10.1016/j.leaqua.2013.11.010

Kafetsios, K., & Loumakou, M. (2007). A comparative evaluation of the effects of trait emotional intelligence and emotion regulation on affect at work and job satisfaction. *International Journal of Work Organization and Emotion, 2*(1), 71–87. doi:10.1504/IJWOE.2007.013616

Kafetsios, K., Nezlek, J. B., & Vassilakou, Th. (2012). Relationships between leaders and subordinates emotion regulation, satisfaction and affect at work. *The Journal of Social Psychology, 152*(4), 436–457. doi:10.1080/00224545.2011.632788 PMID:22822684

Kafetsios, K., Nezlek, J. B., & Vassiou, K. (2011). A multilevel analysis of relationships between leaders and subordinates emotional intelligence and emotional outcomes. *Journal of Applied Social Psychology, 41*(5), 119–1142. doi:10.1111/j.1559-1816.2011.00750.x

Kafetsios, K., & Zampetakis, L. A. (2008). Emotional intelligence and job satisfaction: Testing the mediatory role of positive and negative affect at work. *Personality and Individual Differences, 44*(3), 710–720. doi:10.1016/j.paid.2007.10.004

Kahraman, N., & Hiçdurmaz, D. (2016). Identifying emotional intelligence skills of Turkish clinical nurses according to sociodemographic and professional variables. *Journal of Clinical Nursing, 25*(7-8), 1006–1015. doi:10.1111/jocn.13122 PMID:26914619

Kalleberg, A. L. (1977). Work values and job rewards: A theory of job satisfaction. *American Sociological Review, 42*(1), 124–143. doi:10.2307/2117735

Kanai-Pak, M., Aiken, L. H., Sloane, D. M., & Poghosyan, L. (2008). Poor work environments and nurse inexperience are associated with burnout, job dissatisfaction and quality deficits in Japanese hospitals. *Journal of Clinical Nursing, 17*(24), 3324–3329. doi:10.1111/j.1365-2702.2008.02639.x PMID:19146591

Katz, D., & Kahn, R. (1966). *The social psychology of Organizations*. New York: John Wiley & Sons.

Kaur, D., Sambasivan, M., & Kumar, N. (2015). Impact of emotional intelligence and spiritual intelligence on the caring behavior of nurses: A dimension-level exploratory study among public hospitals in Malaysia. *Applied Nursing Research, 28*(4), 293–298. doi:10.1016/j.apnr.2015.01.006 PMID:26608428

Keltner, D., & Haidt, J. (2001). Social functions of emotions. In T. J. Mayne & G. A. Bonanno (Eds.), *Emotions: Current issues and future directions* (pp. 192–213). New York: Guilford.

Kent, T. W. (2006). Leadership and emotions in health care organizations. *Journal of Health Organization and Management, 20*(1), 49–66. doi:10.1108/14777260610656552 PMID:16703842

Khamisa, N., Peltzer, K., Ilic, D., & Oldenburg, B. (2016). Work related stress, burnout, job satisfaction and general health of nurses: A follow-up study. *International Journal of Nursing Practice, 22*(6), 538–545. doi:10.1111/ijn.12455 PMID:27241867

Khunou, S. H., & Davhana-Maselesele, M. (2016). Level of job satisfaction amongst nurses in the North-West Province, South Africa: Post occupational specific dispensation. *Curationis, 39*(1), 1–10. doi:10.4102/curationis.v39i1.1438 PMID:26974827

Kilroy, S., Flood, P. C., Bosak, J., & Chênevert, D. (2016). Perceptions of high-involvement work practices and burnout: The mediating role of job demands. *Human Resource Management Journal, 26*(4), 408–424. doi:10.1111/1748-8583.12112

Klein, J., Frie, K. G., Blum, K., & von dem Knesebeck, O. (2010). Burnout and perceived quality of care among German clinicians in surgery. *International Journal for Quality in Health Care, 22*(6), 525–530. doi:10.1093/intqhc/mzq056 PMID:20935011

Koning, L. F., & Van Kleef, G. A. (2015). How leaders emotional displays shape followers organizational citizenship behavior. *The Leadership Quarterly*, *26*(4), 489–501. doi:10.1016/j.leaqua.2015.03.001

Kovács, M., Kovács, E., & Hegedűs, K. (2010). Emotion work and burnout: Cross-sectional study of nurses and physicians in Hungary. *Croatian Medical Journal*, *51*(5), 432–442. doi:10.3325/cmj.2010.51.432 PMID:20960593

Kowalski, C., Ommen, O., Driller, E., Ernstmann, N., Wirtz, M. A., Köhler, T., & Pfaff, H. (2010). Burnout in nurses–the relationship between social capital in hospitals and emotional exhaustion. *Journal of Clinical Nursing*, *19*(11-12), 1654–1663. doi:10.1111/j.1365-2702.2009.02989.x PMID:20384668

Kupers, W., & Weibler, J. R. (2008). Emotions in organisation: An integral perspective. *International Journal of Work Organisation and Emotion*, *2*(3), 256–287. doi:10.1504/IJWOE.2008.019426

Landa, J. M. A., López-Zafra, E., Martos, M. P. B., & del Carmen Aguilar-Luzón, M. (2008). The relationship between emotional intelligence, occupational stress and health in nurses: A questionnaire survey. *International Journal of Nursing Studies*, *45*(6), 888–901. doi:10.1016/j.ijnurstu.2007.03.005 PMID:17509597

Landsbergis, P. A. (1988). Occupational stress among health care workers: A test of the job demands-control model. *Journal of Organizational Behavior*, *9*(3), 217–239. doi:10.1002/job.4030090303

Lang, P. J. (1984). The cognitive psychophysiology of emotion: Fear and anxiety. In A. H. Tuma & J. D. Maser (Eds.), *Anxiety and the anxiety disorders* (pp. 131–170). Hillsdale, NJ: Erlbaum.

Laschinger, H. K. S., & Fida, R. (2015). Linking nurses perceptions of patient care quality to job satisfaction: The role of authentic leadership and empowering professional practice environments. *The Journal of Nursing Administration*, *45*(5), 276–283. doi:10.1097/NNA.0000000000000198 PMID:25906136

Lawler, E. J., & Thye, S. R. (1999). Bringing emotions into social exchange theory. *Annual Review of Sociology*, *25*(1), 217–244. doi:10.1146/annurev.soc.25.1.217

Lee, K., & Allen, N. J. (2002). Organizational citizenship behavior and workplace deviance: The role of affect and cognitions. *The Journal of Applied Psychology*, *87*(1), 131–142. doi:10.1037/0021-9010.87.1.131 PMID:11916207

Leiter, M. P., & Laschinger, H. K. S. (2006). Relationships of work and practice environment to professional burnout: Testing a causal model. *Nursing Research*, *55*(2), 137–146. doi:10.1097/00006199-200603000-00009 PMID:16601626

Lewis, K. M. (2000). When leaders display emotion: How followers respond to negative emotional expression of male and female leaders. *Journal of Organizational Behavior*, *21*(2), 221–234. doi:10.1002/(SICI)1099-1379(200003)21:2<221::AID-JOB36>3.0.CO;2-0

Li, H., Zuo, M., Zhao, X., Zhang, B., Gelb, A., Yao, D., ... & Huang, Y. (2016). Abstract PR589: A cross-sectional survey of anesthesiologists' job satisfaction and burnout in Beijing, Tianjin and Hebei of China: Current challenge and possible solutions. *Anesthesia & Analgesia*, *123*(Suppl. 3), 318.

Liang, H. Y., Tang, F. I., Wang, T. F., Lin, K. C., & Yu, S. (2016). Nurse characteristics, leadership, safety climate, emotional labour and intention to stay for nurses: A structural equation modelling approach. *Journal of Advanced Nursing*, 72(12), 3068–3080. doi:10.1111/jan.13072 PMID:27400365

Lin, T. C., Lin, H. S., Cheng, S. F., Wu, L. M., & Ou-Yang, M. C. (2016). Work stress, occupational burnout and depression levels: A clinical study of paediatric intensive care unit nurses in Taiwan. *Journal of Clinical Nursing*, 25(7), 1120–1130. doi:10.1111/jocn.13119 PMID:26914523

Lindqvist, R., Smeds Alenius, L., Griffiths, P., Runesdotter, S., & Tishelman, C. (2015). Structural characteristics of hospitals and nurse-reported care quality, work environment, burnout and leaving intentions. *Journal of Nursing Management*, 23(2), 263–274. doi:10.1111/jonm.12123 PMID:24047463

Little, L. M., Gooty, J., & Williams, M. (2016). The role of leader emotion management in leader–member exchange and follower outcomes. *The Leadership Quarterly*, 27(1), 85–97. doi:10.1016/j.leaqua.2015.08.007

Liu, Y. E., While, A., Li, S. J., & Ye, W. Q. (2015). Job satisfaction and work related variables in Chinese cardiac critical care nurses. *Journal of Nursing Management*, 23(4), 487–497. doi:10.1111/jonm.12161 PMID:24112300

Locke, E. A. (1976). The nature and causes of job satisfaction. In M. Dunette (Ed.), *Handbook of Industrial and Organizational Psychology* (pp. 1297–1349). Chicago: Rand McNally.

Lu, M., Ruan, H., Xing, W., & Hu, Y. (2015). Nurse burnout in China: A questionnaire survey on staffing, job satisfaction, and quality of care. *Journal of Nursing Management*, 23(4), 440–447. doi:10.1111/jonm.12150 PMID:24024567

Lu, Y., Hu, X. M., Huang, X. L., Zhuang, X. D., Guo, P., Feng, L. F., & Hao, Y. T. et al. (2016). Job satisfaction and associated factors among healthcare staff: A cross-sectional study in Guangdong Province, China. *BMJ Open*, 6(7), e011388. doi:10.1136/bmjopen-2016-011388 PMID:27436667

Lucas, V., Spence Laschinger, H. K., & Wong, C. A. (2008). The impact of emotional intelligent leadership on staff nurse empowerment: The moderating effect of span of control. *Journal of Nursing Management*, 16(8), 964–973. doi:10.1111/j.1365-2834.2008.00856.x PMID:19094109

Mann, S. (1999). Emotion at work: To what extent are we expressing, suppressing, or faking it? *European Journal of Work and Organizational Psychology*, 8(3), 347–369. doi:10.1080/135943299398221

Mark, A. (2005). Organizing emotions in health care. *Journal of Health Organization and Management*, 19(4/5), 277–289. doi:10.1108/14777260510615332 PMID:16206913

Martin, R., Guillaume, Y., Thomas, G., Lee, A., & Epitropaki, O. (2016). Leader–Member exchange (LMX) and performance: A meta-analytic review. *Personnel Psychology*, 69(1), 67–121. doi:10.1111/peps.12100

Maruyama, A., Suzuki, E., & Takayama, Y. (2016). Factors affecting burnout in female nurses who have preschool-age children. *Japan Journal of Nursing Science*, 13(1), 123–134. doi:10.1111/jjns.12096 PMID:26477333

Maslach, C., & Jackson, S. (1986). *Maslach Burnout Inventory manual* (2nd ed.). Palo Alto, CA: Consulting Psychologists Press.

Maslach, C., & Leiter, M. P. (2016). Understanding the burnout experience: Recent research and its implications for psychiatry. *World Psychiatry; Official Journal of the World Psychiatric Association (WPA)*, *15*(2), 103–111. doi:10.1002/wps.20311 PMID:27265691

Maslach, C., & Schaufeli, W. B. (1993). Historical and conceptual development of burnout. In W. B. Schaufeli, C. Maslach, & T. Marek (Eds.), *Professional burnout: Recent developments in theory and research* (pp. 1–16). Washington, DC: Taylor and Francis.

Maslow, A. H. (1943). A theory of human motivation. *Psychological Review*, *50*(4), 370–396. doi:10.1037/h0054346

Maslow, A. H. (1970). *Motivation and personality* (2nd ed.). New York: Harper & Row.

Mauno, S., Ruokolainen, M., Kinnunen, U., & De Bloom, J. (2016). Emotional labour and work engagement among nurses: Examining perceived compassion, leadership and work ethic as stress buffers. *Journal of Advanced Nursing*, *72*(5), 1169–1181. doi:10.1111/jan.12906 PMID:26841277

Mayer, J. D., Roberts, R. D., & Barsade, S. G. (2008). Human abilities: Emotional intelligence. *Annual Review of Psychology*, *59*(1), 507–536. doi:10.1146/annurev.psych.59.103006.093646 PMID:17937602

Mccord, M. A., Joseph, D. L., & Grijalva, E. (2014). Blinded by the light: The dark side of traditionally desirable personality traits. *Industrial and Organizational Psychology: Perspectives on Science and Practice*, *7*(1), 130–137. doi:10.1111/iops.12121

Mcmillan, K., Butow, P., Turner, J., Yates, P., White, K., Lambert, S., & Lawsin, C. et al. (2016). Burnout and the provision of psychosocial care amongst Australian cancer nurses. *European Journal of Oncology Nursing*, *22*, 37–45. doi:10.1016/j.ejon.2016.02.007 PMID:27179891

Miao, C., Humphrey, R. H., & Qian, S. (2016). Leader emotional intelligence and subordinate job satisfaction: A meta-analysis of main, mediator, and moderator effects. *Personality and Individual Differences*, *102*, 13–24. doi:10.1016/j.paid.2016.06.056

Montano, D., Reeske, A., Franke, F., & Hüffmeier, J. (2016). Leadership, followers mental health and job performance in organizations: A comprehensive meta-analysis from an occupational health perspective. *Journal of Organizational Behavior*. doi:10.1002/job.2124

Montgomery, A., Spânu, F., Băban, A., & Panagopoulou, E. (2015). Job demands, burnout, and engagement among nurses: A multi-level analysis of ORCAB data investigating the moderating effect of teamwork. *Burnout Research*, *2*(2), 71–79. doi:10.1016/j.burn.2015.06.001 PMID:26877971

Moorman, R. H. (1993). The influence of cognitive and affective based job satisfaction measures on the relationship between satisfaction and organizational citizenship behavior. *Human Relations*, *46*(6), 759–776. doi:10.1177/001872679304600604

Muchinsky, P. M. (2000). Emotions in the workplace: The neglect of organizational behavior. *Journal of Organizational Behavior*, *21*(7), 801–805. doi:10.1002/1099-1379(200011)21:7<801::AID-JOB999>3.0.CO;2-A

Nantsupawat, A., Nantsupawat, R., Kunaviktikul, W., Turale, S., & Poghosyan, L. (2016). Nurse burnout, nurse-reported quality of care, and patient outcomes in Thai hospitals. *Journal of Nursing Scholarship*, *48*(1), 83–90. doi:10.1111/jnu.12187 PMID:26650339

Naz, S., Hashmi, A. M., & Asif, A. (2016). Burnout and quality of life in nurses of a tertiary care hospital in Pakistan. *JPMA. The Journal of the Pakistan Medical Association*, *66*(5), 532–536. PMID:27183930

Nelis, D., Quoidbach, J., Mikolajczak, M., & Hansenne, M. (2009). Increasing emotional intelligence: (How) is it possible? *Personality and Individual Differences*, *47*(1), 36–41. doi:10.1016/j.paid.2009.01.046

Nie, Z., Jin, Y., He, L., Chen, Y., Ren, X., Yu, J., & Yao, Y. (2015). Correlation of burnout with social support in hospital nurses. *International Journal of Clinical and Experimental Medicine*, *8*(10), 19144–191449. PMID:26770546

Niedenthal, P. H., Krauth-Gruber, S., & Ric, F. (2006). *Psychology of Emotion: Interpersonal, Experiential and Cognitive Approaches*. New York: Psychology Press.

Nolen-Hoeksema, S. (2011). *Abnormal Psychology* (5th ed., p. 522). New York: McGraw-Hill.

Nooryan, K., Gasparyan, K., Sharif, F., & Zoladl, M. (2012). Controlling anxiety in physicians and nurses working in intensive care units using emotional intelligence items as an anxiety management tool in Iran. *International Journal of General Medicine*, *5*, 5–10. doi:10.2147/IJGM.S25850 PMID:22259255

Nyberg, A., Bernin, P., & Theorell, T. (2005). *The impact of leadership on the health of subordinates*. Stockholm: National Institute for Working Life.

OKelly, F., Manecksha, R. P., Quinlan, D. M., Reid, A., Joyce, A., OFlynn, K., & Thornhill, J. A. et al. (2016). Rates of self-reported burnout and causative factors amongst urologists in Ireland and the UK: A comparative cross-sectional study. *BJU International*, *117*(2), 363–372. doi:10.1111/bju.13218 PMID:26178315

Owen, D. (2006). Hubris and Nemesis in heads of government. *Journal of the Royal Society of Medicine*, *99*(11), 548–551. doi:10.1258/jrsm.99.11.548 PMID:17082296

Owen, D., & Davidson, J. (2009). Hubris syndrome: An acquired personality disorder? A study of US Presidents and UK Prime Ministers over the last 100 years. *Brain*, *132*(5), 1396–1406. doi:10.1093/brain/awp008 PMID:19213778

Ozyurt, A., Hayran, O., & Sur, H. (2006). Predictors of burnout and job satisfaction among Turkish physicians. *QJM*, *99*(3), 161–169. doi:10.1093/qjmed/hcl019 PMID:16490757

Parkinson, B. (1996). Emotions are social. *British Journal of Psychology*, *87*(4), 663–683. doi:10.1111/j.2044-8295.1996.tb02615.x PMID:8962482

Parkinson, B., Fischer, A. H., & Manstead, A. S. (2004). *Emotion in social relations: Cultural, group, and interpersonal processes*. New York: Psychology Press.

Pedersen, A. F., Andersen, C. M., Olesen, F., & Vedsted, P. (2013). Risk of burnout in Danish GPs and exploration of factors associated with development of burnout: A two-wave panel study. *International Journal of Family Medicine*, *2013*, 1–8. doi:10.1155/2013/603713 PMID:24383000

Perneger, T. V., Deom, M., Cullati, S., & Bovier, P. A. (2012). Growing discontent of Swiss doctors, 1998–2007. *European Journal of Public Health*, 22(4), 478–483. doi:10.1093/eurpub/ckr114 PMID:21948053

Persaud, R. (2005). The drama of being a doctor. *Postgraduate Medical Journal*, 81(955), 276–277. doi:10.1136/pgmj.2004.023796 PMID:15879037

Pescosolido, A. T. (2002). Emergent leaders as managers of group emotion. *The Leadership Quarterly*, 13(5), 583–599. doi:10.1016/S1048-9843(02)00145-5

Pines, A., & Aronson, E. (1988). *Career burnout: Causes and cures*. New York: Free Press.

Pines, A. M. (1993). Burnout: An existential perspective. In W. Schaufel, C. Maslach, an M. Tadeusz (Eds.), Professional burnout: Recent developments in theory and research. Series in applied psychology: Social issues and questions (p. 33-51). Philadelphia, PA: Taylor & Francis.

Piperopoulos, G. (2007). Psychology: Individual, team and organization. 9th edition. Thessaloniki, Greece.

Pirola-Merlo, A., Härtel, C., Mann, L., & Hirst, G. (2002). How leaders influence the impact of affective events on team climate and performance in R & D teams. *The Leadership Quarterly*, 13(5), 561–581. doi:10.1016/S1048-9843(02)00144-3

Pisanti, R., Van Der Doef, M., Maes, S., Meier, L. L., Lazzari, D., & Violani, C. (2016). How changes in psychosocial job characteristics impact burnout in nurses: A longitudinal analysis. *Frontiers in Psychology*, 7. PMID:27507952

Platis, C., Reklitis, P., & Zimeras, S. (2015). Relation between job satisfaction and job performance in healthcare services. *Procedia: Social and Behavioral Sciences*, 175, 480–487. doi:10.1016/j.sbspro.2015.01.1226

Poghosyan, L., Clarke, S. P., Finlayson, M., & Aiken, L. H. (2010). Nurse burnout and quality of care: Cross-national investigation in six countries. *Research in Nursing & Health*, 33(4), 288–298. doi:10.1002/nur.20383 PMID:20645421

Power, M., & Dalgleish, T. (1997). *Cognition and emotion: From order to disorder*. Hove, UK: Psychology Press.

Prins, J. T., Van Der Heijden, F. M. M. A., Hoekstra-Weebers, J. E. H. M., Bakker, A. B., Van de Wiel, H. B. M., Jacobs, B., & Gazendam-Donofrio, S. M. (2009). Burnout, engagement and resident physicians self-reported errors. *Psychology Health and Medicine*, 14(6), 654–666. doi:10.1080/13548500903311554 PMID:20183538

Pu, J., Zhou, X., Zhu, D., Zhong, X., Yang, L., Wang, H., & Xie, P. et al. (2016). Gender differences in psychological morbidity, burnout, job stress and job satisfaction among Chinese neurologists: A national cross-sectional study. *Psychology Health and Medicine*, 1–13. doi:10.1080/13548506.2016.1211717 PMID:27436373

Pugh, S. D. (2001). Service with a smile: Emotional contagion in the service encounter. *Academy of Management Journal*, 44(5), 1018–1027. doi:10.2307/3069445

Purpora, C., & Blegen, M. A. (2015). Job satisfaction and horizontal violence in hospital staff registered nurses: The mediating role of peer relationships. *Journal of Clinical Nursing*, *24*(15-16), 2286–2294. doi:10.1111/jocn.12818 PMID:25939756

Putnam, L. L., & Mumby, D. K. (1993). Organizations, emotion and the myth of rationality. Fineman, S. (Ed.), Emotion in organizations. (pp. 36-57). Thousand Oaks, CA: Sage Publications.

Quattrin, R., Zanini, A., Nascig, E., Annunziata, M. A., Calligaris, L., & Brusaferro, S. (2006, July). Level of burnout among nurses working in oncology in an Italian region. *Oncology Nursing Forum*, *33*(4), 815–820. doi:10.1188/06.ONF.815-820 PMID:16858463

Rafaeli, A., & Sutton, R. I. (1987). Expression of emotion as part of the work role. *Academy of Management Review*, *12*(1), 23–37.

Rafferty, A. M., Clarke, S. P., Coles, J., Ball, J., James, P., McKee, M., & Aiken, L. H. (2007). Outcomes of variation in hospital nurse staffing in English hospitals: Cross-sectional analysis of survey data and discharge records. *International Journal of Nursing Studies*, *44*(2), 175–182. doi:10.1016/j.ijnurstu.2006.08.003 PMID:17064706

Rain, J. S., Lane, I. M., & Steiner, D. D. (1991). A current look at the job satisfaction/life satisfaction relationship: Review and future considerations. *Human Relations*, *44*(3), 287–307. doi:10.1177/001872679104400305

Rajah, R., Song, Z., & Arvey, R. D. (2011). Emotionality and leadership: Taking stock of the past decade of research. *The Leadership Quarterly*, *22*(6), 1107–1119. doi:10.1016/j.leaqua.2011.09.006

Riggio, E. R., & Reichard, J. R. (2008). The emotional and social intelligences of effective leadership: An emotional and social skill approach. *Journal of Managerial Psychology*, *23*(2), 169–185. doi:10.1108/02683940810850808

Rode, J. C. (2004). Job satisfaction and life satisfaction revisited: A longitudinal test of an integrated model. *Human Relations*, *57*(9), 1205–1230. doi:10.1177/0018726704047143

Rodgers, C. (2011). *Hubris syndrome: An emergent outcome of the complex social process of everyday interaction*. London: The Daedalus Trust.

Rowold, J., Borgmann, L., & Bormann, K. (2014). Which leadership constructs are important for predicting job satisfaction, affective commitment, and perceived job performance in profit versus nonprofit organizations? *Nonprofit Management & Leadership*, *25*(2), 147–164. doi:10.1002/nml.21116

Saavedra, R., & Van Dyne, L. (1999). Social exchange and emotional investment in work groups. *Motivation and Emotion*, *23*(2), 105–123. doi:10.1023/A:1021377028608

Safi, M. H., & Kolahi, A. A. (2016). The relationship between job satisfaction with burnout and conflict management styles in employees. *Community Health*, *2*(4), 266–274.

Safi, M. H., Mohamadi, F., Amouzadeh, I., & Arshi, S. (2016). The relationship between manager' leadership style with job satisfaction and burnout in staff of Shomal Health Center of Tehran. *Community Health*, *2*(2), 88–97.

Sansoni, J., De Caro, W., Marucci, A. R., Sorrentino, M., Mayner, L., & Lancia, L. (2016). Nurses' Job satisfaction: An Italian study. *Annali di igiene: medicina preventiva e di comunità, 28*(1), 58. PMID:26980510

Schooley, B., Hikmet, N., Tarcan, M., & Yorgancioglu, G. (2016). Comparing burnout across emergency physicians, nurses, technicians, and health information technicians working for the same organization. *Medicine, 95*(10), e2856. doi:10.1097/MD.0000000000002856 PMID:26962780

Seo, H. S., Kim, H., Hwang, S. M., Hong, S. H., & Lee, I. Y. (2016). Predictors of job satisfaction and burnout among tuberculosis management nurses and physicians. *Epidemiology and Health, 38*.

Shamali, M., Shahriari, M., Babaii, A., & Abbasinia, M. (2015). Comparative study of job burnout among critical care nurses with fixed and rotating shift schedules. *Nursing and Midwifery Studies, 4*(3).

Sharma, J., Dhar, R. L., & Tyagi, A. (2016). Stress as a mediator between work–family conflict and psychological health among the nursing staff: Moderating role of emotional intelligence. *Applied Nursing Research, 30*, 268–275. doi:10.1016/j.apnr.2015.01.010 PMID:25769936

Sherman, G. D., Lee, J. J., Cuddy, A. J., Renshon, J., Oveis, C., Gross, J. J., & Lerner, J. S. (2012). Leadership is associated with lower levels of stress. *Proceedings of the National Academy of Sciences of the United States of America, 109*(44), 17903–17907. doi:10.1073/pnas.1207042109 PMID:23012416

Shirey, M. R. (2006). Authentic leaders creating healthy work environments for nursing practice. *American Journal of Critical Care, 15*(3), 256–267. PMID:16632768

Shirom, A. (2003). Job-related burnout: A review. In J. Quic & L. Tetrick (Eds.), *Handbook of occupational health psychology* (pp. 245–264). Washington, DC: American Psychological Association. doi:10.1037/10474-012

Shirom, A., Nirel, N., & Vinokur, A. D. (2006). Overload, autonomy, and burnout as predictors of physicians quality of care. *Journal of Occupational Health Psychology, 11*(4), 328–342. doi:10.1037/1076-8998.11.4.328 PMID:17059297

Shondrick, S. J., Dinh, J. E., & Lord, R. G. (2010). Developments in implicit leadership theory and cognitive science: Applications to improving measurement and understanding alternatives to hierarchical leadership. *The Leadership Quarterly, 21*(6), 959–978. doi:10.1016/j.leaqua.2010.10.004

Sirsawy, U., Steinberg, W. J., & Raubenheimer, J. E. (2016). Levels of burnout among registrars and medical officers working at Bloemfontein public healthcare facilities in 2013. *South African Family Practice, 58*(6), 213–218. doi:10.1080/20786190.2016.1198088

Sojane, J. S., Klopper, H. C., & Coetzee, S. K. (2016). Leadership, job satisfaction and intention to leave among registered nurses in the North West and Free State provinces of South Africa: Original research. *Curationis, 39*(1), 1–10. doi:10.4102/curationis.v39i1.1585

Solomon, R. C. (2004). Ethical leadership, emotions, and trust: Beyond „charisma. In J. Ciulla (Ed.), *Ethics, the heart of leadership* (pp. 83–102). Westport, CT: Praeger.

Soroush, F., Zargham-Boroujeni, A., & Namnabati, M. (2016). The relationship between nurses clinical competence and burnout in neonatal intensive care units. *Iranian Journal of Nursing and Midwifery Research, 21*(4), 424–429. doi:10.4103/1735-9066.185596 PMID:27563328

Spector, P. E. (1997). *Job satisfaction: Application. assessment, causes, and consequences.* Thousand Oaks, CA: Sage Publications.

Spielberger, C. D. (1983). *State – Trait Anxiety Inventory: A comprehensive bibliography.* Palo Alto, CA: Consultant Psychologists Press.

Squires, M. A. E., Tourangeau, A. N. N., Spence Laschinger, H. K., & Doran, D. (2010). The link between leadership and safety outcomes in hospitals. *Journal of Nursing Management, 18*(8), 914–925. doi:10.1111/j.1365-2834.2010.01181.x PMID:21073565

Stamps, P. L., & Piedmonte, E. B. (1986). *Nurses and work satisfaction: An index for measurement.* Ann Arbor, MI: Health Administration Press Perspectives.

Staw, B. M., Sutton, R. I., & Pelled, L. H. (1994). Employee positive emotion and favorable outcomes at the workplace. *Organization Science, 5*(1), 51–71. doi:10.1287/orsc.5.1.51

Stein, S. J., & Book, H. (2010). *The EQ edge: Emotional intelligence and your success* (Vol. 30). Canada: John Wiley & Sons.

Strömgren, M., Eriksson, A., Bergman, D., & Dellve, L. (2016). Social capital among healthcare professionals: A prospective study of its importance for job satisfaction, work engagement and engagement in clinical improvements. *International Journal of Nursing Studies, 53*, 116–125. doi:10.1016/j.ijnurstu.2015.07.012 PMID:26315780

Sun, Y., Gergen, E., Avila, M., & Green, M. (2016). Leadership and job satisfaction: Implications for leaders of accountants. *American Journal of Industrial and Business Management, 6*(03), 268–275. doi:10.4236/ajibm.2016.63024

Sy, T., Tram, S., & OHara, A. L. (2006). Relation of employee and manager emotional intelligence to job satisfaction and performance. *Journal of Vocational Behavior, 68*(3), 461–473. doi:10.1016/j.jvb.2005.10.003

Tao, H., Ellenbecker, C. H., Wang, Y., & Li, Y. (2015). Examining perception of job satisfaction and intention to leave among ICU nurses in China. *International Journal of Nursing Sciences, 2*(2), 140–148. doi:10.1016/j.ijnss.2015.04.007

Taras, V., Kirkman, B. L., & Steel, P. (2010). Examining the impact of cultures consequences: A three-decade, multilevel, meta-analytic review of Hofstedes Cultural Value Dimensions. *The Journal of Applied Psychology, 95*(3), 405–439. doi:10.1037/a0018938 PMID:20476824

Thompson, E. R., & Phua, F. T. (2012). A brief index of affective job satisfaction. *Group & Organization Management, 37*(3), 275–307. doi:10.1177/1059601111434201

To, M. L., Herman, H. M., & Ashkanasy, N. M. (2015). A multilevel model of transformational leadership, affect, and creative process behavior in work teams. *The Leadership Quarterly, 26*(4), 543–556. doi:10.1016/j.leaqua.2015.05.005

Top, M., Akdere, M., & Tarcan, M. (2015). Examining transformational leadership, job satisfaction, organizational commitment and organizational trust in Turkish hospitals: Public servants versus private sector employees. *International Journal of Human Resource Management, 26*(9), 1259–1282. doi:10.1080/09585192.2014.939987

Trbojevic-Stankovic, J., Stojimirovic, B., Soldatovic, I., Petrovic, D., Nesic, D., & Simic, S. (2015). Work-related factors as predictors of burnout in Serbian nurses working in hemodialysis. *Nephrology Nursing Journal, 42*(6), 553–561. PMID:26875230

Vahidi, M., Namdar Areshtanab, H., & Arshadi Bostanabad, M. (2016). *The relationship between emotional intelligence and perception of job performance among nurses in north west of Iran*. Scientifica.

Vakola, M., Tsaousis, I., & Nikolaou, I. (2004). The role of emotional intelligence and personality variables on attitudes toward organisational change. *Journal of Managerial Psychology, 19*(2), 88–110. doi:10.1108/02683940410526082

Van Dijk, P. A., & Brown, A. K. (2006). Emotional labour and negative job outcomes: An evaluation of the mediating role of emotional dissonance. *Journal of Management & Organization, 12*(2), 101–115. doi:10.5172/jmo.2006.12.2.101

Van Kleef, G. A. (2009). How emotions regulate social life: The emotions as social information (EASI) model. *Current Directions in Psychological Science, 18*(3), 184–188. doi:10.1111/j.1467-8721.2009.01633.x

Van Kleef, G. A., Homan, A. C., & Cheshin, A. (2012). Emotional influence at work: Take it EASI. *Organizational Psychology Review, 2*(4), 311–339. doi:10.1177/2041386612454911

Vifladt, A., Simonsen, B. O., Lydersen, S., & Farup, P. G. (2016). The association between patient safety culture and burnout and sense of coherence: A cross-sectional study in restructured and not restructured intensive care units. *Intensive & Critical Care Nursing: The Official Journal of the British Association of Critical Care Nurses*.

Vinokur-Kaplan, J. X. (1991). Job satisfaction among social workers in public and voluntary child welfare agencies. *Child Welfare, 155*, 81–91.

Waldman, D. A., Balthazard, P. A., & Peterson, S. J. (2011). Leadership and neuroscience: Can we revolutionize the way that inspirational leaders are identified and developed? *The Academy of Management Perspectives, 25*(1), 60–74. doi:10.5465/AMP.2011.59198450

Wallace, J. E., Lemaire, J. B., & Ghali, W. A. (2009). Physician wellness: A missing quality indicator. *Lancet, 374*(9702), 1714–1721. doi:10.1016/S0140-6736(09)61424-0 PMID:19914516

Wang, M. L., & Chang, S. C. (2016). The impact of job involvement on emotional labor to customer-oriented behavior: An empirical study of hospital nurses. *The Journal of Nursing Research, 24*(2), 153–162. doi:10.1097/jnr.0000000000000114 PMID:26551214

Wang, X., Kunaviktikul, W., & Wichaikhum, O. A. (2013). Work empowerment and burnout among registered nurses in two tertiary general hospitals. *Journal of Clinical Nursing, 22*(19-20), 2896–2903. doi:10.1111/jocn.12083 PMID:23834534

Weisinger, H. (1998). *Emotional Intelligence at work: The un-taped edge for success*. San Francisco: Jossey-Bass.

Weiss, H. M. (2002). Conceptual and empirical foundations for the study of affect at work. In R. G. Lord, R. J. Klimoski, and R. Kanfer (Eds.), Emotions in the workplace: Understanding the structure and role of emotions in organizational behavior (pp. 20-63). San Francisco: Jossey Bass.

Welp, A., Meier, L. L., & Manser, T. (2015). Emotional exhaustion and workload predict clinician-rated and objective patient safety. *Frontiers in Psychology*, *5*, 1573. doi:10.3389/fpsyg.2014.01573 PMID:25657627

Wen, J., Cheng, Y., Hu, X., Yuan, P., Hao, T., & Shi, Y. (2016). Workload, burnout, and medical mistakes among physicians in China: A cross-sectional study. *Bioscience trends, 10*(1), 27-33.

Weng, H. C., Chen, H. C., Chen, H. J., Lu, K., & Hung, S. Y. (2008). Doctors emotional intelligence and the patient–doctor relationship. *Medical Education*, *42*(7), 703–711. doi:10.1111/j.1365-2923.2008.03039.x PMID:18588649

Weng, H. C., Hung, C. M., Liu, Y. T., Cheng, Y. J., Yen, C. Y., Chang, C. C., & Huang, C. K. (2011). Associations between emotional intelligence and doctor burnout, job satisfaction and patient satisfaction. *Medical Education*, *45*(8), 835–842. doi:10.1111/j.1365-2923.2011.03985.x PMID:21752080

Williams, E. S., Manwell, L. B., Konrad, T. R., & Linzer, M. (2007). The relationship of organizational culture, stress, satisfaction, and burnout with physician-reported error and suboptimal patient care: Results from the MEMO study. *Health Care Management Review*, *32*(3), 203–212. doi:10.1097/01.HMR.0000281626.28363.59 PMID:17666991

Wong, C. S., & Law, S. K. (2002). The effects of leader and follower emotional intelligence on performance and attitude: An exploratory study. *The Leadership Quarterly*, *13*(3), 243–274. doi:10.1016/S1048-9843(02)00099-1

Xie, Z., Wang, A., & Chen, B. (2011). Nurse burnout and its association with occupational stress in a cross-sectional study in Shanghai. *Journal of Advanced Nursing*, *67*(7), 1537–1546. doi:10.1111/j.1365-2648.2010.05576.x PMID:21261698

Yang, F. H., & Chang, C. C. (2008). Emotional labour, job satisfaction and organizational commitment amongst clinical nurses: A questionnaire survey. *International Journal of Nursing Studies*, *45*(6), 879–887. doi:10.1016/j.ijnurstu.2007.02.001 PMID:17391673

Yoon, H. S., & Sok, S. R. (2016). Experiences of violence, burnout and job satisfaction in Korean nurses in the emergency medical centre setting. *International Journal of Nursing Practice*, *22*(6), 596–604. doi:10.1111/ijn.12479 PMID:27581098

Zaccaro, S. J. A. (2007). Trait-based perspectives of leadership. *The American Psychologist*, *62*(1), 6–16. doi:10.1037/0003-066X.62.1.6 PMID:17209675

Zeidner, M., Matthews, G., & Roberts, R. D. (2004). Emotional intelligence in the workplace: A critical review. *Applied Psychology*, *53*(3), 371–399. doi:10.1111/j.1464-0597.2004.00176.x

Zhu, B., Chen, C. R., Shi, Z. Y., Li, B., Liang, H. X., & Liu, B. (2016). Mediating effect of self-efficacy in relationship between Emotional Intelligence and clinical communication competency of nurses. *International Journal of Nursing Sciences, 3*(2), 162–168. doi:10.1016/j.ijnss.2016.04.003

Zhu, Y., Liu, C., Guo, B., Zhao, L., & Lou, F. (2015). The impact of emotional intelligence on work engagement of registered nurses: The mediating role of organisational justice. *Journal of Clinical Nursing, 24*(15-16), 2115–2124. doi:10.1111/jocn.12807 PMID:25894887

Zopiatis, A., & Constanti, P. (2010). Leadership styles and burnout: Is there an association? *International Journal of Contemporary Hospitality Management, 22*(3), 300–320. doi:10.1108/09596111011035927

ADDITIONAL READING

Bar-On, R. E., & Parker, J. D. (2000). *The handbook of emotional intelligence: Theory, development, assessment, and application at home, school, and in the workplace*. San Francisco: Jossey-Bass.

Bauer, T. N., & Erdogan, B. (Eds.). (2015). *The Oxford handbook of leader-member exchange*. Oxford: Oxford University Press. doi:10.1093/oxfordhb/9780199326174.001.0001

Fleming, K. (2016). The leader's guide to emotional agility (emotional intelligence): How to use soft skills to get hard results. New York: Pearson Higher Ed.

Goleman, D. (2011). *Leadership: The power of emotional intelligence. Selected writings*. More Than Sound.

Goleman, D., Boyatzis, R., & McKee, A. (2002). *Primal leadership: Realizing the power of emotional intelligence*. Boston: Harvard Business School Press.

Lord, R. G., Klimoski, R. J., & Kanfer, R. (Eds.). (2002). *Emotions in the workplace: Understanding the structure and role of emotions in organizational behavior* (Vol. 7). Pfeiffer.

KEY TERMS AND DEFINITIONS

Anxiety: An emotion that resembles an unpleasant state of inner turmoil, which is usually accompanied by somatic complaints.

Burnout: The ultimate depletion that occurs in the physical and mental powers of the individual who wants to achieve unrealistic job objectives.

Emotional Intelligence: The capacity that leaders and subordinates demonstrate when they recognize their own and other people's emotions, when they discriminate between different feelings and label them appropriately, and when they use information relating to emotions in order to guide their own and other's thinking and behavior.

Emotional Labor: The display of emotions toward customers or other people in the working place, that can facilitate the interpersonal communication.

Emotional Regulation: The ability to respond to the ongoing demands of experience with the range of emotions in a manner that is socially tolerable and sufficiently flexible to permit spontaneous reactions as well as the ability to delay spontaneous reactions as needed.

Job Satisfaction: The positive feelings and thoughts that both leaders and subordinates may have towards their job.

Leadership: The ability of an individual-leader or organization to guide other individuals-subordinates, teams or entire organizations.

Chapter 3
The Art and Science in Communication:
Workplace (Cross-Cultural) Communication Skills and Competencies in the Modern Workforce

Ben Tran
Alliant International University, USA

ABSTRACT

One of the challenges facing the modern workforce is the increased diversity of the workforce and similarly complex prospective customers with disparate cultural backgrounds. Language barriers, cultural nuances, and value divergence can easily cause unintended misunderstandings and how low efficiency in internal communication in a multinational environment. It leads to conflict among employees and profit loss in organizational productivity. Therefore, effective communication by people from different cultures stands out significantly in the modern workforce who want to make inroads into international markets, take advantage of multiculturalism, and avoid possible side effects. The purpose of this chapter is on communication, specifically, the art and science in communication, resulting in communication skills and competencies in the modern workforce. The chapter will cover the meaning of communication, language, and history/philosophy of communication and will conclude with factors to be sensitive about when becoming effective cross cultural managers in the modern workforce.

INTRODUCTION

The United States is a diverse country of immigrants, so the promotion of cultural diversity and different cultural heritages (Dong, 1995) are necessary. Ethnocentrism is viewed as lacking acceptance of cultural diversity and intolerance for outgroups (Berry & Kalin, 1995). This lack of acceptance of cultural diversity has a strong tendency to lead to negative stereotypes toward other cultural/ethnic groups, negative prejudice and negative behaviors against these group members. As the world becomes a global village

DOI: 10.4018/978-1-5225-2568-4.ch003

The Art and Science in Communication

and increasingly more people with diverse cultural backgrounds interact with each other constantly, it is imperative to investigate what factors could help overcome ethnocentrism, especially as the modern workforce is expanding overseas (Tran, 2016a, 2016b, 2016c).

Tran (2016) states that one of the challenges facing the modern workforce is the increased diversity of the workforce and similarly complex prospective customers with disparate cultural backgrounds. After all, language barriers, cultural nuances, and value divergence can easily cause unintended misunderstandings and how low efficiency in internal communication in a multinational environment. It leads to conflict among employees and profit loss in organizational productivity. Therefore, effective communication by people from different cultures stands out significantly in the modern workforce who want to make inroads into international markets, take advantage of multiculturalism, and avoid possible side effects.

Therefore, the purpose of this chapter is on communication; specifically, the art and science in communication resulting in communication skills and competencies in the modern workforce. The chapter will cover the meaning of communication, language, and history/philosophy of communication. This chapter will briefly touch upon computer-mediated communication (CMC) in relations to communication in the business environment and the global workplace. The chapter will conclude with factors to be sensitive about when becoming effective cross cultural managers in the modern workforce.

COMMUNICATION

According to Tran (2016a, 2016b, 2016c), Scott (2005) defined communication as sending, receiving, and understanding information and meaning, and claimed that receiving and understanding are the most important operations in the communication process since the response of the receiver defines whether or not the communication attempts are successful. Communication, however, can be defined as the process of transmitting information and common understanding from one person to another (Keyton, 2011). The word communication is derived from the Latin word, *communis* which means common. The definition underscores the fact that unless a common understanding results from the exchange of information, there is actually no communication. The two elements in every communication exchange are the sender and the receiver. The sender initiates the communication. The receiver is the individual to whom the message is sent. The sender encodes the idea by selecting words, symbols, or gestures with which to compose a message. The message is the outcome of the encoding, which takes the form of oral or written verbal and nonverbal symbols (Tran, 2016b).

The message, according to Tran (2016b), is sent through a medium or channel, which is the carrier of the communication. The medium can be a face-to-face conversation, a telephone call, an e-mail, a written report, or a text (via a cell phone). The receiver decodes the received message into meaningful information. Noise is anything that distorts the message. Different perceptions of the message, language barriers, interruptions, emotions, and attitudes are examples of noise. Feedback occurs when the receiver responds to the sender's message by returning the message to the sender. Feedback allows the sender to determine whether the message has been received and understood. The elements in the communication process determine the quality of communication. A problem, commonly known as a barrier (Lunenburg, 2010), in any one of these can reduce communication effectiveness (Keyton, 2011). There are numerous barriers that negatively affect effective communication, of which, the following barriers are detrimental to leaders: emotional barriers, physical barriers, semantic barriers, and psychological barriers (Tran, 2016b).

Hence, Scott (2005) further defined two categories of communication that are related to workplace communication: effective communication and efficient communication. Effective communication is when the message of the sender has a successful decoding from the receiver and efficient communication is when the communication is done effectively at a low cost. Furthermore, Guo and Sanchez (2005) defined communication as the creation or exchange of thoughts, ideas, emotions, and understanding between sender(s) and receiver(s). Guo and Sanchez (2005) found a strong relationship among communication and the efficient and effective performance of the organization. Therefore, communication process is the procedure where a sender and a receiver communicate. This scheme incorporates the encoding-decoding operations and describes the usual transfer of the message. McShane and Von Glinow (2003) have illustrated this process by adding the feedback and communication barriers: environment and personal (factors). Furthermore, there are three types of communication: verbal, nonverbal (Moreau, 2013), and gendered (which will not be covered in this chapter).

In the field of communication (academic degrees and researches), according to Tran (2016a, 2016b), foci are commonly (and traditionally dominant) on rhetoric and interpersonal communication, and some higher educational institutions will offer business communication (commonly known as workplace communication), and fewer higher educational institutions will offer intercultural and international (business) communication. In the field of business, on the other hand, foci are commonly (and traditionally dominant) on administration, accounting, economics, finance, management, and marketing. Thereafter, advertising and public relations, business information systems, corporate management, entrepreneurship, human resources management, operations and enterprise resource management, real estate management, and supply chain management started to establish its presence in academics and research.

The last to join the business field are industrial relations and organizational behavior (with ties to psychology). However, in the field of psychology foci are commonly (and traditionally dominant) in clinical psychology: clinicians, therapists, and counseling. Thereafter, common nonclinical psychology made its presence: abnormal, cognitive, developmental, social, and personality. The last to join the psychology field are industrial and organizational psychology [along with organization development (with ties to business)] and human factor [engineering psychology (with ties to engineering)]. Accordingly, the field of communication, and the practice of communication more often than not, becomes rhetorical and subject to interpretation on what communication is and what communication is not, not to mention effective communication (practices) (Tran, 2016b).

Language of Communication

The origins of human language, according to HistoryWorld (N.Y.), will perhaps remain forever obscure. By contrast, the origin of individual languages has been the subject of very precise study over the past two centuries. There are approximately 5,000 languages spoken in the world today, a third of which are located in Africa, but scholars group them together into relatively few families—probably less than twenty. Languages are linked to each other by shared words or sounds or grammatical constructions. The theory is that the members of each linguistic group have descended from one language, a common ancestor. In many cases, that original language is judged by the experts to have been spoken in surprisingly recent times—as little as a few thousand years ago.

Meaning in Semiotics

From a certain point of view, semiotics appears to be a paradoxical discipline, meaning we find it all around us and, yet, nowhere specifically. It perceives itself as a place of convergence for other disciplines: psychology, sociology, anthropology, and in a broader sense, cognitive sciences, philosophy and especially epistemology, linguistics and the sciences of communication. Moreover, semiotics asks to be applied to objects to different from one another that their enumeration would resemble a surrealist collage (Porcar, 2011). Consequently, the shortest definition is that semiotics is the study of signs.

According to Chandler (2014), in the field of semiotics, Swiss linguist, Ferdinand de Saussure (1857-1913), is the founder not only of linguistics, but also of what is now more usually referred to as semiotics (in his Course in General Linguistics, 1916). Other than Saussure (the usual abbreviation), key figures in the early development of semiotics were the American philosopher Charles Sanders Peirce (sic, pronounced 'purse') (1839-1914) and later Charles William Morris (1901-1979) who developed a behaviorist semiotics. Leading modern semiotic theorists include Roland Barthes (1915-1980), Algirdas Greimas (1917-1992), Yuri Lotman (1922-1993), Christian Metz (1931-1993), Umberto Eco (b 1932) and Julia Kristeva (b 1941). A number of linguists other than Saussure have worked within a semiotic framework, such as Louis Hjelmslev (1899-1966) and Roman Jakobson (1896-1982).

It is difficult to disentangle European semiotics from structuralism in its origins for major structuralists include not only Saussure but also Claude Lévi-Strauss (b. 1908) in anthropology and Jacques Lacan (1901-1981) in psychoanalysis. Structuralism is an analytical method which has been employed by many semioticians and which is based on Saussure's linguistic model. Structuralists seek to describe the overall organization of sign systems as languages—as with Lévi-Strauss and myth, kinship rules and totemism, Lacan and the unconscious and Barthes and Greimas and the grammar of narrative. They engage in a search for deep structures underlying the surface features of phenomena. However, contemporary social semiotics has moved beyond the structuralist concern with the internal relations of parts within a self-contained system, seeking to explore the use of signs in specific social situations. Modern semiotic theory is also sometimes allied with a Marxist approach which stresses the role of ideology (Chandler, 2014).

Semiotics began to become a major approach to cultural studies in the late 1960s, partly as a result of the work of Roland Barthes. The translation into English of his popular essays in a collection entitled Mythologies (Barthes, 1957), followed in the 1970s and 1980s by many of his other writings greatly increased scholarly awareness of this approach. Writing in 1964, Barthes declared that 'semiology aims to take in any system of signs, whatever their substance and limits; images, gestures, musical sounds, objects, and the complex associations of all of these, which form the content of ritual, convention or public entertainment: these constitute, if not languages, at least systems of signification' (Barthes, 1957, p. 9). The adoption of semiotics in Britain was influenced by its prominence in the work of the Centre for Contemporary Cultural Studies (CCCS) at the University of Birmingham while the center was under the direction of the neo-Marxist sociologist Stuart Hall (director 1969-79). Although semiotics may be less central now within cultural and media studies, it remains essential for anyone in the field to understand it. What individual scholars have to assess, of course, is whether or not and how semiotics may be useful in shedding light on any aspect of their concerns. Note that Saussure's term, semiology is sometimes used to refer to the Saussurean tradition, while semiotics sometimes refers to the Peircean tradition, but that nowadays the term semiotics is more likely to be used as an umbrella term to embrace the whole field (Nöth 1990, p. 14; Porcar, 2011).

Semiotics is not widely institutionalized as an academic discipline (Porcar, 2011). It is a field of study involving many different theoretical stances and methodological tools. One of the broadest definitions is that of Umberto Eco who states that "semiotics is concerned with everything that can be taken as a sign" (Eco 1976, p. 7). Semiotics involves the study not only of what we refer to as signs in everyday speech, but of anything which stands for something else. In a semiotic sense, signs assume the form of words, images, sounds, gestures and objects. Contemporary semioticians study signs not in isolation but how meanings are made: as such, being concerned not only with communication but also with the construction and maintenance of reality. Semiotics and that branch of linguistics known as semantics have a common concern with the meaning of signs, but John Sturrock argues that whereas semantics focuses on what words mean, semiotics is concerned with how signs mean (Sturrock, 1986, p. 22). For C. W. Morris, semiotics embraced semantics, along with the other traditional branches of linguistics: (1) semantics is the relationship of signs to what they stand for, (2) syntactics (or syntax) is the formal or structural relations between signs, and (3) pragmatics is the relation of signs to interpreters (Morris, 1938, pp. 6-7; Porcar, 2011).

Meaning in Communication

Semiotics is often employed in the analysis of texts (Bach, 1994). Here it should be noted that a text can exist in any medium and may be verbal, nonverbal, or both, despite the logocentric bias of this distinction. The term text usually refers to a message which has been recorded in some way (e.g., writing, audio recording and video recording) so that it is physically independent of its sender or receiver. A text is an assemblage of signs (such as words, images, sounds and/or gestures) constructed (and interpreted) with reference to the conventions associated with a genre and in a particular medium of communication (Kulczycki, 2014; Porcar, 2011).

The term medium is used in a variety of ways by different theorists, and may include such broad categories as speech and writing or print and broadcasting or relate to specific technical forms within the mass media (radio, television, newspapers, magazines, books, photographs, films and records) or the media of interpersonal communication (telephone, letter, fax, e-mail, video conferencing, computer-based chat systems). Some theorists classify media according to the 'channels' involved (e.g., visual, auditory, tactile, and so forth) (Kulczycki, 2014; Nöth 1990, 175). Human experience is inherently multisensory, and every representation of experience is subject to the constraints and affordances of the medium involved (Bach, 1994). Every medium is constrained by the channels which it utilizes.

For instance, even in the very flexible medium of language words fail us in attempting to represent some experiences, and we have no way at all of representing smell or touch with conventional media. Different media and genres provide different frameworks for representing experience, facilitating some forms of expression and inhibiting others (Bach, 1994; Kulczycki, 2014). The differences between media lead Emile Benveniste to argue that the first principle of semiotic systems is that they are not synonymous: "we are not able to say 'the same thing'" in systems based on different units (Innis, 1986, p. 235) in contrast to Hjelmslev who asserted that "in practice, language is a semiotic into which all other semiotics may be translated" (cited in Genosko, 1994, p. 62).

Meaning in Written (Semantic) Communication

According to Tran (2016b), Carston (2008) claimed that Kent Bach has argued in favor of a view of the semantic component of an utterance ('what is said', as Bach uses this term) as consisting of that information which it provides independent of the speaker's communicative intention (Bach, 1987, pp. 180-181; Bach, 2001, p. 22). This is congruent to the first level Carston (2008) advocates, that is linguistically encoded meaning (LEM), or standing linguistic meaning, Kaplan's semantic character, Grice's formal signification, Perry's meaning. Semantics, in Bach's view then, includes not only encoded linguistic information, but also any context given values of shifting from context to context that arise independently of processes (inferences) geared to the recovery of speaker meaning (so employing pragmatic maxims or principles of some sort). This way of drawing the semantics/pragmatics distinction rests on two other distinctions:

1. A distinction between pronouns which refers semantically ('pure' indexicals) and those which refer pragmatically (demonstrative indexicals). For example, according to the Stanford Encyclopedia of Philosophy (2015), the pronouns 'he', 'she', 'his', and 'hers' appear to have three different types of use: indexical uses (sometimes called deictic or demonstrative uses), bound variable uses, and unbound anaphoric uses (Cappelen & Dever, 2014; Carroll, 1999; Giorgi, 2010; Kaplan 1989, pp. 489–90; Partee 1989; Perry, 2015).
2. A distinction between two kinds of context narrow (or semantic) and broad (or pragmatic, or cognitive). For example, Jeffrey King (2012) argues that the semantic value of a demonstrative in a context is the object such that (a) the speaker intends it to be the demonstrative's semantic value and (b) an attentive hearer would take it to be the speaker's intended semantic value (Cappelen & Dever, 2014; Carroll, 1999; Giorgi, 2010; Littlejohn, 1996; Perry, 2015; The Stanford Encyclopedia of Philosophy, 2015).

With regard to the second of these, Bach (1999) states the following: "There are two sorts of contextual information, one is much more restricted in scope than the other. Information that plays the limited role of combining with linguistic information to determine content [in the sense of fixing (or repairing) it] is restricted to a short list of variables, such as the identity of the speaker and the hearer and the time and place of an utterance. Contextual information in the broad sense is anything that the hearer is to take into account to determine (in the sense of ascertain) the speaker's communicative intention" (p. 39).

Therefore, pronouns that refer semantically are those whose referent is a simply function of narrow (semantic) context. Pronouns that refer pragmatically are those whose referents are a function of broad context (and so are a matter of the speaker's communicative, specifically referential, intention). The following examples, discussed in Bach (1987, p. 176), make the distinction very clear. The semantic ('what is said') of (1a) and (1b) is given by (2a) and (2b), respectively (Carroll, 1999; Littlejohn, 1996):

01a. I am ready to go now.
01b. He was ready to go then.
02a. a is ready to go at t
02b. A certain male was ready to go at a certain time period to the time of utterance.

The proposition in (01a) is the result of applying a standard Kaplanian semantics for *I* and now to a narrow context in which *a* is that parameter which corresponds to the speaker and *t* is the time if utterance parameter. Narrow context does not provide any objective parameters as referents for he and then, so their referents have to be pragmatically inferred, using broad context and maxims or principles geared to the recovery of speaker meaning.

Feedback in Communication

Feedback is any information that individuals receive about their behavior. Feedback can be information related to the productivity of groups in an organization or the performance of a particular individual. Through the feedback process, senders and receivers may adjust their outputs as related to the transmitted information. In the absence of feedback, or in the case where the communication process does not allow for sufficient feedback to develop, or feedback is ignored, a certain amount of feedback will occur spontaneously and tends to take a negative form. In one-way communication, a person sends a one directional message without interaction, whereas an opportunity for feedback results in two way communication between the two individuals who are actively engaged in an effective communication process.

Two-way communication is more accurate when the message is complex, although one-way communication is more efficient, as in the case of the physician's written prescription. To be effective, communication must allow opportunities for feedback. Feedback can take several forms, each with a different intent. Keyton (2002) provides us with three different forms of feedback: (1) descriptive (Feedback that identifies or describes how a person communicates), (2) evaluative (Feedback that provides an assessment of the person who communicates), and (3) prescriptive (Feedback that provides advice about how one should behave or communicate) (Guo & Sanchez, 2005).

In addition to forms and intent, according to Guo and Sanchez (2005), there are also four levels of feedback. Feedback can focus on a group or an individual working with specific tasks or procedures. It can also provide information about relationships within the group or individual behavior within a group (Keyton, 2002). The four levels of feedback include: (1) task or procedural, (2) relational, (3) individual, and (4) group (Guo & Sanchez, 2005).

- **Task or Procedural Feedback:** Feedback at this level involves issues of effectiveness and appropriateness. Specific issues that relate to task feedback include the quantity or quality of a group's output. Procedural feedback refers to whether a correct procedure was used appropriately at the time by the group.
- **Relational Feedback:** Feedback that provides information about interpersonal dynamics within a group. This level of feedback emphasizes how a group gets along while working together. It is effective when it is combined with the descriptive and prescriptive forms of feedback.
- **Individual Feedback:** Feedback that focuses on a particular individual in a group.
- **Group Feedback:** Feedback that focuses on how well the group is performing. Like the questions raised at the individual feedback level, similar questions are asked for the group.

History/Philosophy of Communication

Communication history studies issues related to communication, be it interpersonal, group, organizational, or institutional: this means that all the different levels, means and forms of communication are taken into account (Kulczycki, 2014). Communication history is an interdisciplinary study conducted using various research approaches. Communication history can be said to be a subdiscipline of communicology or communication as a discipline (Kulczycki, 2014). Research on various aspects of communication history this defined can be conducted within various scientific disciplines. Consequently, in reconstructing the state of research into communication history, it is possible to differentiate two periods: (1) an explicit communication history and (2) an implicit communication history, which could be called the prehistory of communication history.

Explicit communication history, according to Kulczycki (2014), existed since the end of the 19th century when the modern understanding of communication appeared, and reached its apex in the middle of the 20th century with the formulation of the first theories of communication (i.e., Claude Shannon's mathematical theory of communication or the theories developed by the Chicago School). Within the explicit communication history, two dominant theoretical approaches concerned with the study of the following: (1) media history and (2) communication theory. The first approach in explicit communication history is the most common in communication history, which is why many scholars identify—on the level of terminology—media history with communication history. The second approach in explicit communication history is relatively young, though certain dominant perspectives can already be indicated (Löblich & Scheu, 2011, pp. 1-22), including the institutional, the biological, and the national. Implicit communication, on the other hand, occurs more often in what the anthropologist Edward Hall referred to as high context cultures. In such cultures, people leave many things unsaid. The context, made up of the environment, the situation, and the parties involved, itself carries messages that complement the spoken word and make up for the things that are left unsaid.

The joining of these two periods was effected in communicology in the 1970s. A communicative reading of Plato's *Phaedrus* and *Symposium* led to an increased interest in rhetoric and semiotics (Craig, 1989, pp. 98-101). This means the emergence of contemporary communication history unfolded along two paths: on the one hand, starting with the history of the medium, and proceeding through media history and the history of communication theory and, on the other hand, through the incorporation of a centuries old tradition of rhetoric and semiotics. A close approach to the tradition of communication research is to be found in Robert T. Craig, who also assumes a constitutive approach to communication (Craig, 1999, pp. 119-161). In the text entitled *Communication Theory as a Field*, Craig showed the correlations between the seven major traditions (rhetorical, semiotic, phenomenological, cybernetic, socio-psychological, sociocultural, and critical). The American scholar, however, did not emphasize the research of the historical development of the concept of communication (Kulczycki, 2014).

COMPUTER-MEDIATED COMMUNICATION (CMC)

The essence of communication is to exchange and share information. In contemporary age, media of communication have various forms and states, especially the network medium. But no matter how special it might be, the nature of network mediated by computers is still information is transmitting and sharing. Computer-mediated communication (CMC), according to Yu (2011), is just a new form of human communication with all the former kinds of communication features included. It absorbs and furthermore extends the advantages of the former formats, embracing the instant interaction of oral communication, the abstract logics of printing dissemination, and the vivid images of movie and television. Additionally, it creates a series of new communication formats, such as Hyper Text, Multimedia, and so forth which are the information organizing methods and cross-space message delivering patterns. Benefiting from the continuous development of technique and mechanism, CMC makes the dream of transmitting information cross space and time come true, which will definitely have a great impact on our social lives.

Communication is a process by which people exchange information or express their thoughts and feelings. It has many formats, such as interpersonal communication, organizational communication, oral communication, small group communication, intercultural communication and so on, but CMC is a kind of communication based on computers and networks. CMC is defined as any communicative transaction that occurs through the use of two or more networked computers (McQuail, 2005). Popular forms of CMC include e-mail, video, audio or text chat, bulletin boards, list-services, and massively multiplayer online game (MMO). These settings are changing rapidly with the development of new technologies.

CMC is a system consisting of human and computer, which means it is alive instead of some rigid facilities. The participation of humans makes themselves creators, users, and ameliorators, furthermore the core of the CMC system, which means that without humans the system would only have a cold apparatus remaining. The combination of humans and computers, or to say networks, forms a complicated information transmitting system aiming at information exchanging and sharing freely. There are some general features of information system in the CMC system, together with some special features of human social system. Hence, according to Yu (2011), Harold Dwight Lasswell's well-known comment on communication is "5W model", including: Who (says), What (to), Whom (in), What Channel (with) and What Effect. According to Lasswell's theory, CMC system, as a new form of communication with its own characteristics, can also be divided into five components (McQuail, 2005):

1. **Subject:** The subject of CMC system is human, called Network Users, who can be creators, providers and recipients of the network,
2. **Host:** In computer networking, a network host is a computer connected to the internet—or more generically—to any type of data network,
3. **Information Resource:** Network information is a summation of all messages transmitted by the computer network and memorized on the network nodes
4. **Channel:** Channels of CMC means a path of networks information transmitting, which outs different subject together, making the transmission of network information smooth, and
5. **Relations and Effects:** Network information resources have potential values more or less. After the process of transmitting and accepting of Network information, there are some social impacts having been produced, and that are the effects of CMC. These effects are the essential part of CMC system, and a presentation of the social functions of CMC.

Computer-Mediated Communication in the Business Environment

CMC applications support a great deal of the collaborative activities in organizations and society. The use of CMC applications is widespread in business and educational institutions (Garton & Wellman, 1995; Markus, 1994), with over 90% of businesses using the Internet, and electronic mail (email) identified as the primary application (Brown, Fuller, & Vician, 2004). A recent survey of 123 large businesses

The Art and Science in Communication

indicates that organizations continue to increase their investment in CMC applications for communication, management, and other collaborative activities (Brownell, Dertnig, & Sirkin, 2002). However, some evidence suggests that it is difficult to ensure broad-based use of these technologies to achieve organizational goals (Naughton, Raymond, Shulman, & Struzzi, 1999).

Organizational dependency on one type of CMC, emails, is particularly salient as it is frequently the foundational communication component of networked organizations (Ahuja & Carley, 1999; Holland & Lockett, 1997), virtual teams (Jarvenpaa & Leidner, 1999; Townsend, DeMarie, & Hendrickson, 1998), and electronic communities (Sproull & Kiesler, 1991). Likewise, educational organizations rely heavily on email and text based messaging components of CMC technologies to facilitate technology mediated and distance education (Belanger & Jordan, 2000; Leidner & Jarvenpaa, 1995; Piccoli, Ahmad, & Ives, 2001). Nonetheless, while email appears to flourish at the organizational level as a successful implementation of CMC technology, anecdotal and empirical evidence reveals uneven and problematic usage at the individual level (Grudin, 1994; Hara & Kling, 2000).

Computer-Mediated Communication in the Global Workplace

In the CMC domain, according to Baumer and van Rensburg (2011) cross-cultural communication is twofold. The Internet and the World Wide Web have shrunk the physical world, fitting it into people's offices and homes as soon as their equipment interfaces with a server. New technological designs, applications, and meanings promote change and influence or alter the status quo (Okan, 2007). Information is often just a mouse click away and online communication overcomes geographical and time limitations. Computer technology changes so quickly that its users are continuously stimulated and challenged by its boundless interactive environments. Digitally influences outlooks, understandings, and cognitive processing routines entice interlocutors as individuals or social groups by allowing them a sense of freedom and equity.

According to Baumer and van Rensburg (2011), CMC is limited by its own qualities as it requires competence in computer application, technical sophistication and communicative proficiency. The Internet dissolves face-to-face (FtF) natural occurring inhibitions while drawing interlocutors into its boundless digital environment. Social interactions are manifested in the first or second virtual world and are supported by animation, graphics, sound and text. FtF interactions are simultaneously occurring cooperatively processes between two or more interlocutors. These interactions require instantaneous and continuous signal transmissions and receptions, while uninterrupted feedback is enhanced by nonverbal cues. In CMC, such cues are limited requiring a high level of interactional control and an awareness of linguistic norms and pragmatic peculiarities (Felix, 2003).

The occurrence of cross-cultural misunderstandings in CMC us common and occurrences are well documented. In particular, people from the same language and cultural background develop similar cognitive processing habits informed by environmental perceptions, observations and agreed norms (Feenberg, 1991). Language manners, such as politeness and other attributes of linguistic interactions are becoming increasing distorted. In FtF, agreed politeness conventions assure interlocutors by means if interactional prompts, making it easy to identify the other's intent. However, group and cultural norms inform politeness: what one interlocutor conveys is not necessarily what the other interlocutors perceive, requiring cautious application of politeness norms among local and across global groups (Pohl, 2004). Particularly in CMC, the singularity of politeness from an English linguistic and cultural perspective seems to enforce incivility towards supposed outgroups.

INTERCULTURAL (CROSS-CULTURAL) COMMUNICATION IN THE MONDERN WORKFORCE

Culture is "the manifold ways of perceiving and organizing the world that are held in common by a group of people and passed on interpersonally and inter-generationally" (Yuan, 2006, p. 5). According to David Victor, it is "the part of behavior that is at once learned and collective", and therefore, "taught rather than instinctive or innate" (2001, p. 30). Starting at birth, "the infant mind is somewhat like a blank tape, waiting to be filled", so culture plays a large part "in the recording process" (Fisher, 1988, p. 45). Handed down from members within the larger community, it is gradually reinforced and imprinted into an individual's mind as time progresses. Culture directly influences the way in which people within the context communicate, and the way in which they perceive each other (Victor, 2001). As a result, one organization's conduct, developed in a particular environment and reflecting the local staff's cultural identity, may not be applicable to another culture. Hence, cross-cultural communication, also known as intercultural communication and transcultural communication, indicates the exchange of ideas, emotions, and information by means of language, words, and body language between people from different cultural backgrounds (Xu, 2007).

Dimensions of Language in the Modern Workforce

The multinational corporation is a business organization whose activities are located in more than two countries and is the organizational form that defines foreign direct investment. This form consists of a country location where the firm is incorporated and of the establishment of branches or subsidiaries in foreign countries. Multinational companies can, obviously, vary in the extent of their multinational activities in terms of the number of countries in which they operate. A large multinational corporation can operate in 100 countries, with hundreds of thousands of employees located outside its home country.

Many MNCs operate in multiple countries and across multiple languages. That is, a single MNC has a language policy that includes a parent company language, a common corporate language, and multiple local (foreign) languages. A parent company language is the language spoken by the majority of parent company employees. It can also be considered the language spoken at company headquarters. This is often an official language of the nation in which the parent company operates. However, if an MNC has moved its headquarters to another country, or if it has undergone an international merger, the parent company language may be replaced by a common corporate language.

A common corporate language (Marschan-Piekkari, Welch, & Welch, 1999) is the language of global operations. This is the language in which official information is transferred between subsidiaries and their parent organizations. Due to the spread of English as a global language of communication, the common corporate language is frequently English (Iseman, 2012; Moreau, 2013; Pikhart, 2011). The local language is the dominant or official language of the organization in which the subsidiary operates, and it is spoken by the locally hired employees, management, and expatriates who speak proficiently. Domestic branches and subsidiaries will likely speak the parent company language.

A local language differs from the parent company language in two respects: an MNC only has one parent company language, and the parent company language plays an important role in global communications and top-down decision making. Local languages spoken in foreign subsidiaries have primarily a geographical or specific market importance; therefore, they are the languages used in local business decisions. Local languages are spoken by the locally hired employees and managers. If the subsidiary is wholly or mostly staffed with expatriate employees, which are parent company employees who are temporarily or permanently assigned to foreign subsidiaries (Tran, 2008), and the language of local operations is likely to be the same as the parent company language.

A global subsidiary staffed with expatriates and local workers may operate in three or four different languages, each with specific functions. For instance, the local employees of a subsidiary of a Japanese electronics company operating in Tijuana, Mexico would speak the local language (Spanish) and possibly the common corporate language (English), but probably not the parent company language (Japanese), while the expatriate managers would speak the parent company language (Japanese), the common corporate language (English), and possibly the local language (Spanish) (Thomas, 2008). Communication between management and the employees may be achieved directly through Spanish, or it may occur indirectly through an intermediary who can speak Spanish and either English or Japanese. Essentially, management at the subsidiary level must be bilingual or multilingual.

Common Corporate Language

According to Tran (2016a, 2016c), whether a corporation has stayed within its national boundaries, or decided to internationalize, there may be considerable pressures to standardize the usage of language within the organization. It must be noted here that language standardization is not used in the traditional sense of language policy and planning literature (Thomas, 2008). Little occurs within business organizations with regard to modifications of the corpus of a language, although most organizations do develop unique terminology (jargon) that reflects the practices, values, and cultures of their respective organizations. According to Thomas (2008), language standardization in organizations refers to status planning and involves decisions as to what language is to be used in boardroom discussions, international communications, research reports, internal documents and memos, manuals, training programs, and daily operations.

Hence, according to Marschan-Piekkari et al. (1999), the choice of promoting a particular language to the status of a common corporate language has many advantages from a management perspective. A common corporate language standardizes conventions for reporting and sharing information between foreign units of the MNC, reduces the potential for miscommunication, and improves access to corporate documents. It also can improve informal communication between units. It is also useful for promoting a common set of corporate values and culture, developing "a sense of belonging to a global 'family'" (Marschan-Piekkari et al., 1999, p. 379).

The need for a common corporate language has been frequently noted by managers as important to communication within the organization and across units of the organization (Tran, 2016a). In an ethnographic study of language policy in Kone Elevators, Charles and Marschan-Piekkari (2002) found that the absence of a common language presented a language barrier that hindered communication between units located in different language regions. Even though English was officially the common corporate language, it was not spoken by many employees in the foreign subsidiaries. As a result, a total of 57% of the employees interviewed in their study saw the lack of a common language as a problem (Thomas, 2008). Furthermore, Palo (1997), who studied the role of language in Finnish MNCs, found that in global communication using English as the common corporate language, nonnative speakers of English (NNSs) preferred to communicate with others NNSs, rather than with native speakers (NSs).

Bartlett and Johnson (1998) offer the proposition that global business English is actually a form of pidgin which is easier for NNSs to understand than it is for NSs, who identify English more with their own culture and communicative strategies. Therefore, NNSs are less judgmental of other speakers. On the other hand, comprehension is often limited, especially in the reading of written documents, which are in formalized Standard English (Charles & Marschan-Piekkari, 2002, p. 16).

Acceptance of Subsidiary Languages

Generally speaking, according to Tran (2016a, 2016c), MNCs communicate with their foreign subsidiaries in multiple languages. Communication between expatriates and headquarter personnel occurs in the parent company language and the common corporate language (Tran, 2008). Communication between locally hired managers and headquarters personnel often occurs in the common corporate language. Within the subsidiary, communication between managers and employees occurs in the local language, and communication between expatriates and locally hired occurs in whichever language communicants are most comfortable with (Thomas, 2008).

However, for competitive advantage, the local language is crucial, especially for interacting with the local market. The subsidiary's use of the local language facilitates communication between the community and the subsidiary and between expatriates and local employees within the subsidiary. It is generally agreed that in order to do business in a foreign country, especially once which peaks a different language or language variety, knowledge of the foreign language and culture is critical for success (Moreau, 2013).

Parent Company Language

According to Tran (2016a, 2016c), in MNCs whose headquarters are based in countries where the language is not English, very often the language of the parent company differs from the language of global operations. The continued maintenance of the parent company language has many benefits for the employees of the parent organization, since it is the language with which they are most comfortable. It has been found to facilitate a strong corporate culture in the home country, but problems often arise regarding how that corporate culture is negotiated between the parent company and its various global subsidiaries (Beechler & Bird, 1999).

Therefore, there remains a gap in the literature on language policy regarding the benefits of an MNC's choice to maintain its parent company language after adopting a common corporate language. However, much has been written about language barriers in parent subsidiary relations. Vihakara (2006) claims that the language barrier is highest in such relations. Charles and Marschan-Piekkari (2002) note that in such cases, important miscommunications occur because expatriates and local employees must exchange information in a language of which neither has perfect grasp.

Feely and Harzing (2002) postulate that when the language barrier is high between parent and subsidiary, the MNC is less likely to control the subsidiary through means of socialization. This has been true of many American MNCs which have often left foreign subsidiary management entirely in the hands of local managers (Garcia & Otheguy, 1994). On the other hand, MNCs may also utilize a higher number of expatriates and expect them to develop skills in the subsidiary language and act as a communicative bridge (Feely & Harzing, 2002; Marschan-Piekkari et al., 1999a; Overmann, 2011).

Finally, Bartlett and Johnson's (1998) research presents the possibility that the native English of some parent companies may not even be the same language as the English of global operations. Bartlett and Johnson (1998) argue that so called global English may actually be pidgin. This could constitute another language barrier—especially in communication between NSs and NNSs of English. Furthermore, nu-

The Art and Science in Communication

merous varieties of English differ greatly from British/American/Australian English. The expectation that English wherever one is in the world is the same may result in serious miscommunications (Tran, 2016a, 2016c)

FUTURE RESEARCH AND RECOMMENDATION

Leadership, according to Giltinane (2013), is complex, comprising many definitions and qualities (Grimm, 2010). One definition of leadership is "a multifaceted process of identifying a goal, motivating other people to act, and providing support and motivation to achieve mutually negotiated goals" (Porter-O'Grady, 2003). Although the practice of leadership has changed considerably over time, the need for leaders and leadership has not (Abu-Tineh, Khasawneh, & Omary, 2009; Bass, 1990; Kouzes & Posner, 1995). A review of the leadership literature reveals an evolving series of schools of thought from *Great Man* and *Trait* theories to *Transformational* leadership. While early theories tend to focus upon the characteristics and behaviors of successful leaders, later theories begin to consider the role of followers and the contextual nature of leadership (Tran, 2014). Consequently, there are 13 different types of leadership styles, divided into four different categories: the classics (autocratic, authoritative, democratic, and laisser-faire), the traditional (transactional, transformational, situational, and charismatic), the modern (affiliative, coaching, exemplary, and visionary/inspirational), and the innovative (servant leadership) (Tran, 2016b).

The link between leadership and competent communication has received limited attention by business and communication scholars alike (Madlock, 2008). According to Holladay and Coombs (1993), leadership is a behavior enacted through communication, specifically strategic communication. Specifically, Holladay and Coombs (1993) suggested that communication shapes the perceptions of a leader's charisma, and communication can be divided into the content of the leader's messages and the presentation of those messages. Similarly, messages sent by leaders are considered to contain both affective and cognitive strategies (Hall & Lord, 1995), and when leaders effectively communicate their vision, they win the confidence of followers, which in turn aids in communication satisfaction between the leader and follower (Pavitt, 1999).

Communicator (Leaders' Communication) Competence

According to Tran (2016b), Harris and Cronen's (1979) research indicated that competent individuals must not only achieve their goals (be effective) but also do so appropriately. In following with this notion, communication competence has been conceptualized to encompass elements of knowledge, motivation, skills, behavior, and effectiveness (Spitzberg, 1983). Spitzberg and Cupach (1981) stated, "competent interaction can be viewed as a form of interpersonal influence, in which an individual is faced with the task of fulfilling communicative functions and goals (effectiveness) while maintaining conversational and interpersonal norms (appropriateness)" (p. 1). Cushman and Craig (1976) argued that communicator competence involves the ability of individuals to display competencies in areas such as listening and negotiating.

Furthermore, Salacuse (2007) indicated that as a result of changing work environments in which employees are more educated and intelligent than past generations, leaders are now required to lead by negotiation. Specifically, Salacuse (2007) noted that in order for leaders to persuade people to follow their vision, they need to communicate effectively by appealing to the interests of the followers. In that competent communicators must employ communicative resources such as language, gestures, and voice (Stohl, 1984), and in order for supervisors to be perceived as competent communicators, they must share and respond to information in a timely manner, actively listen to other points of view, communicate clearly and succinctly to all levels of the organization, and utilize differing communication channels (Shaw, 2005).

According to Tran (2016b), despite the vast amount of research focused on competent communication, there appears to be a lack on prior research directly examining the relationship between supervisor communicator competence and supervisor task and relational leadership styles. However, there does appear to be a limited amount of research examining the influence of supervisors' communicator competence on employee outcomes. One such study was that of Berman and Hellweg (1989), whose findings indicated that the perceived communicator competence of a supervisor was related to their subordinate's satisfaction with that supervisor. Another example was a study by Myers and Kassing (1998), who examined the relationship between subordinate perceptions of their supervisor's communication skills, including communicator competence, and the subordinate's level of organizational identification. Myers and Kassing's findings indicated that supervisor communication competence was a significant predicator of subordinate organizational identification.

Yet another example was a study of Sharbrough, Simmons, and Cantrill (2006), who examined the impact of motivational language on a number of outcomes. Specifically, Sharbrough et al. (2006), found positive relationships between a leader's use of motivational language and their perceived effectiveness, their communication competence, and their subordinates' job and communication satisfaction. The more communication satisfaction perceived by subordinates', the willingness to be led increases, and the more productive the subordinates become (Tran, 2016b).

Communication Satisfaction Between Leaders and Subordinates

Employee satisfaction has been an area examined by business and communication scholars primarily because satisfaction has been positively related to job performance (Gruneberg, 1979). A conceptualization of communication satisfaction was offered by Crino and White (1981) who argued that organizational communication satisfaction involves an individual's satisfaction with various aspects of the communication occurring in the organizations, whereas Putti, Aryee, and Phua (1990) demonstrated that organizational members; communication satisfaction is associated with the amount of information available to them. Although communication provides employees with information that clarifies work tasks and may contribute to communication satisfaction, Anderson and Martin (1995) found that employees engage in communication interactions with coworkers and supervisors to satisfy interpersonal needs of pleasure and inclusion.

Thus, employee communication satisfaction appears to involve a task and relational dimension. Furthermore, prior research indicates that interpersonal interactions involving the exchanging of information and affect between coworkers and between employees and their supervisors can have significant effects on the employees' psychological job outcomes, including job satisfaction, organizational commitment, and burnout (e.g., Pincus, 1986; Postmes, Tanis, & de Wit, 2001; Ray & Miller, 1994). Generally, as employees experience more positive communication relationships, they also experience more positive job outcomes such as job satisfaction (Tran, 2016b).

Job Satisfaction Due to Communication

The most common factors leading to worker stress and dissatisfaction, according to Tran (2016b), are those emanating from the nature of the job itself, within which interpersonal relationships between employees and supervisors take place (Barnett & Brennan, 1997; Rodwell, Kienzle, & Shadur, 1998). According to Korte and Wynne (1996), a deterioration of relationships in organization settings resulting from reduced interpersonal communication between workers and supervisors negatively influences job satisfaction and sometimes leads to employees leaving their jobs. Hence, according to Madlock (2008), early work by Taylor (1970) suggested that worker satisfaction may be attributed to the highest possible earnings with the least amount of fatigue, whereas Locke (1976) defined job satisfaction from an employees' standpoint as "a pleasurable or positive emotional state from the appraisal of one's job or experiences" (p. 1297). Taylor's classical theory prompted a number of studies that revealed differing factors behind job satisfaction. Some of these factors found to mediate job satisfaction include supervisors' displays of nonverbal immediacy (Madlock, 2006a; Richmond & McCroskey, 2000), humor (Avtgis & Taber, 2006), communication satisfaction (Hilgerman, 1998), effects of gender (Madlock, 2006b), and supervisors' communication style (Richmond, McCroskey, Davis, & Koontz, 1980).

CONCLUSION

Communication plays an important role in knowledge management. Employees are the organization's brain cells, and communication represents the nervous system that carries information and shared meaning to vital parts of the organizational body. Effective communication brings knowledge into the organization and disseminates it to employees who require that information. Effective communication minimizes the "silos of knowledge" problem that undermines an organization's potential and, in turn, allows employees to make more informed decisions about corporate actions. Effective communication is one of the most critical goals of organizations (Spillan, Mino, & Rowles, 2002). Recent research evidence suggests that an effective manager is one who spends considerable time on staffing, motivating, and reinforcing activities (Luthans, Welsh, & Taylor, 1988).

Shortell (1991) identified multiple key elements to effective communication in a model developed for physicians and hospital administration to improve their communication abilities to disseminate knowledge within the organization. The following summarizes these key elements:

- An effective communicator must have a desire to communicate, which is influenced both by one's personal values and the expectation that the communication will be received in a meaningful way,
- An effective communicator must have an understanding of how others learn, which includes consideration of differences in how others perceive and process information (i.e., analytic vs. intuitive, abstract vs. concrete, verbal vs. written),
- The receiver of the message should be cued as to the purpose of the message, that is, whether the message is to provide information, elicit a response or reaction, or arrive at a decision,
- The content, importance, and complexity of the message should be considered in determining the manner in which the message is communicated,
- The credibility of the sender affects how the message will be received, and

- The time frame associated with the content of the message (long vs. short) needs to be considered in choosing the manner in which the message is communicated. More precise cues are needed with shorter time frames.

A formula to evaluate an individual's effectiveness in communicating to others can be calculated using Samuel C. Certo's An Index of Communication Effectiveness (ICE): ICE = RIM (Reaction to intended message) / TMS (total number of messages sent) (Certo, 1992). The index of communication effectiveness is a percentage of the reaction to the intended message over the total number of messages sent. If managers find that their index of communication effectiveness is low over time, they should evaluate their communication processes to identify ways to make improvements (Certo, 1992). Research suggests that to improve healthcare organizational communication and cohesion, exchanges between employees and leaders should involve leaders' direct support and encouragement of employees' constructive expressions of dissatisfaction and innovative ideas (Sobo & Sadler, 2002).

Strategic communication is an intentional process of presenting ideas in a clear, concise, and persuasive way. A manager must make an intentional effort to master communication skills and use them strategically, that is, consistently with the organization's values, mission, and strategy. To plan strategic communication, managers must develop a methodology for thinking through and effectively communicating with superiors, staff, and peers. Sperry and Whiteman (2003) provide us with a strategic communication plan, which consists of five components: (1) outcome (the specific result that an individual wants to achieve), (2) context (the organizational importance of the communication), (3) messages (the key information that staff need to know), (4) tactical reinforcement (tactics or methods used to reinforce the message), and (5) feedback (the way the message is received and its impact on the individual, team, unit, or organization). Strategic communication requires forethought about the purpose and outcome of the message. Managers must be able to link the needs of the staff to the organization's mission and deadlines.

ACKNOWLEDGMENT

I would like to dedicate this chapter to William Marc Weisman, M.S. (Marc Weisman), at the State of California, Department of Rehabilitation, in San Francisco, California, who inspired me to write this chapter. Marc Weisman is a Staff Services Manager I with the State of California, Department of Rehabilitation, who manages a team in which I am a member of. Marc is a team manager that I have the pleasure to work under and an opportunity to being mentored by, who demonstrates the behavior and definition of servant leadership, and practices the act of servant leadership. Marc continuously demonstrates the behavior of servant leadership, and practices the act of servant leadership, through the implementation of his knowledge, skills, abilities, wisdom, charm, humor, and charisma. Marc exemplifies his managerial skills and (servant) leadership qualities through his actions with how efficiently he is able to handle and resolve situations at hand.

REFERENCES

Abu-Tineh, A. M., Khasawneh, S. A., & Omary, A. A. (2009). Kouzes and Posners transformational leadership model in practice: The case of Jordanian schools. *Journal of Leadership Education*, *7*(3), 265–283. doi:10.12806/V7/I3/RF10

Ahuja, M. K., & Carley, K. M. (1999). Network structure in virtual organizations. *Organization Science*, *10*(6), 741–757. doi:10.1287/orsc.10.6.741

Anderson, C. M., & Martin, M. M. (1995). The effects of communication motives, interaction involvement, and loneliness on satisfaction: A model of small groups. *Small Group Research*, *26*(1), 118–137. doi:10.1177/1046496495261007

Avtgis, T. A., & Taber, K. R. (2006). I laughed so hard my side hurts, or is that an ulcer? The influence of work humor on job stress, job satisfaction, and burnout among print media employees. *Communication Research Reports*, *23*(1), 13–18. doi:10.1080/17464090500535814

Bach, K. (1987). *Thought and reference*. Oxford: Clarendon Press.

Bach, K. (1994). Meaning, speech acts, and communication. In R. M. Harnish (Ed.), *Introduction to part 1: Basic topics in the philosophy of language*. New York: Prentice-Hall.

Bach, K. (1999). The semantics-pragmatics distinction: What it is and why it matters. In K. Turner (Ed.), *The semantics-pragmatics interface from different points of view* (pp. 65–84). Oxford: Elsevier.

Bach, K. (2001). You dont say. *Synthese*, *128*(1/2), 15–44. doi:10.1023/A:1010353722852

Barnett, R., & Brennan, R. (1997). Change in job conditions, change in psychological distress, and gender: A longitudinal study of dual-earner couples. *Journal of Organizational Behavior*, *18*(3), 253–274. doi:10.1002/(SICI)1099-1379(199705)18:3<253::AID-JOB800>3.0.CO;2-7

Barthes, R. (1957). *Mythologies*. New York: Hill & Wang.

Bartlett, C., & Johnson, C. (1998). Is business English a pidgin? *Language and Intercultural Training*, *16*(1), 4–6.

Bass, B. M. (1990). From transactional to transformational leadership: Learning to share the vision. *Organizational Dynamics*, *18*(3), 19–31. doi:10.1016/0090-2616(90)90061-S

Baumer, M., & van Rensburg, H. (2011). Cross-cultural pragmatic failure in computer-mediated communication. *Coolabah*, *5*, 34–53.

Beechler, S. L., & Bird, A. (Eds.). (1999). *Japanese multinationals abroad*. London: University Press.

Belanger, F., & Jordan, D. H. (2000). *Evaluation and implementation of distance learning: Technologies, tools, and techniques*. Hersey, PA: Idea Group. doi:10.4018/978-1-878289-63-6

Berman, S. J., & Hellweg, S. A. (1989). Perceived supervisor communication competence and supervisor satisfaction as a function of quality circle participation. *Journal of Business Communication*, *26*(2), 103–122. doi:10.1177/002194368902600202

Berry, J., & Kalin, R. (1995). Multicultural and ethnic attitudes in Canada: An overview of the 1991 national survey. *Canadian Journal of Behavioural Science, 27*(3), 301–320. doi:10.1037/0008-400X.27.3.301

Brown, S. A., Fuller, R. M., & Vician, C. (2004). Who's afraid of the virtual world? Anxiety and computer-mediated communication. *Journal of the Association for Information Systems, 5*(2), 79–107.

Cappelen, H., & Dever, J. (2014). *The inessential indexical: On the philosophical insignificance of perspective and the first person: Context and content.* Oxford University Press.

Carroll, D. W. (1999). Psychology of language (3rd ed.). Brooks/Cole Publishing Company.

Carston, R. (2008). Linguistic communication and the semantics/pragmatics distinction. *Synthese, 165*(3), 321–345. doi:10.1007/s11229-007-9191-8

Certo, S. C. (1992). *Modern management: Quality, ethics, and the global environment* (5th ed.). Boston: Allyn and Bacon.

Chandler, D. (2014). *Semiotics for beginners.* Retrieved from http://visual-memory.co.uk/daniel/Documents/S4B/sem01.html

Charles, M., & Marschan-Piekkari, R. (2002). Language training for enhanced horizontal communication: A challenge for MNCs. *Business Communication Quarterly, 65*(2), 9–29. doi:10.1177/108056990206500202

Craig, R. T. (1989). Communication as a practical discipline. In B. Dervin, L. Grossberg, B. J. O'Keefe, & E. A. Wartella (Eds.), *Rethinking communication: Paradigm issues* (Vol. 1, pp. 97–122). London: SAGE publications.

Craig, R. T. (1999). Communication theory as a field. *Journal of Communication, 9*(2), 119–161.

Crino, M. E., & White, M. C. (1981). Satisfaction in communication: An examination of the Downs-Hazen measure. *Psychological Reports, 49*(3), 831–838. doi:10.2466/pr0.1981.49.3.831

Cushman, D. P., & Craig, R. T. (1976). Communication systems: Interpersonal implications. In G. R. Miller (Ed.), *Exploration in interpersonal communication.* Beverly Hills: Sage Publications.

Dong, Q. (1995). *Self, identity, media use and socialization: A student of adolescent Asian immigrants to the United States.* Unpublished doctoral dissertation, Washington State University, Pullman, Washington.

Eco, U. (1976). *A theory of semiotics. Bloomington, IN: Indiana University Press.* London: Macmillan. doi:10.1007/978-1-349-15849-2

Feely, A. J., & Harzing, A. W. (2002). Language management in multicultural companies. *Cross-Cultural Management: An International Journal, 10*(2), 37–52. doi:10.1108/13527600310797586

Feenberg, A. (1991). *Critical theory of technology.* Oxford: Oxford University Press.

Felix, U. (2003). Humanising automated online learning though intelligent feedback. In G. Crisp, D. Thiele, I. Scholten et al. (Eds), *Interact, integrate, impact: Proceedings of the 20th Annual Conference of the Australasian Society of Computers in Learning in Tertiary Education,* Adelaide.

Fisher, G. (1988). *Mindsets: The role of culture and perception in international relations.* Yarmouth, ME: Intercultural Press.

Garcia, O., & Otheguy, R. (1994). The value of speaking a LOTE in U.S. business. *Annals of the American Academy of Political and Social Science: Foreign Language Policy: An Agenda for Change, 532*(3), 99–122. doi:10.1177/0002716294532001008

Garton, L., & Wellman, B. (1995). Social impacts of electronic mail in organizations: A review of the research literature. *Communication Yearbook, 18*, 434–453.

Genosko, G. (1994). *Baudrillard and signs: Signification ablaze.* London: Routledge. doi:10.4324/9780203201145

Giltinane, C. L. (2013). Leadership styles and theories. *Nursing Standard, 27*(41), 35–39. doi:10.7748/ns2013.06.27.41.35.e7565 PMID:23905259

Giorgi, A. (2010). About the speaker: Towards a syntax of indexicality. Oxford University Press.

Grimm, J. W. (2010). Effective leadership: Making the difference. *Journal of Emergency Nursing: JEN, 36*(1), 74–33. doi:10.1016/j.jen.2008.07.012 PMID:20109788

Grudin, J. (1994). Grouware and social dynamics: Eight challenges for developers. *Communications of the ACM, 37*(1), 92–105. doi:10.1145/175222.175230

Gruneberg, M. M. (1979). *Understanding job satisfaction.* New York: John Wiley. doi:10.1007/978-1-349-03952-4

Guo, L. C., & Sanchez, Y. (2005). Workplace communication. In N. Borkowski (Ed.), *Organizational behavior in health care* (pp. 77–110). London: Jones & Bartlett Learning.

Hall, R. J., & Lord, R. G. (1995). Multi-level information-processing explanations of followers leadership perceptions. *The Leadership Quarterly, 6*(3), 265–281. doi:10.1016/1048-9843(95)90010-1

Hara, N., & Kling, R. (2000). Students distress with a web-based distance education course: An ethnographic study of participants experiences. *Information Communication and Society, 3*(4), 557–579. doi:10.1080/13691180010002297

Harris, L., & Cronen, V. E. (1979). A rules-based model for the analysis and evaluation of organizational communication. *Communication Quarterly, 27*(1), 12–28. doi:10.1080/01463377909369320

Hilgerman, R. H. (1988). Communication satisfaction, goal setting, job satisfaction, concertive control, and effectiveness in self-managed teams. Unpublished doctoral dissertation, University of Maine.

HistoryWorld. (N.Y.). (n. d.). *History of language.* Retrieved from http://www.historyworld.net/wrldhis/PlainTextHistories.asp?historyid=ab13

Holladay, S. J., & Coombs, W. T. (1993). Communication visions: An exploration of the role of delivery in the creation of leader charisma. *Management Communication Quarterly, 6*(4), 405–427. doi:10.1177/0893318993006004003

Holland, C. P., & Lockett, A. G. (1997). Mixed mode network structures: The strategic use of electronic communication by organizations. *Organization Science, 8*(5), 475–488. doi:10.1287/orsc.8.5.475

Innis, R. E. (1986). *Semiotics: An introductory reader.* London: Hutchinson.

Iseman, M. (2012). *Top ten countries with which the U.S. trades*. United States Census Bureau.

Jarvenpaa, S. L., & Leidner, D. E. (1999). Communication and trust in global virtual teams. *Organization Science, 10*(6), 791–815. doi:10.1287/orsc.10.6.791

Kaplan, D. (1989). Demonstratives. In J. Almog, P. Perry, H. K. Wettstein, & D. Kaplan (Eds.), *Themes from Kaplan* (pp. 481–563). Oxford University Press.

Keyton, J. (2002). *Communicating in groups: Building relationships for effective decision making* (2nd ed.). Boston: McGraw-Hill.

Keyton, J. (2011). *Communication and organizational culture: A key to understanding work experience*. Thousand Oaks, CA: Sage.

King, J. C. (2012). Anaphora. In G. Russell & D. G. Fara (Eds.), *The Routledge companion to the philosophy of Language*. New York: Routledge.

Korte, W. B., & Wynne, R. (1996). *Telework Penetration, potential and practice in Europe*. Amsterdam: Ohmsha Press.

Kouzes, J. M., & Posner, B. Z. (1995). *The leadership challenge: How to keep getting extraordinary things done in organizations*. San Francisco: Jossey-Bass.

Kulczycki, E. (2014). Communication history and its research subject. *Analele Universitatii din Craiova. Seria Filosofie, 33*(1), 132–155.

Leidner, D. E., & Jarvenpaa, S. L. (1995). The use of information technology to enhance management school education: A theoretical view. *Management Information Systems Quarterly, 19*(3), 265–291. doi:10.2307/249596

Littlejohn, S. W. (1996). *Theories of human communication* (5th ed.). New York: Wadsworth Publishing Company: An International Thomson Publishing Company.

Löblich, M., & Scheu, A. M. (2011). Writing the history of communication studies: A sociology of science approach. *Communication Theory, 21*(1), 1–22. doi:10.1111/j.1468-2885.2010.01373.x

Locke, E. A. (1976). The nature and causes of job satisfaction. In M. D. Dunnette (Ed.), *Handbook of industrial and organizational psychology* (pp. 1297–1349). Chicago: Rand McNally.

Lunenburg, F. C. (2010). Communication: The process, barriers, and improving effectiveness. *Schooling, 1*(1), 1–11.

Madlock, P. E. (2006a). Supervisor' nonverbal immediacy behaviors and their relationship to subordinates' communication satisfaction, job satisfaction, and willingness to collaborate. *Presented at the National Communication Association Convention*, San Antonio, Texas.

Madlock, P. E. (2006b). Do difference in displays of nonverbal immediacy and communication competence between male and female supervisors affect subordinates, job satisfaction. *Ohio Communication Journal, 44*, 61–78.

Madlock, P. E. (2008). The link between leadership style, communicator competence, and employee satisfaction. *Journal of Business Communication, 45*(1), 61–78. doi:10.1177/0021943607309351

Markus, M. L. (1994). Electronic mail as the medium of managerial choice. *Organization Science, 5*(4), 502–527. doi:10.1287/orsc.5.4.502

Marschan-Piekkari, R., Welch, D. E., & Welch, L. S. (1999). Adopting a common corporate language: IHRM implications. *International Journal of Human Resource Management, 10*(3), 377–390. doi:10.1080/095851999340387

McQuail, D. (2005). *McQuail's mass communication theory* (5th ed.). London: Sage Publications.

McShane, S. L., & Von Glinow, M. A. (2003). *Organizational behavior: Emerging realities for the workplace revolution* (2nd ed.). Boston, MA: McGraw-Hill.

Moreau, R. (2013). *The value of foreign languages in business communication.* Retrieved from http://scholarsarchive.jwu.edu/cgi/viewcontent.cgi?article=1016&context=mba_student

Morris, C. W. (1938). *Foundations of the theory of signs.* Chicago: Chicago University Press.

Myers, S. A., & Kassing, J. W. (1998). The relationship between perceived supervisory communication behaviors and subordinate organizational identification. *Communication Research Reports, 15*(1), 71–81. doi:10.1080/08824099809362099

Naughton, K., Raymond, J., Shulman, K., & Struzzi, D. (1999). Cyberslacking. *Newsweek, 134(22),* 62-65.

Nöth, W. (1990). *Handbook of semiotics.* Bloomington, IN: Indiana University Press.

Okan, Z. (2007). *Towards a critical theory of educational technology.* Retrieved from http://files.eric.ed.gov/fulltext/ED500086.pdf

Overmann, M. (2011). *President Obama on the importance of foreign language.* Retrieved from http://www.alliance-exchange.org/policy-monitor/08/22/2011/president-obama-importance-foreign-languages

Palo, U. (1997). *Language skills in inter-unit communication of an internationalizing company: The case of Outokumpu.* Unpublished master's thesis. Helsinki School of Economics, Helsinki, Finland.

Partee, B. (1989). Binding implicit variables in quantified contexts. In C. Wiltshire, B. Music, & R. Graczyk (Eds.), *Papers from Chicago Linguistic Society (CLS) 25* (pp. 342–365). Chicago: Chicago Linguistic Society.

Pavitt, C. (1999). Theorizing about the group communication-leadership relationship: Input-process-output and functional models. In L. R. Frey, D. S. Gouran, & M. S. Poole (Eds.), *The handbook of group communication theory and research* (pp. 313–334). Thousand Oaks, CA: Sage.

Perry, J. (2015). *The problem of the essential indexical and other essays: Extended edition.* Center for the Study of Language and Information.

Piccoli, G., Ahmad, R., & Ives, B. (2001). Web-based virtual learning environments: A research framework and a preliminary assessment of effectiveness in basic IT skills training. *Management Information Systems Quarterly, 25*(4), 401–426. doi:10.2307/3250989

Pikhart, M. (2011). English as a Lingua Franca and its international consequences: Applied linguistics approach. *Bulletin of the Transylvania University of Brasov, Philology & Cultural Studies, 4*(53), 201–204.

Pincus, J. D. (1986). Communication satisfaction, job satisfaction and job performance. *Human Communication Research, 12*(3), 395–419. doi:10.1111/j.1468-2958.1986.tb00084.x

Pohl, G. (2004). Cross-cultural pragmatic failure and implications for language teaching. *Second Language Learning & Teaching, 4*(2), 91–112.

Porcar, C. (2011). Sign and meaning: A semiotic approach to communication. *Journal of Communication and Culture, 1*(1), 20–29.

Porter-OGrady, T. (2003). A different age for leadership, part 1: New context, new content. *The Journal of Nursing Administration, 33*(2), 105–110. doi:10.1097/00005110-200302000-00007 PMID:12584463

Postmes, T., Tanis, M., & de Wit, B. (2001). Communication and commitment in organizations: A social identity approach. *Group Processes & Intergroup Relations, 4*(3), 227–246. doi:10.1177/1368430201004003004

Putti, J. M., Aryee, S., & Phua, J. (1990). Communication relationship satisfaction and organizational commitment. *Group & Organization Studies, 15*(1), 44–52. doi:10.1177/105960119001500104

Ray, E. B., & Miller, K. I. (1994). Social support, home/work stress and burnout: Who can help? *The Journal of Applied Behavioral Science, 30*(3), 357–373. doi:10.1177/0021886394303007

Richmond, V. P., & McCroskey, J. C. (2000). The impact of supervisor and subordinate immediacy on relational and organizational outcomes. *Communication Monographs, 67*(1), 85–95. doi:10.1080/03637750009376496

Richmond, V. P., McCroskey, J. C., Davis, L. M., & Koontz, K. A. (1980). Perceived power as a mediator of management styles and employee satisfaction: A preliminary investigation. *Communication Quarterly, 28*(4), 37–46. doi:10.1080/01463378009369380

Rodwell, J., Kienzle, R., & Shadur, M. (1998). The relationships among work-related perceptions, employee attitudes, and employee perceptions and employee performance: The integral role of communication. *Human Resource Management, 37*(3/4), 277–293. doi:10.1002/(SICI)1099-050X(199823/24)37:3/4<277::AID-HRM9>3.0.CO;2-E

Salacuse, J. W. (2007). *Real leaders negotiate*. Retrieved from https://hbr.org/2008/02/real-leaders-negotiate-1.php

Scott, T. J. (2005). *The concise handbook of manager: A practitioner's approach*. New York: The Haworth Press.

Sharbrough, W. C., Simmons, S. A., & Cantrill, D. A. (2006). Motivating language in industry: Its impact on job satisfaction and perceived supervisor effectiveness. *Journal of Business Communication, 43*(4), 322–343. doi:10.1177/0021943606291712

Shaw, K. (2005). Getting leaders involved in communication strategy: Breaking down the barriers to effective leadership communication. *Strategic Communication Management, 9*, 14–17.

Sobo, E. J., & Sadler, B. L. (2002). Improving organizational communication and cohesion in a healthcare setting through employee-leadership exchange. *Human Organization*, *61*(3), 277–287. doi:10.17730/humo.61.3.fnk9rkekacak6mkx

Sperry, L., & Whiteman, A. (2003). Communicating effectively and strategically. In L. Sperry (Ed.), *Becoming an effective healthcare manager: The essential skills of lead* (pp. 75–98). Baltimore: Health Professions Press.

Spitzberg, B. H. (1983). Communication competence as knowledge, skill, and impression. *Communication Education*, *32*(3), 323–329. doi:10.1080/03634528309378550

Spitzberg, B. H., & Cupach, W. R. (1981). Self-monitoring and relational competence. *Presented at the Speech Communication Association Convention*, Anaheim, California.

Sproull, L. S., & Kiesler, S. (1991). *Connections: New ways of working in the networked organization*. Cambridge, MA: MIT Press.

Stohl, C. (1984). Quality circle and the quality of communication. *Presented at the Speech Communication Association Convention*, Chicago, Illinois.

Sturrock, J. (1986). *Structuralism*. London: Paladin.

Taylor, F. W. (1970). What is scientific management? In H. F. Merrill (Ed.), *Classics in management* (pp. 67–71). New York: American Management Association.

The Stanford Encyclopedia of Philosophy. (2015). *Indexicals*. Stanford's Center for the Study of Language and Information. Retrieved from http://plato.stanford.edu/entries/indexicals/

Thomas, C. A. (2008). Bridging the gap between theory and practice: Language policy in multilingual organisations. *Language Awareness*, *17*(4), 307–325. doi:10.1080/09658410802147295

Townsend, A. M., DeMarie, S. M., & Hendrickson, A. R. (1998). Virtual teams: Technology and workplace of the future. *The Academy of Management Executive*, *12*(3), 17–29.

Tran, B. (2008). *Expatriate selection and retention* [Dissertation]. California School of Professional Psychology at Alliant International University, San Francisco, California.

Tran, B. (2014). The origin of servant leadership: The foundation of leadership. In R. Selladurai and S. Carraher (Eds.). Servant leadership: Research and practice (pp. 262-294). Hershey, PA: IGI Global.

Tran, B. (2016a). Tran, B. (2016). Communication (intercultural and multicultural) at play for cross cultural management within multinational corporations (MNCs). In N. Zakaria, A. N. Abdul-Talib, & N. Osman (Eds.), *Handbook of research on impacts of international business and political affairs on the global economy* (pp. 62-92). Hershey, PA: IGI Global.

Tran, B. (2016b). Communication: The role of the Johari Window on effective leadership communication in multinational corporations (MNCs). In A. H. Normore, M. Javidi, & L. Long (Eds.), *Handbook of research on effective communication, leadership, and conflict resolution* (pp. 405–429). Hershey, PA: IGI Global. doi:10.4018/978-1-4666-9970-0.ch022

Tran, B. (2016c). *Communication (intercultural and multicultural) at play for cross cultural management within multinational corporations (MNCs)*. In International Business: Concepts, Methodologies, Tools, and Applications (pp. 1781–1811). Hershey, PA: IGI Global.

Victor, D. A. (2001). A cross-cultural perspective on gender. In L. Arliss and D. Borisoff (Eds.), Women and men communicating: Challenges and change (pp. 65-77). Long Grove: Waveland Press.

Vihakara, A. (2006). *Patience and understanding: A narrative approach to cross-cultural communication in a Sino-Finnish joint venture*. Turku, Finland: Turku School of Economics and Business Administration.

Xu, Y. (2007). Strategic analysis on cross-cultural human resources management. *Market Modernization*, *19*, 274–275.

Yu, B. (2011). Computer-medicated communication systems. *Triple Cognition Communication Co-Operation*, *9*(2), 531–534.

Yuan, W. (2006). *Intercultural communication and conflict between American and Chinese colleagues in China-based multinational organizations*. Unpublished doctoral dissertation, University of Kentucky, Kentucky.

ADDITONAL READING

Adler, N. J. (1991). *International dimensions of organizational behavior* (2nd ed.). Boston: PWS-Kent Publishing Company.

Ambler, T. (1994). Marketings third paradigm: Guanxi. *Business Strategy Review*, *5*(4), 69–80. doi:10.1111/j.1467-8616.1994.tb00084.x

Argyles, M. (1987). *The psychology of happiness*. London: Methuen.

Bo, Y. (1992). *The ugly chinaman and the crisis of Chinese culture*. Saint Leonards, Australia: Allen & Unwin.

Bond, M. H. (1998). Social psychology across cultures: Two ways forward. In J. G. Adair, D. Betanger, & R. L. Dion (Eds.), *Advances in social science* (Vol. 1). East Sussex, UK: Psychology Press.

Bond, M. H., & Hofstede, G. (1989). The cash value of Confucian values. *Human Systems Management*, *8*, 195–200.

Brislin, R. W., Lonner, W. J., & Thorndike, R. M. (1973). *Cross-cultural research methods*. New York: Wiley.

Bruner, J. (1990). *Acts of meaning*. Cambridge, MA: Harvard University Press.

Carroll, S., & Gannon, M. J. (1997). *Ethical dimensions of international management*. Thousand Oaks, CA: Sage. doi:10.4135/9781483327778

Chan, W. T. (1963). *A source book in chinese philosophy*. Princeton: Princeton University Press.

Chen, M. J. (2001). *Inside Chinese business: A guide for managers worldwide*. Boston: Harvard Business School Press.

Cheng, S. K. S. (1990). Understanding the culture and behavior of east Asians: A Confucian perspective. *The Australian and New Zealand Journal of Psychiatry, 24*(4), 510–515. doi:10.3109/00048679009062907 PMID:2073227

Diener, E., & Diener, M. (1995). Cross-cultural correlates of life satisfaction and self-esteem. *Journal of Personality and Social Psychology, 68*(4), 653–663. doi:10.1037/0022-3514.68.4.653 PMID:7738768

Diener, E., Suh, M., Smith, H., & Shao, L. (1995). National and cultural differences in reported subjective well-being: Why do they occur? *Social Indicators Research, 34*(1), 103–157. doi:10.1007/BF01078966

Earley, P. C. (1997). *Face, harmony, and social structure: An analysis of organizational behavior across cultures*. New York: Oxford University Press.

Fan, Y. (2002). Questioning guanxi: Definition, classification and implications. *International Business Review, 11*(5), 543–561. doi:10.1016/S0969-5931(02)00036-7

Fang, T. (1999). *Chinese business negotiating style*. Thousand Oaks, CA: Sage.

Fang, T. (2002). The moon and the sun of culture: A yin yang approach to cross-cultural management. *Paper presented as a keynote speech at the 2nd Doing Business Across Borders (DBAB) Conference*, Newcastle Business School, Australia.

Francis, L. J., Brown, L. B., Lester, D., & Philipchalk, R. (1998). Happiness as stable extraversion: A cross-cultural examination of the reliability and validity of the oxford happiness inventory among students in the UK, USA, Australia and Canada. *Personality and Individual Differences, 24*(2), 167–171. doi:10.1016/S0191-8869(97)00170-0

Gao, G., Ting-Toomey, S., & Gudykunst, W. B. (1996). Chinese communication processes. In M. H. Bond (Ed.), *The handbook of Chinese psychology* (pp. 280–293). Hong Kong: Oxford University Press.

Gu, Y. G. (1990). Politeness phenomena in modern Chinese. *Journal of Pragmatics, 14*(2), 237–257. doi:10.1016/0378-2166(90)90082-O

Hick, G., & Redding, S. G. (1983). The story of the east Asian economic miracle (pt. 1): Economic theory be damned. *Euro-Asian Business Review, 2*(3/4), 24–32.

Hofheinz, R. Jr, & Calder, K. E. (1982). *The eastasia edge*. New York: Basic Books.

Hofstede, G. (1983). The cultural relativity of organizational practices and theories. *Journal of International Business Studies, 14*(2), 75–89. doi:10.1057/palgrave.jibs.8490867

Hofstede, G. (2002). Dimensions do not exist: A reply to Brebdan McSweeney. *Human Relations, 55*(11), 1355–1361. doi:10.1177/0018726702055011921

Hofstede, G., Neuijen, B., & Ohavy, D. (1990). Measuring organizational cultures: A qualitative and quantitative study across twenty cases. *Administrative Science Quarterly, 35*(6), 286–316. doi:10.2307/2393392

Hsu, F. L. K. (1963). *Clan, caste, and club*. Princeton: Van Nostrand.

Huang, Q. Y., Leonard, J., & Chen, T. (1997). *Business decision making in china.* New York: International Business Press.

Lu, L. (1995). The relationship between subjective well-being and psychosocial variables in Taiwan. *The Journal of Social Psychology, 135*(3), 351-357.

Micholas, A. C. (1991). *Global report on student well-being.* New York: Springer-Verlag.

Myers, D. G., & Diener, E. (1995). Who is happy? *Psychological Science, 6*(1), 10–19. doi:10.1111/j.1467-9280.1995.tb00298.x

KEY TERMS AND DEFINITIONS

Communication: As sending, receiving, and understanding information and meaning.

Communication History: Is the studies of issues related to communication, be it interpersonal, group, organizational, or institutional: this means that all the different levels, means and forms of communication are taken into account.

Cross-Cultural Communication (also known as Intercultural Communication and Trans-Cultural Communication): Is a method that indicates the exchange of ideas, emotions, and information by means of language, words, and body language between people from different cultural backgrounds.

Culture: Is the manifold ways of perceiving and organizing the world that are held in common by a group of people and passed on interpersonally and inter-generationally.

Explicit Communication: Refers to the things we say or write, often messages intended to influence the behavior of others. Explicit communication refers to specific information conveyed in written or spoken words.

Implicit Communication: Refers to the messages we *give off* through our deeds and actions. Implicit communication may or may not be intentional.

Feedback: Any information that individuals receive about their behavior.

Medium: May include such broad categories as speech and writing or print and broadcasting or relate to specific technical forms within the mass media or the media of interpersonal communication.

Message: Is the outcome of the encoding, which takes the form of oral or written verbal and nonverbal symbols.

Nonverbal Communication: Is the sharing of information without using words to encode messages. There are four basic forms of nonverbal communication: proxemics, kinesics, facial and eye behavior, and paralanguage.

Semiotics: Is the study of signs.

Strategic Communication: A communication method that uses the *pushing* and the *delivering* in such a way that being strategic means communicating the best message, through the right channels, measured against well-considered organizational and communications-specific goals.

Verbal Communication: Relies on spoken or written words to share information with others.

Chapter 4
The Misappropriation of Organizational Power and Control:
Managerial Bullying in the Workplace

David Starr-Glass
SUNY Empire State College, USA

ABSTRACT

Workplace bullying has been the focus of much interest and research over the last forty years. This concern reflects the growing awareness of the organizational costs associated with all forms of bullying. Of particular importance is what has been called abusive supervision, which constitutes the most prevalent and destructive form of negative workplace conduct. This chapter understands abusive supervision to be a prototypical example of workplace bullying, rather than a narrower and more restricted expression of it. The chapter reviews workplace bullying, focuses on abusive managerial behavior, and understands such behavior as a misappropriation of legitimate organizational processes and dynamics for own personal ends. Bullying behavior violates the norms of workplace ethics, organizational justice, and the agency role of management. The chapter considers initiatives through which managerial bullying might be identified, remediated, and reduced.

INTRODUCTION

There are multiple definitions and manifestations of workplace bullying, but all center on inappropriate and unwarranted aggression. Aggression is best understood as behavior directed toward another person with the intent to cause harm, although the perpetrator might be unaware of the nature of the harm, its extent, or the personal identity of the target (Anderson & Bushman, 2002; Barling, Dupré, & Kelloway, 2009). Workplace bullying occurs when "an employee's well-being is harmed by an act of aggression perpetrated by one or more members of the organization" (Aquino & Thau, 2009, p. 718). In this context, well-being relates to "a sense of belonging, a feeling that one is a worthy individual, believing that one has the ability to predict and to cognitively control one's environment, and being able to trust others" (p. 718).

Workplace bullying is expressed in different ways and is considered to include a cluster of separate theoretical constructs; however, it has been found that the "meta-analytic research that compares these constructs against a series of consequences has found that, by and large, there is little to no difference in the magnitude of consequences from these different constructs" (Hershcovis, Reich, & Niven, 2015, p. 4). Thus, while workplace bullying can take multiple expressions that might appear distinct, the overall impact and damage produced is uniformly negative.

One of these separate constructs is abusive supervision, defined as the "subordinates' perceptions of the extent to which their supervisors engage in the sustained display of hostile verbal and nonverbal behaviors, excluding physical contact" (Tepper, 2000, p. 178). Subsequently, it was claimed that "abusive supervision excludes reference to the perpetrator's objectives, a feature that sets it apart from the construct definitions for victimization, bullying, supervisor aggression, and supervisor undermining" (Tepper, 2007, p. 284). However, in this chapter, it is argued that all of workplace bullying – including abusive supervision – is indeed predicated on the perpetrator's objectives, which may be deeply personal, psychologically generated, and frequently not consciously recognized by those involved, including the perpetrator. Throughout this chapter, abusive supervision is regarded not only as the most prevalent expression of workplace bullying, but also as the prototypical form of workplace aggression.

From such a perspective, workplace bullying – certainly as expressed through victimization, supervisor aggression, supervisor undermining, and abusive supervision – presents something of an oxymoron. On the one hand, workplace indicates an organizational setting within which participants might be expected to conform to the collective norms of organizational behavior, culture, and citizenship. On the other hand, bullying is an individual and a personal behavior involving manipulation, exploitation, and distortion of organizational power-differentials in ways designed to disempower, marginalize, and distress the targeted individual (Einarsen, 2000; Einarsen, Hoel, Zapf, & Cooper, 2011; Hershcovis et al., 2015). Therefore, workplace bullying represents a dysfunctional clash between organizational and personal objectives; a fundamental conflict between organizational citizenship and individual behavior; and, more crucially, an attempt by the perpetrator, either consciously or unconsciously initiated, to subvert organizational power and authority for his or her self-centered benefit.

Workplace bullying does not simply provide emotional and psychic benefit for the perpetrator; it results in very real costs for the organization within which it occurs. The direct organizational costs include: (a) decreased organizational performance and engagement connected to lowered job satisfaction, life satisfaction, and organizational commitment; (b) increased stress-related absenteeism, sick-days claimed, and rising employee medical and therapeutic intervention costs; (c) increased workforce turnover and intention-to-quit statistics; (d) increased retaliatory and counter-productive behaviors, ranging from deliberate absenteeism and work delays to theft and sabotage; and (e) the very real exposure to criminal liability, litigation, claims for compensation, and potential reputational damage (Bowling & Beehr, 2006; Hershcovis & Barling, 2010; Mitchell & Ambrose, 2007; Restubog, Scott, & Zagenczyk, 2011; Schat & Frone, 2011; Thau & Mitchell, 2010; Yamada, 2013).

These costs may be difficult to quantify, but current estimates show they are significant. For example, it has been estimated that the annual cost of workplace bullying in the United Kingdom is about GBP 13.75 billion (Giga, Hoel, & Lewis, 2008). In the United States, a wide range of cost estimates have been suggested, with Namie and Namie (2009a) providing what seems to be a rather conservative figure of US$64 billion annually. Nonetheless, despite these considerable costs, workplace bullying persists at uncomfortably high levels. A recent meta-analysis of data from North America, Scandinavia, and various other European Union (EU) countries, estimated that on average about 15 percent of all employees had experienced some form of workplace bullying. The average, however, obscures some telling detail: the regional average in North America (26 percent) was significantly higher than in Scandinavia (10 percent) (Nielsen, Matthiesen, & Einarsen, 2010).

This chapter regards workplace bullying not as an isolated phenomenon restricted to individual perpetrators and individual targets, but as involving dyads of organizational participants within an organizational setting. The first section provides a structural framework by examining various definitions of work-related bullying. The following section explores managerial bullying as a dynamic interaction and considers the attributes of perpetrators, targets, and the contribution of national culture. It also argues that managerial bullying is the outcome of a personal misappropriation of legitimate organizational power, authority, and control. The third section advances the misappropriation of power analysis by suggesting a number of recommendations that might prove effective in reducing bullying. The fourth section suggests new research initiatives that might be valuable, while the concluding section briefly reviews the key issues set out in the chapter.

BACKGROUND

Solitary acts of negative or humiliating behavior in the workplace can be unpleasant, but they do not necessarily constitute bullying. Workplace bullying emerges as a pattern of repeated, systematic, and sustained behavior that extends over a considerable period of time and which often intensifies over that period.

Harassment shares many of the characteristics of bullying – indeed, some use the terms synonymously – but researchers, practitioners, and legal systems usually link harassment with verbal and/or physical assaults on those belonging to a legally protected class, which is defined in terms of attributes such as gender, ethnicity, and age. Thus, harassment is normally linked to discriminatory attitudes and practices; in most jurisdictions, it is considered illegal and subject to prosecution. Workplace bullying, by contrast, may or may not be considered illegal in the country within which it takes place. Thus, in most European countries workplace bullying is a criminal offense, whereas in the United States it is not, although a growing number of states have criminalized such behavior (ACAS, 2014; EU-OSHA, 2010; Eurofound, 2015; Lewis, Giga, & Hoel, 2011; Yamada, 2013).

In the United States, attention was first drawn to the issue of workplace harassment by Carol Brodsky (1976) in her book, *The Harassed Worker*, in which she identified sexual harassment, scapegoating, name-calling, physical abuse, and persistent work pressure as significant toxic issues in the workplace. She argued that all of these behaviors – repeatedly and persistently enacted – served to torment, wear down, and frustrate the targeted individual, and ultimately resulted in a climate of pervasive fear, intimidation, and discomfort.

In Scandinavia, which has been an especially productive center of workplace bullying research, Heinz Leymann first explored bullying by referring to it as psychological terror and coining the term mobbing to describe acts of collective bullying (Leymann 1990, 1996; Leymann & Gustafsson, 1996). He suggested that bullying might be quite common in the workplace, but that most of incidents simply went ignored. Subsequently, it was recognized that bullying was not only very prevalent, but that even if ignored it could produce severe anxiety, prolonged misery, and psychological suffering. These outcomes are intensified when bullying is persistent, repetitive, involves significant power difference, or becomes accepted as an inescapable dimension of the working environment (Einarsen, Raknes, & Matthiesen, 1994; Nielsen, Notelaers, & Einarsen, 2011).

What is Workplace Bullying?

Ståle Einarsen, the leading Scandinavian scholar in the field, has defined workplace bullying in a number of ways. In his earlier work, he drew attention to the existence of power imbalances, dominance, and positional vulnerabilities between the actors engaged in bullying behavior, defining workplace bullying as a situation in which individuals "persistently over a period of time perceive themselves to be on the receiving end of negative actions from one or several persons, in a situation where the target of bullying has difficulty in defending him or herself against these actions" (Einarsen & Skogstad, 1996, p. 191). Later, his definition focused on the conduct of the actors involved. Workplace bullying then became defined as a sequence of repeated actions and practices "directed to one or more workers, which are unwanted by the victim, which may be done deliberately or unconsciously, but clearly cause humiliation, offence and distress, and that may interfere with job performance and/or cause an unpleasant working environment" (Einarsen, 1999, p. 17).

This later definition, which informs the present chapter, has three critical elements: (a) bullying is neither an isolated nor an infrequent event – it is the outcome of repeated and persistent behavior and actions; (b) bullying is associated with a hostile intent on the part of the perpetrator, or with targeted individual's perception that the intent is hostile, even although the hostility may be latent, not deliberately projected, or not even consciously recognized; and (c) the consequence of bullying – whether intended, desired, or unforeseen – is the degradation of the targeted individual, of his or her work commitment and performance, and more generally of the organizational environment within which the bullying occurs.

There are a number of problems in comprehensively defining workplace bullying, and while Einarsen's (1999) definition has been contested there is currently no generally accepted alternative. Indeed, the proliferation of definitions – and the splitting of existing constructs into more specific forms of behavior – has increased over the last few years as different forms of abuse have been criminalized, with each requiring a precise legal definition. Among scholars and practitioners, there is general agreement that the proliferation of separate constructs of bullying and harassment has only served to thrown up significant conceptual barriers for those involved with abuse, hostility, and incivility in the workplace (Crawshaw, 2009; Fox & Stallworth, 2009; Hershcovis, 2011).

Workplace bullying can involve any organizational participants, but it is most prevalent in situations where significant power-differentials are involved, with the more powerful person being the perpetrator. An analysis of United Kingdom statistics indicates that as many as 75 percent of all workplace bullying incidents are initiated by perpetrators holding a higher hierarchically position than the targeted individual (Hoel & Cooper, 2000). Similarly, a U.S. survey reveals that most cases of bullying (56 percent) are initiated by supervisors, 33 percent involve those with lateral or horizontal hierarchical positions (peers), while only 11 percent are directed upwards against superiors (Namie, 2014).

DYNAMICS OF BULLYING AND MISAPPROPRIATIONS OF POWER

It is unproductive to view workplace bullying as a static phenomenon in which the perpetrator and the targeted individual are considered separately and disconnected from context within which the bullying occurs (Baillien, Neyens, De Witte, & De Cuyper, 2009; Einarsen et al., 2011; Keashly, 2010). Certainly, for bullying to materialize there needs to be a perpetrator and target, but they must also be brought together and interact within a specific organizational context. Bullying, aggression, and harassment are more productively viewed as the dynamic interaction between the dyad involved, with the organizational context acting to mediate or moderate their behavior (Hershcovis & Rafferty, 2012).

Dynamic Contribution of Perpetrators

It is helpful to understand the dynamics that perpetrators bring to the bullying interaction. However, there is a significant problem: most accounts of bullying come from those who have been targeted; perpetrators tend not to provide insight into their actions and have rarely been the focus of research. Nevertheless, three antecedents of perpetrator engagement have been identified in workplace managerial bullying: protection of self-esteem, lack of social competencies, and micropolitical behavior (Hershcovis et al., 2015; Matthiesen & Einarsen, 2007; Zapf & Einarsen, 2011).

Protection of Self-Esteem

Aggressive behavior is generally associated with bolstering high self-esteem, rather than with low self-esteem; those with low self-esteem tend to avoid active confrontation (Baumeister, Smart, & Boden, 1996). However, bullying behavior can also be motivated by the perpetrator's need to reinforce his or her sense of worth by undermining that of another. For managers, there can be envy of the targeted subordinates' talent, resentment about their perceived standing, or annoyance at their career advancement in the organization. Belittling and berating the target through sustained bullying provides a way of reinforcing the perpetrator's own self-esteem and sense of power. In many cases the perpetrator may have scant conscious recognition of these self-esteem issues; indeed, bullying behavior is often initiated without much prior calculation, premeditation, or strategic agenda.

Lack of Social Competencies

Bullying can also be the product of the perpetrator's lack of social competencies, including emotional intelligence, or of his or her disregard for social convention, consideration of the other, or sense of empathy and social connection. Individuals can indulge in overt aggressive, confrontational, and demeaning behavior without realizing or caring that such behavior is considered socially or culturally inappropriate. When confronted and accused of bullying, managers often defend themselves by claiming that their actions were not intended to cause harm, were appropriate or justified in the situation, or that their actions were misconstrued, misunderstood, or taken out of context. These responses may not originate from a sense of embarrassment, or from a need to defend aggressive behavior; instead, they may reflect a significant lack of social awareness, an inability to empathize, or a lack of concern for others (Jenkins, Winefield, & Sarris, 2010). Some have speculated that these defensive responses may also be designed to obscure deeper and darker traits in the perpetrator, such as Machiavellianism, narcissism, or even psychopathy (Spain, Harms, & Lebreton, 2014).

Micropolitical Behavior

Burns (1961) was among the first to argue that political approaches are as prevalent in organizational life as they are in the governance of the nation state. Organizations and political worlds have valuable resources, benefits, and power that can be redistributed to the advantage of some and the detriment of others (Smeed, Kimber, Millwater, & Ehrich, 2009). In institutional environments, micropolitical activity forms a continuum of behavior, ranging from advocating preferred positions, forming strategic alliances, and creating influential coalitions on the one hand, to "illegitimate, self-interested manipulation" on the other (Hoyle, 1999, p. 126). Most organizational participants soon come to recognize that "formal rules, such as hierarchies and organizational aims, cannot determine actors' behaviors completely... there are always 'scopes of action' of one type or another" (Willner, 2011, p. 160). One of these scopes of action, albeit a pernicious one, is aggression and bullying. When these are utilized, the perpetrator seeks to strengthen his or her power and influence and to weaken others who are seen as rivals. The perpetrator might have no antipathy or personal dislike for the target, and no particular interest in causing distress; rather, the perpetrator considers that bullying and harassment are reasonable and legitimate micropolitical scopes of action, and that the targeted individual is simply collateral damage in accomplishing the desired objectives. It has also been speculated that while bullying might be considered a legitimate form of micropolitical manipulation, it might also be a manifestation of a deeper, darker, and more callus psychological disposition that fails to recognize or respond to the personhood of the target (Furnham, Richards, & Paulhus, 2013; Paulhus & Williams, 2002; Spain et al., 2014).

In listing perpetrator characteristics, there is always a danger that the list can be used as a diagnostic profile to identify potential initiators and to preempt possible managerial bullying. Such considerations, however, are likely to be overly simplistic and may potentially serve to stigmatize and organizationally damage the suspected "proto-perpetrator". Nevertheless, an appreciation of the antecedents of perpetrator bullying behavior is an important starting place for understanding why this kind of behavior might have been initiated and how, once it has emerged, it might be controlled or remediated.

Dynamic Contribution of Targeted Individuals

A more extensive body of research literature exists on those who are the target (the "victims") of bullying. However, it is important to recognize that much of this literature is fragmentary, incomplete, and often contradictory (Aquino & Thau, 2009; Bowling & Beehr, 2006; Matthiesen & Einarsen, 2007; Zapf & Einarsen, 2011). Indeed, much of the bullying literature deals with research conducted in other contexts – notably the schoolyard, and more recently the cyber world – and not the workplace. Non-workplace bullying can potentially contribute to our understanding of this psychologically damaging behavior, but care is needed to distinguish between differently-situated expressions of bullying and not to casually extrapolate such findings into organizational or managerial contexts (Olweus, 2003; Smith, Singer, Hoel, & Cooper, 2003).

It is also important to recognize that workplace bullying behavior is a dynamic process involving the dyadic involvement of perpetrator-target and their organizational environment: this interaction is best viewed from a holistic perspective (Hershcovis & Rafferty, 2012). Nevertheless, some important behavioral and situational generalizations can be made about those who find themselves the target of workplace hostility (Hershcovis et al. 2015; Matthiesen & Einarsen, 2007; Zapf & Einarsen, 2011).

Holding Outsider Status

Those who are perceived as different from the organizational in-group can be devalued and marginalized by their peers and supervisors. Although not inevitable, carrying outsider status can lead to progressive social exclusion and alienation, in which the individual may acquire negative labelling: "loners," "smart-pants," "mischief-makers," "black-sheep," and perhaps ultimately "scapegoats" (Kim & Glomb, 2010). Outsiders usually have poor social networks within the organization and beyond, and may find it difficult to obtain the social support and psychological reassurance to deal with the bullying that they experience. There is also some indication that when supervisors perceive subordinates as differ significantly from themselves relational conflict tends to increase and may finally lead to bullying (Tepper, Moss, & Duffy, 2011).

Social Competencies and Self-Esteem

There is also a general finding that some individuals are more vulnerable to workplace bullying than others. Members of the vulnerable class tend to self-report low levels self-esteem, with this self-perception being present even before the bullying began. They also report having difficulties with social competencies, find confrontation problematic, and conflict management challenging. However, it is important to note that many of these finding are taken from studies in clinical and school settings, and that the extent to which these attributes apply in workplace and organizational context remains unclear (Lind, Glasø, Pallesen, & Einarsen, 2009). Interestingly, a sizable body of research has demonstrated that those who are the targeted for bullying actually exhibit many of the same traits and issues with self-esteem as perpetrators (Hershcovis & Reich, 2013).

Overachievement and Clash With Prevailing Norms

In many work environments, those who are subjected to bullying describe themselves as highly productive, conscientious, and over-achieving compared with their referenced work or organizational group. This self-identification causes targeted individuals considerable distress and frustration, because they believe that they should be praised and rewarded, not subjected to aggression or bullying. This apparently paradoxical situation can be exacerbated if the target has shared his or her perceived superiority and frustration with others; the target's claims of superiority and excellence may spark further resentment, anger, and hostility. When targeted individuals do demonstrate superior performance, they may be considered as violating the accepted organizational norms related to productivity, work-performance, or career advancement. The target's perceived deviance from group-related norms can be heightened when the organizational climate is stressful or unpredictable – when other members of the work-group and their managers are concerns about job security, low levels of job autonomy, and demanding workloads (Baillien, De Cuyper, & De Witte, 2011; De Cuyper, Baillien, & De Witte, 2009). Under these conditions, high output and perceived violation of group-related performance norms can lead to growing social resentment, fear, physical isolation, ostracization, and eventually retaliation in the form of bullying. Indeed, there is growing evidence to indicate that such situational factors – job security, low job autonomy, and demanding workloads – might be among the strongest predictors for harassment and bullying behavior (Bowling & Beehr, 2006).

It is unhelpful to use the characteristics of targeted individuals as a profile for identifying organizational participants who are vulnerable, or at-risk from managerial bullying. A focus on the targeted individuals obscures the reality of the dyadic nature of bullying, and can lead to assigning responsibility – perhaps even to apportioning blame – to isolated actors (specifically to targets), rather than to exploring the complexity and synergistic dynamics at work in the bullying dyad.

Dynamic Contribution of Organizational Culture and Climate

In order to grow and realize their objectives, organizations require a cohesiveness that binds participants together, offers a shared set of aspirations, and provides a collective sense of identity. Organizational culture has been defined as a set of "shared basic assumptions, values, and beliefs that characterize a setting and are taught to newcomers as the proper way to think and feel" (Schneider, Ehrhart, & Macey, 2013, p. 362). These proper ways to think and feel are preserved, reinforced, and communicated through "the myths and stories people tell about how the organization came to be the way it is as it solved problems associated with external adaptation and internal integration" (p. 362).

Organizational culture provides an insight into what organizations believe about themselves, and about the qualities they understand themselves to possess; however, organizational cultures often project idealized visions that are at variance with what organizational participants actually experience. Organizational climate is used to describe what participants directly experience, and how they perceive the ways in which the organization really operates. Organizational climate constitutes the discernable, culturally-embedded, and culturally-mediated enactments that are experienced within the organization; as such, the organizational climate includes attitudes towards aggression and workplace bullying (Martin, 2002; Schneider, Ehrhart, & Macey, 2011; Schein, 2010). Organizational climate is created and shaped by organizational culture, but never mirrors it perfectly. Indeed, there may be an awkward gap and tension between the two.

It is improbably that any competitive organization would want to deliberately create a climate within which harassment and workplace bullying are openly accepted and tolerated. Apart from any ethical or moral concerns, bullying contributes directly to organizational dysfunctionality, a deleterious sense of injustice and organizational dissatisfaction, significant human capital and economic costs, and potential legal exposure (Georgakopoulos, Wilkin, Kent, 2011; Keashly & Neuman, 2004; Tepper, Duffy, Henle, & Lambert, 2006). However, notwithstanding the desire to create a culture that rejects harassment and bullying, organizational climates can exist where these negative patterns of behavior remain unchallenged, or where they are tacitly endorsed. Indeed, the acceptance workplace bullying seems to be extensive. A recent survey concludes that 72 percent of U.S. employers indicated they either tacitly condone or explicitly sustain bullying in the workplace (Namie, 2014, p. 10-12).

Dynamic Contribution of National Culture

A significant mediating factor in recognizing and responding to workplace bullying is the national culture within which the organization is embedded. Organizations attempt to create their own unique cultures and climates; however, in many significant dimensions these mirror the ambient assumptions and values of national culture. That said, there are significant problems in identifying and comparing national cultures, and there is always a danger of projecting unhelpful stereotypes onto those who have specific national or ethnic memberships. Hofstede (2001) proposed one of the most enduring approaches to recognizing national culture, identifying a number of dimensions – including power difference, masculine vs feminine, and individualism vs collectivism – that provides an insight into collectively held national assumptions, beliefs, and values.

Bullying and Power Distance

Many have identified power distance as a crucial element in the prevalence and acceptance of bullying. Power distance measures the extent to which, in a national culture, an unequal distribution of social power is apparent, accepted, and unchallenged. In nations with high power distance, people tend to accept hierarchical social orders in which everybody has an accepted place, and in which differences in power are regarded as natural, inevitable, and largely uncontested. Within such cultures, the use and abuse of power is considered a reality and any resulting unfair treatment tolerated. In societies with low power distance, people believe in a more equal distribution of societal power, demand justification for power inequalities, call for more respect of personal dignity, and are generally more intolerant of bullying behavior (Eurofound, 2015; Giorgi, Leon-Perez, & Arenas, 2015; Jacobson, Hood, & Van Buren, 2014).

Bullying and Individualism

National culture dispositions also significantly impact not only the recognition of workplace bullying, but also the trajectory that research, policies, and legal initiatives have taken in matters of aggression and harassment (Einarsen et al., 2011; Keashly & Jagatic, 2011). For example, in the United States the national culture dimension of individualism is high and the personal qualities of the individual are valued. Organizations and managers tend to value "healthy" competition between individuals, place high expectations of a worker's individual performance, endorse forceful managerial intervention, rely on visionary leadership, and insist on the preservation of a mediating corporate authority. Workplace bullying might be regarded as an aberration, but more often it is discounted or minimized. By contrast, in the Scandinavia countries, where collectivism is a dominant culture value, there is a concern for preserving social consensus, working cooperatively, and providing mutual assistance. In Scandinavia, unlike the United States, bullying is perceived as a disruptive breach of the social and cultural norm and is illegal (Holmberg & Akerblom, 2008; Jacobson et al., 2014).

Misappropriation of Organizational Power and Control

Many workplace landscapes are painted in vibrant and clashing colors. There may be dissent, disagreement, and genuine concerns about the performance of specific organizational members. There might be anguish about how best to realize operational goals, and disagreement about the strategic direction that have been mandated. Managers, and those whom they manage, realize that conflict and disagreement are an integral part of the social and political context of the organization. They realize that conflict can be used constructively to arrive at new and different perspectives which are often valuable. Organizational participants also recognize that although the ultimate outcomes of conflict and dissention are potentially valuable, the active and ongoing process of conflict is usually unpleasant, disruptive, and polarizing (Nicotera & Dorsey, 2006; Tjosvold, Wong, & Chen, 2014).

Organizations fulfill their mission through the orchestrated activities of participants. In almost all settings, management is directly responsible for this orchestration: managers are, as it were, the conductors who coordinate and harmonize the efforts of individual players. Such orchestration requires managerial skill in recognizing and resolving internal conflict in ways that provide optimal benefit for the organization as an entity, and for organizational participants as a collective. Individual managers may adopt different approaches – leading, moderating, negotiating, inspiring, or demanding – yet it is appreciated that: (a) the managerial approach taken rest on the legitimate power, influence, and authority that is organizationally entrusted to the manager; and (b) that the anticipated outcomes of managerial interventions are directed at benefiting the whole organization (Anderson & Brion, 2014; Kramer, 2014).

The scope of managerial involvement – the range of skills that managers need to possess and the degree of power they are required to use – depends on the organizational structure, industrial sector, and task environment. The trend in the latter decades of the 20th century has been for organizational structures to be more horizontal (as opposed to hierarchical), for power distributions to be more even, and for the organizational environment to be more egalitarian. Increasingly, organizations – especially in the service and knowledge-based sectors – have appreciated and adopted internal structures that center on semi-autonomous workgroups, the promotion of creativity, and the cultivation of innovation. Further, there is a growing appreciation that, in such environments, organizational and group effectiveness depends on task-related and socio-emotional processes (Hoegl & Gemuenden, 2001; Priesemuth, Schminke, Ambrose, & Folger, 2014).

Within this setting, managerial bullying – directed at the subordinate and designed, intentionally or unintentionally, to cause personal degradation – is neither warranted nor constructive. Bullying degrades the individual, endangers the task-related cohesiveness of the organizational, and poisons the socio-emotional climate of the work environment. More than that, bullying constitutes a misappropriation of managerial power and control for personal purposes, whether those purposes involve the manager's own sense of psychological identity, a demonstration of personal power, or a furtherance of his or her micropolitical aspirations within the organization. Managerial bullying and abusive supervision, as illegitimate misappropriations of organizational power, violate the manager's duty of agency and demonstrate a personalized reconstruction of legitimate organizational control.

Bullying as a Violation of Agency

Managers operate within a presumed organizational and legal framework of agency. It is acknowledged they also seek to derive personal advantages and benefits that might be at variance with the interest of their principals. This tension necessitates monitoring efforts and policing costs on the part of business owners and shareholders. These efforts usually center on minimizing, not necessarily eliminating, the benefits that managers might otherwise seek to misappropriate (Daily, Dalton, & Cannella, 2003; Lan, & Heracleous, 2010; Uhlaner, 2008). As Geppert and Dörrenbächer (2014) suggest, the perpetual challenge for agency theory in practice is that – despite the simplifications made about human nature, economic rationality, and legal responsibilities – all managerial decisions and behavior are embedded in a more complex matrix of social, economic, and personal self-interest.

Deviation from strict agency theory provides managers with the opportunity to engage in micropolitical considerations to enhance their power, influence, and personal benefits. Although micropolitical activity is both recognized and acknowledged within organizational contexts, such activity must not be seen to violate the norms and boundaries established by organizational governance. Workplace bullying, when initiated by managers against subordinates, constitutes a particularly blunt, aggressive, and negative form of micropolitical manipulation designed to benefit manager-perpetrators at the expense – often at the considerable expense – of their principals, in gross violation of governance norms and normative agency boundaries.

Bullying as a Personal Reconstruction of Control

One of the functions of management is controlling, but control needs to be explained. In the evolution of management, the older understanding of control, which was very much a product of then-existing social norms and ridged hierarchical bureaucratic structures, was that it was synonymous with power, authority, and conforming to organizational objectives (Tannenbaum, 1968). Subordinates were thus "controlled" through a process designed to "help circumscribe idiosyncratic behaviors and keep them conformant with the rational plan of the organization" (Tannenbaum (1962) p. 237). For idiosyncratic behaviors, read individual actions.

The modern and currently accepted understanding of managerial control is that it does not focus on people, but on performance, outputs, and outcomes. The process of controlling compares these non-personal organizational results with those that were originally envisaged, planned, and anticipated (Demartini, 2014). Controlling is a process of adjusting, revising, and aligning outcomes to ensure that they correspond with what had been strategically or operationally planned. Managerial control is presently understood as "supervisory behaviour directed toward subordinates to ensure performance, including setting performance standards and goals, reviewing and providing performance feedback, and taking correcting actions when necessary to ensure performance outcomes" (Chen, Zhang, & Wang, 2014, p. 139).

When initiated by managers, bullying negates – or significantly reduces – their duty of organizational agency. When initiated by managers, bullying represents a regression from control as an organizationally-sanctioned process concerned with outcomes, to a more problematic personally-driven process directed towards individuals. Simply stated, managerial bullying usurps organizationally-bestowed power for personal ends.

SOLUTIONS AND RECOMMENDATIONS

Workplace bullying can easily become a pervasive problem that cannot be easily extinguished by organizational policy or leadership, no matter how well intended. There are strong arguments for organizations creating and monitoring work-environments to ensure that workplace bullying does not occur. Undoubtedly, the efforts and costs related to prevention outweigh those of with dealing with workplace bullying when it materializes, or of ignoring or tacitly accepting its existence. The following suggestions might be useful.

Commitment to a Culture of Non-Aggression

Organizational leaders need to construct and maintain a culture that places value on non-aggression, mutual respect, cooperation, and organizational commitment. Behavior such as aggression, bullying, and harassment must be positioned as destructive to the values, beliefs, and success of the organization. People are the most valuable asset that any organization possesses, but for those human assets to generate economic returns they need to be respected, encouraged, and motivated to contribute to the organization's ongoing success. All participants need to be convinced and reassured that the organization values their membership and that it recognizes, respects, and affirms their human dignity (Gumbus & Meglich, 2012).

HR Policies That Reflect Organizational Culture and Expectations

Corporate policies must reflect the underlying cultural values and beliefs of the organization. However, organizational cultures cannot be based only on rhetorical statements; they need to be created and continuously reinforced by the behavior of organizational participants and the enactments their leaders. In particular, HR management must craft policies that address significant people-related issues in the workplace. There should be clear, unambiguous, published, and enforced HR policies regarding a zero-tolerance for workplace bullying, harassment, and aggressive behavior. It is equally important that HR policies do not merely reflect statutory legal and occupational safety requirements; they must unambiguously identify destructive practices, such as managerial bullying, that might not be classified as illegal in that particular jurisdiction.

Education and Awareness

Although HR policies can map and delineate the territory, it is critical that the actual bullying "territory" is explored by organizational participants themselves. The HR department must promote training and educational programs for managers and their subordinates that allow participants to develop an awareness of bullying, recognize its manifestations, understand its consequences, and appreciate how bullying situations can be resolved. Training should focus on considering the antecedents of bullying and on appreciating the dynamics, processes, and outcomes of this kind of destructive behavior.

A Climate of Openness and Not of Fear

Organizational participants need to sense that they work in a climate in which openness and transparency are valued. The HR department should establish channels of communication for those who experience or witness managerial bullying. Managerial bullying involves power differentials and this can raise issues of fear, intimidation, and reprisal for those who report such conduct. As Morrison (2014) notes, "it is perhaps not surprising that studies have found employees to be more likely to engage in voice when they have a greater sense of psychological safety and more likely to remain silent when they perceive voice to be unsafe" (p. 181). HR departments need to create that sense of psychological safely for all organizational participants; in particular, for those who reveal bullying.

A Process of Recognition and Redress

Adverse criticism from supervisors, fault-finding, and what are perceived as negative comments about performance are unpleasant, but do not normally constitute bullying. It can often be difficult for those who receive such criticism to see it as constructive, or to believe that the manager is challenging rather than provoking. Managers should always present objectives measures to support their criticism and provide remedial options. In cases where there are significant performance issues with employees, managers should involve HR professionals and explore the possibilities for employee retraining, transfer, or possibly termination. The process needs to be open and transparent. It needs to involve others, and it must recognize that all employees are valuable human assets of the organization. The process of dealing with manager-employee conflict needs to respect the human dignity of those involved. It also needs to provide viable and mutually acceptable solutions to resolve the problems encountered.

Coping With and Reappraising Perceived Bullying

When individuals perceive they are the targets of bullying, they should be encouraged to re-evaluate those perceptions. Part of the HR education and training goal should center on helping employees to develop alternative ways of interpreting what they might initially labelled as bullying behavior. Employees should be empowered to re-assess the contexts within which they find themselves, not simply self-identify as "victims" or as individuals locked in a process of victimization. Employees might need to cope with high levels of stress, a sense of being under-appreciated, and concern for their job security. There might be legitimate problems with the employee's performance and the employee should be encouraged to take control, respond constructively, and commit to change. However, in helping employees to reappraise and reconfigure their experiences, it is critical that genuine cases of bullying are not rationalized, excused, or legitimized.

Mediation and Intervention

If it seems clear to the targeted individual and to HR that bullying has indeed occurred, it might be possible to resolve the behavior through mediation. Mediation can involve the organization's HR department, but some HR professions feel that they will be considered biased and elect to employ outside consultants and mediators. Mediation and psycho-therapeutic intervention are expensive, and the outcomes frequently unsuccessful. That notwithstanding, engagement in a remediation process may resolve the bullying and also signal that such behavior is taken seriously by the organization. Mediation and psycho-therapeutic intervention are often most effective in the early stages of bullying; they tend to produce decidedly poorer outcomes when the behavior has escalated (Namie & Namie, 2009b; Saam, 2010). As McCulloch (2010), a practicing mediator, notes: "I'm aware of the arguments against using mediation to resolve allegations of workplace bullying. I'm clear that 'power differences' are a factor in mediation but would argue that this is almost always the case. I'm aware that there are strong arguments to say that mediation risks re-victimising the victim and my response is that victim-villain binaries are usually unhelpful in analysing and resolving problems" (p. 48).

FUTURE RESEARCH DIRECTIONS

The workplace bullying literature is voluminous, but a number of lacunae exist and these suggest possible directions for future research. First, there has been a growing proliferation of constructs for what are regarded as different forms of workplace bullying and harassment (Hershcovis, 2011). Certainly, the variety, scope, and impact of bullying defy a simple and inclusive definition; however, construct proliferation has only served to splinter and isolate research efforts. There is a pressing need for a thoughtful, systematic typology to bring clarity to the field and to encourage collaboration and interdisciplinary efforts.

Second, while the costs associated with various forms of workplace bullying are well-recognized, there is a need for a convincing estimate of the organizational and societal costs associated with these behaviors. This presents several problems: (a) it is difficult to fully identify the direct impact of workplace bullying (absenteeism, stress and mental exhaustion leading to decreased performance, retaliatory employee sabotage, etc.); (b) indirect costs are also involved and borne as economic externalities by society. For example, workplace and abusive managerial bullying can produce damaging psychological fallout for the relatives and non-work acquaintances of targeted individuals: spillover costs or crossover effects (Carlson, Ferguson, Perrewé, & Whitten, 2011; Haines, Marchand, & Harvey, 2006); and (c) even when identified, it is difficult to attribute economic costs to these outcomes. Nevertheless, comprehensive estimates of the full costs of workplace bullying are necessary in order to draw attention to the magnitude of the problem, to make organizations more responsive in reducing these costs, and to catalyze civil society and political efforts in address the issue through legislation.

Third, research is needed to clarify why workplace bullying is initiated. Of particular value would be a fuller appreciation derived from the accounts of those who have actually instigated bullying in the workplace. This research might center on the self-identified psychological needs of perpetrators. Another valuable research area would be the dynamics of the micropolitical contexts in which participants try to optimize personal advantage, benefit, and power. It would also be valuable to know how perpetrators interpret these micropolitical contexts, the dynamics that they believe are in play, and why they instigate bullying to establish power over, with, and through others (see Smeed et al., 2009).

CONCLUSION

Organizations are socially constructed, politically vibrant, mission-driven, and continuously in a process of adapt to changing internal and external environments. As organizations negotiate change and reformulate their fundamental assumptions, it is inevitable that disagreement, dissent, and conflict arise. Organizational conflicts can be transitory and positive, or prolonged and destructive; however, the most insidious and destabilizing forms of conflict are not organizational-centered, but those generated by personal motives.

Creative Conflict

Conflict is creative when forceful debate results in a new consensus that provides benefit for the organization. Conflict and dissention can be abrasive, unpleasant, and not particularly wanted. The crucial factor is whether the conflict serves to facilitate organizational advancement, or whether it has been initiated for provide personal advantage, or individual gratification. Creative conflict is targeted on situations, processes, and outcomes. When directed at individuals it should be designed to improve performance, or to motivate; not to humiliate. Creative conflict and dissention can abrasive, but it can also contribute to organizational health.

Destructive Conflict

Conflict is destructive when it cannot be reconciled, paralyzes the organization, and undermines organizational stability and cohesion. When destructive, conflict and dissention can result in an organizational dysfunctionality that may manifest itself in multiple and seemingly unrelated symptoms. Destructive conflict is often targeted at a particular individual, designed to cause him or her personal harm, and intended to demotivate. Destructive conflict, when repeated, sustained, and pervasive can all too easily be interpreted as bullying.

Although it may be manifested in multiple ways, at its core workplace bullying rests on power differentials, actual or perceived. Some argue that abusive supervision is a special form of workplace bullying; however, this kind of behavior can perhaps be better viewed as prototypical bullying because of its prevalence and because of its reliance on power difference between perpetrator and targeted individual. Keashly (2010) observed that workplace bullying represents a persistent relational aggression, which has the potential to escalate and to draw others into its darkness. She notes that its "effects can be devastating and widespread individually, organizationally and beyond" and that "it is fundamentally a systemic phenomenon, grounded in the organization's culture" (p. 18).

Workplaces bullying, when perpetrated by managers against subordinates, is fundamentally a misappropriation of organizational power and control for the personal benefit of the managers involved. Workplace bullying is organizationally destructive and can result in psychological damage for those targeted, for those who witness or feel complicit in the bullying, and for the target's non-work associates and networks.

Perhaps, with an appreciation of the extensive damage caused, it is time to revisit and reduce bullying in our workplaces. Perhaps, with an appreciation that managerial bullying degrades not only the target but also the environment, it is time to recognize it as a significant threat to organizational success and wellbeing. And perhaps, acknowledging that managerial bullying is a subversion of organizational power, control, and agency it is time for corporate governance to act more vigorously for its elimination.

REFERENCES

ACAS. (2014). *Bullying and harassment at work: A guide for employees*. Advisory, Conciliation and Arbitration Service. Retrieved on September 22, 2015, from: www.acas.org.uk/index.aspx?articleid=794

Anderson, C., & Brion, S. (2014). Perspectives on power in organizations. *Annual Review of Organizational Psychology and Organizational Behavior, 1*(1), 67–97. doi:10.1146/annurev-orgpsych-031413-091259

Anderson, C. A., & Bushman, B. J. (2002). Human aggression. *Annual Review of Psychology, 53*(1), 27–51. doi:10.1146/annurev.psych.53.100901.135231 PMID:11752478

Aquino, K., & Thau, S. (2009). Workplace victimization: Aggression from the targets perspective. *Annual Review of Psychology, 60*(1), 717–741. doi:10.1146/annurev.psych.60.110707.163703 PMID:19035831

Baillien, E., De Cuyper, N., & De Witte, H. (2011). Job autonomy and workload as antecedents of workplace bullying: A two-wave test of Karaseks job demand control model for targets and perpetrators. *Journal of Occupational and Organizational Psychology*, *84*(1), 191–208. doi:10.1348/096317910X508371

Baillien, E., Neyens, I., De Witte, H., & De Cuyper, N. (2009). A qualitative study on the development of workplace bullying: Towards a three way model. *Journal of Community & Applied Social Psychology*, *19*(1), 1–16. doi:10.1002/casp.977

Barling, J., Dupré, K. E., & Kelloway, E. K. (2009). Predicting workplace aggression and violence. *Annual Review of Psychology*, *60*(1), 671–692. doi:10.1146/annurev.psych.60.110707.163629 PMID:18793089

Baumeister, R. F., Smart, L., & Boden, J. M. (1996). Relation of threatened egotism to violence and aggression: The dark side of high self-esteem. *Psychological Review*, *103*(1), 5–33. doi:10.1037/0033-295X.103.1.5 PMID:8650299

Bowling, N. A., & Beehr, T. A. (2006). Workplace harassment from the victims perspective: A theoretical model and meta-analysis. *The Journal of Applied Psychology*, *91*(5), 998–1012. doi:10.1037/0021-9010.91.5.998 PMID:16953764

Brodsky, C. M. (1976). *The harassed worker*. New York: Lexington Books.

Burns, T. (1961). Micropolitics: Mechanisms of institutional change. *Administrative Science Quarterly*, *6*(3), 257–281. doi:10.2307/2390703

Carlson, D. S., Ferguson, M., Perrewé, P. L., & Whitten, D. (2011). The fallout from abusive supervision: An examination of subordinates and their partners. *Personnel Psychology*, *64*(4), 937–961. doi:10.1111/j.1744-6570.2011.01232.x

Chen, C. C., Zhang, A. Y., & Wang, H. (2014). Enhancing the effects of power sharing on psychological empowerment: The roles of management control and power distance orientation. *Management and Organization Review*, *10*(1), 135–156. doi:10.1111/more.12032

Crawshaw, L. (2009). Workplace bullying? Mobbing? Harassment? Distraction by a thousand definitions. *Consulting Psychology Journal: Practice and Research*, *61*(3), 263–267. doi:10.1037/a0016590

Daily, C. M., Dalton, D. R., & Cannella, A. A. (2003). Corporate governance: Decades of dialogue and data. *Academy of Management Review*, *28*(3), 371–382.

De Cuyper, N., Baillien, E., & De Witte, H. (2009). Job insecurity, perceived employability and targets and perpetrators experiences of workplace bullying. *Work and Stress*, *23*(3), 206–224. doi:10.1080/02678370903257578

Demartini, C. (2014). The evolution of the concept of 'management control': Towards a definition of 'performance management system.' In C. Demartini (Ed.), Performance management systems (pp. 9-54). Heidelberg, Germany: Springer-Verlag.

Einarsen, S. (1999). The nature and causes of bullying at work. *International Journal of Manpower*, *20*(1/2), 16–27. doi:10.1108/01437729910268588

Einarsen, S. (2000). Harassment and bullying at work: A review of the Scandinavian approach. *Aggression and Violent Behavior: A Review Journal, 5*(4), 371-401.

Einarsen, S., Hoel, H., Zapf, D., & Cooper, C. L. (2011). The concept of bullying and harassment at work: The European tradition. In S. Einarsen, H. Hoel, D. Zapf, & C. L. Cooper (Eds.), *Bullying and harassment in the workplace. Developments in theory, research, and practice* (2nd ed., pp. 3–39). Boca Raton, FL: CRC Press.

Einarsen, S., Raknes, B. I., & Matthiesen, S. M. (1994). Bullying and harassment at work and their relationships to work environment quality – an exploratory study. *European Work and Organizational Psychologist, 4*(4), 381–401. doi:10.1080/13594329408410497

Einarsen, S., & Skogstad, A. (1996). Bullying at work: Epidemiological findings in public and private organizations. *European Journal of Work and Organizational Psychology, 5*(2), 185–201. doi:10.1080/13594329608414854

EU-OSHA [European Agency for Safety and Health at Work]. (2010). *Workplace violence and harassment: A European picture*. European Risk Observatory Report. Retrieved from https://osha.europa.eu/sites/default/files/publications/documents/en/publications/reports/violence-harassment-TERO09010ENC/violence-harassment-report.pdf

Eurofound. (2015). *Violence and harassment in European workplaces: Causes, impacts and policies*. Dublin, Ireland: Author. Retrieved from http://www.eurofound.europa.eu/sites/default/files/ef_comparative_analytical_report/field_ef_documents/ef1473en.pdf

Fox, S., & Stallworth, L. E. (2009). Building a framework for two internal organizational approaches to resolving and preventing workplace bullying: Alternative dispute resolution and training. *Consulting Psychology Journal: Practice and Research, 61*(3), 220–241. doi:10.1037/a0016637

Furnham, A., Richards, S. C., & Paulhus, D. L. (2013). The Dark Triad of personality: A 10 year review. *Social and Personality Psychology Compass, 7*(3), 199–216. doi:10.1111/spc3.12018

Georgakopoulos, A., Wilkin, L., & Kent, B. (2011). Workplace bullying: A complex problem in contemporary organizations. *International Journal of Business and Social Science, 2*(3), 1–20. Retrieved from http://ijbssnet.com/journals/Vol._2_No._3_[Special_Issue_-_January_2011]/1.pdf

Geppert, M., & Dörrenbächer, C. (2014). Politics and power *within* multinational corporations: Mainstream studies, emerging critical approaches and suggestions for future research. *International Journal of Management Reviews, 16*(2), 226–244. doi:10.1111/ijmr.12018

Giga, S. I., Hoel, H., & Lewis, D. (2008). *The costs of workplace bullying. Research Commissioned by the Dignity at Work Partnership*. Bradford, UK: University of Bradford.

Giorgi, G., Leon-Perez, J. M., & Arenas, A. (2015). Are bullying behaviors tolerated in some cultures? Evidence for a curvilinear relationship between workplace bullying and job satisfaction among Italian workers. *Journal of Business Ethics, 131*(1), 227–237. doi:10.1007/s10551-014-2266-9

Gumbus, A., & Meglich, P. (2012). Lean and mean: Workplace culture and the prevention of workplace bullying. *Journal of Applied Business and Economics, 13*(5), 11–20.

Haines, V. Y., Marchand, A., & Harvey, S. (2006). Crossover of workplace aggression experiences in dual-earner couples. *Journal of Occupational Health Psychology, 11*(4), 305–314. doi:10.1037/1076-8998.11.4.305 PMID:17059295

Hershcovis, M. S. (2011). Incivility, social undermining, bullying…Oh my! A call to reconcile constructs within workplace aggression research. *Journal of Organizational Behavior, 32*(3), 499–519. doi:10.1002/job.689

Hershcovis, M. S., & Barling, J. (2010). Towards a multi-foci approach to workplace aggression: A meta-analytic review of outcomes from different perpetrators. *Journal of Organizational Behavior, 31*(1), 24–44. doi:10.1002/job.621

Hershcovis, M. S., & Rafferty, A. (2012). Predicting abusive supervision. In J. Houdmont, S. Leka, & R. Sinclair (Eds.), *Contemporary occupational health psychology: Global perspectives on research and practice* (Vol. 2, pp. 92–108). Chichester, UK: Wiley-Blackwell. doi:10.1002/9781119942849.ch6

Hershcovis, M. S., & Reich, T. C. (2013). Integrating workplace aggression research: Relational, contextual, and method considerations. *Journal of Organizational Behavior, 34*(S1), 26–42. doi:10.1002/job.1886

Hershcovis, M. S., Reich, T. C., & Niven, K. (2015). *Workplace bullying: Causes, consequences, and intervention strategies*. White Paper prepared by the International Affairs Committee of the Society for Industrial and Organizational Psychology. Bowling Green, OH: SIOP. Retrieved from http://www.siop.org/WhitePapers/WorkplaceBullyingFINAL.pdf

Hoegl, M., & Gemuenden, H. G. (2001). Teamwork quality and the success of innovative projects: A theoretical concept and empirical evidence. *Organization Science, 12*(4), 435–449. doi:10.1287/orsc.12.4.435.10635

Hoel, H., & Cooper, C. L. (2000). *Destructive conflict and bullying at work*. Unpublished report, Manchester School of Management, University of Manchester Institute of Science and Technology, UK.

Hofstede, G. (2001). *Culture's consequences: Comparing values, behaviors, institutions, and organizations across nations* (2nd ed.). London, UK: Sage.

Holmberg, I., & Akerblom, S. (2008). Primus inter pares: Leadership and culture in Sweden. In J. S. Chhokar, F. C. Brodbeck, & R. J. House (Eds.), *Culture and leadership across the world: The GLOBE book of in-depth studies of 25 societies* (pp. 33–74). New York: Erlbaum.

Hoyle, E. (1999). The two faces of micropolitics. *School Leadership & Management, 19*(2), 213–222. doi:10.1080/13632439969249

Jacobson, K. J. L., Hood, J. N., & Van Buren, H. J. III. (2014). Workplace bullying across cultures: A research agenda. *International Journal of Cross Cultural Management, 14*(1), 47–65. doi:10.1177/1470595813494192

Jenkins, M. F., Winefield, H., & Sarris, A. (2010). Listening to the bullies: An exploratory study of managers accused of workplace bullying. *Paper presented at the 7th International Conference on Workplace Bullying*, Cardiff, Wales.

Keashly, L. (2010). Some things you need to know but may have been afraid to ask: A researcher speaks to ombudsmen about workplace bullying. *Journal of the International Ombudsman Association*, *3*(2), 10–23. Retrieved from http://www.ombudsassociation.org/Resources/IOA-Publications/IOA-Journal/Journal-PDFs/JIOAVolume3No2October2010Final.aspx

Keashly, L., & Jagatic, K. (2011). North American perspectives on hostile behaviors and bullying at work. In S. Einarsen, H. Hoel, D. Zapf, & C. L. Cooper (Eds.), *Bullying and harassment in the workplace: Developments in theory, research, and practice* (2nd ed., pp. 41–74). Boca Raton, FL: CRC Press.

Keashly, L., & Neuman, J. H. (2004). Bullying in the workplace: Its impact and management. *Employee Rights and Employment Policy*, *8*(3), 335–373.

Kim, E., & Glomb, T. M. (2010). Get smarty pants: Cognitive ability, personality, and victimization. *The Journal of Applied Psychology*, *95*(5), 889–901. doi:10.1037/a0019985 PMID:20718509

Kramer, R. M. (2014). Power and influence at the top: Effective and ineffective forms of leader behavior. In G. R. Goethals, S. T. Allison, R. M. Kramer, & D. M. Messick (Eds.), *Conceptions of leadership: Enduring ideas and emerging insights* (pp. 223–238). New York: Palgrave Macmillan. doi:10.1057/9781137472038_13

Lan, L.-L., & Heracleous, L. (2010). Rethinking agency theory: The view from law. *Academy of Management Review*, *35*(2), 294–314. doi:10.5465/AMR.2010.48463335

Lewis, D., Giga, S., & Hoel, H. (2011). Discrimination and bullying. In S. Einarsen, H. Hoel, D. Zapf, & C. L. Cooper (Eds.), *Bullying and harassment in the workplace: Development in theory, research, and practice* (2nd ed., pp. 267–281). Boca Raton, FL: CRC Press.

Leymann, H. (1990). Mobbing and psychological terror at workplaces. *Violence and Victims*, *5*(2), 119–126. PMID:2278952

Leymann, H. (1996). The content and development of mobbing at work. *European Journal of Work and Organizational Psychology*, *5*(2), 165–184. doi:10.1080/13594329608414853

Leymann, H., & Gustafsson, A. (1996). Mobbing at work and the development of post-traumatic stress disorders. *European Journal of Work and Organizational Psychology*, *5*(2), 251–276. doi:10.1080/13594329608414858

Lind, K., Glasø, L., Pallesen, S., & Einarsen, S. (2009). Personality profiles among targets and non-targets of workplace bullying. *European Psychologist*, *14*(3), 231–237. doi:10.1027/1016-9040.14.3.231

Martin, J. (2002). *Organizational culture: Mapping the terrain*. Thousand Oaks, CA: Sage. doi:10.4135/9781483328478

Matthiesen, S. B., & Einarsen, S. (2007). Perpetrators and targets of bullying at work: Role stress and individual differences. *Violence and Victims*, *22*(6), 735–753. doi:10.1891/088667007782793174 PMID:18225386

McCulloch, B. (2010). Dealing with bullying behaviours in the workplace: What works – a practitioner's view. *Journal of the International Ombudsman Association, 3*(2), 38–51. Retrieved from http://www.ombudsassociation.org/Resources/IOA-Publications/IOA-Journal/Journal-PDFs/JIOAVolume3No2October2010Final.aspx

Mitchell, M. S., & Ambrose, M. L. (2007). Abusive supervision and workplace deviance and the moderating effects of negative reciprocity beliefs. *The Journal of Applied Psychology, 92*(4), 1159–1168. doi:10.1037/0021-9010.92.4.1159 PMID:17638473

Morrison, E. W. (2014). Employee voice and silence. *Annual Review of Organizational Psychology and Organizational Behavior, 1*(1), 173–197. doi:10.1146/annurev-orgpsych-031413-091328

Namie, G. (2014). *U.S. workplace bullying survey*. Workplace Bullying Institute. Retrieved from http://www.workplacebullying.org/multi/pdf/WBI-2014-US-Survey.pdf

Namie, G., & Namie, R. (2009a). *The bully at work: What you can do to stop the hurt and reclaim your dignity on the job*. Naperville, IL: Sourcebooks.

Namie, G., & Namie, R. (2009b). U.S. workplace bullying: Some basic considerations and consultation interventions. *Consulting Psychology Journal: Practice and Research, 61*(3), 202–219. doi:10.1037/a0016670

Nicotera, A. M., & Dorsey, L. K. (2006). Individual and interactive processes in organizational conflict. In J. G. Oetzel & S. Ting-Toomey (Eds.), *The Sage handbook of conflict communication: Integrating theory, research, and practice* (pp. 293–325). Thousand Oaks, CA: Sage. doi:10.4135/9781412976176.n11

Nielsen, M., Matthiesen, S. B., & Einarsen, S. (2010). The impact of methodological moderators on prevalence rates of workplace bullying. A meta-analysis. *Journal of Occupational and Organizational Psychology, 83*(4), 955–979. doi:10.1348/096317909X481256

Nielsen, M., Notelaers, G., & Einarsen, S. (2011). Measuring exposure to workplace bullying. In S. Einarsen, H. Hoel, D. Zapf, & C. L. Cooper (Eds.), *Bullying and harassment in the workplace: Developments in theory, research, and practice* (2nd ed., pp. 149–174). Boca Raton, FL: CRC Press.

Olweus, D. (2003). Bully/victim problems in school. Basic facts and an effective intervention programme. In S. Einarsen, H. Hoel, D. Zapf, & C. L. Cooper (Eds.), *Bullying and emotional abuse in the workplace* (pp. 62–78). London: Taylor and Francis.

Paulhus, D. L., & Williams, K. M. (2002). The Dark Triad of personality: Narcissism, Machiavellianism, and psychopathy. *Journal of Research in Personality, 36*(6), 556–563. doi:10.1016/S0092-6566(02)00505-6

Priesemuth, M., Schminke, M., Ambrose, M. L., & Folger, R. (2014). Abusive supervision climate: A multiple-mediation model of its impact on group outcomes. *Academy of Management Journal, 57*(5), 1513–1534. doi:10.5465/amj.2011.0237

Restubog, S. L. D., Scott, K. L., & Zagenczyk, T. J. (2011). When distress hits home: The role of contextual factors and psychological distress in predicting employees responses to abusive supervision. *The Journal of Applied Psychology, 96*(4), 713–729. doi:10.1037/a0021593 PMID:21280933

Saam, N. J. (2010). Interventions in workplace bullying: A multilevel approach. *European Journal of Work and Organizational Psychology, 19*(1), 51–75. doi:10.1080/13594320802651403

Schat, A. C. H., & Frone, M. R. (2011). Exposure to psychological aggression at work and job performance: The mediating role of job attitudes and personal health. *Work and Stress, 25*(1), 23–40. doi:10.1080/02678373.2011.563133 PMID:21643471

Schein, E. H. (2010). *Organizational culture and leadership* (4th ed.). San Francisco, CA: Jossey-Bass.

Schneider, B., Ehrhart, M. G., & Macey, W. H. (2011). Perspectives on organizational climate and culture. In S. Zedeck (Ed.), APA handbook of industrial and organizational psychology: Vol. 1. *Building and developing the organization* (pp. 373–414). Washington, DC: American Psychological Association.

Schneider, B., Ehrhart, M. G., & Macey, W. H. (2013). Climate and culture. *Annual Review of Psychology, 64*(1), 361–388. doi:10.1146/annurev-psych-113011-143809 PMID:22856467

Smeed, J. L., Kimber, M., Millwater, J., & Ehrich, L. C. (2009). Power over, with and through: Another look at micropolitics. *Leading & Managing, 15*(1), 26–41.

Smith, P. K., Singer, M., Hoel, H., & Cooper, C. L. (2003). Victimization in the school and the workplace: Are there any links? *British Journal of Psychology, 94*(2), 175–188. doi:10.1348/000712603321661868 PMID:12803813

Spain, S. M., Harms, P., & Lebreton, J. M. (2014). The dark side of personality at work. *Journal of Organizational Behavior, 35*(S1), S41–S60. doi:10.1002/job.1894

Tannenbaum, A. S. (1962). Control in organizations: Individual adjustment and organizational performance. *Administrative Science Quarterly, 7*(2), 236–257. doi:10.2307/2390857

Tannenbaum, A. S. (1968). *Control in organizations*. New York: McGraw-Hill.

Tepper, B. J. (2000). Consequences of abusive supervision. *Academy of Management Journal, 43*(2), 178–190. doi:10.2307/1556375

Tepper, B. J. (2007). Abusive supervision in work organizations: Review, synthesis, and research agenda. *Journal of Management, 33*(3), 261–289. doi:10.1177/0149206307300812

Tepper, B. J., Duffy, M. K., Henle, C. A., & Lambert, L. S. (2006). Procedural injustice, victim, precipitation, and abusive supervision. *Personnel Psychology, 59*(1), 101–123. doi:10.1111/j.1744-6570.2006.00725.x

Tepper, B. J., Moss, S. E., & Duffy, M. K. (2011). Predictors of abusive supervision: Supervisor perceptions of deep-level dissimilarity, relationship conflict, and subordinate performance. *Academy of Management Journal, 54*(2), 279–294. doi:10.5465/AMJ.2011.60263085

Thau, S., & Mitchell, M. S. (2010). Self-gain or self-regulation impairment? Tests of competing explanations of the supervisor abuse and employee deviance relationship through perceptions of distributive justice. *The Journal of Applied Psychology, 95*(6), 1009–1031. doi:10.1037/a0020540 PMID:20718511

Tjosvold, D., Wong, A. S. H., & Chen, N. Y. F. (2014). Constructively managing conflicts in organizations. *Annual Review of Organizational Psychology and Organizational Behavior, 1*(1), 545–568. doi:10.1146/annurev-orgpsych-031413-091306

Uhlaner, L. M. (2008). *The role of ownership in governance: A neglected focus in entrepreneurship and management research* (Inaugural Lecture). Nyenrode Business University, Breukelen, Netherlands. Retrieved from http://www.nyenrode.nl/FacultyResearch/research/Documents/Inaugural%20lectures/uhlaner_inaugural_lecture.pdf

Willner, R. (2011). Micro-politics: An underestimated field of qualitative research in political science. *German Policy Studies*, 7(3), 155-185. Retrieved from https://www.wiso.uni-hamburg.de/fileadmin/sowi/politik/methoden/Roland/GPS_3-2011_Willner.pdf

Yamada, D. (2013). Workplace bullying and the law: A report from the United States. In Japan Institute for Labour Policy and Training Report. In *Workplace bullying and harassment* (pp. 165-185). Tokyo, Japan: JILPT. Retrieved from http://www.jil.go.jp/english/reports/documents/jilpt-reports/no.12.pdf

Zapf, D., & Einarsen, S. (2011). Individual antecedents of bullying: Victims and perpetrators. In S. Einarsen, H. Hoel, D. Zapf, & C. L. Cooper (Eds.), *Bullying and harassment in the workplace: Developments in theory, research, and practice* (2nd ed., pp. 177–200). Boca Raton, FL: CRC Press.

KEY TERMS AND DEFINITIONS

Agency Theory: A presumption that managers (agents) have a legal and fiduciary obligation to protect the rights and economic interests of the owners (principals) of the organization that employs them. To ensure this, owners must establish a system of robust governance and maintain continuous monitoring (policing) of managerial decisions and performance. Policing can be difficult and costly when ownership is separated from direct organizational control, which is often the case with large-scale corporations, fragmented ownership (multiple and dispersed shareholders), and when dealing with strong, professional, and inherently self-interested management.

Bullying: A pattern of consistent, repeated, and predictable negative behavior directed towards a targeted individual. It may manifest itself in many forms including, but not limited to: verbal hostility, abuse, and aggression; constantly ignoring the other, or making belittling suggestions; persistent, unreasonable, and unwarranted criticism; spreading malicious gossip or rumors; unreasonably removing organizational responsibilities and replacing them with demeaning or unpleasant tasks; blatant micromanaging and intrusive monitoring of performance; and repeatedly suggesting that targeted individuals have no value or potential and should quit their jobs.

Crossover Effect: When the psychological damage (lowered self-esteem, anxiety, frustration, and depression) caused to the target of bullying in the primary domain (the workplace) is transferred through that individual to an unrelated secondary domain (the target's home, or personal world) where it adversely impact others (partners, friends, and family members).

Culture: A set of discernible assumptions, attitudes, conceptualizations, and values possessed by members of a specific group that is transmitted through socialization and communication involving key symbols, narratives and stories, and a recalled past.

Harassment: Harassment is generally understood to be negative and psychologically damaging behavior directed towards others primarily because of their membership in legally protected class membership (gender, sexual orientation, disability, age, religion or beliefs, or their racial or ethnic origin).

National Culture: A distinctive set of beliefs, values, and assumptions generally held by members of a national group. National culture difference can be expressed as values on a number of dimensions: power-distance, masculinity-femininity, individualism-collectivism, and uncertainty-avoidance. These dimensions can be quantified and provide country-specific profiles. It is important to recognize that: (a) scores on these dimensions are statistical averages, with considerable individual variance and overlap with other national cultures; and (b) national profiles are useful in predicting behavior, but should not be used to pre-judge or stereotype others.

Targeted Individual: The person towards whom acts of bullying or harassment are directed. Targeting infers that: (a) the hostile acts and behavior are intentional; and (b) the perpetrator has identified a specific individual as the object of his/her abuse. This term is gradually replacing the older designation ("victim"), but both continue to be used interchangeably.

Chapter 5
Welfare Regime:
A Critical Discourse

Chandra Sekhar Patro
GVP College of Engineering (Autonomous), Visakhapatnam, India

ABSTRACT

In the present competitive business environment, it is essential for the management of any organization to precisely manage the welfare services to be provided for their employees. An organization is certainly a place where employees' and employers try to get the maximum from each other. Both, there can be lot more if and when they work together as partners in an organization, and if they have compassion of understanding of each other problems, which is the basic problem in employee welfare. The extreme logic in the wake of providing welfare services is to create proficient, healthy, loyal and satisfied labour force for an organization. The aim of the chapter is to articulate the welfare services administered by the organizations to the employees and their effect on the employees' efficacy and work life. It also examines the various principles and theories of welfare along with measures to improve welfare facilities in the organizations.

INTRODUCTION

Welfare is a driving vigour which secures the labour force and also augments their quality of living. The term welfare suggests the state of well-being and implies wholesomeness of the human being. It is a comprehensive term and refers to the physical, mental, moral, and emotional well-being of an individual (Aswathappa, 2010). According to Hopkins (1955), welfare is fundamentally an attitude of mind on the part of management, influencing the method in which management activities are undertaken. Employers concerned with introducing or extending welfare programmes now or in the future must be concerned not only with the past and current experience, but also with developing trends.

The traditional economic theory defined labour as a factor of production which consists of manual and mental exertion and receives some return by way of wages, salaries, or professional fees (Railkar, 1990). Labour is any physical or intellectual activity applied in industrial production and one who performs it is a worker. The term labour, labourer, workers, or employee are all used to refer to the wage earning

DOI: 10.4018/978-1-5225-2568-4.ch005

Welfare Regime

human agents in various industries and organisations. The term welfare is a relative concept; therefore, it varies from time to time, region to region and from country to country. Welfare helps in keeping the morale and motivation of the employees high so as to retain the employees for longer duration. The welfare measures need not be in monetary terms only but in any kind or forms (Lalitha & Priyanka, 2014).

The concept of 'Employee welfare' is flexible and differs widely with times, regions, industry, country, social values, and customs, the degree of industrialization, the general social economic development of people and political ideologies prevailing at particular moments (Patro, 2015). Coventry and Barker (1988) assert that staff welfare includes providing social club and sports facilities as appropriate, supervising staff and works' canteens, running sick clubs and savings schemes; dealing with superannuation, pension funds and leave grants, making loans on hardship cases; arranging legal aid and giving advice on personal problems; making long service grants; providing assistance to staff transferred to another area and providing fringe benefits. Such facilities enable a worker and his family to lead a good work, family, and social life (Sarma, 1996).

Employee welfare entails all those activities of employer which are directed towards providing the employees with certain facilities and services in addition to wages or salaries. Labour welfare is a state of living of an individual or a group in a desirable relationship with the total environment - ecological, economic, and social (John, 2004). A proper organization and administration of welfare facilities can play a vital role in promoting better working conditions and living standards for industrial workers, and also increase their productivity, especially in developing countries (Kohli & Sharma, 1997).

The very logic behind providing welfare schemes is to create efficient, healthy, loyal and satisfied labour force for the organization. Welfare measures practiced in any organization, aims or should aim, at improving the working and living conditions of employees and their families. Pylee and George (1996) stressed that even one discontented employee or an employee nursing a grievance can eventually infect an entire organization with the germ of discontent which, in turn, will result in lower efficiency, poor morale and reduction in overall production. However, the CLW (1969) defined the phrase to mean such facilities and amenities as adequate canteens, rest and recreation facilities, sanitary and medical facilities arrangements for travel to and from and for accommodation of workers employed at a distance from their homes, and such other services, amenities and facilities including social security measures as contribute to conditions under which workers are employed.

BACKGROUND

The chapter provides an extensive review of available literature in the area of employee welfare to develop a thorough understanding of the conceptual constructs and empirical research. A study by Zacharaiah (1954) in manufacturing undertakings identified that better working conditions and adequate provision of welfare services would contribute to harmonious industrial relations. Saiyadin (1983) revealed that the most predominant theme in the minds of organizations when they think of the voluntary welfare measures was not only the output and efficiency, but also increasing loyalty and morale. In respect of cost, the public sector organizations spend more on transportation and recreation whereas, private sector was found to be spending more on housing. Burchardt (1997) examined the balance between public and private sector welfare activity mainly in five areas such as education, health, housing, personal social services, and income maintenance and social security.

Patro (2012) found that the needs of the employee must be satisfied in order to meet the goals of the organisation. Any organisation would be effective only when there is high degree of co-operation between the employees and their management. Meena and Dangayach (2012) discovered that satisfied employees made positive contributions to the organizational effectiveness and performance. Staff well-being and engagement has direct impact on organizational performance and ultimately organizational success. It is an obvious statement, but high employee satisfaction levels can reduce employee turnover (Sinha, 2013).

Davis and Gibson (1994) emphasized the importance of a comprehensive need both in obtaining the breadth of information needed to design appropriate interventions and also in providing baseline information against which to evaluate programme effectiveness. Harika (2010) argued that the success of these employee welfare activities depend on the approach which has been taken to account in providing such activities to employees and welfare policy should be guided by idealistic morale and human value and such services includes the provision of medical facilities, sanitary and the accommodation of workers employed, amenities and industrial social security measures, training and education facilities, HIV and AIDS risk reduction and counselling services (Lalitha & Priyanka, 2014; Ramana & Reddy, 2015). Welfare services can be used to secure the labour force by providing proper human conditions of work and living through minimizing the hazardous effect on the life of the workers and their family members (Patro, 2016).

Neetha (2001) revealed that gradually the production relations in this industry are becoming increasingly informal and the process of informalisation has led not only to informalisation of workforce, but also to the feminisation and dis-organisation of the workforce. Logasakthi and Rajagopal (2013) revealed that the employees enjoy not only the satisfaction of their jobs but also various facilities given by the firms. Kumar and Yadav (2002) revealed that the overall satisfaction level of workers from labour welfare schemes was low in both the private and state sugar factories. Furthermore, the workers in both sectors ranked the four labour welfare schemes according to their importance as housing scheme, medical scheme, followed by education and recreation schemes.

Aiginger (2005) reassesses the relative impact of labour market regulation on economic performance. Inflexible labour markets combined with high welfare costs are often thought to be the main cause of low growth. The regulation impacts on growth, the impact of regulatory change is, however, less easy to demonstrate. Robinson, Sparrow, Clegg, and Birdi (2006) identified the key behaviours, which were found to be associated with employee engagement. The behaviours included belief in the organisation, desire to work to make things better, understanding of the business context and the 'bigger picture', being respectful of and helpful to colleagues, willingness to 'go the extra mile' and keeping up to date with developments in the field.

Mishra and Bhagat (2007) stated that labour absenteeism can be reduced to a great extent by provision of good housing, health and family care, canteen, educational and training facilities and provision of welfare activities. Joseph, Injodey, and Varghese (2009) point out that the structure of a welfare state rests on its social security fabric. Government, employers, and trade unions have done a lot to promote the betterment of workers' conditions. Employees are highly perishable and need to provide stable welfare facilities for their upgradation and better performance. The social and economic aspects of life of the employees have direct influence on the social and economic development of a nation (Rajkuar, 2014). Nanda and Panda (2013) stated the companies need to adopt better kind of welfare activities which create an effective working environment, maintain better industrial relations and better productivity.

Manzini and Gwandure (2011) reveals that the concept of employee welfare has been used as a strategy of improving productivity of employees by many organisations, since work related problems can lead to

Welfare Regime

poor quality of life for employees and a decline in performance. Satyanarayna and Reddi (2012) stated that the overall satisfaction levels of employees depends on provision of good welfare measures and also suggested that welfare measures enrich the employee standard of living and their satisfaction levels. Bhati and Ashokkumar (2013) concluded in terms of proving that the different welfare provisions provided to the employees working in an organisation under Factories Act, 1948 are having positive relations with employee satisfaction and if these facilities are not present, it sometimes leads to dissatisfaction. Srinivasa (2013) emphasized that labor welfare covers an ample field and connotes a state of well-being, happiness, satisfaction, protection, and enlargement of human resources and also helps to motivation of worker. Reshma and Basavaraj (2013) argued that the prime aim of our nation is to achieve maximum possible economic development so as to achieve higher standard of living for workers in the country.

Sabarirajan, Meharajan, and Arun (2010) argue that welfare measures play an important role in employee satisfaction resulting in improved quality work life. Employee welfare facilities enable workers to live a richer and more satisfactory life. After employees have been hired, trained, and remunerated, they must be retained and maintained to serve the organization better (Laddha, 2012). Mwiti (2007) highlights that naturally welfare services may not directly relate to an employee's job, but the presence or absence of the services is notable through employee performance, attitude, high or low labour turnover. Joseph, Injodey, and Varghese (2009) state the structure of a welfare state rests on its social security fabric. Government, employers and trade unions have done a lot to promote the betterment of worker's conditions. Aziri (2011) observed that job satisfaction is under the influence of a series of factors such as: the nature of work, salary, advancement opportunities, management, work groups and working conditions. Patro (2015) in a comparative analysis of welfare measures in public and private sector found that an employees' welfare facility is the key dimension to smooth employer-employee relationship. These welfare facilities improve the employees' morale and loyalty towards the management thereby increasing their happiness, satisfaction and performance.

SIGNIFICANCE OF SOCIAL SECURITY AND LABOUR WELFARE

The scope of labour welfare, however, cannot offer limited facilities within or near the undertaking, nor can it be so comprehensive as to embrace the whole range of social welfare or social services. Labour welfare has two aspects: negative and positive. On the negative side, labour welfare is concerned with counteracting the baneful effects of the large scale industrial system of production, especially capitalistic, and so far as India is concerned on the personal or family, and social life, of the worker. On the positive side, it deals with the provision of opportunities for the worker and his/her family for a good life as understood in its most comprehensive sense (Moorthy, 1968).

Welfare measures should be provided by the organisations, whether in the public or private sector, as it raises the morale of employees, reduce the risk and insecurity, eliminate turnover and absenteeism, and increase the production and productivity. Thus, improving the quality of working life by providing the employee welfare facilities would go a long way in achieving the goals of the organisation (Patro, 2012). In recent years, implementing necessary employee welfare schemes have become a key factor for the overall growth and development of any organization. The organisations provide welfare measures to their employees to increase their efficiency and reduce the absenteeism.

Social security is one of the pillars on which the structure of welfare state rests, and it constitutes the hard core of social policy in most countries. It is the security that society furnishes through appropriate organisation, against certain risks to which its members are exposed (ILO, 1942). Social security system comprises health and unemployment insurance, family allowances, provident funds, pensions and gratuity schemes, and widows' and survivors' allowances. The concept of social welfare, in its narrow contours, has been equated with economic welfare. General welfare can be brought directly or indirectly into relations with the measuring rod of money (Pigou, 1962; Baumol, 2004). Social welfare alludes to those formally organised and socially sponsored institutions, agencies, and programmes which function to maintain or improve the economic conditions, health or interpersonal competence of some parts or all of a population (Willenskey & Labeaux, 1958).

It was only after India's independence that the problem of employee welfare was given due attention when the socialistic pattern of society was adopted for achieving various socio-economic goals of the country. The Government of India in view of enhancing welfare and wellbeing of employees has established provisions for employee welfare under different labour laws. One of the important laws in this regard is the Factories Act, 1948 which elaborates various provisions in relation to health, safety, and welfare of employees, provisions regarding working hours including weekly hours, daily hours, weekly holidays, regarding employment of young persons, canteen facilities, first aid, shelters, rest rooms and lunchrooms annual leaves with wages and provision regarding employment of women and young persons in every organization (Patro & Raghunath, 2016). Finally, the act makes provision for the employment of welfare officer in manufacturing organizations and service sector also.

OBJECTIVES OF EMPLOYEE WELFARE

The theories of labour welfare have evolved over the years. In the past, the government had to compel industrial organisations to provide basic amenities to their employees (Erasmus, Schenk, & Swanepoel, 2008). Such compulsion was necessary because the employers used to exploit employees and treated them unfairly. With the passage of time, the concept of welfare has undergone changes. Progressive managements today provide welfare facilities voluntarily and with enlightened willingness and enthusiasm (Halal, 1998).

The basic objective of labour welfare is to enable workers to live a richer and more satisfactory life (Monappa, Nambudiri, & Selvaraj, 2012). Labour welfare is in the interest of the labour, the employer, and the society as a whole (Streeck, 2005). In order to increase employee welfare facilities, employers must offer extra incentives in the form of employee welfare schemes, and to make it possible to pursue employees to be more committed to their work. The very logic behind providing welfare schemes is to create efficient, effective and healthy organisation, aims or should aim, at improving the working and living conditions of employees and their families (Patro, 2015). Ramana and Reddy (2015) point out that the common welfare package and schemes that employers provide are categorized as intra-mural and extra-mural. The former is compulsory and an organisation must comply with the laws governing employees' health and safety. However, with regard to extra-mural schemes, it is the prerogative of the organisation and it differs from one organization to another. Implementation of welfare facilities depend on the employer. It is based on the approach of the organisation on how best it has organised the schemes to suit and benefit the workers (Cotton, Sohail, & Scott, 2005).

While statutory welfare facilities are compulsory, non-statutory welfare schemes need to be shaped and driven by a very sound company policy which allows employees to have substantial input into what and how the facilities should be provided without conflicting or undermining the organisation stance and

Welfare Regime

focus. The employer and employee need to work together to make sure that the facilities are provided based on mutual respects and understanding. However, it is pertinent to mention that living wages are not enough and cannot create healthy work environment (Verdon, 2002). Wages are earned and usually used for social economics activities outside the workplace but welfare are provided for by the organisation for healthy and sustainable environment in the workplace (Portney, 2005).

A combination of adequate wages with ample welfare facilities will profoundly yield and achieve good results for the organisation. It is against the backdrop of this that welfare facilities are an important aspect of an organisation social responsibility to the workers. Therefore, organisations have obligations to provide them for the workers. Labour welfare is the voluntary effort of the employer to establish, within the existing industrial system, working and sometimes living and cultural conditions of the employees beyond what is required by law, the custom of the industry and the conditions of the market (Todd, 1933).

All labour welfare measures have the following objectives:

1. Enabling employees to live richer and more satisfactory work lives;
2. Contributing to the efficiency of an employee and productivity of the enterprise;
3. Enhancing the standard of living of employees by indirectly reducing the burden on their purse;
4. Enabling employees to live in tune and harmony with services for workers obtaining in the neighborhood community where similar enterprises are situated;
5. Based on intelligent predictions of the future needs of the industrial workers, designing policies to cushion off and absorb the shocks of industrialization and urbanization to employees;
6. Fostering administratively viable and essentially developmental outlook among the workforce; and
7. Discharging the social responsibilities.

PRINCIPLES OF LABOUR WELFARE

Certain fundamental considerations are involved in the concept of labour welfare. The following are the more important among them.

1. **Social Responsibility of Industry:** This principle is based on the social conception of industry and its role in the society. Employee welfare is neither embroidery on capitalism nor the external dressing of an exploitative management; rather, it is an expression of the assumption by industry of its responsibility for its employees (Bruce, 1961). Organizations are expected to win the co-operation of the workers, provide them security of employment, fair wage, and equal opportunity for personal growth and advancement, and make welfare facilities available to them (John, 2004).
2. **Democratic Values:** The principle of democratic values of labour welfare concedes that employees may have certain unmet needs for no fault of their own, that industry has an obligation to render them help in gratifying those needs, and that workers have a right of determining the manner in which these needs can be met and of participating in the administration of the mechanism of need gratification (John, 2004). The underlying assumption to this approach is that the worker is mature and rational, and is capable of taking decisions individually.
3. **Adequacy of Wages:** This principle implies that employee welfare measures are not a substitute for wages. It will be wrong to argue that since employees are given a variety of labour welfare services, they need be paid only low wages (John, 2004). Right to adequate wage is beyond dispute.

4. **Efficiency:** This principle of labour welfare lays stress on the dictum that to cultivate welfare is to cultivate efficiency. Even those who deny any social responsibility for industry do accept that an enterprise must introduce all such employee welfare measures which promote efficiency (Marshall, 1950). It has been often mentioned that workers' education and training, housing, and diet are the three most important aspects of labour welfare, which always accentuate employee efficiency.
5. **Re-Personalization:** Since industrial organization is rigid and impersonal, the goal of welfare in industry is the enrichment and growth of human personality. The labour welfare movement seeks to bring cheer, comfort, and warmth in the human relationship by treating man as an individual, with quiet distinct needs and aspirations. Social and cultural programs, recreation and other measures designed after taking into consideration the workers' interests go a long way in counteracting the effects of monotony, boredom, and cheerlessness (John, 2004).
6. **Co-Responsibility:** This principle recognizes that the responsibility for labour welfare lies on both employers and workers and not on employers alone (Moorthy, 1968). Employee welfare measures are likely to be of little success unless mutuality of interest and responsibilities are accepted and understood by both the parties, in particular the quality of responsibility at the attitudinal and organizational level.
7. **Totality of Welfare:** The final principle of labour welfare is that the concept of employee welfare must permeate throughout the hierarchy of an organization, and accepted by all levels of functionaries in the enterprise (John, 2004).

THEORIES OF LABOUR WELFARE

The form of labour welfare activities is flexible, elastic, and differs from time to time, region to region, industry to industry, and country to country depending upon the value system, level of education, social customs, degree of industrialization and general standard of the socio-economic development of the nation (Mishra & Bhagat, 2007; Patro & Raghunath, 2016). Eight theories constituting the conceptual frame work of labour welfare activities are the following:

1. **Police Theory:** This is based on the contention that a minimum standard of welfare is necessary for employees. Here the assumption is that without compulsion, employers do not even provide the minimum facilities for workers. Apparently, this theory assumes that, man is self-centered and always tries to achieve his own ends, even at the cost of the welfare of others. According to this theory, owners and managers of industrial undertakings get many opportunities for exploitation of employees. Hence, the state has to intervene to provide minimum standard of welfare to the working class.
2. **Religious Theory:** This is based on the concept that man is essentially a religious animal. Even today, many acts of man are related to religious sentiments and beliefs. These religious feelings sometimes prompt an employer to assume welfare activities in the expectation of future emancipation either in this life or after it. It is an attempt to appeal to the religious sentiments of the employer. It may also be interpreted as if an employer wants to come out purified from his sinful acts of exploitation and profit making.
3. **Philanthropic Theory:** This theory is based on man's love for mankind. Philanthropy means "Loving mankind". Mankind is believed to have an instinctive urge by which he strives to remove

Figure 1. Labour Welfare Theories

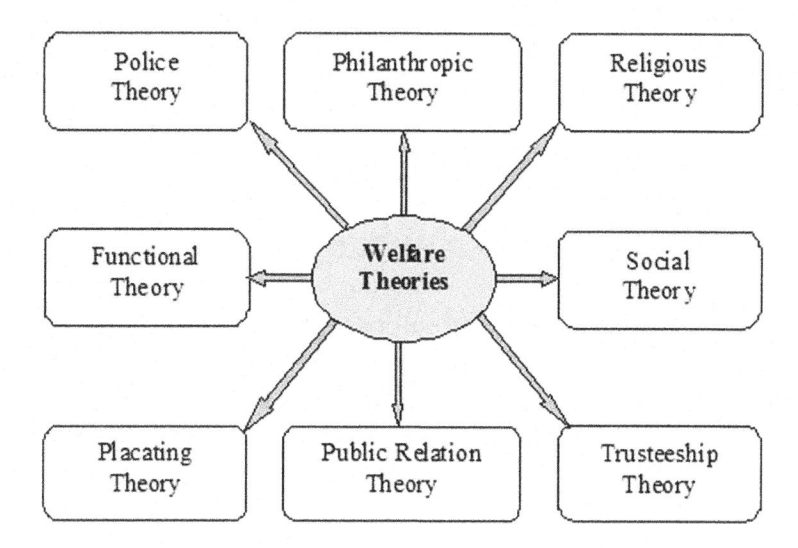

the suffering of others and promote their well-being. In fact, the labour welfare movement began in the early years of the industrial revolution with the support of philanthropists. Mutual help within the society alone will help to promote a peaceful and cooperative atmosphere. The philanthropic theory is common in social welfare rather than in industrial enterprises.

4. **Social Theory:** The social obligation of an industrial establishment has been assuming great significance these days. This theory implies that an organization is morally bound to improve the conditions of the society in addition to improving the condition of its employees. Employee welfare, as mentioned earlier, is gradually becoming social welfare.

5. **Trusteeship Theory:** This is also called the paternalistic theory of employee welfare. According to this the industrialist holds the total industrial estate, properties, and profits accruing from them in a trust. In other words, the employer should hold the industrial assets for himself, for the benefit of his workers, and also for society. The main emphasis of this theory is that employers should provide funds on an ongoing basis for the well-being of their employees.

6. **Placating Theory:** This theory is based on the fact that the employee groups are becoming demanding and are more conscious of their rights and privileges than ever before. Their demand for higher wages and better standards of living cannot be ignored. According to this theory, timely and periodical acts of labour welfare can appease the workers. They are some kind of pacifiers which come with a friendly gesture.

7. **Public Relation Theory:** This theory provides the basis for an atmosphere of goodwill between the employee and management, and also between management and the public. Employee welfare programs under this theory, work as a sort of an advertisement and help an organization to project its good image and build up and promote good and healthy public relations.

8. **Functional Theory:** This is also referred as Efficiency Theory. Here welfare work is used as a means to secure, preserve and develop the efficiency and productivity of employee. It is obvious that if an employer takes good care of his workers, they will tend to become more efficient and will thereby increase production. This theory is a reflection of contemporary support for employee welfare.

It can work well if both the parties have an identical aim in view i.e., higher production through better welfare facilities. This will encourage the employee's participation in welfare programs.

Therefore, the aim and spirit of all these theories is to provide maximum welfare facilities to the employees.

WELFARE MEASURES FOR BETTER EMPLOYEE PERFORMANCE

An employee can be happy with his employment only when he has job satisfaction. The welfare facilities provide better physical and mental health to employees and thus promote a healthy work environment. This makes the employees to pay more attention towards work and thus increases their performance (Patro, 2012, 2015). The chapter focuses on the various dimensions of welfare measures that have an impact on the employees' performance and overall productivity of the organisation. The committee of experts on welfare facilities for industrial works constituted by the ILO (1963) classified welfare amenities into two groups as Intramural and Extramural facilities are discussed.

Intramural Facilities

These welfare amenities are those provided within the premises of the establishments such as sanitary facilities, crèches, rest shelters, canteens, drinking water, prevention of fatigue, health services including occupational safety, administrative arrangements, uniforms and protective clothing, shift allowance, and so forth.

Provision for Safety Measures

The safety measures are the activities and precautions taken to improve safety (i.e., reduce risk related to human health). It includes first aid, risk assessment, insurance, general health and safety advice, and so forth. It is a good practice for all the organizations to practice the safety policies for the improvement of the employee's quality of work life. The organizations should assess systematically any potential risks or hazards to staff, volunteers and public.

Drinking Water and Sanitary Facilities

Drinking water and sanitary facilities are essential for human beings to lead a healthy and quality life at work place. In every organization, effective arrangement shall be made at suitable places for sufficient supply of clean drinking water. Sufficient latrine and urinal accommodation are to be provided at the office or work premises which should be easily accessible to employees. Separate enclosed accommodation should be provided for male and female employees with adequate light and ventilation.

Workmen Compensation

Workmen's compensation act is one of the important social security legislation passed by government of India to give protection to employees. It aims at providing financial protection to workmen in their departments in case of accident resulting to injury, death, and partial or total disablement in the course of duty, by means of payment of compensation by the employers. It is the additional benefit given to the employees other than salary, which gives more satisfaction to lead a healthy life.

Rest Rooms and Locker Facilities

Adequate changing and rest rooms are to be provided for employees in the office or work premises with provisions like water supply, wash basins, toilets, bathrooms, etc. Locker facility should also be provided to the employees to keep their belongings. Separate rest rooms for male and female employees should also be provided. These facilities increase the morale of the employees.

Subsidized Canteen Facilities

Canteen or store facilities includes the cost of food items, quality of food items, variety of items, hygiene, and service of bearers, furniture or seating arrangement in the canteen, drinking water, and so on. Provision of good canteen facilities helps in maintaining good health of the employees which in turn increases their performance.

Grievance Handling Forums

Grievance Handling Forums plays a vital role while providing the welfare measures to the employees in the organizations. Grievance handling means solving the disputes or problems of the employees with the interference of the management, trade unions or enactment of statutory laws by the government. There is a systematic way of dealing with grievance problems. The judgments are to be abided both by the employer and the employees.

Encourage Retention Policies

The current challenge faced today by the organizations is retention of good and talented employees. Recognizing the most talented, skilled and the best employees who can fit within the organization culture and contribute to the organization and retaining them is an important task of the organizations. The retention policies include increments, promotions, incentives, awards, gifts, rewards, job security, performance appraisals, and so on. Retention policies help the employees to feel secure for their job and work for the betterment of the organization.

Other Facilities

The other facilities such as guest house, employee-employer relations, work environment, administrative facilities, first aid and emergency services, etc., also help in motivating the employees towards the management and increase their work efficiency.

Extramural Facilities

These are welfare amenities provided outside the establishment such as maternity benefit, social insurance measures, sports and cultural activities, library or reading room, leave travel facilities, workers co-operatives including consumers' co-operative stores, co-operative credit societies, programs for the welfare of women, youth, and children and transport facilities, and so forth.

Medical and Health Benefits

The health of the employee is of cardinal importance not only to the individual but also to general organizational development. Health care for employees helps to reduce the incidence of sickness and absenteeism, and increases efficiency and productivity. Medical benefits include maternity benefits, medical camps, medical reimbursement, and benefits after retirement, etc. The organizations must also provide medical facilities for the employees and their family members.

Provision of Housing Facilities

Housing facility is the basic human necessity and it needs a very high priority in any scheme of National Planning and Industrial Development. A healthy accommodation includes proper quarter facilities, adequate space, ventilation, electricity facilities, water facility and maintenance facilities such as roads, lighting, drainage systems, lavatories, and other sanitary arrangements should be provided so that the efficiency of the employees increases.

Availability of Education Schemes

Education plays a very important role in motivating and enabling changes necessary for accelerated progress of employees for their mental and physical development. The educational needs in any sector are two-fold (i.e., adult/employees education schemes and schools/colleges for their children). The education centers enable the employees to acquire more knowledge and gain social awareness. The education facilities for children of the employees should also be provided, so that it helps them to obtain better employment opportunities.

Recreation/Sports Activities

Recreation is one of the important dimension of welfare, which relaxes and refreshers the mental and physical fitness of an employee after going through the strings and stresses of daily busy work schedule. In the case of a very few exceptional individuals who find their work so absorbing and satisfying, work itself may be the recreation. These facilities are to be necessarily provided in all organizations whether public or private sector.

Cheaper Transport Facilities

Provision of adequate and cheap transport facilities to the employees residing at long distance from the place of their work is essential as such facilities relieve the workers form strain and anxiety provide relief

Welfare Regime

and relaxation and reduce the absenteeism on account of late arrival. Employees should be enabling to reduce the time spent in travelling between their homes and their work. Transportation is particularly necessary to those employees who work on a shift basis.

Provision of Retirement Benefits

Retirement benefit is one the important activity of providing welfare measures to the employees in the organizations. Retirement benefits include pension, retirement/death gratuity, loan, leave encashment, general provident fund and incentives, contributory provident fund, employee's group insurance schemes, voluntary retirement compensation, etc. These benefits increase the satisfaction level of the employees towards the organizations and motivate them to achieve the organizational objectives.

Other Facilities

The other facilities such as post office, bank facilities, credit cooperative societies, telephone exchange facilities, etc., also help in motivating the employees towards the management and increase their work efficiency.

Thus, labour welfare is very comprehensive and embraces activities provided by employers, State, trade unions and other agencies to help workers and their families to lead a happy work life.

BENEFITS OF EMPLOYEE WELFARE

Employee welfare includes the schemes that benefit the employees working in the company. Although it is a costly procedure for companies, it is nonetheless needed as it helps in the overall development of the employees. The benefits of providing employee welfare schemes include the following:

1. **Higher Efficiency:** Employee welfare schemes act as a morale booster. When the employees get an appreciation for what they do, it helps in increasing the work efficiency of the employees. When completed work is lauded by the organization, it proves lucrative to both the organization as well as the employees. If the work done by the employees is not appreciated, the output might not come as expected (Patro, 2015). Therefore, it is essential to have employee welfare schemes.
2. **Builds Competitive Edge:** Competition is must if an organization wants its employees to work well. In order to form a competitive environment in the work place, it must provide employees with various opportunities. The competitive edge in the work environment can only help in getting the required work from the employees (Sravani, 2016). Therefore, if the healthy work environment or the healthy competition is required within the organization, it is vital to provide employees with welfare facilities.
3. **Timely Results:** If the companies want the employees to give the result on time or deliver the work in time, there needs to be some extra effort by the organization so as to encourage the employees. This is possible by not only encouraging the employees by praising their work but also provide with better welfare schemes. If the extra work is expected from the employees, they should also be given extra benefits by the organization (Patro, 2016). Only then could timely results be expected by the organization.

4. **Better Industrial Relations:** The employees, when benefited, results in good industrial relations as well. Not only is the work output satisfactory, but also the amiable relations are built by the employees when encouraged through various schemes (Sravani, 2016). Therefore, various employee schemes are essential to make employees work in a better manner in the organization.
5. **Improves Mental and Moral Health:** The employees when given different facilities at work; it improves their mental health as well as helping in becoming a good citizen. So, it helps in overall development of the employee. Employee development is equivalent to the development of the organization (Sravani, 2016; Patro, 2015). Therefore, if the organizations want themselves to grow, they need to help employees in their growth.
6. **Social Benefits:** The employees also get various social benefits which are advantageous to the organization also. The social benefits increase the productivity, production as well as the work efficiency of the employees. The good work by the employees also helps in increasing of the remuneration (Sravani, 2016). Finally, this helps in increasing the standard of the employees which is appreciated and accepted by all concerned.
7. **Overall Growth of Employees:** The schemes are a motivating factor to the employees and it helps in the overall growth of the employees. Both the common organizational goal and the personal goals are easily achieved by the employees, which benefits not just the company but also the members working in an organization (Sravani, 2016).
8. **Employee Retention:** The organizations provide training to the employees to get good results. If an employee leaves the organization, it not only affects other employees but also the whole organization. So, the organization has to provide some schemes to retain the employees for a longer time period and that is only possible with the employee welfare schemes (Patro, 2014). The employees would not even think of leaving the company if they obtain sincere appreciation.

DRAWBACKS OF EMPLOYEE WELFARE

The concept of employee welfare has advantages and disadvantages. Some of the disadvantages of employee welfare are as follows:

Welfare Schemes are Driving Force to Work

Neither the money nor the schemes should be the driving force to work for the employees. The employees must be motivated through the work done by others (Sravani, 2016). A competitive environment should be the driving force for the employees to work. Only then can the expected work can be delivered by employees (Patro, 2016).

Financial Burden for the Organization

The organization becomes financially burdened financially as the number of employees increases since a higher budget will be required by the company to equally distribute the schemes among the employees working within an organization. Therefore, in order to equally distribute the schemes among the employees, it is essential for the company to have proper a financial budget to provide employees with the required schemes (Sravani, 2016).

Maintain a Competitive Edge in the Market

To remain in the market, it is essential to keep good employee welfare schemes so as to attract maximum skilled employees within the organization. Every company needs skilled workers to work so that they get better output. In order to do the same, the company will have to have an edge over the welfare schemes too (Sravani, 2016).

Surpass the Old Schemes of the Organization

All other corporate schemes become outdated. When other competitive companies provide employees great and newly developed schemes, the present schemes seems a big failure due to which the other companies has to get the similar beneficial schemes (Sravani, 2016). Therefore, this type of burden is harmful to companies at large.

Employees May Even Leave the Organization

When competitive organizations give better welfare schemes, the employees may choose to reach the organization giving better opportunities (Patro & Raghunath, 2016). This way the employees may even leave the company and move to the next. This also forms one of the disadvantages of the company as well as the employees on the whole (Sravani, 2016).

CONSEQUENCES FOR FAILURE TO PROVIDE WELFARE MEASURES

Statutory welfare facilities are products of the laws regulating provision and implementation of welfare facilities in the workplace (Ridley & Channing, 2008). They are compulsory and important. Therefore, there are consequences for failure to provide welfare facilities as stipulated in the statutes. For instance, in an industry that requires protective apparatus for certain harmful and dangerous jobs (i.e., the chemical industry). The health and safety of the workers are paramount and the necessary safety gadgets must be provided for the workers in addition to other important facilities and services (Patro, 2012). If not provided and there is a mishap or accident in the workplace, the victim may institute legal action against the erring organisation in courts and punitive damages awarded against the organization if found wanting.

Today an organisation is not only considered successful as a result of the profits it has declared, but is also based on the welfare benefits provided employees that were used to make the profits (Schaltegger & Lüdeke-Freund, 2013). Organizational policy now contains numerous welfare facilities and how they are to be provided for the benefits of the employees (Ichniowski, Kochan, Levine, Olson, & Strauss, 1996). The company's annual reports and financial statement now reflect the amount of money being spent on various welfare schemes to employees. Welfare schemes are now statutorily enforceable and every company has a corporate social responsibility to provide these measures for their employees (Joseph, Injodey, & Varghese, 2013).

Pfeffer and Barron (1988) suggest that the employee's organizational positions and how work is structured impacts their place in and relationship to the process of production, implying that externalization has profound implications for individuals' orientations to their jobs. This new relationship is important to understand. If externalization reduces workers' odds of becoming attached to a large, unionized employer, the practice may have consequences for their labor market outcomes and experiences. Morris and Sherman (1981) indicate that organizational commitment has usefulness as a predictor of important behavioral outcomes such as performance (Mowday, Porter, & Dubin, 1974), absenteeism (Steers, 1977) and turnover (Hom, Katerberg, & Hulin, 1979). Much effort has also been directed toward identifying variables that may influence levels of commitment.

However, today varying physical work arrangements, short-duration projects, changing job responsibilities, teams comprised of different types of employees, and movement among multiple employers introduce new dynamics into the workplace. The previous model of conducting business with individuals who were promised life-time employment is no longer valid.

Simultaneously, the Government is no longer asking individuals to remain committed to them for their careers. People now build careers across organizations and display loyalty to themselves, their skills, their professions, and their project teams (Bradach, 1997). Organizations that outsource work will be concerned about the commitment of these employees because their success depends upon employee dedication. With a leaner workforce, absenteeism and tardiness become significant problems. If employees become less committed to organizations due to a lack of reciprocity, they will channel their commitment elsewhere. Employees will assess their skills and experience in terms of marketability versus a singular employment. Finally, organizations that move toward contracting out services will want to ensure that those who provide the services are committed to fulfilling their contracts. Commitment is just as important for the contract employees as for the internal employees (DeLoria, 2001).

MEASURES TO IMPROVE THE WORK LIFE OF EMPLOYEES

Employees are the primary assets of every organisation, so employee needs must be satisfied in order to meet the goals of the organization. Any organization is effective only when there is high degree of co-operation between the employees and their management. The welfare facilities go a long way stimulating interest in the employees to produce their full capacity and pay a good return to management in the long-term.

Motivation of Employees

Motivation is the primitive measure that has to be undertaken in every organization while providing the employee welfare facilities. Many organizations are providing maximum motivation to the employee by providing several employee benefits and welfare facilities by which the employees are feeling happy to work within the organization (Harika, 2010; Patro, 2012). By these welfare activities which is provided directly or indirectly to the employee, the individual is able to work with satisfaction and obedience among the higher authorities and proud to be work within the organization (Kumar & Yadav, 2002).

Remove Dissatisfaction

According to Herzberg, most welfare facilities are hygiene factors which create dissatisfaction to the employees if not provided. Remove dissatisfaction, place an employee in a favourable mood, provide satisfiers, and then motivation will occur (Laddha, 2012). Welfare facilities, besides removing dissatisfaction, help develop loyalty in employees towards the organization (Patro, 2015). Welfare activities may help to minimize social evils, such as alcoholism, gambling, drug addiction, and the like (Sinha, 2013). An employee is likely to fall a victim to any of these if he is dissatisfied or frustrated. Welfare facilities tend to make the employee be happy, cheerful and confident looking.

Employee Retention

The most important challenge faced by the organizations today is retention of talented employees. Recognition of the most talented and skilled employees, and retaining them is an important task of the private organizations. To retain the employees in the organization, certain benefits like increments, promotions, incentives, awards, gifts, rewards, job security, and performance appraisals must be provided by management (Patro, 2014). These policies help the employees to feel secure in their jobs and work for the betterment of the organisation (Rajkuar, 2014). These facilities will attract the employees towards the organisation and will not leave the organisation.

Improvement in Welfare/Safety Facilities

Private sector organisations are lacking in providing certain facilities like housing facilities, transport facilities, canteen or cooperative store facilities, recreational facilities, fair distribution of work, and rest hours (Mishra & Bhagat, 2007). These facilities will help the employees to satisfy their basic needs and live a quality of work life (Bhati & Ashokkumar, 2013). These private organisations should provide allowances such as house rent allowances, dearness allowances, city compensation allowances, transportation reimbursement, transport facility to the work place, canteen facilities, cooperative store facilities, fair distribution of work to the employees, rest hours, working hours, overtime payments, grievance settlement forums and so on according the factories act 1948 (Patro, 2016). By making improvements in providing these facilities employees perform better.

Provision of Welfare Benefits

The management of private sector organisations should concentrate on providing the welfare benefits to the employees inside and outside the work place like health and medical benefits, encourage higher education, provide a children education allowance, festival advance, retirement benefits, leave encashment, provident fund, gratuity, group personal accident insurance, housing loans, and special merit awards so they perform better (Mishra & Bhagat, 2007; Patro, 2015). In many private organisations these facilities are rarely provided (Satyanarayna & Reddi, 2012). These welfare benefits need to be improved as it will help the employees to lead a better quality of work life and helps in overall development of the organisations.

Recruitment of a Welfare Officer

Welfare of the employees is a must for the development of the organization. For this purpose, the management of private sector organizations can appoint a welfare officer to solve all the problems of the employees and maintain good relation between the employee and employer (Mishra & Bhagat, 2007). The individual will be able to bridge the gap between the management and the different level of employees and explain about the welfare facilities provided to the employees and suggest them how to utilize these benefits (Patro, 2015). The management can also think of formulation of a problem-solving committee including the employees and administration for the better solution of the welfare problems of the employees.

Welfare measures should be properly implemented so that they may increase job satisfaction, which in turn may help increase the productivity. The main objective of this study is to remove the dis-satisfaction of the employees towards the organisation for which certain measures are recommended to the management of private sector organisations to improve the quality of work life of the employees.

FUTURE RESEARCH DIRECTIONS

An employee's welfare is the key dimension for smooth employer-employee relationship. The organisations should take necessary steps to solve the problems in those measures so the employee can perform more effectively. New schemes and facilities should be added to existing ones to improve the efficiency and quality of work life of the employees by the management of all organisations. This chapter is expected to help other researchers to consider various welfare schemes that influence the employee's performance and organisational productivity. Further research with regards to other industrial and service sector organisations can be considered as provision of welfare schemes has become important in every type of organization.

CONCLUSION

Every organization whether private or public sector and industrial or service organisations must adopt the welfare schemes for better employee productivity and organisational development. A satisfied employee is the key factor who acts as the organization's ladder for success. Welfare helps in keeping the morale and motivation of the employees high so as to retain the employees for longer durations. The thought of employee welfare has been used by many organizations as a strategy of improving the employee's productivity, especially in the private sector since work related problems can lead to poor quality of life for employees and a decline in performance. The welfare schemes improve the employees' morale and loyalty towards the management thereby increasing their happiness, satisfaction and also their productivity.

India introduced literal industrial policy aimed at increasing industrial growth, promoting modernization, and enhancing technological advancement to make industrial competitive in both domestic and global markets. In this perspective, enterprises should improve their production and productivity which is possible with the satisfaction of labour. Even today's scientific development of modern techno- production methods higher productivity depends on workers. If they are properly directed and fully employed, it makes a great contribution to the prosperity of the enterprise. The high rate of labour absenteeism in Indian industries is indicative of the lack of commitment on the part of the workers. This can be reduced to a great extent by providing adequate housing, health and family care canteens, educational and training facilities, provision of welfare activities enables the workers to live a richer and more satisfactory life and contributes to the productivity of labour, efficiency of the enterprise and helps in maintaining industrial peace. Therefore, steps need to be taken on a larger scale to improve the quality of life of the workers.

REFERENCES

Aiginger, K. (2005). Labour market reforms and economic growth-the European experience in the 1990s. *Journal of Economic Studies (Glasgow, Scotland), 32*(6), 540–573. doi:10.1108/01443580510631414

Aswathappa, K. (2010). *Human Resource Management*. New Delhi, India: Tata McGraw Hill Education Private Limited.

Aziri, B. (2011). Job Satisfaction: A literature review. *Management research and practice, 3*(4), 77-86.

Baumol, W. J. (2004). Welfare Economics and the Theory of the State. In The Encyclopedia of Public Choice (pp. 937-940). Springer US.

Bhati, P. P., & Ashokkumar, M. (2013). Provision of Welfare under Factories Act and its Impact on Employee Satisfaction. *Journal of Business Management & Social Sciences Research, 2*(2), 57–69.

Bradach, J. (1997). *Flexibility: The new social contract between individuals and firms?* Harvard Business School Working Paper.

Bruce, M. (1961). *Coming of the Welfare State*. London, UK: Batsford.

Burchardt, T. (1997). Boundaries between Public and Private Welfare: a typology and map of services. Private Welfare and Public Policy, Burchardt, Hills and Propper, Rowntree Foundation, Jan. 1999). *LSE STICERD Research Paper No. CASE002*.

CLW. (1969). *Report of the Committee on Labour Welfare*. India: Ministry of Labour & Employment, Government of India.

Cotton, A. P., Sohail, M., & Scott, R. E. (2005). Towards improved labour standards for construction of minor works in low income countries. *Engineering, Construction, and Architectural Management, 12*(6), 617–632. doi:10.1108/09699980510634164

Coventry, W. F., & Barker, J. K. (1988). *Management* (International Edition). Heinemann Professional Publishing.

Davis, A., & Gibson, L. (1994). Designing Employee Welfare Provision. *Personnel Review, 23*(7), 33–45. doi:10.1108/00483489410072208

DeLoria, J. E. (2001). A Comparative Study of Employee Commitment: Core and Contract Employees in a Federal Agency [Doctoral Dissertation]. Falls Church, VA.

Erasmus, B., Schenk, H., & Swanepoel, B. (2008). *South African Human Resource Management: Theory & practice* (4th ed.). Cape Town, South Africa: Juta & Co. Ltd.

Halal, W. E. (1998). *The new management: Democracy and enterprise are transforming organizations*. San Francisco, CA: Berrett-Koehler Publishers, Inc.

Harika, V. (2010). *Theories of Labour Welfare*. Retrieved from http://www.scribd.com/doc/52987735/2/THEORIES-OF-LABOURWELFARE

Hom, P., Katerberg, R., & Hulin, C. (1979). Comparative examination of three approaches to the prediction of turnover. *The Journal of Applied Psychology, 64*(3), 280–290. doi:10.1037/0021-9010.64.3.280

Hopkins, R. R. (1955). *Handbook of Industrial Welfare*. Lincoln, UK: Sir Isaac Pitman & Sons.

Ichniowski, C., Kochan, T. A., Levine, D., Olson, C., & Strauss, G. (1996). What works at work: Overview and Assessment. *Industrial Relations, 35*(3), 299–333. doi:10.1111/j.1468-232X.1996.tb00409.x

ILO. (1942). *Approach to Social Security: An International Survey*. Geneva: International Labour Organisation.

ILO. (1963). Labour laws and legislation. *Proceedings of the Asian Regional Conference of International Labour Organisation*.

John, C. P. (2004). *Social Security and Labour Welfare with Special Reference to Construction Workers in Kerala*. Kerala Research Programme on Local Level Development, Centre for Development Studies, Thiruvananthapuram.

Joseph, B., Injodey, J., & Varghese, R. (2009). Labour Welfare in India. *Journal of Workplace Behavioral Health, 24*(1-2), 221–242. doi:10.1080/15555240902849131

Joseph, B., Injodey, J., & Varghese, R. (2013). Labour Welfare in India. In P. A. Kurzman & R. Paul Maiden (Eds.), *Union Contributions to Labor Welfare Policy and Practice: Past, Present and Future* (pp. 225–246). New York: Routledge.

Kohli, A. S., & Sharma, S. R. (1997). *Labour welfare and social security*. New Delhi, India: Anmol Publications Private Limited.

Kumar, S., & Yadav, S. S. (2002). Satisfaction level from labour welfare schemes in sugar factories of Gorakhpur division. *Indian Journal of Economics, 33*(329), 171–188.

Laddha, R. L. (2012). A Study on Employee Welfare Strategies with Special Reference to Solapur Janta Sahakari Bank Ltd, Solapur. *Golden Research Thoughts., 1*(10), 1–4.

Lalitha, K., & Priyanka, T. (2014). A Study on Employee Welfare Measures with Reference to IT Industry. *International Journal of Engineering Technology. Management and Applied Sciences, 2*(7), 191–195.

Logasakthi, K., & Rajagopal, K. (2013). A study on employee health, safety and welfare measures of chemical industry in the view of Sleam region, Tamil Nadu, India. *International Journal of Research in Business Management., 1*(1), 1–10.

Manzini, H., & Gwandure, C. (2011). *The Provision of Employee Assistance Programmes in South Africa Football Clubs*. Johannesburg, South Africa: University of the Witwatersrand.

Marshall, T. H. (1950). *Citizenship and Social class and other Essays*. England, UK: Cambridge University Press.

Meena, M. L., & Dangayach, G. S. (2012). Analysis of Employee Satisfaction in Banking Sector. *International Journal of Humanities and Applied Sciences, 1*(2), 78–81.

Mishra, S., & Bhagat, M. (2007). *Principles for successful implementation of labour welfare activities from police theory to functional theory.* Retrieved from http://www.tesionline.com/intl/indepth.jsp?id=575

Monappa, A., Nambudiri, R., & Selvaraj, P. (2012). *Industrial Relations and Labour Laws* (2nd ed.). New Delhi, India: Tata McGraw-Hill Publishing Company Limited.

Moorthy, M. V. (1968). *Principles of Labour Welfare* (1st ed.). Visakhapatnam, India: Gupta Bros. Books.

Morris, J. H., & Sherman, J. D. (1981). Generalizability of an organizational commitment model. *Academy of Management Journal*, *24*(3), 512–526. doi:10.2307/255572

Mowday, R. T., Porter, L. W., & Dubin, R. (1974). Unit performance, situational factors, and employee attitudes in spatially separated work units. *Organizational Behavior and Human Performance*, *12*(2), 231–248. doi:10.1016/0030-5073(74)90048-8

Mwiti, J. K. (2007). The Role of Welfare Services in Motivation of Staff in Kenyan Parastatals: A case Study of Teachers Service Commission. Jomo: Kenyatta University of Agriculture and Technology.

Nanda, N., & Panda, J.K. (2013). Challenges and effectiveness of industrial relation environment in Indian Industries study on Rourkela Steel Plant. *International Journal of Financial Services and management Research*, *2*(6), 163-174.

Neetha, N. (2001). *Gender and Technology: Impact of flexible Organization and Production on Female Labour in the Tiruppur Knitwear Industry.* Noida, India: V.V. Giri National Labour Institute.

Patro, C. S. (2012). Employee Welfare Activities in Private Sector and Their Impact on Quality of Work Life. *International Journal of Productivity Management and Assessment Technologies*, *1*(2), 18–29. doi:10.4018/ijpmat.2012040102

Patro, C. S. (2014). A Study on the Impact of Employee Retention Policies on Organisation Productivity in Private Sector. *International Journal of Asian Business and Information Management*, *5*(3), 48–63. doi:10.4018/ijabim.2014070104

Patro, C. S. (2015). Employee Welfare Measures in Public and Private Sectors: A Comparative Analysis. *International Journal of Service Science, Management, Engineering, and Technology*, *6*(1), 22–36. doi:10.4018/ijssmet.2015010102

Patro, C. S. (2016). A Study on Adoption of Employee Welfare Schemes in Industrial and Service Organisations: In Contrast with Public and Private Sectors. *International Journal of Service Science, Management, Engineering, and Technology*, *7*(2), 16–33. doi:10.4018/IJSSMET.2016040102

Patro, C. S., & Raghunath, K. M. K. (2016). A Take on Employee Welfare Facilities and Employees Efficiency. *International Journal of Asian Business and Information Management*, *7*(3), 54–70. doi:10.4018/IJABIM.2016070104

Pfeffer, J., & Baron, J. N. (1988). Taking the workers back out: Recent trends in the structuring of employment. *Research in Organizational Behavior*, *10*, 257–303.

Pigou, A. C. (1962). *Economics of Welfare.* London: Macmillan Publishers.

Portney, P. R. (2005). Corporate social responsibility: An Economic and Public Policy Perspective. In B.L. Hay, R.N. Stavins, & R.H.K. Vietor (Eds.), Environmental Protection and the Social Responsibility of Firms-Perspectives from Law, Economics, and Business (pp. 237-242). Washington DC, USA: REF Press book.

Pylee, M. V., & George, A. S. (1996). *Industrial Relations & Personnel Management*. New Delhi, India: Vikas Publishing House Pvt. Ltd.

Railkar, J. S. (1990). *Labour welfare, trade unionism and industrial relations*. Bombay, India: Sheth Publishers Private Limited.

Rajkuar, B. (2014). A Study on Labour Welfare Measures and Social Security in IT Industries with Reference to Chennai. *International Journal of Enterprise Computing and Business Systems*, 4(1), 1–10.

Ramana, T. V., & Reddy, E. L. (2015). A Study on Employee Welfare Measures With Reference to South Central Railways in India. *ZENITH International Journal of Business Economics & Management Research*, 5(1), 1–11.

Reshma, S., & Basavaraj, M. J. (2013). Employee welfare measures in mining industry–A study with reference to statutory welfare measures in NMDC, Donimalai Iron Ore Mine, Bellary district. *EXCEL International Journal of Multidisciplinary Management Studies*, 3(7), 157–164.

Ridley, J., & Channing, J. (2008). *Safety at work*. Oxford, UK: Butterworth-Heinemann.

Robinson, M. A., Sparrow, P. R., Clegg, C., & Birdi, K. (2007). Forecasting future competency requirements: A three-phase methodology. *Personnel Review*, 36(1), 65–90. doi:10.1108/00483480710716722

Sabarirajan, A., Meharajan, T., & Arun, B. (2010). A Study on the Various Welfare Measures and their Impact on QWL Provided by the Textile Mills with reference to Salem District, Tamil Nadu, India. *Asian Journal of Management Research.*, 1(1), 15–24.

Saiyadin, S.M. (1983). *Voluntary Welfare in India, Its objective and Cost*. Lok Udyog.

Sarma, A. M. (1996). *Aspects of labour welfare and social security*. Bombay, India: Himalaya Publishing House.

Satayanarayana, M. R., & Reddi, R. J. (2012). Labour welfare measure in cement industries in India. *International Journal of Physical and Social Sciences*, 2(7), 257–254.

Schaltegger, S., & Lüdeke-Freund, F. (2013). Business cases for sustainability. In *Encyclopedia of Corporate Social Responsibility* (pp. 245–252). Springer Berlin Heidelberg. doi:10.1007/978-3-642-28036-8_744

Sinha, E. (2013). A research work on Employee Satisfaction measurement with special reference to KRIBHCO, Surat. *International Journal of Modern Engineering Research*, 3(1), 523–529.

Sravani, S. (2016). *Employee Welfare Measures: Advantages & Disadvantages*. Retrieved from http://content.wisestep.com/employee-welfare-measures-advantages-disadvantages

Srinivasa, K. T. (2013). A Study on Employees Welfare Facilities Adopted at Bosch Limited, Bangalore. *Research Journal of Management Sciences*, 2(12), 7–11.

Steers, R. M. (1977). Antecedents and outcomes of organizational commitment. *Administrative Science Quarterly*, *22*(1), 46–56. doi:10.2307/2391745 PMID:10236068

Streeck, W. (2005). Industrial relations: From state weakness as strength to state weakness as weakness. Welfare corporatism and the private use of the public interest. In S. Green & W. E. Paterson (Eds.), *Governance in contemporary Germany: The semisoverign state revisited* (pp. 138–164). Cambridge, UK: Cambridge University Press. doi:10.1017/CBO9780511807749.007

Todd, A. J. (1933). *Industry and Society - A Sociological Appraisal of Modern Industrialisation*. New York: H. Holt & Company.

Verdon, N. (2002). *Rural Women Workers in 19th Century England: Gender, Work and Wages*. New York, USA: Boydell Press.

Willenskey, H. L., & Labeaux, C. N. (1958). *Industrial Society and Social Welfare*. New York: Russel Sage Foundation.

Zacharaiah, K. A. (1954). *Industrial relations and personnel problems–A study with particular reference to Bombay*. Bombay, India: Asia Publishing House.

KEY TERMS AND DEFINITIONS

Activities: A pre-determined agreement of program, events or development planned to accrued, accumulate or increase to a given expected outcome.

Efficiency Theory: The welfare work is used as a means to secure, preserve and develop the efficiency and productivity of an employee.

Employee: A person who enters into a contract of employment with another in returns for wages, salaries or other valuable considerations.

Employer: A person or institution that hires employees and offers wages or salaries in exchange of his work or labour.

Job satisfaction: It is the combination of positive or negative feelings that the employees have towards their work and organization.

Paternalistic: The policy of employees of controlling people in a patterned way by providing them with what they need but giving them no freedom of choice.

Welfare: It is an organized effort to ensure the basic well being of people in need. It is also a wide variety of services provided by companies for employee and in some cases for members of employee's families.

Chapter 6
Organizational Learning as a Social Process:
A Social Capital and Network Approach

Jieun You
Yonsei University, South Korea

Junghwan Kim
University of Oklahoma, USA

Sarah M Miller
University of Oklahoma, USA

ABSTRACT

This chapter discusses about application of social capital and network approach to organizational learning research and practice. The shift of organizational learning perspective from a technical or system-structural perspective to a social or interpretative perspective highlights that organizational learning process is socially embedded and is based on social interaction/relationships. Social capital and network theories provides a conceptual framework to explain how organizational learning takes place as well as identifies social and network factors influencing organizational learning. Thus, the chapter provides implications for establishing a conceptual and methodological framework to describe and evaluate an organizational learning process by extensively reviewing the recent organizational learning research adopting social capital and network approach.

INTRODUCTION

Under uncertain and unpredictable environments, individuals and organizations are forced to be continuously committed to learning for their competitiveness. Organizations that do not successfully accomplish their organizational performance and change are threatening their survival. Organizational learning is thought of as one of the key factors determining successful organizational change and innovation even

DOI: 10.4018/978-1-5225-2568-4.ch006

though there is a disagreement on concepts and perspectives of organizational learning (Jimenez-Jimenez & Sanz-Valle, 2011; Lopez, Peon, & Ordas, 2005; Stata & Almond, 1989).

Early organizational learning theories use a technical or systems-structural perspective, which regards learning as a process of acquiring and disseminating information through information processing in a cognitive mechanism embedded in individuals (Daft & Huber, 1987; Easterby-Smith & Araujo, 1999; Hager, 2011). However, recent organizational learning scholars have increasingly paid attention to the social view or interpretative perspective that emphasizes the role of social and organizational contexts in terms of workplace learning (Billett, 1995; Fenwick, 2001; Hager, 2011). Theorists with a social or interpretative perspective claim that learning based on social relationship and interactions a kind of product of social constructs. This argument suggests that in order to understand an organizational learning process, it is important to understand how learners interpret information and build meanings within their social and organizational context (Daft & Huber, 1987; Easterby-Smith & Araujo, 1999).

The recent shift in organizational learning perspectives suggests that social capital/network theory is useful for explaining an organizational learning mechanism and process and how to facilitate organizational learning. Originally coming from sociology, social capital/network has now become a popular concept in various fields. Psychology as well as education, economics, and business pay attention to the importance of social capital/network as a resource of organizational competitiveness (Lesser, 2000). Therefore, scholars have been recently interested in social capital theory and have tried to explain organizational learning by adopting social capital theory (Bogenrieder, 2002; Currah & Wrigley, 2004; Kreiser, 2011). With social capital/network theory, social network analysis provides a valuable and useful tool for identifying and analyzing how organizational learning occurs and how actors interrelate and interact with each other within organizations (Cross, Borgatti, & Parker, 2002; Kilduff & Brass, 2011; Wasserman & Faust, 2009).

Although organizational learning research increasingly highlights the relationship between social capital/network and organizational learning for organizational performance and change, there is limited research to establish an integrative research framework on the relationships among social capital/network, organizational learning and performance. Therefore, this chapter establishes an integrative framework to describe the role of social capital/network in organizational learning by comprehensively reviewing the literature

The purpose of this chapter is to develop a conceptual framework with social capital/network theories and methodology to better understand the relationship between individuals and organizational learning, and how they interact with each other for organizational performance and change. We reviewed a wide range of literature on organizational learning and social capital/network theories. In order to establish the conceptual framework, we conducted an integrative literature review focused on the following topics:

- Concepts, perspectives, and processes of organizational learning
- Concepts and theories of social capital and social networks
- Roles of social capital and networks in organizational learning
- Current organizational learning research with the social capital and social network approach

We then conclude with discussions on the significance of the social capital and network approach to organizational learning, and implications for research and practice based on the findings.

ORGANIZATIONAL LEARNING

As a determinant and/or predictor of organizational success and change, importance of organizational learning is increasingly highlighted in various areas (Bapuji & Crossan, 2004). A great amount of organizational learning research from various fields has been conducted, which repeatedly insists that organizations be constantly involved in organizational learning and enhance their learning capabilities, in order to create competitive advantages and improve organizational performance (Dixon, 1992; Edmonson & Moingeon, 1998; Garvin, 1993; Nonaka, 1994; Stata & Almond, 1989). In spite of scholars' efforts to establish an integrative and cumulative framework, there is still no consensus on the definitions and perspectives of organizational learning (Friedman, Lipshitz, & Popper, 2003).

Concepts of Organizational Learning

Learning has traditionally been regarded as a cognitive process or system within an individual (Simon, 1996), and there have been some arguments on whether organizational learning is just a conceptual metaphor or really exists (Friedman et al., 2003). Although it is now extensively accepted that organizational learning actually exists and is distinguished from individual learning (Fiol & Lyles, 1985; Levitt & March, 1988; Nicolini & Meznar, 1995), the concept of organizational learning is not easy to find a single, clear definition due to diverse understandings of with different perspectives on the concept (Bapuji & Crossan, 2004; Fiol & Lyles, 1985; Friedman et al., 2003; Nicolini & Meznar, 1995).

For instance, Fiol and Lyles (1985) define organizational learning as "the process of improving actions through better knowledge and understanding" (p. 803). Dodgson (1993) also refers to organizational learning as "the way firms build, supplement, and organize knowledge and routines around their activities and within their culture, and adapt and develop organizational efficiency by improving the use of the broad skills of their workforces" (p. 377). Meanwhile, Lundberg (1995) mentions that organizational learning is "an institutionalized process by which organizations and their members notice, interpret, and manage their experience" (p. 12).

Levitt and March (1988) also describe that organizational learning is a process that organizations learn "by encoding inferences from history into routines that guided behavior" (p. 320). Argote (2012) refers to organizational learning as a process "creating, retaining, and transferring knowledge" from an organization's experiences. Despite some differences according to scholars, their definitions suggest that organizational learning is a kind of process where organizations acquire knowledge and understandings from their experiences, acknowledging that organizations themselves have learning capabilities. This interpretation makes us to specifically identify that organizational learning can be characterized by three terms, process, experiences, and knowledge.

Learning as Process

Process is defined, according to Merriam-Webster Dictionary, as: "1) a series of actions that produce something or that lead to a particular result, 2) a series of changes that happen naturally." In most definitions, organizational learning is a process, which means that organizational learning is not a one-time event but a continuous series of actions with a particular goal or objective, such as organizational performance and/or change. Assuming organizations as a social system, a perspective of organizational learning maintains that an organization itself is continuously changing. The concept of communities-of-practice reveals that organizations ceaselessly engage in learning and change process (Brown & Duguid, 1991; Schilling & Kluge, 2009).

Learning From Experiences

As indicated in the definitions of organizational learning, a main resource of organizational learning is an organization's experiences (Argote & Miron-Specktor, 2011). In other words, organizations learn from their experiences, which occurs in two ways. First, organizational learning occurs during trial-and-error from an organization's past experiences (Argote & Miron-Specktor, 2011; Argyris, 1977; Levitt & March, 1988). Organizational learning can obstruct organizational change and innovation, if organizations focus on learning through past experiences and routines. Furthermore, organizations can unlearn existing organizational experiences and routines, and learn new knowledge from other organizations and external environments during the organizational learning process (Argote & Miron-Specktor, 2011; Agyris, 1977; Edmondson, 1996; Hedberg, 1979; March, 1991; Schultz, 2001). In this respect, March (1991) defines organizational learning as a process of exploration to learn new alternatives for competitive advantages, through continuous mutual interaction with changing environments beyond the adaptation process to learn from existing ones.

Organizational Knowledge

According to the definitions of organizational learning, organizational knowledge is inputs in an organizational learning process, and outcomes of organizational learning are changes in organizational knowledge. Argote (2012) claims that the importance of knowledge creation is highlighted more and more in organizational learning research and practice because it is strongly related to an organization's competitive advantage under a knowledge-based economy. In particular, tacit knowledge plays a more critical role in the knowledge creating process (Bennet & Bennet, 2008; Cavusgil, Calantone, & Zhao, 2003; Easterby-Smith & Lyles, 2011; Howells, 2002; Lam, 2000; Nonaka, 1994; Nonaka, von Krogh, & Voelpel, 2006), thus recent organizational learning research focuses on how tacit knowledge is transferred and expanded within and/or across organizations.

Perspectives of Organizational Learning

As suggested in definitions of organizational learning, there is numerous scholarship with varying perspectives on organizational learning. However, perspectives of organizational learning are generally categorized into two perspectives: a technical or systems-structural perspective, and a social or interpretative perspective. The technical view or systems-structural perspective, focuses on the process of acquiring and disseminating information (Daft & Huber, 1987; Easterby-Smith & Araujo, 1999). In the systems-structural perspective, learners – either individuals or organizations – detect and solve problems responding to internal and external environments through information processing (Easterby-Smith & Araujo, 1999). This perspective, hence, emphasizes a cognitive mechanism dealing with information or data and focuses on individual learners, which is influenced by behaviorism (Billett, 1995; Daft & Huber, 1987; Hager, 2011).

The social view, or interpretative perspective, is influenced by sociology and social anthropology, emphasizes the role of social and organizational context in terms of workplace learning (Billett, 1995;

Fenwick, 2001; Hager, 2011). Theorists with a social perspective claim that learning occurs through social interaction and is a by-product of social construct. This suggests that it is important to understand how learners interpret information and build meanings within their social and organizational context, in order to understand workplace learning (Daft & Huber, 1987; Easterby-Smith & Araujo, 1999). While the social perspective claims that learning is a social process through 'legitimate peripheral participation' and occurs in a social context, termed 'situated learning' (Lave & Wenger, 1991), a group, a community or an organization is considered as a unit of analysis (Daft & Huber, 1987; Hager, 2011).

Given a context that recent studies pay attention to social aspects of organizational learning, while the early organizational learning theories focus on information processing through a cognitive system (Akgun, Lynn, & Byrne, 2003; Antonacopoulou & Chiva, 2007; Brandi & Elkjaer, 2011; Esterby-Smith & Araujo, 1999; Gherardi, 2003; Hager, 2011), organizational change research tends to take a social or interpretative perspective rather than a technical or systems-structural perspective (Easterby-Smith & Araujo, 1999; Hager, 2011). Lave and Wenger (1991) argue that employees learn in the organization by participating in social interaction with others, and they explain this process as 'situated learning' and 'legitimate peripheral participation,' and they call these kinds of organization 'communities-of-practice'.

Elkjaer (1999) also explains that organizational learning is "a developmental process that constantly is interpreted and reinterpreted, acted and reacted upon by the individual members and groups involved, including the organization as a whole" (p. 83). This means that learning is a kind of social action where individuals share experiences, goals, visions, and resources with others. In the concept of organizational learning, an organization is a social system where learning agents interrelate and interact with each other, and their learning is socially and culturally embedded in their context (Antonacopoulou & Chiva, 2007; Brandi & Elkjaer, 2011).

Process of Organizational Learning

It is difficult to clearly identify a process of organizational learning because learning is so complex that it is often described as a black box (Friedman et al., 2003). Scholars have tried to open the black box of the organizational learning process, which led to a variety of learning process models, for example, single-loop learning and double-loop learning (Argyris & Schön, 1978), exploitation and exploration (March, 1991), knowledge acquisition, information distribution, information interpretation, and organizational memory (Huber, 1991), and 4I (intuiting, interpreting, integrating, institutionalizing) (Crossan, Lane, & White, 1999). Argote (2012) explains that organizational learning is a three sub-process of creating, retaining, and transferring knowledge. These models imply that organizations go through changes in organizational experiences and knowledge, including routines, cultures, behaviors, and norms throughout the organizational learning process.

The process models of organizational learning proposed by Agyris and Schön (1978) and March (1991) underscore that organizational learning takes place in two different ways. Single-loop learning refers to learning to perform organization's objectives and policies by detecting and correcting errors while double-loop learning questions the organization's objectives and policies (Agyris, 2002; Agyris & Schön, 1978). According to March (1991), exploitative learning is related to 'refinement, choice, production, efficiency, selection, implementation, and execution,' and explorative learning is associated with 'search, variation, risk taking, experimentation, play, flexibility, discovery, and innovation' (p. 71). Conceptually, single-loop learning is similar to exploitation, and double-loop learning is linked to exploration. Agyris and Schön (1978) and March (1991) claim that it is important to balance between the two types of learning for organizational success and competitiveness. Yet, both point out that most organizations tend to be vulnerable to double-loop learning and exploration as they challenge uncertainty (Agyris, 2002; March, 1991).

Organizational learning process models suggested in Huber (1991), Crossan et al. (1999) and Argote (2012), however, focus on a cycle or system that knowledge or information is created, shared and institutionalized in organizations. Huber (1991) and Crossan et al. (1999) stress that knowledge and/or information are interpreted by an organization's culture, norms, structure, and routines, suggesting that organizational contexts are crucial for understanding organizational learning and knowledge.

SOCIAL CAPITAL/NETWORK APPROACH TO ORGANIZATIONAL LEARNING

Research interests in social aspects of organizational learning provoke the application of the social capital and/or network approach in organizational learning. While social capital/network theories and methodology help understand how social relationships and interactions contribute to creating organizational outcomes and benefits within and across organizations (Adler & Kwon, 2002), we focus on here a social capital/network approach to organizational learning.

Concepts of Social Capital

Despite the increasing importance of social capital in various fields, it is not easy to clearly recognize and capture social capital because social capital is invisible, unlike the physical capital (Portes, 1998). This further suggests it is difficult to find a definition of social capital on which most scholars agree. Bourdieu (1985), who originally established the concept of social capital, defines social capital as "the aggregate of the actual or potential resources which are linked to possession of a durable network of more or less institutionalized relationships of mutual acquaintance or recognition" (p. 248). His definition shows that social capital is embedded in a network or relationships, while other forms of capital, such as physical capital and human capital, are embedded in a certain thing or person.

Adler and Kwon (2000) define social capital as "a resource for individual and collective actors created by the configuration and content of network of their more or less durable social relations" (p. 93), which also clarifies that social capital is embedded in the social network among people. Loury (1992) refers to social capital as "naturally occurring social relationships among persons which promote or assist the acquisition of skills and traits valued in the marketplace" (p. 100), which also shows that social capital is placed on social relationships and contributes to acquiring new skills and knowledge which are economically valuable. Burt (1992) defines social capital as "friends, colleagues, and more general contacts through whom you receive opportunities to use your financial and human capital" (p. 9), which suggests that social capital becomes a resource of financial and human capital that produces economic values.

These definitions imply that social capital has some characteristics, which distinguish social capital from other forms of capital. First, social capital is embedded in relationships or networks among actors (Adler & Kwon, 199; Bourdieu, 1985; Loury, 1992; Nahapiet & Ghoshal, 1998). Second, social capital becomes a resource to create other forms of capital, such as physical capital and human capital (Burt, 1992; Coleman, 1990). Third, even though it is hard to capture social capital, it produces economic values in the marketplace like other capital (Coleman, 1990; Nahapiet & Ghoshal, 1998).

Dimensions of Social Capital

Nahapiet and Ghoshal (1998) claim that there are three facets of social capital which particularly influence the development of intellectual capital: structural dimension, cognitive dimension, and relational dimension:

1. **Structural Dimension:** Structure of network or relationship influences exchange and combination of knowledge and information, which affects the development of the cognitive and relational dimension of social capital, as well as intellectual capital. Network tie, network configuration, and appropriable organization are facets of structural dimension which influence access and transfer of resources and information (Nahapiet & Ghoshal, 1998). In particular, Burt (2000) claims that the structural hole, which brokers social capital, is more critical than the density of network, in terms of the network structure in the creation of social capital; while Coleman (1988) asserts that the closure of network, that is, strong ties of network, is more beneficial for social capital (Adler & Kwon, 2000).
2. **Cognitive Dimension:** According to Nahapiet and Ghoshal (1998), social capital theory is based on the belief that intellectual capital, including knowledge, is created and transferred in the social context, which means that socially shared language, code, and even narratives, such as myths, stories, and metaphors, contribute to the creation of collective cognitive perception of actors within a network. It also enables groups or organizations to build their own communication language and code and interpretation mechanism, which are valuable for creating their own intellectual capital.
3. **Relational Dimension:** The relational dimension of social capital plays a critical role in building conditions for exchange and combination of intellectual capital. The relational dimension of social capital is affected by trust, norms, obligations and expectations, and identification (Nahapiet & Ghoshal, 1998). First, Adler and Kwon (2000) distinguish trust from social capital, claiming that trust is a source and an effect of social capital, even though trust is often confused with social capital. Trust allows people to engage in social interaction for exchange and combination and cooperative problem solving (Nahapiet & Ghoshal, 1998). Second, Coleman (1988) claims that effective norms contribute to the security and blindness of community, which can enhance the cooperation and interaction for exchange. Third, obligation and expectation also affect access to parties, anticipation, and motivation for exchange and combination of intellectual capital enhancing the cooperation (Nahapiet & Ghoshal, 1998). Lastly, Nahapiet and Ghoshal (1998) claim that identification allows actors to have belongingness to their community and organization, and also allows them to be involved in collective and cooperative creation of intellectual capital, even though sometimes high identification inhibits creation of intellectual capital.

These dimensions of social capital are interrelated with each other, and they consequently contribute to the creation of new intellectual capital, which is important to enhance organizational competitiveness in the knowledge-based economy.

Social Network Concepts and Analysis

Concepts of Social Network

In explaining social capital, a social network is a significant concept as a location where social capital is embedded and transferred among individual actors within and/or across organizations (Burt, 2000; Lin, 1999; Nahapiet & Ghoshal, 1998). Given the fundamental assumption that social capital is placed on social networks, social networks and social capital are sometimes interchangeably used. Nahapiet and Ghoshal (1998) explain a structure of social networks as a structural dimension of social capital, which affects the development of the cognitive and relational dimension of social capital as well as intellectual capital. Structure of network or relationship influences the exchange and combination of knowledge and information. Network tie, network configuration, and appropriable organization are facets of structural dimension which influence access and transfer of resources and information (Nahapiet & Ghoshal, 1998). In this regard, characteristics of social networks are factors influencing transfer of knowledge in the process of organizational learning. In particular, Burt (2000) claims that the structural hole which brokers social capital is more critical than the density of network, in terms of the network structure in the creation of social capital, while Coleman (1988) asserts that the closure of network; that is, strong ties of network is more beneficial for social capital (Adler & Kwon, 2000).

Social Network Analysis

Social network analysis is a research method that measures and analyzes a social structure and its properties, such as networks of relationships, group, clique, network position, and closeness (Wasserman & Faust, 2009, p. 17). Social network analysis provides methodological usefulness in organizational learning research because it assumes that individual's behavior and attitude are influenced by their social relationship and the social context. Wasserman and Faust (2009) show several perspectives that social network analysis assumes: "First, actors and their actions are viewed as interdependent rather than independent, autonomous units. Second, relational ties (linkages) between actors are channels for transfer or flow of resources. Third, network models focusing on individuals view the network structural environment as providing opportunities for or constraints on individual action. Fourth, network models conceptualize structure (social, economic, political, and so forth) as lasting patterns of relations among actors" (p. 4). These assumptions of social network analysis suggest that it is useful for describing individuals' relationships and some theoretical concepts defined in social network theory.

In addition, social network analysis can be used for testing research models and theories about "relational structures or processes" (Wasserman & Faust, 2009, p. 5). When we recall a process that employees learn and develop their expertise in organizations is based on the social context, it is important to understand how employees interact with each other and share important knowledge and information in an organization. Namely, organizational learning scholars have tried to describe social interaction and relationships among employees and propose some recommendations for facilitating their social interaction and organizational learning through social network (Cross, Parker, Prusak, & Borgatti, 2001; Storberg-Walker & Gubbins, 2007). This implies that social network analysis can play a critical role in better understanding organizational learning that highlights how employees interact and communicate with each other and share their own knowledge and information (Hatala, 2006; Parise, 2007).

According to Kilduff and Tsai (2007), the network approach is distinguished from other traditional research approaches: "(1) Network research focuses on relations and the patterns of relations rather than on attributes of actors; (2) Network research is amenable to multiple levels of analysis, and can, thus, provide micro-macro linkages; (3) Network research can integrate quantitative, qualitative and graphical data, allowing more thorough and in-depth analysis" (p. 19). Given the featuring assumptions in organizational learning theories, the network research approach provides meaningful implications for identifying a complicated organizational learning process.

First, network approach demonstrates how organizational learning occurs, particularly, how social relationship/interaction works for organizational learning. Network research also provides a methodological tool for measuring and analyzing multilevel structures of organizational learning. Organizational learning occurs not just at the individual level or the organizational level but at the individual, group, organizational, and inter-organizational level (Crossan, Lane, White, & Djurfeldt, 1995). Network research, hence, allows organizational learning processes to be identified at multiple levels, and to investigate how organizational learning processes at each level are different and influence each other.

In addition, network research provides an integrative tool for understanding the complex and complicated organizational learning process. Patterns and structures of social relations and interaction vary depending upon the organizational contexts and environmental factors. Moreover, there can be a number of actors and their relations within organizations, which suggests that a single research method, either quantitative or qualitative, cannot fully explain the complicated organizational learning process and factors influencing organizational learning. Given the importance of structures and patterns of social relationships and interactions in organizational learning, data visualization could be helpful for understanding organizational learning patterns. Therefore, network research provides useful methodological tools to effectively identify organizational learning processes and comprehensively explain the whole process of organizational learning.

Roles of Social Capital and Networks in Organizational Learning

Since an organizational learning perspective emphasizes social aspects of learning, the relationship between factors of social capital and social networks – even though the terms social capital or social network are not directly stated – has been continuously and extensively studied and discussed in organizational learning research (Antonacopoulou & Chiva, 2007; Bandi & Elkjaer, 2011; Elkjaer, 1999, 2004; Siemens, 2005). Since Bandura (1977) established a social learning theory, there is an extensive agreement that learning occurs and is reinforced by social relations and interaction with others, which suggests that it is necessary to identify social relationship and interaction, in order to understand a learning process (Reed, Evely, Cundill, Fazey, Glass, Laing, Newig, Parrish, Prell, Raymond, & Stringer, 2006; Salomon & Perkins, 1998).

Given that social capital is embedded in social relations and networks, social capital is an important resource for organizational learning and social network is where learning takes place (Lesser & Prusak, 1999; Nahapiet & Ghoshal, 1998). This suggests that organizational learning is associated with social capital and networks and depends on patterns and characteristics of social capital and networks. Various researchers have demonstrated the roles of social capital and networks in organizational learning (Chen, Liu, & Peng, 2014; Inkpen & Tsang, 2005; Lesser & Prusak, 1999; Reagans & Zuckerman, 2001; Rodes, Lok, Hung, & Fang, 2008; Wasko & Faraj, 2005; Yli-Renko, Autio, & Tontti, 2002; Yli-Renko, Autio, & Sapienza, 2001).

Organizational Learning as a Social Process

Three dimensions of social capital influence organizational learning depending upon characteristics of learning and knowledge. First, the structural dimension of social capital influences knowledge transfer and knowledge creation (Burt, 2000; Gulati, 1999; Reagans & McEvily, 2003; Tsai, 2001; Tsai & Ghoshal, 1998). For example, strong ties among organization's members facilitate and ease knowledge transfer while weak ties promote knowledge creation by encouraging to borrow new ideas and knowledge (Argote, McEvily, & Reagans, 2003; Dyer & Nonaka, 2000; Hansen, 1999; Levin & Cross, 2004; Levin, Cross, & 2002; Reagans & McEvily, 2003; Smith, Collins, & Clark, 2005).

For the network position, individual actors or units in a central position can have a higher absorptive capacity and opportunities for knowledge creation (Tsai, 2001; Reagans & McEvily, 2003). Next, the cognitive dimension of social capital affects knowledge transfer and sharing (Chow & Chan, 2008; Li, 2005; Nahapiet & Ghoshal, 1999; Tsai & Ghoshal, 1998). Shared vision, values, and goals in organizations positively influence knowledge transfer (Chow & Chan, 2008; Li, 2005). Lastly, the relational dimension of social capital promotes knowledge transfer and creation (Chow & Chan, 2008; Li, 2005; Nahapiet & Ghosal, 1998; Inkpen & Tsang, 2005; Levin & Cross, 2004; Sankowska, 2013; Squire, Cousins, & Brown, 2009; Van Wijk, Jansen, & Lyles, 2008). In particular, previous research highlights that trust is a key factor influencing organizational learning – knowledge creation and transfer (Chow & Chan, 2008; Li, 2005; Sankowska, 2013; Squire et al., 2009).

Current Research on Social Capital/Network Approach to Organizational Learning

Despite increased interests in the social capital/network approach to organizational learning, current research on organizational learning with a social capital/network approach is still limited. In particular, although social network analysis provides methodological benefits to explain how organizational learning occurs through social relationships and/or interactions, there is a limited amount of empirical research which adopts social network analysis. This chapter reviews literature of organizational learning research, which has been conducted from 2000 to the present, in order to understand the current state of organizational learning research employing a social capital and network approach. The literature reviewed in this chapter is theoretical/conceptual or empirical research which directly employs concepts, theories, and/or methodologies of social capital and/or social networks because concepts of these aspects still produce confusion and questions among readers. Table 1 shows which topics the current organizational learning research deals with in terms of social capital and networks. Currently, organizational learning research with a social/network approach tends to focus on borrowing theoretical concepts of social capital and/or network, rather than employing social network analysis research method for identifying a process of organizational learning.

As shown in Table 1, the recent organizational learning research concentrates on identifying the impacts of social capital/network factors on organizational learning and performance by conducting empirical research, rather than establishing the theoretical and/or conceptual framework for the relationships between social capital/networks and organizational learning. In particular, given the significance of social networks as a place where organizational learning takes place, and the importance of network properties and characteristics, such as network ties, network position, and closeness, the current research focuses on relationships between social capital/network factors and organizational learning processes for organizational performance and innovation.

Table 1. Organizational learning research with social capital/network approach (2000-present)

	Topic	Author(s)
Theoretical/ Conceptual Research	Social capital, organizational learning, and performance	• Anand, Glick, & Manz (2002) • Kang, Morris, & Snell (2007)
	Social networks and organizational learning	• Bogenrieder (2002) • Currah & Wrigley (2004) • Kreiser (2011) • Inkpen & Tsang (2005) • Jones (2001) • Siemens (2005)
Empirical Research	Network properties and knowledge transfer	• Levin & Cross (2004) • Reagans & McEvily (2003) • Tsai (2001)
	Network properties and organizational learning	• Škerlavaj, Dimovski, & Desouza (2010)
	Social capital/networks and knowledge sharing	• Abrams, Cross, Lesser, & Levin (2003) • Chiu, Hsu, & Wang (2006) • Hansen, Mors, & Løvås (2005) • Wasko & Faraj (2005)
	Social capital/networks, knowledge transfer, and innovation	• Alguezaui & Filieri (2010) • Cavusgil, Calanlone, & Zhao (2003) • Huggins, Johnston, & Thompson (2012) • Maurer, Bartsch, & Ebers (2011)
	Social capital/networks and organizational learning	• Addicott, McGivern & Ferile (2006) • Borgatti & Cross (2003) • Fang, Lee, & Schilling (2010) • Hagedoorn & Duysters (2002) • Lam (2003) • Newell, Tansley, & Huang (2004) • Swift & Hwang (2013) • von Kutzschenbach & Brønn (2010) • Wirtz, Kuan Tambyah, & Mattila (2010) • Yli-Renko, Autio, & Sapienza (2001)
	Social capital/networks, organizational learning, and performance	• Beckman & Haunschild (2002) • Fang, Tsai, & Lin (2010) • Liu, Ghauri, & Sinkovics (2010) • Rhodes, Lok, Hung, & Fang (2008)

Theoretical/Conceptual Research on Social Capital/ Network and Organizational Learning

The theoretical and conceptual research on social capital/networks and organizational learning highlights the roles of social capital/network factors in organizational learning for organizational performance and innovation. The social capital and networks promote organizational learning by facilitating knowledge transfer among individuals and organizations, and the three facets of social capital influence quality and quantity of learning in different ways (Kang, Morris, & Snell, 2007; Inkpen & Tsang, 2005). Inkpen and Tsang (2005) suggest the social capital positively affects organizational learning, while individual-level and organizational-level social capital are interplaying together. Also, network forms – intra-corporate network, strategic alliance, and industrial district – work differently on the relationship between social capital and knowledge transfer. Therefore, it is important to take a strategic approach to social capital development considering network types and learning goals in order to facilitate organizational learning (Inkpen & Tsang, 2005).

Kang, Morris, and Snell (2007) pay attention to the contexts of social relations where organizational learning occurs, which can be called either social capital or social networks. Their study establishes a conceptual framework that shows how the three dimensions of social capital – structural, affective, and cognitive dimension – are related to the exploitation and exploration of organizational learning. Exploitative and explorative learning are not conflicting concepts, but both play a critical role in an organization's value creation, which contributes to organizational performance improvement and organizational change and innovation. However, differences in learning resources and processes between exploitative and explorative learning and the dimensions of social capital, differently influence organizational learning in two types of organizational learning. This means they claimed that organizational learning strategies should consider the relationships between the social capital dimensions and organizational learning for effective organizational learning and value creation.

According to the conceptual framework of Kang et al. (2007)'s study, in terms of the structural dimension, strong and dense networks facilitate exploitative learning while weak and sparse networks promote exploratory learning by opening possible opportunities to import new ideas and/or knowledge into organizations. For the affective dimensions, generalized trust is beneficial for knowledge sharing and exchange, but resilient, dyadic trust enables actors to flexibly adapt to changes in social relations and to resist the existing norms and culture, which allows organizations to build new norms, rules, and culture. Lastly, the cognitive dimension of social relations is associated with a process to build knowledge, common architectural knowledge and common component knowledge (Kang et al., 2007).

In addition, the changing nature of knowledge and increased complexity and complication reinforce the importance of social capital (Anand, Glick, & Manz, 2005). Anand et al. (2005) claim that an organization's social capital plays a critical role in acquiring a large amount of complex and complicated knowledge from outside, which considerably affects organizational competitive advantages. More importantly, depending upon the characteristics of knowledge, organizations should develop social capital and promote organizational learning with strategic and appropriate methods. With regard to this, several theoretical and conceptual research on social capital/networks and organizational learning not only includes a prevailing topic is the application of social capital/network theory in organizational learning research (Jones, 2001; Siemens, 2005) but also identifies network structures to facilitate organizational learning based on social network theory (Bogenrieder, 2002; Currah & Wrigley, 2004; Kreiser, 2011).

Social network itself indicates patterns of relationships among individual actors in organizations, which suggests that understanding and modeling of social networks are critical for identifying how organizational learning takes place, and a beginning point of effective knowledge management (Jones, 2011). In organizational learning, network patterns and structures are critical factors influencing learning, and they differently influence organizational learning depending upon types of knowledge and learning (Bogenrieder, 2002; Currah & Wrigley, 2004; Kreiser, 2011).

For instance, networks with weak restrictions on diversity enables actors to acquire, explore, and create new and innovative ideas and knowledge (Kresier, 2011). In this context, it is important to find network structures to promote cognitive diversity and to encourage other perspectives for organizational learning (Bogenrieder, 2002). Siemens (2005) provides supportive argument that the existing learning theories such as behaviorism, cognitivism, and constructivism have limitations in explaining organizational learning, but connectivism enables us to comprehensively explain how organizational learning contributes to knowledge distribution and creation beyond individual learners.

Empirical Research on Social Capital/Networks and Organizational Learning

Researchers continue to identify the relationships between social capital/network factors and organizational learning. More specific topic and interest areas of empirical studies are described in below:

1. **Network Properties and Knowledge Transfer/Organizational Learning:** Empirical studies currently investigate how network properties such as network position, network ties, and closeness affect an organizational learning process (Levin & Cross, 2004; Reagans & McEvily, 2003; Škerlavaj, Dimovski, & Desouza, 2010; Tsai, 2001). Škerlavaj et al. (2010) examine the role of network properties, including network position, network homophily and proximity, network reciprocity, and transitivity and clustering within a knowledge-intensive organization. Especially, the strength of network ties – strong ties or weak ties – has been considerably studied in terms of characteristics of organizational learning and knowledge (Levin & Cross; Reagans & McEvily, 2003).

2. **Social Capital/Networks and Knowledge Sharing:** The existing empirical research studies consistently demonstrate that social capital and network positively affect knowledge sharing (Abrams, Cross, Lesser, & Levin, 2003; Chiu, Hsu, & Wang, 2006; Hansen, Mors, & Løvås, 2005; Wasko & Faraj, 2005). Abrams et al. (2003) investigate how interpersonal trust develops in informal knowledge-sharing networks. Interpersonal trust plays a critical role in effectively promoting knowledge sharing and creation. From in-depth interviews, they build strategies of managerial behaviors to nurture interpersonal trust: "1) Act with discretion 2) Be consistent between word and deed 3) Ensure frequent and rich communication 4) Engage in collaborative communication 5) Ensure that decisions are fair and transparent 6) Establish and ensure shared vision and language 7) Hold people accountable for trust 8) Create personal connections 9) Give away something of value 10) Disclose your expertise and limitations" (p. 67). Abrams et al. (2003) suggest that trust, a kind of social capital, is not only strongly associated with knowledge sharing, but social capital itself can also be influenced by organizational and relational factors. Chiu et al. (2006) examine individuals' knowledge sharing motivation and behaviors based on the social cognitive theory and the social capital theory. Their research results identify factors of three social capital dimensions, including social interaction ties (structural dimension), trust, norm of reciprocity, identification (relational dimension), shared language and shared vision (cognitive dimension), are associated with the quantity of knowledge sharing and knowledge quality. Hansen et al. (2005) insist that the relationship between network factors and knowledge sharing outcomes can be differently explained depending upon subsets of the social network – within-team network, intersubsidiary network, and transfer network. That is, network size and strength can differently affect knowledge sharing in different types of networks. For example, the dense and strong relationships of within-team networks have a high level of common knowledge, which can negatively influence the team members' knowledge-seeking behaviors from outside.

3. **Social Capital/Networks and Organizational Learning:** Recent empirical studies repeatedly confirm that social capital/network factors have significant relationship with organizational learning throughout the whole process (Addicott, McGivern & Ferile, 2006; Borgatti & Cross, 2003; Fang, Lee, & Schilling, 2010; Hagedorn & Duysters, 2002; Lam, 2003; Newell, Tansley, & Huang, 2004; Swift & Hwang, 2013; von Kutzschenbach & Brønn, 2010; Wirtz, Kuan Tambyah, & Mattila, 2010; Yli-Renko, et al., 2001). Addicott, et al. (2006) and Fang, et al. (2010) show that network and interaction patterns are related to organizational learning, and Fang, et al. (2010) examine the

level of linkage and interaction for balancing exploitative and explorative learning. Borgatti and Cross (2003) examine the relationships between relational characteristics and information seeking and knowledge sharing in social networks, noting the importance of organizational learning as a social process. According to the research results, characteristics of networks and/or relations such as hierarchy proximity, knowing, value, and access have a significant relationship with organizational learning. Borgatti and Cross (2003) claim that it is important to develop and provide social interventions to facilitate the relational factors from their findings. Newell et al. (2004) also investigate the relationship between social capital and knowledge integration, and their study results suggest that both strong ties and weak ties positively affect knowledge integration. The weak ties facilitate importing new knowledge from outside through 'bridging activity', and the strong ties within a team/group help integrate knowledge acquired from the outside (Newell et al., 2004).

4. **Social Capital/Networks, Knowledge Transfer/Organizational Learning, Organizational Performance and Innovation:** Some existing research investigates the relationship among social capital/network factors, organizational learning, and organizational performance and innovation. Organizational performance and innovation is a goal and outcome of organizational learning (Gilley, Gilley, & Eggland, 2002). Thus, the research on the impact of social relations and organizational learning on organizational performance and innovation can reveal the strategic importance of organizational learning – especially as a social process – in organizations (Alguezaui & Filieri, 2010; Cavusgil, Calanlone, & Zhao, 2003; Huggins, Johnston, & Thompson, 2012; Maurer, Bartsch, & Ebers, 2011). Huggins et al. (2012) assert that organizations develop organizational policy to enhance the investment in social capital/network by identifying the significant relationship between network capital investment and organizational innovation. Rhodes et al. (2008) propose an integrative model of organizational learning and social capital on knowledge transfer and organizational performance in their study. The study investigates the effect of organizational learning variables - learning intention, shared values, absorption capacity, and integration capability – and the relationship between the social capital variables – network structure, network stability, and network relational quality - on knowledge transfer and organizational financial performance, and knowledge transfer.

As the importance of organizational learning and the interests in social capital and network increase, organizational learning research is more interested in and employing social capital and network theory. Nevertheless, there are still several limitations in the current organizational learning research adopting social capital and network theory. Most research, in fact, does not consider a multilevel structure of organizational learning. As organizational learning scholars agree, organizational learning occurs at diverse levels (Crossan et al., 2005), and therefore, could have different patterns and forms of network (Inkpen & Tsang, 2005; Hansen, et al., 2005). Given the interdependence among different network units and levels (Crossan et al., 2005; Inkpen & Tsang, 2005), it is important that organizational learning research consider multilevel structures of organizational learning and network.

Although organizational learning is context- and history-based, and social relationship/network is also considerably affected by the organizational and environmental context, most empirical research does not consider social, historical, and cultural contexts within and across organizations (Antonacopoulou & Chiva, 2007; Brandi & Elkjaer, 2011; March, 1991). In addition, there is no consensus on measuring organizational learning and social capital/network factors. Because of disagreements on definitions of organizational learning and complicatedness of social capital/network concepts, the current research uses different measures of learning and social capital and network factors. Furthermore, the current research does not provide practical strategies to nurture social capital and build and expand social network in organizations. The conceptual and theoretical research has tried to establish the integrative framework of the relationships among social capital/network factors, organizational learning, and organizational performance and innovation; yet, there is still a gap between practice and research. Therefore, the empirical research and theoretical research both need to help organizations and practitioners build effective strategies for social capital/network and organizational learning.

IMPLICATIONS FOR FUTURE RESEARCH AND PRACTICE

Existing research highlights that organizational learning can be facilitated under certain types of social network structures. Based on the findings from organizational learning research, this chapter provides several organizational learning strategies for organizational performance and change. One of key strategies we identified was that it is important to nurture social capital and to facilitate appropriate networks for organizational learning in organizations. However, as organizational learning theories suggest, organizational contexts and past experiences are critical factors influencing organizational learning and social networks, which means that understanding of organizational contexts should come prior to building strategies for organizational learning and social capital/networks.

Next, organizations should support informal networks as well as formal networks. With organizational efforts to promote learning in the workplace, many organizations provide a space for workplace learning and social networking through mentoring and communities-of-practice (Douglas & McCauley, 1999). However, relational factors, especially trust in social relationships and networking are neither totally free nor totally planned (Das & Teng, 1998). Given the prevalence and influence of informal learning (Conlon, 2004), organizations also need to promote and support both formal and informal networks.

It is also important to balance exploitative and explorative learning, which requires a different approach to network structures and social relationships (Fang et al., 2010). Although the importance of explorative learning and knowledge creation is repetitively highlighted, organizational competitive advantages come from both knowledge retention and creation. Thus, organizations need to understand characteristics of network structures, such as strong and weak ties and network positions, and to build social networking strategies differently, depending on learning goals and knowledge types for balanced organizational learning.

Since social capital/network theory was adopted in organizational learning research, researchers seek an integrative and comprehensive framework and empirical evidence to show the relationships among social capital/network, organizational learning, and organizational performance. From the current organizational learning research with the social capital/network approach, we suggest three folds of implications for future research.

First, future research needs to apply diverse research methodology to identify and/or measure social capital/networks and organizational learning processes and outcomes (Argote, 2011). For instance, social network analysis can be a useful research method to describe and visualize patterns and structures of social networks and relationships (Wasserman & Faust, 2009). Yet, there is little empirical research adopting social network analysis (Cross et al., 2002). In addition, qualitative research could contribute with an in-depth study to reveal invisible characteristics of social capital and organizational learning processes (Cross et al., 2002; Škerlavaj & Dimovski, 2006).

Second, future research requires to consider the multilevel structures and diverse patterns of social networks and relationships (Inkpen & Tsang, 2005; Hansen et al., 2005), as well as the hierarchical structure of organizational learning levels (Crossan et al., 1995). It also suggests that future research should comprehensively include all the potential factors influencing organizational learning and social capital/networks. This approach would contribute to enhance the reliability of research and help uncover organizational learning processes.

Last, more empirical studies will be conducted in various organizational contexts and settings (Argote, 2011). Organizational contexts and settings are critical factors determining organizational learning and characteristics of social capital and networks. Accumulation of empirical studies enable researchers to establish an integrative and systematic theoretical framework, and also help practitioners develop effective organizational learning strategies appropriate to the organizational contexts. Future empirical research also needs to be performed in new forms of organizations (Argote, 2011). For example, virtual communities are dramatically increasing and emerging as a learning place for geographically dispersed workplaces. Their social relationship and interaction patterns are considerably different from the traditional forms of organizations (Ardichvil, 2008; Argote, 2011; Dubé, Bourhis, & Jacob, 2006). Therefore, the empirical studies in virtual communities would provide new insights and implications for organizational learning research and practice.

CONCLUSION

This chapter explores the relationship between social capital and networks and organizational learning and seeks to establish an integrative and comprehensive understanding of roles of social capital and networks, by reviewing organizational learning research. As a social or interpretative perspective of organizational learning is noticeably emerging, current research that adopts the social capital/network approach in organizational learning is still limited despite increased interests. Given the significance of social capital/networks in organizational learning and performance, researchers' efforts to apply the social capital/network approach to organizational learning in both theoretical and empirical research will provide better explanation of the complicated organizational learning processes and reveal the strategic importance of organizational learning for organizational competitive advantages.

REFERENCES

Abrams, L. C., Cross, R., Lesser, E., & Levin, D. Z. (2003). Nurturing interpersonal trust in knowledge-sharing networks. *The Academy of Management Executive*, *17*(4), 64–77. doi:10.5465/AME.2003.11851845

Addicott, R., McGivern, G., & Ferlie, E. (2006). Networks, organizational management: NHS cancer networks. *Public Money and Management*, *26*(2), 87–94. doi:10.1111/j.1467-9302.2006.00506.x

Adler, P. S., & Kwon, S. W. (2002). Social capital: Prospects for a new concept. *Academy of Management Review*, *27*(1), 17–40.

Akgün, A. E., Lynn, G. S., & Byrne, J. C. (2003). Organizational learning: A socio-cognitive framework. *Human Relations*, *56*(7), 839–868. doi:10.1177/00187267030567004

Alguezaui, S., & Filieri, R. (2010). Investigating the role of social capital in innovation: Sparse versus dense network. *Journal of Knowledge Management, 14*(6), 891–909. doi:10.1108/13673271011084925

Anand, V., Glick, W. H., & Manz, C. C. (2002). Thriving on the knowledge of outsiders: Tapping organizational social capital. *The Academy of Management Executive, 16*(1), 87–101. doi:10.5465/AME.2002.6640198

Antonacopoulou, E., & Chiva, R. (2007). The social complexity of organizational learning: The dynamics of learning and organizing. *Management Learning, 38*(3), 277–295. doi:10.1177/1350507607079029

Ardichvili, A. (2008). Learning and knowledge sharing in virtual communities of practice: Motivators, barriers, and enablers. *Advances in Developing Human Resources, 10*(4), 541–554. doi:10.1177/1523422308319536

Argote, L. (2011). Organizational learning research: Past, present and future. *Management Learning, 42*(4), 439–446. doi:10.1177/1350507611408217

Argote, L. (2012). *Organizational learning: Creating, retaining and transferring knowledge*. New York: Springer.

Argote, L., McEvily, B., & Reagans, R. (2003). Managing knowledge in organizations: An integrative framework and review of emerging themes. *Management Science, 49*(4), 571–582. doi:10.1287/mnsc.49.4.571.14424

Argote, L., & Miron-Spektor, E. (2011). Organizational learning: From experience to knowledge. *Organization Science, 22*(5), 1123–1137. doi:10.1287/orsc.1100.0621

Argyris, C. (1977). Organizational learning and management information systems. *Accounting, Organizations and Society, 2*(2), 113–123. doi:10.1016/0361-3682(77)90028-9

Argyris, C., & Schön, D. A. (1978). *Organizational learning: A theory of action perspective* (Vol. 173). Reading, MA: Addison-Wesley.

Bandura, A. (1977). *Social learning theory*. Englewood Cliffs, NJ: Prentice-Hall.

Bapuji, H., & Crossan, M. (2004). From questions to answers: Reviewing organizational learning research. *Management Learning, 35*(4), 397–417. doi:10.1177/1350507604048270

Beckman, C. M., & Haunschild, P. R. (2002). Network learning: The effects of partners heterogeneity of experience on corporate acquisitions. *Administrative Science Quarterly, 47*(1), 92–124. doi:10.2307/3094892

Bennet, D., & Bennet, A. (2008). Engaging tacit knowledge in support of organizational learning. *Vine, 38*(1), 72–94. doi:10.1108/03055720810870905

Billett, S. (2001). Learning through work: Workplace affordances and individual engagement. *Journal of Workplace Learning, 13*(5), 209–214. doi:10.1108/EUM0000000005548

Bogenrieder, I. (2002). Social architecture as a prerequisite for organizational learning. *Management Learning, 33*(2), 197–212. doi:10.1177/1350507602332003

Borgatti, S. P., & Cross, R. (2003). A relational view of information seeking and learning in social networks. *Management Science, 49*(4), 432–445. doi:10.1287/mnsc.49.4.432.14428

Bourdieu, P. (1985). The forms of capital. In J. G. Richardson (Ed.), *Handbook of theory and research for the sociology of education* (pp. 241–258). New York: Greenwood.

Brandi, U., & Elkjaer, B. (2011). Organizational learning viewed from a social learning perspective. In M. Easterby-Smith & M. A. Lyles (Eds.), *Handbook of organizational learning and knowledge management* (pp. 21–41). Hoboken, NJ: John Wiley & Sons.

Brown, J. S., & Duguid, P. (1991). Organizational learning and communities-of-practice: Toward a unified view of working, learning, and innovation. *Organization Science, 2*(1), 40–57. doi:10.1287/orsc.2.1.40

Burt, R. S. (2000). The network structure of social capital. *Research in Organizational Behavior, 22,* 345–423. doi:10.1016/S0191-3085(00)22009-1

Casey, A. (2005). Enhancing individual and organizational learning a sociological model. *Management Learning, 36*(2), 131–147. doi:10.1177/1350507605052555

Cavusgil, S. T., Calantone, R. J., & Zhao, Y. (2003). Tacit knowledge transfer and firm innovation capability. *Journal of Business and Industrial Marketing, 18*(1), 6–21. doi:10.1108/08858620310458615

Chiu, C. M., Hsu, M. H., & Wang, E. T. (2006). Understanding knowledge sharing in virtual communities: An integration of social capital and social cognitive theories. *Decision Support Systems, 42*(3), 1872–1888. doi:10.1016/j.dss.2006.04.001

Chow, W. S., & Chan, L. S. (2008). Social network, social trust and shared goals in organizational knowledge sharing. *Information & Management, 45*(7), 458–465. doi:10.1016/j.im.2008.06.007

Coleman, J. S. (1988). Social capital in the creation of human capital. *American Journal of Sociology, 94,* S95–S120. doi:10.1086/228943

Cross, R., Borgatti, S. P., & Parker, A. (2002). Making invisible work visible: Using social network analysis to support strategic collaboration. *California Management Review, 44*(2), 25–46. doi:10.2307/41166121

Cross, R., Parker, A., Prusak, L., & Borgatti, S. P. (2001). Knowing what we know: Supporting knowledge creation and sharing in social networks. *Organizational Dynamics, 30*(2), 100–120. doi:10.1016/S0090-2616(01)00046-8

Crossan, M. M., Lane, H. W., & White, R. E. (1999). An organizational learning framework: From intuition to institution. *Academy of Management Review, 24*(3), 522–537.

Crossan, M. M., Lane, H. W., White, R. E., & Djurfeldt, L. (1995). Organizational learning: Dimensions for a theory. *The International Journal of Organizational Analysis, 3*(4), 337–360. doi:10.1108/eb028835

Currah, A., & Wrigley, N. (2004). Networks of organizational learning and adaptation in retail TNCs. *Global Networks, 4*(1), 1–23. doi:10.1111/j.1471-0374.2004.00078.x

Das, T. K., & Teng, B. S. (1998). Between trust and control: Developing confidence in partner cooperation in alliances. *Academy of Management Review, 23*(3), 491–512.

Dixon, N. M. (1992). Organizational learning: A review of the literature with implications for HRD professionals. *Human Resource Development Quarterly, 3*(1), 29–49. doi:10.1002/hrdq.3920030105

Dodgson, M. (1993). Organizational learning: A review of some literatures. *Organization Studies, 14*(3), 375–394. doi:10.1177/017084069301400303

Douglas, C. A., & McCauley, C. D. (1999). Formal developmental relationships: A survey of organizational practices. *Human Resource Development Quarterly, 10*(3), 203–220. doi:10.1002/hrdq.3920100302

Dubé, L., Bourhis, A., & Jacob, R. (2006). Towards a typology of virtual communities of practice. *Interdisciplinary Journal of Information, Knowledge, and Management, 1*(1), 69–93.

Dyer, J. H., & Nobeoka, K. (2000). Creating and managing a high-performance knowledge-sharing network: The Toyota case. *Strategic Management Journal, 21*(3), 345–367. doi:10.1002/(SICI)1097-0266(200003)21:3<345::AID-SMJ96>3.0.CO;2-N

Easterby-Smith, M., & Araujo, L. (1999). Organizational learning: Current debates and opportunities. In M. Easterby-Smith & L. Araujo (Eds.), *Organizational learning and the learning organization: Development in theory and practice* (pp. 1–21). London: Sage. doi:10.4135/9781446218297.n1

Easterby-Smith, M., & Lyles, M. (2011). *The evolving field of organizational learning and knowledge management. Handbook of organizational learning and knowledge management* (pp. 1–20). Chichester, UK: Wiley.

Edmondson, A., & Moingeon, B. (1998). From organizational learning to the learning organization. *Management Learning, 29*(1), 5–20. doi:10.1177/1350507698291001

Edmondson, A. C. (1996). Learning from mistakes is easier said than done: Group and organizational influences on the detection and correction of human error. *The Journal of Applied Behavioral Science, 32*(1), 5–28. doi:10.1177/0021886396321001

Elkjaer, B. (1999). In search of a social learning theory. In M. Easterby-Smith, J. Burgoyne, & L. Araujo (Eds.), *Organizational learning and the learning organization: Development in theory and practice* (pp. 75–91). London: Sage. doi:10.4135/9781446218297.n5

Elkjaer, B. (2004). Organizational learning the third way. *Management Learning, 35*(4), 419–434. doi:10.1177/1350507604048271

Fang, C., Lee, J., & Schilling, M. A. (2010). Balancing exploration and exploitation through structural design: The isolation of subgroups and organizational learning. *Organization Science, 21*(3), 625–642. doi:10.1287/orsc.1090.0468

Fang, S. C., Tsai, F. S., & Lin, J. L. (2010). Leveraging tenant-incubator social capital for organizational learning and performance in incubation programme. *International Small Business Journal, 28*(1), 90–113. doi:10.1177/0266242609350853

Fenwick, T. (2000). Questioning the concept of the learning organization. In C. Paechter, M. Preedy, D. Scott, & J. Soler (Eds.), *Knowledge, power and learning* (pp. 74–88). London: Paul Chapman.

Fiol, C. M., & Lyles, M. A. (1985). Organizational learning. *Academy of Management Review, 10*(4), 803–813.

Friedman, V. J., Lipshitz, R., & Popper, M. (2005). The mystification of organizational learning. *Journal of Management Inquiry, 14*(1), 19–30. doi:10.1177/1056492604273758

Garvin, D. A. (1993). Building a learning organization. *Harvard Business Review, 71*(4), 78. PMID:10127041

Gherardi, S. (2003). Knowing as desiring. Mythic knowledge and the knowledge journey in communities of practitioners. *Journal of Workplace Learning, 15*(7/8), 352–358. doi:10.1108/13665620310504846

Gulati, R. (1999). Network location and learning: The influence of network resources and firm capabilities on alliance formation. *Strategic Management Journal, 20*(5), 397–420. doi:10.1002/(SICI)1097-0266(199905)20:5<397::AID-SMJ35>3.0.CO;2-K

Hagedoorn, J., & Duysters, G. (2002). Learning in dynamic inter-firm networks: The efficacy of multiple contacts. *Organization Studies, 23*(4), 525–548. doi:10.1177/0170840602234002

Hager, P. (2011). Theories of workplace learning. In M. Malloch, L. Cairns, K. Evans, & B. N. O'Connor (Eds.), *The Sage handbook of workplace learning* (pp. 17–31). Thousand Oaks, CA: Sage. doi:10.4135/9781446200940.n2

Hansen, M. T., Mors, M. L., & Løvås, B. (2005). Knowledge sharing in organizations: Multiple networks, multiple phases. *Academy of Management Journal, 48*(5), 776–793. doi:10.5465/AMJ.2005.18803922

Hatala, J. P. (2006). Social network analysis in human resource development: A new methodology. *Human Resource Development Review, 5*(1), 45–71. doi:10.1177/1534484305284318

Hedberg, B. L. T. (1981). How organizations learn and unlearn. In P. C. Nystrom & W. H. Starbuck (Eds.), *Handbook of organizational design* (pp. 3–27). Oxford: Oxford University Press.

Howells, J. R. (2002). Tacit knowledge, innovation and economic geography. *Urban Studies (Edinburgh, Scotland), 39*(5-6), 871–884. doi:10.1080/00420980220128354

Huber, G. P. (1991). Organizational learning: The contributing processes and the literatures. *Organization Science, 2*(1), 88–115. doi:10.1287/orsc.2.1.88

Huber, G. P., & Daft, R. L. (1987). The information environments of organizations. In F. M. Jablin, L. L. Putnam, K. H. Roberts, & L. W. Porter (Eds.), *Handbook of organizational communication: An interdisciplinary perspective* (pp. 130–164). Thousand Oaks, CA: Sage.

Huggins, R., Johnston, A., & Thompson, P. (2012). Network capital, social capital and knowledge flow: How the nature of inter-organizational networks impacts on innovation. *Industry and Innovation, 19*(3), 203–232. doi:10.1080/13662716.2012.669615

Inkpen, A. C., & Tsang, E. W. (2005). Social capital, networks, and knowledge transfer. *Academy of Management Review, 30*(1), 146–165. doi:10.5465/AMR.2005.15281445

Jiménez-Jiménez, D., & Sanz-Valle, R. (2011). Innovation, organizational learning, and performance. *Journal of Business Research, 64*(4), 408–417. doi:10.1016/j.jbusres.2010.09.010

Jones, P. M. (2001). Collaborative knowledge management, social networks, and organizational learning. *Systems. Social and Internationalization Design Aspects of Human-Computer Interaction*, 2, 306–309.

Kang, S. C., Morris, S. S., & Snell, S. A. (2007). Relational archetypes, organizational learning, and value creation: Extending the human resource architecture. *Academy of Management Review*, *32*(1), 236–256. doi:10.5465/AMR.2007.23464060

Kilduff, M., & Brass, D. J. (2010). Organizational social network research: Core ideas and key debates. *The Academy of Management Annals*, *4*(1), 317–357. doi:10.1080/19416520.2010.494827

Kilduff, M., & Tsai, W. (2007). *Social networks and organizations*. Thousand Oaks, CA: Sage.

Kreiser, P. M. (2011). Entrepreneurial orientation and organizational learning: The impact of network range and network closure. *Entrepreneurship Theory and Practice*, *35*(5), 1025–1050. doi:10.1111/j.1540-6520.2011.00449.x

Lam, A. (2000). Tacit knowledge, organizational learning and societal institutions: An integrated framework. *Organization Studies*, *21*(3), 487–513. doi:10.1177/0170840600213001

Lam, A. (2003). Organizational learning in multinationals: R&D networks of Japanese and US MNEs in the UK. *Journal of Management Studies*, *40*(3), 673–703. doi:10.1111/1467-6486.00356

Lave, J., & Wenger, E. (1991). *Situated learning: Legitimate peripheral participation*. New York: Cambridge University Press. doi:10.1017/CBO9780511815355

Lesser, E., & Prusak, L. (1999). Communities of practice, social capital and organizational knowledge. *Information Systems Research*, *1*(1), 3–10.

Lesser, E. L. (2000). *Knowledge and social capital: Foundations and applications*. Woburn, MA: Butterworth-Heinemann.

Levin, D. Z., & Cross, R. (2004). The strength of weak ties you can trust: The mediating role of trust in effective knowledge transfer. *Management Science*, *50*(11), 1477–1490. doi:10.1287/mnsc.1030.0136

Levitt, B., & March, J. G. (1988). Organizational learning. *Annual Review of Sociology*, *14*(1), 319–340. doi:10.1146/annurev.so.14.080188.001535

Li, L. (2005). The effects of trust and shared vision on inward knowledge transfer in subsidiaries intra- and inter-organizational relationships. *International Business Review*, *14*(1), 77–95. doi:10.1016/j.ibusrev.2004.12.005

Lin, N. (1999). Building a network theory of social capital. *Connections*, *22*(1), 28–51.

Liu, C. L. E., Ghauri, P. N., & Sinkovics, R. R. (2010). Understanding the impact of relational capital and organizational learning on alliance outcomes. *Journal of World Business*, *45*(3), 237–249. doi:10.1016/j.jwb.2009.09.005

López, P. S., Peón, M. M. J., & Ordás, J. V. C. (2005). Organizational learning as a determining factor in business performance. *The Learning Organization*, *12*(3), 227–245. doi:10.1108/09696470510592494

Loury, G. (1992). The economics of discrimination: Getting to the core of the problem. *Harvard Journal of African American Public Policy, 1,* 91–110.

Lundberg, C. C. (1995). Learning in and by organizations: Three conceptual issues. *The International Journal of Organizational Analysis, 3*(1), 10–23. doi:10.1108/eb028821

March, J. G. (1991). Exploration and exploitation in organizational learning. *Organization Science, 2*(1), 71–87. doi:10.1287/orsc.2.1.71

Maurer, I., Bartsch, V., & Ebers, M. (2011). The value of intra-organizational social capital: How it fosters knowledge transfer, innovation performance, and growth. *Organization Studies, 32*(2), 157–185. doi:10.1177/0170840610394301

Nahapiet, J., & Ghoshal, S. (1998). Social capital, intellectual capital, and the organizational advantage. *Academy of Management Review, 23*(2), 242–266.

Newell, S., Tansley, C., & Huang, J. (2004). Social capital and knowledge integration in an ERP project team: The importance of bridging and bonding. *British Journal of Management, 15*(S1), S43–S57. doi:10.1111/j.1467-8551.2004.00405.x

Nicolini, D., & Meznar, M. B. (1995). The social construction of organizational learning: Conceptual and practical issues in the field. *Human Relations, 48*(7), 727–746. doi:10.1177/001872679504800701

Nonaka, I. (1994). A dynamic theory of organizational knowledge creation. *Organization Science, 5*(1), 14–37. doi:10.1287/orsc.5.1.14

Parise, S. (2007). Knowledge management and human resource development: An application in social network analysis methods. *Advances in Developing Human Resources, 9*(3), 359–383. doi:10.1177/1523422307304106

Portes, A. (1998). Social capital: Its origins and applications in modern sociology. *Annual Review of Sociology, 22*(1), 1–24. doi:10.1146/annurev.soc.24.1.1

Reagans, R., & McEvily, B. (2003). Network structure and knowledge transfer: The effects of cohesion and range. *Administrative Science Quarterly, 48*(2), 240–267. doi:10.2307/3556658

Reagans, R., & Zuckerman, E. W. (2001). Networks, diversity, and productivity: The social capital of corporate R&D teams. *Organization Science, 12*(4), 502–517. doi:10.1287/orsc.12.4.502.10637

Reed, M. S., Evely, A. C., Cundill, G., Fazey, I., Glass, J., Laing, A., & Stringer, L. C. et al. (2010). What is social learning? *Ecology and Society, 15*(4), 1–10. doi:10.5751/ES-03564-1504r01

Rhodes, J., Lok, P., Yu-Yuan Hung, R., & Fang, S. C. (2008). An integrative model of organizational learning and social capital on effective knowledge transfer and perceived organizational performance. *Journal of Workplace Learning, 20*(4), 245–258. doi:10.1108/13665620810871105

Salomon, G., & Perkins, D. N. (1998). Individual and social aspects of learning. *Review of Research in Education, 23,* 1–24.

Schilling, J., & Kluge, A. (2009). Barriers to organizational learning: An integration of theory and research. *International Journal of Management Reviews, 11*(3), 337–360. doi:10.1111/j.1468-2370.2008.00242.x

Schulz, M. (2001). The uncertain relevance of newness: Organizational learning and knowledge flows. *Academy of Management Journal, 44*(4), 661–681. doi:10.2307/3069409

Siemens, G. (2005). Connectivism: Learning as network-creation. *ASTD Learning News, 10*(1).

Simon, H. A. (1996). *The sciences of the artificial*. Cambridge, MA: The MIT Press.

Škerlavaj, M., Dimovski, V., & Desouza, K. C. (2010). Patterns and structures of intra-organizational learning networks within a knowledge-intensive organization. *Journal of Information Technology, 25*(2), 189–204. doi:10.1057/jit.2010.3

Smith, K. G., Collins, C. J., & Clark, K. D. (2005). Existing knowledge, knowledge creation capability, and the rate of new product introduction in high-technology firms. *Academy of Management Journal, 48*(2), 346–357. doi:10.5465/AMJ.2005.16928421

Squire, B., Cousins, P. D., & Brown, S. (2009). Cooperation and knowledge transfer within buyer–supplier relationships: The moderating properties of trust, relationship duration and supplier performance. *British Journal of Management, 20*(4), 461–477. doi:10.1111/j.1467-8551.2008.00595.x

Stata, R., & Almond, P. (1989). Organizational learning: The key to management innovation. *The Training and Development Sourcebook, 2*, 31–42.

Storberg-Walker, J., & Gubbins, C. (2007). Social networks as a conceptual and empirical tool to understand and do HRD. *Advances in Developing Human Resources, 9*(3), 291–310. doi:10.1177/1523422306304071

Swift, P. E., & Hwang, A. (2013). The impact of affective and cognitive trust on knowledge sharing and organizational learning. *The Learning Organization, 20*(1), 20–37. doi:10.1108/09696471311288500

Tsai, W. (2001). Knowledge transfer in intraorganizational networks: Effects of network position and absorptive capacity on business unit innovation and performance. *Academy of Management Journal, 44*(5), 996–1004. doi:10.2307/3069443

Van Wijk, R., Jansen, J. J., & Lyles, M. A. (2008). Inter-and intra-organizational knowledge transfer: A meta-analytic review and assessment of its antecedents and consequences. *Journal of Management Studies, 45*(4), 830–853. doi:10.1111/j.1467-6486.2008.00771.x

Von Kutzschenbach, M., & Brønn, C. (2010). You cant teach understanding, you construct it: Applying social network analysis to organizational learning. *Procedia: Social and Behavioral Sciences, 4*, 83–92. doi:10.1016/j.sbspro.2010.07.485

Wasko, M. M., & Faraj, S. (2005). Why should I share? Examining social capital and knowledge contribution in electronic networks of practice. *Management Information Systems Quarterly, 29*(1), 35–57.

Wasserman, S., & Faust, K. (2009). *Social network analysis: Methods and applications* (Vol. 8). New York, NY: Cambridge University Press.

Wirtz, J., Kuan Tambyah, S., & Mattila, A. S. (2010). Organizational learning from customer feedback received by service employees: A social capital perspective. *Journal of Service Management, 21*(3), 363–387. doi:10.1108/09564231011050814

Yli-Renko, H., Autio, E., & Sapienza, H. J. (2001). Social capital, knowledge acquisition, and knowledge exploitation in young technology-based firms. *Strategic Management Journal*, *22*(6-7), 587–613. doi:10.1002/smj.183

Yli-Renko, H., Autio, E., & Tontti, V. (2002). Social capital, knowledge, and the international growth of technology-based new firms. *International Business Review*, *11*(3), 279–304. doi:10.1016/S0969-5931(01)00061-0

KEY TERMS AND DEFINITIONS

Exploitative Learning: A learning method to acquire and utilize the existing knowledge from past experiences, routines, and norms of organizations.

Explorative Learning: A learning method used to create new ideas and knowledge to adapt to environmental change through continuous experimental activities.

Organizational Learning: A process in which organizations retain, create, and transfer organizational knowledge from their experiences responding to environmental changes.

Social Capital: Aggregates of actual and potential resources embedded in social relationships and interactions.

Social Network Analysis: A research method to measure and analyze patterns and properties of a social structure where actors interrelate and interact with each other.

Social Networks: Webs of social relationship and social ties where actors interrelate and interact with each other.

Social or Interpretative Perspective: A perspective that organizational learning uses to interpret information and build meanings within their social and organizational context.

Technical or Systems-Structural Perspective: A perspective that organizational learning uses to detect and solve problems responding to the internal and external environments through information processing.

Chapter 7
Performance Appraisal System Effectiveness:
A Conceptual Review

Chandra Sekhar Patro
GVP College of Engineering (Autonomous), Visakhapatnam, India

ABSTRACT

Performance appraisal system (PAS) has been noticed to be one of the most challenging activities of human resource management and is even a destructive effect on the relationship of employees and employers. It not only motivates the employee but also improves the productivity level of an organization. Performance appraisal is considered to be a key instrument and is practiced in almost all types of organizations, but with a few differences. In an effort to change the behaviors and attitudes of employees in the organizations, performance appraisal systems have incorporated the new values and desired behaviors. In this contemporary state the organizations have become more enthusiastic to augment the performance of their employees. The chapter aims at identifying the performance appraisal system undertaken in the organizations and its influence on employees' competency and efficiency. It emphasizes on the problems and consequences faced by the organizations, and also the best practices undertaken for successful execution.

INTRODUCTION

Performance appraisal is one of the Human Resource Management (HRM) tools used to evaluate the job performance of employees. An organization's success or failure can be determined by ways in which performance is managed and effective utilization human resources (Dessler, 2011; Mondy & Martocchio, 2015). Performance Appraisal Systems (PAS) consist of the processes of setting standards and applications, and managing the incidents related to employees' performance appraisal. Assessment of human potential is very difficult, no matter how well the appraisal process is designed and planned. However, the practice continues to generate dissatisfaction among employees and is often viewed as unfair and

DOI: 10.4018/978-1-5225-2568-4.ch007

ineffective. The success of an organization will therefore depend on its ability to measure accurately the performance of its members and use its objectivity to optimize them as a vital resource.

Performance can be defined as, "What is expected to be delivered by an individual or a set of individuals within a time frame, and could be stated in terms of results or efforts, tasks and quality, with specification of conditions under which it is to be delivered" (Kumari & Malhotra, 2012). Performance appraisal is a formal assessment and rating of individuals by their managers usually at an annual review meeting (Armstrong, 2006). Cascio (1998) defined performance appraisal as a process to improve employee's work performance by helping them realize and use their full potential in carrying out the organization's missions and to provide information to employees and managers for use in making work related decisions.

Performance appraisal is the process of identifying, observing, measuring, and developing human performance in organization. The Chartered Institute of Professional Development (CIPD) argues that, 'Performance appraisal is an opportunity for individual employees and those concerned with their performance, typically line managers, to engage in a dialogue about their performance and development, as well as the support required from the manager' (CIPD, 2013). The organizations are run and steered by the employees and it is through them the goals are set and objectives are achieved. Thus, the performance of an organization is dependent upon the total performance of all its employees (Patro, in press). It is a definite instrument in setting job standards, appraising worker's genuine performance comparative to those standards, and providing feedback to the workers with the drive of inspiring the workers to eradicate the insufficiencies in the performance.

HISTORICAL BACKGROUND

The evaluation of job performance has been called by many different names throughout the years as a tool of management, a control process, a critical element in human resources allocation, and many others. The first appraisal systems were just methods for determining whether the salary of the employees in the organizations was fair or not. Later, some empirical studies have shown that reduction or future pay were not the main effects of the process (Cardy & Dobbins, 1994). However, appraisal has been present throughout history and has advanced significantly over time. The earliest evidence of performance appraisal was seen in the 3rd century when a Chinese philosopher Sin Yu criticized a biased rater of the Wei Dynasty on the grounds that the Imperial Rater of Nine Grades rarely rates men by their merits but always rates them according to his likes and dislikes (Patten, 1977).

Furthermore, appraisal was witnessed in 1648 when it was stated the Dublin Evening Post evaluated legislators using a rating scale based on personal qualities (Wiese & Buckley, 1998). Appraisal became a more formal process, firstly in the 1800s, when a General in the US Army submitted an assessment of his soldiers to the War Department. The Army General used a global rating, which defined his men as for example 'a good-natured man' or 'a knave despised by all' (Bellows & Estep, 1954). The first recorded appraisal system in industry was by Robert Owen in New Lanark Mills, Scotland around 1800. He used character books and blocks to rate staff that records each worker's daily report. The blocks were colored differently on every side to represent an assessment of the worker rating them from strong to weak and were displayed in the employee's workplace (Cardy & Dobbins, 1994).

Following the success of the appraisal system, some US corporations tested this technique within their organizations. The tools for rating evolved over time from Global Rating towards Man-to-Man Rating and then to Trait-based Rating. These appraisal tools tended to focus on past actions instead of future goals and were always conducted by the supervisor with little input from the employee (Wiese & Buckley, 1998). Therefore, a change was brought about in the tools used and consequently the critical incident and forced choice methods were introduced. These methods were more advanced and substantive than previous approaches, but their intricacy meant they are not readily used in today's world (Flanagan, 1954).

The popularity of performance appraisal in an industry started growing in the early 1950s (Spriegel, 1962). Smith and Kendall (1963) created the Behaviourally Anchored Rating Scales (BARS) hypothesized to be superior to alternative evaluation methods. This replaced numerical or adjective ratings used in the graphic or trait rating scales, with behavioural examples of actual work behaviours (Schwab, Heneman, & DeCotiis, 1975). One of the most influential events in the evolution of performance appraisal was the legal requirements that changed how appraisals could be conducted. The enactment of the 1964 Civil Rights Act in the United States, which prohibited administrative action on the basis of colr, religious beliefs, sex, and so forth, thus leading to a legal use for performance appraisal. This legal constraint was the final blow to subjective, trait-based approaches (Banner & Cooke, 1984). The practice to formally appraise employees has existed for centuries, but the interest in the area has grown rapidly in the last 40 years. However, performance appraisal became a management tool used widely in businesses around the 1980s (Taylor, 2005).

THEORETICAL REVIEW

For decades, performance appraisal has received considerable attention in the literature from both researchers and practitioners alike. There is a considerable gap between theory and practice, and human resource specialists are not making full use of the psychometric tools available (Bernardin & Klatt, 1985). The main developmental uses include improving work performance, communicating expectations, determining employee potential, and aiding employee counseling. Other common administrative uses included promotions, lay-offs, transfers, terminations, and validations of hiring decisions (Maroney & Buckley, 1992; Patro, in press). The usefulness of performance appraisal as a managerial decision tool depends partly on whether or not the performance appraisal system is able to provide accurate data on employee performance (Poon, 2004). PAS provides an opportunity for the management to recall, as well as to provide, feedback to the employees regarding their performance so that they can correct their mistake in future and acquire new skills (Varkkey, Koshy, & Oburoi, 2008).

According to Vanci-Osam and Askit (2000), an operative appraisal system delivers huge potential advantages to both individual and organization because regular feedback on performance improves the ideas, expectations, and quality of work. Youngcourt, Leiva, and Jones (2007) suggest the common purpose of performance appraisal tends to be targeted at the measurement of individuals and is the central component of performance management; therefore, it is must for an organization. Caruth and Humphreys (2008) add to this viewpoint that a PAS includes characteristics to meet organizational needs and those of its stakeholders.

The most common to almost all purposes of performance appraisal is the concept of improving performance and developing people. Sanjeevni (2012) disclose that the employees perform their duties well and performance appraisal continuously motivates the employees to achieve their goals indirectly helping the organization to achieve its goals. Employees should be praised in public and corrected in private. According to Bateman and Snell (2011), the primary one focuses on motivators such as the nature of the job, duties and responsibilities, and job satisfaction to determine motivation. The second one known as hygiene factors includes working circumstances, compensation, supervision and the policy of an organization.

Kondrasuk (2011) suggested that performance appraisal, even at its best condition, does not work and in the worst case, can damage morale communication and relationship within the organization. Kavanagh, Brown, and Benson (2007) also asserted that in the performance appraisal process it is likely the evaluation is subjectively biased by an individual's emotional state; managers may consider variable codes and standards for different employees which results in an inconsistent, biased, invalid, and unacceptable appraisal. Noe, Hollenberg, Gerhart, and Wright (2009) reported that an employee must understand the employees from her/his own perception and understanding about the organizational systems' fairness based on the system's procedures, outcomes and managers' methods in treating employees when applying those procedures. Sudin (2011) stated that "organizational justice and fairness" are the key elements of performance appraisal that determine the success and acceptance by employees which eventually lead organizations to the achievement of their business goals.

The assessment of employee performance is one of the most common practices in almost every organization; therefore, performance appraisal is an essential procedure for the better performance of employees and the organization itself (Karimi, Malik, & Hussain, 2011). Many businesses regularly use performance appraisal scores to determine the distribution of pay, promotions, and other rewards; however, few organizations attempt to evaluate how employee perceptions of performance appraisal fairness impact employee attitudes and performance (Swiercz, Bryan, Eagle, Bizzotto, & Renn, 2012).

Organizations must take time to question the way things are always done and build a performance appraisal methodology that is fair and effective (Pritchard, 2007). Long, Kowang, Ismail, and Rasid (2013) stated that the employees' perceptions of outcome fairness depend largely on their judgment about the consequences of a decision and the procedure to make such decisions. The understanding and perceptions of performance appraisal purpose have been connected to employee satisfaction with both appraisal and supervisor.

SIGNIFICANCE OF PERFORMANCE APPRAISAL

Performance appraisal was once the unquestioned way of doing things and a formal procedure in which the employees and managers communicated each other for an annual evaluation. The limitations of performance assessment, such as inflated ratings, lack of consistency, and the politics of assessment often lead to their abandonment (Tziner, Latham, Price, & Haccoun, 1996). Poor ratings detract from organizational uses and increase employee mistrust in the performance appraisal system (Tziner & Murphy, 1999). But today, with the widespread emphasis on teamwork, shared leadership, and an ongoing struggle to find and retain qualified employees, it is a model that is falling increasingly out of favor. The success of appraisal scheme depends on how it is perceived by the employees and for whom it is intended, among other factors.

Some facts based on the extant literature are discussed:

1. Performance appraisal acts as a basis for promotion, transfer, or termination of employees in an organization.
2. This helps the employees to recognize their strengths and weaknesses, and enlighten as to what performance is expected from them.

3. It helps in identifying the need for training and development to the employees, and prepares them for meeting the challenge in their current and future employment.
4. Appraisal also helps employees to internalize the norms and values of the organization.
5. Performance Appraisal helps in creating optimistic and healthy environment in an organization.

PERFORMANCE APPRAISAL SYSTEM CHARACTERISTICS

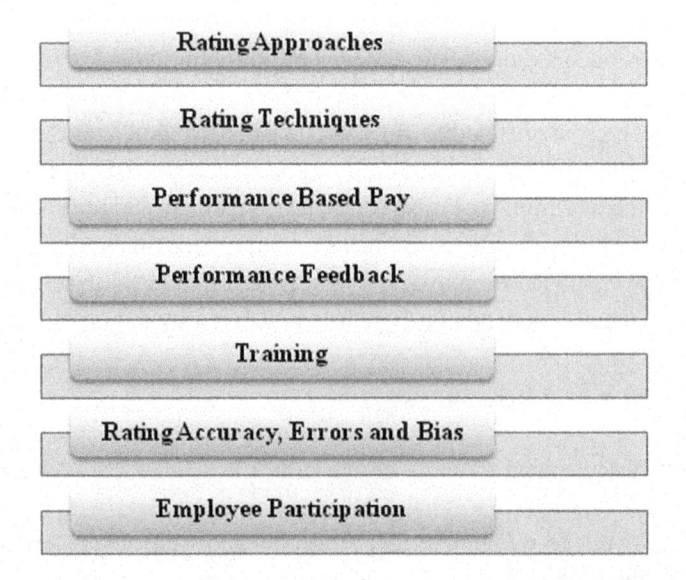

Performance appraisal systems must be effective and successful; otherwise, they are a waste of time and money. What makes them effective is their potential to improve employee performance. However, performance appraisal will only lead to behavioral change if its users accept the system. The following characteristics of performance appraisal have proven to partly determine the effectiveness by affecting acceptance is discussed (see Figure.1):

Rating Approaches

Latham and Wexley (1977) state there are mainly three different rating approaches:

1. The cost-related approach means that profits, product quantity/quality, and return on investment are taken as criteria to appraise an individual.
2. The judgement approach is generally an inadequate measure of individual job performance as it provides no information to the employee why he is effective or ineffective, and these measures are also contaminated by other factors over which the individual has little or no control.

Figure 1. Performance Appraisal System Characteristics

- Rating Approaches
- Rating Techniques
- Performance Based Pay
- Performance Feedback
- Training
- Rating Accuracy, Errors and Bias
- Employee Participation

Performance Appraisal System Effectiveness

3. The behavior approach is a more direct measure of what the employee does or has to change to become more effective.

There are four different single performance appraisal sources possible (Martell & Leavitt, 2002; Dalton, 1996; Berry, 2003):

1. The most common source of performance feedback is the immediate supervisor of the employee because the supervisor is expected to have the basic knowledge and ability to conduct performance appraisal on the subordinates.
2. The second possible source include peers of the employee as they are in a position to observe and often are aware of how well their colleagues perform on the job.
3. Third, performance can be evaluated by the employee. This process is referred to as self-appraisal, and is often conducted when employees work alone or are relatively independent of others.
4. The fourth possible feedback source is subordinates and is thus only suitable for employees who actually have subordinates.

The presented single sources can be combined to multi-source or 360-degree performance appraisal systems. If there is a complete combination of upward, downward, lateral, and self-appraisal, then this system is called 360-degree performance appraisal (Wise, 1998). Even though this system has the potential to improve managerial skills, it is not without problems. This approach is more effective and can be used by the organizations for better results.

Rating Techniques

Rating techniques can be distinguished on basis of several factors (Berry, 2003): using a rating scale, ease of development, quantity and type of information yielded, and the purpose of rating. There as wide variety of different techniques, but the techniques (graphic rating scale, behaviorally anchored rating scale, behavioral observation scale and mixed standard scale) often used by the organizations are discussed.

1. The most common way for a rater to express a judgement of a ratee's job performance is with a Graphic Rating Scale (GRS). Such scales provide a continuum from high to low performance levels concerning an overall performance (Berry, 2003). This technique is simple, easily implemented, and cost-effective. The results are standardized and allow making comparisons between ratees (Parril, 1999).
2. The behaviorally anchored rating scale (BARS) was developed to make the rating task easier what in turn is expected to result in more accurate ratings. BARS use behavioral statements to illustrate multiple levels of performance for each element of performance (Tziner & Kopelman, 2002; Harrell & Wright, 1990). Parrill (1999) identified that if BARS are developed by the same people who will eventually use them, this result in a sensitive understanding, awareness and insight, and anchors are formulated in language or terminology of raters.
3. The behavioural observation scale (BOS) is a procedure that was also based on BARS rationale for reducing subjectivity and error in performance appraisal (Latham and Wexley, 1977). Tziner and Kopelman (2002) additionally state that BOS appears more likely to minimize barriers in the com-

munication process between superiors and subordinates because it pinpoints for both the specific organizational expectations and performance requirements.

4. In the Mixed Standard Scale (MSS), three performance standards (average, superior and inferior performance) are developed per behaviour dimension. The standards for all behavioural dimensions are then randomly sequenced to form a MSS (Benson et al., 1988). This technique aims at ensuring that the rater does not simply use an overall impression of the ratee and produce a rating that contains error (Berry, 2003).

In summary, there is no clear picture of which type of scale is the best. Because different scale formats elicit judgement processes, the acceptability and effectiveness of various formats varies across individuals (Härtel, 1993). According to Jacobs et al. (1980), it is further especially important that the job behaviors included in the rating process are relevant to successful job performance, evaluate the magnitude of importance and frequency of occurrence for behaviour rated.

Performance Based Pay

One widely accepted notion for improving individual performance is tying pay to performance in order to increase productivity (Swiercz, Icenogle, Bryan, & Renn, 1993). Performance based pay is a system which specifically seeks to reward employees for their contribution as individuals or as a part of a group, or to reward employees on account of the organizations overall positive performance (De Silva, 1998). Implementation of a performance based incentive plan proved to lead to the attraction and retention of more productive employees (Banker et al., 2001). Critics argue that performance-based compensation programs encourage competition rather than collaboration (Solmon & Podgursky, 2000). Furthermore, Davis and Landa (1999) state that money will buy only a minimum level of commitment. Therefore, commitment is the key factor in an organizations' success because motivated employees are most likely to make significant contributions to the success of an organization.

Performance Feedback

Generally, feedback to an employee aims at improving performance effectiveness through stimulating behavioral change. The manner in which employees receive feedback on their job performance is a major factor in determining the success of the performance appraisal system (Harris, 1988). As feedback may strike at the core of an individual's personal belief, it is crucial to set conditions of feedback so the ratee is able to tolerate, hear, and own discrepant information (Dalton, 1996). Kondrasuk, Pearson, Tanner, Maruska, and Dwyer (2005) also propose to integrate the process of feedback into the daily interactions of supervisors and subordinate in a way that more frequent but less formal meetings. Furthermore, performance feedback alone generates improvements to ratees` organizational commitment, and particularly to work satisfaction (Tziner & Kopelman, 2002). In summary, giving feedback in an appropriate manner is a key factor in determining the employee's willingness to adapt behaviour.

Training

A rater must be trained to observe, gather, process, and integrate behaviour-relevant information in order to improve performance appraisal effectiveness. Rudner (1992) proposes that training should have three goals:

1. It should familiarize judges with the measure they will be employing.
2. It must ensure that judges understand the sequence of operations they must perform.
3. It should explain how the judges should interpret any normative data given.

Tziner and Kopelman (2002) state that training provides trainees with broad opportunities to practice the specified skills, provide trainees with feedback on their practice, and a comprehensive acquaintance with the appropriate behaviors to be observed, and also avoids errors. Reinke (2003) states there must be an increased focus on the interpersonal issues surrounding appraisal. Harris (1988) points out that continued training is needed in areas such as goal-setting and monitoring performance on a frequent basis, and personal and interactional skills. If implemented this way, employees are less confused, less disappointed concerning measures, and are more aware about the intentions of performance appraisal.

Rating Accuracy, Errors, and Bias

The accuracy of ratings is determined by the reliability and validity of the measurement at hand. Rating accuracy is important, even if insufficient condition for feedback to positively affect future performance (Jelley & Goffin, 2001). Unfortunately, there are several different error phenomena which all poses a threat to the accuracy of ratings (Jacobs et al., 1980). Smith (2001) describes bias as an over or under identification of evaluations relative to performance for some groups because of identification that the rater may have toward his or her own or toward a reference group. Even though bias and errors never can be totally removed, there is a chance to minimize them (Martell & Leavitt, 2002). Concerning the acceptance of a PAS, it is furthermore necessary that appraisees perceive the rating as relatively unbiased, while appraisers must feel able to implement the appraisal system as intended.

Employee Participation

Roberts (2003) proposes genuine employee participation in several aspects of the appraisal process because it has the potential to mitigate may of the dysfunctions of traditional performance appraisal systems as well as to engender a more human and ethical decision-making process. Cox (2000) adds that these positive effects are especially generalisable to the design and implementation of pay systems. In summary, given the appropriate atmosphere and culture in an organization, employee participation will enhance motivation, feelings of fairness and overall acceptance of the performance appraisal process.

BENEFITS OF PERFORMANCE APPRAISAL SYSTEM

An effective performance appraisal system will bring benefits to the staff member being appraised, the manager completing the appraisal and the organization as a whole. The benefits of performance appraisal systems at different levels are discussed below.

Benefits to Organization

Performance appraisal could be an effective source of management information given to employees. Outcomes of performance appraisal can lead to improvements in work performance and, therefore, overall business performance. Martin and Jackson (2002) outlined four different benefits for the organization. These include the targeted training approach, future employee promotion decisions, effective bases for reward decisions, and improved retention of employees. Mullins (1999) states that performance appraisal can help to identify inefficient work practices or reveal potential problems which are restricting the progress of an organization. Derven (1990) believes there is a straight connection between the job of an individual and the strategic goals of the organization and this can directly increase the profitability of the organization. According to Fisher (1995), the benefits include:

1. Improved performance due to effective communication.
2. Increased sense of cohesiveness and better employee-employer relationships.
3. Training and Development needs are identified.
4. Competitive advantage in the market place.
5. Employee satisfaction as a sense that employees are valued is spread.

Benefits to Manager/Supervisor

Performance appraisal provides a clear target of job standards and priorities and ensures more trust on the relationship of manager–worker. The annual meeting gives an opportunity to the manager to formally recognize good performance and this would lead to more motivation from the employees (Derven, 1990). Supervisors focus on behaviors and results, rather than on personalities. Such systems support ongoing communication, feedback and dialogue about organizational goals. For the manager carrying out the appraisal, the benefits include (Fisher, 1995; CIPD, 2012; Jackson & Schuller, 2002):

1. Identification of high performers and poor performers.
2. Identification of strengths, weaknesses and development areas.
3. Better relationship with employees and trust.
4. Stronger knowledge about what is going on in the organization.
5. Facilitate management in decisions including pay rises, promotions, redundancies, etc.

Benefits to Employee

Performance appraisal takes into account the past performance of the employees and focuses on the improvement of the future performance of the employees. It gives the staff the opportunity to express their ideas and expectations for the strategic goals of the company (Mullins, 1999). Employees can understand what is expected from them and the consequences of their performance. Appraisal is a motivation for the employee, who performs well in the present to go on doing so and in the future (Derven, 1990). Additionally, enhancing motivation appraisal is about involvement in the so-called "Big Picture" of responsibility, encouragement, recognition for effective delivery, and effort (Martin & Jackson, 2002). For the employees being appraised, the benefits include (Fisher, 1995; Sudin, 2011; CIPD, 2012):

1. Enhanced relationships with line managers.
2. Increased job satisfaction.
3. Better understanding of management expectations.
4. Greater knowledge of strengths and weaknesses.
5. Helps to align the individual performances with the organizational goals.

CONSEQUENCES OF PERFORMANCE APPRAISAL

Haberstroh (1965) drew two broad conclusions: First, performance reporting is omnipresent and necessary. Second, almost every individual instance of performance reporting has something wrong with it. In this regard, there are several positive and negative consequences of performance appraisal system (Mohrman, Jr., Resnick-West, & Lawler III, 1989). The following list consists of some positive and negative consequences relevant to the performance appraisal.

Positive Consequences

1. The person whose performance is appraised may develop an increased motivation to perform effectively.
2. The self-esteem of the individual being appraised may increase.
3. The job of an individual being appraised may be clarified and better defined.
4. Valuable communication can occur among the individuals taking part in appraisal (subordinate and superior).
5. Rewards such as pay and promotion can be distributed on a fair and credible basis.
6. Organizational goals can be made clearer, and can be more readily accepted.
7. Valuable appraisal information can allow the organization to do better manpower planning, test validation, and development of training programs.

Negative Consequences

1. The self-esteem of an individual being appraised and the individual doing the appraisal may be damaged.
2. Much amount of time may be wasted.
3. The relationship between the individuals involved may deteriorate thereby creating organizational conflicts.
4. Performance motivation may be lowered for many reasons, including the feeling that poor performance means no rewards (i.e. biased evaluation including favoritism towards some employees).
5. Funds may be wasted on forms, training, and a host of support services.

FACTORS INFLUENCING INSTITUTIONALIZATION OF PERFORMANCE APPRAISAL

The chapter focuses on the various organizational, cultural, and political factors that have been influencing and arguably decrementing to some extent the degree of institutionalization of the performance appraisal system. For each of these major factors, a number of sub-factors are referred that can influence positively or negatively in determining the extent of institutionalization of the appraisal system. Therefore, the following discussion is based on each of the three main factors in a theoretical perspective (see Figure 2).

Organizational Factors

In understanding and judging the effectiveness of a PAS, the role played by the organization is crucial (Daley, 1992; Hyde, 1982; Gilbert, 1982; Murphy & Cleveland, 1990). Some essentials that influence how an individual perceives appraisal systems at the organizational level are discussed below.

1. **Implementers Competency and Disposition:** Competency is the capacity that exists in a person that leads to behaviour and meets the job demands within the parameters of the organizational environment and that, in turn, brings about desired results (Galpin, 1997; Boyatzis, 1982). The disposition of implementers is one of the most important components in the policy implementation process. Those responsible in implementing changes in the organization must possess or have access to a wide range of skills, resources, support and knowledge (Van Meter & Van Horn, 1975). Therefore, it is vital that all factors need to be taken into consideration when determining how the competence and disposition of the implementers affect the institutionalization of the performance appraisal system.

Figure 2. Factors Influencing Institutionalization of Performance Appraisal

Organizational Factors
- Implementers Competency and Disposition
- Leadership
- Socialization and Commitment
- Learning History

Cultural Factors
- Avoid Conflicts and Subordinate/Superior Relationships
- Motivation and Reward

Political Factors
- Political Will and Symbolism
- Political Accountability

2. **Leadership:** According to Wart (2003), "effective leadership provides higher-quality and more efficient goods and services; it provides a sense of cohesiveness, personal development, and higher levels of satisfaction among those conducting the work; and it provides an overarching sense of direction and vision, an alignment with the environment, a healthy mechanism for innovation and creativity, and a resource for invigorating the organizational culture". Lawler III (2001) has expressed "without leadership at the top, and a senior management group that models good performance appraisal behavior, it is impossible to have an effective performance management system". Therefore, the leaders' disposition and contribution towards the appraisal system can play a vital role in the success of the appraisal system.

3. **Socialization and Commitment:** When an employee joins an organization, adaptation to the new environment is not automatic or immediate as the individual must experience the phases of socialization. Socialization commonly refers to the efforts of the organization to 'teach the ropes' to the newcomer (Pepper, 1995). In its most general sense, organizational socialization is the process by which an individual acquires the social knowledge and skills necessary to assume an organizational role (Van Maanen & Schein, 1979). When the employee adapts to the organizational rules, norms and values through the socialization process and forms a specific identity, a certain level of commitment could be identified.

4. **Learning History:** Learning in organizations relates to how the organization deliberately changes and adapts over time in terms of structures, functions, values, attitudes and behavior (Barrados & Mayne, 2003). In other words, organization learning inhibits or exhibits the future reforms of the organization. Organizational learning involves improving the action through better knowledge and understanding. In the case of successful learning, the lessons drawn are thereafter stored in the organizational memory in the form of routines and procedures which are applied in the future. Once such rules and procedures are well established, they guide human behaviour as well as shape their preferences, which eventually lead to successful institutionalization.

Cultural Factors

Culture is a pattern of shared basic assumptions the group learned as it solved its problems of external adaptation and internal integration that has worked well enough to be considered valid and, therefore, to be taught to new members as the correct way to perceive, think, and feel in relation to those problem (Schein, 1992). The two broad dimensions used in this respect include "Culture is what organization has" (Deal & Kennedy, 1982; Kanter, 1983; Ouchi, 1981; Peters & Waterman, 1982), and "Culture is what organization is" (Conrad, 1994; Shapiro & Schall, 1990). Furthermore, Jamil (1994) argues that if a culture is what organization has, then there will be several variations among different organizations in a given society. On the contrary, if culture is what organization is, then it is more likely that one will observe more variations across different societies.

1. **Avoid Conflicts and Subordinate/Superior Relationships:** Societal values will have some impact on the nature of the relationship between superiors and subordinates (Murphy & Cleveland, 1995). According to Hofstede (1991), individualism and collectivism express how the individual affiliates himself or herself to the society. Individualism pertains to societies in which the ties between individuals are loose (i.e., everyone is expected to look after themselves and their family). Collectivism as its opposite pertains to societies in which people from birth onwards are integrated

into strong, cohesive in-groups, which throughout a person's lifetime continue to protect them in exchange for unquestionable loyalty (Vallance, 1999). Therefore, having a harmonious relationship between subordinate and superior is given considerable importance.

2. **Motivation and Reward:** Motivation is probably one of the major factors that influence the institutionalization of appraisal systems. According to Pheysey (1993), culture affects motivation through preferences for extrinsic or intrinsic motivators. A person is intrinsically motivated if the individual engages in an activity to feel competent and self-determining in relation to the activity. Extrinsic motivation, by contrast, comes through reward external to the job itself (Deci, 1980; DeVoe & Iyengar, 2004; Hernandez & Iyengar, 2001). Greater satisfaction, commitment and loyalty mean that the individual will stay in the organization longer and will share the values and norms of the organization thereby striving to improve the performance of the organization.

Political Factors

How managers respond to the political environments and how those environments influence the organization is of great importance. For the purpose, two political essentials are considered as discussed below.

1. **Political Will and Symbolism:** Politics is expressed through symbolism. Rather little that is political involves the use of direct force, and though material resources are crucial to the political process, even their distribution is largely shaped through symbolic means (Kertzer, 1988). Symbolism shape political discourse and political struggle is partly a struggle to control such discourse (Drescher, Advid, & Allan, 1982). In the political arena, "action is choice, choice is made in terms of expectations about its consequences, meanings are organized to affect choices, and symbols are curtains that obscure the real politics, or artifacts of an effort to make decisions (March & Olsen, 1989).
2. **Political Accountability:** Political accountability is about how those who are charged with drafting and/or implementing policy owe explanations to the individuals (Glynn & Murphy, 1996). The importance and significance of accountability curtail from the prevailing theoretical contention that accountability forms the preliminary requirement of democratic governance as it assures the continuity of organizational legitimacy, control of financial resources, and employee interests (Ho, 1999). It can be argued that successfully institutionalizing a performance appraisal system is of utmost importance in obtaining bureaucratic accountability or making organization accountable.

DRAWBACKS OF INEFFECTIVE PERFORMANCE APPRAISAL

The appraisal process can become a source of extreme dissatisfaction when employees believe the system is biased, political, or irrelevant and thus are often perceived as both inaccurate and unfair (Skarlicki & Folger, 1997). Cardy and Dobbins (1994) suggested that "with dissatisfaction and feelings of unfairness in process and inequity in evaluations, any performance appraisal system will be doomed to failure". Tziner, Prince, and Murphy (1997) revealed that political considerations in performance appraisal also makes ineffective. Gupta and Swaroop (2012) identified certain drawbacks of ineffective performance appraisal system as discussed.

1. **Unfair Rating:** Employees may consider a performance rating unfair if the rater is considered to be attempting to avoid conflict by inflating ratings; to play favorites; or to yield to political pressures to distort ratings (McCarthy, 1995). If an employee views the PAS as unfair, there is a reduction in motivation to change behavior, a rejection of the usefulness and validity of the information, and an unwillingness to accept decisions based on appraisal information.
2. **Lack of Trust:** For the supervisors, a decrease in trust in the appraisal process results in an increase in the leniency of ratings (Roberts, 1994). Employees are dissatisfied with the ways in which their contributions are appraised. The roots of this dissatisfaction are a lack of transparency, lack of faith, limited opportunities for career development and inconsistent managerial support (Longenecker & Goff, 1992) makes the employees think that their manager does not write appraisals based on employee's performance, but instead bias their decisions based on their personal relations with employees.
3. **Time Consuming Process:** The highly complex questions which they have no answers to or highly complex competencies which they have never heard of confuse them (Longenecker & Goff, 1992). Thus, employees think appraisal is a disturbance to their normal work.
4. **Difficulty in Writing Appraisals:** Many employees have poor language skills and they are unable to communicate their performance in right language and support with data. This difficulty is further increased when they find extremely difficult questions/ terminology in the appraisal (Longenecker & Goff, 1992).
5. **Lack of Feedback After Appraisal:** Many organizations do not provide feedback to employees on their performance (Longenecker & Goff, 1992). In a paper-based appraisal process, the appraisal usually find its place in the human resource closet. Employees desire feedback not only about how they're performing, but also as to where they fit in terms of organizational plans for the future (Gupta & Swaroop, 2012).

As per the extant literature, the following are the causes of employee dissatisfaction: the manager lacked information on the employee's actual performance, lack of regular feedback, and a perception of appraisals being "political". This suggests companies must re-examine this matter to explore issues, perhaps with paper-based processes or an online system. From the views presented here, the roots of dissatisfaction are a lack of transparency, limited opportunities for career development and inconsistent managerial support.

BEST PRACTICES FOR EFFECTIVE PERFORMANCE APPRAISAL

The performance appraisal process has become the heart of the HRM system in the organizations. Appropriate selection and right execution of the performance appraisal tools will benefit both the employees' and the management of the organizations. Murphy and Cleveland (1995) stated that "a system that did nothing more than allow the making of correct promotion decisions would be a good system, even if the indices used to measure performance were inaccurate or measured the wrong set of constructs." The appraisal of employees' performance is really necessary and there is no better way to obtain the benefits. The best practices of a fair performance appraisal process as shown in Figure 3 are discussed below.

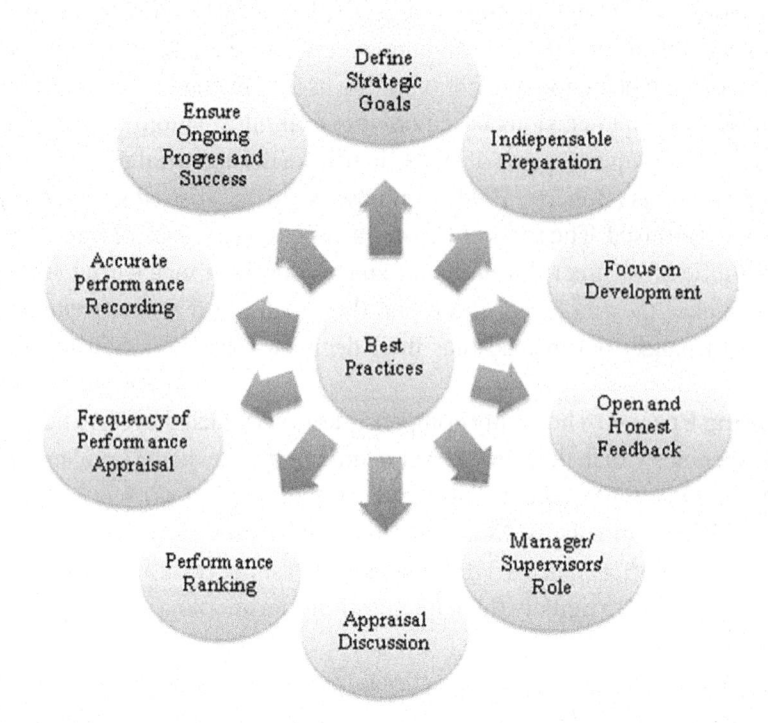

Figure 3. Best Practices for Effective Performance Appraisal

1. **Define Strategic Goals:** Individual goals should draw from strategic direction and overall organizational goals. Typically, the process should start with senior functional managers setting goals for their departments, based upon organization-wide goals that support the business strategy. This could help employees to see how their individual targets relate with the organizations objectives on a higher level (Murphy & Cleveland, 1998). Another aspect is that goals should be written down objectively and clearly so that the expectations of the employee and the manager could be aligned (Latham & Yukl, 1975).
2. **Indispensable Preparation:** Effective appraisal processes require serious preparation work to be done both by the employee and the manager. They should know why appraisal exists and the objectives and the expected results. Obviously, when this information comes from the top it demonstrates management focus and relevance of the process for the overall company performance (Murphy & Cleveland, 1995). Generally, from appraisal discussion the employees can learn where they currently stand versus manager's expectations, and what they could do differently in order to address any performance or behavioral gaps.
3. **Focus on Development:** In performance appraisal process, the HR department should permit time for both parties to discuss development areas and to design learning interventions that will help employees to address their current skills gaps. Use of the GROW model (Whitmore, 1996) could provide a good structure for the development part of the appraisal discussion. It contains Goals (what do you want to be), Reality (where are you now), Option (how could you get there) and Wrap-up (what would you do) and could be used as a basis for effective communication in the appraisal meeting.

4. **Open and Honest Feedback:** The employee believes that objectivity in the assessment process will improve by collecting feedback from different sources and ensures all elements of performance are covered. It helps employees to understand their strengths and weaknesses and the areas in which they need to improve their performance (Lepsinger & Lucia, 1997). Subjective, unsubstantiated comments, vague statements and criticism delivered in a de-motivating manner can compromise the overall process. Credible and specific feedback could play a positive role in boosting individual confidence and motivation (Dechev & Kamphorst, 2010). The best practice can be open and honest feedback from employees to their managers without fear of consequences demonstrates mutual respect.
5. **Manager/Supervisors' Role:** Managing expectations and performance of another person is not an easy task because it requires the manager to know how to achieve goals through the subordinates. Supervisor's attitudes and skills in the appraisal process are crucial - care, empathy, listening, coaching and influencing, asking the right questions, paraphrasing, summarizing, and so forth (Armstrong & Baron, 1998). Managers must understand the psychology of human behaviors by observing employee reactions. They should know what factors could be motivating for each individual, how to coach and develop as well how to resolve conflict situation.
6. **Appraisal Discussion:** Preparation for the appraisal meeting and the atmosphere are important factors for the success of conversation. The manager should begin the discussion with job requirements, strengths and accomplishments observed in the past period. Walters (1995) states the employee should talk 70-80% of the time about how they feel, what achievements they have made, what was not achieved and why, what career objectives they have and how they see their future in the organization. Best practice is at the end of the discussion both parties to reach an agreement based on trust and commitment to fulfilling their own part of the agreement.
7. **Performance Ranking:** Measuring performance of an individual is a very difficult activity. The performance should be measured against defined success criteria, following the same format for everyone. Before the appraisal, the supervisor should gather information on the employee's work performance by seeking input from other people. Information references include feedback from other supervisors, managers and peers (Dechev & Kamphorst, 2010). The supervisor must weigh these and make his/her own assessment of the employee. The evaluation of performance should be based on facts which recognize and acknowledge achievements.
8. **Frequency of Performance Appraisal:** There is a wide spread opinion that an annual meeting to evaluate progress does not have the same benefits as an ongoing dialogue and, formal and informal feedback. Reviewing performance on continuous basis will allow a bad performance or existing issues to be identified and corrective measures to be designed at an earlier stage. Additionally, tasks and targets should be checked out several times a year (Murphy & Cleveland, 1995). Some organizations are moving towards conducting performance reviews twice a year, small numbers of companies do it on more frequent basis.
9. **Accurate Performance Recording:** Documentation is important to support performance decisions, and notes should be written with intent to be shared (Reeves, 2002). The performance log record is kept by manager and employee, and is considered during promotion or development opportunity for the employee. It should be objective, based on observations, comment job-related behaviors only, include achievements and deficiency areas and if applicable disciplinary actions should be logged (Dechev & Kamphorst, 2010). Today online administration in electronic systems are made easy to

remind the managers and employees automatically when reviews are due, late, or incomplete, and HR professionals no longer must track down the missing reports.

10. **Ensure Ongoing Progress and Success:** The performance management process must add value; otherwise, problems with resistance and non-participation will appear. Participation and support from top level and senior management is also important. The effectiveness of the process increases if there is a culture that supports honest communication, where employees can openly consider how to make improvements in order to move forward (Murphy & Cleveland, 1995). Another way of improving efficiency is to make a regular review of the process through surveys and questionnaires or obtain opinions through focus group discussions.

Performance appraisal reports must be based on SWOT (Strengths, Weaknesses, Opportunities, Threats) techniques and provide scope for further career development in the organization. For better results, a 360-degree system of evaluation can be adopted by the organization. Performance of the employees should be evaluated taking all the aspects into consideration and should not be restricted to only one criteria. Performance appraisal is not a one-time affair; for better results, the organization should do the appraisals at frequent intervals. Rating employees based on personal preferences, likes, dislikes must be avoided so that employees gain confidence on the system of appraisal and are motivated to work hard and provide results.

FUTURE IMPLICATIONS

Despite the countless hurdles faced in the implementation of the appraisal system, optimism has been expressed by the organizations. Most accept there lies a long road ahead for the appraisal system to be fully institutionalized across organizations. The need for assessing the performance of employees is believed to be a necessity in this modern age where concepts such as fairness, transparency, accountability, employee development, and mutual involvement are being stressed (Gangwani, 2012). Greater employee participation creates an atmosphere of cooperation, reduces tension and rater – ratee conflict which could be caused by the appraisal (Rankin & Kleiner, 1988). However, the reason for the present lack of institutionalization is mainly because a number of cultural, organizational and political factors are affecting and in most cases hindering the successful implementation of the appraisal system.

Although with the current difficulties, most organizations are in favor of having an appraisal system that can access the employees fairly and are linked to promotion and other rewards. Therefore, the optimism currently shared by most organizations must be taken as a generating force that will push for the appraisal system to succeed in the future. The organization needs to improve the appraisal system accordingly if it is to be successful in carrying out its objective and ensure the system spends more time helping to develop employees, from identifying training needs, providing coaching, and giving more accurate, constructive feedback (Bacal, 1999).

Future researchers may consider exploring the research implications of the organizations practicing the best techniques in making the performance appraisal process more effective. This effort could track differences in the variables, which would help to understand more fully the factors contributing to the effectiveness of performance appraisal system in different organizational sectors.

CONCLUSION

In today's global hypercompetitive scenario, human resources must be very committed to the organization and the organization must be committed to the employee and their overall manpower of the organization. The PAS plays a very vital role in the organization in achieving the goals of the organization. Management must participate with the workforce to achieve the objectives and goal of the organization. The ultimate purpose of the PAS is to allow employees to improve continuously. The predetermined goal of an organization can be achieved through the efforts of human resources and the performance evaluation and feedback with the employees can help in gaining the results for the organization as a whole. The various techniques of performance appraisal can be deployed in the corporation for the betterment of the organization and wellness of the organization.

The fairness of a PAS has been recognized as an important effect on the success of any organization because perceived fairness is connected to the acceptance of appraisal system and eventually, the performance of employees and organization. The understanding and perceptions of performance appraisal purpose have been connected to employee satisfaction with both appraisal and supervisor. The main job of human resources is to judge the behavior of employees and overall performance within the organization so as to ensure the accomplishment of tasks.

The process of performance appraisal must be conducted for the benefit of management while simultaneously motivating employees. Therefore, the purpose of performance appraisal may affect all dimensions of employee's perception and reactions toward performance appraisal. Finally, this will directly affect the organization as the performance of an organization is the performance of its employees.

REFERENCES

Armstrong, M. (2006). *A Handbook of Human Resource Management Practice* (10th ed.). London: Kogan Page, Ltd.

Armstrong, M., & Baron, A. (1998). *Performance management: The new realities*. London: Institute of Personnel and Development.

Bacal, R. (1999). *Performance management*. New York: McGraw-Hill.

Banker, R. D., Lee, S. Y., Potter, G., & Srinivasan, D. (2000). An empirical analysis of continuing improvements following the implementation of a performance-based compensation plan. *Journal of Accounting and Economics*, *30*(3), 315–350. doi:10.1016/S0165-4101(01)00016-7

Banner, D., & Cooke, R. (1984). Ethical Dilemmas in Performance Appraisal. *Journal of Business Ethics*, *3*(4), 327–333. doi:10.1007/BF00381756

Barrados, M., & Mayne, J. (2003). Can Public Sector Organisations Learn? *OECD Journal on Budgeting*, *3*(3), 87–103. doi:10.1787/budget-v3-art17-en

Bateman, T., & Snell, S. (2011). Management: Leading and Collaborating in a Competitive World (6th ed.). Boston: McGraw-Hill companies, Inc.

Bellows, R. M., & Estep, M. F. (1954). *Employment Psychology: The Interview*. New York: Rinehart.

Benson, P. G., Buckley, M. R., & Hall, S. (1988). Mixed Standard Scale. *Journal of Management, 14*(3), 415–423. doi:10.1177/014920638801400305

Bernardin, H., & Klatt, L. (1985). Managerial Appraisal systems: Has practice "caught-up" with the state of the art? *The Personnel Administrator, 30*, 79–86.

Berry, L. M. (2003). *Employee Selection*. Belmont, CA: Thomson/Wadsworth.

Boyatzis, R. (1982). *The Competent Manager*. New York: Wiley.

Campbell, D., Campbell, K., & Chia, H. (1998). Merit pay, performance appraisal, and individual motivation: An analysis and alternative. *Human Resource Management, 37*(2), 131–146. doi:10.1002/(SICI)1099-050X(199822)37:2<131::AID-HRM4>3.0.CO;2-X

Cardy, R. L., & Dobbins, G. H. (1994). *Performance appraisal: Alternative perspectives*. Cincinnati, OH: South Western Publishing Company.

Caruth, D. L., & Humphreys, J. H. (2008). Performance Appraisal; essential characteristics for strategic control. *Measuring Business Excellence, 12*(3), 24–32. doi:10.1108/13683040810900377

Cascio, W. F. (1998). *Managing Human Resources*. Boston: McGraw Hill Publishing Company.

CIPD. (2012). *Strategic HR*. Chartered Institute of Personnel and Development. Retrieved from http://www.cipd.co.uk/hr-topics/strategic-hr.aspx

Conrad, C. (1994). *Strategic organizational communication: Toward the twenty-first century* (3rd ed.). Fort Worth, TX: Harcourt Brace College Publishers.

Cox, A. (2000). The importance of employee participation in determining pay system effectiveness. *International Journal of Management Reviews, 2*(4), 357–375. doi:10.1111/1468-2370.00047

Daley, D. M. (1992). *Performance Appraisal in the Public Sector: Techniques and Applications*. Westport, CT: Quorum Books.

Dalton, M. (1996). Multirater Feedback and Conditions for Change. *Consulting Psychology Journal, 48*(1), 12–16. doi:10.1037/1061-4087.48.1.12

Davis, T., & Landa, M. (1999). A Contrary Look at performance Appraisal. *Canadian Manager, Fall*, 18-28. Retrieved from http://www.thefreelibrary.com/A+contrary+look+at+employee+performance+appraisal.-a058436540

De Silva, S. (1998). *Performance-Related and Skill-Based Pay: An Introduction*. Geneva: International Labour Office.

De Voe, S. E., & Iyengar, S. S. (2004). Managers theories of subordinates: A cross-cultural examination of manager perceptions of motivation and appraisal of performance. *Organizational Behavior and Human Decision Processes, 93*(1), 47–61. doi:10.1016/j.obhdp.2003.09.001

Deal, T. E., & Kennedy, A. A. (1982). *Corporate cultures: The rites and rituals of corporate life*. Reading, MA: Addison-Wesley Publishing.

Dechev, Z., & Kamphorst, J. J. A. (2010). Effective Performance Appraisal – A study into the relation between employer satisfaction and optimizing business results. Unpublished dissertation, Erasmus University, Rotterdam.

Deci, E. (1980). *The Psychology of Self Determination*. Lexington, MA: Lexington Books.

Derven, M. G. (1990). The paradox of performance appraisal. *The Personnel Journal*, *69*, 107–111.

Dessler, G. (2011). *Human Resource Management*. New Jersey: Prentice-Hall.

Drescher, S., Sabean, D., & Sharlin, A. (1982). *Political Symbolism in Modern Europe*. London: Transaction Books.

Fisher, M. (1995). *Performance Appraisals*. London: Kogan Page, Limited.

Flanagan, J. C. (1954). The critical incidents technique. *Psychological Bulletin*, *51*(4), 327–358. doi:10.1037/h0061470 PMID:13177800

Folger, R., Konovsky, M., & Cropanzano, R. (2002). A due process metaphor for performance appraisal. In B. M. Staw & L. L. Cummings (Eds.), *Research in Organizational Behavior* (Vol. 14, pp. 129–177). Greenwich, CT: JAI Press.

Galpin, T. J. (1997). *Making Strategy Work: Building Sustainable Growth Capability*. San Francisco: Jossey-Bass Publishers.

Gangwani, S. (2012). Employee Survey on Performance Appraisal System. International. *Journal of Social Sciences & Interdisciplinary Research*, *1*(6), 124–141.

Gilbert, G. R. (1982). Performance Appraisal and Organizational Practices: A Post Reform Review. *Public Personnel Management*, *11*(4), 318–321. doi:10.1177/009102608201100405

Glynn, J. J., & Murphy, M. P. (1996). Public Management: Failing Accountabilities and Failing Performance Review. *International Journal of Public Sector Management*, *9*(5/6), 125–137. doi:10.1108/09513559610146492

Gupta, V., & Swaroop, A. (2012). Comparative study of performance appraisal on two Pharmaceutical organizations in Madhya Pradesh. *International Journal of Engineering Sciences & Management*, *2*(2), 248–260.

Haberstroh, C. J. (1965). Organizational Design and Systems Analysis. In J. G. March (Ed.), *Handbook of Organizations* (pp. 1171–1212). Chicago: Rand McNally.

Harrell, A., & Wright, A. (1990). Empirical Evidence on the Validity and Reliability of Behaviourally Anchored Rating Scales for Auditors. *A Journal of Practice & Theory*, *9*(3), 134-149.

Harris, C. (1988). A Comparison of Employee Attitude Toward Two Performance Appraisal Systems. *Public Personnel Management*, *17*(4), 443–456. doi:10.1177/009102608801700408

Härtel, C. E. J. (1993). Rating Format Research Revisited: Format Effectiveness and Acceptability depend on Rater Characteristics. *The Journal of Applied Psychology*, *78*(2), 212–217. doi:10.1037/0021-9010.78.2.212

Hernandez, M. R., & Iyengar, S. S. (2001). What drives whom? A cultural perspective on human agency. *Social Cognition, 19*(3), 269–294. doi:10.1521/soco.19.3.269.21468

Ho, K. L. (1999). Bureaucratic Accountability in Malaysia: Control Mechanisms and Critical Concerns. In H.-K. Wong & H. S. Chan (Eds.), *The Handbook of Comparative Public Administration in the Asia-Pacific Basin* (pp. 23–45). New York: Marcel Dekker.

Hofstede, G. (1991). *Cultures and Organizations - Software of the mind*. London: McGraw-Hill Book Company.

Hyde, A. (1982). Performance Appraisal in the Post Reform Era. *Public Personnel Management, 11*(4), 294–305. doi:10.1177/009102608201100402

Jackson, S., & Schuler, R. (2002). *Managing Human Resources through Strategic Partnership* (8th ed.). Toronto: Thompson.

Jacobs, R., Kafry, D., & Zedeck, S. (1980). Expectations of behaviorally anchored rating scales. *Personnel Psychology, 33*(3), 595–640. doi:10.1111/j.1744-6570.1980.tb00486.x

Jelley, R. B., & Goffin, R. D. (2001). Can Performance-Feedback Accuracy Be Improved? Effects of Rater Priming and Rating Scale Format on Rating Accuracy. *The Journal of Applied Psychology, 86*(1), 134–144. doi:10.1037/0021-9010.86.1.134 PMID:11302225

Kanter, R. M. (1983). *The change masters: Innovation & entrepreneurship in the American corporation*. New York: Touchstone.

Karimi, R., Malik, M. I., & Hussain, S. (2011). Examining the relationship of performance appraisal system and employee satisfaction. *International Journal of Business and Social Science, 2*(22), 243–247.

Kavanagh, P., Benson, J., & Brown, M. (2007). Understanding performance appraisal fairness. *Asia Pacific Journal of Human Resources, 45*(2), 89–99. doi:10.1177/1038411107079108

Kertzer, D. I. (1988). *Ritual, Politics, and Power*. London: Yale University Press.

Kondrasuk, J. N. (2011). So what would an ideal performance appraisal look like? *The Journal of Applied Business and Economics, 12*(1), 57.

Kondrasuk, J. N., Pearson, D., Tanner, K., Maruska, E., & Dwyer, J. (2005). An elusive panacea: The ideal performance appraisal. In S. Reddy (Ed.), *Performance Appraisals: A Critical View* (pp. 3–12). Hyderabad, India: Institute of Chartered Financial Analysts of India.

Kumari, N., & Malhotra, R. (2012). Effective Performance Management System for Enhancing Growth. *Global Management Journal, 4*(1/2), 77–85.

Latham, G. P., & Wexley, K. N. (1977). Behavioural Observation Scales For Performance Appraisal Purposes. *Personnel Psychology, 30*(2), 255–268. doi:10.1111/j.1744-6570.1977.tb02092.x

Latham, G. P., & Yukl, G. A. (1975). A review of research on the application of goal setting in organizations. *Academy of Management Journal, 18*(4), 824–845. doi:10.2307/255381

Lawler, E. E. III. (2001). Performance Management. In L. Carter, D. Giber, & M. Goldsmith (Eds.), *Best Practices in Organization Development and Change*. San Francisco: Jossey-Bass/Pfeiffer.

Lepsinger, R., & Lucia. (1997). *360 degree feedback and performance appraisal. ABI/INFORM Global*, 62.

Long, C. S., Kowang, T. O., Ismail, W. K. W., & Rasid, S. Z. A. (2013). A Review on Performance Appraisal System: An Ineffective and Destructive Practice? *Middle-East Journal of Scientific Research, 14*(7), 887–891.

Longenecker, C. O., & Goff, S. J. (1992). Performance appraisal effectiveness: A matter of perspective. *SAM Advanced Management Journal, 57*(2), 17.

March, J. G., & Olsen, J. P. (1989). *Rediscovering Institutions - The Organizational Basis of Politics*. New York: The Free Press.

Maroney, B. P., & Buckely, M. R. (1992). Does research in performance appraisal influence the practice of performance appraisal? Regretfully not! *Public Personnel Management, 21*(2), 185–196. doi:10.1177/009102609202100206

Martell, R.F., & Leavitt, K.N. (2002). Reducing the Performance-Cue Bias in Work behaviour Ratings: Can Groups Help? *Journal of Applied Psychology, 87* 6), 1032-1041.

Martin, M., & Jackson, T. (2002). *Personnel practice* (3rd ed.). London: CIPD Publishing.

McCarthy, B. J. (1995). *Rater Motivation In Performance Appraisal*. Unpublished doctoral dissertation, The University Of WI, Madison.

Mohrman, A. M. Jr, Resnick-West, S. M., & Lawler, E. E. III. (1989). *Designing Performance Appraisal Systems - Aligning Appraisals and Organizational Realities*. San Francisco: Jossey Bass Publishers.

Mondy, R. W. D., & Martocchio, J. J. (2015). *Human Resource Management* (14th ed.). New Jersey: Prentice Hall.

Mullins, L. (1999). *Management and organizational behavior* (9th ed.). London: Financial Times / Prentice Hall.

Murphy, K. R., & Cleveland, J. N. (1990). *Performance Appraisal: An Organizational Perspective*. Boston: Allyn and Bacon.

Murphy, K. R., & Cleveland, J. N. (1995). *Understanding Performance Appraisal: Social, Organizational, and Goal-Based Perspectives*. Thousand Oaks, CA: Sage Publications.

Noe, R. A., Hollenberg, J. R., Gerhart, B., & Wright, P. M. (2009). *Fundamentals of Human Resource Management* (4th ed.). New York: Mc Graw Hill.

Ouchi, W. G. (1981). *Theory Z: How American business can meet the Japanese challenge*. Reading, MA: Addison-Wesley. doi:10.1016/0007-6813(81)90031-8

Parrill, S. (1999). *Revisiting Rating Format Research: Computer-Based Rating Formats and Components of Accuracy*. Unpublished manuscript, Virginia Polytechnic and State Institute, Blacksburg, VA.

Patro, C.S. (in press). Performance Appraisal-A Controversial Human Resource Tool. In *Encyclopedia of Information Sciences*.

Patten, T. H. (1977). *Pay: Employee compensation and incentive plan*. London: Free Press.

Pepper, G. L. (1995). *Communicating in Organizations: A Cultural Approach*. New York: McGraw-Hill.

Peters, T. J., & Waterman, R. H. Jr. (1982). *In search of excellence: Lessons from America's best-run companies*. New York: Warner Books.

Pheysey, D. C. (1993). *Organizational Cultures: Types and Transformations*. London: Routledge. doi:10.4324/9780203028568

Poon, J. (2004). Effects of performance appraisal politics on job satisfaction and turnover intention. *Personnel Review*, *33*(3), 322–334. doi:10.1108/00483480410528850

Pritchard, C. W. (2007). *101 Strategies for recruiting success: where, when, and how to find the right people every time*. New York: AMACOM Division American Management Association.

Rankin, G. D., & Kleiner, B. H. (1988). Effective performance appraisal. *Industrial Management & Data Systems*, *88*(1/2), 13–17. doi:10.1108/eb057500

Reeves, J. (2002). *Performance management in education*. London: Sage Publications.

Reinke, S. J. (2003). Does The Form Really Matter? Leadership, Trust, and Acceptance of the Performance Appraisal Process. *Review of Public Personnel Administration*, *23*(1), 23–37. doi:10.1177/0734371X02250109

Roberts, G. E. (1994). Barriers to Municipal Government Performance Appraisal Systems: Evidence from a Survey of Municipal Personnel Administrators. *Public Personnel Management*, *23*(2), 225–236. doi:10.1177/009102609402300205

Roberts, G. E. (2003). Employee Performance Appraisal System Participation: A Technique that Works. *Public Personnel Management*, *30*(1), 89–98. doi:10.1177/009102600303200105

Rudner, L. M. (1992). Reducing Errors Due to the Use of Judges. *Practical Assessment, Research & Evaluation*, *7*(26), 241–271.

Sanjeevni, G. (2012). Employee Survey on Performance Appraisal System. *International Journal of Social Sciences and Interdisciplinary Research*, *1*(6), 124–141.

Schein, E. H. (1992). *Organizational Culture and Leadership*. San Francisco: Jossey-Bass Publishers.

Schwab, D. P., Heneman, H. G., & DeCotiis, T. A. (1975). Behaviorally anchored rating scales: A review of the literature. *Personnel Psychology*, *28*(4), 549–562. doi:10.1111/j.1744-6570.1975.tb01392.x

Shapiro, G. L., & Schall, M. S. (1990). Rhetorical rules and organization-cultures: Identification, maintenance, and change. *Human Resource Development Quarterly*, *1*(4), 321–337. doi:10.1002/hrdq.3920010403

Skarlicki, D. P., & Folger, R. (1997). Retaliation in the Workplace: The Roles of Distributive, Procedural and Interactional Justice. *The Journal of Applied Psychology*, *82*(3), 434–443. doi:10.1037/0021-9010.82.3.434

Smith, P. C., & Kendall, L. M. (1963). Retranslation of expectations: An approach to the construction of unambiguous anchors for rating scales. *The Journal of Applied Psychology*, *47*(2), 149–155. doi:10.1037/h0047060

Smith, R., DiTomaso, N., Farris, G. F., & Cordero, R. (2001). Favouritism, Bias, and error in performance ratings of scientists and engineers: The effects of power, status, and numbers. *Sex Roles*, *45*(5-6), 337–358. doi:10.1023/A:1014309631243

Solmon, L. C., & Podgursky, M. (2000). *The Pros and Cons of Performance-based Compensation*. Santa Monica, CA: The Milken Family Foundation.

Spriegel, W. R. (1962). Company practices in appraisal of managerial performance. *Personnel*, *39*, 77–83.

Sudin, S. (2011). Fairness of and Satisfaction with performance appraisal process. *Journal of Global Management*, *2*(1), 66–83.

Swiercz, P. M., Bryan, N. B., Eagle, B. W., Bizzotto, V., & Renn, R. W. (2012). Predicting employee attitudes and performance from perceptions of performance appraisal fairness. *Business Renaissance Quarterly*, *7*(1), 25–46.

Swiercz, P. M., Icenogle, M. L., Bryan, N. B., & Renn, R. W. (1993). *Do perceptions of performance appraisal fairness predict employee attitudes and performance? In Academy of Management Proceedings* (Vol. 1, pp. 304–308). New York: Academy of Management.

Taylor, S. (2005). *People Resourcing* (3rd ed.). London: Chartered Institute of Personnel and Development.

Taylor, S., & Beechler, S. (1995). Human resources management system integration and adaptation in multinational firms. *Advances in International Comparative Management*, *8*, 115–174.

Tziner, A., & Kopelman, R. E. (2002). Is there a Preferred Performance Rating Format? A Non-psychometric Perspective. *Applied Psychology*, *51*(3), 479–503. doi:10.1111/1464-0597.00104

Tziner, A., Latham, G. P., Price, B. S., & Haccoun, R. (1996). Development and validation of a questionnaire for measuring perceived political considerations in performance appraisal. *Journal of Organizational Behavior*, *17*(2), 179–190. doi:10.1002/(SICI)1099-1379(199603)17:2<179::AID-JOB740>3.0.CO;2-Z

Tziner, A., Prince, B., & Murphy, K. (1997). PCPAQ – The Questionnaire for Measuring the Perceived Political Considerations in Performance Appraisal: Some New Evidence Regarding Its Psychometric Properties. *Journal of Social Behavior and Personality*, *12*, 189–200.

Vallance, S. (1999). Performance appraisal in Singapore, Thailand and the Philippines: A cultural perspective. *Australian Journal of Public Administration*, *58*(4), 78–95. doi:10.1111/1467-8500.00129

Van Maanen, J., & Schein, E. H. (1979). Toward a theory of organizational socialization. In B. M. Straw (Ed.), *Research in organization behaviour: An annual series of analytical essays and critical reviews* (Vol. 1, pp. 209–264). Greenwich, CT: Jai Press.

Vanci-Osam, U., & Aksit, T. (2000). Do intentions and perceptions always meet? A case study regarding the use of a teacher appraisal scheme in an English language teaching environment. *Teaching and Teacher Education*, *16*(2), 1–15. doi:10.1016/S0742-051X(99)00058-X

VanMeter, D. S., & VanHorn, C. E. (1975). The Policy Implementation Process: A Conceptual Framework. *Administration & Society*, *6*(4), 445–487. doi:10.1177/009539977500600404

Varkkey, B., Koshy, A., & Oburoi, P. (2008). *Apollo Unstopable: The transformation journey of Apollo Tyres, Ltd*.

Walters, M. (1995). *The Performance Management Handbook (Developing Practice)*. London: Chartered Institute of Personnel.

Wart, M. V. (2003). Public-Sector leadership theory: An assessment. *Public Administration Review*, *63*(2), 214–228. doi:10.1111/1540-6210.00281

Whitmore, J. (2010). *Coaching for performance: growing human potential and purpose: the principles and practice of coaching and leadership*. London: Nicholas Brealey Publishing.

Wiese, D. S., & Buckley, M. R. (1998). The evolution of the performance appraisal process. *Journal of Management History*, *4*(3), 233–249. doi:10.1108/13552529810231003

Wise, P. G. (1998). Rating differences in Multi-Rater Feedback. *Proceedings of the International Personnel Management Association Assessment Council`s Conference on Professional Personnel Assessment*, Chicago, IL.

Youngcourt, S. S., Leiva, P. I., & Jones, R. G. (2007). Perceived purposes of performance appraisal: Correlates of individual-and position-focused purposes on attitudinal outcomes. *Human Resource Development Quarterly*, *18*(3), 315–343. doi:10.1002/hrdq.1207

KEY TERMS AND DEFINITIONS

360-Degree Appraisal: This approach involves gathering performance information from individuals on all sides of the manager - above, beside, below and so forth.

Appraise: An individual being evaluated on work performance.

Appraiser: An individual responsible for evaluating an individual's work performance.

Behaviorally Anchored Rating Scales (BARS): Behaviorally Anchored Rating Scales is a formatted performance appraisal method based on making rates on behaviors or sets of indicators to determine the effectiveness or ineffectiveness of employees work performance.

Performance Appraisal: It facilitates the management in hauling out the administrative decisions relating to promotions, firings, layoffs and pay increases.

Performance Management: It is the process of directing and supporting individuals to work as effectively as possible in streak with the needs of the organization.

Trait Focused Appraisals: It motivates employees to be competitive in a fair manner and yet be available for helping out colleagues if need be. It considers attributes like helpfulness, dependability, punctuality, etc for being appraised by the organization.

Work Performance: It is an accomplishment of the assigned tasks for achieving organization's goal.

Chapter 8
The Significance of Job Satisfaction in Modern Organizations

Kijpokin Kasemsap
Suan Sunandha Rajabhat University, Thailand

ABSTRACT

This chapter explains the relationship between job satisfaction and organizational constructs in modern organizations; job satisfaction, job performance, and adaptability; job satisfaction and negative organizational issues; and the importance of job satisfaction in the health care industry. Job satisfaction is an attitude that employees have about their work and job-related activities. Job satisfaction is important from the perspective of maintaining employees within the organization. High job satisfaction effectively leads to the improved organizational productivity, decreased employee turnover, and reduced job stress in modern organizations. Job satisfaction leads to a positive ambience at the workplace and is essential to ensure the higher revenues for the organization. Organizations should create the systematic management and leadership strategies to increase the high levels of job satisfaction of their employees. When employees are satisfied with their jobs, they will energetically deliver the higher levels of job performance.

INTRODUCTION

Job satisfaction is the sense of inner fulfillment and pride achieved when performing a particular job (Kasemsap, 2017a) regarding the concept of organizational psychology (Hauff, Richter, & Tressin, 2015). Ensuring the satisfaction of employees in the organization is one of the most important tasks for organizational management (Özpehlivan & Acar, 2015). The features of the work and work environment can predict job satisfaction in modern organizations (Brawley & Pury, 2016). Satisfied employees will have more time to transfer their positive emotions to the customers toward improving organizational profits (Yee, Guo, & Yeung, 2015). Job satisfaction is an affective reaction to a job that results from the incumbent's comparison of actual outcomes with those that are desired, expected, and deserved (Castaneda & Scanlan, 2014).

DOI: 10.4018/978-1-5225-2568-4.ch008

Job satisfaction, regardless of occupation or sector of employment, has been an issue of concern and of thorough research during the past decades (Ioannou et al., 2015). Job satisfaction is the individual's positive feelings about his or her job and its characteristic structure. Employees' job satisfactions have gained the increasing attentions from many researchers and practitioners in organizational study and the particular focus are given into searching the answer to understand why people are more satisfied with their jobs than others (Long & Xuan, 2014). Job-provided development opportunities are significantly related to satisfaction with growth opportunities, which is related to the citizenship behaviors of interpersonal helping, personal industry, and loyal boosterism (Jawahar, 2012).

This chapter focuses on the literature review through a thorough literature consolidation of job satisfaction. The extensive literature of job satisfaction provides a contribution to practitioners and researchers by explaining the challenges and implications of job satisfaction in order to maximize the impact of job satisfaction in modern organizations.

Background

In recent years, job satisfaction has attracted the attention of cross-national and intercultural researchers (Hauff et al., 2015). Job satisfaction can be defined by the level of satisfaction the person receives through job rewarding, especially when it involves the awards that fuel the intrinsic motivation of the employee (Statt, 2004). Employee satisfaction is considered as achievable when the employees are satisfied with certain factors related to their job, such as style of management, work culture, and teamwork empowerment (Hashim, 2015). Promoting psychological empowerment, job satisfaction, and organizational citizenship behavior can increase organizational performance in modern organizations (Kasemsap, 2013a).

Job satisfaction of the working-age person plays one of the most important tasks in terms of its motivation, performance, and work efficiency. Job satisfaction is associated with both social and psychological natures in the modern workplace (Malloy & Penprase, 2010). There are many studies that consider the relationships between job satisfaction and organizational culture (Lovas, 2007), between job satisfaction and the leadership style of the working group (Havig, Skogstad, Veenstra, & Romoren, 2011), between job satisfaction and life satisfaction (Bowling, Eschleman, & Wang, 2010), between job satisfaction and teamwork (Kalisch, Lee, & Rochman, 2010), between job satisfaction and perceived supervisor support (Gok, Karatuna, & Karaca, 2015), between job satisfaction and the sense of personal fulfillment (Kaliski, 2007), between job satisfaction and organizational justice (Kasemsap, 2012a), between job satisfaction and organizational citizenship behavior (Kasemsap, 2013b), and between job satisfaction and job involvement (Kasemsap, 2013c).

According to Herzberg et al. (1959), job satisfaction's antecedents can be clustered in real motivational factors (e.g., achievement, recognition, work, responsibility, promotion, and growth), and hygiene factors (e.g., pay, company policy, good relationships with co-workers, and supervision). The popular categorization distinguishes between extrinsic and intrinsic job characteristics, and can be traced back to the Herzberg's differentiation between motivators (intrinsic aspects) and hygiene factors (extrinsic aspects) (Kaasa, 2011). Job characteristics model defines five job characteristics (i.e., task identity, task significance, skills variety, autonomy, and feedback) that lead to the higher job satisfaction (Hackman & Oldham, 1976). Autonomy is the only working feature that is directly associated with the perceived responsibility of the employee, toward enhancing the intrinsic motivation (Belias, Koustelios, Sdrolias, & Aspridis, 2015). Job characteristics, rewards, and employee engagement are positively correlated with job satisfaction in the modern workplace (Kasemsap, 2013d).

ADVANCED ISSUES OF JOB SATISFACTION IN MODERN ORGANIZATIONS

This section indicates the relationship between job satisfaction and organizational constructs in modern organizations; job satisfaction, job performance, and adaptability; job satisfaction and negative organizational issues; and the importance of job satisfaction in the health care industry.

Relationship Between Job Satisfaction and Organizational Constructs in Modern Organizations

The predictors of the job–life satisfaction relationship vary across cultures and that such cross-cultural variations are correlates with cultural values and beliefs (Georgellis & Lange, 2012). Warr (2007) indicated the comprehensive issues job features that are positively related to job satisfaction include opportunity for personal control (e.g., employee discretion, autonomy, and self-determination); opportunity for skill use (e.g., skills utilization and opportunities for learning); externally generated goals (e.g., job demands, workload, and work-family conflict); variety in job content and location; environmental clarity (e.g., information about the future and the required behavior); communication with others (e.g., quantity and quality of interactions); availability of money (e.g., income level); physical security (e.g., good working conditions); valued social position (e.g., status in society and task significance); supportive supervision (e.g., leader consideration and supportive management); career outlook (e.g., job security, opportunities for promotion, and advancement); and equity (e.g., fairness in individual's employment relationship and morality in an employer's relationship with society).

The dimensions of organizational culture, organizational learning, and knowledge management have mediated positive effect on job satisfaction in the modern workplace (Kasemsap, 2014a). Job satisfaction is recognized as the global attitudinal judgment which requires employees to conclude their experiences (Grube, Schroer, Hentzschel, & Hertel, 2008). Psychosocial work environment factors (e.g., information about decisions concerning the workplace, social support, and influence) have the significant impacts on the level of job satisfaction (Sell & Cleal, 2011). Satisfaction with work–life balance provides the holistic measure of employees' contentment with the relationships between personal, work, and family in their lives (Cahill, McNamara, Pitt-Catsouphes, & Valcour, 2015). The increased tenure improves job satisfaction for the most satisfied male and female workers (Chaudhuri, Reilly, & Spencer, 2015). Men have the highest hours-of-work satisfaction if they work full-time without overtime hours but neither their job satisfaction nor their life satisfaction are affected by how many hours they work (Booth & van Ours, 2008).

Leadership behavior, perceived organizational support, and job satisfaction lead to the improved organizational commitment (Kasemsap, 2012b). Leadership style, leadership behavior, and organizational culture have a positive relationship with job satisfaction (Kasemsap, 2012c). Leadership behavior of supervisor is positively associated with subordinate job satisfaction and organizational commitment (Westlund, 2010). Trust in leader has a direct effect on job satisfaction (Gibson & Petrosko, 2014). Rowold et al. (2014) indicated that the leadership style of an employee's supervisor promotes the organizational commitment and job satisfaction in the workplace. Job satisfaction can promote the supervisor–employee relationships (Volmer, Niessen, Spurk, Linz, & Abele, 2011). Factors (e.g., the extent to which a supervisor delegates and gives autonomy to employees) can affect the employees' evaluations of their jobs (Alegre, Mas-Machuca, & Berbegal-Mirabent, 2016).

The relationship between pro-social motivation and job satisfaction is moderated by the perceived usefulness of the job for society and other people (Kjeldsen & Andersen, 2013). Whitman et al. (2010) indicated the significant relationships are found between unit-level job satisfaction and unit-level criteria, including productivity, customer satisfaction, withdrawal, and organizational citizenship behavior. Job satisfaction reflects the on-the-job utility of workers and affects both the behavior of workers and the productivity of firms (Artz, 2008). The core self-evaluations interact with organizational socialization tactics to affect job satisfaction and work engagement (Song, Chon, Ding, & Gu, 2015).

Job satisfaction refers to the employees' attitudes toward the job, the relevant environment, and their overall emotional response to their job roles (Diener, 2000) and is one of the most effective indicators of vocational happiness (Zhang, Wu, Miao, Yan, & Peng, 2014). There are positive relationships among job satisfaction, well-being, happiness, and quality of life (Platania, Santisi, Magnano, & Ramaci, 2015). Workplace satisfaction implies the achievement evaluations and workplace success, and it is positively correlated with well-being (Avram, Ionescu, & Mincu, 2015). Happiness in the form of good emotions, well-being, and positive attitudes has been attracting the attention throughout psychology research (Fisher, 2010). To promote organizational commitment to organizational goals, organizations must clearly define their objectives (Patterson et al., 2005). Affective commitment is a potential mediator between job satisfaction and job performance (Zhang & Zheng, 2009). Affective commitment moderates the relationship between strain-based conflict and job satisfaction, whereas normative commitment moderates the relationship between time-based conflict and job satisfaction (Buonocore & Russo, 2013).

Rewards, organizational justice, and perceived organizational support lead to the enhanced job satisfaction (Kasemsap, 2013e). Process-based rewards represent a reward system that compensates new product development (NPD) teams for finishing the specified procedures that are the important approach to accomplishing the project goals (Li, Chu, & Lin, 2010). NPD teams respond to reward structures in a manner that minimizes their own risk and thus reward structures that are effective in facilitating job satisfaction are those that describe the minimal risk to them (Sarin & Majahan, 2001). Process-based rewards decrease project members' pressure to attain the expected performance and thus under this reward structure team members will feel more satisfied with their jobs (Carbonell & Rodríguez-Escudero, 2016). However, the low level of satisfaction from rewards is associated with the increased levels of stress (Mateescu & Chraif, 2015).

Job Satisfaction, Job Performance, and Adaptability

The relationship between job performance (e.g., productivity) and job satisfaction has been the focus of study in the psychological literature (Judge, Bono, Thoresen, & Patton, 2001). Job satisfaction is a better predictor of job performance (Kasemsap, 2013f) when individuals experience the low job ambivalence, as compared to when individuals experience the high job ambivalence (Ziegler, Hagen, & Diehl, 2012). The important predictors of overall employee performance are employee engagement and job satisfaction (Dalal, Baysinger, Brummel, & LeBreton, 2012). Satisfaction with supervision has a significant impact on job satisfaction (Mardanov, Maertz, & Sterrett, 2008). There is a stronger relationship between satisfaction with supervision and contextual performance compared to task performance (Edwards, Bell, Arthur, & Decuir, 2008).

Adaptability of employees is the significant factor that affects various organizational outcomes (Cullen, Edwards, Casper, & Gue, 2013), such as job satisfaction and job performance (Stokes, Schneider, & Lyons, 2010). The highly adaptable individuals perceive more control over workplace uncertainty and feel confident to overcome obstacles, reducing the impact of the negative emotions generated by instability and experiencing overall lower work stress (Fiori, Bollmann, & Rossier, 2015). Mastering adaptive performance as a criterion is essential for the usefulness of job performance models which can be utilized by practitioners at the forefront of the changing workplace (Sony & Mekoth, 2016). The adaptable employee is an important asset for the organization (Chebat & Kollias, 2000) and customer (Ahearne, Mathieu, & Rapp, 2005) because it leads to the increased organization performance (Nesbit & Lam, 2014) and the enhanced customer satisfaction (Keillor, Pettijohn, & d'Amico, 2011).

Job Satisfaction and Negative Organizational Issues

The low level of job satisfaction is reflected by the reduced stability, discipline, responsibility, lower power, fluctuation, and lack of staff (Hajdukova, Klementova, & Klementova, 2015). Job burnout is a kind of reaction that develops against stress and is related to individual's profession in the workplace (Aliyev & Tunc, 2015). Job-related tension is related to job burnout, which decreases the employees' levels of job satisfaction and organizational commitment (Chong & Monroe, 2015). The direct relationship between job satisfaction and turnover intention is stronger in the private than public organizations (de Moura, Abrams, Retter, Gunnarsdottir, & Ando, 2009).

The weakened psychological presence is correlated with the weakened affective evaluations of work (e.g., job satisfaction) through its effect on affective-motivational states, such as work engagement and work addiction (Karanika-Murray, Pontes, Griffiths, & Biron, 2015). A person who lacks self-approval and views himself or herself in a negative way will be dissatisfied with his or her job (Tavousi, 2015). Work-family conflict affects employees' personal happiness and life satisfaction as well as their levels of job stress, job satisfaction, and organizational commitment (Efeoğlu & Sanal, 2015). Workplace stress and the perception of the perilous workplace safety have a negative impact on job satisfaction, thus increasing the employee turnover intention (Malek, Fahrudin, & Kamil, 2009).

Job insecurity is a feeling based on the individual's subjective perception and explanation of changes in his or her job environment (Mauno, Kinnunen, Makikangas, & Natti, 2005). Job insecurity not only results in employees' negative attitudes about their job and organization, reduces individual and organizational job performance, and destroys employees' physical and mental health, but also reduces employees' job satisfaction (Green, 2011).

From the point of emotion processes theory, job insecurity acts as a chronic stressor toward moderating the effect of individuals manage emotion and reducing job satisfaction (Ouyang, Sang, Li, & Peng, 2015). Job satisfaction decreases with perceived job insecurity among union workers in the public sector and primarily when tenure with an employer is high (Artz & Kaya, 2014). Job insecurity lowers the employees' level of organizational commitment (Rosenblatt, Talmud, & Ruvio, 1999) and increases employee turnover intention (Lambert, Hogan, & Barton, 2001). The employees' perceptions of job insecurity are associated with the national level of unemployment (Erlinghagen, 2008).

Employees reporting the higher rates of abusive supervision are less satisfied with their job, have the lower levels of commitment to their organization, and have the higher turnover intentions (Tepper, 2000). Abusive supervision is related to the reduced employee creativity (Liu, Liao, & Loi, 2012), the decrease in the perceived organizational support (Shoss, Eisenberger, Restubog, & Zagenczyk, 2013), an increase in employees' organizational deviance (Tepper, Henle, Lambert, Giacalone, & Duffy, 2008), and the lowered employee performance (Harris, Kacmar, & Zivnuska, 2007). By diminishing abusive supervisory behavior, or hiring individuals who do not exhibit the psychopathic traits, organizations will be able to enhance employees' job satisfaction, toward reducing employee turnover intention (Mathieu & Babiak, 2016).

Importance of Job Satisfaction in the Health Care Industry

Understanding the determinants of job satisfaction are the significant factors that help reduce the problem of nurse attrition (Ravari, Bazargan, Vanaki, & Mirzael, 2012). Job satisfaction of nurses is correlated with productivity, turnover, absenteeism, and patient outcomes (Prosen & Piskar, 2015). Job rotation and internal marketing help the nursing personnel acquire knowledge, skills, and insights while enhancing their job satisfaction and organizational commitment (Chen, Wu, Chang, & Lin, 2015). Nursing dissatisfaction is associated with the high rates of nurses leaving the profession, poor morale, and poor patient outcomes (Hayes, Bonner, & Pryor, 2010).

As the nursing workforce is aging and increasing numbers of nurses are leaving the workforce due to retirement, the retention of younger nurses is critical to ensure the future supply of nurses (Kenny, Reeve, & Hall, 2016). Nursing care quality is directly related to work environment and job satisfaction (Boev, Xue, & Ingersoll, 2015). Nurse job satisfaction is associated with a positive nursing work environment (Gabriel, Erickson, Moran, Diefendoff, & Bromley, 2013). Work environments perceived as favorable by the nursing staff are related to fewer adverse nurse-sensitive patient outcomes and increased patient satisfaction (Manojlovich, Antonakos, & Ronis, 2009).

Nursing administrators should emphasize the perspectives that positively affect their nurses' levels of job satisfaction, as it will result in the less staff turnover and the greater patient care in health care settings (Tao, Ellenbecker, Wang, & Li, 2015). Promoting nurses' job satisfaction and occupational commitment are essential to increase nurses' intention to stay and for strategies to emphasize the nursing shortage (Wang, Tao, Ellenbecker, & Liu, 2012).

Nurses with positive evaluation and expectation toward self and others tend to report the higher job satisfaction (Chang, Li, Wu, & Wang, 2010). Nursing resources and patient satisfaction are important to nurses' job satisfaction (Kaunonen, Salin, & Aalto, 2015). Nurse leaders should recognize the retention strategies related to the job satisfaction predictors of various age groups (Klaus, Ekerdt, & Gajewski, 2012). Nurse leaders must be aware of the role preceptors' authentic leadership plays in promoting work engagement and job satisfaction of new nurses (Giallonardo, Wong, & Iwasiw, 2010).

FUTURE RESEARCH DIRECTIONS

The classification of the extensive literature in the domains of job satisfaction will provide the potential opportunities for future research. Social capital is the network of relationships among people, firms, and institutions in a society, together with associated norms of behavior, trust, and cooperation that enable a society to effectively function (Kasemsap, 2014b). Social capital can increase the performance of diverse groups, the growth of entrepreneurial firms, superior managerial performance, enhanced supply chain relations, the value derived from strategic alliances, and the evolution of communities (Kasemsap, 2017b). Organizations should create a supportive and innovative climate to encourage employee to behave in the interactive ways toward enhancing good employee behavior (Kasemsap, 2016a). Effective leadership inspires and empowers employees to realize their fullest potential and manage their potentials to achieve common goals (Kasemsap, 2017c). Promoting job satisfaction through effective social capital, organizational climate, and leadership in modern organizations would be beneficial for future research directions.

Cultural environments relate to beliefs, practices, customs, and behaviors that are common to everyone that is living within a certain population (Kasemsap, 2016b). Membership in a culture adapts to new cultural contexts while transporting elements of one culture to another (Kasemsap, 2015a). Cross culture is a business environment where participants from different countries or regions interact, bringing different values, viewpoints, and business practices (Kasemsap, 2015b). Considering the association between job satisfaction and culture in cross-cultural work settings should be further studied.

CONCLUSION

This chapter revealed the relationship between job satisfaction and organizational constructs in modern organizations; job satisfaction, job performance, and adaptability; job satisfaction and negative organizational issues; and the importance of job satisfaction in the health care industry. Job satisfaction is an attitude that employees have about their work and job-related activities. Job satisfaction is important from the perspective of maintaining employees within the organization. Employee satisfaction is of utmost importance for employees to remain happy and also deliver their level best. Satisfied employees are the ones who are extremely loyal toward their organization and stick to it even in the worst scenario. Job satisfaction is a matter of great significance for employers.

High job satisfaction effectively leads to the improved organizational productivity, decreased employee turnover, and reduced job stress in modern organizations. Organizations benefit a lot from satisfied employees in the following ways (e.g., the lower employee turnover, higher productivity, punctuality, better worked morale, and reduction in conflicts). Job satisfaction leads to a positive ambience at the workplace and is essential to ensure the higher revenues for the organization. Organizations should create the systematic management and leadership strategies to increase the high levels of job satisfaction of their employees. When employees are satisfied with their jobs, they will energetically deliver the higher levels of job performance.

REFERENCES

Ahearne, M., Mathieu, J., & Rapp, A. (2005). To empower or not to empower your sales force? An empirical examination of the influence of leadership empowerment behavior on customer satisfaction and performance. *The Journal of Applied Psychology*, *90*(5), 945–955. doi:10.1037/0021-9010.90.5.945 PMID:16162066

Alegre, I., Mas-Machuca, M., & Berbegal-Mirabent, J. (2016). Antecedents of employee job satisfaction: Do they matter? *Journal of Business Research*, *69*(4), 1390–1395. doi:10.1016/j.jbusres.2015.10.113

Aliyev, R., & Tunc, E. (2015). Self-efficacy in counseling: The role of organizational psychological capital, job satisfaction, and burnout. *Procedia: Social and Behavioral Sciences*, *190*, 97–105. doi:10.1016/j.sbspro.2015.04.922

Artz, B. (2008). The role of firm size and performance pay in determining employee job satisfaction brief: Firm size, performance pay, and job satisfaction. *Labour, 22*(2), 315–343. doi:10.1111/j.1467-9914.2007.00398.x

Artz, B., & Kaya, I. (2014). Job insecurity and job satisfaction in the United States: The case of public sector union workers. *Industrial Relations Journal, 45*(2), 103–120. doi:10.1111/irj.12044

Avram, E., Ionescu, D., & Mincu, C. L. (2015). Perceived safety climate and organizational trust: The mediator role of job satisfaction. *Procedia: Social and Behavioral Sciences, 187*, 679–684. doi:10.1016/j.sbspro.2015.03.126

Belias, D., Koustelios, A., Sdrolias, L., & Aspridis, G. (2015). Job satisfaction, role conflict and autonomy of employees in the Greek banking organization. *Procedia: Social and Behavioral Sciences, 175*, 324–333. doi:10.1016/j.sbspro.2015.01.1207

Boev, C., Xue, Y., & Ingersoll, G. L. (2015). Nursing job satisfaction, certification and healthcare associated infections in critical care. *Intensive & Critical Care Nursing, 31*(5), 276–284. doi:10.1016/j.iccn.2015.04.001 PMID:26169234

Booth, A. L., & van Ours, J. C. (2008). Job satisfaction and family happiness: The part-time work puzzle. *The Economic Journal, 118*(526), F77–F99. doi:10.1111/j.1468-0297.2007.02117.x

Bowling, N. A., Eschleman, K. J., & Wang, Q. (2010). A meta-analytic examination of the relationship between job satisfaction and subjective well-being. *Journal of Occupational and Organizational Psychology, 83*(4), 915–934. doi:10.1348/096317909X478557

Brawley, A. M., & Pury, C. L. S. (2016). Work experiences on MTurk: Job satisfaction, turnover, and information sharing. *Computers in Human Behavior, 54*, 531–546. doi:10.1016/j.chb.2015.08.031

Buonocore, F., & Russo, M. (2013). Reducing the effects of work–family conflict on job satisfaction: The kind of commitment matters. *Human Resource Management Journal, 23*(1), 91–108. doi:10.1111/j.1748-8583.2011.00187.x

Cahill, K. E., McNamara, T. K., Pitt-Catsouphes, M., & Valcour, M. (2015). Linking shifts in the national economy with changes in job satisfaction, employee engagement and work–life balance. *Journal of Behavioral and Experimental Economics, 56*, 40–54. doi:10.1016/j.socec.2015.03.002

Carbonell, P., & Rodríguez-Escudero, A. I. (2016). The individual and joint effects of process control and process-based rewards on new product performance and job satisfaction. *BRQ Business Research Quarterly, 19*(1), 26–39. doi:10.1016/j.brq.2015.04.001

Castaneda, G. A., & Scanlan, J. M. (2014). Job satisfaction in nursing: A concept analysis. *Nursing Forum, 49*(2), 130–138. doi:10.1111/nuf.12056 PMID:24383666

Chang, Y. H., Li, H. H., Wu, C. M., & Wang, P. C. (2010). The influence of personality traits on nurses' job satisfaction in Taiwan. *International Nursing Review, 57*(4), 478–484. doi:10.1111/j.1466-7657.2010.00825.x PMID:21050200

Chaudhuri, K., Reilly, K. T., & Spencer, D. A. (2015). Job satisfaction, age and tenure: A generalized dynamic random effects model. *Economics Letters, 130*, 13–16. doi:10.1016/j.econlet.2015.02.017

Chebat, J. C., & Kollias, P. (2000). The impact of empowerment on customer contact employees' roles in service organizations. *Journal of Service Research*, *3*(1), 66–81. doi:10.1177/109467050031005

Chen, S. Y., Wu, W. C., Chang, C. S., & Lin, C. T. (2015). Job rotation and internal marketing for increased job satisfaction and organisational commitment in hospital nursing staff. *Journal of Nursing Management*, *23*(3), 297–306. doi:10.1111/jonm.12126 PMID:23981132

Chong, V. K., & Monroe, G. S. (2015). The impact of the antecedents and consequences of job burnout on junior accountants' turnover intentions: A structural equation modelling approach. *Accounting and Finance*, *55*(1), 105–132. doi:10.1111/acfi.12049

Cullen, K. L., Edwards, B. D., Casper, W. C., & Gue, K. R. (2013). Employees' adaptability and perceptions of change-related uncertainty: Implications for perceived organizational support, job satisfaction, and performance. *Journal of Business and Psychology*, *29*(2), 269–280. doi:10.1007/s10869-013-9312-y

Dalal, R. S., Baysinger, M., Brummel, B. J., & LeBreton, J. M. (2012). The relative importance of employee engagement, other job attitudes, and trait affect as predictors of job performance. *Journal of Applied Social Psychology*, *42*(Suppl. 1), E295–E325. doi:10.1111/j.1559-1816.2012.01017.x

de Moura, G. R., Abrams, D., Retter, C., Gunnarsdottir, S., & Ando, K. (2009). Identification as an organizational anchor: How identification and job satisfaction combine to predict turnover intention. *European Journal of Social Psychology*, *39*(4), 540–557. doi:10.1002/ejsp.553

Diener, E. (2000). Subjective well-being: The science of happiness and a proposal for a national index. *The American Psychologist*, *55*(1), 34–43. doi:10.1037/0003-066X.55.1.34 PMID:11392863

Edwards, B. D., Bell, S. T., Arthur, W. Jr, & Decuir, A. D. (2008). Relationships between facets of job satisfaction and task and contextual performance. *Applied Psychology*, *57*(3), 441–465. doi:10.1111/j.1464-0597.2008.00328.x

Efeoğlu, I. E., & Sanal, M. (2015). The effects of work-family conflict on job stress, job satisfaction, and organizational commitment: A study in Turkish pharmaceutical industry. In B. Christiansen (Ed.), *Handbook of research on global business opportunities* (pp. 213–228). Hershey, PA: IGI Global. doi:10.4018/978-1-4666-6551-4.ch010

Erlinghagen, M. (2008). Self-perceived job insecurity and social context: A multi-level analysis of 17 European countries. *European Sociological Review*, *24*(2), 183–197. doi:10.1093/esr/jcm042

Fiori, M., Bollmann, G., & Rossier, J. (2015). Exploring the path through which career adaptability increases job satisfaction and lowers job stress: The role of affect. *Journal of Vocational Behavior*, *91*, 113–121. doi:10.1016/j.jvb.2015.08.010

Fisher, C. D. (2010). Happiness at work. *International Journal of Management Reviews*, *12*(4), 384–412. doi:10.1111/j.1468-2370.2009.00270.x

Gabriel, A. S., Erickson, R. J., Moran, C. M., Diefendoff, J. M., & Bromley, G. E. (2013). A multilevel analysis of the effects of the practice environment scale of the nursing work index on nurse outcomes. *Research in Nursing & Health*, *36*(6), 567–581. doi:10.1002/nur.21562 PMID:24122833

Georgellis, Y., & Lange, T. (2012). Traditional versus secular values and the job–life satisfaction relationship across Europe. *British Journal of Management, 23*(4), 437–454. doi:10.1111/j.1467-8551.2011.00753.x

Giallonardo, L. M., Wong, C. A., & Iwasiw, C. L. (2010). Authentic leadership of preceptors: Predictor of new graduate nurses' work engagement and job satisfaction. *Journal of Nursing Management, 18*(8), 993–1003. doi:10.1111/j.1365-2834.2010.01126.x PMID:21073571

Gibson, D., & Petrosko, J. (2014). Trust in leader and its effect on job satisfaction and intent to leave in a healthcare setting. *New Horizons in Adult Education and Human Resource Development, 26*(3), 3–19. doi:10.1002/nha3.20069

Gok, S., Karatuna, I., & Karaca, P. O. (2015). The role of perceived supervisor support and organizational identification in job satisfaction. *Procedia: Social and Behavioral Sciences, 177,* 38–42. doi:10.1016/j.sbspro.2015.02.328

Green, F. (2011). Unpacking the misery multiplier: How employability modifies the impacts of unemployment and job insecurity on life satisfaction and mental health. *Journal of Health Economics, 30*(2), 265–276. doi:10.1016/j.jhealeco.2010.12.005 PMID:21236508

Grube, A., Schroer, J., Hentzschel, C., & Hertel, G. (2008). The event reconstruction method: An efficient measure of experience-based job satisfaction. *Journal of Occupational and Organizational Psychology, 81*(4), 669–689. doi:10.1348/096317907X251578

Hackman, J., & Oldham, G. R. (1976). Motivation through the design of work: Test of a theory. *Organizational Behavior and Human Performance, 16*(2), 250–279. doi:10.1016/0030-5073(76)90016-7

Haile, G. A. (2015). Workplace job satisfaction in Britain: Evidence from linked employer–employee data. *Labour, 29*(3), 225–242. doi:10.1111/labr.12054

Hajdukova, A., Klementova, J., & Klementova, J. Jr. (2015). The job satisfaction as a regulator of the working behaviour. *Procedia: Social and Behavioral Sciences, 190,* 471–476. doi:10.1016/j.sbspro.2015.05.028

Harris, K. J., Kacmar, K. M., & Zivnuska, S. (2007). An investigation of abusive supervision as a predictor of performance and the meaning of work as a moderator of the relationship. *The Leadership Quarterly, 18*(3), 252–263. doi:10.1016/j.leaqua.2007.03.007

Hashim, R. (2015). Levels of job satisfaction among engineers in a Malaysian local organization. *Procedia: Social and Behavioral Sciences, 195,* 175–181. doi:10.1016/j.sbspro.2015.06.430

Hauff, S., Richter, N. F., & Tressin, T. (2015). Situational job characteristics and job satisfaction: The moderating role of national culture. *International Business Review, 24*(4), 710–723. doi:10.1016/j.ibusrev.2015.01.003

Havig, A. K., Skogstad, A., Veenstra, M., & Romoren, T. I. (2011). The effects of leadership and ward factors on job satisfaction in nursing homes: A multilevel approach. *Journal of Clinical Nursing, 20*(23/24), 3532–3542. doi:10.1111/j.1365-2702.2011.03697.x PMID:21564362

Hayes, B., Bonner, A., & Pryor, J. (2010). Factors contributing to nurse job satisfaction in the acute hospital setting: A review of recent literature. *Journal of Nursing Management, 18*(7), 804–814. doi:10.1111/j.1365-2834.2010.01131.x PMID:20946216

Herzberg, F., Mausner, B., & Snyderman, B. B. (1959). *The motivation to work*. New York: John Wiley & Sons.

Huang, Q., & Gamble, J. (2015). Social expectations, gender and job satisfaction: Front-line employees in China's retail sector. *Human Resource Management Journal, 25*(3), 331–347. doi:10.1111/1748-8583.12066

Ioannou, P., Katsikavali, V., Galanis, P., Velonakis, E., Papadatou, D., & Sourtzi, P. (2015). Impact of job satisfaction on Greek nurses' health-related quality of life. *Safety and Health at Work, 6*(4), 324–328. doi:10.1016/j.shaw.2015.07.010 PMID:26929845

Jawahar, I. M. (2012). Mediating role of satisfaction with growth opportunities on the relationship between employee development opportunities and citizenship behaviors and burnout. *Journal of Applied Social Psychology, 42*(9), 2257–2284. doi:10.1111/j.1559-1816.2012.00939.x

Judge, T. A., Bono, J. E., Thoresen, C. J., & Patton, G. K. (2001). The job satisfaction-job performance relationship: A qualitative and quantitative review. *Psychological Bulletin, 127*(3), 376–407. doi:10.1037/0033-2909.127.3.376 PMID:11393302

Kaasa, A. (2011). Work values in European countries: Empirical evidence and explanations. *Review of International Comparative Management, 12*(5), 852–862.

Kalisch, B. J., Lee, H., & Rochman, M. (2010). Nursing staff teamwork and job satisfaction. *Journal of Nursing Management, 18*(8), 938–947. doi:10.1111/j.1365-2834.2010.01153.x PMID:21073567

Kaliski, B. S. (2007). *Encyclopedia of business and finance*. Detroit, MI: Macmillan Reference.

Karanika-Murray, M., Pontes, H. M., Griffiths, M. D., & Biron, C. (2015). Sickness presenteeism determines job satisfaction via affective motivational states. *Social Science & Medicine, 139*, 100–106. doi:10.1016/j.socscimed.2015.06.035 PMID:26183017

Kasemsap, K. (2012a). Factor affecting organizational citizenship behavior of passenger car plant employees in Thailand. *Silpakorn University Journal of Social Sciences, Humanities, and Arts, 12*(2), 129–159.

Kasemsap, K. (2012b). Conceptual framework: A causal model of leadership behavior, perceived organizational support, job satisfaction, and organizational commitment of plastic plant employees in Thailand. *International Journal of Advances in Management, Technology & Engineering Sciences, 2*(3-1), 17–20.

Kasemsap, K. (2012c). Conceptual framework: Determination of causal model of leadership style, leadership behavior, organizational culture, and job satisfaction of petrochemical plant employees in Thailand. *International Journal of Advances in Management, Technology & Engineering Sciences, 2*(3-2), 20–24.

Kasemsap, K. (2013a). *Innovative human resource practice: A unified framework and causal model of psychological empowerment, job satisfaction, organizational citizenship behavior, and organizational performance*. Paper presented at the 2nd International Conference on Humanity, History and Society (ICHHS '13), Bangkok, Thailand.

Kasemsap, K. (2013b). Innovative human resource practice: A synthesized framework and causal model of leader-member exchange, organizational justice, job satisfaction, and organizational citizenship behavior. *International Journal of e-Education, e-Business, e-. Management Learning, 3*(1), 13–17. doi:10.7763/IJEEEE.2013.V3.185

Kasemsap, K. (2013c). Strategic human resource management: A synthesized framework and causal model of job involvement, job satisfaction, knowledge-sharing behavior, and job performance. *International Journal of Advances in Management, Technology & Engineering Sciences, 2*(6-2), 73–77.

Kasemsap, K. (2013d). *Strategic human resource practice: A systematic framework and causal model for job characteristics, rewards and recognition, employee engagement, and job satisfaction.* Paper presented at the 2013 Global Information and Management Symposium (GIAMS '13), Bangkok, Thailand.

Kasemsap, K. (2013e). *Innovative human resource practice: A functional framework and causal model of organizational rewards, organizational justice, perceived organizational support, and job satisfaction.* Paper presented at the 2nd International Conference on Economics, Business Innovation (ICEBI '13), Copenhagen, Denmark.

Kasemsap, K. (2013f). *Strategic human resource practice: A functional framework and causal model of leadership behavior, job satisfaction, organizational commitment, and job performance.* Paper presented at the 2nd International Conference on Global Business Environment: Role of Education and Technology (ICGBE '13), Bangkok, Thailand.

Kasemsap, K. (2014a). The role of knowledge management on job satisfaction: A systematic framework. In B. Tripathy & D. Acharjya (Eds.), *Advances in secure computing, Internet services, and applications* (pp. 104–127). Hershey, PA: IGI Global. doi:10.4018/978-1-4666-4940-8.ch006

Kasemsap, K. (2014b). The role of social capital in higher education institutions. In N. Baporikar (Ed.), *Handbook of research on higher education in the MENA region: Policy and practice* (pp. 119–147). Hershey, PA: IGI Global. doi:10.4018/978-1-4666-6198-1.ch007

Kasemsap, K. (2015a). The role of cultural dynamics in the digital age. In B. Christiansen & J. Koeman (Eds.), *Nationalism, cultural indoctrination, and economic prosperity in the digital age* (pp. 295–312). Hershey, PA: IGI Global. doi:10.4018/978-1-4666-7492-9.ch014

Kasemsap, K. (2015b). The roles of cross-cultural perspectives in global marketing. In J. Alcántara-Pilar, S. del Barrio-García, E. Crespo-Almendros, & L. Porcu (Eds.), *Analyzing the cultural diversity of consumers in the global marketplace* (pp. 37–59). Hershey, PA: IGI Global. doi:10.4018/978-1-4666-8262-7.ch003

Kasemsap, K. (2016a). A unified framework of organizational perspectives and knowledge management and their impact on job performance. In A. Normore, L. Long, & M. Javidi (Eds.), *Handbook of research on effective communication, leadership, and conflict resolution* (pp. 267–297). Hershey, PA: IGI Global. doi:10.4018/978-1-4666-9970-0.ch015

Kasemsap, K. (2016b). Cultural perspectives and cultural dynamics: Advanced issues and approaches. *International Journal of Art, Culture and Design Technologies, 5*(1), 35–47. doi:10.4018/IJACDT.2016010103

Kasemsap, K. (2017a). Examining the roles of job satisfaction and organizational commitment in the global workplace. In P. Ordoñez de Pablos & R. Tennyson (Eds.), *Handbook of research on human resources strategies for the new millennial workforce* (pp. 148–176). Hershey, PA: IGI Global. doi:10.4018/978-1-5225-0948-6.ch008

Kasemsap, K. (2017b). The fundamentals of social capital. In G. Koç, M. Claes, & B. Christiansen (Eds.), *Cultural influences on architecture* (pp. 259–292). Hershey, PA: IGI Global. doi:10.4018/978-1-5225-1744-3.ch010

Kasemsap, K. (2017c). Management education and leadership styles: Current issues and approaches. In N. Baporikar (Ed.), *Innovation and shifting perspectives in management education* (pp. 166–193). Hershey, PA: IGI Global. doi:10.4018/978-1-5225-1019-2.ch008

Kaunonen, M., Salin, S., & Aalto, P. (2015). Database nurse staffing indicators: Explaining risks of staff job dissatisfaction in outpatient care. *Journal of Nursing Management*, *23*(5), 546–556. doi:10.1111/jonm.12169 PMID:24373115

Keillor, B. D., Pettijohn, C. E., & d'Amico, M. (2011). The relationship between attitudes toward technology, adaptability, and customer orientation among professional salespeople. *Journal of Applied Business Research*, *17*(4), 31–40. doi:10.19030/jabr.v17i4.2090

Kenny, P., Reeve, R., & Hall, J. (2016). Satisfaction with nursing education, job satisfaction, and work intentions of new graduate nurses. *Nurse Education Today*, *36*, 230–235. doi:10.1016/j.nedt.2015.10.023 PMID:26556705

Kjeldsen, A. M., & Andersen, L. B. (2013). How pro-social motivation affects job satisfaction: An international analysis of countries with different welfare state regimes. *Scandinavian Political Studies*, *36*(2), 153–176. doi:10.1111/j.1467-9477.2012.00301.x

Klaus, S. F., Ekerdt, D. J., & Gajewski, B. (2012). Job satisfaction in birth cohorts of nurses. *Journal of Nursing Management*, *20*(4), 461–471. doi:10.1111/j.1365-2834.2011.01283.x PMID:22591148

Lambert, E. G., Hogan, N. L., & Barton, S. M. (2001). The impact of job satisfaction on turnover intent: A test of a structural measurement model using a national sample of workers. *The Social Science Journal*, *38*(2), 233–250. doi:10.1016/S0362-3319(01)00110-0

Li, C. R., Chu, C. P., & Lin, C. J. (2010). The contingent value of exploratory and exploitative learning for new product development performance. *Industrial Marketing Management*, *39*(7), 1186–1197. doi:10.1016/j.indmarman.2010.02.002

Liu, D., Liao, H., & Loi, R. (2012). The dark side of leadership: A three-level investigation of the cascading effect of abusive supervision on employee creativity. *Academy of Management Journal*, *55*(5), 1187–1212. doi:10.5465/amj.2010.0400

Long, C. S., & Xuan, S. S. (2014). Human resources development practices and employees' job satisfaction. In P. Ordóñez de Pablos & R. Tennyson (Eds.), *Strategic approaches for human capital management and development in a turbulent economy* (pp. 117–128). Hershey, PA: IGI Global. doi:10.4018/978-1-4666-4530-1.ch008

Lovas, L. (2007). Relationship of organizational culture and job satisfaction in the public sector. *Studia Psychologica*, *49*(3), 215–221.

Malek, M. D., Fahrudin, A., & Kamil, I. S. M. (2009). Occupational stress and psychological well-being in emergency services. *Asian Social Work and Policy Review*, *3*(3), 143–154. doi:10.1111/j.1753-1411.2009.00030.x

Malloy, T., & Penprase, B. (2010). Nursing leadership style and psychosocial work environment. *Journal of Nursing Management*, *18*(6), 715–725. doi:10.1111/j.1365-2834.2010.01094.x PMID:20840366

Manojlovich, M., Antonakos, C. L., & Ronis, D. L. (2009). Intensive care units, communication between nurses and physicians, and patients' outcomes. *American Journal of Critical Care*, *18*(1), 21–30. doi:10.4037/ajcc2009353 PMID:19116401

Mardanov, I. T., Maertz, C. P., & Sterrett, J. L. (2008). Leader-member exchange and job satisfaction: Cross-industry comparisons and predicted employee turnover. *The Journal of Leadership Studies*, *2*(2), 63–82. doi:10.1002/jls.20062

Mateescu, A., & Chraif, M. (2015). The relationship between job satisfaction, occupational stress and coping mechanism in educational and technical organizations. *Procedia: Social and Behavioral Sciences*, *187*, 728–732. doi:10.1016/j.sbspro.2015.03.153

Mathieu, C., & Babiak, P. (2016). Corporate psychopathy and abusive supervision: Their influence on employees' job satisfaction and turnover intentions. *Personality and Individual Differences*, *91*, 102–106. doi:10.1016/j.paid.2015.12.002

Mauno, S., Kinnunen, U., Makikangas, A., & Natti, J. (2005). Psychological consequences of fixed-term employment and perceived job insecurity among health care staff. *European Journal of Work and Organizational Psychology*, *14*(3), 209–237. doi:10.1080/13594320500146649

Nesbit, P. L., & Lam, E. (2014). Cultural adaptability and organizational change: A case study of a social service organization in Hong Kong. *Contemporary Management Research*, *10*(4), 303–324. doi:10.7903/cmr.12186

Ouyang, Z., Sang, J., Li, P., & Peng, J. (2015). Organizational justice and job insecurity as mediators of the effect of emotional intelligence on job satisfaction: A study from China. *Personality and Individual Differences*, *76*, 147–152. doi:10.1016/j.paid.2014.12.004

Özpehlivan, M., & Acar, A. Z. (2015). Assessment of a multidimensional job satisfaction instrument. *Procedia: Social and Behavioral Sciences*, *210*, 283–290. doi:10.1016/j.sbspro.2015.11.368

Patterson, M. G., West, M. A., Shackleton, V. J., Dawson, J. F., Lawthom, R., Maitlis, S., & Wallace, A. M. et al. (2005). Validating the organizational climate measure: Links to managerial practices, productivity and innovation. *Journal of Organizational Behavior*, *26*(4), 379–408. doi:10.1002/job.312

Platania, S., Santisi, G., Magnano, P., & Ramaci, T. (2015). Job satisfaction and organizational well-being queried: A comparison between the two companies. *Procedia: Social and Behavioral Sciences*, *191*, 1436–1441. doi:10.1016/j.sbspro.2015.04.406

Prosen, M., & Piskar, F. (2015). Job satisfaction of Slovenian hospital nursing workforce. *Journal of Nursing Management*, *23*(2), 242–251. doi:10.1111/jonm.12121 PMID:23869437

Ravari, A., Bazargan, M., Vanaki, Z., & Mirzael, T. (2012). Job satisfaction among Iranian hospital-based practicing nurses: Examining the influence of self-expectation, social interaction and organisational situations. *Journal of Nursing Management*, *20*(4), 522–533. doi:10.1111/j.1365-2834.2010.01188.x PMID:22591154

Rosenblatt, Z., Talmud, I., & Ruvio, A. (1999). A gender-based framework of the experience of job insecurity and its effects on work attitudes. *European Journal of Work and Organizational Psychology*, *8*(2), 197–217. doi:10.1080/135943299398320

Rowold, J., Borgmann, L., & Bormann, K. (2014). Which leadership constructs are important for predicting job satisfaction, affective commitment, and perceived job performance in profit versus nonprofit organizations? *Nonprofit Management & Leadership*, *25*(2), 147–164. doi:10.1002/nml.21116

Sarin, S., & Majahan, V. (2001). The effect of reward structures on the performance of cross-functional product development teams. *Journal of Marketing*, *65*(2), 35–53. doi:10.1509/jmkg.65.2.35.18252

Sell, L., & Cleal, B. (2011). Job satisfaction, work environment, and rewards: Motivational theory revisited. *Labour*, *25*(1), 1–23. doi:10.1111/j.1467-9914.2010.00496.x

Shoss, M. K., Eisenberger, R., Restubog, S. L. D., & Zagenczyk, T. J. (2013). Blaming the organization for abusive supervision: The roles of perceived organizational support and supervisor's organizational embodiment. *The Journal of Applied Psychology*, *98*(1), 158–168. doi:10.1037/a0030687 PMID:23205496

Song, Z., Chon, K., Ding, G., & Gu, C. (2015). Impact of organizational socialization tactics on newcomer job satisfaction and engagement: Core self-evaluations as moderators. *International Journal of Hospitality Management*, *46*, 180–189. doi:10.1016/j.ijhm.2015.02.006

Sony, M., & Mekoth, N. (2016). The relationship between emotional intelligence, frontline employee adaptability, job satisfaction and job performance. *Journal of Retailing and Consumer Services*, *30*, 20–32. doi:10.1016/j.jretconser.2015.12.003

Statt, D. A. (2004). *The Routledge dictionary of business management*. New York: Routledge.

Stokes, C. K., Schneider, T. R., & Lyons, J. B. (2010). Adaptive performance: A criterion problem. *Team Performance Management: An International Journal*, *16*(3/4), 212–230. doi:10.1108/13527591011053278

Tao, H., Ellenbecker, C. H., Wang, Y., & Li, Y. (2015). Examining perception of job satisfaction and intention to leave among ICU nurses in China. *International Journal of Nursing Sciences*, *2*(2), 140–148. doi:10.1016/j.ijnss.2015.04.007

Tavousi, M. N. (2015). Dispositional effects on job stressors and job satisfaction: The role of core evaluations. *Procedia: Social and Behavioral Sciences*, *190*, 61–68. doi:10.1016/j.sbspro.2015.04.917

Tepper, B. J. (2000). Consequences of abusive supervision. *Academy of Management Journal*, *43*(2), 178–190. doi:10.2307/1556375

Tepper, B. J., Henle, C. A., Lambert, L. S., Giacalone, R. A., & Duffy, M. K. (2008). Abusive supervision and subordinates' organization deviance. *The Journal of Applied Psychology*, *93*(4), 721–732. doi:10.1037/0021-9010.93.4.721 PMID:18642979

Volmer, J., Niessen, C., Spurk, D., Linz, A., & Abele, A. E. (2011). Reciprocal relationships between leader–member exchange (LMX) and job satisfaction: A cross-lagged analysis. *Applied Psychology*, *60*(4), 522–545. doi:10.1111/j.1464-0597.2011.00446.x

Wang, L., Tao, H., Ellenbecker, C. H., & Liu, X. (2012). Job satisfaction, occupational commitment and intent to stay among Chinese nurses: A cross-sectional questionnaire survey. *Journal of Advanced Nursing*, *68*(3), 539–549. doi:10.1111/j.1365-2648.2011.05755.x PMID:21722170

Warr, P. (2007). *Work, happiness, and unhappiness*. Mahwah, NJ: Lawrence Erlbaum Associates.

Westlund, S. (2013). Leading techies: Assessing project leadership styles most significantly related to software developer job satisfaction. In R. Colomo-Palacios (Ed.), *Enhancing the modern organization through information technology professionals: Research, studies, and techniques* (pp. 200–215). Hershey, PA: IGI Global. doi:10.4018/978-1-4666-2648-5.ch014

Whitman, D. S., van Rooy, D. L., & Viswesvaran, C. (2010). Satisfaction, citizenship behaviors, and performance in work units: A meta-analysis of collective construct relations. *Personnel Psychology*, *63*(1), 41–81. doi:10.1111/j.1744-6570.2009.01162.x

Yee, R. W. Y., Guo, Y., & Yeung, A. C. L. (2015). Being close or being happy? The relative impact of work relationship and job satisfaction on service quality. *International Journal of Production Economics*, *169*, 391–400. doi:10.1016/j.ijpe.2015.08.021

Zhang, J., Wu, Q., Miao, D., Yan, X., & Peng, J. (2014). The impact of core self-evaluations on job satisfaction: The mediator role of career commitment. *Social Indicators Research*, *116*(3), 809–822. doi:10.1007/s11205-013-0328-5

Zhang, J., & Zheng, W. (2009). How does satisfaction translate into performance? An examination of commitment and cultural values. *Human Resource Development Quarterly*, *20*(3), 331–351. doi:10.1002/hrdq.20022

Ziegler, R., Hagen, B., & Diehl, M. (2012). Relationship between job satisfaction and job performance: Job ambivalence as a moderator. *Journal of Applied Social Psychology*, *42*(8), 2019–2040. doi:10.1111/j.1559-1816.2012.00929.x

ADDITIONAL READING

Agypt, B., & Rubin, B. A. (2012). Time in the new economy: The impact of the interaction of individual and structural temporalities on job satisfaction. *Journal of Management Studies, 49*(2), 403–428. doi:10.1111/j.1467-6486.2011.01021.x

Akinyemi, O., & Atilola, O. (2013). Nigerian resident doctors on strike: Insights from and policy implications of job satisfaction among resident doctors in a Nigerian teaching hospital. *The International Journal of Health Planning and Management, 28*(1), e46–e61. doi:10.1002/hpm.2141 PMID:22961749

Avery, R. E., Smillie, L. D., & Fife-Schaw, C. R. (2015). Employee achievement orientations and personality as predictors of job satisfaction facets. *Personality and Individual Differences, 76*, 56–61. doi:10.1016/j.paid.2014.11.037

Bergheim, K., Nielsen, M. B., Mearns, K., & Eid, J. (2015). The relationship between psychological capital, job satisfaction, and safety perceptions in the maritime industry. *Safety Science, 74*, 27–36. doi:10.1016/j.ssci.2014.11.024

Chang, M., & Cheng, C. (2014). How balance theory explains high-tech professionals' solutions of enhancing job satisfaction. *Journal of Business Research, 67*(9), 2008–2018. doi:10.1016/j.jbusres.2013.10.010

Chen, I. H., Brown, R., Bowers, B. J., & Chang, W. Y. (2015). Job demand and job satisfaction in latent groups of turnover intention among licensed nurses in Taiwan nursing homes. *Research in Nursing & Health, 38*(5), 342–356. doi:10.1002/nur.21667 PMID:26012950

Cheng, C. Y., Liou, S. R., Tsai, H. M., & Chang, C. H. (2015). Job stress and job satisfaction among new graduate nurses during the first year of employment in Taiwan. *International Journal of Nursing Practice, 21*(4), 410–418. doi:10.1111/ijn.12281 PMID:24666722

Chung, Y., & Chun, J. (2015). Workplace stress and job satisfaction among child protective service workers in South Korea: Focusing on the buffering effects of protective factors. *Children and Youth Services Review, 57*, 134–140. doi:10.1016/j.childyouth.2015.08.007

Cotti, C. D., Haley, M. R., & Miller, L. A. (2014). Workplace flexibilities, job satisfaction and union membership in the US workforce. *British Journal of Industrial Relations, 52*(3), 403–425. doi:10.1111/bjir.12025

Davis, R. S. (2013). Unionization and work attitudes: How union commitment influences public sector job satisfaction. *Public Administration Review, 73*(1), 74–84. doi:10.1111/j.1540-6210.2012.02609.x

Dierdorff, E. C., & Morgeson, F. P. (2013). Getting what the occupation gives: Exploring multilevel links between work design and occupational values. *Personnel Psychology, 66*(3), 687–721. doi:10.1111/peps.12023

Felstead, A., Gallie, D., Green, F., & Inanc, H. (2015). Fits, misfits and interactions: Learning at work, job satisfaction and job-related well-being. *Human Resource Management Journal*, *25*(3), 294–310. doi:10.1111/1748-8583.12071

Fila, M. J., Paik, L. S., Griffeth, R. W., & Allen, D. (2014). Disaggregating job satisfaction: Effects of perceived demands, control, and support. *Journal of Business and Psychology*, *29*(4), 639–649. doi:10.1007/s10869-014-9358-5

Gabriel, A. S., Diefendorff, J. M., Chandler, M. M., Moran, C. M., & Greguras, G. J. (2014). The dynamic relationships of work affect and job satisfaction with perceptions of fit. *Personnel Psychology*, *67*(2), 389–420. doi:10.1111/peps.12042

Gambacorta, R., & Iannario, M. (2013). Measuring job satisfaction with CUB models. *Labour*, *27*(2), 198–224. doi:10.1111/labr.12008

Gurková, E., Čáp, J., Žiaková, K., & Ďurišková, M. (2012). Job satisfaction and emotional subjective well-being among Slovak nurses. *International Nursing Review*, *59*(1), 94–100. doi:10.1111/j.1466-7657.2011.00922.x

Hasegawa, H., & Ueda, K. (2016). Analysis of job satisfaction: The case of Japanese private companies. *Labour*, *30*(1), 109–134. doi:10.1111/labr.12064

Hirschi, A. (2011). Vocational identity as a mediator of the relationship between core self-evaluations and life and job satisfaction. *Applied Psychology*, *60*(4), 622–644. doi:10.1111/j.1464-0597.2011.00450.x

Homberg, F., McCarthy, D., & Tabvuma, V. (2015). A meta-analysis of the relationship between public service motivation and job satisfaction. *Public Administration Review*, *75*(5), 711–722. doi:10.1111/puar.12423

Hsu, L. C., & Liao, P. W. (2016). From job characteristics to job satisfaction of foreign workers in Taiwans construction industry: The mediating role of organizational commitment. *Human Factors and Ergonomics in Manufacturing & Service Industries*, *26*(2), 243–255. doi:10.1002/hfm.20624

Iseke, A. (2014). The part-time job satisfaction puzzle: Different types of job discrepancies and the moderating effect of family importance. *British Journal of Industrial Relations*, *52*(3), 445–469. doi:10.1111/bjir.12019

Kurland, H., & Hasson-Gilad, D. R. (2015). Organizational learning and extra effort: The mediating effect of job satisfaction. *Teaching and Teacher Education*, *49*, 56–67. doi:10.1016/j.tate.2015.02.010

Lau, W. M., Pang, J., & Chui, W. (2011). Job satisfaction and the association with involvement in clinical activities among hospital pharmacists in Hong Kong. *International Journal of Pharmacy Practice*, *19*(4), 253–263. doi:10.1111/j.2042-7174.2010.00085.x PMID:21733013

Linz, S. J., & Semykina, A. (2012). What makes workers happy? Anticipated rewards and job satisfaction. *Industrial Relations*, *51*(4), 811–844. doi:10.1111/j.1468-232X.2012.00702.x

McCrae, J. S., Scannapieco, M., & Obermann, A. (2015). Retention and job satisfaction of child welfare supervisors. *Children and Youth Services Review*, *59*, 171–176. doi:10.1016/j.childyouth.2015.11.011

Mueller, K., Voelkle, M. C., & Hattrup, K. (2011). On the relationship between job satisfaction and non-response in employee attitude surveys: A longitudinal field study. *Journal of Occupational and Organizational Psychology*, *84*(4), 780–798. doi:10.1348/096317910X526777

Purpora, C., & Blegen, M. A. (2015). Job satisfaction and horizontal violence in hospital staff registered nurses: The mediating role of peer relationships. *Journal of Clinical Nursing*, *24*(15/16), 2286–2294. doi:10.1111/jocn.12818 PMID:25939756

Qu, H., & Zhao, X. (2012). Employees' work–family conflict moderating life and job satisfaction. *Journal of Business Research*, *65*(1), 22–28. doi:10.1016/j.jbusres.2011.07.010

Semykina, A., & Linz, S. J. (2013). Job satisfaction and perceived gender equality in advanced promotion opportunities: An empirical investigation. *Kyklos*, *66*(4), 591–619. doi:10.1111/kykl.12038

Shirom, A., Toker, S., Melamed, S., Berliner, S., & Shapira, I. (2012). Life and job satisfaction as predictors of the incidence of diabetes. *Applied Psychology: Health and Well-Being*, *4*(1), 31–48. PMID:26286969

Shiu, E., Hassan, L. M., & Parry, S. (2015). The moderating effects of national age stereotyping on the relationships between job satisfaction and its determinants: A study of older workers across 26 countries. *British Journal of Management*, *26*(2), 255–272. doi:10.1111/1467-8551.12091

Smith, J. C. (2015). Pay growth, fairness, and job satisfaction: Implications for nominal and real wage rigidity. *The Scandinavian Journal of Economics*, *117*(3), 852–877. doi:10.1111/sjoe.12091

Spagnoli, P., Caetano, A., & Santos, S. C. (2012). Satisfaction with job aspects: Do patterns change over time? *Journal of Business Research*, *65*(5), 609–616. doi:10.1016/j.jbusres.2011.02.048

Stromgren, M., Eriksson, A., Bergman, D., & Dellve, L. (2016). Social capital among healthcare professionals: A prospective study of its importance for job satisfaction, work engagement and engagement in clinical improvements. *International Journal of Nursing Studies*, *53*, 116–125. doi:10.1016/j.ijnurstu.2015.07.012 PMID:26315780

Tabvuma, V., Bui, H. T. M., & Homberg, F. (2014). Adaptation to externally driven change: The impact of political change on job satisfaction in the public sector. *Public Administration Review*, *74*(3), 384–395. doi:10.1111/puar.12204 PMID:25598554

Taylor, J. (2014). Public service motivation, relational job design, and job satisfaction in local government. *Public Administration*, *92*(4), 902–918. doi:10.1111/j.1467-9299.2012.02108.x

Tepret, N. Y., & Tuna, K. (2015). Effect of management factor on employee job satisfaction: An application in telecommunication sector. *Procedia: Social and Behavioral Sciences*, *195*, 673–679. doi:10.1016/j.sbspro.2015.06.264

KEY TERMS AND DEFINITIONS

Autonomy: The level of freedom and discretion allowed to an employee over his or her job.

Burnout: The state of having no enthusiasm because of working too hard.

Job Characteristics: The aspects specific to a job (e.g., knowledge, skills, physical demands, and working conditions) that can be recognized, defined, and evaluated.

Job Performance: The accomplishment of a given task measured against the standards of accuracy, completeness, cost, and speed.

Job Satisfaction: The sense of inner fulfillment and pride achieved when performing a particular job.

Motivation: The internal and external factors that stimulate desire and energy in people to be continually interested and committed to a job, role or subject, or to make an effort to attain a goal.

Promotion: The advancement of an employee's position within the organization.

Reward: Something given in exchange for good behavior or good work.

Work-Family Conflict: The opposition resulting from the perceived differences between individual's work and their family life.

Chapter 9
Communication and Job Satisfaction

Libi Shen
University of Phoenix, USA

Larry Austin
University of Phoenix, USA

ABSTRACT

In a business organization, communication is imperative for employers to express their thoughts, ideas, policies, and goals to their employees. Different organizational leaders or managers have various communication styles. Effective communication between employers and employees would not only boost employees' morale and job performance, but also demonstrate employers' successful leadership. Are communication and job satisfaction related? How should employers communicate so that their employees have higher job satisfaction, better engagement, lower turnover, and stronger long-term commitment? The purpose of this chapter is to explore the relationship between communication and employees' job satisfaction. This chapter attempts to provide business executives, company leaders, and scholar-practitioners suggestions with regard to developing effective communication strategies for better company management.

INTRODUCTION

Employers need to communicate with their employees to reach their goals. Clear communication is critical for leadership success. Froschheiser (2015) indicated that clear communication is the golden thread tying six basic functions (i.e., leading, planning, organizing, staffing, controlling, and communicating) of the management. Communication is essential, because it can create positive changes within an organization. As Maxwell (2001) expressed,

Only with good communication can a team succeed – it doesn't matter whether that team is a family, a company, a ministry, or a ball club. Effective teams have teammates who are constantly talking to one another. Communication increases commitment and connection, they in turn fuel action (p. 197).

DOI: 10.4018/978-1-5225-2568-4.ch009

Communication is important for both employers and employees in a company. An "open, honest, and regular communication is essential to keeping employees motivated and productive" (DuFrene & Lehman 2014, p. 443). A timely communication from the employers may reduce miscommunication and employees' job stress.

Researchers have defined six leadership styles that create harmony and boost performance: visionary, coaching, affiliative, democratic, pacesetting, and commanding (Coleman, Boyatzis, & McKee, 2002; Goleman, 2002). Leadership styles mediate relations between communication styles and leadership outcomes (De Vries, Bakker-Pieper, & Oostenveld, 2010). Garg and Jain (2013) outlined four levels of work efficiency related to people's skills. Low-relationship/low-task managers were considered unattached and would often delegate authority; low-relationship/high-task managers were viewed as authoritarian with little regard for suggestions from others; high-relationship/low-task managers were considered ineffective and would have difficulty maintaining order; high-relationship/high-task managers were considered as the most efficient (Garg & Jain, 2013). It is obvious that work efficiency is associated with leadership and communication styles.

What is the impact of effective communication in an organization? Effective communication is "intentional, goal-oriented and coherent with an organization's strategy" (Garcia, 2012, p. 42). Effective communication is rational, logical, and persuasive, which benefits industrial relations, organizational change, and relaxation (Choudhardy & Rathore, 2013). Effective communication contributes to higher employee satisfaction and engagement, lower turnover, and stronger long-term commitment (DuFrene & Lehman, 2014). Effective leaders need to know how to communicate with all stakeholders of an organization including managers, employees, investors, and customers (Anthony, 2015).

The problem is that not all managers are effective communicators. Communication involves more than leadership styles; emotional intelligence, attitudes, methods of expression, and strategies used all matter. What is the relationship between employers' communication styles and employees' job satisfaction? What strategies best facilitate communications between employers and employees? How do employers communicate to their employees so they can improve company management and reach their goals? The purpose of this chapter is to explore the relationship between communication and employees' job satisfaction as well as to provide business executives, company leaders, and scholar-practitioners recommendations on effective communication strategies for better organizational management.

BACKGROUND

The trend for employees' job satisfaction has fluctuated for the past 10 years, starting from 77% in 2005, 86% in 2009, 81% in 2012 and 2013, and 88% in 2015 (SHRM, 2016). Based on SHRM (2016), the top 12 aspects or contributors to employee job satisfaction included the following: (1) respectful treatment of all employees at all levels (67%); (2) overall compensation/pay (63%); (3) overall benefits (60%); (4) job security (58%), (5) trust between employees and senior management (55%) and opportunities to use skills and abilities at work (55%); (6) the organization's financial stability as well as the relationship with immediate supervisors (53%); (7) a feeling safety in the work environment (e.g., physical safety, taking measures to prevent violence in the workplace, acts of terrorism) (50%); (8) immediate supervisor's showing respect for the ideas of others (50%); (9) the work itself (whether the work is interesting, challenging, exciting) (48%); management's recognition of employee job performance (48%), communication between employees and senior management (48%); (10) career advancement opportunities within the organization (47%); (11) autonomy and independence to make decisions (46%); and (12) management's communication of organizational goals and strategies (45%). These statistics showed the importance of the interpersonal dynamics in the workplace.

It was apparent that employees' relationships with management played a significant role in employee job satisfaction, because respect, trust, relationship, recognition, communication, autonomy, and independence are key words on the list. In SHRM's (2016) further study of 581-590 participants' satisfaction ranking with relation to the management, the manager's communication of organizational goals and strategies, respectful treatment of all employees at all levels, and communication between employee and senior management stood out as the top three on the list. Communication has played a pivotal role in job satisfaction, as reported by SHRM (2016).

With the rise of flexible work arrangements, globalization and technological advances that make it possible for knowledge workers to work from virtually anywhere; strengthening communication efforts is a critical function of a successful organization. It is also important for organizations to pay attention to what communication methods are most conducive for their particular environment, the purpose of the exchange and their staff's preference. Choosing the wrong communication technique could influence the effectiveness of the message and, thus, possibly affect its end goal (SHRM, 2016, p. 28).

LITERATURE REVIEW

Definitions, Theories, and Models of Communication

The word communication came from the Latin word *commūnicāre*, which means to share. Communication is the process of transmitting information and common understanding from one person to another (Keyton, 2011). Communication was defined as "an act of will directed toward a living entity that reacts" (Garcia, 2012, p.42). Communication is the process of giving, receiving, imparting, or exchanging information/news. In other words, when an employer uses language(s) to express his/her ideas, thoughts, concerns, opinions, hopes, suggestions, or goals to the employees, it is a communication.

The first major model of communication was developed by Claude Elwood Shannon in *A Mathematical Theory of Communication*. He studied the quantification, storage, and communication of information with the information theory. Shannon (1948) explained how best to encode the information that a sender wanted to transmit. The initial model is a linear model consisting of sender, channel, and receiver. Communication was viewed as the process of sending and receiving messages or transferring information from sender to the receiver. Later, Shannon and Weaver (1949) constructed the model of communication based on the following elements: an information source (which produces a message), a transmitter (which encodes the message into signals), a channel (which adapts to the signals for transmission), a receiver (which decodes the message from the signal), and a destination (where the message arrives). They argued that there are three problems for communication: the technical problem (i.e., how accurately can the message be transmitted), the semantic problem (i.e., how precisely is the meaning being conveyed), and the effectiveness problem (i.e. how effectively does the received meaning affect the behavior).

In 1954, Wilbur Schramm proposed that people should also examine the impact of the original message on the target message, besides the components of message, source/encoder, form, channel/medium, destination/receiver/decoder, and receiver. Communication is a two-way process in this model. Communication includes acts that confer knowledge and experiences, give advice and commands, and ask questions (Schramm, 1954). Communication is the process of information transmission governed by three levels of semiotic rules: syntactic, pragmatic, and semantic rules (Schramm, 1954). Communication, which consists of a message and feedback, is the social interaction between two or more agents who share a common set of signs and semiotic rules. Encoding and decoding are two important parts of the communication process; encoding is done by a sender (transmitter) who sends data (message) to a receiver, and the receiver decodes the data. Culture, beliefs, experiences, social background, values and rules are all fields of experience that influence the understanding of the message.

In 1960, David Berlo expanded Shannon and Weaver's (1949) linear model of communication to the Sender-Message-Channel-Receiver (SMCR) Model of Communication. In Berlo's model, there were five elements within both the source/encoder and the receiver/decoder, which affect the fidelity of the message. Both the source and the receiver consist of communication, skills, attitudes, knowledge, social system, and culture. The message involves content, elements, treatment, structure, and code. Additionally, there were five senses (i.e., hearing, seeing, touching, smelling, and tasting) in the channel, whatever communication people do (Communication Theory, 2016).

In 1970, Dean Barnlund proposed a transactional model of communication. This model revealed a two-way continuous transaction in which two individuals are simultaneously engaging in the sending and receiving of messages. A sender and a receiver are linked reciprocally, while there are three types of noises that influence communications in the transactional model: external noise, physiological noise, and psychological noise (Barnlund, 2008). Communication is the passage of information, which travels from one individual to another; the information becomes separate from the communication itself. It focuses on how an individual communicates as the determining factor of the way the message will be interpreted. Factors that impact the meanings in this transactional model include channels, communicators, environment, and overlap of communicator understanding (Barnlund, 2008). This type of communication is also called the constitutive model or the constructionist view of communication. In the Constructionist Model, the process of communication cannot be separated from its social and historical context.

In the Constitutive Meta model, Craig (1999) argued that there are seven different traditions which can engage each other in dialogue rather than ignore each other. Those seven traditions included: Rhetorical (which views communication as the practical art of discourse); Semiotic (which perceives communication as the mediation by signs); Phenomenological (which considers communication as the experience of dialogue with others); Cybernetic (which regards communication as the flow of information); Socio-psychological (which views communication as the interaction of individuals); Socio-cultural (which views communication as the production and reproduction of the social order), and Critical (which views communication as the process in which all assumptions can be challenged) (Craig, 1999). Each of these views clearly defined against the others to describe different communication behaviors.

Additionally, Littlejohn and Foss (2009) described that in constitutive view of communication,

Communication is seen not only as creating meaning but as creating, or constituting, social entities (personal relationships and organizations, respectively). In other words, personal relationships and organizations are seen as made of or made from communication. This is a fundamentally constitutive view because communication is theorized not as merely one factor that influences the formation of the social entities but rather as the very essence of their nature (p. 177).

Over the years, the theories of communication have continued to evolve and develop. The rapid growth of social media, computers, telephone, television, movies, and the Internet has changed the way people communicate. Technology has not only changed people's thoughts and behaviors, but also influenced their communication styles.

Communication Styles

Communication can be verbal (e.g., using languages, sounds, tone of voice), non-verbal (e.g., using posture, facial expressions, body language), written (e.g., using memos, notes, emails, letters, blogs, text messages, journals), and visual (e.g., using signs, symbols, pictures, photos, posters). In this chapter, the researchers focus on the verbal communication. DeVries, Bakker-Pieper, and Oostenveld (2010) once noted, "communication styles were strongly and differentially related to knowledge sharing behaviors, perceived leader performance, satisfaction with the leader, and subordinate's team commitment" (p.367). According to Newton (2011), there are five communication styles: assertive, aggressive, passive-aggressive, submissive, and manipulative. People might use different styles in different situations, or they might use their default style. In the following, Newton's (2011) five communication styles were illustrated.

The Assertive Style of Communication is the most effective one because it involves achieving goals without hurting people; being protective of one's own rights while being respectful of people's rights; being socially and emotionally expressive; making choices and taking responsibility for them; asking directly for help while accepting the possibility of rejection; accepting compliments; coping with criticism, using a medium pitch or volume when speaking; using good eye contact and an open posture; and being respect of others.

The Aggressive Style of Communication is an ineffective communication style since the person communicating often behaves as if his/her needs are the most important ones. The behaviors in this style include: threating, frightening, hostility, loudness, demanding, belligerent, explosive, unpredictable, intimidating, bullying, willing to achieve goals at other's expense, out to win, loud volume, scowl, frown, invading others' personal space, posture bigger than others, and big gestures.

The Passive-Aggressive Style of Communication allows the person to outwardly appear passive, but actually acts out his/her anger in an indirect way, or behind the scenes. Passive aggressive people often feel resentful or powerless to express their feelings. This style of behavior often includes sarcastic, unreliable, complaining, devious, unreliable, sulky, patronizing, gossips, indirect aggressive, two-faced, sweet voice, asymmetrical posture, quick, looks sweet and innocent, and pretending to be warm and friendly.

The Submissive Style of Communication is about pleasing other people and avoiding conflict. The behaviors in this style include being apologetic, avoiding confrontation, finding difficulty in taking decisions, constantly yielding to the preferences of others, opting out, feeling like a victim, blaming others for events, refusing compliments, inexpressive of feelings and desires, and speaking with a soft voice.

The Manipulative Style of Communication is scheming, calculating, and shrewd. People who use this style are cunning, controlling of others, skillful at influencing or controlling others to their own advantage, creating fake tears, making others feel obliged or sorry for them, controlling of others in an insidious way, hiding an underlying message while speaking with high pitch voice and making people feel guilty and frustrated.

To strengthen human relationships, reduce stress from conflict, and decrease anxiety in life, it is suggested to practice the assertive communication style (Newton, 2011). An effective leader would act according to one or more of those communication styles to leadership. Newton (2011) believed that a good understanding of the five basic styles of communication will help people learn to react effectively when confronted with difficult people, as well as being aware of them when they are not behaving in the right way.

Definitions and Theories of Job Satisfaction

Job satisfaction was defined in various ways. Job satisfaction is "any number of psychological, physiological, and environmental circumstances that causes a person to say that I am satisfied with my job" (Hoppock's remark, as cited in Ali, 2016, p.101). Job satisfaction is "a pleasure or positive emotional state resulting from the appraisal of one's job or job experiences" (Locke, 1976, p. 1300). Job satisfaction is "the employees' attitudes towards the jobs which include cognitive and behavioral aspects such as work environment, subordinates, supervision, salary, job development, etc." (Sulaiman & Seng, 2016, p. 45).

Dugguh and Ayaga (2014) pointed out that job satisfaction is influenced by three factors: environmental (e.g., communication, employee recognition), individual (e.g., emotions, genetics, personality), and psychological (e.g., one's life, family, community) factors. The extrinsic job satisfaction categories include "pay, company policies, job security, relations with others and physical working conditions" (Yoke & Panatik, 2016, p. 807). The intrinsic factors that influence job satisfaction are promotional opportunities, recognition, achievement, and responsibility. The theories of job satisfaction are related to motivation. There are several models related to job satisfaction: Maslow's (1943) hierarchy of needs, Herzberg's motivator-hygiene theory, Locke's (1976) Range of Affect Theory, the Job Characteristics Model, and the Dispositional Approach.

Maslow (1934, pp. 2-3) believed that "any motivated behavior, either preparatory or consummatory, must be understood to be a channel through which many basic needs may be simultaneously expressed or satisfied. Typically, an act has more than one motivation." In Maslow's (1943) *Theory of Motivation*, there are five levels of needs: the physiological needs (e.g., water, salt, sugar, protein, fat, calcium, oxygen, temperature, foods, and shelter), the safety needs (e.g., security, stability, and freedom from fear), the love needs (e.g., acceptance, affection, belonging, and affiliation), the esteem needs (e.g., approval, recognition, self-respect, self-esteem), and the need for self-actualization (e.g., self-fulfillment). When people's basic needs are satisfied, they will be motivated for next level of needs.

Herzberg's (1966) motivator-hygiene theory suggested that job satisfaction and job dissatisfaction are not on two opposite ends of the same continuum, because they are different and independent. There is a neutral feeling between satisfied and dissatisfied; employees might be neither satisfied nor dissatisfied. The motivation factors, such as pay, benefits, recognition, and achievement need to be met for employees' satisfaction; however, the hygiene factors (e.g., working conditions, job security, company policies, company structure, interaction with colleagues, and quality of management) are associated with job dissatisfaction (Herzberg, 1966).

Locke's (1976) Affect Theory revealed that job satisfaction is determined by a discrepancy between what one wants in a job and what one has in a job. How much one values a given facet of work moderates how satisfied or dissatisfied one becomes when expectations are or aren't met. The Job Characteristics Model (JMC) involved five major characteristics: skill variety, task identity, task significance, autonomy, and feedback, which influenced three psychological states (i.e., core job dimensions, critical psychological states, and personal and work outcomes) (Hackman & Oldham, 1975).

The Dispositional Approach model showed that job satisfaction is tied to personality. Judge, Locke, and Durham (1997) believed that self-esteem, self-efficacy, emotional stability, and locus of control comprised a broad personality construct, and these four affective constructs are related to job satisfaction. In sum, the aforementioned theories and models provide the foundation for job satisfaction. How do employers measure employees' job satisfaction?

Measurement of Job Satisfaction

Factors that contributed to employees' job satisfaction can also be viewed through the items or categories in the instrument for measuring job satisfaction. For example, in Johnson's (1955) Job Satisfaction Questionnaire, the followings were used to measure job satisfaction: physical and mental exertion, relations with associates, relations with employer, job security, advancement, finances, interest, emotional involvement in the job, job information and status, physical surroundings and work conditions, future, goals, progress toward goals, and evaluation in retrospect. In the Minnesota Satisfaction Questionnaire (MSQ), Weiss et al., (1967) included ability utilization, achievement, activity, advancement, authority, company policies, compensation, co-workers, creativity, independence, moral values, recognition, responsibility, security, social service, social status, supervision- human relations, supervision-technical, variety, and working conditions in the job satisfaction measurement. The newer version of Minnesota Satisfaction Questionnaire consisted of the nature of work, compensation and benefits, attitudes toward supervisors, relations with co-workers, and opportunities for promotion as well as co-workers, achievement, activity, advancement, authority, company policies, compensation, moral values, creativity, independence, security, social service, social status, recognition, responsibility, supervision-human relations, supervision-technical, variety, working conditions.

In Sigrist's (2010) study, he used Minnesota Satisfaction Questionnaire (MSQ) to measure high school principals' job satisfaction, and the categories in MSQ included: social service, achievement, activity, variety, ability utilization, moral values, responsibility, co-workers, creativity, authority, independence, supervision-human relations, working conditions, company policies and practices, social status, recognition, supervision-technical, security, compensation, and advancement.

In the Job Descriptive Index (JDI), pay and benefit, work itself, promotion opportunity, supervision, and coworkers were used by Smith, Kendall, & Hullin (1969) as the major categories for job satisfaction measurement. In the Job Diagnostic Survey (JDS), Hackman and Oldham (1975) had the nature of the job and job tasks, motivation, personality, psychological states (cognition and feelings about job tasks), relation to the job growth, pay security, social, supervision, and global satisfaction in the categories. The Michigan Organizational Assessment Questionnaire Subscale covered demographics, general attitudes, job facets (importance and contingency), task and role characteristics, work group functioning, supervising behavior, intergroup relations, influence structure, individual differences and outcomes, compensation and performance evaluation in the job satisfaction instrument (Jenkins, Nadler, Lawler, & Cammann, 1975).

In the Job in General Scale (JIG), Ironson et al., (1989) listed pleasant, bad, ideal, waste of time, good, undesirable, worthwhile, worse than most, acceptable, superior, better than most, disagreeable, makes me content, Inadequate, excellent, rotten, enjoyable, and poor as measurement categories. In the Faces Scale developed in 1950s, job satisfaction was measured by requesting the participants to choose a face. In Yeoh's (2007) Facet Satisfaction Scale (FSS), pay, promotion, supervisors, co-workers, the work, benefits, procedures, and physical work conditions were included.

A survey of 5,000 households conducted by Cheng, Kan, Levanon, and Ray (2014) revealed the ranking of job satisfaction from the most to the least satisfied: people at work, interest in work, commute to work, physical environment, supervisor, quality of equipment, vacation policy, overall satisfaction, job security, sick day policy, health plan, family leave plan, flex/time plan, work/life balance, wages, retirement plan, communication channel, work load, growth potential, recognition, performance review, training programs, bonus plan, promotion policy. It appears that employees are more satisfied with job components that are related to people and the work environment, instead of promotion policy, bonus plan, training programs, performance review, and recognition. The job satisfaction index presented by Happiness Research Institute (2015) showed the following categories as impacting to job satisfaction: a sense of purpose at work, managers' leadership, being able to influence working conditions, achievements, work/life balance, and colleagues.

By surveying the job satisfaction of 600 U.S.-based employees in 2015, SHRM (2016) presented a report in eight areas: career development, benefits, work environment, engagement opinions, compensation, employee relationships with management, conditions for engagement, and engagement behaviors. It can be concluded that survey questionnaires for job satisfaction are broad, and many factors have contributed to employees' job satisfaction. However, communication is not apparent in some job satisfaction measurement or instrument. Does communication play a role in employees' job satisfaction? What role does communication play in job satisfaction?

Communication and Job Satisfaction

In the past four decades, many researchers have explored the relationship between communication and employees' job satisfaction (e.g., Abugre, 2011; Akpinar, Torun, Okur, & Akpinar, 2013; Ali & Haider, 2012; Awad & Alhashemi, 2012; Burke & Wilcox, 1969; Carriere & Bourque, 2009; Chitrao, 2014; Czech & Forward, 2013; De Nobile & McCormick, 2008; De Vries, Van den Hooff, & De Ridder, 2006; Farahbod, Salimi, & Dorostkar, 2013; Goris, 2007; Ilozor, Ilozor, & Carr, 2001; Ismail, Mohd Sani, & Mohamad, 2014; Iyer & Israel, 2012; Kumar & Giri, 2009; Mădălina & Cătălin, 2016; Madlock, 2008; Madlock & Kennedy-Lightsey, 2010; Miles, Patrick, & King, 1996; Muchinsky, 1977; Orpen, 1997; Proctor, 2014; Rajhans, 2012; Ramirez, 2010; Rodwell, Kienzle, & Shadur, 1998; Sharma, 2015; Steingrímsdóttir, 2011; Swan & Futrell, 1978; Thomas, Zolin, & Hartman, 2009; Tourani & Rast, 2012).

Some researchers proved that effective organizational communication has been shown to positively impact employee satisfaction, performance, and engagement levels (De Nobile & McCormick, 2008; Goris, 2007; Iyer & Israel, 2012; Kumar & Giri, 2009; Orpen, 1997). Others have found significant relationships between communication and job stress (e.g., Chen, Silverthorne, & Hung, 2006; De Nobile, McCormick, & Hoekman, 2013; Diggens & Chesson, 2014; Harville, 1992; Jones, 2014; Ray & Miller, 1991; Rodwell, Kienzle, & Shadur, 1998).

As early as 1969, Ronald Burke and Douglas Wilcox administered a questionnaire survey to 323 people to explore the effects of different patterns and degrees of openness in superior-subordinate communication on subordinate job satisfaction. They discovered that different patterns and degrees of openness in super-subordinate communication affected five areas of work satisfaction (i.e., satisfaction with company, satisfaction with job, satisfaction with performance appraisal, helping relationship, and satisfaction with supervisor) (Burke & Wilcox, 1969). Their findings revealed that the greater the level of openness of superior or subordinate, the greater the satisfaction on those five variables (Burke & Wilcox, 1969).

Muchinsky (1977) adopted Roberts and O'Reilly's (1974) questionnaire to survey 695 employees on the relationships among organizational communication, organizational climate, and job satisfaction. He found that certain dimensions of organizational communications were closely tied to organizational climate and job satisfaction (Muchinsky, 1977). The highly relevant organizational communication variables included trust, influence, desire for interaction, accuracy, directionality downward/lateral, and satisfaction with communication; whereas, the job satisfaction variables consisted of satisfaction with work, supervision, pay, promotions, and co-workers. Satisfaction with communication was significantly and positively correlated with those dimensions of job satisfaction (Munchinsky, 1977). Swan and Futrell (1978) adopted Smith, Kendall, and Hulin's (1969) Job Description Index to survey 431 salesmen and found that goal clarity (i.e., accomplishments, results expected, priorities) had significant effects on job satisfaction. In other words, clear communication of job goals is related to job satisfaction factors, such as work, pay, supervision, promotion, and co-workers.

Ray and Miller (1991) believed that supportive communication can help clarify role expectations, reduce uncertainty, and increase perceptions for personal control in an organization. They surveyed 60 elementary school teachers and found that "satisfaction" was influenced by role conflict, role ambiguity, and exhaustion, while "affect" was influenced by exhaustion and participation in decision making (Ray & Miller, 1991). Role conflict and ambiguity had negative impact on job satisfaction (Ray & Miller, 1991).

On the other hand, some researchers learned that communication might not be effective to all. Harville (1992) surveyed 351 employees in a workshop and discovered that higher level jobs had significantly lower communication requirements than lower level jobs. In other words, the more the employers communicate on job requirements, the higher satisfaction the general employees have, but not for high-apprehensive employees. Orpen (1997) who gathered data from 135 managers of 21 companies found that the quality of communication in the companies influence both job satisfaction and work motivation. Rodwell, Kienzle, and Shadur (1998) examined organizational communication in the human resources management context from 329 employees in an Austrian technology company. They found that communication enhanced teamwork, job satisfaction, and commitment; however, it was not related to job performance (Rodwell, Kienzle, & Shadur, 1998).

In general, job satisfaction is associated with communication. Goris (2007) conducted a study of 302 employees in two companies to examine the influence of communication satisfaction on job congruence, job performance, and job satisfaction. He found that satisfaction with communication is the main predictor of both job performance and job satisfaction, but not for job congruence (Goris, 2007). In De Nobile and McCormick's (2008) study of 356 staff from 52 Catholic primary schools in Australia, there were significant relationships between organizational communication and job satisfaction. They concluded that supportive, democratic, cultural, and open communication was related to job satisfaction (De Nobile & McCormick, 2008). Madlock (2008) conducted a survey to 220 employees from different companies to explore the influence of communicator competence and relational leadership styles on job satisfaction. There was strong evidence that supervisors' communicator competence was a strong predictor of employee job and communication satisfaction (Madlock, 2008).

Kumar and Giri (2009) also investigated the relationship between organizational communication and job satisfaction. They collected questionnaires from 380 employees in Indian organizations, and found the significant correlation between communication and job satisfaction (Kumar & Giri, 2009). They believed that trust and communication satisfaction were related to pay, promotion, supervision, and fringe benefits (Kumar & Giri, 2009).

In Ali and Haider's (2012) study of 143 bank employees, they proved that internal organizational communication was an important factor that impact employees' job satisfaction. Their three dimensions of internal organizational communication (i.e., communication climate, formal communication, and informal communication) proved to have great impact on job satisfaction (Ali & Haider, 2012). Czech and Forward (2013) asked 154 fulltime employees to determine relationships among communication, leadership, and job satisfaction. Their findings revealed that the employees rated higher satisfaction when supervisors were honest and clear in their intentions, and involved employees in collaboration and decision-making in the organizations; however, income did not play a significant role in job satisfaction. "Money alone cannot compensate for a negative communication climate, feckless leadership, or enervating relationships at work" (Czech & Forward, 2013, p. 20).

Ismail, Mohd Sani, and Mohamad (2014) surveyed 129 employees in an organization regarding the relationship between communication openness in performance appraisal and job satisfaction. They confirmed that communication openness in performance appraisal systems was an important predictor of job satisfaction. By examining the relationship among effective organizational communication, employee attitudes, happiness, and job satisfaction from university staff, Proctor (2014, p. i) summarized that "effective bi-directional communication between employees, supervisors, and management improves attitude and happiness thereby affecting job satisfaction." In Sharma's (2015) study of 463 non-faculty staff in a higher education to examine the relationship between organizational communication and staff's perceptions of level of communication and job satisfaction, that staff members' level of satisfaction was related to personal feedback, relationship to supervisors, horizontal and informal communication, organizational integration, media quality, organizational perspective, and communication climate.

Mădălina and Cătălin (2016, p. 109) assumed that "a healthy communication determines the motivation of the staff, the increase of the productivity and individual and organizational performances" and proved that there is a positive correlation between the organizational communication (e.g., personal feedback, organizational integration, organizational perspective, and relationship with supervisors) and job satisfaction. Shmailan (2016) further examined how factors such as job fit, good communication, appreciation, and clear objectives contribute to employees' job satisfaction. He concluded that employee satisfaction linked to employee engagement directly; "employee satisfaction makes good business sense and increases productivity and career enhancement" (p.6).

Based on the review of previous research studies, it is obvious the relationship between communication and job satisfaction from year 1969 to year 2016 was significant. Employer's communication may contribute to either job satisfaction or job stress. In general, satisfaction with communication was the main predictor of both job performance and work satisfaction (Goris, 2007). Three dimensions of internal organizational communications, such as communication climate, formal communication, and informal communication influenced employees' job satisfaction significantly (Ali & Haider, 2012). Aspects of organizational communication (e.g., support, openness, access, participation in decision making, and load) were associated with domains of occupational stress at schools (De Nobile, McCormick, & Hoekman, 2013).

Additionally, communication effectiveness was greatly affected by leadership styles; communications became more effective when proactive leadership methods were employed (Czech & Forward, 2013). The most favorable results for generating subordinate satisfaction occur when supervisors combine high relational communication skills with task-oriented behavior (Madlock, 2008; Orpen, 1997). The most effective leaders increase employee satisfaction and commitment by combining communication competency with subordinate mentoring (Burke & Wilcox, 1969; Madlock & Kennedy-Lightsey, 2010). In fact, supervisor leadership styles and communication proficiency significantly influence subordinate satisfaction levels (Burke & Wilcox, 1969; Madlock, 2008). Awad and Alhashemi (2012) indicated that a culture of open and honest organizational communication generates favorable emotional connections (e.g., pleasure, inclusion, affection, and relaxation) between managers and employees, which would influence employee commitment levels.

ISSUES, CONTROVERSIES, PROBLEMS

The aforementioned review provided evidence that communication and job satisfaction are related. In the following, issues, controversies, and problems on communication and job satisfaction will be illustrated.

More Communication, More Stress?

The first issue is that employers need to consider not only the quality of communication, but also the influence of communication. It is not necessary that more communication, more job satisfaction. Research studies have shown both effects. Increasing the quality of organizational communications and evaluating how an increased message load can affect employee satisfaction and performance are equally important. De Nobile, McCormick, and Hoekman (2013) found that, although open communication within organizations created a more enjoyable working environment for the employees, stress increased as communication demands increased.

Perceptions of communication effectiveness regarding participation and employee input when decisions are made are often inconsistent (Rodwell, Kienzle, & Shadur, 1998). In organizations where work involved high stress settings, increased communication and teamwork also increased employee perceptions of added job stress (Rodwell, Kienzle, & Shadur, 1998). In occupations with potential high levels of emotional stress, as in health care settings, added communication and training to improve communication efficiency seems to elevate employee stress and burnout (Diggens & Chesson, 2014). Miles, Patrick, and King (1996) also found that organizations with lean operations, possibly resulting from downsizing, could experience work role ambiguity as employees perform multiple tasks. Additionally, increased organizational demands resulting from greater levels of communication might cause lower levels of employee satisfaction and higher levels of stress in organizations with high role ambiguity. Harville (1992) and Ray and Miller (1991) pointed out that, even though increased communication generally increased employee satisfaction, those who experience communication apprehension might suffer from elevated levels of stress and avoid situations where communication opportunities.

Thomas, Zolin, and Hartman (2009) described that worker's trust is more reliant upon communication quality at lower and mid managerial levels, while communication quantity is more important at top management levels. Although effective organizational communication fosters greater organizational commitment, cultural differences may also affect the level of organizational commitment (Chen, Silverthorne, & Hung, 2006). Organizational communication quality must remain consistent over time (Ramirez, 2010). What should the employers do if their communications cause employees' job stress?

Communication Is Not a Major Category in Job Satisfaction Measurement

The major factors contributing to job satisfaction were viewed in different ways over the years. Although there are some similarities, the instrument for measuring job satisfaction is not consistent. Table 1 showed the inconsistency of categories in job satisfaction, and the lack of "communication" as measuring item in the instrument of job satisfaction measurement.

Table 1. Examples of job satisfaction categories

Year	Instrument	Categories
Johnson (1955)	Job Satisfaction Questionnaire	physical and mental exertion, relations with associates, relations with employer, job security, advancement, finances, interest, emotional involvement in the job, job information and status, physical surroundings and work conditions, future, goals, progress toward goals, and evaluation in retrospect
Weiss et al. (1967)	Minnesota Satisfaction Questionnaire (MSQ)	ability utilization, achievement, activity, advancement, authority, company policies, compensation, co-workers, creativity, independence, moral values, recognition, responsibility, security, social service, social status, supervision-human relations, supervision-technical, variety, and working conditions
Smith, Kendall, & Hullin (1969)	Job Descriptive Index (JDI)	pay and benefit, work itself, promotion opportunity, supervision, and coworkers
Hackman & Oldham (1975)	Job Diagnostic Survey (JDS)	the nature of the job and job tasks, motivation, personality, psychological states (cognition and feelings about job tasks), relation to the job growth, pay security, social, supervision, and global satisfaction
Jenkins et al. (1975)	Michigan Organizational Assessment	demographics, general attitudes, job facets (importance and contingency), task and role characteristics, work group functioning, supervising behavior, intergroup relations, influence structure, individual differences and outcomes, compensation and performance evaluation
Ironson et al., (1989)	Job in General Scale (JIG)	pleasant, bad, ideal, waste of time, good, undesirable, worthwhile, worse than most, acceptable, superior, better than most, disagreeable, makes me content, Inadequate, excellent, rotten, enjoyable, and poor
Yeoh (2007)	Facet Satisfaction Scale (FSS)	pay, promotion, supervisors, co-workers, the work, benefits, procedures, and physical work conditions
Happiness Research Institute (2015)	Job Satisfaction Index (JSI)	purpose, leadership, influence, achievements, work/life balance, colleagues
Society for Human Resource Management (2016)	Employee Job Satisfaction	career development, benefits, work environment, compensation, employee relationships with management, conditions for engagement, engagement opinions, engagement behaviors

In most instances, communication is not apparent or included in job satisfaction measurement. Should communication be listed as one of the category for job satisfaction? Additionally, how do employers measure employees' job satisfaction if the measurement instrument is inconsistent?

Barriers to Effective Human Communication

Communication is essential for organizational management. Communication could become ineffective if there are barriers during the message transmission. Robbins, Judge, Millett, and Boyle (2011) explained that barriers for effective communication included: (a) physical barriers, (b) system design fault, (c) attitudinal barriers, (d) ambiguity of words/phrases, (e) individual linguistic ability, (f) physiological barriers, (g) bypassing, (h) technological multi-tasking and absorbency, and (i) fear of being criticized.

According to Robbins, Judge, Millett, and Boyle (2011), physical barriers include staff in different location, poor equipment, staff shortage, etc. System design includes unclear organizational structure, inefficient information systems, lack of supervision or training, lack of clarity in roles and responsibilities. Attitudinal barriers consist of poor management, lack of consultation with employees, personality conflicts, lack of motivation, dissatisfaction at work, insufficient training, resistance to the ideas, and so forth. Ambiguity of words refers to words sounding the same but have different meanings. Individual

Communication and Job Satisfaction

linguistic ability involves the use of jargon or difficult words in communication. Physiological barriers consist of sickness, poor eyesight, or hearing difficulties. Bypassing exists when the communicators do not attach same symbolic meanings to their words. Technological multi-tasking is physically and cognitively connect with individuals facing condensed communication in text message, email, and social updates. Fear of being criticized prevents good communication as well. Practice will make it perfect. Barriers to communication can also be categorized as organizational, physical, cultural, linguistic, and interpersonal (Effective Communications, 2013).

Do all employers notice the barriers of effective communication while they are ordering their employees to complete the tasks? It is vital for employers to understand the goals, mission, beliefs, and values of the organization. It is also essential for the employers to understand all kinds of barriers, such as physical barriers, cultural differences, information overload, lack of source credibility, semantics, gender differences, poor listening, emotions, language problem, silence, communication apprehension, political correctness, uses of jargon, acronyms, and nonverbal signals in language and so forth. A company or an organization would not progress successfully, if there are communication barriers between employers and employees.

Positive or Negative Tone?

Another issue is that not all managers communicate in an effective and positive way. To find out the problem with employers' communication, the researchers collected some employers' words from their previous employees. The ways they talked, especially their tones, were not considered favorable, positive, or effective. Here are a few clips.

"Why should I tell somebody that they are doing a good job when that's what I'm paying them to do anyway?" "Do you realize how much I pay people to use the toilet? It's a lot of money if you add it all up." "You should already be at your desk and working as soon as you are on the clock; if you're just walking in the door, you are late." "Do you realize that if you talk about something personal for five minutes, you've cost me a lot of money? I'm paying you to talk about work, not about your own personal things." "Here at work, every second must be productive and work related." "I don't believe people can learn anything about sales, either you're a born salesperson or you're not. You can't teach a person how to sell." "You're sitting in a million dollar chair, and you're going to earn the right to sit in that chair, or I'll find someone else who can." "I never tell anyone when they do a good job, because if I do, they will ask for more money." "So you're not happy with the way things are running around here? Keep it up and I'll ship all your jobs to China, and then we'll see how much complaining you'll do." "What I say goes." "Oh you think you're just so great. What makes you an authority on anything?" "Do it my way, or hit the highway." "You guys are going to shape up, or I'm going to kick your ass." "I only want people on my team that are going full time and give it their all. There are some slackers in our midst and you know who you are." "The best part about only paying commissions on sales is that if the person doesn't work out, I don't have to pay them." "I don't have any time to spare for poor performers. If you want to get my attention, you'll be a winner. I don't associate with losers."

It seems that those managers or employers were using the aggressive style of communication or negative tone in the companies. How would employees react if their employers all speak like that? How should leaders, managers, executives, supervisors, and employers communicate with their employees?

SOLUTIONS AND RECOMMENDATIONS

How do we solve the aforementioned problems? In the following, solutions and recommendations for communication and job satisfaction are presented for both employers and employees.

Develop Effective Communication Strategies and Skills

Organizational leaders must develop communication strategies for multiple levels. Developing effective communication skills is essential to effective leadership. Three important levels for organizational communication that impact employee job satisfaction include formal, informal, and internal settings (Ali & Haider, 2012). The three levels of organizational communication may be implemented when discussing job responsibilities, deadlines, job expectations, communication freedom, communication regularity, social groups, supplying appropriate communication equipment, career development, continuous training, work reviews, and salary expectations (Ilozor, Ilozor, and Carr, 2001). Employee feedback on the informal level was found to reduce job stress and improve worker performance. Sharma (2015) stressed that the type and quality of communication feedback in an educational organization positively affected employee perceptions of job satisfaction.

Respectful Communication

Respectful treatment of all employees in all levels was rated the most important factor for job satisfaction two years in a row (SHRM, 2016). To effectively communicate with others, the sender must transmit his/her message in a way that can be accurately and happily received by the intended recipient. If a message is interwoven with emotional expression, like sarcasm or anger, the intended recipient may respond to the poor emotional component rather than focusing on the message content itself. In other words, the emotional component should completely support the intended message content to produce desired results.

How do supervisors or employers demonstrate respectful communication? The language the supervisors used should be polite, respectful, positive, and constructive. Supervisors should provide employees with ongoing, accurate, and timely feedback regarding their job performance positively and respectfully. Job termination should not be considered as the only option when dealing with an underperforming employee. Employees should be allowed to discuss any problems they have at work and the steps they might take to improve before a decision to terminate their employment is made.

Supervisors should examine the details of an employee's work to determine whether poor job performance is due to a lack of ability, motivation, or a combination of both. If an ability problem exists, does the problem stem from a lack of skill or from a dependency on others? If an underperforming employee lacks a personal skill, they may be reassigned to a different role within the organization where they may be more effective.

Honesty and Trust

Providing truthful feedback to the employee and praising the employee for nice job performance is essential. Building trust between employers and employees is mandatory. It is absolutely important that company managers do not lie or exaggerate when dealing with their subordinates. They need to check employees' working status as well as job satisfaction constantly. Supervisor and employee's communication may play a critical role in establishing employees' attitudes and behaviors at work.

Research showed that honest communication between supervisors and employees lowered stress levels and increased job satisfaction (Jones, 2014; Muchinsky, 1977; Proctor, 2014; Rajhans, 2012; Tourani & Rast, 2012). Open and honest communication during formal performance appraisals positively affected employee attitudes and behavior (Ismail, Mohd Sani, & Mohamad, 2014). Employee satisfaction and commitment increased proportionally along with the level of organizational commitment to open communication policies (Akpinar, Torun, Okur, & Akpinar, 2013; Carriére & Bourque, 2009; Rodwell, Kienzle, & Shadur, 1998). Chitrao (2014) found that face-to-face communication is important at all levels within organizations to motivate employees and better serve customers.

To be effective, subordinates must be able to trust their supervisors. When people are afraid of speaking openly and honestly with supervisors, communication will suffer. Supervisors must create a safe environment to foster honest and open communication. If subordinates know that they have nothing to fear when communicating bad news, company leaders can make better management decisions when the information they receive is not filtered to remove bad news. Additionally, company leaders should be approachable if they desire to engender trust with their employees. Managers must interact with employees to build relationships to support honest communication.

Clear Instruction and Accurate Information

Effective communication involves accurate transmission of an intended message. In environments where employees do not receive continuous information, rumors and hearsay rule the day. Maxwell (1999) believed that effective communicators follow four basic truths: simplify the message, see the person, show the truth, and seek a response. Regardless of face-to-face or remote meetings, supervisors must provide accurate information regarding company policies, training, and goals.

Supervisors have the responsibility to ensure that employees completely understand company policies and goals. If employers do not understand the procedures, the employers should provide guidance. By providing employee guidance, company leaders can describe policies in detail which cannot be misunderstood. In addition, regardless of work locations, the employer should visit the employees on a regular basis to ensure that employees have no hidden problems or issues that hinder work effectiveness. Supervisor activities in large organizations should be coordinated and in line with company policies so that supervisor activities do not conflicted with the directives of other supervisors.

Show Attractive Charisma and Positive Attitude

Maxwell (1999) defined charisma as the ability to draw people to a person. He stated that people enjoy leaders who enjoy life; "If you want to attract people, you need to be like the people you enjoy being with" (Maxwell, 1999, p.10). He suggested the employers to put ten on every person's head, give people hope, and share themselves with the employees (Maxwell, 1999). The employees will like the employers when the employers help them think more highly of themselves, encourage them, and share their life journeys with them.

Communication success often depends upon the attitudes displayed by the managers. Employee job satisfaction and organizational commitment is often influenced by supervisor attitudes toward their subordinates. Managers need to exhibit respect while communicating with employees; attitudes toward subordinates directly affect the perceptions of the entire workforce, and ultimately the success of the organization (Abugre, 2011). "Attitudes have the power to lift up or tear down a team" (Maxwell, 2001). It is always a great challenge for employees to deal with negative attitudes from their managers in a workplace. A company manager should stay positive and avoid pessimism because it might promote depression, discourage action, lead to fear, cause the anxiety, impede health, and turn minor mistakes into setbacks in the workplace. An optimistic manager would create a positive and cheerful environment for his/her employees and the employees would feel ease or happy to stay in the company.

Harrell (2003, p. 17) believed that "A person with a negative attitude has the same power to influence others as a person with a positive attitude. The difference appears in the results." Positive attitudes would help increase productivity and keep up morale; whereas, negative attitudes increase stress, dismantle teamwork, and cripple productivity (Harrell, 2003). It is important to build lasting and supportive relationships in the company. The attitudes to build mutual supportive relationships include: (a) accept others unconditionally, (b) earn trust by being trustworthy, (c) do nice things without expecting anything in return, (d) be loyal and honor them, (e) listen to others not to form judgements but to understand their point of view (Harrell, 2003).

Cultivate Emotional Intelligence

Employers should be aware of their display of emotions while communicating with their employees. Employers with high levels of emotional intelligence should understand that their subordinates are not out to victimize them. Comments about how much salary employers are forced to pay as their employees take toilet breaks can appear insensitive, trivial, and not reflect respect for personal needs. Even truthful and accurate feedback regarding employee performance must be provided with total respect and understanding of employee needs.

The ways leaders communicate to their employees affects their leadership and job performance. The leaders' communication skills are related to their emotional intelligence. Emotional intelligence can be cultivated and trained. There are four dimensions of emotional intelligence: self-awareness, self-management, social awareness, and relationship management (Coleman, Boyatzis, & McKee, 2002). A leader's success depends on their levels of emotional intelligence. Emotional intelligence allows leaders to deal with their frustration in effective manner without having emotional breakdown on the job.

Satija and Khan (2013) found that self-regulation, motivation, self-awareness, empathy, and social awareness are related to effective leadership. Self-regulation requires personal accountability of emotions such as how one feels and reacts to situations. Self-regulation influences engagement skills, because it enables individuals to deal with difficult people in a tactful manner to maintain order at work (Darvish & Nasrollahi, 2011). Positive emotions are required in a leadership position. Motivation which holds up effective morale helps people overcome disappointments and seeking for assurance within the organization. Self-awareness enhances high emotional intelligence to modify behaviors along with incorporating self-confidence. Self-awareness requires knowing self (Goleman, 1998). Goleman (1998) indicated that self-awareness enables leaders to become assertive when managing themselves to stay committed to the organization's goals purpose along with enhancing work ethics. Emotional intelligence produces effective mindfulness skills within leaders concerning knowing who they are and having a deep perception of their own feelings and emotions (Wren, 1995). Leaders who have self-awareness are honest with themselves and others concerning strengths and weaknesses (Darvish & Nasrollahi, 2011).

Communication and Job Satisfaction

Additionally, understanding the emotions of others requires patience and effective listening skills. Emotional intelligence allows leaders to empathize with their employees in the organization to promote job satisfaction (Darvish & Nasrollahi, 2011). Social awareness allows effective leaders to know what is and is not acceptable within the organization. Goleman (1995) mentioned that social awareness helps leaders to know what their followers are thinking along with listening to new ideas and delegating work duties to build up self-esteem and confidence in others. Social awareness results in productive relationship within the workplace (Darvish & Nasrollahi, 2011). Leaders with high emotional intelligence understand issues within the workplace better and demonstrate more effective problem solving skills.

Emotional intelligence assisted individuals in making effective decisions when under hectic conditions such as dealing with difficult people and working in a hostile environment by maintaining a positive attitude when faced with adversity (Caruso, Mayer, & Salovey, 2002). Emotional intelligence can influence an organization's culture and structure in any profession, such as consulting, educating, and counseling along with meeting environmental demands, which can place pressure on one's stress level (Seal, Boyatzis, & Bailey, 2006). Leaders who lack emotional intelligence tend to suffer mentally from life stressors, such as depression, anxiety, and other mood disorders (Boyatis & Goleman, 2006). High level of emotional intelligence allows individuals to examine negative situations before determining their actions, which can improve leadership effectiveness (Brackett, Rivers, & Salovey, 2011). Good relationships form because of a supporting network of professionals who care about thoughts and emotions of others without controlling the way one should feel (Goleman, 1998; Satija & Khan, 2013). It is important for both employers and employees to develop emotional intelligence, since great leadership works through the emotions.

Undertake Communication Skills Training

Training is learning. Some employers do not possess good management skills and still believe that if they give instructions or commands, employees will obey. In an organization, employers should enforce a policy where all employees understand that on the job discrimination will not be tolerated and while ensuring that each employee is promoted based upon his/her merits, and not because a supervisor liked that employee more. If the mangers or employers do not have good management skills, they should take training, or attend a workshop for effective leadership to learn practical communication skills. Managers need adequate training so that they can communicate with employees well. Effective communication skills need to be constantly developed and practiced.

There are communication skills training websites, conferences, or courses on the Internet. For example, American Management Association (2016) has AMA's Communication Skills Seminars to help people connect with people more effectively. It focuses on face-to-face communication. *Communication Skills Training* by AdValue (2016) is another example. It focuses on interpersonal communication skills and could be used in the workplace with managers and coworkers. Its goal is to help people improve interpersonal communication skills to become a more effective communicator. For instance, McPheat's (2010) MTD effective communication skills training book was designed to help new and experienced managers maximize their potential by refining their leadership or management skills through communication skills training. Additionally, Garber (2008) proposed 50 communication activities, ice breakers, and exercises to help people become aware of communication challenges and to improve communication between human beings, which is a self-help guide for improving communication skills.

FUTURE RESEARCH DIRECTIONS

This chapter focused solely on the relationship between communication and job satisfaction. Future research can be focused on communication skills and strategies employers use to successfully communicate with their employees. Future research can also be focused on the relationship among communication, job performance, and successful company management. More studies should be done to set up the communication models for 21st century and to establish standardized instrument for measuring job satisfaction.

CONCLUSION

Communication is an essential component for every organization or company. Communication and job satisfaction are closely tied. A successful manager listens, motivates, inspires, and provides support to his/her employees. An effective manager knows how to communicate with his or her employees. Company policies to ensure clear and concise communication at all levels must be developed by employers and understood by all employees. Although various problems can appear from many levels of an organization within different types of activity, clear and honest communication policies may reduce misunderstandings that result in problems. Employers must provide opportunities for employees to speak openly and honestly. Employees must not be placed in a position to fear retaliation if they communicate bad news. Supervisors must also ensure that all subordinates are treated fairly and with respect. Leaders should go through training and workshops to make sure they know the ways to lead, to monitor, and to communicate effectively. Employees should learn to communicate with their employers as well; they should communicate to learn the job expectations so as to comply with job requirements. Employees' job satisfaction leads to employer's leadership success. Both employers and employees should be honest, open-minded, and respectful to each other.

REFERENCES

Abugre, J. B. (2011). Perceived satisfaction in sustained outcomes of employee communication in Ghanaian organizations. *Journal of Management Policy and Practice, 12*(7), 37–49.

AdValue. (2016). *Communication Skills Training*. Retrieved from: http://www.advalue-project.eu/content_files/EN/33/AdValue_Communication_skills_EN.pdf

Akoinar, A. T., Torun, E., Okur, M. E., & Akipinar, O. (2013). The effect of organizational communication and job satisfaction on organizational commitment in small businesses. *Interdisciplinary Journal of Research in Business, 3*(4), 27–32.

Ali, A., & Haider, J. (2012). Impact of internal organizational communications on employee job satisfaction – Case of some Pakistani banks. *Global Advanced Research Journal of Management and Business Studies, 1*(x), 38–44.

Ali, W. (2016). Understanding the concept of job satisfaction, measurements, theories and its significance in the recent organizational environment: A theoretical framework. *Archives of Business Research, 4*(1), 100–111. doi:10.14738/abr.41.1735

American Management Association. (2016). *Communication skills: August to December 2016*. Retrieved from: http://www.amanet.org/training/seminars/booklets/communication-skills.pdf

Anthony, L. (2015). *Effective communication & leadership*. Retrieved from http://smallbusiness.chron.com/effective-communication-leadership-5090.html

Awad, T. A., & Alhashemi, S. E. (2012). Assessing the effect of interpersonal communications on employees commitment and satisfaction. *International Journal of Islamic and Middle Eastern Finance and Management, 5*(2), 134–156. doi:10.1108/17538391211233425

Barnlund, D. C. (2008). A transactional model of communication. In C. D. Mortensen (Ed.), *Communication theory* (2nd ed., pp. 47–57). New Brunswick, NJ: Transaction.

Berlo, D. K. (1960). *The process of communication*. New York: Holt, Rinehart, & Winston.

Boyatzis, R. E., & Goleman, D. (2006). *Emotional and Social Competency Inventory*. Boston, MA: The Hay Group.

Brackett, M. A., Rivers, S. E., & Salovey, P. (2011). Emotional intelligence: implication of personal, social, academic, and workplace success. *Social and Personality psychological compass, 5*(1), 88-103. doi:10.1111/j.1751-9004.2010.00334

Burke, R. J., & Wilcox, D. S. (1969). Effects of different patterns and degrees of openness in superior-subordinate communication on subordinate job satisfaction. *Academy of Management Journal (pre-1986), 12*(3), 319-326.

Carriere, J., & Bourque, C. (2009). The effects of organizational communication on job satisfaction and organizational commitment in a land ambulance service and the mediating role of communication satisfaction. *Career Development International, 14*(1), 29–49. doi:10.1108/13620430910933565

Caruso, D. R., Mayer, J. D., & Salovey, P. (2002). Relation of an ability measure of emotional intelligence to personality. *Journal of Personality Assessment, 79*(2), 306–320. Retrieved from http://www.unh.edu/emotional_intelligence/EI%20Assets/Reprints...EI%20Proper/EI2002CarusoMayerSaloveyMEIS.pdf doi:10.1207/S15327752JPA7902_12 PMID:12425393

Chen, J., Silverthorne, C., & Hung, J. (2006). Organization communication, job stress, organizational commitment, and job performance of accounting professionals in Taiwan and America. *Leadership and Organization Development Journal, 27*(4), 242–249. doi:10.1108/01437730610666000

Cheng, B., Kan, M., Levanon, G., & Ray, R. L. (2014). Job satisfaction: 2014 Edition. Retrieved from https://hcexchange.conference-board.org/attachment/The-annual1.pdf

Chitrao, P. (2014). Internal communication satisfaction as an employee motivation tool in the retail sector in Pune. *The European Journal of Social & Behavioural Sciences, 10*, 1541-1552.

Choudhary, N. K., & Rathore, N. S. (2013). Role of effective communication in total quality management. *The International Journal of Scientific & Engineering Research, 4*(7), 2083–2090.

Coleman, D., Boyatzis, R., & McKee, A. (2002). *Primal leadership: Realizing the power of emotional intelligence.* Boston, MA: Harvard Business School Press.

Communication Theory. (2016). Berlo's SMCR model of communication. Retrieved from http://communicationtheory.org/berlos-smcr-model-of-communication/

Craig, R. T. (1999, May). Communication Theory. *International Communication Association, 9*(2), 119–161. doi:10.1111/j.1468-2885.1999.tb00355

Czech, K., & Forward, G.L. (2013). Communication, leadership, and job satisfaction: Perspectives on supervisor-subordinate relationships. *Studies in media and Communication, 1*(2), 11-24.

Darvish, H., & Nasrollahi, A. A. (2011). Studying the relations between emotional intelligence and occupational stress: A case study at Payame Noor University. *Economic Science, 2,* 38-49. Retrieved from http://www.upg-bulletin-se.ro/archive/2011-2/4.%20Darvish_Nasrollahi.pdf

De Nobile, J., McCormick, J., & Hoekman, K. (2013). Organizational communication and occupational stress in Australian Catholic primary schools. *Journal of Educational Administration, 51*(6), 744–767. doi:10.1108/JEA-09-2011-0081

De Nobile, J. J., & McCormick, J. (2008). Organizational communication and job satisfaction in Australian Catholic Primary Schools. *Educational Management Administration & Leadership, 36*(1), 101–122. doi:10.1177/1741143207084063

De Vries, R. E., Bakker-Pieper, A., & Oostenveld, W. (2010). Leadership = communication? The relations of leaders communication styles with leadership styles, knowledge sharing and leadership outcomes. *Journal of Business and Psychology, 25*(3), 367–380. doi:10.1007/s10869-009-9140-2 PMID:20700375

De Vries, R. E., Van den Hooff, B., & DeRidder, J. A. (2006). Explaining knowledge sharing: The role of team communication styles, job satisfaction, and performance beliefs. *Communication Research, 33*(2), 115–135. doi:10.1177/0093650205285366

Diggens, J., & Chesson, T. (2014). Do factors of emotion-focused patient care and communication impact job stress, satisfaction and burnout in radiation therapists? *Journal of Radiotherapy in Practice, 13*(01), 4–17. doi:10.1017/S146039691300006X

DuFrene, D. D., & Lehman, C. M. (2014). Navigating change: Employee communication in times of instability. *Business and Professional Communication Quarterly, 77*(4), 443–452. doi:10.1177/2329490614544736

Dugguh, S. I., & Ayaga, D. (2014). Job satisfaction theories: Traceability to employee performance in organizations. *IOSR Journal of Business and Management, 16*(5), 11-18.

Effective Communications. (2013). Communication skills. Retrieved from http://www.free-management-ebooks.com/dldebk-pdf/fme-effective-communication.pdf

Farahbod, F., Salimi, S. B., & Dorostkar, K. R. (2013). Impact of organizational communication in job satisfaction and organizational commitment. *Interdisciplinary Journal of Contemporary Research in Business, 5*(4), 419–430.

Froschheiser, L. (2015). Communication: The most important key to leadership success. Retrieved from http://www.reliableplant.com/Read/12675/communication-most-important-key-to-leadership-success

Garber, P. R. (2008). *50 communications activities, icebreakers, and exercises.* Amherst, MA: HRD Press, Inc. Retrieved from https://www2.cortland.edu/dotAsset/c1a635f6-a099-4ede-8f15-79b86e315088.pdf

Garcia, H. F. (2012). Leadership communications: Planning for the desired reaction. *Strategy and Leadership, 40*(6), 42–45. doi:10.1108/10878571211278886

Garg, S., & Jain, S. (2013). Mapping leadership styles of public and private sector leaders using Blake and mouton leadership model. *Drishtikon: A Management Journal, 4*(1), 48-64. Retrieved from http://search.proquest.com/docview/1477998237?accountid=35812

Goleman, D. (1995). *Working with emotional intelligence.* New York: Bantam Books.

Goleman, D. (1998). *Emotional intelligence: why can it matter.* New York: Bantam Books.

Goleman, D., Boyatzis, R., & McKee, A. (2002). *Primal leadership: Realizing the power of emotional intelligence.* Boston, MA: Harvard Business School Press.

Goris, J. R. (2007). Effects of satisfaction with communication on the relationship between individual-job congruence and job performance/satisfaction. *Journal of Management Development, 26*(8), 737–752. doi:10.1108/02621710710777255

Hackman, J., & Oldham, G. R. (1975). Development of the job diagnostic survey. *The Journal of Applied Psychology, 60*(2), 159–170. doi:10.1037/h0076546

Happiness Research Institute (2015). Job satisfaction index 2015: What drives job satisfaction?

Harrell, K. (2003). *Attitude is everything.* New York: Harper Business.

Harville, D. L. (1992). Person/Job fit model of communication apprehension in organizations. *Management Communication Quarterly, 6*(2), 150–165. doi:10.1177/0893318992006002002

Herzberg, F. (1966). *Work and the Nature of Man.* Cleveland, OH: World Publishing.

Hua, W., & Omar, B. (2016). Examining communication satisfaction, Confucian work dynamism and job satisfaction: A comparative study of international and domestic hotels in Hainan, China. *The Journal of the South East Asia Research Centre for Communications and Humanities, 8*(1), 105–127.

Ilozor, D. B., Ilozor, B. D., & Carr, J. (2001). Management communication strategies determine job satisfaction in telecommuting. *Journal of Management Development, 20*(6), 495–507. doi:10.1108/02621710110399783

Ironson, G. H., Smith, P. C., Brannick, M. T., Gibson, W. M., & Paul, K. B. (1989). Construction of a job in general scale: A comparison of global, composite, and specific measures. *The Journal of Applied Psychology, 74*(2), 193–200. doi:10.1037/0021-9010.74.2.193

Ismail, A., Mohd Sani, R., & Mohamad, M. H. (2014). Communication openness in performance appraisal systems enhancing job satisfaction. *Journal of Public Administration. Finance and Law, 5*, 98–109.

Iyer, S., & Israel, D. (2012). Structural equation modeling for testing the impact of organization communication satisfaction on employee engagement. *South Asian Journal of Management, 19*(1), 51–81.

Jenkins, G. D., Nadler, D. A., Lawler, E. E. III, & Cammann, C. (1975). Standardized observation: An approach to measuring the nature of jobs. *The Journal of Applied Psychology, 60*(2), 171–181. doi:10.1037/h0076541

Johnson, G. H. (1955). An instrument for the measurement of job satisfaction. *Personnel Psychology: The Study of People at Work, 8*(1), 27–37. doi:10.1111/j.1744-6570.1955.tb01185.x

Jones, E. A. (2014). *Employees' perceptions of supervisor communication and job stress in the work environment* [Doctoral dissertation].

Judge, T. A., Locke, E. A., & Durham, C. C. (1997). The dispositional causes of job satisfaction: A core evaluations approach. *Research in Organizational Behavior, 19*, 151–188.

Keyton, J. (2011). *Communication and organizational culture: A key to understanding work experience.* Thousand Oaks, CA: Sage.

Kumar, B. P., & Giri, V. N. (2009). Examining the relationship of organizational communication and job satisfaction in Indian organizations. *Journal of Creative Communications, 4*(3), 177–184. doi:10.1177/097325861000400303

Littlejohn, S. W., & Foss, K. A. (Eds.). (2009). Encyclopedia of communication theory. Thousand Oaks, CA: SAGE Publications, Inc.

Locke, E. A. (1976). The nature and causes of job satisfaction. In M. D. Dunnette (Ed.), *Handbook of Industrial and Organizational Psychology* (pp. 1297–1349). Chicago: Rand McNally.

Mădălina, S.S., & Cătălin, B.M. (2016). Enhancing job satisfaction through organizational communication. *Annals of the Constantin Brancusi University of Targu Jiu, Economy Series, 109-114.*

Madlock, P. E. (2008). The link between leadership style, communicator competence, and employee satisfaction. *Journal of Business Communication, 45*(1), 61–78. doi:10.1177/0021943607309351

Madlock, P. E., & Kennedy-Lightsey, C. (2010). The effects of supervisors verbal aggressiveness and mentoring on their subordinates. *Journal of Business Communication, 47*(1), 42–62. doi:10.1177/0021943609353511

Maslow, A. H. (1943). A theory of human motivation. [&type=pdf]. *Psychological Review, 50*(4), 370–396. Retrieved from http://citeseerx.ist.psu.edu/viewdoc/download?doi=10.1.1.318.2317&rep=rep1 doi:10.1037/h0054346

Maxwell, J. C. (1999). *The 21 indispensable qualities of a leader: Becoming the person others will want to follow*. Nashville, GA: Thomas Nelson Publishers.

Maxwell, J. C. (2001). *The 17 indisputable laws of teamwork*. Nashiville, TN: Thomas Nelson Publishers.

McPheat, S. (2010). *MTD training: Effective communication skills*. MTD Training & Ventus Publishing. Retrieved from http://promeng.eu/downloads/training-materials/ebooks/soft-skills/effective-communication-skills.pdf

Miles, E. W., Patrick, S. L., & King, W. C. Jr. (1996). Job level as a systemic variable in predicting the relationship between supervisory communication and job satisfaction. *Journal of Occupational and Organizational Psychology, 69*(3), 277–292. doi:10.1111/j.2044-8325.1996.tb00615.x

Muchinsky, P.M. (1977). Organizational communication: Relationships to organizational climate and job satisfaction. *Academy of Management Journal (pre-1986), 20*(4), 592-607.

Newton, C. (2011). The five communication styles. Retrieved from http://www.clairenewton.co.za/my-articles/the-five-communication-styles.html

Orpen, C. (1997). The interactive effects of communication quality and job involvement on managerial job satisfaction and work motivation. *The Journal of Psychology, 131*(5), 519–522. doi:10.1080/00223989709603540

Proctor, C. (2014). Effective organizational communication affects employee attitude, happiness, and job satisfaction (master's thesis). Retrieved from https://www.suu.edu/hss/comm/masters/capstone/thesis/proctor-c.pdf

Rajhans, K. (2012). Effective organizational communication: A key to employee motivation and performance. *Interscience Management Review, 2*(2), 81–85.

Ramirez, D. L. (2010). *Organizational communication satisfaction and job satisfaction within university foodservice* [Master's thesis]. Retrieved from http://krex.k-state.edu/dspace/bitstream/handle/2097/14123/danielramirez2012.pdf?sequence=1

Ray, E. B., & Miller, K. I. (1991). The influence of communication structure and social support on job stress and burnout. *Management Communication Quarterly, 4*(4), 506–527. doi:10.1177/0893318991004004005

Robbins, S., Judge, T., Millett, B., & Boyle, M. (2011). Organizational Behavior (6th ed.). Pearson, French's Forest, NSW.

Roberts, K. H., & OReilly, C. A. (1974). Measuring organizational communication. *The Journal of Applied Psychology, 59*(3), 321–326. doi:10.1037/h0036660

Rodwell, J.J., Kienzle, R., & Shadur, M.A. (1998). The relationships among work-related perceptions, employee attitudes, and employee performance: The integral role of communication. *Human Resource Management (1986-1998), 37*(3-4), 277-293.

Satija, S., & Khan, W. (2013). Emotional intelligence as a predictor of occupational stress among working professionals. *Aweshkar Research Journal, 15*(1), 79–97.

Schramm, W. (1954). How communication works. In W. Schramm (Ed.), *The process and effects of communication* (pp. 3–26). Urbana, Illinois: University of Illinois Press.

Seal, C. R., Boyatzis, R. E., & Bailey, J. R. (2006). Fostering emotional and social intelligence in organizations. *Organizational Management Journal, 3*(3), 190–209. doi:10.1057/omj.2006.19

Shannon, C. E. (1948). A mathematical theory of communication. *The Bell System Technical Journal, 27*(3), 1–55. doi:10.1002/j.1538-7305.1948.tb01338.x

Shannon, C. E., & Weaver, W. (1949). *The mathematical theory of communication.* Urbana, Illinois: University of Illinois Press.

Sharma, P. R. (2015). *Organizational communication: Perceptions of staff members' level of communication satisfaction and job satisfaction* (Doctoral dissertation). Retrieved from http://dc.etsu.edu/cgi/viewcontent.cgi?article=3854&context=etd

Shmailan, A. S. B. (2016). The relationship between job satisfaction, job performance and employee engagement: An explorative study. *Issues in Business Management and Economics, 4*(1), 1–8.

SHRM. (2016). *Employee job satisfaction and engagement: Revitalizing a changing workforce.* A research report by the society for human resource management. Retrieved from https://www.shrm.org/hr-today/trends-and-forecasting/research-and-surveys/Documents/2016-Employee-Job-Satisfaction-and-Engagement-Report.pdf

Sigrist, R. D. (2010). *Job satisfaction at Missouri High School principals as measured by the Minnesota Satisfaction Questionnaire* [Doctoral dissertation]. The University of Missouri-Columbia, Missouri. Retrieved from https://mospace.umsystem.edu/xmlui/bitstream/handle/10355/8284/research.pdf?sequence=3

Smith, P. C., Kendall, L. M., & Hulin, C. L. (1969). *The Measurement of Satisfaction in Work and Retirement.* Chicago, IL: Rand McNally.

Steingrímsdóttir, H. (2011). *The relationship between internal communication & job satisfaction* [Master's thesis]. Retrieved from http://studenttheses.cbs.dk/bitstream/handle/10417/3240/hrund_steingrimsdottir.pdf?sequence=1

Sulaiman, M. R., & Seng, L. C. (2016). Leadership and job satisfaction among foreign seafarers in maritime industry: Human leadership. *International Research Journal of Interdisciplinary & Multidisciplinary Studies, 2*(2), 44–57.

Swan, J. E., & Futrell, C. M. (1978). Does clear communication relate to job satisfaction and self-confidence among salespeople? *Journal of Business Communication, 15*(4), 39–52. doi:10.1177/002194367801500404

Thomas, G. F., Zolin, R., & Hartman, J. K. (2009). The central role of communication in developing trust and its effect on employee involvement. *Journal of Business Communication, 46*(3), 287–310. doi:10.1177/0021943609333522

Tourani, A., & Rast, S. (2012). Effect of employees' communication and participation on employees' job satisfaction: An empirical study on airline companies in Iran. *Proceedings of the 2012 2nd International Conference on Economics, Trade and Development IPEDR* (Vol. 36, pp. 52-56). Singapore: IACSIT Press.

Weiss, D. J., Dawis, R. V., England, G. W., & Lofquist, L. H. (1967). *Manual for the Minnesota satisfaction questionnaire*. Work Adjustment Project Industrial Relations Center, University of Minnesota.

Wren, J. T. (1995). *The leader's companion: Insights on leadership through the ages*. New York: The Free Press.

Yeoh. (2007). The facet satisfaction scale: Enhancing the measurement of job satisfaction [Master's thesis]. Retrieved from http://digital.library.unt.edu/ark:/67531/metadc3899/m2/1/high_res_d/thesis.pdf

Yoke, L. B., & Panatik, S. A. (2016). The mediatory role of job satisfaction between emotional intelligence and job performance. *International Business Management, 10*(6), 806–812.

KEY TERMS AND DEFINITIONS

Communication: The process of giving, receiving, imparting, or exchanging information/news.
Emotional Intelligence: The ability to recognize and monitor one's own and other's emotions.
Job Satisfaction: The level of fulfillment one experiences in the work place.
Job Satisfaction Measurement: The instrument used to measure employees' job satisfaction.
Leadership: The ability of a person to provide guidance, direction, and motivation to a group of people or organization.
Management: The coordination of organizational activities.
Motivation: Factors that provide inspiration to achieve the goals.
Organizational Communication: The methods used to transmit and receive information within an organization.
Stress: The feeling or the emotional state we have under pressure or during difficulties.

Chapter 10
Emotional Intelligence and Job Stress

Germaine D. Washington
Calvary University, USA

Libi Shen
University of Phoenix, USA

ABSTRACT

Substance abuse professionals work with chemically dependent addicts and disgruntled coworkers. They experience more occupational stress and employee turnover than social workers, community support workers, and youth care workers. Three of 37 substance abuse agencies in Kansas City, Missouri have reported extremely high employee turnover rates and occupational stress. How do substance abuse professionals perceive the relationship between emotional intelligence and job stress? What are substance abuse professionals' definitions of emotional intelligence and job stress? How does emotional intelligence affect job stress in the substance abuse profession? Why do higher levels of emotional intelligence reduce people's job stress and improve their job performance? The purposes of this chapter are to explore substance abuse professionals' definitions of emotional intelligence and job stress, and their viewpoints on the relationship between emotional intelligence and job stress.

INTRODUCTION

Occupational stress is common in the workplace. Based on a 2013 *Work Stress Survey*, a total of 83% of Americans were stressed by at least one issue at work, which was an increase of 10% compared to 73% in 2012 (Swartz, 2013). A small amount of stress may be healthy, but too much stress could be dangerous to people's mental and physical health. Levinson (2008) reported that too much stress could damage brain cells, which impair thinking and judgment. Ducharme, Knudsen, and Roman (2008) also indicated that stress and exhaustion have been associated with stress-related illness. Workplace stress is a significant contributor to both health problems and healthcare costs with US$125-190 billion of healthcare cost a year (Blanding, 2015). Additionally, occupational stress creates unpleasant feelings that affect work performance and job satisfaction (Satija & Khan, 2013).

DOI: 10.4018/978-1-5225-2568-4.ch010

Emotional Intelligence and Job Stress

In the past two decades, many researchers have studied emotional intelligence and job stress and most researchers have found significant relationships between emotional intelligence and occupational stress (e.g., Darvish & Nasrollahi, 2011; Dedovic et al., 2009; Gardner & Stough, 2002; Goswami & Talukdar, 2013; Iqbal & Abbasi, 2013; Reynolds & O'Dwyer, 2008; Schultz et al., 2007). Some researchers believed that emotional intelligence improves leadership and job satisfaction (Brackett, Rivers, & Salovey, 2011; Darvish & Nasrollahi, 2011; Ducharme et al., 2008; Vorkapic & Mustapic, 2012). For example, emotional intelligence enables leaders to attain interpersonal effectiveness and seek to obtain information regarding what happens within the workplace (Darvish & Nasrollahi, 2011).

Emotional intelligence could guide the way humans behave, such as obtaining an emotional common foundation (Ducharme et al., 2008; Vorkapic & Mustapic, 2012), and allowing leaders to empathize with employees within organizations to promote job satisfaction (Darvish & Nasrollahi, 2011). Emotional intelligence allows individuals to examine negative situations before making decisions for actions which can enhance leadership effectiveness (Brackett, Rivers, & Salovey, 2011).

In contrast, Charniss, Extein, Goleman, and Weissber (2006) stated that emotional intelligence fails to elaborate on the management of emotions concerning awareness along with a growing body of conflicting perceptions of cognitive abilities controlled by one's thinking and feeling. Charniss et al. (2006) indicated that emotional intelligence fails to provide evidence that lack of emotional intelligence prevents one from managing other people along with professional's performance capabilities. Law, Long, and Song (2004) offered evidence that emotional intelligence lacks clarification if it has any relations or separations from one's personality. Van Rooy, Viswesvaran, and Pluta (2005) provided further insights regarding how emotional intelligence fails to decipher if the processing of emotional information has the ability assist one in making sense of altered moods and cognition.

Substance abuse professions experience more occupational stress and employee burnout than any other human service professions, such as social workers, community support workers, and youth care workers (Ducharme et al., 2008). Three of 37 substance abuse agencies in Kansas City, Missouri, USA have reported extremely high turnover rates and occupational stress (Meeting report, 2013). How do substance abuse professionals perceive emotional intelligence and job stress? The purposes of this chapter are to explore substance abuse professionals' definitions of emotional intelligence and job stress, and their viewpoints on the relationship between emotional intelligence and job stress.

It is significant to explore substance abuse professionals' perceptions and viewpoints concerning emotional intelligence and job stress, because it might help these professionals to understand the importance of emotional intelligence and find ways to minimize stress in an intense working environment. It might raise awareness and contribute to substance abuse professionals' knowledge on what they should do to avoid overload and pressure. This study might help supervisors of substance abuse agencies rethink the problem of job stress and come up with some leadership strategies to cope with the problem. This study might help the world to realize the role emotional intelligence plays on job stress, not limited to the substance abuse professionals.

BACKGROUND

Theories of Emotional Intelligence

Charles Darwin was one of the first writers to make use of emotional intelligence. In *The Expression of Emotions in Man and Animals*, Darwin (1872) classified three chief principles of expression: the principle of serviceable associated habits, the principle of antithesis, and the principle of actions due to the constitution of nervous system. Darwin (1872) believed the "expression in itself, or the language of the emotions, as it has sometimes been called, is certainly of importance for the welfare of mankind" (p.219). Emotional expression involved the importance of survival and adaptation in Darwin's thought (Dulewicz & Higgs, 2000).

Later, Salovey and Mayer (1990) defined Emotional Intelligence as the ability to recognize and scrutinize one's own emotion and the feelings of others in order to guide thought processes and actions. They believed that emotional intelligence is a personality factor that can modify moods to enhance job skills effectiveness and to develop good relationships with others (Salovey & Mayer, 1990). There are four types of abilities in emotional intelligence: perceiving emotions, using emotions, understanding emotions, and managing emotions in Salovey and Mayer's (1990) model. Perceiving emotions involves understanding facial expressions and non-verbal guess; using emotions involves making use of feeling to generate cognitive and rational decisions; understanding emotional involves interpreting why an individual feels a particular way; and managing emotions involves responding to our own and others' feelings properly (Salovey & Mayer, 1990).

Daniel Goleman (1995), the author of the *New York Times* bestseller book *Emotional Intelligence*, defined emotional intelligence as self-awareness and discipline regarding one's own emotions along with capturing and understanding the emotions of others. Goleman (1995) argued that emotional intelligence enables individuals to have intrapersonal and interpersonal skills within the workplace. Intrapersonal skills involve internal communication such as modifying one's mood or feelings, whereas interpersonal skills enable individuals to communicate effectively with others concerning their emotions and feeling (Goleman, 1995).

Based on Goleman (1998), emotional intelligence includes self-confidence, social awareness, self-control, and influence. Emotional intelligence enables professionals to work in different types of environments without experiencing emotional breakdowns or exhaustion. Goleman (1998) mentioned that professionals are responsible for their own thoughts and feelings, such as if workers think negatively they would become less motivated in the workplace because of destructive emotions; the same holds true for positive thoughts as well. Professionals with effective emotional intelligence show high levels of compassion for others and prevent conflict or major differences within relationships (Goleman, 1998). Goleman (1998) believed that building emotional intelligence is a learned behavior that is constantly practiced. For example, being aware of own feelings, being aware of other's emotions, having good communication skills by effective listening and provide feedback, seeing adversity and diversity as opportunity, leading by a positive example and holding others accountable for their actions, and always embracing change are good strategies for cultivating emotional intelligence.

Goleman (1998) supported the theory of *"Knowing thyself: Plumbing the unconscious"* as it provides the expression of being different and paying close attention to feelings and emotions along with self-acceptance. Understanding the self, such as one's reactions to stressful situations, is important, because personal emotions were used as signals and they play a crucial role in stress management. Goleman (1998) mentioned that self-awareness allows individuals to channel their emotions for mood regulating purposes, while self-regulation allows one to control impulses while working under pressure or dealing with others. Another theory is *"Empathic mindfulness: Sensing other's feeling and perspectives"* that indicates the importance understanding others' emotions along with openness to change. This approach provided an enlightened view of conflict management, such as being able to listen well and understand others' needs. The empathic theory applied to this study because it emphasized developing and building relationships with others.

Researchers continued to explore and develop the theories of emotional intelligence. Goleman, Boyatzis, and McKee (2002) proposed that the leadership competencies of emotional intelligence are: Self-awareness (i.e., emotional self-awareness, accurate self-assessment, self-confidence), self-management (i.e., self-control, transparency, adaptability, achievement, initiative, optimism), social awareness (i.e., empathy, organizational awareness, service), and relationship management (i.e., inspiration, influence, developing others, change catalyst, conflict management, teamwork and collaboration). They stressed that the key to make primal leadership work for everyone depends on "the leadership competencies of emotional intelligence: how leaders handle themselves and their relationships" (Goleman, Boyatzis, & McKee, 2002, p. 6). In other words, leaders with higher levels of emotional intelligence know how to augment the benefits of primal leadership, and it would drive the emotions of their employees in the right direction.

According to Seal, Boyatzis, and Bailey's (2006) study, *Fostering Emotional and Social Intelligence in Organizations*, they found the distinctions between emotional and social intelligence; social intelligence focuses on monitoring one's own emotions and feelings, while emotional intelligence focuses on understanding and regulating emotions under stress and pressure. Additionally, Charniss, Extein, Goleman, and Weissberg (2006) explored several major underpinnings that relate to emotional intelligence, such as perception of emotions, awareness of emotions, and management of emotions, etc., which clarify the role of social-emotional core abilities.

Charniss et al. (2006) described five personality traits related to emotional intelligence: extroversion (i.e., positive energy), agreeableness (i.e., cooperation), neuroticism (i.e., negative emotions), openness (i.e., appreciation for new ideas), and conscientiousness (i.e., effective planning and self-discipline). Newman, Joseph, and MacCann (2010) supported that these five personality traits, also known as five-factor model (FFM), provided guidance concerning emotional regulations along with cognitive abilities that affects job performance. In Newman, Joseph, and MacCann's (2010) study, *The Importance of Emotion Regulation and Emotional Labor Context*, emotional competence is a self-assessment tool for psychological growth.

How does emotional intelligence help in the workplace? The functions of emotional intelligence were examined and supported by several researchers. For instance, Connor and Slear (2009) explained that emotional intelligence helps people access past and present emotions, especially when working with others, and maturity has a great consideration when learning how to deal with difficult people in the workplace. In fact, understanding one's emotions allows individuals to nurture feelings, such as sadness, fear, enjoyment, shame, and surprise, and enhances the process of handling relationship (Connor

& Slear, 2009). Additionally, emotional intelligence enables individuals to maintain motivation when working with difficult people and prevent burnout (Connor & Slear, 2009).

Brackett, Rivers, and Salovey (2011) argued that lack of emotional intelligence would cause mental illness, such as depression and anxiety, and physical illness, such as heart disease and stroke. Emotional intelligence promotes positive social functioning by assisting individuals to target each other's emotions along with communication and behavior enhancement (Brackett et al., 2011). Emotional intelligence assists in developing personal relationships without minimizing inter-personality sensitivity and reflecting closeness with others, such as feeling comfortable with oneself around others (Brackett et al., 2011). Emotional intelligence enables individuals to develop self-control when dealing with difficult people and situations, along with incorporating a level of distress tolerance (Brackett et al., 2011). It is apparent that personal growth, social relationship, and people's mental/physical health are all associated with emotional intelligence.

Theories of Occupational Stress

The theories of occupational stress evolved three decades ago. The major theories for occupational stress included Hobfoll's (1989) *Conservation of Resource Theory*, Ursin and Eriksen's (2004) *Cognitive Activation Theory of Stress and Preservative Cognition*, Karasek's (1979) *Job Demand-Control Theory*, and Lazarus' (2000) *Transactional Model of Stress*. These theories provided the incentives or foundations of occupational stress. These theories were examined as follows.

Conservation of Resource Theory referred to social, physical, psychological, or organizational aspects of the workplace (Hobfoll, 1989). The *Conservation of Resource Theory* represented the objects, personal characteristics, conditions, and energies valued by people while the imbalance of larger environmental demands over resources produces tension (Hobfoll, 1989). Based on the *Conservation of Resource Theory*, individuals accumulate resources so they can accommodate and withstand threats such as self-worth, optimism, money, status, and social support (Hobfoll, 1989). Resources like reputation allow people to encounter and secure additional resources, which can improve performance and attract promotions (Hobfoll, 1989).

In the *Cognitive Activation Theory of Stress and Preservative Cognition,* repetitive experience with a motivation allows individuals to adapt and control themselves (Ursin & Eriksen, 2004). Ursin and Eriksen (2004) stated that arousal and stress are important to the brain's operational responses, which could alarm the individual of a particular strain to ignite the response, coping, and adaptation signals. According to *Cognitive Activation Theory of Stress and Preservative Cognition*, appraisals made by individuals affect determinations of expectancies, which can be divided into either motivation or outcome expectancies (Ursin & Eriksen, 2004). The *Cognitive Activation Theory of Stress and Preservative Cognition* involved the development of future expectancies through appraisal along with determining how a person responds to stressors (Ursin & Eriksen, 2004).

The *Job Demand-Control Theory* implied self-control within the workplace (Karasek, 1979). Even though job demands can place physical and psychological strain on individuals, a person's stress level can affect how s/he deals with excessive strain (Karasek, 1979). This theory implies that the amount of personal strain individuals experience at their jobs may determine whether they have control over the demands they face while control can moderate stress one experiences in the workplace (Karasek, 1979). The Job Demand-Control Theory indicated that low control produces high job stress and high control produces low job stress; therefore, perceptions of control depend on the coping and adaptation responses of the individual.

Additionally, Lazarus (2000) defined the *Transactional Model of Stress* as the environmental demands affecting personal resources to threaten the well-being of individual. Stress is the result of transaction between an individual and their environment (Lazarus, 2000). There are three types of appraisals: harm/loss (something that has already happened), threat (possibility of future harm), and challenge (where the individual engages in the command) (Lazarus, 2000). The appraisal process offers an informal pathway to isolate emotions associated with trauma; appraisals can be associated with different types of emotions, which might lead to different levels to environmental stress (Lazarus, 2000).

The Impact of Job Stress

Job stress has caused extensive expenditure to organizations and professionals over the years. What is job stress and what causes job stress? What is the impact of job stress? How does job stress affect workers? Is job stress associated with workers' health? Adaramola (2012) stated that occupational stress exists when employees' goals do not match the work requirements of the employer or when they do not meet the needs of the employer. There are two types of occupational stress, physical and psychosocial (Pasca & Wagner, 2011). Physical stress in the workplace can result from poor equipment, temperature, or noise that prevents individuals from working productively; psychosocial stress can result from workplace demands, poor relations with co-workers or employees, lack of self-control, and inadequate support from management; these typically occur within the first three years of employment (Pasca & Wagner, 2011).

Over the years, the impact of job stress has been explored by many researchers (e.g., Archer, Fredriksson, Schut, & Kostrzewa, 2011; Chao, 2011; Cotton & Hart, 2003; Dedovic et al., 2009; Kiani, Samavatyan, & Pourabion, 2011; Nabirye, Brown, Pryor, & Maples, 2011; Oginska-Bulik, 2005; Perkins & Sprang, 2013; Rees & Cooper, 1992; Yamada, McEwen, & Pavlides, 2003). Job stress is associated with workers' physical health. Two decades ago, Karasek and Theorell (1990) investigated occupational stress among 300 healthcare workers in Ohio, and 35% of the workers have indicated that they experienced occupational stress with severe body aches and pains. In a study of 250 human service workers in a mental health clinic, Rees and Cooper (1992) found that employee absenteeism increased when workers experienced stress in the workplace and that produced physical illnesses.

In a stress management study of 330 participants, Oginska-Bulik (2005) found that occupational stress could generate poor health conditions, such as migraines and lower back pain in 37.5% of human service workers. Oginska-Bulik (2005) stated that occupational stress could cause negative effects on the body including poor decision-making and mobility issues. Occupational stress can produce physical pains such as headache, neck pain, and back pain, because bodily tension may occur which increases absenteeism when the mind is distressed (Schmidt & Neubach, 2007). Dedovic et al. (2009) found that extensive job stress can affect the body's ability to fight infections or diseases which could incorporate chronic health conditions such as depression, anxiety, insomnia, asthma, ulcers, migraine headaches, and cardiovascular illness just to name a few.

In recent years, researchers have found more evidence that job stress is associated with workers' physical health. Archer, Fredriksson, Schuts, and Kostrzewa (2011) surveyed 537 human service workers, and 30-50% reported that workplace stress produced adverse physical effects, such as aging and imbalanced immune systems. Job stress can induce serious health problems, and the chronic job stress may generate diseases, such as cancer and diabetes with possible fatal outcomes. Nabirye, Brown, Pryor, and

Maples (2011) indicated that people who respond to job stress in a negative manner might experience detrimental health problems that affect their mental and physical well-being. Many professionals have become chemically dependent on medications to cope with job stress, which would eventually produce additional mental and physical health consequences (Dedorvic, D'Aguiar, & Pruessner, 2009).

Job stress is also associated with mental health. Nixon, Mazzola, Bauer, Krueger, and Spector (2011) indicated that heart disease, stroke, homicide, suicide, and many other physical and mental illnesses occur because ongoing pressures and strain can appear in the workplace due to job stress. Nixon et al. (2008) reported that extreme and ongoing job stress could cause chemical imbalances in the brain, which would produce an onset of different mental health deficits such as depression, anxiety, posttraumatic stress disorders (PTSD), and schizophrenia. Dedorvic et al. (2009) surveyed 219 service workers and 27% reported occupational stress induced mental health issues that complicated their careers and overall well-being. They found that job stress could negatively affect brain function and induce individuals to make irrational workplace decisions (Dedorvic et al., 2009)

In fact, biological mechanism has contributed to an individual's ability to gain resilience from high occupational stressed events. Biological mechanisms determine a person's coping response when encountering stress, such as managing to overcome stressful obligations through social support, avoidance, and problem-focused mechanisms (Chao, 2011). Individuals who exhibited effective defense mechanisms usually show healthier psychological maturity, advanced workplace capacity, and life contentment (Plaude & Rascevska, 2011). Dedovic, D' Aguiar, and Pruessner (2009) manifested that hormonal reactions to occupational stress may negatively affect the immune system which can increase the onset of mental and physical diseases. Chao (2011) further reported that hormone increases during the fight or flight response, which could determine if a stressed employee might quit. Additionally, job stress has led health declines in professionals, but usually overlooked due to the demands of a certain economic class (Kiani, Samavatyan, & Pourabion, 2011).

Job stressors can develop into serious health hazards if individuals do not learn to de-escalate emotions to prevent mental breakdowns (Yamada, McEwen, & Pavlides, 2003). What do leaders do when their employees have high levels of job stress? How do employees react if they experience job stress? Do leaders with high level of emotional intelligence manage their companies well? Do people with high levels of emotional intelligence help them deal with job stress?

Research Studies on Emotional Intelligence and Job Stress

Many researchers have found significant relationships between emotional intelligence and occupational stress for years (e.g., Darvish & Nasrollahi, 2011; Gardner & Stough, 2002; Goswami & Talukdar, 2013; Levinson, 2008; Newman, Joseph, & MacCann, 2010; Reynolds & O'Dwyer, 2008; Satija & Khan, 2013). Some researchers uncovered the importance of emotional maturity as a stress coping skill (Levinson, 2008; Satija & Khan, 2013). Others have examined the relationship between emotional intelligence and leadership (Gardner & Stough, 2002; Palmer, Walls, Burgess, & Stough, 2000).

Two decades ago, Wharton (1993) examined if emotional labor affects employees in the banking and hospital settings negatively, and suggested the performance of emotional labor does not have negative consequences. However, through a quantitative correlation study of 300 professionals, Palmer, Walls, Burgess, and Stough (2000) investigated if higher levels of emotional intelligence related to transformational or transactional leadership; they discovered that emotional intelligence affects the competency of transformational leadership. Gardner and Stough (2002) examined if emotional intelligence predicts transformational, transactional, and laissez-faire leadership styles. Through a quantitative correlation and regression method with a sample of over 200 professionals, they discovered that emotional intelligence highly correlated with transformational leadership (Gardner & Stough, 2002).

In a quantitative correlation study with a moderate sample of over 50 people, King and Gardner (2006) explored if individuals with high emotional intelligence can deal with challenges from individuals with low emotional intelligence in the workplace; they discovered that emotional intelligence influences skills in managing emotional reactions. Leaders who lack emotional intelligence tend to suffer mentally from depression, anxiety, and other mood disorders (Boyatis & Goleman, 2006). Emotional intelligence affects performance, known as behavioral competencies, which also affects emotional effectiveness within high-stress organizations (Seal, Boyatzis, & Bailey, 2006). People who worked in large organizations with emotional intelligence have a tendency to improve work performance with social and communication skills (Seal et al., 2006). People with higher levels of emotional intelligence accept change more easily and show more leadership traits during major transitions (Seal et al., 2006).

Schultz et al. (2007) believed that people with high levels of emotional intelligence could work effectively when under severe occupation stress and pressure. In a quantitative correlational study with more than 150 school professionals, Reynolds and O'Dwyer (2008) found that high levels of emotional intelligence and coping skills predict leadership effectiveness, while other characteristics, such as gender, years of experience, level of education, and job satisfaction hold constant. According to Levinson (2008), high stress levels decreased substance abuse professionals' emotional intelligence and low emotional intelligence affected their job performance.

Mikolajczak, Roy, Verstrynge, and Luminet (2009) argued that emotional intelligence prevents certain emotions from surfacing, such as self-blame and other self-defeating beliefs that would cause stress. They also examined how emotional intelligence can have huge impact on the mood and memory, along with a person's ability to recall certain events and to determine which coping skills to use to adapt to different situations (Mikolajczak et al., 2009). A high level of emotional intelligence allows people to process negative information without mental breakdown or confusion (Mikolajczak et al., 2009). According to Dedovic et al. (2009), those who had high levels of emotional intelligence ignited positive responses facing occupational stress because they have elevated body's defenses against infections and diseases. This helped motivate professionals to complete complex tasks as well as deal with difficult coworkers.

Newman et al. (2010) explained that different levels of emotional intelligence could be used to predict certain behaviors in the workplace with; emotional intelligence can elevate substance abuse professionals' motivation to improve workplace performance and to increase job sustainability. Emotional intelligence affects job performance when exhaustion surfaces; professionals who work at high-stress jobs in a low emotional intelligence environment may experience burnout (Newman, et al., 2010). Salami (2010) proposed that people with higher emotional intelligence are better equipped to handle workplace challenges such as layoffs, because they are not prone to exhibit decreased productivity, lack of commitment, distrust, and overall workplace meltdowns. People who lack emotional intelligence in a stressful workplace may exhibit counterproductive and bullying behavior, such as spreading negative rumors, character assassinations of peers and leaders, and missing organizational citizenship behavior (Salami, 2010).

Five years ago, Darvish and Nasrollahi (2011) examined the relationship between emotional intelligence and occupational stress among Payam Noor University's staff, and discovered that emotional intelligence positively influenced occupational stress, which improved employee performance. In a quantitative correlation study of 250 engineers, Goswami and Talukdar (2013) investigated whether emotional intelligence influenced job stress among engineers in public sector organizations; they discovered that emotional intelligence has a positive impact on job stress as well.

However, in Nabirye, Brown, Pryor, and Maples' (2011) study of human service professionals, not all occupational stressors lead to unhealthy consequence as people respond to stress differently, due to different emotional intelligence levels. People with high levels of emotional intelligence take job demands more positively; they experience healthy occupational stress that can lead to positive outcome (Nabirye et al., 2011). Nabirye et al. (2011) mentioned that moderate occupational stress coupled with helpful emotional intelligence could improve work performance based on their study of 356 adult care workers. Individuals with high emotional intelligence are best able to gain control and maintain strength during unexpected events in the workplace; high emotional intelligence can lead to high self-esteem and confidence (Pasca & Wagner, 2011).

It appears that emotional intelligence which facilitates affective management of feelings during stressful situations helps prevent mental and physical breakdowns, release job stress, and improve job performance. Is emotional intelligence a predictor for job performance? Iqbal and Abbasi (2013) mentioned that emotional intelligence is a powerful predictor of job performance, because in stressful work environment people with good emotional intelligence know how to make adjustments when handling lengthy work assignments with short deadlines. Job performance is an important factor when considering employment issues because workers must maintain a proficient level of motivation, not only to satisfy their job duties, but also to work well with others (Iqbal and Abbasi, 2013). Emotional intelligence and job performance go hand and hand because workers' emotional intelligence levels would provide an indication of employees' efficiency in the workplace.

Substance Abuse Professionals

The substance abuse profession is an industry consisting of drug and alcohol counseling services to individuals who suffer from chemical dependency or abuse. Substance abuse professionals are state certified professionals who evaluate individuals with drug and alcohol problems using therapy, group education, follow-up testing, and aftercare. The role of substance abuse agencies is to provide health insurance that would cover mental health services to maintain healthy employees.

Even though all human service occupations experience tension and pressure, substance abuse professionals are more likely to contemplate quitting due to workplace exhaustion, which in turn affects leadership skills. As Vorkapic and Mustapic (2012) highlighted, the substance abuse profession has a higher burnout rate than any other people-oriented profession in the United States. Substance abuse professionals usually experience high absenteeism and turnover in the workplace because of stress and vulnerability (Vorkapic & Mustapic, 2012). Oser et al. (2013, p. 17) further indicated, "substance abuse professionals are the most vulnerable to burnout because of low pay and emotional stress."

Additionally, some researchers found that workers in high stress professions are more likely to experience physical and mental exhaustion. Oginska-Bulik (2005) explained that high stress professions, such as human services, could cause employees' physical and mental exhaustion resulting from ongoing stress while working with difficult populations. Burnout syndrome occurs when lack of interest becomes a factor within a profession driven by stress (Oginska-Bulik, 2005). Human service professions such as counselors, case managers, and other healthcare workers experience occupational stress on a regular basis; therefore, elevated levels of emotional intelligence may ease mental and physical health outcomes

Emotional Intelligence and Job Stress

(Oginska-Bulik, 2005). Importantly, Schulz et al. (2007) emphasized that human high level of emotional strain along with unhealthy work-related behaviors linked to workplace stress.

In their study of 389 health professional participants, a total of 38.2% reported experiencing emotional exhaustion along with burnout due to job stress (Schultz et al. 2007). Unrelieved job stress may escalate to high levels of mental and physical suffering and affliction (Schultz et al., 2007). Human services occupations can experience increased rates of turnover and burnout (Ducharme et al., 2008). They provided reasons why service workers such as counselors experience intensive stress; their success depends on their abilities to sustain maturity while dealing with difficult people (Ducharme et al., 2008). The aforementioned review has provided relevant research studies in the field and background information for emotional intelligence, job stress, and substance abuse professionals. In the following, methodology and findings of this study will be presented.

MAIN FOCUS OF THE CHAPTER

Methodology

The purpose of this chapter was to explore substance abuse professionals' definitions, perceptions, and viewpoints regarding the relationship between emotional intelligence and job stress. A qualitative method with a case study design was adopted for this study. The participants were 18 voluntary substance abuse professionals from three similar substance abuse treatment agencies in the metropolitan area of Kansas City, Missouri. Four research questions guided this study: (a) What are substance abuse professionals' definitions of emotional intelligence and job stress?; (b) How do higher levels of emotional intelligence help people deal with job stress?; (c) How does job stress negatively affect peoples' emotional intelligence from substance abuse professionals' viewpoints?; and (d) Why do higher levels of emotional intelligence reduce people's job stress and improve their job performance?

Eight open-ended interview questions were used to gather data. The interview questions included: (a) what is your definition of emotional intelligence? (b) What is your definition of job stress? (c) In your opinion, what is the relationship between emotional intelligence and job stress? (d) From your perspective, how do higher levels of emotional intelligence help people deal with job stress? (e) How does job stress affect a person's emotional intelligence from your point of view? (f) How does good emotional intelligence improve skill building and job satisfaction in the workplace? (g) How do you deal with occupational stress? (h) In your opinion, why do higher levels of emotional intelligence reduce people's job stress and improve job performance? NVivo 10 was used to process and analyze interview data.

Results

The findings of this study were illustrated as follows. The definitions of emotional intelligence included four categories: ignoring silliness, ability to identify emotions/feelings, expressing emotions, and cognitive skills. The definition of job stress involved high demands/expectations, overwhelmed feelings, inability to cope, and pressure. The relationship between emotional intelligence and job stress consisted of level of control, supportive network, finding solutions, awareness of job stress, and effective responses to job stress. The ways high emotional intelligence helped deal with job stress involved appropriate behavior, motivating self-care, reduction of anxiety, good decision-making skills, improved job retention/performance, and understanding feelings. The ways job stress affected emotional intelligence involved chronic stress, avoidance attitude, workplace conflict, hard to recognize true feelings, overwhelmed pressures, and negative stress/mental responses.

The ways emotional intelligence increased job stress consisted of building supportive relationships, positive coping skills, self-control, stress reduction, conflict management, promotion, and better pay. Job stress management involved exercise, vacation, support from family/friends, meditation/pray, communication with boss/coworkers, and avoiding drama. Reasons for high emotional intelligence reducing job stress and improve job performance are regulating emotions, understanding emotions, positive attitudes, self-discipline, adapting to change, and relaxation.

In this study, certain themes recurred from participants' responses to various interview questions relating to emotional intelligence and job stress. There were eight significant emergent themes: emotional awareness, elevated job obligations, awareness of job strain, self-care, negative mental responses, increased support system, physical activity, and understanding/identifying feelings. In the following, eight themes were described with examples.

Emotional Awareness

Some participants perceived that being aware of how one feels is a manifestation of emotional intelligence. SAP 1 stated, "Emotional intelligence is being able to identify your own emotional state and the emotional state of others." SAP 2 mentioned, "I believe that emotional intelligence is a measure of one's ability to identify and describe emotional states" and SAP 4 stated, "Emotional intelligence is the ability to recognize own and other's emotions." SAP 6 mentioned, "Emotional intelligence to me is the ability to recognize emotion in self and others." SAP 8 said, "Emotional intelligence is being able identify and control your emotions by using cognitive skills."

Elevated Job Obligations

Many participants believed that increases in job demands are their definition of job stress, because heavy obligations could place enormous pressure on professionals. SAP 1 believed that, "Job stress is being overwhelmed with obligations on your time and attention in the workplace." In SAP 2's viewpoint, "Job stress is related to the pressure placed upon employees by the demands of their position in the work environment." In SAP 4's perspective, "Job stress is the expectations that we place on ourselves and others" and SAP 5 stated, "The definition is job stress would be the pressure we put on ourselves from the natural demands of employment." SAP 10 mentioned, "job duties, coworkers, etc., to the degree that an individual has a difficult time dealing with demanding situations."

Awareness of Job Strain

Some participants perceived the relationship between emotional intelligence and job stress as acknowledging and understanding that job stress continuously happens and one needs to respond appropriately. SAP 5 stated, "The more you know about your own job stress and emotions, the more you have control over them." On the other hand, SAP 7 mentioned, "Being aware of what causes job stress for you and what effects your emotions could help you understand how both are related." SAP 8 stated that the relationship between emotional intelligence and job stress is "being able to identify that you are having job stress and realizing there is something you can do about it."

Self-Care

Many participants noted that emotional intelligence motivates professionals to practice effective self-care to help them deal with job stress. SAP 10 said, "Having a higher level of emotional intelligence will motivate a person to cope with their emotional responses to job stress in a healthier way." SAP 2 mentioned, "Emotional intelligence can allow one to make stress a motivator to practice self-care, rather than allowing stress to be a hindrance." SAP 6 stated, "It helps people aware of themselves and others, knowing that something is wrong and being willing to take care of you." SAP 8 stated, "Emotional intelligence is something you are able to learn and use as it will make it easier to realize where the stress is coming from and how to take care of self."

Negative Mental Responses

Some participants believed that job stress greatly affect one's mental stability and emotional intelligence; this could lead to burnout in the workplace. SAP 10 stated, "Job stress affects one's emotional intelligence in different ways such as some people become angry and others may become weak and passive in the workplace." SAP 11 said, "Job stress can cause anxiety for some people." SAP 12 mentioned, "Job stress taxes one's emotional intelligence; as you become more stressed, you may become less rational" and SAP 14 stated, "Job stress can weaken people mentally, which can affect job performance."

Increased Support System

Many participants believed that emotional intelligence encourages professionals to build a supportive network, which could elevate work skills and produce job contentment. SAP 1 stated, "Emotional intelligence can enable people to build a supportive network of coworkers that will increase your job satisfaction." SAP 4 mentioned, "We can reduce stress, build reliable relationships, and continue to work on the foundation as a team." SAP 6 noted, "Because we can use our knowledge of our own feelings and others to reduce conflict and build trusting relationships." SAP 18 indicated, "You are able to make good decisions if you have emotional intelligence and be able to work with anybody."

Physical Activity

Some participants regarded exercises as the best way to deal with job stress. SAP 1 stated, "It is important to seek a therapist and do some relaxation exercises." SAP 2 stated, "It is important to exercise at least two times weekly." SAP 3 stated, "It is important to work out or walk your dog." SAP 5 explained, "One can play music or take a short walk." SAP 18 believed that, "People should not take their workplace problems home and they should work out every day."

Understanding/ Identifying Feelings

Many participants indicated that higher levels of emotional intelligence enable professionals to realize and classify emotions, which allows workers to decrease stress and elevate job performance. SAP 4 mentioned, "Higher emotional intelligence allows people to understand themselves as they would able to perform better in the workplace." SAP 6 stated, "If you can understand feeling, you can know when to back down and provide others space and empathy." SAP 9 indicated, "If you have higher levels of emotional intelligence, you will be able to identify and label emotions." SAP 10 said, "Higher levels of emotional intelligence reduce job stress and improve job performance because the individual is able to understand people's emotional responses." SAP 16 stated, "Higher levels of emotional intelligence allow a person to understand emotions to where one can manage and deal with difficult people and tasks." SAP 17 said, "I believe that emotional intelligence can increase job performance because you are not stressed out and you have the mental ability to understand emotions along with knowing the job stress will happen."

ISSUES, CONTROVERSIES, PROBLEMS

Substance abuse professionals play a vital role in the lives of people with chemical dependency issues; therefore, the health and well-being of substance abuse professionals are extremely important in providing optimal treatment services. To provide optimal service, substance abuse professionals have to communicate not only their clients, but also their supervisors regarding issues. After exploring substance abuse professionals' viewpoints and thoughts for this study, a few issues and problems were surfaced.

First, substance abuse professionals invest significant amount of emotional time in constructing their therapeutic relationships with clients. Since chemically dependent people were a difficult population to serve, professionals become emotionally overwhelmed as their clients experienced high relapse rates. The circumstance that professionals face in workplace might cause stress and pose a problem with job performance.

Second, some substance abuse professionals experience fatigue, burnout, and exhaustion when managing large clients' caseloads. Substance abuse professionals normally have a caseload of 30 or more clients with intensified problems. Employee burnout occurs when they have excessive stress. Stressors on the job in addiction treatment services can produce burnout amongst professionals and potentially create associated issues, such as job ineffectiveness, absenteeism, interpersonal conflict, lower productivity, reduced organizational commitment, job dissatisfaction, and employee turnover in the workplace. Researchers have discovered that substance abuse professionals who fail to identify when stress levels are out of control, may experience burnout and exhaustion (Ducharme et al., 2008; Vorkapic & Mustapic, 2012; Perkins & Sprang, 2013).

Third, the stress of substance abuse professionals came from three sources: their supervisors, their clients, and the Department of Mental Health. Most substance abuse professionals have histories of drug and alcohol addiction, which may cause workers to get emotionally involved with their client's treatment programs. The Missouri Department of Mental Health performs annual audits with all client files to determine if client problems and interventions match. State oversight might create additional pressure on substance abuse workers. Substance abuse professionals might be stressful if they do not meet their supervisors' expectations.

Fourth, some substance abuse professionals have reported symptoms of depression and anxiety at work. When substance abuse professionals experience intense pressure, some failed to maintain good work attendance due to their need to decompress. These professionals tend to use up sick leave and vacation time because of stress and exhaustion (Vorkapic & Mustapic, 2012). Most substance abuse professionals mentioned that they do not have time to attend self-care meetings or get EAP assistance because of demanding pressures of the job. Additionally, substance abuse agencies place enormous amounts of pressure on substance abuse professionals, resulting in workers being afraid of taking time off for self-care (Perkins & Sprang, 2013).

Fifth, substance abuse professionals must be state certified or licensed to work in treatment programs. They have to take difficult state exams in addition to hectic work shifts to assist in positively changing lives. However, substance abuse professionals usually experience poor working environments, demanding job descriptions, low pay, and ongoing conflict between clients and coworkers (Ducharme et al. 2008; Perkins & Sprang, 2013). Agency supervisors tend to overlook the pressures and stress that staff experience because of billing and other financial obligations such as weekly or monthly reports and quotas (Ducharme et al. 2008; Vorkapic & Mustapic, 2013).

SOLUTIONS AND RECOMMENDATIONS

Stress Management Tools

Job stress occurs in both the employee and the employer within the workplace. Organizations must identify job adversity and discover solutions to assist with workplace problems. The state of Missouri is required to provide job satisfaction surveys to substance abuse professionals to aid in decreasing employee turnover. Beyond that, making use of different stress management tools is useful for recapturing good health (Nixon et al., 2011). The Occupational Stress Inventory Revised (OSI-R) identifies ways of looking at the amount of stress people encounter from the workplace, which is a measure of three coping resources: occupational regulation, psychological strain, and occupational stress (Khurshid, Butt, & Muzaffar, 2012).

Some employee assistance programs use OSI-R as a source to identify job hardship, which assists in developing interventions to produce change (Khurshid et al., 2012). According to Schaefer and Moos (1996), stress management is a tool to relieve stress in order to improve one's overall well-being. Using stress management can alleviate possible illnesses, both mentally and physically. Stress management in a hectic workplace is extremely important because it allows professionals to relax and to maintain productivity and sustainability. Occupational turnover decreases when stress is addressed in an appropriate manner, because people learn how to relax when their body and mind experienced exertion (Shoptaw, Stein, & Rawson, 2000).

Recommendations for Substance Abuse Professionals' Leaders

Based on the research findings, the following recommendations were made for substance abuse professionals. Managers of substance abuse professions must understand that emotions are the inevitable when individuals lose control. An enormous amount of stress in the workplace can be caused by demanding workloads. Clinical supervisors should understand that emotional intelligence is a learned skill and can lead to on-the-job success (Goleman, 1995). Clinical supervisors must not assume that all substance abuse professionals have high emotional intelligence just because they help a difficult population of consumers who may be stricken with addiction and mental illnesses.

Clinical supervisors must be able to determine suitable workloads and maintain reasonable expectations of others in the workplace to reduce stress and burnout. Clinical supervisors must assume that substance abuse professionals may experience emotional imbalances, and stress can control substance abuse professionals' well-being. Clinical supervisors must understand that job stress can cost employees their happiness and health; this could also affect the organization to lose money and time due to low productivity. The following strategies were recommended for clinical supervisors of agencies A, B, and C:

- Clinical supervisors should implement quarterly mandatory in-service trainings for all employees regarding job stress awareness held by the State of Missouri's Occupational Safety and Health Administration.
- Clinical directors should incorporate weekly one-on-one supervision meetings with all employees regarding their job description to identify and discuss stressful occupational demands along with developing personal interventions to decrease workplace stressors to become more productive.
- Clinical directors should hire a psychologist or chaplain within the organization's Employee Assistance Program (EAP) to assist employees with mental health or spirituality counseling needs along with gaining information regarding mindfulness, emotional control, and interpersonal efficiency to obtain the tools to practice emotional regulation.
- The board of directors of all three agencies should collaborate to raise money to implement an all-expense paid employee retreat at the Tan-Tar-A Resort in Osage Beach, Missouri once a year for substance abuse professionals working for Agency A, B, or C. The retreat should include stress management activities along with meet and greet sessions for support system building purposes. The recommended retreat should be designed to gain and maintain employee morale.

Recommendations for Substance Abuse Professionals

Due the high demands of the job, quarterly retreats may ensure employee satisfaction. Lowering the demands of contact hours and quotas releases additional stress in which the agency's motivation and productivity elevates. Exploring different avenues for substance abuse professionals to address occupational stress could help balance the demands of the job and employee retention. Implementing monthly trainings on self-care may educate substance abuse professionals to understand why stress levels are high in the workplace (Vorkapic & Mustapic, 2012; Perkins & Sprang, 2013). Intensive professional development skills concerning emotional intelligence and quality improvement may help substance abuse professional succeed in their every job duties assist counselors with to perform everyday job demands effectively (Ducharme et al., 2008).

Based on the findings, substance abuse professionals should understand that workplace stress in normal; however, excessive job stress can be damaging both mentally and physically. Substance abuse professionals must understand that persistent self-care is important when helping and working with people in stressful situations. Substance abuse professionals must understand that they cannot control everything or everyone in their work environment; however, this does not imply that workers are powerless when facing difficult situations.

Emotional Intelligence and Job Stress

Substance abuse professionals must not assume that taking control of their stress does not mean quitting their jobs or leaving the substance abuse field; however, they should understand that it is about taking control of what matters most: their emotions (Darvish & Nasrollahi, 2011). Substance abuse professionals should be open-minded at understanding that people have different feelings; therefore, attending emotional awareness groups or conferences may help broaden employee's horizons in cases regarding empathy and positive interaction. Substance abuse professionals should be willing to attend training sessions on learning how to identify warning signs and symptoms of excessive workplace stress, and to address problems in a timely manner.

The following recommendations are for the substance abuse professionals:

- Substance abuse professionals should consider meeting with a mental health provider that is not affiliated with the workplace (EAP) on a regular basis if additional processing or prescribed medications are needed to gain and maintain mental stability.
- Substance abuse professionals should review their job description on a consistent basis to determine if certain assignment, or a particular employee position, is too overwhelming thereby decreasing effective job performance. Substance abuse professionals should also consider using a journal to record daily feelings and behaviors to process with mental health provider, site supervisor, or self-tracking for awareness purposes.
- Substances abuse professionals should consider participating in regular physical activities three to six times per week to maintain mental and physical health along with improving their nutrition intake.
- Substance abuse professionals should participate in peer-to-peer support groups, develop within the organization, to discuss feelings and emotions of themselves and others to reduce workplace stress and to enhance morale.

FUTURE RESEARCH DIRECTIONS

There were some limitations in this study. The first limitation of the study involved a limited range of feedback because the responses came from a small sample of 18 participants in three substance abuse agencies. The second limitation was that some participants' responses were similar regarding to the perceptions and opinions of emotional intelligence and job stress. The third limitation was that this was a case study with small sample size, so it cannot be generalized to a large population.

Future researchers can broaden their work to collect more data from diverse population of participants in different agencies to provide additional insights. Researchers can also consider exploring lived experience of their participants concerning emotional intelligence and job stress with surveys, which would enable them to gather rich information for statistical analysis. Future researchers may consider focusing on a larger sample size to uncover participants' actual work environment, how job stress has affected them in the workplace, how long they have been dealing with job stress, and how different levels of emotional intelligence affect their job performance.

For future research, the researchers can: (a) Change the method from qualitative to quantitative to gather a statistical data and to compare findings; (b) change the design from a case study to a narrative inquiry or a phenomenology to gain a deeper understanding of the essence of the topic, and to explore the life stories and experiences of participants; and (c) broaden the geographical location from one city to many cities and from one state to multiple states.

CONCLUSION

The purposes of this study are to explore substance abuse professionals' definitions of emotional intelligence and job stress, and their viewpoints on the relationship between emotional intelligence and job stress. The purposive sample used for this case study consisted of 18 substance abuse professionals from three substance abuse agencies. All substance abuse professionals were employed at one of three agencies in Kansas City, Missouri. Participants responded to open-ended questions in the face-to-face interviews. Demographic information was collected. NVivo 10 software was used to enter and code participants' data as well as to retrieve themes. Research questions, major findings, implications, and contributions of the study were summed up as follows.

The first research question asked, "What are substance abuse professionals' definition of emotional intelligence and job stress?" The emergent theme of emotional awareness is apparent because many substance abuse professionals perceived that identifying one's own feelings and emotional state is the definition of emotional intelligence. This finding supports Satija and Khan (2013) finding, as they mentioned emotional intelligence is the process of self-regulation and self-awareness along with empathy, which required accountability of emotions. Additionally, substance abuse professionals perceived the definition of job stress as having elevated job demands, which supports Cotton and Hart (2003) finding that organizational job demands influence stress levels and performance. The findings of this study also support Adaramola (2012) research findings who noted that job stress exists when employees' professional goals do not match the purpose of the employer.

The second research question asked, "How do higher levels of emotional intelligence help people deal with job stress?" Some substance abuse professionals believed that emotional intelligence could assist people in dealing with job stress by knowing when one is under job stress; this supports Cotton and Hart's (2003) research finding that people must be aware when job stress is happening to allow them to deal with stress effectively. Many substance abuse professionals also believed that making use of self-care techniques such as relaxation, seeking therapy, and building a supportive networking system are ways of making adjustments to deal with job stress. The finding supports Iqbal and Abbasi's (2013) research finding on emotional intelligence as a powerful predictor of job stress, because people with high emotional intelligence know how to make adjustments when facing pressure at work.

The third research question asked, "How does job stress negatively affect people's emotional intelligence from substance abuse professionals' viewpoints?" Many substance abuse professionals believed that negative mental responses could affect one's emotional intelligence such as anxiety, depression, sadness, anger, or passive behaviors. The finding is consistent with Cotton and Hart's (2003) research finding, in which job stress has inflicted professionals' mental well-being for centuries because of workplace pressures. This finding also supports the finding of Nixon et al. (2008), in which extreme and ongoing job stress could cause chemical imbalances in the brain and may produce different mental health deficits such as depression, anxiety, posttraumatic stress disorder (PTSD), and schizophrenia.

The fourth research question asked, "Why do higher levels of emotional intelligence reduce people's job stress and improve job performance?" Many substance abuse professionals mentioned that increased support systems and physical activity could reduce stress and improve performance. This finding is consistent with Darvish and Nasrollahi's (2011) finding that emotional intelligence enables professionals to practice interpersonal effectiveness to seek out and obtain support within the workplace. Some substance abuse professionals also perceived that physical activity could reduce stress and improve performance, which supports Dedovic, D'Aguiar, and Pruessner's (2009) research finding on physical activities reduce stress and decrease chances of the onset of different diseases. Additionally, some substance abuse professionals believed that understanding feelings of self and others could reduce stress and improve work performance. This finding supports Goleman's (1998) finding that people have feelings of anger at work from time to time; however, it is the leader's responsibility to regulate composure when undesirable situations occur. As Goleman (1998) described, emotional intelligence enables professionals to imagine the depth of other's feelings, to hold productive conversations, and to solve problems.

The theoretical implications derived from the interpretation of the findings were as follows. In this study, substance abuse professionals believed that emotional intelligence could assist people in knowing when they are under significant job strain. This finding is consistent with Ursin and Eriksen's (2004) *Cognitive Activation Theory of Stress and Preservative Cognition*, which indicated how the brain alarms an individual's response system when undergoing stain to incorporate coping or adaptation skills. The fact that many substance abuse professionals believed that increased support systems could reduce stress and improve performance supports Hobfoll's (1989) *Conservation of Resource Theory*, as individuals accumulate resources such as self-worth, optimism, money, status, and social support to accommodate and withstand threats.

The finding that negative mental responses could affect one's stress level on the job by producing anxiety, depression, sadness, anger, or passivity behaviors is consistent with Karasek's (1979) *Job Demand-Control Theory* in which one's stress level can impact how a person deals with excessive strain, even though job demands can place physical and psychological strain on individuals. The findings of the study also support the transactional model of stress by Lazarus (2000), who indicated that environmental demands could affect the well-being of individuals.

This study may contribute to employees' understanding of how different emotional intelligence levels influence occupational stress levels, which might also affect one's job performance. This study may raise the awareness or provide the workforce with reasons why people in human services experience burnout with fewer than five years of employment. This study may remind clinical supervisors within all three agencies the importance of self-care.

More individuals are entering into the substance abuse field because of employment opportunities and high turnover. Occasionally, substance abuse professionals need to decompress; therefore, stress management programs should be part of the organization. Clinical supervisors should approach the situation with understanding as opposed to an industrial paradigm of leadership. Satija and Khan (2013) emphasized that job satisfaction should be the main priority in any organization. Due to the high demands of the job, quarterly retreats may ensure employee satisfaction. Exploring the value of investing in an in-house on staff psychologist may increase emotional intelligence and reduce employee turnover. Lowering the demands of contact hours and quotas may release additional stress in which the agency's motivation and productivity may also increase. Training in intensive professional development skills concerning emotional intelligence and quality improvement may help substance abuse professionals succeed in their every job duties and in performing everyday job demands effectively.

Staff shortage due to a growing number of turnovers of substance abuse professionals adds to the urgency of stress management programs. The themes extracted from this qualitative case study offer insights on what would be essential for clinical supervisors to pay attention to for the next generation of substance abuse professionals. Clinical supervisors should consider implementing fitness program, stress management and emotional awareness conferences, along with stress management activities to add to employee's job description. At every annual performance evaluation, substance abuse professionals must present proof that they participated in several stress management activities in order to receive a descent performance evaluation. Implementing such programs could lead to less stress for substance abuse professionals, increased job satisfaction, improved job performance, less burnout, and lower employee turnover.

REFERENCES

Adaramola, S. S. (2012). Job stress and productivity increase. *Work (Reading, Mass.)*, *41*, 2955–2958. doi:10.3233/WOR-2012-0547-2955 PMID:22317168

Archer, T., Freddriksson, A., Schutz, E., & Kostrzewa, R. M. (2011). Influence of physical exercise on neuroimmunological functioning and health: Aging and stress. *Neurotox*, *20*(1), 69–83. doi:10.1007/s12640-010-9224-9 PMID:20953749

Blanding, M. (2015). Workplace stress responsible for up to $190B in annual U.S. healthcare costs. *Forbes*. Retrieved from http://www.forbes.com/sites/hbsworkingknowledge/2015/01/26/workplace-stress-responsible-for-up-to-190-billion-in-annual-u-s-heathcare-costs/#326009864333

Boyatzis, R. E., & Goleman, D. (2006). *Emotional and Social Competency Inventory*. Boston: The Hay Group.

Boyatzis, R. E., Goleman, D., & Rhee, K. S. (2000). Clustering competence in emotional intelligence: Insights from the Emotional Competence Inventory. In Bar-On and J. Parker (Eds.), The Handbook of Emotional Intelligence: Theory, development, assessment, and application at home, school, and in the workplace. San Francisco, CA: Jossey-Bass.

Brackett, M. A., Rivers, S. E., & Salovey, P. (2011). Emotional intelligence: implication of personal, social, academic, and workplace success. *Social and Personality psychological compass, 5*(1), 88-103. doi:10.1111/j.1751-9004.2010.00334

Caruso, D. R., Mayer, J. D., & Salovey, P. (2002). Relation of an ability measure of emotional intelligence to personality. *Journal of Personality Assessment*, *79*(2), 306–320. Retrieved from http://www.unh.edu/emotional_intelligence/EI%20Assets/Reprints...EI%20Proper/EI2002CarusoMayerSaloveyMEIS.pdf doi:10.1207/S15327752JPA7902_12 PMID:12425393

Chao, C. R. (2011). Managing stress and maintaining well-being: Social support, problem-focused, coping, and avoidant coping. *Journal of Counseling and Development*, *89*(3), 338–348. doi:10.1002/j.1556-6678.2011.tb00098.x

Charniss, C. (2010). Emotional intelligence: Toward clarification of a concept. *Industrial and Organizational Psychology: Perspectives on Science and Practice*, *3*(2), 110–126. doi:10.1111/j.1754-9434.2010.01231.x

Charniss, C., Extein, M., Goleman, D., & Weissberg, R. P. (2006). Emotional intelligence: What does the research really indicate? *Educational Psychologist*, *41*(4), 239–245. Retrieved from http://alliance.la.asu.edu/temporary/students/katie/MultipleIntelligenceEmotional.Pdf doi:10.1207/s15326985ep4104_4

Connor, B., & Slear, S. (2009). Emotional intelligence and anxiety; Emotional intelligence and resiliency. *The International Journal of Learning*, *16*(1), 249–260.

Cotton, P., & Hart, P. M. (2003). Occupational well-being and performance: A review of organizational health research. *Australian Psychologist*, *38*(2), 118–127. doi:10.1080/00050060310001707117

Darvish, H., & Nasrollahi, A. A. (2011). Studying the relations between emotional intelligence and occupational stress: A case study at Payame Noor University. *Economic Science, 2*, 38-49. Retrieved from http://www.upg-bulletin-se.ro/archive/2011-2/4.%20Darvish_Nasrollahi.pdf

Darwin, C. R. (1872). *The expression of the emotions in man and animals* (1st ed.). London: John Murray. doi:10.1037/10001-000

Dedovic, K., DAguiar, C., & Pruessner, J. C. (2009). What stress does to your brain: A review of neuroimaging studies. *Canadian Journal of Psychiatry*, *54*(1), 6–15. doi:10.1177/070674370905400104 PMID:19175975

Ducharme, L. J., Knudsen, H. K., & Roman, P. M. (2008). Emotional exhaustion and turnover intention in human services occupations: The protective role of co-working support. *Sociological Spectrum*, *28*(1), 81–104. doi:10.1080/02732170701675268

Dulewicz, V., & Higgs, M. (2000). Emotional intelligence: A review and evaluation study. *Journal of Managerial Psychology*, *15*(4), 341–372. doi:10.1108/02683940010330993

Gardner, L., & Stough, C. (2002). Examining the relationship between leadership and emotional intelligence in senior level managers. *Leadership and Organization Development Journal*, *2*(2), 68–78. doi:10.1108/01437730210419198

Goleman, D. (1995). *Working with emotional intelligence*. New York: Bantam Books.

Goleman, D. (1998). *Emotional intelligence: why can it matter?* New York: Bantam Books.

Goswami, K., & Talukdar, R. R. (2013). Relation between emotional intelligence and job stress among engineers at managerial level at public sector organization. *IOSR Journal of Humanities and Social Science*, *7*(3), 44–47. doi:10.9790/0837-0734447

Hobfoll, S. E. (1989). Conservation of resources: A new attempt at conceptualizing stress. *The American Psychologist*, *44*(3), 513–524. doi:10.1037/0003-066X.44.3.513 PMID:2648906

Iqbal, F., & Abbasi, F. (2013). Relationship between emotional intelligence and job burnout among universities professors. *Journal of Psychology*, *2*(2), 219-229. Retrieved from http://www.ajssh.leena-luna.co.jp/AJSSHPDFs/Vol.2(2)/AJSSH2013 (2.2-24).pdf

Jackson, S. E., Schwab, R. L., & Schuler, R. S. (1986). Toward an understanding of the burnout phenomenon. *The Journal of Applied Psychology, 71*(4), 630–640. doi:10.1037/0021-9010.71.4.630 PMID:3804935

Karasek, R. A. (1979). Job demands, job decisions latitude, and mental strain: Implications for job redesign. *Administrative Science Quarterly, 24*(2), 285–307. doi:10.2307/2392498

Karasek, R. A., & Theorell, T. (1990). *Healthy work: Stress, productivity and the reconstruction of working life*. New York: Basic Books.

Khurshid, F., Butt, Z. U., & Muzaffer, B. (2012). Occupational stress and turnover intensions among the non-governmental organizations employees. *Language in India, 12*(1), 100–115.

Kiani, F., Samavatyan, S., & Pourabion, S. (2011). Job stress and the rate of reported incidents among workers of Isfahan Steel Company: The role mediator work pressure. *Iran Occupational Health, 8*(3), 23-31. Retrieved from http://www.sid.ir/en/ViewPaper.asp?ID=249815&vDate=FALL%202011&vEnd=31&vJournal=IRAN+OCCUPATIONAL+HEALTH+JOURNAL&vNo=3&vStart=23&vVolume=8&vWriter=KIANI%20F.,SAMAVATYAN%20S.,POURABIAN%20S

King, M., & Gardner, D. (2006). Emotional intelligence and occupational stress among professional staff in New Zealand. *The International Journal of Organizational Analysis, 14*(3), 186–203. doi:10.1108/19348830610823392

Lazarus, R. S. (2000). Toward better research on stress and coping. *The American Psychologist, 55*(6), 665–673. doi:10.1037/0003-066X.55.6.665 PMID:10892209

Levinson, M. H. (2008). General semantics and emotional intelligence. *A Review of General Semantics, 65*(3), 243-251. Retrieved from http://www.generalsemantics.org/wp-content/uploads/2011/05/2006-conference/levinson.pdf

Mikolajczak, K. M., Roy, E., Verstrynge, V., & Luminet, O. (2009). An exploration of the moderating effect of trait emotional intelligence on memory and attention in neutral and stress conditions. *British Journal of Psychology, 100*(4), 699–715. Retrieved from http://www.vikalpa.com/pdf/articles/2010/vol-35-1jan-mar-53-61.pdf doi:10.1348/000712608X395522 PMID:19236794

Mulvey, K. P., Hubbard, S., & Hayashi, S. (2003). A national study of the substance abuse treatment workforce. *Journal of Substance Abuse Treatment, 24*(3), 51–57. Retrieved from http://www.attcnetwork.org/wfs/documents/mulvey_article.pdf doi:10.1016/S0740-5472(02)00322-7 PMID:12646330

Nabirye, R. C., Brown, K. C., Pryor, E. R., & Maples, E. H. (2011). Occupational stress, job satisfaction and job performance among hospital nurses in Kampala, Uganda. *Journal of Nursing Management, 19*(6), 760–768. doi:10.1111/j.1365-2834.2011.01240.x PMID:21899629

Newman, D. A., Joseph, D. A., & MacCann, C. (2010). Emotional intelligence and job performance: The importance of emotion regulation and emotional labor context. *Industrial and Organizational Psychology: Perspectives on Science and Practice, 3*(2), 159–164. doi:10.1111/j.1754-9434.2010.01218.x

Nixon, A. E., Mazzola, J. J., Bauer, J., Krueger, J. R., & Spector, P. E. (2011). Can work make use sick? A meta-analysis of the relationship between job stressors and physical symptoms. *Work and Stress, 25*(1), 1–22. doi:10.1080/02678373.2011.569175

Oginska-Bulik, N. (2005). Emotional intelligence in the workplace: Exploring its effects on occupational stress and health outcomes in human service worker. *International Journal of Occupational Medicine and Environmental Health, 18*(2), 167–175. Retrieved from http://www.imp.lodz.pl/upload/oficyna/artykuly/pdf/full/Ogi8-02-05.pdf PMID:16201208

Oser, C., Biebel, P., Pullen, E., & Kathi, L. H. (2013). Causes, consequences, and prevention of burnout among substance abuse treatment counselors: A rural versus urban comparison. *Journal of Psychoactive Drugs, 45*(1), 17–27. doi:10.1080/02791072.2013.763558 PMID:23662328

Palmer, B., Walls, M., Burgess, Z., & Stough, C. (2000). Emotional intelligence and effective leadership. *Leadership and Organization Development Journal, 21*(1), 5–10. Retrieved from http://www.carmineleo.com/files/3713/5946/8640/ei-leadership.pdf

Pasca, R., & Wagner, S. L. (2011). Occupational stress in the multicultural workplace. *Journal of Immigrant and Minority Health, 13*(4), 697–705. doi:10.1007/s10903-011-9457-6 PMID:21394456

Perkins, E. B., & Sprang, G. (2013). Results from the Pro-QOL-IV for substance abuse counselors working with offenders. *International Journal of Mental Health and Addiction, 11*(2), 199–213. doi:10.1007/s11469-012-9412-3

Plaude, A., & Rascevska, M. (2011). The association of cognition abilities, emotional intelligence, defense mechanisms and coping with employment and unemployment. *Baltic Journal of Psychology, 12*(1), 83–101.

Rees, D. W., & Cooper, C. L. (1992). Occupational stress in health service workers in the UK. *Stress Medicine, 8*(2), 79–90. doi:10.1002/smi.2460080205

Reynolds, C., & O'Dwyer, L. M. (2008). Examining the relationship among emotional intelligence, coping with stress mechanisms for stress, and leadership effectiveness for middle school principals. *Journal of School Leadership, 18*, 472–500. Retrieved from http://eric.ed.gov/?id=EJ888561

Salami, S. O. (2010). Conflict resolution strategies and organizational citizenship behavioral: The Moderating role of trait emotional intelligence. *Social Behavior and Personality: An International Journal, 38*(1), 75–86. doi:10.2224/sbp.2010.38.1.75

Salovey, P., & Mayer, J. D. (1990). Emotional intelligence. *Imagination, Cognition and Personality, 9*(3), 185–211. Retrieved from http://www.unh.edu/emotional_intelligence/EIAssets/EmotionalIntelligenceProper/EI1990%20Emotional%20Intelligence.pdf doi:10.2190/DUGG-P24E-52WK-6CDG

Salovey, P., Mayer, J. D., Caruso, D., & Seung, H. Y. (2008). *Emotional intelligence: Perspectives on educational and positive psychology*. New York: Oxford University Press.

Satija, S., & Khan, W. (2013). Emotional intelligence as a predictor of occupational stress among working professionals. *Aweshkar Research Journal, 15*(1), 79–97.

Schmidt, K. H., & Neubach, B. (2007). Self-control demands. A source of stress at work. *International Journal of Stress Management, 14*(4), 398–416. doi:10.1037/1072-5245.14.4.398

Seal, C. R., Boyatzis, R. E., & Bailey, J. R. (2006). Fostering emotional and social intelligence in organizations. *Organizational Management Journal, 3*(3), 190–209. doi:10.1057/omj.2006.19

Seeds, P. M., & Dozois, D. J. A. (2010). Prospective evaluation of a cognitive vulnerability-stress model for depression: The interaction of schema self-structures and negative life events. *Journal of Chemical Psychology, 66*(12), 1307–1323. doi:10.1002/jclp.20723 PMID:20715020

Shoptaw, S., Stein, A., & Rawson, R. A. (2000). Burnout in substance abuse counselors: Impact of environment, attitudes, and client with HIV. *Journal of Substance Abuse Treatment, 19*(2), 117–126. doi:10.1016/S0740-5472(99)00106-3 PMID:10963923

Swartz, J. (2013). Workplace stress on the rise with 83% of Americans frazzled by something at work. Corinthian Colleges, Inc. Retrieved from http://globenewswire.com/news-release/2013/04/09/536945/10027728/en/Workplace-Stress-on-the-Rise-With-83-of-Americans-Frazzled-by-Something-at-Work.html

Ursin, H., & Eriksen, H. R. (2004). The cognitive activation theory of stress. *Psychoneuroendoctrinology, 29*(5), 567–592. doi:10.1016/S0306-4530(03)00091-X PMID:15041082

Vorkapic, S. T., & Mustapic, J. (2012). Internal and external factors in professional burnout of substance abuse professionals in Croatia. *Annali dellIstituto Superiore di Sanita, 48*(2), 189–197. doi:10.4415/ANN_12_02_12

Yamada, K., McEwen, B. S., & Pavlides, C. (2003). Site and time dependent effects of acute stress on hippocampal long-term potentiation in freely behaving rats. *Experimental Brain research, 152*(1), 52-59. doi:10.1007%2Fs00221-003-1519-0

KEY TERMS AND DEFINITIONS

Burnout: A state of emotional and physical exhaustion due to ongoing stress and demands.

Emotional Awareness: Being aware of one's feelings and emotions.

Emotional Exhaustion: The process of physical and mental depletion from ongoing job demands.

Emotional Intelligence: The ability to recognize one's emotions/feelings and the emotions/feelings of others.

Employee Turnover: Employee's job lost and replacements within an organization in a short time frame.

Occupational Stress: Pressure or tension mentally and physically in the workplace due to heavy workload or hostile work environment.

Substance Abuse Profession: An industry consists of drug and alcohol counseling services to individuals who suffer from chemical dependency or abuse.

Substance Abuse Professionals: The state certified professionals who evaluate individuals with drug and alcohol problems by using therapy, group education, follow-up testing, and aftercare.

Chapter 11
Experienced Stress and the Value of Rest Stops in the Transportation Field:
Stress and Transportation

Ville Pietiläinen
University of Lapland, Finland

Rauno Rusko
University of Lapland, Finland

Ilkka Salmi
University of Lapland, Finland

Raimo Jänkälä
University of Lapland, Finland

ABSTRACT

Work-related stress has been a long-term research focus in the field of industrial-organizational (I-O) psychology. Transportation is marginal, but an interesting context for the study as the field contains many specific characteristics related to stress phenomena. This chapter investigates the contents of and connection between work-related stress and rest stops' value in the transportation field, specifically in a lightly settled area with long geographic distances. Professional truck drivers in Finland serve as the target group for this study. The working conditions of truck drivers are unique compared to other branches where the work is not so mobile. In addition to how the truck is equipped, the services and facilities at rest stops are important elements in wellbeing. Based on the qualitative content analysis, this study offers in-depth information concerning work-related stress as an experienced phenomenon in the transportation field. Work management and legislation are highlighted as primary results while a dangerous work environment as well as isolation and loneliness are listed as secondary research results associated with work-related stress and the value of rest stops. Recommendations for future research and practical implications are proposed.

DOI: 10.4018/978-1-5225-2568-4.ch011

INTRODUCTION

Industrial–organizational (I-O) psychology is a relevant part of contemporary studies of the workplace. However, until recently, I-O psychology was neglected in, for example, psychology textbooks and courses (Maynard et al., 2002). The area was first labeled economic/business psychology, illustrating its link to business studies. In 1973, the field of I-O psychology was delineated by the American Psychological Association (Stryker et al., 2012). Since the 1980s, the Scandinavian focus on I-O psychology has rested on the physical and mental health of workers and the relationship between stress and mental health (Erez, 1994). According to the Four European Working Survey conducted in 2005, a total of one-fifth of European workers reported ill-health outcomes (Eurofound, 2007). In line with the survey, studies conducted by the likes of Hakanen (2008) and Belkić (2004, 2008), to mention a few, have covered topics such as work engagement and the relationship between occupational stress and cardiovascular disease.

In Finland, I-O psychology is often referred to as work and organizational psychology (WO), and it has a long tradition in the country. Research topics have mostly been negatively driven—such as work-related stress and burnout (e.g., Mauno, 2012), but since the turn of the millennium, positive issues such as work engagement have also gained momentum. In addition, the Finnish Institute of Occupational Health (FIOH) has actively studied and promoted well-being at work.

According to Katzell and Austin (1992), I-O psychology is a dynamic field that has made contributions to both the science of behavior and to industrial society. However, they pointed to a disjunction between theory and practice as a problem of I-O psychology (Katzell & Austin, 1992). To address this issue, the present chapter combines practical experiences and theory with a focus on one industry: transportation. In other words, this chapter considers transportation and the I-O psychology of professional truck drivers. Work in the transportation sector has several specific features, which have effects on the health and wellbeing of the drivers. In particular, the workplace is mobile, such that how trucks are equipped affects the wellbeing of drivers. Another factor influencing the wellbeing of these professional drivers involves the services offered at rest stops (see, e.g., Pandi-Perumal, 2006).

Epistemologically, this study concentrates on work-related stress as an experienced phenomenon focusing on the contents of and connections between the work-related stress and rest stops' value in the transportation field. Specifically, the emphasis is on lightly settled areas with long geographic distances. As an example of such an area, the study considers truck drivers working in Finland. The approaches to stress within the chosen empirical context are discussed below.

LITERATURE REVIEW

Work-related stress has been addressed abundantly in the organizational context. It has been concluded through numerous studies that prolonged and intense stress can create negative effects on people's mental and physical health (Johnson et al., 2005). Stress occurs when an employee experiences a demand (or a threat) that exceeds his or her abilities to successfully cope with it (Colligan & Higgins, 2005). This results in problems for one's psychological balance. An employee's response to stress has a direct relation to the characteristics of that specific situation.

Work-related stress and wellbeing research has emphasized the high-tech field (e.g., Moen et al., 2016) on the one hand, and social professions, particularly health care (e.g., Dendaas, 2011), on the other. However, research has also focused on professional drivers as an example of a high-strain occupation with physical and mental occupational demands that can lead to absenteeism and the decreased productivity of both drivers and organizations (Kompier & di Martino, 1995). Work-related stress is a primary cause of the health problems experienced by professional drivers (Chung & Wu, 2013).

As an underlying assumption, three dimensions contribute to stress. First, the conditions that create stress are referred to as stressors, which vary in duration of occurrence and severity (Joseph, 2013). Cooper and Marshall (1976) identified five main sources of stress at work: the work itself (i.e., working conditions and work overload), role in the organization (possible role conflicts), career development (lack of job security, promotion possibilities), relationships at work (with leader or co-workers), and organizational structure and climate (i.e., little or no involvement in decision-making). Other sources of stress may include work-life balance, the amount of control and autonomy in the workplace, and levels of commitment from the employee to the organization and vice versa (Johnson et al., 2005). Second, strains are physiological and psychological responses to job stressors. Strains can be illustrated as negative thoughts or unpleasant feelings toward work conditions. Third, adverse health outcomes, such as cardiovascular disease or depression, are consequences caused by exposure to job stressors. (Hurrell, Nelson, & Simmons, 1998.)

The connections between the three stress-inducing dimensions have been approached from various psychometric-emphasized perspectives. The effort–reward imbalance (ERI; Siegrist, 1996) and the job demand–control (JDC) models (Karasek, 1979) are considered to be the most thorough approaches. The JDC model primarily concentrates on the interaction between job demands and job control. Demands refer to sources of stressors in the work environment, such as excessive work and time pressure, while job control is related to authority over decisions and skill utilization (Fillion et al., 2007). Johnson and Hall (1988) later presented a third dimension—social support at work—to the model. The new dimension formed the JDCS (job–demand–control–support) model. Social support refers to having co-workers in the workplace, and according to the model, employees who encounter high job demand connected with low job control and low social support are at risk of experiencing organizational stress.

In contrast, according to the ERI model, when employees' perceptions of the rewards from working do not match their perceptions of the effort made, this can create an imbalance that affects wellbeing and related behavior (Fillion et al., 2007; Siegrist, 1996). Siegrist (1996) stated that work-related stress can manifest, for instance, when an employee has no promotion prospects or experiences high work pressure or low job security. Among professional drivers, the three dimensions of work-related stress have varied as the work content and environment have changed. A general paradox appears to be that professional drivers' wellbeing at work has decreased while the available vehicles and ancillary equipment have improved and working time has been reduced (Louit-Martinod, Chanut-Guieu, Kornig, & Méhaut, 2016). In the United Kingdom, the most extensive, longstanding study targeting professional bus drivers revealed that poor cabin ergonomics, inappropriate rotational shift patterns, and running times were the primary stressors several decades ago.

However, emerging stressors, including traffic and violent passengers, have come to have a primary negative influence on driver's wellbeing (Tse, Flin, & Mearns, 2006.) The stressors in the past mainly related to job design practices, while the emerging stressors highlight the physical environment. Another broad study focusing on professional bus drivers identified the significance of reasonable physical demands and flexible job design practices for lower stress; however, they also emphasized the physical and psychological outcomes of stressors, especially in relation to drivers' sleep (Chung & Wu, 2013).

As corroborative research results, professional bus drivers appear to have an increased risk of coronary heart disease (Wang & Lin, 2001) and arteriosclerosis, especially with long-term shift driving (Chen et al., 2010). Chung and Wong (2011) connected problems related to job-design practices with drivers' long working hours, irregular driving schedules, and low work control. As a stressor associated with organizational issues, they highlighted the company safety culture, referring to the practices that specify how disorders and incidents during driving are reported and responded to; a good safety culture is linked to a low level of depression in drivers. Furthermore, Strahan, Watson, and Lennon (2008) emphasized a company's safety culture as a tool for predicting driver fatigue, which can lead to near misses (i.e., narrowly avoiding other vehicles, incidents on the road).

Chung and Wong (2011) also distinguished between some strains associated with work-related stress, such as the driver's age and body mass index. Jex (1998) added that work-related stress can also be caused by issues like driving tasks and work overload. Finally, Rowden et al. (2011) concluded that drivers' work-related stress can be related to other domains, such as domestic life. This spillover effect can include, for instance, task overload at home. Spillover of stress can also occur from domestic life to work (Eckenrode & Gore, 1990). Rowden et al. (2011) concluded that drivers' awareness of their emotional responses to different driving events should be increased by creating strategies of self-regulation of emotions and coping when facing stressful situations on the job.

A few stress studies related to professional drivers have been specifically targeted to the truck drivers. Ulhôa et al. (2011) recognized that cortisol levels were higher on off days among truck drivers who worked irregular shifts compared to those who worked day shifts. They also proposed that irregular shifts impair recovery from work and prolong truck drivers' stress response. Hartley, Arnold, Smythe, and Hansen (1994) suggested that solo truck drivers may experience more fatigue, manifested in delayed reactions and a decreased ability to engage in controlled mental efforts compared to a two-person truck crew. Hentschel and Bijleveld (1993) argued that technical improvements related to the heavy transportation vehicles may have a positive effect on work-related stress.

However, they also emphasized the differences in truck drivers' personality; according to them, this partly explains how drivers react to the stressors, such as a risk of car accident on the road. Finally, Shattell, Apostolopoulos, and Griffin (2010) concluded that truck drivers can face work stressors, such as social isolation and constant driving hazards (e.g., sudden weather changes, poor road conditions) that can ultimately lead to risky behaviors, such as the use of intoxicants or drugs abuse.

In summary, work-related stress among professional drivers is a well-identified phenomenon. However, research on this topic has emphasized psychometric stress measurements. Accordingly, the focus has been on the extent and relationships of the parameters of work-related stress. In contrast, little research information is available on the ways in which professional drivers experience work-related stress. Furthermore, the previous research has mainly concentrated on the urban environment, that is, bus drivers in metropolitan and city areas. We propose that professional truck driving in a lightly settled area with long geographic distances may highlight different stressors, strains, and outcomes compared to passenger transportation in the urban areas.

For instance, tolerating solitude, a lack of social stimulus, and surviving independently during challenging situations may be the stressors associated with driver strains among long-distance drivers (c.f., Hill & Boyle, 2007). Furthermore, we suggest the rest stops and service stations' services and especially services encouraging for physical exercise may have a mitigating influence on experienced stress. As an empirical research aim, we highlight the two following questions: In what ways do the professional truck drivers experience work-related stress? What is the value of incentives of rest stops and service stations in decreasing work-related stress?

Experiences Stress and the Value of Rest Stops in the Transportation Field

METHODS

Research Design

This study examines data on professional truck drivers working in Finland. As characteristics of the country, low population density, varying contrast in lightness and darkness, and long geographic distances form the context for the truck driving profession. Finland is one of five Nordic countries and the northernmost country in the European Union (EU). Furthermore, it is one of the most sparsely populated countries in Europe (EU, 2016). These features represent a challenge for Finnish transportation. Finnish transportation firms and their truck drivers must cope with long distances to export and import goods to/from the different parts of the EU and sparsely populated areas of Finland.

The total passenger-kilometers travelled in Finland was over 90,000 million in 2012. According to the forecast estimates, the volume will be approximately 112,000 million by 2030. Finnish domestic freight traffic volume was approximately 33,000 million kilometer-tons in 2012. The share of freight traffic attributable to roadways was 67% in 2012 (Ristikartano et al., 2014).

The present study follows case study strategy (Yin, 2013), which allows the use of several methods to find answers to the research questions. The data employed in this study are presented in Table 1. An inquiry conducted in summer 2015 by one of the authors was the main source of the study data. This comprehensive inquiry consisted of several quantitative and qualitative questions related to drivers' well-being, experienced stress, and rest stop services. The inquiry was directed toward two organizations—the largest union of professional drivers in Finland and the largest association of Finnish drivers of motor caravans. The organizers of these associations provided the link to the inquiry to their members, which numbered about 30,000 professional and leisure drivers.

As a result, 1,528 drivers responded to the questionnaire, of which 498 were professional truck drivers (Table 2). The inquiry was part of a project focusing on long-distance drivers' opportunities for physical exercise and ways to maintain their wellbeing on the road, particularly at rest stops. These themes are linked with the physical and mental health of drivers on the road; thus, it is also related to the working conditions and experienced stress of truck drivers, which represent the main themes of this study.

This study concentrates on the responses of the 498 professional truck drivers. To address our first research question, we analyzed the inquiry's open-ended question related to work-related stress as research data. In this question, the truck drivers were asked whether they had experienced any stress during their work, and if they had, in what ways the stress occurred. The concept of work-related stress was not explicated to the drivers in a precise way, as the study focuses on stress as an experienced phenomenon.

Table 1. The Rules for Driving Times and Rest Periods in Finland (Salanne et al., 2013)

Driving time per day:	9 hours
Driving time per week:	56 hours
Driving time per 2 weeks:	90 hours
Rest period for a day:	11 hours
Rest period for a week:	45 hours
Break after 4.5 hours of driving:	45 minutes

Table 2. Sources of empirical material

Type of Empirical Material	Number of Units	Location
Inquiry	498 out of 1,528 respondents were professional truck drivers	Finland
Observation sessions at the rest stops	7 in the study (9 in the project)	Northern Rovaniemi 2 Rovaniemi 1 Tervola 2 Oulu 1 Northern Ii 1
Short interviews (3–14 minutes)	8 out of 15 interviews of the project focused on professional truck drivers	
Long interviews (over 15 minutes)	3 interviews of truck drivers out of 9 interviews	Rovaniemi

However, to ensure the truck drivers could understand the open-ended question, stress was characterized as a feeling of strain or an experience of the burdensome situations during driving or at the rest stops.

In this study, the truck drivers' observations and interviews were used as supplementary data for the inquiry. The supplemental data were not primarily targeted to experienced stress during the data gathering phase; however, they were considered meaningful for the study because they enhanced the general impression of the truck-driving profession. The interviews also offered some in-depth information on the experienced stress that the truck drivers described in the survey's open-ended question. For instance, in the interviews, some drivers explicated how weather conditions or traffic jams increased their feeling of strain or in what ways they experienced loneliness on the road. In this way, the supplementary data offered an opportunity for the authors to ensure that the inferences drawn from the open-ended question in the inquiry were reliable.

The items associated with the value of the service stations' incentives were identified from the data in the responses to the second research question. The need for rest stops was investigated via the following two items: "I do usually feel tired during the driving" (reversed item)" and "There are sufficiently appropriate rest and service stops for the heavy transportation in Finland." The rest stops' incentivizing value were examined with the following seven items: "I do take sufficiently breaks during driving" (reversed item)," "I usually feel that I am in good physical shape as I step out of the truck at the rest stop area," "The rest stop areas are designed in a way that enhances the drivers' opportunities for physical exercise," "I have found opportunities to stimulate drivers' vitality at the rest stop areas," "I try to stretch or engage in some physical exercises at the rest stop areas," "I usually have social interactions at the rest stop (i.e., talking with other people)," and "There is a sufficient supply of services at the rest stop areas." The questions were classified with a five-point scale (5 = I totally agree, 1 = I totally disagree). In the inquiry, along with the quantitative questions, the truck drivers were openly asked if they had any ideas about ways in which the rest stop areas and included services should be developed. In this way, the possible connection between rest stops' incentives and experienced stress was highlighted by identifying all the utterances in which the rest stop areas and work-related stress were mentioned in the same context.

Analysis

Qualitative content analysis was utilized when analyzing the open-ended questions of the questionnaire concerning work-related stress along with the short and long interviews. Content analysis is widely used in health studies (Shieh & Shannon, 2005). It focuses on the characteristics of language as communication while paying attention to the content or contextual meaning of the text (McTavish & Pirro 1990; Tesch, 1990). The goal of content analysis is to produce knowledge and understanding concerning the phenomenon in question by categorizing the raw data into different concepts. The authors chose the content analysis approach because we wanted to present the results of the analysis in a compact, general form.

There are three different approaches that may be chosen in qualitative content analysis: conventional, directed, and summative content analysis (Shieh & Shannon, 2005). In conventional content analysis, categories originate from the raw data during analysis. In contrast, in directed content analysis prior theories are used to form the coding scheme before analyzing the data. Finally, in summative content analysis, the data are approached as keywords that are identified before and during data analysis. For this study, conventional content analysis was chosen because there were no specific theoretical frameworks in place beforehand. Thus, we avoided preconceived categories and allowed categories to be derived from the data.

Conventional content analysis, like the other approaches to content analysis, proceeds step by step. First, all data are read multiple times to create a sense of the data as a whole (Tesch, 1990). Second, data are read word by word to derive codes by highlighting the words that represent key concepts (cf., Morgan, 1993). In the third step, notes on impressions are made, and a preliminary analysis of the text is carried out. Here, labels for codes from the text start to emerge. Fourth, codes are categorized based on the relationships and linkages between them (Shieh & Shannon, 2005). Categories are used to organize codes into meaningful groups (Patton, 2002). Categories are then combined into fewer categories. Finally, definitions for each category and code are produced. Words and sentences are considered for the unit of analysis.

The number of answers in the analysis did not directly correspond to the number of the truck drivers in the data due to the multiple classifications of the answers. Some answers could have been classified under two or more themes. For instance, the following response was classified into contents that illustrate: a) work management and b) traffic conditions: "Sometimes the work can be stressful. But the strain relies on the day. If someone [the other driver or a person in the delivery chain] gets sick, the number and the quality of the work may change. If you add the tight timetables and bad traffic conditions to that, you may suffer from stress."

The possibility of inadequate interpretations of the truck drivers' answers was circumvented using a cross-validation during the content classification. Each content was documented as a content card in .doc format by one of the study's authors. The other authors then had the opportunity to read the content cards and make propositions for revision if they disagreed with the contents included in the cards. A deficiency related to the participants' representativeness was identified from the open-ended answers, and this may have had some influence on study's reliability. The answers revealed that some of the respondents were already retired from the truck-driving profession. Furthermore, a few answers appeared to represent bus drivers or leisure drivers, even though the questions were targeted to professional truck drivers. The respondents that did not appear to be truck drivers were excluded from the analysis. Nonetheless, there is a possibility that some answers that did not represent professional truck drivers remained in the data. However, we consider this as a minor defect since the potential number of drivers other than truck drivers was substantially low in the answers.

RESULTS

A total of sixty-two percent ($n = 310$) of the truck drivers expressed work-related stress in their answers, while a total of 38% ($n = 188$) of the drivers reported that they did not experience any stress. Some of the "unstressed" drivers also specified arguments for working in the transportation field in their answers. In these cases, long-distance driving was seen in a romantic light: It was a symbol of liberty and a counterbalance to an office job in which people were considered to be enslaved by the administration and bureaucracy. The respondents that did not experience stress also highlighted driving as "a way to relax" and "an opportunity to spend some time with oneself." The latter statement also proposed that seeing loneliness or independence in a positive light are natural characteristics of the long-distance drivers.

The thematic classification of stressors and the connection between them are presented in Picture 1. A dangerous work environment, isolation, and loneliness, as well as work management and legislation, were the fundamental dimensions of stress that captured the main contents of the drivers' answers. Weather conditions, traffic jams, and inappropriate road conditions, as well as some other stressors, such as the driver's vitality, police activities, and wild animals on the road, had a moderate or minor influence on experienced stress. Work management and legislation can be considered to represent a single key stressor, as it is tightly connected with the other stress dimensions. The experienced stress contents, as well as the connections between them, are discussed below.

Work Management and Legislation

Work management and legislation had two sub-contents, namely insufficient timetables (14% of the drivers) and rigid work structures (6% of the drivers). The drivers mainly considered that these stressors were caused by the unsuccessful work management and legislation that overemphasized financial baselines and boundary conditions in the transportation field. For drivers, the financial requirements—leading to overly tight timetables—have remarkably diminished the occupation's core value, namely a sense of liberty:

Twenty years ago, I fell in love with this field. Then, I felt that within the [transportation] field, you always have your liberty. People respected you, asking "What are you carrying in the shipment?" and

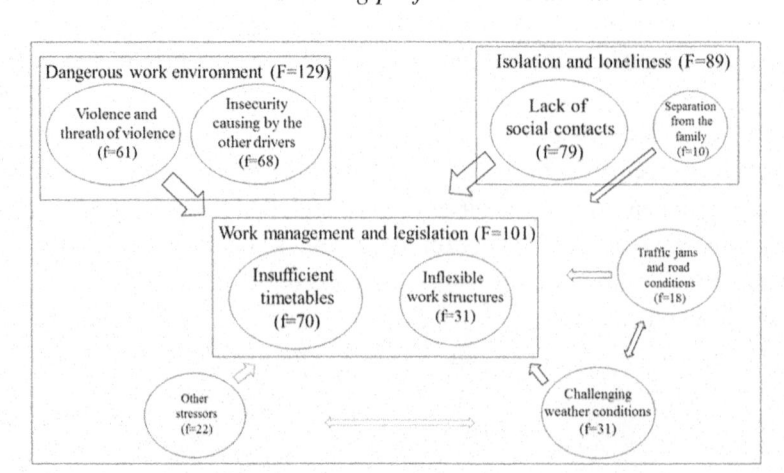

Figure 1. Experienced work-related stress among professional truck drivers

"Where are you headed?" But nowadays you always have to hurry. And you are harshly controlled. Being on the road does not cause me stress, but the stupid decisions of the politicians do. The drivers are forced to burn themselves out.

The tight timetables were commonly criticized in the drivers' responses. However, the drivers also highlighted some specific deficiencies related to the schedules. First, along with the legislation, time management made the drivers more dependent on the clock, in turn suppressing their opportunities to attend to the work's qualitative aspects, such as driving or customer service. Second, a strict timetable—causing experienced stress—could increase the risk of traffic accidents. In stress mode, as some drivers pointed out, "small mistakes may have unpredictable influences." Along with strictness, the drivers considered inflexibility to be a fundamental weakness of time management. For instance, it appeared that changing weather and traffic conditions were not sufficiently taken into account in the job design. As a specific characteristic of Finland, the drivers considered the early winters to be a challenge for time management:

You're tired, but you cannot plan your work. You have to hurry... There is no space for any exceptions [in the timetable]... It's impossible to stay on a schedule in every weather... It's [inevitable] that you are slower during the wintertime.

Along with the weather and traffic conditions, drivers emphasized the irregular working rhythm as a stressor. For some drivers, many subsequent days on the road resulted in mental oppression. In contrast, some drivers desired more working hours. For both of these driver groups, work management appeared to be a rigid system of control. Decreased vitality was the primary effect of dogmatic task management. Drivers who experienced inflexibility suffered from sleep deprivation and had difficulty recovering after a working day. Consequently, inflexibility shadowed these drivers' leisure time as well. In the most extreme situations, such inflexibility had some tragicomic features. In one drivers' description, he almost managed to arrive home on schedule. Only a few miles before arrival, he noticed that the time was up for that day. He then had to spend nine hours off the road before driving home. Finally, the dogmatic work management had some influence on loneliness and social activities. Some drivers described that long, irregular working days, as well as tiredness, created challenges for planning social events.

A Dangerous Work Environment

A dangerous work environment was another stressor that the drivers negatively experienced. This stressor had two primary contents, as follows: violence or the threat of violence and insecurity caused by the other drivers. A total of 61 drivers (12%) had faced direct violence toward them or a threatening situation. The number is remarkable, as some conditions caused by the other drivers also referred to violent behavior toward truck drivers. The experienced violence was partly connected with the work management and legislation. Some of the drivers reported that they had limited opportunities to avoid threatening situations if they endeavored to follow the timetable. Violence primarily occurred at night. Although the drivers perceived the risk of violence was lower in cargo transportation lines compared to transportation lines for people, they identified two possible situations for violence: First, some drivers were afraid to take rest breaks at the night time, particularly in isolated parking areas. In some answers, the risk was associated with the growing immigrant population that were claimed to be lodging around the truck stops.

In contrast, some truck drivers with an immigrant background reported the racist behavior among the native population had increased. Second, the risk of violence increased at the shipment loading and unloading areas in the gloom:

I don't dare to stop alone at a wooded parking area in the dark... You cannot have a break in every parking area at night time... Forested parking areas are dangerous places to take a nap. Sometimes suspicious people are lurking there.

Night-time delivery tasks in town centers involve a risk of violence... During the [shipment] unloading [tasks], I have faced situations in which some people exploited the gloom and would come to threaten and harassing you... Sometimes, at night, I have been forced to change the delivery route if there were some dubious characters moving around [at the shipment unloading area].

Dangerous situations caused by the other drivers (14% of the drivers) were the only stressors that were not linked to the work management and legislation. As an exception, the truck drivers described a few situations in which other drivers appeared to be irritating them on purpose. For instance, other drivers would occasionally pass the truck and then aggressively hit the brake in front of the vehicle. The respondents suggested that such behavior was the result of increasing traffic. However, the truck drivers ascribed the most general risk situations caused by the other drivers to drug and alcohol misuse, as well as to suicidal drivers. Furthermore, according to the respondents, the general discipline of traffic had decreased, while carelessness toward others had increased:

Nowadays I feel that I'm a target to the suicides. Too many crashes with cars and trucks happen without explanation... I don't spend time on the road that much anymore. I was in a fatal car accident in which a drunk driver hit the nose of my truck.

The general discipline in traffic has given way to utter recklessness, causing me stress and irritation. Many drivers have an entirely careless style. For instance, they can just accelerate in a particular area in which there are extra warnings about elks... Some people take idiotic risks in the passing situations. For these drivers, a double barrier line appears to be permission to overtake freely... The drivers that come too near [do not maintain a safe distance] cause danger... Some drivers talk on the phone or type messages while driving on the wrong side of the road line [at the same time].

Isolation and Loneliness

Isolation and loneliness were emphasized as a stressor in 89 (18% of the truck drivers) answers. In contrast, as described earlier in this chapters, many truck drivers also had a positive bias toward loneliness. For some drivers, an opportunity to be alone was an essential reason for becoming a professional truck driver. As a stressor, however, an experience of isolation was a serious problem. Loneliness was experienced as a mental burden, especially in situations in which the drivers had to spend extended periods of time in the vehicle. However, solitude was not limited to working hours. Many truck drivers experienced that they did not have a lot of social contact during their leisure time either. The reasons for social problems in leisure time were strongly associated with work management and legislation issues. Some truck drivers experienced they did not have sufficient time for friends and social activities after a driving period.

These drivers expressed they were too tired to spend time with other people. Furthermore, a concern of the drivers' family members was highlighted in some of the answers, as the drivers experienced that they could not carry out all of their obligations as a husband or wife and as a parent:

A driver's work is lonely and more stressful than people used to think. Perhaps it's more mentally than physically burdensome... You go into seclusion when you are in the box [a driver's cabin] alone... Under these long and irregular working times, it's sometimes totally impossible to meet people... You are too tired to meet people after a long working period.

The truck drivers also described some strategies for loneliness management. A primary tool for that was social phone calls on the road and at rest stops. The drivers were rather satisfied with these distant connections, as they experienced that the phone calls had a positive influence on their solitude. However, loneliness management may be connected with traffic safety, as the drivers actively used cell phones while driving. For instance, it was not clear how high or low the drivers' vitality was or did they use hands-free devices during the phone calls. Along with social calls, the drivers endeavored to relieve loneliness by listening to the radio and engaging in discussions with people in the shipments' loading and unloading areas.

Other Stressors

The truck drivers mentioned weather conditions (6% of the drivers) as a moderate stressor. Characteristic of Finland, the wet, dark season during the late autumn and early winter was challenging for drivers. Furthermore, some of the drivers also reported that traffic jams had increased. However, these stressors may also have been connected with work management and legislation. The winter season and traffic jams were not necessarily that stressful as such, but these parameters could emerge as stressors if they were not taken into account in the planning of the drivers' timetables:

I have noticed that I'm drained when the dark season arrives in autumn. Then, my neck also gets stiff even though I don't recognize that I'm tensing it while driving... The risk of accidents increases in slippery conditions. Then, it's not necessarily even you who will make a mistake. Anyone can make mistakes [under these circumstances].

A few drivers criticized the Finnish road conditions. They argued that the facility service did not pay sufficient attention to deficiencies, such as potholes and rocks on the road. Three drivers also reported that wild animals can pass through the fence along the road. Furthermore, four drivers were not satisfied with the police activities and control system. They supported the idea of flexible speed limits that would change according to the weather conditions instead of invariable traffic signs. However, these stressors were restricted only to a few answers, indicating that the road network and police control system have a rather high quality in Finland.

The Connection Between Work-Related Stress and Service Stations' Incentives

The survey items relating to the value of the service stations' incentives are presented in Table 3. In the responses to the first two items, the need for rest stops appeared to be obvious. A significant proportion

Table 3. The Value of the Rest Stops' Incentives

	Mean
1. I do usually feel tired during driving (reversed item)	3.0
2. There are sufficiently appropriate rest and service stops for heavy transportation in Finland	2.7
3. I do keep sufficient breaks during driving (reversed item)	2.7
4. I usually feel that I am in good physical shape as I step out of the truck at the rest stop area	3.3
5. The rest stop areas are designed in a way that enhances drivers' opportunities for physical exercise	2.5
6. I have found opportunities to stimulate drivers' vitality at the rest stop areas	2.1
7. There is a sufficient service supply available in the rest stop areas	2.9
8. I try to stretch or engage in some physical exercises at the rest stop areas	3.1
9. I usually engage in social interactions at the rest stop (i.e., talking with other people)	3.0

of the respondents (31% of the drivers) reported that they were considerably or moderately tired during the driving. Furthermore, they were rather discontent with the number of opportunities for rest stops. When arriving at parking areas, most of the truck drivers felt that they were physically in a reasonable shape (item 4). However, they were rather disappointed in the rest stops' physical facility services, as well as the enhancement of the drivers' vitality (items 5–7). In general, they were not willing to actively execute physical exercises or social activities at the rest stop (items 8–9).

In summary, the gap between the truck drivers' vitality and sufficient opportunities for the rest stops illustrates the need for the development of service areas. However, the results did not reveal the reasons for the truck drivers' inactive behavior at the rest stops. A possible explanation and a connection with the experienced stress were sought in the truck drivers' open-ended answers related to the development of rest stops and service stations.

The truck drivers' propositions for improvements for service stations' were primarily targeted to the number of rest stops and the frequency of service stations (19% of the drivers). As things currently stand, the drivers could not always plan their routes and rest stops in the way the legislation required. Night was considered to be the main challenge as many service stations were closed at this time. The truck drivers also complained that the service stations' parking areas were primarily planned for passenger cars' needs, and there was not always sufficient space for heavy transportation. Some of the drivers also mentioned that the guidance into the service areas was defective:

Definitely, there should be more rest stops. Nowadays, you always have to hurry so that you can find the [appropriate] place for that damn break. And you must find it [the place] in ten minutes... There is lack of services, especially at the night time... It should be mentioned in the guidance signs if the parking area is not suitable for heavy transportation.

The propositions related to the rest stop services included three main elements. First, the truck drivers ought to have access to healthier, higher-quality food (15% of the drivers) instead of fast food. The truck drivers also assumed that unhealthy meals could have an adverse influence on their vitality and health, which had the potential to cause some dangerous situations on the road. Second, the drivers reported defects in service stations' general cleanness and aesthetic impression (14% of the drivers). Primarily, they complained about the insufficient numbers and the untidiness of the washrooms. The truck drivers also highlighted the need for stimulating and relaxing experiences at the rest stops. For instance, water views or nature trails were stressed in the answers. Third, they required more separate rooms for rest and freshening up (13% of the drivers). They also proposed that the rest stop services should be developed as a subscription system that included all necessary facilities for truck drivers:

Outside of lunch time, there is no healthy food available... The rest stops are untidy because there are not [sufficient] garbage cans and facility services... The rest stops could be located along the water and in places where the landscape is impressive... And not directly beside the noisy highway... I would pay for decent rooms in which you could shower or sit in the sauna. And take a nap. A subscription system for [truck drivers'] services should be developed.

Services that would require an active orientation of the truck drivers were not highlighted in the answers. Only a few drivers sought physical exercise, such as opportunities for stretching or doing pull-ups during the breaks. After a driving session, the truck drivers mainly felt they were too tired for active exercise.

DISCUSSION

Previous studies have comprehensively identified the concept of work-related stress as a psychometric phenomenon among professional drivers. In these studies, professional drivers, mainly working in an urban environment, have been examined as an example of a high-strain occupation with physical and mental occupational demands. The present study offers in-depth information about how professional drivers experience work-related stress in a lightly settled area with long geographic distances. Instead of statistical description of the connections between the stressors, strains, and health outcomes, the study focused on highlighting the reasons underpinning the stress dimensions.

The stressors described in this study included both job design practices and the physical environment. Contextually, this research result is consistent with one of the most extensive studies related to professional drivers (Chung & Wu, 2013). The result partly differs from another long-term study associated with the professional drivers in the United Kingdom in which the job design practices were considered moribund, and the issues related to the drivers' physical environment were seen as emerging stressors (Tse et al., 2006). The data presented in this study highlighted the meaning of job design practices, which were tightly connected with the other stressors. Insecurity causing by the other drivers was the only stressor that was not associated with job design practices. The explication for the different research results can be found in the driving environment. Despite some professional similarities, working with passengers in a metropolitan area is a different profession compared to cargo transportation in a lightly settled area with long geographic distances.

The stressors related to the job design, illustrated as work management and legislation in this study, culminated in the questions of flexibility. It has been found in previous stress and wellbeing research (e.g., Halpern, 2005) that flexible managerial decisions, such as those concerning work schedule policies, can reduce stress among working adults. Halpern (2005) explained that with time-flexible arrangements, workers reported less stress and higher commitment to their employers. Normal office workers' job and work environments differ a quite a lot from professional drivers' job and work environments; here, as stated above, normal "office parameters" do not apply. Thus, it will be vital to study what changes can be made with flexible time schedules and other measures to reduce stress among drivers.

CONCLUSION

Limitations of the Study

The limitations related to the analytical setting and data gathering have been discussed in the methods section. The chosen methodology revealed work-related stress as a phenomenon as though the truck drivers illustrated it during a single moment. Hence, the method did not offer an analytical key to the question of how a stress experience develops and transforms over time among professional truck drivers. A long-term inquiry and interviews would have been required to capture work-related stress as a process. As a contextual limitation, we found only a vague connection between the experienced stress and the value of the rest stops' incentives. This result was partly due to the inappropriate use of the rest stops. With the tight timetables and inflexible work conditions, the drivers did not always have an opportunity to benefit from the rest stop as they would have preferred. Consequently, a comprehensive examination related to the connection between experienced stress and the value of the rest stops' incentives would first require legislation and work management to be developed in a more flexible direction.

Recommendations for Future Research

Within the field of I-O psychology, experienced stress in the transportation field has been a marginal aim of study. As work-related stress research emphasizes psychometric approaches in the high-tech field and healthcare professions, professional drivers have been examined as an example of a high-strain occupation with physical and mental occupational demands. Because professional drivers' work includes many specific stressors and strains, the transportation field should remain as a research focus in the future.

More precisely, the research tradition associated with the professional drivers does not offer in-depth information about the context of flexible work management that would also ensure the drivers' equality. According to the data presented in this study, we propose that this dual endeavor should be the aim of future research. A company's safety culture (Chung & Wong, 2011; Shattell et. al., 2010), emphasizing disorder and incident documentation during driving, opens some avenues for research. However, additional data related to the contents, situations, and effects of drivers' independent decisions on the road are needed.

An essential research issue related to drivers' stress reduction relates to drivers themselves: They spend a lot of time working alone and have to rely on their own decisions in stressful working situations. It has been stated in the literature (e.g., Dolbier et al., 2001; Lovelace et al., 2007) that people can reduce their stress level and enhance their wellbeing independently. Lovelace et al. (2007) referred to self-leadership, which they found to be a vital factor for managing stress among leaders. This study has revealed some aspects of driver's stress management (e.g., strategies for coping with loneliness), although this topic was not the core of the investigation. Thus, future studies should concentrate on how drivers manage their stress and the support they receive from organization to improve those skills.

Recommendations for Practitioners

For professional truck drivers, self-leadership includes strategies like self-goal-setting, self-talk, and self-reward, which act as stress management "tools." Dolbier et al. (2001) agreed about the effects of self-leadership; this concept was related to greater perceived wellness and less work stress in their study of corporate employees. As drivers' jobs mostly involve solitary work, it can become crucial for them to be able to lead themselves to deal with work stress and maintain a good state of wellbeing. Rowden et al. (2011) also emphasized drivers' awareness of their own stress experiences as a vital platform to improve self-leadership skills by self-regulation of emotions in stressful work situations.

General Managerial Implications

Strictly framed legislation and management practices may ensure equal working conditions for professional drivers. However, rigorous rules may also pay insufficient attention to the situational variables that arise during the driving work, such as dangerous weather conditions or incidents caused by the other drivers, thereby suppressing the drivers' initiative and ability to make judgements based on the situation. Furthermore, inflexible legislation and management may alienate the drivers from one of the work's core values—independence and an experience of freedom. According to the data described in this study, a need for more adaptive management practices exists.

Despite its limitations, this study can put forward the preliminary suggestion that even minor improvements in rest stops and the supply of services may have a positive influence on drivers' experienced stress. The main requirements involve a need for fresh and healthy food and sufficient opportunities for rest and bathing. As a characteristic of a sparsely settled area with long geographic distances, the sufficiency of service station networks, particularly at night, can also be considered as an essential area for development and research in the future.

The results of this study may be important to other professions as well. For instance, the security field shares some of the same work characteristics with the transportation field. Security guards, like truck drivers, can face loneliness, isolation, and serious safety issues (e.g., possible incidents of violence) at work and thus, experience high levels of work stress (c.f. Oginska-Bulik, 2005). To cope with these types of stressors, security guards can exercise self-leadership strategies to manage their stress at work. Furthermore, managerial decisions can help to support security guards by creating training opportunities for them to exercise how to handle stressful situations. Despite the confluences between transportation and some other fields, it may be too risky to make further generalizations based on the results of this study.

REFERENCES

Belkić, K., Landsbergis, P., Schnall, P., & Baker, D. (2004). Is job strain a major source of cardiovascular disease risk? *Scandinavian Journal of Work, Environment & Health, 30*(2), 85–128. doi:10.5271/sjweh.769 PMID:15127782

Belkić, K., & Savić, Č. (2008). The occupational stress index: An approach derived from cognitive ergonomics applicable to clinical practice. *Scandinavian Journal of Work, Environment & Health, 34*, 169–175. PMID:18728906

Chen, C.-C., Shiu, L.-J., Li, Y.-L., Tung, K.-Y., Chan, K.-Y., Yeh, C.-J., & Wong, R.-H. et al. (2010). Shift work and arteriosclerosis risk in professional bus drivers. *AEP, 20*(1), 60–66. PMID:19804986

Chung, Y.-S., & Wong, J.-T. (2011). Developing effective professional bus driver health programs: An investigation of self-rated health. *Accident; Analysis and Prevention, 43*(6), 2093–2103. doi:10.1016/j.aap.2011.05.032 PMID:21819839

Chung, Y.-S., & Wu, H.-L. (2013). Stress, strain, and health outcomes of professional drivers: An application of the effort reward imbalance model on Taiwanese public transport drivers. *Transportation Research Part F: Traffic Psychology and Behaviour, 19*, 97–107. doi:10.1016/j.trf.2013.03.002

Colligan, T. W., & Higgins, E. M. (2005). Workplace stress: Etiology and consequences. *Journal of Workplace Behavioral Health, 21*(2), 89–97. doi:10.1300/J490v21n02_07

Cooper, C. L., & Marshall, J. (1976). Occupational sources of stress: A review of the literature relating to coronary heart disease and mental ill health. *Journal of Occupational Psychology, 49*(1), 11–28. doi:10.1111/j.2044-8325.1976.tb00325.x

Dendaas, N. (2011). Environmental congruence and work-related stress in acute care hospital medical/surgical units: A descriptive, correlational study. *Health Environments Research & Design Journal, 5*(1), 23–42. doi:10.1177/193758671100500103 PMID:22322634

Dolbier, C. L., Soderstrom, M., & Steinhardt, M. A. (2001). The relationships between self-leadership and enhanced psychological, health, and work outcomes. *The Journal of Psychology, 135*(5), 469–485. doi:10.1080/00223980109603713 PMID:11804002

Eckenrode, J., & Gore, S. (1990). In J. Eckenrode & S. Gore (Eds.), *Stress Between Work and Family* (pp. 1–16). New York: Springer. doi:10.1007/978-1-4899-2097-3_1

Erez, M. (1994). Towards a Model of Cross-Cultural I/O Psychology. In M.D. Dunnette, L. Hough, & H. Triandis (Eds.), *Handbook of Industrial and Organizational Psychology* (Vol. 4, pp. 569–607). Palo Alto, CA: Consulting Psychologists Press.

Eriksson, P., & Kovalainen, A. (2015). *Qualitative Methods in Business Research*. Thousand Oaks, CA: Sage.

European Foundation for the Improvement of Living and Working Conditions. (2007). *Fourth European Survey of Working Conditions*. Luxembourg: Publications Office of the European Union. Retrieved from http://www.eurofound.europa.eu/publications/htmlfiles/ef0698.htm

European Union. (2016). About the EU. Finland. Reviewed from http://europa.eu/about-eu/countries/member-countries/finland/index_en.htm

Fillion, L., Trembley, I., Truchon, M., Côté, D., Struthers, C. W., & Dupuis, R. (2007). Job satisfaction and emotional distress among nurses providing palliative care: Empirical evidence for an integrative occupational stress-model. *International Journal of Stress Management, 14*(1), 1–25. doi:10.1037/1072-5245.14.1.1

Hakanen, J. J., Schaufeli, W. B., & Ahola, K. (2008). The Job Demands-Resources model: A three-year cross-lagged study of burnout, depression, commitment, and work engagement. *Work and Stress*, *22*(3), 224–241. doi:10.1080/02678370802379432

Halpern, D. F. (2005). How time-flexible work policies can reduce stress, improve health, and save money. *Stress and Health*, *21*(3), 157–168. doi:10.1002/smi.1049

Hartley, L. R., Arnold, P. K., Smythe, G., & Hansen, J. (1994). Indicators of fatigue in truck drivers. *Applied Ergonomics*, *25*(3), 143–156. doi:10.1016/0003-6870(94)90012-4 PMID:15676962

Hentschel, U., Bijleveld, C. C., Kiessling, M., & Hosemann, A. (1993). Stress-related psychophysiological reactions of truck drivers in relation to anxiety, defense, and situational factors. *Accident; Analysis and Prevention*, *25*(2), 115–121. doi:10.1016/0001-4575(93)90050-7 PMID:8471109

Hill, J. D., & Boyle, L. N. (2007). Driver stress as influenced by driving maneuvers and roadway conditions. *Transportation Research Part F: Traffic Psychology and Behaviour*, *10*(3), 177–186. doi:10.1016/j.trf.2006.09.002

Hurrell, J., Nelson, D., & Simmons, B. (1998). Measuring job stressors and strains: Where we have been, where we are, and where we need to go. *Journal of Professional Health Psychology*, *3*, 368–389. PMID:9805282

Jex, S. M. (1998). *Stress and job performance: Theory, research, and implications for managerial practice*. Thousand Oaks, CA: Sage.

Jick, T. D. (1979). Mixing qualitative and quantitative methods: Triangulation in action. *Administrative Science Quarterly*, *24*(4), 602–611. doi:10.2307/2392366

Johnson, J. V., & Hall, E. M. (1988). Job strain, work place social support, and cardiovascular disease: A cross-sectional study of a random sample of the Swedish working population. *American Journal of Public Health*, *78*(10), 1336–1342. doi:10.2105/AJPH.78.10.1336 PMID:3421392

Johnson, S., Cooper, C., Cartwright, S., Taylor, I., Taylor, P., & Millet, C. (2005). The experience of work-related stress across occupations. *Journal of Managerial Psychology*, *20*(2), 178–187. doi:10.1108/02683940510579803

Joseph, T. D. (2013). Work related stress. *European Journal of Business and Social Sciences*, *1*(10), 73–80.

Karasek, R. (1979). Job demands, job decision latitude, and mental strain—Implications for job redesign. *Administrative Science Quarterly*, *24*(2), 285–308. doi:10.2307/2392498

Katzell, R. A., & Austin, J. T. (1992). From then to now: The development of industrial-organizational psychology in the United States. *The Journal of Applied Psychology*, *77*(6), 803–835. doi:10.1037/0021-9010.77.6.803

Kompier, M. A. J., & di Stefano, V. (1995). Review of stress bus drivers occupational and stress prevention. *Stress Medicine*, *11*(1), 253–262. doi:10.1002/smi.2460110141

Louit-Martinod, N., Chanut-Guieu, C., Kornig, C., & Méhaut, P. (2016). "A plus dans le bus": Work-related stress among French bus drivers. *Journal of Workplace Rights*, *3*(23), 1–14.

Lovelace, K. J., Manz, C. C., & Alves, J. C. (2007). Work stress and leadership development: The role of self-leadership, shared leadership, physical fitness and flow in managing demands and increasing job control. *Human Resource Review*, *17*(4), 374–387. doi:10.1016/j.hrmr.2007.08.001

Mauno, S., Ruokolainen, M., & Kinnunen, U. (2013). Does aging make employees more resilient to job stress? Age as a moderator in the job stressor–well-being relationship in three Finnish occupational samples. *Aging & Mental Health*, *17*(4), 411–422. doi:10.1080/13607863.2012.747077 PMID:23215801

Maynard, D. C., Bachiochi, P. D., & Luna, A. C. (2002). An evaluation of industrial/organizational psychology teaching modules for use in introductory psychology. *Teaching of Psychology*, *29*(1), 39–43. doi:10.1207/S15328023TOP2901_10

McTavish, D. G., & Pirro, E. B. (1990). Contextual content analysis. *Quality & Quantity*, *24*(3), 245–265. doi:10.1007/BF00139259

Moen, P., Kelly, E., Fan, W., Lee, S.-R., Almeida, D., Kossek, E., & Buxton, O. (2016). Does a flexibility/support organizational initiative improve high-tech employees well-being? Evidence from the work, family, and health network. *American Sociological Review*, *81*(1), 134–164. doi:10.1177/0003122415622391

Morgan, D. L. (1993). Qualitative content analysis: A guide to paths not taken. *Qualitative Health Research*, *3*(1), 112–121. doi:10.1177/104973239300300107 PMID:8457790

Oginska-Bulik, N. (2005). The role of personal and social resources in preventing adverse health outcomes in employees of uniformed professions. *International Journal of Occupational Medicine and Environmental Health*, *18*(3), 233–240. PMID:16411561

Pandi-Perumal, S. R., Verster, J. C., Kayumov, L., Lowe, A. D., Santana, M. G., Pires, M. L. N., & Mello, M. T. et al. (2006). Sleep disorders, sleepiness and traffic safety: A public health menace. *Brazilian Journal of Medical and Biological Research*, *39*(7), 863–871. doi:10.1590/S0100-879X2006000700003 PMID:16862276

Patton, M. Q. (2002). *Qualitative research and evaluation methods*. Thousand Oaks, CA: Sage.

Ristikartano, J., Iikkanen, P., Tervonen, J., & Lapp, T. (2014). Nationwide Road Traffic Forecast 2030. Finnish Transport Agency, Planning Department. Research reports of the Finnish Transport Agency.

Rowden, P., Matthews, G., Watson, B., & Biggs, H. (2011). The relative impact of work-related stress, life stress and driving environment stress on driving outcomes. *Accident; Analysis and Prevention*, *43*(4), 1332–1340. doi:10.1016/j.aap.2011.02.004 PMID:21545862

Salanne, I., Rönkkö, S., Tikkanen, M., & Perttula, P. (2013). *Ajo-ja lepoaikasäädösten vaikutukset. Trafin julkaisuja 22/2013*. Retrieved from http://www.trafi.fi/filebank/a/1388410753/ea7ed86abe9be-b74a4773eb2c 3783f67/139

Shattell, M., Apostolopoulos, Y., Sönmez, S., & Griffin, M. (2010). Occupational stressors and the mental health of truckers. *Issues in Mental Health Nursing*, *31*(9), 561–568. doi:10.3109/01612840.2010.488783 PMID:20701418

Shieh, H.-F., & Shannon, S. E. (2005). Three approaches to qualitative content analysis. *Qualitative Health Research*, *15*(9), 1277–1288. doi:10.1177/1049732305276687 PMID:16204405

Siegrist, J. (1996). Adverse health effects of high effort – Low reward conditions at work. *Journal of Professional Health Psychology, 1*, 27–41. PMID:9547031

Strahan, C., Watson, B. C., & Lennon, A. (2008). Can organisational safety climate and occupational stress predict work-related driver fatigue? *Transportation Research Part F: Traffic Psychology and Behaviour, 11*(6), 418–426. doi:10.1016/j.trf.2008.04.002

Stryker, R., Docka-Filipek, D., & Wald, P. (2012). Employment Discrimination Law and Industrial Psychology: Social Science as Social Authority and the Co-Production of Law and Science. *Law & Social Inquiry, 37*(4), 777–814. doi:10.1111/j.1747-4469.2011.01277.x

Tesch, R. (1990). *Qualitative research: Analysis types and software tools*. Bristol: Falmer.

Tse, J., Flin, R., & Mearns, K. (2006). Bus driver well-being review: 50 years of research. *Transportation Research Part F: Traffic Psychology and Behaviour, 9*(2), 89–114. doi:10.1016/j.trf.2005.10.002

Ulhôa, M., Araújo, M., Elaine, C., Kantermann, T., & Skene, D. (2011). When does stress end? Evidence of a prolonged stress reaction in shiftworking truck drivers. *Chronobiology International, 28*(9), 810–818. doi:10.3109/07420528.2011.613136 PMID:22080787

Wang, P., & Lin, R. (2001). Coronary heart disease risk factors in urban bus drivers. *Public Health, 115*(4), 261–264. doi:10.1016/S0033-3506(01)00456-5 PMID:11464297

Yin, R. K. (2013). *Case study research: Design and methods*. Thousand Oaks, CA: Sage publications.

KEY TERMS AND DEFINITIONS

Effort-Reward Imbalance (ERI) Model: In the ERI model, when employees' perceptions of the rewards from working do not match their perceptions of the effort made, this can create an imbalance that affects well-being and related behavior.

Experienced Stress: An experienced stress in the context of truck drivers is based on hurry, time tables, social life, imperfect facilities of food and rest, and possibilities to sleep during the long breaks.

Job Demand-Control (JDC) Model: The JDC model primarily concentrates on the interaction between job demands and job control.

Qualitative Content Analysis: Qualitative techniques for contextualized interpretations of various documents.

Rest Stop: A rest area that has several synonyms, including travel plaza, service area, service station, and service plaza. A rest stop is a public facility located next to a highway, expressway, or freeway. It provides opportunities for drivers and passengers to rest, eat, or refuel.

Self-Leadership: Self-leadership includes strategies such as self-goal-setting, self-talk, and self-reward, which act as stress management tools.

Work-Related Stress: A stress that is associated with the work content and environment.

Chapter 12
The Relationship Between Social Problem Solving Ability and Burnout Level:
A Field Study Among Health Professionals

Efe Ibrahim Efeoğlu
Adana Science and Technology University, Turkey

Sevgi Ozcan
Cukurova University, Turkey

ABSTRACT

The aim of this study is to identify the relationship between social problem solving ability and burnout level of health professionals in a southeast city of Turkey. Material and Method: Data were collected using a self-reported questionnaire with the Short Form of Social Problem Solving Inventory and Maslach Burnout Inventory. A total number of 356 health professionals participated in the study. Results: Of all the participants; 44.1% were nurses, 27.0% were doctors and 28.9% consisted of other health professionals. Functional social problem solving dimensions were negatively correlated with emotional exhaustion and depersonalization and positively correlated with personal accomplishment. Conclusion: There is a negative correlation between social problem solving ability and burnout levels of health professionals. Evaluating social problem skills may allow to identify the ones who may be at risk for burnout; and improving their social problem solving skills may protect them from burnout.

INTRODUCTION

The term social problem solving refers to the process of problem solving as it occurs in the natural environment or "real world" (D'Zurilla & Nezu, 1982). As indicated by D'Zurilla et al. (2004), in this definition the term social does not mean a limitation in the study of problem solving to any particular type of problem. It is used to draw attention to the problem solving that influences one's adaptive functioning in the real life social environment. That means the study of social problem solving deals with all

DOI: 10.4018/978-1-5225-2568-4.ch012

types of problems that might affect a person's functioning, including impersonal problems (e.g., insufficient finances, stolen property), personal or intrapersonal problems (emotional, behavioral, cognitive, or health problems), interpersonal problems (e.g., marital conflicts, family disputes) as well as broader community and societal problems (e.g., crime, racial discrimination) (D'Zurilla et al., 2004). D'Zurilla et al. (2004) built social problem process on five dimensions as demonstrated in Figure 1.

As the figure shows, problem-solving outcomes in the real world are assumed to be largely determined by two general, partially independent processes: (a) problem orientation and (b) problem solving style. Problem orientation has two dimensions – positive and negative – while there are three problem-solving styles: rational, impulsivity/carelessness, and avoidance styles. Constructive or effective problem solving is described as a process in which positive problem orientation facilitates rational problem solving which, in turn, is likely to produce positive outcomes. Dysfunctional or ineffective problem solving is shown as a process in which negative problem orientation contributes to impulsivity-carelessness style or avoidance style, which are both likely to produce negative outcomes (D'Zurilla et al., 2004).

Social problem solving is embedded within transactionalism and the stress and coping paradigm. At any given point in time, a variable can serve as an antecedent, a mediator, a moderator, or a consequence in the social problem solving process (Lazarus, 1981). However, the related literature includes a few studies on moderators and mediators of social problem solving.

Rich and Bonner (2004) forward three main concepts which affect social problem solving;

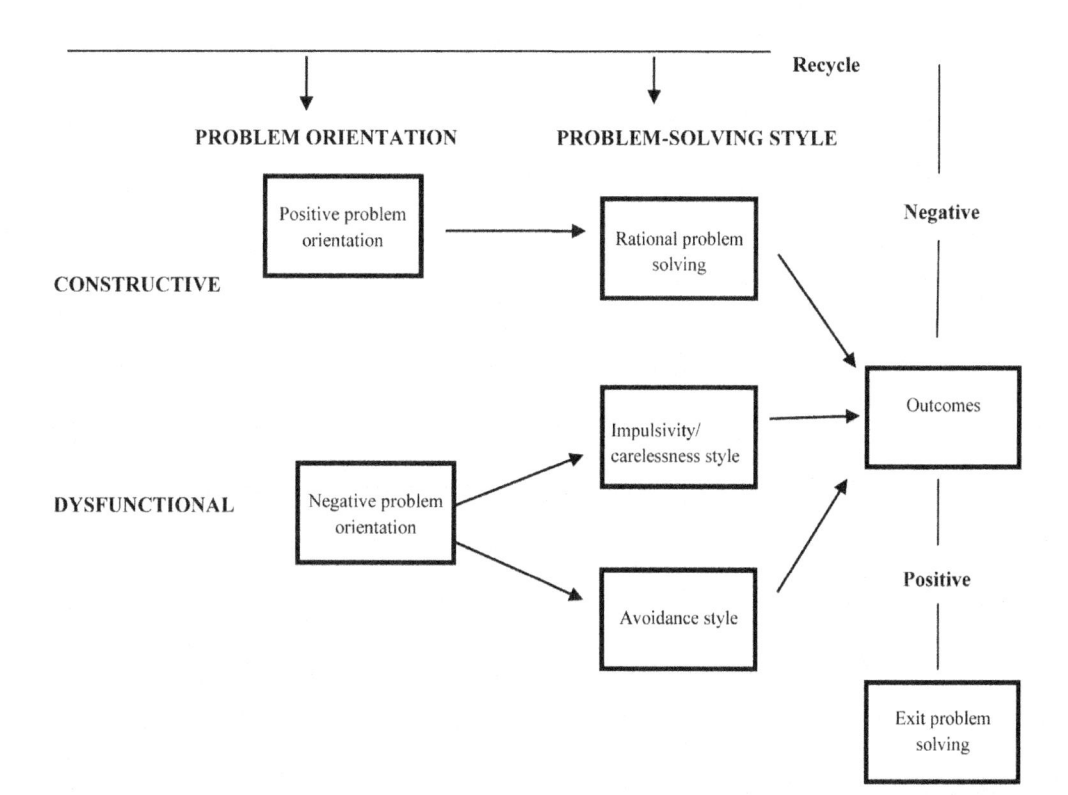

Figure1. Indicates problem solving process (2004)

- **Genetic and Early Childhood Influences:** Although there are not many studies that investigate direct contributions of genetic factors to social problem solving, there are several studies which indicate that genetic may play a role in it (Taylor & Aspinvall, 1996; Kendler et. al., 1991). However, studies indicate that parental role models, child rearing practices, and day-to-day interactions between parents and children have the potential to teach both a general orientation to everyday problems and the skills necessary for solving them (Gauvain, 2001)
- **Personality:** In the investigation of the effects of super traits (neuroticsm, positive and negative affectivity, optimism-pessimism, hope, and perfectionism), social problem solving, researchers point out there is a correlation between super traits and social problem solving. For instance, according to Suls et al. (1998), high scorers on neuroticism experience more stressful life than low scorers. In addition, negative emotions generate negative consequences. The same correlation also exists with other five-factor model members (Watson & Hubbard, 1996; McMurran et al., 2001).
- **Contextual Variables:** According to research, it is clear that one's biosocial context also influences social problem solving. Life span development, ethnicity, gender, and social relationships are factors that can be considered contextual variables. Social problem solving represents an important general coping process that, when effective, serves to increase situational coping and behavioral competence (D'Zurilla & Nezu, 1999), and also has been hypothesized to be an important general coping strategy that can reduce or prevent the negative effects of major and minor stressful life events on overall psychological well-being.

For example, a large number of studies have been conducted with a view to investigating the relationship between social problem solving and depression on different group of people such as college students (Nezu, 1985; Cheng, 2001; Marx & Schulze,1991; Elliot et al., 1995, Pretorious & Diedricks, 1994; Reinecke et al., 2001), adult patients with major depressive disorder (Marx et al., 1992), clinically depressed adults (Nezu, 1986a), adults (D'Zurilla et al., 1998), and adolescent girls (Frye & Goodman, 2000). There are also studies investigating the relationship between social problem solving and suicide risk, which is also a psychological situation. Although there are a few studies which report no significant relationships between problem solving and depression (Blankstein et al., 1992; Haaga et al., 1995), most studies indicate a significant relationship between problem solving and depression or negative affectivity.

For example, in their study with college students, Schotte and Clum (1982) found that the combination of high stress and poor problem solving skills caused hopelessness and suicidal intent. Similar results have been revealed in different studies with different groups which show that there is a significant relationship between social problem solving and suicide risk (Schote & Clum, 1982; Biggam & Power, 1998; Pollock & Williams, 2001). Similar to the studies regarding depression and suicide risk, researchers also conducted studies to explore if there is a relationship between social problem solving and anxiety. Most studies on the issue show that there is also a significant relationship between problem solving and anxiety (Zebb & Beck, 1998; Bond et al., 2002).

Stress is one of the most investigated issues which has been considered within a social problem solving context. These studies have evaluated moderating role of problem solving regarding the deleterious effects of stressful life events (Nezu et al., 2004). Various studies have aimed to find answers to the question whether problem solving moderated the stress-distress relationship. According to some studies, problem solving is a significant moderator of the relationship between stressful events and consequent psychological distress. For example, people who have poor problem solving skills have experienced significantly higher levels of psychological distress, such as depression under similar levels of high stress (Cheng, 2001; Nezu & Ronan, 1988).

However, burnout is also a psychological syndrome in response to chronic emotional and interpersonal stressors on the job (Li et al., 2015). It was first defined as a combination of personal and environmental variables that lead to a syndrome which involves the experience of emotional exhaustion, depersonalization, and feelings of reduced personal accomplishment among people who care for others in their line of work (Maslach & Jackson, 1981). They also indicated that burnout among workers might deteriorate work quality and cause irrevocable consequences for the staff, clients, and larger institutions with which they interact.

Burnout is a contagious phenomenon which may cross over from one person to another. It is particularly seen in professions that require face-to-face relationship and communication with people (Yavuzyılmaz et al., 2007). In today's work life, burnout has reached critical levels and has been associated with various forms of job withdrawal and absenteeism, intention to leave the job, and actual turnover (Maslach et al., 2001). Although there are different models of burnout in the literature depending on its definitions, the Three-Factor Model is the most widely used by researchers (Maslach & Jackson, 1981).

According to this model, burnout is a multidimensional syndrome consisting of three cognitive and affective components: emotional exhaustion, depersonalization, and lack of accomplishment. In this model, emotional exhaustion represents the basic individual stress dimensions of burnout, referring to feelings of being overextended and perceived depletion of one's emotional and physical resources. Depersonalization represents the interpersonal context of burnout; it refers to a negative, callous, or excessively detached response to various aspects of the job. Accomplishment represents the self-evaluative dimension of burnout, referring to feelings of incompetence and a lack of achievement and productivity at work (Maslach et. al., 2001).

One of the most striking reasons why burnout is so important for health professionals is the fact that it is a pervasive international problem affecting the healthcare workforce worldwide. A burned out health professional is cynical and exhausted and feels ineffective in his or her work (Leiter et al., 2013; Leiter et al., 2011). In parallel with this situation, health professionals with burnout pay less attention to their patients in providing routine care.

Review of the related extant literature indicates the factors that cause burnout among healthcare employees as excessive bureaucratic tasks and hours at work, insufficient income, workload, lack of support, work-related stress, work-family conflict, low self-efficacy, and environmental factors such as lack of information about changes (Peckham, 2015). Reducing burnout results in improved quality, safety, and efficiency and lower turnover rates (Epstein & Krasner, 2013). There are also some factors to be taken into consideration in the prevention of burnout with the prominent ones include high-quality leadership (Day & Lord, 1988: Bassi & McMurrer, 2007), supervisory and social support (Li et al., 2015), mentorship programs (Parkerson et al., 1990), and career counseling (Fares et al., 2016).

Social problem solving ability has also been viewed as one of the coping strategies in managing the burnout situation. Many studies support that higher social problem solving ability relates to higher psychological wellbeing and general health (Dreer et al., 2005; Paul-Odouard 2006). Various studies report that social problem solving interventions have been effective in reducing burnout (Eskin et al., 2012; Mynors-Wallis et al., 2000). Eliott et al. (1996) state that employee burnout stems from inefficient social problem solving skills, and maintains that negative problem solving orientations hinder problem solving attempts, place the individual at risk for developing burnout over time, and reinforce their negative problem solving orientation.

They examined problem solving orientations among nurses in their study. The researchers found that nurses with positive problem solving orientations had more confidence in their problem solving abilities, and were less likely to burnout than their peers who had negative problem solving orientations and tended to cope with work stressors using emotion focused coping strategies (Eliott et al., 1996). Similarly, Elliott et al. (1995) found, in a sample of 94 undergraduate psychology students, that a positive problem solving orientation was significantly associated with greater positive mood on a daily basis, heightened positive mood during final examinations, and lower negative mood when recalling stressful situations.

MATERIAL AND METHOD

The questionnaires were administered to the participants before a meeting held for the health professionals working in the Turkish province of Osmaniye and they were collected at the end of the meeting. A total of 356 questionnaires with complete data were analyzed.

- **Socio-Demographic Data Form:** The form developed by the researchers aimed to obtain data related to the socio-demographic and professional features of the health professionals.
- **Maslach Burnout Inventory:** The instrument, developed by Maslach and Jackson, is a Likert type scale and consists of 22 items and 3 sub-scales in total. Of these scales, emotional exhaustion subscale consists of nine items, depersonalization subscale includes five items and personal accomplishment subscale has eight items. Scale items are rated ranging from '1 never' to '7 always'. Some changes were made in the inventory translated into Turkish by Ergin (1992); and the 7-point scale in the original form was arranged as a five-point scale ranging from '0 never' to '4 always'. Emotional exhaustion (EE) subscale expresses the state of employees' feeling tired and worn out due to excessive exposure to psychological and emotional stress in business. In this subscale; there are eight items related to tiredness, weariness, lack of energy end exhaustion of emotional sources; and they are listed as the 1st, 2nd, 3rd, 6th, 8th, 13th, 16th and 20th items.

Depersonalization (DP) subscale includes expressions concerning an individual's treatment toward the recipients of his/her care and service in an indifferent, strict, and deprived of emotion way without considering the fact that individuals are human beings, not objects. Depersonalization subscale including six items consists of the 5th, 10th, 11th, 15th, 21st, and 22nd items.

Personal Accomplishment (PA) subscale describes the state of an individual's feeling competent and successful in his/ her job, in his/her relationships with the people s/he meets as a part of his job and the care and service s/he provides for them. This scale consists of eight items and includes the 9th, 12th, 14th, 17th, 18th and 19th items.

The studies on the issue indicate that exhaustion is a feeling felt at low, medium and high levels and it becomes a concept as a continuous variable. High score in emotional exhaustion and depersonalization subscales and low score in personal accomplishment subscales reflect high level of exhaustion. While medium level exhaustion reflects the medium level scores for each of the three subscales, low level reflects the low scores in emotional exhaustion and depersonalization subscales and high scores in personal accomplishment subscale. Three different exhaustion scores are calculated for each participant.

- **Social Problem Solving Inventory Short Form:** The study utilized Social Problem Solving Inventory-Short Form developed by D'Zurilla et al. (2004) with the aim of collecting data related to the social problem solving skills.

The Social Problem Solving Inventory-Short Form (SPSI-SF) consists of two dimensions as 'problem orientation' and 'problem solving styles'. The two problem-orientation dimensions are positive problem orientation and negative problem orientation; and the three subscales of the problem-solving style are rational problem solving, impulsivity-carelessness style, and avoidance style.

The 25-item inventory consists of five subscales in total. The items are rated ranging from 0 (not appropriate at all) to 4 (totally appropriate) on a five-point scale. The inventory provides both an overall total score and a total score for each subscale. There are no reverse-scored items in the inventory. Total score for each subscale is obtained by simply adding up the scores of items in that subscale. However, it is necessary to implement a formula in order to obtain an overall total score from the scale. Scores obtained from the inventory range between 0 and 100. While a high score indicates that social problem solving skill is at a 'good' level, low scores indicate a 'poor' level of social problem solving skill.

Of the subscales, positive problem orientation and rational problem solving represent a constructive approach; however, negative problem orientation, impulsivity-carelessness style, and avoidance style represent dysfunctional approach. Explanations for each subscale are presented below:

1. **Positive Problem Orientation (PPO):** It can be defined as a constructive problem solving cognitive set. This 5-item subscale (the 4th, 5th, 13th, 15th, and 22nd items) measures characteristics such as a positive view related to solving problems, self-efficacy and anticipation for a positive consequence.
2. **Negative Problem Orientation (NPO):** This 5-item subscale (the 1st, 3rd, 7th, 8th, and 11th items) consists of characteristics such as dysfunctional cognitive-emotional schemas in social problem solving, viewing problems as threatening factors, low self-efficacy, anticipating negative consequences and low frustration tolerance.
3. **Rational Problem Solving (RPS):** RPS is the constructive subscale among the problem-solving styles. In the implementation of effective problem solving skills, it includes setting realistic and systematic applications, which are thought over and debated on. These are the problem definition and formulation, the generation of alternative solutions, the decision making and the solution implementation and verification. There are 5 items (the 12th, 16th, 19th, 21st, and 23rd items) in this subscale.
4. **Impulsivity-Carelessness Style (ICS):** It is one of the dysfunctional problem solving styles. It consists of narrowed, impulsive, careless, rash and incomplete behaviors in problem solving process. There are a total of five items (the 2nd, 14th, 20th, 24th, and 25th items) in this subscale.
5. **Avoidance Style (AS):** This is another dysfunctional problem solving style. Procrastination, passivity or inaction and attempting to shift the responsibility to other people are examples of behavioral activities which are found in avoidance style. There are 5 items (the 6th, 9th, 10th, 17th and 18th items) in this subscale.

SPSI-SF OVERALL TOTAL SCORE = PP0 + RPS + (20- NPO) + (20-ICS) + (20- AS)

Turkish adaption of this inventory and validity and reliability analysis were performed by Eskin and Aycan (2009). Internal consistency and test-retest reliability coefficients obtained for the scale ranged from good to perfect. Internal consistency coefficients were found to be between 62 and 92. Internal consistency reliability coefficients were; 67 in the Positive Problem Orientation, 78 in the Negative Problem Orientation, 75 in the Rational Problem Solving Style, 62 in the Impulsivity-Carelessness Problem Solving Style and 75 in the Avoidance Problem Solving Style. The test-retest reliability coefficients ranged from 60 to 84. Test-retest reliability coefficients included the following; 61 in the Positive Problem Orientation, 73 in the Negative Problem Orientation, 66 in the Rational Problem Solving Style, 66 in the Impulsivity-Carelessness Problem Solving Style and 72 in the Avoidance Problem Solving Style.

RESULTS

Of all the participants, a total of 44.1% were nurses, 27.0% were doctors, and 28.9% consisted of other health professionals. The mean age was 36.1 ± 8.1 years (18-58). While years of experience in profession was found to be 12.77 ± 8.12 (1-36) years on the average, years of experience in their current institution was found to be 4.93 ± 5.55 (1-30) years on the average (median 4).

NPO scores for women and ICS scores for men were found to be significantly higher. It was found that ICS, AS, and SPSI scores varied depending on age groups, which stemmed from the group over 40. ICS and AS scores of the participants at the age of 40 and above were significantly high while their SPSI score was significantly low. NPO scores of the nurses were detected to be significantly higher in comparison to the scores of other health professionals. NPO scores of the married participants were significantly higher in comparison to the scores of the participants who were not married.

Emotional exhaustion score was significantly higher for doctors, for family health center employees, and for those whose job tenure was between 11 and 20 years. Depersonalization score was significantly higher for men, for those under the age of 30, for doctors, for family health center employees, and for the ones whose job tenure was between 11 and 20 years. In the personal accomplishment subscale, no significant difference was found among the groups in terms of socio-demographic characteristics.

In the correlation analysis between emotional exhaustion, depersonalization and personal accomplishment subscale scores and SPSI and its subscales, the following relationships were found:

A negative relationship between EE and PPO, RPS, SPSI and a positive relationship with the NPO,
A negative relationship between DP and PPO, RPS and SPSI and a positive relationship with NPO, ICS,
A positive relationship between PA and PPO, RPS, SPSI and a negative relationship with NPO.

DISCUSSION

The most important result of our study is that social problem solving ability was significantly correlated to all three dimensions of burnout. Functional social problem solving dimensions (PPO, RPS, SPSI) were negatively correlated with EE and DP and positively correlated with PA. NPO was positively correlated with EE and DP, and negatively correlated with PA. ICS was positively correlated with only DP. These results of our study are consistent with those of Huey (2007), which was conducted with 78

Table 1. Demographic Features of the Participants

	N	%
Gender		
Female	226	63.5
Male	130	36.5
Age (Years)		
<30	88	24.7
31-39	144	40.4
≥40	124	34.8
Marital Status		
Single	68	19.1
Married	288	80.9
Occupation		
Doctor	96	27.0
Nurse-Midwife	157	44.1
Others	103	28.9
Work Setting		
Family Health Center (FHC)	154	43.3
Public Health Center (PHC)	107	30.1
Others	95	26.7
Total Professional Experience (Years)		
1-10	156	43.8
11-20	124	34.8
≥21	76	21.3
Average Time in Current Institution (Years)		
1-5	279	78.4
≥6	77	21.6

mental health professionals. Huey found that AS was positively correlated with EE and DP. Unlike this finding, the present study found no relationship between AS and burnout, which might result from the socio-cultural differences of the participants.

According to Maslach, patient contacts are emotionally charged by their nature because health care professionals deal with troubled people who are in need. To deal with emotional demands and perform efficiently and well, professionals may adopt techniques of detachment. When patients are treated in a more remote way, it becomes easier to do one's job without suffering strong psychological discomfort. A functional way to achieve this is to develop an attitude of detached concern which is the medical profession's ideal blending of compassion with emotional distance. A dysfunctional way to do this is depersonalization. The finding that revealed no relationship between AS and EE and DP in this study is considered to indicate that this style was used functionally.

Table 2. Burnout Scores According the Demographic Features

		Burnout		
		Emotional Exhaustion	Depersonalization	Personal Accomplishment
Gender	Female	10.41	4.63	22.42
	Male	11.06	6.02	21.98
	p	.225	.001	.530
Age (years)	<30	10.05	5.81	22.09
	31-39	10.81	5.10	22.24
	≥40	10.88	4.70	22.41
	p	.459	.020	.589
Marital status	Single	10.25	5.32	22.09
	Married	10.74	5.09	22.30
	p	.479	.537	.803
Occupation	Doctor	13.02	6.82	21.70
	Nurse-Midwife	10.64	4.79	22.29
	Others	8.44	4.10	22.75
	P	.000	.000	.065
Work setting	Family Health Center	11.84	5.75	22.27
	Public Health Center	9.21	4.53	22.20
	Others	10.33	4.82	22.32
	P	.001	.011	.940
Total professional experience (years)	1-10	9.76	5.08	22.27
	11-20	11.63	5.88	22.14
	≥21	10.87	4.04	22.45
	p	.042	.002	.619

Schauefi analyzed the studies and compared the mean burnout scores of various professions. They found that, compared with physicians, nurses experience slightly less EE but much less DP and PA. In our study, the EE score was significantly higher for doctors, for family health center employees and for those whose job tenure was between 11 and 20 years; and DP score was significantly higher for men, for those under the age of 30, for doctors, for family health center employees, and for those whose job tenure was between 11 and 20 years.

According to Schauefi, differences in depersonalization reflect different professional roles and attitudes. Men report higher depersonalization scores than women. A study among Japanese health care facilities showed that burnout scores were significantly higher among direct care staff members compared with facility directors, middle managers and other types of staff per-sonnel. As Schaufeli states, "it appears that compared with those who are not involved in direct care, burnout levels are higher in health care workers who deal intensively with patients on a daily basis". McManus, Winder and Gordon (2002) showed that high levels of depersonalization protect doctors from future stress. It is stated that

Table 3. Social Problem Solving Scores According to the Demographic Features

		Positive Problem Orientation	Negative Problem Orientation	Rationale Problem Solving	Careless/Impulsive Style	Avoidant Style	SPSI
Gender	Female	10.74	6.68	13.95	5.95	4.34	67.72
	Male	10.52	5.64	13.74	6.74	4.83	67.05
	p	.531	.020	.611	.047	.251	.476
Age	<30	10.92	6.95	14.25	6.06	4.00	68.16
	31-39	10.55	6.02	13.87	5.62	4.02	68.76
	≥40	10.60	6.16	13.61	7.09	5.47	65.50
	p	.771	.432	.472	.015	.004	.037
Marital Status	Single	10.68	7.25	13.68	6.13	4.62	66.35
	Married	10.66	6.08	13.92	6.26	4.50	67.74
	p	.675	.029	.533	.951	.944	.394
Title	Doctor	10.53	6.16	13.88	5.83	4.54	67.88
	Nurse-Midwife	10.48	7.07	13.88	6.06	4.39	66.83
	Others	11.06	5.26	13.86	6.88	4.69	68.09
	p	.205	.001	.996	.191	.859	.608
The place they work	FHC	10.71	6.08	13.90	6.10	4.58	67.86
	PHC	10.55	6.64	13.77	6.71	4.92	66.06
	Others	10.69	6.28	13.95	5.94	3.97	68.45
	p	.941	.308	.955	.215	.121	.158
Average time in their profession	1-10	10.78	6.64	14.00	6.31	4.29	67.53
	11-20	10.61	5.86	14.13	5.73	4.32	68.82
	≥21	10.50	6.32	13.20	6.92	5.30	65.16
	p	.698	.288	.104	.117	.089	.051

Table 4. Correlation between burn-out and social problem solving scores

	PPO	NPO	RPS	ICS	AS	SPSI	EE	DP	PA
PPO	1	-.333**	.546**	.027	-.134*	.583**	-.242**	-.204**	.474**
NPO	-.333**	1	-.170**	.278**	.311**	-.667**	.261**	.250**	-.249**
RPS	.546**	-.170**	1	-.147**	-.210**	.638**	-.111*	-.165**	.324**
ICS	.027	.278**	-.147**	1	.434**	-.602**	.076	.141**	-.059
AS	-.134*	.311**	-.210**	.434**	1	-.678**	.048	.103	-.096
SPSI	.583**	-.667**	.638**	-.602**	-.678**	1	-.227**	-.269**	.362**
EE	-.242**	.261**	-.111*	.076	.048	-.227**	1	.605**	-.245**
DP	-.204**	.250**	-.165**	.141**	.103	-.269**	.605**	1	-.270**
PA	.474**	-.249**	.324**	-.059	-.096	.362**	-.245**	-.270**	1

**. Correlation is significant at the 0.01 level (2-tailed).
*. Correlation is significant at the 0.05 level (2-tailed).

depersonalization should also be recognized as adaptive, but increased professional efficacy can be maladaptive, increasing future stress and burnout.

Burnout is observed more often among younger health care professionals than those aged 30 or 40, and it is known that burnout is negatively related to work experience. However, the present study found that depersonalization scores were higher in those whose job tenure was between 11 and 20 years. In addition, this group, whose overall problem solving scores were also high, is considered to prefer DP adaptively and protectively.

Another result of the study was that NPO score was significantly higher for women, for nurses and for those who were married. ICS scores for men were found to be significantly higher. Studies across different age samples suggest that women tend to score higher on negative problem orientation than men, whereas men tend to score higher on avoidance and impulsivity/carelessness styles than women. ICS and AS scores of the participants aged 40 and higher were significantly high while their SPSI score was significantly low. These were unexpected results. However, these results suggest that responding more quickly or avoiding/waiting to various demands appears to be adaptive and protective for the participants at the age of 40 and above.

The present study should be considered in the light of a few limitations. First, our study included health care professionals who worked under government service obligation. Second, all of our data were self-reported and the extent of underreporting or over reporting cannot be determined. Third, the development level of the city where the study was conducted is relatively low. The results of this study demonstrate that social problem solving ability is significantly correlated with burnout dimensions among healthcare professionals. Evaluating social problem skills may allow identifying the ones who may be at risk for burnout, and improving their social problem solving skills may protect them from burnout. We hope our study will raise awareness about improvement of social problem solving skills of the healthcare professionals, and will act as a guide for the steps to be taken on this particular issue.

REFERENCES

Bassi, L., & McMurrer, D. (2007). Maximizing your return through people. *Harvard Business Review*, *85*(3), 115–123. PMID:17348175

Biggam, F. H., & Power, K. G. (1998). The quality of perceived parenting experienced by a group of Scottish incarcerated young offenders and its relation to psychological distress. *Journal of Adolescence*, *21*(2), 161–176. doi:10.1006/jado.1997.0139 PMID:9585494

Blankstein, K. R., Flett, G. L., & Johnston, M. E. (1992). Depression, Problem-Solving Ability, and Problem-Solving Appraisals. *Journal of Clinical Psychology*, *48*(6), 749–759. doi:10.1002/1097-4679(199211)48:6<749::AID-JCLP2270480609>3.0.CO;2-V PMID:1452764

Bond, D. S., Lyle, R. M., Tappe, M. K., Seehafer, R. S., & DZurilla, T. J. (2002). Moderate aerobic exercise, Tai Chi, and social problem-solving ability in relation to psychological stress. *International Journal of Stress Management*, *9*(4), 329–343. doi:10.1023/A:1019934417236

Chang, E. C., D'Zurilla, T., & Sanna, L. J. (2004). *Social Problem Solving: Theory, Research, and Training*. Washington, DC: American Psychological Association. doi:10.1037/10805-000

Cheng, S. K. (2001). Life stress, problem solving, perfectionism, and depressive symptoms in Chinese. *Cognitive Therapy and Research*, 25(3), 303–310. doi:10.1023/A:1010788513083

D' Zurilla, T. J. et al.. (2004). Social problem solving: theory and assessment. In E. C. Chang, T. J. D' Zurilla, & L. J. Sanna (Eds.), *Social Problem Solving: Theory, Research and Training* (pp. 11–27). Washington, DC: American Psychological Association. doi:10.1037/10805-001

D'Zurilla, T. J., & Nezu, A. M. (1982). Social problem solving in adults. In P. C. Kendall (Ed.), *Advances in Cognitive-Behavioral Research and Therapy* (Vol. 1, pp. 201–274). New York: Academic Press. doi:10.1016/B978-0-12-010601-1.50010-3

D'Zurilla, T. J., & Nezu, A. M. (1999). *Problem-solving therapy: A social competence approach to clinical intervention*. New York: Springer.

D'Zurilla, T. J., Nezu, A. M., & Maydeu-Olivares, A. (2004). Social problem solving: Theory and assessment. In E. C. Chang, T. J. D'Zurilla, & L. J. Sanna (Eds.), *Social problem solving: Theory, research, and training* (pp. 11–27). Washington, DC: American Psychological Association. doi:10.1037/10805-001

Day, D. V., & Lord, R. G. (1988). Executive leadership and organizational performance: Suggestions for a new theory and methodology. *Journal of Management*, 14(3), 453–464. doi:10.1177/014920638801400308

Dreer, L. E., Elliott, T. R., Fletcher, D. C., & Swanson, M. (2005). Social problem solving abilities and psychological adjustment of persons in low vision rehabilitation. *Rehabilitation Psychology*, 50(3), 232–238. doi:10.1037/0090-5550.50.3.232

DZurilla, T. J., Chang, E. C., Nottingham, E. J., & Faccini, L. (1998). Social problem-solving deficits and hopelessness, depression, and suicidal risk in college students and psychiatric inpatients. *Journal of Clinical Psychology*, 54(8), 1091–1107. doi:10.1002/(SICI)1097-4679(199812)54:8<1091::AID-JCLP9>3.0.CO;2-J PMID:9840781

Eisdorfer, C. (1981). *Critique of the stress and coping paradigm. Models for Clinical Psychopathology*. New York: Spectrum Publications, Inc. doi:10.1007/978-94-015-7129-6

Elliott, T. R., Sherwin, E., Harkins, S. W., & Marmarosh, C. (1995). Self-appraised problem-solving ability, affective states, and psychological distress. *Journal of Counseling Psychology*, 42(1), 105–115. doi:10.1037/0022-0167.42.1.105

Elliott, T. R., Shewchuk, R., Hagglund, K., Rybarczyk, B., & Harkins, S. (1996). Occupational burnout, tolerance for stress, and coping among nurses in rehabilitation units. *Rehabilitation Psychology*, 41(4), 267–284. doi:10.1037/0090-5550.41.4.267

Epstein, R. M., & Krasner, M. S. (2013). Physician resilience: What it means, why it matters, and how to promote it. *Academic Medicine*, 88(3), 301–303. doi:10.1097/ACM.0b013e318280cff0 PMID:23442430

Ergin, C. (1992). *Doktor ve Hemşirelerde Tükenmişlik ve Maslach Tükenmişlik Ölçeğinin Uyarlanması* (pp. 143–154). Ankara, Turkey: Türk Psikologlar Derneği Yayınları.

Eskin, M., & Aycan, Z. (2009). The adaptation of the revised social problem solving inventory into Turkish (Tr-SPSI-R): A reliability and validity analysis. *Türk Psiko Yaz*, 12, 11–13.

Eskin, M., Kurt, I., & Demirkiran, F. (2012). Does social problem-solving training reduce psychological distress in nurses employed in an academic hospital. *Journal of Basic and Applied Scientific Research*, *2*(10), 10450–10458.

Fares, J., Tabosh, H., Saadeddin, Z., Mouhayyar, C., & Aridi, H. (2016). Stress, Burnout and Coping Strategies in Preclinical Medical Students. *North American Journal of Medical Sciences*, *8*(2), 75–81. doi:10.4103/1947-2714.177299 PMID:27042604

Frye, A. A., & Goodman, S. H. (2000). Which social problem-solving components buffer depression in adolescent girls? *Cognitive Therapy and Research*, *24*(6), 637–650. doi:10.1023/A:1005583210589

Gauvain, M. (2001). *The Social Context of Cognitive Development*. New York: Guilford Press.

Haaga, D. A., Fine, J. A., Terrill, D. R., Stewart, B. L., & Beck, A. T. (1995). Social problem-solving deficits, dependency, and depressive symptoms. *Cognitive Therapy and Research*, *19*(2), 147–158. doi:10.1007/BF02229691

Kendall, P. C., & Watson, D. (Eds.). (1989). *Anxiety and depression: Distinctive and overlapping features. Personality, Psychopathology, and Psychotherapy*. San Diego, CA: Academic Press.

Kendler, K. S., Kessler, R. C., Heath, A. C., Neale, M. C., & Eaves, L. J. (1991). Coping: A genetic epidemiological investigation. *Psychological Medicine*, *21*(02), 337–346. doi:10.1017/S0033291700020444 PMID:1876639

Leiter, M. P., Laschinger, H. K. S., Day, A., & Oore, D. G. (2011). The impact of civility interventions on employee social behavior, distress, and attitudes. *The Journal of Applied Psychology*, *96*(6), 1258–1274. doi:10.1037/a0024442 PMID:21744942

Li, L., Ruan, H., & Yuan, W. J. (2015). The relationship between social support and burnout among ICU nurses in Shanghai: A cross-sectional study. *Clinical Nursing Research*, *2*(2), 45–50.

Marx, E. M., & Schulze, C. C. (1991). Interpersonal problem-solving in depressed students. *Journal of Clinical Psychology*, *47*(3), 361–367. doi:10.1002/1097-4679(199105)47:3<361::AID-JCLP2270470307>3.0.CO;2-L PMID:2066404

Marx, E. M., Williams, J. M., & Claridge, G. C. (1992). Depression and social problem solving. *Journal of Abnormal Psychology*, *101*(1), 78–86. doi:10.1037/0021-843X.101.1.78 PMID:1537977

Maslach, C., & Jackson, S. E. (1981). The measurement of experienced burnout. *Journal of Organizational Behavior*, *2*(2), 99–113. doi:10.1002/job.4030020205

Maslach, C., Schaufeli, W. B., & Leiter, M. P. (2001). Job burnout. *Annual Review of Psychology*, *52*(1), 397–422. doi:10.1146/annurev.psych.52.1.397 PMID:11148311

McMurran, M., Egan, V., Blair, M., & Richardson, C. (2001). The relationship between social problem-solving and personality in mentally disordered offenders. *Personality and Individual Differences*, *30*(3), 517–524. doi:10.1016/S0191-8869(00)00050-7

Mynors-Wallis, L. M., Gath, D. H., Day, A., & Baker, F. (2000). Randomised controlled trial of problem solving treatment, antidepressant medication, and combined treatment for major depression in primary care. *BMJ (Clinical Research Ed.), 320*(7226), 26–30. doi:10.1136/bmj.320.7226.26 PMID:10617523

Nezu, A. M. (1985). Differences in psychological distress between effective and ineffective problem solvers. *Journal of Counseling Psychology, 32*(1), 135–138. doi:10.1037/0022-0167.32.1.135

Nezu, A. M. (1986). Cognitive appraisal of problem solving effectiveness: Relation to depression and depressive symptoms. *Journal of Clinical Psychology, 42*(1), 42–48. doi:10.1002/1097-4679(198601)42:1<42::AID-JCLP2270420106>3.0.CO;2-2 PMID:3950013

Leiter, M.P., Hakanen, J.J., Ahola, K., Toppinen-Tanner, S., Koskinen, A., & Väänänen, A. (2013). Organizational predictors and health consequences of changes in burnout: A 12-year cohort study. *Journal of Organizational Behavior, 34*(7), 959–973.

Parkerson, G. R. Jr, Broadhead, W. E., & Tse, C. K. (1990). The health status and life satisfaction of fi rst-year medical students. *Academic Medicine, 65*(9), 586–588. doi:10.1097/00001888-199009000-00009 PMID:2400477

Paul-Odouard, R. (2006). *Emotional intelligence, social problem solving, and demographics as predictors of well-being in women with multiple roles* [Dissertation]. University of Adelphi.

Peckham, C. (2015, January 26). *Medscape Physician Lifestyle Report 2015* [Infographic]. Retrieved from http://www.medscape.com/features/slideshow/lifestyle/2015/public/overview

Pollock, L. R., & Williams, J. M. G. (2001). Effective problem solving in suicide attempters depends on specific autobiographical recall. *Suicide & Life-Threatening Behavior, 31*(4), 386–396. doi:10.1521/suli.31.4.386.22041 PMID:11775714

Pretorius, T. B., & Diedricks, M. (1994). Problem-solving appraisal, social support and stress-depression relationship. *South African Journal of Psychology. Suid-Afrikaanse Tydskrif vir Sielkunde, 24*(2), 86–90. doi:10.1177/008124639402400206

Reinecke, M. A., DuBois, D. L., & Schultz, T. M. (2001). Social problem solving, mood, and suicidality among inpatient adolescents. *Cognitive Therapy and Research, 25*(6), 743–756. doi:10.1023/A:1012971423547

Rich, A. R., & Bonner, R. L. (2004). *Mediators and Moderators of Social Problem Solving*. Tampa, FL: University of South Florida. doi:10.1037/10805-002

Rich, A. R., Bonner, R. L., Chang, E. C., D'Zurilla, T. J., & Sanna, L. J. (Eds.). (2004). *Social problem solving: Theory, research, and Training*. Washington, DC: American Psychological Association. Doi: doi:10.1037/10805-002

Schaufeli, W. B. (2007). Burnout in health care. In P. Carayan (Ed.), *Handbook of Human Factors and Ergonomics in Health Care and Patient Safety* (pp. 217–232). Mahwah, NJ: Lawrence Erlbaum Association.

Schotte, D. E., & Clum, G. A. (1982). Suicide ideation in a college population: A test of a model. *Journal of Consulting and Clinical Psychology, 50*(5), 690–696. doi:10.1037/0022-006X.50.5.690 PMID:7142542

Solam, T. H. (2007). *Occupational Stress, Social Problem Solving, and Burnout among Mental Health-Professionals in HIV/AIDS Care*. Faculty of Drexel University Clinical Psychology.

Suls, J., Green, P., & Hillis, S. (1998). Emotional reactivity to everyday problems, affective inertia, and neuroticism. *Personality and Social Psychology Bulletin, 24*(2), 127–136. doi:10.1177/0146167298242002

Taylor, S. E., & Aspinwall, L. G. (1996). Mediating and moderating processes in psychosocial stress: Appraisal, coping, resistance, and vulnerability. In H. B. Kaplan (Ed.), *Psychosocial Stress: Perspectives on structure, theory, life course, and methods* (pp. 71–110). San Diego, CA: Academic Press.

Watson, D., & Hubbard, B. (1996). Adaptational style and dispositional structure: Coping in the context of the Five-Factor model. *Journal of Personality, 64*(4), 737–774. doi:10.1111/j.1467-6494.1996.tb00943.x

Yavuzyılmaz, A., Topbaş, M., Çan, E., Çan, G., & Özgün, Ş. (2007). Trabzon İl Merkezindeki Sağlık Ocakları Çalışanlarında Tükenmişlik Sendromu ile İş Doyumu Düzeyleri ve İlişkili Faktörler. *TAF Preventive Medicine Bulletin, 6*(1), 41–50.

Zebb, B. J., & Beck, J. G. (1998). Worry Versus Anxiety Is There Really a Difference? *Behavior Modification, 22*(1), 45–61. doi:10.1177/01454455980221003 PMID:9567736

Chapter 13
Understanding Diversity in Virtual Work Environments:
A Comparative Case Study

Marta Alicja Tomasiak
Thompson Reuters, UK

Petros Chamakiotis
University of Sussex, UK

ABSTRACT

This chapter presents a comparative case study which was conducted with the aim of understanding how diversity can be managed in the context of the virtual work environment. The authors argue that the unique characteristics of virtuality might influence how diversity is managed in the virtual, computer-mediated environment. In view of this, a comparative case study involving qualitative interviews with participants from two contrasting environments—a face-to-face one and a virtual one—is presented. The findings of the study show what types of diversity are found to be important in the virtual workplace and also start to unpack the relationship between some of the unique characteristics of virtuality and diversity within the context of this study. The contributions of the study are discussed and recommendations to both future researchers and also practitioners are provided.

INTRODUCTION

In recent years, the development of information and communications technology (ICT) has enabled organizations to deploy virtual teams (VTs) in their effort to reach out to global expertise and resources and, by extension, improve their overall competitiveness and performance (Algesheimer, Dholakia, & Gurău, 2011; Ebrahim, Ahmed, & Taha, 2009; Nemiro, Bradley, Beyerlein, & Beyerlein, 2008; Tong, Yang, & Teo, 2013; Workman, 2007). VTs are known for these unique benefits but also for their unprecedented challenges in the literature. Scholars in the field of Industrial-Organizational (I-O) psychology as well as in kindred fields, such as information systems (IS), agree that diversity and heterogeneity feature as unique characteristics of VTs and virtual organizations (Chamakiotis, Dekoninck, & Panteli,

DOI: 10.4018/978-1-5225-2568-4.ch013

2013; Martin, 2014). The notion of diversity is based on respect, acceptance, and equality for all. It recognizes individual differences and involves understanding of not only the way of being, but also the way of knowing (Patrick & Kumar, 2012). There are different types of diversity in the extant literature, for example, it can be demographic (i.e., sex, race or age) or based on personal attributes such as status, experience, expertise, or lifestyle (Williams & O'Reilly, 1998). Diversity in the workplace mainly concerns the visible characteristics (i.e., race, gender) or job-related attributes (i.e., educational background and tenure) (Ibid.).

With regards to the virtual environment in particular, diversity plays a crucial role because it helps to produce greater solutions to problems (Comfort & Franklin, 2014). However, working in the virtual environment involves working without physical proximity, across cultures and time zones, which can be very challenging (Klitmøller, Schneider, & Jonsen, 2015). According to recent research studies, VTs are expected to dominate the global workforce by 2020 (de Kare-Silver, 2011). For many organizations, success will depend on how adaptable teams are in the light of ICT and globalization, which is seen as affecting the way in which people do their jobs (Pierce & Hansen, 2013). But why is the study of diversity in the virtual context important?

Managing diversity in the workplace is important as it can impact on the establishment of good working relationships and the levels of trust between co-workers (Phillips, Northcraft, & Neale, 2006). On one hand, good relationships between co-workers are critical because they often can affect group performance, attendance, and employee turnover and therefore organizational performance (Dumas, Phillips, & Rothbard, 2013). On the other hand, the notion of trust is related to relationships at work because its lack is likely to diminish performance and increase employee turnover. Godar and Ferris (2004) argue that trust constitutes the cement that binds the team together to work towards the common goal.

In the context of VTs, the literature posits that developing trust among diverse members is challenging, with factors such as uncommon backgrounds between VT members and lack of physical proximity contributing to this (Coppola, Hiltz, & Rotter, 2004; Crisp & Jarvenpaa, 2013; DeRosa, Hantula, Kock, & D'Arcy, 2004; Jarvenpaa & Leidner, 1999; Panteli & Duncan, 2004). Given the dispersed nature of work, members of VTs are known to develop swift trust, rather than competency- and emotional-based trust (Crisp & Jarvenpaa, 2013). The concept of swift trust describes the creation and development of trust relations in short-term VTs, in the absence of pre-existing working relationships among workers (Germain & McGuire, 2014). It is different from the traditional form of trust in that it is competence-based, rather than integrity-based.

Following from the above commentary, a theoretical gap emerges as to how this increased diversity can be managed in the virtual context. What types of diversity are important in the virtual environment? What are the factors influencing diversity in the virtual environment and how do they relate to those influencing diversity in the traditional workplace? Which of the unique characteristics of virtuality influence diversity and how? This chapter seeks to address these questions by focusing on a comparative case study involving interviews with workers from two contrasting research sites—a traditional, collocated one and a virtual, computer-mediated one. This study is important to scholars and practitioners alike, as well as to educators and students whose work involves collaboration in virtual environments characterized by increased diversity and heterogeneity. In what follows, a literature review on the above topics is presented.

BACKGROUND

The Notion of Diversity

With the constantly increasing levels of globalization, the interaction between people of diverse backgrounds, beliefs, and cultures is greater than ever before (Jackson, Joshi, & Erhardt, 2003). Development and use of the ICT now allows organizations to operate on a global scale, which, on the other hand, increases the level of competition in the market. Therefore, in order to survive in this global, ICT-enabled, virtual environment, organizations must maximize and capitalize on workplace diversity (Ibid.). Scholars highlight that, in order for managers and human resources (HR) practitioners to get the best results, understanding the effects of visible attributes among staff is more important than ever before (e.g. Williams & O'Reilly, 1998).

Diversity has been referred to as a situation in which the actors involved differ with respect to some attributes (Jackson, Stone, & Alvarez, 1992). Scholars distinguish between personal and demographic attributes, with the former involving status, expertise or style, and the latter being sex, age, or race (Williams & O'Reilly, 1998). Jackson et al. (2003) support this view by using the notion of diversity to refer to the distribution of attributes (both visible and non-visible) among members of a work group. Furthermore, some scholars argue that individual differences among independent individuals are rooted in their distinctive geographical regions, ethnic groups, culture, age, gender and related characteristics (CIPD, 2015).

What is clear in the extant literature is that diversity is not a unitary construct. Different researchers have defined the notion of diversity in various ways. These definitions range from narrow to very broad. The former tends to represent the Equal Employment Opportunity (EEO) Act which describes diversity in terms of gender, age, religion, race, national origin, and disability (DHS, 2016). The latter, on the other hand, usually include values, personality, language, beliefs, sexual orientation, tenure with the organization, and economic status (Wentling & Palma-Rivas, 1998). Furthermore, Leonard-Barton and Swap (1999) argue that team members' diverse backgrounds, different cultures, and intellectual capabilities can lead to higher levels of performance.

Scholars and practitioners are agreed on the view that diversity in the workplace can help organizations to develop a competitive advantage as long as it is managed appropriately (e.g., Williams & O'Reilly, 1998). Indeed, a diverse working environment has the potential to (a) enable organizations to develop a competitive advantage, and to (b) provide opportunities for employee productivity (Saxena, 2014). Furthermore, diversity can be useful in problem-solving and decision-making situations, and it can also enable access to new consumer markets, enhance product development, and improve competition at the global level (Fine, 1996).

As stated by Egan (2011) in her article in *The Forbes Insights* about diversity and inclusion on a global scale in the workplace, diversity could play an important part of the business strategy. An example of a company is Coca-Cola Co., which believes that differences among their staff members make the company stronger in the market by enhancing creativity and innovation which play a crucial role for the company's economic growth (Coca-Cola Co., 2014). These findings have been echoed by scholars who have examined how creativity and innovation play out in the VT context; Chamakiotis, Dekoninck, and Panteli (2013) highlight that diversity and heterogeneity, as they refer to it, has the potential to improve a VT's creativity significantly, although they can also have a negative influence.

It follows that effectively managing diversity is essential in both collocated and VT environments. Fine (1996) sees diversity as a resource that is available to managers for their use in enhancing organizational effectiveness. Following this viewpoint, diversity is seen a managerial tool that can be manipulated to achieve organizational goals. Bassett-Jones (2005) use the term 'diversity management' to refer to the planned and systematic commitment of organizations to retain and recruit members with diverse abilities and backgrounds.

The relevant literature posits four reasons for which organizations attempt to manage diversity: (a) improving productivity and remaining competitive (which is found to be the most common one); (b) forming better work relationships among employees; (c) enhancing social responsibility; and (d) addressing legal concerns (Wentling & Palma-Rivas, 1998). An interesting view is offered by Leach (1995) who argues that team leaders should not 'manage' diversity, but they should instead 'work' with diversity, as this requires individuals to be curious, patient, respectful of others and willing to learn from each other.

Managing diversity involves creating a work environment that is inclusive of everyone. In order to create a successful diverse environment, organizations should focus on personal awareness among staff as they must be aware of their personal differences and biases (Roosevelt, 2001). However, some scholars argue that managing diversity is more than just simply being aware of individual differences in the workplace. It involves recognizing the value of differences, combating discrimination, and promoting inclusiveness (Jackson et al., 2003) and when managed ineffectively, it can actually result in decreased performance (Williams & O'Reilly, 1998). This is because individuals from different cultural backgrounds often communicate and make decisions differently, including different verbal and non-verbal communication styles (Shachaf, 2008), which is particularly relevant in the virtual environment.

Previous studies on the notion of diversity in the workplace and organizational performance have found that culturally diverse workgroups have lower levels of cohesion and integration, due to the lack of shared understanding among team members (Ibid.). These misunderstandings are typically caused by slower pace of speech, translation problems, and reduced accuracy in communication. Mattson (2003) adds that language and vocal accents can often cause misunderstandings which are more impactful than the differences in the language itself. Non-verbal forms of communication can be also misunderstood between those of different cultures, and those who speak different languages. Bassett-Jones (2005) argues that diversity accounts not only for misunderstanding, but also for conflict in the workplace, and can result in absenteeism, poor quality, low morale, and loss of competitiveness.

Having examined diversity and its importance in the workplace, the authors now turn to discuss in more detail diversity in relation to virtual work environments (e.g., VTs) and the unique characteristics of virtuality.

Diversity in Virtual Work Environments

The VT literature, as well as the wider literature on virtuality and computer-mediated communication (CMC) systems (e.g., Panteli, 2009), argues that the unique characteristics of virtuality, for example, geographical dispersion, computer-mediation, lack of face-to-face (F2F) interaction make it difficult for team members to develop trust and cohesion and deliver their tasks effectively in the virtual environment (e.g., Ebrahim et al., 2009). Among these characteristics is that of physically collocated subgroups within VT environments. These may raise additional boundaries, reinforcing the negative effects of diversity in VTs, and thus impacting the development of trust, as well as VT cohesion overall (Panteli & Davison, 2005).

Understanding Diversity in Virtual Work Environments

Indeed, the topic of trust development is a popular one within the VT literature (Coppola et al., 2004; Crisp & Jarvenpaa, 2013; DeRosa et al., 2004; Jarvenpaa & Leidner, 1999; Panteli & Duncan, 2004). Some of these authors highlight that swift trust is important in VTs given their temporary (in some cases) character (e.g. Crisp & Jarvenpaa, 2013). Trust has also been closely associated with diversity, with recent findings arguing, for instance, that functional diversity does not exert any influences on trust and, in contrast, has the potential to lead to higher levels of VT performance (Pinjani & Palvia, 2013).

Further to trust and diversity, prominent position within the virtual literature has 'media richness theory' (MRT) which sees different ICTs as differing in terms of their degree of synchronicity from synchronous (thus, very rich) through to asynchronous (thus, lean) (e.g., Workman, Kahnweiler, & Bommer, 2003). Researchers highlight that specific tasks are better accomplished via asynchronous ICTs and others via more synchronous ones in the virtual environment. For instance, synchronous ICTs can be appropriate for complex tasks that require direct feedback, interdependence and increases levels of certainty (Hambley, O'Neill, & Kline, 2007). Further to the type of ICTs used, it has also been shown that individuals who communicate in a language different from their native language tend to choose asynchronous over synchronous ICTs to level out the differences in levels of language proficiencies. For example, when using email communication, they have possibility to delay their feedback, giving them more time to think about the message they want to convey (Klitmøller et al., 2015).

Staples and Zhao (2006) posit—in a comparative, experimental study of cultural diversity they conducted between virtual and F2F teams—that heterogeneous teams in general (i.e., both virtual and F2F teams) experienced lower levels of satisfaction and overall team cohesion, though, interestingly, virtual heterogeneous teams exhibited higher performance levels in comparison to F2F heterogeneous teams. In a similar study with a global corporation involving VTs, Shachaf (2008) unpacked the role played by cultural diversity; on one hand, it improved the overall decision-making process within the team environment, but it raised communication-related challenges.

On the other hand, she found that cultural diversity influenced significantly ICT selection within the team, which, by extension, mitigated the negative impact it had on communication matters. Some of these findings are corroborated further by Paul, Seetharaman, Samarah, and Mykytyn (2004) who argue that "collaborative conflict management style positively impacted satisfaction with the decision making process, perceived decision quality, and perceived participation of the VTs" (p. 303). Conflict management has indeed been recognized as a significant challenge in the context of VTs where member interactions are predominantly ICT-mediated (e.g. Zornoza, Ripoll, & Peiró, 2002).

Overall, and further to what has been discussed so far, researchers have identified links between diversity/heterogeneity and, not only conflict management, but also creativity/innovation (e.g. Chamakiotis et al., 2013, as stated earlier). But how is diversity managed within this context? Researchers recognize that leadership constitutes a significant concern among practitioners working in VTs, mainly because of the added challenges of having to exercise leadership remotely, oftentimes with no F2F interaction. The literature on VT leadership argues that rather than having one central leader, it may be necessary that different members share different leadership responsibilities (e.g. Chamakiotis & Panteli, 2010; Hill, 2005; Hoch & Kozlowski, 2014).

What this literature review has shown is that despite the importance of diversity, there is limited evidence of how it can be managed in the virtual environment and within a VT context in particular. The relevant VT literature posits a number of unique characteristics which have been found by researchers in the field to affect traditional management practices. However, what we do not know is how these influence diversity and its management. With this gap in mind, the chapter next presents a comparative case study with the purpose of addressing the above gap.

A COMPARATIVE CASE STUDY

Research Approach

A comparative case study approach (Saunders, Lewis, & Thornhill, 2009) was used in order to address the above gap and aims, because, unlike a survey design, case studies aim for an in-depth understanding of the context which surrounds the phenomenon under investigation (Yin, 2008). As Cassel and Symon (2011) argue, survey research is too static to capture complex and active organizational phenomena worthy of qualitative approaches. Case study research, on the other hand, is a useful approach where it is important to understand social relation processes, behaviors and attitudes in their natural context and has also been seen as fruitful in studies entailing technology and IS (Cavaye, 1996) as it is the case with the study presented here. For this study, a comparative case study was deemed suitable as it was considered suitable for identifying what is it that influences diversity and its management in the virtual environment. Presented next are the research sites in which the comparative case study was conducted.

Research Sites

Case A, an example of a physically collocated work environment, involved a UK-based coffee shop, referred to here as Coffee Hut (CH; a pseudonym). Work in the selected coffee shop is standardized and repetitive—everyone is performing similar duties. There is a shared responsibility for meeting weekly targets and everyone holds himself or herself mutually accountable for meeting them. There is a high level of demographic diversity with the majority of staff being from different countries, although diversity was lower in terms of age for example.

Case B, an example of a virtual work environment, involved a UK-based recruitment office, referred to here as William's Recruitment Agency (WRA; a pseudonym). Working patterns in the selected recruitment office are less repetitive and, although all staff members work together, there is no collective sense of responsibility. Everyone is in charge of retaining staff in different areas of business. Staff members are given monthly targets they have to meet and it is only their individual responsibility to meet those tasks. Diversity in this organization is linked to job-related characteristics, such as educational background as well as ethnic.

Data Collection and Analysis

In-depth, semi-structured interviews were conducted to gather rich, qualitative data that aimed to understand human behavior within the selected organizational contexts. Qualitative data are better suited to answering the how and why questions that were of relevance to this study (Cassell & Symon, 2011). In particular, a total of 10 semi-structured interviews were conducted (five from each of the two cases), each lasting an average of 40 minutes. The interviews were audio-recorded with the participants' written consent and in line with the ethical procedure required by the institution in which the authors are based. An interview guide was developed, which acted as a starting point and guided the interview with each

Understanding Diversity in Virtual Work Environments

participant (see the Appendix for the interview guide). The interviewees in both environments (collocated and virtual) were asked about their day-to-day experiences of working and collaborating with others. The goal was to explore what types of diversity were evident in the two environments, to understand how these were managed, and to elicit what was unique about diversity in the virtual environment in particular. The interviews were conducted in an informal environment of the participants' choice, at a time suitable for them, ensuring they would be comfortable being interviewed and recorded. These were mostly at the participants' homes or public places.

Data analysis occurred as the data were being collected. An inductive approach was taken in analyzing the interview data, which allowed for the emergence of themes without developing a priori hypotheses based on the authors' review of the relevant literature. Rather, the analysis was conducted with the research gap in mind as previously discussed. Thus, the researchers' aim was to identify themes that would enable them address the above gap. In particular, the authors adopted a thematic analysis approach, as suggested by Braun and Clarke (2006), involving the following stages: (a) interview transcription; (b) search for initial codes based on several readings of the interview dataset; (c) collocating similar codes into wider themes; and (d) writing up the emerged.

Coding was performed manually with the use of colored pens, highlighters and post-it notes. Some of the common codes that emerged in both environments were: training, miscommunication, misunderstanding, non-verbal cues and trust. In writing up the analysis, pseudonyms were given to each participant in order for their anonymity to be protected. Overall, this approach enabled flexibility in terms of identifying codes and relating them with existing themes from the literature. Having described in detail how the data were collected and analyzed, the chapter continues with a discussion of the emerged findings.

Research Findings

In this section, the authors present the findings from the two cases, beginning with Case A, the selected coffee shop.

Case A: Coffee Hut (CH)

Presented first are the participants from Case A (Table 1).

CH is busy on a regular basis and staff are under a lot of pressure, insofar that employees compare their workplace to a factory:

Table 1. Case A Participants

Pseudonym	Age Group	Nationality	Gender	Educational Background	Spoken Languages	Work Experience*
Daniel	26-35	Greek	Male	Bachelor	English, Greek	0-2
Barney	26-35	British	Male	High School	English	0-2
Alex	26-35	Italian	Male	High School	English, Italian	2-4
Ella	16-25	Polish	Female	High School	English, Polish	0-2
Sofia	16-25	Columbian	Female	High School	English, Spanish	0-2

* In years

It's a very busy store—it's like a factory and it gets very chaotic. (Alex)

Performance is measured collectively based on the coffee shop's overall performance; however, everyone has different tasks and responsibilities within the group. The level of employee turnover is relatively high, with a large part of the staff resigning after a number of weeks in the coffee shop because they cannot keep up with the pressure:

I have been here for 2 years and I could see people coming for 3 months, 2 weeks but never really longer. (Alex)

The section continues with the themes that emerged from the analysis.

Training and Routines

Work at CH is standardized and monotonous, as per the interviewees' perceptions; therefore, it is more skills-focused rather than knowledge-focused. There are no entry skills or certifications required to apply for a job at CH; rather, employees undergo a weeklong training once recruited. The training process consists of learning the routines of the job, which involve following step-by-step detailed ways of carrying out every activity at work:

The job is indeed very routinized, you need to undergo three months training during which you learn the routines—and there are quite a few of them. There is a routine for everything, how you collect dirty mugs from tables, how you wash them, order in which you wash them; different routines for making coffees... Not much thinking is required really. (Barney)

Moreover, there is collective responsibility of meeting weekly sales targets; hence, staff are made aware of the importance of working collectively as a team. Following the standardized working methods outlined during the training period is therefore critical:

There are different positions and each involves a different routine process that needs to be followed ... you need to follow the routines and do what is expected from you, otherwise there will be consequences. (Daniel)

Training was found to be an important factor because inadequate training might lead to a conflict between staff members and decrease group performance:

When you are on bar and someone is on the till and you get the order wrong because someone on the till didn't get it right, you get really annoyed at that person so this can lead to conflict, especially on a busy day. (Sofia)

Importance of F2F Communication

Interactions between staff are mainly based on F2F communication; however, non-verbal cues such as body language and gestures were found to be of critical importance within the F2F working environment:

Sometimes when it gets really busy I just show people different sizes of drinks with my hands (small, medium, large) instead of trying to shout through the crowd. (Daniel)

This was found to have a significant effect on customer experience overall:

And then you can tell from the voice, from the face you can tell if they are in a hurry, if they are angry or if they want to engage in a conversation, so I think F2F interaction and the body language is really important. (Daniel)

Lack of Communication

The 'factory'-like environment with set routines characterizing the type of work at the CH means that work is largely task-related and customer-focused, diminishing significantly the staff's opportunities to develop social bonds and speak about their lives outside the job:

Exchange of information is only work-related (if there is any at all) but as for the personal exchange of information not really because when it's busy you don't have the time to talk about personal life and socialize ... and what usually happens when it's really busy, you don't talk at all for the entire shift. (Daniel)

Lack of communication is also triggered by separation of responsibilities and by having to follow the routines:

There is not much communication needed. There are three different positions in the store and if you are placed on till, that's where you will probably be for the rest of your day ... and you don't really need to communicate much with the rest of the team unless you need something from them. (Sofia)

If you have to focus on customers and the routine of the job, you can't focus on anything else. (Alex)

Miscommunication

Language in terms of different levels of spoken proficiencies was found to cause many misunderstandings and miscommunication between workers, as well as decreased staff morale.

Language is sometimes an obstacle because some people I work with don't speak English very well. (Ella)

You don't need to speak the language well as long as you know the language of the job. (Alex)

I feel bad by asking over and over again to repeat and it makes you feel not stupid, but uncomfortable because you can't understand someone. (Daniel)

Miscommunication is often resolved by increasing, and capitalizing on, non-verbal communication, for example by using body language and gestures.

I often use gestures when someone doesn't understand me well ... Sometimes I find it really hard to understand what someone of the people are saying. (Sofia)

Group Identity: Similarity

There is a shared responsivity for meeting weekly sales targets and everyone holds themselves mutually accountable for meeting them. Everyone's contribution to the group success is considered equally important. Hence, workers feel strongly connected to the group as a whole, rather than to particular individuals within this group. Therefore, no in-groups emerged in this environment.

I like everyone, I can't say I like someone more than others because I don't really know others well and you can't really get to know them well because there is never enough time. (Barney)

Workers mainly seek similarities in others based on their cultural background, shared life experience and similar work ethics, all of which act as a link that integrates them together.

We are all foreign so we understand each other and help each other; for example when someone has a problem like to ask about something he doesn't understand because he doesn't speak English well—we help each other because we understand the situation ... It makes me feel like home because I used to work in places when they are only English people and I felt like they were all against me because I was 'different'. (Ella)

Presented next are the findings from Case B, the virtual setting of the study.

Case B: William's Recruitment Agency

Presented first in this section are the participants in Case B (Table 2).

The job itself is not standardized and it requires flexibility and interpersonal as well as strong communication skills. However, many interviewees described it as repetitive to some degree. Workers are given monthly targets to meet and their performance is being evaluated on a monthly basis:

Little training is provided for recruiters prior starting the job, they often learn through trial-and-error approach and seek assistance from their more experienced co-workers to share their knowledge. Share

Table 2. Case B Participants

Pseudonym	Age Group	Nationality	Gender	Educational Background	Spoken Languages	Work Experience*
Emma	16-25	Luxembourger	Female	Bachelor	English, French, German, Spanish	0-2
Lucas	26-35	Lithuanian	Male	Bachelor	English, Lithuanian, Russian	2-4
Chris	26-35	Polish	Male	Bachelor	English, Polish, Russian, French	2-4
Adrien	26-35	French	Male	Bachelor	English, French	2-4
Carol	36-45	English	Female	Bachelor	English	2-4

* In years

Understanding Diversity in Virtual Work Environments

experiences on how they communicate with people, how they write to people. It's easier when you start so you know what to do. (Emma)

Channels of Communication

Recruiters have a daily, F2F interaction with other workers in the office. However, much of their time is spent in the virtual environment in search of potential candidates that would fill in the positions available.

On average, I would say that I spend about 7 hours a day glued to my desk, sending emails and calling people. (Carol)

Their virtual collaborations are mainly based on written means of communication and oral communication (over the phone), but due to the disperse nature of work, they are usually unaware of who is on the other side of the screen or line.

We use emails and telephones on a regular basis. (Lukas)

Email featured as a dominant means of communication; often participants referred to it as their 'favorite' means:

It's much easier to when you communicate by email because before sending it, you proofread it like twice. (Lukas)

Communication via Skype was found to be important because it gives people opportunity to see each other. However, Skype alone was not considered to be enough as there is typically a need to put things in in an email following the Skype call:

Sometimes we use Skype for business, it's much easier to communicate when using this because you can actually see the person but in most cases we need to have a proof of our conversation, so we still have to write an email to sum up and have a clear statement. (Chris)

Work Relationships

The recruitment company has a few offices across the UK, but communication (F2F or virtual) exchange between those working in different offices happens rarely and they get to see each other only a few times a year—if at all.

You know the company has many more employees but you don't really get to see them so you don't really have any connection to them. (Emma)

I've met a few other people from other offices, but we don't talk to each other unless it's a business-related manner. This is probably one of the things we could probably improve. (Lukas)

Therefore, similarity and attraction among office staff is based only on their F2F and everyday interactions. Interviewees felt stronger connection to particular individuals within a group of workers in the office, rather than to the group of workers as a whole in their office.

I have 2-3 members of staff that could be considered as my buddies, we occasionally meet after work. (Chris)

Their similarity was based on shared work ethics, life experiences and interests.

We have the same attitude at work, I'm trying to treat my work seriously and use positive attitude when it comes to solving issues, but not everyone is on the same page, some people tend to be just lazy and closed-minded. (Chris)

Challenges of Virtual Collaborations

On top of the challenges coming from working with physically collocated colleagues, recruiters also face challenges arising from their virtual collaborations with others. First are challenges relative miscommunication and language-related issues. For instance, low levels of language proficiency in terms of the spoken and written communication seemed to account for numerous misunderstanding and misinterpretations.

Sometimes people are using online language translation services which can be very misleading and sometimes results can be quite funny, for instance someone saying 'of course you did good I am the sucker' which probably in their mother language sounded a bit different. (Chris)

We are 'equal opportunities' employer but people are sometimes different on their resumes. Sometimes you call them and they are not very fluent in English so we have problems of understanding them over the phone. (Lukas)

However, participants were found to have developed ways to overcome these; for example, by asking for clarifications, which, in turn, slowed down the communication process overall:

Usually we are trying to guess what was meant, if we are not able to do this we are asking for clarification of paraphrasing. (Chris)

Second was the issue of physical contact, which featured as an important issue for participants in this case study. The flexible nature of work and being able to work from home has many advantages; however, working from home and communicating exclusively via CMC systems led to feelings of isolation and reinforced the need for some level of F2F, human interaction:

I prefer working in the office because you get that interaction with people ... I think it's easier when you have any questions to ask someone to help you, than sending them and email and waiting for response and maybe they will reply a few hours later and you might need a response immediately. (Emma)

80% of the time when we communicate we use body language but in a virtual environment it's very different and this lack of seeing the body language is one of the key challenges we face. Especially in recruitment when you hire people and you can't to see them - that's the troublesome. (Lukas)

Thirdly, response time was found to be an important challenge because it prevents people from moving forward and making progress, which causes frustration and irritation:

I find it really frustrating when I am working on something important and the other side isn't communicating well after that first initial contact. (Carol)

Fourthly, virtual collaborations sometimes did not allow for trust to develop. Rather than allowing for it to develop slowly over time, it was being coerced upon workers. High levels of trust are difficult to build because of the lack of F2F interaction and also because of not being able to see the person in real life:

Working virtually, considering that it's mainly based on computer-mediated communication, I would say there are more barriers to develop trust because sometimes I need more time to elaborate on what's been said and I need more time to understand something. (Adrien)

I have no choice but to trust that the person I recommended for the role will do their best at the later stage. (Carol)

DISCUSSION

This study was initiated with the aim of improving understanding around how diversity can be managed in the modern virtual environment. This section begins by outlining the different types of diversity that were identified in the two organizations before discussing the study's contributions to the literature.

Types of Diversity

The study identified two different types of diversity—visible and job-related—which are discussed next in an attempt to contextualize the emerged findings. Visible types of diversity include cultural, age, sex and linguistic (Williams & O'Reilly, 1998). At the cultural level, diversity was high in both workplaces, consisting of workers from countries all around Europe. Therefore, the linguistic type of diversity was also high in both environments. The majority of respondents at the CH—4 out of 5—spoke two languages (mother tongue and English) and their level of English proficiency ranged from limited working proficiency to full working proficiency.

As for the WRA, proficiency of English language amongst staff was between full professional proficiency and bilingual proficiency. When compared to the collocated environment, language diversity at the WRA was found to be much higher, with 3 respondents speaking 3 or more languages fluently. In terms of the remaining two, one respondent was bilingual and one spoke only English as a native language. Age diversity varied; it was found to be low at the CH and high at the WRA. Workers at the coffee shop were found to be of similar age, ranging between 18 and 25. In comparison, age gap amongst staff was significantly higher at the recruitment agency (i.e., between 20 and 50 years). Diversity in terms of gender was high in both environments, with three male and two female respondents in each workplace.

Job-related diversity emerged from the data analysis too; this was educational and knowledge-related. These were found to be low at the CH. Only one respondent was a university graduate, whereas the remaining 4 terminated their studies at the secondary school level. The majority of respondents worked there for less than 2 years and did not have any work experience prior to that job, thus, knowledge emanating from experience was found to be low. In contrast, both types of job-related diversity were high at the WRA.

All respondents were university graduates, with the majority having been in their current posts between 2 and 4 years. Only one respondent who worked at the WRA for less than 2 years did not have any other work experience prior to taking up that role. The remaining interviewees had other full- and part-time jobs in the past (mostly in customer service). Thus, diversity in terms of knowledge emanating from experience was high at the WRA. Having outlined the types of diversity that were posited in the study, the authors move on to discuss the contributions of the study to the literature.

Theoretical Contributions

The contributions to the field of I-O psychology and kindred fields, such as IS and management, are discussed here. Findings show that channels of communication—different between the two environments—were strongly influenced by language diversity, which was ultimately triggered by high cultural diversity. Insofar as MRT (Workman et al., 2003) is concerned, workers at the CH used the richest type of communication, that is F2F communication which allows for direct exchange of information in real-time. As already mentioned, there was a high variety of language diversity amongst staff, which led to major miscommunication issues.

The language used in the workplace was English and levels of spoken proficiency between staff ranged from elementary to full working proficiency. This dis-commonality in terms of levels of the language spoken caused misunderstandings due to lack of pertinent vocabulary and strong voice accents of some workers, confirming existing literature (Mattson, 2003). What the present study has further shown is that this diminished staff morale, their self-esteem and increased task-conflict, as, on some occasions, employees were unable to exchange work-related information without obstacles. In such situations, when there was a high level of uncertainty, workers would switch to non-verbal communication (body language) which was found to be of critical importance for, ultimately, achieving their goals.

These findings add to MRT which argues that when complex tasks need to be solved, the richest media of communication are most effective as they allow for picking up on non-verbal cues, which, in turn, diminishes level of uncertainty. However, at the WRA workers used asynchronous communication on a regular basis (emails), synchronous (telephone) and, occasionally, richer media such as Skype. The study adds to the MRT by showing that when clarification needed to be in place, for example, in cases where language diversity got on the way, email (i.e., lean media) featured as the preferred way of communication.

Furthermore, these findings on, for example, diversity-related misunderstandings in the virtual environment also contribute to the emerging body of literature on emotion and conflict in VTs (e.g., Ayoko, Konrad, & Boyle, 2011; Baralou & McInnes, 2013; Billings & Watts, 2010; Glikson & Erez, 2013; Kankanhalli, Tan, & Wei, 2007; Zornoza et al., 2002) by explaining what is it that actually triggers conflict in this context. Additionally, Bassett-Jones (2005) argues that diversity accounts not only for misunderstandings, but also for conflict in the workplace, and can result in absenteeism, poor quality, low morale and loss of competitiveness. The study presented here shows that, in the collocated environment, less proficient members' morale was lowered because of the difficulty of understanding information fully.

Language diversity in the context of virtual collaborations was found to have a noteworthy impact on the quality of online collaborations. Findings show that diversity in terms of language was the reason behind many misunderstandings and miscommunication between individuals. Similar to the CH, both parties involved in the communication process had different levels of English fluency. Miscommunication associated with lean media was due to misinterpretations of the message, due to the lack of voice sound and other non-verbal cues. Moreover, some non-proficient speakers used online translation services when writing emails, which caused confusion when translated incorrectly.

However, even though email communication was also associated with time-delays, it was still the preferred method of communication. This is consistent with a study conducted by Klitmøller et al. (2015) who found that individuals who do not share the same native language will tend to choose asynchronous (written) communication over synchronous (oral). Further to confirming these existing findings, the study here demonstrates that asynchronous communication in these cases enables virtual colleagues to respond at a slower pace, which gives them more time to think of the message they want to communicate.

According to the MRT, the best way of communication when complex tasks need to be solved is via rich media (e.g., telephone) (Workman et al., 2003). However, the findings of the study show that language-related diversity in fact decreased communication effectiveness when a rich medium was used, instead of increasing it. The use of email—an example of a lean medium—gave rise to the use of translation services and spelling checks. Moreover, with response delays, the participants in the study had more time to reflect on the message and make changes to the wording used. Thus, the findings from the study contradict the above theory which states that the best way to communicate when complex tasks need to be solved is through rich media, mainly because of the added benefit of allowing for extra time to think, which asynchronous media can offer. When clarification needed to be in place, the participants used emails when dealing with language diversity. Hence, lean communication, as opposed to rich, raised certainty levels.

Moreover, emails reduced verbal misunderstandings caused by vocal accents and lack of pertinent vocabulary—both of which were present communications over the telephone, as these did not allow for time to reflect on what individuals tried communicating. In addition, emails allowed for proofreading before sending it. Even when other rich media were used, individuals followed up the conversations with emails to increase their levels of certainty. These findings corroborate Klitmøller et al. (2015) who argue that those whose level of language proficiency is not proficient enough are more likely to choose asynchronous, over synchronous, media because of a fear of picking up the phone.

What these findings have also demonstrated is that workers lacked human interaction and non-verbal cues, such as body language, in their virtual collaborations. Therefore, even though they were allowed to work from home, they still preferred to come into the office on a regular basis to maintain that human interaction. This is consistent with the theory of anonymity and deindividuation which states that when individuals communicate through CMC, and are virtually anonymous, their personalities become deinviduated (Yilmaz & Peña, 2014). Taking into account the nature of work in the case of the WRA—online recruitment—virtual anonymity might be important because it removes any personal biases caused by stereotyping and cultural differences. However, virtual anonymity on a regular basis can also lead to social isolation, corroborating existing VT literature (Hinds, Neeley, & Cramton, 2014; Morgan & Symon, 2002).

Another theme which emerged in both environments involved relationships at work. The findings show that workers in both environments developed group identity, however these relationships were affected by different types of diversity in the two environments. In the collocated one, workers developed group identity, rather than creating bonds with specific individuals in their teams. This group identity was strongly based on cultural diversity (the fact that they were all non-UK citizens) and age similarity amongst workers—both of which can be categorized as surface-level diversity.

However, the findings have also shown that workers found it difficult to create bonds at the personal level, due to the—as they themselves put it—'factory-like' nature of work at the CH. They did not have time to get to know one other and creating common bond usually takes time as it is based on deep-level diversity. Taking a group perspective also means that social categorization did not take place and therefore no in-groups or out-groups emerged. This is consistent with studies arguing that when work is standardized, there are fewer opportunities for cultural diversity to trigger categorization process and creation of in-groups and out-groups (Pelled, Eisenhardt, & Xin, 1999).

The findings support this theory and highlight the fact that the 'factory-like' environment not only diminishes cultural differences between staff, but it more importantly diminishes any opportunity for the development of work relationships at personal level to develop. This is because the standardized nature of work removes flexibility of work and reduces communication to a minimum, as workers do not need to exchange information.

At the recruitment agency, however, workers developed both group identity and common bond with particular individuals. Categorization at the group level took place as workers did not feel any connection with workers in other offices around the UK. At the group level, common identity was caused by intragroup comparisons to other offices around the UK. Workers identified themselves as members of one office and compared themselves with other groups of offices in the country. Findings show that this intragroup comparison was based on lack of physical contact with other workers, what made communication style between them more business-like.

The findings also show that these participants felt detached from the rest of the company, which is what prevented them from creating work relationships with workers outside their office. Within the office, however, even though workers felt connected to their group as a whole, in-groups also emerged as individuals felt more attracted to few individuals. This was triggered by similarity in terms of attitudes and shared values. Moreover, the study demonstrates that creating that interaction at a personal level was triggered by factors of flexibility and also by the ability to exchange information. None of these factors were present in the collocated environment.

What was surprising to find was the fact that group trust in the collocated environment did not emerge as a separate theme. Taking the nature of work and its continuity—the fact that the job process is designed in a way that everyone's input is connected to the next person—it would seem that trust would be an important factor for staff relations. However, the findings show otherwise. When asked about shared trust, participants often referred to 'consequences' which resulted in not getting the job done.

Thus, even though success is measured through collective performance, they are still being evaluated at the individual level. As already discussed, no in-groups or out-groups emerged due to lack of communication between staff members. Following this rationale, lack of communication—and therefore the absence of informational and value diversity—meant that workers did not get a chance to get to know one another which, in turn, diminished trust as this is typically built through open communication.

In the virtual workplace, on the contrary, workers felt that trust was forced upon them in their online collaborations, which is consistent with a theory of swift trust (Crisp & Jarvenpaa, 2013). These findings add to the noteworthy body of literature on trust in the virtual environment, notably in the context of globally dispersed VTs (Coppola et al., 2004; DeRosa et al., 2004; Jarvenpaa & Leidner, 1999; Panteli & Duncan, 2004). In other words, workers had to develop and maintain trust at the work-related level, without having a chance to see their colleagues F2F.

However, levels of trust were often distorted by language diversity (which was ultimately triggered by high level of cultural diversity), inability to see the respondent, and challenges emanating from using CMC as a main source of correspondence. This is consistent with existing findings suggesting that language barriers lower team members' trustworthiness and lead to misunderstandings; less proficient members feel insecure and are often faced with frustration by more proficient members (Klitmøller et al., 2015).

SOLUTIONS AND RECOMMENDATIONS

A number of practical recommendations emerge from this study which could be of interest to HR practitioners and managers as well as others working in the modern virtual, and highly diverse workplace. Choosing the right ICTs is not enough. In order to diminish the potential negative effects of language diversity in virtual collaborations, full training should be provided to individuals prior to joining their team, regardless of their field of expertise and years of experience. Managers should not assume that all individuals have strong interpersonal and writing skills, and that all will therefore be able to deal with language-related misunderstandings and miscommunication effectively, because most of the F2F techniques of dealing with language dis-commonality may not apply in the virtual context. For example, given that CMC may obscure body language, the emphasis when communicating virtually could be placed on the tone of voice (e.g., when using the telephone), as it might be useful in communicating what cannot be transferred otherwise.

The findings here suggest that requesting frequent clarifications might put the non-proficient speakers in an uncomfortable position, and diminish their confidence; thus, it is not advised. It is proposed that virtual workers use simple and direct information, as well as try to avoid using complex sentences, slang and jokes that may be difficult to be understood. Instead, they could speak at a slower pace when communicating with colleagues across different countries. Therefore, the training process should encompass pertinent ways of approaching people and resolving conflict, writing skills and other mechanisms that may prove useful when trying to deal with linguistic barriers in the virtual environment. Moreover, workers should be allowed to take advantage of their linguistic skills and—if possible—communicate with others in their native language. This would decrease levels of uncertainty and increase levels of job satisfaction, as employees who feel trusted and valued are more likely perform well and stay with the company in the long term.

Finally, managers should incorporate more physical contact between members of staff across other offices across the country (or the locations involved more generally). This would strengthen organizational culture and organizational commitment, as employees would not only consider themselves part of a group, but also part of the wider company. A way of achieving this would be by creating online social portals for employees as well as other types social events which everyone would be able to join on a regular basis.

FUTURE RESEARCH DIRECTIONS

The study presented here has limitations which also give rise to future research directions. For instance, due to the exploratory character of this study, a relatively small number of interviewees participated. This has the limitation that the findings might not be relevant to other contexts, industries, or organizations that differ to the ones studied here. To overcome this issue of limited statistical generalizability, researchers could focus on larger populations and adopt other research approaches (e.g., quantitative methodologies).

Furthermore, the study hints at contributions that have highlighted important areas of interest within the wider literature on virtuality and VTs. These include the well-researched area of trust, and swift trust in particular (Crisp & Jarvenpaa, 2013; Germain & McGuire, 2014), as well as issues of language, misunderstandings and conflict (Billings & Watts, 2010; Kankanhalli et al., 2007; Zornoza et al., 2002). Noted last here is the fact that not all virtual workplaces are the same and therefore they cannot be treated equally.

The literature on virtuality (e.g., Panteli, 2009) highlights that virtual configurations may vary, for example, between virtual social networks, CMC systems, local VTs, global VTs, and so on. In view of this, the authors envisage that the future of the present collection could focus on investigations of diversity—and other issues recommended above—within these different contexts that the literature on virtuality has identified.

CONCLUSION

The study presented here was driven by a need to understand diversity in virtual workplaces. Therefore, the authors adopted a comparative case study approach and examined diversity in two contrasting work environments—a collocated, F2F, and a virtual one. The findings show what types of diversity were found to be important in the virtual workplace and which of the unique characteristics of virtuality might influence diversity—by, for example, leading to misunderstandings or issues of identity and belongingness. In the earlier sections, the authors have shown how these findings contribute to the extant literature and they have also provided recommendations for both practitioners and future researchers interested in the area of diversity in the modern virtual workplace.

REFERENCES

Algesheimer, R., Dholakia, U. M., & Gurău, C. (2011). Virtual Team Performance in a Highly Competitive Environment. *Group & Organization Management, 36*(2), 161–190. doi:10.1177/1059601110391251

Ayoko, O. B., Konrad, A. M., & Boyle, M. V. (2011). Online work: Managing conflict and emotions for performance in virtual teams. *European Management Journal, 30*(2), 156–174. doi:10.1016/j.emj.2011.10.001

Baralou, E., & McInnes, P. (2013). Emotions and the spatialisation of social relations in text-based computer-mediated communication. *New Technology, Work and Employment, 28*(2), 160–175. doi:10.1111/ntwe.12012

Bassett-Jones, N. (2005). The Paradox of Diversity Management, Creativity and Innovation. *Creativity and Innovation Management, 14*(2), 169–175. doi:10.1111/j.1467-8691.00337.x

Billings, M., & Watts, L. A. (2010). *Understanding dispute resolution online: using text to reflect personal and substantive issues in conflict*. London: ACM Press. doi:10.1145/1753326.1753542

Braun, V., & Clarke, V. (2006). Using thematic analysis in psychology. *Qualitative Research in Psychology, 3*(2), 77–101. doi:10.1191/1478088706qp063oa

Cassell, C., & Symon, G. (2011). Assessing good qualitative research in the work psychology field: A narrative analysis: Good qualitative research. *Journal of Occupational and Organizational Psychology, 84*(4), 633–650. doi:10.1111/j.2044-8325.2011.02009.x

Cavaye, A. L. M. (1996). Case study research: A multi-faceted research approach for IS. *Information Systems Journal, 6*(3), 227–242. doi:10.1111/j.1365-2575.1996.tb00015.x

Chamakiotis, P., Dekoninck, E. A., & Panteli, N. (2013). Factors Influencing Creativity in Virtual Design Teams: An Interplay between Technology, Teams and Individuals: Factors Influencing Creativity in Virtual Design Teams. *Creativity and Innovation Management, 22*(3), 265–279. doi:10.1111/caim.12039

Chamakiotis, P., & Panteli, N. (2010). E-Leadership Styles for Global Virtual Teams. In P. Yoong (Ed.), *Leadership in the Digital Enterprise: Issues and Challenges* (pp. 143–161). Hershey, PA: IGI Global. Retrieved from http://www.igi-global.com/chapter/leadership-styles-global-virtual-teams/37093

CIPD. (2015). Diversity in the workplace: an overview. Retrieved from http://www.cipd.co.uk/hr-resources/factsheets/diversity-workplace-overview.aspx

Coca-Cola Co. (2014). Retrieved from http://www.coca-colacompany.com/our-company/diversity/global-diversity-mission

Comfort, J., & Franklin, P. (2014). *The mindful international manager: how to work effectively across cultures* (2nd ed.). London, Philadelphia: Kogan Page Limited.

Coppola, N. W., Hiltz, S. R., & Rotter, N. G. (2004). Building trust in virtual teams. *IEEE Transactions on Professional Communication, 47*(2), 95–104. doi:10.1109/TPC.2004.828203

Crisp, C. B., & Jarvenpaa, S. L. (2013). Swift Trust in Global Virtual Teams. *Journal of Personnel Psychology, 12*(1), 45–56. doi:10.1027/1866-5888/a000075

De Kare-Silver, M. (2011). Changes to the Workplace and in the Workforce. In M. de Kare-Silver (Ed.), *E-Shock 2020* (pp. 115–124). London: Palgrave Macmillan UK. Retrieved from http://link.springer.com/10.1057/9780230343368_13

DeRosa, D. M., Hantula, D. A., Kock, N., & DArcy, J. (2004). Trust and leadership in virtual teamwork: A media naturalness perspective. *Human Resource Management, 43*(2-3), 219–232. doi:10.1002/hrm.20016

DHS. (2016). Equal Employment Opportunity and Diversity Division. Retrieved from https://www.dhs.gov/about-office-equal-employment-opportunity-and-diversity-division

Dumas, T. L., Phillips, K. W., & Rothbard, N. P. (2013). Getting Closer at the Company Party: Integration Experiences, Racial Dissimilarity, and Workplace Relationships. *Organization Science, 24*(5), 1377–1401. doi:10.1287/orsc.1120.0808

Ebrahim, N. A., Ahmed, S., & Taha, Z. (2009). Virtual Teams: A Literature Review. *Australian Journal of Basic and Applied Sciences, 3*(3), 2653–2669.

Egan, M. E. (2011). *Global Diversity and Inclusion: Fostering Innovation Through a Diverse Workforce.* Retrieved from http://images.forbes.com/forbesinsights/StudyPDFs/Innovation_Through_Diversity.pdf

Fine, M. G. (1996). Cultural Diversity in the Workplace: The State of the Field. *Journal of Business Communication, 33*(4), 485–502. doi:10.1177/002194369603300408

Germain, M.-L., & McGuire, D. (2014). The Role of Swift Trust in Virtual Teams and Implications for Human Resource Development. *Advances in Developing Human Resources, 16*(3), 356–370. doi:10.1177/1523422314532097

Glikson, E., & Erez, M. (2013). Emotion display norms in virtual teams. *Journal of Personnel Psychology, 12*(1), 22–32. doi:10.1027/1866-5888/a000078

Godar, S. H., & Ferris, S. P. (Eds.). (2004). *Virtual and collaborative teams: process, technologies and practice.* Hershey, PA: Idea Group Publications. doi:10.4018/978-1-59140-204-6

Hambley, L. A., ONeill, T. A., & Kline, T. J. B. (2007). Virtual Team Leadership: Perspectives From the Field. *International Journal of e-Collaboration, 3*(1), 40–64. doi:10.4018/jec.2007010103

Hill, N. S. (2005). Leading Together, Working Together: The Role of Team Shared Leadership in Building Collaborative Capital in Virtual Teams. In *Advances in Interdisciplinary Studies of Work Teams* (Vol. 11, pp. 183–209). Bingley: Emerald. Retrieved from http://www.emeraldinsight.com/10.1016/S1572-0977(05)11007-3

Hinds, P. J., Neeley, T. B., & Cramton, C. D. (2014). Language as a lightning rod: Power contests, emotion regulation, and subgroup dynamics in global teams. *Journal of International Business Studies, 45*(5), 536–561. doi:10.1057/jibs.2013.62

Hoch, J. E., & Kozlowski, S. W. J. (2014). Leading virtual teams: Hierarchical leadership, structural supports, and shared team leadership. *The Journal of Applied Psychology, 99*(3), 390–403. doi:10.1037/a0030264 PMID:23205494

Jackson, S. E., Joshi, A., & Erhardt, N. L. (2003). Recent Research on Team and Organizational Diversity: SWOT Analysis and Implications. *Journal of Management, 29*(6), 801–830. doi:10.1016/S0149-2063(03)00080-1

Jackson, S. E., Stone, V. K., & Alvarez, E. B. (1992). Socialization amidst diversity — the impact of demographics on work team oldtimers and newcomers. *Research in Organizational Behavior, 15*, 45–109.

Jarvenpaa, S. L., & Leidner, D. E. (1999). Communication and trust in global virtual teams. *Organization Science, 10*(6), 791–815. doi:10.1287/orsc.10.6.791

Kankanhalli, A., Tan, B. C. Y., & Wei, K. K. (2007). Conflict and performance in global virtual teams. *Journal of Management Information Systems*, *23*(3), 237–274. doi:10.2753/MIS0742-1222230309

Klitmøller, A., Schneider, S. C., & Jonsen, K. (2015). Speaking of global virtual teams: Language differences, social categorization and media choice. *Personnel Review*, *44*(2), 270–285. doi:10.1108/PR-11-2013-0205

Leach, J. (1995). *A practical guide to working with diversity: The process, the tools, the resources*. New York: AMACOM.

Leonard-Barton, D., & Swap, W. C. (1999). *When sparks fly: igniting creativity in groups*. Boston: Harvard Business School Press.

Martin, G. C. (2014). The Effects Of Cultural Diversity In The Workplace. *Journal of Diversity Management*, *9*(2), 89. doi:10.19030/jdm.v9i2.8974

Mattson, S. (2003). Cultural Diversity in the Workplace: How the Meaning of Work Can Affect the Way We Work. *AWHONN Lifelines*, *7*(2), 154–158. doi:10.1177/1091592303253868 PMID:12735224

Morgan, S. J., & Symon, G. (2002). Computer-Mediated Communication and Remote Management: Integration or Isolation? *Social Science Computer Review*, *20*(3), 302–311. doi:10.1177/089443930202000307

Nemiro, J. E., Bradley, L., Beyerlein, M. M., & Beyerlein, S. (2008). *The Handbook of High-Performance Virtual Teams: A Toolkit for Collaborating Across Boundaries*. San Francisco: Jossey-Bass.

Panteli, N. (2009). Virtual Social Networks: A New Dimension for Virtuality Research. In N. Panteli (Ed.), *Virtual Social Networks: Mediated, Massive and Multiplayer Sites*. Hampshire, UK: Palgrave-Macmillan. doi:10.1057/9780230250888_1

Panteli, N., & Davison, R. M. (2005). The Role of Subgroups in the Communication Patterns of Global Virtual Teams. *IEEE Transactions on Professional Communication*, *48*(2), 191–200. doi:10.1109/TPC.2005.849651

Panteli, N., & Duncan, E. (2004). Trust and temporary virtual teams: Alternative explanations and dramaturgical relationships. *Information Technology & People*, *17*(4), 423–441. doi:10.1108/09593840410570276

Patrick, H. A., & Kumar, V. R. (2012). Managing Workplace Diversity: Issues and Challenges. *SAGE Open*, *2*(2). doi:10.1177/2158244012444615

Paul, S., Seetharaman, P., Samarah, I., & Mykytyn, P. P. (2004). Impact of heterogeneity and collaborative conflict management style on the performance of synchronous global virtual teams. *Information & Management*, *41*(3), 303–321. doi:10.1016/S0378-7206(03)00076-4

Pelled, L. H., Eisenhardt, K. M., & Xin, K. R. (1999). Exploring the Black Box: An Analysis of Work Group Diversity, Conflict, and Performance. *Administrative Science Quarterly*, *44*(1), 1. doi:10.2307/2667029

Phillips, K. W., Northcraft, G. B., & Neale, M. A. (2006). Surface-Level Diversity and Decision-Making in Groups: When Does Deep-Level Similarity Help? *Group Processes & Intergroup Relations*, *9*(4), 467–482. doi:10.1177/1368430206067557

Pierce, E., & Hansen, S. W. (2013). Technology, Trust and Effectiveness in Virtual Teams. *The International Journal of Management and Business*, *4*(1), 33–56.

Pinjani, P., & Palvia, P. (2013). Trust and knowledge sharing in diverse global virtual teams. *Information & Management*, *50*(4), 144–153. doi:10.1016/j.im.2012.10.002

Roosevelt, T. R. (2001). *Elements of a successful diversity process: Part I*. American Institute for Managing Diversity.

Saunders, M., Lewis, P., & Thornhill, A. (2009). *Research methods for business students*. Essex, UK: Pearson Education.

Saxena, A. (2014). Workforce Diversity: A Key to Improve Productivity. *Procedia Economics and Finance*, *11*, 76–85. doi:10.1016/S2212-5671(14)00178-6

Shachaf, P. (2008). Cultural diversity and information and communication technology impacts on global virtual teams: An exploratory study. *Information & Management*, *45*(2), 131–142. doi:10.1016/j.im.2007.12.003

Staples, D. S., & Zhao, L. (2006). The Effects of Cultural Diversity in Virtual Teams Versus Face-to-Face Teams. *Group Decision and Negotiation*, *15*(4), 389–406. doi:10.1007/s10726-006-9042-x

Tong, Y., Yang, X., & Teo, H. H. (2013). Spontaneous virtual teams: Improving organizational performance through information and communication technology. *Business Horizons*, *56*(3), 361–375. doi:10.1016/j.bushor.2013.01.003

Wentling, R. M., & Palma-Rivas, N. (1998). Current status and future trends of diversity initiatives in the workplace: Diversity experts perspective. *Human Resource Development Quarterly*, *9*(3), 235–253. doi:10.1002/hrdq.3920090304

Williams, K. Y., & O'Reilly, C. A. (1998). Demography And Diversity In Organizations: A Review Of 40 Years Of Research. *Research in Organizational Behavior*, *20*, 77–140.

Workman, M. (2007). The proximal virtual team continuum: A study of performance. *Journal of the American Society for Information Science and Technology*, *58*(6), 794–801. doi:10.1002/asi.20545

Workman, M., Kahnweiler, W., & Bommer, W. (2003). The effects of cognitive style and media richness on commitment to telework and virtual teams. *Journal of Vocational Behavior*, *63*(2), 199–219. doi:10.1016/S0001-8791(03)00041-1

Yilmaz, G., & Peña, J. (2014). The Influence of Social Categories and Interpersonal Behaviors on Future Intentions and Attitudes to Form Subgroups in Virtual Teams. *Communication Research*, *41*(3), 333–352. doi:10.1177/0093650212443696

Yin, R. K. (2008). *Case study research: Design and methods*. Thousand Oaks, CA: Sage Publications, Inc.

Zornoza, A., Ripoll, P., & Peiró, J. M. (2002). Conflict management in groups that work in two different communication contexts: Face-to-Face and Computer-Mediated Communication. *Small Group Research*, *33*(5), 481–508. doi:10.1177/104649602237167

KEY TERMS AND DEFINITIONS

Computer-Mediated Communication (CMC): Communication (usually between organizational members) which is accomplished via technology due to the members being in different locations (geographically dispersed).

Face-to-Face (F2F): The richest form of communication, when individuals are physically collocated and their interactions are not mediated by technology.

Heterogeneity: Diversity/variety in terms of culture, nationality, educational background, work experience, etc. Also, something that comes in different shapes and sizes.

Human Resources (HR): The personnel of an organization/firm.

Industrial-Organizational (I-O) Psychology: A field of study that draws on psychology to study human behavior in organizations.

Information and Communication Technology (ICT): A term used to describe several types of technologies used for information and communication purposes.

Information Systems (IS): A field of study focused on the management of information and associated technologies in organizations and in society at large.

Virtual Teams (VTs): Teams whose members are dispersed (not necessarily global) and who communicate via technology to accomplish an organizational task.

APPENDIX

Interview Guide

Section 1: Questions Relative to Participants' Background

- Could you tell me a little about yourself?
- Why did you decide to work in this profession? What do you do?
- What do you like and dislike the most about your current working environment? Why?

Section 2: Questions Relative to Diversity

- What is diversity to you?
- What is your view on diversity in the workplace?
- How do you think cultural diversity affects performance?
- Tell me about a time when there was a conflict/misunderstanding between you and some of your workmates.
- What do you think is the role of stereotypes?
- Tell me about a time when you think that diversity helped you achieve a better outcome? (e.g. seeing 'the bigger picture', creating better ideas).
- Do you think language differences set limits and boundaries for some activities in the workplace?
- Are there any members of staff you feel a strong connection with? Is it based on your personal values/ethnicity/age/language spoken?
- Do you tend to be more motivated and get more work done when you're working with people you feel connection with or do you get less work done because they're being too distractive?
- Tell me about a time when you disliked someone or just didn't get along with that person. What was the reason?

Section 3: Questions Relative to the Virtual Environment

- What experience do you have of working in a virtual environment?
- What means of communication do you use? How frequent do you use them?
- What are the challenges you face?
- Do you think working in a virtual environment minimizes the chances of interpersonal interaction with other staff members?
- Why did you decide to work in the virtual environment instead of collocated? What makes it different?
- What kinds of experiences have you had in relating with people whose backgrounds are different than yours (educational/cultural background)?
- Would you like to work from home on a regular basis? Do you think working from home affects performance?
- Do you have any examples of stories to share about diversity in your virtual collaborations?
- Is there anything else you would like to add?

Chapter 14
Diversity in the Workplace:
How to Achieve Gender Diversity in the Workplace

Carola Hieker
Richmond, The American University in London, UK

Maia Rushby
Diversity-in-Leadership, UK

ABSTRACT

The 'diversity in the workforce' chapter looks at the current status of gender diversity in the workplace and describes initiatives that are commonly designed and implemented by organizations for their female workforce and their senior leaders in pursuit of gender parity. It is emphasized that one or two interventions in isolation will not guarantee gender parity but that a combination of interventions is necessary, depending on the size and complexity of the organization. Furthermore, it is underlined that if these interventions are perceived as attractive by senior leaders then the senior leaders should be encouraged to invest time and resources in pursuing them. It will raise their commitment to become diversity champions, which is key for sustainable change. Examples from finance and professional service firms illustrate how some of the described interventions are used to enhance diversity.

INTRODUCTION: GENDER DIVERSITY IN THE WORKPLACE

There is much extant literature regarding the struggle to achieve gender diversity in the workplace such as publications, websites, blogs, and organizations all with a point of view and ideas on why current initiatives on gender diversity are difficult to achieve (Dobbin & Kalev, 2016) and what could be done to make a change (Hewlett, Marshall, & Sherbin, 2011). However, this chapter aims to give a structured overview of commonly used interventions in business with a specific look at gender diversity in leadership roles. A critical overview is offered of current literature as well as analysis on trends based on formal and informal interviews with HR professionals and senior leaders (both male and female) in private organizations.

DOI: 10.4018/978-1-5225-2568-4.ch014

Diversity in the Workplace

Current Status of Gender Diversity

In 2014, the World Economic Forum predicted it would be 80 years before gender parity could be achieved, according to economic, educational, health-based and political indicators. However, in 2015 the forecast increased to 117 years (World Economic Forum Global Gender Gap Report, 2015). From the same report, it can be seen that no countries are at gender parity in their workforce (see Figure 1).

Further reviewing the workforce detail in America (Figure 2), a total of 57% of women participate in the labor force compared with 69.2% of men. And of this working population, twice the percentage of women are working part time (26% of women versus 13% of men), which means the majority of the full-time workforce is male and the majority of the part-time population is female. (US Department for Labor, 2014).

A closer look at seniority in the workplace regarding the average representation of women in Financial Services in 20 global markets shows that 60% of total employees are women; however, only 25% of middle managers are women reducing to only 19% of senior level leaders who are women (PwC, 2013). The situation is similar in S&P 500 companies where 45% of the labor force are women of which 37% of middle managers are female and 19% of the board seats are held by women (only 4% of CEOs of S&P 500 companies are women) (Catalyst, 2015).

One of the key messages from these statistics is that diversity (more specifically gender diversity) in the workplace has been measured for years, and while small incremental improvements have occurred in some areas, organizations still struggle to see significant shifts in female representation in the workplace, especially at the most senior levels. With the demand to improve gender diversity across most global organizations, many different terms are used. The term 'gender intelligence' (Gray & Annis, 2013) is a more recent term used in organizations to understand the different approach of men and women to decision-making, problem solving, and communication. However, because the main focus lies on the differences between men and women, there is the risk that it can foster potentially existing stereotypes.

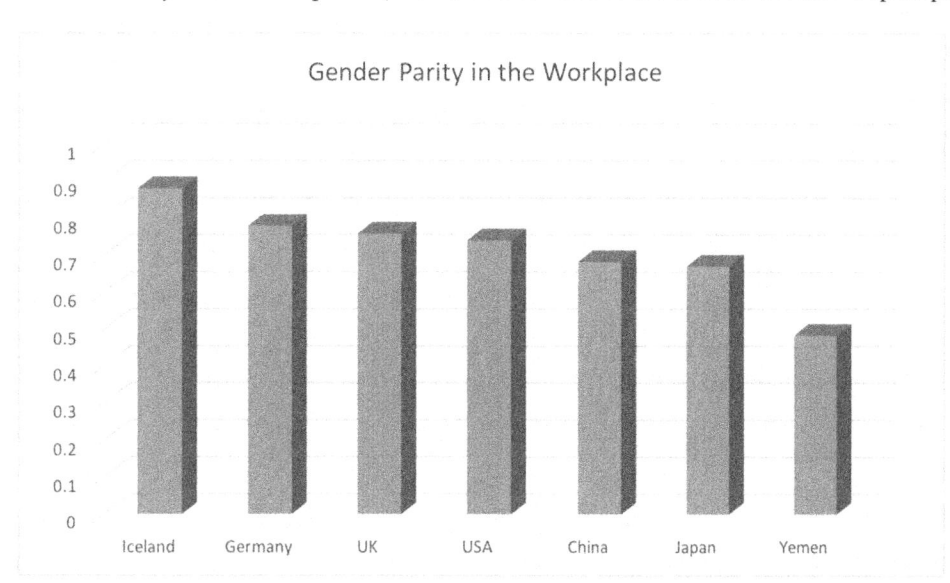

Figure 1. Gender Parity in the Workplace (World Economic Forum Global Gender Gap Report, 2015)

Figure 2. Percentage Participation in the US Workforce, (US Department for Labor, 2014)

[Bar chart: Percentage Participation in the US Workforce, showing Men and Women with Full Time, Part Time, and Not Working categories]

In addition, examining the long list of literature explaining gender differences published over decades, (Gray, 2004) it is questionable if the claim that an understanding of gender differences will help on the way to gender parity.

In 2014, the management consultancy McKinsey & Company introduced the term 'mind-set' into the diversity discussion and suggested that 'moving mind-sets' is important to increase gender diversity in the workplace (McKinsey, 2014). Expanding on this term, some organizations refer to *'diversity of mind-set'* as a more forward thinking and inclusive concept which focuses on the senior leaders' openness and curiosity. It also implies that a mind-set is not actually set and can change by being challenged and confronted with different assumptions and beliefs. Additionally, the term 'diversity of mind-set' is a good reminder that even though the main focus of organization is currently on the equality of gender diversity is much broader and includes such factors as race, culture, age, language, and sexual orientation.

BACKGROUND

The Benefits of Diversity

The benefits of having a diverse workforce for organizational success are widely discussed (US Chamber of Commerce Foundation 2014; Leong, 2015). It is documented that diversity improves decision making, creativity, innovation, flexibility, and as a result long term sustainability (Burrel, 2016).

Benefits of a Diverse Workforce

- Most businesses involve a diverse set of clients, customers, and/or other stakeholders and companies must remain attractive and be able to relate to them

Diversity in the Workplace

- Exceptional talent is hard to find – diverse organizations are likely to attract people from more sources and retain them for longer
- Expectations around diversity are increasing, from stakeholders, shareholders and governments
- Organizations with highly diverse boards and senior leadership teams generally outperform those with low diversity.

In terms of the financial benefit, there is evidence showing that having at least one woman on the board of a company will improve its financial performance. For example, companies have seen an average return on investment of 14% since 2005 compared to 11% for all male boards (Credit Suisse Research, 2015). And a McKinsey study in 2015 calculated that tackling gender inequality and boosting women's opportunities in the labor market could add US$12 million to annual global Gross Domestic Product (GDP) over the next decade (McKinsey Global Institute, 2015). Analyzing the wealth of statistics, many reports have been published since 2000 (e.g., see Woetzel et al., 2015; Gadhia, 2016; World Economic Forum, 2015).

However, the application or development of theoretical models to explain the benefits of diversity and what inhibits diversity is limited. One theory that explains the positive impact of diversity on organizational success is that it reduces the risk of so-called "group-think" which occurs in homogenous groups where conformity reigns. As a result, the group is at risk of overestimating its own power and morality. There is also the risk of group-think where the group follows one strong leader without critical reflection. Diversity is critical to avoid group-think by allowing for differing perspectives on ideas, offering unique insights into problems and at the same time creating opportunities for innovation (Sunstein & Hastie, 2015).

In addition, Kahneman's System 1 and System 2 thinking has been taken into consideration to explain the benefits of diversity (Burrel, 2016). System 1 thinking is rapid, intuitive, automatic, and emotional and is very powerful and predominant in homogenous groups whereas System 2 thinking is slow, calculating and deliberative. It is claimed that diversity in a workforce enhances System 2 thinking, which is an important safeguard and reduces risk (Kahneman, 2012).

The Challenges of Diversity

Research shows the important role that unconscious biases play in influencing the way that women are seen in the workplace, and how it can hinder their progress. In the famous Howard/Heidi research, the same resume was used once with the name Howard and once with the name Heidi. The feedback was that Howard would be an excellent person to have within the company as he got things done and was likeable, whereas Heidi was seen as equally qualified but was said to be more selfish and less desirable (Routson, 2009). This first research was conducted in 2005, and more than a decade later, the same results were seen in a rerun of the experiment at the Oslo School of Management. In the usually egalitarian country of Norway, the experiment showed how deeply unconscious biases are ingrained and how these biases contribute to the slow progress to achieve gender parity (Oslo School of Management, 2015).

Another psychological theory which is helpful to understand better what hinders diversity is *Social Identity Theory*. This theory suggests that members of an 'in-group' become organized into networks of social relations that are driven by the principles of similarity - attraction and social categorization (Van der Zee et al., 2004). In a research project with university students, Swan and Wyer (1997) showed that when women were a minority both genders perceived the female minority group as having lower social status. Therefore, both men and women tried to distinguish themselves apart from the female minority group. This finding did not affect men when they were in the minority. Applying these findings to organizations, social identity theory can go some way to explain why organizations struggle with their ambition for gender parity when they are 'stuck' with women in a minority. If women are a minority, they are perceived by men and women to be of lower status and lower capability. Therefore, men and even women themselves avoid to be connected with the lower status group.

In addition, Duguid (2011) describes other patterns that make it difficult to 'break through' the boundary of women being a minority. One phenomenon she observed is the concern of more senior women in organizations that a moderately-qualified female peer will reinforce negative stereotypes. She refers to this as the 'collective threat'; consequently, women might not support each other in the best way possible. The same applies for the 'competitive threat' describing the concern of women in organization that a highly qualified female peer might be more valued than themselves (Duguid, 2011). These research findings show that in addition to work-life balance and demographic challenges, there are also a variety of psychological reasons which make it difficult to achieve gender parity.

The Value of Role Models

The above psychological barriers that hinder the increase in the percentage of women in a business environment show the importance of *role models*. Role models develop and hone the ambitions of women and are typically senior female leaders who have successful careers and are happy to share their experiences of handling difficult situations in support of other women. In their research, Sealy and Singh (2009) underline the benefits of female role models and distinguish between behavioral value which focuses more on the narrative of the role model and how this can help the next generation of female leaders to learn from the role model's own experience; and symbolic value which gives rise to increased optimism, commitment to stay, reduced stereotyping, higher self-ratings and higher career satisfaction.

Both values were acknowledged by one female accountant in a consumer goods company when she stated after listening to one of the female senior leaders at a town hall event: "I had heard about her before and knew that she was a very senior member in the sales team but listening to her life story, her narrative and some personal examples on what she is proud of and where she still has to compromise was hugely inspiring. I realized how important it is to be true to myself and that if I sometimes lack the self-confidence I still have to be brave and take the risk. I also learned that my drive for perfectionism which makes it hard for me to delegate will stop me in the long run from moving on in my career". This quote shows how role models can motivate the female workforce and support them to become more resilient on the way up the corporate ladder. It also demonstrates that organizations need to give these senior female leaders a platform to share their learning to inspire the next generation.

MAIN FOCUS OF THE CHAPTER: CURRENT INTERVENTIONS AND CRITICAL REFLECTION ON THEIR EFFECTIVENESS

Interventions to Promote Diversity

As mentioned above, organizations have a high interest in achieving gender parity and as a consequence they invest in a variety of different interventions to make this happen. Often bigger organizations have

Diversity in the Workplace

dedicated diversity and inclusions teams who work closely together with senior leaders, HR and talent teams on setting and working towards their diversity targets. Historically, most of these interventions have focused on supporting and changing the minority groups to become more successful in a white male dominated workforce. However, more recently it has been recognized that sustainable change will not be achieved unless the mind-set of the senior leaders changes. Therefore, many organizations are investing in their senior leaders to encourage and support them to foster and manage diversity.

The following section describes and analyzes the main interventions that are used and accepted in organizations today. It initially examines interventions for women in the workplace, then moves on to consider interventions to change the mindset of the senior leaders. Each intervention will be discussed and the effectiveness critically reflected upon.

Interventions Used to Support Women in the Workplace

Over the last few decades, many organizations have designed programs to support and develop their female workforce to be best equipped for challenges in a male dominated working environment. In the following section there will be an overview of these interventions. To illustrate the impact these interventions have within organizations, the Dilts model of change is used (Dilts, 1996). It will be shown that most of these interventions focus on changing the behavior and competence level. This approach fits well with global initiatives such as the LeanIn campaign championed by Sheryl Sandberg (Sandberg, 2013), which proclaim the idea that if women are well trained, motivated, and brave to take a risk, gender parity will be a natural consequence.

Flexible Working

One of the most powerful interventions affecting the most numbers of people in the effort to improve diversity is the introduction of flexible working. Flexible working is a way of working that allows an employee to work more effectively by adapting the working practice to suit their personal needs as well as being acceptable to the organization, for example part time working, working from home and job-share to name but a few.

Having more flexibility to organize working life around personal schedules and those of family has proven to improve motivation and commitment, especially for working mothers. Clarke (2016) claims this is the case for female senior leaders as well; flexible working hours can keep women in top jobs. As one female director who reduced her working hours from 100% to 80% highlighted:

Of course, I often work more than 80% as our work is project-based and cannot always be scheduled according to my day off from work. However, the freedom of taking some time off and spending it with my family or just having some time for myself makes a big difference to me and I feel I am less exhausted and therefore more present when I am at work.

Looking at these quotes it is no surprise that the decision of Marissa Mayer CEO of Yahoo to ban working from home for Yahoo staff in 2013 was seen as returning to stone age (Goudreau, 2013). There might not be a direct correlation but the decision did not help Yahoo to improve its financial success over the three years since the decision was made (Levin, 2016).

Networking Platforms

As shown in the example of Maria, the ability to develop a sustainable network is a quality of a successful leader (Ibarra, 2007). Networking is not just seen as an important competence of a leader but is also critical for the success of the organization (Giovagnoli & Stover, 2004). It is common for organizations to offer a platform for groups to meet, to share information, ideas and experiences – an opportunity to network. Networking platforms are often established for diverse groups of people, who tend to be in the minority. Therefore, networking events for women are often the first intervention that companies initiate when they become more active in the Diversity and Inclusion (D&I) arena. While the events may be popular with participants, they do not appear to have contributed to improved gender diversity within organizations. However, this is not a reason to dismiss these events in general. Women often report that they appreciate the opportunity to meet female peers and exchange ideas on challenges in their daily work. In addition, listening to the narrative of senior female leaders – the above described role models – who are willing to share their life-line, with insights into how they handled the ups and downs in their career and what was most helpful for them, is seen by the female workforce as inspiring and motivating.

One observation made about the limited effectiveness of women-only networking events is that meeting and networking with other women might not make a difference to the career progression of a potential female leader. After coming back from a networking lunch with other female colleagues, Mary said: "I really enjoyed the lunch, I met some interesting women and we had an informative exchange on work related topics as well as some really nice personal conversation. Emotionally, it was good to realize that most of them have similar challenges and I will try to stay in touch with some of them. However, as we were all women with similar background this wasn't an event that helped me with my career. My biggest challenge at the moment is to be more visible with senior (usually male) leaders and to build up my stakeholder network".

Training the Female Workforce

While flexible working and networking can be categorized primarily on the Dilts change level of 'environment', the focus on training is mainly to improve the skillset and competences of female employees. Women-only training programs are a popular intervention in support of increasing the number of women in organizations, and in addition to the benefit of improving skills and capabilities, there is the more intangible goodwill aspect that is particularly appreciated by women, i.e. the organization values me because they are investing in my development.

Often the focus of these programs is to improve the women's leadership presence and to reflect on the female's individual brand. This is in response to the commonly received feedback that women experience in their annual performance appraisal that whilst being strong on content, women score lower on envisioning – the ability to 'develop a new strategic direction for an enterprise" (Ibarra & Obodaru, 2009 p. 62). Negotiation training is also a popular 'off-the-shelf' option since Linda Babcock's book in 2003 titled, *Women Don't Ask* (Babcock & Laschever, 2003) in which the authors underline that women often expect to be rewarded for working hard and achieving good outcomes but are less inclined to ask for what they want.

The discussion about the effectiveness of women-only training programs in promoting gender diversity is continuous. Experience shows that women in a women-only group are more open to show their vulnerability, share their experiences, and therefore might learn and change with more ease. However,

Diversity in the Workplace

a good program might be equally useful for men, and there is limited networking opportunity if the course is hosted for a minority group. Women quite often would benefit more from the recognition and sponsorship of men who are regularly absent from this type of training.

As Laura wrote down in one of her feedback sheets, "I really enjoyed the program and took a lot out of it. However, I don't think the topics we discussed are female specific and we all would have benefitted from a more diverse participant group which means having men in the room as well". Some female leaders get impatient with these interventions as they feel that are often just 'tick the box' activities on the diversity and inclusion agenda and have no impact on improving gender diversity.

When women appear to need more training to be in line for promotion, there is an implicit assumption that the men are more naturally talented. As Sue, a successful manager in a large hospital who had participated in many different female high potential program pointed out: "I sometimes wonder what it is exactly that I can't do, as I constantly get offered more leadership training and support but do not seem to move forward in my career as I would like to" (Diversity-in-Leadership, 2013).

Returnship® Programs

The term returnship® was first used by Goldman Sachs in 2008 in the USA (Goldman Sachs, 2016) to describe a program which focuses on professionals, usually women who are interested in restarting their career after an extended absence from the workforce. Goldman Sachs even trademarked the term returnship® and by doing this started a trend with other global banks and professional service firms. Usually a returnship® program is a paid short-term employment contract with an opportunity to make the role permanent at the end of the contract. In general, returnship programs try to attract women who left the workplace to have children and have been away for at least two years; the participants are usually highly educated, experienced workers (Fishman Cohen, 2012).

Fishman Cohen emphasizes that having an internal champion for the program as well as the identification of current employees who are good role models is key for the success of the returnship program (Fishman Cohen, 2012). Companies also offer numerous networking opportunities so the returner can 'fast track' the development of a network in a short period of time to be successful in the longer term. Most companies claim they offer more than 60% of the returners a permanent position, but there is no research to substantiate this or to suggest how long the average returner remains or moves on in their career.

Coaching to Feed the Female Pipeline

1. Maternity Coaching (Predominantly in Europe)

Statistics show that organizations often lose female talent at the point when they have children and they do not return to work after having their child. This is mainly the case in Europe where in European Union countries both parents have a legal right to take time-off (up to four months) after the birth of their child and return to their employer in the same or similar role (EUR-Lex, 2016). To reduce the number of talented female employees leaving at this point in their careers, some of the leading professional service firms and financial institutions offer 'maternity coaching' within their European operations. Maternity coaching is usually offered as a series of 1:1 coaching sessions, held before, during, and after maternity leave, or can be done in small groups, largely depending on the seniority of the female employee.

2. Coaching for High Potential Females

Research shows the percentage of female representation in organizations reduces with seniority. Even with the support of the above mentioned interventions, women still struggle to move on in their careers and reach the level of seniority they would like. To address this issue, organizations increasingly offer 1:1 coaching for female senior leaders. A suitable time for 1:1 coaching is before promotion or during a transition to a bigger role or a role with a different scope; however, being an intervention at the individual level, it is relatively high cost and usually only available for high potential women.

Potential topics for the first session are to establish trust and clarify the individual's objectives, as well as to introduce a first reflection on self-perception and consider what the coachee's desired individual 'brand' looks like. The involvement of the line manager is essential for the success of this type of coaching program and, therefore, the set-up of the second coaching session includes the line manager. The coach in this 'trio-session' assumes the role of a facilitator who explores strengths and development needs of the female coachee and invites the line manager to offer his/her perception as well as that of senior management. The opportunity to get facilitated 'live' feedback in a protected environment is usually seen as a very powerful intervention and gives the female leader helpful feedback and ideas to build into their individual action plan.

In addition to a facilitated trio session, quite often a diagnostic tool can help the coach and coachee to understand the underlying beliefs that drive behaviors and offer a different perspective and language upon which to discuss areas for development for the female coachee. As Gabi, a manager in the automotive industry with ambitions and the potential to reach the board level expressed it:

I had so many appraisals with my boss over the years but he was never really clear about what he really wanted to see from me to support my promotion case. I wished I had had this trio-session with my coach and line manager many years earlier, then I would have had more clarity around what is really expected. The way the coach continued exploring what people expect from me and listening to the answer was truly insightful.

Following the trio session, Gabi worked with her coach on her belief that senior leaders might not be interested in her opinion and then on the behavior level she became more pro-active in approaching clients. In addition, she actively developed her stakeholder network, asked for a mentor/sponsor, and involved herself in the graduate recruitment process which provided more visibility outside her department. To reflect on limiting beliefs and unconscious barriers and therefore to achieve a change on the Dilts belief level (Dilts, 1996), tools such as the 'Immunity to Change map' (Kegan & Lahey, 2009) and a variety of diagnostics were used by the coach to raise Gabi's self-awareness. Her peers and senior management noticed the changes and the year after she was promoted to Head of Manufacturing. Gabi's case shows that 1:1 coaching can contribute to improving diversity at senior levels in an organization, and it also develops and prepares female leaders to become active role models.

3. Peer Coaching

The benefits of peer coaching are well-researched, especially its use in teacher training (Hooker, 2013). In recent years, this intervention has been recognized as a valuable tool for personal development in general as well as for supporting female employees. A typical time to introduce peer coaching is after

Diversity in the Workplace

training events where female participants have already had some time together to establish trust and get to know each other. Alternatively, it is sometimes introduced for a cohort of women who are promoted in the same round or change jobs and take on significantly more responsibility at a similar time.

Peer coaching can be a valuable opportunity for participants to take 'cases' for discussion; for example, conflict with team members, situations where they feel particularly challenged, or simply an opportunity to reflect on their career progress. Peers become a trusted sounding board, offering each other different perspectives and ideas that encourage them to practice their coaching style and learn from alternative approaches. After approximately four facilitated coaching sessions, the peer group should be robust enough to continue their meetings without an external facilitator. Often these peer coaching groups come to a natural end after one to two years, but some of the group members stay close and continue supporting each other over their career.

A big advantage of peer coaching is that female employees create a network, learn from each other, and support each other, therefore making a change for themselves and their environment. When the peer coaching group moves on without a facilitator, it becomes a low-cost intervention for the organization. However, it needs to be marketed and positioned correctly as the success is highly dependent on the involvement of the peers. As Elizabeth put it:

I was quite skeptical when HR invited me to join a peer coaching group after my promotion. However, I was positively surprised. With the support of the facilitator, we became a trusted group who respected each other and were able to give insightful feedback. We worked on 'real-life' cases and I benefited from it immensely when I took forward a case involving a long-term conflict in my team. My peers and I worked on different options considering how to handle the situation and I had the opportunity to reflect on which option worked best for me without being pushed into a decision or overwhelmed with 'good advice.'

Summary of Interventions for Women

Many organizations offer a portfolio of interventions to support and encourage women to stay active in the workplace and quite often these programs also become the competitive advantage for recruitment. The competition for talent is fierce, especially in technology; Facebook CEO Mark Zuckerberg introduced four months paid leave for all new parents globally from 2016 which was immediately followed by eBay announcing that it would extend maternity leave to six months' full pay and paternity to leave to four months. These decisions were made in an environment where only 12% of private sector employees in the US receive any kind of paid family leave (US Department of Labor, 2014).

In summary, reviewing all the interventions on the Dilts Model (Figure 3), it can be seen that general initiatives such as flexible working or training mainly reach change on the lower levels of environment, behavior and competence while interventions that focus on the individual's needs, such as 1:1 coaching, can achieve a change on the belief level. However, the change on one level might trigger changes on the other levels as well. As the interventions discussed above target different levels, a combination of these complementary interventions make change more sustainable.

Interventions Used to Support Senior Leaders

While a combination of interventions to support women in the workplace is helpful to build up the skills and capabilities of the female pipeline, statistics show that they do not make a significant change

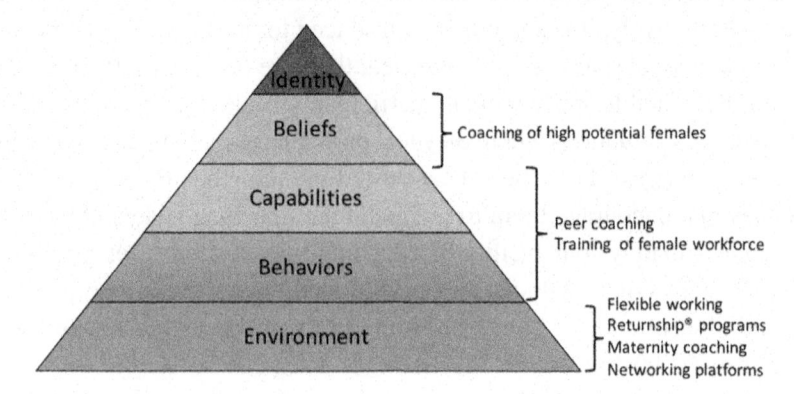

Figure 3. Dilts pyramid showing the change level impact of interventions to support women in the workplace

[Pyramid diagram with levels from top to bottom: Identity, Beliefs, Capabilities, Behaviors, Environment]

- Coaching of high potential females (Identity, Beliefs)
- Peer coaching; Training of female workforce (Capabilities, Behaviors)
- Flexible working; Returnship® programs; Maternity coaching; Networking platforms (Environment)

to the number of women employed in senior positions. The objective 'to change the women' is too one-dimensional; for sustainable change, a diversity-of-mindset of the senior leadership group must be achieved. In the following section current interventions to achieve this 'diverse mind-set' in the leadership team will be described to make senior leaders become diversity champions.

Gender Diversity and Unconscious Biases

Acknowledging that people are "terrible at evaluating people objectively" (Burrell, 2016 p. 71), everyone is subject to biases, formed and shaped from childhood through all life experiences, including exposure to patterns of behavior in the workplace. Unfortunately, many types of bias such as maternal bias or likability bias (McKinsey, 2015) contribute to the difficulty that women have in progressing equally in the workplace. Many organizations invest in programs to raise awareness of unconscious bias in the workplace which help to reduce the long term impact. An effective way to reach larger number of employees is to use actors in creative role plays that illustrate the extent to which bias is present, but as Alex, a workshop participant said after an unconscious bias workshop 'it was fun, I even recognized other people's bias and some bias that I might have as well, but I am nor sure it will change anything because we don't notice when our biases have an impact on our behavior in the day-to-day work".

Managing Diverse Teams Training

As referenced above, the potential of diverse teams to achieve better results and make sustainable change is now well documented. However, to bring diverse teams to top performance they need to be well led – the very difference that feeds creativity and high performance can also create communication barriers (Polzer, 2008). Ibarra and Hansen (2011) emphasize that a collaborative leadership style works well for diverse groups especially when innovation and creativity are critical. Acknowledging that leading diverse groups is a challenge for any leader, organizations often offer training on how to 'manage a diverse team'. Managing diverse teams training programs allow an organization to align their organizational values with their commitments to diversity and inclusion, as well as building the link between being a collaborative leader, an emotionally intelligent leader and an authentic leader (Goffee & Jones, 2015).

Diversity in the Workplace

Shadow Coaching

As Alex in the example above mentioned after his unconscious bias training – the nature of them being unconscious – or as Banahji and Greenwald (2013) state, 'blind' makes it very difficult to be aware of, track, and change these biases through training. One option is to raise awareness of the leader's personal unconscious biases through shadow coaching, a process where 1:1 observation of the senior leader is at its core.

In shadow coaching, the senior manager reflects with an external coach on potential biases which might exist. In a next step, the coach observes the senior manager in different situations; for example, interacting with peers, team members, and/or clients and gives feedback on what they have noticed. The coach should not have too much background information about the people involved, and due to their neutrality in the interactions, 'holding up the mirror' is very insightful. The coach can feedback on observed behaviors: for example, the place where the senior manager chooses to sit at the table, or how language and body language changes depending on who is in the room and/or what is the ratio of listening and talking. All this information can help to unravel the individual's blind spot(s). A useful tool to support the shadow coaching process is a variation of the Johari model which was developed by Luft and Ingham in the 1950s (Johari Window, 2016).

Using the Johari Window in Figure 4 above, blind and unconscious are both unknown to us. However, in the blind quadrant, blind spots are often visible to people around us; therefore, awareness can be achieved through peer feedback or line manager feedback, for example during the performance evaluation process. In contrast, biases in the unconscious quadrant are neither obvious to oneself nor to the people around us.

To achieve sustainable behavioral change, it is important to locate the root cause of the (often unconscious) behavior, beliefs, and biases. In support of this goal, shadow coaching programs are often accompanied by 360 Feedback given by peers, subordinates, and leaders who all interact with the manager in different situations. Hearing the perceptions of others, coupled with shadow observations, can support the senior leader to discover what motivates his/her behavior which in turn leads to a much higher degree of self-awareness. Based on the rich feedback material, the coach and senior manager can reflect on what potentially triggers the bias that influences behavior, and together they can develop an action plan to recognize the bias and change the associated behavior.

Figure 4. The Johari Window

	Known to self	Unknown to self
Known to others	*Open*	*Blind*
Unknown to others	*Hidden*	*Unconscious*

Establishing the Mentor Role

A mentor is 'someone who will advise, provide feedback on how to improve, be a role model, and teach the ropes for navigating through corporate politics to gain access to influential networks that is seen as key to getting ahead' (Catalyst, 2016). Mentors are usually more experienced although don't have to be in the same organization or have a similar background; they can offer experience of a particular industry, maybe a target company, or could merely be someone admired and respected for their achievements. A person can have more than one mentor, and with the explosion of social media, the benefits of 'virtual mentors' are being realized, each with specific experience and expertise in different areas (Iyer & Murphy, 2016). The important criteria to look for in a good mentor is someone who is willing to afford time to discuss interests and career goals, and assist as a guide to challenge one's thinking in a supportive and sometimes challenging manner.

While mentoring is encouraged within organizations, the support is often rather informal except for the initial introduction of senior leaders to their mentees. This is especially the case when mentor frameworks are established between companies. The benefit of mentoring is shown in the case of Angela, a senior director in public services who was participating in a mentorship program where high potential female leaders were linked with senior leaders of other organizations. Phil, her mentor, a managing director in a global pharmaceutical firm, over time developed into a sparring partner for Angela and his seniority and external perspective helped her in several difficult situations at work.

I trusted him from the beginning; he didn't have his own agenda so it was different than talking to my line manager, I could share my frustrations and self-doubts as well as my successes without constantly reflecting about the impact it would have on my career.

Introducing the Sponsor's Role

For many years, the term mentoring and sponsoring was used synonymously (Hieker & Rushby, 2015). However, recent literature distinguishes between these two roles (Ibarra, 2015) acknowledging the need of female employees to have a senior leader in the organization who agrees to take responsibility to support his/her protégé to progress and be promoted to a more senior position. There is more accountability involved in sponsoring than in mentoring. "Sponsorship is key to advancement whereas mentoring is good for building a network and confidence" (Gadhia, 2016). To make the protégé successful, the sponsor must be proactive as "sponsoring is a very targeted thing. It has to do with fighting to get somebody a promotion, mentioning their name in an appointments meeting, and making sure that the person that you're sponsoring gets the next assignment, and gets visible and developmental assignments" (Ibarra, 2015).

Sponsoring is increasingly seen as a pre-requisite for progression in organizations, and because men predominantly have male networks and women have mostly female or mixed networks, coupled with the fact that men are more likely to hold leadership positions, women may end up with less access to senior level sponsorship (McKinsey, 2015). In an environment where meetings may not happen naturally the matching process of sponsor and protégé is even more key, and needs to be carefully facilitated.

Diversity in the Workplace

When protégés were questioned about their expectations of a sponsor, a total of 74% of a cohort of high potential men and women responded 'provide honest feedback, specifically by suggesting ways to narrow gaps in skills and experience' and 41% said they expect their sponsor to "be willing to defend me"', (Hewlett, Marshall, & Sherbin, 2011 p. 133). Sponsoring is so critical for the career advancement of high potential women that global organizations invest large amounts of time and resources to ensure the quality and effectiveness of their programs.

1. Sponsor Programs

Recognizing the importance of a sponsor, organizations have increasingly started to implement sponsor programs to facilitate the bringing together of sponsor and protégé and ensure the sponsor relationship is valuable and productive. These programs can be effective in raising the profile of women and giving them the opportunity to interact with leaders more senior than them. However, to make a sponsor program successful, it is important the objectives are aligned with organizational values and strategy to ensure that leaders and managers believe in and invest time in the relationship; and an effective matching process must be in place to ensure that the sponsor and protégé respect and trust each other.

Another critical ingredient of a sponsor program is the involvement of the line manager. Quite often the protégé's line manager may not know the sponsor as the sponsor will be more senior in the organization; as a result, the line manager may feel vulnerable and suspicious about the special support that their team member is receiving without their knowledge. Therefore, it is important that early in the sponsor relationship, there is a trio-session with the sponsor, protégé and their line manager to be explicit about each other's expectations and responsibilities.

2. Sponsor Supervision

Because the most effective sponsors are the highest-level leaders in an organization, it is assumed that the behaviors and the competences of a good leader are internalized and therefore training is perceived as neither needed nor accepted with this target group. However, as the sponsor role is a different role to their normal line manager role, it is necessary to support the senior leader to become the best sponsor possible. The structured process of sponsor supervision helps organizations to develop best-in-class sponsors to foster a more diverse workforce.

Sponsor supervision is based on the industry accepted practice of supervising coaches and consultants. Supervision is a 'collaborative learning practice to continually build the capacity of the coach through reflective dialogue and to benefit his or her clients and the overall system' (ICF, 2016). A critical part of the sponsor supervision process is to help sponsor and protégé to create a meaningful and challenging dialogue. Initially, this is most effectively done with a facilitated trio session where the supervisor will encourage both parties to be clear on their expectations of a successful sponsoring relationship and how to make the most of the time together.

Summary of Interventions to Support Senior Leaders

Offering interventions to support senior leaders to promote diversity in the workplace is not as well established or outspoken as supporting the women. However, examining the Dilts level of change model, the interventions described above show that using a portfolio of interventions to support the senior leaders would have a more sustainable impact on all levels. Again, this diagram shows the primary level of change whilst the full impact will be greater.

SOLUTIONS AND RECOMMENDATIONS: OUTLOOK FOR GENDER DIVERSITY

As shown above, to work towards gender parity it is important to implement interventions which address both the development of the female workforce as well as the diversity mindset of the senior leaders. However, while the approach to train and support female employees is widely used, just a few organizations invest in interventions which work towards a 'diverse mind-set' for senior leaders. However, even if an organization has put these interventions in place this is not a guarantee for change. Senior leaders themselves have to visibly demonstrate and communicate their commitment.

As Dobbin states, "Once it was clear that top mangers were watching, women started to get more premier assignments" (Dobbin, 2016, p. 60). One way to 'watch' the progress of diversity is to set targets. Targets have been discussed for a long time by many in the spirit of 'what gets measured gets delivered'. As Sandra Peterson, J&J's group world-wide chairman said in an interview with the *Wall Street Journal* in 2015: "Until you actually put metrics on these things—the way you do everything else business leaders are measured against—you don't get the right outcomes," (Feintzeig, 2015).

Some organizations and government also use quotas, for example the German government passed legislation stating that all large organizations have to have a minimum of 30% female representation at board level (Smale & Miller, 2015). Other companies ensure that there is at least one female on all short lists for jobs. In the United Kingdom, the 'Women in Finance Charter' in 2016 (Harriet Baldwin & HM Treasury, 2016) recommends all financial service companies set internal targets for gender diversity and publish their progress externally on an annual basis.

FUTURE RESEARCH DIRECTION

As stated above, most research on diversity in the workplace over the last few decades has focused on gender differences and has attempted to understand why the desired change toward gender parity is not achieved. However, in recent years there has been a growing number of articles that focus on interven-

Figure 5. Dilts pyramid showing the change level impact of interventions to support senior leaders

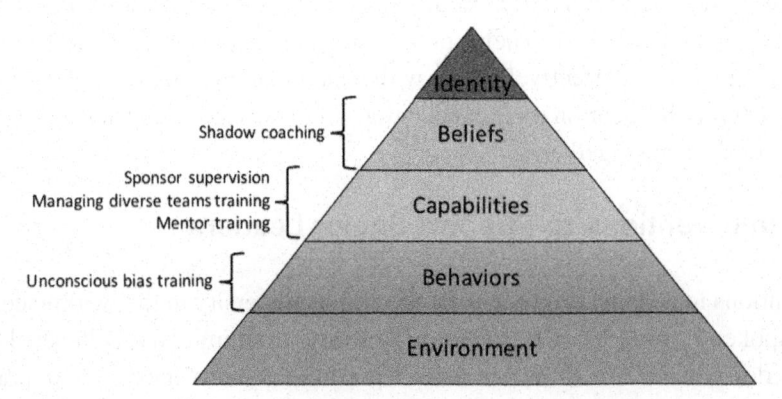

Diversity in the Workplace

Table 1. Case Study 1: When a Diverse Workforce is Not Well-Managed

When Helen received the phone call from her boss Tom in China, she was delighted to hear that he had put her forward to participate in the 'Next Generation Leader Program', an 18-month high potential program to prepare her for promotion to Senior Leader. She felt that she had finally received recognition for all the years of hard work that she had committed to the organization. Helen had been with the company for nearly 20 years, being based in the US, India, and China. Over this period, her career had progressed continuously, and now she was being given the opportunity to enter the circle of the top 200 of this global firm; what a privilege and an achievement!
After studying economics in Germany, Helen had done an internship with the company and had had a fantastic career so far. She explained it this way: "I changed jobs at least every three years and was challenged by a new environment. I lived and worked abroad, worked in sales, marketing and product development so I always felt that I was learning and growing; I always through that this was the company for me for life!".
However, at the age of 43, something else happened in Helen's life. Having been told that they could not have children, she and her husband had adopted a small baby-boy when they lived in China. The situation worked out really well because her husband was an artist who had taken on most of the childcare allowing Helen to excel in her career. Now at age 43, she was told that she was pregnant with a baby-girl!
During the following months, one major event followed another: Helen and her family relocated back to Germany, she started a new job with her new boss Mark, she attended her first leadership training on the 'Next Generation Leader Program' and she gave birth to a little baby-girl. Unfortunately, due to the timing of the birth, she missed the second module of the program, but with a good network of peers from the program and support from the talent team, she was confident to catch up when returning to work.
Helen planned to stay at home for six months to help her and her family to settle back into life in Germany. She had the discipline to manage her time – she was well-known as a role model in this area, and as her husband worked mainly from home, she felt that the logistics were well set up and there would be no need for additional support or maternity coaching.
However, while Helen felt that she had organized her home life effectively, the relationship with her new boss Mark became more and more tense. Even though Mark was very friendly and supportive when he heard that she was pregnant, he had been clear from the beginning that he would not treat her differently than her peers. This did not bother Helen at first as she had operated in a male-dominated environment for the past 20 years and had not expected anything different. Nevertheless, when Helen said she would like to take up her right to stay at home for six months, Mark said she had 'forced' him to organize a replacement during her maternity leave which would cost the department money. Unfortunately, Mark saw this as proof of his perception that Helen did not have the right attitude to work.
A few weeks after returning from maternity leave, Mark openly challenged the fact that Helen was taking part in the 'Next Generation Leader Program', and a couple of months later when they had their first appraisal session together, Helen learned that Mark had downgraded her assessment on her leadership and team skills. He said that she was perceived as too aggressive, not consensus oriented, and too tough.
Surprised as well as annoyed, Helen challenged the appraisal with the HR department, given that she had always been praised for her confident and effective leadership style in the past. She refused to sign the appraisal and argued that what might be seen as confident and present for her male colleagues was seen as aggressive and not consensus oriented for her. To support Helen through this difficult time, the HR Manager offered her some coaching to handle the difficult situation with her boss better.
Meanwhile the 'Next Generation Leader Program' had finished. A natural step in the process was that successful participants would be sponsored for promotion by their line manager, supported by the talent development team within 6-9 months. However, Mark decided to withdraw his support for Helen's promotion and HR made it clear that at this stage there were no other options for promotion.
During the coaching sessions, Helen took the opportunity to reflect on how she might sometimes be perceived, and what she could do to change this perception. However, feeling frustrated with the support that HR had given her and disappointed that nobody had questioned the assessment that her new boss had given her, Helen soon started to feel undervalued and she started to look for jobs outside the company. As a senior female leader in the automotive industry, she was quickly recognized for her global experience and achievements and received many different offers.
Helen finally left her employer of 18 years with a sense of sadness.

tions that do work (Paddison, 2013), as well as looking at the best supportive environments for diverse teams (Haas & Mortensen, 2016) and which leadership styles are most effective to foster diversity (Ibarra & Hansen, 2011).

In addition, Dobbin and Kalev (2016, p. 59) examine "which diversity efforts actually succeed" and emphasize the importance to frame interventions in a positive way. They show that when senior managers invest their own time and resources to improve diversity, they begin to think of themselves as diversity champions. This is explained with the cognitive dissonance theory (Pepitone & Festinger, 1959) as people have a strong tendency to reduce any dissonance between their beliefs and their action. If a senior manager acts as a sponsor, actively supports the female workforce and opens doors for female leaders, they will conclude that this is important for them as an individual and the organization.

Table 2. Case Study 2: The Right Intervention at the Right Time

> Anna was furious as she left the office after a conversation with her boss, Matt. She had been back from her second maternity for six months, and in that time had reconnected with her key clients and managed to win several big deals. The feedback from senior management and peers was very positive and based on her performance of the last six months she was convinced she deserved to be on the list of the Managing Director (MD) promotion candidates this year. In addition, with her fantastic track record of over-satisfied clients and of winning deals before her maternity break, her former boss Richard had said that she could trust him with the MD promotion when she returned.
>
> Now, due to the financial crisis, Richard had been made redundant and Matt was very clear that he could not stick to Richard's promises as there was only space for one MD promotion this year. The fact that Anna nearly cried when Matt told her his decision made her even more furious. She knew that he would say that she was too emotional and not ready for the promotion due to showing her emotion and her frustration. "Of course I felt under pressure. If I hadn't been pregnant I would have become MD last year, and now I have been told that no matter how hard I work I won't be promoted because of the limited size of the MD positions available. Also, I could continue to to win big deals and be the 'golden girl' but have no guarantee that I will be put forward next year either".
>
> Concurrently, the bank had become more conscious of the fact that more men than women were being promoted to MD, and started to pilot a program where their high potential promotion candidates would be supported with one-to-one coaching. Matt suggested Anna to take part in this program, and after being very cynical at the start Anna finally agreed.
>
> The coaching turned out to be a true success for Anna. She learned to step back in emotional situations, and by taking an observer role she managed to handle difficult situations better. As part of the coaching, Anna received some 360° feedback – the coach had conducted 6 half-standardized interviews with her peers and seniors. The reflection on the anonymized feedback helped Anna to understand where she could change behavior and develop clear action steps. In addition, she realized how much goodwill was around her to make her successful. She learned to see senior management more as a resource for being sparring partners and felt less 'left alone'. A final breakthrough came when the coach facilitated a dialog between her and her boss. During this session it became clear to both Matt and Anna that they had developed an unhealthy pattern of communication where he became patronizing and she became rebellious. Talking about this pattern and ways to improve their communication, they developed a level of trust that they never previously experiences, which deepened their relationship.
>
> The following year, Matt put Anna forward as an MD promotion candidate. She had raised her visibility with senior management and was seen as a key talent within. She was successful. Reflecting back on her journey Anna said: "without the coaching I would have left the organization. The coach held up the mirror in a respectful way and helped me to acknowledge my feelings and refocus when I felt self-pity or anger of having 'missed' the first opportunity for promotion. Even more important, I developed a trusting relationship with Matt, and he often picks my brain when he wants to understand a client deal better which I really appreciate."

Taking the above into consideration, a key message for organizations is: whatever you are doing, do it whole-heartedly with the maximum involvement of senior managers. As Groysberg and Connolly (2012, p. 70) highlight, diversity in the workplace needs to be approached as the senior managers/leaders 'personal mission'. Building on this concept, it is recommended that future research will focus less on the parameters of individual interventions but more on the marketing and communication of the implemented initiatives. The research questions should explore what can be done to make initiatives interesting, how to create a positive aura about being an advocate for diversity and how to encourage senior leaders to invest their own time and resources in the quest for true diversity.

Therefore, more qualitative research is needed on what leaders are doing already to make the mix work in their organizations (Groysberg & Connolly, 2013), and what they can do more of. Additionally, research should be conducted around the correlation of emotional intelligence and the concept of 'diversity of mind-set'; assuming that the emotional intelligence components of self-awareness, empathy, social skill and self-regulation (Goleman, 1998) could to be necessary preconditions for 'diversity of mind-set' research to validate this hypothesis is needed. Finally, based on the recognition that the existence of role models accelerates the desired change, research on how to create more visible role models and how to make it more attractive for women to become role models is desired.

In conclusion, gender parity will continue to be a challenge and will need to be pro-actively pursued for the foreseeable future. Each organization must review its needs and consider which interventions will work best, but at some point linking success to real recognition and reward will probably need to

Diversity in the Workplace

feature to really have an impact. Most of the references in this chapter have referred to gender diversity; however, diversity is far more multi-dimensional in scope.

It was found that while gender diverse companies were 15% more likely to outperform companies who were less gender-diverse, research showed that companies which were ethnically diverse were a staggering 35% more likely to outperform a company less ethnically diverse (McKinsey, 2015). Gender diversity is obviously easier to see and easier to measure, so it is a good place to start when trying to improve the diversity of a workforce. It seems that if an organization gets gender diversity right, then other diversity will follow – the message will be given that the environment and culture are accepting of a diverse set of people, ideas, and practices.

Voices of Experience: In Financial Services, Barclays

The Voices of Experience sections contain insights from financial service industry as well as professional service firms as these companies have a tradition of investing resources in a variety of diversity programs.

Table 3. Barclays Program Design

As a global business, Barclays recognizes that women are crucial to the world economy, so the design of their programs examine the needs and aspirations of women both internally and externally to ensure that they are supported to growth and succeed. Here are some examples of programs that Barclays invest in to support and promote women, looking specifically as programs available to all employees, men, and women: • Taking flexible working to the next level, in June 2015 Barclays launched a Dynamic Working campaign globally. With a tag line 'How do you work your life', it encourages colleagues to have an open dialogue with their line managers about what will make them more productive and engaged. It is not about a set of policies but more importantly about having a culture where colleagues feel confident about bringing their whole selves to work and working with line managers to design work patterns that help them be successful at work and outside. • There are many training and development opportunities for women, to enable them to think about their career aspirations and set their own goals promote their career development. For example, the Women@Barclays is an online portal which has tools and resources to support career development- right from understanding one's strength to articulating and acting on career development goals. The portal is helpful for managers too, providing a wealth of information to raise awareness and share resources and tips for better gender intelligence and leading diverse teams. • Making the bridge between internal and external, Barclays is a founding member of the United Nations HeForShe global campaign to engage one billion men in the advancement of women's rights. They are calling on all male colleagues to become active participants in the HeForShe campaign - questioning old norms, stereotypes and gender based roles to partnering in the workplace and at home to have a better balance for both. Mark McLane, Head of Global Diversity and Inclusion at Barclays says "For Barclays, gender balance, particularly at senior leadership levels, is the foundation of sustainable success as we all know that diverse teams have better outcomes"

Table 4. Voices of Experience: In Financial Services, UBS

Carolanne Minashi, Global Head of Diversity & Inclusion for UBS, is very clear that diversity is a business issue and needs to be managed like a business issue. She underlines that three basic tools must be established: • Having a clear vision of where you want to be, with thoughtful aspirational targets based on real data and predictive analytics which gives purpose and generates belief to achieve the objectives • Management Accountability in measuring the progress– utilizing the internal processes available that are used for other leadership objectives • Metrics – available direct the senior leaders being held accountable, real-time and frequently enough so they can amend and adapt their approach to create the maximum leverage. Carolanne emphasizes that "to attempt to 'shift the culture' without these three things in place is, in my opinion, almost impossible, but on their own are inadequate. The three foundation tools need to be combined with an execution strategy that provides a roadmap for Leaders of not just what needs to change but how it needs to change".

Table 5. Voices of Experience: In Professional Service Firms, PwC

Diversity matters at PwC because of the increasingly diverse world that has become deeply interconnected. This impacts the firm in two ways: 1) their clients expect to see diversity in their people; and 2) a lack of diversity in more senior roles brings into question the integrity, fairness and equity of their people, processes and therefore the culture of the firm.

Given the opportunity that diversity presents, PwC is acting to cultivate an inclusive culture in which difference flourishes. They have learnt that diversity has to be regarded as a business strategy and not just an (HR) initiative, and that a variety of stakeholders, tools, techniques and interventions must be mobilized and supported. Here is a flavor of some of the interventions that have helped PwC to enhance diversity across the firm:

- Tackling unconscious bias is still a priority, but has now progressed from unconscious bias training that was seen as intellectually fascinating but had limited success, towards inclusive leadership development embedded across the curriculum of their leadership training.
- Breakthrough' is the PwC flagship women's leadership program that targets talented female senior managers. The key to the success of the program is that every woman attends the program accompanied by a senior level sponsor (a significant number who are males). Both are developed, learn about gender intelligence and, for the males, they begin to see and experience the organization through a different lens
- Many of the outcomes of the programs are brought together with target setting which has undoubtedly supported the progress of women at PwC. The next step is to put these targets in the public domain, encouraged by the PwC signature to the UK HM Treasury's Charter for Women in Financial Services which aims to strengthen leadership accountability.

Sarah Churchman, Head of Talent, Inclusion and Wellbeing at PwC: "We truly believe that a working environment which allows our people to be themselves, to be different and so maximize their potential, whatever their background, is good for all - our clients, our people themselves and the wider communities in which we operate. Gender balance is a critical part of this strategy."

Table 6. Voices of Experience: In the Global Law Firm of Linklaters

In 2012, Linklaters introduced its global Women's Leadership Program for female senior associates with the aim of developing and retaining talented female associates, and ultimately ensuring there is a greater proportion of female partners to act as role models and mentors for the next generation. The program is a key part of the firm's gender diversity strategy and runs in conjunction with Cranfield School of Management.

A key element in the program design was establishing a sponsor relationship between each participant and a senior partner in the firm. Female associates are matched with senior partners who are based in different practice areas and countries. The partners do not know the associates before the sponsoring relationship, but understand the workings of the firm and so can offer valuable advice and guidance. Sponsees (Linklaters term for protégé) have highlighted the benefits of the sponsoring relationship, but the most encouraging feedback comes from the sponsors. They recognize that the involvement in the program has helped them to increase their diversity competence through exposure to and experience of the perspective of female associates. One male sponsor said he had never previously considered how challenging it could be for a woman to navigate taking time out for maternity leave and the impact this could potentially have on her career, either perceived or real.

From the outset, the Women's Leadership Program was not about 'fixing the women' and to further strengthen their commitment to diversity, Linklaters has established the firm's position on setting gender targets and having strong leadership accountability for diversity and inclusion, introducing the role of Global Diversity Partner.

"I think it's an absolutely fantastic thing and I am incredibly proud of what the firm is doing; I have enjoyed being part of it. It has been great to have the opportunity to get to know somebody I would not otherwise have had any opportunity or reason to come across." Fiona Hobbs, Partner and Global Diversity Partner.

REFERENCES

Annis, B., & Merron, K. (2014). *Gender intelligence: Breakthrough strategies for increasing diversity and improving your bottom line eBook: Barbara Annis, Keith Merron*. Harper Business.

Association, P. (2015, June 8). "Queen bee syndrome" among women at work is a myth, study finds. *The Guardian*. Retrieved from https://www.theguardian.com/world/2015/jun/07/queen-bee-syndrome-women-work-myth-research-columbia-business-school

Babcock, L., & Laschever, S. (2003). *Women don't ask: Negotiation and the gender divide*. Princeton: Princeton University Press.

Baldwin, H., & Treasury, H. M. (2015, November 4). Link bonuses to appointment of senior women, says review. *UK Government*. Retrieved from https://www.gov.uk/government/news/link-bonuses-to-appointment-of-senior-women-says-review

Baldwin, H., & Treasury, H. M. (2016, July 11). *Women in finance charter*. Retrieved from https://www.gov.uk/government/publications/women-in-finance-charter

Banaji, M., & Greenwald, A. (2013). *Blindspot: Hidden biases of good people*. New York: Delacorte Press.

Bloomberg. (2015, March 10). Germany's quota on women in the boardroom could backfire. *Bloomberg*. Retrieved from https://www.bloomberg.com/view/articles/2015-03-10/germany-s-quota-on-women-in-the-boardroom-could-backfire

Bohnet, I. (2016, April 18). How to take the bias out of interviews. *HBR.org*. Retrieved from https://hbr.org/2016/04/how-to-take-the-bias-out-of-interviews

Burrell, L. (2016). We just can't handle diversity. *Harvard Business Review, 94*(7), 70–74. PMID:27491197

Carter, N. M., & Silva, C. (2010). *Mentoring: Necessary But Insufficient for Advancement the Promise of Future Leadership: Highly Talented Employees in the Pipeline*. Retrieved from http://www.catalyst.org/system/files/Mentoring_Necessary_But_Insufficient_for_Advancement_Final_120610.pdf

Catalyst. (2016a, February 3). *Women in S&P 500 companies*. Retrieved from http://www.catalyst.org/knowledge/women-sp-500-companies

Catalyst. (2016b, June 14). *Sponsorship/Mentoring*. Retrieved from http://www.catalyst.org/knowledge/topics/sponsorshipmentoring

Clarke, C. (2016, March 15). *How flexible working hours can keep women in top jobs*. Retrieved from/ https://uk.news.yahoo.com/flexible-working-hours-keep-women-071600453.html

Credit Suisse. (2016). *Diversity programs*. Retrieved from https://www.credit-suisse.com/uk/en/careers/campus-recruiting/our-business/internship-programs-emea/diversity-programs.html

Credit Suisse Research. (2015, June 10). *Diversity on board!* Retrieved from https://www.credit-suisse.com/us/en/articles/articles/news-and-expertise/2015/06/en/diveristy-on-board.html

Dilts, R. B. (1996). *Visionary leadership skills: Creating a world to which people want to belong*. New York: Meta Publications.

Diversity-in-Leadership. (2013). *INSIGHTS*. Retrieved from http://diversity-in-leadership.com/insights/

Dobbin, F., & Kalev, A. (2016). Why diversity programs fail. *Harvard Business Review*, *94*(6), 70–76. PMID:27491197

Duguid, M. (2011). Female tokens in high-prestige work groups: Catalysts or inhibitors of group diversification? *Organizational Behavior and Human Decision Processes*, *116*(1), 104–115. doi:10.1016/j.obhdp.2011.05.009

EUR-Lex. (2016). Retrieved from http://eur-lex.europa.eu/legal-content/EN/TXT/?uri=URISERV:em0031

Feintzeig, R. (2015, September 30). More companies say targets are the key to diversity. *WSJ.com*. Retrieved from http://www.wsj.com/articles/more-companies-say-targets-are-the-key-to-diversity-1443600464

WEForum. (2016). *Global gender gap report 2015*. Retrieved from https://www.weforum.org/reports/global-gender-gap-report-2015/

Gadhia, J.-A. (2016). *Harnessing the talents of women in financial services empowering productivity*. Retrieved from http://uk.virginmoney.com/virgin/assets/pdf/Virgin-Money-Empowering-Productivity-Report.pdf

Giovagnoli, M., & Stover, D. R. (2004). How leadership networks strengthen people and organizations. *Leader to Leader*, *2004*(32), 56–62. doi:10.1002/ltl.77

Goffee, R., & Jones, G. (2015). *Why should anyone be led by you? What it takes to be an authentic leader*. Boston: Harvard Business Review Press.

Goldman Sachs. (2016). Returnship program. Retrieved from: http://www.goldmansachs.com/careers/experienced-professionals/returnship/

Goleman, D. (2004). What makes a leader? *Emotional intelligence*. Retrieved from https://hbr.org/2004/01/what-makes-a-leader

Goudreau, J. (2013, February 25). Back to the stone age? New Yahoo CEO Marissa Mayer bans working from home. *Forbes*. Retrieved from http://www.forbes.com/sites/jennagoudreau/2013/02/25/back-to-the-stone-age-new-yahoo-ceo-marissa-mayer-bans-working-from-home/#166133f563d0

GOV.UK. (2014, November 12). *Flexible working*. Retrieved from https://www.gov.uk/flexible-working/overview

Gray, J., & Annis, B. (2013). *Work with me: How gender intelligence can help you succeed at work and in life*. London: Piatkus Books.

Gray, J. A. (2004). *Men are from mars, women are from Venus*. Chicago: Turtleback Books.

Groysberg, B., & Connolly, K. (2013). Great leaders who make the mix work. *Harvard Business Review*, *91*(9), 68–76.

Groysberg, B. G., & Bell, D. (2013). Dysfunction in the boardroom. *Harvard Business Review*, *91*(9).

Haas, M., & Mortensen, M. (2016). The secrets of great teamwork. *Harvard Business Review*, *94*(6), 70–76. PMID:27491197

Hewlett, S. A., Marshall, M., & Sherbin, L. (2011). The relationship you need to get right. *Harvard Business Review*, *89*(10), 131–134.

Hieker, C., & Rushby, M. (2016, February 11). *How mentor supervision can give you the best mentors*. Retrieved from https://www.trainingjournal.com/articles/feature/how-mentor-supervision-can-give-you-best-mentors

Hooker, T. (2013). Peer coaching: A review of the literature. *Waikato Journal of Education*, *18*(2). doi:10.15663/wje.v18i2.166

Ibarra, H. (2015, March 30). *Women are Over-Mentored (but under-sponsored)*. Retrieved from https://hbr.org/2010/08/women-are-over-mentored-but-un/

Ibarra, H., & Hansen, M. (2011). Are you a collaborative leader? *Harvard Business Review*, *89*(7/8), 68–74. PMID:21800471

Ibarra, H., & Hunter, M. (2007). How leaders create and use networks. *Harvard Business Review*, *85*(1), 40–47. PMID:17286073

Ibarra, H., & Obodaru, O. (2009). Women and the vision thing. *Harvard Business Review*, *87*(1), 62–70. PMID:19227409

ICF. (2016). *Coaching supervision - individual Credentialing*. Retrieved from http://coachfederation.org/credential/landing.cfm?ItemNumber=4259&_ga=1.232862494.1633684418.1466783891

Iyer, B., & Murphy, W. (2016, April 26). *The benefits of virtual mentors*. Retrieved from https://hbr.org/2016/04/the-benefits-of-virtual-mentors

Johari Window. (2016). In *Wikipedia*. Retrieved from https://en.wikipedia.org/wiki/Johari_window

Kahneman, D. (2012). *Thinking, fast and slow*. London: Penguin Press/Classics.

Kegan, R., & Lahey, L. L. (2009). *Immunity to change: How to overcome it and unlock the potential in yourself and your organization*. Boston: Harvard Business Review Press.

Kegan, R., & Laskow Lahey, L. (2001). The Real Reason People Won't Change. *Harvard Business Review*, *79*(10), 84–92.

LeanIn. L. 2016. (2016). *Get our tips for managers*. Retrieved from http://leanin.org/tips/managers

Leong, C. W. (2015, October 5). *Why gender diversity makes good business sense*. Retrieved from: http://www.cnbc.com/2015/10/05/why-gender-diversity-makes-good-business-sense.html

Levin, S. (2016, April 13). By the numbers: Why big-name businesses are bidding for Yahoo. *The Guardian*. Retrieved from https://www.theguardian.com/technology/2016/apr/12/yahoo-bid-marissa-mayer-daily-mail-verizon

McKinsey. (2012). *Unlocking the full potential of women at work organization*. Retrieved from http://www.mckinsey.com/business-functions/organization/our-insights/unlocking-the-full-potential-of-women-at-work

McKinsey. (2014, January). *Moving mind-sets on gender diversity: McKinsey global survey results*. Retrieved from: http://www.mckinsey.com/business-functions/organization/our-insights/moving-mind-sets-on-gender-diversity-mckinsey-global-survey-results

McKinsey. (2015, January). *Why Diversity Matters*. Retrieved from http://www.mckinsey.com/business-functions/organization/our-insights/why-diversity-matters

McKinsey, & LeanIn. (2015). *Women in the workplace 2015*. Retrieved from http://womenintheworkplace.com/ui/pdfs/Women_in_the_Workplace_2015.pdf?v=5

Murphy, W., & Ayer, B. (2016, April 26). *The benefits of virtual mentors*. Retrieved from https://hbr.org/2016/04/the-benefits-of-virtual-mentors

Oslo School of Management and Agenda. (2015, April 9). *Men who dislike female leaders* (YouTube video) Retrieved from https://www.youtube.com/watch?v=Ad1giiCO6k0

Paddison, D. (2013). Guided sponsorship: The ultimate tool for internal talent sourcing. *Leader to Leader*, *2013*(67), 13–18. doi:10.1002/ltl.20056

Pepitone, A., & Festinger, L. (1959). A theory of cognitive dissonance. *The American Journal of Psychology*, *72*(1), 153. doi:10.2307/1420234

Perlberg, H. (2012, July 31). Stocks perform better if women are on company boards. Retrieved from http://www.bloomberg.com/news/articles/2012-07-31/women-as-directors-beat-men-only-boards-in-company-stock-return

Polzer, J. T. (2008). Making diverse teams click. *Harvard Business Review*. Retrieved from https://hbr.org/2008/07/making-diverse-teams-click

PwC. (2013). *Mending the Gender Gap*. Retrieved from https://www.pwc.com/us/en/financial-services/publications/assets/pwc-advancing-women-in-financial-services.pdf

Routson, J. (2009, November 1). *Heidi Roizen: Networking is more than collecting lots of names*. Retrieved from https://www.gsb.stanford.edu/insights/heidi-roizen-networking-more-collecting-lots-names

Sandberg, S. (2013). *Lean in: Women, work, and the will to lead*. New York: Knopf Doubleday Publishing Group.

Sandberg, S. (2015). *Lean in: Women, work, and the will to lead*. London: Ebury Press.

Sealy, R. H. V., & Singh, V. (2009). The importance of role models and demographic context for senior womens work identity development. *International Journal of Management Reviews*. doi:10.1111/j.1468-2370.2009.00262.x

Smale, A., & Miller, C. C. (2015, March 11). Germany sets gender quota in boardrooms. *NY Times*. Retrieved from http://www.nytimes.com/2015/03/07/world/europe/german-law-requires-more-women-on-corporate-boards.html?_r=1

Sunstein, C. R., & Hastie, R. (2014). *Wiser: Getting beyond Groupthink to make groups smarter*. Boston: Harvard Business Review Press.

Swan, S., & Wyer, R. S. (1997). Gender stereotypes and social identity: How being in the minority affects judgments of self and others. *Personality and Social Psychology Bulletin, 23*(12), 1265–1276. doi:10.1177/01461672972312004

UK Government, Department for Business, Innovation & Skills. (2015). *Improving the gender balance on British boards.* Retrieved from https://www.gov.uk/government/uploads/system/uploads/attachment_data/file/482059/BIS-15-585-women-on-boards-davies-review-5-year-summary-october-2015.pdf

U.S. Chamber of commerce foundation. (2014, June 4). Diversity makes good business sense. Retrieved from https://www.uschamberfoundation.org/blog/post/diversity-makes-good-business-sense/31773

US Department of Labor Women's Bureau. (2014). *Women's bureau (WB) - recent facts.* Retrieved from https://www.dol.gov/wb/stats/latest_annual_data.htm#age

Van Der Zee, K., Atsma, N., & Brodbeck, F. (2004). The influence of social identity and personality on outcomes of cultural diversity in teams. *Journal of Cross-Cultural Psychology, 35*(3), 283–303. doi:10.1177/0022022104264123

Woetzel, J., Manyika, J., Dobbs, R., ... (2015, September). *How advancing women's equality can add $12 trillion to global growth.* Retrieved from http://www.mckinsey.com/global-themes/employment-and-growth/how-advancing-womens-equality-can-add-12-trillion-to-global-growth

KEY TERMS AND DEFINITIONS

Coaching: A development process where a professional coach works with a client to pursue a personal and/or professional goal.

Diversity and Inclusion: Collective name for a team within an organization who focus on enhancing diversity in the workplace and inclusion of people from different backgrounds.

Diversity of Mindset: The ability to think and see the value of diversity in different situations with the emotional intelligence to understand different points of view and take them into consideration.

Gender Diversity: The proportion of men versus women in a given group.

Gender Intelligence: The awareness of gender difference and the ability to take these into consideration in decision making.

Gender Parity: Where the number of men and women in a given group is the same.

Group Think: A phenomenon that occurs when a homogenous group reinforce each other in their thinking without critically reflecting upon their decisions. It can also occur when a strong leader sets the frame and group members follow to please.

Peer Coaching: A structured setting where an experienced coach encourages peers to coach each other guided by coaching ground rules.

Role Model: Someone who is seen as having all the right attributes and is looked up to as someone to emulate.

Social Identity Theory: The explanation of why members of an 'in-group' prefer and select others on based on the principles of similarity.

Sponsor Supervision: The practice of a professional supervisor offering the space for a sponsor to reflect on how to make most of the sponsor relationship both for the sponsor and the protégé.

Unconscious Bias: The thinking and judgments made automatically based on preformed ways of perceiving the world.

Chapter 15
The Diversity Management for Employment of the Persons With Disabilities:
Evidence of Vocational Rehabilitation in the United States and Japan

Kai Seino
Toyo University, National Institute of Vocational Rehabilitation, Japan

Tomohiro Takezawa
National Institute of Vocational Rehabilitation, Japan

Aoi Nomoto
Chiba University, Japan

Heike Boeltzig-Brown
University of Massachusetts-Boston, USA

ABSTRACT

The purpose of this chapter is to discuss the latest knowledge of effective diversity management—from businesses and academia—with regard to the employment of persons with disabilities. From a broad perspective, this knowledge is found in the field of industrial-organizational psychology. From a more narrow perspective, and based on evidence from a substantial study, the knowledge of vocational rehabilitation has relevance for persons with disabilities. Vocational rehabilitation is the practice of providing employment supports that will build win-win relationships between employers and persons with disabilities. This chapter reviews recent findings documenting the effective employment and management of persons with disabilities, and summarizes effective actions and workplace considerations for the employment of persons with disabilities.

DOI: 10.4018/978-1-5225-2568-4.ch015

INTRODUCTION

This chapter focuses on diversity management in industries and organizations in the employment of people with disabilities in the United States (USA) and Japan. Diversity in the labor market has previously focused on race or gender. However, diversity now is "any and/or every dimension of attributes one may have" (Taniguchi, 2008, p. 69), and includes disabilities (within that dimension). Employment of individuals was previously an issue that fell under the welfare domain in both the USA and Japan. However, employment of people with disabilities is now becoming an industrial and/or organizational issue. Globally, the United Nation's Convention on the Rights of Persons with Disabilities in 2006, the nationwide promotion of Employment First in the USA, the amendment of the Disabled Persons Employment Quota System and the enforcement of the Comprehensive Support for Disabled Persons Act in Japan, have facilitated protection of the rights of people with disabilities in society and emphasizes a shift from welfare to employment.

This chapter has two objectives. The first is to contribute to the development of companies and society by introducing effective management of people with disabilities in the labor market. The second is to contribute to the promotion of attaining independence, social participation, rehabilitation, and right through the employment of people with disabilities. In order to achieve both these objectives simultaneously, research from the field of vocational rehabilitation focusing on employment support for people with disabilities is required. This is because vocational rehabilitation concentrates not only employment for the sake of social contribution by an employer, but is also an accumulation of studies, utilizing many methods, with the goal of constructing a "Win-Win relationship" between an employer and a person with disabilities.

However, there has been little cooperation (interaction) between the field of vocational rehabilitation research and the field of industrial/organizational research. Therefore, reporting the findings from vocational rehabilitation research in this chapter may also contribute to the promotion of industrial/organizational research. Based on this background, in this chapter, we report findings and examples of effective practices for organizations and industries hiring individuals with disabilities, from the field of vocational rehabilitation research. This chapter's objective is to clarify effective employment management for people with disabilities in the workplace, from both the USA and Japan; therefore, we identified the following research questions and keywords:

1. What is effective employment management for people with disabilities from the field of vocational rehabilitation research?
2. What are good examples of employment management of people with disabilities conducted by companies?

Additionally, the following three keywords were common in both USA and Japanese studies:

1. Evidence from vocational rehabilitation
2. Customized employment
3. Universal design

Regarding the third keyword, "universal design," effective management with consideration of those with cognitive and physical function disabilities, is not only effective for affected individuals, but also for those who have experienced a change in their cognitive or physical abilities due to aging. Therefore, we included the keyword "universal design" to examine the possibility of a general application of employment management of people with disabilities. The content of this chapter not only contributes to increasing the understanding of people with disabilities from the point of view of company executives, human resources, managers, and government personnel, but also provides beneficial knowledge to researchers and students of industrial/organizational psychology.

BACKGROUND

Diversity is defined in the Oxford Advanced Learner's Dictionary as "a range of many people or things that are very different from each other," and "the quality or fact of including a range of many people or things" (p. 443). Although diversity has traditionally been defined as differences in gender, race, and age, the definition has since broadened. According to the United Nations High Commissioner for Refugees (UNHCR), diversity refers to "different values, attitudes, cultural perspectives, beliefs, ethnic background, nationality, sexual orientation, gender identity, ability, health, social status, skill, and other specific personal characteristics" (UNHCR, 2011), and Taniguchi (2008) defines diversity as "any and/or every dimension of attributes one may have" (p. 69).

Biodiversity, a shortened version of the word biological diversity, was created by Walter Rosen, and is defined as "constructed of genetic diversity, human-derived diversity, and ecosystem diversity" (Simon, Reece, & Dickey, p. 476), and is essential to human life. Diversity in the sense of the modern meaning was used in Regents of the University of California v. Bakke, a landmark decision made by the Supreme Court of the United States. Allan Bakke, a white man, sued the University of California after having been rejected for admission to the Davis School of Medicine twice, despite testing higher than some minority students who had been admitted via the racial quotas set by the school. The Supreme Court ruled in favor of Bakke, ruling the quota unconstitutional, and that Bakke be admitted. However, Justice Lewis Powell, Jr. argued that although the racial quota did violate the Civil Rights Act, "the goal of achieving a diverse student body is sufficiently compelling to justify consideration of race in admissions decisions under some circumstances" (Cornell University Law School, n. d.).

Furthermore, in the USA the Genetic Information Nondiscrimination Act was established in 2008, banning discrimination based on genetic information in health insurance and employment fields. Diversity now does not only include the traditional demographical information (such as sex, age, and education) but also psychographic information such as personality traits, life style, and sexual orientation. Diversity drew attention in the USA after the publication of *Workforce 2000: Work and Workers for the 21st Century,* by Johnson and Packer (1987). It estimated the demographics of the workforce in the year 2000, and proposed that the workforce would be older, and have higher participation by women and minorities, resulting in the need for a shift in the employment environment to embrace the change (Figure 1).

The term "Diversity Management" was founded by Roosevelt Thomas (Roosevelt Thomas Consulting & Training, n. d.), who defined diversity as referring to "any collective mixture characterized by differences, similarities, and related tensions and complexities" ("Definitions of Diversity," n. d.) and introduced strategic categories to conduct diversity management:

1. Managing diverse talent
2. Managing all strategic mixtures

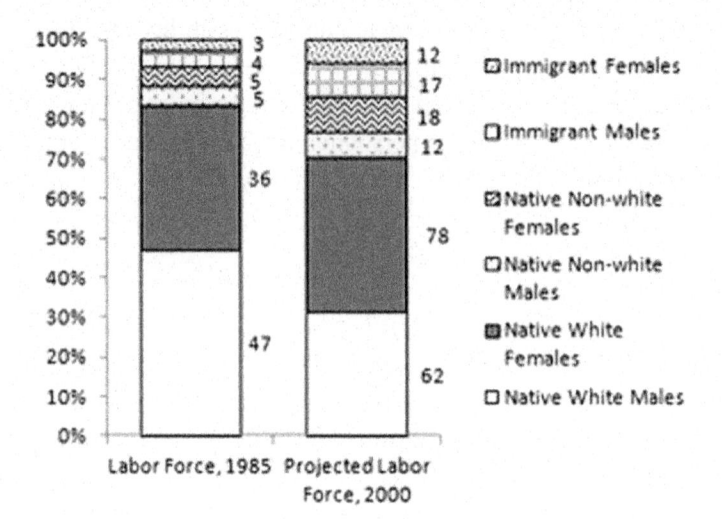

Figure 1. Estimates made in Workforce 2000

[Bar chart showing Labor Force, 1985 vs Projected Labor Force, 2000 with categories: Immigrant Females, Immigrant Males, Native Non-white Females, Native Non-white Males, Native White Females, Native White Males. 1985 values: 47, 36, 5, 5, 4, 3. 2000 values: 62, 78, 12, 18, 17, 12.]

3. Managing relationships
4. Managing representation.

Diversity management in Japan drew attention after 2000 following the establishment of the Equal Employment Opportunity Law of 1986. Diversity management in Japan has focused largely on the employment of women. The Japanese Business Federation's (*Keidanren*, formerly *Nikkeiren*) Diversity Work Rule Collegium defined diversity management as "a strategy to maximize diverse personnel, to take in diverse attributes (such as sex, age, and nationalities), values, and ideas, without being held to previous standards or norms, and meet the changes of the business environment swiftly and flexibly for company growth and personal happiness" (Japanese Ministry of Education, Culture, Science and Technology, 2012).

In recent years, diversity management has finally begun expanding to facilitate the careers of people of all ages, including persons with disabilities (Keidanren, 2016). Negative aspects related to diversity management have also been reported. Ellison and Mullin (2014) compared working environments of men only, women only, and both over a span of eight years, and reported that although diversity enabled 41% more success, individuals were less happy. However, Cox and Blake (1991) supported diversity management's superiority in six fields, specifically, marketing, creativity, problem solving quality, organizational flexibility, cost, and attracting human resources. McMahon (2010) reported that work performance may also be influenced by work environment (i.e., whether or not work the environment is stable), and not just diversity management.

It is important to note that, in some diversity management policies, disability as a dimension of diversity is forgotten. For example, Ball and colleagues (2005) reported that of the top 100 companies on *Fortune Magazine's* 2003 list of the 500 most profitable companies in the nation, a total of 10 companies did not include disability in their diversity policies, despite referencing groups protected by civil rights laws. Numerous state laws in the USA, as well as the Americans with Disabilities Act (ADA) of 1990, as amended have designated persons with disabilities to these protected groups, and therefore should be referenced. In reality, even as of 2016, in the diversity section of the Fortune 500 website, there is still only data with regard to gender and race, and persons with disabilities are not mentioned.

Furthermore, we should be aware that the collective group of persons with disabilities is different from other groups related to diversity. There is no "group norm," as they have difficulty having a sense of group membership, and disability in and of itself is very diverse (e.g., physical disability, mental disability, etc.). For example, two people with the same disability may exhibit different symptoms, and their degree of disability will most likely be different as well. Group membership is difficult, not only because disability itself is diverse, but also because some people may feel that the disability is the only element they have in common, and are therefore not members of the same group. In addition, Jones (2002) has pointed out that the desire to be part of a particular group is contingent on the group being viewed as positive. Therefore, group self-identification may be diminished, as discrimination against various disabilities still exit.

On a more fundamental note, the International Classification of Functioning, Disability, and Health (ICF) introduced a basic model of disability, the biopsychosocial model, which synthesizes the medical and social aspects of disability (ICF, 2002). In the medical aspect, the person with the disability requires treatment or intervention to better the individual. The social aspect proposes that society at large is in need of change, and demands environmental accommodation for the individual. Lederer and colleagues (2014) also identified disability in the workplace as "a relational concept resulting from the interaction of multiple dimensions that overlap and influence each other" (p. 259) at the individual, organizational, and societal levels.

Discrimination and prejudices must not be forgotten when discussing persons with disabilities. It may not be difficult to accommodate for a disability that is "visible," but many people have disabilities and/or symptoms that are not "visible" (e.g., mental disabilities). In recent years, the term "neurodiversity" has been created as a dimension of diversity to include individuals with no physical defect or impairment, but do need some accommodation and/or support (in the workplace). This includes individuals with autism and autism spectrum disorder (April 2016). Unfortunately, stereotypes of persons with disabilities not being able to work still exist. Fassinger (2008) stresses that small issues, or micro-inequities (e.g., not being promoted once), lead to bigger problems over time, becoming a cumulative disadvantage (e.g., becoming depressed after not being promoted several times) that needs to be resolved.

The use of a number of interventions, collectively called disability diversity training, is gradually increasin in an effort to reduce such prejudices and improve intergroup relations. However, there is still little empirical data validating the effectiveness of diversity training (Philips, Deiches, Morrison, Chan, & Bezyak, 2016; Horwitz & Horwitz, 2007), and perceptions that people hold prior to training may still persist. Specifically, Rynes and Rosen (1995) reported that only 33% (30% answered quite successful and 3% answered extremely successful) of participants of diversity training believed it would be successful in the long run. These issues will hopefully be addressed in the future.

EFFECTIVE EMPLOYMENT MANAGEMENT PRACTICES FOR PERSONS WITH DISABILITIES

Disability and Diversity Management in the United States

Attracting and maintaining a diverse workforce is critical in today's competitive labor market. We live in a global and interconnected world in which our workforce is becoming increasingly diverse and that poses both challenges and opportunities for employers. The idea is that having a more diverse workforce helps companies remain competitive. It also helps companies to become more reflective of the diverse communities and the customers they serve. Employers recognize and leverage diversity and inclusion in order to remain competitive and achieve better business results. This is part of building high-performing business organizations. Incorporating disability into companies' diversity and inclusion policies and practices helps employers improve their bottom line (U.S. Business Leadership Network (USBLN), 2012).

Large businesses develop a diversity and inclusion (D&I) strategy and dedicate staff positions to managing the D&I aspect of their business operations. Indeed, the area of "diversity and inclusion" is a relatively new focus for employers, and employers that have D&I personnel are challenged to create clear competencies that individuals in these positions must achieve (Lahiri, 2010). Lahiri discusses the emergence of the D&I practitioners over the last decade and that this has become an important part of companies' strategic global business growth. These practitioners are charged with creating universally designed workplaces that benefit all employees, including people with disabilities, and ultimately the employer.

There is evidence that employers are implementing disability-inclusive practices/policies but more must be done (Erickson, 2013, 2014; Linkow, Barrington, Bruyere, Figueroa, & Wright, 2013; USBLN, 2012; Young & Kan, 2015). Erickson (2013, 2014), for example, based on a survey of 675 HR professionals (23% response rate), identified a range of practices related to recruitment and hiring, accessibility and accommodations, and retention and advancement. More than half of the respondents reported that their organization included people with disabilities in their diversity and inclusion plans (58.8%), required sub-contractors to adhere to non-discrimination requirements (57.2%), and had relationships with community disability organizations (53.9%).

In terms of accessibility and accommodations, nearly three-quarters reported having a designated office or person to address accommodation questions (74.1%). Allowing employees to exceed the maximum medical leave duration as an accommodation (71.2%) and having a grievance procedure to address accommodations issues (65.7%) were the next most often reported practices. Having a return to work or disability management program for employees who are ill/injured or become disabled (76.4%), encouraging flexible work arrangements for all employees (such as flextime, part-time, telecommuting) (56.6%), and encouraging employees to confidentially disclose their disability (in staff surveys for example) (41.0%) were the top three retention and advancement practices reported by Human Resource (HR) professionals.

Erickson concluded that, beyond the most frequently reported practices/policies, a large proportion of employers had not implemented any or only a few of the practices/policies and that more needed to be done (see also Young & Kan, 2015). While the knowledge base on disability-inclusive practices/policies is increasing, little is known about their effectiveness in terms of improving employment outcomes of people with disabilities. Studies have mostly measured effectiveness in terms of perceived effectiveness by HR professionals and others knowledgeable about the practice/policy under investigation (e.g.,

Erickson, 2013, 2014; Young & Kan, 2015). Erickson, von Schrader, Bruyere, VanLooy, and Matteson (2014), for example, surveyed a total of 339 organizations about 10 disability-specific recruitment and hiring practices/policies. They found that nearly three-quarters had implemented at least one of the ten practices/policies but that there was no large-scale adoption across organizations.

Larger organizations (500+ employees), federal contractors, and non-profit organizations were significantly more likely to implement many of the listed practices/policies than their counterparts. Organizations with a history of hiring people with disabilities were significantly more likely to have each of the listed practices/policies in place compared to organizations without such histories or track records. Conversely, having these practices/policies in place increased the likelihood of organizations hiring people with disabilities. The practices/policies that had the greatest impact on the recruitment and hiring of people with disabilities included (in order): internships for people with disabilities, strong senior management commitment, explicit organizational goals regarding people with disabilities, actively recruiting people with disabilities, including people with disabilities in diversity and inclusion plans, considering people with disabilities' goals in management performance assessment, and relationships with community organizations (see also Young & Kan, 2015).

Measuring effectiveness of disability-inclusive practices/policies is challenging because of voluntary self-identification. The problem with measuring effectiveness is that self-identification is voluntary and that in the absence of disability data on job applicants and employees, employers do not know how they are doing (Young & Kan, 2015). This is particularly challenging for federal contractors. In 2013, the U.S. Department of Labor's Office of Federal Contract Compliance Program passed regulations that, effective March 2014, requires businesses that want to contract with the federal government to fill a total of 7% of their job positions with people with disabilities (U.S. Department of Labor, n. d.). Compliance with this so-called "utilization goal" depends on the self-identification of job applicants/employees and their comfort level.

Despite these challenges, research indicates that some employers are making an effort to track disability data and that they are in a better position to assess effectiveness of their practices/policies compared to their counterparts (e.g., Erickson, von Schrader, Bruyere, & VanLooy, 2014). Erickson et al. (2014), based on a survey of 675 employers about their data collection efforts, found that the majority of employers track general HR data, such as employee performance/productivity (93%), number of work-related injuries (91%) and lost work days (83%). As for disability-specific data, the top three types of data collected by employers were: information on accommodations (32%), number of job applicants hired (29%), and number of job applicants (23%).

Other data points on which employers were less likely to collect disability data included: employment and retention (18%), grievances (17%), compensation equity (14%), and turnover rate (11%). The researchers concluded that "employers are only now beginning to consider inclusion a disability measure among their recruitment, hiring, and retention HR analytics" (p. 12).

Research also indicates that strategies targeted at a particular diverse group of employees may be transferable to other diverse groups (Hall, Boeltzig, Hamner, Timmons, & Fesko, 2006; Timmons, Hall, Fesko, & Migliore, 2011; The National Center on Workforce and Disability/Adult (NCWD/Adult), 2008a, 2008b).

Timmons et al. (2011), for example, studied workplace strategies of U.S. companies seeking to recruit and retain older workers ages 50+. They found that the strategies these companies were using not only benefited older workers but also workers with disabilities. Results were based on interviews with 18 employers (their HR or diversity program representatives) in 13 U.S. states, as well as in-depth case studies of 5 of the 18 companies. Transferable recruitment strategies included: employee referral, collaboration with community partners, recruitment from a volunteer pool, formal recruitment programs among businesses, and placement agencies focused on specific populations. Transferable retention strategies included: job flexibility, comprehensive benefits packages that go beyond standard health and pension components, professional growth and development opportunities, and other workplace accommodations, such as physical modifications.

DISCUSSION

Based on this work, the researchers identified characteristics of a universally designed workplace that benefits all employees. Originally developed to promote architectural access for people with disabilities, universal design refers to the "design of products and environments to be usable by all people, to the greatest extent possible, without the need for adaptation or specialization" (Definition by Roy L. Mace, The Center for Universal Design). Timmons et al. (2011) identified a total of six characteristics of a universally designed workplace: 1) creating an inclusive organizational culture, 2) flexible workplace policies and practices, 3) effective supervision and management, 4) a welcoming and accessible environment, 5) clear and consistent communication, and 6) recruiting, hiring, orienting, and maintaining a diverse workforce that maximizes each employee's performance. There is evidence that companies both in the USA (Linkow et al., 2013) and Japan (Hirano, Matsumoto, & Nose, 2004) are incorporating a focus on universal design into their operations. Future research should investigate these employer efforts and evaluate them in terms of their effectiveness in increasing workplace access for all.

A REVIEW OF EVIDENCE OF VOCATIONAL REHABILITATION IN JAPAN

Introduction and Background

In recent years, the number of individuals with disabilities working in companies in Japan has increased due to systems that assist people with disabilities and improvement of employment support services (Conference on community employment support, 2014). However, many problems have been highlighted regarding community employment support (Conference on the promotion of employment of people with disabilities though the cooperation of welfare, education, 2007). Low competitive employment rates (i.e., employment in companies and not welfare institutions) and low employment transition rates (i.e., ratio of transition from welfare education services to employment) for people with disabilities in welfare and education institutions have been reported (Ministry of Health, Labour, and Welfare, 2014).

Therefore, in order to facilitate the employment of people with disabilities and promote diversity in companies, more effective practices regarding transition from work preparation to employment, and accommodation of a long-term support system after obtaining employment is required from healthcare, welfare, and education related fields. Such a transition to employment from healthcare, welfare, and education fields requires effort from labor field supporters, who specialize in the understanding of labor markets and companies. More specifically, labor field supporters are staff members from the National Institute of Vocational Rehabilitation, the Public Employment Security Office, and employment support institutions. However, the effect of "employment support" in such related fields has yet to be organized, except for some Individual Placement and Support (IPS) approaches in mental health fields (Haruna & Tomei, 2012).

Based on the above, this section's objective is to organize known effective approaches of the broadly interpreted "employment support" practiced in Japan, from studies and research, as evidence of vocational rehabilitation, and provide background information of employment management for individuals with disabilities to companies and government organizations.

Method

Related literature in both English and Japanese were gathered and analyzed for this literature review. Specifically, for employment support in Japan, a full-text search was conducted on 17th June 2014 using the NDL-OPAC (National Diet Library) and CiNii (National Institute of Informatics) databases. Search terms are given in Table 1. Literature searches were also conducted using the academic journal "Vocational Rehabilitation" and proceedings of the conference on vocational rehabilitation research (Japan Organization for Employment of the Elderly, Persons with Disabilities and Job Seekers). Literature search was restricted to literature published after 2006. Only quantitative studies were selected after reviewing either abstract or full manuscript.

Next, a hand search of the extracted literature and cited literature was conducted, and the approaches of employment support in each field were analyzed. In this review, we interpreted "employment support" broadly, and extracted approaches based on the hierarchy structure of individual characteristics on employment, proposed by Matsui (2004), that had an effect on employment. The hierarchy structures were "performance of duties," "performance of vocational life," "performance of daily life," and "management of disease/disorder."

Approaches of "Employment Support" in Each Field

The approaches extracted from literature were organized by the type of disability covered and by the level of evidence. Categorization of the level of evidence was based on that of the Agency for Health Care Policy and Research (AHCPR, 1993; see Table 2).

Furthermore, prospective studies with intervention were categorized as IIb, and cross-sectional studies with no intervention as III. Results are shown in Table 3. Each disability was counted, even when more than one type of disability was covered. With regards to the type of disability covered, mental disorders and higher brain dysfunction was most prevalent in the healthcare field, all disabilities and mental disorders in the welfare field, and all disabilities and intellectual disability was most prevalent

Table 1. Search terms

Field	Search Term Combination
Healthcare	(employment support or vocational rehabilitation) and (medical care or hospital or health)
Welfare	(employment support or vocational rehabilitation) and (welfare or employment transition or sustained employment)
Education	(disability or disability*) and (employment support or vocational rehabilitation or career education or career counseling) and (education or special needs)

*Although both words here are "disability," we used different characters in Japanese to expand search results.

Table 2. Levels of evidence and content

Ia	Meta-analysis
Ib	Randomized controlled trial
IIa	Well controlled study without randomization
IIb	Well-designed quasi-experimental study
III	Non-experimental descriptive studies (comparative studies, correlation studies)
IV	Expert committee opinion, and/or clinical experience of respected authorities

Table 3. Overview of approach of each field

Literature		Field			
		Healthcare	Welfare	Education	Other
Number of Literature		30	50	78	11
Number of approach		30	54	141	11
Disability	All disabilities	0	12	37	3
	Physical	3	2	12	0
	Intellectual	0	4	32	0
	Mental	16	14	0	3
	Higher brain dysfunction	9	2	0	3
	Developmental	2	6	13	1
	Intractable disease	1	1	1	0
	Co-occurring	0	0	2	0
	Unknown	1	14	30	1
	Other	-	-	17	-
Level of evidence	IIa	1	0	0	0
	IIb	2	2	0	0
	III	4	0	1	2
	IV	0	0	12	0
	Other (Practical study, etc.)	23	52	128	9

in the education field. With regards to the level of evidence, studies of levels IIa, IIb, and III were most prevalent in the healthcare field, studies of levels IIb in the welfare field, and studies of levels III and IV were most prevalent in the education field. In general, many studies of levels IV and below, such as practical studies, were reported.

Table 4 shows the overview of studies that were categorized as level a or b, with clear intervention methods and effects. In the healthcare field, various approaches were conducted alongside drug treatment. As a result, improvement was seen in more fundamental elements to facilitate employment that were related to "management of disease/disorder," such cognitive functions and symptoms. In the welfare field, a more comprehensive employment support program was implemented. As a result, approach was

Table 4. Summary of high evidence level research

Author	Participants	Study design	Intervention	Results
Sato et al (2014)	109 patients with schizophrenia spectrum disorder	Non-randomized controlled trial	Cognitive Rehabilitation: Training using computers (cognitive rehabilitation and supported employment group; 52 people, supported employment group; 57 people)	Verbal memory, psychiatric symptoms, interpersonal relationships, social functions, and cognitive functions significantly improved. However, the groups did not differ significantly in employment rate and wages earned.
Tashiro et al (2013)	12 patients with depression remission	One group pre-test, post-test	Integrated Return to work Support Program (IRSP): 30 subprograms such as Bright Light Therapy, Exercise Therapy, Cognitive Therapy, Behavioral Therapy, and Social Life Program Therapy was conducted for 6.5 hours every day.	Return to work/Employment rate was 100%, relapse/exacerbation rate was 0% 4-38 months after the program. Significant improvement was seen for depression assessment indexes (HAM-D17, BDI-II).
Tajima et al (2010)	55 people taking a leave of absence due to depression	One group pre-test, post-test	Group Cognitive Behavioral Therapy (GCBT) to return to work: Strengthen return to work readiness by learning the basis of CBT, was conducted 9 times, each time was 100 minutes a week.	Significant improvement was seen for dysphoria symptoms (BDI-II), nonfunctional cognition (DAS24-J), and self-esteem (SE).
Kitagwa et al (2011)	28 patients with depression	One group pre-test, post-test	Return to work Support Program: 12 weeks of Cognitive Rehabilitation, 12-16 weeks of Work Therapy, 12 weeks, 60 minutes a week of GCBT.	Cognitive function tests (such as WCST, TMT-A, and ALVT) significantly improved. Of 29 different patients, 21 returned to work within a year after finishing the program (72.4%), and 5 relapsed/exacerbated within a year after finishing the program (17.2%).
National Institute of Vocational Rehabilitation (2011)	90 patients with intractable diseases	Prospective study	Intractable disease model project: Coherent approach such as job preparation, employment, job adjustment sustaining employment, and career-building. Peer and/or advocate group counseling, employment seminars were also conducted.	Employment using Promotion of Employment of Persons with Disabilities Act was significantly greater. Work-related problems were significantly related to approaches.
	34 people with developmental disorders	Prospective study	Developmental disorder model project: Work support such as accompanying to work, on-the-job training, employment seminars.	General work-related problems were significantly related to various approaches.

associated with more practical elements such as "performance of duties" and "performance of work achievements" (specifically employment rates work duties).

Discussion

Regarding the method of employment support for the employment of people with disabilities, "employment support" in healthcare, welfare, and education fields was related to the expertise of each field. Furthermore, characteristics of disability covered by each field were also implicated. Concerning the level of evidence, some experimental design studies were found in healthcare and welfare fields. However, many studies were individual observations (such as practical/case studies) and were at the "building specialist consensus stage" (i.e., creating definitions). Studies examining the effect of employment support with higher levels of evidence are needed in the future.

As for the implications for employment management of people with disabilities, there were many studies (a total of four studies describing support for people with mental disorders in medical institutions) as evidence of support methods confirmed in this section. Further, the content of the support improved mental symptoms, cognitive functions, and other functions, through individual/group training and numerous other programs. All support in medical institutions was found in training or programs prior to employment/rehabilitation.

From the results of this review, support directly related to employment management of people with disabilities in organizations could not be found. However, many psychiatric diseases are chronic, and even those that are not chronic, still require some ongoing support. Therefore, medical treatment and/or support are still needed after obtaining a job in companies. Hence, organizations employing people with disorders accommodating considerations for hospital visits, and constructing a system so that organizations can ask for help or support when needed, may be considered effective for people with mental disorders to experience stable and long-term employment.

Research from the National Institute of Vocational Rehabilitation implicated ongoing efforts and counseling, from before to after employment, would improve work issues for people with intractable diseases and developmental disorders. It would seem that workers receiving ongoing and comprehensive support from employment support institutions would face fewer problems related to employment. Therefore, it would be effective for companies to actively encourage individuals with disabilities who want employment/rehabilitation to use such services of employment support institutions.

A REVIEW OF EMPLOYMENT PRACTICES FOR PERSONS WITH DEVELOPMENTAL DISABILITIES IN JAPAN

Introduction and Background

As mentioned above, "Universal Design" is an approach for diversity management. For example, creating a cognitive disability-friendly workplace can lead to a workplace that has low cognitive load for all employees. Overall, companies should strive to construct a work environment that "enables every member of the work force to perform to his or her potential" (Arimura, 2009). In this section, we focus on developmental disorder as an example of cognitive disability. By reviewing research on employment management examples in Japan, we wish to provide evidence that cognitive disability-friendly management results in diversity management.

Method

We searched for studies that focused primarily on employment management procedures for individuals with developmental disorders. To do so, we used the search terms "Developmental Disorders" and "Employment Management" using the database CiNii (http://ci.nii.ac.jp/). Four studies were identified;

however, one (Ayukawa, 2011) was excluded from analysis because the study focused on procedures of legal employment management.

Results

Aoki (2008) reported an example of employment management of an employee diagnosed with Asperger's syndrome. The management technique described can be classified into four categories: "Consideration for imagination disorder," "Consideration for cognitive load," "Construction of a support system," and "Management of motivation." It is difficult for individuals with autism spectrum disorders, including Asperger's syndrome, to deal with vagueness and an undecided future. These individuals find it difficult to resolve vagueness with imagination. To address "Consideration for imagination disorder," management carried out at least five interviews, and talked about working conditions repeatedly, to fill the gap between the actual workplace environment and what the employee with Asperger's syndrome thought.

In addition, management visualized information using pictures and documents, as well as oral explanation, when they instructed duties or suggested an improvement of duties, and avoided sudden changes or addition of duties. "Consideration for cognitive load" means controlling the quantity of information handled at one time, and attempting to lower the load of information processed in the brain. Considering cognitive load becomes important because some people with developmental disorders have difficulty processing numerous information sources at one time. Specifically, management assigned one, and only one supervisor to a person with developmental disabilities to instruct any and all duties. They also gradually increased work difficulty, starting with easy tasks, and gradually extending work hours (starting with 5–6 hours), depending on the degree of achievement.

In addition, management facilitated the acquisition of supplemental means to reduce recognition load by instructing employees with disabilities to write down work content, work points, and questions. To address "Construction of a support system," management emphasized enhancing the employee's strengths, explained the characteristics of the employee's disability to neighboring employees, and created a notebook to facilitate communication between the company and employee's home, when needed. The fourth category, "Management of motivation," was the employment management technique that Aoki regarded as most important. There are people with developmental disorders who have a strong unease for work because they did not receive appropriate support in school life, and experienced numerous failures.

Therefore, it is important for the employee him/herself to steadily acquire successful experiences in his/her career, to enhance self-esteem, while also being aware that "he/she is a valuable member of the workforce to both the company and themselves" (Aoki, 2008). Aoki introduced examples such as commending the employee for achievements, promoting awareness as part of the company by giving the employee a business card, comparing the employee's past and present achievements at regular intervals to increase the employee's confidence, and making it easy to experience success by creating aims that he/she can definitely accomplish.

Sano (2011) pointed out that people with autism spectrum disorder were not suitable for customer duties. In addition, he stated that consideration for communication was "key to continue working," because relationships are also necessary in line work found in the manufacturing industry. He insisted on consideration for cognitive load by assigning a job coach and restricting work at the beginning and gradually increasing it. People with autism spectrum disorder tend to have a limited range of interests, so it is comparatively easy to strengthen such areas, while it is difficult to strengthen areas outside of this range, because they feel distress in making such efforts. Sano, as well as Yamada (2014), pointed out that approaches that maximize his/her strengths are more effective than emphasizing the overcoming of weaker characteristics (e.g., communication).

Takezawa (2015) extracted a total of 33 instances of people with developmental disorders from a database that recorded employment examples of people with disabilities. Six categories were found for employment management: "The allotment of duties that maximize the employee's strength," "Consideration for communication," "Consideration for imagination," "Visual support," "Consideration for mental health," and "Construction of a sustainable support system for sharing information." These categories are similar to that from previous studies. "The allotment of duties that maximize the employee's strength" means assigning duties that capitalize on employee strengths.

As Sano (2011) previously pointed out, people with autism spectrum disorder have a limited range of interest. However, their knowledge on the domain of interest tends to be far richer than people without developmental disorders. Maximizing this wealth of knowledge in the workplace would be Yamada's (2014) "approach to maximize strengths." More specifically, Takezawa reports an example of an employee with developmental disorders who had "persistence to follow a certain procedure" be assigned office work, such as confirming monthly attendance records and requests. Such work that requires the employee to follow a certain procedure was performed better, more precisely, and was enjoyed more than other employees who would have found the work too monotonous and/or uninteresting.

With respect to "Consideration for communication," examples included permitting an earlier break time that did not overlap with other employees, for those that were uncomfortable with communicating with other employees. Communication for people with developmental disorders falls under the area Sano (2011) stressed as "weaker characteristics that are hard to strengthen." Rather than expect the employee to resolve issues on communication, it is fundamental to build a workplace environment that prevents such trouble from occurring in the first place. With respect to "Consideration for imagination" and "Visual support," similar considerations were reported as those that Aoki suggested in "Consideration for imagination disorder" and "Consideration for cognitive load." With regard to "Consideration for mental health," similar considerations were reported as those Aoki pointed out in "Management of motivation."

However, some individuals with developmental disorders gain high academic achievement in school life, and they are resistant towards receiving support in their work life. In that case, Takezawa suggests the need to assign duties that give a sense of accomplishment, along with subtle consideration as it becomes necessary. With respect to "Construction of a sustainable support system for sharing information," an example of cooperation with job support organizations was extracted, in addition to the cooperation with home that Aoki highlighted.

In the above-mentioned review, accommodation of nonphysical workplace environment was examined, such as how to assign duties, how to instruct duties, and building a social support network. However, consideration for employees with developmental disorders is also possible by accommodating the physical workplace environment. An example of such physical accommodation is "Job-Related Assistive Technologies." However, assistive technologies for people with developmental disorders are hardly known in Japan. Actually, in the above-mentioned CiNii database, there were no hits when we entered the search terms "Developmental Disorders" and "Job-Related Assistive Technologies."

Only one study (Enomoto, Ishiwata, & Inoue, 2013) was significant with the search terms "Developmental Disorders" and "Technologies." Enomoto et al. (2013) investigated the use of job-related assistive technologies in 503 business establishments which had received commendation on the employment of people with disabilities. Of the 29 locations that replied, none had implemented the use of job-related assistive technologies. Meanwhile, active development of job-related assistive technologies for people with developmental disorders is happening abroad. For example, Montgomey, Storey, Post, et al. (2011) reported an employee with autism spectrum disorder who had difficulties memorizing job goals, used a system that alerted job goals by sound at regular time intervals (e.g. "Did you finish wiping the table?").

As a result, the employee was less likely to be told by other staff members to work more, and ultimately, work time of the employee increased. Kandalaft et al. (2013) reported that performance of judging emotions from others' facial expressions and voice improved for people with autism spectrum disorders after social skill training, such as practicing a job interview using virtual reality. In recent years, a meta study (Lang et al., 2014) on assistive technologies for people with autism spectrum disorders has appeared. However, in the study group reviewed, research remains at the evidence level of the comparison of pre-to-post assistive technology use. In other words, in the present conditions, accumulation of evidence is not yet adequate.

Discussion

As a result of the review of management procedures for people with developmental disorders in Japan, although examples of effective employment management techniques were found, it is clear that objective inspection of effects has not yet been performed. Additionally, job-related assistive technologies have failed to attract attention as an object of study. However, despite case study-like examination, it is easy to imagine that the introduced employment management techniques may effectively function not only for people with developmental disorders, but also for people without developmental disorders.

For example, techniques of how to instruct duties to an employee with developmental disorders that are easy to recognize (e.g., "Instruct each duty after having prioritized it," "Instruct the next work after one is completed and do not convey vague plans") would also be easy for individuals without developmental disorders to recognize. Therefore, constructing an effective management procedure method for employees with cognitive disorders leads to clarifying a workplace environment where cognitive load is lessened for all employees. It is necessary to clarify the effect of management procedures for people with cognitive disorders, by conducting a high-level research design, which would lead to universally designing the workplace environment and contribute to diversity management.

BEST PRACTICES IN WORKPLACE IMPROVEMENT FOR PERSONS WITH DISABILITIES IN JAPAN

Introduction and Background

In addition to evidence provided by empirical research, case studies of actual work places describing effective management of individuals with disabilities are also informative. The proceedings of workplace improvement case studies, annually issued by the Japan Organization for Employment of the Elderly, Persons with Disabilities and Job Seekers (JEED), provides helpful, effective management strategies for use in the workplace. JEED is an organization that facilitates employment of people with disabilities as stipulated by the Promotion of Employment of Persons with Disabilities Act.

JEED is a quasi-official organization that offers free employment support services to people with disabilities, companies, and related organizations. JEED recruits successful workplace case studies of various improvement/efforts, such as employment management and workplace environment accommodation for people with disabilities, to publish, and commends the most outstanding case example, in order to promote employment and job retention. A total of 19 issues have been published from 1992 to 2015, with the best company approaches and useful tools for the employment of people with disabilities awarded the outstanding performance and encouragement awards.

Objective and Method

Based on the above background, this section's objective is to provide background information of effective employment management of people with disabilities by introducing successful case studies of workplace improvement in companies of Japan. Outlines are given of successful workplace improvement case studies from 2004 to 2015 that were awarded the highest award and are posted on the JEED website.

Results

Practice 1: Approaches for People With Disabilities That Experience More Difficulty in Employment: Individuals With Mental Disorders, Developmental Disorders, and Higher Brain Dysfunction

Here we introduce approaches of job retention for people with mental and developmental disorders, conducted by an insurance special subsidiary company (JEED, 2016). A special subsidiary company is defined as a company that has adopted a system of special considerations for people with disorders, and meets certain requirements. Workers employed in the subsidiary company can be ascribed to the parent company, and are calculated in the parent company's employment rate. Duties performed by employees in this subsidiary company were office work for the parent company, such as using computers and organizing paper work. The company's case example of improvement was as follows.

For an employee with mental disorders, the company understood his/her characteristics and made appropriate assignment transfers. His/her superior offered support, after building trust by creating a comfortable environment for him/her to seek guidance, and talking to him/her on a daily basis, enabling him/her to further his/her career. For an employee with higher brain dysfunction, work accuracy improved after understanding his/her characteristics and practicing appropriate accommodation. For an employee with developmental disorders, support from his/her superiors and senior colleagues enabled a system where he/she could perform to his/her full potential.

Efforts made in this company included all employees understanding each other's disabilities to construct support networks inside and outside the company; one-on-one advice from senior colleagues and training workshops/liaison meetings for senior colleagues; strengthening of cooperation between employment support institutions, medical institutions, and families; and strengthening systems by accumulating accommodation techniques into "human care examples" books. As a result of these approaches, 37 employees with mental disorders retained their jobs. They were able to work with confidence, were motivated to try new assignments, expanded their work, displayed a decrease in mistakes, and their time management skills improved.

Practice 2: Approaches to Issues People With Disabilities Face: Career Building and Aging

Here we introduce approaches conducted by a department store special subsidiary company that improved selling efficiency and created assignments by constructing an employment management system for people with disabilities (JEED, 2013). Duties performed by people with disorders here were light duties, such as box folding, writing expense sheets, sealing/stamping documents, printing, bookbinding, stocking shelves, and labeling. Approaches conducted here included creating in-house assignments by breaking down and reconstructing existing assignments; practicing duties anchored by employees with disabilities; maintaining training workshops for employees with disabilities; improving communication skills of employees with disabilities; and support from in-house job coaches.

Specifically, in-house personnel were appointed to be in charge of employees with disabilities, and created light assignments by breaking down and reconstructing existing assignments previously conducted by each store between distributions. As a result, the burden for each sales person was reduced and selling efficiency improved. Additionally, a work procedure was determined through discussion within teams, and skill improvement was conducted based on work in which each employee was already excelled. As a result, employee's confidence and motivation improved. On some occasions, "on-the-job training in other companies" was set up for employees with developmental disorders.

As a result, employees were able to rediscover their own issues and goals, which improved their ability to adapt during work. To improve communication, employees took initiative in explaining and instructing work, and using the cafeteria when students from special needs schools and university students came for job training. As a result, employees developed awareness and a sense of responsibility as personnel in charge of job training, as well as natural improvement of communication skills through the accumulation of these experiences. In-house job coaches also supported the independence of employees with disabilities, and helped employees adjust their own assignments themselves. This lead to an improvement in the trust of clientele, because employees were able to perform business transactions single-handedly. Employees also acquired the skills to voluntarily resolve problems on-site, without the support of job coaches.

Practice 3: Approaches for People With Hearing Disabilities

Here we introduce approaches conducted by a department store that increased work by developing job fields for people with disabilities (JEED, 2009). Duties performed by people with hearing disability were checking quality, writing expense sheets, and putting price tags on expensive merchandise, such as clocks and jewelry. Approaches included developing new job fields focused on the strengths of people with hearing disability; using support systems designed for job retention; creating a task manual to increase task efficiency; developing skills; supporting communication; and environmental accommodation and safety management using subsidies.

In further detail, all quality checks of group businesses were assigned to employees with hearing disability, focusing on their superior concentration and accuracy. By matching the strengths of people with hearing disability and task content, task efficiency of group business increased. This led to more new job contracts. Additionally, effective assessment of compatibility between the company and the person with the disability became possible by using a trial employment system before official employment.

Moreover, all people with hearing disability participated in creating a task manual, that explained all task flow photographically, and all characters had phonetics to make it easier to read.

As a result, tasks were standardized and accuracy increased. Productivity and goal management was conducted through "self-assessment tables" and "performance assessment tables." Based on the data, successful employees were rewarded, while less successful were provided guidance. As a result, employee's skills improved and the working level as a whole improved. In addition, meetings/training workshops took place every Saturday to acquire job knowledge/skill and improve working levels. Furthermore, a sign language dictionary was created for 100 technical terms that previously did not have sign phrases, and a sign language translator was dispatched using subsidies.

The company also spread awareness by having sign language courses for employees with no hearing disability. Efforts focusing on sign language improved sign language skills of employees with no hearing disability, and smooth communication became possible without a translator to mediate. Electronic panels, patlites, and flashlights were also installed using subsidies. By conducting evacuation drills using these, an environment where people with hearing disability could work safely was accommodated.

Discussion

This section introduced three successful case studies of work place improvement in companies. Although we only introduced three examples, many more efforts have been conducted by various types of businesses. In the three examples introduced, a wide range of management efforts, tailored to the company situation, task content, and characteristics and strengths of people with disabilities, were conducted. In addition, two of the examples were special subsidiary companies. A special subsidiary company is a system unique to Japan, which a parent company sets up to accommodate people with disabilities independently from the parent company.

Therefore, the majority of the employees in special subsidiary companies are people with disabilities. From the perspective of aiming toward competitive employment of the USA, employment in special subsidiary companies may be perceived as discriminatory, and this cannot be completely denied. Further examination and discussion is needed after an accurate understanding of working conditions in special subsidiary accompanies. However, as introduced in the case studies, by demonstrating the strengths of special subsidiary companies, such as accommodating people with disabilities and sensitive long-term efforts, implementation has facilitated the employment where people with disabilities were able to work safely.

Many commonalities were found with customized employment in the USA. That is, matching employee characteristics and tasks, creating assignments by breaking down and reconstructing existing assignments, and contributing to companies through productivity and task effectiveness. Although customized employment in the USA is workplace cultivation before job application, the examples in Japan introduced here can be perceived as customized employment within the company with affirmative action (i.e., an employment rate system, special subsidiary company) after employment. This difference may reflect the different culture between Japan and U.S. companies, and the different employment rate system for people with disabilities.

Efforts made in the given case studies included employees with disabilities supporting each other, improving independence and confidence, and creating a manual, with people with disabilities taking lead. These efforts could lead to peer-support and empowerment of people with disabilities, and are important efforts for the recovery and rehabilitation of people with disabilities, as well as improving employment management and productivity. In addition, support from superiors and senior colleagues, training workshops and spreading awareness to employees with no disabilities, and support from peers, were also reported. These are all efforts for standardization of natural support in supported employment.

Although there was no verification through research, and levels of evidence were low, many of the efforts of employment management of people with disabilities were confirmed and effectiveness was implicated, in the case studies introduced. Management of people with disabilities in other companies may move forward effectively by using these case studies as a reference. However, limitations include no objective verification, and caution is needed, as the case studies reported were efforts that were awarded, and made by forward-thinking, highly motivated companies, and therefore do not reflect average efforts. Conducting objective research on organizational/individual factors, and the effect of people with disabilities/organization on management is important in the future. As a result, standardization and generalization of employment management, and improvement of the quality of employment management for society as a whole, is expected.

GENERAL DISCUSSION

Clarifying what an effective diversity management for people with disabilities in the workplace was the main issue raised in this study. In order to clarify this issue, we reviewed studies/practice outcomes on employment management of people with disabilities in the USA and Japan. As a result, improvement in productivity, and characteristics of universal design for employment management in U.S. companies was confirmed. In addition, treatment, training, and support services from case studies of employment support and other related organizations in Japan were also reported. Thus, many U.S. studies reported meso-level studies focused on organizations and management, and their efforts were not restricted to people with disabilities, but seem to discuss effective employment management that may be applicable to all employees.

Conversely, many studies in Japan were micro-level studies which were focused on the person with the disability, and almost no studies had a universal perspective akin to the U.S. studies, but discussed employment management, medical care, education, and employment support services for people with disabilities. By integrating information from Japan and the U.S., meso-level and micro-level methods of support and the whole concept of organization/workplace employment management for people with disabilities that may be highly effective, was implicated. Macro-level influences, such as bills and systems of international organizations, as well as country, county, and local government bodies, should also be examined.

Limitations include the review of studies on employment management of people with disabilities in the USA and Japan from a certain perspective, and thus, do not cover all studies. Studies on employment of people with disabilities are conducted in many fields, such as various fields of psychology, welfare, labor policies, and rehabilitation, making it difficult to cover studies from all fields. Many studies in Japan were case studies and few studies had high levels of evidence. In addition, most of the studies reported in Japan focused on support organizations, and very few focused on organization and management of companies. Furthermore, in both Japan and the U.S., there seems to be no consensus yet on whether diversity including people with disabilities is effective for management. However, promoting employment of people with disabilities from a macro-level perspective, such as through social and employment policies would be important.

FUTURE RESEARCH DIRECTIONS

For further research, macro-level, micro-level, and meso-level efforts on effective employment management for people with disabilities from an organizational management perspective, and verification using experimental data is important. More specifically, international trends regarding the rights of people with disabilities, and influences of systems and policies of each country, need to be considered in macro-level studies; examination of effects of management policies/systems of company organizations are needed for meso-level studies; and factors of managers, administrators, superiors, peers, and employees with disabilities, and efforts made on-the-spot are needed for micro-level studies.

Hard and soft accommodation for people with disabilities can lead to a safe and efficient work environment for employees without disabilities. Therefore, examining the achievement attained from the employment of people with disabilities studies with the framework of universal design is possible. These universal designs are not only essential knowledge for employees, but also for managers and administrators of the modern labor market, which is inevitably becoming more diverse (gender, age, race, etc.), due to internationalization and a decrease in the labor force.

CONCLUSION

This chapter clarified effective methods of employment of people with disabilities, an attribute of diversity, by reviewing literature of the USA and Japan. As a result of the review, the following emerged as effective employment management practices. That is to say that affirmative action and reasonable accommodation, such as employment quotas and special subsidiary companies for people with disabilities, were confirmed to be effective at the macro-level; mission and systems of organizations/workplaces, soft and hard environmental accommodations, and a cooperation system between support institutions and families were confirmed to be effective at the meso-level; and natural support from superiors and peers in the workplace, and creating task manuals and tools were confirmed to be effective at the micro-level.

The following emerged as successful examples of employment management for persons with disabilities introduced in companies: (1) matching appropriate tasks (with strengths and characteristics, and creating assignments), (2) consideration for a variety of aspects (communication, imagination, mental health, cognitive load, motivation, task efficiency, independence, and developing skills), (3) accumulating knowledge for support, (4) constructing a support system (both inside and outside the workplace, and building trust so it is easy to ask for advice), and (5) well-equipped environment and safety measures.

These efforts had many commonalities with achievements of customized employment of the USA and supported employment in both the USA and Japan. In order to promote such company employment of people with disabilities, and guarantee work quality, efforts of the company alone is not enough. Governments and employment support organizations will need to support companies and contribute to practical management. Furthermore, experimental verification of employment of people with disabilities is hoped for in the future. From a philosophical standpoint, it is clear that promoting employment for people with disabilities is important for the independence and rights of people with disabilities.

However, in order for companies to employ people with disabilities, employ them long-term, and expand, it is essential for employees with disabilities to contribute to the organization/management, and for it not to be considered a social contribution or paternalistic employment. For that, realizing a society where people with disabilities can perform to their best abilities and strengths is needed. Additionally, it is essential for governments and employment support organizations to support companies and work together with them. A workplace where employees with disabilities can perform to their full potential is also a pleasant workplace for employees without disabilities. Therefore, effective universal employment management will contribute to employees succeeding, regardless of disability, and enhance the development/continuation of companies and career advancement of workers.

REFERENCES

Aoki, K. (2008). The employment management of people with developmental disorders in Advantest green Co., Ltd. *Vocational rehabilitation network, 62,* 9-13.

April, L. (2016, September 27). Neurodiversity: An untapped talent powerhouse for contingent workforce programs. Retrieved from www.zenithtalent.com/recruiting-and-staffing-blog/neurodiversity-contingent-workforce

Ayukawa, K. (2011). The employment management question and answer of the employee with mental disorders or developmental disorders: Business correspondence. *Labor Circumstances, 48,* 20–35.

Ball, P., Monaco, G., Schmeling, J., Schartz, H., & Blanck, P. (2005). Disability as a diversity in Fortune 100 companies. *Behavioral Sciences & the Law, 23*(1), 97–121. doi:10.1002/bsl.629 PMID:15706604

Cornell University Law School. (n. d.). Retrieved from https://www.law.cornell.edu/supremecourt/text/438/265

Cox, T. H. Jr, & Blake, S. B. (1991). Managing cultural diversity: Implications for organizational competitiveness. *The Academy of Management Executive, 5*(3), 45–56. doi:10.5465/AME.1991.4274465

Definitions of diversity. (n. d.). Retrieved from: http://www.rthomasconsulting.com/#/definitions-of-diversity/4539543895

Ellison, S. F., & Mullin, W. P. (2014). Diversity, social goods provision, and performance in the firm. *Journal of Economics & Management Strategy, 23*(2), 465–481. doi:10.1111/jems.12051

Enomoto, Y., Ishiwata, R., & Inoue, T. (2013). Installing Assistive Technology into the Work Place of Persons with Developmental Disorders. *Journal of Society of Plant Engineers Japan, 25,* 76–81.

Equal Employment Opportunity Commission. (n. d.). Retrieved from https://www.eeoc.gov/eeoc/

Erickson, W. (2013). *Employer practices and policies regarding the employment of persons with disabilities. Research Brief.* Ithaca, NY: Cornell University. Retrieved from http://digitalcommons.ilr.cornell.edu/cgi/viewcontent.cgi?article=1328&context=edicollect

Erickson, W. (2014). *Disability inclusive recruitment and hiring practices and policies: Who has them and what difference does it really make? Research Brief.* Ithaca, NY: Cornell University. Retrieved from http://digitalcommons.ilr.cornell.edu/cgi/viewcontent.cgi?article=1353&context=edicollect

Erickson, W. A., von Schrader, S., Bruyere, S. M., & VanLooy, S. A. (2014). The employment environment: Employer perspectives, policies, and practices regarding the employment of persons with disabilities. *Rehabilitation Counseling Bulletin, 57*(4), 195–208. doi:10.1177/0034355213509841

Erickson, W. A., von Schrader, S., Bruyere, S. M., VanLooy, S. A., & Matteson, S. (2014). Disability-inclusive employer practices and hiring of individuals with disabilities *Rehabilitation Research. Policy, and Evaluation, 28*(4), 309–328.

Fassinger, R. E. (2008). Workplace diversity and public policy. *The American Psychologist, 63*(4), 252–268. doi:10.1037/0003-066X.63.4.252 PMID:18473610

Hall, A. C., Boeltzig, H., Hamner, D., Timmons, J. C., & Fesko, S. (2006). *Analysis of Change: A Four Year Longitudinal Study of One-Stop Systems Serving Adults with Disabilities. Report submitted to the Office of Disability and Employment (ODEP)*. U.S. Department of Labor.

Hirano, T., Matsumoto, K., & Nose, K. (2004). *Universal design for workplace. Fujitsu Scientific & Technical Journal, 41*(1), 97-104. Retrieved from http://www.fujitsu.com/global/documents/about/resources/publications/fstj/archives/vol41-1/paper13.pdf

Hornby, A. S., Turnbull, J., Lea, D., Parkinson, D., Phillips, P., Francis, B., & Ashby, M. et al. (Eds.). (2010). *Oxford advanced learner's dictionary of current English* (8th ed.). Oxford: Oxford University Press.

Horwitz, S. K., & Horwitz, I. B. (2007). The effects of team diversity on team outcomes: A meta-analytic review of team demography. *Journal of Management, 33*(6), 987–1015. doi:10.1177/0149206307308587

Japan Organization for Employment of the Elderly. Persons with Disabilities and Job Seekers (2009). *Workplace improvement enthusiast casebook for hearing persons with a disability*. Retrieved from: http://www.jeed.or.jp/disability/data/handbook/ca_ls/h20_kaizen_jirei.html

Japan Organization for Employment of the Elderly, Persons with Disabilities and Job Seekers (2013). *Workplace improvement enthusiast casebook about the correspondence to the career up of the persons with disabilities and an age-related problem*. Retrieved from http://www.jeed.or.jp/disability/data/handbook/ca_ls/h24_kaizen_jirei.html

Japanese Ministry of Education, Culture, Science and Technology. (2012). Retrieved from www.mext.go.jp/b_menu/shingi/008/toushin/030301/02.htm

Johnson, W. B., & Packer, A. E. (1987). *Workforce 2000: Work and workers for the 21st century*. Indianapolis: Hudson Institute.

Jones, M. A. (2002). Deafness as culture: A psychosocial perspective. *Disability Studies Quarterly, 22*(2), 51–60. doi:10.18061/dsq.v22i2.344

Kandalaft, M. R., Didehbani, N., Krawczyk, D. C., Allen, T. T., & Chapman, S. B. (2013). Virtual reality social cognition training for young adults with high-functioning autism. *Journal of Autism and Developmental Disorders, 43*(1), 34–44. doi:10.1007/s10803-012-1544-6 PMID:22570145

Keidanren. (2016). Retrieved from https://www.keidanren.or.jp/en/

Lahiri, I. (2008). *Creating a competency model for diversity and inclusion practitioners. Research Report Number R-1420-08-RR*. New York: The Conference Board, Inc. Retrieved from https://www.conference-board.org/pdf_free/councils/TCBCP005.pdf

Lancioni and N. N. Singh (Ed.), *Assistive Technologies for People with Diverse Abilities* (pp. 157–190). New York: Springer.

Lang, R., Ramdoss, S., Raulston, T., Carnet, A., Sigafoos, J., Didden, R., & O'Reilly, M. F. et al. (2014). Assistive Technology for People with Autism Spectrum Disorders. In G. E. doi:10.1007/978-1-4899-8029-8_6

Lederer, V., Loisel, P., Rivard, M., & Champagne, F. (2014). Exploring the diversity of conceptualizations of work (dis)ability: A scoping review of published definitions. *Journal of Occupational Rehabilitation*, 24(2), 242–267. doi:10.1007/s10926-013-9459-4 PMID:23884716

Linkow, P., Barrington, L., Bruyere, S., Figueroa, I., & Wright, M. (2013). *Leveling the playing field. Attracting, engaging, and advancing people with disabilities. Research Report R-1510-12-RR*. New York: The Conference Board, Inc. Retrieved from http://digitalcommons.ilr.cornell.edu/cgi/viewcontent.cgi?article=1292&context=edicollect

McMahon, A. M. (2010). Does workplace diversity matter? A survey of empirical studies on diversity and firm performance, 2000-09. *Journal of Diversity Management*, 5(2), 37–48.

Montgomey, J., Storey, K., & Post, M. (2011). The use of auditory prompting systems for increasing independent performance of students with autism in employment training. *International Journal of Rehabilitation Research. Internationale Zeitschrift fur Rehabilitationsforschung. Revue Internationale de Recherches de Readaptation*, 34(4), 330–335. doi:10.1097/MRR.0b013e32834a8fa8 PMID:21885987

Philips, B. N., Deiches, J., Morrison, B., Chan, F., & Bezyak, J. L. (2016). Disability diversity training in the workplace: Systematic review and future directions. *Journal of Occupational Rehabilitation*, 26(3), 264–275. doi:10.1007/s10926-015-9612-3 PMID:26519035

Rynes, S., & Rosen, B. (1995). A field survey of factors affecting the adoption and perceived success of diversity training. *Personnel Psychology*, 48(2), 247–270. doi:10.1111/j.1744-6570.1995.tb01756.x

Sano, H. (2011). The employment management question and answer of the employee with mental disorders or developmental disorders: Basic knowledge. *Labor Circumstances*, 48, 6–18.

Simon, E. J., Reece, J. B., & Dickey, J. L. (2009). *Essential Campbell Seibutsugaku* [Campbell Essential Biology] (4th ed.). San Francisco: Benjamin Cummings.

Takezawa, T. (2015). The introduction of employment management: Model of employment cases based on reference service from JEED for persons with developmental disabilities. *Vocational Rehabilitation*, 29, 63–68.

Taniguchi, M. (2008). Soshiki ni okeru diversity management [Diversity in organizations] (in Japanese). *Japanese Journal of Labour Studies*, 574, 69–84.

The Center for Universal Design. (2008). About UD (webpage). Retrieved from https://www.ncsu.edu/ncsu/design/cud/about_ud/about_ud.htm

The International Classification of Functioning, Disability and Health (ICF). (2002). *Towards a common language for functioning, disability and health.* Retrieved from http://www.who.int/classifications/icf/icfbeginnersguide.pdf

The National Center on Workforce and Disability/Adult (NCWD/A). (2008a). *Recruitment and retention of older workers: Considerations for employers*. Boston: Institute for Community Inclusion, UMass Boston.

The National Center on Workforce and Disability/Adult (NCWD/A). (2008b). *Recruitment and retention of older workers: Application to people with disabilities*. Boston: Institute for Community Inclusion, UMass Boston.

Timmons, J. C., Hall, A. C., Fesko, S. L., & Migliore, A. (2011). Retaining the older workforce: Social policy considerations for the universally designed workplace. *Journal of Aging & Social Policy, 23*(2), 119–140. doi:10.1080/08959420.2011.551623 PMID:21491303

United Nations High Commissioner for Refugees (UNHCR). (2011). *UNHCR Age, gender, and diversity policy*. Retrieved from http://www.unhcr.org/protection/women/4e7757449/unhcr-age-gender-diversity-policy-working-peopl

U.S. Business Leadership Network (USBLN). (2012). *Leading practices on disability inclusion*. Alexandria, VA: U.S. BLN.

U.S. Department of Labor (U.S. DOL). (n. d.). *Fact sheet: New Regulations on Section 503 of the Rehabilitation Act of 1973.*

Yamada, M. (2014). Positioning of Employment of Persons with Disabilities in Diversity and Business Ethics: To make the Most of the Characteristics of Disabilities. Japan Society for Business Ethics Study, 21, 43-56.

Young, M. B., & Kan, M. (2015). *Do ask, Do tell: Encouraging employees with disabilities to self-identify. Research Report R-1569-14-RR*. New York: The Conference Board, Inc. Retrieved from http://askearn.org/docs/Do%20Ask%20Do%20Tell.pdf

KEY TERMS AND DEFINITIONS

Diversity: Any dimension of attributes one may have.

Employment First: A U.S. movement of employment support for persons with disabilities, where integrated employment is preferred over welfare-based employment.

Natural Support: Providing natural or planned support to persons with disabilities in the workplace.

Special Subsidiary Company: A company that has special accommodations for persons with disabilities using a system unique to Japan. The employment rate of persons with disabilities is calculated in the parent company's employment rate.

Universal Design: Design of an environment that is user-friendly to a diverse population.

Chapter 16
Employer Branding and Internet Security

Ewa Maria Matuska
Pomeranian Academy, Poland

Joanna Grubicka
Pomeranian Academy, Poland

ABSTRACT

This chapter promotes the concept of employer branding (EB) as special kind of value management being part of strategic human resources management (SHRM) and including elements of cyber security. Employees' and organization's shared values (EVPs) bring opportunity to create common sense of identity, which prevents potentially aversive behavior towards company's reputation. Chapter's background positions EB and EVP in process of SHRM, introduces the view of EB as architectural frame for core organizational values, and describes popular Internet tools of EB. The background is closed by descriptions of common Internet threats, their implications to overall organization's information security, as well as useful Internet security systems. Chapter concludes with recommendations regarding enhancing EB by better controlling company's information security. As a new research area is proposed sub-discipline of cyber security in management, with special dedication to SHRM.

INTRODUCTION

Organizations operating on a current competitive market are assessed not only through products or services, but also, increasingly, through their image as an employer – so called employer's brand (Botha et al, 2011). When public image of a company is highly rated on the market, the company is perceived as an attractive place to work and becomes the employer of choice for employees. Employer branding (EB) is an intentional human capital development strategy and important part of overall human resources management in company (Minchington, 2013). Demographic changes and deepening shortages between supply and demand on labor market causes that companies around the globe try to attract and retain talents - best employees. EB is here considered the accurate hr tool to recruit new talents and to bind most effective, creative and engaged workers. However, the question arises:

DOI: 10.4018/978-1-5225-2568-4.ch016

Is EB adequately used by different stakeholders of organizations' to achieve planned aims?

When we plan EB, first we need to define core organizational values which in a best way exemplify company's Employer's Value Proposition (EVP). EVP must be attractive for future or current coworkers both in a mental sense, as the best result of cognitive benchmarking of different job offers, as well as in an emotional sense (i.e. it is perceived as authentic, unique, positively challenging, exciting, etc.). EVP should be wide enough to attract sufficiently big scope of different individuals, but at the same time - has to be precisely described to be easily distinguished from similar proposals of competitors. And it is a really challenging task for hr departments when it is very hard to control the communication and behavior of own employees, including their activities on open social networks. Hierarchically, EB as an element of hr strategy is subordinated to overall company's HRM policy. This policy should involve basic humanistic values including truth, trust, transparency, loyalty, etc. However, any officially promoted values will not be shared in an organization if there is perceived disagreement between theory and practice. Only people can decide whether they want to internalize some work content in form of shared organizational values or not. Thus, value management (VM) should be the basis for successful EB strategy, and the same - definition of company's EVP - delivers the argumentation for her VM.

EB represents also marketing and public relation tool aimed at promoting the company as an attractive and good work place for current and future employees. Its aim is to show the company as a socially responsible business for a wide range of different stakeholders. Marketing is an intentional activity to sell something on the market – and in case of EB – to sell the job place(s). This pragmatic aspect puts EB strategy into kind of a conflict: on the one hand EB loudly says about values, and on the other hand – strives for its own benefits. This ethically "double-bind" situation locates EB activities at problematic position in a space of all hr processes. Present, future and former employees of the company carefully observe EB's promotion and collect their own opinions and conclusions about it. They can keep these opinions to themselves, or can share them with others - doing it directly (face-to face), or by using different distant communicators. Especially, the latter channel spreads information very fast and widely. Internet and social networks are today the main communication tools and EB's efficiency mainly depends on a responsible usage of Information Communication Technology (ICT) and social networks. Employer branding, so carefully developed by organizations, can be easily compromised by unconcerned or hostile Internet activity of different stakeholders (both internal and external), including current and former employees, unsatisfied customers, and competitors.

The notion of employer brand serves, in authors' opinion, as a platform to discuss main pros and cons of using the Internet in the process of implementation of employer branding strategy. Their aim is to summarize the results of the recent academic literature regarding employer brand by using cyber security perspective for analyzing the overall efficiency of employer branding in contemporary digital times. The list of possible e-threats and risks of careless (or even hostile) use of social media and Internet serves as the argumentation for including organizational internal information security policy into general EB strategy.

BACKGROUND

Scientists mostly trace the foundations of employer branding in aspects of organizational behavior (OB) such as the concept of psychological contract and customer relationship management (Beaumont & Graeme, 2003, p. 7; Dunmore, 2002, p. 195; Rosethorn, 2009, p. 4). Reviewing literature, the first impression is employer branding encompasses almost everything human resource management (HRM) in organization is expected to handle with (Edwards, 2010; Figurska & Matuska, 2013). More recent views, especially those interpreting data collected from global surveys, locate employer brand as closely related to strategic management (Minchington, 2013, pp. 2–3) and with strategic human resource management (SHRM). In a frame of the latter one we can enumerate at least three key areas of SHRM strictly connected with employer branding: talent, value and competence management. The idea of this chapter is to consider possible links between value management and employer brand with the explanation of the role of responsible using of Internet in (and through) the company. Although a number of scholars in the fields of management, marketing, and psychology have contributed to different interpretations and perspectives of EB, it is still hard to find works binding the issues of employer brand and Internet security.

Employer Brand and Employer Branding Concepts

Organizations oriented on gaining business success and striving for innovation aim to attract and retain most effective employees – "talents" (Michaels et al., 2001), and EB is the way to gain it. Employer brand, seen from the perspective of employees, simply means an employer of choice. It can be assumed that the more expressive, better employer brand the organization possesses, the more attractive place to work for employees it is. Employer brand of specific organization obviously is determined by many factors including: attractiveness of the sector, company's reputation, quality of products and service, location, work environment, pay, economic conditions, employee benefits, people and culture, work/life balance and corporate social responsibility (Kelly Services, 2013).Looking at the concept's origin, employer brand notion first was introduced in 1990s in works of Ambler and Barrow (1996, p. 187), who described it as "the package of functional, economic, and psychological benefits provided by employment, and identified with the employing company." Since that time, employer branding has mostly been referred both to human resources management and to marketing, which mutually derive from their work. In a line with above, employer branding usually is defined as "the process of building an identifiable and unique employer identity, and the employer brand as a concept of the firm that differentiates it from its competitors" (Backhaus & Tikoo, 2004).

Depending on at which stakeholders the initiatives in the field of employer branding are addressed, EB is divided into internal and external (Bigram SA.,2013a, Bigram SA.,2013b). Internal employer branding communicates to existing and leaving employees and is implemented by means of benefits and development/outplacement programs of corporate culture. Companies should keep in mind that employed workers are their first opinion leaders and ambassadors. Current and former employees largely create reputation of the company in the environment. External employer branding is addressed at future employees: professionals, graduates and other stakeholders. This kind of EB is implemented via public relation and marketing means, including: ICT channels, co-operation with opinion-leading media, image-enhancing recruitment projects, etc. Summing up, the main objective of EB is to build positive internal and public image of the organization as a good place to work, as well as to observe and adequately respond to trends emerging on the labor market. Employer brand is a planned result of the special kind of managerial intentional activity - employer branding. However, in literature both notions: employer brand and employer branding are often used interchangeably.

Most popular definitions of both notions are presented in Table 1.

Comparing diversity of definitions of employer brand existing already in literature, we can conclude that they are dominated by organizational behavior (OB) concepts explaining employees' perception, emo-

Table 1. Employer brand and Employer branding definitions. Source: elaboration on basis of literature

Employer Brand - An Employee Perspective	Employer Branding - An Organization's Perspective
"… the two-way deal between an organization and its people – the reason they choose to join and the reasons they choose – and are permitted – to stay" (Rosethorn, 2009)	"Development and communication of an organization's culture as an employer in the marketplace. It is the package of functional, economic and psychological benefits provided by employment and identified with the employing company" (Ambler & Barrow, 1996)
"… a set of attributes that make an organization distinctive and attractive to those people who will feel an affinity with it and deliver their best performance within it." (CIPD, 2006)	"A targeted long term strategy to manage awareness and perceptions of employees, potential employees and related stakeholders with regards to a particular firm" (Sullivan, 2004)
"… the image of the organization as a great place to work in the minds of current employees and key stakeholders in the external market (active and passive candidates, clients, customers and other key stakeholders)" (SHRM, 2008)	"A process of building an identifiable and unique identity of the employer" (Backhaus & Tikoo, 2004)
"A complex concept based on various intangible factors, including perception, image versus identity, and the ability to differentiate between them" (Randstad, 2013)	"The efforts of the organization in communicating internal and external stakeholders of what makes it both desirable and distinctive employer" (Jenner & Taylor, 2008, p. 7)
"A sum of the key qualities current and prospective employees identify with organization as an employer, such as: economic (compensation and benefits), functional (e.g. learning new skills) or psychological (e.g. sense of identity and status)" (Mosley, 2009, p. 4)	"Attracting talented people to the organization and ensuring that both existing and potential employees will identify with the company (its brand, mission) and deliver the desired by the company results" (Martin, 2008, p. 19)

tions, motifs, way of thinking, decisions, etc. All of it suggests that employer brand focuses on individual level of organizational participation mechanisms (point of view of particular employees). In relation to conceptualization of employer branding, we realize managerial perspective. An employer branding is perceived as one of management processes addressed at human resources - both those already employed, as well as at those potentially ready to join the organization. Thus, employer branding strategies include different group organizational participation mechanisms and are focused more on organization's perspective. The cross analysis of the definitions listed above discovers some elements in common such as: target groups, objectives of employer branding and communiqué transmitted in the process of shaping the brand of the employer. The interpretation done from organizational behavior (OB) perspective also helps to recognize mutual links between employees' perception and employer branding image (Dukerich & Carter, 2000). Employee's personal perception determines the psychological contract between a particular employee (potential or already engaged with company) and an employer, and tracks his/her employment/de-recruitment decision (Wellin 2013, p. 33). Explaining mutual relations of both notions: employer brand and employer branding, it is necessary to mention specific type of reinforcement: the more coherent the efforts of organization directed on employer branding are – the stronger (which means: more recognizable by stakeholders) employer brand is. Because of above reasons, the regular feed-back within organization (both from employer branding and from current HR processes) is simply necessary.

According to some authors, the common field for the employer brand and employer branding is the sense of identity in the organization shared by different groups of stakeholders. Identity of the organization "… refers broadly to what members perceive, feel and think about their organizations. It is assumed to be a collective, commonly shared understanding of the organization's distinctive values and characteristics" (Hatch & Schultz, 2007, p. 327). Identity can be also defined as a symbolic, collective interpretation of employees about what the organization is and what it wants to be. To be successful on the way to build common identity of employees and the organization, the following things are required:

definition, implementing and internalization of the same (or at least similar) values; the same on the side of the company and the employees.

And this is the real challenge for the employer branding strategy.

EB and Value Management: EVP

As we have assumed above, the basis for employer brand and employer branding strategy is sharing organizational (of corporation) and personal (of employees') values which promise to build the common sense of the organizational identity. The first step to prepare EB strategy for the company is to identify its specific corporate values (i.e. EVP - Employer Value Proposition). These values will help to answer the question of why the person, considering the new employment place, should not only just choose a given organization, but also convince those already employed that it is worth staying in a current job place. In other words, EVP provides a reason to believe it makes sense to work for the company. The most popular way of checking determinants of company's EB is to make regular analysis of attributes that attract and/or retain talents in the company via benchmarking to similar organizations (Hieronimus at al., 2005, p.13). This can be perceived as the process of mapping values. The key role of values in EB is indicated by for example K. Backhaus and S. Tikoo, assuming it is a three-step process (Backhous & Tikoo, 2004, pp. 502–503):

1. **Creation of an Employer Brand:** Represents a specific employee value proposition, which is to communicate what the organization has to offer to employees;
2. **External Marketing of Employer Brand:** The company directs the message to the labor market – for candidates, recruitment agencies and other target groups;
3. **Internal Marketing:** The aim is to develop human resources, which will adhere to the values and pursue the objectives set by the organization.

Also, Nigel Wright Consultancy when describing EB external strategy focuses on five key values to the potential applicant (Nigel Wright Recruitment, 2013, p. 6):

- **Interest Value:** The extent to which an individual is attracted to an employer that provides an exciting work environment, has fresh work practices, and makes use of its employees' creativity;
- **Social Value:** The extent to which an individual is attracted to an employer that provides a working environment that is fun, happy, and provides a supportive team atmosphere;
- **Economic Value:** The extent to which an individual is attracted to an employer that provides above average salary, an attractive overall compensation package, job security and promotion opportunities;
- **Development Value:** The extent to which an individual is attracted to an employer that provides recognition, self-worth, and confidence coupled with career-enhancing experiences and a base for future employability;
- **Application Value:** The extent to which the employer provides an opportunity for the employee to apply what they have learned and to develop others in a customer orientated and humanitarian environment.
- Trying to identify EB success factors we come back once again to the values. According to Menor (2010) to attract and retain most "talented" employees we have to provide:

- **Balanced Work and Personal Life:** Work-life balance is becoming more and more important for building employees' loyalty and results in higher level of their retention;
- **Competitive Compensation Package:** To make employees feel appropriately and fairly paid for the work they do, HR specialists should investigate what other organizations offer their employees in terms of salary and benefits, as well as in terms of compensation package and benefits for the particular position;
- **Treat Each Employee with Respect and as an Individual:** Each employee expects respect and recognition of the team member's contribution in the success of the organization;
- **Positive Work Environment:** The best way to build positive work environment and retain the best employees in the company is to make it as easy as possible for people to do their jobs;
- **Eradicate Favoritism:** Favoring certain employees causes dissatisfaction among team members, decreases their morale and productivity, which is reflected in the finance results of the company. Therefore equal treatment of all employees and avoiding favoritism is essential for the retention of key employees in the organization;
- **Communication and Availability:** Active listening to employees and clear communication of expectations, goals and rules to be followed, gives them honest feedback and helps to feel recognized and important;
- **Employee Empowerment:** Employees who have a sense of responsibility and ownership, and whose ideas are often recognized, feel important to the organization, work harder, complain less and are willing to stay in this company for longer;
- **Placing the Right Talent for the Right Job:** Employees should be placed in the environment that can be truly useful, making the world around them a better place for all stakeholders of their organizations;
- **Celebrate Successes and Make the Workplace Fun:** Sharing small successes with employees is a great way of making the workplace fun;
- **Workplace Flexibility:** It is hard to manage workplace flexibility (which means giving employees the option to work flexible hours) therefore flexibility policy should be well defined and implemented accordingly.

Analyzing statements made above, it can be concluded that majority of authors focuses on an external EB trying to identify values which potentially will be appreciated by jobseekers. To attract new talents through exposition of desirable (from the point of view of the candidates) values is the aim of successful recruitment. However, it is necessary to remark that personal values are passing the evolution together with assimilating new cultural trends, generation's priorities, business impacts, etc. That's why it is necessary to observe trends on external labor market and understand changes in workforce priorities. Already recruited talents will be checking their own expectations with the reality and comparing the employer with the offers of competitive companies. Employees evaluate company's organizational culture, managing style, preferred communication manners, information flow, attractiveness of wages and benefits, working conditions, career perspectives, etc. They collect their observations and share conclusions with the surrounding. Because of it, it is necessary to take care about current employees via studying their work satisfaction levels and opinions about the company. For overall efficiency of HRM processes it is recommended to measure employees personal values, to differentiate, understand them and to compare them with corporate values systematically (Kelly et al., 2005; Stahl et al., 2012).

Thus, internal EB should be more articulated in the activities of strategic HRM and the proportion of attention which is focused on external and internal EB should be at least equal.

EB in Frame of Strategic Human Resources Management

The observations collected in recent global reports (for example Employer Brand International, Minchington 2013) suggest EB has crucial strategic value for total company's success, as it attracts, recruits and binds talents - the employees with the most desired competencies, who promise innovation. Here we have to explain the notions of "competence" and "competency", which are commonly used to evaluate the chances for good (best) performance in an organization, and are indirectly connected with employer brand. Although both terms in HRM dictionaries usually have basically the same meaning, it is worth signalizing the main differences between them:

- **Competence (pl: competencies):** Is understood as employees' worthy performance, is a function of the ratio of valuable accomplishments to effective behavior (Gilbert 1996, p. 17). This term is usually used to describe individual /team level of performance;
- **Competency:** Are those human characteristics: knowledge, skills, mindsets, thought patterns, motives, values - that used singularly, or in various combinations, result in a successful performance of the whole organization (Dubois 1998, p.5). This term, also named "core competency," is the matter analyzed usually on corporate level, and determines whether company is able to reach the brand of its products/ services, as well as – an employer brand.

Employees' competence and corporate competency meet at general organization's performance as their common goal is to enhance company's market competitive position. They both are controlled by "competence management" - a central strategy of overall HRM in a company. Attracting most desired competencies within company promises success of EB strategy. But, employees' competence has to fit company's vision of organizational culture represented by incorporated values, including those exemplified in company's mission, as so called "core values". Therefore, "competence management" should be accompanied by "value management". During selection of candidates attention should be paid not only to recruiting best abilities and skills (talents), but also to choosing best motivations to take the job. And just motivation, as behavioral component of competence (observable as attitude demonstrated at work) is mostly determined by specific personal values. Positive verification of work motifs of the candidate represents the most complicated part of successful recruitment. This is also the final test for the efficiency of external EB. Recruited employee's competence should fit company's competency. Authors of the chapter consider it as an essence of the mission of employer brand. Employer branding has also reciprocal positive psychological and sociological impact on organizational culture and increases employees' satisfaction and morale.

Searching for common base of competence and employer branding, once again we conclude values contributing in organizational culture (see Figure 1).

The holistic approach to employer brand offers the concept of strategic human resources management (SHRM), or human capital management (HCM), which sees workers of organizations as potential to create value (Hesketh, 2014). According to this approach: "Human capital management in the organization is based on the optimal investing in the people and their resources gradually emerging fields where they can identify their own values, as consistent with the core strategy of the organization and its accompany-

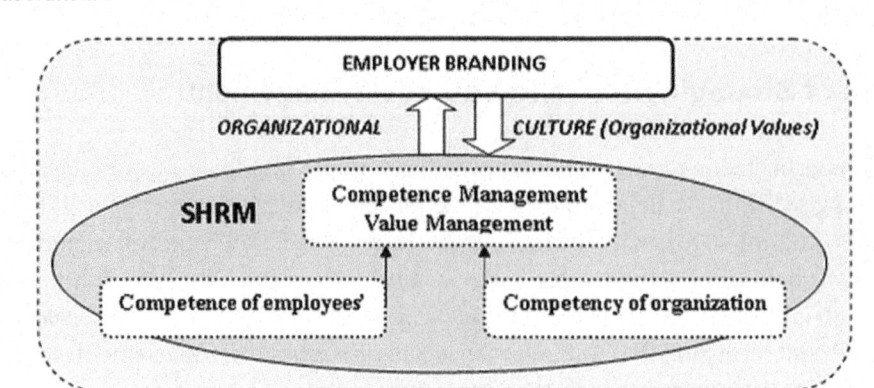

Figure 1 Employer branding based on competence management and value management
Source: own elaboration.

ing business model"(Hesketh 2014, p. 31). Employees are kind of capital, which respectively invested in the organization creates value on a similar basis as financial capital. The common task of company's services is to evaluate this impact in numbers, to describe how much money the company saves via own employer branding activities. The relationship among flow rate of employees, financial performance and the market value has been already well verified in many studies (review of Xiang et al, 2012). They prove economic sense of employer branding. Similarly, the connection of employee's satisfaction and customers' satisfaction proves that employer branding positively influences customer's service level and customer satisfaction. Via this, the economic value of the company is also secondary reinforced.

All of it changes the look at the integration of overall business strategy and human resources management strategy and explains why the latter one grows to the level of the company's key strategy. In line with such an interpretation there is also the assumption that efficiency of EB is determined by value management process which should be included into SHRM.

The concept of SHRM perceives staff as a resource of organization which have to be protected from exploitation and to be invested in their development. Popular strategies of HRM, however, are unfortunately mostly reactive, which means - they are focused mainly on monitoring changes of staff resources and run to take an appropriate response from those changes. Therefore, employer branding, as a tool of SHRM, has the task to save company from danger like for example the lack of demanded overall competency, and acts towards attracting new talents. In this approach EB is focused mostly only on one HRM process: recruitment/selection of candidates. However, regular task of HRM is also to look after employees during the time of their employment in the company. Thus, hr programs like: system of remuneration, plans of development, quality work or work-life balance - should collect data proving good EB. It is worth noticing that "competency gap", both already happened, or predicted in close future, frequently is caused by voluntary departure of talented staff. This suggests EB should regularly inspect satisfaction and try to enhance motivation of employees, and it explains also why activities of EB should be part of general pro-active SHRM.

This means that EB should not only react to already happened situation, but first – predict future probable problems. One of crucial problems is to understand how low level of employees' engagement can be solved via EB. In the latest presentation prepared by Deloitte Consultancy "New model for talent management Agenda for 2015" it is stated: "Employee engagement is your employer brand" (Bershin, 2014), and that current talents at work are not looking for career, but for experience. It means "a talent" plans to stay with the company as long as it delivers the valuable for him/her professional experience. Later - he/ she is ready to leave the company and look for a better work place. Data obtained in recent Gallup Report are alarming: "The state of the global workplace shows that only 13% of global workforce is "highly engaged," 63% "disengaged," and 24% "actively non-engaged" during working (Gallup Report, 2013, p. 12). Engagement in work is an important part of corporate competency and consists of the sum of adequate work attitude of particular employees'. Here we are not talking about the qualification or skills of workforce, but about their behavior - motivation.

The question arises: *Why talents selected by companies so carefully, are not enough engaged in working?*

The answer, according to Josh Bershin from Deloitte, lies in critical ratings of key intra-organizational fields, given by employees.

On a scale from 1 to 5 the average evaluations given by employees were the following (Bershin 2015): senior leadership - 2,8; own career opportunities - 2,9; company culture - 3,1; work-life balance - 3,2. Similar observation, done by Glassdoor research on cc 20 000 respondents) shows that: "only 54% of employees would recommend the company to a friend"; "in the high-technology industry, two-thirds of all workers believe they could find a better job in less than 60 days if they only took the time to look" (Dice, 2014).

The conclusion of Josh Bershin is that organizations definitely should change their HRM approach. They can't any longer be focused on traditional issues like: "employees' performance management", but should start to think how to build the new kind of organization - "an irresistible organization", which people simply will not want to leave. He explains: "The employee-work contract has changed: people are operating more like free agents than in the past. In short, the balance of power has shifted from employer to employee, forcing business leaders to learn how to build an organization that engages employees as sensitive, passionate, creative contributors" (Bershin, 2015, p. 148).

Referring all above to the EB strategy, it can be stated it is high time to revise traditional offer based on the vision of attractive "career path" and offer something much more – the commitment, self- development, cooperation, shared sense of identity, common values, etc. Only if people themselves want to stay with an organization, will they probably also be loyal to it and will spread its good reputation in surroundings. If they feel disappointed, frustrated, or harmed – they can easily act against the company's image. It is their free will to do it, and they want - they have an availability to do it. The power of Internet brings one of easy tools.

Internet as the Main Tool of EB

Companies have public image whether they care about it, or not. And even if they seriously work for employer brand, their effort does not always bring desirable results.

Today Google collects all formal and informal information about companies, both the information which is put on the site as company's EB operations being part of SHRM, as well as the information sent individually by its employees. The brand is intentionally created by HR specialists, who use variety of online tools for their external and internal EB, but it is also shaped by the activity of many non - functional people: employees, ex-employees, customers, etc.

Using Internet tools in a responsible way is the obligation of HR department workers, especially recruiters and public relation officers. Nowadays e-recruitment has become a natural process in SHRM and plays first role in external EB. Technologies supporting recruitment not only optimize costs, ensure speed and accuracy of the selection, but also make recruitment process more attractive to candidates. Also, many activities on the field of internal EB commonly use Internet potential.

The most fruitful EB tool currently are considered social media which have demonstrated spectacular growth over the last five years: from 14% of use in 2009 - to 58% of use in 2014 (Minchington 2014). The actions undertaken to enhance EB according to the last Employer Branding Global Trends Study Report (Minchington, 2014) are ranked (from most to less frequent) in a following way:

- Social media are 58% of all EB activities; career website development - 56%; recruitment advertising/ employer marketing- 52%; recruitment branding – 45%; developing EB strategy – 39%; defining EVP's -39%; employee referral program – 36%; current employee research – 35%; employer brand positioning – 29%; audit of current employer brand – 24%; retention initiatives- 23%; mobile career sites – 21%; focus groups with current employees – 19%; employer brand forums with external stakeholders are 15% of all EB activities.

Above data confirm that more sophisticated Internet skills are today a key part of hr officers' competencies. But they also confirm that external EB constantly stays dominant in a spectrum of all EB activities. Activities addressed at potential candidates from external labor market are located on higher positions comparing to initiatives addressed at the current employees. But just the latter ones, including: referral program, current employee research, retention initiatives, focus groups with employees, etc., seem to be crucial in preventing possible defamatory messages about reputation of the company.

Managers have to be aware of the growth of digitalization of their own workforce. It requires, especially hr managers, to rethink organizational structures, ways of influence and control. This is the reason the individual Internet activity of currently employed people should be (more or less) monitored and controlled by hr departments.

An important hr task is also to provide employees' with adequate skills for safe Internet use. Another new task for hr is to take care about implementation of the efficient preventive IT system defending different kinds of aversive behavior, both from outside of the company, and from the inside. The issue of Internet security in context of EB should be considered in relation to current employees first. We can try to avoid potential "wastes" of EB, although we can't control workers' behavior in Internet totally.

However, what to do with Internet activity of ex-employees' addressed at company's EB?

The "post–exit" activity of de-recruited people is critical to organization's brand and reputation, and these people widely use potential of Internet against their former workplaces.

Here it is worth mentioning a relatively new and fast popularized Internet platform – so called "user-generated content" (UGC). UGS is defined as "Any form of content such as blogs, wikis, discussion forums, posts, chats, tweets, podcasts, digital images, video, audio files, advertisements and other forms of media that was created by users of an online system or service, often made available via social media websites" (Chua et al, 2014). Examples of globally well recognizable employer's UGC sites represent: Glassdoor, Vault, JobAdvisor, CareerSupport365, and many other. UGCs have the high potential to sway perception and opinion about job places and one of the newest frontiers of them is the anonymous ranking of companies. According to data collected by CareerSupport365, out of almost 500 people who lost their jobs, it was found that (CareerSupport365, 2013):

- 92% were very likely to visit a job site in the first week they were made redundant or retrenched;
- 91% felt 'down about themselves' and attributed their feelings mostly to their displacement;

- 88% of former employees felt more likely to still talk poorly about their employer within 13 weeks of losing their job;
- 65% of respondents, aged from 25 to 45, were aware of Glassdoor and or similar sites;
- 85% of those who knew of Glassdoor and or similar sites were likely to visit the sites and rank their former employer;
- 90% of employees had not received any outplacement or career transition support upon being laid off;
- 89% of those laid off employees said they would have felt 'much more positive' towards their employer had their former employer provided them with outplacement or career transition support;
- 95% of people would have felt 'far less inclined' to post adverse comments about their own former employers
- 74% of respondents put weight behind most online UGC ratings.

The same source, CareerSupport365 (2013) found a high propensity for disgruntled employees to visit UGC platforms with the aim to rank their former employers poorly within a short time of losing their job.

All of it means that employers need to pre-empt how they behave towards all employees, but especially, what they propose to workers who are planned to be de-recruited in close future. They should include the offer of some form of outplacement support to such employees. It may significantly help to mitigate the potential media attacks against former employer. Treating employees with dignity, regardless of their position in the organization, is not only morally and ethically right, but it is strategic in business sense. Employers should remember that anyone has the potential to speak their mind, and it is very easy to do via the Internet.

Internet Threats Against Company Reputation

These days the power of the Internet is not to be underestimated and its impact can be visible in all areas of business activity, which plays a remarkable role in creating the image of a company. It is hard to imagine a company that could function without the support of such a tool as the Internet. It provides us with all the essential information, which quite often is the basis to undertake strategic decisions in company's activity. On the one hand the tool that has such a powerful potential can only improve the company's activity and become a source of a number of benefits. On the other hand, there is a negative side of the Internet that destroys the company.

Visible from the level of search engines negative contents such as unfavorable opinions or defamatory comments are a real threat to a company's reputation. In the era of common access to games forums, social networks as well as opinion-shaping websites, a negative opinion of one disappointed client can reach hundreds of people looking for the information on the activity of a given company.

Undoubtedly, belittling the problem of negative contents as well as recognizing the threat too late, can be related with significant financial losses, and quite often can lead to the company's bankruptcy (Dąbrowska et al, 2009). New more accessible information technologies are indispensable for the development of a company, but at the same time they involve a number of threats. Nowadays, apart from traditional forms of reaching a client, for example through advertisements in the media the image of a company in the Internet is becoming extremely important. It is connected with inside and outside threats of local network. Most typical types of local network outside threats include:

- Cracking into computers of local network in order to gain access passwords;
- Cracking into company's server and access to company's data: list of partners, income, business plans, projects;
- Cracking into network and disturbing its activity;
- Cracking in order to get the list of e-mail addresses of the company and its partners in order to send viruses and spam or spam through e-mails.

Types of local network inside threats are following (Polaczek, 2006):

- Sharing confidential data through a company's worker via the Internet link;
- Visiting www services with the content not connected to the company's activity (entertainment, pornographic sites, etc.);
- Downloading from the Internet various software that could include viruses or destabilize the work of user's computer. Using such software is not necessarily a threat to a network but can simply be illegal.

The factor that destructively influences the condition of small companies and big corporations is *cyberslacking*. The workers find interesting places in the Internet such as IRC channels, discussions lists and chats, to which they devote their valuable time within working hours in order to deal with their private matters. Overusing the network is visible most often in such areas as: visiting web pages devoted to work and hobby, looking for current information, planning holidays and days-off, doing the shopping or active participation in discussion lists and chat-rooms.

One of negative effects of cyberslacking is decrease in worker's efficiency, which contributes to making financial losses by an employer. Moreover, cyberslacking can be a threat to protection of company's resources. First of all, it can lead to threat the security of employer's information systems. If employees enter suspicious web pages, they download files of different kinds by the means of Internet search engines, which in turn can lead to infecting the information system of the company with viruses. Since the procedure of sending e-mail messages with infected content in the form of attachments is incredibly popular, even simple checking the private mail by an employee poses a risk for an employer. Systems infected by viruses or spying software are easy goals for cyber criminals.

Hackers' attacks are the biggest threat for Internet systems, particularly the systems using data, generating high costs, but they also negatively influence the company's reputation and discourage clients. A successful DoS (denial of service) or DDos (distributed denial of service) attack can damage critical for the activity services leading to serious consequences for the company. A DoS type of attack is one of a more efficient ways of immobilizing network server. The main goal of such an attack is partly blocking the access to certain services for example www or e-mail as well as total immobilization of a server. The attack is based on sending in a short time a big number of questions to a network server. The server is trying to answer each of the questions, whereas the hacker without waiting for the answer from the server keeps sending the next questions. It leads to the situation in which the server is "flooded" with the questions and cannot answer them in time (Kępa et al., 2012). The system is increasingly overloaded and when the number of questions exceeds the calculative possibilities of the system what follows is its blockade.

However, because of easiness of detecting the perpetrator as well as relatively easy methods of protection, it is being improved all the time which results in creating an upgraded version – DdoS. DoS takes place in a hacker's computer, whereas DDoS attack happens in a scattered way, which means from many computers at the same time. The computers are situated in different places and their users are not aware that they are being involved in an attack for an Internet system. Such a computer is first infected with a virus, kind of "Trojan's horse" or logical bomb which gets activated only when detecting a clear signal from an aggressor and begins the process of destruction. Detecting such a virus is relatively hard because it either gets activated only at the moment of attack, and afterwards it becomes dormant, or after an attack it uninstalls and deletes itself.

Viruses and hackers' attacks can also lead to leak of information important to the company, often confidential, and above all - personal data processed by a company. And it is direct responsibility of HRM departments to secure this sensitive kind of data. The leak of information or data can be also the result of sending company's documents via private e-mail or storing them on private data carriers.

And it is employer's responsibility to be liable for downloading through the Internet illegal files that violates intellectual property rights and saving them by employees on the disc of company's computer. Illegal contents of the disc and violating copy rights can result in employer's being responsible for that not only in terms of civil but also criminal liability. Cybercriminals develop their techniques such as identity thefts, applying socio-technology developed APT attacks (advanced persistent threats) or dramatic DDos-s.

The smaller company's budget to protect IT is, the easier it may be for a company to become a victim of a cyber-attack. That is why companies should consider applying DDos protection as an integral part of its general IT security policy. It is equally important as the protection against harmful software, directed attacks, leak of data and similar threats.

How to Enhance Organizational E-Security

Network is a universal centre of information and knowledge which is important in company's activity and no one needs to be convinced how important security of awaiting threats coming from inside and outside of company's local network is. In order to fight the threats it is not enough to inform employees about existing threats orally or in writing.

It is necessary to implement in company's IT systems special secure programs and solutions, as well as to train staff how to use them in a responsible way. Some tools can act independently and need only monitoring from side of ITC internal specialists, others – need close cooperation of employees.

The solution to the companies that have a constant access to the Internet is so-called *Firewall*. The task of this blockade is to prevent non-authorized access to the company network from outside as well as establish the policy of security of employees' computers. The security policy to the great extent limits the possibility of "harming" the company's computers by their employees. It is based on allocating the authorization to each computer in terms of the access to the Internet, for example blocking the SMTP ports different than company's server. Efficiently used blockade not only supports local systems detecting threats such as anti-viruses, anti-spam etc. but also helps to detect potential threat by registering the number of crack trials into so-called logs. It also reduces by-side effects of an outside attack in a way that part of the movement is strictly designed to so-called allowed movement only to trusted services and servers.

Also applying the programs to analyze the movement in networks, so-called sniffers, can contribute to increasing security. Examples of sniffers are the following:

- **Tcpdump:** It provides capturing and storing packets;
- **Ettercap:** A powerful sniffer to capture and analyze movement as well as to make advanced attacks;
- **Wireshark:** Advanced tool to capture and save data in the network;
- **Snort:** Used by network administrators, it has a wide range of mechanisms of detecting cracks;
- **Dsniff:** A packet of advanced tools to capture data and make attacks.

It is necessary to mention personal data processing which is an important part of hr processes. Companies are responsible for creation of the overall information security policy and for the formulation of instructions how to manage information systems used to process personal data. All companies that process any personal data are obliged to act on the basis of the defined law rules[1]. They have to document all this processed kind of data, as well as to deliver all necessary technical and organizational conditions which guarantee that devices and information systems used to process personal data are efficient and secure.

This documentation should describe the way of processing personal data as well as technical and organizational measures providing protection of processed personal data suitable to the threats and category of the data being protected. The law regulation usually also includes information on basic technical and organizational conditions which devices and information systems used to process personal data should follow. The limits, aimed at protecting against leak of personal data, are for example: blocking access to some websites, as well as some types of files which should be clearly described in an information security policy and should be applied by an employer.

Moreover, employer should create the internal regulation of using the Internet, software and computer equipment in a company (Grubicka & Matuska, 2015). He has the right to include in own regulations special bans related for example to such issues like:

- Using the Internet, software and equipment for personal reasons;
- Using private e-mail;
- Using private data carriers and installing there business-related files.

However, it has to be emphasized that an employee is here obliged to follow the regulations, as well as should be obedient to all existing work regulations.

Another way of reducing cyberslacking is installing in the employees' computers professional software monitoring the movement in the Internet. There is a lot of software on the market; for example on Polish market we can find such popular tools as: *PC Szpieg, Statlook, SpectorSoft, Oko Szefa, Detektyw* - the systems of efficiency and information security audit that collect the information on working applications and browsed websites.

Employer has the right to control the work of own workforce in order to evaluate its efficiency. It is a duty of an employee to be available for an employer within work hours and working for him and in the situations when an employee does not work, but undertakes activities for personal reasons it means a violation of respective article of labor law legislation.[2] Undertaking controlling activities by an employer is additionally justified by the responsibility he has for employees' activities towards the third party[3](Białas, 2006).

However, in order to monitor employees, certain conditions must be met. First of all, monitoring can be introduced only with one aim, for example: employer's technology security system or preventing such employees' activities that could expose an employer to damage. When implementing monitoring, an employer must also meet the conditions of processing personal data defined in the regulation on personal data protection. An employer, when applying monitoring, has to inform the employees about that fact by including this information in the regulations, verbally or by means of e-mail.

Data transmission security is composed of integrity and confidentiality. Integrity means care about the fact that nobody changes the data while transmitting it whereas confidentiality is connected with keeping the information in secret so as only the one who should can get familiar with it. The data between web application and a client (search engine) are sent in an open text, which makes it possible to overhear it. Introducing system of coding (SSL) will prevent not only an unauthorized person from overhearing the transmission, but also unauthorized change of the content sent through the network. When there is no SSL in company's IT system, coding a potential cybercriminal can:

- Overhear the transmission and gain the information such as an ID and a password of the person logging in, cookies' content, data content seen on the screen of a system user,
- Change in any way the content of the information sent between a user and a system.

Coding the data transmission has a vital role in e-commerce and should be treated as an investment in reputation and clients' trust (Kępa et al, 2012). The certificate trusted and signed by trusted certification centre (CA) tells the clients that the information about the server and more exactly about the company as its administrator was checked by an independent subject and that the company is actually the one it claims to be. Besides, the company that holds a SSL certificate makes a better image, whereas its site is resistant to forgery. The site can be copied, however it is not that easy to forge a reliable SSL certificate. The probability that a hacker could pretend to be a trustworthy member of a company and get hold of such a certificate is not that high.

In e-commerce systems it is essential to send e-mails to their users. Unfortunately, protecting e-mail communication is troublesome. In order to code messages for clients there must be mechanisms serving coding on both sides, for example: PGP, GPG or mail application that serves certain standard, for example: S/MIME in Microsoft Outlook. The necessity to possess certain programs is one thing, but on the other hand there is a problem of exchanging coding keys. In case of sending confidential data to a client when using e-mail a good solution seems to be to send them in an attachment form as a safe PDF file (Kępa et al, 2012). The client can decide on the password to attachments in e-commerce service earlier. It cannot be the same password as one uses to log in, though. Passwords should not be stored in an open form, whereas the password to protect PDF will have to be stored in such a way as in this case it is not possible to use hash. There are free libraries accessible for PHP and PHP classes used to create PDF files secured by the password. Under no circumstances should passwords be sent by an e-mail. The exception is the situation when the sent password is one of many elements of logging, i.e. when there is nothing one can do about it or when one does not possess a token or such a piece of information. If a user forgets the password and wants to retrieve it he should be sent a link to reset or a link to a web page where he could generate a new password giving answers to earlier defined questions as well as its validity should be limited, for example it should last one day. Here are the examples of using simple security protection techniques:

- The programs installed on all the servers in a company are configured in such a way that one can reach a suitable level of access control to information systems;
- All the transmission and data gathered on carriers are to be coded;

- Archiving the data twice a day.

The control of access to business information should take into account both the needs of their usage while working, as well as security requirements. The number and quantity of IT security systems are increasing and also cybercriminals use more and more sophisticated methods. Usually smaller companies, which frequently are equipped with relatively weaker and sometimes even outdated security systems, become aims of cybercriminals' attacks. Because of it systems of security should constantly be developed in response to new threats (Kifner,1999).

Access to business information, which is the basis of functioning of each company, should be in harmony with policy of information security. The document should define the principles of allocating specific employees suitable levels of access and information, confidentiality clause or secrecy (Grubicka & Matuska, 2012). A good support for traditional IT security system is current monitoring of network movement, which in its easiest form enables administrators to capture anomalies and prevent real threats more efficiently.

It is worth keeping calm and thinking about consequences and advantages of efficient and legal way of doing one's job. Depending on the way and kind of given content, private activity of an employee can influence the strengthening of company's image, or - it can become a kind of threat for its employer branding efforts.

SOLUTIONS AND RECOMMENDATIONS

Recent studies deliver a new set of parameters that is available both to sociologists and economists, which might be defined as an input to effective employer branding. These parameters are both organizational, as well as technical markers and promote widening of the view on the range of activities which should be undertaken by employer branding within strategic human resources management of organizations oriented on sustainable development.

Firstly, the scope of EB activities should be focused on value management conducted together with competence management. In today's turbulent times, when it is hard to attract new talents, it is high time to concentrate on already employed human resources and treat them as the first source of competitive advantage. At least equal attention should be given both to internal and to external EB, and especially recommended is not neglecting internal EB activities addressed at staff who is considered to be fired in close future.

Secondly, definition of talents has to be perceived in a broader sense – talents are not only fresh graduates, young and mobile people with not very clearly specified expectations towards employers. Talents are also people already working in organizations, although maybe they need investment in developing of their professional competencies. This investment is worthwhile because it promises the coherence of personal and corporate values and sharing common identity of organization. Such employees (at least in majority) will probably be more engaged in their work and will not be keen to act against company's reputation, thus also its EB activities, have chance to be more effective.

Thirdly, effective EB necessarily needs delivering adequate information security systems, including Internet danger prevention. It is in a vital company's interest in the light of risks posed by Internet aversive activities of staff, especially actions undertaken by dismissed employees feeling sense of grievance against their employer, as well as on the side of unsatisfied customers. Cyber security, fast developing engineering new branch, provides hard data about real danger coming from Internet and how possible it is to protect from it. Today, this technical knowledge is not to be underestimated when we plan to be effective with employer branding activities.

That's why Internet security knowledge and skills (at least on a basic level) should be also demonstrated by staff of HR departments, not only by IT specialists engaged by companies. Consequently, the scope of competencies demanded from HR officers responsible for EB should cover also a set of technical skills connected with secure use of Internet. This kind of knowledge and skills has to be also obligatory spread among all workers of the company during internal trainings and HR officers should monitor and control how employees implement agreed Internet security instructions.

FUTURE RESEARCH DIRECTIONS

Growing complex binds between technology and peoples' activity imply cyber security is a science which should be deeper involved also into management seen as a kind of social research, and obligatory – in practical use of hr activities consisting of employer branding.

Recent research explains how intensively over a few recent years Internet activities undertaken as external employer branding have grown. Also, the research documenting Internet activities of people on UGCs platforms sheds new light on EB strategy. On the other hand, current changes on labor market, global mobility of workforce and growth of digitalization demand fresh human resources approaches.

The new human resource management surely has to focus not only on developing theory of human capital management, but also on including elements of some engineering new branches such as cyber security in management. The latter one should be also addressed at intercultural issues in order to respond to more complex communication realities with its most probable conflict areas. Multicultural organizations have to seek of how to improve overall organizational information security, especially when they are aspiring for employer branding.

CONCLUSION

In today's turbulent times it is very hard to plan efficient pro-active business strategies promising success on the market. Organizations acting in a globalizing world, where geographical boundaries are becoming increasingly less relevant, are confronted with the fact that social and communication skills of the workforce are changing rapidly. They can be used both for favorable and hostile intentions towards employer. Thus, also human resources management practices, including employer branding, need redefinition and implementing new practices and techniques.

A useful "navigation system" can be value management and competence management executed within strategic human resources management (SHRM). Employer branding as part of SHRM tries to deliver talents - most competitive asset for organizations. But to build employer brand during commonly observed scarcity of talents is not easy, which is why talents for the organization have to be considered not only potential, new employees, but first – people already employed. Consequently, external and internal EB activities have to be balanced, and investment in development of own staff – should be seen in categories of enhancing own competitive assets. As a result of such an approach the sense of the organizational identity which proves that corporate values are shared by employees should also grow. And this is why value management and competence management refer directly to efficiency of employer branding.

It is also necessary to remember that EB communications are under sustainable verification, both on the side of external, as well as internal stakeholders. It is essential to respect the power of Internet. Today Internet is a dominant tool of EB and intentionally used promotes good reputation of the organization well. But it can be also easily used by different stakeholders as a weapon against this reputation. Because of it, the cyber security as the new technical knowledge, is strongly recommended to use to enhance the efficiency of organization's EB activities.

REFERENCES

Ambler, T., & Barrow, S. (1996). The employer brand. *Journal of Brand Management*, *4*(3), 185–206. doi:10.1057/bm.1996.42

Backhaus, K., & Tikoo, S. (2004). Conceptualizing and researching employer branding. *Career Development International*, *9*(5), 501–517. doi:10.1108/13620430410550754

Beaumont, Ph., & Graeme, M. (2003). *Branding and People Management: What is a Name?* London: CIPD.

Berłowski, P., & Turłukowska, J. (2013). *Internal and external employer branding- benefits from the consistent development of the company's image as an employer on the example of Poland Mars.* Wolters Kluwer Business. Retrieved from http://www.kadry.abc.com.pl

Bershin, J. (2014). The *Talent Agenda for 2015. What comes after "Integrated Talent Management"?* Deloitte Consuting LLP. Retrieved from http://www.slideshare.net/jbersin/talent-management-revisited

Bershin, J. (2015). Becoming Irresistible: A New Model for Employee Engagement. *Deloitte Review*, *16*. Retrieved from http://d27n205l7rookf.cloudfront.net/wp-content/uploads/2015/01/DR16_becoming_irresistible

Białas, A. (2006). *Security information and services in modern institutions and the company.* Warsaw: Scientific Technical Publishing.

Bigram, S. A. (2013a). *Internal Employer Branding. Bigram SA Personnel Consulting.* Retrieved from http://www.bigram.pl

Bigram, S. A. (2013b). *External Employer Branding.* Bigram SA Personnel Consulting. Retrieved from http://www.bigram.pl

Botha, A., Bussin, M., & De Swardt, L. (2011). An employer brand predictive model for talent attraction and retention: original research. *SA Journal of Human Resource Management*, *9*(1), 1-12. Retrieved from http://reference.sabinet.co.za/sa_epublication_article/sajhrm_v9_n1_a26

CareerSupport365. (2013). Market Research: Attitudes towards Employers After Losing Their Job and The Associated Risks to Employer Branding. Retrieved from http://careersupport365.com/wp-content/uploads/2013/06/Employee_Attitudes.pdf

Chua, T. S., Juanzi, L., & Moens, M. F. (2014). *Mining user generated content*. Chapman and Hall/CRC.

CIPD. (2006). *Chartered Institute of Professional Development*. Retrieved from http://www.cipd.co.uk

Dąbrowska, A., Janoś-Kresło, M. & Wódkowski, A. (2009). *E - services and information society*. Warsow: Difin.

Dice. (2014). *Dice Tech salary survey results—2014*. Retrieved from http://resources.dice.com/report/dice-tech-salary-survey-results-2014

Dubois, D. (1998). The competency casebook. Amherst, MA: HRD & Silver Spring MD: International Society for Performance Improvement.

Dukerich, J. M., & Carter, S. M. (2000). Distorted Images and Reputation Repair.

Dunmore, M. (2002). *Inside-Out Marketing: How to Create an Internal Marketing Strategy*. London: Kogan Page.

Edwards, M. R. (2010). An integrative review of employer branding and OB theory. *Personnel Review*, *39*(1), 5–23. doi:10.1108/00483481011012809

Figurska, I., & Matuska, E. (2013). Employer branding as human resources strategy. *Human Resources Management & Ergonomics*, VIII(2), 35-51. Retrieved from https://frcatel.fri.uniza.sk/hrme/files/2013/2013_2_03.pdf

Gilbert, T. F. (1996). *Human Competence: Engineering Worthy Performance*. Washington, D.C: International Society for Performance Improvement.

Griffin, L. & Clarke, T. (2008). Employer Branding. Your Customers Know Your Brand & Values. Do Your Employees? *Bridge Partners Insights*.

Grubicka, J., & Matuska, E. (2012). Consumer safety of e-market participant. In H. Lisiak & W. Stach (Eds.), Security of contemporary world. History and public safety (pp. 45-54). Poznań: Institute of Scientific Publishing - Maiuscula.

Grubicka, J., & Matuska, E. (2015). Sustainable entrepreneurship in conditions of un(safety) globalization and technological convergence, *The International Journal Entrepreneurship and Sustainability Issues*. Retrieved from http://jssidoi.org/jesi/aims-and-scope-of-research doi:10.9770/jesi.2015.2.4(2)

Hatch, M. J., & Schultz, M. (2007). Relations between Organizational Culture, Identity and Image. *European Journal of Marketing*, *31*(5/6).

Hesketh, A. (2014). *Managing the value of your talent. A new framework for human capital measurement, Valuing your Talent - Research report July*. London: Chartered Institute of Personnel and Development. Retrieved from www.valuingyourtalent.co.uk

Hieronimus, F., Schaefer, K., & Schroeder, J. (2005). Using branding to attract talent. *The McKinsey Quarterly*, 3.

Jenner, S. J., & Taylor, S. (2008). *Employer Branding – Fad or the Future of HR? Research insight*. London: Chartered Institute of Personnel and Development.

Kelly, Ch., Kocourek, P., McGaw, N., & Samuelson, J. (2005). *Deriving Value from Corporate Values*, The Aspen Institute and Booz Allen Hamilton, Inc. Retrieved from https://www.aspeninstitute.org/sites/default/files/content/docs/bsp/VALUE%2520SURVEY%2520FINAL.PDF

Kelly Services. (2013). *Building a Strong Employer Brand at all times for sustainable organization*. Retrieved from www.kellyservices.com.my

Kępa, L., Tomasik, P., & Dobrzyński, S. (2012). *Security of e-commerce system, or how to run a business without the risk of the Internet*. Gliwice: Helion.

Kifner, T. (1999). *Security and data protection* (pp. 26–54). Gliwice: Helion.

Knox, S., & Freeman, C. H. (2006). Measuring and Managing Employer Brand Image in the Service Industry. *Journal of Marketing Management, 22*, 695–716.

Martin, G. (2008). Employer Branding – Time for Some Long and 'Hard' Reflections? *Research insight*. London: Chartered Institute of Personnel and Development. Retrieved from http://www.therecruiterslounge.com/2010/08/17/10-strategic-tips-for-employee-retention/

Martin, G., Beaumont, P., Doig, R., & Pate, J. (2005). Branding: A new performance discourse for HR? *European Management Journal, 23*(1).

Michaels, E., Handfield-Jones, H., & Axelrod, B. (2001). *The war for talent*. Harvard Business Press.

Minchington, B. (2013). *The Rise of Employer Brand Leadership, Second Ed., Oct. 2013*. Retrieved from http://www.employerbrandinginternational.com

Minchington, B. (2014). *Employer Branding Global Trends Study Report*. Retrieved from www.slideshare.net/brettminch/2014-employer-branding-global-trends-survey-report-by-employer-brand-international.pdf

Moroko, L., & Uncles, M. D. (2008). Uncles M.D.: Characteristics of successful employer brands. *Journal of Brand Management, 16*(3), 160–175. doi:10.1057/bm.2008.4

Mosley, R. (2009). *Employer Brand. The Performance Driver No Business Can Ignore*. Shoulders of Giants Publication.

Nigel Wright Recruitment. (2013). *Employer Branding Report*. Retrieved from http://www.nigelwright.com/media/1531/employer-branding-report.pdf

Polaczek, T. (2006). *Information security audit*. Gliwice: Helion.

Randstad (2013). *Employer Branding. Perception being reality. Results Randstad Award 2013. Global Report*. (online): http://www.randstadaward.ca

Report, D. (2015). *Global Human Capital Trends 2015. Leading in the new world of work*, Deloitte University Press. Retrieved from http://www2.deloitte.com/content/dam/Deloitte/at/Documents/human-capital/hc-trends-2015.pdf

Report, G. (2013). *The state of global workplace. Employee engagement insights for business leaders worldwide.* Gallup Report. Retrieved from http://www.securex.be/export/sites/default/.content/download-gallery/nl/brochures/Gallup-state-of-the-GlobalWorkplaceReport_20131.pdf

Rosethorn, H. (2009). *The Employer Brand. Keeping Faith with the Deal.* Farnham: Gower Publishing Limited.

Rosethorn, H. (2009). *The Employer Brand. Keeping Faith with the Deal.* Farnham: Gower Publishing Limited.

Schultz, M., Hatch, M. J., & Larsen, M. H. (Eds.), *The Expressive Organization: Linking Identity, Reputation, and the Corporate Brand* (pp. 97–112). Oxford: Oxford University Press.

SHRM. (2008). The Employer Brand: A Strategic Tool to Attract, Recruit and Retain Talent. *Society for Human Resources Management, April/June.* Retrieved from http://www.shrm.org/research/articles/articles/documents/08-0201staffinginsert_final.pdf

Stahl, G. Björkman, I., Farndale, E., Morris, S. S., Paauwe, J., Stiles, P., Trevor, J., & Wright, P. (2012). Six principles of effective global talent management. *Sloan Management Review, 53*(2), 25-42. Retrieved from http://epub.wu.ac.at/id/eprint/3616

Sullivan, J. (2004). The 8 Elements of a Successful Employment Brand. *ER Daily.* Retrieved from http://www.ere.net/2004/02/23/the-8-elements-of-a-successful-employment-brand

Wellin, M. (2013). Managing psychological contract. Using the Personal Deal to Increase Business Performance. Warsow: Wolters Kluwer.

Xiang, X., Zhan, Z., & Yanling, L. (2012). *The Impact of Employer Brand on Corporate Financial Performance.* Singapore: IACSIT Press. Doi:10.7763/IPCSIT.2012.V52.80

KEY TERMS AND DEFINITIONS

Advanced Persistent Threat (APT): Is a network attack in which an unauthorized person gains access to a network and stays there undetected for a long period of time. The intention of an APT attack is usually to steal data of organization.

Competence Management: The main stream of strategic Human Resources Management, the process of delivering and to developing staff's most useful competencies in organization striving to gain high performance for a significant period of time.

Cyberslacking: A term describing the increased use of the Internet on company computers by employees during their work time, but for personal use or entertainment.

Cybersecurity in Management: The new research and practice field aimed to provide secure IT systems used for implementation regular tasks connected with management and performed by using Internet.

Denial of Service (Dos): an attempt to make a machine or network resource unavailable to its intended user.

Distributed Denial of Service (DdoS): Form of electronic attack involving multiple computers, which send repeated HTTP requests or pings to a server to load it down and render it inaccessible for a period of time.

Employer Brand: Achieved positive public and internal image of the organization as a good place to work with it, the positive result of employer branding strategy.

Employer Branding: An element of strategic Human Resources Management and Marketing aimed to attract and retain employees with most valuable competencies.

Employer Value Proposition (EVP): A set of benefits and offerings provided by an organization to employee in return for the input of his/ her competencies used during work performance.

Firewall: Computer, device connecting company local Network with global network (Internet).

Strategic Human Resources Management: Proactive human resource management filling all typical HR processes such as staff's recruitment, development, assessment, remuneration, etc., with the goal to maximize mutual benefits for both the employee and employer

Value Management: The part of strategic Human Resources Management focused on recognizing and satisfying personal values of employees and customers and matching them with defined corporate values. The aim of VM is to achieve desirable balance between the wants and needs of different stakeholders and the organizational resources needed to satisfy them.

ENDNOTES

[1] In case of the Polish law this regulation is described in § 3 of the Regulation No, done by the Ministry of Internal Affairs and Administration, dated on April 29. 2004.
[2] In Poland: art.22 § 1 of Labor Code.
[3] In Poland: art. 120 of Labor Code.

Chapter 17
National Ethical Institutions and Social Entrepreneurship

Etayankara Muralidharan
MacEwan University, Canada

Saurav Pathak
Kansas State University, USA

ABSTRACT

Using insights from institutional theory, the chapter proposes understanding ethics as national institutions that deeply influence social entrepreneurship. Moreover, the chapter proposes that low behavioral ethical standards (normative ethical institutions) provide opportunities for individuals to establish social enterprises. Furthermore, it proposes that high public-sector ethical standards (regulatory ethical institutions) and values of unselfishness (cognitive ethical institutions) facilitate and motivate individuals to establish social enterprises. The chapter also explores the combined effects of public-sector ethical standards and low behavioral ethics, public-sector ethical standards and societal unselfishness, and low behavioral ethics and unselfishness, on the creation of social enterprises. The chapter contributes to cross-cultural comparative entrepreneurship by suggesting, through a multilevel framework, the effects of societal-level ethical institutions on the creation of social enterprises.

BACKGROUND

Although the study of entrepreneurship and the study of business ethics have become important lines of inquiry, study of the intersection of entrepreneurship and ethics remains relatively new (Harris, Sapienza, & Bowie, 2009). In particular, examining what ethical factors drive socially responsible behaviors is a burgeoning area of interest among research scholars (Bacq, Hartog, & Hoogendoorn, 2014). Extant scholarship has examined ethical standards primarily at the individual level. Similarly, at the firm level, few studies have examined conceptually the mechanisms through which variation in societal-level institutions may specifically influence corporate social performance among firms (Jackson & Apostolakou, 2010). Some studies have empirically examined the role and effect of societal-level institutions across

DOI: 10.4018/978-1-5225-2568-4.ch017

large datasets of countries (Habisch, Jonker, Wegner, & Schmidpeter, 2004; Ioannou & Serafeim, 2012; Jackson & Apostolakou, 2010; Jamali, Sidani, & El-Asmar, 2009).

In the case of social entrepreneurship (SE), a growing line of inquiry among scholars investigating the intersection of entrepreneurship and ethics is the ethical or moral factors that drive social enterprises (Bacq et al., 2014). Scholarly discourses on SE appear to dwell on discussions that demand more ethical and socially inclusive capitalistic behaviors (Dacin, Dacin, & Tracey, 2011). Some examples include consumers increasingly looking for more ethically sourced and manufactured goods (Nicholls & Opal, 2005); increasing expectations for multinational organizations to behave in ethically and socially responsible ways (Friedman & Miles, 2001); and politicians under increasing obligation to pursue and implement policies that promote social equality, and reduce the harmful effects of business activities on the environment (Bernauer & Caduff, 2004). Extant research on entrepreneurship and ethics adopts the perspective of either entrepreneurship and ethics or entrepreneurship and society. The former perspective deals with the ethics of individual entrepreneurs, and the latter concerns questions related to social and economic implications of entrepreneurship (Hannafey, 2003).

Some of the key constructs scholars use to understand the influence of ethics on social entrepreneurship are ethical attitudes reflected in the responses to questions about right and wrong (Bucar, Glas, & Hisrich, 2003); a system of value principles or practices and the ability to determine right from wrong (Payne & Joyner, 2006); perceived importance of ethics, measured by obligations to stockholders and stakeholders (Shafer, Fukukawa, & Lee, 2007); and ethical attitudes in response to issues, concerns, and activities involving standards in society for what is morally right and virtuous (Franke & Nadler, 2008). Further, the Global Entrepreneurship Monitor's (GEM) research report on SE reports an average of 3.2% of new social entrepreneurial activity (or new social enterprises established or under establishment) across the 58 GEM economies (Bosma, Schøtt, Terjesen, & Kew, 2016). The report suggests this activity ranges from 0.3% in South Korea, to 10.1% in Peru. The reported cross-country variance suggests possible societal-level differences in countries, which have resulted in differences in the establishment rates of social enterprises.

These items imply the following observations. First, extant scholarship that has attempted to link ethics with social entrepreneurship has been using constructs interchangeably; therefore, the measures of ethics described above are similar, and capture all aspects of ethics. Second, national or societal-level differences may contribute to the differences in the establishment rates of social enterprises. This chapter addresses the identified gaps by proposing that ethics be viewed through different lenses, by developing an understanding of national or societal-level ethical institutions, and attempting to predict their influence on the creation of social enterprises. Further, the chapter uses the institutional configuration perspective (Stephan, Uhlaner, & Stride, 2014) to understand the joint effects of societal-level institutions. It suggests a multilevel theoretical framework to understand the effects of societal-level ethical antecedents, and to predict the creation of social enterprises. In so doing, the chapter distinguishes one form of ethics from the other, and provides a framework for understanding the effects of ethical institutions at the societal level on the creation of social enterprises. The chapter further contributes to the calls for research to examine the effects of context on entrepreneurship (Welter, 2011).

The chapter is organized as follows. In the next section, a brief discussion of SE precedes discussions on context and its relevance to entrepreneurial research. Then, societal institutions (or institutions at the national level) and research on the interface between ethics and social entrepreneurship are discussed. There follows a discussion of the suggested conceptual framework, and development of propositions related to the effect of societal-level ethical institutions on the creation of social enterprises. Finally, discussion of and elaboration on the propositions leads to suggestions for future avenues of research.

SOCIAL ENTREPRENEURSHIP

Entrepreneurship involves the identification, evaluation, and exploitation of opportunities that are present in society (Shane & Venkataraman, 2000). Typically, such situations represent opportunities to bring new products or services into existence in society, such that individuals or firms can sell their outputs at prices higher than their cost of production (for a detailed review on opportunities and entrepreneurship, please refer to Eckhardt and Shane, 2003). However, the understanding in this definition is that the fundamental objectives of such entrepreneurial activities involve profit generation, and these profits help entrepreneurs to build their personal wealth (Certo & Miller, 2008). In the recent past, SE, a subdiscipline in the area of entrepreneurship, has been gaining attention among both academics and practitioners working in the area of entrepreneurship, due to its potential to address societal problems such as poverty and illiteracy (Certo & Miller, 2008; DeLeon, 1996; Estrin, Mickiewicz, & Stephan, 2013a).

As defined in the literature, SE involves the recognition, evaluation, and exploitation of opportunities presented in society that result in social value. SE creates value by bringing about catalytic changes in society (Waddock & Post, 1991). Organizations that have a particular social, environmental or community objective create such value (Bosma et al., 2016). This social value essentially addresses the basic and long-standing needs and concerns of society, in contrast to personal or shareholder wealth (Austin, Stevenson, & Wei-Skillern, 2006). Social value has little to do with profits, but instead involves the fulfillment of basic and long-standing needs such as food, water, shelter, education, and medical services, to those members of society who are in need. In order to better understand SE, Austin et al. (2006) distinguished between two types of entrepreneurship: commercial entrepreneurship (CE) and SE. In their framework, CE represents the identification, evaluation, and exploitation of opportunities in societies that result in profits; whereas SE refers to the identification, evaluation, and exploitation of opportunities in societies that result in social value. Opportunity awareness and recognition is an important ability of an entrepreneur running any form of enterprise (social or commercial) to exercise when either supply or demand for a value-creating product or service exists in society (Kirzner, 1973).

SE has gained both academic and practitioner interest due to its potential for addressing societal problems such as poverty and illiteracy (Estrin et al., 2013a; Seelos & Mair, 2005). A social entrepreneur is an individual running an enterprise, working for his or her own account, while primarily pursuing prosocial goals—that is, goals that are set to benefit individuals in society other than the entrepreneur (Bierhoff, 2002). The occupational definition of entrepreneurship explains the first part of the definition above: working for one's own account (Hébert & Link, 1988). This definition, however, does not specify the types of goals that entrepreneurs can pursue, such as economic wealth versus social value, and hence the definition applies to both commercial and social entrepreneurs (Stephan et al., 2014). The focus on prosocial goals and social value creation, over economic wealth creation, differentiates social from commercial entrepreneurs and their respective enterprises, and is consistent with recent definitions of SE (Mair & Marti, 2006; Zahra, Gedajlovic, Neubaum, & Shulman, 2009).

In summary, through an acute understanding of social needs, social entrepreneurs fulfill these needs creatively through their enterprises. This focus on social value is consistent across the various definitions of SE (Peredo & McLean, 2006), as opposed to the focus on private or economic wealth that differentiates them from CE. The study of SE spreads through politics and the media (Dey, 2006), and it legitimizes and gives identity to social entrepreneurs and their enterprises, those individuals who run enterprises concerned with a variety of issues including poverty, concerns about the natural environment, and social inequality (Dacin et al., 2011). Therefore, it is important to understand social entrepreneurial behavior in the context in which such entrepreneurs operate.

CONTEXT AND ENTREPRENEURSHIP RESEARCH

While in Latin, "context" means to weave together or to make a connection (Rousseau & Fried, 2001), in management research it refers to the conditions external to a phenomenon that facilitate it or constrain it (Welter, 2011). Some examples that define context refer to surroundings associated with specific phenomena that help illustrate them (Capelli & Sherer, 1991) and stimuli that exist in the surrounding external environment (Mowday & Sutton, 1993). Context also includes situational opportunities and constraints that influence or affect behavior (Johns, 2006). Consideration of context in entrepreneurship is not new (Welter, 2011). Any economic behavior can be understood better within the context in which it is observed (Low & MacMillan, 1988). Contexts may be social (Granovetter, 1985), spatial (Katz & Steyaert, 2004), or institutional (Polanyi, 1957). Scholars studying entrepreneurial phenomena have therefore suggested recognizing the importance of the context in which entrepreneurship occurs. Researchers "have a tendency to underestimate the influence of external factors and overestimate the influence of internal or personal factors when making judgements about the behavior of other individuals" (Gartner, 1995, p. 70). This chapter examines societal institutions or dimensions of institutional context for their influence on SE.

Societal Institutions

A society's institutional context consists of stable rules, social norms, and cognitive structures (Scott, 1995). It sets the framework for market transactions by defining the "rules of the game" (North, 1990, p. 1) and by specifying the conditions under which firms are legitimate (Meyer & Rowan, 1977; Spencer & Gomez, 2004). Extant research reveals that institutional contexts influence a firm's strategic activities, the growth of foreign partnerships (Steensma, Tihanyi, Lyles, & Dhanaraj, 2005), and differences in entrepreneurial activities (Bruton, Fried, & Manigart, 2005; Busenitz, Gomez, & Spencer, 2000; Casson, 1992).

Institutions are therefore key aspects of social structure, which provide strong guidelines and constraints for behavior (North, 1991, 2005; Scott, 2005, 2008). They are taken-for-granted rules that are either explicit and perceived by individuals, or acting as implicit guidelines for individual behavior and actions (Powell & DiMaggio, 1991). Institutions are further divided into formal and informal institutions (North, 1990). Formal institutions are explicit, objective incentives and constraints, the consequence of government regulation of individual and organizational actions (Bruton, Ahlstrom, & Li, 2010; Scott, 1995, 2005, 2008). Formal institutions are more related to the political and economic environment that creates or restricts opportunities for entrepreneurship (Welter, 2011).

Some examples include laws and regulations for market entry and exit, or private property regulations (Welter, 2011). Informal institutions are more implicit, culturally transmitted, and socially constructed (Stephan et al., 2014). These institutions include the norms and attitudes of individuals in a society, and influence opportunity recognition, opportunity exploitation, and access to resources (Welter, 2011). Some examples include the values of trust, in-group collectivism, and the value society generally accords to entrepreneurship (Pathak & Muralidharan, 2014; Welter & Smallbone, 2008).

Scott's (1995, 2005) work further divides institutions into a three-pillar framework that considers formal institutions regulatory, and further differentiates informal institutions into cognitive and normative. Cognitive and normative arguably correspond to the concepts of cultural values and practices in cross-cultural research (Javidan, House, Dorfman, Hanges, & De Luque, 2006). Regulatory institutions include laws, regulations, and government policies that facilitate certain behaviors and constrain others (Busenitz et al., 2000). Normative institutions essentially define the various behaviors and values expected of individuals or organizations (Scott, 1995). These are often visible through shared norms about the appropriate behaviors in a particular profession (Bruton et al., 2005).

These institutions basically describe social obligations and expectations for appropriate actions, modeled on existing dominant practices or norms in a given society (Bruton et al., 2010; Javidan et al., 2006; Scott, 2005; Stephan & Uhlaner, 2010). Finally, cognitive institutions reflect how certain knowledge sets have become institutionalized and form part of a shared social understanding or shared values (Zucker, 1991). Specifically, these institutions include the culturally shared understandings in society closely associated with cultural values (Bruton et al., 2010; Javidan et al., 2006; Scott, 2005; Stephan & Uhlaner, 2010, Stephan et al., 2014). In summary, institutions can be described as widely diffused practices, regulations, or rules of social interaction, which have become entrenched in society, in the sense that it is difficult to choose alternative practices, technologies, or rules (Lawrence, Hardy, & Phillips, 2002). Ethics are now examined as societal or national-level institutions, in order to understand ethical antecedents of social entrepreneurship.

Ethics

A survey of literature by Harris et al. (2009) reveals that existing academic literature connecting ethics and entrepreneurship falls into one of three areas: entrepreneurial ethics, entrepreneurship and society, and social venturing (or SE). While the literature covering entrepreneurial ethics is primarily concerned with the ethical dilemmas involved in setting up new enterprises, the literature on ethics and entrepreneurship adopts a broader view of entrepreneurship, exploring the role of new enterprises in the relationship between business and society (Harris et al., 2009). Social venturing, or SE, is considered an important topic at the intersection of ethics and entrepreneurship, and covers six broad areas of research (Harris et al., 2009): defining SE, discussing ethical concerns in setting up a social venture, covering the measurement of the performance of a social enterprise, examining disenfranchised entrepreneurs, discussing the differences between social ventures and traditional ventures, and discussing the role of purpose in a social venture. This research has paid scant attention to societal-level ethical attitudes (Franke & Nadler, 2008).

Societal-level ethical attitudes comprise people's cognitive, affective, and behavioral predispositions to respond to issues, concerns, and activities involving standards in society for what is morally right and virtuous (Franke & Nadler, 2008). While various frameworks of ethical decision-making (see Ferrell, Gresham, & Fraedrich, 1989; Hunt & Vitell, 2006; Srnka, 2004) suggest that ethical judgements depend on the nature of the consequences of the issue and personal traits of the decision maker, national culture is also an important influencer (Franke & Nadler, 2008). Extant literature has examined various aspects of ethical attitudes, such as sensitivity to the presence of ethical concerns (Sparks & Hunt, 1998), process of moral development in discussions on ethical concerns (Goolsby & Hunt, 1992), and the correctness of particular behaviors in situations involving dilemmas (Volkema, 2004).

Besides discussions on societal-level attitudes, extant research has also examined the influence of ethics as antecedents of different variations of social responsibility. In understanding the corporate ethical values of managers, Singhapakdi, Kraft, Vitell, and Rallapalli (1995) suggest that for managers to act ethically and socially responsibly, they should believe that ethics and social responsibility are important aspects of organizational effectiveness. Questions of what is right and wrong reflect ethical attitudes of managers (Bucar et al., 2003).

At the firm level, actions of firms reflect attitudes concerning ethical concerns (Longenecker, Moore, Petty, Palich, & McKinney, 2006). Ethical frameworks are also considered to be systems of value principles or practices, and the ability to distinguish between right and wrong (Joyner & Payne, 2002; Payne & Joyner, 2006). Researchers have also examined the perceived importance of ethics in terms of the obligations that firms have toward various stockholders and stakeholders (Shafer et al., 2007). The high ethical standards that drive several professions, such as advertising, marketing, and medical services, also reflect their emphasis on ethics (Valentine & Fleischman, 2008). Finally, respect and concern for the environment are also the measure of ethical standards (Cambra-Fierro, Hart, & Polo-Redondo, 2008). Extant research also refers to the various traits or characteristics that comprise or define ethical leadership (Resick et al., 2011).

While all extant research has merit in associating ethical attitudes or drivers of ethics with performing socially responsible behaviors, the understanding of all types of ethics assumes ethics to be universal. The above discussion focuses on the individual level. In regard to ethical attitudes at the societal level, research is limited to the understanding of national culture as a driver of societal-level ethical attitudes. While ethical attitudes at the firm or individual level have been considered as drivers of ethically or socially responsible behaviors, this chapter attempts first to establish societal-level ethical attitudes as societal or national-level institutions, and then to predict their influence on SE. The understanding gained from this study of societal-level ethical institutions in the establishment of social enterprises can also extend to predicting socially responsible behaviors by commercial enterprises.

Societal Ethical Institutions and Social Entrepreneurship

Insights drawn from institutional theory and institutional configuration perspective establish ethical attitudes as societal-level institutions, in order to discuss the mechanism by which these institutions jointly influence SE (Stephan et al., 2014). The influence of formal institutions on entrepreneurship has been well researched, with several studies analyzing the effects of the formal and regulatory frameworks (e.g., Acs & Karlsson, 2002; Davidsson, Hunter, & Klofsten, 2006; Karlsson & Acs, 2002; Klapper, Lewin, & Delgado, 2009). For example, changes in technology policies, political factors or forces, and various regulations, can have decisive impacts on the occurrence and creation of new opportunities (Shane, 2003). A typical example of new opportunities being created for entrepreneurs is changes in the regulations in Eastern and Central European countries that permitted private organizations to lawfully exist (Smallbone & Welter, 2009).

The other area of research examines the influence of informal institutions on entrepreneurship. This group of studies specifically examines the role of informal institutions across countries. Some of the research that falls into this category includes studies comparing different institutional profiles (Busenitz et al., 2000; Manolova, Eunni, & Gyoshev, 2008); study of entrepreneurial cognitions across differ-

National Ethical Institutions and Social Entrepreneurship

ent national cultures (Busenitz & Lau, 1996; Mitchell, Smith, Seawright, & Morse, 2000; Mitchell et al., 2002); the impact of national cultures on entrepreneurship (Hayton, George, & Zahra, 2002; Tan, 2002); and cross-country study of the impact of postmaterialism on entrepreneurship (Uhlaner, Thurik, & Hutjes, 2002).

Like the case of commercial entrepreneurship, SE needs to be studied in the social context in which it is embedded (Mair & Marti, 2006). Drawing from institutional theory suggests that individuals in society are embedded within larger social structures, which comprise different institutions that strongly influence individual decision-making (Campbell, 2007). As discussed in the section on societal institutions, Scott (1995) classified North's formal and informal dimensions of institutions into three pillars: regulative, normative, and cognitive. So far, scholarly research has mainly examined the influence of formal institutions on SE (Dacin, Dacin, & Matear, 2010; Estrin et al., 2013a; Mair & Marti, 2009; Zahra et al., 2009).

Different disciplines define comparative entrepreneurship research differently, depending on whether they use formal or informal institutions to predict the existence of entrepreneurship (Bruton et al., 2010; Jones, Coviello, & Tang, 2011). For example, cross-national comparative entrepreneurship research, based on institutional economics, examines formal institutions (Autio & Acs, 2010; Estrin, Korosteleva, & Mickiewicz, 2013b); cross-cultural psychology and sociology entrepreneurship research examines informal institutions (Autio, Pathak, & Wennberg, 2013; Stephan et al., 2014). While scholars in other research areas have suggested the possibility of joint influences (formal and informal institutions to predict phenomena) (Carney, Gedajlovic, & Yang, 2009; North, 2005), scholarly studies integrating and using both formal institutions and informal institutions in comparative entrepreneurship research are limited (Stephan & Uhlaner, 2010; Stephan et al., 2014).

Inputs from institutional theory (North, 2005; Scott, 1995) are used to develop societal-level ethical antecedents of the creation of social enterprise. In the process, the institutional configuration perspective is used to develop the conceptual framework. From the institutional configuration perspective, incentives and constraints provided by both informal and formal institutions jointly influence behavior of an individual or a firm (Stephan et al., 2014). Furthermore, individual mental models of entrepreneurs influence the type of firm; extant research suggests that the firm is an extension of the individual entrepreneur's ego (Muralidharan & Pathak, 2016; Zahra, Korri, & Yu, 2005). Researchers in the area of strategy equate a firm's objectives to the goals and vision of the founding individuals (Katz & Gartner, 1988). Therefore, the exploration in this chapter occurs at the firm level, given the intricate link between individual entrepreneurs' personal objectives and the goals of the firms they establish (Zahra et al., 2005).

In summary, both formal and informal institutions are integrated into a framework to propose the impact of societal-level public-sector ethical attitudes (as a formal-regulatory institution), societal-level behavioral ethical attitudes (as an informal-normative institution), and societal-level unselfishness values (as an informal-cognitive institution), and their interplay in the creation of social enterprises. These societal or national-level institutions are considered opportunities and facilitators of SE in the proposed framework, as demonstrated in Figure 1. The subsequent sections discuss each of the predictors and their interplay, to predict the creation of social enterprises.

Public-Sector Ethics (Regulatory Institution) and Social Entrepreneurship

Public-sector ethics relate to integrity, bribery, and favoritism in the public sector (Kaufmann, 2004). The Global Competitiveness Report of the World Economic Forum measures the following factors that

Figure 1.

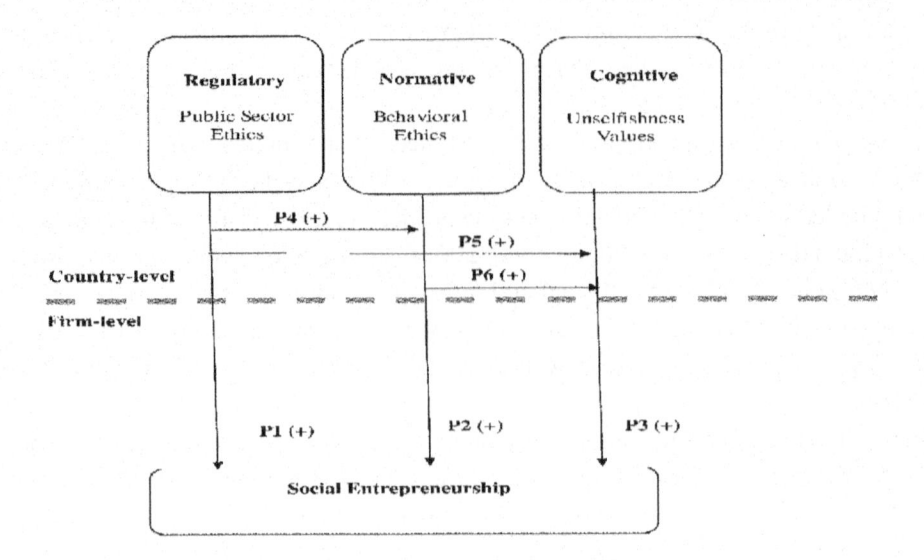

```
    ┌──────────┐   ┌──────────┐   ┌──────────┐
    │Regulatory│   │Normative │   │Cognitive │
    │Public Sec│   │Behavioral│   │Unselfish-│
    │tor Ethics│   │  Ethics  │   │ness Vals │
    └────┬─────┘   └────┬─────┘   └────┬─────┘
         │  P4(+)       │               │
         │──────────────▶               │
Country-level    P5(+)  │               │
         │──────────────────────────────▶
                   P6(+)│               │
                        │───────────────▶
- - - - - - - - - - - - - - - - - - - - - - - -
Firm-level
         │              │               │
         │ P1(+)        │ P2(+)         │ P3(+)
         ▼              ▼               ▼
         ┌─────────────────────────────────┐
         │    Social Entrepreneurship      │
         └─────────────────────────────────┘
```

could potentially define public-sector ethics: honesty of politicians, government favoritism in procurement, diversion of public funds, trust in the postal service, extent of bribing in issuing permits, siphoning utilities, and cheating on or avoiding taxes. Public-sector ethics is posited as a societal-level regulatory institution. The institutional support perspective (Stephan et al., 2014) is used to understand the effect of public-sector ethics, and suggests that societies with more active governments, bureaucracy, and public-sector institutions will support, and thus enhance, SE (Evans, 1996; Korosec & Berman, 2006; Zahra & Wright, 2011).

Extant research suggests that national governments, through their bureaucracy and public-sector institutions, participate in addressing social concerns in society by providing both tangible and intangible resources, thereby providing support to social entrepreneurs (Evans, 1996; Korosec & Berman, 2006; Zahra & Wright, 2011). Tangible support arrives through funding and easy access to information, and intangible support through all forms of assistance in performing transactions related to setting up and running a social enterprise in a sustainable manner. Some examples of tangible resource support include donations, grants, and subsidies. Intangible resource support may include assistance with accessing and completion of grant and funding applications, obtaining necessary permits to obtain resources, and providing a networking platform for managing operations in a smooth and uninterrupted manner (Korosec & Berman, 2006; Meyskens, Carsrud, & Cardozo, 2010).

The ethical standards of the government bureaucracy and public-sector institutions are formal societal-level institutions that can facilitate or constrain social entrepreneurial activities. Low ethical standards in these institutions in society could create barriers to entry or operational barriers to obtaining clearances and permits to start social ventures for individuals with social objectives. Such contexts may also delay access to resources required to start and operate their enterprises. Barriers could increase the transaction costs involved for social entrepreneurs to start and manage their ventures in a sustainable manner (Nicholls, 2006), and hence these barriers would constitute institutional constraints for such activities.

In summary, an important role of the government and its constituencies is to provide public resources, and also to take care of the welfare of its citizens. As discussed earlier in this chapter, social entrepreneurs create enterprises that address societal concerns and needs. This implies that social entrepreneurs, the government, and public institutions are natural partners in addressing societal concerns and needs (Zahra & Wright, 2011). Extant research has found a positive association between government support and the creation of non-profit enterprises (Saxton & Benson, 2005). The established bureaucracy and public-sector bodies translate government objectives into action. Higher ethical standards of the government and the public sector may enhance social entrepreneurs' resources, and reduce transaction costs in commencing and managing their social enterprises in a sustainable manner (Nicholls, 2006; Stephan et al., 2014). A culture of high ethical standards in the government and its constituencies is a reflection of a society's regulatory institution, an indication of the government support for social entrepreneurs in the creation and management of their enterprises. Since entrepreneurs' personal objectives and the goals of the enterprises they form are intricately linked (Zahra et al., 2005), it is proposed:

Proposition 1: Public-sector ethics in society is positively associated with the creation of social enterprises.

Behavioral Ethics (Normative Institution) and Social Entrepreneurship

Justifiable behaviors are the accepted norms or practices of behavior of individuals in society. Behavioral ethics encompass morally justifiable actions, norms, or practices in society. The World Values Survey, using the following parameters that could potentially reflect behavioral ethical norms in society, measures the extent to which individuals consider the following as normal: claiming benefits to which they are not entitled; avoiding paying for public transportation; cheating on taxes; and accepting bribes in the course of duty. Since these are norms and practices that occur in daily life, they may qualify behavioral ethics as societal or national-level normative institutions.

Extant research considers entrepreneurship a function of available opportunity and motivated individuals (Aldrich & Zimmer, 1986). Entrepreneurial activity is therefore a product of the individual entrepreneur and the opportunity provided by the environment (Shane & Venkataraman, 2000). Scholars agree that opportunities exist when there are imperfections in the market, or in conditions of imperfect competition (Alvarez & Barney, 2010). While market imperfections could present opportunities for commercial entrepreneurs, opportunities for social entrepreneurs are different (Corner & Ho, 2010). Opportunities for social entrepreneurs stem from activities that create social value for society. Examples of such opportunities for SE include philanthropic activities, facilitating fair-trade importing, and self-help systems such as the microfinance movement (Hockerts, 2006).

Opportunities for social entrepreneurs are therefore embedded in society (Robinson, 2006). Lack of a favorable context could also provide opportunities of which firms can take advantage, such as institutional voids in developing economies (Mair & Marti, 2009; Puffer, McCarthy, & Boisot, 2010). In particular, a low behavioral ethical standard in society may be an opportunity for motivated social entrepreneurs, through their social enterprises, to pursue change and create social value. The presence of low behavioral standards in society is an opportunity for prosocial entrepreneurs, just as demographical, technological, and regulatory changes in society can result in opportunities for commercial enterprises (Drucker, 1985; Hall & Rosson, 2006). Examples of low ethical standards discussed earlier reflect unethical norms and practices, such as bribing at all levels in the administration, tax evasion by individuals, excessive levels of pollution, or not adhering to civic or regulatory standards in society. These societal concerns or opportunities act as motivational stimulants for entrepreneurs ranking high for prosocial motivations (Stephan et al., 2014). Existing scholarship linking entrepreneurship and society suggests that social entrepreneurs, through their social enterprises, can stimulate positive change in society by helping to discard existing social norms (i.e., low behavioral ethical standards in this study), and helping to create new ones (Harris et al., 2009).

In summary, entrepreneurship is a combined product of the individual and the context that provides an opportunity to act entrepreneurially (Shane & Venkataraman, 2000). As mentioned earlier in the chapter, SE is the recognition and exploitation of opportunities that stem from the long-standing needs or concerns of society, which may warrant change (Austin et al., 2006). Societal norms can create incentives for entrepreneurial activities (Baumol, 1990). Behavioral ethics are morally justifiable actions in society, and low behavioral ethics in society are norms that provide opportunities for change in society for prosocial entrepreneurs, through their agency. Again, based on the intricate link between entrepreneurs' personal objectives and the goals of the enterprises they form (Zahra et al., 2005), it is proposed:

Proposition 2: Unethical behavior in society is positively associated with the creation of social enterprises.

Unselfishness (Cognitive Institution) and Social Entrepreneurship

Unselfishness is a cultural value in society, whereby individuals attach importance to others, and therefore actively value doing good for society, as opposed to private gain (Dacin et al., 2010; Kanungo, 2001; Zahra et al., 2009). The World Values Survey reports the percentage of respondents in a country who believe that unselfishness is an important value that they encourage their children to learn at home. Since these are values that are shared and cultural-cognitive, unselfishness is a societal-level cognitive institution. Unselfishness as a societal value plays an important role in motivating individuals to pursue socially important goals through their agency. Motivation, as established in the literature, is an important driver of entrepreneurship (Shane, Locke, & Collins, 2003).

Furthermore, research suggests that an individual's values play an important role in career decision-making (Knafo & Sagiv, 2004; Noseleit, 2010). This insight can extend to understanding the drivers of career decision-making by individuals pursuing a career in SE (Roccas, Sagiv, Schwartz, & Knafo, 2002). Scholars have used insights from aggregate trait theory to understand the drivers of cross-cultural differences in individual career choices to engage in commercial entrepreneurship (Davidsson & Wiklund, 1997; Uhlaner & Thurik, 2007). Applying this insight from aggregate trait theory suggests that societal values reflect the importance of certain values for a society's inhabitants—that is, the aggregate of goals which are personally important to those inhabitants (Schwartz, 2006). When applied to SE, aggregate trait perspective maintains that the greater the number of individuals in a society who hold values consistent with SE, the greater the number will be of individuals in that society motivated to engage in social entrepreneurial activities (Stephan et al., 2014).

Extant research has also established that SE is based on ethical motives and moral responsibility considerations (Mair & Martí, 2006). Therefore, individuals who score high for prosocial values will be more inclined to become social entrepreneurs (Stephan et al., 2014). Unselfishness is a key ethical value that motivates such individuals to become social entrepreneurs, as this value differentiates them from commercial entrepreneurs, by virtue of their objective of actively doing good for members of the society, as opposed to pursuing initiatives solely to generate personal profits (Dacin et al., 2010; Grant & Berry, 2011; Grant & Sumanth, 2009; Zahra et al., 2009). This argument is also in line with extant research that suggests that social entrepreneurs create value for the benefit of the collective, as opposed to individual monetary gain (Bacq et al., 2014).

In summary, societal cultural values reflect the importance of certain values for individuals in a society—that is, the aggregate of personally important goals that those individuals hold (Schwartz, 2006). The aggregate trait perspective (Davidsson & Wiklund, 1997; Uhlaner & Thurik, 2007) has been used to understand why differences in values across cultures predict differences in individual career choices for commercial entrepreneurship. This insight extends to understanding the drivers of career choices of social entrepreneurs. SE is primarily based on ethical motives and moral responsibility (Mair & Marti, 2006). Unselfishness is a moral value that distinguishes social entrepreneurs from commercial entrepreneurs, by the importance they attach to actively doing good for society, as opposed to individual gain (Dacin et al., 2010). The societal value of unselfishness drives the prosocial motivation of such individuals to help or contribute to other people through their enterprises (Grant & Berry, 2011). Finally, given the intricate link between an entrepreneurs' personal objectives and the goals of the enterprises they form (Zahra et al., 2005), it is proposed:

Proposition 3: Unselfishness in society is positively associated with the creation of social enterprises.

Behavioral Ethics and Public-Sector Ethics

As discussed earlier in the chapter, entrepreneurial activities are a function of "*opportunity* structures and *motivated* entrepreneurs" (Aldrich & Zimmer, 1986, p. 3). The activity is an outcome of the fit between the individual and the opportunity (Shane & Venkataraman, 2000). Davidsson's (2015) review, which shows limited progress in understanding the role of opportunities and individuals, suggests the connection between "external enablers" and "actors" for new venture creation. High public-sector ethics in the environment would be an external enabler that would act as a strong motivational stimulant (Stephan et al., 2014) for individuals with high prosocial motivations (Grant & Berry, 2011; Grant & Sumanth, 2009) to engage in activities or form organizations that lead to social change.

While low behavioral ethics in the environment would elicit entrepreneurial responses from individuals who want to create social change, high public-sector ethical standards in the environment may serve to enhance or support the responses that such prosocial entrepreneurs may have to create social value. High public-sector ethical standards tend to alleviate the challenges that such entrepreneurs face, due to high transaction costs they may have to incur to establish and manage their social enterprises in contexts where public-sector ethical standards are low. This insight of a synergy between public enterprises and private agency appears in political science and development economics literature (Skocpol, 2008; Woolcock & Narayan, 2000). It is therefore suggested that high regulatory public-sector ethical standards reinforce the positive effects of the normative low behavioral ethical standards in society, and consequently enable SE. Hence it is proposed:

Proposition 4: Public-sector ethics moderate the relationship between unethical behavior in society and the creation of social enterprises; the relationship is stronger when both unethical behavior and public-sector ethical standards in society are high.

Unselfishness and Public-Sector Ethics

As discussed in relation to Proposition 4, entrepreneurial action has often been considered a product of the individual and a situation that provides an opportunity to act entrepreneurially (Shane & Venkataraman, 2000). Again, Davidsson's (2015) review, in understanding the role of opportunities and individuals, suggests the strong linkage between "external enablers" and "entrepreneurs" for new venture creation. Thus, widespread unselfishness values in a society, based on the aggregate trait hypothesis (Davidsson & Wiklund, 1997; Uhlaner & Thurik, 2007), may not be sufficient to stimulate a large number of individuals to become social entrepreneurs (Stephan et al., 2014), unless there are external enablers for these individuals to act upon those values.

Using the same arguments leading to Proposition 4, high public-sector ethical standards may serve to act as external enablers. High public-sector ethical standards tend to act as motivational stimulants (Stephan et al., 2014) for individuals with high unselfishness values, and hence a prosocial bent, to set up social enterprises with social objectives. High public-sector ethical standards help reduce transaction costs that prosocial entrepreneurs incur in setting up and managing their social enterprises. Hence it is proposed:

Proposition 5: Public-sector ethics moderate the relationship between unselfishness in society and the creation of social enterprises; the relationship is stronger when both unselfishness in society and public-sector ethical standards are high.

Behavioral Ethics and Unselfishness

Propositions 4 and 5 illustrate that entrepreneurial action is a product of the individual and his or her context (Shane & Venkataraman, 2000). Widespread unselfishness as a moral value in society may not be sufficient to motivate a large number of individuals in society to become social entrepreneurs, unless there is sufficient opportunity in society for them to create social change through their enterprises (Stephan et al., 2014). Bornstein's (2004) series of biographies of social entrepreneurs highlights how moral values of social entrepreneurs motivated them to act after they were sufficiently exposed to human suffering. Low behavioral ethical standards in society would be an opportunity that triggers individuals who score high for unselfishness values to pursue social change. Individuals in society are more likely to establish social enterprises in such situations. Individuals are more likely to engage in SE in societies where there is greater social need and demand for SE (when behavioral ethical standards in society are low), and a high proportion of prosocial individuals (those with high unselfishness values). Hence it is proposed:

Proposition 6: Unethical behavior moderates the relationship between unselfishness in society and the creation of social enterprises; the relationship is stronger when both unselfishness and unethical behavior in society are high.

DISCUSSION

Extant reviews by scholars suggest that entrepreneurship and ethics have generally been treated as separate fields of study. This conceptual study contributes to the intersection of entrepreneurship and business ethics, which remains in relatively early stages (Harris et al., 2009). There is limited research that examines how the ethical context of a society influences entrepreneurial actions. This study has attempted to address that gap, specifically by defining the ethical context of a society along the three dimensions of institutional theory: regulatory, normative, and cognitive; then by examining the influence of these ethical dimensions on the creation or establishment of social enterprises.

Insights from institutional theory are used to establish public-sector ethical standards of a society, behavioral ethical standards of a society, and unselfishness values of a society, as regulatory, normative, and cognitive institutions, respectively. Thereafter, the discussion establishes that behavioral ethical practices (or low behavioral ethical standards) provide opportunities for social entrepreneurs, through their enterprises, to bring about social change in society. Unselfishness is established as a societal value and a key driver of the prosocial motivations of social entrepreneurs setting up social enterprises. Then, it is suggested that for successful entry and establishment of their social enterprises, such prosocial individuals would require easy accessibility and the support of public-sector institutions to facilitate transactions in establishing and running their enterprises. Therefore, presence of high ethical standards in such public institutions would help reduce the transaction costs associated with social entrepreneurs starting and managing enterprises.

A mixed-determinant, multilevel model (presented in Figure 1) (Kozlowski & Klein, 2000; Stephan et al., 2014) is proposed, in which the three societal-level institutions (regulatory, normative, and cognitive) are represented. The proposed model represents the effects of public-sector ethical standards (the regulatory dimension), behavioral ethical norms and practices (the normative dimension), and societal unselfishness value (the cognitive dimension), alone and in combination, in relation to the probability of establishment of a social enterprise. While the presence of postmaterialist cultural values of unselfishness increases the supply of potential social entrepreneurs (Stephan et al., 2014), and low behavioral ethical standards in society provide the opportunity for such individuals to create social change, government support through high public-sector ethical standards serves as a strong enabler for lowering transaction costs and providing access to resources that social entrepreneurs need to establish and manage social enterprises in a sustainable manner (Nicholls, 2006). Given that entrepreneurs' personal objectives and the goals of the enterprises they form are intricately linked (Zahra et al., 2005), the probability determination is explored at the firm level.

The propositions in this chapter suggest joint institutional configurations of formal and informal institutions. Propositions using the institutional configuration perspective enable better integration of research on formal and informal institutions, and go beyond the debate on whether formal or informal institutions are more important for outcomes (Stephan et al., 2014). While theorizing the effect of configuration is a common practice in strategic management and psychology research (Short, Payne, & Ketchen, 2008; Tett & Burnett, 2003), it is limited in institutional theory research (Scott, 2005) and in comparative entrepreneurship research (Bruton et al., 2010; Jones et al., 2011; Stephan et al., 2014). The propositions offer a wider perspective by suggesting that formal and informal institutions can also have additive and mutually reinforcing influences on the creation of social enterprises (Stephan et al., 2014), as proposed between public-sector ethics and behavioral ethical standards, between public-sector ethics and unselfishness values, and between behavioral ethical standards and unselfishness values.

The chapter makes the following contributions to extant literature on entrepreneurship and societal institutions. First, the use of institutional theory as a framework is growing in all areas of management research, as the framework captures issues that the concept of culture cannot (Busenitz et al., 2000; Hoskisson, Eden, Lau, & Wright, 2000). Further, inconsistencies in research that uses Hofstede's measures of culture have prompted scholars to incorporate institutional arguments in their studies (Mueller & Thomas, 2001). Kostova (1997), for example, proposed the concept of a country institutional profile to explain how a society's institutional context influences its domestic business activity. Many entrepreneurship scholars use this concept to explore why levels of entrepreneurship vary by country (Busenitz et al., 2000). The institutional framework has been used to understand the effects of societal ethical context on social entrepreneurship. Classifying societal ethics along the three dimensions of institutional theory provides a benchmark to identify societal-level ethics as either regulatory, normative, or cognitive institutions.

Second, the institutional framework for ethics suggests a more contextualized understanding of the effect of societal-level ethics on SE at the individual level. While practitioners acknowledge the influence of context, academic research on the influence of context on SE is limited (Bacq & Janssen 2011; Estrin, et al., 2013b; Nicholls, 2010). Scholars have observed that socially responsible behaviors, represented by the rates of SE, vary significantly across countries (Lepoutre, Justo, Terjesen, & Bosma, 2013). The proposed framework in this chapter suggests that this variance may also be due to differences in a country's ethical attitudes. These societal-level ethical attitudes may also influence and contribute to discussions of the national entrepreneurship framework conditions, assumed to be resource-allocation mechanisms driven by opportunity discovery and pursuits at the individual or firm level, the results or outcomes of which are regulated by societal-level institutions (Ács, Autio, & Szerb, 2014).

Third, this conceptual study uses a multilevel theoretical framework to understand and propose how societal ethical attitudes influence SE at the firm level, given the intricate link between entrepreneurs' personal goals and the goals of the enterprises they form (Zahra et al., 2005). While societal culture is basically a collective-level construct, entrepreneurship is fundamentally an individual or team-level construct (Baumol, 1990). Using a multilevel theoretical design helps to avoid ecological and individualistic fallacies (Autio et al., 2013). The proposed framework in this chapter therefore contributes to multicountry comparative entrepreneurship research. This study is also in line with the recent calls by academic scholars for greater examination of the impact of context on entrepreneurial behavior (Welter, 2011; Zahra & Wright, 2011). The chapter specifically suggests that societal ethical contexts can serve as opportunities for individual social change agents to establish social enterprises, and addresses how these ethical contexts can enable or facilitate entry into social entrepreneurial activity.

FUTURE RESEARCH DIRECTIONS

The proposed framework is multilevel in design and conceptual in nature, to examine the influence of societal-level ethical institutions on SE. Future research may need to empirically test the framework proposed in this chapter, using advanced quantitative methods. Doing so will also respond to the call by scholars for the advancement of SE research through quantitative methods (Dacin et al., 2011; Short, Moss, & Lumpkin, 2009). Only three types of ethics have been conceptualized in this chapter. Future research may identify more ethical institutions at the societal level, and examine their influences on SE, as well as on socially responsible behaviors (Jones, 1999). Zahra et al. (2009), building on the research by Hayek (1945), Kirzner (1973), and Schumpeter (1934), identified three types of social entrepreneurs: social bricoleurs, social constructionists, and social engineers. Future research may examine the effect of the societal ethical institutions on these social entrepreneurial types.

CONCLUSION

Extant research has largely examined ethics in terms of the extent to which context influences ethical attitudes of entrepreneurs, or how entrepreneurs react to ethical dilemmas. The activities of social entrepreneurs have been examined from the point of view of individual motivation of such entrepreneurs. This chapter attempts to establish how societal ethical contexts can serve as an opportunity for social entrepreneurs, and how such contexts can facilitate establishment of social enterprises by such individuals. It suggests that societal-level ethical institutions, along the regulatory, normative, and cognitive dimensions, influence the probability of establishing social enterprises. Low behavioral ethical standards in society—a normative institution—serve as an opportunity for social entrepreneurs to establish social enterprises. Societal unselfishness values provide the supply of social entrepreneurs. High public-sector ethical standards in society enable or facilitate individual success in social entrepreneurial endeavors. The chapter also proposes additive or reinforcing effects of public-sector ethics and behavioral ethical standards, public-sector ethics and unselfishness values, and behavioral ethical standards and unselfishness values, on the creation of social enterprises. In clearly identifying different types of societal-level ethical institutions, the chapter contributes to the sought-after literature that examines the effect of context on entrepreneurial behavior.

REFERENCES

Ács, Z. J., Autio, E., & Szerb, L. (2014). National systems of entrepreneurship: Measurement issues and policy implications. *Research Policy, 43*(3), 476–494. doi:10.1016/j.respol.2013.08.016

Acs, Z. J., & Karlsson, C. (2002). Introduction to institutions, entrepreneurship and firm growth: From Sweden to the OECD. *Small Business Economics, 19*(3), 183–187. doi:10.1023/A:1019634716768

Aldrich, H., & Zimmer, C. (1986). Entrepreneurship through social networks. In D. Sexton & R. Smilor (Eds.), *The art and science of entrepreneurship* (pp. 3–23). Cambridge, MA: Ballinger Publishing Co.

Alvarez, S. A., & Barney, J. B. (2010). Entrepreneurship and epistemology: The philosophical underpinnings of the study of entrepreneurial opportunities. *The Academy of Management Annals, 4*(1), 557–583. doi:10.1080/19416520.2010.495521

Austin, J., Stevenson, H., & Wei-Skillern, J. (2006). Social and commercial entrepreneurship: Same, different, or both? *Entrepreneurship Theory and Practice, 30*(1), 1–22. doi:10.1111/j.1540-6520.2006.00107.x

Autio, E., & Acs, Z. (2010). Intellectual property protection and the formation of entrepreneurial growth aspirations. *Strategic Entrepreneurship Journal, 4*(3), 234–251. doi:10.1002/sej.93

Autio, E., Pathak, S., & Wennberg, K. (2013). Consequences of cultural practices for entrepreneurial behaviors. *Journal of International Business Studies, 44*(4), 334–362. doi:10.1057/jibs.2013.15

Bacq, S., Hartog, C., & Hoogendoorn, B. (2014). Beyond the moral portrayal of social entrepreneurs: An empirical approach to who they are and what drives them. *Journal of Business Ethics*.

Bacq, S., & Janssen, F. (2011). The multiple faces of social entrepreneurship: A review of definitional issues based on geographical and thematic criteria. *Entrepreneurship & Regional Development, 23*(5-6), 373–403. doi:10.1080/08985626.2011.577242

Baumol, W. J. (1990). Entrepreneurship: Productive, unproductive, and destructive. *Journal of Political Economy, 98*(5), 893–921. doi:10.1086/261712

Bernauer, T., & Caduff, L. (2004). In whose interest? Pressure group politics, economic competition and environmental regulation. *Journal of Public Policy, 24*(01), 99–126. doi:10.1017/S0143814X04000054

Bierhoff, H.-W. (2002). *Pro-social behaviour*. Hove, UK: Psychology Press.

Bornstein, D. (2004). *How to change the world: Social entrepreneurs and the power of new ideas*. Oxford, UK: Oxford University Press.

Bosma, N., Terjesen, S. A., Schøtt, T., & Kew, P. (2016). *Global Entrepreneurship Monitor 2015 to 2016: Special Report on Social Entrepreneurship*. Retrieved from http://ssrn.com/abstract=2786949

Bruton, G. D., Ahlstrom, D., & Li, H. L. (2010). Institutional theory and entrepreneurship: Where are we now and where do we need to move in the future? *Entrepreneurship Theory and Practice, 34*(3), 421–440. doi:10.1111/j.1540-6520.2010.00390.x

Bruton, G. D., Fried, V. H., & Manigart, S. (2005). Institutional influences on the worldwide expansion of venture capital. *Entrepreneurship Theory and Practice, 29*(6), 737–760. doi:10.1111/j.1540-6520.2005.00106.x

Bucar, B., Glas, M., & Hisrich, R. D. (2003). Ethics and entrepreneurs: An international comparative study. *Journal of Business Venturing, 18*(2), 261–281. doi:10.1016/S0883-9026(01)00083-0

Busenitz, L. W., Gomez, C., & Spencer, J. W. (2000). Country institutional profiles: Unlocking entrepreneurial phenomena. *Academy of Management Journal, 43*(5), 994–1003. doi:10.2307/1556423

Busenitz, L. W., & Lau, C. M. (1996). A cross-cultural cognitive model of new venture creation. *Entrepreneurship: Theory and Practice, 20*(4), 25–40.

Cambra-Fierro, J., Hart, S., & Polo-Redondo, Y. (2008). Environmental respect: Ethics or simply business? A study in the small and medium enterprise (SME) context. *Journal of Business Ethics, 82*(3), 645–656. doi:10.1007/s10551-007-9583-1

Campbell, J. L. (2007). Why would corporations behave in socially responsible ways? An institutional theory of corporate social responsibility. *Academy of Management Review, 32*(3), 946–967. doi:10.5465/AMR.2007.25275684

Capelli, P., & Sherer, P. D. (1991). The missing role of context in OB: The need for a meso-level approach. *Research in Organizational Behavior, 13*, 55–110.

Carney, M., Gedajlovic, E., & Yang, X. (2009). Varieties of Asian capitalism: Toward an institutional theory of Asian enterprise. *Asia Pacific Journal of Management, 26*(3), 361–380. doi:10.1007/s10490-009-9139-2

Casson, M. (1992). Internalization theory and beyond. In P. J. Buckley (Ed.), *New directions in international business. Research priorities for the 1990s* (pp. 4–27). Brookfield, VT: Edward Elgar.

Certo, S. T., & Miller, T. (2008). Social entrepreneurship: Key issues and concepts. *Business Horizons, 51*(4), 267–271. doi:10.1016/j.bushor.2008.02.009

Corner, P. D., & Ho, M. (2010). How opportunities develop in social entrepreneurship. *Entrepreneurship Theory and Practice, 34*(4), 635–659. doi:10.1111/j.1540-6520.2010.00382.x

Dacin, M. T., Dacin, P. A., & Tracey, P. (2011). Social entrepreneurship: A critique and future directions. *Organization Science, 22*(5), 1203–1213. doi:10.1287/orsc.1100.0620

Dacin, P. A., Dacin, M. T., & Matear, M. (2010). Social entrepreneurship: Why we dont need a new theory and how we move forward from here. *The Academy of Management Perspectives, 24*(3), 37–57. doi:10.5465/AMP.2010.52842950

Davidsson, P. (2015). Entrepreneurial opportunities and the entrepreneurship nexus: A re-conceptualization. *Journal of Business Venturing, 30*(5), 674–695. doi:10.1016/j.jbusvent.2015.01.002

Davidsson, P., Hunter, E., & Klofsten, M. (2006). Institutional forces: The invisible hand that shapes venture ideas? *International Small Business Journal, 24*(2), 115–131. doi:10.1177/0266242606061834

Davidsson, P., & Wiklund, J. (1997). Values, beliefs and regional variations in new firm formation rates. *Journal of Economic Psychology, 18*(2), 179–199. doi:10.1016/S0167-4870(97)00004-4

DeLeon, L. (1996). Ethics and entrepreneurship. *Policy Studies Journal: the Journal of the Policy Studies Organization, 24*(3), 495–510. doi:10.1111/j.1541-0072.1996.tb01642.x

Dey, P. (2006). The rhetoric of social entrepreneurship: Paralogy and new language games in academic discourse. In C. Steyaert & D. Hjorth (Eds.), *Entrepreneurship as social change: A third movements of entrepreneurship* (pp. 121–144). Cheltenham, UK: Edward Elgar. doi:10.4337/9781847204424.00015

Drucker, P. (1985). *Innovation and entrepreneurship: Practice and principles*. New York: Harper & Row Publishers.

Eckhardt, J. T., & Shane, S. A. (2003). Opportunities and entrepreneurship. *Journal of Management, 29*(3), 333–349. doi:10.1177/014920630302900304

Estrin, S., Korosteleva, J., & Mickiewicz, T. (2013b). Which institutions encourage entrepreneurial growth aspirations? *Journal of Business Venturing, 28*(4), 564–580. doi:10.1016/j.jbusvent.2012.05.001

Estrin, S., Mickiewicz, T., & Stephan, U. (2013a). Entrepreneurship, social capital, and institutions: Social and commercial entrepreneurship across nations. *Entrepreneurship Theory and Practice, 37*(3), 479–504. doi:10.1111/etap.12019

Evans, P. (1996). Government action, social capital and development: Reviewing the evidence on synergy. *World Development, 24*(6), 1119–1132. doi:10.1016/0305-750X(96)00021-6

Ferrell, O., Gresham, L. G., & Fraedrich, J. (1989). A synthesis of ethical decision models for marketing. *Journal of Macromarketing, 9*(2), 55–64. doi:10.1177/027614678900900207

Franke, G. R., & Nadler, S. S. (2008). Culture, economic development, and national ethical attitudes. *Journal of Business Research*, *61*(3), 254–264. doi:10.1016/j.jbusres.2007.06.005

Friedman, A. L., & Miles, S. (2001). Socially responsible investment and corporate social and environmental reporting in the UK: An exploratory study. *The British Accounting Review*, *33*(4), 523–548. doi:10.1006/bare.2001.0172

Gartner, W. B. (1995). Aspects of organizational emergence. In I. Bull, H. Thomas, & G. Willard (Eds.), *Entrepreneurship: Perspectives on theory building* (pp. 67–86). Oxford, UK: Pergamon.

Goolsby, J. R., & Hunt, S. D. (1992). Cognitive moral development and marketing. *Journal of Marketing*, *56*(1), 55–68. doi:10.2307/1252132

Granovetter, M. (1985). Economic action and social structure: The problem of embeddedness. *American Journal of Sociology*, *91*(3), 481–510. doi:10.1086/228311

Grant, A. M., & Berry, J. W. (2011). The necessity of others is the mother of invention: Intrinsic and prosocial motivations, perspective taking, and creativity. *Academy of Management Journal*, *54*(1), 73–96. doi:10.5465/AMJ.2011.59215085

Grant, A. M., & Sumanth, J. J. (2009). Mission possible? The performance of prosocially motivated employees depends on manager trustworthiness. *The Journal of Applied Psychology*, *94*(4), 927–944. doi:10.1037/a0014391 PMID:19594235

Habisch, A., Jonker, J., Wegner, M., & Schmidpeter, R. (2004). *Corporate social responsibility across Europe*. Berlin: Springer.

Hall, J., & Rosson, P. (2006). The impact of technological turbulence on entrepreneurial behavior, social norms and ethics: Three internet-based cases. *Journal of Business Ethics*, *64*(3), 231–248. doi:10.1007/s10551-005-5354-z

Hannafey, F. T. (2003). Entrepreneurship and ethics: A literature review. *Journal of Business Ethics*, *46*(2), 99–110. doi:10.1023/A:1025054220365

Harris, J. D., Sapienza, H. J., & Bowie, N. E. (2009). Ethics and entrepreneurship. *Journal of Business Venturing*, *24*(5), 407–418. doi:10.1016/j.jbusvent.2009.06.001

Hayek, F. A. (1945). The use of knowledge in society. *The American Economic Review*, *35*(4), 519–530.

Hayton, J. C., George, G., & Zahra, S. A. (2002). National culture and entrepreneurship: A review of behavioral research. *Entrepreneurship Theory and Practice*, *26*(4), 33.

Hébert, R. F., & Link, A. N. (1988). *The entrepreneur: Mainstream views & radical critiques*. New York: Praeger Publishers.

Hockerts, K. (2006). Entrepreneurial opportunity in social purpose ventures. In J. Mair, J. Robinson, & K. Hockerts (Eds.), *Social entrepreneurship* (pp. 142–154). London, UK: Palgrave. doi:10.1057/9780230625655_10

Hoskisson, R. E., Eden, L., Lau, C. M., & Wright, M. (2000). Strategy in emerging economies. *Academy of Management Journal*, *43*(3), 249–267. doi:10.2307/1556394

Hunt, S. D., & Vitell, S. J. (2006). The general theory of marketing ethics: A revision and three questions. *Journal of Macromarketing, 26*(2), 143–153. doi:10.1177/0276146706290923

Ioannou, I., & Serafeim, G. (2012). What drives corporate social performance quest: The role of nation-level institutions. *Journal of International Business Studies, 43*(9), 834–864. doi:10.1057/jibs.2012.26

Jackson, G., & Apostolakou, A. (2010). Corporate social responsibility in Western Europe: An institutional mirror or substitute? *Journal of Business Ethics, 94*(3), 371–394. doi:10.1007/s10551-009-0269-8

Jamali, D., Sidani, Y., & El-Asmar, K. (2009). A three country comparative analysis of managerial CSR perspectives: Insights from Lebanon, Syria and Jordan. *Journal of Business Ethics, 85*(2), 173–192. doi:10.1007/s10551-008-9755-7

Javidan, M., House, R. J., Dorfman, P. W., Hanges, P. J., & De Luque, M. S. (2006). Conceptualizing and measuring cultures and their consequences: A comparative review of GLOBEs and Hofstedes approaches. *Journal of International Business Studies, 37*(6), 897–914. doi:10.1057/palgrave.jibs.8400234

Johns, G. (2006). The essential impact of context on organizational behaviour. *Academy of Management Review, 31*(2), 386–408. doi:10.5465/AMR.2006.20208687

Jones, M. T. (1999). The institutional determinants of social responsibility. *Journal of Business Ethics, 20*(2), 163–170. doi:10.1023/A:1005871021412

Jones, M. V., Coviello, N., & Tang, Y. K. (2011). International entrepreneurship research (1989–2009): A domain ontology and thematic analysis. *Journal of Business Venturing, 26*(6), 632–659. doi:10.1016/j.jbusvent.2011.04.001

Joyner, B. E., & Payne, D. (2002). Evolution and implementation: A study of values, business ethics and corporate social responsibility. *Journal of Business Ethics, 41*(4), 297–311. doi:10.1023/A:1021237420663

Kanungo, R. N. (2001). Ethical values of transactional and transformational leaders. *Canadian Journal of Administrative Sciences/Revue Canadienne des Sciences de l'Administration, 18*(4), 257-265.

Karlsson, C., & Acs, Z. J. (2002). Introduction to institutions, entrepreneurship and firm growth: The case of Sweden. *Small Business Economics, 19*(2), 63–67. doi:10.1023/A:1016202618249

Katz, J., & Gartner, W. B. (1988). Properties of emerging organizations? *Academy of Management Review, 13*(3), 429–441.

Katz, J., & Steyaert, C. (2004). Entrepreneurship in society: Exploring and theorizing new forms and practices of entrepreneurship. *Entrepreneurship and Regional Development, 16*(3), 179–250.

Kaufmann, D. (2004). *Corruption, governance and security: Challenges for the rich countries and the world.*

Kirzner, I. (1973). *Competition and entrepreneurship.* Chicago: The University of Chicago Press.

Klapper, L., Lewin, A., & Delgado, J. M. (2009). *The impact of the business environment on the business creation process* (Policy Research Working Paper 4937). Washington, DC: The World Bank.

Knafo, A., & Sagiv, L. (2004). Values and work environment: Mapping 32 occupations. *European Journal of Psychology of Education*, *19*(3), 255–273. doi:10.1007/BF03173223

Korosec, M. L., & Berman, E. M. (2006). Municipal support for social entrepreneurship. *Public Administration Review*, *66*(3), 448–462. doi:10.1111/j.1540-6210.2006.00601.x

Kostova, T. (1997). Country institutional profiles: Concept and measurement. *Academy of Management Proceedings*, *1997*(1), 180-184.

Kozlowski, S. W., & Klein, K. J. (2000). A multilevel approach to theory and research in organizations: Contextual, temporal, and emergent processes. In K. J. Klein & S. W. Kozlowski (Eds.), *Multilevel theory, research and methods in organizations* (pp. 3–90). San Francisco: Jossey Bass.

Lawrence, T. B., Hardy, C., & Phillips, N. (2002). Institutional effects of interorganizational collaboration: The emergence of proto-institutions. *Academy of Management Journal*, *45*(1), 281–290. doi:10.2307/3069297

Lepoutre, J., Justo, R., Terjesen, S., & Bosma, N. (2013). Designing a global standardized methodology for measuring social entrepreneurship activity: The Global Entrepreneurship Monitor social entrepreneurship study. *Small Business Economics*, *40*(3), 693–714. doi:10.1007/s11187-011-9398-4

Longenecker, J. G., Moore, C. W., Petty, J. W., Palich, L. E., & McKinney, J. A. (2006). Ethical attitudes in small businesses and large corporations: Theory and empirical findings from a tracking study spanning three decades. *Journal of Small Business Management*, *44*(2), 167–183. doi:10.1111/j.1540-627X.2006.00162.x

Low, M. B., & MacMillan, I. C. (1988). Entrepreneurship: Past research and future challenges. *Journal of Management*, *14*(2), 139–161. doi:10.1177/014920638801400202

Mair, J., & Martí, I. (2006). Social entrepreneurship research: A source of explanation, prediction, and delight. *Journal of World Business*, *41*(1), 36–44. doi:10.1016/j.jwb.2005.09.002

Mair, J., & Martí, I. (2009). Entrepreneurship in and around institutional voids: A case study from Bangladesh. *Journal of Business Venturing*, *24*(5), 419–435. doi:10.1016/j.jbusvent.2008.04.006

Manolova, T. S., Eunni, R. V., & Gyoshev, B. S. (2008). Institutional environments for entrepreneurship: Evidence from emerging economies in Eastern Europe. *Entrepreneurship Theory and Practice*, *32*(1), 203–218. doi:10.1111/j.1540-6520.2007.00222.x

Meyer, J. W., & Rowan, B. (1977). Institutionalized organizations: Formal structure as myth and ceremony. *American Journal of Sociology*, *83*(2), 340–363. doi:10.1086/226550

Meyskens, M., Carsrud, A. L., & Cardozo, R. N. (2010). The symbiosis of entities in the social engagement network: The role of social ventures. *Entrepreneurship & Regional Development*, *22*(5), 425–455. doi:10.1080/08985620903168299

Mitchell, R. K., Busenitz, L., Lant, T., McDougall, P. P., Morse, E. A., & Smith, J. B. (2002). Toward a theory of entrepreneurial cognition: Rethinking the people side of entrepreneurship research. *Entrepreneurship Theory and Practice*, *27*(2), 93–104. doi:10.1111/1540-8520.00001

Mitchell, R. K., Smith, B., Seawright, K. W., & Morse, E. A. (2000). Cross-cultural cognitions and the venture creation decision. *Academy of Management Journal, 43*(5), 974–993. doi:10.2307/1556422

Mowday, R., & Sutton, R. (1993). Organizational behavior: Linking individuals and groups to organizational contexts. *Annual Review of Psychology, 44*(1), 195–229. doi:10.1146/annurev.ps.44.020193.001211 PMID:19090760

Mueller, S. L., & Thomas, A. S. (2001). Culture and entrepreneurial potential: A nine country study of locus of control and innovativeness. *Journal of Business Venturing, 16*(1), 51–75. doi:10.1016/S0883-9026(99)00039-7

Muralidharan, E., & Pathak, S. (2016). (in press). Informal institutions and international entrepreneurship. *International Business Review*. doi:10.1016/j.ibusrev.2016.07.006

Nicholls, A. (2006). *Social entrepreneurship: New models of sustainable social change*. Oxford: Oxford University Press.

Nicholls, A. (2010). The legitimacy of social entrepreneurship: Reflexive isomorphism in a pre-paradigmatic field. *Entrepreneurship Theory and Practice, 34*(4), 611–633. doi:10.1111/j.1540-6520.2010.00397.x

Nicholls, A., & Opal, C. (2005). *Fair trade: Market-driven ethical consumption*. London: Sage.

North, D. C. (1990). *Institutions, institutional change and economic performance*. Cambridge, UK: Cambridge University Press. doi:10.1017/CBO9780511808678

North, D. C. (1991). Institutions, transaction costs, and the rise of merchant empires. In J. D. Tracy (Ed.), *The political economy of merchant empires* (pp. 22–40). Cambridge, UK: Cambridge University Press. doi:10.1017/CBO9780511665288.002

North, D. C. (2005). *Understanding the process of economic change*. Princeton: Princeton University Press. doi:10.1515/9781400829484

Noseleit, F. (2010). The entrepreneurial culture: Guiding principles of the self-employed. In A. Freytag & R. Thurik (Eds.), *Entrepreneurship and culture* (pp. 41–54). Berlin: Springer. doi:10.1007/978-3-540-87910-7_3

Pathak, S., & Muralidharan, E. (2014). *Societal-level collectivism and trust: Influence on social and commercial entrepreneurship*.

Payne, D., & Joyner, B. E. (2006). Successful US entrepreneurs: Identifying ethical decision-making and social responsibility behaviors. *Journal of Business Ethics, 65*(3), 203–217. doi:10.1007/s10551-005-4674-3

Peredo, A. M., & McLean, M. (2006). Social entrepreneurship: A critical review of the concept. *Journal of World Business, 41*(1), 56–65. doi:10.1016/j.jwb.2005.10.007

Polanyi, K. (1957). *The great transformation: The political and economic origin of our time*. Boston: Beacon Hill.

Powell, W. W., & DiMaggio, P. J. (1991). *The new institutionalism in organizational analysis*. Chicago: University of Chicago Press.

Puffer, S. M., McCarthy, D. J., & Boisot, M. (2010). Entrepreneurship in Russia and China: The impact of formal institutional voids. *Entrepreneurship Theory and Practice, 34*(3), 441–467. doi:10.1111/j.1540-6520.2009.00353.x

Resick, C. J., Martin, G. S., Keating, M. A., Dickson, M. W., Kwan, H. K., & Peng, C. (2011). What ethical leadership means to me: Asian, American, and European perspectives. *Journal of Business Ethics, 101*(3), 435–457. doi:10.1007/s10551-010-0730-8

Robinson, J. (2006). Navigating social and institutional barriers to markets: How social entrepreneurs identify and evaluate opportunities. In J. Mair, J. Robinson, & K. Hockerts (Eds.), *Social entrepreneurship* (pp. 95–120). New York: Palgrave Macmillan. doi:10.1057/9780230625655_7

Roccas, S., Sagiv, L., Schwartz, S. H., & Knafo, A. (2002). The big five personality factors and personal values. *Personality and Social Psychology Bulletin, 28*(6), 789–801. doi:10.1177/0146167202289008

Rousseau, D., & Fried, Y. (2001). Location, location, location: Contextualizing organizational research. *Journal of Organizational Behavior, 22*(1), 1–13. doi:10.1002/job.78

Saxton, G. D., & Benson, M. A. (2005). Social capital and the growth of the non-profit sector. *Social Science Quarterly, 86*(1), 16–35. doi:10.1111/j.0038-4941.2005.00288.x

Schumpeter, J. A. (1934). *The theory of economic development: An inquiry into profits, capital, credit, interest and the business cycle.* Cambridge, MA: Harvard University Press.*(Reprinted in 1962.)*

Schwartz, S. H. (2006). A theory of cultural value orientations: Explication and applications. *Comparative Sociology, 5*(2), 137–182. doi:10.1163/156913306778667357

Scott, W. R. (1995). *Institutions and organizations.* Thousand Oaks, CA: Sage.

Scott, W. R. (2005). Institutional theory: Contributing to a theoretical research program. In K. G. Smith & M. A. Hitts (Eds.), *Great minds in management: The process of theory development* (pp. 460–485). Oxford, UK: Oxford University Press. doi:10.4135/9781412952552.n155

Scott, W. R. (2008). Approaching adulthood: The maturing of institutional theory. *Theory and Society, 37*(5), 427–442. doi:10.1007/s11186-008-9067-z

Seelos, C., & Mair, J. (2005). Social entrepreneurship: Creating new business models to serve the poor. *Business Horizons, 48*(3), 241–246. doi:10.1016/j.bushor.2004.11.006

Shafer, W. E., Fukukawa, K., & Lee, G. M. (2007). Values and the perceived importance of ethics and social responsibility: The US versus China. *Journal of Business Ethics, 70*(3), 265–284. doi:10.1007/s10551-006-9110-9

Shane, S., Locke, E. A., & Collins, C. J. (2003). Entrepreneurial motivation. *Human Resource Management Review, 13*(2), 257–279. doi:10.1016/S1053-4822(03)00017-2

Shane, S., & Venkataraman, S. (2000). The promise of entrepreneurship as a field of research. *Academy of Management Review, 25*(1), 217–226.

Shane, S. A. (2003). *A general theory of entrepreneurship: The individual-opportunity nexus.* Northampton, MA: Edward Elgar Publishing. doi:10.4337/9781781007990

Short, J. C., Moss, T. W., & Lumpkin, G. T. (2009). Research in social entrepreneurship: Past contributions and future opportunities. *Strategic Entrepreneurship Journal, 3*(2), 161–194. doi:10.1002/sej.69

Short, J. C., Payne, G. T., & Ketchen, D. J. Jr. (2008). Research on organizational configurations: Past accomplishments and future challenges. *Journal of Management, 34*(6), 1053–1079. doi:10.1177/0149206308324324

Singhapakdi, A., Kraft, K. L., Vitell, S. J., & Rallapalli, K. C. (1995). The perceived importance of ethics and social responsibility on organizational effectiveness: A survey of marketers. *Journal of the Academy of Marketing Science, 23*(1), 49–56. doi:10.1007/BF02894611

Skocpol, T. (2008). Bringing the state back in: Retrospect and prospect. The 2007 Johan Skytte Prize Lecture. *Scandinavian Political Studies, 31*(2), 109–124. doi:10.1111/j.1467-9477.2008.00204.x

Smallbone, D., & Welter, F. (2009). *Entrepreneurship and small business development in post-Soviet economies*. London: Routledge.

Sparks, J. R., & Hunt, S. D. (1998). Marketing researcher ethical sensitivity: Conceptualization, measurement, and exploratory investigation. *Journal of Marketing, 62*(2), 92–109. doi:10.2307/1252163

Spencer, J. W., & Gómez, C. (2004). The relationship among national institutional structures, economic factors, and domestic entrepreneurial activity: A multicountry study. *Journal of Business Research, 57*(10), 1098–1107. doi:10.1016/S0148-2963(03)00040-7

Srnka, K. J. (2004). Culture's role in marketers' ethical decision making: An integrated theoretical framework. *Academy of Marketing Science Review, 2004*, 1.

Steensma, H. K., Tihanyi, L., Lyles, M. A., & Dhanaraj, C. (2005). The evolving value of foreign partnerships in transitioning economies. *Academy of Management Journal, 48*(2), 213–235. doi:10.5465/AMJ.2005.16928394

Stephan, U., & Uhlaner, L. M. (2010). Performance-based vs socially supportive culture: A cross-national study of descriptive norms and entrepreneurship. *Journal of International Business Studies, 41*(8), 1347–1364. doi:10.1057/jibs.2010.14

Stephan, U., Uhlaner, L. M., & Stride, C. (2014). Institutions and social entrepreneurship: The role of institutional voids, institutional support, and institutional configurations. *Journal of International Business Studies, 46*(3), 308–331. doi:10.1057/jibs.2014.38

Tan, J. (2002). Culture, nation, and entrepreneurial strategic orientations: Implications for an emerging economy. *Entrepreneurship: Theory and Practice, 26*(4), 96–111.

Tett, R. P., & Burnett, D. D. (2003). A personality trait-based interactionist model of job performance. *The Journal of Applied Psychology, 88*(3), 500–517. doi:10.1037/0021-9010.88.3.500 PMID:12814298

Uhlaner, L., & Thurik, R. (2007). Postmaterialism influencing total entrepreneurial activity across nations. *Journal of Evolutionary Economics, 17*(2), 161–185. doi:10.1007/s00191-006-0046-0

Uhlaner, L. M., Thurik, A. R., & Hutjes, J. (2002, April 15-16). Post-materialism and entrepreneurial activity: a macro view. *Proceedings, Small Business and Entrepreneurship Development Conference*, University of Nottingham.

Valentine, S., & Fleischman, G. (2008). Professional ethical standards, corporate social responsibility, and the perceived role of ethics and social responsibility. *Journal of Business Ethics, 82*(3), 657–666. doi:10.1007/s10551-007-9584-0

Volkema, R. J. (2004). Demographic, cultural, and economic predictors of perceived ethicality of negotiation behavior: A nine-country analysis. *Journal of Business Research, 57*(1), 69–78. doi:10.1016/S0148-2963(02)00286-2

Waddock, S. A., & Post, J. E. (1991). Social entrepreneurs and catalytic change. *Public Administration Review, 51*(5), 393–401. doi:10.2307/976408

Welter, F. (2011). Contextualizing entrepreneurship—conceptual challenges and ways forward. *Entrepreneurship Theory and Practice, 35*(1), 165–184. doi:10.1111/j.1540-6520.2010.00427.x

Welter, F., & Smallbone, D. (2008). Womens entrepreneurship from an institutional perspective: The case of Uzbekistan. *The International Entrepreneurship and Management Journal, 4*(4), 505–520. doi:10.1007/s11365-008-0087-y

Woolcock, M., & Narayan, D. (2000). Social capital: Implications for development theory, research, and policy. *The World Bank Research Observer, 15*(2), 225–249. doi:10.1093/wbro/15.2.225

Zahra, S. A., Gedajlovic, E., Neubaum, D. O., & Shulman, J. M. (2009). A typology of social entrepreneurs: Motives, search processes and ethical challenges. *Journal of Business Venturing, 24*(5), 519–532. doi:10.1016/j.jbusvent.2008.04.007

Zahra, S. A., Korri, J. S., & Yu, J. (2005). Cognition and international entrepreneurship: Implications for research on international opportunity recognition and exploitation. *International Business Review, 14*(2), 129–146. doi:10.1016/j.ibusrev.2004.04.005

Zahra, S. A., & Wright, M. (2011). Entrepreneurships next act. *The Academy of Management Perspectives, 25*(4), 67–83. doi:10.5465/amp.2010.0149

Zucker, L. G. (1991). Postscript: Micro foundations of institutional thought. In W. E. Powell & P. J. DiMaggio (Eds.), *The new institutionalism in organizational analysis* (pp. 103–107). Chicago, IL: University of Chicago Press.

Chapter 18
Factors Related to Readjustment to Daily Life:
A Study of Repatriates in Japanese Multinational Enterprises

Yoko Naito
Tokai University, Japan

ABSTRACT

This study explores issues arising from cross-cultural transitions, focusing on Japanese multinational enterprises (MNEs) and readjustment to daily life in general after international assignments. Employee readjustment to the home country needs to study from two perspectives: work and private life. However, most studies of repatriates focus on the work aspect, and few focus on the aspect of private life. Using structural equation modeling based on the questionnaire data, this study empirically examines nine variables that may possibly affect readjustment to daily life in general after returning to Japan. In this process, this study deals with "readjustment to daily life in general" from a viewpoint outside the organization. Based on these findings, this chapter suggests emphasizing management practices that provide assistance and support to repatriates in their readjustment to daily life in general, along with the importance of readjustment to the organization.

INTRODUCTION

Migrations and exchanges of people across cultural borders have rapidly increased since the second half of the 20th century. These changes in the social environment have led to a rapid increase in the number of people who live in non-native cultures and interact with the people in the host countries. These interactions inspire people to become aware of and interested in different cultures and in many things and customs of their home countries. At the same time, many people experience culture shock involving psychological stress and other difficulties while they are in non-native cultures. The challenges and problems associated with interactions in a host country cannot be resolved easily. When individuals who have been socialized in their home cultures begin to have contact with people in a host culture, they are

DOI: 10.4018/978-1-5225-2568-4.ch018

influenced by cultural differences in numerous ways as they confront a variety of challenges. Particularly when they remain in a host culture for several years, people gradually adjust to the culture through their experiences (Gudykunst & Kim, 2003).

The difficulties that people experience during stays in host cultures are not necessarily alleviated after they return home. In general, people return home after spending time in different countries and are confronted by unexpected challenges after they return (Brabant, Palmer, & Gramling, 1990; Gullahorn & Gullahorn, 1963; Lazarova & Caligiuri, 2001; Mesmer-Magnus & Viswesvaran, 2008). A stay in a host culture involves experiencing a different cultural context, and reentry similarly involves experiences of readjustment to the home environment, which has changed over time (Gama & Pedersen, 1977; Gullahorn & Gullahorn, 1963; Sussman, 1986). Returning to the home country is not generally regarded as difficult, but from a practical standpoint it is not easy. People returning home reportedly experience readjustment problems, commonly referred to as reentry shock (Black, Gregersen, Mendenhall, & Stroh, 1999; Brabant et al., 1990; Gullahorn & Gullahorn, 1963; Kim, 2001; Uehara, 1986). Some people who have experienced the transition claimed that the difficulties of reentry are more challenging than their adjustments to the host cultures (e.g., Adler, 2002; Mesmer-Magnus & Viswesvaran, 2008; Stroh, Black, Mendenhall, & Gregersen, 2004).

This study focuses on one aspect of the readjustment of repatriates of multinational enterprises (MNEs); namely, readjustment to daily life in general.[1] It examines factors associated with readjustment and suggests organizational practices that might facilitate their readjustment. Previous relevant studies in Japan have pointed out a lack of organizational career support for repatriates (Yashiro, 2015). This study focused on daily life because aspects of daily life have a ripple effect on the work aspects described below.

Mainly based on a literature review, Naito (2012b) suggested factors that might influence repatriates' readjustment to daily life in general. The present study reports the results of an analysis based on a questionnaire survey to examine the factors identified by that review. The following some sections present a condensed version of Naito (2012b) and quote a part of Naito (2016). This paper is mainly based on Naito (2015; in Japanese, "Kaigai haken kininsya no seikatsu ippan eno saitekiou: Nikkei takokuseki kigyou deno chosa kara" [Factors related to readjustment to daily life: A study of repatriates in Japanese multi-national enterprises], *Journal of the Faculty of Political Science and Economics*, 47, 159-177, Tokai University) which has been translated here into English, and uses a part of Naito (2016).

BACKGROUND

A growing number of studies of adjustment to host cultures have been conducted as the number of people living in foreign countries has grown. However, readjustment research, which addresses the circumstances and problems faced by repatriates returning to their home cultures, is scarcely represented in the literature (Szkudlarek, 2010).

Adjustment to Host Cultures and Readjustment to Home Cultures

The problems of culture shock experienced during a stay in a host culture are widely known. Nevertheless, difficulties related to reentry shock or reverse culture shock experienced upon returning home are not well known (Brabant et al., 1990; Gullahorn & Gullahorn, 1963). In early studies of readjustment, Gullahorn and Gullahorn (1963), for example, found that the readjustment of overseas returnees followed

Factors Related to Readjustment to Daily Life

a process equivalent to that of adjusting to a host culture. A subsequent study of readjustment by Black, Gregersen, and Mendenhall (1992) identified some characteristics of readjustment processes that differ from those of adjustment to a host culture.

Gudykunst (2005) defined adjustment to a host culture as circumstances in which an individual feels comfortable and behaves in a socially appropriate manner with members of the host country. Church (1982) argued that adjustment to a host culture refers to the psychological well-being that an individual feels and that they obtain a sense of professional accomplishment and satisfaction by socially interacting with the local people. Bennett (1998) argued it is necessary to experience the accompanying sense of loss and change for adjustment to the new context to occur. It is emphasized that the transitional experiences include value changes and social changes attributable to life changes as well as intercultural movement. Bennett (1998) also noted that these experiences typically involve a sense of loss and change with shocks.

Martin and Harrell (2004) defined readjustment to the home culture as a process of reintegrating into the home cultural context after a stay in a host culture. According to Adler (2002), readjustment is not easy, but it is an experience resembling adjustment to a host country. It involves readjustment to the home environment when at work, when not at work, and when interacting again with home-country residents. Black et al. (1992) argued that mal-readjustment usually arises from gaps between a returnee's expectations and the realities of his or her circumstances after reentry.[2] Storti (2003) emphasized that, unlike the general perception that returning to the home country means returning to familiar places, being with familiar people, and using customary forms of interaction, actual homecoming is a surprising and unexpected experience because of the changes that have occurred in the home country and its people while the individual was away. During a stay in a foreign culture, changes continue to occur in the home country. Therefore, reentry to the home country is not just a "homecoming", and it is similar to starting a new life while handling a variety of difficulties. Although individuals' extents of awareness vary, some studies have found that the severity of reentry shock relates to the extent of changes that occurred in the home country (Martin, 1984; Martin & Nakayama, 2004).

The differences between adjustment and readjustment and both definitions are as follows. The process of adjusting to a host culture is that of a gradual acclimation to a new and unfamiliar cultural environment. Adjustment occurs when individuals maintain stable psychological conditions and use appropriate behaviors in the hosts' cultural contexts. In the studies of adjustment, research was verified and conducted on personal matters and responses, such as stress in a host country or acculturation through contact with foreign cultures (Kim, 2001; Martin & Nakayama, 2004). In contrast, readjustment refers to a process of reintegration into the home country, which is often regarded as a familiar social context (Martin & Harrell, 2004). As in the case of adjustment to a host culture, readjustment requires psychological and behavioral acclimation to the home culture. Moreover, the characteristics of readjustment that differ from those of adjustment have been identified. One important characteristic is that readjustment is complicated by the mistaken impression that returning home is easy, despite the contrasting reality.

Readjustment to Daily Life of Corporate Repatriates

Readjustment research addresses the problems faced by a variety of individuals who return from foreign countries (Szkudlarek, 2010; Ward, Bochner, & Furnham, 2001), including corporate repatriates (Black, 1992; Harvey, 1989; Lazarova & Caligiuri, 2001; Murray, 1973; Stevens, Oddou, Furuya, Bird, & Mendenhall, 2006), repatriates by "self-initiated expatriates" (Jokinen, Brewster, & Suutari, 2008; Tharenou & Caulfield, 2010), returnees belong to organization unrelated to commercial companies such as researchers (Cox, 2004; Gama & Pedersen, 1977; Gullahorn & Gullahorn, 1963), students after study abroad (Rohrlich & Martin, 1991; Uehara, 1986), those of immigrants, and their family members (including spouses and children) (Isa, 2000; Kidder, 1992; Miyoshi, 2009). Figure 1 shows the types of repatriates and returnees that have been studied by readjustment research as summarized above.

Among the previously described topics of research on readjustment, this study investigated repatriates who spent time in host countries on international assignments by their companies. Most corporate repatriates must confront unique problems during repatriation that particularly differ from those of other returnees such as students or immigrants. After their overseas assignments, corporate repatriates are not always free to decide their repatriation matters such as the repatriation date and place of work according to their intentions or convenience. In general, the difficulty and severity of repatriation tends to relate to particular circumstances including the business management decisions of their companies and work-related problems during repatriation. Therefore, corporate repatriates tend to face unique problems different from the other repatriates and returnees (Adler, 1981).

READJUSTMENT TO DAILY LIFE IN GENERAL

Literature on the Readjustment of Corporate Repatriates

In their overseas companies and offices, expatriates learn about different cultures, engage in work activities, and acquire new technologies, knowledge, and skills (Black et al., 1999; Guo, Rammal, & Dowling, 2016; Kraimer, Bolino, & Mead, 2016; Shiraki, 2006). Corporate repatriates' approach to readjustment requires addressing work and daily life factors because repatriates tend to have considerable difficulty and anxiety about both of these aspects after they return home (Black et al., 1999; Shiraki & Nagai, 2002; Umezawa, 2001). Furthermore, the work and private or daily life aspects are different things for repatriates, but those are closely related each other.[3]

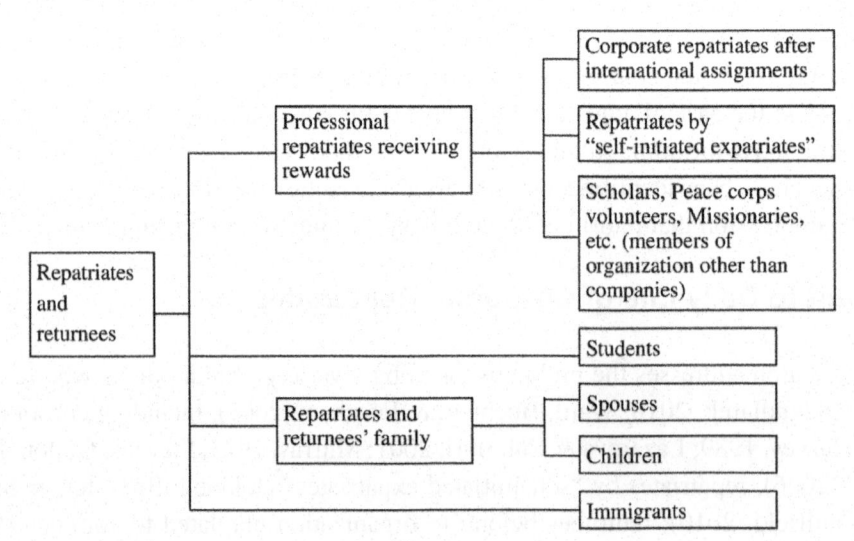

Figure 1. Types of repatriates and returnees in readjustment research

Factors Related to Readjustment to Daily Life

Therefore, it is important to examine readjustment from a perspective outside the organization (namely, from the perspective of the repatriate's private or daily life), as well as the readjustment viewed within the organization. Nevertheless, studies on corporate repatriates have tended to focus on readjustment to the workplace and on the individual's role in the organization, rather than on the impact of repatriation on the worker's private and daily life (Lazarova & Caligiuri, 2001; Murray, 1973; Naito, 2011, 2012a; Stevens et al., 2006). By examining the aspects of daily life, we might gain a clearer understanding of individuals' readjustments.

However, few empirical studies have focused on readjustment to daily life in general. Here are some exceptional studies as follows. Furusawa (2011) focused on factors related to the human resources (HR) practices of Japanese companies and examined three dependent variables: readjustment, use of knowledge and skills, and career improvements. The study presumed that HR practices are not strongly related to readjustment.[4] This point needs further examination using factors other than HR practices that might influence readjustment. Black (1994) previously examined a variety of factors in Japanese companies and found that four variables (age, length of overseas assignment, time after return from assignment, and clarity about the repatriation process) possibly influenced readjustment to the general environment.

An earlier study by Black (1992) examined data from repatriates of US companies and found a positive relationship between two variables: gaps between the expectations and the reality regarding general nonwork and readjustment to the nonwork (general) environment. These findings suggest that five factors (age, length of overseas assignment, time after return from assignment, clarity about the repatriation process, and gaps) comprehensively might influence readjustment to daily life along with other factors that will influence readjustment to life in Japan. Furthermore, because of the correlations among the variables identified by the previous studies, it would be valuable to verify the process using a path model.

Thus, this study specifically focused on corporate repatriates after their overseas assignments, examined a wide range of variables that might influence readjustment to daily life, and investigated how these variables related to each other.

Research Questions: Factors Related to Readjustment to Daily Life

This study examined aspects of Japanese corporate repatriates' readjustment to daily life in general (the dependent variable). To identify and assess the factors influencing the readjustment to daily life, this study considered the following nine independent variables (presented in italics in this section) because they are supposed to influence readjustment to daily life based on previous studies (Naito, 2012b). Two research questions are addressed to assess the influences of the variables on readjustment to daily life in general and develop a readjustment path model illustrating the relationships among the variables.

Regarding *age*, older repatriates might readjust more easily than younger repatriates to daily life in the home country because they presumably have had longer contact with the home environment. Some studies have found that *age* and readjustment are related. Black (1994) found that age related to readjustment such that older repatriates readjusted relatively more easily to daily life. Gullahorn and Gullahorn (1963) argued that relatively young people have difficulties readjusting to the home environment, whereas older people have easier readjustments.

Some studies have found that a longer *length of overseas assignment* makes readjustment more difficult because repatriates are less familiar with events in the home country (Black, 1994; Black & Gregersen, 1991). In other words, the longer the *length of overseas assignment*, the more difficult the readjustment because the cultural identity of the repatriate and the environment of the home country have changed during the overseas' stay (Kidder, 1992; Sussman, 2000, 2001; Uehara, 1986). Thus, repatriates with longer overseas assignments tend to have relatively more difficulties acclimating to the home country's environment and the length of the most recent assignment is expected to negatively influence repatriates' readjustments to daily life.

Sojourners, such as expatriates who lived in host cultures for extended periods, tended to adjust gradually to the host countries (Kim, 2001). Other studies similarly considered reentry shock and proposed that returnees acclimate to the home culture over time (Adler, 2002; Gullahorn & Gullahorn, 1963). Black and Gregersen (1991) found that the *length of time after return* from assignment may influenced readjustment such that a longer period after returning related to fewer readjustment difficulties. Therefore, the length of time after return from assignment was expected to relate with repatriates' readjustment to daily life in general positively.

Organizations that provide repatriation orientations and guidance help to inform repatriates of the changes that have taken place in the home country and in the organization during their international assignments. Some studies stressed the importance of implementing these orientations for repatriates (Black et al., 1992; Isogai, Hayashi, & Uno, 1999; Szkudlarek & Sumpter, 2015). Therefore, the organizational practice of *repatriation orientation/guidance* is assumed in this study to facilitate repatriates' readjustments to daily life. Some studies found that the clarity of the repatriation process positively related to readjustment, but the conceptualization is rather vague. This study therefore examined *repatriation orientation/guidance*.

Gaps between life expectations and reality are the gaps between repatriates' expectations of what daily life will be like in the home country after they return and the actual conditions experienced in the home country after returning (Gregersen & Stroh, 1997). Several studies have found that a high level of match between expectations and reality might influence well-being readjustment, and that reducing the gaps between expectations and reality enhanced readjustment to nonwork (Black, 1992, 1993; Gregersen & Stroh, 1998). Consequently, the *gaps between life expectations and reality* are expected to influence repatriates' readjustments to daily life in general.

Most expatriates are accompanied by family members when they sojourn overseas. These family members begin new lives as repatriates after returning to the home country and likely face *family-related problems*, such as problems with the children's education or, more recently problems finding employment or re-employment for spouses which has been argued in Japan (Isa, 2000; Miyoshi, 2009). These problems have generally been treated as family problems in the literature (Harvey, 1989; Isa, 2000) where positive correlations have been found between spousal readjustment to daily life and repatriate readjustments, suggesting that the family situation might influence repatriates' readjustments (Black & Gregersen, 1991; Gregersen & Stroh, 1997; Howe-Walsh, 2013).

It is often difficult for repatriates to personally decide at their own discretion when to return home. However, repatriates tend to consider their overseas stays as temporary. Some of them might want to return home, depending on their family situations, personal career developments and other factors, before their organizations notify them of their repatriation. Therefore, it might be difficult for organizations to meet repatriates' requests to return home, if they can, readjustment to daily life may improve after repatriation. For this reason, the desire to return home is supposed to influence readjustments to daily life in general.

Regarding the *length of time to prepare to return* to the home country, repatriation is effectively a relocation to another country, which involves time-consuming preparations, such as administrative tasks, changes of residence, and building the foundations of a new life. The relocation requires adequate preparation (Kim, 2001), and some studies have found that the preparations for return are important

Factors Related to Readjustment to Daily Life

to readjustment (Sussman, 2001). When the situation is an intraorganizational transfer, and the change specifically involves a change in place of residence, companies tend to unofficially inform the employees being relocated in advance of official notifications. In the case of overseas assignments, the employees are often informed months in advance. Therefore, it is reasonable that, when the length of time between the announcement and actual repatriation (i.e., length of time to prepare to return) is relatively short, employees have relatively less time to prepare to return, and readjustment to daily life in general is relatively poor.

Expatriates can learn about changes happening at home by visiting the home country during their assignments. Because temporary home leaves tend to enable them to obtain information about their home countries, readjustment after repatriation could be smoother than if they did not have temporary home leaves (Harvey & Novicevic, 2006; Stroh, Black, Mendenhall, & Gregersen, 2004). This finding supports a presumption that the *frequency of home visits* influences readjustment to daily life in general.

This study presumed that the nine variables described above influence readjustment to daily life in general, and addressed the following research questions:

- **RQ1:** Which type of path model for readjustment to daily life in general is adequate for the data?
- **RQ2:** How do the 10 variables (9 independent variables and 1 dependent variable) directly and indirectly relate to each other?

The next section first describes the methods used to address the research questions followed by explanation of the extents of the relationships of the independent variables to readjustment to daily life in general. Then, the results of the structural equation model (SEM) that examined the relationships among the 10 variables are reported. Last is an explanation of the model of the data that was developed based on the analytical results.

METHODS

Before developing the questionnaire for this study, the author visited eight Japanese major multinational enterprises (MNEs) and discussed the experiences of expatriation and repatriation with HR staff and employees. The questionnaire was administered after it was revised based on those discussions.[5]

Measures

The dependent variable, readjustment to daily life in general, was measured with a modified scale based on Black (1994) measuring the extent of acclimation to the home environment. Response options were on a Likert-type scale where 1 = *not acclimated at all* to 7 = *well acclimated* on the following items (Cronbach's α = 0.92).

1. Living costs and price levels in Japan.
2. Current housing conditions.
3. Dietary experiences in Japan.
4. Shopping in Japan.
5. Opportunities to use entertainment and leisure facilities in Japan.

6. Overall life in Japan.

Black's (1994) original documents regarding readjustment to daily life in general and gaps between life expectations and reality (Black, 1992), written in English, were translated into Japanese using back-translation (Brislin, 1980; Brislin, Lonner, & Thorndike, 1973). The nine independent variables and their items used in the study are as follows. The values of the inversely scaled items were reversed for analysis.

- **Age:** Five-year age groups were created for the analysis.
- **Length of Overseas Assignment:** The responses on duration in years and months were converted into months.
- **Length of Time After Return:** The responses on duration in years and months were converted into months.
- **Repatriation Orientation/Guidance:** Responses to the question, "Did you receive repatriation orientation/guidance provided by your company at the time of your most recent repatriation?" were used to measure this variable. The response options were: 1 = *no orientation/guidance provided*, 2 = *received guidance in written form*, 3 = *received guidance in face-to-face meeting(s)*, and 4 = *received repatriation orientation*, coded as 0 = *no orientation/guidance provided* and 1= *orientation/guidance provided*.
- **Gaps Between Life Expectations and Reality:** The variable was constructed of responses to two items based on Black (1992): "How similar or different is your actual life after returning home from your expectations before returning home [regarding living conditions] / [regarding residential environment]?" (Cronbach's α = 0.89). The response options were: 1 = *reality matched expectations* to 4 = *reality did not match expectations* (inversely scaled).
- **Family Problems:** Responses to the question, "Did your family experience problems living in Japan after returning home?" measured the extent of family problems. Response options were: 1 = *some problems* and 2 = *no problems*. The responses were transformed into dummy variables.[6]
- **Desire to Return Home:** Responses to the question, "How much did you want to return home?" were used to measure the extent of the respondents' desires to do so. Response options were: 1 = *strongly wanted to return home* through 5 = *did not want to return home* (inversely scaled).
- **Length of Time to Prepare to Return:** The variable was measured by the number provided in response to the question, "How many months in advance did you receive notice of repatriation?"
- **Frequency of Home Visits:** The question asked for the number of times the respondent had visited home during the overseas assignment.

Statistical software programs SPSS (version 15), R (version 3.1.3), and AMOS (version 7) were used for the statistical analysis.

Research Procedures

The questionnaire was distributed to 233 employees at Japan-based MNEs through the HR departments of the seven participating MNEs. The employees with experience in overseas assignments lasting six months or longer who had returned home within two years of the survey were eligible to participate in the study. Responses were returned directly to the author in provided self-addressed stamped envelopes and 192 (82.40%) valid responses were received.[7] This paper assigns the length of time since the return to the home country as within two years. This duration was set to avoid respondent memory bias to within two years, since certain duration is needed to identify influences on readjustment to daily life after returning home.

RESULTS AND DISCUSSION

Participants

The largest age group in the sample was 41–45 years old (33.33%), and 99.48% were male. The average employment tenure in the companies was 19.77 years (standard deviation (SD) = 7.47) at the time the questionnaire was administered. The mean frequency of overseas assignments was 1.33 times (SD = 0.61), and the mean length of overseas assignment was 4.38 years (SD = 2.71). The most destinations were the US (31.25%, $n = 60$), followed by China (23.96%, $n = 46$) and Germany (8.85%, $n = 17$).

The situation regarding the repatriates' family members was as follows.

- Accompanied by the entire nuclear family (57.59%, $n = 110$).
- Accompanied by some nuclear family members (3.14%, $n = 6$).
- Unaccompanied (all family members remained at home) (26.18%, $n = 50$).
- Single (13.09%, $n = 26$).

The total number of repatriates accompanied by family members was 116 (spouse only = 42, children only = 1, spouse and children = 72, no response = 1). The scores on two variables, repatriation orientation/guidance and family problems, were separately summed. Regarding repatriation orientation/guidance, a total of 137 (71.35%) respondents reported that it was provided and 54 (28.13%) respondents reported that it was not provided. Regarding family problems, 74 (38.54%) respondents reported some problems and 118 (61.46%) respondents reported no problems. The following section presents the results of the analysis and discusses the variables that directly and indirectly related to readjustment to daily life in general.

Correlations Among the Variables

Table 1 shows the correlations among the variables. First, five variables had statistically significant correlations with readjustment to daily life in general: (1) length of overseas assignment, (2) length of time after return, (3) repatriation orientation/guidance, (4) gaps between life expectations and reality, and (5) family problems. Repatriates who had adjusted well to daily life in general had shorter lengths of overseas assignments, longer times after returning from their assignments, had received repatriation orientation/guidance, had smaller gaps between expectations and reality regarding daily life, and had fewer family problems after returning home.

Second, the following correlations among variables other than readjustment to daily life in general were statistically significant.

- Age correlated with length of overseas assignment, length of time to prepare to return, and frequency of home visits.

Table 1. Correlations among the variables [a,b]

	M	SD	1	2	3	4	5	6	7	8	9
2	52.50	32.47	.22**								
3	12.97	6.78	-.04	.04							
4	.72	.45	-.03	-.14 (-.13)	.00						
5	1.95	.68	.01	-.21**	-.02	.25** (.27)					
6	.61	.49	-.04 (-.05)	-.27** (-.31)	-.01 (-.02)	.10 (.16)	.29** (.32)				
7	2.77	1.24	.07	.21**	.01	.10	.18*	-.11			
8	4.29	3.27	-.16*	.02	.05	-.08 (-.09)	.00	.02 (.03)	.05		
9	4.16	4.61	.18*	.31**	-.12	-.02 (-.04)	-.05	-.08 (-.11)	.20**	-.18*	
10	5.58	1.13	-.02	-.37**	.21**	.16* (.17)	.51**	.34** (.35)	.06	.04	-.12

* = $p < .05$, ** = $p < .01$; $n = 192$, M = mean, SD = standard deviation

[a] Values are Pearson's correlation coefficients. Note that the correlations between two values were derived from bi-serial correlation coefficients and those of binary valuables were derived from tetrachoric correlation coefficients using R (version 3.1.3). The tetrachoric correlation coefficients that differ from the Pearson's correlation coefficients are in parentheses.

[b] 1 = age, 2 = length of overseas assignment, 3 = length of time after return, 4 = repatriation orientation/guidance, 5 = gaps between life expectations and reality, 6 = family problems, 7 = desire to return, 8 = length of time to prepare to return, 9 = frequency of home visits, 10 = readjustment to daily life in general

- Length of overseas assignment correlated with gaps between life expectations and reality, family problems, desire to return home, and frequency of home visits.
- Repatriation orientation/guidance correlated with gaps between life expectations and reality.
- Gaps between life expectations and reality correlated with family problems and desire to return home.
- Desire to return home correlated with frequency of home visits.
- Length of time to prepare to return correlated with frequency of home visits.

These relationships among variables are accounted for in the following path model using SEM.

Structural Equation Model (SEM)

An adequate model was sought to achieve the best fit with the data using SEM. This model provided a visual presentation of the variables' direct and indirect relationships to readjustment to daily life in general. This approach contributes to a more complete understanding of readjustment because few studies of readjustment have employed path analysis. The relationships among the variables in the SEM are considered based on the results of a multiple regression analysis and the correlations among the variables.

Direct Paths to Readjustment to Daily Life in General

Before drawing the path diagram, a multiple regression analysis was performed to determine which of the nine variables had strong possible influences on readjustment to daily life in general (Table 2) and to avoid spurious correlations of the nine independent variables. Four variables significantly related to readjustment to daily life in general: length of overseas assignment, length of time after return, gaps between life expectations and reality, and family problems.[8] Because these four variables might directly influence readjustment to daily life in general, they directly link to readjustment, indicated by arrows in the SEM.

Indirect Paths to Readjustment to Daily Life in General

Indirect influences are present when path variables relate to readjustment to daily life in general through their relationships to other variables. These were examined based on the correlations found among the variables. Rational influences among paths were presumed as follows.

1. Age → length of overseas assignment implies that older repatriates tend to be assigned overseas postings for longer periods than are younger repatriates because they are engaged in management at higher positions with more responsibility. Conversely, younger repatriates work shorter periods in overseas assignments. Such reverse interpretations might be applied to other relationships among these variables.
2. Age → length of time to prepare to return implies that older repatriates have shorter periods to prepare to return home because they are more accustomed to company life in their higher positions.

Table 2. Results of the multiple regression analysis

Independent Variable	Dependent Variable Readjustment to Daily Life in General		
	B	t	p-value
Age	.06	.89	
Length of overseas assignment	-.30	4.46	***
Length of time after return	.23	3.83	***
Repatriation orientation/guidance	.00	.03	
Gaps between life expectations and reality	.40	6.07	***
Family problems	.16	2.47	*
Desire to return	.05	.83	
Length of time to prepare to return	.05	.76	
Frequency of home visits	.02	.24	
Adjusted R^2	.39		
R^2	.42		
F	13.70***		

$* = p < .05, ** = p < .01, *** = p < .001, n = 192$

3. Length of overseas assignment → frequency of home visits suggests that repatriates assigned for longer periods have more opportunities to visit home. In many cases, companies conventionally permit temporary home leaves, such as once per year.
4. Length of overseas assignment → gaps between life expectations and reality suggests that repatriates assigned to longer overseas assignments experience larger gaps between their expectations and the realities at home.
5. Length of overseas assignment → family problems suggests that repatriates assigned to longer overseas assignments might have more problems associated with their family members because they might be generally less familiar with events in their home countries.
6. Length of overseas assignment → desire to return home, related to (4) and (5) above, suggests that longer overseas assignments might create stronger desires to return home in general, particularly because international assignments last a relatively long time.
7. Family problems → gaps between life expectations and reality implies that family members experience problems before or after returning home that the repatriates did not anticipate, which might increase the gaps between life expectations and reality.
8. Desire to return home → gaps between life expectations and reality implies that repatriates who have strong desires to return home think more realistically about the return than do those who have weak desires to return home, which would reduce the gaps.
9. Repatriation orientation/guidance → gaps between life expectations and reality suggests that providing guidance for repatriation contributes to repatriates' abilities to obtain knowledge about the home environment.
10. Length of time to prepare to return → frequency of home visits implies that a shorter length of time to prepare to return involves fewer home visits. Some repatriates have fixed periods of assignment, such as a one-year assignment for which the return date is pre-determined (Table 3)[9]. In that case, these repatriates might not need temporary home leaves.
11. Frequency of home visits → desire to return home implies that repatriates who use more temporary home leaves have stronger desires to return home for various reasons, such as matters related to family members in the home country.

Table 3. Cross table of length of overseas assignment and length of time to prepare to return

Length of Overseas Assignment		1 Month	2 Months	3 Months	4 Months	5 Months	6 Months	Longer Than 6 Months	Total
Up to	1 year	4	4	3	1	0	0	8	20
	2 years	1	5	9	1	1	0	0	17
	3 years	6	9	12	2	2	3	3	37
	4 years	1	8	12	1	1	3	3	29
	longer	2	9	32	6	6	26	8	39
Total		14	35	68	11	10	32	22	192

Time for Preparations to Return

Factors Related to Readjustment to Daily Life

Results of Structural Equation Model Analysis

Figure 2 shows the SEM analysis reported above, which was adequate to the data ($\chi 2 = 20.49$ (*ns*), CFI = 1.00, RMSEA = 0.00, GFI = 0.98, AGFI = 0.96).[10]

First, the SEM results show the variables that directly influenced readjustment to daily life in general: length of overseas assignment, length of time after return, gaps between life expectations and reality, and family problems.

Figure 2 (i), length of overseas assignment → readjustment to daily life in general indicates that repatriates with shorter overseas assignments have more successfully adjusted to daily life in general. This finding also could be interpreted to mean that the longer the length of overseas assignment, the poorer the readjustment to daily life in general.

Figure 2 (ii), length of time after return → readjustment to daily life in general means that repatriates who are home longer after returning from the assignment have more successfully adjusted to daily life in general. The results of (i) and (ii) imply that changes occurring over time also significantly relate to readjustment to daily life in general, which agrees with Naito (2012a) regarding readjustment to the organization.[11]

Figure 2 (iii), gaps between life expectations and reality → readjustment to daily life in general indicates that repatriates with smaller gaps have more successfully adjusted to daily life in general. This result implies that thinking of the return to the home country as 'just returning home' rather than entering the new environment, tends to create gaps, resulting in repatriation problems. Therefore, it is important that organizations, managers, and colleagues provide helpful information in advance to prevent repatriates from developing expectations that radically differ from the real situations at home (Black, 1992; Stroh, Gregersen, & Black, 1998).

Figure 2. Results of the SEM (structural equation modeling)

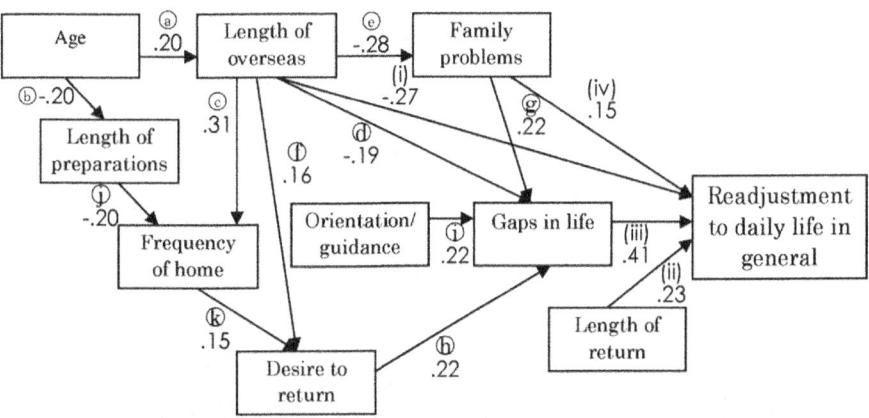

$\chi^2 = 20.49$ (*ns*), CFI = 1.00, RMSEA = .00, GFI = .98, AGFI = .96

Values under the arrows are standard path coefficients, all of which are statistically significant ($p < .05$).

Error variables omitted, $n = 180$

Figure 2 (iv), family problems → readjustment to daily life in general suggests that repatriates with no family problems accompanying their returns home have more successfully adjusted to daily life in general. The descriptive statistics indicate that family members accompanied more than one-half of the respondents and that more than 80% of the sample was married. In other words, many repatriates begin their new lives together with their family members after they return home. Family situations, including matters related to children's education, spousal employment, and matters that vary and depend on particular situations, require organizations (employers) to provide support to family members as well as to the repatriated employees to ensure successful repatriation (Howe-Walsh, 2013). Therefore, matters of children's education and spousal employment should be addressed with the repatriated employees' family needs in mind.

The second issue based on the path model concerns the variables that indirectly influenced readjustment to daily life in general. Those five variables are: age, repatriation orientation/guidance, desire to return home, length of time to prepare to return, and frequency of home visits. The paths of these five variables link to readjustment to daily life in general through their relationships to other variables.[12] Those relationships are discussed in the previous section (Indirect Paths to Readjustment to Daily Life in General), and these discussions are coherent findings of the analysis. Figure 2 shows 11 paths connecting the variables that might be indirect influences.

As described above, the four variables with the largest path coefficients directly relate to adjustment to daily life in general. Two of the four variables, (length of overseas assignment and family problems) are factors that respectively have direct and indirect relationships to adjustment to daily life in general. For example, Figure 2 shows four paths (indicated by arrows), which are (c), (d), (e), and (f), that begin at length of overseas assignment and link to variables other than adjustment to daily life in general. One arrow (g) connects family problems to adjustment to daily life in general. These paths represent indirect relationships to adjustment to daily life in general through other variables.

CONCLUSION, SOLUTIONS, AND RECOMMENDATIONS

This study investigated issues related to readjustment to daily life among repatriates of Japanese MNEs, as seen from outside the organization; therefore, it differs from the conventional studies of readjustment to the organization. The author analyzed the variables empirically, investigated the relationships among them, and presented a path model of those variables with direct and indirect relationships to the readjustment to daily life in general variable.

This model shows that the multiple factors could promote readjustment to daily life in general. This illustrates the importance of examining measures by assessing a variety of factors, and paying attention to the process through which these factors may influence the readjustment. Furthermore, it is important that companies and organizations provide support to their repatriates and their family members by specifically focusing on the lengths of overseas assignments, lengths of time after they have returned home, gaps between their expectations and reality, and family problems. It is also necessary for repatriates to pay attention to these issues. However, issues around the length of time after returning home from assignment appear to be resolved naturally by elapsed time after the return.

Based on the above discussion, this study proposes two management policies to support repatriates' readjustment to daily life in general. First, HR staff, managers, and colleagues should provide information to repatriates that is useful to aspects of daily life in addition to work duties. This would contribute to decreasing the gaps that repatriates have between their expectations of and the reality at home. Providing guidance about daily life in general could be useful to repatriates who are returning after long overseas assignments. It is also important to consider their desires to return home, particularly among expatriates on long international assignments. Second, companies and organizations should help repatriates' family members with matters such as school selections for children and career developments for spouses. Specifically, when overseas assignments are long, it is also important to provide sufficient and appropriate assistance and support to each family.

FUTURE RESEARCH DIRECTIONS

Two issues should be examined by future studies. First, it is strongly believed that qualitative research would help to elucidate relationships between the two aspects of the readjustment (work and non-work) and thereby contribute to the knowledge on readjustment. That approach would help us to gain an in-depth understanding. Second, comparative studies across cultures and countries and other aspects of social context would further illuminate the issues and the interpretations of findings, which would enable the discovery and identification of issues unique to the context of Japanese companies.

ACKNOWLEDGMENT

This research is supported by a fellowship grant of the Department of Political Economic Science, Tokai University, and JSPS KAKENHI Grants-in-Aid for Scientific Research (C) 26380531.

REFERENCES

Adler, N. J. (1981). Reentry: Managing cross-cultural transitions. *Group and Organization Studies*, *6*(3), 341–356. doi:10.1177/105960118100600310

Adler, N. J. (2002). *Cross-cultural transitions: Expatriate entry and reentry. International dimensions of organizational behavior* (pp. 284–300). Mason, OH: South-Western.

Bennett, J. (1998). Transition shock: Putting culture shock in perspective. In M. J. Bennett (Ed.), *Basic concepts of intercultural communication: Selected readings* (pp. 215–224). Yarmouth, ME: Intercultural Press.

Black, J. S. (1992). Coming home: The relationship of expatriate expectations with repatriation adjustment and job performance. *Human Relations*, *45*(2), 177–192. doi:10.1177/001872679204500205

Black, J. S. (1993). The role of expectations during repatriation for Japanese managers. *Research in Personnel and Human Resource Management*, *3*, 339–358.

Black, J. S. (1994). Okaerinasai: Factors related to Japanese repatriation adjustment. *Human Relations*, *47*(12), 1489–1508. doi:10.1177/001872679404701203

Black, J. S., & Gregersen, H. B. (1991). When Yankee comes home: Factors related to expatriate and spouse repatriation adjustment. *Journal of International Business Studies, 22*(4), 671–695. doi:10.1057/palgrave.jibs.8490319

Black, J. S., Gregersen, H. B., & Mendenhall, M. E. (1992). Toward a theoretical framework of repatriation adjustment. *Journal of International Business Studies, 23*(4), 737–760. doi:10.1057/palgrave.jibs.8490286

Black, J. S., Gregersen, H. B., Mendenhall, M. E., & Stroh, L. K. (1999). *Globalizing people through international assignments*. Reading, MA: Addison-Wesley.

Brabant, S., Palmer, C. E., & Gramling, R. (1990). Returning home: An empirical investigation of cross-cultural reentry. *International Journal of Intercultural Relations, 14*(4), 387–404. doi:10.1016/0147-1767(90)90027-T

Brislin, R. W. (1980). Translation and content analysis of oral and written material. In H. C. Triandis & J. W. Berry (Eds.), Handbook of cross-cultural psychology: Methodology (Vol. 2, pp. 389–444). Boston, MA: Allyn & Bacon.

Brislin, R. W., Lonner, W., & Thorndike, R. M. (1973). *Cross-cultural research methods* (pp. 32–45). New York: John Wiley & Sons.

Church, A. T. (1982). Sojourner adjustment. *Psychological Bulletin, 91*(3), 540–572. doi:10.1037/0033-2909.91.3.540

Cox, J. B. (2004). The role of communication, technology, and cultural identity in repatriation adjustment. *International Journal of Intercultural Relations, 28*(3–4), 201–219. doi:10.1016/j.ijintrel.2004.06.005

Furusawa, M. (2011). Nihonkigyouno kaigaihakensya ni taisuru jintekishigenn kanrino kenkyu [Human resource management for expatriates of Japanese corporations]. *Osaka Shogyodigaku Ronshu, 6*(3), 1–22.

Gama, E. M. P., & Pedersen, P. (1977). Readjustment problems of Brazilian returnees from graduate studies in the United States. *International Journal of Intercultural Relations, 1*(4), 46–58. doi:10.1016/0147-1767(77)90031-1

Gregersen, H. B., & Stroh, L. K. (1997). Coming home to the arctic cold: Antecedents to Finnish expatriate and spouse repatriation adjustment. *Personnel Psychology, 50*(3), 635–654. doi:10.1111/j.1744-6570.1997.tb00708.x

Gudykunst, W. B. (2005). An anxiety/uncertainty management (AUM) theory of stranger's intercultural adjustment. In W. B. Gudykunst (Ed.), *Theorizing about intercultural communication* (pp. 419–457). Thousand Oaks, CA: Sage.

Gudykunst, W. B., & Kim, Y. Y. (2003). *Communicating with strangers: An approach to intercultural communication*. New York: McGraw-Hill.

Gullahorn, J. T., & Gullahorn, J. E. (1963). An extension of the U-curve hypothesis. *The Journal of Social Issues, 19*(3), 33–47. doi:10.1111/j.1540-4560.1963.tb00447.x

Guo, Y., Rammal, H. G., & Dowling, P. J. (2016). Global talent management and staffing in MNEs: An introduction to the edited volume of international business and management. In Global talent management and staffing in MNEs (International Business and Management, Vol. 32; pp. xv–xxiv). Bingley, UK: Emerald Group. doi:10.1108/S1876-066X20160000032014

Harvey, M., & Novicevic, M. M. (2006). The evolution from repatriation of managers in MNEs to "patriation" in global organizations. In G. K. Stahl & I. Björkman (Eds.), *Handbook of research in international human resource management* (pp. 323–343). Cheltenham, UK: Edward Elgar. doi:10.4337/9781845428235.00024

Harvey, M. G. (1989). Repatriation of corporate executives: An empirical study. *Journal of International Business Studies*, *20*(1), 131–144. doi:10.1057/palgrave.jibs.8490355

Howe-Walsh, L. (2013). Repatriation: Furthering the research agenda through the lens of commitment, uncertainty reduction and social cognitive career theories. *International Journal of Business and Management*, *8*(16), 1–10. doi:10.5539/ijbm.v8n16p1

Isa, M. (2000). *Joseino kikoku tekio mondaino kenkyu: Ibunka juyo to kikoku tekio mondaino jisshoteki kenkyu* [Readjustment issues among female returnees: Empirical study of acceptance of different cultures and readjustment issues]. Tokyo, Japan: Taga Shuppan.

Isogai, T. Y., Hayashi, Y., & Uno, M. (1999). Identity issues and reentry training. *International Journal of Intercultural Relations*, *23*(3), 493–525. doi:10.1016/S0147-1767(99)00007-3

Jokinen, T., Brewster, C., & Suutari, V. (2008). Career capital during international work experiences: Contrasting self-initiated expatriate experiences and assigned expatriation. *International Journal of Human Resource Management*, *19*(6), 979–998. doi:10.1080/09585190802051279

Kidder, L. H. (1992). Requirements for being Japanese. *International Journal of Intercultural Relations*, *16*(4), 383–393. doi:10.1016/0147-1767(92)90029-T

Kim, Y. Y. (2001). *Becoming intercultural: An integrative theory of communication and cross-cultural adaptation*. Thousand Oaks, CA: Sage.

Kraimer, M., Bolino, M., & Mead, B. (2016). Themes in expatriate and repatriate research over four decades: What do we know and what do we still need to learn? *Annual Review of Organizational Psychology and Organizational Behavior*, *3*(1), 83–109. doi:10.1146/annurev-orgpsych-041015-062437

Lazarova, M., & Caligiuri, P. (2001). Retaining repatriates: The role of organizational support practices. *Journal of World Business*, *36*(4), 389–401. doi:10.1016/S1090-9516(01)00063-3

Martin, J. N. (1984). The intercultural reentry: Conceptualization and directions for future research. *International Journal of Intercultural Relations*, *8*(2), 115–134. doi:10.1016/0147-1767(84)90035-X

Martin, J. N., & Harrell, T. (2004). Intercultural reentry of students and professionals: Theory and practice. In D. Landis, J. M. Bennett, & M. J. Bennett (Eds.), *Handbook of intercultural training* (pp. 309–336). Thousand Oaks, CA: Sage. doi:10.4135/9781452231129.n13

Martin, J. N., & Nakayama, T. K. (2004). *Understanding intercultural transitions. Intercultural communication in contexts* (pp. 266–302). New York: McGraw-Hill.

Mesmer-Magnus, J. R., & Viswesvaran, C. (2008). Expatriate management: A review and directions for research in expatriate selection, training, and repatriation. In M. M. Harris (Ed.), *Handbook of research in international human resource management* (pp. 183–206). New York: Lawrence Erlbaum Associates.

Miyoshi, K. (2009). *Tenkinto kikon joseino kyaria keisei* [*Relocation and married women's career development*]. Tokyo, Japan: Hakuto-Shobo.

Murray, J. A. (1973). International personnel repatriation: Cultural shock in reverse. *MSU Business Topics*, *21*(3), 59–66.

Naito, Y. (2009). Kaigai karano kininkatei niokeru mondai to sonoshien: Nikkei ote takokusekikigyo no kininsha heno chosa kara [Issues of international repatriation and organizational support: A study of repatriates at large Japanese multinational corporations]. *Journal of International Business*, *1*(1), 1–17.

Naito, Y. (2011). Soshikisaishakaika niokeru johonyushukoi to soshikitekio: Kaigaikininsha wo taishotosita moderu no kochiku to kensho [Repatriation as an organizational re-socialization: An empirical study of an information acquisition model for repatriation adjustment in large Japanese MNCs]. *Organization Science*, *45*(1), 93–110.

Naito, Y. (2012a). Kaigaihaken karano kinin: Soshiki heno saitekio to sonoketteiyoin [Repatriation after overseas assignments: Readjustment to organizations and its determinants]. *The Japanese Journal of Labour Studies*, *626*, 75–88.

Naito, Y. (2012b). Kaigaikara no kikokusha no saitekio: Kigyo no kaigaihaken niyoru kininsha no seikatutekio wo chusintoshite [Readjustment of returnees from foreign countries: Focusing on readjustment to the daily life of corporate repatriates]. *Sauvage: Graduate students' bulletin, Graduate School of International Media, Communication and Tourism Studies. Hokkaido University*, *8*, 45–56.

Naito, Y. (2015). Kaigai haken kininsya no seikatsu ippan eno saitekiou: Nikkei takokuseki kigyou deno chosa kara [Factors related to readjustment to daily life: A study of repatriates in Japanese multi-national enterprises]. *Journal of the Faculty of Political Science and Economics*, *47*, 159–177.

Naito, Y. (2016). Multiple aspects of readjustment experienced by international repatriates in multinational enterprises: A perspective of changes occurring over time and changes due to cultural differences. In Y. Guo, H. G. Rammal, & P. J. Dowling (Eds.), Global talent management and staffing in MNEs (International Business and Management, Vol. 32; pp. 101–124). Bingley, UK: Emerald Group. doi:10.1108/S1876-066X20160000032004

Rohrlich, B., & Martin, J. N. (1991). Host country and reentry adjustment of student sojourners. *International Journal of Intercultural Relations*, *15*(2), 163–182. doi:10.1016/0147-1767(91)90027-E

Shiraki, M. (2006). Takokuseki naibu rodoshijo no jisshobunseki [Experimental analysis of internal labor market in MNEs]. Kokusai jintekishigenkanri no hikaku bunseki: Takokuseki naibu roudoushijo no shitenkara [The comparative analysis of international HRM] (pp. 33–102). Tokyo, Japan: Yuhikaku.

Shiraki, M., & Nagai, H. (2002). Chosa kekka no gaiyo: Kaigai hakensha chosa kekka [The results of survey: The research results of expatriates]. *Kokusai idosha no shakaiteki togo ni kansuru kenkyu* [*The Survey of Social Integration for International Transfer*], *305*, 73–103.

Stevens, M. J., Oddou, G., Furuya, N., Bird, A., & Mendenhall, M. (2006). HR factors affecting repatriate job satisfaction and job attachment for Japanese managers. *International Journal of Human Resource Management, 17*(5), 831–841. doi:10.1080/09585190600640844

Storti, C. (2003). *The art of coming home*. Yarmouth, ME: Intercultural Press.

Stroh, L. K., Black, J. S., Mendenhall, M. E., & Gregersen, H. B. (2004). *International assignments: An integration of strategy, research, and practice*. Mahwah, NJ: Lawrence Erlbaum Associates.

Stroh, L. K., Gregersen, H. B., & Black, J. S. (1998). Closing the gap: Expectations versus reality among repatriates. *Journal of World Business, 33*(3), 111–124. doi:10.1016/S1090-9516(98)90001-3

Sussman, N. M. (1986). Reentry research and training: Methods and implications. *International Journal of Intercultural Relations, 10*(2), 235–254. doi:10.1016/0147-1767(86)90008-8

Sussman, N. M. (2000). The dynamic nature of cultural identity throughout cultural transitions: Why home is not so sweet. *Personality and Social Psychology Review, 4*(4), 355–373. doi:10.1207/S15327957P-SPR0404_5

Sussman, N. M. (2001). Repatriation transitions: Psychological preparedness, cultural identity, and attributions among American managers. *International Journal of Intercultural Relations, 25*(2), 109–123. doi:10.1016/S0147-1767(00)00046-8

Szkudlarek, B. (2010). Reentry: A review of the literature. *International Journal of Intercultural Relations, 34*(1), 1–21. doi:10.1016/j.ijintrel.2009.06.006

Szkudlarek, B., & Sumpter, D. M. (2015). What, when, and with whom? Investigating expatriate reentry training with a proximal approach. *Human Resource Management, 54*(6), 1037–1057. doi:10.1002/hrm.21647

Templer, K. J., Tay, C., & Chandrasekar, N. A. (2006). Motivational cultural intelligence, realistic job preview, realistic living conditions preview, and cross-cultural adjustment. *Group & Organization Management, 31*(1), 154–173. doi:10.1177/1059601105275293

Tharenou, P., & Caulfield, N. (2010). Will I stay or will I go? Explaining repatriation by self-initiated expatriates. *Academy of Management Journal, 53*(5), 1009–1028. doi:10.5465/AMJ.2010.54533183

Uehara, A. (1986). The nature of American student reentry adjustment and perceptions of the sojourn experience. *International Journal of Intercultural Relations, 10*(4), 415–438. doi:10.1016/0147-1767(86)90043-X

Umezawa, T. (2001). Kiningono mondaito kaigaikinmuno saikibou [Issues after repatriation and renewed desire to undertake overseas assignments]. In The Japan Institute for Labour Policy and Training (Ed.), Nihon kigyouno kaigaihakensha: Shokugyoto seikatsuno jittai [Expatriates of Japanese companies: Survey of work and life aspects] (pp. 129–149). Tokyo, Japan: The Japan Institute for Labour Policy and Training.

Ward, C., Bochner, S., & Furnham, A. (2001). *The psychology of culture shock*. London: Routledge.

Yashiro, A. (2015). Jinji no kokusaika. [Globalization of human resources] In H. Sato, H. Fujimura, & A. Yashiro (Eds.), *Atarashii jinjiroumu kanri* [Contemporary human resource management]. (pp. 26–31). Tokyo, Japan: Yuhikaku Publishing.

ADDITIONAL READING

Burmeister, A., Deller, J., Osland, J., Szkudlarek, B., Oddou, G., & Blakeney, R. (2015). The microprocesses during repatriate knowledge transfer: The repatriates perspective. *Journal of Knowledge Management, 19*(4), 735–755. doi:10.1108/JKM-01-2015-0011

Cerdin, J.-L., Abdeljalil, M., & Brewster, C. (2014). Qualified immigrants success: Exploring the motivation to migrate and to adjust. *Journal of International Business Studies, 45*(2), 151–168. doi:10.1057/jibs.2013.45

Cerdin, J.-L., & Brewster, C. (2014). Talent management and expatriation: Bridging two streams of research and practice. *Journal of World Business, 49*(2), 245–252. doi:10.1016/j.jwb.2013.11.008

Haslberger, A., Brewster, C., & Hippler, T. (2014). *Repatriation adjustment: Individual and organizational perspectives. Managing performance abroad: A new model for understanding expatriate adjustment* (pp. 161–181). New York, NY: Routledge.

Howe-Walsh, L. (2015). Bank stems the loss of employees returning from abroad: Talent-management system helps to keep people loyal. *Human Resource Management International Digest, 23*(2), 25–27. doi:10.1108/HRMID-01-2015-0005

Lazarova, M. (2015). Taking stock of repatriation research. In D. G. Collings, G. T. Wood, & P. M. Caligiuri (Eds.), *The Routledge companion to international human resource management* (pp. 378–398). London, UK: Routledge.

Naito, Y. (2016). Multiple aspects of readjustment experienced by international repatriates in multinational enterprises: A perspective of changes occurring over time and changes due to cultural differences. In Y. Guo, H. G. Rammal, & P. J. Dowling (Eds.), Global talent management and staffing in MNEs (International Business and Management, Vol. 32; pp. 101–124). Bingley, UK: Emerald Group. doi:10.1108/S1876-066X20160000032004

KEY TERMS AND DEFINITIONS

Adjustment: The process of adjusting to a host culture, which comprises becoming gradually acclimated to a new and unfamiliar cultural environment, such as when living in a foreign country. Adjustment occurs when individuals maintain stable psychological conditions and can use appropriate behaviors in the host countries' cultural contexts.

Daily Life in General: The nonwork or private life aspect of daily life. Nonwork refers to the aspects of daily life that do not require or involve work for money. It involves the division between work and private life. For individuals, the nonwork and work aspects are two opposing aspects of daily lives.

International Assignment: These assignments occur when an organization or company dispatches employees from the home country to a different country for work and business operations at overseas offices or companies. These employees are defined as "expatriates."

Japanese MNEs: Since about the 1980s, the major Japanese companies have become active in direct investing in foreign countries and Japanese excellent companies have gradually developed globally and as multinational entities.

Readjustment: It is the process of reintegration into the home country environment. It is often regarded as 'familiar' but the reality is not always the case. As in the case of adjustment to a host culture, readjustment requires becoming behaviorally and psychologically acclimated to the home culture.

Reentry or Repatriation to the Home Country: Reentry is more than coming home because it is similar to starting a new life, although it unexpectedly entails surmounting numerous difficulties.

Repatriates: Employees who were assigned return home to their countries or regions by their employers (the home organization or company) after working on assignments in different countries or regions.

ENDNOTES

[1] In this paper, individuals who return to their home countries after foreign assignments are termed "repatriates," which differentiates them from returnees, who return home from foreign countries after study abroad and so on.

[2] Although a gap between the expectations and the reality has been suggested to exist during an overseas stay (Templer, Tay, & Chandrasekar, 2006), it often has been reported that returnees and the people around them tend not to expect such a gap during their repatriation (Black et al., 1992; Martin, 1984; Storti, 1997).

[3] Naito (2009) reported comparably high correlations between readjustments to the company and daily life for repatriates ($r = .68$). Based on this, it was assumed that a satisfactory private daily life statistically correlates with readjustment to the company.

[4] Furusawa (2011) found that HR policy, as an independent variable, significantly relate to three dependent variables: readjustment to daily life (adjusted $R^2 = 0.08$), utilization of knowledge and skills (adjusted $R^2 = 0.27$), and improvement to the career (adjusted $R^2 = 0.18$). The author speculate that HR policy is a relatively weaker influence level to Readjustment to daily life, because the adjusted R2 value of Readjustment to daily life is smaller than the other two.

[5] The author visited the HR departments of the eight participating companies and discussed this study with HR staff members on November 24 and 27, 2006; January 12, 2007; and March 8, 2007. Regarding the pilot survey, a request to evaluate a draft questionnaire was made to the HR staff and repatriates of seven companies by email, post, and/or telephone between December 2006 and February 2007. The responses collected from 22 repatriates of three companies by mail or personally by the author during a visit in February 2007 comprised the pilot survey. Through this process, the author received detailed comments and suggestions about the questions, accuracy of the terms, and unclear or inappropriate statements in the questionnaire. Based on these comments and evaluations, a revised questionnaire was examined by the HR staff of the companies. Then, the final questionnaire was administered to repatriates of seven companies in person or by post in March through April of 2007. Empirical studies by the author include the present study and Naito (2012a), which used data obtained from questionnaire surveys (excluding data from a pilot survey

due to lack of items for analysis), Naito (2009), and Naito (2011), which used data from questionnaire surveys and pilot studies. Naito (2009) addressed and analyzed the problems that repatriates face in work duties and lifestyle, focusing on recognition gaps and difficulties in repatriation, and proposed organizational practices and support for repatriates based on an analysis of comments by the participating repatriates. Naito (2011) presented and discussed the key concept of organizational resocialization as the transitional process before and after international assignments. Naito (2011) found that obtaining information through interactions with company staff (specifically, managers) at a workplace might improve readjustment to the organization, and reducing the gaps might facilitate readjustment. Naito (2012a) classified factors in terms of changes over time and changes due to cultural differences, focused on the characteristics of repatriation, and presented factors that might influence repatriates' readjustments to the organization through a comprehensive analysis. Naito (2011, 2012a) differ from the present study in that the former examined readjustments to the organization and the latter focused on readjustment to aspects of daily life outside the organization. Further, Naito (2016) was mainly based on Naito (2012a) to study readjustment to the organization/work and partially relied on Naito (2015) to study readjustment to daily life/nonwork (translated into English).

[6] Thirty-one participants did not answer this question, mainly because they were single. Therefore, their answers were coded as "found no problems." There were no participants (repatriates) who were accompanied by family members other than the spouse and children.

[7] The way in which the companies observed in this study were chosen is explained in Naito (2012a).

[8] It was determined that there is no multicollinearity because the Variance Inflation Factor (VIF) values were 1.02–1.32.

[9] For assignments less than one year, the data indicate that eight participants (40%) had seven months or more in which to prepare to return (see Table 3). The frequency of home visits of these eight participants was that six of them had no temporary home leave and two of them had home leave one time. The overall distribution of the frequency of home visits was: zero (14.06%, $n = 27$), one (18.75%, $n = 36$), two (9.90%, $n = 19$), three (15.63%, $n = 30$), four (10.42%, $n = 20$), five (6.25%, $n = 12$), and six or more (25.00%, $n = 48$).

[10] Some of the submitted questionnaires had missing data ($n = 12$). The path analysis was performed on $n = 180$, which excluded the cases with missing data.

[11] While living in a different culture, expatriates experience changes in their behaviors, interpersonal interactions, and cultural identities (Isogai et al., 1999; Kidder, 1992). Their situations at home also change along with the changes that occur over time during their international assignments. Compared to domestic assignments, it is difficult to update changes at home while working in a foreign country (Black et al., 1992). In this context, repatriates experience many types of reentry shock (Uehara, 1986). However, the difficulties that they face after returning home tend to decrease over time (Gullahorn & Gullahorn, 1963) and repatriates eventually acclimate to living at home after they return.

[12] For example, regarding repatriation orientation/guidance → gaps between life expectations and reality → readjustment to daily life in general, a path (indicated by an arrow) starting at repatriation orientation/guidance directly links to gaps between life expectations and reality, and a path starting at gaps between life expectations and reality is linked to readjustment to daily life in general. This finding suggests that repatriation orientation/guidance influences readjustment to daily life in general via the gaps between life expectations and reality and repatriation orientation/guidance might indirectly influence readjustment to daily life in general.

Chapter 19

Investigation of Ergonomic Risk Factors in Snacks Manufacturing in Central India:
Ergonomics in Unorganized Sector

Prabir Mukhopadhyay
Indian Institute of Information Technology Design and Manufacturing, Jabalpur, India

ABSTRACT

Hand-made snacks (locally known as papadam) manufacturing is a popular profession in Central India employing a large number of women workers The objective of this study was to identify the ergonomic risk factors for Work related musculoskeletal disorders (WMSDs) in this sector. Direct observation, activity analysis was applied along with postural analysis methods. Pre and post exercise heart rate was measured by the 10 beats method. Lower back (30%), upper arm (30%) and shoulder were the zones where maximum post work pain and discomfort was reported in the dough cutting section. The maximum post work heart rate was at 116.3 beats per minute in the dough cutting section. High REBA score of 15/15 was observed in the grading, kneading and dough cutting sections. Similarly the RULA scores were very high at 7/7 in majority of the sections. Strain Index scores were very high at 60.8 in the dough cutting section.

INTRODUCTION

Hand-made smacks manufacturing as a profession employs a large number of rural and urban women in Central India who otherwise does not have any other avenues of earning an income. These women are most illiterate and supplement their family income by working in these labour intensive manufacturing units. As these units require a significant amount of forceful exertions in awkward postures and involves frequent repetitive movements, it leads to different types of Work Related Musculoskeletal Disorders which manifests themselves in the form of pain and numbness in different body parts. These contribute to a decline in productivity and quality of work. To date there has not been an investigation on the

DOI: 10.4018/978-1-5225-2568-4.ch019

magnitude and the nature of the problem and the feasibility of any ergonomic design intervention for this sector. For any successful ergonomic intervention, it is imperative to identify the hazards and the levels of risk implicit in performing the required tasks. This research was an attempt in that direction.

LEARNING OBJECTIVES

After completing this chapter the reader will gain an insight into the following:

1. Ergonomic risk factors related to WMSD in the informal sector like hand-made snacks manufacturing involving women
2. The process of identifying the risk factors for WMSD in this sector
3. Directions for ergonomic solutions for the risk factors identified

BACKGROUND

Work related musculoskeletal disorders (WMSDs) are the single largest category of illness globally (Messing et al., 1998) affecting the back and upper extremities. The risk factors for such disorders have been found to be repetitive motions, forceful exertions, non-neutral body positions and vibrations. This has been substantiated by the works of Kattel et al. (1996), and Wiker et al. (1989) wherein it was stressed that poor work space layout and/or hand tool design forces workers to adopt awkward postures over long periods of time; thus, these are risk factors for the occurrence of WMSDs. Therefore, WMSDs are a proven health concern among workers worldwide (Kattel et al., 1996, Wiker et al., 1989). It is important to acknowledge the risk factors for WMSDs, including awkward postures, repetitive movements, and forceful exertions, be identified (Mukhopadhyay et. Al., 2006) before workers develop WMSDs, as they can result in decreased productivity and decreased quality of work as previously mentioned.

Globally, WMSDs have been found to account for huge losses in industry. For example, in the United Kingdom an estimated 9,466,000 working days (HSE, 2015) was lost due to WMSDs, which accounts for an average of 17.1 days lost ineach case. Similarly, in the United States (BLS, 2001), WMSDs were responsible for maximum temporary work disability after a common cold. It has been found that WMSDs (BLS, 2001) cost US$215 billion in 1991 in the USA, C$26 billion in Canada in 1998, and 38 billion Euros in Germany in 2002 (European Agency for Safety and Health at Work, 2014).

In Canada, WMSD problems resulted in lower productivity in manufacturing sectors causing approximately 34% of the annual lost time (Xu et al., 2012). However, there was no data available for the unorganized sector globally. In the Indian context, such data linking WMSDs and productivity remain unavailable.

WMSDs have been found to be especially prevalent in unorganized occupational sectors, since risk factors and control measures are less well understood in the informal economy (Mukhopadhyay, 2007). Such unorganized sectors form the backbone of the developing economies such as in India. The recent trend in India reflects an increase in the number of women workforce in these sectors for various reasons, one of which is supplementing the family income. Most of these sectors are related to agriculture, handicrafts, and hand-made snacks where a significant amount of physical labour is required. These sectors are an important means of livelihood for many people throughout India and are a major source of employment for the rural and semi-urban women (Mukhopadhyay & Ghosal, 2008).

One such sector is the hand-made snacks manufacturing in central India. Statistical data regarding the injury rate, occupational health hazards, and other ergonomic issues related to this profession is not yet available. The extant literature contains almost no data on different ergonomic issues relevant to this particular profession in India. Hence, the little work done in similar sectors in the western countries and in India form the only source of data for the people employed in this profession in India.

For example, it was discovered there were relatively higher rates of incidences of WMSDs (Messing et al., 1998) in females compared to their male counterparts in areas such as garment manufacturing, packaging, textile and electronic manufacturing, poultry, healthcare, food processing, grocery and cashiers in studies done on workers in the industrialized world. Contradicting this study, in a comparative study on the prevalence of WMSDs among male and female industrial workers, Punnette and Herbert (2000) could not conclude whether or not female workers were at increased risk for WMSDs compared to their male counterpart when exposed to the same ergonomic stressors.

In another investigation on female hair dressers (Hanvold et al., 2015), it was reported that work with prolonged arm elevation (greater than 70 degrees) was associated with shoulder pain and indicated the importance of early prevention strategies however there were no directions for ergonomic intervention. Petit et al. (2015), in a study on identification of risk factors for carpal tunnel syndrome among women employees in different manufacturing units, inferred that the incidence of the syndrome was higher in women compared to men. The group, however, did not probe into other ergonomic risk factors for WMSDs. There were mixed results in other comparative studies on the prevalence of WMSDs between male and female working groups.

For example, Dahlberg et al. (2004) reported that in the metal industry the self-reported incidences of WMSDs were found to be more common among women compared to men. In a study on female nurses (Rotenberg et al., 2008), it was found that for any investigation into the female well-being, particularly WMSDs, one must consider the total workload both at work as well as at home or the results are inconclusive. Vanderwal et al. (2011) studied the effects of the long- and short-handled hoe design in Gambia and inferred that women agricultural workers in general preferred the short-handled hoe over the long-handled hoe. However, the group did not investigate in to the WMSD issues associated in the profession.

In an investigation on the prevalence of musculoskeletal symptoms and ergonomic risk factors (Ozturk & Esin, 2011) among female sewing operators, it was observed that both intensity of pain and postural risk factors for WMSDs was quite high with the final RULA score at 6.7. The group, however, did not investigate any other ergonomic risk factors. It was found by another group (Rutanen et al., 2014) that six months of physical exercise among symptomatic (musculoskeletal symptoms) menopausal women decreased the symptoms and increased their working capability. Courville et al. (1991), in a comparative study of male and female mechanics, reported that the lack of appropriate gender specific tools for the females forced them to exert more strength in an uncomfortable posture compared to their male counterpart, thus leading to enhanced symptoms of musculoskeletal pain in different parts of the body. All these studies have been conducted in the western world.

In the Indian context, very little work has been reported in the literature. At present, the majority of studies conducted (Sen & Kar, 1984, Sen & Chakraborty, 1984) focused on the agricultural and allied sectors. A study on bamboo manufacturers (Sen & Kar, 1986) focused exclusively on energy expenditure and the nutritional status of the workers. Unfortunately, other major ergonomic risk factors like posture and repetitive movements were not investigated. In another study on agricultural workers in eastern

India, the emphasis was on ergonomic tool design for ploughs; however, risk factors were not reported or studied. In a study on butchers, tailors, and weavers in eastern India (Gangyopadhyay et al., 2003), repetitive activities were found to be contributory factor in occupational injury; again, there was no investigation into postural risk factors that play a major role in the genesis of WMSDs (Mukhopadhyay & Ghosal, 2008).

In the fishing industry in western India (Saha et al., 2006), the nature of work such as blanching, packaging, and grading was found to have a significant impact on injury causation. In the same industry (Nag & Nag, 2007), women complained of musculoskeletal pain and discomfort in the lower back, followed by the knee, upper back, calf muscles and other areas of the body. Again, there were no investigations on ergonomic risk factors, with no probe into postural risk factors or repetitiveness. Interview technique and injury data from primary health centres were the only sources for data collection.

The little work that has been done in some sectors, like semi-precious stone polishing (Patel,2006) and food processing (Raut & Kakhoen, 2006) have all focused on improving working conditions through improvement of ventilation, illumination, and so forth. These studies focused primarily on data collection techniques and comprised of interviews and questionnaires. No ergonomic assessment for different risk factors for WMSDs was conducted. For example, Nag et al. (1986) analysed different sitting postures of Indian women and inferred that sitting on the floor with the legs extended was relaxing with less muscle activity compared to any other postures. However, they did not investigate the risk factors for WMSDs in working women.

Singh et al. (2012) designed a hand operated maize dehusk-sheller to be operated by farm women, but like others there were no investigation into the ergonomic risk factors for WMSDs in the profession. In another study (Nag et al., 2004), the effect of shift work on female VDT-cum telephone operators were investigated. It was found that overlapping schedule of rotating shift work including night shifts were risk factors for different problems like digestion, cognitive ability; however, there was no mention of WMSDs.

In another study by Mukhopadhyay and Ghosal (2008), a workstation was developed for the manual incenses stick workers in western India. However, there was no investigation on the ergonomic risk factors for WMSDs in this profession. Direct observation and activity analysis (using still photography) was used for collecting data from the field. The majority of works done in other sectors have either focused on the redesign of tools or workstations, or the design of personal protective equipment. The few studies which have investigated risk factors (in manufacturing industry and not traditional craft) have been in a controlled environment and not in the field.

ISSUES/PROBLEMS

Hand-made snacks manufacturing is a sector where risk factors like awkward posture repetitive activities and forceful exertions, and so forth for WMSDs seem to be present (McCann, 1998). To date there has not been an investigation on the magnitude and the nature of the problem. For any successful ergonomic intervention, it is imperative to identify the hazards and the levels of risk implicit in performing the required tasks (Kilbom 1994; Mukhopadhyay et al., 2007). This research was an attempt in that direction.

STUDY DESIGN

Overview

Hand-made snacks are very popular all over India and are manufactured mainly in central India. It is made of chick peas and is circular in shape and very thin. One needs to either roast or fry it in oil to make it crispy before consumption. One such large manufacturing unit in central India was selected for the study. The uniqueness of this profession is that it is dominated only by females and there are no male employees. It is a labour intensive job with very few machinery being used in the entire manufacturing unit. There were seven different sections in which seven different tasks were performed namely; grading, cleaning, grinding, kneading, dough cutting, rolling, and packaging.

Workers were recruited separately for working in different sections and there were no systems of transferring workers from one section to another once they were recruited and trained. Keeping this in mind workers were selected from all the seven different sections and this selection was done randomly. A total of 25 workers were selected from each of these seven sections for the ergonomic analysis. Environmental parameters were recorded in each of these sections and total ten readings of different environmental parameters were recorded.

Questionnaire and Interview

A questionnaire was developed along the lines of Sinclair et al. (1975) to get an insight into the nature and the quantum of various ergonomic issues in different sections. A list of required information was made for this purpose. Next, closed- and open-ended questions were framed to extract the required information from the subjects. There were six trial versions of the questionnaire which was pilot tested on the users to produce the final version to be used for collecting the required information. The questionnaire was comprised of questions such as experience in the profession, problems faced while working, pain and / or discomfort in different body parts, duration of work, and normal daily activity.

Direct Observation and Activity Analysis

Drury's (1990) direct observation and activity analysis was applied specific to this sector after modifications (Mukhopadhyay & Srivastava, 2010a). This was essential as the activities in this sector was quite different compared to other organized sectors like banking or manufacturing for which the original method was devised. Subjects were observed in each of the seven sections mentioned before. The key elements observed included the posture assumed, number of repetitive movements, types of load being handled, and the movement pattern of the workers in each section. Data obtained from this was used for assessing different ergonomic risk factors for WMSDs on the lines of similar studies conducted in the unorganized sectors such as incense sticks manufacturing (Mukhopadhyay & Ghosal, 2008), and stone carving (Mukhopadhyay & Srivastava, 2010a, b).

Photography of Different Sections

Still and video photography of different sections on similar lines by other investigators in similar situations like incense sticks manufacturing, stone carving, and butchers (Mukhopadhyay & Ghosal, 2008, Mukhopadhyay & Srivastava, 2010a, b; Mukhopadhyay et al., 2015) were done with focus on posture, repetitive movement of the different body parts, nature of work and the type of load being handled. These photographs were later analysed in the laboratory. The still photographs were used for identification of different postural risk factors. The video photography was used to analyse repetitive movements and the duration of different sections at specific awkward postures.

Measurement of Physiological Parameters

Heart rate was measured by the 10 beats method at the beginning of work and at the end of 30 minutes of work for each of the seven different sections. This was again on the lines of similar studies carried out in the unorganized sectors like stone carving (Mukhopadhyay & Srivastava, 2010a, b).

Measurement of Psychophysical Parameters

A modified Body Part Discomfort Map (BPD) from Corlett and Bishop (1976) was applied to identify discomfort in different parts and was developed along the lines of Mukhopadhyay and Srivastava (2010 a, b). The workers were asked to rate one specific zone in their body where they had the maximum discomfort after 30 minutes of working. A 10 centimeter Visual Analogue Scale (VAS) was also used to obtain an insight into the level of discomfort in the shoulder-arm area following 30 minutes of work. Borg's scale for Rated Perceived Exertion (RPE) was also used parallel to get an insight into the amount of effort involved in the particular section and was also taken at the end of 30 minutes of work. These were all in line with previous work done in similar sectors (Mukhopadhyay & Srivastava, 2010a, b; Sen et al., 1986).

Measurement of Environmental Parameters

Radiant heat was measured by Vernon's Globe, Dry Bulb, and Wet Bulb Temperature by the Whirling Psychrometer. All thermal the parameters were recorded every hour for 10 hours and the mean of all the readings was calculated. Separate measurements were taken for all the seven different sections as they were performed at different places. This process was used to understand and measure the effect of environmental heat on physiological parameters like heart rate and the psychophysical parameters like Rated Perceived Exertion (RPE) and Visual Analogue Scale (VAS) on the lines of similar investigations (Sen & Kar, 2006) on agricultural workers working under the sun and on stone carving units (Mukhopadhyay & Srivastava, 2010 a) in shades.

SOLUTIONS AND RECOMMENDATIONS

Physical Characteristics of the Subjects

Twenty-five female subjects were selected in each of the seven different sections (Table 1). The mean age was maximum in the grinding section at 44.8 years (SD = 8.3) with age ranging from 30 to 57 years. Minimum mean age was observed in the packaging section at 37.2 years (SD = 10.9) with age ranging from 22 to 65 years. The mean height of the worker's max maximum in packaging section at 163.9 centimeters (SD = 9.8) with height ranging from 146 to 182 centimeters. The minimum mean height was observed in kneading section at 154.7 cm (SD = 6.9) with height ranging from 144 to 169cm.

Similarly, the maximum mean weight was observed in rolling sections at 60.4 kilograms (SD=14.2) with weight ranging from 43-84 kilograms. The minimum mean weight was again observed in cleaning/straining section at only 49.4 kilograms (SD = 8.5) with weight ranging from 20 to 60 kilograms. Maximum experienced workers were observed in grading section with mean experience at 17.5 years (SD=9.5) and experience ranging from 1 to 40 years. The minimum mean experience of the workers was observed in the dough cutting section at 9.3 years (SD = 6.6) with experience ranging from 1 to 24 years.

Body Part Discomfort

The body part discomfort map (Table 2) indicated discomfort in varying proportion in different parts of the body for different section. Discomfort was maximum in the lower back (30%) for cleaning/straining, kneading and rolling sections. Similar discomfort (30%) was also reported in the upper arm and shoulder in dough cutting section. In the grinding section maximum discomfort (25%) was reported in

Table 1. Mean (Standard Deviation) Physical Characteristics of the Subjects (n=25 in each activity)

Sections	Physical Characteristics			
	Age (years)	Height (cm)	Weight (kg)	Experience (years)
Grading	41.5(13.3)	157(6.5)	55.9(6.3)	17.5(9.5)
	22-63	146-170	46-72	1-40
Cleaning/straining	41.6(15.1)	156.6(7.6)	49.4(8.5)	13.2(8.1)
	21-66	144-170	20-60	1-31
Grinding	44.8(8.3)	154.8(8.8)	60.2(12.7)	12.9(9.7)
	30-57	143-171	41-88	1-31
Kneading	44.2(8.1)	154.7(6.9)	50(1.3)	15.5(8.2)
	30-65	144-169	25-72	1-30
Dough cutting	39(9.7)	155.4(8.1)	57.8(12.1)	9.3(6.6)
	24-59	144-169	40-90	1-24
Rolling	40.3(1.2)	159.2(7.1)	60.4(14.2)	12.9(9.7)
	23-65	146-170	43-84	1-31
Packing	37.2(10.9)	163.9(9.8)	57.8(12)	13.2(8.1)
	22-65	146-182	44-90	1-31

Table 2. Body Part Discomfort (%) in Different Parts at Different Sections after One Hour of Work (n=25 in each activity)

Sections	Body Parts					
	Neck	Shoulder	Upper Arm	Forearm	Upper Back	Lower Back
Grading	10	15	10	20	20	25
Cleaning/straining	20	10	10	10	20	30
Grinding	5	25	10	25	20	15
Kneading	5	15	10	20	20	30
Dough cutting	10	30	30	10	10	10
Rolling	20	10	10	05	25	30
Packing	05	10	15	20	25	25

the shoulder and forearm region. 25% discomfort was reported in the upper back in the rolling and the packaging section respectively. Discomfort was minimum (5%) in the neck region for grinding, kneading and packaging section, and in the forearm for the rolling section.

Qualitative Data

The workers were normally employed for eight hours a day for six days with one day off every week. Working hours at times were extended when there were demand for snacks and in such cases the workers were paid for the extra hours they worked. The workers suffered from pain in different parts of the body for almost all the sections of the manufacturing unit, but in general for all the units pain in the lower back, upper arm, and lower arm was very common. For those working in the dough cutting unit the pain was at time intense at the end of the day's work such that they needed to take a day off due to the intense pain. This happened mainly when there was demand for extra work (October-November) during the festive season (extending to twelve to fourteen hours at a stretch). It was also found that workers in the higher age group ranging from 45 years to 65 years were the maximum affected.

Work Process

Manufacturing of snacks comprised of seven different sections (grading, cleaning/straining, grinding, kneading, dough cutting, rolling and packaging) each having dedicated work force. Grading involved inspecting the grain (chick peas) and separating out the grains on the basis of their quality for the purpose of snacks manufacturing (Figure 1).

This was done manually and then poured into the machine. Grains of different quality were separated out as the best ones (larger in size) were used for snacks manufacturing and the smaller grains were taken away for other usage. This phase was followed by the cleaning phase, (Figure 2) wherein any foreign particles were cleaned manually by spreading the grain on a clean piece of cloth on the floor.

After this the grains were given a wash in plain water if required and dried subsequently. The grinding phase (Figure 3) followed next with the cleaned grains being unloaded in an automatic grinder which reduced the grains into a fine powder.

Figure 1. Inspection and grain separation

Figure 2. Manual cleaning of the grains

Figure 3. Grinding

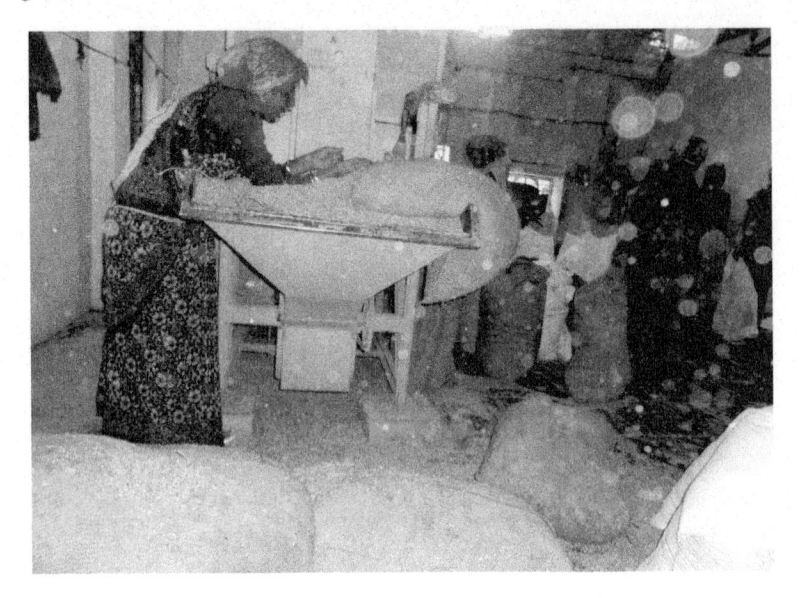

The next section was kneading (Figure 4) in which the powder was manually mixed with water and the semisolid substance was poured into a kneading machine manually to ensure that it was further mixed to make the dough soft.

This was followed by cutting the dough (Figure 5) into smaller pieces which was again manually done with the help of a hinged blade attached to metallic tables.

Rolling of the dough (Figure 6) followed this section where the small pieces of dough were manually rolled with the help of a wooden roller to form circular papadams.

Figure 4. Kneading phase

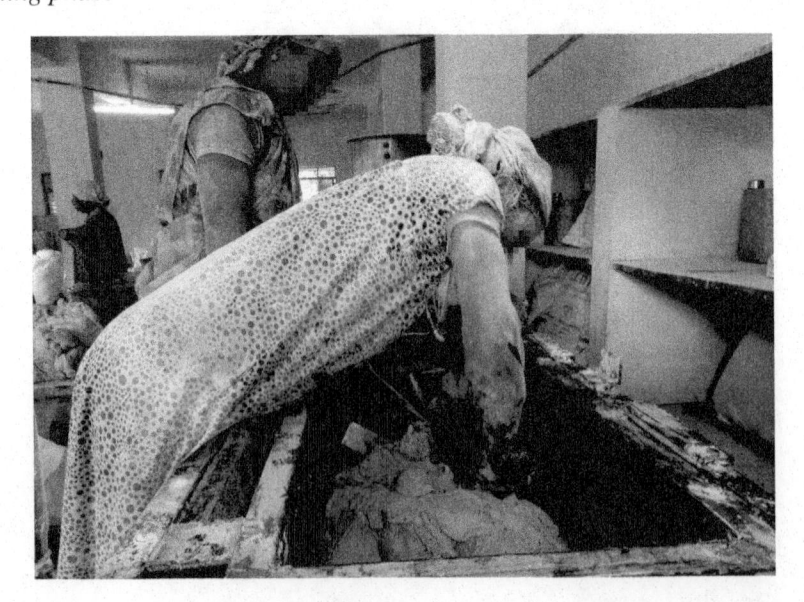

Figure 5. Dough cutting

The last phase involved drying of these snacks in direct sunlight (Figure 7) and packing them in plastic packets (Figure 8) which were then sealed manually with the help of thermal sealer. Most of the sections took place indoors except for rolling the snacks where the workers had the option to work outdoors as well.

Postural Analysis of Musculoskeletal Risk Factors

Different techniques were applied for postural analysis of Work Related Musculoskeletal risk factors. These methods were the OVAKO working posture, Rapid Entire Body Assessment (REBA) and Rapid Upper Limb Assessment Method (RULA). Strain Index (SI) was applied to investigate injury risk to the distal upper extremities. Quick Exposure Checklist (QEC) was also applied to assess musculoskeletal risk. In order to understand and measure the work load on hand musculature Threshold Limit Value (TLV) for hand activity was applied as well. All the postural analysis was done in the actual working condition and this was further validated by the still and digital photography recordings (taken in the actual working conditions) by analysing them in the laboratory.

Figure 6. Rolling the snacks

Figure 7. Sun drying of the snacks

Investigation of Ergonomic Risk Factors in Snacks Manufacturing in Central India

Figure 8. Packaging of the snacks

OVAKO Working Posture

The postural analysis method devised by Karhu (1977) was applied (Table 3). Extremely vulnerable postures with a score of 6 were observed in the back for the cleaning/straining section, and the dough cutting section. Similar vulnerable posture was observed in the arms in the dough cutting section with a score of 6. Such high scores of 6 were also observed for the force/weight handle for the sections like grading, grinding and dough cutting. Vulnerable postures with scores of 5 was also observed for the back in the cleaning/straining section, in the arms for the grading, cleaning/straining, and grinding sections, and for the force/weight handled for the cleaning/straining and kneading sections respectively. Other postures which had a high score of 4 were the back for grading and rolling section, arms for the rolling section, and the legs for the dough cutting section demanding immediate ergonomic intervention.

Rapid Entire Body Assessment (REBA) and Rapid Upper Limb Assessment (RULA) Working Posture Analysis

The postural analysis method (REBA) devised by Hignet and McAtamney (2000) and that (RULA) devised by McAtamney & Corlett (1993) was applied. The sections in the manufacturing units involved high intensity and awkward postures involving the entire body. That is the reason for applying the REBA

Table 3. OVAKO Working Posture Analysis for Different Body Parts at Different Sections

Sections	Body Parts				
	Head	Back	Arms	Legs	Force/Weight
Grading	2	4	5	3	6
Cleaning/ straining	2	6	5	2	5
Grinding	2	5	5	2	6
Kneading	2	6	3	2	5
Dough cutting	2	6	6	4	6
Rolling	2	4	4	2	3
Packing	2	2	3	3	2

method for analysis. RULA was applied due to the fact that for some sections of the manufacturing units there was intense involvement of the upper limb compared with the lower limb. As it was difficult to isolate the two different types of activities both REBA and RULA was applied (Table 4) on the lines of other researchers working in similar sectors like stone carving (Mukhopadhyay & Srivastava, 2010b) and bamboo handicraft manufacturing unit (Sen & Kar, 1984). The REBA scores were very high (15/15) in the grading, kneading, and dough cutting section indicating immediate ergonomic intervention. The REBA scores were also high (12/12) in the cleaning/straining section and the grinding section indicating immediate intervention as well. The RULA scores were very high (7/7) for grading, cleaning/straining, grinding, kneading and dough cutting sections warranting early intervention.

Strain Index (SI)

The job risk analysis method; Strain Index (SI) devised by Moore & Garg (1995) was applied. SI scores were extremely high (60.8) for the dough cutting section, very high (27) for the grading section, it was high for the grinding (13.5) and kneading (18) sections warranting immediate intervention (Table 4).

Table 4. Postural Analysis and Repetitiveness Scores for Different Sections

Sections	REBA	RULA	SI
Grading	15/15	7/7	27
Cleaning/ straining	12/12	7/7	6.8
Grinding	12/12	7/7	13.5
Kneading	15/15	7/7	18
Dough cutting	15/15	7/7	60.8
Rolling	4/4	4/4	6
Packing	6/6	3/3	3.4

REBA= Rapid Entire Body Assessment
RULA= Rapid Upper Limb Assessment
SI= Strain Index

Quick Exposure Checklist (QEC)

The QEC method devised by Li and Buckle (1999) was applied for assessing musculoskeletal risk in the different sections of the manufacturing unit (Table 5). For interpreting the results of QEC, the method of David et al. (2005) was adopted. The scores were very high (50) for the back in the grading section, grinding section (56), kneading section (56), dough cutting section (56). The scores were moderate for the back (26) for the rolling and the packaging sections. The scores for the wrist/hand were very high (46) for the cleaning/straining section, grinding section, kneading section and dough cutting section.

They were high for the wrist/hand in the grading section (38), rolling section (34), and packaging section (34). For the neck the scores were very high for all the sections ranging from 16-18, with 18 in the kneading, dough cutting and rolling section, and 16 in the grading, cleaning/straining and grinding sections respectively. The scores were low for driving for all the sections and for vibration also it was low for almost all the sections at 1, except for kneading where it was 4 but within the category of low risk. The scores for work pace was high (9) for cleaning/straining, grinding and kneading sections. It was moderate for grading (4) and rolling (4). It was low for the dough cutting and rolling section at 1. The scores for stress were very high at 16 for grading, cleaning/straining, grinding, and kneading sections. It was high at 9 for the packaging section and was moderate at 4 for the rolling section.

American Conference of Governmental Industrial Hygienist (ACGIH) Threshold Limit Value (TLV) for Hand Activity

The Threshold Limit Value (TLV) method devised by Lalko and Armstrong (1997) was applied for assessing the job strain. In the grading, cleaning/straining, grinding, and dough cutting sections (Table 6), the TLV was high (1) for both the hands and it was high (0.8) in the kneading section for both the hands warranting immediate intervention in these sections. In the rolling and packaging sections the TLV values for both the hand (0.3) were within the action limit of 0.56 and hence considered relatively safe.

Table 5. Quick Exposure Checklist (QEC) for Different Sections

Sections	Back	Shoulder/Arm	Wrist/Hand	Neck	Driving	Vibration	Work Pace	#St
Grading	50	48	38	16	1	1	4	16
Cleaning/Straining	44	44	46	16	1	1	9	16
Grinding	56	56	46	16	1	1	9	16
Kneading	56	48	46	18	1	4	9	16
Dough cutting	56	56	46	18	1	1	1	16
Rolling	26	30	34	18	1	1	1	4
Packing	26	34	40	16	1	1	4	9

#St= Stress

Table 6. American Conference of Governmental Industrial Hygienists (ACGIH) Threshold Limit Value for Hand Activity

Sections	Hand Activity Level (HAL)		Normalized Peak Force (NPF)		NPF/HAL	
	*L	#R	*L	#R	*L	#R
Grading	9	9	9	9	1	1
Cleaning/straining	10	10	10	10	1	1
Grinding	8	8	8	8	1	1
Kneading	10	10	8	8	0.8	0.8
Dough cutting	10	10	10	10	1	1
Rolling	6	6	2	2	0.3	0.3
Packing	4	4	1	1	0.3	0.3

*L= Left Hand
#R= Right Hand

Physiological Parameter

The mean pre-exercise heart rate (Table 7) was the minimum in the packaging and the rolling sections at 82.2 beats per minute. The maximum pre-exercise heart rate was observed in the cleaning/straining section at 85.4 beats per minute. To obtain further insights into whether there were any differences in the mean pre-exercise heart rates across different sections a One-Way Independent Analysis of Variance (ANOVA) was applied for the pre-exercise heart rate across all seven sections. The ANOVA results was not significant ($p < 0.740$), indicating similar pre-exercise heart rate among all the workers in the different sections.

The mean post-exercise heart rate (Table 7) was the minimum in the packaging section at 98.5 beats per minute and it was the maximum in the dough cutting section at 116.3 beats per minute. To gain further insights into the differences in the mean post exercise heart rates across the different sections, a One-Way Independent ANOVA was applied for post exercise heart rate across all the seven sections. The ANOVA results were highly significant ($p<0.001$). A Post Hoc Student-Newman-Keuls (SNK) test was applied on the post exercise heart rates. The SNK test indicated that the mean heart rate in the dough cutting section was significantly different from the other sections.

Mean post-exercise heart rates in packaging and sealing, kneading, rolling, and grinding sections were similar and placed in the same group. On similar lines, the mean post exercise heart rates in the kneading, rolling, grinding and grading section were also similar. Following similar trend the mean heart rates in rolling, grinding, grading and cleaning sections were similar and grouped together. To test for a significant change in the heart rate from the pre-exercise level to the post exercise level in the different sections an independent t-test was applied for the pre- and post-exercise heart rates for each of the seven sections. The t-test was highly significant for both pre and post exercise heart rates in all the seven sections like; grading: $p < 0.001$, ($t(24) = -9.540$), cleaning: $p < 0.001$, ($t(24) = -11.003$), grinding: $p < 0.001$, ($t(24) = -10.241$), kneading = $p < 0.001$, ($t(24) = -8.800$), dough cutting = $p < 0.001$, ($t(24) = -18.813$), rolling = $p < 0.001$, ($t(24) = -12.373$), packaging and sealing = $p < 0.001$, ($t(24) = -6.844$).

Table 7. Mean Pre- and Post-Exercise Heart Rates (after 30 minutes) in Different Activities (n = 25 for each activity)

Sections	Heart Rate (Beats/Minute)					
	Pre-Exercise			Post Exercise		
	Mean	SD	Min-Max	Mean	SD	Min-Max
Grading	84.2	8.6	66-99	103.8	2.9	98-108
Cleaning/straining	85.4	8.1	70-99	104.7	5.1	98-121
Grinding	84.6	8.2	70-99	102.2	7.3	91-120
Kneading	84.3	8.4	70-90	100.4	3.4	90-110
Dough cutting	84.6	8.6	66-99	116.3	6.1	101-130
Rolling	82.2	4.9	70-90	101.1	4.2	93-111
Packing	82.2	8.5	70-99	98.5	5.7	84-111

Psychophysical Parameters

Mean Rated Perceived Exertion (RPE) values (Table 8) were maximum in the dough cutting section (19.3 = very very hard) and it was minimum in the packaging section (7.2 = very very light). A One-Way Independent ANOVA was applied on the RPE scores. RPE scores were highly significant (p < 0.001) across the different sections. Post Hoc SNK test was then applied on the RPE scores. The SNK test revealed different mean RPE values for all the seven sections.

Mean discomfort score on the Visual Analogue Scale (VAS) was maximum (9.2) in the dough cutting section (Table 8) and minimum (1.0) in the packaging and the grinding sections. To gain further insights a One-Way Independent ANOVA was applied on the VAS scores. VAS scores were again highly significant (p<0.001). To gain further insights a Post Hoc SNK test was then applied on the VAS scores. The SNK test revealed that the mean VAS scores were similar in the grinding and the packaging sec-

Table 8. Mean Scores on Rated Perceived Exertion (RPE) and Visual Analogue Scale (VAS) for different sections after 30 minutes of work (n = 25 for each activity)

Sections	RPE			VAS		
	Mean	SD	Min-Max	Mean	SD	Min-Max
Grading	11.1	0.4	10-12	2.6	0.5	2-3.3
Cleaning/straining	12.6	0.6	12-14	4.9	0.7	3.6-6.3
Grinding	9.4	0.5	9-10	1.0	0.5	0.1-1.9
Kneading	11.5	0.5	11-12	2.9	0.5	2.1-3.9
Dough cutting	19.3	0.7	18-20	9.2	0.6	8.1-10
Rolling	12.2	0.7	11-14	5.3	0.7	4-6.8
Packing	7.2	1.1	6-9	1.0	0.6	0.1-2

tions and hence placed in the same group. The mean VAS scores for all other sections were significantly different from one another and placed in separate groups.

Environmental Parameters

Different environmental parameters were measured in all the seven different sections (Table 9). The maximum mean globe temperature was observed in the rolling section at 32° C (SD = 2.5) with temperature ranging from 29.1° C to 38.1° C. The minimum mean globe temperature was observed in the grinding section at 21.4°C (SD = 1.9) with temperature ranging from 18.6°C to 25.2°C. The maximum mean dry bulb temperature was in the dough cutting section at 22.6°C (SD = 1.1) with temperature ranging from 21.1°C to 24.1°C. The minimum mean dry bulb temperature was in the cleaning/straining section at 17.8°C (SD = 0.8) with temperature ranging from 16.5°C to 19.2°C. The maximum mean wet bulb temperature was observed in the dough cutting section at 12.1°C (SD = 1.3) with temperature ranging from 10.5°C to 14.1°C. The minimum mean wet bulb temperature was in the packaging section at 11.4°C (SD = 1.1) with temperature ranging from 9.7°C to 13.2°C.

Ergonomic Issues

The mean age of the subjects in majority of the sections indicated that the users were in the middle age category (40 years and above). The weight of the female subjects was 50 kilograms and above in majority of the sections and in the Indian context this is considered to be normal (Kinare et al., 2000). The experience of the workers in different sections varied which was substantiated by a high standard deviation (8 and above in majority of the sections) which again ensured the sample was homogenous comprised of novice and experienced workers.

The Body Part Discomfort Map revealed maximum discomfort in the lower and upper back which in many of the sections which could be attributed to repeated bending forward accompanied by torso twisting. The shoulder, upper ram, and forearm was next affected which was due to forward flexion and abduction of the shoulder arm system leading to strain in the gleno-humeral joint which triggered

Table 9. Environmental Parameters in Different Sections (n = 10)

Sections	Globe (°C) Mean (SD)	Globe (°C) (Min-Max)	*DB (°C) Mean (SD)	*DB (°C) (Min-Max)	#WB (°C) Mean (SD)	#WB (°C) (Min-Max)
Grading	22.2(3.1)	(19.8-29.7)	17.9(0.7)	(16.8-19.1)	11.8(1.2)	(9.9-14.5)
Cleaning/Straining	22.1(1.7)	(20.3-26.1)	17.8(0.8)	(16.5-19.2)	11.5(1.5)	(10.1-15.3)
Grinding	21.4(1.9)	(18.6-25.2)	18.1(0.8)	(17.1-19.6)	11.6(1.2)	(10.3-13.9)
Kneading	25.9(2)	(22.5-29.1)	18(0.5)	(17.2-18.9)	11.9(0.8)	(10.9-13.5)
Dough cutting	26.2(2.1)	(22.9-29.1)	22.6(1.1)	(21.1-24.1)	12.1(1.3)	(10.5-14.1)
Rolling	32(2.5)	(29.1-38.1)	20.7(1.8)	(17.5-23.1)	11.7(0.9)	(10-12.9)
Packing	24.3(1.7)	(22.3-27.3)	19.6(1.9)	(16.2-22.3)	11.4(1.1)	(9.7-13.2)

*DB = Dry Bulb
#WB = Wet Bulb

discomfort. Forearm discomfort could be attributed to repeated rotation of the forearm along with load lifting especially in rolling, dough cutting and kneading sections. These were along the lines of those reported by others in experiments in controlled environment (Mukhopadhyay et al., 2007; O'Sullivan & Gallwey, 2005).

The work schedule of eight hours in majority of the sections was hectic and there was only one day off in the entire week. The problem of musculoskeletal disorders and pain escalated in some of the sections like dough cutting, grinding, and rolling sections which involved either maximum force exertion and/or repetitive movements with almost no recovery time. The age group that was the maximum affected (45 to 65 years) is the prime age at which menopause develops. The literature has proven evidence (Blumel et al., 2013) to suggest that post- menopausal women are at increased risk of WMSDs.

The results of the questionnaire only substantiated the findings of the different methods discussed above. For example, the long and extended working hours of 8-10 hours could be attributed to the cause of pain in different body parts for many of the sections. Pain in the lower back and shoulder arm system could be attributed to awkward postures for prolong period associated with load handling which has been explained before. The elderly workers complaining of pain in different body parts can be attributed to the duration of risk factors for WMSDs they have been exposed to already setting the stage for WMSD onset, which is probably difficult to reverse at this point of time except if they are given voluntary retirement from service with all due benefits.

Absence of multitasking and job rotation among the different sections was one major ergonomic issue which needs to be addressed. This implied that workers involved in heavy physical work as depicted in the sections like dough cutting would have to continue working in that section for her entire career. In the long run this would not only expose her to WMSDs but also lead to boredom and fatigue doing the same task repeatedly. There should be job rotation amongst the different sections so that workers are not exposed to one hazardous area comprising of multiple risk factors for WMSDs like force, repetition etc. for long. This type of job design approach has been followed in the manufacturing sector before (Michalos et al., 2013).

Postural analysis by different methods indicates that majority of the postures in the different sections are at risk and demands immediate intervention as they are above the normal limit. This was expected as the workers were working in awkward postures deviating from neutral position for prolong period, which was accompanied by static muscular loading of the different limbs. These findings were along the lines of the work done by Sen (1965) and Mukhopadhyay & Srivastava (2010, a, b) in similar sectors like stone carving, brick manufacturing and in the controlled environment (Mukhopadhyay et al., 2007, O'Sullivan & Gallwey, 2005.). Thus, working under such conditions there is a degradation of the quality of work and productivity. The occupational health and safety of the workers under such circumstances are at risk for the development of WMSDs.

The High Strain Index score for majority of the sections substantiated the fact repetitive activities were involved in majority of the sections as a risk factor for WMSDs. This was further substantiated by an elevated TLV for the majority of the sections for both the hands. Thus, looking at this trend it could be inferred there are substantial repetitive movements of the upper limbs without adequate rest. Such activities lead to micro were and tear of the softer tissues of the body which do not get adequate rest for recovery. Ultimately this wear and tear builds up with the passage of time setting the stage for WMSDs in the long run. These were supported by similar studies in controlled environment (Mukhopadhyay et al., 2007; O'Sullivan & Gallwey, 2005) where it has been demonstrated that at different awkward postures of the shoulder arm system and at different grip and torque forces, accompanied by repetitive twisting, bending forward or load lifting were significant risk factors in the genesis of WMSDs.

High QEC values for the back, shoulder/arm, wrist/hand, and neck only substantiated the previous findings from postural analysis that due to awkward postures and repetitive activities without adequate rest and recovery these parts were vulnerable to musculoskeletal injury in the long run. The neck in majority of the sections were either forward flexed or rotated from neutral rendering them vulnerable to injury as well. The QEC indicated very high work pace in some sections like cleaning/straining, grinding, kneading which was expected as work in these sections had to be done very fast to meet the production target and there was complete absence of any mechanization.

The overall stress scores were very high which again was as expected as the tasks in the sector involved awkward, repetitive postures for long period of time without any rest. The only QEC variables which were low were driving and vibration. This was again expected as none of the women knew driving, and all of them walked to their place of work. There was no significant vibration from any of the little equipment used in this unit thus this variable also had a low score.

The relative duration and the force exerted in the dough cutting section was critical and this was substantiated by an elevated heart rate well above the pre-exercise value, thus categorizing it as a moderately heavy work (Lui et al., 2014; Sen, 1965). The radiant heat and the dry bulb and wet bulb temperature in this section was low as the work was carried out in the month of February which is in the winter months. This could be one of the reasons why the heart rate did not rise further even though the workload was apparently high. In the warm summer months with an increase in the radiant heat, dry bulb, and wet bulb temperature, would further increase the cardiovascular load on the workers thus leading to a decline in productivity in the long run. This was also applicable for other sections where the post exercise heart rates exhibited an increased value which was significant for all the sections.

This was substantiated by an elevated RPE score for the dough cutting section (very, very hard) and increased discomfort score on the VAS scale which was due to the fact that such sections were coupled with awkward postures and forceful exertions without adequate rest period. but the corresponding RPE and discomfort scores on VAS especially for cleaning/straining section and the rolling section were elevated and hence demands careful monitoring. Borgs RPE indicated a high score (very, very hard) in the dough cutting unit which was further substantiated by an elevated Discomfort Score on VAS for the same section.

This could be attributed to the involvement of more and more forearm and upper arm musculatures in performing these sections. Similarly, for the rolling section the RPE score was close to "fairly light" which was again reflected in a VAS score close to average. For the grinding section which was mainly automated, the RPE scores were very light accompanied by a very low discomfort score. This was evident as there as minimal load of the working in this section except for the fact that they had to pour the grains into the machine.

Mean Globe, Dry-Bulb, and Wet-Bulb temperatures were measured in the cooler winter months and were all within the normal limit. Thus as mentioned before it did not increase the cardiovascular load even in the sections like dough cutting which involved heavy force exertion (Lui et al., 2014).

FUTURE RESEARCH DIRECTIONS

There is a dearth of data related to the ergonomic risk factors associated with work related musculoskeletal disorders typical of such home-made snacks manufacturing in the country. In these units, the female workers must work in awkward postures involving static position of different body parts for prolong periods, associated with heavy manual material handling and repetitive activities of different body parts. There were no concepts of small breaks in between sections which could have led to recovery of the micro wear and tear of the softer tissues. This study presents the different ergonomic risk factors in different types of sections, including their nature and the quantum. These data might be useful to identify and control the high risk sections in these sectors well before they develop into work-related musculoskeletal disorders especially at the design stage while using biomechanical models.

The different ergonomic intervention in this sector could be categorised under three different headings. The first one could be the ergonomic design of different tools associated with manufacturing. For example, for the purpose of lifting the heavy bags small trolleys or carts could be designed along with detachable tongs with proper grip so that all the fingers of the palm could be used to evenly distribute the load on all the muscles. For spreading the grains instead of using the hands small metallic or wooden spreaders in the shape of a duck's leg could be designed. The second intervention could be that many of the work surface height need to be re-designed with reference to the worker's anthropometric dimensions. For example, in the kneading section as the section involves bending forward the height of the machine top could be brought down at the trochanter height of the subjects which would ease such bending movements.

CONCLUSION

The findings from this study indicates the majority of the working postures, processes, and the environment in which the work took place were potential risk factors in the genesis of WMSDs and injury in the long-run. This, in turn, would affect the productivity and the quality of the work which would decrease the profit margin of the particular industry. These risk factors must be controlled at the level of tools, workstation, and work process design to ensure effective control. It seems the stakeholders of this particular sector are unaware of the above issues and its relationship with the profit generating capacity of the industry. A health workforce is an asset of any organization, and if the organization has to pay huge sum for its employee medical benefit, then the organization cannot make profits. This awareness needs to be spread among the stakeholders of this sector.

Ergonomic analysis of the snacks manufacturing sector revealed different risk factors which in the long run if left unattended could lead to WMSDs. This sector is a major source of employment for the local women force. Thus, it is important that this profession be made much more attractive by making the working conditions a little more humane. Over the long-term this would increase productivity, promote occupational health and safety of the workers and at the same time increase profit of the industry which, in turn, would make the profession attractive.

LIMITATIONS OF RESEARCH

The particular sector in which the research was conducted is an unorganized sector, with no benefits for the workers and under no rules and regulations. There were no data on record about accident rates, productivity, and others associated with the sector which would act as a point of reference for the current research. Getting permission to conduct such a research was extremely difficult and, hence, the tenure of the entire research was restricted to only three months. A longer duration spanning over a year or more would help in assessing the impact of the changes suggested in this research related to increased productivity, and enhanced occupational health and safety of the workers.

ACKNOWLEDGMENT

Acknowledgement is owed to all those who volunteered for this project. Acknowledgement is also owed to undergraduate students Mr. Parag Nawani and Mr. Pratik Sahu for their assistance with the photographs.

REFERENCES

Chedraui, P., Blümel, J. E., Baron, G., Belzares, E., Bencosme, A., Calle, A., & Hernandez-Bueno, J. A. (2008). Impaired quality of life among middle aged women: A multicentre Latin American study. *Maturitas*, *61*(4), 323–329. doi:10.1016/j.maturitas.2008.09.026 PMID:19010618

Courville, J., Vézina, N., & Messing, K. (1991). Comparison of the work activity of two mechanics: A woman and a man. *International Journal of Industrial Ergonomics*, *7*(2), 163–174. doi:10.1016/0169-8141(91)90045-N

Dahlberg, R., Karlqvist, L., Bildt, C., & Nykvist, K. (2004). Do work technique and musculoskeletal symptoms differ between men and women performing the same type of work tasks? *Applied Ergonomics*, *35*(6), 521–529. doi:10.1016/j.apergo.2004.06.008 PMID:15374759

David, G., Buckle, P., & Woods, V. (2005). *Further development of the usability and validity of the Quick Exposure Check (QEC)*. Health & Safety Executive.

Drury, C. G. (1990). Methods for direct observation for performance. In J. R. Wilson & E. N. Corlett (Eds.), *Evaluation of Human Work* (pp. 35–37). London: Taylor and Francis.

Gangopadhyay, S., Ray, A., Das, A., Das, T., Ghoshal, G., Banerjee, P., & Bagchi, S. (2003). A study on upper extremity cumulative trauma disorder in different unorganised sectors of West Bengal, India. *Journal of Occupational Health*, *45*(6), 351–357. doi:10.1539/joh.45.351 PMID:14676414

Hanvold, T. N., Wærsted, M., Mengshoel, A. M., Bjertness, E., & Veiersted, K. B. (2015). Work with prolonged arm elevation as a risk factor for shoulder pain: A longitudinal study among young adults. *Applied Ergonomics*, *47*, 43–51. doi:10.1016/j.apergo.2014.08.019 PMID:25479973

Hignett, S., & McAtamney, L. (2000). Rapid entire body assessment (REBA). *Applied Ergonomics*, *31*(2), 201–205. doi:10.1016/S0003-6870(99)00039-3 PMID:10711982

Karhu, O., Kansi, P., & Kuorinka, I. (1977). Correcting working postures in industry: A practical method for analysis. *Applied Ergonomics*, *8*(4), 199–201. doi:10.1016/0003-6870(77)90164-8 PMID:15677243

Kattel, B. P., Fredericks, T. K., Fernandez, J. E., & Lee, D. C. (1996). The effect of upper-extremity posture on maximum grip strength. *International Journal of Industrial Ergonomics*, *18*(5), 423–429. doi:10.1016/0169-8141(95)00105-0

Kilbom, Å. (2000). Repetitive work of the upper extremity: Part II—The scientific basis (knowledge base) for the guide. *Elsevier Ergonomics Book Series*, *1*, 151–178. doi:10.1016/S1572-347X(00)80011-7

Kinare, A. S., Natekar, A. S., Chinchwadkar, M. C., Yajnik, C. S., Coyaji, K. J., Fall, C. H., & Howe, D. T. (2000). Low midpregnancy placental volume in rural Indian women: A cause for low birth weight? *American Journal of Obstetrics and Gynecology*, *182*(2), 443–448. doi:10.1016/S0002-9378(00)70237-7 PMID:10694350

Kumar, S. (2001). Theories of musculoskeletal injury causation. *Ergonomics*, *44*(1), 17–47. doi:10.1080/00140130120716 PMID:11214897

Latko, W. A., Armstrong, T. J., Foulke, J. A., Herrin, G. D., Rabourn, R. A., & Ulin, S. S. (1997). Development and evaluation of an observational method for assessing repetition in hand tasks. *American Industrial Hygiene Association Journal*, *58*(4), 278–285. doi:10.1080/15428119791012793 PMID:9115085

Li, G., & Buckle, P. (2000, July). Evaluating Change in Exposure to Risk for Musculoskeletal Disorders—A Practical Tool. *Proceedings of the Human Factors and Ergonomics Society Annual Meeting* (Vol. 44, No. 30, pp. 5-407). Thousand Oaks, CA: SAGE Publications. doi:10.1177/154193120004403001

Lui, B., Cuddy, J. S., Hailes, W. S., & Ruby, B. C. (2014). Seasonal heat acclimatization in wildland firefighters. *Journal of Thermal Biology*, *45*, 134–140. doi:10.1016/j.jtherbio.2014.08.009 PMID:25436962

McCann, M. (1996). Hazards in cottage industries in developing countries. *American Journal of Industrial Medicine*, *30*(2), 125–129. doi:10.1002/(SICI)1097-0274(199608)30:2<125::AID-AJIM2>3.0.CO;2-# PMID:8844041

Messing, K., Tissot, F., Saurel-Cubizolles, M. J., Kaminski, M., & Bourgine, M. (1998). Sex as a variable can be a surrogate for some working conditions: Factors associated with sickness absence. *Journal of Occupational and Environmental Medicine*, *40*(3), 250–260. doi:10.1097/00043764-199803000-00007 PMID:9531096

Michalos, G., Makris, S., & Chryssolouris, G. (2013). The effect of job rotation during assembly on the quality of final product. *CIRP Journal of Manufacturing Science and Technology*, *6*(3), 187–197. doi:10.1016/j.cirpj.2013.03.001

Mukhopadhyay, P. (2006). Looking Beyond the Horizon: Ergonomics in India. *Ergonomics in Design: The Quarterly of Human Factors Applications*, *14*(3), 4–35. doi:10.1177/106480460601400302

Mukhopadhyay, P., & Ghosal, S. (2008). Ergonomic design intervention in manual incense sticks manufacturing. *The Design Journal*, *11*(1), 65–80. doi:10.2752/175630608X317913

Mukhopadhyay, P., O'Sullivan, L. W., & Gallwey, T. J. (2007). Effects of upper arm articulations on shoulder-arm discomfort profile in a pronation task. *Occupational Ergonomics*, *7*(3), 169–181.

Mukhopadhyay, P., & Srivastava, S. (2010a). Ergonomic design issues in some craft sectors of Jaipur. *The Design Journal*, *13*(1), 99–124. doi:10.2752/146069210X12580336766446

Mukhopadhyay, P., & Srivastava, S. (2010b). Evaluating ergonomic risk factors in non-regulated stone carving units of Jaipur. *Work (Reading, Mass.)*, *35*(1), 87–99. PMID:20164628

Nag, A., & Nag, P. K. (2004). Do the work stress factors of women telephone operators change with the shift schedules? *International Journal of Industrial Ergonomics*, *33*(5), 449–461. doi:10.1016/j.ergon.2003.11.004

Nag, P. K., Chintharia, S., Saiyed, S., & Nag, A. (1986). EMG analysis of sitting work postures in women. *Applied Ergonomics*, *17*(3), 195–197. doi:10.1016/0003-6870(86)90006-2 PMID:15676585

Nag, P. K., & Nag, A. (2007). Hazards and health complaints associated with fish processing activities in India—Evaluation of a low-cost intervention. *International Journal of Industrial Ergonomics*, *37*(2), 125–132. doi:10.1016/j.ergon.2006.10.012

OSullivan, L. W., & Gallwey, T. J. (2005). Forearm torque strengths and discomfort profiles in pronation and supination. *Ergonomics*, *48*(6), 703–721. doi:10.1080/00140130500070954 PMID:16087504

Öztürk, N., & Esin, M. N. (2011). Investigation of musculoskeletal symptoms and ergonomic risk factors among female sewing machine operators in Turkey. *International Journal of Industrial Ergonomics*, *41*(6), 585–591. doi:10.1016/j.ergon.2011.07.001

Patel, J. (2006). Silicosis among agate workers: Efforts to promote acceptance of safer technology. *Asian-Pacific Newsletter on Occupational Health and Safety*, *13*(1), 16–18.

Petit, A., Ha, C., Bodin, J., Rigouin, P., Descatha, A., Brunet, R., & Roquelaure, Y. et al. (2015). Risk factors for carpal tunnel syndrome related to the work organization: A prospective surveillance study in a large working population. *Applied Ergonomics*, *47*, 1–10. doi:10.1016/j.apergo.2014.08.007 PMID:25479968

Punnett, L., & Herbert, R. (2000). Work-related musculoskeletal disorders: Is there a gender differential, and if so, what does it mean. *Women & Health*, *38*(6), 474–492.

Raut, P., & Kahkonen, E. (2006). How to improve occupational health, safety and environment by applying cleaner production in industry. *Asian-Pacific Newsletter on Occupational Health and Safety*, *13*(3), 64–67.

Rotenberg, L., Portela, L. F., Banks, B., Griep, R. H., Fischer, F. M., & Landsbergis, P. (2008). A gender approach to work ability and its relationship to professional and domestic work hours among nursing personnel. *Applied Ergonomics*, *39*(5), 646–652. doi:10.1016/j.apergo.2008.02.013 PMID:18405878

Rutanen, R., Luoto, R., Raitanen, J., Mansikkamäki, K., Tomás, E., & Nygård, C. H. (2014). Short- and long-term effects of a physical exercise intervention on work ability and work strain in symptomatic menopausal women. *Safety and Health at Work*, *5*(4), 186–190. doi:10.1016/j.shaw.2014.08.003 PMID:25516810

Saha, A., Nag, A., & Nag, P. K. (2006). Occupational injury proneness in Indian women: A survey in fish processing industries. *Journal of Occupational Medicine and Toxicology (London, England)*, *1*(1), 1. doi:10.1186/1745-6673-1-23 PMID:16968532

Sen, R. N. (1965). Physical environmental factors affecting health of workers in industry. *Indian Labour J*, *6*, 735–746.

Sen, R. N., & Chakraborty, D. (1984). A new ergonomic design of a 'desi' plough'. *Indian Journal of Physiology and Allied Sciences*, *38*, 97–105.

Sen, R. N., & Kar, A. (1984). An ergonomic study on bamboo handicraft workers. *Indian Journal of Physiology and Allied Sciences*, *38*, 69–77.

Sinclair, M. A. (1975). Questionnaire design. *Applied Ergonomics*, *6*(2), 73–80. doi:10.1016/0003-6870(75)90299-9 PMID:15677171

Singh, S. P., Singh, S., & Singh, P. (2012). Ergonomics in developing hand operated maize dehusker–sheller for farm women. *Applied Ergonomics*, *43*(4), 792–798. doi:10.1016/j.apergo.2011.11.014 PMID:22142989

Stanton, N. A., Hedge, A., Brookhuis, K., Salas, E., & Hendrick, H. W. (Eds.). (2004). *Handbook of Human Factors and Ergonomics Methods*. New York: CRC Press. doi:10.1201/9780203489925

Steven Moore, J., & Garg, A. (1995). The strain index: A proposed method to analyze jobs for risk of distal upper extremity disorders. *American Industrial Hygiene Association*, *56*(5), 443–458. doi:10.1080/15428119591016863 PMID:7754975

Vanderwal, L., Rautiainen, R., Kuye, R., Peek-Asa, C., Cook, T., Ramirez, M., & Donham, K. et al. (2011). Evaluation of long-and short-handled hand hoes for land preparation, developed in a participatory manner among women vegetable farmers in The Gambia. *Applied Ergonomics*, *42*(5), 749–756. doi:10.1016/j.apergo.2010.12.002 PMID:21236415

Waddell, G. (1987). 1987 Volvo Award in Clinical Sciences: A new clinical model for the treatment of low-back pain. *Spine*, *12*(7), 632–644. doi:10.1097/00007632-198709000-00002 PMID:2961080

Wiker, S. F., Chaffin, D. B., & Langolf, G. D. (1989). Shoulder posture and localized muscle fatigue and discomfort. *Ergonomics*, *32*(2), 211–237. doi:10.1080/00140138908966080 PMID:2714248

Xu, Z., Ko, J., Cochran, D. J., & Jung, M. C. (2012). Design of assembly lines with the concurrent consideration of productivity and upper extremity musculoskeletal disorders using linear models. *Computers & Industrial Engineering*, *62*(2), 431–441. doi:10.1016/j.cie.2011.10.008

Yelin, E. H., Henke, C. J., & Epstein, W. V. (1986). Work disability among persons with musculoskeletal conditions. *Arthritis and Rheumatism*, *29*(11), 1322–1333. doi:10.1002/art.1780291104 PMID:3778541

Compilation of References

Abarghouei, M. R., Sorbi, M. H., Abarghouei, M., Bidaki, R., & Yazdanpoor, S. (2016). A study of job stress and burnout and related factors in the hospital personnel of Iran. *Electronic Physician*, *8*(7), 2625–2632. doi:10.19082/2625 PMID:27648189

Abdo, S. A. M., El-Sallamy, R. M., El-Sherbiny, A. A. M., & Kabbash, I. A. (2015). Burnout among physicians and nursing staff working in the emergency hospital of Tanta University, Egypt. *Eastern Mediterranean Health Journal*, *21*(12), 906. PMID:26996364

Abrams, L. C., Cross, R., Lesser, E., & Levin, D. Z. (2003). Nurturing interpersonal trust in knowledge-sharing networks. *The Academy of Management Executive*, *17*(4), 64–77. doi:10.5465/AME.2003.11851845

Abugre, J. B. (2011). Perceived satisfaction in sustained outcomes of employee communication in Ghanaian organizations. *Journal of Management Policy and Practice*, *12*(7), 37–49.

Abu-Tineh, A. M., Khasawneh, S. A., & Omary, A. A. (2009). Kouzes and Posners transformational leadership model in practice: The case of Jordanian schools. *Journal of Leadership Education*, *7*(3), 265–283. doi:10.12806/V7/I3/RF10

Acaray, A., & Akturan, A. (2015). The relationship between organizational citizenship behaviour and organizational silence. *Procedia: Social and Behavioral Sciences*, *207*, 472–482. doi:10.1016/j.sbspro.2015.10.117

ACAS. (2014). *Bullying and harassment at work: A guide for employees*. Advisory, Conciliation and Arbitration Service. Retrieved on September 22, 2015, from: www.acas.org.uk/index.aspx?articleid=794

Ács, Z. J., Autio, E., & Szerb, L. (2014). National systems of entrepreneurship: Measurement issues and policy implications. *Research Policy*, *43*(3), 476–494. doi:10.1016/j.respol.2013.08.016

Acs, Z. J., & Karlsson, C. (2002). Introduction to institutions, entrepreneurship and firm growth: From Sweden to the OECD. *Small Business Economics*, *19*(3), 183–187. doi:10.1023/A:1019634716768

Adaramola, S. S. (2012). Job stress and productivity increase. *Work (Reading, Mass.)*, *41*, 2955–2958. doi:10.3233/WOR-2012-0547-2955 PMID:22317168

Addicott, R., McGivern, G., & Ferlie, E. (2006). Networks, organizational management: NHS cancer networks. *Public Money and Management*, *26*(2), 87–94. doi:10.1111/j.1467-9302.2006.00506.x

Adler, N. J. (1981). Reentry: Managing cross-cultural transitions. *Group and Organization Studies*, *6*(3), 341–356. doi:10.1177/105960118100600310

Adler, N. J. (2002). *Cross-cultural transitions: Expatriate entry and reentry. International dimensions of organizational behavior* (pp. 284–300). Mason, OH: South-Western.

Compilation of References

Adler, P. S., & Kwon, S. W. (2002). Social capital: Prospects for a new concept. *Academy of Management Review*, *27*(1), 17–40.

Adriaenssens, J., De Gucht, V., & Maes, S. (2015). Determinants and prevalence of burnout in emergency nurses: A systematic review of 25 years of research. *International Journal of Nursing Studies*, *52*(2), 649–661. doi:10.1016/j.ijnurstu.2014.11.004 PMID:25468279

AdValue. (2016). *Communication Skills Training*. Retrieved from: http://www.advalue-project.eu/content_files/EN/33/AdValue_Communication_skills_EN.pdf

Ahearne, M., Mathieu, J., & Rapp, A. (2005). To empower or not to empower your sales force? An empirical examination of the influence of leadership empowerment behavior on customer satisfaction and performance. *The Journal of Applied Psychology*, *90*(5), 945–955. doi:10.1037/0021-9010.90.5.945 PMID:16162066

Ahmadi, S., Nami, Y., & Barvarz, R. (2014). The relationship between spirituality in the workplace and organizational citizenship behavior. *Procedia: Social and Behavioral Sciences*, *114*, 262–264. doi:10.1016/j.sbspro.2013.12.695

Ahuja, M. K., & Carley, K. M. (1999). Network structure in virtual organizations. *Organization Science*, *10*(6), 741–757. doi:10.1287/orsc.10.6.741

Aiginger, K. (2005). Labour market reforms and economic growth-the European experience in the 1990s. *Journal of Economic Studies (Glasgow, Scotland)*, *32*(6), 540–573. doi:10.1108/01443580510631414

Akgün, A. E., Lynn, G. S., & Byrne, J. C. (2003). Organizational learning: A socio-cognitive framework. *Human Relations*, *56*(7), 839–868. doi:10.1177/00187267030567004

Akman, O., Ozturk, C., Bektas, M., Ayar, D., & Armstrong, M. A. (2016). Job satisfaction and burnout among paediatric nurses. *Journal of Nursing Management*, *24*(7), 923–933. doi:10.1111/jonm.12399 PMID:27271021

Akoinar, A. T., Torun, E., Okur, M. E., & Akipinar, O. (2013). The effect of organizational communication and job satisfaction on organizational commitment in small businesses. *Interdisciplinary Journal of Research in Business*, *3*(4), 27–32.

Aldrich, H., & Zimmer, C. (1986). Entrepreneurship through social networks. In D. Sexton & R. Smilor (Eds.), *The art and science of entrepreneurship* (pp. 3–23). Cambridge, MA: Ballinger Publishing Co.

Alegre, I., Mas-Machuca, M., & Berbegal-Mirabent, J. (2016). Antecedents of employee job satisfaction: Do they matter? *Journal of Business Research*, *69*(4), 1390–1395. doi:10.1016/j.jbusres.2015.10.113

Alexandrova-Karamanova, A., Todorova, I., Montgomery, A., Panagopoulou, E., Costa, P., Baban, A., & Mijakoski, D. et al. (2016). Burnout and health behaviors in health professionals from seven European countries. *International Archives of Occupational and Environmental Health*, *89*(7), 1059–1075. doi:10.1007/s00420-016-1143-5 PMID:27251338

Algesheimer, R., Dholakia, U. M., & Gurău, C. (2011). Virtual Team Performance in a Highly Competitive Environment. *Group & Organization Management*, *36*(2), 161–190. doi:10.1177/1059601110391251

Alguezaui, S., & Filieri, R. (2010). Investigating the role of social capital in innovation: Sparse versus dense network. *Journal of Knowledge Management*, *14*(6), 891–909. doi:10.1108/13673271011084925

Al-Hamdan, Z., Oweidat, I. A., Al-Faouri, I., & Codier, E. (2016). Correlating emotional intelligence and job performance among Jordanian hospitals' registered nurses. *Nursing Forum*. PMID:27194022

Alharbi, J., Wilson, R., Woods, C., & Usher, K. (2016). The factors influencing burnout and job satisfaction among critical care nurses: A study of Saudi critical care nurses. *Journal of Nursing Management*, *24*(6), 708–717. doi:10.1111/jonm.12386 PMID:27189515

Ali, A., & Haider, J. (2012). Impact of internal organizational communications on employee job satisfaction – Case of some Pakistani banks. *Global Advanced Research Journal of Management and Business Studies*, *1*(x), 38–44.

Ali, W. (2016). Understanding the concept of job satisfaction, measurements, theories and its significance in the recent organizational environment: A theoretical framework. *Archives of Business Research*, *4*(1), 100–111. doi:10.14738/abr.41.1735

Aliyev, R., & Tunc, E. (2015). Self-efficacy in counseling: The role of organizational psychological capital, job satisfaction, and burnout. *Procedia: Social and Behavioral Sciences*, *190*, 97–105. doi:10.1016/j.sbspro.2015.04.922

Altuntas, S., & Baykal, U. (2010). Relationship between nurses' organizational trust levels and their organizational citizenship behaviors. *Journal of Nursing Scholarship*, *42*(2), 186–194. doi:10.1111/j.1547-5069.2010.01347.x PMID:20618602

Alvarez, S. A., & Barney, J. B. (2010). Entrepreneurship and epistemology: The philosophical underpinnings of the study of entrepreneurial opportunities. *The Academy of Management Annals*, *4*(1), 557–583. doi:10.1080/19416520.2010.495521

Alves, D. F. S., & Guirardello, E. B. (2016). Safety climate, emotional exhaustion and job satisfaction among Brazilian paediatric professional nurses. *International Nursing Review*, *63*(3), 328–335. doi:10.1111/inr.12276 PMID:27265871

Ambler, T., & Barrow, S. (1996). The employer brand. *Journal of Brand Management*, *4*(3), 185–206. doi:10.1057/bm.1996.42

American Management Association. (2016). *Communication skills: August to December 2016*. Retrieved from: http://www.amanet.org/training/seminars/booklets/communication-skills.pdf

Anand, V., Glick, W. H., & Manz, C. C. (2002). Thriving on the knowledge of outsiders: Tapping organizational social capital. *The Academy of Management Executive*, *16*(1), 87–101. doi:10.5465/AME.2002.6640198

Andela, M., Truchot, D., & Van der Doef, M. (2015). Job stressors and burnout in hospitals: The mediating role of emotional dissonance. *International Journal of Stress Management*, *23*(3), 298–317. doi:10.1037/str0000013

Anderson, C. A., & Bushman, B. J. (2002). Human aggression. *Annual Review of Psychology*, *53*(1), 27–51. doi:10.1146/annurev.psych.53.100901.135231 PMID:11752478

Anderson, C. M., & Martin, M. M. (1995). The effects of communication motives, interaction involvement, and loneliness on satisfaction: A model of small groups. *Small Group Research*, *26*(1), 118–137. doi:10.1177/1046496495261007

Anderson, C., & Brion, S. (2014). Perspectives on power in organizations. *Annual Review of Organizational Psychology and Organizational Behavior*, *1*(1), 67–97. doi:10.1146/annurev-orgpsych-031413-091259

Ang, S. Y., Dhaliwal, S. S., Ayre, T. C., Uthaman, T., Fong, K. Y., Tien, C. E., & Della, P. (2016). *Demographics and Personality Factors Associated with Burnout among Nurses in a Singapore Tertiary Hospital*. BioMed Research International.

Annis, B., & Merron, K. (2014). *Gender intelligence: Breakthrough strategies for increasing diversity and improving your bottom line eBook: Barbara Annis, Keith Merron*. Harper Business.

Anthony, L. (2015). *Effective communication & leadership*. Retrieved from http://smallbusiness.chron.com/effective-communication-leadership-5090.html

Antonacopoulou, E., & Chiva, R. (2007). The social complexity of organizational learning: The dynamics of learning and organizing. *Management Learning*, *38*(3), 277–295. doi:10.1177/1350507607079029

Antonakis, J., Ashkanasy, N. M., & Dasborough, M. T. (2009). Does leadership need emotional intelligence? *The Leadership Quarterly*, *20*(2), 247–261. doi:10.1016/j.leaqua.2009.01.006

Compilation of References

Aoki, K. (2008). The employment management of people with developmental disorders in Advantest green Co., Ltd. *Vocational rehabilitation network, 62*, 9-13.

April, L. (2016, September 27). Neurodiversity: An untapped talent powerhouse for contingent workforce programs. Retrieved from www.zenithtalent.com/recruiting-and-staffing-blog/neurodiversity-contingent-workforce

Aquino, K., & Thau, S. (2009). Workplace victimization: Aggression from the targets perspective. *Annual Review of Psychology, 60*(1), 717–741. doi:10.1146/annurev.psych.60.110707.163703 PMID:19035831

Archer, T., Freddriksson, A., Schutz, E., & Kostrzewa, R. M. (2011). Influence of physical exercise on neuroimmunological functioning and health: Aging and stress. *Neurotox, 20*(1), 69–83. doi:10.1007/s12640-010-9224-9 PMID:20953749

Ardichvili, A. (2008). Learning and knowledge sharing in virtual communities of practice: Motivators, barriers, and enablers. *Advances in Developing Human Resources, 10*(4), 541–554. doi:10.1177/1523422308319536

Argote, L. (2011). Organizational learning research: Past, present and future. *Management Learning, 42*(4), 439–446. doi:10.1177/1350507611408217

Argote, L. (2012). *Organizational learning: Creating, retaining and transferring knowledge*. New York: Springer.

Argote, L., McEvily, B., & Reagans, R. (2003). Managing knowledge in organizations: An integrative framework and review of emerging themes. *Management Science, 49*(4), 571–582. doi:10.1287/mnsc.49.4.571.14424

Argote, L., & Miron-Spektor, E. (2011). Organizational learning: From experience to knowledge. *Organization Science, 22*(5), 1123–1137. doi:10.1287/orsc.1100.0621

Argyris, C. (1977). Organizational learning and management information systems. *Accounting, Organizations and Society, 2*(2), 113–123. doi:10.1016/0361-3682(77)90028-9

Argyris, C., & Schön, D. A. (1978). *Organizational learning: A theory of action perspective* (Vol. 173). Reading, MA: Addison-Wesley.

Arigoni, F., Bovierb, P. A., & Sappinoa, A. P. (2010). Trend in burnout among Swiss doctors. *Swiss Medical Weekly, 9*, 140.

Arli, S. K., Bakan, A. B., & Erisik, E. (2016). An investigation of the relationship between nurses' views on spirituality and spiritual care and their level of burnout. *Journal of Holistic Nursing*.

Armstrong, M. (2006). *A Handbook of Human Resource Management Practice* (10th ed.). London: Kogan Page, Ltd.

Armstrong, M., & Baron, A. (1998). *Performance management: The new realities*. London: Institute of Personnel and Development.

Arora, S., Ashrafian, H., Davis, R., Athanasiou, T., Darzi, A., & Sevdalis, N. (2010). Emotional intelligence in medicine: A systematic review through the context of the ACGME competencies. *Medical Education, 44*(8), 749–764. doi:10.1111/j.1365-2923.2010.03709.x PMID:20633215

Artz, B. (2008). The role of firm size and performance pay in determining employee job satisfaction brief: Firm size, performance pay, and job satisfaction. *Labour, 22*(2), 315–343. doi:10.1111/j.1467-9914.2007.00398.x

Artz, B., & Kaya, I. (2014). Job insecurity and job satisfaction in the United States: The case of public sector union workers. *Industrial Relations Journal, 45*(2), 103–120. doi:10.1111/irj.12044

Arvey, R. D., Renz, G. L., & Watson, T. W. (1998). Emotionality and job performance: Implications for personnel selection. *Research in Personnel and Human Resources Management, 16*, 103–147.

Aryee, S., Chen, Z. X., Sun, L., & Debrah, Y. A. (2007). Antecedents and outcomes of abusive supervision: Test of a trickle-down model. *The Journal of Applied Psychology, 92*(1), 191–201. doi:10.1037/0021-9010.92.1.191 PMID:17227160

Ashforth, B. E., & Humphrey, R. H. (1995). Emotion in the workplace: A reappraisal. *Human Relations, 48*(2), 97–125. doi:10.1177/001872679504800201

Ashkanasy, N. M. (2003). Emotions in organizations: A multilevel perspective. *Research in Multi-level Issues, 2*, 9–54. doi:10.1016/S1475-9144(03)02002-2

Ashkanasy, N. M., & Cooper, C. L. (Eds.). (2008). *Research companion to emotion in organizations*. Cheltenham, UK: Edward Elgar. doi:10.4337/9781848443778

Ashkanasy, N. M., Härtel, C. E., & Daus, C. S. (2002). Diversity and emotion: The new frontiers in organizational behavior research. *Journal of Management, 28*(3), 307–338. doi:10.1177/014920630202800304

Ashkanasy, N. M., Härtel, C. E., & Zerbe, W. J. (Eds.). (2000). *Emotions in the workplace: Research, theory, and practice*. Greenwood Publishing Group.

Association, P. (2015, June 8). "Queen bee syndrome" among women at work is a myth, study finds. *The Guardian*. Retrieved from https://www.theguardian.com/world/2015/jun/07/queen-bee-syndrome-women-work-myth-research-columbia-business-school

Aswathappa, K. (2010). *Human Resource Management*. New Delhi, India: Tata McGraw Hill Education Private Limited.

Atefi, N., Lim Abdullah, K., Wong, L. P., & Mazlom, R. (2015). Factors influencing job satisfaction among registered nurses: A questionnaire survey in Mashhad, Iran. *Journal of Nursing Management, 23*(4), 448–458. doi:10.1111/jonm.12151 PMID:24102706

Austin, J., Stevenson, H., & Wei-Skillern, J. (2006). Social and commercial entrepreneurship: Same, different, or both? *Entrepreneurship Theory and Practice, 30*(1), 1–22. doi:10.1111/j.1540-6520.2006.00107.x

Autio, E., & Acs, Z. (2010). Intellectual property protection and the formation of entrepreneurial growth aspirations. *Strategic Entrepreneurship Journal, 4*(3), 234–251. doi:10.1002/sej.93

Autio, E., Pathak, S., & Wennberg, K. (2013). Consequences of cultural practices for entrepreneurial behaviors. *Journal of International Business Studies, 44*(4), 334–362. doi:10.1057/jibs.2013.15

Avolio, J. B. (2005). *Leadership development in balance: Made/Born. NJ*. Hillsdale: Erlbaum.

Avram, E., Ionescu, D., & Mincu, C. L. (2015). Perceived safety climate and organizational trust: The mediator role of job satisfaction. *Procedia: Social and Behavioral Sciences, 187*, 679–684. doi:10.1016/j.sbspro.2015.03.126

Avtgis, T. A., & Taber, K. R. (2006). I laughed so hard my side hurts, or is that an ulcer? The influence of work humor on job stress, job satisfaction, and burnout among print media employees. *Communication Research Reports, 23*(1), 13–18. doi:10.1080/17464090500535814

Awad, T. A., & Alhashemi, S. E. (2012). Assessing the effect of interpersonal communications on employees commitment and satisfaction. *International Journal of Islamic and Middle Eastern Finance and Management, 5*(2), 134–156. doi:10.1108/17538391211233425

Ayoko, O. B., Konrad, A. M., & Boyle, M. V. (2011). Online work: Managing conflict and emotions for performance in virtual teams. *European Management Journal, 30*(2), 156–174. doi:10.1016/j.emj.2011.10.001

Ayukawa, K. (2011). The employment management question and answer of the employee with mental disorders or developmental disorders: Business correspondence. *Labor Circumstances, 48*, 20–35.

Compilation of References

Aziri, B. (2011). Job Satisfaction: A literature review. *Management research and practice, 3*(4), 77-86.

Babcock, L., & Laschever, S. (2003). *Women don't ask: Negotiation and the gender divide*. Princeton: Princeton University Press.

Bacal, R. (1999). *Performance management*. New York: McGraw-Hill.

Bach, K. (1987). *Thought and reference*. Oxford: Clarendon Press.

Bach, K. (1994). Meaning, speech acts, and communication. In R. M. Harnish (Ed.), *Introduction to part 1: Basic topics in the philosophy of language*. New York: Prentice-Hall.

Bach, K. (1999). The semantics-pragmatics distinction: What it is and why it matters. In K. Turner (Ed.), *The semantics-pragmatics interface from different points of view* (pp. 65–84). Oxford: Elsevier.

Bach, K. (2001). You dont say. *Synthese, 128*(1/2), 15–44. doi:10.1023/A:1010353722852

Backhaus, K., & Tikoo, S. (2004). Conceptualizing and researching employer branding. *Career Development International, 9*(5), 501–517. doi:10.1108/13620430410550754

Bacq, S., Hartog, C., & Hoogendoorn, B. (2014). Beyond the moral portrayal of social entrepreneurs: An empirical approach to who they are and what drives them. *Journal of Business Ethics*.

Bacq, S., & Janssen, F. (2011). The multiple faces of social entrepreneurship: A review of definitional issues based on geographical and thematic criteria. *Entrepreneurship & Regional Development, 23*(5-6), 373–403. doi:10.1080/08985626.2011.577242

Bagshaw, M. (2000). Emotional intelligence–training people to be affective so they can be effective. *Industrial and Commercial Training, 32*(2), 61–65. doi:10.1108/00197850010320699

Baillien, E., De Cuyper, N., & De Witte, H. (2011). Job autonomy and workload as antecedents of workplace bullying: A two-wave test of Karaseks job demand control model for targets and perpetrators. *Journal of Occupational and Organizational Psychology, 84*(1), 191–208. doi:10.1348/096317910X508371

Baillien, E., Neyens, I., De Witte, H., & De Cuyper, N. (2009). A qualitative study on the development of workplace bullying: Towards a three way model. *Journal of Community & Applied Social Psychology, 19*(1), 1–16. doi:10.1002/casp.977

Bakker, A. B., Demerouti, E., & Verbeke, W. (2004). Using the job demands-resources model to predict burnout and performance. *Human Resource Management, 43*(1), 83–104. doi:10.1002/hrm.20004

Baldwin, H., & Treasury, H. M. (2015, November 4). Link bonuses to appointment of senior women, says review. *UK Government*. Retrieved from https://www.gov.uk/government/news/link-bonuses-to-appointment-of-senior-women-says-review

Baldwin, H., & Treasury, H. M. (2016, July 11). *Women in finance charter*. Retrieved from https://www.gov.uk/government/publications/women-in-finance-charter

Ballinger, G. A., & Rockmann, K. W. (2010). Chutes versus ladders: Anchoring events and a punctuated-equilibrium perspective on social exchange relationships. *Academy of Management Review, 35*(3), 373–391. doi:10.5465/AMR.2010.51141732

Ball, P., Monaco, G., Schmeling, J., Schartz, H., & Blanck, P. (2005). Disability as a diversity in Fortune 100 companies. *Behavioral Sciences & the Law, 23*(1), 97–121. doi:10.1002/bsl.629 PMID:15706604

Banaji, M., & Greenwald, A. (2013). *Blindspot: Hidden biases of good people*. New York: Delacorte Press.

Bandura, A. (1977). *Social learning theory*. Englewood Cliffs, NJ: Prentice-Hall.

Banker, R. D., Lee, S. Y., Potter, G., & Srinivasan, D. (2000). An empirical analysis of continuing improvements following the implementation of a performance-based compensation plan. *Journal of Accounting and Economics*, *30*(3), 315–350. doi:10.1016/S0165-4101(01)00016-7

Banner, D., & Cooke, R. (1984). Ethical Dilemmas in Performance Appraisal. *Journal of Business Ethics*, *3*(4), 327–333. doi:10.1007/BF00381756

Bapuji, H., & Crossan, M. (2004). From questions to answers: Reviewing organizational learning research. *Management Learning*, *35*(4), 397–417. doi:10.1177/1350507604048270

Baralou, E., & McInnes, P. (2013). Emotions and the spatialisation of social relations in text-based computer-mediated communication. *New Technology, Work and Employment*, *28*(2), 160–175. doi:10.1111/ntwe.12012

Barling, J., Dupré, K. E., & Kelloway, E. K. (2009). Predicting workplace aggression and violence. *Annual Review of Psychology*, *60*(1), 671–692. doi:10.1146/annurev.psych.60.110707.163629 PMID:18793089

Barling, J., Slater, F., & Kevin Kelloway, E. (2000). Transformational leadership and emotional intelligence: An exploratory study. *Leadership and Organization Development Journal*, *21*(3), 157–161. doi:10.1108/01437730010325040

Barnett, R., & Brennan, R. (1997). Change in job conditions, change in psychological distress, and gender: A longitudinal study of dual-earner couples. *Journal of Organizational Behavior*, *18*(3), 253–274. doi:10.1002/(SICI)1099-1379(199705)18:3<253::AID-JOB800>3.0.CO;2-7

Barnlund, D. C. (2008). A transactional model of communication. In C. D. Mortensen (Ed.), *Communication theory* (2nd ed., pp. 47–57). New Brunswick, NJ: Transaction.

Barrados, M., & Mayne, J. (2003). Can Public Sector Organisations Learn? *OECD Journal on Budgeting*, *3*(3), 87–103. doi:10.1787/budget-v3-art17-en

Barrett, L. F. (2004). Feelings or words? Understanding the content in self-report ratings of experienced emotion. *Journal of Personality and Social Psychology*, *87*(2), 266–281. doi:10.1037/0022-3514.87.2.266 PMID:15301632

Barthes, R. (1957). *Mythologies*. New York: Hill & Wang.

Bartlett, C., & Johnson, C. (1998). Is business English a pidgin? *Language and Intercultural Training*, *16*(1), 4–6.

Bass, B. M. (1990). From transactional to transformational leadership: Learning to share the vision. *Organizational Dynamics*, *18*(3), 19–31. doi:10.1016/0090-2616(90)90061-S

Bass, B. M., & Avolio, B. J. (1994). *Improving organizational effectiveness through transformational leadership*. Thousand Oaks, CA: Sage Publications.

Bassett-Jones, N. (2005). The Paradox of Diversity Management, Creativity and Innovation. *Creativity and Innovation Management*, *14*(2), 169–175. doi:10.1111/j.1467-8691.00337.x

Bassi, L., & McMurrer, D. (2007). Maximizing your return through people. *Harvard Business Review*, *85*(3), 115–123. PMID:17348175

Bateman, T., & Snell, S. (2011). *Management: Leading and Collaborating in a Competitive World* (6th ed.). Boston: McGraw-Hill companies, Inc.

Baumeister, R. F., Smart, L., & Boden, J. M. (1996). Relation of threatened egotism to violence and aggression: The dark side of high self-esteem. *Psychological Review*, *103*(1), 5–33. doi:10.1037/0033-295X.103.1.5 PMID:8650299

Baumer, M., & van Rensburg, H. (2011). Cross-cultural pragmatic failure in computer-mediated communication. *Coolabah*, *5*, 34–53.

Baumol, W. J. (2004). Welfare Economics and the Theory of the State. In The Encyclopedia of Public Choice (pp. 937-940). Springer US.

Baumol, W. J. (1990). Entrepreneurship: Productive, unproductive, and destructive. *Journal of Political Economy*, *98*(5), 893–921. doi:10.1086/261712

Beaumont, Ph., & Graeme, M. (2003). *Branding and People Management: What is a Name?* London: CIPD.

Beckman, C. M., & Haunschild, P. R. (2002). Network learning: The effects of partners heterogeneity of experience on corporate acquisitions. *Administrative Science Quarterly*, *47*(1), 92–124. doi:10.2307/3094892

Beechler, S. L., & Bird, A. (Eds.). (1999). *Japanese multinationals abroad*. London: University Press.

Beheshtifar, M., Borhani, H., & Moghadam, M. N. (2012). Destructive role of employee silence in organizational success. *International Journal of Academic Research in Business and Social Sciences*, *2*(11), 275–282.

Belanger, F., & Jordan, D. H. (2000). *Evaluation and implementation of distance learning: Technologies, tools, and techniques*. Hersey, PA: Idea Group. doi:10.4018/978-1-878289-63-6

Belias, D., Koustelios, A., Sdrolias, L., & Aspridis, G. (2015). Job satisfaction, role conflict and autonomy of employees in the Greek banking organization. *Procedia: Social and Behavioral Sciences*, *175*, 324–333. doi:10.1016/j.sbspro.2015.01.1207

Belkić, K., Landsbergis, P., Schnall, P., & Baker, D. (2004). Is job strain a major source of cardiovascular disease risk? *Scandinavian Journal of Work, Environment & Health*, *30*(2), 85–128. doi:10.5271/sjweh.769 PMID:15127782

Belkić, K., & Savić, Č. (2008). The occupational stress index: An approach derived from cognitive ergonomics applicable to clinical practice. *Scandinavian Journal of Work, Environment & Health*, *34*, 169–175. PMID:18728906

Bellows, R. M., & Estep, M. F. (1954). *Employment Psychology: The Interview*. New York: Rinehart.

Bendersky, C., & Shah, N. P. (2013). The downfall of extraverts and rise of neurotics: The dynamic process of status allocation in task groups. *Academy of Management Journal*, *56*(2), 387–406. doi:10.5465/amj.2011.0316

Bennet, D., & Bennet, A. (2008). Engaging tacit knowledge in support of organizational learning. *Vine*, *38*(1), 72–94. doi:10.1108/03055720810870905

Bennett, J. (1998). Transition shock: Putting culture shock in perspective. In M. J. Bennett (Ed.), *Basic concepts of intercultural communication: Selected readings* (pp. 215–224). Yarmouth, ME: Intercultural Press.

Bennett, R. J., & Robinson, S. L. (2000). Development of a measure of workplace deviance. *The Journal of Applied Psychology*, *85*(3), 349–360. doi:10.1037/0021-9010.85.3.349 PMID:10900810

Benson, P. G., Buckley, M. R., & Hall, S. (1988). Mixed Standard Scale. *Journal of Management*, *14*(3), 415–423. doi:10.1177/014920638801400305

Bergeron, D. M. (2007). The potential paradox of organizational citizenship behavior: Good citizens at what cost? *Academy of Management Review*, *32*(4), 1078–1095. doi:10.5465/AMR.2007.26585791

Berlo, D. K. (1960). *The process of communication*. New York: Holt, Rinehart, & Winston.

Berłowski, P., & Turłukowska, J. (2013). *Internal and external employer branding- benefits from the consistent development of the company's image as an employer on the example of Poland Mars*. Wolters Kluwer Business. Retrieved from http://www.kadry.abc.com.pl

Berman, S. J., & Hellweg, S. A. (1989). Perceived supervisor communication competence and supervisor satisfaction as a function of quality circle participation. *Journal of Business Communication, 26*(2), 103–122. doi:10.1177/002194368902600202

Bernardin, H., & Klatt, L. (1985). Managerial Appraisal systems: Has practice "caught-up" with the state of the art? *The Personnel Administrator, 30*, 79–86.

Bernauer, T., & Caduff, L. (2004). In whose interest? Pressure group politics, economic competition and environmental regulation. *Journal of Public Policy, 24*(01), 99–126. doi:10.1017/S0143814X04000054

Berry, J., & Kalin, R. (1995). Multicultural and ethnic attitudes in Canada: An overview of the 1991 national survey. *Canadian Journal of Behavioural Science, 27*(3), 301–320. doi:10.1037/0008-400X.27.3.301

Berry, L. M. (2003). *Employee Selection*. Belmont, CA: Thomson/Wadsworth.

Bershin, J. (2014). The *Talent Agenda for 2015. What comes after "Integrated Talent Management"?* Deloitte Consuting LLP. Retrieved from http://www.slideshare.net/jbersin/talent-management-revisited

Bershin, J. (2015). Becoming Irresistible: A New Model for Employee Engagement. *Deloitte Review, 16*. Retrieved from http://d27n205l7rookf.cloudfront.net/wp-content/uploads/2015/01/DR16_becoming_irresistible

Bhati, P. P., & Ashokkumar, M. (2013). Provision of Welfare under Factories Act and its Impact on Employee Satisfaction. *Journal of Business Management & Social Sciences Research, 2*(2), 57–69.

Białas, A. (2006). *Security information and services in modern institutions and the company*. Warsaw: Scientific Technical Publishing.

Bierhoff, H.-W. (2002). *Pro-social behaviour*. Hove, UK: Psychology Press.

Biggam, F. H., & Power, K. G. (1998). The quality of perceived parenting experienced by a group of Scottish incarcerated young offenders and its relation to psychological distress. *Journal of Adolescence, 21*(2), 161–176. doi:10.1006/jado.1997.0139 PMID:9585494

Bigram, S. A. (2013a). *Internal Employer Branding. Bigram SA Personnel Consulting*. Retrieved from http://www.bigram.pl

Bigram, S. A. (2013b). *External Employer Branding*. Bigram SA Personnel Consulting. Retrieved from http://www.bigram.pl

Biksegn, A., Kenfe, T., Matiwos, S., & Eshetu, G. (2016). Burnout status at work among health care professionals in a tertiary hospital. *Ethiopian journal of health sciences, 26*(2), 101-108.

Bilal, A., & Ahmed, H. M. (2016). *Organizational structure as a determinant of job burnout. An exploratory study on Pakistani pediatric nurses*. Workplace Health & Safety.

Billett, S. (2001). Learning through work: Workplace affordances and individual engagement. *Journal of Workplace Learning, 13*(5), 209–214. doi:10.1108/EUM0000000005548

Billings, M., & Watts, L. A. (2010). *Understanding dispute resolution online: using text to reflect personal and substantive issues in conflict*. London: ACM Press. doi:10.1145/1753326.1753542

Black, J. S. (1992). Coming home: The relationship of expatriate expectations with repatriation adjustment and job performance. *Human Relations, 45*(2), 177–192. doi:10.1177/001872679204500205

Black, J. S. (1993). The role of expectations during repatriation for Japanese managers. *Research in Personnel and Human Resource Management, 3*, 339–358.

Black, J. S. (1994). Okaerinasai: Factors related to Japanese repatriation adjustment. *Human Relations, 47*(12), 1489–1508. doi:10.1177/001872679404701203

Black, J. S., & Gregersen, H. B. (1991). When Yankee comes home: Factors related to expatriate and spouse repatriation adjustment. *Journal of International Business Studies, 22*(4), 671–695. doi:10.1057/palgrave.jibs.8490319

Black, J. S., Gregersen, H. B., & Mendenhall, M. E. (1992). Toward a theoretical framework of repatriation adjustment. *Journal of International Business Studies, 23*(4), 737–760. doi:10.1057/palgrave.jibs.8490286

Black, J. S., Gregersen, H. B., Mendenhall, M. E., & Stroh, L. K. (1999). *Globalizing people through international assignments*. Reading, MA: Addison-Wesley.

Blanding, M. (2015). Workplace stress responsible for up to $190B in annual U.S. healthcare costs. *Forbes*. Retrieved from http://www.forbes.com/sites/hbsworkingknowledge/2015/01/26/workplace-stress-responsible-for-up-to-190-billion-in-annual-u-s-heathcare-costs/#326009864333

Blankstein, K. R., Flett, G. L., & Johnston, M. E. (1992). Depression, Problem-Solving Ability, and Problem-Solving Appraisals. *Journal of Clinical Psychology, 48*(6), 749–759. doi:10.1002/1097-4679(199211)48:6<749::AID-JCLP2270480609>3.0.CO;2-V PMID:1452764

Blau, P. M. (1964). *Exchange and power in social life*. New York: John Wiley & Sons.

Bloomberg. (2015, March 10). Germany's quota on women in the boardroom could backfire. *Bloomberg*. Retrieved from https://www.bloomberg.com/view/articles/2015-03-10/germany-s-quota-on-women-in-the-boardroom-could-backfire

Boev, C., Xue, Y., & Ingersoll, G. L. (2015). Nursing job satisfaction, certification and healthcare associated infections in critical care. *Intensive & Critical Care Nursing, 31*(5), 276–284. doi:10.1016/j.iccn.2015.04.001 PMID:26169234

Bogenrieder, I. (2002). Social architecture as a prerequisite for organizational learning. *Management Learning, 33*(2), 197–212. doi:10.1177/1350507602332003

Bogler, R., & Somech, A. (2004). Influence of teacher empowerment on teachers' organizational commitment, professional commitment and organizational citizenship behavior in schools. *Teaching and Teacher Education, 20*(3), 277–289. doi:10.1016/j.tate.2004.02.003

Bohnet, I. (2016, April 18). How to take the bias out of interviews. *HBR.org*. Retrieved from https://hbr.org/2016/04/how-to-take-the-bias-out-of-interviews

Bolino, M. C., & Turnley, W. H. (2005). The personal costs of citizenship behavior: The relationship between individual initiative and role overload, job stress, and work–family conflict. *The Journal of Applied Psychology, 90*(4), 740–748. doi:10.1037/0021-9010.90.4.740 PMID:16060790

Bollaert, H., & Petit, V. (2010). Beyond the dark side of executive psychology: Current research and new directions. *European Management Journal, 28*(5), 362–376. doi:10.1016/j.emj.2010.01.001

Bolton, S. C. (2004). *Emotion management in the workplace*. Basingstoke, UK: Palgrave Macmillan.

Bond, D. S., Lyle, R. M., Tappe, M. K., Seehafer, R. S., & DZurilla, T. J. (2002). Moderate aerobic exercise, Tai Chi, and social problem-solving ability in relation to psychological stress. *International Journal of Stress Management, 9*(4), 329–343. doi:10.1023/A:1019934417236

Bono, E. J., Foldes, H. J., Vinson, G., & Muros, P. J. (2007). Workplace emotions: The role of supervision and leadership. *The Journal of Applied Psychology*, *92*(5), 1357–1367. doi:10.1037/0021-9010.92.5.1357 PMID:17845090

Booth, A. L., & van Ours, J. C. (2008). Job satisfaction and family happiness: The part-time work puzzle. *The Economic Journal*, *118*(526), F77–F99. doi:10.1111/j.1468-0297.2007.02117.x

Borgatti, S. P., & Cross, R. (2003). A relational view of information seeking and learning in social networks. *Management Science*, *49*(4), 432–445. doi:10.1287/mnsc.49.4.432.14428

Bornstein, D. (2004). *How to change the world: Social entrepreneurs and the power of new ideas*. Oxford, UK: Oxford University Press.

Bosma, N., Terjesen, S. A., Schøtt, T., & Kew, P. (2016). *Global Entrepreneurship Monitor 2015 to 2016: Special Report on Social Entrepreneurship*. Retrieved from http://ssrn.com/abstract=2786949

Botha, A., Bussin, M., & De Swardt, L. (2011). An employer brand predictive model for talent attraction and retention: original research. *SA Journal of Human Resource Management*, *9*(1), 1-12. Retrieved from http://reference.sabinet.co.za/sa_epublication_article/sajhrm_v9_n1_a26

Bourdieu, P. (1985). The forms of capital. In J. G. Richardson (Ed.), *Handbook of theory and research for the sociology of education* (pp. 241–258). New York: Greenwood.

Bovier, P. A., Arigoni, F., Schneider, M., & Gallacchi, M. B. (2009). Relationships between work satisfaction, emotional exhaustion and mental health among Swiss primary care physicians. *European Journal of Public Health*, *19*(6), 611–617. doi:10.1093/eurpub/ckp056 PMID:19403785

Bowling, N. A., & Beehr, T. A. (2006). Workplace harassment from the victims perspective: A theoretical model and meta-analysis. *The Journal of Applied Psychology*, *91*(5), 998–1012. doi:10.1037/0021-9010.91.5.998 PMID:16953764

Bowling, N. A., Eschleman, K. J., & Wang, Q. (2010). A meta-analytic examination of the relationship between job satisfaction and subjective well-being. *Journal of Occupational and Organizational Psychology*, *83*(4), 915–934. doi:10.1348/096317909X478557

Bowling, N. A., Wang, Q., & Li, H. Y. (2012). The moderating effect of core self-evaluations on the relationships between job attitudes and organisational citizenship behavior. *Applied Psychology*, *61*(1), 97–113. doi:10.1111/j.1464-0597.2011.00458.x

Boyatzis, R. E., Goleman, D., & Rhee, K. S. (2000). Clustering competence in emotional intelligence: Insights from the Emotional Competence Inventory. In Bar-On and J. Parker (Eds.), The Handbook of Emotional Intelligence: Theory, development, assessment, and application at home, school, and in the workplace. San Francisco, CA: Jossey-Bass.

Boyatzis, R. (1982). *The Competent Manager*. New York: Wiley.

Boyatzis, R. E., & Goleman, D. (2006). *Emotional and Social Competency Inventory*. Boston, MA: The Hay Group.

Brabant, S., Palmer, C. E., & Gramling, R. (1990). Returning home: An empirical investigation of cross-cultural reentry. *International Journal of Intercultural Relations*, *14*(4), 387–404. doi:10.1016/0147-1767(90)90027-T

Brackett, M. A., Rivers, S. E., & Salovey, P. (2011). Emotional intelligence: implication of personal, social, academic, and workplace success. *Social and Personality psychological compass*, *5*(1), 88-103. doi:10.1111/j.1751-9004.2010.00334

Bradach, J. (1997). *Flexibility: The new social contract between individuals and firms?* Harvard Business School Working Paper.

Brandi, U., & Elkjaer, B. (2011). Organizational learning viewed from a social learning perspective. In M. Easterby-Smith & M. A. Lyles (Eds.), *Handbook of organizational learning and knowledge management* (pp. 21–41). Hoboken, NJ: John Wiley & Sons.

Braun, S., Aydin, N., Frey, D., & Peus, C. V. (2015). Leader narcissism predicts followers' malicious envy and counterproductive work behaviors. In Academy of Management Proceedings (vol. 2015, No. 1, pp. 16115). New York: Academy of Management.

Braun, V., & Clarke, V. (2006). Using thematic analysis in psychology. *Qualitative Research in Psychology*, *3*(2), 77–101. doi:10.1191/1478088706qp063oa

Brawley, A. M., & Pury, C. L. S. (2016). Work experiences on MTurk: Job satisfaction, turnover, and information sharing. *Computers in Human Behavior*, *54*, 531–546. doi:10.1016/j.chb.2015.08.031

Brief, A. P., & Weiss, H. M. (2002). Organizational behavior: Affect in the workplace. *Annual Review of Psychology*, *53*(1), 279–307. doi:10.1146/annurev.psych.53.100901.135156 PMID:11752487

Brill, P. L. (1984). The need for an operational definition of burnout. *Family & Community Health*, *6*(4), 12–24. doi:10.1097/00003727-198402000-00005 PMID:10264597

Briner, R. (1999). The neglect and importance of emotion at work. *European Journal of Work and Organizational Psychology*, *8*(3), 323–346. doi:10.1080/135943299398212

Brislin, R. W. (1980). Translation and content analysis of oral and written material. In H. C. Triandis & J. W. Berry (Eds.), Handbook of cross-cultural psychology: Methodology (Vol. 2, pp. 389–444). Boston, MA: Allyn & Bacon.

Brislin, R. W., Lonner, W., & Thorndike, R. M. (1973). *Cross-cultural research methods* (pp. 32–45). New York: John Wiley & Sons.

Britt, T. W., McKibben, E. S., Greene-Shortridge, T. M., Odle-Dusseau, H. N., & Herleman, H. A. (2012). Self-engagement moderates the mediated relationship between organizational constraints and organizational citizenship behaviors via rated leadership. *Journal of Applied Social Psychology*, *42*(8), 1830–1846. doi:10.1111/j.1559-1816.2012.00920.x

Brodsky, C. M. (1976). *The harassed worker*. New York: Lexington Books.

Brotheridge, C. M., & Grandey, A. A. (2002). Emotional labor and burnout: Comparing two perspectives of people work. *Journal of Vocational Behavior*, *60*(1), 17–39. doi:10.1006/jvbe.2001.1815

Brotheridge, C. M., & Lee, R. T. (2003). Development and validation of the emotional labour scale. *Journal of Occupational and Organizational Psychology*, *76*(3), 365–379. doi:10.1348/096317903769647229

Brown, J. S., & Duguid, P. (1991). Organizational learning and communities-of-practice: Toward a unified view of working, learning, and innovation. *Organization Science*, *2*(1), 40–57. doi:10.1287/orsc.2.1.40

Brown, M. E., Treviño, L. K., & Harrison, D. A. (2005). Ethical leadership: A social learning perspective for construct development and testing. *Organizational Behavior and Human Decision Processes*, *97*(2), 117–134. doi:10.1016/j.obhdp.2005.03.002

Brown, S. A., Fuller, R. M., & Vician, C. (2004). Who's afraid of the virtual world? Anxiety and computer-mediated communication. *Journal of the Association for Information Systems*, *5*(2), 79–107.

Bruce, M. (1961). *Coming of the Welfare State*. London, UK: Batsford.

Bruton, G. D., Ahlstrom, D., & Li, H. L. (2010). Institutional theory and entrepreneurship: Where are we now and where do we need to move in the future? *Entrepreneurship Theory and Practice, 34*(3), 421–440. doi:10.1111/j.1540-6520.2010.00390.x

Bruton, G. D., Fried, V. H., & Manigart, S. (2005). Institutional influences on the worldwide expansion of venture capital. *Entrepreneurship Theory and Practice, 29*(6), 737–760. doi:10.1111/j.1540-6520.2005.00106.x

Bryman, A. S., Stephens, M., & Campo, C. (1996). The importance of context: Qualitative research and the study of leadership. *The Leadership Quarterly, 7*(3), 353–370. doi:10.1016/S1048-9843(96)90025-9

Bucar, B., Glas, M., & Hisrich, R. D. (2003). Ethics and entrepreneurs: An international comparative study. *Journal of Business Venturing, 18*(2), 261–281. doi:10.1016/S0883-9026(01)00083-0

Buonocore, F., & Russo, M. (2013). Reducing the effects of work–family conflict on job satisfaction: The kind of commitment matters. *Human Resource Management Journal, 23*(1), 91–108. doi:10.1111/j.1748-8583.2011.00187.x

Burchardt, T. (1997). Boundaries between Public and Private Welfare: a typology and map of services. Private Welfare and Public Policy, Burchardt, Hills and Propper, Rowntree Foundation, Jan. 1999). *LSE STICERD Research Paper No. CASE002.*

Burch, T. C., & Guarana, C. L. (2014). The comparative influences of transformational leadership and leader–member exchange on follower engagement. *The Journal of Leadership Studies, 8*(3), 6–25. doi:10.1002/jls.21334

Burke, R. J., & Wilcox, D. S. (1969). Effects of different patterns and degrees of openness in superior-subordinate communication on subordinate job satisfaction. *Academy of Management Journal (pre-1986), 12*(3), 319-326.

Burns, T. (1961). Micropolitics: Mechanisms of institutional change. *Administrative Science Quarterly, 6*(3), 257–281. doi:10.2307/2390703

Burrell, L. (2016). We just can't handle diversity. *Harvard Business Review, 94*(7), 70–74. PMID:27491197

Burt, R. S. (2000). The network structure of social capital. *Research in Organizational Behavior, 22*, 345–423. doi:10.1016/S0191-3085(00)22009-1

Busenitz, L. W., Gomez, C., & Spencer, J. W. (2000). Country institutional profiles: Unlocking entrepreneurial phenomena. *Academy of Management Journal, 43*(5), 994–1003. doi:10.2307/1556423

Busenitz, L. W., & Lau, C. M. (1996). A cross-cultural cognitive model of new venture creation. *Entrepreneurship: Theory and Practice, 20*(4), 25–40.

Butler, E. A., Egloff, B., Wlhelm, F. H., Smith, N. C., Erickson, E. A., & Gross, J. J. (2003). The social consequences of expressive suppression. *Emotion (Washington, D.C.), 3*(1), 48–67. doi:10.1037/1528-3542.3.1.48 PMID:12899316

Cable, D. M., & Judge, T. A. (1996). Person-organization fit, job choice decisions, and organizational entry. *Organizational Behavior and Human Decision Processes, 67*(3), 294–311. doi:10.1006/obhd.1996.0081

Cahill, K. E., McNamara, T. K., Pitt-Catsouphes, M., & Valcour, M. (2015). Linking shifts in the national economy with changes in job satisfaction, employee engagement and work–life balance. *Journal of Behavioral and Experimental Economics, 56*, 40–54. doi:10.1016/j.socec.2015.03.002

Cambra-Fierro, J., Hart, S., & Polo-Redondo, Y. (2008). Environmental respect: Ethics or simply business? A study in the small and medium enterprise (SME) context. *Journal of Business Ethics, 82*(3), 645–656. doi:10.1007/s10551-007-9583-1

Compilation of References

Campbell, D., Campbell, K., & Chia, H. (1998). Merit pay, performance appraisal, and individual motivation: An analysis and alternative. *Human Resource Management, 37*(2), 131–146. doi:10.1002/(SICI)1099-050X(199822)37:2<131::AID-HRM4>3.0.CO;2-X

Campbell, J. L. (2007). Why would corporations behave in socially responsible ways? An institutional theory of corporate social responsibility. *Academy of Management Review, 32*(3), 946–967. doi:10.5465/AMR.2007.25275684

Capelli, P., & Sherer, P. D. (1991). The missing role of context in OB: The need for a meso-level approach. *Research in Organizational Behavior, 13*, 55–110.

Cappelen, H., & Dever, J. (2014). *The inessential indexical: On the philosophical insignificance of perspective and the first person: Context and content.* Oxford University Press.

Carbonell, P., & Rodríguez-Escudero, A. I. (2016). The individual and joint effects of process control and process-based rewards on new product performance and job satisfaction. *BRQ Business Research Quarterly, 19*(1), 26–39. doi:10.1016/j.brq.2015.04.001

Cardy, R. L., & Dobbins, G. H. (1994). *Performance appraisal: Alternative perspectives.* Cincinnati, OH: South Western Publishing Company.

CareerSupport365. (2013). Market Research: Attitudes towards Employers After Losing Their Job and The Associated Risks to Employer Branding. Retrieved from http://careersupport365.com/wp-content/uploads/2013/06/Employee_Attitudes.pdf

Carlson, D. S., Ferguson, M., Perrewé, P. L., & Whitten, D. (2011). The fallout from abusive supervision: An examination of subordinates and their partners. *Personnel Psychology, 64*(4), 937–961. doi:10.1111/j.1744-6570.2011.01232.x

Carney, M., Gedajlovic, E., & Yang, X. (2009). Varieties of Asian capitalism: Toward an institutional theory of Asian enterprise. *Asia Pacific Journal of Management, 26*(3), 361–380. doi:10.1007/s10490-009-9139-2

Carriere, J., & Bourque, C. (2009). The effects of organizational communication on job satisfaction and organizational commitment in a land ambulance service and the mediating role of communication satisfaction. *Career Development International, 14*(1), 29–49. doi:10.1108/13620430910933565

Carroll, D. W. (1999). Psychology of language (3rd ed.). Brooks/Cole Publishing Company.

Carston, R. (2008). Linguistic communication and the semantics/pragmatics distinction. *Synthese, 165*(3), 321–345. doi:10.1007/s11229-007-9191-8

Carter, N. M., & Silva, C. (2010). *Mentoring: Necessary But Insufficient for Advancement the Promise of Future Leadership: Highly Talented Employees in the Pipeline.* Retrieved from http://www.catalyst.org/system/files/Mentoring_Necessary_But_Insufficient_for_Advancement_Final_120610.pdf

Caruso, D. R., Mayer, J. D., & Salovey, P. (2002, April 9). Emotional intelligence and emotional leadership. *Proceedings of the Kravis-de Roulet Leadership Conference,* Claremont. McKenna.

Caruso, D. R., Mayer, J. D., & Salovey, P. (2002). Relation of an ability measure of emotional intelligence to personality. *Journal of Personality Assessment, 79*(2), 306–320. Retrieved from http://www.unh.edu/emotional_intelligence/EI%20Assets/Reprints...EI%20Proper/EI2002CarusoMayerSaloveyMEIS.pdf doi:10.1207/S15327752JPA7902_12 PMID:12425393

Caruth, D. L., & Humphreys, J. H. (2008). Performance Appraisal; essential characteristics for strategic control. *Measuring Business Excellence, 12*(3), 24–32. doi:10.1108/13683040810900377

Cascio, W. F. (1998). *Managing Human Resources.* Boston: McGraw Hill Publishing Company.

Casey, A. (2005). Enhancing individual and organizational learning a sociological model. *Management Learning*, *36*(2), 131–147. doi:10.1177/1350507605052555

Cassell, C., & Symon, G. (2011). Assessing good qualitative research in the work psychology field: A narrative analysis: Good qualitative research. *Journal of Occupational and Organizational Psychology*, *84*(4), 633–650. doi:10.1111/j.2044-8325.2011.02009.x

Casson, M. (1992). Internalization theory and beyond. In P. J. Buckley (Ed.), *New directions in international business. Research priorities for the 1990s* (pp. 4–27). Brookfield, VT: Edward Elgar.

Castaneda, G. A., & Scanlan, J. M. (2014). Job satisfaction in nursing: A concept analysis. *Nursing Forum*, *49*(2), 130–138. doi:10.1111/nuf.12056 PMID:24383666

Catalyst. (2016a, February 3). *Women in S&P 500 companies*. Retrieved from http://www.catalyst.org/knowledge/women-sp-500-companies

Catalyst. (2016b, June 14). *Sponsorship/Mentoring*. Retrieved from http://www.catalyst.org/knowledge/topics/sponsorshipmentoring

Cavaye, A. L. M. (1996). Case study research: A multi-faceted research approach for IS. *Information Systems Journal*, *6*(3), 227–242. doi:10.1111/j.1365-2575.1996.tb00015.x

Cavusgil, S. T., Calantone, R. J., & Zhao, Y. (2003). Tacit knowledge transfer and firm innovation capability. *Journal of Business and Industrial Marketing*, *18*(1), 6–21. doi:10.1108/08858620310458615

Certo, S. C. (1992). *Modern management: Quality, ethics, and the global environment* (5th ed.). Boston: Allyn and Bacon.

Certo, S. T., & Miller, T. (2008). Social entrepreneurship: Key issues and concepts. *Business Horizons*, *51*(4), 267–271. doi:10.1016/j.bushor.2008.02.009

Chamakiotis, P., & Panteli, N. (2010). E-Leadership Styles for Global Virtual Teams. In P. Yoong (Ed.), *Leadership in the Digital Enterprise: Issues and Challenges* (pp. 143–161). Hershey, PA: IGI Global. Retrieved from http://www.igi-global.com/chapter/leadership-styles-global-virtual-teams/37093

Chamakiotis, P., Dekoninck, E. A., & Panteli, N. (2013). Factors Influencing Creativity in Virtual Design Teams: An Interplay between Technology, Teams and Individuals: Factors Influencing Creativity in Virtual Design Teams. *Creativity and Innovation Management*, *22*(3), 265–279. doi:10.1111/caim.12039

Chambers, R., & Campbell, I. (1996). Anxiety and depression in general practitioners: Associations with type of practice, fundholding, gender and other personal characteristics. *Family Practice*, *13*(2), 170–173. doi:10.1093/fampra/13.2.170 PMID:8732330

Chandler, D. (2014). *Semiotics for beginners*. Retrieved from http://visual-memory.co.uk/daniel/Documents/S4B/sem01.html

Chang, C. S. (2014). Moderating effects of nurses' organizational justice between organizational support and organizational citizenship behaviors for evidence-based practice. *Worldviews on Evidence-Based Nursing*, *11*(5), 332–340. doi:10.1111/wvn.12054 PMID:25132135

Chang, C. S., & Chang, H. C. (2010). Motivating nurses' organizational citizenship behaviors by customer-oriented perception for evidence-based practice. *Worldviews on Evidence-Based Nursing*, *7*(4), 214–225. doi:10.1111/j.1741-6787.2010.00188.x PMID:20345521

Compilation of References

Chang, E. C., D'Zurilla, T., & Sanna, L. J. (2004). *Social Problem Solving: Theory, Research, and Training*. Washington, DC: American Psychological Association. doi:10.1037/10805-000

Chang, Y. H., Li, H. H., Wu, C. M., & Wang, P. C. (2010). The influence of personality traits on nurses' job satisfaction in Taiwan. *International Nursing Review*, *57*(4), 478–484. doi:10.1111/j.1466-7657.2010.00825.x PMID:21050200

Chao, C. R. (2011). Managing stress and maintaining well-being: Social support, problem-focused, coping, and avoidant coping. *Journal of Counseling and Development*, *89*(3), 338–348. doi:10.1002/j.1556-6678.2011.tb00098.x

Chao, G. T., O'Leary-Kelly, A. M., Wolfe, S., Klein, H. J., & Gardner, P. D. (1994). Organizational socialization: Its content and consequences. *The Journal of Applied Psychology*, *779*(5), 730–743. doi:10.1037/0021-9010.79.5.730

Chao, M. C., Jou, R. C., Liao, C. C., & Kuo, C. W. (2015). Workplace stress, job satisfaction, job performance, and turnover intention of health care workers in rural Taiwan. *Asia-Pacific Journal of Public Health*, *27*(2), NP1827–NP1836. doi:10.1177/1010539513506604 PMID:24174390

Charles, M., & Marschan-Piekkari, R. (2002). Language training for enhanced horizontal communication: A challenge for MNCs. *Business Communication Quarterly*, *65*(2), 9–29. doi:10.1177/108056990206500202

Charniss, C. (2010). Emotional intelligence: Toward clarification of a concept. *Industrial and Organizational Psychology: Perspectives on Science and Practice*, *3*(2), 110–126. doi:10.1111/j.1754-9434.2010.01231.x

Charniss, C., Extein, M., Goleman, D., & Weissberg, R. P. (2006). Emotional intelligence: What does the research really indicate? *Educational Psychologist*, *41*(4), 239–245. Retrieved from http://alliance.la.asu.edu/temporary/students/katie/MultipleIntelligenceEmotional.Pdf doi:10.1207/s15326985ep4104_4

Chatzipanteli, P. S. (1998). *Human resource management*. Athens: Metaixmio Publications.

Chaudhuri, K., Reilly, K. T., & Spencer, D. A. (2015). Job satisfaction, age and tenure: A generalized dynamic random effects model. *Economics Letters*, *130*, 13–16. doi:10.1016/j.econlet.2015.02.017

Chebat, J. C., & Kollias, P. (2000). The impact of empowerment on customer contact employees' roles in service organizations. *Journal of Service Research*, *3*(1), 66–81. doi:10.1177/109467050031005

Chedraui, P., Blümel, J. E., Baron, G., Belzares, E., Bencosme, A., Calle, A., & Hernandez-Bueno, J. A. (2008). Impaired quality of life among middle aged women: A multicentre Latin American study. *Maturitas*, *61*(4), 323–329. doi:10.1016/j.maturitas.2008.09.026 PMID:19010618

Chen, C. C., Zhang, A. Y., & Wang, H. (2014). Enhancing the effects of power sharing on psychological empowerment: The roles of management control and power distance orientation. *Management and Organization Review*, *10*(1), 135–156. doi:10.1111/more.12032

Chen, C.-C., Shiu, L.-J., Li, Y.-L., Tung, K.-Y., Chan, K.-Y., Yeh, C.-J., & Wong, R.-H. et al. (2010). Shift work and arteriosclerosis risk in professional bus drivers. *AEP*, *20*(1), 60–66. PMID:19804986

Cheng, B., Kan, M., Levanon, G., & Ray, R. L. (2014). Job satisfaction: 2014 Edition. Retrieved from https://hcexchange.conference-board.org/attachment/The-annual1.pdf

Cheng, S. K. (2001). Life stress, problem solving, perfectionism, and depressive symptoms in Chinese. *Cognitive Therapy and Research*, *25*(3), 303–310. doi:10.1023/A:1010788513083

Chen, J., Silverthorne, C., & Hung, J. (2006). Organization communication, job stress, organizational commitment, and job performance of accounting professionals in Taiwan and America. *Leadership and Organization Development Journal*, *27*(4), 242–249. doi:10.1108/01437730610666000

Chen, S. H., Yu, H. Y., Hsu, H. Y., Lin, F. C., & Lou, J. H. (2013). Organisational support, organisational identification and organisational citizenship behaviour among male nurses. *Journal of Nursing Management, 21*(8), 1072–1082. doi:10.1111/j.1365-2834.2012.01449.x PMID:23409728

Chen, S. Y., Wu, W. C., Chang, C. S., & Lin, C. T. (2015). Job rotation and internal marketing for increased job satisfaction and organisational commitment in hospital nursing staff. *Journal of Nursing Management, 23*(3), 297–306. doi:10.1111/jonm.12126 PMID:23981132

Cherniss, C. (1980a). *Staff burnout: Job stress in the human services*. Beverly Hills, CA: Sage Publications.

Cherniss, C. (1980b). *Professional burnout in human service Organizations*. New York: Praeger.

Cherniss, C., Goleman, D., Emmerling, R., Cowan, K., & Adler, M. (1998). *Bringing emotional intelligence to the workplace*. New Brunswick, NJ: Consortium for Research on Emotional Intelligence in Organizations, Rutgers University.

Cheung, M. F. Y., & Law, M. C. C. (2008). Relationships of organizational justice and organizational identification: The mediating effects of perceived organizational support in Hong Kong. *Asia Pacific Business Review, 14*(2), 213–231. doi:10.1080/13602380701430879

Chitrao, P. (2014). Internal communication satisfaction as an employee motivation tool in the retail sector in Pune. *The European Journal of Social & Behavioural Sciences, 10*, 1541-1552.

Chiu, C. M., Hsu, M. H., & Wang, E. T. (2006). Understanding knowledge sharing in virtual communities: An integration of social capital and social cognitive theories. *Decision Support Systems, 42*(3), 1872–1888. doi:10.1016/j.dss.2006.04.001

Chiu, C. Y. C., Balkunid, P., & Weinberg, F. (2016). *When managers become leaders: The role of manager network centralities, social power, and followers' perception of leadership. The Leadership Quarterly*. Claremont, CA: Lawrence Erlbaum Associates Publishers.

Chong, V. K., & Monroe, G. S. (2015). The impact of the antecedents and consequences of job burnout on junior accountants' turnover intentions: A structural equation modelling approach. *Accounting and Finance, 55*(1), 105–132. doi:10.1111/acfi.12049

Choudhary, N. K., & Rathore, N. S. (2013). Role of effective communication in total quality management. *The International Journal of Scientific & Engineering Research, 4*(7), 2083–2090.

Chou, L. P., Li, C. Y., & Hu, S. C. (2014). Job stress and burnout in hospital employees: Comparisons of different medical professions in a regional hospital in Taiwan. *BMJ Open, 4*(2), e004185. doi:10.1136/bmjopen-2013-004185 PMID:24568961

Chou, T. L., Chang, L. I., & Chung, M. H. (2015). The mediating and moderating effects of sleep hygiene practice on anxiety and insomnia in hospital nurses. *International Journal of Nursing Practice, 21*(Suppl. 2), 9–18. doi:10.1111/ijn.12164 PMID:26125570

Chou, T., Jiang, J. J., Klein, G., & Chou, S. T. (2013). Organizational citizenship behavior of information system personnel: The influence of leader-member exchange. In M. Khosrow-Pour (Ed.), *Managing information resources and technology: Emerging applications and theories* (pp. 284–299). Hershey, PA: IGI Global. doi:10.4018/978-1-4666-3616-3.ch019

Chow, C. W. C., Lai, J. Y. M., & Loi, R. (2015). Motivation of travel agents' customer service behavior and organizational citizenship behavior: The role of leader-member exchange and internal marketing orientation. *Tourism Management, 48*, 362–369. doi:10.1016/j.tourman.2014.12.008

Chow, W. S., & Chan, L. S. (2008). Social network, social trust and shared goals in organizational knowledge sharing. *Information & Management, 45*(7), 458–465. doi:10.1016/j.im.2008.06.007

Compilation of References

Chua, T. S., Juanzi, L., & Moens, M. F. (2014). *Mining user generated content*. Chapman and Hall/CRC.

Chung, Y.-S., & Wong, J.-T. (2011). Developing effective professional bus driver health programs: An investigation of self-rated health. *Accident; Analysis and Prevention*, *43*(6), 2093–2103. doi:10.1016/j.aap.2011.05.032 PMID:21819839

Chung, Y.-S., & Wu, H.-L. (2013). Stress, strain, and health outcomes of professional drivers: An application of the effort reward imbalance model on Taiwanese public transport drivers. *Transportation Research Part F: Traffic Psychology and Behaviour*, *19*, 97–107. doi:10.1016/j.trf.2013.03.002

Church, A. T. (1982). Sojourner adjustment. *Psychological Bulletin*, *91*(3), 540–572. doi:10.1037/0033-2909.91.3.540

Çınar, O., & Karcıoğlu, F. (2015). The relationship between cyber loafing and organizational citizenship behavior: A survey study in Erzurum/Turkey. *Procedia: Social and Behavioral Sciences*, *207*, 444–453. doi:10.1016/j.sbspro.2015.10.114

CIPD. (2006). *Chartered Institute of Professional Development*. Retrieved from http://www.cipd.co.uk

CIPD. (2012). *Strategic HR*. Chartered Institute of Personnel and Development. Retrieved from http://www.cipd.co.uk/hr-topics/strategic-hr.aspx

CIPD. (2015). Diversity in the workplace: an overview. Retrieved from http://www.cipd.co.uk/hr-resources/factsheets/diversity-workplace-overview.aspx

Clarke, C. (2016, March 15). *How flexible working hours can keep women in top jobs*. Retrieved from/ https://uk.news.yahoo.com/flexible-working-hours-keep-women-071600453.html

CLW. (1969). *Report of the Committee on Labour Welfare*. India: Ministry of Labour & Employment, Government of India.

Coca-Cola Co. (2014). Retrieved from http://www.coca-colacompany.com/our-company/diversity/global-diversity-mission

Codier, E., Kooker, B. M., & Shoultz, J. (2008). Measuring the emotional intelligence of clinical staff nurses: An approach for improving the clinical care environment. *Nursing Administration Quarterly*, *32*(1), 8–14. doi:10.1097/01.NAQ.0000305942.38816.3b PMID:18160858

Coleman, D., Boyatzis, R., & McKee, A. (2002). *Primal leadership: Realizing the power of emotional intelligence*. Boston, MA: Harvard Business School Press.

Coleman, J. S. (1988). Social capital in the creation of human capital. *American Journal of Sociology*, *94*, S95–S120. doi:10.1086/228943

Colfax, R. S., Rivera, J. J., & Perez, K. T. (2010). Applying Emotional Intelligence (EQ-I) in the workplace: Vital to global business success. *Journal of International Business Research, 9*.

Colligan, T. W., & Higgins, E. M. (2005). Workplace stress: Etiology and consequences. *Journal of Workplace Behavioral Health*, *21*(2), 89–97. doi:10.1300/J490v21n02_07

Comfort, J., & Franklin, P. (2014). *The mindful international manager: how to work effectively across cultures* (2nd ed.). London, Philadelphia: Kogan Page Limited.

Communication Theory. (2016). Berlo's SMCR model of communication. Retrieved from http://communicationtheory.org/berlos-smcr-model-of-communication/

Connelly, S., & Gooty, J. (2015). Leading with emotion: An overview of the special issue on leadership and emotions. *The Leadership Quarterly*, *26*(4), 485–488. doi:10.1016/j.leaqua.2015.07.002

Connor, B., & Slear, S. (2009). Emotional intelligence and anxiety; Emotional intelligence and resiliency. *The International Journal of Learning*, *16*(1), 249–260.

Conrad, C. (1994). *Strategic organizational communication: Toward the twenty-first century* (3rd ed.). Fort Worth, TX: Harcourt Brace College Publishers.

Cooper, C. L., & Marshall, J. (1976). Occupational sources of stress: A review of the literature relating to coronary heart disease and mental ill health. *Journal of Occupational Psychology, 49*(1), 11–28. doi:10.1111/j.2044-8325.1976.tb00325.x

Cooper, C., Rout, U., & Faragher, B. (1989). Mental health, job satisfaction, and job stress among general practitioners. *British Medical Journal, 298*(6670), 366–370. doi:10.1136/bmj.298.6670.366 PMID:2493939

Cooper, R. K., & Sawaf, A. (1997). *Emotional Intelligence in business*. London: Orion Business.

Cooper-Thomas, H. D., Vianen, A. V., & Anderson, N. (2004). Changes in person-organization fit: The impact of socialization tactics on perceived and actual P-O fit. *European Journal of Work and Organizational Psychology, 13*(1), 52–78. doi:10.1080/13594320344000246

Coppola, N. W., Hiltz, S. R., & Rotter, N. G. (2004). Building trust in virtual teams. *IEEE Transactions on Professional Communication, 47*(2), 95–104. doi:10.1109/TPC.2004.828203

Cornell University Law School. (n. d.). Retrieved from https://www.law.cornell.edu/supremecourt/text/438/265

Corner, P. D., & Ho, M. (2010). How opportunities develop in social entrepreneurship. *Entrepreneurship Theory and Practice, 34*(4), 635–659. doi:10.1111/j.1540-6520.2010.00382.x

Cottingham, M. D., Erickson, R. J., & Diefendorff, J. M. (2015). Examining mens status shield and status bonus: How gender frames the emotional labor and job satisfaction of nurses. *Sex Roles, 72*(7-8), 377–389. doi:10.1007/s11199-014-0419-z

Cotton, A. P., Sohail, M., & Scott, R. E. (2005). Towards improved labour standards for construction of minor works in low income countries. *Engineering, Construction, and Architectural Management, 12*(6), 617–632. doi:10.1108/09699980510634164

Cotton, P., & Hart, P. M. (2003). Occupational well-being and performance: A review of organizational health research. *Australian Psychologist, 38*(2), 118–127. doi:10.1080/00050060310001707117

Courville, J., Vézina, N., & Messing, K. (1991). Comparison of the work activity of two mechanics: A woman and a man. *International Journal of Industrial Ergonomics, 7*(2), 163–174. doi:10.1016/0169-8141(91)90045-N

Coventry, W. F., & Barker, J. K. (1988). *Management* (International Edition). Heinemann Professional Publishing.

Cox, A. (2000). The importance of employee participation in determining pay system effectiveness. *International Journal of Management Reviews, 2*(4), 357–375. doi:10.1111/1468-2370.00047

Cox, J. B. (2004). The role of communication, technology, and cultural identity in repatriation adjustment. *International Journal of Intercultural Relations, 28*(3–4), 201–219. doi:10.1016/j.ijintrel.2004.06.005

Cox, T. H. Jr, & Blake, S. B. (1991). Managing cultural diversity: Implications for organizational competitiveness. *The Academy of Management Executive, 5*(3), 45–56. doi:10.5465/AME.1991.4274465

Craig, R. T. (1989). Communication as a practical discipline. In B. Dervin, L. Grossberg, B. J. O'Keefe, & E. A. Wartella (Eds.), *Rethinking communication: Paradigm issues* (Vol. 1, pp. 97–122). London: SAGE publications.

Craig, R. T. (1999). Communication theory as a field. *Journal of Communication, 9*(2), 119–161.

Craig, R. T. (1999, May). Communication Theory. *International Communication Association, 9*(2), 119–161. doi:10.1111/j.1468-2885.1999.tb00355

Compilation of References

Crawshaw, L. (2009). Workplace bullying? Mobbing? Harassment? Distraction by a thousand definitions. *Consulting Psychology Journal: Practice and Research, 61*(3), 263–267. doi:10.1037/a0016590

Credit Suisse Research. (2015, June 10). *Diversity on board!* Retrieved from https://www.credit-suisse.com/us/en/articles/articles/news-and-expertise/2015/06/en/diveristy-on-board.html

Credit Suisse. (2016). *Diversity programs.* Retrieved from https://www.credit-suisse.com/uk/en/careers/campus-recruiting/our-business/internship-programs-emea/diversity-programs.html

Crino, M. E., & White, M. C. (1981). Satisfaction in communication: An examination of the Downs-Hazen measure. *Psychological Reports, 49*(3), 831–838. doi:10.2466/pr0.1981.49.3.831

Crisp, C. B., & Jarvenpaa, S. L. (2013). Swift Trust in Global Virtual Teams. *Journal of Personnel Psychology, 12*(1), 45–56. doi:10.1027/1866-5888/a000075

Crossan, M. M., Lane, H. W., & White, R. E. (1999). An organizational learning framework: From intuition to institution. *Academy of Management Review, 24*(3), 522–537.

Crossan, M. M., Lane, H. W., White, R. E., & Djurfeldt, L. (1995). Organizational learning: Dimensions for a theory. *The International Journal of Organizational Analysis, 3*(4), 337–360. doi:10.1108/eb028835

Cross, R., Borgatti, S. P., & Parker, A. (2002). Making invisible work visible: Using social network analysis to support strategic collaboration. *California Management Review, 44*(2), 25–46. doi:10.2307/41166121

Cross, R., Parker, A., Prusak, L., & Borgatti, S. P. (2001). Knowing what we know: Supporting knowledge creation and sharing in social networks. *Organizational Dynamics, 30*(2), 100–120. doi:10.1016/S0090-2616(01)00046-8

Cullen, K. L., Edwards, B. D., Casper, W. C., & Gue, K. R. (2013). Employees' adaptability and perceptions of change-related uncertainty: Implications for perceived organizational support, job satisfaction, and performance. *Journal of Business and Psychology, 29*(2), 269–280. doi:10.1007/s10869-013-9312-y

Currah, A., & Wrigley, N. (2004). Networks of organizational learning and adaptation in retail TNCs. *Global Networks, 4*(1), 1–23. doi:10.1111/j.1471-0374.2004.00078.x

Cushman, D. P., & Craig, R. T. (1976). Communication systems: Interpersonal implications. In G. R. Miller (Ed.), *Exploration in interpersonal communication*. Beverly Hills: Sage Publications.

Czech, K., & Forward, G.L. (2013). Communication, leadership, and job satisfaction: Perspectives on supervisor-subordinate relationships. *Studies in media and Communication, 1*(2), 11-24.

D' Zurilla, T. J. et al.. (2004). Social problem solving: theory and assessment. In E. C. Chang, T. J. D' Zurilla, & L. J. Sanna (Eds.), *Social Problem Solving: Theory, Research and Training* (pp. 11–27). Washington, DC: American Psychological Association. doi:10.1037/10805-001

D'Zurilla, T. J., & Nezu, A. M. (1982). Social problem solving in adults. In P. C. Kendall (Ed.), *Advances in Cognitive-Behavioral Research and Therapy* (Vol. 1, pp. 201–274). New York: Academic Press. doi:10.1016/B978-0-12-010601-1.50010-3

Dąbrowska, A., Janoś-Kresło, M. & Wódkowski, A. (2009). *E - services and information society*. Warsow: Difin.

Dacin, M. T., Dacin, P. A., & Tracey, P. (2011). Social entrepreneurship: A critique and future directions. *Organization Science, 22*(5), 1203–1213. doi:10.1287/orsc.1100.0620

Dacin, P. A., Dacin, M. T., & Matear, M. (2010). Social entrepreneurship: Why we dont need a new theory and how we move forward from here. *The Academy of Management Perspectives, 24*(3), 37–57. doi:10.5465/AMP.2010.52842950

Dahlberg, R., Karlqvist, L., Bildt, C., & Nykvist, K. (2004). Do work technique and musculoskeletal symptoms differ between men and women performing the same type of work tasks? *Applied Ergonomics*, *35*(6), 521–529. doi:10.1016/j.apergo.2004.06.008 PMID:15374759

Daily, C. M., Dalton, D. R., & Cannella, A. A. (2003). Corporate governance: Decades of dialogue and data. *Academy of Management Review*, *28*(3), 371–382.

Dalal, R. S., Baysinger, M., Brummel, B. J., & LeBreton, J. M. (2012). The relative importance of employee engagement, other job attitudes, and trait affect as predictors of job performance. *Journal of Applied Social Psychology*, *42*(Suppl. 1), E295–E325. doi:10.1111/j.1559-1816.2012.01017.x

Dalal, R. S., Lam, H., Weiss, H. M., Welch, E. R., & Hulin, C. L. (2009). A within-person approach to work behavior and performance: Concurrent and lagged citizenship-counterproductivity associations, and dynamic relationships with affect and overall job performance. *Academy of Management Journal*, *52*(5), 1051–1066. doi:10.5465/AMJ.2009.44636148

Daley, D. M. (1992). *Performance Appraisal in the Public Sector: Techniques and Applications*. Westport, CT: Quorum Books.

DallOra, C., Griffiths, P., Ball, J., Simon, M., & Aiken, L. H. (2015). Association of 12 h shifts and nurses job satisfaction, burnout and intention to leave: Findings from a cross-sectional study of 12 European countries. *BMJ Open*, *5*(9), e008331. doi:10.1136/bmjopen-2015-008331 PMID:26359284

Dalton, M. (1996). Multirater Feedback and Conditions for Change. *Consulting Psychology Journal*, *48*(1), 12–16. doi:10.1037/1061-4087.48.1.12

Darvish, H., & Nasrollahi, A. A. (2011). Studying the relations between emotional intelligence and occupational stress: A case study at Payame Noor University. *Economic Science, 2*, 38-49. Retrieved from http://www.upg-bulletin-se.ro/archive/2011-2/4.%20Darvish_Nasrollahi.pdf

Darwin, C. R. (1872). *The expression of the emotions in man and animals* (1st ed.). London: John Murray. doi:10.1037/10001-000

Dasborough, M. T., & Ashkanasy, N. M. (2002). Emotion and attribution of intentionality in leader–member relationships. *The Leadership Quarterly*, *13*(5), 615–634. doi:10.1016/S1048-9843(02)00147-9

Das, T. K., & Teng, B. S. (1998). Between trust and control: Developing confidence in partner cooperation in alliances. *Academy of Management Review*, *23*(3), 491–512.

David, G., Buckle, P., & Woods, V. (2005). *Further development of the usability and validity of the Quick Exposure Check (QEC)*. Health & Safety Executive.

Davidovitz, R., Mikulincer, M., Shaver, P. R., Izsak, R., & Popper, M. (2007). Leaders as attachment figures: Leaders attachment orientations predict leadership-related mental representations and followers performance and mental health. *Journal of Personality and Social Psychology*, *93*(4), 632–650. doi:10.1037/0022-3514.93.4.632 PMID:17892336

Davidsson, P. (2015). Entrepreneurial opportunities and the entrepreneurship nexus: A re-conceptualization. *Journal of Business Venturing*, *30*(5), 674–695. doi:10.1016/j.jbusvent.2015.01.002

Davidsson, P., Hunter, E., & Klofsten, M. (2006). Institutional forces: The invisible hand that shapes venture ideas? *International Small Business Journal*, *24*(2), 115–131. doi:10.1177/0266242606061834

Davidsson, P., & Wiklund, J. (1997). Values, beliefs and regional variations in new firm formation rates. *Journal of Economic Psychology*, *18*(2), 179–199. doi:10.1016/S0167-4870(97)00004-4

Davis, T., & Landa, M. (1999). A Contrary Look at performance Appraisal. *Canadian Manager, Fall*, 18-28. Retrieved from http://www.thefreelibrary.com/A+contrary+look+at+employee+performance+appraisal.-a058436540

Davis, A., & Gibson, L. (1994). Designing Employee Welfare Provision. *Personnel Review*, *23*(7), 33–45. doi:10.1108/00483489410072208

Day, D. V., & Lord, R. G. (1988). Executive leadership and organizational performance: Suggestions for a new theory and methodology. *Journal of Management*, *14*(3), 453–464. doi:10.1177/014920638801400308

De Cuyper, N., Baillien, E., & De Witte, H. (2009). Job insecurity, perceived employability and targets and perpetrators experiences of workplace bullying. *Work and Stress*, *23*(3), 206–224. doi:10.1080/02678370903257578

De Hoogh, A. H., & Den Hartog, D. N. (2009). Neuroticism and locus of control as moderators of the relationships of charismatic and autocratic leadership with burnout. *The Journal of Applied Psychology*, *94*(4), 1058–1067. doi:10.1037/a0016253 PMID:19594244

De Kare-Silver, M. (2011). Changes to the Workplace and in the Workforce. In M. de Kare-Silver (Ed.), *E-Shock 2020* (pp. 115–124). London: Palgrave Macmillan UK. Retrieved from http://link.springer.com/10.1057/9780230343368_13

de Moura, G. R., Abrams, D., Retter, C., Gunnarsdottir, S., & Ando, K. (2009). Identification as an organizational anchor: How identification and job satisfaction combine to predict turnover intention. *European Journal of Social Psychology*, *39*(4), 540–557. doi:10.1002/ejsp.553

De Nobile, J. J., & McCormick, J. (2008). Organizational communication and job satisfaction in Australian Catholic Primary Schools. *Educational Management Administration & Leadership*, *36*(1), 101–122. doi:10.1177/1741143207084063

De Nobile, J., McCormick, J., & Hoekman, K. (2013). Organizational communication and occupational stress in Australian Catholic primary schools. *Journal of Educational Administration*, *51*(6), 744–767. doi:10.1108/JEA-09-2011-0081

De Silva, S. (1998). *Performance-Related and Skill-Based Pay: An Introduction*. Geneva: International Labour Office.

De Voe, S. E., & Iyengar, S. S. (2004). Managers theories of subordinates: A cross-cultural examination of manager perceptions of motivation and appraisal of performance. *Organizational Behavior and Human Decision Processes*, *93*(1), 47–61. doi:10.1016/j.obhdp.2003.09.001

De Vries, R. E., Bakker-Pieper, A., & Oostenveld, W. (2010). Leadership = communication? The relations of leaders communication styles with leadership styles, knowledge sharing and leadership outcomes. *Journal of Business and Psychology*, *25*(3), 367–380. doi:10.1007/s10869-009-9140-2 PMID:20700375

De Vries, R. E., Van den Hooff, B., & DeRidder, J. A. (2006). Explaining knowledge sharing: The role of team communication styles, job satisfaction, and performance beliefs. *Communication Research*, *33*(2), 115–135. doi:10.1177/0093650205285366

Deal, T. E., & Kennedy, A. A. (1982). *Corporate cultures: The rites and rituals of corporate life*. Reading, MA: Addison-Wesley Publishing.

Dechev, Z., & Kamphorst, J. J. A. (2010). Effective Performance Appraisal – A study into the relation between employer satisfaction and optimizing business results. Unpublished dissertation, Erasmus University, Rotterdam.

Deci, E. (1980). *The Psychology of Self Determination*. Lexington, MA: Lexington Books.

Dedovic, K., DAguiar, C., & Pruessner, J. C. (2009). What stress does to your brain: A review of neuroimaging studies. *Canadian Journal of Psychiatry*, *54*(1), 6–15. doi:10.1177/070674370905400104 PMID:19175975

Definitions of diversity. (n. d.). Retrieved from: http://www.rthomasconsulting.com/#/definitions-of-diversity/4539543895

DeLeon, L. (1996). Ethics and entrepreneurship. *Policy Studies Journal: the Journal of the Policy Studies Organization*, *24*(3), 495–510. doi:10.1111/j.1541-0072.1996.tb01642.x

DeLoria, J. E. (2001). *A Comparative Study of Employee Commitment: Core and Contract Employees in a Federal Agency* [Doctoral Dissertation]. Falls Church, VA.

Demartini, C. (2014). The evolution of the concept of 'management control': Towards a definition of 'performance management system.' In C. Demartini (Ed.), Performance management systems (pp. 9-54). Heidelberg, Germany: Springer-Verlag.

Demir, K. (2015). Teachers' organizational citizenship behaviors and organizational identification in public and private preschools. *Procedia: Social and Behavioral Sciences*, *174*, 1176–1182. doi:10.1016/j.sbspro.2015.01.734

Denat, Y., Gokce, S., Gungor, H., Zencir, C., & Akgullu, C. (2016). Relationship of anxiety and burnout with extrasystoles in critical care nurses in Turkey. *Pakistan Journal of Medical Sciences*, *32*(1), 196. PMID:27022374

Dendaas, N. (2011). Environmental congruence and work-related stress in acute care hospital medical/surgical units: A descriptive, correlational study. *Health Environments Research & Design Journal*, *5*(1), 23–42. doi:10.1177/193758671100500103 PMID:22322634

DeRosa, D. M., Hantula, D. A., Kock, N., & DArcy, J. (2004). Trust and leadership in virtual teamwork: A media naturalness perspective. *Human Resource Management*, *43*(2-3), 219–232. doi:10.1002/hrm.20016

Derven, M. G. (1990). The paradox of performance appraisal. *The Personnel Journal*, *69*, 107–111.

Dey, P. (2006). The rhetoric of social entrepreneurship: Paralogy and new language games in academic discourse. In C. Steyaert & D. Hjorth (Eds.), *Entrepreneurship as social change: A third movements of entrepreneurship* (pp. 121–144). Cheltenham, UK: Edward Elgar. doi:10.4337/9781847204424.00015

DHS. (2016). Equal Employment Opportunity and Diversity Division. Retrieved from https://www.dhs.gov/about-office-equal-employment-opportunity-and-diversity-division

Di Fabio, A., & Palazzeschi, L. (2012). Organizational justice: Personality traits or emotional intelligence? An empirical study in an Italian hospital context. *Journal of Employment Counseling*, *49*(1), 31–42. doi:10.1002/j.2161-1920.2012.00004.x

Dice. (2014). *Dice Tech salary survey results—2014*. Retrieved from http://resources.dice.com/report/dice-tech-salary-survey-results-2014

Diefendorff, J. M., Erickson, R. J., Grandey, A. A., & Dahling, J. J. (2011). Emotional display rules as work unit norms: A multilevel analysis of emotional labor among nurses. *Journal of Occupational Health Psychology*, *16*(2), 170–186. doi:10.1037/a0021725 PMID:21244168

Diefendorff, J., Brown, D., Kamin, A., & Lord, R. (2002). Examining the roles of job involvement and work centrality in predicting organizational citizenship behaviors and job performance. *Journal of Organizational Behavior*, *23*(1), 93–108. doi:10.1002/job.123

Diener, E. (2000). Subjective well-being: The science of happiness and a proposal for a national index. *The American Psychologist*, *55*(1), 34–43. doi:10.1037/0003-066X.55.1.34 PMID:11392863

Diggens, J., & Chesson, T. (2014). Do factors of emotion-focused patient care and communication impact job stress, satisfaction and burnout in radiation therapists? *Journal of Radiotherapy in Practice*, *13*(01), 4–17. doi:10.1017/S146039691300006X

Dilts, R. B. (1996). *Visionary leadership skills: Creating a world to which people want to belong*. New York: Meta Publications.

Diversity-in-Leadership. (2013). *INSIGHTS*. Retrieved from http://diversity-in-leadership.com/insights/

Dixon, N. M. (1992). Organizational learning: A review of the literature with implications for HRD professionals. *Human Resource Development Quarterly*, *3*(1), 29–49. doi:10.1002/hrdq.3920030105

Dobbin, F., & Kalev, A. (2016). Why diversity programs fail. *Harvard Business Review*, *94*(6), 70–76. PMID:27491197

Dodgson, M. (1993). Organizational learning: A review of some literatures. *Organization Studies*, *14*(3), 375–394. doi:10.1177/017084069301400303

Dolbier, C. L., Soderstrom, M., & Steinhardt, M. A. (2001). The relationships between self-leadership and enhanced psychological, health, and work outcomes. *The Journal of Psychology*, *135*(5), 469–485. doi:10.1080/00223980109603713 PMID:11804002

Dong, Q. (1995). *Self, identity, media use and socialization: A student of adolescent Asian immigrants to the United States*. Unpublished doctoral dissertation, Washington State University, Pullman, Washington.

Douglas, C. A., & McCauley, C. D. (1999). Formal developmental relationships: A survey of organizational practices. *Human Resource Development Quarterly*, *10*(3), 203–220. doi:10.1002/hrdq.3920100302

Dreer, L. E., Elliott, T. R., Fletcher, D. C., & Swanson, M. (2005). Social problem solving abilities and psychological adjustment of persons in low vision rehabilitation. *Rehabilitation Psychology*, *50*(3), 232–238. doi:10.1037/0090-5550.50.3.232

Drescher, S., Sabean, D., & Sharlin, A. (1982). *Political Symbolism in Modern Europe*. London: Transaction Books.

Drucker, P. (1985). *Innovation and entrepreneurship: Practice and principles*. New York: Harper & Row Publishers.

Drury, C. G. (1990). Methods for direct observation for performance. In J. R. Wilson & E. N. Corlett (Eds.), *Evaluation of Human Work* (pp. 35–37). London: Taylor and Francis.

Dubé, L., Bourhis, A., & Jacob, R. (2006). Towards a typology of virtual communities of practice. *Interdisciplinary Journal of Information, Knowledge, and Management*, *1*(1), 69–93.

Dubois, D. (1998). The competency casebook. Amherst, MA: HRD & Silver Spring MD: International Society for Performance Improvement.

Ducharme, L. J., Knudsen, H. K., & Roman, P. M. (2008). Emotional exhaustion and turnover intention in human services occupations: The protective role of co-working support. *Sociological Spectrum*, *28*(1), 81–104. doi:10.1080/02732170701675268

DuFrene, D. D., & Lehman, C. M. (2014). Navigating change: Employee communication in times of instability. *Business and Professional Communication Quarterly*, *77*(4), 443–452. doi:10.1177/2329490614544736

Dugguh, S. I., & Ayaga, D. (2014). Job satisfaction theories: Traceability to employee performance in organizations. *IOSR Journal of Business and Management*, *16*(5), 11-18.

Duguid, M. (2011). Female tokens in high-prestige work groups: Catalysts or inhibitors of group diversification? *Organizational Behavior and Human Decision Processes*, *116*(1), 104–115. doi:10.1016/j.obhdp.2011.05.009

Dukerich, J. M., & Carter, S. M. (2000). Distorted Images and Reputation Repair.

Dulewicz, V., & Higgs, M. (2000). Emotional intelligence: A review and evaluation study. *Journal of Managerial Psychology*, *15*(4), 341–372. doi:10.1108/02683940010330993

Dumas, T. L., Phillips, K. W., & Rothbard, N. P. (2013). Getting Closer at the Company Party: Integration Experiences, Racial Dissimilarity, and Workplace Relationships. *Organization Science*, *24*(5), 1377–1401. doi:10.1287/orsc.1120.0808

Dunmore, M. (2002). *Inside-Out Marketing: How to Create an Internal Marketing Strategy*. London: Kogan Page.

Dutton, J. E., & Dukerich, J. M. (1991). Keeping an eye on the mirror: Image and identity in organisational adaptation. *Academy of Management Journal*, *34*(3), 517–554. doi:10.2307/256405

Dyer, J. H., & Nobeoka, K. (2000). Creating and managing a high-performance knowledge-sharing network: The Toyota case. *Strategic Management Journal*, *21*(3), 345–367. doi:10.1002/(SICI)1097-0266(200003)21:3<345::AID-SMJ96>3.0.CO;2-N

DZurilla, T. J., Chang, E. C., Nottingham, E. J., & Faccini, L. (1998). Social problem-solving deficits and hopelessness, depression, and suicidal risk in college students and psychiatric inpatients. *Journal of Clinical Psychology*, *54*(8), 1091–1107. doi:10.1002/(SICI)1097-4679(199812)54:8<1091::AID-JCLP9>3.0.CO;2-J PMID:9840781

D'Zurilla, T. J., & Nezu, A. M. (1999). *Problem-solving therapy: A social competence approach to clinical intervention*. New York: Springer.

Easterby-Smith, M., & Araujo, L. (1999). Organizational learning: Current debates and opportunities. In M. Easterby-Smith & L. Araujo (Eds.), *Organizational learning and the learning organization: Development in theory and practice* (pp. 1–21). London: Sage. doi:10.4135/9781446218297.n1

Easterby-Smith, M., & Lyles, M. (2011). *The evolving field of organizational learning and knowledge management. Handbook of organizational learning and knowledge management* (pp. 1–20). Chichester, UK: Wiley.

Ebrahim, N. A., Ahmed, S., & Taha, Z. (2009). Virtual Teams: A Literature Review. *Australian Journal of Basic and Applied Sciences*, *3*(3), 2653–2669.

Eckenrode, J., & Gore, S. (1990). In J. Eckenrode & S. Gore (Eds.), *Stress Between Work and Family* (pp. 1–16). New York: Springer. doi:10.1007/978-1-4899-2097-3_1

Eckhardt, J. T., & Shane, S. A. (2003). Opportunities and entrepreneurship. *Journal of Management*, *29*(3), 333–349. doi:10.1177/014920630302900304

Eco, U. (1976). *A theory of semiotics. Bloomington, IN: Indiana University Press*. London: Macmillan. doi:10.1007/978-1-349-15849-2

Edelwich, J., & Brodsky, A. (1980). *Burn-out: Stages of disillusionment in the helping professions* (Vol. 255). New York: Human Sciences Press.

Edmondson, A. C. (1996). Learning from mistakes is easier said than done: Group and organizational influences on the detection and correction of human error. *The Journal of Applied Behavioral Science*, *32*(1), 5–28. doi:10.1177/0021886396321001

Edmondson, A., & Moingeon, B. (1998). From organizational learning to the learning organization. *Management Learning*, *29*(1), 5–20. doi:10.1177/1350507698291001

Edwards, B. D., Bell, S. T., Arthur, W. Jr, & Decuir, A. D. (2008). Relationships between facets of job satisfaction and task and contextual performance. *Applied Psychology*, *57*(3), 441–465. doi:10.1111/j.1464-0597.2008.00328.x

Edwards, M. R. (2010). An integrative review of employer branding and OB theory. *Personnel Review*, *39*(1), 5–23. doi:10.1108/00483481011012809

Efeoğlu, I. E., & Sanal, M. (2015). The effects of work-family conflict on job stress, job satisfaction, and organizational commitment: A study in Turkish pharmaceutical industry. In B. Christiansen (Ed.), *Handbook of research on global business opportunities* (pp. 213–228). Hershey, PA: IGI Global. doi:10.4018/978-1-4666-6551-4.ch010

Effective Communications. (2013). Communication skills. Retrieved from http://www.free-management-ebooks.com/dldebk-pdf/fme-effective-communication.pdf

Efkarpidis, A., Efkarpidis, P., & Zyga, S. (2012). A study of the emotional intelligence of employees at a district hospital of Greece. *International Journal of Caring Sciences*, *5*(1), 36–42.

Egan, M. E. (2011). Global Diversity and Inclusion: Fostering Innovation Through a Diverse Workforce. Retrieved from http://images.forbes.com/forbesinsights/StudyPDFs/Innovation_Through_Diversity.pdf

Einarsen, S. (2000). Harassment and bullying at work: A review of the Scandinavian approach. *Aggression and Violent Behavior: A Review Journal*, *5*(4), 371-401.

Einarsen, S. (1999). The nature and causes of bullying at work. *International Journal of Manpower*, *20*(1/2), 16–27. doi:10.1108/01437729910268588

Einarsen, S., Hoel, H., Zapf, D., & Cooper, C. L. (2011). The concept of bullying and harassment at work: The European tradition. In S. Einarsen, H. Hoel, D. Zapf, & C. L. Cooper (Eds.), *Bullying and harassment in the workplace. Developments in theory, research, and practice* (2nd ed., pp. 3–39). Boca Raton, FL: CRC Press.

Einarsen, S., Raknes, B. I., & Matthiesen, S. M. (1994). Bullying and harassment at work and their relationships to work environment quality – an exploratory study. *European Work and Organizational Psychologist*, *4*(4), 381–401. doi:10.1080/13594329408410497

Einarsen, S., & Skogstad, A. (1996). Bullying at work: Epidemiological findings in public and private organizations. *European Journal of Work and Organizational Psychology*, *5*(2), 185–201. doi:10.1080/13594329608414854

Eisdorfer, C. (1981). *Critique of the stress and coping paradigm. Models for Clinical Psychopathology*. New York: Spectrum Publications, Inc. doi:10.1007/978-94-015-7129-6

Elkjaer, B. (1999). In search of a social learning theory. In M. Easterby-Smith, J. Burgoyne, & L. Araujo (Eds.), *Organizational learning and the learning organization: Development in theory and practice* (pp. 75–91). London: Sage. doi:10.4135/9781446218297.n5

Elkjaer, B. (2004). Organizational learning the third way. *Management Learning*, *35*(4), 419–434. doi:10.1177/1350507604048271

Elliott, T. R., Sherwin, E., Harkins, S. W., & Marmarosh, C. (1995). Self-appraised problem-solving ability, affective states, and psychological distress. *Journal of Counseling Psychology*, *42*(1), 105–115. doi:10.1037/0022-0167.42.1.105

Elliott, T. R., Shewchuk, R., Hagglund, K., Rybarczyk, B., & Harkins, S. (1996). Occupational burnout, tolerance for stress, and coping among nurses in rehabilitation units. *Rehabilitation Psychology*, *41*(4), 267–284. doi:10.1037/0090-5550.41.4.267

Ellison, S. F., & Mullin, W. P. (2014). Diversity, social goods provision, and performance in the firm. *Journal of Economics & Management Strategy*, *23*(2), 465–481. doi:10.1111/jems.12051

Enomoto, Y., Ishiwata, R., & Inoue, T. (2013). Installing Assistive Technology into the Work Place of Persons with Developmental Disorders. *Journal of Society of Plant Engineers Japan*, *25*, 76–81.

Epstein, R. M., & Krasner, M. S. (2013). Physician resilience: What it means, why it matters, and how to promote it. *Academic Medicine*, *88*(3), 301–303. doi:10.1097/ACM.0b013e318280cff0 PMID:23442430

Equal Employment Opportunity Commission. (n. d.). Retrieved from https://www.eeoc.gov/eeoc/

Erasmus, B., Schenk, H., & Swanepoel, B. (2008). *South African Human Resource Management: Theory & practice* (4th ed.). Cape Town, South Africa: Juta & Co. Ltd.

Erez, M. (1994). Towards a Model of Cross-Cultural I/O Psychology. In M.D. Dunnette, L. Hough, & H. Triandis (Eds.), *Handbook of Industrial and Organizational Psychology* (Vol. 4, pp. 569–607). Palo Alto, CA: Consulting Psychologists Press.

Ergin, C. (1992). *Doktor ve Hemşirelerde Tükenmişlik ve Maslach Tükenmişlik Ölçeğinin Uyarlanması* (pp. 143–154). Ankara, Turkey: Türk Psikologlar Derneği Yayınları.

Erickson, W. (2013). *Employer practices and policies regarding the employment of persons with disabilities. Research Brief*. Ithaca, NY: Cornell University. Retrieved from http://digitalcommons.ilr.cornell.edu/cgi/viewcontent.cgi?article=1328&context=edicollect

Erickson, W. (2014). *Disability inclusive recruitment and hiring practices and policies: Who has them and what difference does it really make? Research Brief*. Ithaca, NY: Cornell University. Retrieved from http://digitalcommons.ilr.cornell.edu/cgi/viewcontent.cgi?article=1353&context=edicollect

Erickson, R., & Grove, W. (2007). Why emotions matter: Age, agitation, and burnout among registered nurses. *Online Journal of Issues in Nursing*, *13*(1), 1–13.

Erickson, W. A., von Schrader, S., Bruyere, S. M., & VanLooy, S. A. (2014). The employment environment: Employer perspectives, policies, and practices regarding the employment of persons with disabilities. *Rehabilitation Counseling Bulletin*, *57*(4), 195–208. doi:10.1177/0034355213509841

Erickson, W. A., von Schrader, S., Bruyere, S. M., VanLooy, S. A., & Matteson, S. (2014). Disability-inclusive employer practices and hiring of individuals with disabilities *Rehabilitation Research. Policy, and Evaluation*, *28*(4), 309–328.

Eriksson, P., & Kovalainen, A. (2015). *Qualitative Methods in Business Research*. Thousand Oaks, CA: Sage.

Erlinghagen, M. (2008). Self-perceived job insecurity and social context: A multi-level analysis of 17 European countries. *European Sociological Review*, *24*(2), 183–197. doi:10.1093/esr/jcm042

Ersoy, N. C., Derous, E., Born, M. P., & van der Molen, H. T. (2015). Antecedents of organizational citizenship behavior among Turkish white-collar employees in The Netherlands and Turkey. *International Journal of Intercultural Relations*, *49*, 68–79. doi:10.1016/j.ijintrel.2015.06.010

Eskin, M., & Aycan, Z. (2009). The adaptation of the revised social problem solving inventory into Turkish (Tr-SPSI-R): A reliability and validity analysis. *Türk Psiko Yaz*, *12*, 11–13.

Eskin, M., Kurt, I., & Demirkiran, F. (2012). Does social problem-solving training reduce psychological distress in nurses employed in an academic hospital. *Journal of Basic and Applied Scientific Research*, *2*(10), 10450–10458.

Estiri, M., Nargesian, A., Dastpish, F., & Sharifi, S. M. (2016). The impact of psychological capital on mental health among Iranian nurses: Considering the mediating role of job burnout. *SpringerPlus*, *5*(1), 1377. doi:10.1186/s40064-016-3099-z PMID:27610296

Estrin, S., Korosteleva, J., & Mickiewicz, T. (2013b). Which institutions encourage entrepreneurial growth aspirations? *Journal of Business Venturing*, *28*(4), 564–580. doi:10.1016/j.jbusvent.2012.05.001

Compilation of References

Estrin, S., Mickiewicz, T., & Stephan, U. (2013a). Entrepreneurship, social capital, and institutions: Social and commercial entrepreneurship across nations. *Entrepreneurship Theory and Practice*, *37*(3), 479–504. doi:10.1111/etap.12019

Etzion, D. (1987). *Burning out in management: A comparison of women and men in matched organizational positions*. Tel Aviv University, Faculty of Management, The Leon Recanati Graduate School of Business Administration.

EU-OSHA [European Agency for Safety and Health at Work]. (2010). *Workplace violence and harassment: A European picture*. European Risk Observatory Report. Retrieved from https://osha.europa.eu/sites/default/files/publications/documents/en/publications/reports/violence-harassment-TERO09010ENC/violence-harassment-report.pdf

EUR-Lex. (2016). Retrieved from http://eur-lex.europa.eu/legal-content/EN/TXT/?uri=URISERV:em0031

Eurofound. (2015). *Violence and harassment in European workplaces: Causes, impacts and policies*. Dublin, Ireland: Author. Retrieved from http://www.eurofound.europa.eu/sites/default/files/ef_comparative_analytical_report/field_ef_documents/ef1473en.pdf

European Foundation for the Improvement of Living and Working Conditions. (2007). *Fourth European Survey of Working Conditions*. Luxembourg: Publications Office of the European Union. Retrieved from http://www.eurofound.europa.eu/publications/htmlfiles/ef0698.htm

European Union. (2016). About the EU. Finland. Reviewed from http://europa.eu/about-eu/countries/member-countries/finland/index_en.htm

Evans, P. (1996). Government action, social capital and development: Reviewing the evidence on synergy. *World Development*, *24*(6), 1119–1132. doi:10.1016/0305-750X(96)00021-6

Fang, C., Lee, J., & Schilling, M. A. (2010). Balancing exploration and exploitation through structural design: The isolation of subgroups and organizational learning. *Organization Science*, *21*(3), 625–642. doi:10.1287/orsc.1090.0468

Fang, S. C., Tsai, F. S., & Lin, J. L. (2010). Leveraging tenant-incubator social capital for organizational learning and performance in incubation programme. *International Small Business Journal*, *28*(1), 90–113. doi:10.1177/0266242609350853

Farahbod, F., Salimi, S. B., & Dorostkar, K. R. (2013). Impact of organizational communication in job satisfaction and organizational commitment. *Interdisciplinary Journal of Contemporary Research in Business*, *5*(4), 419–430.

Fares, J., Tabosh, H., Saadeddin, Z., Mouhayyar, C., & Aridi, H. (2016). Stress, Burnout and Coping Strategies in Preclinical Medical Students. *North American Journal of Medical Sciences*, *8*(2), 75–81. doi:10.4103/1947-2714.177299 PMID:27042604

Farzianpour, F., Abbasi, M., Foruoshani, A. R., & Pooyan, E. J. (2016). The relationship between Hofstede Organizational Culture and employees job burnout in hospitals of Tehran University of Medical Sciences 20142015. *Materia Socio-Medica*, *28*(1), 26. doi:10.5455/msm.2016.28.26-31 PMID:27047263

Fassinger, R. E. (2008). Workplace diversity and public policy. *The American Psychologist*, *63*(4), 252–268. doi:10.1037/0003-066X.63.4.252 PMID:18473610

Feely, A. J., & Harzing, A. W. (2002). Language management in multicultural companies. *Cross-Cultural Management: An International Journal*, *10*(2), 37–52. doi:10.1108/13527600310797586

Feenberg, A. (1991). *Critical theory of technology*. Oxford: Oxford University Press.

Feintzeig, R. (2015, September 30). More companies say targets are the key to diversity. *WSJ.com*. Retrieved from http://www.wsj.com/articles/more-companies-say-targets-are-the-key-to-diversity-1443600464

Felix, U. (2003). Humanising automated online learning though intelligent feedback. In G. Crisp, D. Thiele, I. Scholten et al. (Eds), *Interact, integrate, impact: Proceedings of the 20th Annual Conference of the Australasian Society of Computers in Learning in Tertiary Education*, Adelaide.

Fenwick, T. (2000). Questioning the concept of the learning organization. In C. Paechter, M. Preedy, D. Scott, & J. Soler (Eds.), *Knowledge, power and learning* (pp. 74–88). London: Paul Chapman.

Ferrell, O., Gresham, L. G., & Fraedrich, J. (1989). A synthesis of ethical decision models for marketing. *Journal of Macromarketing*, *9*(2), 55–64. doi:10.1177/027614678900900207

Figurska, I., & Matuska, E. (2013). Employer branding as human resources strategy. *Human Resources Management & Ergonomics*, VIII(2), 35-51. Retrieved from https://frcatel.fri.uniza.sk/hrme/files/2013/2013_2_03.pdf

Fillion, L., Trembley, I., Truchon, M., Côté, D., Struthers, C. W., & Dupuis, R. (2007). Job satisfaction and emotional distress among nurses providing palliative care: Empirical evidence for an integrative occupational stress-model. *International Journal of Stress Management*, *14*(1), 1–25. doi:10.1037/1072-5245.14.1.1

Fine, M. G. (1996). Cultural Diversity in the Workplace: The State of the Field. *Journal of Business Communication*, *33*(4), 485–502. doi:10.1177/002194369603300408

Fineman, S. (Ed.). (2000). *Emotion in organizations* (2nd ed.). London: Sage.

Fiol, C. M., & Lyles, M. A. (1985). Organizational learning. *Academy of Management Review*, *10*(4), 803–813.

Fiori, M., Bollmann, G., & Rossier, J. (2015). Exploring the path through which career adaptability increases job satisfaction and lowers job stress: The role of affect. *Journal of Vocational Behavior*, *91*, 113–121. doi:10.1016/j.jvb.2015.08.010

Fisher, C. D. (2010). Happiness at work. *International Journal of Management Reviews*, *12*(4), 384–412. doi:10.1111/j.1468-2370.2009.00270.x

Fisher, G. (1988). *Mindsets: The role of culture and perception in international relations*. Yarmouth, ME: Intercultural Press.

Fisher, M. (1995). *Performance Appraisals*. London: Kogan Page, Limited.

Flanagan, J. C. (1954). The critical incidents technique. *Psychological Bulletin*, *51*(4), 327–358. doi:10.1037/h0061470 PMID:13177800

Folger, R., Konovsky, M., & Cropanzano, R. (2002). A due process metaphor for performance appraisal. In B. M. Staw & L. L. Cummings (Eds.), *Research in Organizational Behavior* (Vol. 14, pp. 129–177). Greenwich, CT: JAI Press.

Force, L. M. (2008). *The influence of causal attribution on work exhaustion and turnover intention of traditional discipline engineers in the United States*. ProQuest.

Fox, S., & Stallworth, L. E. (2009). Building a framework for two internal organizational approaches to resolving and preventing workplace bullying: Alternative dispute resolution and training. *Consulting Psychology Journal: Practice and Research*, *61*(3), 220–241. doi:10.1037/a0016637

Franke, G. R., & Nadler, S. S. (2008). Culture, economic development, and national ethical attitudes. *Journal of Business Research*, *61*(3), 254–264. doi:10.1016/j.jbusres.2007.06.005

Freshman, B., & Rubino, L. (2002). Emotional intelligence: A core competency for health care administrators. *The Health Care Manager*, *20*(4), 1–9. doi:10.1097/00126450-200206000-00002 PMID:12083173

Compilation of References

Freudenberger, H. J. (1974). Staff burn-out. *The Journal of Social Issues*, *30*(1), 159–165. doi:10.1111/j.1540-4560.1974.tb00706.x

Friedman, A. L., & Miles, S. (2001). Socially responsible investment and corporate social and environmental reporting in the UK: An exploratory study. *The British Accounting Review*, *33*(4), 523–548. doi:10.1006/bare.2001.0172

Friedman, V. J., Lipshitz, R., & Popper, M. (2005). The mystification of organizational learning. *Journal of Management Inquiry*, *14*(1), 19–30. doi:10.1177/1056492604273758

Froschheiser, L. (2015). Communication: The most important key to leadership success. Retrieved from http://www.reliableplant.com/Read/12675/communication-most-important-key-to-leadership-success

Frye, A. A., & Goodman, S. H. (2000). Which social problem-solving components buffer depression in adolescent girls? *Cognitive Therapy and Research*, *24*(6), 637–650. doi:10.1023/A:1005583210589

Fujino, Y., Tanaka, M., Yonemitsu, Y., & Kawamoto, R. (2015). The relationship between characteristics of nursing performance and years of experience in nurses with high emotional intelligence. *International Journal of Nursing Practice*, *21*(6), 876–881. doi:10.1111/ijn.12311 PMID:24712344

Furnham, A., Richards, S. C., & Paulhus, D. L. (2013). The Dark Triad of personality: A 10 year review. *Social and Personality Psychology Compass*, *7*(3), 199–216. doi:10.1111/spc3.12018

Furusawa, M. (2011). Nihonkigyouno kaigaihakensya ni taisuru jintekishigenn kanrino kenkyu [Human resource management for expatriates of Japanese corporations]. *Osaka Shogyodigaku Ronshu*, *6*(3), 1–22.

Gabel Shemueli, R., Dolan, S. L., Suárez Ceretti, A., & Nuñez del Prado, P. (2015). Burnout and engagement as mediators in the relationship between work characteristics and turnover Intentions across two Ibero-American nations. *Stress and Health*. PMID:26680339

Gabriel, A. S., Erickson, R. J., Moran, C. M., Diefendoff, J. M., & Bromley, G. E. (2013). A multilevel analysis of the effects of the practice environment scale of the nursing work index on nurse outcomes. *Research in Nursing & Health*, *36*(6), 567–581. doi:10.1002/nur.21562 PMID:24122833

Gadhia, J.-A. (2016). *Harnessing the talents of women in financial services empowering productivity*. Retrieved from http://uk.virginmoney.com/virgin/assets/pdf/Virgin-Money-Empowering-Productivity-Report.pdf

Galletta, M., Portoghese, I., DAloja, E., Mereu, A., Contu, P., Coppola, R. C., & Campagna, M. et al. (2016). Relationship between job burnout, psychosocial factors and health care-associated infections in critical care units. *Intensive & Critical Care Nursing*, *34*, 51–58. doi:10.1016/j.iccn.2015.11.004 PMID:26961918

Galpin, T. J. (1997). *Making Strategy Work: Building Sustainable Growth Capability*. San Francisco: Jossey-Bass Publishers.

Gama, E. M. P., & Pedersen, P. (1977). Readjustment problems of Brazilian returnees from graduate studies in the United States. *International Journal of Intercultural Relations*, *1*(4), 46–58. doi:10.1016/0147-1767(77)90031-1

Gangopadhyay, S., Ray, A., Das, A., Das, T., Ghoshal, G., Banerjee, P., & Bagchi, S. (2003). A study on upper extremity cumulative trauma disorder in different unorganised sectors of West Bengal, India. *Journal of Occupational Health*, *45*(6), 351–357. doi:10.1539/joh.45.351 PMID:14676414

Gangwani, S. (2012). Employee Survey on Performance Appraisal System. International. *Journal of Social Sciences & Interdisciplinary Research*, *1*(6), 124–141.

Gao, Y. Q., Pan, B. C., Sun, W., Wu, H., Wang, J. N., & Wang, L. (2012). Anxiety symptoms among Chinese nurses and the associated factors: A cross sectional study. *BMC Psychiatry*, *12*(1), 1. doi:10.1186/1471-244X-12-141 PMID:22978466

Garber, P. R. (2008). *50 communications activities, icebreakers, and exercises*. Amherst, MA: HRD Press, Inc. Retrieved from https://www2.cortland.edu/dotAsset/c1a635f6-a099-4ede-8f15-79b86e315088.pdf

Garcia, H. F. (2012). Leadership communications: Planning for the desired reaction. *Strategy and Leadership*, *40*(6), 42–45. doi:10.1108/10878571211278886

Garcia, O., & Otheguy, R. (1994). The value of speaking a LOTE in U.S. business. *Annals of the American Academy of Political and Social Science: Foreign Language Policy: An Agenda for Change*, *532*(3), 99–122. doi:10.1177/0002716294532001008

Garcia-Prieto, P., Mackie, D. M., Tran, V., & Smith, E. R. (2007). Intergroup emotions in workgroups: Some emotional antecedents and consequences of belonging. *Research on Managing Groups and Teams*, *10*, 145–184. doi:10.1016/S1534-0856(07)10007-4

Gardner, L., & Stough, C. (2002). Examining the relationship between leadership and emotional intelligence in senior level managers. *Leadership and Organization Development Journal*, *2*(2), 68–78. doi:10.1108/01437730210419198

Garg, S., & Jain, S. (2013). Mapping leadership styles of public and private sector leaders using Blake and mouton leadership model. *Drishtikon: A Management Journal*, *4*(1), 48-64. Retrieved from http://search.proquest.com/docview/1477998237?accountid=35812

Gartner, W. B. (1995). Aspects of organizational emergence. In I. Bull, H. Thomas, & G. Willard (Eds.), *Entrepreneurship: Perspectives on theory building* (pp. 67–86). Oxford, UK: Pergamon.

Garton, L., & Wellman, B. (1995). Social impacts of electronic mail in organizations: A review of the research literature. *Communication Yearbook*, *18*, 434–453.

Garvin, D. A. (1993). Building a learning organization. *Harvard Business Review*, *71*(4), 78. PMID:10127041

Gauvain, M. (2001). *The Social Context of Cognitive Development*. New York: Guilford Press.

Genosko, G. (1994). *Baudrillard and signs: Signification ablaze*. London: Routledge. doi:10.4324/9780203201145

Georgakopoulos, A., Wilkin, L., & Kent, B. (2011). Workplace bullying: A complex problem in contemporary organizations. *International Journal of Business and Social Science*, *2*(3), 1–20. Retrieved from http://ijbssnet.com/journals/Vol._2_No._3_[Special_Issue_-_January_2011]/1.pdf

George, J. M. (2000). Emotions and leadership: The role of emotional intelligence. *Human Relations*, *53*(8), 1027–1055. doi:10.1177/0018726700538001

Georgellis, Y., & Lange, T. (2012). Traditional versus secular values and the job–life satisfaction relationship across Europe. *British Journal of Management*, *23*(4), 437–454. doi:10.1111/j.1467-8551.2011.00753.x

Geppert, M., & Dörrenbächer, C. (2014). Politics and power *within* multinational corporations: Mainstream studies, emerging critical approaches and suggestions for future research. *International Journal of Management Reviews*, *16*(2), 226–244. doi:10.1111/ijmr.12018

Germain, M.-L., & McGuire, D. (2014). The Role of Swift Trust in Virtual Teams and Implications for Human Resource Development. *Advances in Developing Human Resources*, *16*(3), 356–370. doi:10.1177/1523422314532097

Gherardi, S. (2003). Knowing as desiring. Mythic knowledge and the knowledge journey in communities of practitioners. *Journal of Workplace Learning*, *15*(7/8), 352–358. doi:10.1108/13665620310504846

Ghodratollah, B., Matin, H. Z., & Amighi, F. (2011). The relationship between empowerment and organizational citizenship behavior of the pedagogical organization employees. *Iranian Journal of Management Studies*, *4*(2), 53–62.

Compilation of References

Giallonardo, L. M., Wong, C. A., & Iwasiw, C. L. (2010). Authentic leadership of preceptors: Predictor of new graduate nurses' work engagement and job satisfaction. *Journal of Nursing Management*, *18*(8), 993–1003. doi:10.1111/j.1365-2834.2010.01126.x PMID:21073571

Giannouli, V. (2014). *Emotional leadership in health care units: Relationships of leaders-subordinates.* Unpublished master's thesis,. Hellenic Open University, Patras, Greece.

Gibson, D., & Petrosko, J. (2014). Trust in leader and its effect on job satisfaction and intent to leave in a healthcare setting. *New Horizons in Adult Education and Human Resource Development*, *26*(3), 3–19. doi:10.1002/nha3.20069

Giga, S. I., Hoel, H., & Lewis, D. (2008). *The costs of workplace bullying. Research Commissioned by the Dignity at Work Partnership*. Bradford, UK: University of Bradford.

Gilbert, G. R. (1982). Performance Appraisal and Organizational Practices: A Post Reform Review. *Public Personnel Management*, *11*(4), 318–321. doi:10.1177/009102608201100405

Gilbert, S., Laschinger, H. K. S., & Leiter, M. (2010). The mediating effect of burnout on the relationship between structural empowerment and organizational citizenship behaviours. *Journal of Nursing Management*, *18*(3), 339–348. doi:10.1111/j.1365-2834.2010.01074.x PMID:20546475

Gilbert, T. F. (1996). *Human Competence: Engineering Worthy Performance*. Washington, D.C: International Society for Performance Improvement.

Giltinane, C. L. (2013). Leadership styles and theories. *Nursing Standard*, *27*(41), 35–39. doi:10.7748/ns2013.06.27.41.35.e7565 PMID:23905259

Giorgi, A. (2010). About the speaker: Towards a syntax of indexicality. Oxford University Press.

Giorgi, G., Leon-Perez, J. M., & Arenas, A. (2015). Are bullying behaviors tolerated in some cultures? Evidence for a curvilinear relationship between workplace bullying and job satisfaction among Italian workers. *Journal of Business Ethics*, *131*(1), 227–237. doi:10.1007/s10551-014-2266-9

Giovagnoli, M., & Stover, D. R. (2004). How leadership networks strengthen people and organizations. *Leader to Leader*, *2004*(32), 56–62. doi:10.1002/ltl.77

Glasø, L., & Einarsen, S. (2008). Emotion regulation in leader-follower relationships. *European Journal of Work and Organizational Psychology*, *17*(4), 482–500. doi:10.1080/13594320801994960

Glikson, E., & Erez, M. (2013). Emotion display norms in virtual teams. *Journal of Personnel Psychology*, *12*(1), 22–32. doi:10.1027/1866-5888/a000078

Glomb, T. M., Bhave, D. P., Miner, A. G., & Wall, M. (2011). Doing good, feeling good: Examining the role of organizational citizenship behaviors in changing mood. *Personnel Psychology*, *64*(1), 191–223. doi:10.1111/j.1744-6570.2010.01206.x

Glynn, J. J., & Murphy, M. P. (1996). Public Management: Failing Accountabilities and Failing Performance Review. *International Journal of Public Sector Management*, *9*(5/6), 125–137. doi:10.1108/09513559610146492

Godar, S. H., & Ferris, S. P. (Eds.). (2004). *Virtual and collaborative teams: process, technologies and practice*. Hershey, PA: Idea Group Publications. doi:10.4018/978-1-59140-204-6

Goffee, R., & Jones, G. (2015). *Why should anyone be led by you? What it takes to be an authentic leader*. Boston: Harvard Business Review Press.

Goh, Y. S., Lee, A., Chan, S. W. C., & Chan, M. F. (2015). Profiling nurses job satisfaction, acculturation, work environment, stress, cultural values and coping abilities: A cluster analysis. *International Journal of Nursing Practice*, *21*(4), 443–452. doi:10.1111/ijn.12318 PMID:24754648

Gok, S., Karatuna, I., & Karaca, P. O. (2015). The role of perceived supervisor support and organizational identification in job satisfaction. *Procedia: Social and Behavioral Sciences*, *177*, 38–42. doi:10.1016/j.sbspro.2015.02.328

Goldman Sachs. (2016). Returnship program. Retrieved from: http://www.goldmansachs.com/careers/experienced-professionals/returnship/

Goleman, D. (2004). What makes a leader? *Emotional intelligence*. Retrieved from https://hbr.org/2004/01/what-makes-a-leader

Goleman, D. (1995). *Emotional Intelligence: Why it can matter more than IQ*. London: Bloomsbury.

Goleman, D. (1995). *Working with emotional intelligence*. New York: Bantam Books.

Goleman, D. (1998). *Emotional intelligence: why can it matter*. New York: Bantam Books.

Goleman, D. (1998). *Emotional intelligence: why can it matter?* New York: Bantam Books.

Goleman, D. (1998a). *Working with Emotional Intelligence*. London: Bloomsbury.

Goleman, D. (1998b). What makes a leader? *Harvard Business Review*, *76*(6), 93–102. PMID:10187249

Goleman, D. (2001). An EI-based theory of performance. In C. Cherniss & D. Goleman (Eds.), *The Emotionally Intelligent workplace. How to select for, measure, and improve Emotional Intelligence in individuals, groups, and organizations* (pp. 27–44). San Francisco, CA: Jossey-Bass.

Goleman, D., Boyatzis, R., & McKee, A. (2001). Primal leadership: The hidden driver of great performance. *Harvard Business Review*, *79*(11), 42–53.

Golfenshtein, N., & Drach-Zahavy, A. (2015). An attribution theory perspective on emotional labour in nurse–patient encounters: A nested cross-sectional study in paediatric settings. *Journal of Advanced Nursing*, *71*(5), 1123–1134. doi:10.1111/jan.12612 PMID:25558788

Gonzalez, J. A., & Chakraborty, S. (2012). Image and similarity: An identity orientation perspective to organizational identification. *Leadership and Organization Development Journal*, *33*(1), 51–65. doi:10.1108/01437731211193115

Goolsby, J. R., & Hunt, S. D. (1992). Cognitive moral development and marketing. *Journal of Marketing*, *56*(1), 55–68. doi:10.2307/1252132

Gooty, J., Thomas, J., & Connelly, S. (2015) The leader–member exchange relationship: a cross-level examination of emotions and emotion-related phenomena. In K. Niven and H. Madrid (Chairs). *Emotions and Leadership: How leader emotion influences followers*. Annual Meeting of the Academy of Management, Vancouver, Canada.

Gooty, J., Connelly, S., Griffith, J., & Gupta, A. (2010). Leadership, affect and emotions: A state of the science review. *The Leadership Quarterly*, *21*(6), 979–1004. doi:10.1016/j.leaqua.2010.10.005

Gorgi, H. A., Ahmadi, A., Shabaninejad, H., Tahmasbi, A., Baratimarnani, A., & Mehralian, G. (2015). The impact of emotional intelligence on managers' performance: Evidence from hospitals located in Tehran. *Journal of Education and Health Promotion*, *4*.

Goris, J. R. (2007). Effects of satisfaction with communication on the relationship between individual-job congruence and job performance/satisfaction. *Journal of Management Development*, *26*(8), 737–752. doi:10.1108/02621710710777255

Compilation of References

Gosseries, O., Demertzi, A., Ledoux, D., Bruno, M. A., Vanhaudenhuyse, A., Thibaut, A., & Schnakers, C. et al. (2012). Burnout in healthcare workers managing chronic patients with disorders of consciousness. *Brain Injury : [BI]*, *26*(12), 1493–1499. doi:10.3109/02699052.2012.695426 PMID:22725684

Goswami, K., & Talukdar, R. R. (2013). Relation between emotional intelligence and job stress among engineers at managerial level at public sector organization. *IOSR Journal of Humanities and Social Science*, *7*(3), 44–47. doi:10.9790/0837-0734447

Goudreau, J. (2013, February 25). Back to the stone age? New Yahoo CEO Marissa Mayer bans working from home. *Forbes*. Retrieved from http://www.forbes.com/sites/jennagoudreau/2013/02/25/back-to-the-stone-age-new-yahoo-ceo-marissa-mayer-bans-working-from-home/#166133f563d0

Gourzoulidis, G., Kontodimopoulos, N., Kastanioti, C., Bellali, T., Goumas, K., Voudigaris, D., & Polyzos, N. (2015). Do self-perceptions of emotional intelligence predict health-related quality of life? A case study in hospital managers in Greece. *Global Journal of Health Science*, *7*(1), 210. PMID:25560350

GOV.UK. (2014, November 12). *Flexible working*. Retrieved from https://www.gov.uk/flexible-working/overview

Graen, G. B., & Scandura, T. A. (1987). Toward a psychology of dyadic organizing. *Research in Organizational Behavior*, *9*, 175–208.

Grandey, A. A. (2008). Emotions at work: A review and research agenda. In Handbook of Organizational Behavior (pp. 235-261).

Grandey, A. A. (2000). Emotional regulation in the workplace: A new way to conceptualize emotional labor. *Journal of Occupational Health Psychology*, *5*(1), 95–110. doi:10.1037/1076-8998.5.1.95 PMID:10658889

Granovetter, M. (1985). Economic action and social structure: The problem of embeddedness. *American Journal of Sociology*, *91*(3), 481–510. doi:10.1086/228311

Grant, A. M., & Berry, J. W. (2011). The necessity of others is the mother of invention: Intrinsic and prosocial motivations, perspective taking, and creativity. *Academy of Management Journal*, *54*(1), 73–96. doi:10.5465/AMJ.2011.59215085

Grant, A. M., & Sumanth, J. J. (2009). Mission possible? The performance of prosocially motivated employees depends on manager trustworthiness. *The Journal of Applied Psychology*, *94*(4), 927–944. doi:10.1037/a0014391 PMID:19594235

Gray, J. A. (2004). *Men are from mars, women are from Venus*. Chicago: Turtleback Books.

Gray, J., & Annis, B. (2013). *Work with me: How gender intelligence can help you succeed at work and in life*. London: Piatkus Books.

Greco, P., Laschinger, H. K. S., & Wong, C. (2006). Leader empowering behaviours, staff nurse empowerment and work engagement/burnout. *Nursing Leadership*, *19*(4), 41–56. doi:10.12927/cjnl.2006.18599 PMID:17265673

Green, F. (2011). Unpacking the misery multiplier: How employability modifies the impacts of unemployment and job insecurity on life satisfaction and mental health. *Journal of Health Economics*, *30*(2), 265–276. doi:10.1016/j.jhealeco.2010.12.005 PMID:21236508

Greenglass, E. R., Burke, R. J., & Fiksenbaum, L. (2001). Workload and burnout in nurses. *Journal of Community & Applied Social Psychology*, *11*(3), 211–215. doi:10.1002/casp.614

Gregersen, H. B., & Stroh, L. K. (1997). Coming home to the arctic cold: Antecedents to Finnish expatriate and spouse repatriation adjustment. *Personnel Psychology*, *50*(3), 635–654. doi:10.1111/j.1744-6570.1997.tb00708.x

Griffin, L. & Clarke, T. (2008). Employer Branding. Your Customers Know Your Brand & Values. Do Your Employees? *Bridge Partners Insights*.

Grimm, J. W. (2010). Effective leadership: Making the difference. *Journal of Emergency Nursing: JEN, 36*(1), 74–33. doi:10.1016/j.jen.2008.07.012 PMID:20109788

Grisales Romero, H., Muñoz, Y., Osorio, D., & Robles, E. (2016). Burnout syndrome in nursing personnel of a referral hospital in Ibague, Colombia, 2014. *Enfermería Global, 15*(1), 244–257. doi:10.6018/eglobal.15.1.212851

Gross, J. J. (1999). Emotion regulation: Past, present, future. *Cognition and Emotion, 13*(5), 551–573. doi:10.1080/026999399379186

Gross, J. J. (2007). Emotion regulation: Conceptual foundations. In J. J. Gross (Ed.), *Handbook of Emotion Regulation* (pp. 3–26). New York: Guilford.

Gross, J. J., & John, O. P. (2003). Individual differences in two emotion regulation processes: Implications for affect, relationships, and well being. *Journal of Personality and Social Psychology, 85*(2), 348–362. doi:10.1037/0022-3514.85.2.348 PMID:12916575

Groysberg, B. G., & Bell, D. (2013). Dysfunction in the boardroom. *Harvard Business Review, 91*(9).

Groysberg, B., & Connolly, K. (2013). Great leaders who make the mix work. *Harvard Business Review, 91*(9), 68–76.

Grube, A., Schroer, J., Hentzschel, C., & Hertel, G. (2008). The event reconstruction method: An efficient measure of experience-based job satisfaction. *Journal of Occupational and Organizational Psychology, 81*(4), 669–689. doi:10.1348/096317907X251578

Grubicka, J., & Matuska, E. (2012). Consumer safety of e-market participant. In H. Lisiak & W. Stach (Eds.), Security of contemporary world. History and public safety (pp. 45-54). Poznań: Institute of Scientific Publishing - Maiuscula.

Grubicka, J., & Matuska, E. (2015). Sustainable entrepreneurship in conditions of un(safety) globalization and technological convergence, *The International Journal Entrepreneurship and Sustainability Issues*. Retrieved from http://jssidoi.org/jesi/aims-and-scope-of-research doi:10.9770/jesi.2015.2.4(2)

Grudin, J. (1994). Grouware and social dynamics: Eight challenges for developers. *Communications of the ACM, 37*(1), 92–105. doi:10.1145/175222.175230

Gruneberg, M. M. (1979). *Understanding job satisfaction*. New York: John Wiley. doi:10.1007/978-1-349-03952-4

Guay, R. P., & Choi, D. (2015). To whom does transformational leadership matter more? An examination of neurotic and introverted followers and their organizational citizenship behavior. *The Leadership Quarterly, 26*(5), 851–862. doi:10.1016/j.leaqua.2015.06.005

Gudykunst, W. B. (2005). An anxiety/uncertainty management (AUM) theory of stranger's intercultural adjustment. In W. B. Gudykunst (Ed.), *Theorizing about intercultural communication* (pp. 419–457). Thousand Oaks, CA: Sage.

Gudykunst, W. B., & Kim, Y. Y. (2003). *Communicating with strangers: An approach to intercultural communication*. New York: McGraw-Hill.

Gulati, R. (1999). Network location and learning: The influence of network resources and firm capabilities on alliance formation. *Strategic Management Journal, 20*(5), 397–420. doi:10.1002/(SICI)1097-0266(199905)20:5<397::AID-SMJ35>3.0.CO;2-K

Compilation of References

Güleryüz, G., Güney, S., Aydın, E. M., & Aşan, Ö. (2008). The mediating effect of job satisfaction between emotional intelligence and organisational commitment of nurses: A questionnaire survey. *International Journal of Nursing Studies*, *45*(11), 1625–1635. doi:10.1016/j.ijnurstu.2008.02.004 PMID:18394625

Gullahorn, J. T., & Gullahorn, J. E. (1963). An extension of the U-curve hypothesis. *The Journal of Social Issues*, *19*(3), 33–47. doi:10.1111/j.1540-4560.1963.tb00447.x

Gumbus, A., & Meglich, P. (2012). Lean and mean: Workplace culture and the prevention of workplace bullying. *Journal of Applied Business and Economics*, *13*(5), 11–20.

Guo, Y., Rammal, H. G., & Dowling, P. J. (2016). Global talent management and staffing in MNEs: An introduction to the edited volume of international business and management. In Global talent management and staffing in MNEs (International Business and Management, Vol. 32; pp. xv–xxiv). Bingley, UK: Emerald Group. doi:10.1108/S1876-066X20160000032014

Guo, J., Chen, J., Fu, J., Ge, X., Chen, M., & Liu, Y. (2016). Structural empowerment, job stress and burnout of nurses in China. *Applied Nursing Research*, *31*, 41–45. doi:10.1016/j.apnr.2015.12.007 PMID:27397817

Guo, L. C., & Sanchez, Y. (2005). Workplace communication. In N. Borkowski (Ed.), *Organizational behavior in health care* (pp. 77–110). London: Jones & Bartlett Learning.

Gupta, V., & Swaroop, A. (2012). Comparative study of performance appraisal on two Pharmaceutical organizations in Madhya Pradesh. *International Journal of Engineering Sciences & Management*, *2*(2), 248–260.

Haaga, D. A., Fine, J. A., Terrill, D. R., Stewart, B. L., & Beck, A. T. (1995). Social problem-solving deficits, dependency, and depressive symptoms. *Cognitive Therapy and Research*, *19*(2), 147–158. doi:10.1007/BF02229691

Haas, M., & Mortensen, M. (2016). The secrets of great teamwork. *Harvard Business Review*, *94*(6), 70–76. PMID:27491197

Haberstroh, C. J. (1965). Organizational Design and Systems Analysis. In J. G. March (Ed.), *Handbook of Organizations* (pp. 1171–1212). Chicago: Rand McNally.

Habisch, A., Jonker, J., Wegner, M., & Schmidpeter, R. (2004). *Corporate social responsibility across Europe*. Berlin: Springer.

Hackman, J., & Oldham, G. R. (1975). Development of the job diagnostic survey. *The Journal of Applied Psychology*, *60*(2), 159–170. doi:10.1037/h0076546

Hackman, J., & Oldham, G. R. (1976). Motivation through the design of work: Test of a theory. *Organizational Behavior and Human Performance*, *16*(2), 250–279. doi:10.1016/0030-5073(76)90016-7

Hagedoorn, J., & Duysters, G. (2002). Learning in dynamic inter-firm networks: The efficacy of multiple contacts. *Organization Studies*, *23*(4), 525–548. doi:10.1177/0170840602234002

Hager, P. (2011). Theories of workplace learning. In M. Malloch, L. Cairns, K. Evans, & B. N. O'Connor (Eds.), *The Sage handbook of workplace learning* (pp. 17–31). Thousand Oaks, CA: Sage. doi:10.4135/9781446200940.n2

Haile, G. A. (2015). Workplace job satisfaction in Britain: Evidence from linked employer–employee data. *Labour*, *29*(3), 225–242. doi:10.1111/labr.12054

Haines, V. Y., Marchand, A., & Harvey, S. (2006). Crossover of workplace aggression experiences in dual-earner couples. *Journal of Occupational Health Psychology*, *11*(4), 305–314. doi:10.1037/1076-8998.11.4.305 PMID:17059295

Hajdukova, A., Klementova, J., & Klementova, J. Jr. (2015). The job satisfaction as a regulator of the working behaviour. *Procedia: Social and Behavioral Sciences*, *190*, 471–476. doi:10.1016/j.sbspro.2015.05.028

Hakanen, J. J., Schaufeli, W. B., & Ahola, K. (2008). The Job Demands-Resources model: A three-year cross-lagged study of burnout, depression, commitment, and work engagement. *Work and Stress*, *22*(3), 224–241. doi:10.1080/02678370802379432

Halal, W. E. (1998). *The new management: Democracy and enterprise are transforming organizations*. San Francisco, CA: Berrett-Koehler Publishers, Inc.

Halbesleben, J. R. B., Bowler, W. M., Bolino, M. C., & Turnley, W. H. (2010). Organizational concern, prosocial values, or impression management? How supervisors attribute motives to organizational citizenship behavior. *Journal of Applied Social Psychology*, *40*(6), 1450–1489. doi:10.1111/j.1559-1816.2010.00625.x

Halbesleben, J. R., & Buckley, M. R. (2004). Burnout in organizational life. *Journal of Management*, *30*(6), 859–879. doi:10.1016/j.jm.2004.06.004

Hall, A. C., Boeltzig, H., Hamner, D., Timmons, J. C., & Fesko, S. (2006). *Analysis of Change: A Four Year Longitudinal Study of One-Stop Systems Serving Adults with Disabilities. Report submitted to the Office of Disability and Employment (ODEP)*. U.S. Department of Labor.

Hall, J., & Rosson, P. (2006). The impact of technological turbulence on entrepreneurial behavior, social norms and ethics: Three internet-based cases. *Journal of Business Ethics*, *64*(3), 231–248. doi:10.1007/s10551-005-5354-z

Hall, R. J., & Lord, R. G. (1995). Multi-level information-processing explanations of followers leadership perceptions. *The Leadership Quarterly*, *6*(3), 265–281. doi:10.1016/1048-9843(95)90010-1

Halpern, D. F. (2005). How time-flexible work policies can reduce stress, improve health, and save money. *Stress and Health*, *21*(3), 157–168. doi:10.1002/smi.1049

Hambley, L. A., ONeill, T. A., & Kline, T. J. B. (2007). Virtual Team Leadership: Perspectives From the Field. *International Journal of e-Collaboration*, *3*(1), 40–64. doi:10.4018/jec.2007010103

Hannafey, F. T. (2003). Entrepreneurship and ethics: A literature review. *Journal of Business Ethics*, *46*(2), 99–110. doi:10.1023/A:1025054220365

Hanrahan, N. P., Aiken, L. H., McClaine, L., & Hanlon, A. L. (2010). Relationship between psychiatric nurse work environments and nurse burnout in acute care general hospitals. *Issues in Mental Health Nursing*, *31*(3), 198–207. doi:10.3109/01612840903200068 PMID:20144031

Hansen, M. T., Mors, M. L., & Løvås, B. (2005). Knowledge sharing in organizations: Multiple networks, multiple phases. *Academy of Management Journal*, *48*(5), 776–793. doi:10.5465/AMJ.2005.18803922

Hanvold, T. N., Wærsted, M., Mengshoel, A. M., Bjertness, E., & Veiersted, K. B. (2015). Work with prolonged arm elevation as a risk factor for shoulder pain: A longitudinal study among young adults. *Applied Ergonomics*, *47*, 43–51. doi:10.1016/j.apergo.2014.08.019 PMID:25479973

Happiness Research Institute (2015). Job satisfaction index 2015: What drives job satisfaction?

Hara, N., & Kling, R. (2000). Students distress with a web-based distance education course: An ethnographic study of participants experiences. *Information Communication and Society*, *3*(4), 557–579. doi:10.1080/13691180010002297

Hare, R. (1986). *The social construction of emotions*. New York: Basil Blackwell.

Harika, V. (2010). *Theories of Labour Welfare*. Retrieved from http://www.scribd.com/doc/52987735/2/THEORIES-OF-LABOURWELFARE

Harker, L., & Keltner, D. (2001). Expressions of positive emotion in womens college yearbook pictures and their relationship to personality and life outcomes across adulthood. *Journal of Personality and Social Psychology, 80*(1), 112–124. doi:10.1037/0022-3514.80.1.112 PMID:11195884

Harrell, A., & Wright, A. (1990). Empirical Evidence on the Validity and Reliability of Behaviourally Anchored Rating Scales for Auditors. *A Journal of Practice & Theory, 9*(3), 134-149.

Harrell, K. (2003). *Attitude is everything*. New York: Harper Business.

Harris, C. (1988). A Comparison of Employee Attitude Toward Two Performance Appraisal Systems. *Public Personnel Management, 17*(4), 443–456. doi:10.1177/009102608801700408

Harris, J. D., Sapienza, H. J., & Bowie, N. E. (2009). Ethics and entrepreneurship. *Journal of Business Venturing, 24*(5), 407–418. doi:10.1016/j.jbusvent.2009.06.001

Harris, K. J., Kacmar, K. M., & Zivnuska, S. (2007). An investigation of abusive supervision as a predictor of performance and the meaning of work as a moderator of the relationship. *The Leadership Quarterly, 18*(3), 252–263. doi:10.1016/j.leaqua.2007.03.007

Harris, L., & Cronen, V. E. (1979). A rules-based model for the analysis and evaluation of organizational communication. *Communication Quarterly, 27*(1), 12–28. doi:10.1080/01463377909369320

Härtel, C. E. J. (1993). Rating Format Research Revisited: Format Effectiveness and Acceptability depend on Rater Characteristics. *The Journal of Applied Psychology, 78*(2), 212–217. doi:10.1037/0021-9010.78.2.212

Hartley, L. R., Arnold, P. K., Smythe, G., & Hansen, J. (1994). Indicators of fatigue in truck drivers. *Applied Ergonomics, 25*(3), 143–156. doi:10.1016/0003-6870(94)90012-4 PMID:15676962

Harvey, M. G. (1989). Repatriation of corporate executives: An empirical study. *Journal of International Business Studies, 20*(1), 131–144. doi:10.1057/palgrave.jibs.8490355

Harvey, M., & Novicevic, M. M. (2006). The evolution from repatriation of managers in MNEs to "patriation" in global organizations. In G. K. Stahl & I. Björkman (Eds.), *Handbook of research in international human resource management* (pp. 323–343). Cheltenham, UK: Edward Elgar. doi:10.4337/9781845428235.00024

Harvey, P., Stoner, J., Hochwarter, W., & Kacmar, C. (2007). Coping with abusive supervision: The neutralizing effects of ingratiation and positive affect on negative employee outcomes. *The Leadership Quarterly, 18*(3), 264–280. doi:10.1016/j.leaqua.2007.03.008

Harville, D. L. (1992). Person/Job fit model of communication apprehension in organizations. *Management Communication Quarterly, 6*(2), 150–165. doi:10.1177/0893318992006002002

Hashim, R. (2015). Levels of job satisfaction among engineers in a Malaysian local organization. *Procedia: Social and Behavioral Sciences, 195*, 175–181. doi:10.1016/j.sbspro.2015.06.430

Hatala, J. P. (2006). Social network analysis in human resource development: A new methodology. *Human Resource Development Review, 5*(1), 45–71. doi:10.1177/1534484305284318

Hatch, M. J., & Schultz, M. (2007). Relations between Organizational Culture, Identity and Image. *European Journal of Marketing, 31*(5/6).

Hauff, S., Richter, N. F., & Tressin, T. (2015). Situational job characteristics and job satisfaction: The moderating role of national culture. *International Business Review, 24*(4), 710–723. doi:10.1016/j.ibusrev.2015.01.003

Havig, A. K., Skogstad, A., Veenstra, M., & Romoren, T. I. (2011). The effects of leadership and ward factors on job satisfaction in nursing homes: A multilevel approach. *Journal of Clinical Nursing*, *20*(23/24), 3532–3542. doi:10.1111/j.1365-2702.2011.03697.x PMID:21564362

Hayek, F. A. (1945). The use of knowledge in society. *The American Economic Review*, *35*(4), 519–530.

Hayes, B., Bonner, A., & Pryor, J. (2010). Factors contributing to nurse job satisfaction in the acute hospital setting: A review of recent literature. *Journal of Nursing Management*, *18*(7), 804–814. doi:10.1111/j.1365-2834.2010.01131.x PMID:20946216

Hayes, B., Douglas, C., & Bonner, A. (2015). Work environment, job satisfaction, stress and burnout among haemodialysis nurses. *Journal of Nursing Management*, *23*(5), 588–598. doi:10.1111/jonm.12184 PMID:24372699

Hayton, J. C., George, G., & Zahra, S. A. (2002). National culture and entrepreneurship: A review of behavioral research. *Entrepreneurship Theory and Practice*, *26*(4), 33.

Hébert, R. F., & Link, A. N. (1988). *The entrepreneur: Mainstream views & radical critiques*. New York: Praeger Publishers.

Hedberg, B. L. T. (1981). How organizations learn and unlearn. In P. C. Nystrom & W. H. Starbuck (Eds.), *Handbook of organizational design* (pp. 3–27). Oxford: Oxford University Press.

Heffernan, M., Quinn Griffin, M. T., McNulty, S. R., & Fitzpatrick, J. J. (2010). Self-compassion and emotional intelligence in nurses. *International Journal of Nursing Practice*, *16*(4), 366–373. doi:10.1111/j.1440-172X.2010.01853.x PMID:20649668

Henriksen, K., & Dayton, E. (2006). Organizational silence and hidden threats to patient safety. *Health Services Research*, *41*(4), 1539–1554. doi:10.1111/j.1475-6773.2006.00564.x PMID:16898978

Hentschel, U., Bijleveld, C. C., Kiessling, M., & Hosemann, A. (1993). Stress-related psychophysiological reactions of truck drivers in relation to anxiety, defense, and situational factors. *Accident; Analysis and Prevention*, *25*(2), 115–121. doi:10.1016/0001-4575(93)90050-7 PMID:8471109

Hernandez, M. R., & Iyengar, S. S. (2001). What drives whom? A cultural perspective on human agency. *Social Cognition*, *19*(3), 269–294. doi:10.1521/soco.19.3.269.21468

Hershcovis, M. S., Reich, T. C., & Niven, K. (2015). *Workplace bullying: Causes, consequences, and intervention strategies*. White Paper prepared by the International Affairs Committee of the Society for Industrial and Organizational Psychology. Bowling Green, OH: SIOP. Retrieved from http://www.siop.org/WhitePapers/WorkplaceBullyingFINAL.pdf

Hershcovis, M. S. (2011). Incivility, social undermining, bullying…Oh my! A call to reconcile constructs within workplace aggression research. *Journal of Organizational Behavior*, *32*(3), 499–519. doi:10.1002/job.689

Hershcovis, M. S., & Barling, J. (2010). Towards a multi-foci approach to workplace aggression: A meta-analytic review of outcomes from different perpetrators. *Journal of Organizational Behavior*, *31*(1), 24–44. doi:10.1002/job.621

Hershcovis, M. S., & Rafferty, A. (2012). Predicting abusive supervision. In J. Houdmont, S. Leka, & R. Sinclair (Eds.), *Contemporary occupational health psychology: Global perspectives on research and practice* (Vol. 2, pp. 92–108). Chichester, UK: Wiley-Blackwell. doi:10.1002/9781119942849.ch6

Hershcovis, M. S., & Reich, T. C. (2013). Integrating workplace aggression research: Relational, contextual, and method considerations. *Journal of Organizational Behavior*, *34*(S1), 26–42. doi:10.1002/job.1886

Herzberg, F. (1966). *Work and the Nature of Man*. Cleveland, OH: World Publishing.

Herzberg, F., Mausner, B., & Snyderman, B. B. (1959). *The motivation to work*. New York: John Wiley & Sons.

Compilation of References

Hesketh, A. (2014). *Managing the value of your talent. A new framework for human capital measurement, Valuing your Talent - Research report July*. London: Chartered Institute of Personnel and Development. Retrieved from www.valuingyourtalent.co.uk

Hewlett, S. A., Marshall, M., & Sherbin, L. (2011). The relationship you need to get right. *Harvard Business Review*, *89*(10), 131–134.

Heydari, A., Kareshki, H., & Armat, M. R. (2016). Is nurses professional competence related to their personality and emotional intelligence? A cross-sectional study. *Journal of Caring Sciences*, *5*(2), 121–132. doi:10.15171/jcs.2016.013 PMID:27354976

Hieker, C., & Rushby, M. (2016, February 11). *How mentor supervision can give you the best mentors*. Retrieved from https://www.trainingjournal.com/articles/feature/how-mentor-supervision-can-give-you-best-mentors

Hieronimus, F., Schaefer, K., & Schroeder, J. (2005). Using branding to attract talent. *The McKinsey Quarterly*, *3*.

Hignett, S., & McAtamney, L. (2000). Rapid entire body assessment (REBA). *Applied Ergonomics*, *31*(2), 201–205. doi:10.1016/S0003-6870(99)00039-3 PMID:10711982

Hilgerman, R. H. (1988). Communication satisfaction, goal setting, job satisfaction, concertive control, and effectiveness in self-managed teams. Unpublished doctoral dissertation, University of Maine.

Hill, N. S. (2005). Leading Together, Working Together: The Role of Team Shared Leadership in Building Collaborative Capital in Virtual Teams. In *Advances in Interdisciplinary Studies of Work Teams* (Vol. 11, pp. 183–209). Bingley: Emerald. Retrieved from http://www.emeraldinsight.com/10.1016/S1572-0977(05)11007-3

Hill, C. W. L., & Jones, G. R. (2004). *Strategic management theory: An integrated approach* (6th ed.). Boston: Houghton Mifflin Company.

Hiller, N. J., & Hambrick, D. C. (2005). Conceptualizing executive hubris: The role of (hyper-) core self-evaluations in strategic decision making. *Strategic Management Journal*, *26*(4), 297–319. doi:10.1002/smj.455

Hill, J. D., & Boyle, L. N. (2007). Driver stress as influenced by driving maneuvers and roadway conditions. *Transportation Research Part F: Traffic Psychology and Behaviour*, *10*(3), 177–186. doi:10.1016/j.trf.2006.09.002

Hinds, P. J., Neeley, T. B., & Cramton, C. D. (2014). Language as a lightning rod: Power contests, emotion regulation, and subgroup dynamics in global teams. *Journal of International Business Studies*, *45*(5), 536–561. doi:10.1057/jibs.2013.62

Hirano, T., Matsumoto, K., & Nose, K. (2004). *Universal design for workplace. Fujitsu Scientific & Technical Journal*, *41*(1), 97-104. Retrieved from http://www.fujitsu.com/global/documents/about/resources/publications/fstj/archives/vol41-1/paper13.pdf

HistoryWorld. (N.Y.). (n. d.). *History of language*. Retrieved from http://www.historyworld.net/wrldhis/PlainTextHistories.asp?historyid=ab13

Hobfoll, S. E. (1989). Conservation of resources: A new attempt at conceptualizing stress. *The American Psychologist*, *44*(3), 513–524. doi:10.1037/0003-066X.44.3.513 PMID:2648906

Hoch, J. E., & Kozlowski, S. W. J. (2014). Leading virtual teams: Hierarchical leadership, structural supports, and shared team leadership. *The Journal of Applied Psychology*, *99*(3), 390–403. doi:10.1037/a0030264 PMID:23205494

Hochschild, A. R. (1979). Emotion work, feeling rules, and social structure. *American Journal of Sociology*, *85*(3), 551–575. doi:10.1086/227049

Hochschild, A. R. (1983). *The managed heart: Commercialization of human feeling*. Berkeley: University of California Press.

Hockerts, K. (2006). Entrepreneurial opportunity in social purpose ventures. In J. Mair, J. Robinson, & K. Hockerts (Eds.), *Social entrepreneurship* (pp. 142–154). London, UK: Palgrave. doi:10.1057/9780230625655_10

Hoegl, M., & Gemuenden, H. G. (2001). Teamwork quality and the success of innovative projects: A theoretical concept and empirical evidence. *Organization Science*, *12*(4), 435–449. doi:10.1287/orsc.12.4.435.10635

Hoel, H., & Cooper, C. L. (2000). *Destructive conflict and bullying at work*. Unpublished report, Manchester School of Management, University of Manchester Institute of Science and Technology, UK.

Hofstede, G. (1991). *Cultures and Organizations - Software of the mind*. London: McGraw-Hill Book Company.

Hofstede, G. (2001). *Culture's consequences: Comparing values, behaviors, institutions, and organizations across nations* (2nd ed.). London, UK: Sage.

Hogan, R. L., & McKnight, M. A. (2007). Exploring burnout among university online instructors: An initial investigation. *The Internet and Higher Education*, *10*(2), 117–124. doi:10.1016/j.iheduc.2007.03.001

Ho, K. L. (1999). Bureaucratic Accountability in Malaysia: Control Mechanisms and Critical Concerns. In H.-K. Wong & H. S. Chan (Eds.), *The Handbook of Comparative Public Administration in the Asia-Pacific Basin* (pp. 23–45). New York: Marcel Dekker.

Holladay, S. J., & Coombs, W. T. (1993). Communication visions: An exploration of the role of delivery in the creation of leader charisma. *Management Communication Quarterly*, *6*(4), 405–427. doi:10.1177/0893318993006004003

Holland, C. P., & Lockett, A. G. (1997). Mixed mode network structures: The strategic use of electronic communication by organizations. *Organization Science*, *8*(5), 475–488. doi:10.1287/orsc.8.5.475

Holmberg, I., & Akerblom, S. (2008). Primus inter pares: Leadership and culture in Sweden. In J. S. Chhokar, F. C. Brodbeck, & R. J. House (Eds.), *Culture and leadership across the world: The GLOBE book of in-depth studies of 25 societies* (pp. 33–74). New York: Erlbaum.

Hom, P., Katerberg, R., & Hulin, C. (1979). Comparative examination of three approaches to the prediction of turnover. *The Journal of Applied Psychology*, *64*(3), 280–290. doi:10.1037/0021-9010.64.3.280

Hong, E., & Lee, Y. S. (2016). The mediating effect of emotional intelligence between emotional labour, job stress, burnout and nurses turnover intention. *International Journal of Nursing Practice*, *22*(6), 625–632. doi:10.1111/ijn.12493 PMID:27653752

Hooker, T. (2013). Peer coaching: A review of the literature. *Waikato Journal of Education*, *18*(2). doi:10.15663/wje.v18i2.166

Hooper, C., Craig, J., Janvrin, D. R., Wetsel, M. A., & Reimels, E. (2010). Compassion satisfaction, burnout, and compassion fatigue among emergency nurses compared with nurses in other selected inpatient specialties. *Journal of Emergency Nursing: JEN*, *36*(5), 420–427. doi:10.1016/j.jen.2009.11.027 PMID:20837210

Hopkins, R. R. (1955). *Handbook of Industrial Welfare*. Lincoln, UK: Sir Isaac Pitman & Sons.

Hornby, A. S., Turnbull, J., Lea, D., Parkinson, D., Phillips, P., Francis, B., & Ashby, M. et al. (Eds.). (2010). *Oxford advanced learner's dictionary of current English* (8th ed.). Oxford: Oxford University Press.

Horowitz, C. R., Suchman, A. L., Branch, W. T., & Frankel, R. M. (2003). What do doctors find meaningful about their work? *Annals of Internal Medicine*, *138*(9), 772–775. doi:10.7326/0003-4819-138-9-200305060-00028 PMID:12729445

Compilation of References

Horwitz, S. K., & Horwitz, I. B. (2007). The effects of team diversity on team outcomes: A meta-analytic review of team demography. *Journal of Management, 33*(6), 987–1015. doi:10.1177/0149206307308587

Hoskisson, R. E., Eden, L., Lau, C. M., & Wright, M. (2000). Strategy in emerging economies. *Academy of Management Journal, 43*(3), 249–267. doi:10.2307/1556394

House, R. J. (1996). Path-goal theory of leadership: Lessons, legacy and a reformulated theory. *The Leadership Quarterly, 7*(3), 323–352. doi:10.1016/S1048-9843(96)90024-7

Howard, M. C. (2009). Emotional intelligence as a predictor of job satisfaction, organizational commitment, and occupational commitment among human service workers. *Dissertation Abstracts International, 69*(12B), 7842.

Howells, J. R. (2002). Tacit knowledge, innovation and economic geography. *Urban Studies (Edinburgh, Scotland), 39*(5-6), 871–884. doi:10.1080/00420980220128354

Howe-Walsh, L. (2013). Repatriation: Furthering the research agenda through the lens of commitment, uncertainty reduction and social cognitive career theories. *International Journal of Business and Management, 8*(16), 1–10. doi:10.5539/ijbm.v8n16p1

Hoyle, E. (1999). The two faces of micropolitics. *School Leadership & Management, 19*(2), 213–222. doi:10.1080/13632439969249

Hsiung, H. H., Lin, C. W., & Lin, C. S. (2012). Nourishing or suppressing? The contradictory influences of perception of organizational politics on organizational citizenship behaviour. *Journal of Occupational and Organizational Psychology, 85*(2), 258–276. doi:10.1111/j.2044-8325.2011.02030.x

Huang, Q., & Gamble, J. (2015). Social expectations, gender and job satisfaction: Front-line employees in China's retail sector. *Human Resource Management Journal, 25*(3), 331–347. doi:10.1111/1748-8583.12066

Hua, W., & Omar, B. (2016). Examining communication satisfaction, Confucian work dynamism and job satisfaction: A comparative study of international and domestic hotels in Hainan, China. *The Journal of the South East Asia Research Centre for Communications and Humanities, 8*(1), 105–127.

Huber, G. P. (1991). Organizational learning: The contributing processes and the literatures. *Organization Science, 2*(1), 88–115. doi:10.1287/orsc.2.1.88

Huber, G. P., & Daft, R. L. (1987). The information environments of organizations. In F. M. Jablin, L. L. Putnam, K. H. Roberts, & L. W. Porter (Eds.), *Handbook of organizational communication: An interdisciplinary perspective* (pp. 130–164). Thousand Oaks, CA: Sage.

Huggins, R., Johnston, A., & Thompson, P. (2012). Network capital, social capital and knowledge flow: How the nature of inter-organizational networks impacts on innovation. *Industry and Innovation, 19*(3), 203–232. doi:10.1080/13662716.2012.669615

Humphrey, R. (2015). The influence of leader emotional intelligence on employees' job satisfaction: a meta-analysis. *Proceedings of the International Leadership Association 17th Annual Global Conference*.

Humphrey, R. H. (2002). The many faces of emotional leadership. *The Leadership Quarterly, 13*(5), 493–504. doi:10.1016/S1048-9843(02)00140-6

Humphrey, R. H. (2008). The right way to lead with emotional labor. In R. H. Humphrey (Ed.), *Affect and emotion: New directions in management theory and research* (pp. 1–17). Charlotte, NC: Information Age Publishing.

Humphrey, R. H., Ashforth, B. E., & Diefendorff, J. M. (2015). The bright side of emotional labor. *Journal of Organizational Behavior*, *36*(6), 749–769. doi:10.1002/job.2019

Humphrey, R. H., Burch, G. F., & Adams, L. L. (2016). The benefits of merging leadership research and emotions research. *Frontiers in Psychology*, 7. PMID:27458415

Hunt, S. D., & Vitell, S. J. (2006). The general theory of marketing ethics: A revision and three questions. *Journal of Macromarketing*, *26*(2), 143–153. doi:10.1177/0276146706290923

Hurrell, J., Nelson, D., & Simmons, B. (1998). Measuring job stressors and strains: Where we have been, where we are, and where we need to go. *Journal of Professional Health Psychology*, *3*, 368–389. PMID:9805282

Hyde, A. (1982). Performance Appraisal in the Post Reform Era. *Public Personnel Management*, *11*(4), 294–305. doi:10.1177/009102608201100402

Ibarra, H. (2015, March 30). *Women are Over-Mentored (but under-sponsored)*. Retrieved from https://hbr.org/2010/08/women-are-over-mentored-but-un/

Ibarra, H., & Hansen, M. (2011). Are you a collaborative leader? *Harvard Business Review*, *89*(7/8), 68–74. PMID:21800471

Ibarra, H., & Hunter, M. (2007). How leaders create and use networks. *Harvard Business Review*, *85*(1), 40–47. PMID:17286073

Ibarra, H., & Obodaru, O. (2009). Women and the vision thing. *Harvard Business Review*, *87*(1), 62–70. PMID:19227409

ICF. (2016). *Coaching supervision - individual Credentialing*. Retrieved from http://coachfederation.org/credential/landing.cfm?ItemNumber=4259&_ga=1.232862494.1633684418.1466783891

Ichniowski, C., Kochan, T. A., Levine, D., Olson, C., & Strauss, G. (1996). What works at work: Overview and Assessment. *Industrial Relations*, *35*(3), 299–333. doi:10.1111/j.1468-232X.1996.tb00409.x

Ilies, R., Nahrgang, J. D., & Morgeson, F. P. (2007). Leader-member exchange and citizenship behaviors: A meta-analysis. *The Journal of Applied Psychology*, *92*(1), 269–277. doi:10.1037/0021-9010.92.1.269 PMID:17227168

ILO. (1942). *Approach to Social Security: An International Survey*. Geneva: International Labour Organisation.

ILO. (1963). Labour laws and legislation. *Proceedings of the Asian Regional Conference of International Labour Organisation*.

Ilozor, D. B., Ilozor, B. D., & Carr, J. (2001). Management communication strategies determine job satisfaction in telecommuting. *Journal of Management Development*, *20*(6), 495–507. doi:10.1108/02621710110399783

Im Kim, Y., Geun, H. G., Choi, S., & Lee, Y. S. (2016). The impact of organizational commitment and nursing organizational culture on job satisfaction in Korean American registered nurses. *Journal of Transcultural Nursing*.

Inkpen, A. C., & Tsang, E. W. (2005). Social capital, networks, and knowledge transfer. *Academy of Management Review*, *30*(1), 146–165. doi:10.5465/AMR.2005.15281445

Innis, R. E. (1986). *Semiotics: An introductory reader*. London: Hutchinson.

Ioannou, I., & Serafeim, G. (2012). What drives corporate social performance quest: The role of nation-level institutions. *Journal of International Business Studies*, *43*(9), 834–864. doi:10.1057/jibs.2012.26

Ioannou, P., Katsikavali, V., Galanis, P., Velonakis, E., Papadatou, D., & Sourtzi, P. (2015). Impact of job satisfaction on Greek nurses' health-related quality of life. *Safety and Health at Work*, *6*(4), 324–328. doi:10.1016/j.shaw.2015.07.010 PMID:26929845

Compilation of References

Iqbal, F., & Abbasi, F. (2013). Relationship between emotional intelligence and job burnout among universities professors. *Journal of Psychology, 2*(2), 219-229. Retrieved from http://www.ajssh.leena-luna.co.jp/AJSSHPDFs/Vol.2(2)/AJSSH2013 (2.2-24).pdf

Ironson, G. H., Smith, P. C., Brannick, M. T., Gibson, W. M., & Paul, K. B. (1989). Construction of a job in general scale: A comparison of global, composite, and specific measures. *The Journal of Applied Psychology, 74*(2), 193–200. doi:10.1037/0021-9010.74.2.193

Isa, M. (2000). *Joseino kikoku tekio mondaino kenkyu: Ibunka juyo to kikoku tekio mondaino jisshoteki kenkyu* [Readjustment issues among female returnees: Empirical study of acceptance of different cultures and readjustment issues]. Tokyo, Japan: Taga Shuppan.

Iseman, M. (2012). *Top ten countries with which the U.S. trades*. United States Census Bureau.

Ismail, A., Mohd Sani, R., & Mohamad, M. H. (2014). Communication openness in performance appraisal systems enhancing job satisfaction. *Journal of Public Administration. Finance and Law, 5*, 98–109.

Isogai, T. Y., Hayashi, Y., & Uno, M. (1999). Identity issues and reentry training. *International Journal of Intercultural Relations, 23*(3), 493–525. doi:10.1016/S0147-1767(99)00007-3

Iyer, B., & Murphy, W. (2016, April 26). *The benefits of virtual mentors*. Retrieved from https://hbr.org/2016/04/the-benefits-of-virtual-mentors

Iyer, S., & Israel, D. (2012). Structural equation modeling for testing the impact of organization communication satisfaction on employee engagement. *South Asian Journal of Management, 19*(1), 51–81.

Jackson, G., & Apostolakou, A. (2010). Corporate social responsibility in Western Europe: An institutional mirror or substitute? *Journal of Business Ethics, 94*(3), 371–394. doi:10.1007/s10551-009-0269-8

Jackson, S. E., Joshi, A., & Erhardt, N. L. (2003). Recent Research on Team and Organizational Diversity: SWOT Analysis and Implications. *Journal of Management, 29*(6), 801–830. doi:10.1016/S0149-2063(03)00080-1

Jackson, S. E., Schwab, R. L., & Schuler, R. S. (1986). Toward an understanding of the burnout phenomenon. *The Journal of Applied Psychology, 71*(4), 630–640. doi:10.1037/0021-9010.71.4.630 PMID:3804935

Jackson, S. E., Stone, V. K., & Alvarez, E. B. (1992). Socialization amidst diversity — the impact of demographics on work team oldtimers and newcomers. *Research in Organizational Behavior, 15*, 45–109.

Jackson, S., & Schuler, R. (2002). *Managing Human Resources through Strategic Partnership* (8th ed.). Toronto: Thompson.

Jacobson, K. J. L., Hood, J. N., & Van Buren, H. J. III. (2014). Workplace bullying across cultures: A research agenda. *International Journal of Cross Cultural Management, 14*(1), 47–65. doi:10.1177/1470595813494192

Jacobs, R., Kafry, D., & Zedeck, S. (1980). Expectations of behaviorally anchored rating scales. *Personnel Psychology, 33*(3), 595–640. doi:10.1111/j.1744-6570.1980.tb00486.x

Jadoo, S. A. A., Aljunid, S. M., Dastan, I., Tawfeeq, R. S., Mustafa, M. A., Ganasegeran, K., & AlDubai, S. A. R. (2015). Job satisfaction and turnover intention among Iraqi doctors-a descriptive cross-sectional multicentre study. *Human Resources for Health, 13*(1), 1. PMID:25588887

Jamali, D., Sidani, Y., & El-Asmar, K. (2009). A three country comparative analysis of managerial CSR perspectives: Insights from Lebanon, Syria and Jordan. *Journal of Business Ethics, 85*(2), 173–192. doi:10.1007/s10551-008-9755-7

Jang, H. M., Park, J. Y., Choi, Y. J., Park, S. W., & Lim, H. N. (2016). Effect of general hospital nurses perception of patient safety culture and burnout on safety management activities. *Journal of Korean Academy of Nursing Administration*, *22*(3), 239–250. doi:10.11111/jkana.2016.22.3.239

Jansen, K. J., & Kristof-Brown, A. (2006). Toward a multidimensional theory of person-environment fit. *Journal of Managerial Issues*, *18*(2), 193–212.

Japan Organization for Employment of the Elderly, Persons with Disabilities and Job Seekers (2013). *Workplace improvement enthusiast casebook about the correspondence to the career up of the persons with disabilities and an age-related problem*. Retrieved from http://www.jeed.or.jp/disability/data/handbook/ca_ls/h24_kaizen_jirei.html

Japan Organization for Employment of the Elderly. Persons with Disabilities and Job Seekers (2009). *Workplace improvement enthusiast casebook for hearing persons with a disability*. Retrieved from: http://www.jeed.or.jp/disability/data/handbook/ca_ls/h20_kaizen_jirei.html

Japanese Ministry of Education, Culture, Science and Technology. (2012). Retrieved from www.mext.go.jp/b_menu/shingi/008/toushin/030301/02.htm

Jarvenpaa, S. L., & Leidner, D. E. (1999). Communication and trust in global virtual teams. *Organization Science*, *10*(6), 791–815. doi:10.1287/orsc.10.6.791

Javidan, M., House, R. J., Dorfman, P. W., Hanges, P. J., & De Luque, M. S. (2006). Conceptualizing and measuring cultures and their consequences: A comparative review of GLOBEs and Hofstedes approaches. *Journal of International Business Studies*, *37*(6), 897–914. doi:10.1057/palgrave.jibs.8400234

Jawahar, I. M. (2012). Mediating role of satisfaction with growth opportunities on the relationship between employee development opportunities and citizenship behaviors and burnout. *Journal of Applied Social Psychology*, *42*(9), 2257–2284. doi:10.1111/j.1559-1816.2012.00939.x

Jelley, R. B., & Goffin, R. D. (2001). Can Performance-Feedback Accuracy Be Improved? Effects of Rater Priming and Rating Scale Format on Rating Accuracy. *The Journal of Applied Psychology*, *86*(1), 134–144. doi:10.1037/0021-9010.86.1.134 PMID:11302225

Jena, R. K., & Goswami, R. (2013). Exploring the relationship between organizational citizenship behavior and job satisfaction among shift workers in India. *Global Business and Organizational Excellence*, *32*(6), 36–46. doi:10.1002/joe.21513

Jenkins, M. F., Winefield, H., & Sarris, A. (2010). Listening to the bullies: An exploratory study of managers accused of workplace bullying. *Paper presented at the 7th International Conference on Workplace Bullying*, Cardiff, Wales.

Jenkins, G. D., Nadler, D. A., Lawler, E. E. III, & Cammann, C. (1975). Standardized observation: An approach to measuring the nature of jobs. *The Journal of Applied Psychology*, *60*(2), 171–181. doi:10.1037/h0076541

Jenner, S. J., & Taylor, S. (2008). *Employer Branding – Fad or the Future of HR? Research insight*. London: Chartered Institute of Personnel and Development.

Jex, S. M. (1998). *Stress and job performance: Theory, research, and implications for managerial practice*. Thousand Oaks, CA: Sage.

Jian, Z., Kwan, H. K., Qiu, Q., Liu, Z. Q., & Yim, F. H. K. (2012). Abusive supervision and frontline employees' service performance. *Service Industries Journal*, *32*(5), 683–698. doi:10.1080/02642069.2011.614338

Jick, T. D. (1979). Mixing qualitative and quantitative methods: Triangulation in action. *Administrative Science Quarterly*, *24*(4), 602–611. doi:10.2307/2392366

Compilation of References

Jiménez-Jiménez, D., & Sanz-Valle, R. (2011). Innovation, organizational learning, and performance. *Journal of Business Research*, *64*(4), 408–417. doi:10.1016/j.jbusres.2010.09.010

Johari Window. (2016). In *Wikipedia*. Retrieved from https://en.wikipedia.org/wiki/Johari_window

John, C. P. (2004). *Social Security and Labour Welfare with Special Reference to Construction Workers in Kerala*. Kerala Research Programme on Local Level Development, Centre for Development Studies, Thiruvananthapuram.

Johns, G. (2006). The essential impact of context on organizational behaviour. *Academy of Management Review*, *31*(2), 386–408. doi:10.5465/AMR.2006.20208687

Johnson, G. H. (1955). An instrument for the measurement of job satisfaction. *Personnel Psychology: The Study of People at Work*, *8*(1), 27–37. doi:10.1111/j.1744-6570.1955.tb01185.x

Johnson, J. V., & Hall, E. M. (1988). Job strain, work place social support, and cardiovascular disease: A cross-sectional study of a random sample of the Swedish working population. *American Journal of Public Health*, *78*(10), 1336–1342. doi:10.2105/AJPH.78.10.1336 PMID:3421392

Johnson, S., Cooper, C., Cartwright, S., Taylor, I., Taylor, P., & Millet, C. (2005). The experience of work-related stress across occupations. *Journal of Managerial Psychology*, *20*(2), 178–187. doi:10.1108/02683940510579803

Johnson, W. B., & Packer, A. E. (1987). *Workforce 2000: Work and workers for the 21st century*. Indianapolis: Hudson Institute.

Jokinen, T., Brewster, C., & Suutari, V. (2008). Career capital during international work experiences: Contrasting self-initiated expatriate experiences and assigned expatriation. *International Journal of Human Resource Management*, *19*(6), 979–998. doi:10.1080/09585190802051279

Jones, E. A. (2014). *Employees' perceptions of supervisor communication and job stress in the work environment* [Doctoral dissertation].

Jones, M. A. (2002). Deafness as culture: A psychosocial perspective. *Disability Studies Quarterly*, *22*(2), 51–60. doi:10.18061/dsq.v22i2.344

Jones, M. T. (1999). The institutional determinants of social responsibility. *Journal of Business Ethics*, *20*(2), 163–170. doi:10.1023/A:1005871021412

Jones, M. V., Coviello, N., & Tang, Y. K. (2011). International entrepreneurship research (1989–2009): A domain ontology and thematic analysis. *Journal of Business Venturing*, *26*(6), 632–659. doi:10.1016/j.jbusvent.2011.04.001

Jones, P. M. (2001). Collaborative knowledge management, social networks, and organizational learning. *Systems. Social and Internationalization Design Aspects of Human-Computer Interaction*, *2*, 306–309.

Joseph, B., Injodey, J., & Varghese, R. (2009). Labour Welfare in India. *Journal of Workplace Behavioral Health*, *24*(1-2), 221–242. doi:10.1080/15555240902849131

Joseph, B., Injodey, J., & Varghese, R. (2013). Labour Welfare in India. In P. A. Kurzman & R. Paul Maiden (Eds.), *Union Contributions to Labor Welfare Policy and Practice: Past, Present and Future* (pp. 225–246). New York: Routledge.

Joseph, T. D. (2013). Work related stress. *European Journal of Business and Social Sciences*, *1*(10), 73–80.

Joyner, B. E., & Payne, D. (2002). Evolution and implementation: A study of values, business ethics and corporate social responsibility. *Journal of Business Ethics*, *41*(4), 297–311. doi:10.1023/A:1021237420663

Judge, T. A., Locke, E. A., & Durham, C. C. (1997). The dispositional causes of job satisfaction: A core evaluations approach. *Research in Organizational Behavior, 19*, 151–188.

Judge, T. A., Thoresen, C. J., Bono, J. E., & Patton, G. K. (2001). The job satisfaction–job performance relationship: A qualitative and quantitative review. *Psychological Bulletin, 127*(3), 376–407. doi:10.1037/0033-2909.127.3.376 PMID:11393302

Kaasa, A. (2011). Work values in European countries: Empirical evidence and explanations. *Review of International Comparative Management, 12*(5), 852–862.

Kafetsios, K. (2003). Emotional Intelligence abilities: Theory and application in occupational settings. *Greek Business Academy, 2*, 16–25.

Kafetsios, K., Anagnostopoulos, F., Lempesis, E., & Valindra, A. (2014). Doctors emotion regulation and patient satisfaction: A social-functional perspective. *Health Communication, 29*(2), 205–214. doi:10.1080/10410236.2012.7381 50 PMID:23537402

Kafetsios, K., Athanasiadou, M., & Dimou, N. (2014). Leaders and subordinates attachment orientations, emotion regulation capabilities and affect at work: A multilevel analysis. *The Leadership Quarterly, 25*(3), 512–527. doi:10.1016/j.leaqua.2013.11.010

Kafetsios, K., & Loumakou, M. (2007). A comparative evaluation of the effects of trait emotional intelligence and emotion regulation on affect at work and job satisfaction. *International Journal of Work Organization and Emotion, 2*(1), 71–87. doi:10.1504/IJWOE.2007.013616

Kafetsios, K., Nezlek, J. B., & Vassilakou, Th. (2012). Relationships between leaders and subordinates emotion regulation, satisfaction and affect at work. *The Journal of Social Psychology, 152*(4), 436–457. doi:10.1080/00224545.2011.632788 PMID:22822684

Kafetsios, K., Nezlek, J. B., & Vassiou, K. (2011). A multilevel analysis of relationships between leaders and subordinates emotional intelligence and emotional outcomes. *Journal of Applied Social Psychology, 41*(5), 119–1142. doi:10.1111/j.1559-1816.2011.00750.x

Kafetsios, K., & Zampetakis, L. A. (2008). Emotional intelligence and job satisfaction: Testing the mediatory role of positive and negative affect at work. *Personality and Individual Differences, 44*(3), 710–720. doi:10.1016/j.paid.2007.10.004

Kahneman, D. (2012). *Thinking, fast and slow*. London: Penguin Press/Classics.

Kahraman, N., & Hiçdurmaz, D. (2016). Identifying emotional intelligence skills of Turkish clinical nurses according to sociodemographic and professional variables. *Journal of Clinical Nursing, 25*(7-8), 1006–1015. doi:10.1111/jocn.13122 PMID:26914619

Kalisch, B. J., Lee, H., & Rochman, M. (2010). Nursing staff teamwork and job satisfaction. *Journal of Nursing Management, 18*(8), 938–947. doi:10.1111/j.1365-2834.2010.01153.x PMID:21073567

Kaliski, B. S. (2007). *Encyclopedia of business and finance*. Detroit, MI: Macmillan Reference.

Kalleberg, A. L. (1977). Work values and job rewards: A theory of job satisfaction. *American Sociological Review, 42*(1), 124–143. doi:10.2307/2117735

Kanai-Pak, M., Aiken, L. H., Sloane, D. M., & Poghosyan, L. (2008). Poor work environments and nurse inexperience are associated with burnout, job dissatisfaction and quality deficits in Japanese hospitals. *Journal of Clinical Nursing, 17*(24), 3324–3329. doi:10.1111/j.1365-2702.2008.02639.x PMID:19146591

Kandalaft, M. R., Didehbani, N., Krawczyk, D. C., Allen, T. T., & Chapman, S. B. (2013). Virtual reality social cognition training for young adults with high-functioning autism. *Journal of Autism and Developmental Disorders*, *43*(1), 34–44. doi:10.1007/s10803-012-1544-6 PMID:22570145

Kane, R. E., Magnusen, M. J., & Perrewe, P. L. (2012). Differential effects of identification on extra-role behavior. *Career Development International*, *17*(1), 25–42. doi:10.1108/13620431211201319

Kang, S. C., Morris, S. S., & Snell, S. A. (2007). Relational archetypes, organizational learning, and value creation: Extending the human resource architecture. *Academy of Management Review*, *32*(1), 236–256. doi:10.5465/AMR.2007.23464060

Kankanhalli, A., Tan, B. C. Y., & Wei, K. K. (2007). Conflict and performance in global virtual teams. *Journal of Management Information Systems*, *23*(3), 237–274. doi:10.2753/MIS0742-1222230309

Kanter, R. M. (1983). *The change masters: Innovation & entrepreneurship in the American corporation*. New York: Touchstone.

Kanungo, R. N. (2001). Ethical values of transactional and transformational leaders. *Canadian Journal of Administrative Sciences/Revue Canadienne des Sciences de l'Administration*, *18*(4), 257-265.

Kaplan, D. (1989). Demonstratives. In J. Almog, P. Perry, H. K. Wettstein, & D. Kaplan (Eds.), *Themes from Kaplan* (pp. 481–563). Oxford University Press.

Karadal, H., & Saygin, M. (2013). An investigation of the relationship between social loafing and organizational citizenship behavior. *Procedia: Social and Behavioral Sciences*, *99*, 206–215. doi:10.1016/j.sbspro.2013.10.487

Karanika-Murray, M., Pontes, H. M., Griffiths, M. D., & Biron, C. (2015). Sickness presenteeism determines job satisfaction via affective motivational states. *Social Science & Medicine*, *139*, 100–106. doi:10.1016/j.socscimed.2015.06.035 PMID:26183017

Karasek, R. A. (1979). Job demands, job decisions latitude, and mental strain: Implications for job redesign. *Administrative Science Quarterly*, *24*(2), 285–307. doi:10.2307/2392498

Karasek, R. A., & Theorell, T. (1990). *Healthy work: Stress, productivity and the reconstruction of working life*. New York: Basic Books.

Karatepe, O. M., & Olugbade, O. A. (2009). The effects of job and personal resources on hotel employees' work engagement. *International Journal of Hospitality Management*, *28*(4), 504–512. doi:10.1016/j.ijhm.2009.02.003

Karau, S. J., & Williams, K. D. (1993). Social loafing: A meta-analytic review and theoretical integration. *Journal of Personality and Social Psychology*, *65*(4), 681–706. doi:10.1037/0022-3514.65.4.681

Karhu, O., Kansi, P., & Kuorinka, I. (1977). Correcting working postures in industry: A practical method for analysis. *Applied Ergonomics*, *8*(4), 199–201. doi:10.1016/0003-6870(77)90164-8 PMID:15677243

Karimi, R., Malik, M. I., & Hussain, S. (2011). Examining the relationship of performance appraisal system and employee satisfaction. *International Journal of Business and Social Science*, *2*(22), 243–247.

Karlsson, C., & Acs, Z. J. (2002). Introduction to institutions, entrepreneurship and firm growth: The case of Sweden. *Small Business Economics*, *19*(2), 63–67. doi:10.1023/A:1016202618249

Kasa, M., & Hassan, Z. (2015). The role of flow between burnout and organizational citizenship behavior (OCB) among hotel employees in Malaysia. *Procedia: Social and Behavioral Sciences*, *211*, 199–206. doi:10.1016/j.sbspro.2015.11.084

Kasemsap, K. (2012b). Conceptual framework: A causal model of leadership behavior, perceived organizational support, job satisfaction, and organizational commitment of plastic plant employees in Thailand. *International Journal of Advances in Management, Technology & Engineering Sciences, 2*(3-1), 17–20.

Kasemsap, K. (2012c). Conceptual framework: Determination of causal model of leadership style, leadership behavior, organizational culture, and job satisfaction of petrochemical plant employees in Thailand. *International Journal of Advances in Management, Technology & Engineering Sciences, 2*(3-2), 20–24.

Kasemsap, K. (2013a). *Innovative human resource practice: A unified framework and causal model of psychological empowerment, job satisfaction, organizational citizenship behavior, and organizational performance.* Paper presented at the 2nd International Conference on Humanity, History and Society (ICHHS '13), Bangkok, Thailand.

Kasemsap, K. (2013b). Practical framework: Formation of causal model of job involvement, organizational commitment, organizational citizenship behavior, and organizational performance. *International Journal of Advances in Management, Technology & Engineering Sciences, 2*(6-1), 22–26.

Kasemsap, K. (2013c). Strategic human resource management: A synthesized framework and causal model of job involvement, job satisfaction, knowledge-sharing behavior, and job performance. *International Journal of Advances in Management, Technology & Engineering Sciences, 2*(6-2), 73–77.

Kasemsap, K. (2013d). *Strategic human resource practice: A systematic framework and causal model for job characteristics, rewards and recognition, employee engagement, and job satisfaction.* Paper presented at the 2013 Global Information and Management Symposium (GIAMS '13), Bangkok, Thailand.

Kasemsap, K. (2013e). *Innovative human resource practice: A functional framework and causal model of organizational rewards, organizational justice, perceived organizational support, and job satisfaction.* Paper presented at the 2nd International Conference on Economics, Business Innovation (ICEBI '13), Copenhagen, Denmark.

Kasemsap, K. (2013f). *Strategic human resource practice: A functional framework and causal model of leadership behavior, job satisfaction, organizational commitment, and job performance.* Paper presented at the 2nd International Conference on Global Business Environment: Role of Education and Technology (ICGBE '13), Bangkok, Thailand.

Kasemsap, K. (2012). Factor affecting organizational citizenship behavior of passenger car plant employees in Thailand. *Silpakorn University Journal of Social Sciences, Humanities, and Arts, 12*(2), 129–159.

Kasemsap, K. (2013a). Innovative human resource practice: A synthesized framework and causal model of leader-member exchange, organizational justice, job satisfaction, and organizational citizenship behavior. *International Journal of e-Education, e-Business, e-. Management Learning, 3*(1), 13–17. doi:10.7763/IJEEEE.2013.V3.185

Kasemsap, K. (2014a). The role of knowledge management on job satisfaction: A systematic framework. In B. Tripathy & D. Acharjya (Eds.), *Advances in secure computing, Internet services, and applications* (pp. 104–127). Hershey, PA: IGI Global. doi:10.4018/978-1-4666-4940-8.ch006

Kasemsap, K. (2014b). The role of social capital in higher education institutions. In N. Baporikar (Ed.), *Handbook of research on higher education in the MENA region: Policy and practice* (pp. 119–147). Hershey, PA: IGI Global. doi:10.4018/978-1-4666-6198-1.ch007

Kasemsap, K. (2015). The roles of cross-cultural perspectives in global marketing. In J. Alcántara-Pilar, S. del Barrio-García, E. Crespo-Almendros, & L. Porcu (Eds.), *Analyzing the cultural diversity of consumers in the global marketplace* (pp. 37–59). Hershey, PA: IGI Global. doi:10.4018/978-1-4666-8262-7.ch003

Compilation of References

Kasemsap, K. (2015a). The role of cultural dynamics in the digital age. In B. Christiansen & J. Koeman (Eds.), *Nationalism, cultural indoctrination, and economic prosperity in the digital age* (pp. 295–312). Hershey, PA: IGI Global. doi:10.4018/978-1-4666-7492-9.ch014

Kasemsap, K. (2016a). The roles of organizational justice, social justice, and organizational culture in global higher education. In N. Ololube (Ed.), *Handbook of research on organizational justice and culture in higher education institutions* (pp. 83–115). Hershey, PA: IGI Global. doi:10.4018/978-1-4666-9850-5.ch004

Kasemsap, K. (2016b). Promoting service quality and customer satisfaction in global business. In U. Panwar, R. Kumar, & N. Ray (Eds.), *Handbook of research on promotional strategies and consumer influence in the service sector* (pp. 247–276). Hershey, PA: IGI Global. doi:10.4018/978-1-5225-0143-5.ch015

Kasemsap, K. (2016c). Cultural perspectives and cultural dynamics: Advanced issues and approaches. *International Journal of Art, Culture and Design Technologies*, 5(1), 35–47. doi:10.4018/IJACDT.2016010103

Kasemsap, K. (2016d). A unified framework of organizational perspectives and knowledge management and their impact on job performance. In A. Normore, L. Long, & M. Javidi (Eds.), *Handbook of research on effective communication, leadership, and conflict resolution* (pp. 267–297). Hershey, PA: IGI Global. doi:10.4018/978-1-4666-9970-0.ch015

Kasemsap, K. (2016e). The roles of organizational change management and resistance to change in the modern business world. In A. Goksoy (Ed.), *Organizational change management strategies in modern business* (pp. 143–171). Hershey, PA: IGI Global. doi:10.4018/978-1-4666-9533-7.ch008

Kasemsap, K. (2016f). Utilizing complexity theory and complex adaptive systems in global business. In Ş. Erçetin & H. Bağcı (Eds.), *Handbook of research on chaos and complexity theory in the social sciences* (pp. 235–260). Hershey, PA: IGI Global. doi:10.4018/978-1-5225-0148-0.ch018

Kasemsap, K. (2017a). Examining the roles of job satisfaction and organizational commitment in the global workplace. In P. Ordoñez de Pablos & R. Tennyson (Eds.), *Handbook of research on human resources strategies for the new millennial workforce* (pp. 148–176). Hershey, PA: IGI Global. doi:10.4018/978-1-5225-0948-6.ch008

Kasemsap, K. (2017b). Management education and leadership styles: Current issues and approaches. In N. Baporikar (Ed.), *Innovation and shifting perspectives in management education* (pp. 166–193). Hershey, PA: IGI Global. doi:10.4018/978-1-5225-1019-2.ch008

Kasemsap, K. (2017c). The fundamentals of social capital. In G. Koç, M. Claes, & B. Christiansen (Eds.), *Cultural influences on architecture* (pp. 259–292). Hershey, PA: IGI Global. doi:10.4018/978-1-5225-1744-3.ch010

Kasemsap, K. (2017d). Organizational learning: Advanced issues and trends. In A. Bencsik (Ed.), *Knowledge management initiatives and strategies in small and medium enterprises* (pp. 42–66). Hershey, PA: IGI Global. doi:10.4018/978-1-5225-1642-2.ch003

Kasemsap, K. (2017e). Advocating problem-based learning and creative problem-solving skills in global education. In C. Zhou (Ed.), *Handbook of research on creative problem-solving skill development in higher education* (pp. 351–377). Hershey, PA: IGI Global. doi:10.4018/978-1-5225-0643-0.ch016

Kasemsap, K. (2017f). Investigating the roles of neuroscience and knowledge management in higher education. In S. Mukerji & P. Tripathi (Eds.), *Handbook of research on administration, policy, and leadership in higher education* (pp. 112–140). Hershey, PA: IGI Global. doi:10.4018/978-1-5225-0672-0.ch006

Kasemsap, K. (2017g). Mastering cognitive neuroscience and social neuroscience perspectives in the information age. In M. Dos Santos (Ed.), *Applying neuroscience to business practice* (pp. 82–113). Hershey, PA: IGI Global. doi:10.4018/978-1-5225-1028-4.ch005

Kattel, B. P., Fredericks, T. K., Fernandez, J. E., & Lee, D. C. (1996). The effect of upper-extremity posture on maximum grip strength. *International Journal of Industrial Ergonomics*, *18*(5), 423–429. doi:10.1016/0169-8141(95)00105-0

Katz, D., & Kahn, R. (1966). *The social psychology of Organizations*. New York: John Wiley & Sons.

Katzell, R. A., & Austin, J. T. (1992). From then to now: The development of industrial-organizational psychology in the United States. *The Journal of Applied Psychology*, *77*(6), 803–835. doi:10.1037/0021-9010.77.6.803

Katz, J., & Gartner, W. B. (1988). Properties of emerging organizations? *Academy of Management Review*, *13*(3), 429–441.

Katz, J., & Steyaert, C. (2004). Entrepreneurship in society: Exploring and theorizing new forms and practices of entrepreneurship. *Entrepreneurship and Regional Development*, *16*(3), 179–250.

Kaufmann, D. (2004). *Corruption, governance and security: Challenges for the rich countries and the world*.

Kaunonen, M., Salin, S., & Aalto, P. (2015). Database nurse staffing indicators: Explaining risks of staff job dissatisfaction in outpatient care. *Journal of Nursing Management*, *23*(5), 546–556. doi:10.1111/jonm.12169 PMID:24373115

Kaur, D., Sambasivan, M., & Kumar, N. (2015). Impact of emotional intelligence and spiritual intelligence on the caring behavior of nurses: A dimension-level exploratory study among public hospitals in Malaysia. *Applied Nursing Research*, *28*(4), 293–298. doi:10.1016/j.apnr.2015.01.006 PMID:26608428

Kavanagh, P., Benson, J., & Brown, M. (2007). Understanding performance appraisal fairness. *Asia Pacific Journal of Human Resources*, *45*(2), 89–99. doi:10.1177/1038411107079108

Kazemipour, F., Amin, S. M., & Pourseidi, B. (2012). Relationship between workplace spirituality and organizational citizenship behavior among nurses through mediation of affective organizational commitment. *Journal of Nursing Scholarship*, *44*(3), 302–310. doi:10.1111/j.1547-5069.2012.01456.x PMID:22804973

Keashly, L. (2010). Some things you need to know but may have been afraid to ask: A researcher speaks to ombudsmen about workplace bullying. *Journal of the International Ombudsman Association*, *3*(2), 10–23. Retrieved from http://www.ombudsassociation.org/Resources/IOA-Publications/IOA-Journal/Journal-PDFs/JIOAVolume3No2October2010Final.aspx

Keashly, L., & Jagatic, K. (2011). North American perspectives on hostile behaviors and bullying at work. In S. Einarsen, H. Hoel, D. Zapf, & C. L. Cooper (Eds.), *Bullying and harassment in the workplace: Developments in theory, research, and practice* (2nd ed., pp. 41–74). Boca Raton, FL: CRC Press.

Keashly, L., & Neuman, J. H. (2004). Bullying in the workplace: Its impact and management. *Employee Rights and Employment Policy*, *8*(3), 335–373.

Kegan, R., & Lahey, L. L. (2009). *Immunity to change: How to overcome it and unlock the potential in yourself and your organization*. Boston: Harvard Business Review Press.

Kegan, R., & Laskow Lahey, L. (2001). The Real Reason People Won't Change. *Harvard Business Review*, *79*(10), 84–92.

Keidanren. (2016). Retrieved from https://www.keidanren.or.jp/en/

Keillor, B. D., Pettijohn, C. E., & d'Amico, M. (2011). The relationship between attitudes toward technology, adaptability, and customer orientation among professional salespeople. *Journal of Applied Business Research*, *17*(4), 31–40. doi:10.19030/jabr.v17i4.2090

Kelly Services. (2013). *Building a Strong Employer Brand at all times for sustainable organization*. Retrieved from www.kellyservices.com.my

Kelly, Ch., Kocourek, P., McGaw, N., & Samuelson, J. (2005). *Deriving Value from Corporate Values*, The Aspen Institute and Booz Allen Hamilton, Inc. Retrieved from https://www.aspeninstitute.org/sites/default/files/content/docs/bsp/VALUE%2520SURVEY%2520FINAL.PDF

Keltner, D., & Haidt, J. (2001). Social functions of emotions. In T. J. Mayne & G. A. Bonanno (Eds.), *Emotions: Current issues and future directions* (pp. 192–213). New York: Guilford.

Kendall, P. C., & Watson, D. (Eds.). (1989). *Anxiety and depression: Distinctive and overlapping features. Personality, Psychopathology, and Psychotherapy*. San Diego, CA: Academic Press.

Kendler, K. S., Kessler, R. C., Heath, A. C., Neale, M. C., & Eaves, L. J. (1991). Coping: A genetic epidemiological investigation. *Psychological Medicine*, *21*(02), 337–346. doi:10.1017/S0033291700020444 PMID:1876639

Kenny, P., Reeve, R., & Hall, J. (2016). Satisfaction with nursing education, job satisfaction, and work intentions of new graduate nurses. *Nurse Education Today*, *36*, 230–235. doi:10.1016/j.nedt.2015.10.023 PMID:26556705

Kent, T. W. (2006). Leadership and emotions in health care organizations. *Journal of Health Organization and Management*, *20*(1), 49–66. doi:10.1108/14777260610656552 PMID:16703842

Kępa, L., Tomasik, P., & Dobrzyński, S. (2012). *Security of e-commerce system, or how to run a business without the risk of the Internet*. Gliwice: Helion.

Kertzer, D. I. (1988). *Ritual, Politics, and Power*. London: Yale University Press.

Keyton, J. (2002). *Communicating in groups: Building relationships for effective decision making* (2nd ed.). Boston: McGraw-Hill.

Keyton, J. (2011). *Communication and organizational culture: A key to understanding work experience*. Thousand Oaks, CA: Sage.

Khamisa, N., Peltzer, K., Ilic, D., & Oldenburg, B. (2016). Work related stress, burnout, job satisfaction and general health of nurses: A follow-up study. *International Journal of Nursing Practice*, *22*(6), 538–545. doi:10.1111/ijn.12455 PMID:27241867

Khunou, S. H., & Davhana-Maselesele, M. (2016). Level of job satisfaction amongst nurses in the North-West Province, South Africa: Post occupational specific dispensation. *Curationis*, *39*(1), 1–10. doi:10.4102/curationis.v39i1.1438 PMID:26974827

Khurshid, F., Butt, Z. U., & Muzaffer, B. (2012). Occupational stress and turnover intensions among the non-governmental organizations employees. *Language in India*, *12*(1), 100–115.

Kiani, F., Samavatyan, S., & Pourabion, S. (2011). Job stress and the rate of reported incidents among workers of Isfahan Steel Company: The role mediator work pressure. *Iran Occupational Health*, *8*(3), 23-31. Retrieved from http://www.sid.ir/en/ViewPaper.asp?ID=249815&vDate=FALL%202011&vEnd=31&vJournal=IRAN+OCCUPATIONAL+HEALTH+JOURNAL&vNo=3&vStart=23&vVolume=8&vWriter=KIANI%20F.,SAMAVATYAN%20S.,POURABIAN%20S

Kidder, L. H. (1992). Requirements for being Japanese. *International Journal of Intercultural Relations*, *16*(4), 383–393. doi:10.1016/0147-1767(92)90029-T

Kifner, T. (1999). *Security and data protection* (pp. 26–54). Gliwice: Helion.

Kilbom, Å. (2000). Repetitive work of the upper extremity: Part II—The scientific basis (knowledge base) for the guide. *Elsevier Ergonomics Book Series*, *1*, 151–178. doi:10.1016/S1572-347X(00)80011-7

Kilduff, M., & Brass, D. J. (2010). Organizational social network research: Core ideas and key debates. *The Academy of Management Annals*, *4*(1), 317–357. doi:10.1080/19416520.2010.494827

Kilduff, M., & Tsai, W. (2007). *Social networks and organizations*. Thousand Oaks, CA: Sage.

Kilroy, S., Flood, P. C., Bosak, J., & Chênevert, D. (2016). Perceptions of high-involvement work practices and burnout: The mediating role of job demands. *Human Resource Management Journal*, *26*(4), 408–424. doi:10.1111/1748-8583.12112

Kim, E., & Glomb, T. M. (2010). Get smarty pants: Cognitive ability, personality, and victimization. *The Journal of Applied Psychology*, *95*(5), 889–901. doi:10.1037/a0019985 PMID:20718509

Kim, Y. Y. (2001). *Becoming intercultural: An integrative theory of communication and cross-cultural adaptation*. Thousand Oaks, CA: Sage.

Kinare, A. S., Natekar, A. S., Chinchwadkar, M. C., Yajnik, C. S., Coyaji, K. J., Fall, C. H., & Howe, D. T. (2000). Low midpregnancy placental volume in rural Indian women: A cause for low birth weight? *American Journal of Obstetrics and Gynecology*, *182*(2), 443–448. doi:10.1016/S0002-9378(00)70237-7 PMID:10694350

King, J. C. (2012). Anaphora. In G. Russell & D. G. Fara (Eds.), *The Routledge companion to the philosophy of Language*. New York: Routledge.

King, M., & Gardner, D. (2006). Emotional intelligence and occupational stress among professional staff in New Zealand. *The International Journal of Organizational Analysis*, *14*(3), 186–203. doi:10.1108/19348830610823392

Kirzner, I. (1973). *Competition and entrepreneurship*. Chicago: The University of Chicago Press.

Kjeldsen, A. M., & Andersen, L. B. (2013). How pro-social motivation affects job satisfaction: An international analysis of countries with different welfare state regimes. *Scandinavian Political Studies*, *36*(2), 153–176. doi:10.1111/j.1467-9477.2012.00301.x

Klapper, L., Lewin, A., & Delgado, J. M. (2009). *The impact of the business environment on the business creation process* (Policy Research Working Paper 4937). Washington, DC: The World Bank.

Klaus, S. F., Ekerdt, D. J., & Gajewski, B. (2012). Job satisfaction in birth cohorts of nurses. *Journal of Nursing Management*, *20*(4), 461–471. doi:10.1111/j.1365-2834.2011.01283.x PMID:22591148

Klein, J., Frie, K. G., Blum, K., & von dem Knesebeck, O. (2010). Burnout and perceived quality of care among German clinicians in surgery. *International Journal for Quality in Health Care*, *22*(6), 525–530. doi:10.1093/intqhc/mzq056 PMID:20935011

Klitmøller, A., Schneider, S. C., & Jonsen, K. (2015). Speaking of global virtual teams: Language differences, social categorization and media choice. *Personnel Review*, *44*(2), 270–285. doi:10.1108/PR-11-2013-0205

Knafo, A., & Sagiv, L. (2004). Values and work environment: Mapping 32 occupations. *European Journal of Psychology of Education*, *19*(3), 255–273. doi:10.1007/BF03173223

Knox, S., & Freeman, C. H. (2006). Measuring and Managing Employer Brand Image in the Service Industry. *Journal of Marketing Management*, *22*, 695–716.

Kohli, A. S., & Sharma, S. R. (1997). *Labour welfare and social security*. New Delhi, India: Anmol Publications Private Limited.

Kompier, M. A. J., & di Stefano, V. (1995). Review of stress bus drivers occupational and stress prevention. *Stress Medicine*, *11*(1), 253–262. doi:10.1002/smi.2460110141

Kondrasuk, J. N. (2011). So what would an ideal performance appraisal look like? *The Journal of Applied Business and Economics*, *12*(1), 57.

Kondrasuk, J. N., Pearson, D., Tanner, K., Maruska, E., & Dwyer, J. (2005). An elusive panacea: The ideal performance appraisal. In S. Reddy (Ed.), *Performance Appraisals: A Critical View* (pp. 3–12). Hyderabad, India: Institute of Chartered Financial Analysts of India.

Koning, L. F., & Van Kleef, G. A. (2015). How leaders emotional displays shape followers organizational citizenship behavior. *The Leadership Quarterly*, *26*(4), 489–501. doi:10.1016/j.leaqua.2015.03.001

Korosec, M. L., & Berman, E. M. (2006). Municipal support for social entrepreneurship. *Public Administration Review*, *66*(3), 448–462. doi:10.1111/j.1540-6210.2006.00601.x

Korte, W. B., & Wynne, R. (1996). *Telework Penetration, potential and practice in Europe*. Amsterdam: Ohmsha Press.

Kostova, T. (1997). Country institutional profiles: Concept and measurement. *Academy of Management Proceedings*, *1997*(1), 180-184.

Kouzes, J. M., & Posner, B. Z. (1995). *The leadership challenge: How to keep getting extraordinary things done in organizations*. San Francisco: Jossey-Bass.

Kovács, M., Kovács, E., & Hegedűs, K. (2010). Emotion work and burnout: Cross-sectional study of nurses and physicians in Hungary. *Croatian Medical Journal*, *51*(5), 432–442. doi:10.3325/cmj.2010.51.432 PMID:20960593

Kowalski, C., Ommen, O., Driller, E., Ernstmann, N., Wirtz, M. A., Köhler, T., & Pfaff, H. (2010). Burnout in nurses–the relationship between social capital in hospitals and emotional exhaustion. *Journal of Clinical Nursing*, *19*(11-12), 1654–1663. doi:10.1111/j.1365-2702.2009.02989.x PMID:20384668

Kozlowski, S. W., & Klein, K. J. (2000). A multilevel approach to theory and research in organizations: Contextual, temporal, and emergent processes. In K. J. Klein & S. W. Kozlowski (Eds.), *Multilevel theory, research and methods in organizations* (pp. 3–90). San Francisco: Jossey Bass.

Kraimer, M., Bolino, M., & Mead, B. (2016). Themes in expatriate and repatriate research over four decades: What do we know and what do we still need to learn? *Annual Review of Organizational Psychology and Organizational Behavior*, *3*(1), 83–109. doi:10.1146/annurev-orgpsych-041015-062437

Kramer, R. M. (2014). Power and influence at the top: Effective and ineffective forms of leader behavior. In G. R. Goethals, S. T. Allison, R. M. Kramer, & D. M. Messick (Eds.), *Conceptions of leadership: Enduring ideas and emerging insights* (pp. 223–238). New York: Palgrave Macmillan. doi:10.1057/9781137472038_13

Kreiser, P. M. (2011). Entrepreneurial orientation and organizational learning: The impact of network range and network closure. *Entrepreneurship Theory and Practice*, *35*(5), 1025–1050. doi:10.1111/j.1540-6520.2011.00449.x

Kristof-Brown, A. L., Zimmerman, R. D., & Johnson, E. C. (2005). Consequences of individuals' fit at work: A meta-analysis of person-job, person-organization, person-group, and person-supervisor fit. *Personnel Psychology*, *58*(2), 281–342. doi:10.1111/j.1744-6570.2005.00672.x

Kuhnel, J., Sonnentag, S., & Bledow, R. (2012). Resources and time pressure as day-level antecedents of work engagement. *Journal of Occupational and Organizational Psychology*, *85*(1), 181–198. doi:10.1111/j.2044-8325.2011.02022.x

Kulczycki, E. (2014). Communication history and its research subject. *Analele Universitatii din Craiova. Seria Filosofie*, *33*(1), 132–155.

Kumar, B. P., & Giri, V. N. (2009). Examining the relationship of organizational communication and job satisfaction in Indian organizations. *Journal of Creative Communications*, *4*(3), 177–184. doi:10.1177/097325861000400303

Kumari, N., & Malhotra, R. (2012). Effective Performance Management System for Enhancing Growth. *Global Management Journal*, *4*(1/2), 77–85.

Kumar, S. (2001). Theories of musculoskeletal injury causation. *Ergonomics*, *44*(1), 17–47. doi:10.1080/00140130120716 PMID:11214897

Kumar, S., & Yadav, S. S. (2002). Satisfaction level from labour welfare schemes in sugar factories of Gorakhpur division. *Indian Journal of Economics*, *33*(329), 171–188.

Kupers, W., & Weibler, J. R. (2008). Emotions in organisation: An integral perspective. *International Journal of Work Organisation and Emotion*, *2*(3), 256–287. doi:10.1504/IJWOE.2008.019426

Laddha, R. L. (2012). A Study on Employee Welfare Strategies with Special Reference to Solapur Janta Sahakari Bank Ltd, Solapur. *Golden Research Thoughts.*, *1*(10), 1–4.

Lahiri, I. (2008). *Creating a competency model for diversity and inclusion practitioners. Research Report Number R-1420-08-RR*. New York: The Conference Board, Inc. Retrieved from https://www.conference-board.org/pdf_free/councils/TCBCP005.pdf

Lai, J. Y. M., Lam, L. W., & Lam, S. S. K. (2013). Organizational citizenship behavior in work groups: A team cultural perspective. *Journal of Organizational Behavior*, *34*(7), 1039–1056.

Lalitha, K., & Priyanka, T. (2014). A Study on Employee Welfare Measures with Reference to IT Industry. *International Journal of Engineering Technology. Management and Applied Sciences*, *2*(7), 191–195.

Lam, A. (2000). Tacit knowledge, organizational learning and societal institutions: An integrated framework. *Organization Studies*, *21*(3), 487–513. doi:10.1177/0170840600213001

Lam, A. (2003). Organizational learning in multinationals: R&D networks of Japanese and US MNEs in the UK. *Journal of Management Studies*, *40*(3), 673–703. doi:10.1111/1467-6486.00356

Lambert, E. G., Hogan, N. L., & Barton, S. M. (2001). The impact of job satisfaction on turnover intent: A test of a structural measurement model using a national sample of workers. *The Social Science Journal*, *38*(2), 233–250. doi:10.1016/S0362-3319(01)00110-0

Lancioni and N. N. Singh (Ed.), *Assistive Technologies for People with Diverse Abilities* (pp. 157–190). New York: Springer.

Landa, J. M. A., López-Zafra, E., Martos, M. P. B., & del Carmen Aguilar-Luzón, M. (2008). The relationship between emotional intelligence, occupational stress and health in nurses: A questionnaire survey. *International Journal of Nursing Studies*, *45*(6), 888–901. doi:10.1016/j.ijnurstu.2007.03.005 PMID:17509597

Landsbergis, P. A. (1988). Occupational stress among health care workers: A test of the job demands- control model. *Journal of Organizational Behavior*, *9*(3), 217–239. doi:10.1002/job.4030090303

Lang, P. J. (1984). The cognitive psychophysiology of emotion: Fear and anxiety. In A. H. Tuma & J. D. Maser (Eds.), *Anxiety and the anxiety disorders* (pp. 131–170). Hillsdale, NJ: Erlbaum.

Lang, R., Ramdoss, S., Raulston, T., Carnet, A., Sigafoos, J., Didden, R., & O'Reilly, M. F. et al. (2014). Assistive Technology for People with Autism Spectrum Disorders. In G. E. doi:10.1007/978-1-4899-8029-8_6

Lan, L.-L., & Heracleous, L. (2010). Rethinking agency theory: The view from law. *Academy of Management Review*, *35*(2), 294–314. doi:10.5465/AMR.2010.48463335

Laschinger, H. K. S., & Fida, R. (2015). Linking nurses perceptions of patient care quality to job satisfaction: The role of authentic leadership and empowering professional practice environments. *The Journal of Nursing Administration*, *45*(5), 276–283. doi:10.1097/NNA.0000000000000198 PMID:25906136

Latham, G. P., & Wexley, K. N. (1977). Behavioural Observation Scales For Performance Appraisal Purposes. *Personnel Psychology*, *30*(2), 255–268. doi:10.1111/j.1744-6570.1977.tb02092.x

Latham, G. P., & Yukl, G. A. (1975). A review of research on the application of goal setting in organizations. *Academy of Management Journal*, *18*(4), 824–845. doi:10.2307/255381

Latko, W. A., Armstrong, T. J., Foulke, J. A., Herrin, G. D., Rabourn, R. A., & Ulin, S. S. (1997). Development and evaluation of an observational method for assessing repetition in hand tasks. *American Industrial Hygiene Association Journal*, *58*(4), 278–285. doi:10.1080/15428119791012793 PMID:9115085

Lau, D. C., & Lam, L. W. (2008). Effects of trusting and being trusted on team citizenship behaviours in chain stores. *Asian Journal of Social Psychology*, *11*(2), 141–149. doi:10.1111/j.1467-839X.2008.00251.x

Lave, J., & Wenger, E. (1991). *Situated learning: Legitimate peripheral participation*. New York: Cambridge University Press. doi:10.1017/CBO9780511815355

Lavelle, J. J., Brockner, J., Konovsky, M. A., Price, K. H., Henley, A. B., Taneja, A., & Vinekar, V. (2009). Commitment, procedural fairness, and organizational citizenship behavior: A multifoci analysis. *Journal of Organizational Behavior*, *30*(3), 337–357. doi:10.1002/job.518

Lawler, E. E. III. (2001). Performance Management. In L. Carter, D. Giber, & M. Goldsmith (Eds.), *Best Practices in Organization Development and Change*. San Francisco: Jossey-Bass/Pfeiffer.

Lawler, E. J., & Thye, S. R. (1999). Bringing emotions into social exchange theory. *Annual Review of Sociology*, *25*(1), 217–244. doi:10.1146/annurev.soc.25.1.217

Lawrence, T. B., Hardy, C., & Phillips, N. (2002). Institutional effects of interorganizational collaboration: The emergence of proto-institutions. *Academy of Management Journal*, *45*(1), 281–290. doi:10.2307/3069297

Law, S. K., Wong, C., & Chen, X. Z. (2005). The construct of organizational citizenship behavior: Should we analyze after we have conceptualized? In D. Turnipseed (Ed.), *Handbook of organizational citizenship behavior* (pp. 47–65). New York: Nova Science Publishers.

Lazarova, M., & Caligiuri, P. (2001). Retaining repatriates: The role of organizational support practices. *Journal of World Business*, *36*(4), 389–401. doi:10.1016/S1090-9516(01)00063-3

Lazarus, R. S. (2000). Toward better research on stress and coping. *The American Psychologist*, *55*(6), 665–673. doi:10.1037/0003-066X.55.6.665 PMID:10892209

Leach, J. (1995). *A practical guide to working with diversity: The process, the tools, the resources*. New York: AMACOM.

LeanIn. L. 2016. (2016). *Get our tips for managers*. Retrieved from http://leanin.org/tips/managers

Lederer, V., Loisel, P., Rivard, M., & Champagne, F. (2014). Exploring the diversity of conceptualizations of work (dis)ability: A scoping review of published definitions. *Journal of Occupational Rehabilitation*, *24*(2), 242–267. doi:10.1007/s10926-013-9459-4 PMID:23884716

Lee, K., & Allen, N. J. (2002). Organizational citizenship behavior and workplace deviance: The role of affect and cognitions. *The Journal of Applied Psychology*, *87*(1), 131–142. doi:10.1037/0021-9010.87.1.131 PMID:11916207

Leidner, D. E., & Jarvenpaa, S. L. (1995). The use of information technology to enhance management school education: A theoretical view. *Management Information Systems Quarterly, 19*(3), 265–291. doi:10.2307/249596

Leiter, M.P., Hakanen, J.J., Ahola, K., Toppinen-Tanner, S., Koskinen, A., & Väänänen, A. (2013). Organizational predictors and health consequences of changes in burnout: A 12-year cohort study. *Journal of Organizational Behavior, 34*(7), 959–973.

Leiter, M. P., & Laschinger, H. K. S. (2006). Relationships of work and practice environment to professional burnout: Testing a causal model. *Nursing Research, 55*(2), 137–146. doi:10.1097/00006199-200603000-00009 PMID:16601626

Leiter, M. P., Laschinger, H. K. S., Day, A., & Oore, D. G. (2011). The impact of civility interventions on employee social behavior, distress, and attitudes. *The Journal of Applied Psychology, 96*(6), 1258–1274. doi:10.1037/a0024442 PMID:21744942

Leonard-Barton, D., & Swap, W. C. (1999). *When sparks fly: igniting creativity in groups*. Boston: Harvard Business School Press.

Leong, C. W. (2015, October 5). *Why gender diversity makes good business sense*. Retrieved from: http://www.cnbc.com/2015/10/05/why-gender-diversity-makes-good-business-sense.html

LePine, J. A., Erez, A., & Johnson, D. E. (2002). The nature and dimensionality of organizational citizenship behaviour: A critical review and meta-analysis. *The Journal of Applied Psychology, 87*(1), 52–65. doi:10.1037/0021-9010.87.1.52 PMID:11916216

Lepoutre, J., Justo, R., Terjesen, S., & Bosma, N. (2013). Designing a global standardized methodology for measuring social entrepreneurship activity: The Global Entrepreneurship Monitor social entrepreneurship study. *Small Business Economics, 40*(3), 693–714. doi:10.1007/s11187-011-9398-4

Lepsinger, R., & Lucia. (1997). *360 degree feedback and performance appraisal*. ABI/INFORM Global, 62.

Lesser, E. L. (2000). *Knowledge and social capital: Foundations and applications*. Woburn, MA: Butterworth-Heinemann.

Lesser, E., & Prusak, L. (1999). Communities of practice, social capital and organizational knowledge. *Information Systems Research, 1*(1), 3–10.

Levin, S. (2016, April 13). By the numbers: Why big-name businesses are bidding for Yahoo. *The Guardian*. Retrieved from https://www.theguardian.com/technology/2016/apr/12/yahoo-bid-marissa-mayer-daily-mail-verizon

Levin, D. Z., & Cross, R. (2004). The strength of weak ties you can trust: The mediating role of trust in effective knowledge transfer. *Management Science, 50*(11), 1477–1490. doi:10.1287/mnsc.1030.0136

Levinson, M. H. (2008). General semantics and emotional intelligence. *A Review of General Semantics, 65*(3), 243-251. Retrieved from http://www.generalsemantics.org/wp-content/uploads/2011/05/2006-conference/levinson.pdf

Levitt, B., & March, J. G. (1988). Organizational learning. *Annual Review of Sociology, 14*(1), 319–340. doi:10.1146/annurev.so.14.080188.001535

Lewis, D., Giga, S., & Hoel, H. (2011). Discrimination and bullying. In S. Einarsen, H. Hoel, D. Zapf, & C. L. Cooper (Eds.), *Bullying and harassment in the workplace: Development in theory, research, and practice* (2nd ed., pp. 267–281). Boca Raton, FL: CRC Press.

Lewis, K. M. (2000). When leaders display emotion: How followers respond to negative emotional expression of male and female leaders. *Journal of Organizational Behavior, 21*(2), 221–234. doi:10.1002/(SICI)1099-1379(200003)21:2<221::AID-JOB36>3.0.CO;2-0

Leymann, H. (1990). Mobbing and psychological terror at workplaces. *Violence and Victims*, *5*(2), 119–126. PMID:2278952

Leymann, H. (1996). The content and development of mobbing at work. *European Journal of Work and Organizational Psychology*, *5*(2), 165–184. doi:10.1080/13594329608414853

Leymann, H., & Gustafsson, A. (1996). Mobbing at work and the development of post-traumatic stress disorders. *European Journal of Work and Organizational Psychology*, *5*(2), 251–276. doi:10.1080/13594329608414858

Li, H., Zuo, M., Zhao, X., Zhang, B., Gelb, A., Yao, D., ... & Huang, Y. (2016). Abstract PR589: A cross-sectional survey of anesthesiologists' job satisfaction and burnout in Beijing, Tianjin and Hebei of China: Current challenge and possible solutions. *Anesthesia & Analgesia, 123*(Suppl. 3), 318.

Liang, H. Y., Tang, F. I., Wang, T. F., Lin, K. C., & Yu, S. (2016). Nurse characteristics, leadership, safety climate, emotional labour and intention to stay for nurses: A structural equation modelling approach. *Journal of Advanced Nursing*, *72*(12), 3068–3080. doi:10.1111/jan.13072 PMID:27400365

Lian, H., Ferris, D. L., & Brown, D. J. (2012). Does power distance exacerbate or mitigate the effects of abusive supervision? It depends on the outcome. *The Journal of Applied Psychology*, *97*(1), 107–123. doi:10.1037/a0024610 PMID:21766996

Li, C. R., Chu, C. P., & Lin, C. J. (2010). The contingent value of exploratory and exploitative learning for new product development performance. *Industrial Marketing Management*, *39*(7), 1186–1197. doi:10.1016/j.indmarman.2010.02.002

Lievens, F., Conway, J. M., & de Corte, W. (2008). The relative importance of task, citizenship and counterproductive performance to job performance ratings: Do rater source and team-based culture matter? *Journal of Occupational and Organizational Psychology*, *81*(1), 11–27. doi:10.1348/096317907X182971

Li, G., & Buckle, P. (2000, July). Evaluating Change in Exposure to Risk for Musculoskeletal Disorders—A Practical Tool. *Proceedings of the Human Factors and Ergonomics Society Annual Meeting* (Vol. 44, No. 30, pp. 5-407). Thousand Oaks, CA: SAGE Publications. doi:10.1177/154193120004403001

Li, L. (2005). The effects of trust and shared vision on inward knowledge transfer in subsidiaries intra-and inter-organizational relationships. *International Business Review*, *14*(1), 77–95. doi:10.1016/j.ibusrev.2004.12.005

Li, L., Ruan, H., & Yuan, W. J. (2015). The relationship between social support and burnout among ICU nurses in Shanghai: A cross-sectional study. *Clinical Nursing Research*, *2*(2), 45–50.

Lin, C. C., & Peng, T. K. (2010). From organizational citizenship behaviour to team performance: The mediation of group cohesion and collective efficacy. *Management and Organization Review*, *6*(1), 55–75. doi:10.1111/j.1740-8784.2009.00172.x

Lind, K., Glasø, L., Pallesen, S., & Einarsen, S. (2009). Personality profiles among targets and non-targets of workplace bullying. *European Psychologist*, *14*(3), 231–237. doi:10.1027/1016-9040.14.3.231

Lindqvist, R., Smeds Alenius, L., Griffiths, P., Runesdotter, S., & Tishelman, C. (2015). Structural characteristics of hospitals and nurse-reported care quality, work environment, burnout and leaving intentions. *Journal of Nursing Management*, *23*(2), 263–274. doi:10.1111/jonm.12123 PMID:24047463

Linkow, P., Barrington, L., Bruyere, S., Figueroa, I., & Wright, M. (2013). *Leveling the playing field. Attracting, engaging, and advancing people with disabilities. Research Report R-1510-12-RR*. New York: The Conference Board, Inc. Retrieved from http://digitalcommons.ilr.cornell.edu/cgi/viewcontent.cgi?article=1292&context=edicollect

Lin, N. (1999). Building a network theory of social capital. *Connections*, *22*(1), 28–51.

Lin, T. C., Lin, H. S., Cheng, S. F., Wu, L. M., & Ou-Yang, M. C. (2016). Work stress, occupational burnout and depression levels: A clinical study of paediatric intensive care unit nurses in Taiwan. *Journal of Clinical Nursing, 25*(7), 1120–1130. doi:10.1111/jocn.13119 PMID:26914523

Littlejohn, S. W., & Foss, K. A. (Eds.). (2009). Encyclopedia of communication theory. Thousand Oaks, CA: SAGE Publications, Inc.

Littlejohn, S. W. (1996). *Theories of human communication* (5th ed.). New York: Wadsworth Publishing Company: An International Thomson Publishing Company.

Little, L. M., Gooty, J., & Williams, M. (2016). The role of leader emotion management in leader–member exchange and follower outcomes. *The Leadership Quarterly, 27*(1), 85–97. doi:10.1016/j.leaqua.2015.08.007

Liu, C. L. E., Ghauri, P. N., & Sinkovics, R. R. (2010). Understanding the impact of relational capital and organizational learning on alliance outcomes. *Journal of World Business, 45*(3), 237–249. doi:10.1016/j.jwb.2009.09.005

Liu, D., Liao, H., & Loi, R. (2012). The dark side of leadership: A three-level investigation of the cascading effect of abusive supervision on employee creativity. *Academy of Management Journal, 55*(5), 1187–1212. doi:10.5465/amj.2010.0400

Liu, X. Y., & Wang, J. (2013). Abusive supervision and organizational citizenship behaviour: Is supervisor–subordinate Guanxi a mediator? *International Journal of Human Resource Management, 24*(7), 1471–1489. doi:10.1080/09585192.2012.725082

Liu, Y. E., While, A., Li, S. J., & Ye, W. Q. (2015). Job satisfaction and work related variables in Chinese cardiac critical care nurses. *Journal of Nursing Management, 23*(4), 487–497. doi:10.1111/jonm.12161 PMID:24112300

Löblich, M., & Scheu, A. M. (2011). Writing the history of communication studies: A sociology of science approach. *Communication Theory, 21*(1), 1–22. doi:10.1111/j.1468-2885.2010.01373.x

Locke, E. A. (1976). The nature and causes of job satisfaction. In M. Dunette (Ed.), *Handbook of Industrial and Organizational Psychology* (pp. 1297–1349). Chicago: Rand McNally.

Locke, E. A. (1976). The nature and causes of job satisfaction. In M. D. Dunnette (Ed.), *Handbook of industrial and organizational psychology* (pp. 1297–1349). Chicago: Rand McNally.

Logasakthi, K., & Rajagopal, K. (2013). A study on employee health, safety and welfare measures of chemical industry in the view of Sleam region, Tamil Nadu, India. *International Journal of Research in Business Management., 1*(1), 1–10.

Loi, R., Mao, Y., & Ngo, H. Y. (2009). Linking leader-member exchange and employee work outcomes: The mediating role of organizational social and economic exchange. *Management and Organization Review, 5*(3), 401–422. doi:10.1111/j.1740-8784.2009.00149.x

Long, C. S., Kowang, T. O., Ismail, W. K. W., & Rasid, S. Z. A. (2013). A Review on Performance Appraisal System: An Ineffective and Destructive Practice? *Middle-East Journal of Scientific Research, 14*(7), 887–891.

Long, C. S., & Xuan, S. S. (2014). Human resources development practices and employees' job satisfaction. In P. Ordóñez de Pablos & R. Tennyson (Eds.), *Strategic approaches for human capital management and development in a turbulent economy* (pp. 117–128). Hershey, PA: IGI Global. doi:10.4018/978-1-4666-4530-1.ch008

Longenecker, C. O., & Goff, S. J. (1992). Performance appraisal effectiveness: A matter of perspective. *SAM Advanced Management Journal, 57*(2), 17.

Compilation of References

Longenecker, J. G., Moore, C. W., Petty, J. W., Palich, L. E., & McKinney, J. A. (2006). Ethical attitudes in small businesses and large corporations: Theory and empirical findings from a tracking study spanning three decades. *Journal of Small Business Management*, *44*(2), 167–183. doi:10.1111/j.1540-627X.2006.00162.x

López-Domínguez, M., Enache, M., Sallan, J. M., & Simo, P. (2013). Transformational leadership as an antecedent of change-oriented organizational citizenship behavior. *Journal of Business Research*, *66*(10), 2147–2152. doi:10.1016/j.jbusres.2013.02.041

López, P. S., Peón, M. M. J., & Ordás, J. V. C. (2005). Organizational learning as a determining factor in business performance. *The Learning Organization*, *12*(3), 227–245. doi:10.1108/09696470510592494

Louit-Martinod, N., Chanut-Guieu, C., Kornig, C., & Méhaut, P. (2016). "A plus dans le bus": Work-related stress among French bus drivers. *Journal of Workplace Rights*, *3*(23), 1–14.

Loury, G. (1992). The economics of discrimination: Getting to the core of the problem. *Harvard Journal of African American Public Policy*, *1*, 91–110.

Lovas, L. (2007). Relationship of organizational culture and job satisfaction in the public sector. *Studia Psychologica*, *49*(3), 215–221.

Lovelace, K. J., Manz, C. C., & Alves, J. C. (2007). Work stress and leadership development: The role of self-leadership, shared leadership, physical fitness and flow in managing demands and increasing job control. *Human Resource Review*, *17*(4), 374–387. doi:10.1016/j.hrmr.2007.08.001

Low, M. B., & MacMillan, I. C. (1988). Entrepreneurship: Past research and future challenges. *Journal of Management*, *14*(2), 139–161. doi:10.1177/014920638801400202

Lucas, V., Spence Laschinger, H. K., & Wong, C. A. (2008). The impact of emotional intelligent leadership on staff nurse empowerment: The moderating effect of span of control. *Journal of Nursing Management*, *16*(8), 964–973. doi:10.1111/j.1365-2834.2008.00856.x PMID:19094109

Lui, B., Cuddy, J. S., Hailes, W. S., & Ruby, B. C. (2014). Seasonal heat acclimatization in wildland firefighters. *Journal of Thermal Biology*, *45*, 134–140. doi:10.1016/j.jtherbio.2014.08.009 PMID:25436962

Lu, M., Ruan, H., Xing, W., & Hu, Y. (2015). Nurse burnout in China: A questionnaire survey on staffing, job satisfaction, and quality of care. *Journal of Nursing Management*, *23*(4), 440–447. doi:10.1111/jonm.12150 PMID:24024567

Lundberg, C. C. (1995). Learning in and by organizations: Three conceptual issues. *The International Journal of Organizational Analysis*, *3*(1), 10–23. doi:10.1108/eb028821

Lunenburg, F. C. (2010). Communication: The process, barriers, and improving effectiveness. *Schooling*, *1*(1), 1–11.

Lu, Y., Hu, X. M., Huang, X. L., Zhuang, X. D., Guo, P., Feng, L. F., & Hao, Y. T. et al. (2016). Job satisfaction and associated factors among healthcare staff: A cross-sectional study in Guangdong Province, China. *BMJ Open*, *6*(7), e011388. doi:10.1136/bmjopen-2016-011388 PMID:27436667

Lyu, Y., Zhu, H., Zhong, H. J., & Hu, L. (2016). Abusive supervision and customer-oriented organizational citizenship behavior: The roles of hostile attribution bias and work engagement. *International Journal of Hospitality Management*, *53*, 69–80. doi:10.1016/j.ijhm.2015.12.001

MacKenzie, S. B., Podsakoff, P. M., & Podsakoff, N. P. (2011). Challenge-oriented organizational citizenship behaviors and organizational effectiveness: Do challenge-oriented behaviors really have an impact on the organization's bottom line? *Personnel Psychology*, *64*(3), 559–592. doi:10.1111/j.1744-6570.2011.01219.x

Mădălina, S.S., & Cătălin, B.M. (2016). Enhancing job satisfaction through organizational communication. *Annals of the Constantin Brancusi University of Targu Jiu, Economy Series, 109-114.*

Madlock, P. E. (2006a). Supervisor' nonverbal immediacy behaviors and their relationship to subordinates' communication satisfaction, job satisfaction, and willingness to collaborate. *Presented at the National Communication Association Convention*, San Antonio, Texas.

Madlock, P. E. (2006b). Do difference in displays of nonverbal immediacy and communication competence between male and female supervisors affect subordinates, job satisfaction. *Ohio Communication Journal, 44*, 61–78.

Madlock, P. E. (2008). The link between leadership style, communicator competence, and employee satisfaction. *Journal of Business Communication, 45*(1), 61–78. doi:10.1177/0021943607309351

Madlock, P. E., & Kennedy-Lightsey, C. (2010). The effects of supervisors verbal aggressiveness and mentoring on their subordinates. *Journal of Business Communication, 47*(1), 42–62. doi:10.1177/0021943609353511

Mael, F., & Ashforth, B. (1992). Alumni and their alma maters: A partial test of the reformulated model of organizational identification. *Journal of Organizational Behavior, 13*(2), 103–123. doi:10.1002/job.4030130202

Magdalena, S. M. (2014). The effects of organizational citizenship behavior in the academic environment. *Procedia: Social and Behavioral Sciences, 127*, 738–742. doi:10.1016/j.sbspro.2014.03.346

Mair, J., & Martí, I. (2006). Social entrepreneurship research: A source of explanation, prediction, and delight. *Journal of World Business, 41*(1), 36–44. doi:10.1016/j.jwb.2005.09.002

Mair, J., & Martí, I. (2009). Entrepreneurship in and around institutional voids: A case study from Bangladesh. *Journal of Business Venturing, 24*(5), 419–435. doi:10.1016/j.jbusvent.2008.04.006

Malek, M. D., Fahrudin, A., & Kamil, I. S. M. (2009). Occupational stress and psychological well-being in emergency services. *Asian Social Work and Policy Review, 3*(3), 143–154. doi:10.1111/j.1753-1411.2009.00030.x

Malloy, T., & Penprase, B. (2010). Nursing leadership style and psychosocial work environment. *Journal of Nursing Management, 18*(6), 715–725. doi:10.1111/j.1365-2834.2010.01094.x PMID:20840366

Mann, S. (1999). Emotion at work: To what extent are we expressing, suppressing, or faking it? *European Journal of Work and Organizational Psychology, 8*(3), 347–369. doi:10.1080/135943299398221

Manojlovich, M., Antonakos, C. L., & Ronis, D. L. (2009). Intensive care units, communication between nurses and physicians, and patients' outcomes. *American Journal of Critical Care, 18*(1), 21–30. doi:10.4037/ajcc2009353 PMID:19116401

Manolova, T. S., Eunni, R. V., & Gyoshev, B. S. (2008). Institutional environments for entrepreneurship: Evidence from emerging economies in Eastern Europe. *Entrepreneurship Theory and Practice, 32*(1), 203–218. doi:10.1111/j.1540-6520.2007.00222.x

Manzini, H., & Gwandure, C. (2011). *The Provision of Employee Assistance Programmes in South Africa Football Clubs*. Johannesburg, South Africa: University of the Witwatersrand.

March, J. G. (1991). Exploration and exploitation in organizational learning. *Organization Science, 2*(1), 71–87. doi:10.1287/orsc.2.1.71

March, J. G., & Olsen, J. P. (1989). *Rediscovering Institutions - The Organizational Basis of Politics*. New York: The Free Press.

Mardanov, I. T., Maertz, C. P., & Sterrett, J. L. (2008). Leader-member exchange and job satisfaction: Cross-industry comparisons and predicted employee turnover. *The Journal of Leadership Studies, 2*(2), 63–82. doi:10.1002/jls.20062

Compilation of References

Mark, A. (2005). Organizing emotions in health care. *Journal of Health Organization and Management, 19*(4/5), 277–289. doi:10.1108/14777260510615332 PMID:16206913

Markus, M. L. (1994). Electronic mail as the medium of managerial choice. *Organization Science, 5*(4), 502–527. doi:10.1287/orsc.5.4.502

Maroney, B. P., & Buckely, M. R. (1992). Does research in performance appraisal influence the practice of performance appraisal? Regretfully not! *Public Personnel Management, 21*(2), 185–196. doi:10.1177/009102609202100206

Marschan-Piekkari, R., Welch, D. E., & Welch, L. S. (1999). Adopting a common corporate language: IHRM implications. *International Journal of Human Resource Management, 10*(3), 377–390. doi:10.1080/095851999340387

Marshall, T. H. (1950). *Citizenship and Social class and other Essays*. England, UK: Cambridge University Press.

Martell, R.F., & Leavitt, K.N. (2002). Reducing the Performance-Cue Bias in Work behaviour Ratings: Can Groups Help? *Journal of Applied Psychology, 87* 6), 1032-1041.

Martin, G. (2008). Employer Branding – Time for Some Long and 'Hard' Reflections? *Research insight.* London: Chartered Institute of Personnel and Development. Retrieved from http://www.therecruiterslounge.com/2010/08/17/10-strategic-tips-for-employee-retention/

Martin, G. C. (2014). The Effects Of Cultural Diversity In The Workplace. *Journal of Diversity Management, 9*(2), 89. doi:10.19030/jdm.v9i2.8974

Martin, G., Beaumont, P., Doig, R., & Pate, J. (2005). Branding: A new performance discourse for HR? *European Management Journal, 23*(1).

Martin, J. (2002). *Organizational culture: Mapping the terrain*. Thousand Oaks, CA: Sage. doi:10.4135/9781483328478

Martin, J. N. (1984). The intercultural reentry: Conceptualization and directions for future research. *International Journal of Intercultural Relations, 8*(2), 115–134. doi:10.1016/0147-1767(84)90035-X

Martin, J. N., & Harrell, T. (2004). Intercultural reentry of students and professionals: Theory and practice. In D. Landis, J. M. Bennett, & M. J. Bennett (Eds.), *Handbook of intercultural training* (pp. 309–336). Thousand Oaks, CA: Sage. doi:10.4135/9781452231129.n13

Martin, J. N., & Nakayama, T. K. (2004). *Understanding intercultural transitions. Intercultural communication in contexts* (pp. 266–302). New York: McGraw-Hill.

Martin, M., & Jackson, T. (2002). *Personnel practice* (3rd ed.). London: CIPD Publishing.

Martin, R., Guillaume, Y., Thomas, G., Lee, A., & Epitropaki, O. (2016). Leader–Member exchange (LMX) and performance: A meta-analytic review. *Personnel Psychology, 69*(1), 67–121. doi:10.1111/peps.12100

Maruyama, A., Suzuki, E., & Takayama, Y. (2016). Factors affecting burnout in female nurses who have preschool-age children. *Japan Journal of Nursing Science, 13*(1), 123–134. doi:10.1111/jjns.12096 PMID:26477333

Marx, E. M., & Schulze, C. C. (1991). Interpersonal problem-solving in depressed students. *Journal of Clinical Psychology, 47*(3), 361–367. doi:10.1002/1097-4679(199105)47:3<361::AID-JCLP2270470307>3.0.CO;2-L PMID:2066404

Marx, E. M., Williams, J. M., & Claridge, G. C. (1992). Depression and social problem solving. *Journal of Abnormal Psychology, 101*(1), 78–86. doi:10.1037/0021-843X.101.1.78 PMID:1537977

Maslach, C., & Jackson, S. (1986). *Maslach Burnout Inventory manual* (2nd ed.). Palo Alto, CA: Consulting Psychologists Press.

Maslach, C., & Jackson, S. E. (1981). The measurement of experienced burnout. *Journal of Organizational Behavior*, *2*(2), 99–113. doi:10.1002/job.4030020205

Maslach, C., & Leiter, M. P. (2016). Understanding the burnout experience: Recent research and its implications for psychiatry. *World Psychiatry; Official Journal of the World Psychiatric Association (WPA)*, *15*(2), 103–111. doi:10.1002/wps.20311 PMID:27265691

Maslach, C., & Schaufeli, W. B. (1993). Historical and conceptual development of burnout. In W. B. Schaufeli, C. Maslach, & T. Marek (Eds.), *Professional burnout: Recent developments in theory and research* (pp. 1–16). Washington, DC: Taylor and Francis.

Maslach, C., Schaufeli, W. B., & Leiter, M. P. (2001). Job burnout. *Annual Review of Psychology*, *52*(1), 397–422. doi:10.1146/annurev.psych.52.1.397 PMID:11148311

Maslow, A. H. (1943). A theory of human motivation. *Psychological Review*, *50*(4), 370–396. doi:10.1037/h0054346

Maslow, A. H. (1970). *Motivation and personality* (2nd ed.). New York: Harper & Row.

Mateescu, A., & Chraif, M. (2015). The relationship between job satisfaction, occupational stress and coping mechanism in educational and technical organizations. *Procedia: Social and Behavioral Sciences*, *187*, 728–732. doi:10.1016/j.sbspro.2015.03.153

Mathieu, C., & Babiak, P. (2016). Corporate psychopathy and abusive supervision: Their influence on employees' job satisfaction and turnover intentions. *Personality and Individual Differences*, *91*, 102–106. doi:10.1016/j.paid.2015.12.002

Matthiesen, S. B., & Einarsen, S. (2007). Perpetrators and targets of bullying at work: Role stress and individual differences. *Violence and Victims*, *22*(6), 735–753. doi:10.1891/088667007782793174 PMID:18225386

Mattson, S. (2003). Cultural Diversity in the Workplace: How the Meaning of Work Can Affect the Way We Work. *AWHONN Lifelines*, *7*(2), 154–158. doi:10.1177/1091592303253868 PMID:12735224

Mauno, S., Kinnunen, U., Makikangas, A., & Natti, J. (2005). Psychological consequences of fixed-term employment and perceived job insecurity among health care staff. *European Journal of Work and Organizational Psychology*, *14*(3), 209–237. doi:10.1080/13594320500146649

Mauno, S., Ruokolainen, M., & Kinnunen, U. (2013). Does aging make employees more resilient to job stress? Age as a moderator in the job stressor–well-being relationship in three Finnish occupational samples. *Aging & Mental Health*, *17*(4), 411–422. doi:10.1080/13607863.2012.747077 PMID:23215801

Mauno, S., Ruokolainen, M., Kinnunen, U., & De Bloom, J. (2016). Emotional labour and work engagement among nurses: Examining perceived compassion, leadership and work ethic as stress buffers. *Journal of Advanced Nursing*, *72*(5), 1169–1181. doi:10.1111/jan.12906 PMID:26841277

Maurer, I., Bartsch, V., & Ebers, M. (2011). The value of intra-organizational social capital: How it fosters knowledge transfer, innovation performance, and growth. *Organization Studies*, *32*(2), 157–185. doi:10.1177/0170840610394301

Maxwell, J. C. (1999). *The 21 indispensable qualities of a leader: Becoming the person others will want to follow*. Nashville, GA: Thomas Nelson Publishers.

Maxwell, J. C. (2001). *The 17 indisputable laws of teamwork*. Nashiville, TN: Thomas Nelson Publishers.

Mayer, J. D., Roberts, R. D., & Barsade, S. G. (2008). Human abilities: Emotional intelligence. *Annual Review of Psychology*, *59*(1), 507–536. doi:10.1146/annurev.psych.59.103006.093646 PMID:17937602

Maynard, D. C., Bachiochi, P. D., & Luna, A. C. (2002). An evaluation of industrial/organizational psychology teaching modules for use in introductory psychology. *Teaching of Psychology*, *29*(1), 39–43. doi:10.1207/S15328023TOP2901_10

McCann, M. (1996). Hazards in cottage industries in developing countries. *American Journal of Industrial Medicine*, *30*(2), 125–129. doi:10.1002/(SICI)1097-0274(199608)30:2<125::AID-AJIM2>3.0.CO;2-# PMID:8844041

McCarthy, B. J. (1995). *Rater Motivation In Performance Appraisal*. Unpublished doctoral dissertation, The University Of WI, Madison.

Mccord, M. A., Joseph, D. L., & Grijalva, E. (2014). Blinded by the light: The dark side of traditionally desirable personality traits. *Industrial and Organizational Psychology: Perspectives on Science and Practice*, *7*(1), 130–137. doi:10.1111/iops.12121

McCulloch, B. (2010). Dealing with bullying behaviours in the workplace: What works – a practitioner's view. *Journal of the International Ombudsman Association*, *3*(2), 38–51. Retrieved from http://www.ombudsassociation.org/Resources/IOA-Publications/IOA-Journal/Journal-PDFs/JIOAVolume3No2October2010Final.aspx

McKinsey, & LeanIn. (2015). *Women in the workplace 2015*. Retrieved from http://womenintheworkplace.com/ui/pdfs/Women_in_the_Workplace_2015.pdf?v=5

McKinsey. (2012). *Unlocking the full potential of women at work organization*. Retrieved from http://www.mckinsey.com/business-functions/organization/our-insights/unlocking-the-full-potential-of-women-at-work

McKinsey. (2014, January). *Moving mind-sets on gender diversity: McKinsey global survey results*. Retrieved from: http://www.mckinsey.com/business-functions/organization/our-insights/moving-mind-sets-on-gender-diversity-mckinsey-global-survey-results

McKinsey. (2015, January). *Why Diversity Matters*. Retrieved from http://www.mckinsey.com/business-functions/organization/our-insights/why-diversity-matters

McMahon, A. M. (2010). Does workplace diversity matter? A survey of empirical studies on diversity and firm performance, 2000-09. *Journal of Diversity Management*, *5*(2), 37–48.

Mcmillan, K., Butow, P., Turner, J., Yates, P., White, K., Lambert, S., & Lawsin, C. et al. (2016). Burnout and the provision of psychosocial care amongst Australian cancer nurses. *European Journal of Oncology Nursing*, *22*, 37–45. doi:10.1016/j.ejon.2016.02.007 PMID:27179891

McMurran, M., Egan, V., Blair, M., & Richardson, C. (2001). The relationship between social problem-solving and personality in mentally disordered offenders. *Personality and Individual Differences*, *30*(3), 517–524. doi:10.1016/S0191-8869(00)00050-7

McPheat, S. (2010). *MTD training: Effective communication skills*. MTD Training & Ventus Publishing. Retrieved from http://promeng.eu/downloads/training-materials/ebooks/soft-skills/effective-communication-skills.pdf

McQuail, D. (2005). *McQuail's mass communication theory* (5th ed.). London: Sage Publications.

McShane, S. L., & Von Glinow, M. A. (2003). *Organizational behavior: Emerging realities for the workplace revolution* (2nd ed.). Boston, MA: McGraw-Hill.

McTavish, D. G., & Pirro, E. B. (1990). Contextual content analysis. *Quality & Quantity*, *24*(3), 245–265. doi:10.1007/BF00139259

Meena, M. L., & Dangayach, G. S. (2012). Analysis of Employee Satisfaction in Banking Sector. *International Journal of Humanities and Applied Sciences*, *1*(2), 78–81.

Mesmer-Magnus, J. R., & Viswesvaran, C. (2008). Expatriate management: A review and directions for research in expatriate selection, training, and repatriation. In M. M. Harris (Ed.), *Handbook of research in international human resource management* (pp. 183–206). New York: Lawrence Erlbaum Associates.

Messing, K., Tissot, F., Saurel-Cubizolles, M. J., Kaminski, M., & Bourgine, M. (1998). Sex as a variable can be a surrogate for some working conditions: Factors associated with sickness absence. *Journal of Occupational and Environmental Medicine*, *40*(3), 250–260. doi:10.1097/00043764-199803000-00007 PMID:9531096

Meyer, J. W., & Rowan, B. (1977). Institutionalized organizations: Formal structure as myth and ceremony. *American Journal of Sociology*, *83*(2), 340–363. doi:10.1086/226550

Meyskens, M., Carsrud, A. L., & Cardozo, R. N. (2010). The symbiosis of entities in the social engagement network: The role of social ventures. *Entrepreneurship & Regional Development*, *22*(5), 425–455. doi:10.1080/08985620903168299

Miao, C., Humphrey, R. H., & Qian, S. (2016). Leader emotional intelligence and subordinate job satisfaction: A meta-analysis of main, mediator, and moderator effects. *Personality and Individual Differences*, *102*, 13–24. doi:10.1016/j.paid.2016.06.056

Michaels, E., Handfield-Jones, H., & Axelrod, B. (2001). *The war for talent*. Harvard Business Press.

Michalos, G., Makris, S., & Chryssolouris, G. (2013). The effect of job rotation during assembly on the quality of final product. *CIRP Journal of Manufacturing Science and Technology*, *6*(3), 187–197. doi:10.1016/j.cirpj.2013.03.001

Mikolajczak, K. M., Roy, E., Verstrynge, V., & Luminet, O. (2009). An exploration of the moderating effect of trait emotional intelligence on memory and attention in neutral and stress conditions. *British Journal of Psychology*, *100*(4), 699–715. Retrieved from http://www.vikalpa.com/pdf/articles/2010/vol-35-1jan-mar-53-61.pdf doi:10.1348/000712608X395522 PMID:19236794

Miles, E. W., Patrick, S. L., & King, W. C. Jr. (1996). Job level as a systemic variable in predicting the relationship between supervisory communication and job satisfaction. *Journal of Occupational and Organizational Psychology*, *69*(3), 277–292. doi:10.1111/j.2044-8325.1996.tb00615.x

Milliken, F. J., Morrison, E. W., & Hewlin, P. F. (2003). An exploratory study of employee silence: Issues that employees don't communicate upward and why. *Journal of Management Studies*, *40*(6), 1453–1476. doi:10.1111/1467-6486.00387

Minchington, B. (2013). *The Rise of Employer Brand Leadership, Second Ed., Oct. 2013*. Retrieved from http://www.employerbrandinginternational.com

Minchington, B. (2014). *Employer Branding Global Trends Study Report*. Retrieved from www.slideshare.net/brettminch/2014-employer-branding-global-trends-survey-report-by-employer-brand-international.pdf

Mishra, S., & Bhagat, M. (2007). *Principles for successful implementation of labour welfare activities from police theory to functional theory*. Retrieved from http://www.tesionline.com/intl/indepth.jsp?id=575

Mitchell, M. S., & Ambrose, M. L. (2007). Abusive supervision and workplace deviance and the moderating effects of negative reciprocity beliefs. *The Journal of Applied Psychology*, *92*(4), 1159–1168. doi:10.1037/0021-9010.92.4.1159 PMID:17638473

Mitchell, R. K., Busenitz, L., Lant, T., McDougall, P. P., Morse, E. A., & Smith, J. B. (2002). Toward a theory of entrepreneurial cognition: Rethinking the people side of entrepreneurship research. *Entrepreneurship Theory and Practice*, *27*(2), 93–104. doi:10.1111/1540-8520.00001

Mitchell, R. K., Smith, B., Seawright, K. W., & Morse, E. A. (2000). Cross-cultural cognitions and the venture creation decision. *Academy of Management Journal*, *43*(5), 974–993. doi:10.2307/1556422

Compilation of References

Miyoshi, K. (2009). *Tenkinto kikon joseino kyaria keisei* [*Relocation and married women's career development*]. Tokyo, Japan: Hakuto-Shobo.

Moen, P., Kelly, E., Fan, W., Lee, S.-R., Almeida, D., Kossek, E., & Buxton, O. (2016). Does a flexibility/support organizational initiative improve high-tech employees well-being? Evidence from the work, family, and health network. *American Sociological Review*, *81*(1), 134–164. doi:10.1177/0003122415622391

Mohrman, A. M. Jr, Resnick-West, S. M., & Lawler, E. E. III. (1989). *Designing Performance Appraisal Systems - Aligning Appraisals and Organizational Realities*. San Francisco: Jossey Bass Publishers.

Monappa, A., Nambudiri, R., & Selvaraj, P. (2012). *Industrial Relations and Labour Laws* (2nd ed.). New Delhi, India: Tata McGraw-Hill Publishing Company Limited.

Montano, D., Reeske, A., Franke, F., & Hüffmeier, J. (2016). Leadership, followers mental health and job performance in organizations: A comprehensive meta-analysis from an occupational health perspective. *Journal of Organizational Behavior*. doi:10.1002/job.2124

Montgomery, A., Spânu, F., Băban, A., & Panagopoulou, E. (2015). Job demands, burnout, and engagement among nurses: A multi-level analysis of ORCAB data investigating the moderating effect of teamwork. *Burnout Research*, *2*(2), 71–79. doi:10.1016/j.burn.2015.06.001 PMID:26877971

Montgomey, J., Storey, K., & Post, M. (2011). The use of auditory prompting systems for increasing independent performance of students with autism in employment training. *International Journal of Rehabilitation Research. Internationale Zeitschrift fur Rehabilitationsforschung. Revue Internationale de Recherches de Readaptation*, *34*(4), 330–335. doi:10.1097/MRR.0b013e32834a8fa8 PMID:21885987

Moorman, R. H. (1993). The influence of cognitive and affective based job satisfaction measures on the relationship between satisfaction and organizational citizenship behavior. *Human Relations*, *46*(6), 759–776. doi:10.1177/001872679304600604

Moorthy, M. V. (1968). *Principles of Labour Welfare* (1st ed.). Visakhapatnam, India: Gupta Bros. Books.

Moreau, R. (2013). *The value of foreign languages in business communication*. Retrieved from http://scholarsarchive.jwu.edu/cgi/viewcontent.cgi?article=1016&context=mba_student

Morgan, D. L. (1993). Qualitative content analysis: A guide to paths not taken. *Qualitative Health Research*, *3*(1), 112–121. doi:10.1177/104973239300300107 PMID:8457790

Morgan, S. J., & Symon, G. (2002). Computer-Mediated Communication and Remote Management: Integration or Isolation? *Social Science Computer Review*, *20*(3), 302–311. doi:10.1177/089443930202000307

Moroko, L., & Uncles, M. D. (2008). Uncles M.D.: Characteristics of successful employer brands. *Journal of Brand Management*, *16*(3), 160–175. doi:10.1057/bm.2008.4

Morris, C. W. (1938). *Foundations of the theory of signs*. Chicago: Chicago University Press.

Morris, J. H., & Sherman, J. D. (1981). Generalizability of an organizational commitment model. *Academy of Management Journal*, *24*(3), 512–526. doi:10.2307/255572

Morrison, E. W. (2014). Employee voice and silence. *Annual Review of Organizational Psychology and Organizational Behavior*, *1*(1), 173–197. doi:10.1146/annurev-orgpsych-031413-091328

Morrison, E. W., & Milliken, F. J. (2000). Organizational silence: A barrier to change and development in a pluralistic world. *Academy of Management Review*, *25*(4), 706–725.

Mosley, R. (2009). *Employer Brand. The Performance Driver No Business Can Ignore*. Shoulders of Giants Publication.

Mowday, R. T., Porter, L. W., & Dubin, R. (1974). Unit performance, situational factors, and employee attitudes in spatially separated work units. *Organizational Behavior and Human Performance*, *12*(2), 231–248. doi:10.1016/0030-5073(74)90048-8

Mowday, R., & Sutton, R. (1993). Organizational behavior: Linking individuals and groups to organizational contexts. *Annual Review of Psychology*, *44*(1), 195–229. doi:10.1146/annurev.ps.44.020193.001211 PMID:19090760

Muchinsky, P.M. (1977). Organizational communication: Relationships to organizational climate and job satisfaction. *Academy of Management Journal (pre-1986)*, *20*(4), 592-607.

Muchinsky, P. M. (2000). Emotions in the workplace: The neglect of organizational behavior. *Journal of Organizational Behavior*, *21*(7), 801–805. doi:10.1002/1099-1379(200011)21:7<801::AID-JOB999>3.0.CO;2-A

Mueller, S. L., & Thomas, A. S. (2001). Culture and entrepreneurial potential: A nine country study of locus of control and innovativeness. *Journal of Business Venturing*, *16*(1), 51–75. doi:10.1016/S0883-9026(99)00039-7

Mukhopadhyay, P. (2006). Looking Beyond the Horizon: Ergonomics in India. *Ergonomics in Design: The Quarterly of Human Factors Applications*, *14*(3), 4–35. doi:10.1177/106480460601400302

Mukhopadhyay, P., & Ghosal, S. (2008). Ergonomic design intervention in manual incense sticks manufacturing. *The Design Journal*, *11*(1), 65–80. doi:10.2752/175630608X317913

Mukhopadhyay, P., O'Sullivan, L. W., & Gallwey, T. J. (2007). Effects of upper arm articulations on shoulder-arm discomfort profile in a pronation task. *Occupational Ergonomics*, *7*(3), 169–181.

Mukhopadhyay, P., & Srivastava, S. (2010a). Ergonomic design issues in some craft sectors of Jaipur. *The Design Journal*, *13*(1), 99–124. doi:10.2752/146069210X12580336766446

Mukhopadhyay, P., & Srivastava, S. (2010b). Evaluating ergonomic risk factors in non-regulated stone carving units of Jaipur. *Work (Reading, Mass.)*, *35*(1), 87–99. PMID:20164628

Mullins, L. (1999). *Management and organizational behavior* (9th ed.). London: Financial Times / Prentice Hall.

Mulvey, K. P., Hubbard, S., & Hayashi, S. (2003). A national study of the substance abuse treatment workforce. *Journal of Substance Abuse Treatment*, *24*(3), 51–57. Retrieved from http://www.attcnetwork.org/wfs/documents/mulvey_article.pdf doi:10.1016/S0740-5472(02)00322-7 PMID:12646330

Muralidharan, E., & Pathak, S. (2016). (in press). Informal institutions and international entrepreneurship. *International Business Review*. doi:10.1016/j.ibusrev.2016.07.006

Murphy, W., & Ayer, B. (2016, April 26). *The benefits of virtual mentors*. Retrieved from https://hbr.org/2016/04/the-benefits-of-virtual-mentors

Murphy, K. R., & Cleveland, J. N. (1990). *Performance Appraisal: An Organizational Perspective*. Boston: Allyn and Bacon.

Murphy, K. R., & Cleveland, J. N. (1995). *Understanding Performance Appraisal: Social, Organizational, and Goal-Based Perspectives*. Thousand Oaks, CA: Sage Publications.

Murray, J. A. (1973). International personnel repatriation: Cultural shock in reverse. *MSU Business Topics*, *21*(3), 59–66.

Mwiti, J. K. (2007). The Role of Welfare Services in Motivation of Staff in Kenyan Parastatals: A case Study of Teachers Service Commission. Jomo: Kenyatta University of Agriculture and Technology.

Myers, S. A., & Kassing, J. W. (1998). The relationship between perceived supervisory communication behaviors and subordinate organizational identification. *Communication Research Reports, 15*(1), 71–81. doi:10.1080/08824099809362099

Mynors-Wallis, L. M., Gath, D. H., Day, A., & Baker, F. (2000). Randomised controlled trial of problem solving treatment, antidepressant medication, and combined treatment for major depression in primary care. *BMJ (Clinical Research Ed.), 320*(7226), 26–30. doi:10.1136/bmj.320.7226.26 PMID:10617523

Nabirye, R. C., Brown, K. C., Pryor, E. R., & Maples, E. H. (2011). Occupational stress, job satisfaction and job performance among hospital nurses in Kampala, Uganda. *Journal of Nursing Management, 19*(6), 760–768. doi:10.1111/j.1365-2834.2011.01240.x PMID:21899629

Nag, A., & Nag, P. K. (2004). Do the work stress factors of women telephone operators change with the shift schedules? *International Journal of Industrial Ergonomics, 33*(5), 449–461. doi:10.1016/j.ergon.2003.11.004

Nag, P. K., Chintharia, S., Saiyed, S., & Nag, A. (1986). EMG analysis of sitting work postures in women. *Applied Ergonomics, 17*(3), 195–197. doi:10.1016/0003-6870(86)90006-2 PMID:15676585

Nag, P. K., & Nag, A. (2007). Hazards and health complaints associated with fish processing activities in India—Evaluation of a low-cost intervention. *International Journal of Industrial Ergonomics, 37*(2), 125–132. doi:10.1016/j.ergon.2006.10.012

Nahapiet, J., & Ghoshal, S. (1998). Social capital, intellectual capital, and the organizational advantage. *Academy of Management Review, 23*(2), 242–266.

Naito, Y. (2016). Multiple aspects of readjustment experienced by international repatriates in multinational enterprises: A perspective of changes occurring over time and changes due to cultural differences. In Y. Guo, H. G. Rammal, & P. J. Dowling (Eds.), Global talent management and staffing in MNEs (International Business and Management, Vol. 32; pp. 101–124). Bingley, UK: Emerald Group. doi:10.1108/S1876-066X20160000032004

Naito, Y. (2009). Kaigai karano kininkatei niokeru mondai to sonoshien: Nikkei ote takokusekikigyo no kininsha heno chosa kara [Issues of international repatriation and organizational support: A study of repatriates at large Japanese multinational corporations]. *Journal of International Business, 1*(1), 1–17.

Naito, Y. (2011). Soshikisaishakaika niokeru johonyushukoi to soshikitekio: Kaigaikininsha wo taishotosita moderu no kochiku to kensho [Repatriation as an organizational re-socialization: An empirical study of an information acquisition model for repatriation adjustment in large Japanese MNCs]. *Organization Science, 45*(1), 93–110.

Naito, Y. (2012a). Kaigaihaken karano kinin: Soshiki heno saitekio to sonoketteiyoin [Repatriation after overseas assignments: Readjustment to organizations and its determinants]. *The Japanese Journal of Labour Studies, 626*, 75–88.

Naito, Y. (2012b). Kaigaikara no kikokusha no saitekio: Kigyo no kaigaihaken niyoru kininsha no seikatutekio wo chusintoshite [Readjustment of returnees from foreign countries: Focusing on readjustment to the daily life of corporate repatriates]. *Sauvage: Graduate students' bulletin, Graduate School of International Media, Communication and Tourism Studies. Hokkaido University, 8*, 45–56.

Naito, Y. (2015). Kaigai haken kininsya no seikatsu ippan eno saitekiou: Nikkei takokuseki kigyou deno chosa kara [Factors related to readjustment to daily life: A study of repatriates in Japanese multi-national enterprises]. *Journal of the Faculty of Political Science and Economics, 47*, 159–177.

Namie, G. (2014). *U.S. workplace bullying survey*. Workplace Bullying Institute. Retrieved from http://www.workplacebullying.org/multi/pdf/WBI-2014-US-Survey.pdf

Namie, G., & Namie, R. (2009a). *The bully at work: What you can do to stop the hurt and reclaim your dignity on the job*. Naperville, IL: Sourcebooks.

Namie, G., & Namie, R. (2009b). U.S. workplace bullying: Some basic considerations and consultation interventions. *Consulting Psychology Journal: Practice and Research, 61*(3), 202–219. doi:10.1037/a0016670

Nanda, N., & Panda, J.K. (2013). Challenges and effectiveness of industrial relation environment in Indian Industries study on Rourkela Steel Plant. *International Journal of Financial Services and management Research, 2*(6), 163-174.

Nantsupawat, A., Nantsupawat, R., Kunaviktikul, W., Turale, S., & Poghosyan, L. (2016). Nurse burnout, nurse-reported quality of care, and patient outcomes in Thai hospitals. *Journal of Nursing Scholarship, 48*(1), 83–90. doi:10.1111/jnu.12187 PMID:26650339

Naughton, K., Raymond, J., Shulman, K., & Struzzi, D. (1999). Cyberslacking. *Newsweek, 134(22)*, 62-65.

Naz, S., Hashmi, A. M., & Asif, A. (2016). Burnout and quality of life in nurses of a tertiary care hospital in Pakistan. *JPMA. The Journal of the Pakistan Medical Association, 66*(5), 532–536. PMID:27183930

Neetha, N. (2001). *Gender and Technology: Impact of flexible Organization and Production on Female Labour in the Tiruppur Knitwear Industry*. Noida, India: V.V. Giri National Labour Institute.

Nelis, D., Quoidbach, J., Mikolajczak, M., & Hansenne, M. (2009). Increasing emotional intelligence: (How) is it possible? *Personality and Individual Differences, 47*(1), 36–41. doi:10.1016/j.paid.2009.01.046

Nemiro, J. E., Bradley, L., Beyerlein, M. M., & Beyerlein, S. (2008). *The Handbook of High-Performance Virtual Teams: A Toolkit for Collaborating Across Boundaries*. San Francisco: Jossey-Bass.

Nesbit, P. L., & Lam, E. (2014). Cultural adaptability and organizational change: A case study of a social service organization in Hong Kong. *Contemporary Management Research, 10*(4), 303–324. doi:10.7903/cmr.12186

Newell, S., Tansley, C., & Huang, J. (2004). Social capital and knowledge integration in an ERP project team: The importance of bridging and bonding. *British Journal of Management, 15*(S1), S43–S57. doi:10.1111/j.1467-8551.2004.00405.x

Newman, D. A., Joseph, D. A., & MacCann, C. (2010). Emotional intelligence and job performance: The importance of emotion regulation and emotional labor context. *Industrial and Organizational Psychology: Perspectives on Science and Practice, 3*(2), 159–164. doi:10.1111/j.1754-9434.2010.01218.x

Newton, C. (2011). The five communication styles. Retrieved from http://www.clairenewton.co.za/my-articles/the-five-communication-styles.html

Newton, S. K., & Nowak, L. I. (2013). Attitudes and work environment factors influencing the information technology professionals' work behaviors. *International Journal of Human Capital and Information Technology Professionals, 4*(4), 46–65. doi:10.4018/ijhcitp.2013100104

Newton, S. K., Nowak, L. I., & Blanton, J. E. (2012). The relationship between the fulfillment of the IT professional's psychological contract and their organizational citizenship and innovative work behaviors. In *Human resources management: Concepts, methodologies, tools, and applications* (pp. 1085–1105). Hershey, PA: IGI Global. doi:10.4018/978-1-4666-1601-1.ch067

Nezu, A. M. (1985). Differences in psychological distress between effective and ineffective problem solvers. *Journal of Counseling Psychology, 32*(1), 135–138. doi:10.1037/0022-0167.32.1.135

Nezu, A. M. (1986). Cognitive appraisal of problem solving effectiveness: Relation to depression and depressive symptoms. *Journal of Clinical Psychology*, *42*(1), 42–48. doi:10.1002/1097-4679(198601)42:1<42::AID-JCLP2270420106>3.0.CO;2-2 PMID:3950013

Ng, S. M., Ke, G. N., & Raymond, W. (2014). The mediating role of work locus of control on the relationship among emotional intelligence, organisational citizenship behaviours, and mental health among nurses. *Australian Journal of Psychology*, *66*(4), 207–215. doi:10.1111/ajpy.12049

Ng, T. W. H., Lam, S. S. K., & Feldman, D. C. (2016). Organizational citizenship behavior and counterproductive work behavior: Do males and females differ? *Journal of Vocational Behavior*, *93*, 11–32. doi:10.1016/j.jvb.2015.12.005

Nicholls, A. (2006). *Social entrepreneurship: New models of sustainable social change*. Oxford: Oxford University Press.

Nicholls, A. (2010). The legitimacy of social entrepreneurship: Reflexive isomorphism in a pre-paradigmatic field. *Entrepreneurship Theory and Practice*, *34*(4), 611–633. doi:10.1111/j.1540-6520.2010.00397.x

Nicholls, A., & Opal, C. (2005). *Fair trade: Market-driven ethical consumption*. London: Sage.

Nicolini, D., & Meznar, M. B. (1995). The social construction of organizational learning: Conceptual and practical issues in the field. *Human Relations*, *48*(7), 727–746. doi:10.1177/001872679504800701

Nicotera, A. M., & Dorsey, L. K. (2006). Individual and interactive processes in organizational conflict. In J. G. Oetzel & S. Ting-Toomey (Eds.), *The Sage handbook of conflict communication: Integrating theory, research, and practice* (pp. 293–325). Thousand Oaks, CA: Sage. doi:10.4135/9781412976176.n11

Niedenthal, P. H., Krauth-Gruber, S., & Ric, F. (2006). *Psychology of Emotion: Interpersonal, Experiential and Cognitive Approaches*. New York: Psychology Press.

Nielsen, M., Matthiesen, S. B., & Einarsen, S. (2010). The impact of methodological moderators on prevalence rates of workplace bullying. A meta-analysis. *Journal of Occupational and Organizational Psychology*, *83*(4), 955–979. doi:10.1348/096317909X481256

Nielsen, M., Notelaers, G., & Einarsen, S. (2011). Measuring exposure to workplace bullying. In S. Einarsen, H. Hoel, D. Zapf, & C. L. Cooper (Eds.), *Bullying and harassment in the workplace: Developments in theory, research, and practice* (2nd ed., pp. 149–174). Boca Raton, FL: CRC Press.

Nie, Z., Jin, Y., He, L., Chen, Y., Ren, X., Yu, J., & Yao, Y. (2015). Correlation of burnout with social support in hospital nurses. *International Journal of Clinical and Experimental Medicine*, *8*(10), 19144–191449. PMID:26770546

Nigel Wright Recruitment. (2013). *Employer Branding Report*. Retrieved from http://www.nigelwright.com/media/1531/employer-branding-report.pdf

Nikmaram, S., Yamchi, G. H., Shojaii, S., Zahrani, M. A., & Alvani, S. M. (2012). Study on relationship between organizational silence and commitment in Iran. *World Applied Sciences Journal*, *17*(10), 1271–1277.

Nixon, A. E., Mazzola, J. J., Bauer, J., Krueger, J. R., & Spector, P. E. (2011). Can work make use sick? A meta-analysis of the relationship between job stressors and physical symptoms. *Work and Stress*, *25*(1), 1–22. doi:10.1080/02678373.2011.569175

Noe, R. A., Hollenberg, J. R., Gerhart, B., & Wright, P. M. (2009). *Fundamentals of Human Resource Management* (4th ed.). New York: Mc Graw Hill.

Nolen-Hoeksema, S. (2011). *Abnormal Psychology* (5th ed., p. 522). New York: McGraw-Hill.

Nonaka, I. (1994). A dynamic theory of organizational knowledge creation. *Organization Science*, *5*(1), 14–37. doi:10.1287/orsc.5.1.14

Nooryan, K., Gasparyan, K., Sharif, F., & Zoladl, M. (2012). Controlling anxiety in physicians and nurses working in intensive care units using emotional intelligence items as an anxiety management tool in Iran. *International Journal of General Medicine*, *5*, 5–10. doi:10.2147/IJGM.S25850 PMID:22259255

North, D. C. (1990). *Institutions, institutional change and economic performance*. Cambridge, UK: Cambridge University Press. doi:10.1017/CBO9780511808678

North, D. C. (1991). Institutions, transaction costs, and the rise of merchant empires. In J. D. Tracy (Ed.), *The political economy of merchant empires* (pp. 22–40). Cambridge, UK: Cambridge University Press. doi:10.1017/CBO9780511665288.002

North, D. C. (2005). *Understanding the process of economic change*. Princeton: Princeton University Press. doi:10.1515/9781400829484

Noseleit, F. (2010). The entrepreneurial culture: Guiding principles of the self-employed. In A. Freytag & R. Thurik (Eds.), *Entrepreneurship and culture* (pp. 41–54). Berlin: Springer. doi:10.1007/978-3-540-87910-7_3

Nöth, W. (1990). *Handbook of semiotics*. Bloomington, IN: Indiana University Press.

Nyberg, A., Bernin, P., & Theorell, T. (2005). *The impact of leadership on the health of subordinates*. Stockholm: National Institute for Working Life.

Oginska-Bulik, N. (2005). Emotional intelligence in the workplace: Exploring its effects on occupational stress and health outcomes in human service worker. *International Journal of Occupational Medicine and Environmental Health*, *18*(2), 167–175. Retrieved from http://www.imp.lodz.pl/upload/oficyna/artykuly/pdf/full/Ogi8-02-05.pdf PMID:16201208

Oginska-Bulik, N. (2005). The role of personal and social resources in preventing adverse health outcomes in employees of uniformed professions. *International Journal of Occupational Medicine and Environmental Health*, *18*(3), 233–240. PMID:16411561

Okan, Z. (2007). *Towards a critical theory of educational technology*. Retrieved from http://files.eric.ed.gov/fulltext/ED500086.pdf

OKelly, F., Manecksha, R. P., Quinlan, D. M., Reid, A., Joyce, A., OFlynn, K., & Thornhill, J. A. et al. (2016). Rates of self-reported burnout and causative factors amongst urologists in Ireland and the UK: A comparative cross-sectional study. *BJU International*, *117*(2), 363–372. doi:10.1111/bju.13218 PMID:26178315

Olweus, D. (2003). Bully/ victim problems in school. Basic facts and an effective intervention programme. In S. Einarsen, H. Hoel, D. Zapf, & C. L. Cooper (Eds.), *Bullying and emotional abuse in the workplace* (pp. 62–78). London: Taylor and Francis.

Oplatka, I. (2009). Organizational citizenship behavior in teaching: The consequences for teachers, pupils, and the school. *International Journal of Educational Management*, *23*(5), 375–389. doi:10.1108/09513540910970476

Organ, D. W. (1988). *Organizational citizenship behavior: The good soldier syndrome*. Lexington, MA: Lexington Books.

Organ, D. W., Podsakoff, P. M., & MacKenzie, S. B. (2006). *Organizational citizenship behavior: Its nature, antecedents, and consequences*. London, UK: Sage Publications.

Orpen, C. (1997). The interactive effects of communication quality and job involvement on managerial job satisfaction and work motivation. *The Journal of Psychology*, *131*(5), 519–522. doi:10.1080/00223989709603540

Oser, C., Biebel, P., Pullen, E., & Kathi, L. H. (2013). Causes, consequences, and prevention of burnout among substance abuse treatment counselors: A rural versus urban comparison. *Journal of Psychoactive Drugs*, *45*(1), 17–27. doi:10.1080/02791072.2013.763558 PMID:23662328

Oslo School of Management and Agenda. (2015, April 9). *Men who dislike female leaders* (YouTube video) Retrieved from https://www.youtube.com/watch?v=Ad1giiCO6k0

OSullivan, L. W., & Gallwey, T. J. (2005). Forearm torque strengths and discomfort profiles in pronation and supination. *Ergonomics*, *48*(6), 703–721. doi:10.1080/00140130500070954 PMID:16087504

Ouchi, W. G. (1981). *Theory Z: How American business can meet the Japanese challenge*. Reading, MA: Addison-Wesley. doi:10.1016/0007-6813(81)90031-8

Ouyang, Z., Sang, J., Li, P., & Peng, J. (2015). Organizational justice and job insecurity as mediators of the effect of emotional intelligence on job satisfaction: A study from China. *Personality and Individual Differences*, *76*, 147–152. doi:10.1016/j.paid.2014.12.004

Overmann, M. (2011). *President Obama on the importance of foreign language*. Retrieved from http://www.alliance-exchange.org/policy-monitor/08/22/2011/president-obama-importance-foreign-languages

Owen, D. (2006). Hubris and Nemesis in heads of government. *Journal of the Royal Society of Medicine*, *99*(11), 548–551. doi:10.1258/jrsm.99.11.548 PMID:17082296

Owen, D., & Davidson, J. (2009). Hubris syndrome: An acquired personality disorder? A study of US Presidents and UK Prime Ministers over the last 100 years. *Brain*, *132*(5), 1396–1406. doi:10.1093/brain/awp008 PMID:19213778

Özçelik, G., & Fındıklı, M. A. (2014). The relationship between internal branding and organizational citizenship behaviour: The mediating role of person-organization fit. *Procedia: Social and Behavioral Sciences*, *150*, 1120–1128. doi:10.1016/j.sbspro.2014.09.127

Özdemir, Y., & Ergun, S. (2015). The relationship between organizational socialization and organizational citizenship behavior: The mediating role of person-environment fit. *Procedia: Social and Behavioral Sciences*, *207*, 432–443. doi:10.1016/j.sbspro.2015.10.113

Özpehlivan, M., & Acar, A. Z. (2015). Assessment of a multidimensional job satisfaction instrument. *Procedia: Social and Behavioral Sciences*, *210*, 283–290. doi:10.1016/j.sbspro.2015.11.368

Öztürk, N., & Esin, M. N. (2011). Investigation of musculoskeletal symptoms and ergonomic risk factors among female sewing machine operators in Turkey. *International Journal of Industrial Ergonomics*, *41*(6), 585–591. doi:10.1016/j.ergon.2011.07.001

Ozyurt, A., Hayran, O., & Sur, H. (2006). Predictors of burnout and job satisfaction among Turkish physicians. *QJM*, *99*(3), 161–169. doi:10.1093/qjmed/hcl019 PMID:16490757

Paddison, D. (2013). Guided sponsorship: The ultimate tool for internal talent sourcing. *Leader to Leader*, *2013*(67), 13–18. doi:10.1002/ltl.20056

Palmer, B., Walls, M., Burgess, Z., & Stough, C. (2000). Emotional intelligence and effective leadership. *Leadership and Organization Development Journal*, *21*(1), 5–10. Retrieved from http://www.carmineleo.com/files/3713/5946/8640/ei-leadership.pdf

Palo, U. (1997). *Language skills in inter-unit communication of an internationalizing company: The case of Outokumpu*. Unpublished master's thesis. Helsinki School of Economics, Helsinki, Finland.

Pandi-Perumal, S. R., Verster, J. C., Kayumov, L., Lowe, A. D., Santana, M. G., Pires, M. L. N., & Mello, M. T. et al. (2006). Sleep disorders, sleepiness and traffic safety: A public health menace. *Brazilian Journal of Medical and Biological Research*, *39*(7), 863–871. doi:10.1590/S0100-879X2006000700003 PMID:16862276

Panteli, N. (2009). Virtual Social Networks: A New Dimension for Virtuality Research. In N. Panteli (Ed.), *Virtual Social Networks: Mediated, Massive and Multiplayer Sites*. Hampshire, UK: Palgrave-Macmillan. doi:10.1057/9780230250888_1

Panteli, N., & Davison, R. M. (2005). The Role of Subgroups in the Communication Patterns of Global Virtual Teams. *IEEE Transactions on Professional Communication*, *48*(2), 191–200. doi:10.1109/TPC.2005.849651

Panteli, N., & Duncan, E. (2004). Trust and temporary virtual teams: Alternative explanations and dramaturgical relationships. *Information Technology & People*, *17*(4), 423–441. doi:10.1108/09593840410570276

Parise, S. (2007). Knowledge management and human resource development: An application in social network analysis methods. *Advances in Developing Human Resources*, *9*(3), 359–383. doi:10.1177/1523422307304106

Parker, S. K., & Axtell, C. M. (2001). Seeing another viewpoint: Antecedents and outcomes of employee perspective taking. *Academy of Management Journal*, *44*(6), 1085–1100. doi:10.2307/3069390

Parkerson, G. R. Jr, Broadhead, W. E., & Tse, C. K. (1990). The health status and life satisfaction of first-year medical students. *Academic Medicine*, *65*(9), 586–588. doi:10.1097/00001888-199009000-00009 PMID:2400477

Parkinson, B. (1996). Emotions are social. *British Journal of Psychology*, *87*(4), 663–683. doi:10.1111/j.2044-8295.1996.tb02615.x PMID:8962482

Parkinson, B., Fischer, A. H., & Manstead, A. S. (2004). *Emotion in social relations: Cultural, group, and interpersonal processes*. New York: Psychology Press.

Parrill, S. (1999). *Revisiting Rating Format Research: Computer-Based Rating Formats and Components of Accuracy*. Unpublished manuscript, Virginia Polytechnic and State Institute, Blacksburg, VA.

Partee, B. (1989). Binding implicit variables in quantified contexts. In C. Wiltshire, B. Music, & R. Graczyk (Eds.), *Papers from Chicago Linguistic Society (CLS) 25* (pp. 342–365). Chicago: Chicago Linguistic Society.

Pasca, R., & Wagner, S. L. (2011). Occupational stress in the multicultural workplace. *Journal of Immigrant and Minority Health*, *13*(4), 697–705. doi:10.1007/s10903-011-9457-6 PMID:21394456

Patel, J. (2006). Silicosis among agate workers: Efforts to promote acceptance of safer technology. *Asian-Pacific Newsletter on Occupational Health and Safety*, *13*(1), 16–18.

Pathak, S., & Muralidharan, E. (2014). *Societal-level collectivism and trust: Influence on social and commercial entrepreneurship*.

Patrick, H. A., & Kumar, V. R. (2012). Managing Workplace Diversity: Issues and Challenges. *SAGE Open*, *2*(2). doi:10.1177/2158244012444615

Patro, C.S. (in press). Performance Appraisal-A Controversial Human Resource Tool. In *Encyclopedia of Information Sciences*.

Patro, C. S. (2012). Employee Welfare Activities in Private Sector and Their Impact on Quality of Work Life. *International Journal of Productivity Management and Assessment Technologies*, *1*(2), 18–29. doi:10.4018/ijpmat.2012040102

Patro, C. S. (2014). A Study on the Impact of Employee Retention Policies on Organisation Productivity in Private Sector. *International Journal of Asian Business and Information Management*, *5*(3), 48–63. doi:10.4018/ijabim.2014070104

Compilation of References

Patro, C. S. (2015). Employee Welfare Measures in Public and Private Sectors: A Comparative Analysis. *International Journal of Service Science, Management, Engineering, and Technology*, 6(1), 22–36. doi:10.4018/ijssmet.2015010102

Patro, C. S. (2016). A Study on Adoption of Employee Welfare Schemes in Industrial and Service Organisations: In Contrast with Public and Private Sectors. *International Journal of Service Science, Management, Engineering, and Technology*, 7(2), 16–33. doi:10.4018/IJSSMET.2016040102

Patro, C. S., & Raghunath, K. M. K. (2016). A Take on Employee Welfare Facilities and Employees Efficiency. *International Journal of Asian Business and Information Management*, 7(3), 54–70. doi:10.4018/IJABIM.2016070104

Patten, T. H. (1977). *Pay: Employee compensation and incentive plan*. London: Free Press.

Patterson, M. G., West, M. A., Shackleton, V. J., Dawson, J. F., Lawthom, R., Maitlis, S., & Wallace, A. M. et al. (2005). Validating the organizational climate measure: Links to managerial practices, productivity and innovation. *Journal of Organizational Behavior*, 26(4), 379–408. doi:10.1002/job.312

Patton, M. Q. (2002). *Qualitative research and evaluation methods*. Thousand Oaks, CA: Sage.

Paulhus, D. L., & Williams, K. M. (2002). The Dark Triad of personality: Narcissism, Machiavellianism, and psychopathy. *Journal of Research in Personality*, 36(6), 556–563. doi:10.1016/S0092-6566(02)00505-6

Paul-Odouard, R. (2006). *Emotional intelligence, social problem solving, and demographics as predictors of well-being in women with multiple roles* [Dissertation]. University of Adelphi.

Paul, S., Seetharaman, P., Samarah, I., & Mykytyn, P. P. (2004). Impact of heterogeneity and collaborative conflict management style on the performance of synchronous global virtual teams. *Information & Management*, 41(3), 303–321. doi:10.1016/S0378-7206(03)00076-4

Pavalache-Ilie, M. (2014). Organizational citizenship behaviour, work satisfaction and employees' personality. *Procedia: Social and Behavioral Sciences*, 127, 489–493. doi:10.1016/j.sbspro.2014.03.296

Pavitt, C. (1999). Theorizing about the group communication-leadership relationship: Input-process-output and functional models. In L. R. Frey, D. S. Gouran, & M. S. Poole (Eds.), *The handbook of group communication theory and research* (pp. 313–334). Thousand Oaks, CA: Sage.

Payne, D., & Joyner, B. E. (2006). Successful US entrepreneurs: Identifying ethical decision-making and social responsibility behaviors. *Journal of Business Ethics*, 65(3), 203–217. doi:10.1007/s10551-005-4674-3

Peckham, C. (2015, January 26). *Medscape Physician Lifestyle Report 2015* [Infographic]. Retrieved from http://www.medscape.com/features/slideshow/lifestyle/2015/public/overview

Pedersen, A. F., Andersen, C. M., Olesen, F., & Vedsted, P. (2013). Risk of burnout in Danish GPs and exploration of factors associated with development of burnout: A two-wave panel study. *International Journal of Family Medicine*, 2013, 1–8. doi:10.1155/2013/603713 PMID:24383000

Pelled, L. H., Eisenhardt, K. M., & Xin, K. R. (1999). Exploring the Black Box: An Analysis of Work Group Diversity, Conflict, and Performance. *Administrative Science Quarterly*, 44(1), 1. doi:10.2307/2667029

Pepitone, A., & Festinger, L. (1959). A theory of cognitive dissonance. *The American Journal of Psychology*, 72(1), 153. doi:10.2307/1420234

Pepper, G. L. (1995). *Communicating in Organizations: A Cultural Approach*. New York: McGraw-Hill.

Peredo, A. M., & McLean, M. (2006). Social entrepreneurship: A critical review of the concept. *Journal of World Business*, 41(1), 56–65. doi:10.1016/j.jwb.2005.10.007

Perkins, E. B., & Sprang, G. (2013). Results from the Pro-QOL-IV for substance abuse counselors working with offenders. *International Journal of Mental Health and Addiction, 11*(2), 199–213. doi:10.1007/s11469-012-9412-3

Perlberg, H. (2012, July 31). Stocks perform better if women are on company boards. Retrieved from http://www.bloomberg.com/news/articles/2012-07-31/women-as-directors-beat-men-only-boards-in-company-stock-return

Perneger, T. V., Deom, M., Cullati, S., & Bovier, P. A. (2012). Growing discontent of Swiss doctors, 1998–2007. *European Journal of Public Health, 22*(4), 478–483. doi:10.1093/eurpub/ckr114 PMID:21948053

Perry, J. (2015). *The problem of the essential indexical and other essays: Extended edition*. Center for the Study of Language and Information.

Persaud, R. (2005). The drama of being a doctor. *Postgraduate Medical Journal, 81*(955), 276–277. doi:10.1136/pgmj.2004.023796 PMID:15879037

Pescosolido, A. T. (2002). Emergent leaders as managers of group emotion. *The Leadership Quarterly, 13*(5), 583–599. doi:10.1016/S1048-9843(02)00145-5

Peters, T. J., & Waterman, R. H. Jr. (1982). *In search of excellence: Lessons from America's best-run companies*. New York: Warner Books.

Petit, A., Ha, C., Bodin, J., Rigouin, P., Descatha, A., Brunet, R., & Roquelaure, Y. et al. (2015). Risk factors for carpal tunnel syndrome related to the work organization: A prospective surveillance study in a large working population. *Applied Ergonomics, 47*, 1–10. doi:10.1016/j.apergo.2014.08.007 PMID:25479968

Pfeffer, J., & Baron, J. N. (1988). Taking the workers back out: Recent trends in the structuring of employment. *Research in Organizational Behavior, 10*, 257–303.

Pheysey, D. C. (1993). *Organizational Cultures: Types and Transformations*. London: Routledge. doi:10.4324/9780203028568

Philips, B. N., Deiches, J., Morrison, B., Chan, F., & Bezyak, J. L. (2016). Disability diversity training in the workplace: Systematic review and future directions. *Journal of Occupational Rehabilitation, 26*(3), 264–275. doi:10.1007/s10926-015-9612-3 PMID:26519035

Phillips, K. W., Northcraft, G. B., & Neale, M. A. (2006). Surface-Level Diversity and Decision-Making in Groups: When Does Deep-Level Similarity Help? *Group Processes & Intergroup Relations, 9*(4), 467–482. doi:10.1177/1368430206067557

Piccoli, G., Ahmad, R., & Ives, B. (2001). Web-based virtual learning environments: A research framework and a preliminary assessment of effectiveness in basic IT skills training. *Management Information Systems Quarterly, 25*(4), 401–426. doi:10.2307/3250989

Pierce, E., & Hansen, S. W. (2013). Technology, Trust and Effectiveness in Virtual Teams. *The International Journal of Management and Business, 4*(1), 33–56.

Pigou, A. C. (1962). *Economics of Welfare*. London: Macmillan Publishers.

Pikhart, M. (2011). English as a Lingua Franca and its international consequences: Applied linguistics approach. *Bulletin of the Transylvania University of Brasov, Philology & Cultural Studies, 4*(53), 201–204.

Pincus, J. D. (1986). Communication satisfaction, job satisfaction and job performance. *Human Communication Research, 12*(3), 395–419. doi:10.1111/j.1468-2958.1986.tb00084.x

Pines, A. M. (1993). Burnout: An existential perspective. In W. Schaufel, C. Maslach, an M. Tadeusz (Eds.), Professional burnout: Recent developments in theory and research. Series in applied psychology: Social issues and questions (p. 33-51). Philadelphia, PA: Taylor & Francis.

Compilation of References

Pines, A., & Aronson, E. (1988). *Career burnout: Causes and cures*. New York: Free Press.

Pinjani, P., & Palvia, P. (2013). Trust and knowledge sharing in diverse global virtual teams. *Information & Management*, *50*(4), 144–153. doi:10.1016/j.im.2012.10.002

Piperopoulos, G. (2007). Psychology: Individual, team and organization. 9th edition. Thessaloniki, Greece.

Pirola-Merlo, A., Härtel, C., Mann, L., & Hirst, G. (2002). How leaders influence the impact of affective events on team climate and performance in R & D teams. *The Leadership Quarterly*, *13*(5), 561–581. doi:10.1016/S1048-9843(02)00144-3

Pisanti, R., Van Der Doef, M., Maes, S., Meier, L. L., Lazzari, D., & Violani, C. (2016). How changes in psychosocial job characteristics impact burnout in nurses: A longitudinal analysis. *Frontiers in Psychology*, 7. PMID:27507952

Platania, S., Santisi, G., Magnano, P., & Ramaci, T. (2015). Job satisfaction and organizational well-being queried: A comparison between the two companies. *Procedia: Social and Behavioral Sciences*, *191*, 1436–1441. doi:10.1016/j.sbspro.2015.04.406

Platis, C., Reklitis, P., & Zimeras, S. (2015). Relation between job satisfaction and job performance in healthcare services. *Procedia: Social and Behavioral Sciences*, *175*, 480–487. doi:10.1016/j.sbspro.2015.01.1226

Plaude, A., & Rascevska, M. (2011). The association of cognition abilities, emotional intelligence, defense mechanisms and coping with employment and unemployment. *Baltic Journal of Psychology*, *12*(1), 83–101.

Podsakoff, N. P., Podsakoff, P. M., MacKenzie, S. B., Maynes, T. D., & Spoelma, T. M. (2014). Consequences of unit-level organizational citizenship behaviors: A review and recommendations for future research. *Journal of Organizational Behavior*, *35*(Suppl. 1), S87–S119. doi:10.1002/job.1911

Podsakoff, P. M., MacKenzie, S. B., Paine, J. B., & Bachrach, D. G. (2000). Organizational citizenship behaviors: A critical review of the theoretical and empirical literature and suggestions for future research. *Journal of Management*, *26*(3), 513–563. doi:10.1177/014920630002600307

Poghosyan, L., Clarke, S. P., Finlayson, M., & Aiken, L. H. (2010). Nurse burnout and quality of care: Cross-national investigation in six countries. *Research in Nursing & Health*, *33*(4), 288–298. doi:10.1002/nur.20383 PMID:20645421

Pohl, G. (2004). Cross-cultural pragmatic failure and implications for language teaching. *Second Language Learning & Teaching*, *4*(2), 91–112.

Polaczek, T. (2006). *Information security audit*. Gliwice: Helion.

Polanyi, K. (1957). *The great transformation: The political and economic origin of our time*. Boston: Beacon Hill.

Pollock, L. R., & Williams, J. M. G. (2001). Effective problem solving in suicide attempters depends on specific autobiographical recall. *Suicide & Life-Threatening Behavior*, *31*(4), 386–396. doi:10.1521/suli.31.4.386.22041 PMID:11775714

Polzer, J. T. (2008). Making diverse teams click. *Harvard Business Review*. Retrieved from https://hbr.org/2008/07/making-diverse-teams-click

Poon, J. (2004). Effects of performance appraisal politics on job satisfaction and turnover intention. *Personnel Review*, *33*(3), 322–334. doi:10.1108/00483480410528850

Popescu, A. M., Deaconu, A., & Popescu, T., (2015). Organization's age and organizational citizenship behavior (OCB), performance criteria at SMEs level. Case study - Bucharest – Ilfov development region. *Procedia Economics and Finance*, *22*, 645–654. doi:10.1016/S2212-5671(15)00278-6

Porcar, C. (2011). Sign and meaning: A semiotic approach to communication. *Journal of Communication and Culture, 1*(1), 20–29.

Porter-OGrady, T. (2003). A different age for leadership, part 1: New context, new content. *The Journal of Nursing Administration, 33*(2), 105–110. doi:10.1097/00005110-200302000-00007 PMID:12584463

Portes, A. (1998). Social capital: Its origins and applications in modern sociology. *Annual Review of Sociology, 22*(1), 1–24. doi:10.1146/annurev.soc.24.1.1

Portney, P. R. (2005). Corporate social responsibility: An Economic and Public Policy Perspective. In B.L. Hay, R.N. Stavins, & R.H.K. Vietor (Eds.), Environmental Protection and the Social Responsibility of Firms-Perspectives from Law, Economics, and Business (pp. 237-242). Washington DC, USA: REF Press book.

Postmes, T., Tanis, M., & de Wit, B. (2001). Communication and commitment in organizations: A social identity approach. *Group Processes & Intergroup Relations, 4*(3), 227–246. doi:10.1177/1368430201004003004

Powell, W. W., & DiMaggio, P. J. (1991). *The new institutionalism in organizational analysis.* Chicago: University of Chicago Press.

Power, M., & Dalgleish, T. (1997). *Cognition and emotion: From order to disorder.* Hove, UK: Psychology Press.

Pretorius, T. B., & Diedricks, M. (1994). Problem-solving appraisal, social support and stress-depression relationship. *South African Journal of Psychology. Suid-Afrikaanse Tydskrif vir Sielkunde, 24*(2), 86–90. doi:10.1177/008124639402400206

Priesemuth, M., Schminke, M., Ambrose, M. L., & Folger, R. (2014). Abusive supervision climate: A multiple-mediation model of its impact on group outcomes. *Academy of Management Journal, 57*(5), 1513–1534. doi:10.5465/amj.2011.0237

Prins, J. T., Van Der Heijden, F. M. M. A., Hoekstra-Weebers, J. E. H. M., Bakker, A. B., Van de Wiel, H. B. M., Jacobs, B., & Gazendam-Donofrio, S. M. (2009). Burnout, engagement and resident physicians self-reported errors. *Psychology Health and Medicine, 14*(6), 654–666. doi:10.1080/13548500903311554 PMID:20183538

Pritchard, C. W. (2007). *101 Strategies for recruiting success: where, when, and how to find the right people every time.* New York: AMACOM Division American Management Association.

Proctor, C. (2014). Effective organizational communication affects employee attitude, happiness, and job satisfaction (master's thesis). Retrieved from https://www.suu.edu/hss/comm/masters/capstone/thesis/proctor-c.pdf

Prosen, M., & Piskar, F. (2015). Job satisfaction of Slovenian hospital nursing workforce. *Journal of Nursing Management, 23*(2), 242–251. doi:10.1111/jonm.12121 PMID:23869437

Puffer, S. M., McCarthy, D. J., & Boisot, M. (2010). Entrepreneurship in Russia and China: The impact of formal institutional voids. *Entrepreneurship Theory and Practice, 34*(3), 441–467. doi:10.1111/j.1540-6520.2009.00353.x

Pugh, S. D. (2001). Service with a smile: Emotional contagion in the service encounter. *Academy of Management Journal, 44*(5), 1018–1027. doi:10.2307/3069445

Pu, J., Zhou, X., Zhu, D., Zhong, X., Yang, L., Wang, H., & Xie, P. et al. (2016). Gender differences in psychological morbidity, burnout, job stress and job satisfaction among Chinese neurologists: A national cross-sectional study. *Psychology Health and Medicine*, 1–13. doi:10.1080/13548506.2016.1211717 PMID:27436373

Punnett, L., & Herbert, R. (2000). Work-related musculoskeletal disorders: Is there a gender differential, and if so, what does it mean. *Women & Health, 38*(6), 474–492.

Compilation of References

Purpora, C., & Blegen, M. A. (2015). Job satisfaction and horizontal violence in hospital staff registered nurses: The mediating role of peer relationships. *Journal of Clinical Nursing*, *24*(15-16), 2286–2294. doi:10.1111/jocn.12818 PMID:25939756

Putnam, L. L., & Mumby, D. K. (1993). Organizations, emotion and the myth of rationality. Fineman, S. (Ed.), Emotion in organizations. (pp. 36-57). Thousand Oaks, CA: Sage Publications.

Putti, J. M., Aryee, S., & Phua, J. (1990). Communication relationship satisfaction and organizational commitment. *Group & Organization Studies*, *15*(1), 44–52. doi:10.1177/105960119001500104

PwC. (2013). *Mending the Gender Gap*. Retrieved from https://www.pwc.com/us/en/financial-services/publications/assets/pwc-advancing-women-in-financial-services.pdf

Pylee, M. V., & George, A. S. (1996). *Industrial Relations & Personnel Management*. New Delhi, India: Vikas Publishing House Pvt. Ltd.

Quattrin, R., Zanini, A., Nascig, E., Annunziata, M. A., Calligaris, L., & Brusaferro, S. (2006, July). Level of burnout among nurses working in oncology in an Italian region. *Oncology Nursing Forum*, *33*(4), 815–820. doi:10.1188/06.ONF.815-820 PMID:16858463

Rafaeli, A., & Sutton, R. I. (1987). Expression of emotion as part of the work role. *Academy of Management Review*, *12*(1), 23–37.

Rafferty, A. M., Clarke, S. P., Coles, J., Ball, J., James, P., McKee, M., & Aiken, L. H. (2007). Outcomes of variation in hospital nurse staffing in English hospitals: Cross-sectional analysis of survey data and discharge records. *International Journal of Nursing Studies*, *44*(2), 175–182. doi:10.1016/j.ijnurstu.2006.08.003 PMID:17064706

Railkar, J. S. (1990). *Labour welfare, trade unionism and industrial relations*. Bombay, India: Sheth Publishers Private Limited.

Rain, J. S., Lane, I. M., & Steiner, D. D. (1991). A current look at the job satisfaction/life satisfaction relationship: Review and future considerations. *Human Relations*, *44*(3), 287–307. doi:10.1177/001872679104400305

Rajah, R., Song, Z., & Arvey, R. D. (2011). Emotionality and leadership: Taking stock of the past decade of research. *The Leadership Quarterly*, *22*(6), 1107–1119. doi:10.1016/j.leaqua.2011.09.006

Rajhans, K. (2012). Effective organizational communication: A key to employee motivation and performance. *Interscience Management Review*, *2*(2), 81–85.

Rajkuar, B. (2014). A Study on Labour Welfare Measures and Social Security in IT Industries with Reference to Chennai. *International Journal of Enterprise Computing and Business Systems*, *4*(1), 1–10.

Ramana, T. V., & Reddy, E. L. (2015). A Study on Employee Welfare Measures With Reference to South Central Railways in India. *ZENITH International Journal of Business Economics & Management Research*, *5*(1), 1–11.

Ramirez, D. L. (2010). *Organizational communication satisfaction and job satisfaction within university foodservice* [Master's thesis]. Retrieved from http://krex.k-state.edu/dspace/bitstream/handle/2097/14123/danielramirez2012.pdf?sequence=1

Randstad (2013). *Employer Branding. Perception being reality. Results Randstad Award 2013. Global Report.* (online): http://www.randstadaward.ca

Rankin, G. D., & Kleiner, B. H. (1988). Effective performance appraisal. *Industrial Management & Data Systems*, *88*(1/2), 13–17. doi:10.1108/eb057500

Raut, P., & Kahkonen, E. (2006). How to improve occupational health, safety and environment by applying cleaner production in industry. *Asian-Pacific Newsletter on Occupational Health and Safety, 13*(3), 64–67.

Ravari, A., Bazargan, M., Vanaki, Z., & Mirzael, T. (2012). Job satisfaction among Iranian hospital-based practicing nurses: Examining the influence of self-expectation, social interaction and organisational situations. *Journal of Nursing Management, 20*(4), 522–533. doi:10.1111/j.1365-2834.2010.01188.x PMID:22591154

Ray, E. B., & Miller, K. I. (1991). The influence of communication structure and social support on job stress and burnout. *Management Communication Quarterly, 4*(4), 506–527. doi:10.1177/0893318991004004005

Ray, E. B., & Miller, K. I. (1994). Social support, home/work stress and burnout: Who can help? *The Journal of Applied Behavioral Science, 30*(3), 357–373. doi:10.1177/0021886394303007

Reagans, R., & McEvily, B. (2003). Network structure and knowledge transfer: The effects of cohesion and range. *Administrative Science Quarterly, 48*(2), 240–267. doi:10.2307/3556658

Reagans, R., & Zuckerman, E. W. (2001). Networks, diversity, and productivity: The social capital of corporate R&D teams. *Organization Science, 12*(4), 502–517. doi:10.1287/orsc.12.4.502.10637

Reed, M. S., Evely, A. C., Cundill, G., Fazey, I., Glass, J., Laing, A., & Stringer, L. C. et al. (2010). What is social learning? *Ecology and Society, 15*(4), 1–10. doi:10.5751/ES-03564-1504r01

Rees, D. W., & Cooper, C. L. (1992). Occupational stress in health service workers in the UK. *Stress Medicine, 8*(2), 79–90. doi:10.1002/smi.2460080205

Reeves, J. (2002). *Performance management in education*. London: Sage Publications.

Reinecke, M. A., DuBois, D. L., & Schultz, T. M. (2001). Social problem solving, mood, and suicidality among inpatient adolescents. *Cognitive Therapy and Research, 25*(6), 743–756. doi:10.1023/A:1012971423547

Reinke, S. J. (2003). Does The Form Really Matter? Leadership, Trust, and Acceptance of the Performance Appraisal Process. *Review of Public Personnel Administration, 23*(1), 23–37. doi:10.1177/0734371X02250109

Report, D. (2015). *Global Human Capital Trends 2015. Leading in the new world of work*, Deloitte University Press. Retrieved from http://www2.deloitte.com/content/dam/Deloitte/at/Documents/human-capital/hc-trends-2015.pdf

Report, G. (2013). *The state of global workplace. Employee engagement insights for business leaders worldwide*. Gallup Report. Retrieved from http://www.securex.be/export/sites/default/.content/download-gallery/nl/brochures/Gallup-state-of-the-GlobalWorkplaceReport_20131.pdf

Reshma, S., & Basavaraj, M. J. (2013). Employee welfare measures in mining industry–A study with reference to statutory welfare measures in NMDC, Donimalai Iron Ore Mine, Bellary district. *EXCEL International Journal of Multidisciplinary Management Studies, 3*(7), 157–164.

Resick, C. J., Martin, G. S., Keating, M. A., Dickson, M. W., Kwan, H. K., & Peng, C. (2011). What ethical leadership means to me: Asian, American, and European perspectives. *Journal of Business Ethics, 101*(3), 435–457. doi:10.1007/s10551-010-0730-8

Restubog, S. L. D., Scott, K. L., & Zagenczyk, T. J. (2011). When distress hits home: The role of contextual factors and psychological distress in predicting employees responses to abusive supervision. *The Journal of Applied Psychology, 96*(4), 713–729. doi:10.1037/a0021593 PMID:21280933

Reynolds, C. A., Shoss, M. K., & Jundt, D. K. (2015). In the eye of the beholder: A multi-stakeholder perspective of organizational citizenship and counterproductive work behaviors. *Human Resource Management Review*, *25*(1), 80–93. doi:10.1016/j.hrmr.2014.06.002

Reynolds, C., & O'Dwyer, L. M. (2008). Examining the relationship among emotional intelligence, coping with stress mechanisms for stress, and leadership effectiveness for middle school principals. *Journal of School Leadership*, *18*, 472–500. Retrieved from http://eric.ed.gov/?id=EJ888561

Rhodes, J., Lok, P., Yu-Yuan Hung, R., & Fang, S. C. (2008). An integrative model of organizational learning and social capital on effective knowledge transfer and perceived organizational performance. *Journal of Workplace Learning*, *20*(4), 245–258. doi:10.1108/13665620810871105

Rich, A. R., & Bonner, R. L. (2004). *Mediators and Moderators of Social Problem Solving*. Tampa, FL: University of South Florida. doi:10.1037/10805-002

Richmond, V. P., & McCroskey, J. C. (2000). The impact of supervisor and subordinate immediacy on relational and organizational outcomes. *Communication Monographs*, *67*(1), 85–95. doi:10.1080/03637750009376496

Richmond, V. P., McCroskey, J. C., Davis, L. M., & Koontz, K. A. (1980). Perceived power as a mediator of management styles and employee satisfaction: A preliminary investigation. *Communication Quarterly*, *28*(4), 37–46. doi:10.1080/01463378009369380

Ridley, J., & Channing, J. (2008). *Safety at work*. Oxford, UK: Butterworth-Heinemann.

Riggio, E. R., & Reichard, J. R. (2008). The emotional and social intelligences of effective leadership: An emotional and social skill approach. *Journal of Managerial Psychology*, *23*(2), 169–185. doi:10.1108/02683940810850808

Ristikartano, J., Iikkanen, P., Tervonen, J., & Lapp, T. (2014). Nationwide Road Traffic Forecast 2030. Finnish Transport Agency, Planning Department. Research reports of the Finnish Transport Agency.

Robbins, S., Judge, T., Millett, B., & Boyle, M. (2011). Organizational Behavior (6th ed.). Pearson, French's Forest, NSW.

Roberts, G. E. (1994). Barriers to Municipal Government Performance Appraisal Systems: Evidence from a Survey of Municipal Personnel Administrators. *Public Personnel Management*, *23*(2), 225–236. doi:10.1177/009102609402300205

Roberts, G. E. (2003). Employee Performance Appraisal System Participation: A Technique that Works. *Public Personnel Management*, *30*(1), 89–98. doi:10.1177/009102600303200105

Roberts, K. H., & OReilly, C. A. (1974). Measuring organizational communication. *The Journal of Applied Psychology*, *59*(3), 321–326. doi:10.1037/h0036660

Robinson, J. (2006). Navigating social and institutional barriers to markets: How social entrepreneurs identify and evaluate opportunities. In J. Mair, J. Robinson, & K. Hockerts (Eds.), *Social entrepreneurship* (pp. 95–120). New York: Palgrave Macmillan. doi:10.1057/9780230625655_7

Robinson, M. A., Sparrow, P. R., Clegg, C., & Birdi, K. (2007). Forecasting future competency requirements: A three-phase methodology. *Personnel Review*, *36*(1), 65–90. doi:10.1108/00483480710716722

Roccas, S., Sagiv, L., Schwartz, S. H., & Knafo, A. (2002). The big five personality factors and personal values. *Personality and Social Psychology Bulletin*, *28*(6), 789–801. doi:10.1177/0146167202289008

Rode, J. C. (2004). Job satisfaction and life satisfaction revisited: A longitudinal test of an integrated model. *Human Relations*, *57*(9), 1205–1230. doi:10.1177/0018726704047143

Rodgers, C. (2011). *Hubris syndrome: An emergent outcome of the complex social process of everyday interaction.* London: The Daedalus Trust.

Rodwell, J.J., Kienzle, R., & Shadur, M.A. (1998). The relationships among work-related perceptions, employee attitudes, and employee performance: The integral role of communication. *Human Resource Management (1986-1998), 37*(3-4), 277-293.

Rodwell, J., Kienzle, R., & Shadur, M. (1998). The relationships among work-related perceptions, employee attitudes, and employee perceptions and employee performance: The integral role of communication. *Human Resource Management, 37*(3/4), 277–293. doi:10.1002/(SICI)1099-050X(199823/24)37:3/4<277::AID-HRM9>3.0.CO;2-E

Rohrlich, B., & Martin, J. N. (1991). Host country and reentry adjustment of student sojourners. *International Journal of Intercultural Relations, 15*(2), 163–182. doi:10.1016/0147-1767(91)90027-E

Roosevelt, T. R. (2001). *Elements of a successful diversity process: Part I.* American Institute for Managing Diversity.

Rosenblatt, Z., Talmud, I., & Ruvio, A. (1999). A gender-based framework of the experience of job insecurity and its effects on work attitudes. *European Journal of Work and Organizational Psychology, 8*(2), 197–217. doi:10.1080/135943299398320

Rosethorn, H. (2009). *The Employer Brand. Keeping Faith with the Deal.* Farnham: Gower Publishing Limited.

Rotenberg, L., Portela, L. F., Banks, B., Griep, R. H., Fischer, F. M., & Landsbergis, P. (2008). A gender approach to work ability and its relationship to professional and domestic work hours among nursing personnel. *Applied Ergonomics, 39*(5), 646–652. doi:10.1016/j.apergo.2008.02.013 PMID:18405878

Rotundo, M., & Sackett, P. R. (2002). The relative importance of task, citizenship, and counterproductive performance to global ratings of job performance: A policy-capturing approach. *The Journal of Applied Psychology, 87*(1), 66–80. doi:10.1037/0021-9010.87.1.66 PMID:11916217

Rousseau, D., & Fried, Y. (2001). Location, location, location: Contextualizing organizational research. *Journal of Organizational Behavior, 22*(1), 1–13. doi:10.1002/job.78

Routson, J. (2009, November 1). *Heidi Roizen: Networking is more than collecting lots of names.* Retrieved from https://www.gsb.stanford.edu/insights/heidi-roizen-networking-more-collecting-lots-names

Rowden, P., Matthews, G., Watson, B., & Biggs, H. (2011). The relative impact of work-related stress, life stress and driving environment stress on driving outcomes. *Accident; Analysis and Prevention, 43*(4), 1332–1340. doi:10.1016/j.aap.2011.02.004 PMID:21545862

Rowold, J., Borgmann, L., & Bormann, K. (2014). Which leadership constructs are important for predicting job satisfaction, affective commitment, and perceived job performance in profit versus nonprofit organizations? *Nonprofit Management & Leadership, 25*(2), 147–164. doi:10.1002/nml.21116

Rudner, L. M. (1992). Reducing Errors Due to the Use of Judges. *Practical Assessment, Research & Evaluation, 7*(26), 241–271.

Rutanen, R., Luoto, R., Raitanen, J., Mansikkamäki, K., Tomás, E., & Nygård, C. H. (2014). Short-and long-term effects of a physical exercise intervention on work ability and work strain in symptomatic menopausal women. *Safety and Health at Work, 5*(4), 186–190. doi:10.1016/j.shaw.2014.08.003 PMID:25516810

Rynes, S., & Rosen, B. (1995). A field survey of factors affecting the adoption and perceived success of diversity training. *Personnel Psychology, 48*(2), 247–270. doi:10.1111/j.1744-6570.1995.tb01756.x

Saam, N. J. (2010). Interventions in workplace bullying: A multilevel approach. *European Journal of Work and Organizational Psychology*, *19*(1), 51–75. doi:10.1080/13594320802651403

Saavedra, R., & Van Dyne, L. (1999). Social exchange and emotional investment in work groups. *Motivation and Emotion*, *23*(2), 105–123. doi:10.1023/A:1021377028608

Sabarirajan, A., Meharajan, T., & Arun, B. (2010). A Study on the Various Welfare Measures and their Impact on QWL Provided by the Textile Mills with reference to Salem District, Tamil Nadu, India. *Asian Journal of Management Research.*, *1*(1), 15–24.

Safi, M. H., & Kolahi, A. A. (2016). The relationship between job satisfaction with burnout and conflict management styles in employees. *Community Health*, *2*(4), 266–274.

Safi, M. H., Mohamadi, F., Amouzadeh, I., & Arshi, S. (2016). The relationship between manager' leadership style with job satisfaction and burnout in staff of Shomal Health Center of Tehran. *Community Health*, *2*(2), 88–97.

Saha, A., Nag, A., & Nag, P. K. (2006). Occupational injury proneness in Indian women: A survey in fish processing industries. *Journal of Occupational Medicine and Toxicology (London, England)*, *1*(1), 1. doi:10.1186/1745-6673-1-23 PMID:16968532

Saiyadin, S.M. (1983). *Voluntary Welfare in India, Its objective and Cost.* Lok Udyog.

Salacuse, J. W. (2007). *Real leaders negotiate.* Retrieved from https://hbr.org/2008/02/real-leaders-negotiate-1.php

Salami, S. O. (2010). Conflict resolution strategies and organizational citizenship behavioral: The Moderating role of trait emotional intelligence. *Social Behavior and Personality: An International Journal*, *38*(1), 75–86. doi:10.2224/sbp.2010.38.1.75

Salanne, I., Rönkkö, S., Tikkanen, M., & Perttula, P. (2013). *Ajo-ja lepoaikasäädösten vaikutukset. Trafin julkaisuja 22/2013.* Retrieved from http://www.trafi.fi/filebank/a/1388410753/ea7ed86abe9beb74a4773eb2c 3783f67/139

Salomon, G., & Perkins, D. N. (1998). Individual and social aspects of learning. *Review of Research in Education*, *23*, 1–24.

Salovey, P., & Mayer, J. D. (1990). Emotional intelligence. *Imagination, Cognition and Personality*, *9*(3), 185–211. Retrieved from http://www.unh.edu/emotional_intelligence/EIAssets/EmotionalIntelligenceProper/EI1990%20Emotional%20Intelligence.pdf doi:10.2190/DUGG-P24E-52WK-6CDG

Salovey, P., Mayer, J. D., Caruso, D., & Seung, H. Y. (2008). *Emotional intelligence: Perspectives on educational and positive psychology.* New York: Oxford University Press.

Sandberg, S. (2013). *Lean in: Women, work, and the will to lead.* New York: Knopf Doubleday Publishing Group.

Sanjeevni, G. (2012). Employee Survey on Performance Appraisal System. *International Journal of Social Sciences and Interdisciplinary Research*, *1*(6), 124–141.

Sano, H. (2011). The employment management question and answer of the employee with mental disorders or developmental disorders: Basic knowledge. *Labor Circumstances*, *48*, 6–18.

Sansoni, J., De Caro, W., Marucci, A. R., Sorrentino, M., Mayner, L., & Lancia, L. (2016). Nurses' Job satisfaction: An Italian study. *Annali di igiene: medicina preventiva e di comunità*, *28*(1), 58. PMID:26980510

Sarin, S., & Majahan, V. (2001). The effect of reward structures on the performance of cross-functional product development teams. *Journal of Marketing*, *65*(2), 35–53. doi:10.1509/jmkg.65.2.35.18252

Sarma, A. M. (1996). *Aspects of labour welfare and social security.* Bombay, India: Himalaya Publishing House.

Satayanarayana, M. R., & Reddi, R. J. (2012). Labour welfare measure in cement industries in India. *International Journal of Physical and Social Sciences, 2*(7), 257–254.

Satija, S., & Khan, W. (2013). Emotional intelligence as a predictor of occupational stress among working professionals. *Aweshkar Research Journal, 15*(1), 79–97.

Saunders, M., Lewis, P., & Thornhill, A. (2009). *Research methods for business students*. Essex, UK: Pearson Education.

Saxena, A. (2014). Workforce Diversity: A Key to Improve Productivity. *Procedia Economics and Finance, 11*, 76–85. doi:10.1016/S2212-5671(14)00178-6

Saxton, G. D., & Benson, M. A. (2005). Social capital and the growth of the non-profit sector. *Social Science Quarterly, 86*(1), 16–35. doi:10.1111/j.0038-4941.2005.00288.x

Schaltegger, S., & Lüdeke-Freund, F. (2013). Business cases for sustainability. In *Encyclopedia of Corporate Social Responsibility* (pp. 245–252). Springer Berlin Heidelberg. doi:10.1007/978-3-642-28036-8_744

Schat, A. C. H., & Frone, M. R. (2011). Exposure to psychological aggression at work and job performance: The mediating role of job attitudes and personal health. *Work and Stress, 25*(1), 23–40. doi:10.1080/02678373.2011.563133 PMID:21643471

Schaufeli, W. B. (2007). Burnout in health care. In P. Carayan (Ed.), *Handbook of Human Factors and Ergonomics in Health Care and Patient Safety* (pp. 217–232). Mahwah, NJ: Lawrence Erlbaum Association.

Schein, E. H. (1992). *Organizational Culture and Leadership*. San Francisco: Jossey-Bass Publishers.

Schein, E. H. (2010). *Organizational culture and leadership* (4th ed.). San Francisco, CA: Jossey-Bass.

Schilling, J., & Kluge, A. (2009). Barriers to organizational learning: An integration of theory and research. *International Journal of Management Reviews, 11*(3), 337–360. doi:10.1111/j.1468-2370.2008.00242.x

Schmidt, K. H., & Neubach, B. (2007). Self-control demands. A source of stress at work. *International Journal of Stress Management, 14*(4), 398–416. doi:10.1037/1072-5245.14.4.398

Schneider, B., Ehrhart, M. G., & Macey, W. H. (2011). Perspectives on organizational climate and culture. In S. Zedeck (Ed.), APA handbook of industrial and organizational psychology: Vol. 1. *Building and developing the organization* (pp. 373–414). Washington, DC: American Psychological Association.

Schneider, B., Ehrhart, M. G., & Macey, W. H. (2013). Climate and culture. *Annual Review of Psychology, 64*(1), 361–388. doi:10.1146/annurev-psych-113011-143809 PMID:22856467

Schooley, B., Hikmet, N., Tarcan, M., & Yorgancioglu, G. (2016). Comparing burnout across emergency physicians, nurses, technicians, and health information technicians working for the same organization. *Medicine, 95*(10), e2856. doi:10.1097/MD.0000000000002856 PMID:26962780

Schotte, D. E., & Clum, G. A. (1982). Suicide ideation in a college population: A test of a model. *Journal of Consulting and Clinical Psychology, 50*(5), 690–696. doi:10.1037/0022-006X.50.5.690 PMID:7142542

Schramm, W. (1954). How communication works. In W. Schramm (Ed.), *The process and effects of communication* (pp. 3–26). Urbana, Illinois: University of Illinois Press.

Schultz, M., Hatch, M. J., & Larsen, M. H. (Eds.), *The Expressive Organization: Linking Identity, Reputation, and the Corporate Brand* (pp. 97–112). Oxford: Oxford University Press.

Compilation of References

Schulz, M. (2001). The uncertain relevance of newness: Organizational learning and knowledge flows. *Academy of Management Journal, 44*(4), 661–681. doi:10.2307/3069409

Schumpeter, J. A. (1934). *The theory of economic development: An inquiry into profits, capital, credit, interest and the business cycle*. Cambridge, MA: Harvard University Press.*(Reprinted in 1962.)*

Schwab, D. P., Heneman, H. G., & DeCotiis, T. A. (1975). Behaviorally anchored rating scales: A review of the literature. *Personnel Psychology, 28*(4), 549–562. doi:10.1111/j.1744-6570.1975.tb01392.x

Schwartz, S. H. (2006). A theory of cultural value orientations: Explication and applications. *Comparative Sociology, 5*(2), 137–182. doi:10.1163/156913306778667357

Scott, T. J. (2005). *The concise handbook of manager: A practitioner's approach*. New York: The Haworth Press.

Scott, W. R. (1995). *Institutions and organizations*. Thousand Oaks, CA: Sage.

Scott, W. R. (2005). Institutional theory: Contributing to a theoretical research program. In K. G. Smith & M. A. Hitts (Eds.), *Great minds in management: The process of theory development* (pp. 460–485). Oxford, UK: Oxford University Press. doi:10.4135/9781412952552.n155

Scott, W. R. (2008). Approaching adulthood: The maturing of institutional theory. *Theory and Society, 37*(5), 427–442. doi:10.1007/s11186-008-9067-z

Seal, C. R., Boyatzis, R. E., & Bailey, J. R. (2006). Fostering emotional and social intelligence in organizations. *Organizational Management Journal, 3*(3), 190–209. doi:10.1057/omj.2006.19

Sealy, R. H. V., & Singh, V. (2009). The importance of role models and demographic context for senior womens work identity development. *International Journal of Management Reviews*. doi:10.1111/j.1468-2370.2009.00262.x

Seeds, P. M., & Dozois, D. J. A. (2010). Prospective evaluation of a cognitive vulnerability-stress model for depression: The interaction of schema self-structures and negative life events. *Journal of Chemical Psychology, 66*(12), 1307–1323. doi:10.1002/jclp.20723 PMID:20715020

Seelos, C., & Mair, J. (2005). Social entrepreneurship: Creating new business models to serve the poor. *Business Horizons, 48*(3), 241–246. doi:10.1016/j.bushor.2004.11.006

Sell, L., & Cleal, B. (2011). Job satisfaction, work environment, and rewards: Motivational theory revisited. *Labour, 25*(1), 1–23. doi:10.1111/j.1467-9914.2010.00496.x

Sen, R. N. (1965). Physical environmental factors affecting health of workers in industry. *Indian Labour J, 6*, 735–746.

Sen, R. N., & Chakraborty, D. (1984). A new ergonomic design of a 'desi'plough'. *Indian Journal of Physiology and Allied Sciences, 38*, 97–105.

Sen, R. N., & Kar, A. (1984). An ergonomic study on bamboo handicraft workers. *Indian Journal of Physiology and Allied Sciences, 38*, 69–77.

Seo, H. S., Kim, H., Hwang, S. M., Hong, S. H., & Lee, I. Y. (2016). Predictors of job satisfaction and burnout among tuberculosis management nurses and physicians. *Epidemiology and Health, 38*.

Seppälä, T., Lipponen, J., Bardi, A., & Pirttilä-Backman, A. M. (2012). Change-oriented organizational citizenship behaviour: An interactive product of openness to change values, work unit identification, and sense of power. *Journal of Occupational and Organizational Psychology, 85*(1), 136–155. doi:10.1111/j.2044-8325.2010.02010.x

Serim, H., Demirbağ, O., & Yozgat, U. (2014). The effects of employees' perceptions of competency models on employability outcomes and organizational citizenship behavior and the moderating role of social exchange in this effect. *Procedia: Social and Behavioral Sciences, 150*, 1101–1110. doi:10.1016/j.sbspro.2014.09.125

Shachaf, P. (2008). Cultural diversity and information and communication technology impacts on global virtual teams: An exploratory study. *Information & Management, 45*(2), 131–142. doi:10.1016/j.im.2007.12.003

Shafer, W. E., Fukukawa, K., & Lee, G. M. (2007). Values and the perceived importance of ethics and social responsibility: The US versus China. *Journal of Business Ethics, 70*(3), 265–284. doi:10.1007/s10551-006-9110-9

Shamali, M., Shahriari, M., Babaii, A., & Abbasinia, M. (2015). Comparative study of job burnout among critical care nurses with fixed and rotating shift schedules. *Nursing and Midwifery Studies, 4*(3).

Shane, S. A. (2003). *A general theory of entrepreneurship: The individual-opportunity nexus*. Northampton, MA: Edward Elgar Publishing. doi:10.4337/9781781007990

Shane, S., Locke, E. A., & Collins, C. J. (2003). Entrepreneurial motivation. *Human Resource Management Review, 13*(2), 257–279. doi:10.1016/S1053-4822(03)00017-2

Shane, S., & Venkataraman, S. (2000). The promise of entrepreneurship as a field of research. *Academy of Management Review, 25*(1), 217–226.

Shannon, C. E. (1948). A mathematical theory of communication. *The Bell System Technical Journal, 27*(3), 1–55. doi:10.1002/j.1538-7305.1948.tb01338.x

Shannon, C. E., & Weaver, W. (1949). *The mathematical theory of communication*. Urbana, Illinois: University of Illinois Press.

Shapiro, G. L., & Schall, M. S. (1990). Rhetorical rules and organization-cultures: Identification, maintenance, and change. *Human Resource Development Quarterly, 1*(4), 321–337. doi:10.1002/hrdq.3920010403

Sharbrough, W. C., Simmons, S. A., & Cantrill, D. A. (2006). Motivating language in industry: Its impact on job satisfaction and perceived supervisor effectiveness. *Journal of Business Communication, 43*(4), 322–343. doi:10.1177/0021943606291712

Sharma, P. R. (2015). *Organizational communication: Perceptions of staff members' level of communication satisfaction and job satisfaction* (Doctoral dissertation). Retrieved from http://dc.etsu.edu/cgi/viewcontent.cgi?article=3854&context=etd

Sharma, J., Dhar, R. L., & Tyagi, A. (2016). Stress as a mediator between work–family conflict and psychological health among the nursing staff: Moderating role of emotional intelligence. *Applied Nursing Research, 30*, 268–275. doi:10.1016/j.apnr.2015.01.010 PMID:25769936

Shattell, M., Apostolopoulos, Y., Sönmez, S., & Griffin, M. (2010). Occupational stressors and the mental health of truckers. *Issues in Mental Health Nursing, 31*(9), 561–568. doi:10.3109/01612840.2010.488783 PMID:20701418

Shaw, K. (2005). Getting leaders involved in communication strategy: Breaking down the barriers to effective leadership communication. *Strategic Communication Management, 9*, 14–17.

Sherman, G. D., Lee, J. J., Cuddy, A. J., Renshon, J., Oveis, C., Gross, J. J., & Lerner, J. S. (2012). Leadership is associated with lower levels of stress. *Proceedings of the National Academy of Sciences of the United States of America, 109*(44), 17903–17907. doi:10.1073/pnas.1207042109 PMID:23012416

Shieh, H.-F., & Shannon, S. E. (2005). Three approaches to qualitative content analysis. *Qualitative Health Research, 15*(9), 1277–1288. doi:10.1177/1049732305276687 PMID:16204405

Compilation of References

Shiraki, M. (2006). Takokuseki naibu rodoshijo no jisshobunseki [Experimental analysis of internal labor market in MNEs]. Kokusai jintekishigenkanri no hikaku bunseki: Takokuseki naibu roudoushijo no shitenkara [The comparative analysis of international HRM] (pp. 33–102). Tokyo, Japan: Yuhikaku.

Shiraki, M., & Nagai, H. (2002). Chosa kekka no gaiyo: Kaigai hakensha chosa kekka [The results of survey: The research results of expatriates]. *Kokusai idosha no shakaiteki togo ni kansuru kenkyu* [*The Survey of Social Integration for International Transfer*], *305*, 73–103.

Shirey, M. R. (2006). Authentic leaders creating healthy work environments for nursing practice. *American Journal of Critical Care*, *15*(3), 256–267. PMID:16632768

Shirom, A. (2003). Job-related burnout: A review. In J. Quic & L. Tetrick (Eds.), *Handbook of occupational health psychology* (pp. 245–264). Washington, DC: American Psychological Association. doi:10.1037/10474-012

Shirom, A., Nirel, N., & Vinokur, A. D. (2006). Overload, autonomy, and burnout as predictors of physicians quality of care. *Journal of Occupational Health Psychology*, *11*(4), 328–342. doi:10.1037/1076-8998.11.4.328 PMID:17059297

Shmailan, A. S. B. (2016). The relationship between job satisfaction, job performance and employee engagement: An explorative study. *Issues in Business Management and Economics*, *4*(1), 1–8.

Shondrick, S. J., Dinh, J. E., & Lord, R. G. (2010). Developments in implicit leadership theory and cognitive science: Applications to improving measurement and understanding alternatives to hierarchical leadership. *The Leadership Quarterly*, *21*(6), 959–978. doi:10.1016/j.leaqua.2010.10.004

Shoptaw, S., Stein, A., & Rawson, R. A. (2000). Burnout in substance abuse counselors: Impact of environment, attitudes, and client with HIV. *Journal of Substance Abuse Treatment*, *19*(2), 117–126. doi:10.1016/S0740-5472(99)00106-3 PMID:10963923

Short, J. C., Moss, T. W., & Lumpkin, G. T. (2009). Research in social entrepreneurship: Past contributions and future opportunities. *Strategic Entrepreneurship Journal*, *3*(2), 161–194. doi:10.1002/sej.69

Short, J. C., Payne, G. T., & Ketchen, D. J. Jr. (2008). Research on organizational configurations: Past accomplishments and future challenges. *Journal of Management*, *34*(6), 1053–1079. doi:10.1177/0149206308324324

Shoss, M. K., Eisenberger, R., Restubog, S. L. D., & Zagenczyk, T. J. (2013). Blaming the organization for abusive supervision: The roles of perceived organizational support and supervisor's organizational embodiment. *The Journal of Applied Psychology*, *98*(1), 158–168. doi:10.1037/a0030687 PMID:23205496

SHRM. (2008). The Employer Brand: A Strategic Tool to Attract, Recruit and Retain Talent. *Society for Human Resources Management, April/June*. Retrieved from http://www.shrm.org/research/articles/articles/documents/08-0201staffinginsert_final.pdf

SHRM. (2016). *Employee job satisfaction and engagement: Revitalizing a changing workforce.* A research report by the society for human resource management. Retrieved from https://www.shrm.org/hr-today/trends-and-forecasting/research-and-surveys/Documents/2016-Employee-Job-Satisfaction-and-Engagement-Report.pdf

Siegrist, J. (1996). Adverse health effects of high effort – Low reward conditions at work. *Journal of Professional Health Psychology*, *1*, 27–41. PMID:9547031

Siemens, G. (2005). Connectivism: Learning as network-creation. *ASTD Learning News*, *10*(1).

Sigrist, R. D. (2010). *Job satisfaction at Missouri High School principals as measured by the Minnesota Satisfaction Questionnaire* [Doctoral dissertation]. The University of Missouri-Columbia, Missouri. Retrieved from https://mospace.umsystem.edu/xmlui/bitstream/handle/10355/8284/research.pdf?sequence=3

Simon, E. J., Reece, J. B., & Dickey, J. L. (2009). *Essential Campbell Seibutsugaku* [Campbell Essential Biology] (4th ed.). San Francisco: Benjamin Cummings.

Simon, H. A. (1996). *The sciences of the artificial*. Cambridge, MA: The MIT Press.

Sinclair, M. A. (1975). Questionnaire design. *Applied Ergonomics*, *6*(2), 73–80. doi:10.1016/0003-6870(75)90299-9 PMID:15677171

Singhapakdi, A., Kraft, K. L., Vitell, S. J., & Rallapalli, K. C. (1995). The perceived importance of ethics and social responsibility on organizational effectiveness: A survey of marketers. *Journal of the Academy of Marketing Science*, *23*(1), 49–56. doi:10.1007/BF02894611

Singh, S. P., Singh, S., & Singh, P. (2012). Ergonomics in developing hand operated maize dehusker–sheller for farm women. *Applied Ergonomics*, *43*(4), 792–798. doi:10.1016/j.apergo.2011.11.014 PMID:22142989

Sinha, E. (2013). A research work on Employee Satisfaction measurement with special reference to KRIBHCO, Surat. *International Journal of Modern Engineering Research*, *3*(1), 523–529.

Sirsawy, U., Steinberg, W. J., & Raubenheimer, J. E. (2016). Levels of burnout among registrars and medical officers working at Bloemfontein public healthcare facilities in 2013. *South African Family Practice*, *58*(6), 213–218. doi:10.1080/20786190.2016.1198088

Skarlicki, D. P., & Folger, R. (1997). Retaliation in the Workplace: The Roles of Distributive, Procedural and Interactional Justice. *The Journal of Applied Psychology*, *82*(3), 434–443. doi:10.1037/0021-9010.82.3.434

Škerlavaj, M., Dimovski, V., & Desouza, K. C. (2010). Patterns and structures of intra-organizational learning networks within a knowledge-intensive organization. *Journal of Information Technology*, *25*(2), 189–204. doi:10.1057/jit.2010.3

Skocpol, T. (2008). Bringing the state back in: Retrospect and prospect. The 2007 Johan Skytte Prize Lecture. *Scandinavian Political Studies*, *31*(2), 109–124. doi:10.1111/j.1467-9477.2008.00204.x

Smale, A., & Miller, C. C. (2015, March 11). Germany sets gender quota in boardrooms. *NY Times*. Retrieved from http://www.nytimes.com/2015/03/07/world/europe/german-law-requires-more-women-on-corporate-boards.html?_r=1

Smallbone, D., & Welter, F. (2009). *Entrepreneurship and small business development in post-Soviet economies*. London: Routledge.

Smeed, J. L., Kimber, M., Millwater, J., & Ehrich, L. C. (2009). Power over, with and through: Another look at micropolitics. *Leading & Managing*, *15*(1), 26–41.

Smith, K. G., Collins, C. J., & Clark, K. D. (2005). Existing knowledge, knowledge creation capability, and the rate of new product introduction in high-technology firms. *Academy of Management Journal*, *48*(2), 346–357. doi:10.5465/AMJ.2005.16928421

Smith, P. C., & Kendall, L. M. (1963). Retranslation of expectations: An approach to the construction of unambiguous anchors for rating scales. *The Journal of Applied Psychology*, *47*(2), 149–155. doi:10.1037/h0047060

Smith, P. C., Kendall, L. M., & Hulin, C. L. (1969). *The Measurement of Satisfaction in Work and Retirement*. Chicago, IL: Rand McNally.

Smith, P. K., Singer, M., Hoel, H., & Cooper, C. L. (2003). Victimization in the school and the workplace: Are there any links? *British Journal of Psychology*, *94*(2), 175–188. doi:10.1348/000712603321661868 PMID:12803813

Smith, R., DiTomaso, N., Farris, G. F., & Cordero, R. (2001). Favouritism, Bias, and error in performance ratings of scientists and engineers: The effects of power, status, and numbers. *Sex Roles*, *45*(5-6), 337–358. doi:10.1023/A:1014309631243

Snape, E., & Redman, T. (2010). HRM practices, organizational citizenship behaviour, and performance: A multi-level analysis. *Journal of Management Studies*, *47*(7), 1219–1247.

Sobo, E. J., & Sadler, B. L. (2002). Improving organizational communication and cohesion in a healthcare setting through employee-leadership exchange. *Human Organization*, *61*(3), 277–287. doi:10.17730/humo.61.3.fnk9rkekacak6mkx

Sojane, J. S., Klopper, H. C., & Coetzee, S. K. (2016). Leadership, job satisfaction and intention to leave among registered nurses in the North West and Free State provinces of South Africa: Original research. *Curationis*, *39*(1), 1–10. doi:10.4102/curationis.v39i1.1585

Solam, T. H. (2007). *Occupational Stress, Social Problem Solving, and Burnout among Mental HealthProfessionals in HIV/AIDS Care*. Faculty of Drexel University Clinical Psychology.

Solmon, L. C., & Podgursky, M. (2000). *The Pros and Cons of Performance-based Compensation*. Santa Monica, CA: The Milken Family Foundation.

Solomon, R. C. (2004). Ethical leadership, emotions, and trust: Beyond „charisma. In J. Ciulla (Ed.), *Ethics, the heart of leadership* (pp. 83–102). Westport, CT: Praeger.

Soltani, S., Elkhani, N., & Bardsiri, V. K. (2014). The effects of perceived organizational support and organizational citizenship behaviors on continuance intention of enterprise resource planning. *International Journal of Enterprise Information Systems*, *10*(2), 81–102. doi:10.4018/ijeis.2014040105

Song, Z., Chon, K., Ding, G., & Gu, C. (2015). Impact of organizational socialization tactics on newcomer job satisfaction and engagement: Core self-evaluations as moderators. *International Journal of Hospitality Management*, *46*, 180–189. doi:10.1016/j.ijhm.2015.02.006

Sony, M., & Mekoth, N. (2016). The relationship between emotional intelligence, frontline employee adaptability, job satisfaction and job performance. *Journal of Retailing and Consumer Services*, *30*, 20–32. doi:10.1016/j.jretconser.2015.12.003

Soroush, F., Zargham-Boroujeni, A., & Namnabati, M. (2016). The relationship between nurses clinical competence and burnout in neonatal intensive care units. *Iranian Journal of Nursing and Midwifery Research*, *21*(4), 424–429. doi:10.4103/1735-9066.185596 PMID:27563328

Spain, S. M., Harms, P., & Lebreton, J. M. (2014). The dark side of personality at work. *Journal of Organizational Behavior*, *35*(S1), S41–S60. doi:10.1002/job.1894

Sparks, J. R., & Hunt, S. D. (1998). Marketing researcher ethical sensitivity: Conceptualization, measurement, and exploratory investigation. *Journal of Marketing*, *62*(2), 92–109. doi:10.2307/1252163

Spector, P. E. (1997). *Job satisfaction: Application. assessment, causes, and consequences*. Thousand Oaks, CA: Sage Publications.

Spector, P. E., & Fox, S. (2010). Counterproductive work behavior and organisational citizenship behavior: Are they opposite forms of active behavior? *Applied Psychology*, *59*(1), 21–39. doi:10.1111/j.1464-0597.2009.00414.x

Spence, J. R., Ferris, D. L., Brown, D. J., & Heller, D. (2011). Understanding daily citizenship behaviors: A social comparison perspective. *Journal of Organizational Behavior*, *32*(4), 547–571. doi:10.1002/job.738

Spencer, J. W., & Gómez, C. (2004). The relationship among national institutional structures, economic factors, and domestic entrepreneurial activity: A multicountry study. *Journal of Business Research*, *57*(10), 1098–1107. doi:10.1016/S0148-2963(03)00040-7

Sperry, L., & Whiteman, A. (2003). Communicating effectively and strategically. In L. Sperry (Ed.), *Becoming an effective healthcare manager: The essential skills of lead* (pp. 75–98). Baltimore: Health Professions Press.

Spielberger, C. D. (1983). *State – Trait Anxiety Inventory: A comprehensive bibliography*. Palo Alto, CA: Consultant Psychologists Press.

Spitzberg, B. H., & Cupach, W. R. (1981). Self-monitoring and relational competence. *Presented at the Speech Communication Association Convention*, Anaheim, California.

Spitzberg, B. H. (1983). Communication competence as knowledge, skill, and impression. *Communication Education*, *32*(3), 323–329. doi:10.1080/03634528309378550

Spriegel, W. R. (1962). Company practices in appraisal of managerial performance. *Personnel*, *39*, 77–83.

Sproull, L. S., & Kiesler, S. (1991). *Connections: New ways of working in the networked organization*. Cambridge, MA: MIT Press.

Squire, B., Cousins, P. D., & Brown, S. (2009). Cooperation and knowledge transfer within buyer–supplier relationships: The moderating properties of trust, relationship duration and supplier performance. *British Journal of Management*, *20*(4), 461–477. doi:10.1111/j.1467-8551.2008.00595.x

Squires, M. A. E., Tourangeau, A. N. N., Spence Laschinger, H. K., & Doran, D. (2010). The link between leadership and safety outcomes in hospitals. *Journal of Nursing Management*, *18*(8), 914–925. doi:10.1111/j.1365-2834.2010.01181.x PMID:21073565

Sravani, S. (2016). *Employee Welfare Measures: Advantages & Disadvantages*. Retrieved from http://content.wisestep.com/employee-welfare-measures-advantages-disadvantages

Srinivasa, K. T. (2013). A Study on Employees Welfare Facilities Adopted at Bosch Limited, Bangalore. *Research Journal of Management Sciences*, *2*(12), 7–11.

Srnka, K. J. (2004). Culture's role in marketers' ethical decision making: An integrated theoretical framework. *Academy of Marketing Science Review*, *2004*, 1.

Stahl, G. Björkman, I., Farndale, E., Morris, S. S., Paauwe, J., Stiles, P., Trevor, J., & Wright, P. (2012). Six principles of effective global talent management. *Sloan Management Review*, *53*(2), 25-42. Retrieved from http://epub.wu.ac.at/id/eprint/3616

Stamps, P. L., & Piedmonte, E. B. (1986). *Nurses and work satisfaction: An index for measurement*. Ann Arbor, MI: Health Administration Press Perspectives.

Stanton, N. A., Hedge, A., Brookhuis, K., Salas, E., & Hendrick, H. W. (Eds.). (2004). *Handbook of Human Factors and Ergonomics Methods*. New York: CRC Press. doi:10.1201/9780203489925

Staples, D. S., & Zhao, L. (2006). The Effects of Cultural Diversity in Virtual Teams Versus Face-to-Face Teams. *Group Decision and Negotiation*, *15*(4), 389–406. doi:10.1007/s10726-006-9042-x

Stata, R., & Almond, P. (1989). Organizational learning: The key to management innovation. *The Training and Development Sourcebook*, *2*, 31–42.

Statt, D. A. (2004). *The Routledge dictionary of business management*. New York: Routledge.

Staw, B. M., Sutton, R. I., & Pelled, L. H. (1994). Employee positive emotion and favorable outcomes at the workplace. *Organization Science*, *5*(1), 51–71. doi:10.1287/orsc.5.1.51

Compilation of References

Steensma, H. K., Tihanyi, L., Lyles, M. A., & Dhanaraj, C. (2005). The evolving value of foreign partnerships in transitioning economies. *Academy of Management Journal*, *48*(2), 213–235. doi:10.5465/AMJ.2005.16928394

Steers, R. M. (1977). Antecedents and outcomes of organizational commitment. *Administrative Science Quarterly*, *22*(1), 46–56. doi:10.2307/2391745 PMID:10236068

Steingrímsdóttir, H. (2011). *The relationship between internal communication & job satisfaction* [Master's thesis]. Retrieved from http://studenttheses.cbs.dk/bitstream/handle/10417/3240/hrund_steingrimsdottir.pdf?sequence=1

Stein, S. J., & Book, H. (2010). *The EQ edge: Emotional intelligence and your success* (Vol. 30). Canada: John Wiley & Sons.

Stephan, U., & Uhlaner, L. M. (2010). Performance-based vs socially supportive culture: A cross-national study of descriptive norms and entrepreneurship. *Journal of International Business Studies*, *41*(8), 1347–1364. doi:10.1057/jibs.2010.14

Stephan, U., Uhlaner, L. M., & Stride, C. (2014). Institutions and social entrepreneurship: The role of institutional voids, institutional support, and institutional configurations. *Journal of International Business Studies*, *46*(3), 308–331. doi:10.1057/jibs.2014.38

Steven Moore, J., & Garg, A. (1995). The strain index: A proposed method to analyze jobs for risk of distal upper extremity disorders. *American Industrial Hygiene Association*, *56*(5), 443–458. doi:10.1080/15428119591016863 PMID:7754975

Stevens, M. J., Oddou, G., Furuya, N., Bird, A., & Mendenhall, M. (2006). HR factors affecting repatriate job satisfaction and job attachment for Japanese managers. *International Journal of Human Resource Management*, *17*(5), 831–841. doi:10.1080/09585190600640844

Stohl, C. (1984). Quality circle and the quality of communication. *Presented at the Speech Communication Association Convention*, Chicago, Illinois.

Stokes, C. K., Schneider, T. R., & Lyons, J. B. (2010). Adaptive performance: A criterion problem. *Team Performance Management: An International Journal*, *16*(3/4), 212–230. doi:10.1108/13527591011053278

Storberg-Walker, J., & Gubbins, C. (2007). Social networks as a conceptual and empirical tool to understand and do HRD. *Advances in Developing Human Resources*, *9*(3), 291–310. doi:10.1177/1523422306304071

Storti, C. (2003). *The art of coming home*. Yarmouth, ME: Intercultural Press.

Strahan, C., Watson, B. C., & Lennon, A. (2008). Can organisational safety climate and occupational stress predict work-related driver fatigue? *Transportation Research Part F: Traffic Psychology and Behaviour*, *11*(6), 418–426. doi:10.1016/j.trf.2008.04.002

Streeck, W. (2005). Industrial relations: From state weakness as strength to state weakness as weakness. Welfare corporatism and the private use of the public interest. In S. Green & W. E. Paterson (Eds.), *Governance in contemporary Germany: The semisovereign state revisited* (pp. 138–164). Cambridge, UK: Cambridge University Press. doi:10.1017/CBO9780511807749.007

Stroh, L. K., Black, J. S., Mendenhall, M. E., & Gregersen, H. B. (2004). *International assignments: An integration of strategy, research, and practice*. Mahwah, NJ: Lawrence Erlbaum Associates.

Stroh, L. K., Gregersen, H. B., & Black, J. S. (1998). Closing the gap: Expectations versus reality among repatriates. *Journal of World Business*, *33*(3), 111–124. doi:10.1016/S1090-9516(98)90001-3

Strömgren, M., Eriksson, A., Bergman, D., & Dellve, L. (2016). Social capital among healthcare professionals: A prospective study of its importance for job satisfaction, work engagement and engagement in clinical improvements. *International Journal of Nursing Studies*, *53*, 116–125. doi:10.1016/j.ijnurstu.2015.07.012 PMID:26315780

Stryker, R., Docka-Filipek, D., & Wald, P. (2012). Employment Discrimination Law and Industrial Psychology: Social Science as Social Authority and the Co-Production of Law and Science. *Law & Social Inquiry*, *37*(4), 777–814. doi:10.1111/j.1747-4469.2011.01277.x

Sturrock, J. (1986). *Structuralism*. London: Paladin.

Sudin, S. (2011). Fairness of and Satisfaction with performance appraisal process. *Journal of Global Management*, *2*(1), 66–83.

Sulaiman, M. R., & Seng, L. C. (2016). Leadership and job satisfaction among foreign seafarers in maritime industry: Human leadership. *International Research Journal of Interdisciplinary & Multidisciplinary Studies*, *2*(2), 44–57.

Sullivan, J. (2004). The 8 Elements of a Successful Employment Brand. *ER Daily*. Retrieved from http://www.ere.net/2004/02/23/the-8-elements-of-a-successful-employment-brand

Suls, J., Green, P., & Hillis, S. (1998). Emotional reactivity to everyday problems, affective inertia, and neuroticism. *Personality and Social Psychology Bulletin*, *24*(2), 127–136. doi:10.1177/0146167298242002

Sunstein, C. R., & Hastie, R. (2014). *Wiser: Getting beyond Groupthink to make groups smarter*. Boston: Harvard Business Review Press.

Sun, Y., Gergen, E., Avila, M., & Green, M. (2016). Leadership and job satisfaction: Implications for leaders of accountants. *American Journal of Industrial and Business Management*, *6*(03), 268–275. doi:10.4236/ajibm.2016.63024

Sussman, N. M. (1986). Reentry research and training: Methods and implications. *International Journal of Intercultural Relations*, *10*(2), 235–254. doi:10.1016/0147-1767(86)90008-8

Sussman, N. M. (2000). The dynamic nature of cultural identity throughout cultural transitions: Why home is not so sweet. *Personality and Social Psychology Review*, *4*(4), 355–373. doi:10.1207/S15327957PSPR0404_5

Sussman, N. M. (2001). Repatriation transitions: Psychological preparedness, cultural identity, and attributions among American managers. *International Journal of Intercultural Relations*, *25*(2), 109–123. doi:10.1016/S0147-1767(00)00046-8

Swan, J. E., & Futrell, C. M. (1978). Does clear communication relate to job satisfaction and self-confidence among salespeople? *Journal of Business Communication*, *15*(4), 39–52. doi:10.1177/002194367801500404

Swan, S., & Wyer, R. S. (1997). Gender stereotypes and social identity: How being in the minority affects judgments of self and others. *Personality and Social Psychology Bulletin*, *23*(12), 1265–1276. doi:10.1177/01461672972312004

Swartz, J. (2013). Workplace stress on the rise with 83% of Americans frazzled by something at work. Corinthian Colleges, Inc. Retrieved from http://globenewswire.com/news-release/2013/04/09/536945/10027728/en/Workplace-Stress-on-the-Rise-With-83-of-Americans-Frazzled-by-Something-at-Work.html

Swiercz, P. M., Bryan, N. B., Eagle, B. W., Bizzotto, V., & Renn, R. W. (2012). Predicting employee attitudes and performance from perceptions of performance appraisal fairness. *Business Renaissance Quarterly*, *7*(1), 25–46.

Swiercz, P. M., Icenogle, M. L., Bryan, N. B., & Renn, R. W. (1993). *Do perceptions of performance appraisal fairness predict employee attitudes and performance?* In Academy of Management Proceedings (Vol. 1, pp. 304–308). New York: Academy of Management.

Swift, P. E., & Hwang, A. (2013). The impact of affective and cognitive trust on knowledge sharing and organizational learning. *The Learning Organization, 20*(1), 20–37. doi:10.1108/09696471311288500

Sy, T., Tram, S., & OHara, A. L. (2006). Relation of employee and manager emotional intelligence to job satisfaction and performance. *Journal of Vocational Behavior, 68*(3), 461–473. doi:10.1016/j.jvb.2005.10.003

Szkudlarek, B. (2010). Reentry: A review of the literature. *International Journal of Intercultural Relations, 34*(1), 1–21. doi:10.1016/j.ijintrel.2009.06.006

Szkudlarek, B., & Sumpter, D. M. (2015). What, when, and with whom? Investigating expatriate reentry training with a proximal approach. *Human Resource Management, 54*(6), 1037–1057. doi:10.1002/hrm.21647

Takezawa, T. (2015). The introduction of employment management: Model of employment cases based on reference service from JEED for persons with developmental disabilities. *Vocational Rehabilitation, 29*, 63–68.

Tangirala, S., & Ramanujam, R. (2008). Employee silence on critical issues: The cross level effects procedural justice climate. *Personnel Psychology, 61*(1), 37–68. doi:10.1111/j.1744-6570.2008.00105.x

Taniguchi, M. (2008). Soshiki ni okeru diversity management [Diversity in organizations] (in Japanese). *Japanese Journal of Labour Studies, 574*, 69–84.

Tan, J. (2002). Culture, nation, and entrepreneurial strategic orientations: Implications for an emerging economy. *Entrepreneurship: Theory and Practice, 26*(4), 96–111.

Tannenbaum, A. S. (1962). Control in organizations: Individual adjustment and organizational performance. *Administrative Science Quarterly, 7*(2), 236–257. doi:10.2307/2390857

Tannenbaum, A. S. (1968). *Control in organizations.* New York: McGraw-Hill.

Tao, H., Ellenbecker, C. H., Wang, Y., & Li, Y. (2015). Examining perception of job satisfaction and intention to leave among ICU nurses in China. *International Journal of Nursing Sciences, 2*(2), 140–148. doi:10.1016/j.ijnss.2015.04.007

Taras, V., Kirkman, B. L., & Steel, P. (2010). Examining the impact of cultures consequences: A three-decade, multilevel, meta-analytic review of Hofstedes Cultural Value Dimensions. *The Journal of Applied Psychology, 95*(3), 405–439. doi:10.1037/a0018938 PMID:20476824

Tavousi, M. N. (2015). Dispositional effects on job stressors and job satisfaction: The role of core evaluations. *Procedia: Social and Behavioral Sciences, 190*, 61–68. doi:10.1016/j.sbspro.2015.04.917

Taylor, F. W. (1970). What is scientific management? In H. F. Merrill (Ed.), *Classics in management* (pp. 67–71). New York: American Management Association.

Taylor, S. (2005). *People Resourcing* (3rd ed.). London: Chartered Institute of Personnel and Development.

Taylor, S. E., & Aspinwall, L. G. (1996). Mediating and moderating processes in psychosocial stress: Appraisal, coping, resistance, and vulnerability. In H. B. Kaplan (Ed.), *Psychosocial Stress: Perspectives on structure, theory, life course, and methods* (pp. 71–110). San Diego, CA: Academic Press.

Taylor, S., & Beechler, S. (1995). Human resources management system integration and adaptation in multinational firms. *Advances in International Comparative Management, 8*, 115–174.

Templer, K. J., Tay, C., & Chandrasekar, N. A. (2006). Motivational cultural intelligence, realistic job preview, realistic living conditions preview, and cross-cultural adjustment. *Group & Organization Management, 31*(1), 154–173. doi:10.1177/1059601105275293

Tepper, B. J. (2000). Consequences of abusive supervision. *Academy of Management Journal, 43*(2), 178–190. doi:10.2307/1556375

Tepper, B. J. (2007). Abusive supervision in work organizations: Review, synthesis, and research agenda. *Journal of Management, 33*(3), 261–289. doi:10.1177/0149206307300812

Tepper, B. J., Carr, J. C., Breaux, D. M., Geider, S., Hu, C., & Hua, W. (2009). Abusive supervision, intentions to quit, and employees' workplace deviance: A power/dependence analysis. *Organizational Behavior and Human Decision Processes, 109*(2), 156–167. doi:10.1016/j.obhdp.2009.03.004

Tepper, B. J., Duffy, M. K., Henle, C. A., & Lambert, L. S. (2006). Procedural injustice, victim, precipitation, and abusive supervision. *Personnel Psychology, 59*(1), 101–123. doi:10.1111/j.1744-6570.2006.00725.x

Tepper, B. J., Duffy, M. K., Hoobler, J. M., & Ensley, M. D. (2004). Moderators of the relationship between coworkers' organizational citizenship behavior and fellow employees' attitudes. *The Journal of Applied Psychology, 89*(3), 455–465. doi:10.1037/0021-9010.89.3.455 PMID:15161405

Tepper, B. J., Duffy, M. K., & Shaw, J. D. (2001). Personality moderators of the relationships between abusive supervision and subordinates' resistance. *The Journal of Applied Psychology, 86*(5), 974–983. doi:10.1037/0021-9010.86.5.974 PMID:11596813

Tepper, B. J., Henle, C. A., Lambert, L. S., Giacalone, R. A., & Duffy, M. K. (2008). Abusive supervision and subordinates' organization deviance. *The Journal of Applied Psychology, 93*(4), 721–732. doi:10.1037/0021-9010.93.4.721 PMID:18642979

Tepper, B. J., Moss, S. E., & Duffy, M. K. (2011). Predictors of abusive supervision: Supervisor perceptions of deep-level dissimilarity, relationship conflict, and subordinate performance. *Academy of Management Journal, 54*(2), 279–294. doi:10.5465/AMJ.2011.60263085

Tesch, R. (1990). *Qualitative research: Analysis types and software tools*. Bristol: Falmer.

Tett, R. P., & Burnett, D. D. (2003). A personality trait-based interactionist model of job performance. *The Journal of Applied Psychology, 88*(3), 500–517. doi:10.1037/0021-9010.88.3.500 PMID:12814298

Tharenou, P., & Caulfield, N. (2010). Will I stay or will I go? Explaining repatriation by self-initiated expatriates. *Academy of Management Journal, 53*(5), 1009–1028. doi:10.5465/AMJ.2010.54533183

Thau, S., & Mitchell, M. S. (2010). Self-gain or self-regulation impairment? Tests of competing explanations of the supervisor abuse and employee deviance relationship through perceptions of distributive justice. *The Journal of Applied Psychology, 95*(6), 1009–1031. doi:10.1037/a0020540 PMID:20718511

The Center for Universal Design. (2008). About UD (webpage). Retrieved from https://www.ncsu.edu/ncsu/design/cud/about_ud/about_ud.htm

The International Classification of Functioning, Disability and Health (ICF). (2002). Towards a common language for functioning, disability and health. Retrieved from http://www.who.int/classifications/icf/icfbeginnersguide.pdf

The National Center on Workforce and Disability/Adult (NCWD/A). (2008a). *Recruitment and retention of older workers: Considerations for employers*. Boston: Institute for Community Inclusion, UMass Boston.

The National Center on Workforce and Disability/Adult (NCWD/A). (2008b). *Recruitment and retention of older workers: Application to people with disabilities*. Boston: Institute for Community Inclusion, UMass Boston.

Compilation of References

The Stanford Encyclopedia of Philosophy. (2015). *Indexicals*. Stanford's Center for the Study of Language and Information. Retrieved from http://plato.stanford.edu/entries/indexicals/

Thomas, C. A. (2008). Bridging the gap between theory and practice: Language policy in multilingual organisations. *Language Awareness*, *17*(4), 307–325. doi:10.1080/09658410802147295

Thomas, G. F., Zolin, R., & Hartman, J. K. (2009). The central role of communication in developing trust and its effect on employee involvement. *Journal of Business Communication*, *46*(3), 287–310. doi:10.1177/0021943609333522

Thompson, E. R., & Phua, F. T. (2012). A brief index of affective job satisfaction. *Group & Organization Management*, *37*(3), 275–307. doi:10.1177/1059601111434201

Timmons, J. C., Hall, A. C., Fesko, S. L., & Migliore, A. (2011). Retaining the older workforce: Social policy considerations for the universally designed workplace. *Journal of Aging & Social Policy*, *23*(2), 119–140. doi:10.1080/08959 420.2011.551623 PMID:21491303

Tjosvold, D., Wong, A. S. H., & Chen, N. Y. F. (2014). Constructively managing conflicts in organizations. *Annual Review of Organizational Psychology and Organizational Behavior*, *1*(1), 545–568. doi:10.1146/annurev-orgpsych-031413-091306

Todd, A. J. (1933). *Industry and Society - A Sociological Appraisal of Modern Industrialisation*. New York: H. Holt & Company.

To, M. L., Herman, H. M., & Ashkanasy, N. M. (2015). A multilevel model of transformational leadership, affect, and creative process behavior in work teams. *The Leadership Quarterly*, *26*(4), 543–556. doi:10.1016/j.leaqua.2015.05.005

Tong, Y., Yang, X., & Teo, H. H. (2013). Spontaneous virtual teams: Improving organizational performance through information and communication technology. *Business Horizons*, *56*(3), 361–375. doi:10.1016/j.bushor.2013.01.003

Top, M., Akdere, M., & Tarcan, M. (2015). Examining transformational leadership, job satisfaction, organizational commitment and organizational trust in Turkish hospitals: Public servants versus private sector employees. *International Journal of Human Resource Management*, *26*(9), 1259–1282. doi:10.1080/09585192.2014.939987

Tourani, A., & Rast, S. (2012). Effect of employees' communication and participation on employees' job satisfaction: An empirical study on airline companies in Iran. *Proceedings of the 2012 2nd International Conference on Economics, Trade and Development IPEDR* (Vol. 36, pp. 52-56). Singapore: IACSIT Press.

Townsend, A. M., DeMarie, S. M., & Hendrickson, A. R. (1998). Virtual teams: Technology and workplace of the future. *The Academy of Management Executive*, *12*(3), 17–29.

Tran, B. (2008). *Expatriate selection and retention* [Dissertation]. California School of Professional Psychology at Alliant International University, San Francisco, California.

Tran, B. (2014). The origin of servant leadership: The foundation of leadership. In R. Selladurai and S. Carraher (Eds.). Servant leadership: Research and practice (pp. 262-294). Hershey, PA: IGI Global.

Tran, B. (2016a). Tran, B. (2016). Communication (intercultural and multicultural) at play for cross cultural management within multinational corporations (MNCs). In N. Zakaria, A. N. Abdul-Talib, & N. Osman (Eds.), *Handbook of research on impacts of international business and political affairs on the global economy* (pp. 62-92). Hershey, PA: IGI Global.

Tran, B. (2016b). Communication: The role of the Johari Window on effective leadership communication in multinational corporations (MNCs). In A. H. Normore, M. Javidi, & L. Long (Eds.), *Handbook of research on effective communication, leadership, and conflict resolution* (pp. 405–429). Hershey, PA: IGI Global. doi:10.4018/978-1-4666-9970-0.ch022

Tran, B. (2016c). *Communication (intercultural and multicultural) at play for cross cultural management within multinational corporations (MNCs)*. In International Business: Concepts, Methodologies, Tools, and Applications (pp. 1781–1811). Hershey, PA: IGI Global.

Trbojevic-Stankovic, J., Stojimirovic, B., Soldatovic, I., Petrovic, D., Nesic, D., & Simic, S. (2015). Work-related factors as predictors of burnout in Serbian nurses working in hemodialysis. *Nephrology Nursing Journal*, *42*(6), 553–561. PMID:26875230

Tsai, W. (2001). Knowledge transfer in intraorganizational networks: Effects of network position and absorptive capacity on business unit innovation and performance. *Academy of Management Journal*, *44*(5), 996–1004. doi:10.2307/3069443

Tsai, Y., & Wu, S. W. (2010). The relationships between organisational citizenship behaviour, job satisfaction and turnover intention. *Journal of Clinical Nursing*, *19*(23/24), 3564–3574. doi:10.1111/j.1365-2702.2010.03375.x PMID:20964747

Tse, J., Flin, R., & Mearns, K. (2006). Bus driver well-being review: 50 years of research. *Transportation Research Part F: Traffic Psychology and Behaviour*, *9*(2), 89–114. doi:10.1016/j.trf.2005.10.002

Tziner, A., & Kopelman, R. E. (2002). Is there a Preferred Performance Rating Format? A Non-psychometric Perspective. *Applied Psychology*, *51*(3), 479–503. doi:10.1111/1464-0597.00104

Tziner, A., Latham, G. P., Price, B. S., & Haccoun, R. (1996). Development and validation of a questionnaire for measuring perceived political considerations in performance appraisal. *Journal of Organizational Behavior*, *17*(2), 179–190. doi:10.1002/(SICI)1099-1379(199603)17:2<179::AID-JOB740>3.0.CO;2-Z

Tziner, A., Prince, B., & Murphy, K. (1997). PCPAQ – The Questionnaire for Measuring the Perceived Political Considerations in Performance Appraisal: Some New Evidence Regarding Its Psychometric Properties. *Journal of Social Behavior and Personality*, *12*, 189–200.

U.S. Business Leadership Network (USBLN). (2012). *Leading practices on disability inclusion*. Alexandria, VA: U.S. BLN.

U.S. Chamber of commerce foundation. (2014, June 4). Diversity makes good business sense. Retrieved from https://www.uschamberfoundation.org/blog/post/diversity-makes-good-business-sense/31773

U.S. Department of Labor (U.S. DOL). (n. d.). *Fact sheet: New Regulations on Section 503 of the Rehabilitation Act of 1973*.

Uçanok, B., & Karabatı, S. (2013). The effects of values, work centrality, and organizational commitment on organizational citizenship behaviors: Evidence from Turkish SMEs. *Human Resource Development Quarterly*, *24*(1), 89–129. doi:10.1002/hrdq.21156

Uehara, A. (1986). The nature of American student reentry adjustment and perceptions of the sojourn experience. *International Journal of Intercultural Relations*, *10*(4), 415–438. doi:10.1016/0147-1767(86)90043-X

Uhlaner, L. M. (2008). *The role of ownership in governance: A neglected focus in entrepreneurship and management research* (Inaugural Lecture). Nyenrode Business University, Breukelen, Netherlands. Retrieved from http://www.nyenrode.nl/FacultyResearch/research/Documents/Inaugural%20lectures/uhlaner_inaugural_lecture.pdf

Uhlaner, L. M., Thurik, A. R., & Hutjes, J. (2002, April 15-16). Post-materialism and entrepreneurial activity: a macro view. *Proceedings, Small Business and Entrepreneurship Development Conference*, University of Nottingham.

Uhlaner, L., & Thurik, R. (2007). Postmaterialism influencing total entrepreneurial activity across nations. *Journal of Evolutionary Economics*, *17*(2), 161–185. doi:10.1007/s00191-006-0046-0

UK Government, Department for Business, Innovation & Skills. (2015). *Improving the gender balance on British boards.* Retrieved from https://www.gov.uk/government/uploads/system/uploads/attachment_data/file/482059/BIS-15-585-women-on-boards-davies-review-5-year-summary-october-2015.pdf

Ulhôa, M., Araújo, M., Elaine, C., Kantermann, T., & Skene, D. (2011). When does stress end? Evidence of a prolonged stress reaction in shiftworking truck drivers. *Chronobiology International, 28*(9), 810–818. doi:10.3109/07420528.2011.613136 PMID:22080787

Ulke, H. E., & Bilgic, R. (2011). Investigating the role of the big five on the social loafing of information technology workers. *International Journal of Selection and Assessment, 19*(3), 301–312. doi:10.1111/j.1468-2389.2011.00559.x

Umezawa, T. (2001). Kiningono mondaito kaigaikinmuno saikibou [Issues after repatriation and renewed desire to undertake overseas assignments]. In The Japan Institute for Labour Policy and Training (Ed.), Nihon kigyouno kaigaihakensha: Shokugyoto seikatsuno jittai [Expatriates of Japanese companies: Survey of work and life aspects] (pp. 129–149). Tokyo, Japan: The Japan Institute for Labour Policy and Training.

United Nations High Commissioner for Refugees (UNHCR). (2011). *UNHCR Age, gender, and diversity policy.* Retrieved from http://www.unhcr.org/protection/women/4e7757449/unhcr-age-gender-diversity-policy-working-peopl

Ursin, H., & Eriksen, H. R. (2004). The cognitive activation theory of stress. *Psychoneuroendoctrinology, 29*(5), 567–592. doi:10.1016/S0306-4530(03)00091-X PMID:15041082

US Department of Labor Women's Bureau. (2014). *Women's bureau (WB) - recent facts.* Retrieved from https://www.dol.gov/wb/stats/latest_annual_data.htm#age

Vahidi, M., Namdar Areshtanab, H., & Arshadi Bostanabad, M. (2016). *The relationship between emotional intelligence and perception of job performance among nurses in north west of Iran.* Scientifica.

Vakola, M., & Bouradas, D. (2005). Antecedents and consequences of organizational silence: An empirical investigation. *Employee Relations, 27*(5), 441–458. doi:10.1108/01425450510611997

Vakola, M., Tsaousis, I., & Nikolaou, I. (2004). The role of emotional intelligence and personality variables on attitudes toward organisational change. *Journal of Managerial Psychology, 19*(2), 88–110. doi:10.1108/02683940410526082

Valentine, S., & Fleischman, G. (2008). Professional ethical standards, corporate social responsibility, and the perceived role of ethics and social responsibility. *Journal of Business Ethics, 82*(3), 657–666. doi:10.1007/s10551-007-9584-0

Vallance, S. (1999). Performance appraisal in Singapore, Thailand and the Philippines: A cultural perspective. *Australian Journal of Public Administration, 58*(4), 78–95. doi:10.1111/1467-8500.00129

Van Der Zee, K., Atsma, N., & Brodbeck, F. (2004). The influence of social identity and personality on outcomes of cultural diversity in teams. *Journal of Cross-Cultural Psychology, 35*(3), 283–303. doi:10.1177/0022022104264123

Van Dijk, P. A., & Brown, A. K. (2006). Emotional labour and negative job outcomes: An evaluation of the mediating role of emotional dissonance. *Journal of Management & Organization, 12*(2), 101–115. doi:10.5172/jmo.2006.12.2.101

Van Kleef, G. A. (2009). How emotions regulate social life: The emotions as social information (EASI) model. *Current Directions in Psychological Science, 18*(3), 184–188. doi:10.1111/j.1467-8721.2009.01633.x

Van Kleef, G. A., Homan, A. C., & Cheshin, A. (2012). Emotional influence at work: Take it EASI. *Organizational Psychology Review, 2*(4), 311–339. doi:10.1177/2041386612454911

Van Maanen, J., & Schein, E. H. (1979). Toward a theory of organizational socialization. In B. M. Straw (Ed.), *Research in organization behaviour: An annual series of analytical essays and critical reviews* (Vol. 1, pp. 209–264). Greenwich, CT: Jai Press.

van Scotter, J. R., & Motowidlo, S. J. (1996). Interpersonal facilitation and job dedication as separate facets of contextual performance. *The Journal of Applied Psychology, 81*(5), 525–531. doi:10.1037/0021-9010.81.5.525

van Vianen, A., Shen, C., & Chuang, A. (2011). Person-organization and person-supervisor fits: Employee commitments in China context. *Journal of Organizational Behavior, 32*(6), 906–926. doi:10.1002/job.726

Van Wijk, R., Jansen, J. J., & Lyles, M. A. (2008). Inter-and intra-organizational knowledge transfer: A meta-analytic review and assessment of its antecedents and consequences. *Journal of Management Studies, 45*(4), 830–853. doi:10.1111/j.1467-6486.2008.00771.x

Vanci-Osam, U., & Aksit, T. (2000). Do intentions and perceptions always meet? A case study regarding the use of a teacher appraisal scheme in an English language teaching environment. *Teaching and Teacher Education, 16*(2), 1–15. doi:10.1016/S0742-051X(99)00058-X

Vanderwal, L., Rautiainen, R., Kuye, R., Peek-Asa, C., Cook, T., Ramirez, M., & Donham, K. et al. (2011). Evaluation of long-and short-handled hand hoes for land preparation, developed in a participatory manner among women vegetable farmers in The Gambia. *Applied Ergonomics, 42*(5), 749–756. doi:10.1016/j.apergo.2010.12.002 PMID:21236415

VanMeter, D. S., & VanHorn, C. E. (1975). The Policy Implementation Process: A Conceptual Framework. *Administration & Society, 6*(4), 445–487. doi:10.1177/009539977500600404

Varkkey, B., Koshy, A., & Oburoi, P. (2008). *Apollo Unstopable: The transformation journey of Apollo Tyres, Ltd.*

Verdon, N. (2002). *Rural Women Workers in 19th Century England: Gender, Work and Wages*. New York, USA: Boydell Press.

Victor, D. A. (2001). A cross-cultural perspective on gender. In L. Arliss and D. Borisoff (Eds.), Women and men communicating: Challenges and change (pp. 65-77). Long Grove: Waveland Press.

Vifladt, A., Simonsen, B. O., Lydersen, S., & Farup, P. G. (2016). The association between patient safety culture and burnout and sense of coherence: A cross-sectional study in restructured and not restructured intensive care units. *Intensive & Critical Care Nursing: The Official Journal of the British Association of Critical Care Nurses*.

Vigoda-Gadot, E., & Cohen, A. (2004). *Citizenship and management in public administration: Integrating behavioral theories and managerial thinking*. London, UK: Edward Elgar Publishing.

Vihakara, A. (2006). Patience and understanding: A narrative approach to cross-cultural communication in a Sino-Finnish joint venture. Turku, Finland: Turku School of Economics and Business Administration.

Vinokur-Kaplan, J. X. (1991). Job satisfaction among social workers in public and voluntary child welfare agencies. *Child Welfare, 155*, 81–91.

Volkema, R. J. (2004). Demographic, cultural, and economic predictors of perceived ethicality of negotiation behavior: A nine-country analysis. *Journal of Business Research, 57*(1), 69–78. doi:10.1016/S0148-2963(02)00286-2

Volmer, J., Niessen, C., Spurk, D., Linz, A., & Abele, A. E. (2011). Reciprocal relationships between leader–member exchange (LMX) and job satisfaction: A cross-lagged analysis. *Applied Psychology, 60*(4), 522–545. doi:10.1111/j.1464-0597.2011.00446.x

Compilation of References

Von Kutzschenbach, M., & Brønn, C. (2010). You cant teach understanding, you construct it: Applying social network analysis to organizational learning. *Procedia: Social and Behavioral Sciences*, *4*, 83–92. doi:10.1016/j.sbspro.2010.07.485

Vorkapic, S. T., & Mustapic, J. (2012). Internal and external factors in professional burnout of substance abuse professionals in Croatia. *Annali dellIstituto Superiore di Sanita*, *48*(2), 189–197. doi:10.4415/ANN_12_02_12

Waddell, G. (1987). 1987 Volvo Award in Clinical Sciences: A new clinical model for the treatment of low-back pain. *Spine*, *12*(7), 632–644. doi:10.1097/00007632-198709000-00002 PMID:2961080

Waddock, S. A., & Post, J. E. (1991). Social entrepreneurs and catalytic change. *Public Administration Review*, *51*(5), 393–401. doi:10.2307/976408

Waldman, D. A., Balthazard, P. A., & Peterson, S. J. (2011). Leadership and neuroscience: Can we revolutionize the way that inspirational leaders are identified and developed? *The Academy of Management Perspectives*, *25*(1), 60–74. doi:10.5465/AMP.2011.59198450

Wallace, J. E., Lemaire, J. B., & Ghali, W. A. (2009). Physician wellness: A missing quality indicator. *Lancet*, *374*(9702), 1714–1721. doi:10.1016/S0140-6736(09)61424-0 PMID:19914516

Walters, M. (1995). *The Performance Management Handbook (Developing Practice)*. London: Chartered Institute of Personnel.

Walz, S. M., & Niehoff, B. P. (2000). Organizational citizenship behaviors: Their relationship to organizational effectiveness. *Journal of Hospitality & Tourism Research (Washington, D.C.)*, *24*(3), 301–319. doi:10.1177/109634800002400301

Wang, L., Tao, H., Ellenbecker, C. H., & Liu, X. (2012). Job satisfaction, occupational commitment and intent to stay among Chinese nurses: A cross-sectional questionnaire survey. *Journal of Advanced Nursing*, *68*(3), 539–549. doi:10.1111/j.1365-2648.2011.05755.x PMID:21722170

Wang, M. L., & Chang, S. C. (2016). The impact of job involvement on emotional labor to customer-oriented behavior: An empirical study of hospital nurses. *The Journal of Nursing Research*, *24*(2), 153–162. doi:10.1097/jnr.0000000000000114 PMID:26551214

Wang, P., & Lin, R. (2001). Coronary heart disease risk factors in urban bus drivers. *Public Health*, *115*(4), 261–264. doi:10.1016/S0033-3506(01)00456-5 PMID:11464297

Wang, X., Kunaviktikul, W., & Wichaikhum, O. A. (2013). Work empowerment and burnout among registered nurses in two tertiary general hospitals. *Journal of Clinical Nursing*, *22*(19-20), 2896–2903. doi:10.1111/jocn.12083 PMID:23834534

Ward, C., Bochner, S., & Furnham, A. (2001). *The psychology of culture shock*. London: Routledge.

Warr, P. (2007). *Work, happiness, and unhappiness*. Mahwah, NJ: Lawrence Erlbaum Associates.

Wart, M. V. (2003). Public-Sector leadership theory: An assessment. *Public Administration Review*, *63*(2), 214–228. doi:10.1111/1540-6210.00281

Wasko, M. M., & Faraj, S. (2005). Why should I share? Examining social capital and knowledge contribution in electronic networks of practice. *Management Information Systems Quarterly*, *29*(1), 35–57.

Wasserman, S., & Faust, K. (2009). *Social network analysis: Methods and applications* (Vol. 8). New York, NY: Cambridge University Press.

Watson, D., & Hubbard, B. (1996). Adaptational style and dispositional structure: Coping in the context of the Five-Factor model. *Journal of Personality*, *64*(4), 737–774. doi:10.1111/j.1467-6494.1996.tb00943.x

WEForum. (2016). *Global gender gap report 2015*. Retrieved from https://www.weforum.org/reports/global-gender-gap-report-2015/

Weisinger, H. (1998). *Emotional Intelligence at work: The un-taped edge for success*. San Francisco: Jossey-Bass.

Weiss, H. M. (2002). Conceptual and empirical foundations for the study of affect at work. In R. G. Lord, R. J. Klimoski, and R. Kanfer (Eds.), Emotions in the workplace: Understanding the structure and role of emotions in organizational behavior (pp. 20-63). San Francisco: Jossey Bass.

Weiss, D. J., Dawis, R. V., England, G. W., & Lofquist, L. H. (1967). *Manual for the Minnesota satisfaction questionnaire*. Work Adjustment Project Industrial Relations Center, University of Minnesota.

Wellin, M. (2013). Managing psychological contract. Using the Personal Deal to Increase Business Performance. Warsow: Wolters Kluwer.

Welp, A., Meier, L. L., & Manser, T. (2015). Emotional exhaustion and workload predict clinician-rated and objective patient safety. *Frontiers in Psychology, 5*, 1573. doi:10.3389/fpsyg.2014.01573 PMID:25657627

Welter, F. (2011). Contextualizing entrepreneurship—conceptual challenges and ways forward. *Entrepreneurship Theory and Practice, 35*(1), 165–184. doi:10.1111/j.1540-6520.2010.00427.x

Welter, F., & Smallbone, D. (2008). Womens entrepreneurship from an institutional perspective: The case of Uzbekistan. *The International Entrepreneurship and Management Journal, 4*(4), 505–520. doi:10.1007/s11365-008-0087-y

Wen, J., Cheng, Y., Hu, X., Yuan, P., Hao, T., & Shi, Y. (2016). Workload, burnout, and medical mistakes among physicians in China: A cross-sectional study. *Bioscience trends, 10*(1), 27-33.

Weng, H. C., Chen, H. C., Chen, H. J., Lu, K., & Hung, S. Y. (2008). Doctors emotional intelligence and the patient–doctor relationship. *Medical Education, 42*(7), 703–711. doi:10.1111/j.1365-2923.2008.03039.x PMID:18588649

Weng, H. C., Hung, C. M., Liu, Y. T., Cheng, Y. J., Yen, C. Y., Chang, C. C., & Huang, C. K. (2011). Associations between emotional intelligence and doctor burnout, job satisfaction and patient satisfaction. *Medical Education, 45*(8), 835–842. doi:10.1111/j.1365-2923.2011.03985.x PMID:21752080

Wentling, R. M., & Palma-Rivas, N. (1998). Current status and future trends of diversity initiatives in the workplace: Diversity experts perspective. *Human Resource Development Quarterly, 9*(3), 235–253. doi:10.1002/hrdq.3920090304

Westlund, S. (2013). Leading techies: Assessing project leadership styles most significantly related to software developer job satisfaction. In R. Colomo-Palacios (Ed.), *Enhancing the modern organization through information technology professionals: Research, studies, and techniques* (pp. 200–215). Hershey, PA: IGI Global. doi:10.4018/978-1-4666-2648-5.ch014

White, L., & Yanamandrama, V. (2012). Why do some business relationships persist despite dissatisfaction? A social exchange review. *Asia Pacific Management Review, 17*(3), 301–319.

Whitman, D. S., van Rooy, D. L., & Viswesvaran, C. (2010). Satisfaction, citizenship behaviors, and performance in work units: A meta-analysis of collective construct relations. *Personnel Psychology, 63*(1), 41–81. doi:10.1111/j.1744-6570.2009.01162.x

Whitmore, J. (2010). *Coaching for performance: growing human potential and purpose: the principles and practice of coaching and leadership*. London: Nicholas Brealey Publishing.

Wiese, D. S., & Buckley, M. R. (1998). The evolution of the performance appraisal process. *Journal of Management History, 4*(3), 233–249. doi:10.1108/13552529810231003

Wiker, S. F., Chaffin, D. B., & Langolf, G. D. (1989). Shoulder posture and localized muscle fatigue and discomfort. *Ergonomics*, *32*(2), 211–237. doi:10.1080/00140138908966080 PMID:2714248

Willenskey, H. L., & Labeaux, C. N. (1958). *Industrial Society and Social Welfare*. New York: Russel Sage Foundation.

Williams, E. S., Manwell, L. B., Konrad, T. R., & Linzer, M. (2007). The relationship of organizational culture, stress, satisfaction, and burnout with physician-reported error and suboptimal patient care: Results from the MEMO study. *Health Care Management Review*, *32*(3), 203–212. doi:10.1097/01.HMR.0000281626.28363.59 PMID:17666991

Williams, K. Y., & O'Reilly, C. A. (1998). Demography And Diversity In Organizations: A Review Of 40 Years Of Research. *Research in Organizational Behavior*, *20*, 77–140.

Williams, L. J., & Anderson, S. E. (1991). Job satisfaction and organizational commitment as predictors of organizational citizenship and in-role behaviors. *Journal of Management*, *17*(3), 601–617. doi:10.1177/014920639101700305

Willner, R. (2011). Micro-politics: An underestimated field of qualitative research in political science. *German Policy Studies*, *7*(3), 155-185. Retrieved from https://www.wiso.uni-hamburg.de/fileadmin/sowi/politik/methoden/Roland/GPS_3-2011_Willner.pdf

Wirtz, J., Kuan Tambyah, S., & Mattila, A. S. (2010). Organizational learning from customer feedback received by service employees: A social capital perspective. *Journal of Service Management*, *21*(3), 363–387. doi:10.1108/09564231011050814

Wise, P. G. (1998). Rating differences in Multi-Rater Feedback. *Proceedings of the International Personnel Management Association Assessment Council's Conference on Professional Personnel Assessment*, Chicago, IL.

Woetzel, J., Manyika, J., Dobbs, R., ... (2015, September). *How advancing women's equality can add $12 trillion to global growth*. Retrieved from http://www.mckinsey.com/global-themes/employment-and-growth/how-advancing-womens-equality-can-add-12-trillion-to-global-growth

Wong, C. S., & Law, S. K. (2002). The effects of leader and follower emotional intelligence on performance and attitude: An exploratory study. *The Leadership Quarterly*, *13*(3), 243–274. doi:10.1016/S1048-9843(02)00099-1

Woolcock, M., & Narayan, D. (2000). Social capital: Implications for development theory, research, and policy. *The World Bank Research Observer*, *15*(2), 225–249. doi:10.1093/wbro/15.2.225

Workman, M. (2007). The proximal virtual team continuum: A study of performance. *Journal of the American Society for Information Science and Technology*, *58*(6), 794–801. doi:10.1002/asi.20545

Workman, M., Kahnweiler, W., & Bommer, W. (2003). The effects of cognitive style and media richness on commitment to telework and virtual teams. *Journal of Vocational Behavior*, *63*(2), 199–219. doi:10.1016/S0001-8791(03)00041-1

Wren, J. T. (1995). *The leader's companion: Insights on leadership through the ages*. New York: The Free Press.

Xiang, X., Zhan, Z., & Yanling, L. (2012). *The Impact of Employer Brand on Corporate Financial Performance*. Singapore: IACSIT Press. Doi:10.7763/IPCSIT.2012.V52.80

Xie, Z., Wang, A., & Chen, B. (2011). Nurse burnout and its association with occupational stress in a cross-sectional study in Shanghai. *Journal of Advanced Nursing*, *67*(7), 1537–1546. doi:10.1111/j.1365-2648.2010.05576.x PMID:21261698

Xu, Y. (2007). Strategic analysis on cross-cultural human resources management. *Market Modernization*, *19*, 274–275.

Xu, Z., Ko, J., Cochran, D. J., & Jung, M. C. (2012). Design of assembly lines with the concurrent consideration of productivity and upper extremity musculoskeletal disorders using linear models. *Computers & Industrial Engineering*, *62*(2), 431–441. doi:10.1016/j.cie.2011.10.008

Yamada, D. (2013). Workplace bullying and the law: A report from the United States. In Japan Institute for Labour Policy and Training Report. In *Workplace bullying and harassment* (pp. 165-185). Tokyo, Japan: JILPT. Retrieved from http://www.jil.go.jp/english/reports/documents/jilpt-reports/no.12.pdf

Yamada, K., McEwen, B. S., & Pavlides, C. (2003). Site and time dependent effects of acute stress on hippocampal long-term potentiation in freely behaving rats. *Experimental Brain research*, *152*(1), 52-59. doi:10.1007%2Fs00221-003-1519-0

Yamada, M. (2014). Positioning of Employment of Persons with Disabilities in Diversity and Business Ethics: To make the Most of the Characteristics of Disabilities. Japan Society for Business Ethics Study, 21, 43-56.

Yang, F. H., & Chang, C. C. (2008). Emotional labour, job satisfaction and organizational commitment amongst clinical nurses: A questionnaire survey. *International Journal of Nursing Studies*, *45*(6), 879–887. doi:10.1016/j.ijnurstu.2007.02.001 PMID:17391673

Yaniv, E., & Farkas, F. (2005). The impact of person-organization fit on the corporate brand perception of employees and of customers. *Journal of Change Management*, *5*(4), 447–461. doi:10.1080/14697010500372600

Yashiro, A. (2015). Jinji no kokusaika. [Globalization of human resources] In H. Sato, H. Fujimura, & A. Yashiro (Eds.), *Atarashii jinjiroumu kanri* [Contemporary human resource management]. (pp. 26–31). Tokyo, Japan: Yuhikaku Publishing.

Yavuzyılmaz, A., Topbaş, M., Çan, E., Çan, G., & Özgün, Ş. (2007). Trabzon İl Merkezindeki Sağlık Ocakları Çalışanlarında Tükenmişlik Sendromu ile İş Doyumu Düzeyleri ve İlişkili Faktörler. *TAF Preventive Medicine Bulletin*, *6*(1), 41–50.

Yee, R. W. Y., Guo, Y., & Yeung, A. C. L. (2015). Being close or being happy? The relative impact of work relationship and job satisfaction on service quality. *International Journal of Production Economics*, *169*, 391–400. doi:10.1016/j.ijpe.2015.08.021

Yelin, E. H., Henke, C. J., & Epstein, W. V. (1986). Work disability among persons with musculoskeletal conditions. *Arthritis and Rheumatism*, *29*(11), 1322–1333. doi:10.1002/art.1780291104 PMID:3778541

Yeoh. (2007). The facet satisfaction scale: Enhancing the measurement of job satisfaction [Master's thesis]. Retrieved from http://digital.library.unt.edu/ark:/67531/metadc3899/m2/1/high_res_d/thesis.pdf

Yildirim, O. (2015). The impact of organizational communication on organizational citizenship behavior: Research findings. *Procedia: Social and Behavioral Sciences*, *150*, 1095–1100. doi:10.1016/j.sbspro.2014.09.124

Yilmaz, G., & Peña, J. (2014). The Influence of Social Categories and Interpersonal Behaviors on Future Intentions and Attitudes to Form Subgroups in Virtual Teams. *Communication Research*, *41*(3), 333–352. doi:10.1177/0093650212443696

Yin, R. K. (2013). *Case study research: Design and methods*. Thousand Oaks, CA: Sage publications.

Yli-Renko, H., Autio, E., & Sapienza, H. J. (2001). Social capital, knowledge acquisition, and knowledge exploitation in young technology-based firms. *Strategic Management Journal*, *22*(6-7), 587–613. doi:10.1002/smj.183

Yli-Renko, H., Autio, E., & Tontti, V. (2002). Social capital, knowledge, and the international growth of technology-based new firms. *International Business Review*, *11*(3), 279–304. doi:10.1016/S0969-5931(01)00061-0

Yoke, L. B., & Panatik, S. A. (2016). The mediatory role of job satisfaction between emotional intelligence and job performance. *International Business Management*, *10*(6), 806–812.

Yoon, H. S., & Sok, S. R. (2016). Experiences of violence, burnout and job satisfaction in Korean nurses in the emergency medical centre setting. *International Journal of Nursing Practice*, *22*(6), 596–604. doi:10.1111/ijn.12479 PMID:27581098

Young, M. B., & Kan, M. (2015). *Do ask, Do tell: Encouraging employees with disabilities to self-identify. Research Report R-1569-14-RR*. New York: The Conference Board, Inc. Retrieved from http://askearn.org/docs/Do%20Ask%20 Do%20Tell.pdf

Youngcourt, S. S., Leiva, P. I., & Jones, R. G. (2007). Perceived purposes of performance appraisal: Correlates of individual-and position-focused purposes on attitudinal outcomes. *Human Resource Development Quarterly, 18*(3), 315–343. doi:10.1002/hrdq.1207

Yuan, W. (2006). *Intercultural communication and conflict between American and Chinese colleagues in China-based multinational organizations*. Unpublished doctoral dissertation, University of Kentucky, Kentucky.

Yu, B. (2011). Computer-medicated communication systems. *Triple Cognition Communication Co-Operation, 9*(2), 531–534.

Zaccaro, S. J. A. (2007). Trait-based perspectives of leadership. *The American Psychologist, 62*(1), 6–16. doi:10.1037/0003-066X.62.1.6 PMID:17209675

Zacharaiah, K. A. (1954). *Industrial relations and personnel problems–A study with particular reference to Bombay*. Bombay, India: Asia Publishing House.

Zahra, S. A., Gedajlovic, E., Neubaum, D. O., & Shulman, J. M. (2009). A typology of social entrepreneurs: Motives, search processes and ethical challenges. *Journal of Business Venturing, 24*(5), 519–532. doi:10.1016/j.jbusvent.2008.04.007

Zahra, S. A., Korri, J. S., & Yu, J. (2005). Cognition and international entrepreneurship: Implications for research on international opportunity recognition and exploitation. *International Business Review, 14*(2), 129–146. doi:10.1016/j.ibusrev.2004.04.005

Zahra, S. A., & Wright, M. (2011). Entrepreneurships next act. *The Academy of Management Perspectives, 25*(4), 67–83. doi:10.5465/amp.2010.0149

Zapf, D., & Einarsen, S. (2011). Individual antecedents of bullying: Victims and perpetrators. In S. Einarsen, H. Hoel, D. Zapf, & C. L. Cooper (Eds.), *Bullying and harassment in the workplace: Developments in theory, research, and practice* (2nd ed., pp. 177–200). Boca Raton, FL: CRC Press.

Zebb, B. J., & Beck, J. G. (1998). Worry Versus Anxiety Is There Really a Difference? *Behavior Modification, 22*(1), 45–61. doi:10.1177/01454455980221003 PMID:9567736

Zeidner, M., Matthews, G., & Roberts, R. D. (2004). Emotional intelligence in the workplace: A critical review. *Applied Psychology, 53*(3), 371–399. doi:10.1111/j.1464-0597.2004.00176.x

Zhang, J., Wu, Q., Miao, D., Yan, X., & Peng, J. (2014). The impact of core self-evaluations on job satisfaction: The mediator role of career commitment. *Social Indicators Research, 116*(3), 809–822. doi:10.1007/s11205-013-0328-5

Zhang, J., & Zheng, W. (2009). How does satisfaction translate into performance? An examination of commitment and cultural values. *Human Resource Development Quarterly, 20*(3), 331–351. doi:10.1002/hrdq.20022

Zhu, B., Chen, C. R., Shi, Z. Y., Li, B., Liang, H. X., & Liu, B. (2016). Mediating effect of self-efficacy in relationship between Emotional Intelligence and clinical communication competency of nurses. *International Journal of Nursing Sciences, 3*(2), 162–168. doi:10.1016/j.ijnss.2016.04.003

Zhu, Y., Liu, C., Guo, B., Zhao, L., & Lou, F. (2015). The impact of emotional intelligence on work engagement of registered nurses: The mediating role of organisational justice. *Journal of Clinical Nursing, 24*(15-16), 2115–2124. doi:10.1111/jocn.12807 PMID:25894887

Ziegler, R., Hagen, B., & Diehl, M. (2012). Relationship between job satisfaction and job performance: Job ambivalence as a moderator. *Journal of Applied Social Psychology*, *42*(8), 2019–2040. doi:10.1111/j.1559-1816.2012.00929.x

Zopiatis, A., & Constanti, P. (2010). Leadership styles and burnout: Is there an association? *International Journal of Contemporary Hospitality Management*, *22*(3), 300–320. doi:10.1108/09596111011035927

Zornoza, A., Ripoll, P., & Peiró, J. M. (2002). Conflict management in groups that work in two different communication contexts: Face-to-Face and Computer-Mediated Communication. *Small Group Research*, *33*(5), 481–508. doi:10.1177/104649602237167

Zucker, L. G. (1991). Postscript: Micro foundations of institutional thought. In W. E. Powell & P. J. DiMaggio (Eds.), *The new institutionalism in organizational analysis* (pp. 103–107). Chicago, IL: University of Chicago Press.

About the Contributors

Bryan Christiansen Since 2004, has progressively held the positions of President, CEO, and then Chairman in PryMarke, LLC, a Michigan, USA-based Business Analytics and Management Consultancy. Bryan has also been an Adjunct Business Professor at Capella University, DeVry University, and Ellis University (formerly Ellis College of New York Institute of Technology) in the USA, and a Senior Business Lecturer at Gumushane University in Turkey. Born in Washington, DC and raised in Asia, Bryan is fluent in Chinese, Japanese, Spanish, and Turkish, and has traveled to 40 countries during his 28-year business career involving Global 1000 firms. Bryan holds a Bachelor's degree in Marketing from the University of the State of New York and an MBA degree from Capella University. Bryan will complete his Doctor of Business Administration degree (DBA) from Middlesex University in London, England in 2020.

Harish C. Chandan is Professor of Business at Argosy University, Atlanta. He was interim chair of the business program in 2011. He received President's award for excellence in teaching in 2007, 2008 and 2009. His teaching philosophy is grounded in the learner needs and life-long learning. His research interests include research methods, leadership, marketing, and organizational behavior. He has published 20 peer-reviewed articles in business journals and five chapters in business reference books. Dr. Chandan has presented conference papers at Academy of Management, International Academy of Business and Management, Southeast Association of Information Systems, and Academy of International Business. Prior to joining Argosy, Dr. Chandan managed optical fiber and cable product qualification laboratories for Lucent Technologies, Bell Laboratories. During his career with Lucent, he had 40 technical publications, a chapter in a book and five patents.

* * *

Larry Austin received his MBA and EdD from University of Phoenix. He is an educational consultant, curriculum designer, and online instructor. Dr. Austin's research interests include educational leadership, instructional technology, management, business administration, and cultural awareness. Email: larryaustin@email.phoenix.edu

Heike Boeltzig-Brown, PhD, is a senior research associate and program developer at the Institute for Community Inclusion (IC), School for Global Inclusion and Social Development at UMass Boston. Heike's research interests are disability, employment, and information and communication technology. At the ICI, she has directed research activities under the Vocational Rehabilitation Research and Training Center, funded by the U.S. Department of Education. Before joining the ICI, Heike conducted cross-national comparative research on disability and employment at Stirling University in Scotland. Between May 2012 and December 2015, Heike was working for the ICI remotely from Tokyo, where she collaborated with researchers from the National Institute of Vocational Rehabilitation (NIVR) and others on research on public VR service delivery in the US and Japan. More recently, Heike's work focuses on disability and career services for students with disabilities in Japan. Heike also directs the Duskin Disability Leadership Program at UMass Boston.

Petros Chamakiotis, Ph.D., is a Lecturer (Assistant Professor) in Information Systems in the School of Business, Management and Economics at the University of Sussex, UK; and the Secretary of the IFIP Working Group 9.5 on Virtuality & Society. He earned his PhD from the University of Bath, UK, with the support of an EPSRC scholarship, and he formerly held research and visiting positions at the University of Valencia, Spain, and at Royal Holloway and Birkbeck—two colleges of the University of London, UK. His research addresses two main areas: (a) the management of virtual teams and other virtual configurations (e.g. cloud computing) with an emphasis on issues of leadership, creativity and innovation; and (b) the implications of information and communication technologies for work-life boundaries. His research has appeared as chapters in books and encyclopedias, as articles in journals, and as online videos. Further, Petros has given presentations at conferences in Germany, Spain, Greece, Croatia, India, the USA, the UK, Cyprus, Israel, the Netherlands, Canada, Finland, and Ireland. Prior to becoming an academic, he worked in junior management positions in Madrid, Spain. Petros speaks English, Greek and Spanish fluently.

Efe Efeoglu, Ph.D Assistant Professor of Management., worked as manager at different levels of management in multinational companies more than 10 years. His last position in a multinational environment was as assistant manager, in charge of management & leadership skills training in banking. Efeoglu has been teaching at university since 2009. He has been conducting research on a variety of topics related with organizational behaviour subjects mostly micro and meso level. He has a particular interest on leadership. His other research areas include communication, and cultural influences on interpersonal communication. He has papers on Organizational Citizenship, Organizational Justice, Organizational Cynism, Emotional Intelligence, Work & Family Conflict. Currently, he is the head of International Affairs Office and Assistant Professor at Adana Science and Technology University where he teaches courses on Management & Organization, Human Resources Management, Organizational Behaviour and Organizational Communication in Adana, Turkey. He also has been working as freelance trainer for companies.

About the Contributors

Vaitsa Giannouli received her PhD in Neuroscience from the School of Medicine, Aristotle University of Thessaloniki. She is a cognitive psychologist and neuropsychologist. She is currently a research fellow at Aristotle University of Thessaloniki (AUTh), Greece. She has received numerous accolades and scholarships for her work as an undergraduate and graduate student. She is working as a research assistant and is involved in several cross-cultural research projects focusing on issues of cognition, emotion and lifespan development.

Joanna Grubicka Ph.D - math graduate, doctorate in technical sciences completed at Systems Research Institute Polish Academy of Sciences, lecturer at Plant Security Engineering in National Security Institute at Pomeranian Academy in Slupsk. The main area of academic interests is application of calculus of probability, statistics in reliability engineering, risk analysis and computer systems security.

Carola Hieker is a senior executive coach with over 20 years of experience in leadership development. As a founding partner of diversity-in-leadership (www.diversity-in-leadership) and hilcoaching (www.hilcoaching.com) her main clients are global companies in the Financial Services Sector as well as Professional Services Firms. Next to her work as a coach and consultant she is a Professor for Organisational Behaviour at Richmond, The American University in London UK and supervises on a pro-bono base the Ashoka UK team, an organization which supports worldwide social entrepreneurs. Carola has university degrees as Diploma Psychology (corresponding to M.A. in Psychology) and Dr. Phil (corresponding to Ph.D. in Psychology.); she also completed a Diploma in Systemic Management at Birbeck University and is an Ashridge Certified Supervisor (Master level). In addition, she is certified in NLP, Transactional Analysis, Gestalt and Systemic Consulting and qualified to interpret the Myers-Briggs Type Indicator MBTI Step I and Step II, the Firo B diagnostics, and the Leadership Effectiveness Analyses as a 360' FB tool as well as accredited in the use of Hogan Personality Inventory, Hogan Development Survey (HDS) as well as Hogan Motives, Values and Preferences Inventory (MVPI). Her publication in the International Coaching Psychology Review details on reflexive questions in a coaching psychology context; her publication in 'Coaching at work' focuses on the benefits of mentor supervision and she spoke recently on the International Supervision Conference in Oxford about the topic of 'Power in Coaching and Supervision'.

Kijpokin Kasemsap received his BEng degree in Mechanical Engineering from King Mongkut's University of Technology, Thonburi, his MBA degree from Ramkhamhaeng University, and his DBA degree in Human Resource Management from Suan Sunandha Rajabhat University. Dr. Kasemsap is a Special Lecturer in the Faculty of Management Sciences, Suan Sunandha Rajabhat University, based in Bangkok, Thailand. Dr. Kasemsap is a Member of the International Economics Development and Research Center (IEDRC), the International Foundation for Research and Development (IFRD), and the International Innovative Scientific and Research Organization (IISRO). Dr. Kasemsap also serves on the International Advisory Committee (IAC) for the International Association of Academicians and Researchers (INAAR). Dr. Kasemsap is the sole author of over 250 peer-reviewed international publications and book chapters on business, education, and information technology. Dr. Kasemsap is included in the TOP 100 Professionals–2016 and in the 10th edition of 2000 Outstanding Intellectuals of the 21st Century by the International Biographical Centre, Cambridge, England.

Junghwan Kim is an Assistant Professor of Adult and Higher Education and a Faculty Affiliate in the Center for Social Justice at the University of Oklahoma, Norman. Dr. Kim received his Ph.D. from the Pennsylvania State University, University Park, and M.A. and B.A. from Yonsei University, Seoul, South Korea. He has expertise across three fields (1) Adult, Community, and Lifelong Education, (2) Continuing Higher Education, and (3) Human Resource Development.

Ewa Matuska - PhD in Psychology, graduate of Gdansk University (Poland) and Charles' University in Praque (Czech Rep.). Assistant Professor at Pomeranian Academy, Institute of Safety, Chair of Management, Slupsk - Poland. Experienced manager and HR practitioner. Member of Polish Association of Human Resources Management and a vice - president of the board in international academic network "Human Potential Development in Central and Eastern EU", joining higher schools from Poland, Slovakia, Lithuania, Czech Rep. and Hungary. About 60 scientific publications in area of HRM and labor market. Scientific interests: change management, competence & talent management, innovation, personal safety, psychosocial work threats.

Sarah Miller is a doctoral student in the Adult and Higher Education program and a Graduate Student Research Fellow at the Center for Social Justice at the University of Oklahoma. She received her Masters in Human Relations at the University of Oklahoma. Her professional interests include workplace learning, organizational change and development, layoff survivors, and the multi-generational workforce.

Prabir Mukhopadhyay: Associate Professor in the area of Human Factors at the Design Discipline at Indian Institute of Information Technology Design and Manufacturing Jabalpur, India. PhD in Industrial Ergonomics from the University of Limerick, Ireland.

Etayankara Muralidharan is currently an Assistant Professor at MacEwan University School of Business in Canada. He received his PhD from the University of Manitoba in Canada. His research interests are in organizational crisis management, emerging market multinationals, entrepreneurship. His research has been recently published in Journal Business Ethics, International Business Review, Thunderbird International Business Review, Management Research Review, International Journal of Innovation & Technology Management, Current Topics in Management and has been presented at and appeared in the proceedings of the Academy of Management, Academy of International Business, Babson Entrepreneurship Conference (BCERC) and the Administrative Sciences Association of Canada.

Aoi Nomoto has a B.A. and a M.A. from Chiba University, and is currently a PhD student at Chiba University. She has been an assistant Research Investigator at the National Institute of Vocational Rehabilitation (NIVR) since 2014.

About the Contributors

Yoko Naito is an associate professor of Human Resource Management in the Department of Business Administration, School of Political Science and Economics at Tokai University, and an adjunct researcher at the Institute for Transnational Human Resource Management at Waseda University, Japan. She obtained her Ph. D. in 2013 and was awarded the Ohtsuka memorial Award in 2014 from Hokkaido University. Her research interests are IHRM strategies in multi-national enterprises, with a focus on management of international repatriates and foreign employees, their knowledge sharing/ transfer, socialization/ adjustment, career effectiveness, and work life balance. Before she joined academia, she worked in the manufacturing and banking industries.

Sevgi Ozcan was born in Mersin, Turkey, in 1969. She received special training in family medicine at University of Cukurova, and is currently working at the Department of Family Medicine as an Associate Professor. Her professional interests focus on medical education, healthy life counselling, management of psychosocial problems and chronic diseases in primary care. She serves as an associate editor for Turkish Journal of Family Medicine and Primary Care (TJFMPC). She is a member of Turkish Association of Family Physicians (TAHUD) and European Academy of Teachers in General Practice (EURACT). She is married and has two children.

Saurav Pathak is currently an Assistant Professor in Entrepreneurship at Kansas State University. Prior to KSU. He was the Rick and Joan Berquist Professor of Innovation and Entrepreneurship at Michigan Tech University from 2011-14. He has two doctoral degrees – first in Mechanical Engineering from the University of Florida (2007) and the second in Entrepreneurship from the Imperial College Business School, London (2011). His research revolves around cross-country comparative entrepreneurship (both commercial and social) and focuses on examining the contextual influences on individual-level entrepreneurial behaviors. He has published over fifteen research articles in top tier entrepreneurship and management journals.

Maia Rushby is an executive coach with over 20 years of business experience in international blue-chip organisations, Unilever, PwC Consulting and IBM. She has held regional and global leadership positions and has lived and worked in Asia, Europe and the Middle East which has given her deep insight and practical knowledge into the value and challenges of working in diverse environments. As a founding partner of diversity-in-leadership (www.diversity-in-leadership.com), she leverages this international experience to develop the mind-sets of leaders across a variety of sectors. Earlier in her career, Maia qualified as a chartered management accountant and chartered management consultant, both of which give her the necessary business acumen to design and deliver leadership development programmes across organisations. In addition, Maia has a diploma in executive coaching, NLP and hypnosis and is a trained values coach specializing in NLP with values. In her publication in Training Journal on 'How mentor supervision can give you the best mentors' Maia outlines the concept of mentor supervision and how it can be used to introduce best practice techniques to ensure the quality of the process, focussing on developing the mentoring skills of the senior leaders.

Ilkka Salmi serves as a University Teacher in Applied Psychology at the University of Lapland, Finland. Salmi is also a PhD student concentrating on leadership of well-being in knowledge-intensive work. His other areas of interest are positive conflict management and self-leadership.

Kai Seino: B.S. from Waseda University and M.M.G (Media and Governance) and Ph.D. from Keio University. 2001- Intern. Staff Training Course of Psychiatric Rehabilitation at the University of Tokyo Hospital, 2007- Research Fellowship for Young Scientists. Japan Society for the Promotion of Science, 2007- Visiting Researcher. National Center of Neurology and Psychiatry,2009- Assistant Professor. Toyo University,2014- Staff Research Investigator. National Institute of Vocational Rehabilitation, 2015- Senior Researcher. Keio Research Institute at SFC, an Editorial Board Member of Japan Society of Vocational Rehabilitation, a Member of Association of People Supporting Employment First.

Chandra Sekhar Patro is currently an Assistant Professor in Gayatri Vidya Parishad College of Engineering (Autonomous), India and doing his Ph.D. in Faculty of Commerce and Management Studies, Andhra University, India. He has post-graduate degree in Master of Commerce (M.Com.) from Andhra University, Master in Financial Management (MFM) from Pondicherry University, and also MBA (HR & Finance) from JNT University. Mr. Patro has over 9 years of teaching experience in higher education. Mr. Patro has gained very good knowledge in Human Resource Management and Accountancy/Finance subjects. He has published number of research papers in reputed National and International Journals and also presented papers in National and International Conferences.

Libi Shen has a Ph.D in Instruction and Learning from University of Pittsburgh, PA, and an outstanding dissertation award from International Reading Association. She started her teaching career in 1989. Currently, she is an online faculty for University of Phoenix. Libi is a contributing author for the following books: Technology in the Classroom for Now and the Future; Educational, Behavioral, Psychological Considerations in Niche Online Communities; Cases on Critical and Qualitative Perspectives in Online Higher Education; Online Tutor 2.0: Methodologies and Case Studies for Successful Learning; Emerging Priorities and Trends in Distance Education: Communication, Pedagogy, and Technology; Identification, Evaluation, and Perceptions of Distance Education Experts; and Cybersecurity Breaches and Issues Surrounding Online Threat Protection. Her research interests include reading skills, curriculum design, distance education, and instructional technology.

David Starr-Glass is a faculty member of the University of New York in Prague, Czech Republic, and a senior mentor with the International Programs (Prague Unit) of the State University of New York, Empire State College. He teaches a wide range of business related areas at the undergraduate level, in both blended and online distance learning formats. He also serves as the supervisor for undergraduate dissertations, mentoring final year students in designing and writing their work. David has a wide range of managerial and educational experience and has earned three master's degrees: business administration (Notre Dame de Namur University, California), organizational psychology (Birkbeck College, University of London), and flexible education and online learning (University of Southern Queensland, Australia). David has contributed more than a dozen chapters to edited books and published about sixty peer-reviewed journal articles in the international business, online distance learning, and mentoring literature. When not in Prague, he lives in Jerusalem where he teaches economic and business related courses with a number of local colleges.

About the Contributors

Tomohiro Takezawa – 2007 - Researcher. Research Institute of National Rehabilitation Center for Persons with Disabilities 2010- Research Associate. Research and Education Program for Life Science, University of Fukui 2012- Researcher. National Institute of Vocational Rehabilitation.

Marta Alicja Tomasiak is a Senior Human Resources Associate at Thompson Reuters in London, UK. She recently graduated from the University of Sussex, UK, with a BSc in Business with Human Resource Management. Prior to starting this research, she obtained experience of working with highly diverse teams, which is what inspired her to focus on the issue of diversity in the workplace. She is particularly interested in the different types of diversity that play an important role in changing the workplace, specifically within virtual collaboration environments.

Ben Tran is a Senior Vocational Rehabilitation Counselor, Qualified Rehabilitation Professional (QRP), with the State of California's Department of Rehabilitation. Dr. Tran received his Doctor of Psychology (Psy.D) in Organizational Psychology from California School of Professional Psychology at Alliant International University in San Francisco, California, United States of America. Dr. Tran's research interests include domestic and expatriate recruitment, selection, retention, evaluation, training, and disability and accommodation, assistive technology, gender, business and organizational ethics, organizational/international organizational behavior, knowledge management, and minorities in multinational organizations. Dr. Tran can be reach at tranconsulting@gmail.com.

Germaine Washington received her Doctor of Management in Organizational Leadership from University of Phoenix. She has worked in the field of drug and alcohol addiction for 19 years. She is currently working at Calvary University as a professor of Management and Business Administration for the graduate program, and a director for the Department of Business Administration. Her research interests include management, organizational leadership, business administration, management systems, emotional intelligence, and occupational stress.

Jieun You is a senior researcher in the Institute of Educational Research at Yonsei University. She received her Ph.D degree in Workforce Development and Education from the Ohio State University. Her current research interests include: 1) social capital/network approach in human resource development and organizational learning, 2) informal learning, 3) measurement and evaluation in workplace learning, and 4) organizational change and development.

Index

360-Degree Appraisal 180

A

abusive supervision 1, 3, 7-9, 30, 87-88, 96, 101, 185
accommodation 111-112, 118, 120, 337-338, 340, 346-349, 352
action 23, 92, 123, 136, 139, 158, 201, 216, 316, 319, 323, 350, 352, 387, 389-390, 439
activities 2, 5-7, 68-70, 75, 96, 110-112, 115-116, 118, 120-121, 124, 126, 131, 134, 155-156, 181, 187, 215, 217, 225, 243-244, 256-260, 315, 358, 363-364, 366, 370, 372-374, 380-383, 386-389, 393, 406, 428-429, 438, 443-445
activity 1, 23, 92, 96, 110-111, 121, 207, 218, 236-237, 243, 290, 358-359, 365-369, 372-373, 380, 387, 389, 391-392, 425, 428-429, 435, 439
adaptability 27, 181, 183-184, 187, 229
adjustment 4, 29, 404-405, 416, 422-423
Advanced Persistent Threat (APT) 377
Agency Theory 96, 108
aggression 26, 87-88, 91-95, 97, 101, 108
anxiety 6, 24, 26, 30-33, 35, 58, 89, 108, 120, 205, 216-217, 230-233, 235, 237, 239, 242-243, 270, 406
Appraise 158, 180
Appraiser 180
attitude 2, 23, 26, 31, 110, 113, 139, 181, 187, 210, 215-217, 236, 275, 294, 363, 365
autonomy 93-94, 182-183, 200, 203, 206, 251

B

behavior 1-8, 23-28, 30-31, 36-37, 58, 62, 66, 70, 73, 76, 86-92, 94-99, 101, 108-109, 134, 139, 173, 182-186, 200, 203, 205-207, 210, 215, 228, 230, 233, 235, 250-251, 257-258, 260, 267, 288, 305, 313, 316-319, 357-360, 365-366, 382, 385, 387, 392-393
Behaviorally Anchored Rating Scales (BARS) 180

bullying 87-101, 108-109, 205, 233
burnout 24, 26, 29-33, 35, 58, 74, 185, 200, 211, 227, 230, 233-235, 237-238, 240, 243-244, 248, 250, 268, 271-272, 274-276, 278

C

coaching 73, 172, 202, 315-317, 319, 331
communication 7, 58, 60-76, 86, 98, 108, 159, 164, 183, 201-206, 208-218, 225, 228, 230, 233, 236, 254, 271, 286-287, 290-298, 305, 309, 318, 324, 340, 345-346, 349-350, 352, 358, 362, 371, 373
Communication History 67, 86
competence management 359, 363-364, 372-374, 377
computer-mediated communication (CMC) 61, 67, 286, 305
conflict 5, 60-61, 88, 93, 95-96, 99-101, 172, 183-185, 200, 205, 209, 228-229, 236-239, 271, 286-287, 290, 296-297, 299-300, 317, 358, 373
content analysis 249, 254-255, 267
Counterproductive Work Behavior 1, 3, 5, 23
cross-cultural communication 69-70, 86
Cross-Cultural Communication (also known as Intercultural Communication and Trans-Cultural Communication) 86
Crossover Effect 108
culture 4, 7-8, 70-72, 86, 88-89, 94-95, 97-98, 101, 108-109, 119, 134, 137, 143, 163, 167, 182-183, 187, 204, 210, 217, 252, 262, 285, 299, 305, 310, 325, 336, 340, 350, 359, 362-363, 365, 383-384, 387, 391-392, 403-405, 408, 422-423
Cybersecurity in Management 377
cyberslacking 368, 370, 377

D

daily life in general 403-404, 406-413, 415-417, 422
Denial of Service (Dos) 377
dissent 95

Index

Distributed Denial of Service (DdoS) 378
diversity 60-61, 143, 228, 283-289, 295-300, 305-306, 308-316, 318, 321-325, 331, 333-340, 344, 347, 351-352, 356, 359
diversity and inclusion 285, 314-315, 318, 331, 338-339
Diversity of Mindset 331
duty 96-97, 119, 347, 370, 387

E

efficiency 1, 4, 9, 23, 27, 31, 60-61, 111, 113, 119-121, 126, 131, 134, 136, 156, 182, 202, 211, 234, 271, 349, 352, 358, 362-364, 368, 370, 374
Efficiency Theory 131
Effort-Reward Imbalance (ERI) Model 267
emotion 24-29, 33, 35, 37, 58, 185, 228-229, 236, 272, 296
emotion regulation 24, 26-28, 33, 35, 229
emotional awareness 236, 241-242, 244, 248
emotional exhaustion 29-31, 235, 248, 268, 271-272, 274
emotional intelligence 24-27, 33, 35, 58, 91, 202, 216-217, 225-230, 232-243, 248, 324, 331
emotional labor 24, 26, 28-29, 33, 35, 58, 229, 232
Emotional Regulation 28, 59
employee turnover 1, 9, 112, 181, 185-187, 226, 238-239, 243-244, 248, 284, 290
employer 23, 111, 114-115, 119, 123, 125, 131, 183, 185, 203, 207, 210, 215, 218, 231, 239, 242, 294, 315, 334, 338, 340, 357-374, 378
employer brand 358-361, 363-365, 373, 378
employer branding 357-361, 363-364, 366, 372-374, 378
Employer Value Proposition (EVP) 378
Employment First 334, 356
employment support 334, 340-344, 347-348, 351-353, 356
empowerment 31, 182, 350
engagement 1, 3, 6-9, 29, 31, 88, 91, 99, 112, 182, 184-186, 201-202, 208, 210, 216, 250, 364-365
Ergonomics 251, 425
evidence 7, 26, 36-37, 69, 75, 93, 146, 157, 209, 211, 227, 231, 287, 311, 333, 338, 340-342, 344, 347, 351, 443
experienced stress 231, 249, 252-254, 256-257, 260, 262-263, 267
Explicit communication 67, 86
exploitative learning 136, 143, 155
explorative learning 136, 143, 146, 155

F

Face-to-Face (F2F) 286, 305
feedback 8, 31, 61-62, 66, 69, 76, 86, 97, 157-158, 162-164, 169, 172-173, 182, 204, 206, 210, 214, 216, 228, 241, 287, 311, 314-317, 319-321
Finland 249-250, 253-254, 257, 259
Firewall 369, 378
function 4, 8, 65, 114, 186, 203, 232, 334, 347, 367, 387, 389

G

gender diversity 308-310, 314-315, 318, 322, 325, 331
Gender Intelligence 309, 331
gender parity 308-313, 322, 324, 331
Group Think 331

H

harassment 89-92, 94-95, 97-99, 108-109
health professionals 268, 271-272, 274-275
healthcare 24, 27-28, 32-33, 35-36, 76, 226, 231, 234, 262, 271, 278, 340-344, 427
heterogeneity 35, 283-285, 287, 305
history of communication 67
hospital 27, 32-33, 35, 75, 232, 315, 344
human resource 4, 156, 158, 338, 359, 373, 378
human resources (HR) 285, 305, 407

I

Implicit communication 67, 86
Industrial-Organizational (I-O) Psychology 249, 283, 305
Information and Communication Technology (ICT) 305
Information Systems (IS) 283, 305
injury 119, 427-428, 435, 444-445
intention 1, 4, 7-8, 65, 185-186, 271, 377
International Assignment 423
international assignments 403, 406, 408, 417
interpretative perspective 132-133, 135-136, 147, 155

J

Japan 333-334, 336, 340-341, 344, 346-348, 350-352, 356, 403-404, 407-408
Japanese MNEs 416, 423
Job Characteristics 182, 200, 206
Job Demand-Control (JDC) Model 267
job performance 5, 7, 74, 90, 156-157, 162, 181, 183-185, 187, 200-202, 209-210, 214, 216, 218, 226, 229, 233-238, 241, 243-244

561

job satisfaction 1-2, 4-6, 9, 24, 26, 28-31, 33, 35-36, 59, 74-75, 88, 113, 118, 126, 131, 158, 181-187, 200-203, 206-212, 214-215, 217-218, 225-227, 233, 235, 237, 239, 243-244, 299
job satisfaction measurement 207-208, 211-212, 225

L

language diversity 295-297, 299
Leader-Member Exchange Theory 23
leaders 6, 8, 23-29, 31-33, 35-37, 58-59, 61, 73-74, 76, 97-98, 186, 201-202, 210, 213-218, 227, 229, 232-233, 239, 262, 286, 308-310, 312-324, 359, 365
leadership 1, 3, 6, 8-9, 23-27, 30-33, 35-37, 59, 73-74, 76, 95, 97, 159, 181-183, 186-187, 201-202, 205, 208-210, 214, 216-218, 225, 227, 229, 232-234, 243, 271, 287, 308, 314-315, 318, 320, 323, 338, 365, 384
legislation 100, 118, 249, 256-263, 322, 370

M

mediation 99, 204
medium 61, 64, 67, 86, 203, 205, 272, 291, 297
message 61-62, 64, 66, 68, 76, 86, 203-205, 211-215, 287, 297, 324-325
motivation 2, 4, 6, 8, 30, 73, 111, 113, 124, 126, 158, 163-165, 182, 184, 200, 206-207, 209-210, 212, 214, 216, 225, 230, 233-234, 240, 243, 313, 345-346, 349, 352, 363-365, 388-389, 393

N

national culture 89, 94-95, 109, 383-384
natural support 351-352, 356
nonverbal communication 86
nonwork 407-408, 422

O

occupational health 250, 427, 443, 445-446
occupational stress 210, 226-227, 230-235, 239-240, 243, 248, 250
Organizational Citizenship Behavior 1, 3, 5-7, 23, 182, 184, 233
organizational climate 93-94, 187, 208
organizational communication 7, 68, 74, 76, 208-211, 214, 225
organizational culture 8, 94, 98, 182-183, 299, 340, 362-363
organizational effectiveness 2, 23, 112, 286, 384

organizational identification 1, 3, 5-6, 9, 23, 74
organizational information security 373
organizational learning 8, 132-137, 139-147, 155, 183
organizational learning process 132-133, 135-137, 140

P

pain 31, 231, 425, 427-429, 432, 443
paternalistic 131, 352
peer coaching 316-317, 331
performance appraisal 156-166, 168-170, 172-173, 180, 208, 210, 314
Performance appraisal system (PAS) 156
performance management 158, 180, 365
Person-Organization Fit 23
persons with disabilities 333-334, 336-338, 341, 347, 352, 356
productivity 1-2, 5-6, 9, 27, 31, 33, 60-61, 66, 93, 111-113, 118, 120, 126, 131, 156, 162, 181, 184, 186-187, 210, 216, 233, 238-240, 243, 251, 271, 285-286, 339, 350-351, 425-426, 443-446
promotion 60, 96, 164, 169, 172, 182-183, 200, 207-209, 236, 251, 315-317, 320, 334, 340, 347, 358

Q

qualitative content analysis 249, 254-255, 267

R

readjustment 403-413, 415-417, 423
Reentry or Repatriation to the Home Country 423
repatriates 403-408, 411, 415-417, 423
repatriation 406-409, 411, 415-416, 423
rest stop 253-254, 260-262, 267
rest stops 249-250, 252-254, 259-263
reward 5, 162, 164, 184, 200, 251, 324
role model 312, 320, 331

S

satisfaction 1-2, 4-9, 24, 26, 28-33, 35-37, 59, 73-75, 88, 112-113, 118-119, 121, 124, 126, 131, 158-159, 162, 173, 181-187, 200-203, 205-212, 214-215, 217-218, 225-227, 233, 235, 237, 239-240, 243-244, 287, 299, 312, 362-364, 405
self-leadership 262-263, 267
semiotics 63-64, 67, 86
social capital 6, 132-133, 137-147, 155, 186-187
Social Identity Theory 5, 311-312, 331
social network analysis 133, 139, 141, 146, 155

Index

social networks 93, 139-141, 143, 146-147, 155, 300, 358, 367
social or interpretative perspective 132-133, 135-136, 147, 155
social problem solving 268-271, 273-274, 278
social process 132, 136
social relationship 133, 139-140, 145, 147, 155, 230
socialization 4, 23, 72, 108, 184
special subsidiary company 348-350, 356
Sponsor Supervision 321, 332
strategic communication 73, 76, 86
strategic human resources management 357, 363, 372-373, 377-378
stress 5, 29-32, 75, 99-100, 137, 181, 184-185, 187, 202, 205, 208, 210-211, 214-217, 225-227, 229-244, 248-263, 267, 269-271, 276, 278, 403, 405, 439, 444
subordinates 6-8, 24-26, 28, 31-33, 35-36, 58-59, 74, 88, 91, 93, 97-98, 101, 206, 214-216, 218, 319
substance abuse profession 226, 234, 248
substance abuse professionals 226-227, 233-235, 238-244, 248

T

targeted individual 88-92, 99, 101, 108-109
technical or systems-structural perspective 133, 135-136, 155
Trait Focused Appraisals 180
transportation 111, 121, 125, 249-250, 252-254, 256-257, 260-263, 387
truck drivers 249-250, 252-263, 267

U

unconscious bias 318-319, 332
universal design 334-335, 340, 344, 351-352, 356
unselfishness values 385, 390-391, 393

V

value management 357-359, 361, 363-364, 372-374, 378
verbal communication 86, 205
victimization 88, 99
virtual environment 284-289, 293, 295-296, 299, 306
virtual organizations 283
Virtual Teams (VTs) 283, 305

W

welfare 110-126, 131, 228, 334, 340-344, 351, 386
welfare facilities 110-115, 118, 123-125
WMSDs 425-429, 443-445
work performance 157-158, 164, 180, 226, 233-234, 243, 336, 378
work-family conflict 183, 185, 200, 271
work-related stress 249-254, 256, 259, 261-262, 267, 271

Purchase Print + Free E-Book or E-Book Only

Purchase a print book through the IGI Global Online Bookstore and receive the e-book for free or purchase the e-book only! Shipping fees apply.

www.igi-global.com

Recommended Reference Books

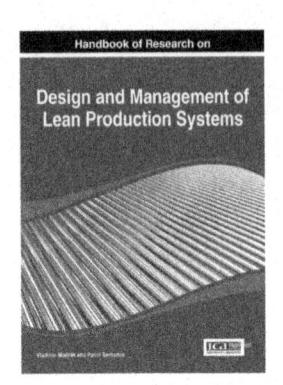

Handbook of Research on Design and Management of Lean Production Systems
ISBN: 978-1-4666-5039-8
© 2014; 487 pp.
List Price: $260

Handbook of Research on Business Ethics and Corporate Responsibilities
ISBN: 978-1-4666-7476-9
© 2015; 508 pp.
List Price: $212

Integrating Social Media into Business Practice, Applications, Management, and Models
ISBN: 978-1-4666-6182-0
© 2014; 325 pp.
List Price: $180

Handbook of Research on Strategic Performance Management and Measurement Using Data Envelopment Analysis
ISBN: 978-1-4666-4474-8
© 2014; 735 pp.
List Price: $276

Emerging Trends in Smart Banking: Risk Management Under Basel II and III
ISBN: 978-1-4666-5950-6
© 2014; 290 pp.
List Price: $156

Computer-Mediated Marketing Strategies: Social Media and Online Brand Communities
ISBN: 978-1-4666-6595-8
© 2015; 406 pp.
List Price: $156

*IGI Global now offers the exclusive opportunity to receive a free e-book with the purchase of the publication in print, or purchase any e-book publication only. You choose the format that best suits your needs. This offer is only valid on purchases made directly through IGI Global's Online Bookstore and not intended for use by book distributors or wholesalers. Shipping fees will be applied for hardcover purchases during checkout if this option is selected.

Should a new edition of any given publication become available, access will not be extended on the new edition and will only be available for the purchased publication. If a new edition becomes available, you will not lose access, but you would no longer receive new content for that publication (i.e. updates). The free e-book is only available to single institutions that purchase printed publications through IGI Global. Sharing the free e-book is prohibited and will result in the termination of e-access.

Publishing Information Science and Technology Research Since 1988

IGI GLOBAL DISSEMINATOR of KNOWLEDGE

www.igi-global.com | Sign up at www.igi-global.com/newsletters | facebook.com/igiglobal | twitter.com/igiglobal

Stay Current on the Latest Emerging Research Developments

Become an IGI Global Reviewer for Authored Book Projects

The overall success of an authored book project is dependent on quality and timely reviews.

In this competitive age of scholarly publishing, constructive and timely feedback significantly decreases the turnaround time of manuscripts from submission to acceptance, allowing the publication and discovery of progressive research at a much more expeditious rate. Several IGI Global authored book projects are currently seeking highly qualified experts in the field to fill vacancies on their respective editorial review boards:

Applications may be sent to:
development@igi-global.com

Applicants must have a doctorate (or an equivalent degree) as well as publishing and reviewing experience. Reviewers are asked to write reviews in a timely, collegial, and constructive manner. All reviewers will begin their role on an ad-hoc basis for a period of one year, and upon successful completion of this term can be considered for full editorial review board status, with the potential for a subsequent promotion to Associate Editor.

If you have a colleague that may be interested in this opportunity,
we encourage you to share this information with them.

InfoSci®-Books
A Database for Progressive Information Science and Technology Research

www.igi-global.com

Maximize Your Library's Book Collection!

Invest in IGI Global's InfoSci®-Books database and gain access to hundreds of reference books at a fraction of their individual list price.

The InfoSci®-Books database offers unlimited simultaneous users the ability to precisely return search results through more than 68,000 full-text chapters from nearly 3,000 reference books in the following academic research areas:

Business & Management Information Science & Technology • Computer Science & Information Technology
Educational Science & Technology • Engineering Science & Technology • Environmental Science & Technology
Government Science & Technology • Library Information Science & Technology • Media & Communication Science & Technology
Medical, Healthcare & Life Science & Technology • Security & Forensic Science & Technology • Social Sciences & Online Behavior

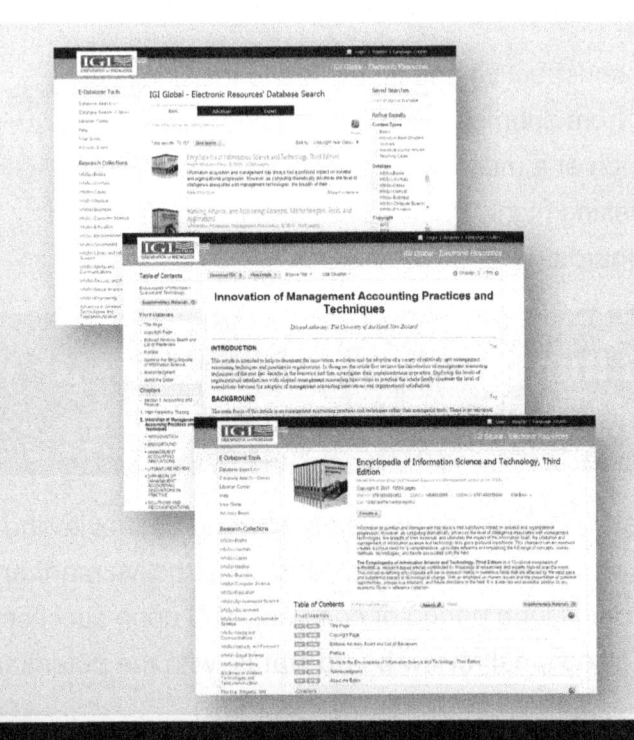

Peer-Reviewed Content:
- Cutting-edge research
- No embargoes
- Scholarly and professional
- Interdisciplinary

Award-Winning Platform:
- Unlimited simultaneous users
- Full-text in XML and PDF
- Advanced search engine
- No DRM

Librarian-Friendly:
- Free MARC records
- Discovery services
- COUNTER4/SUSHI compliant
- Training available

To find out more or request a free trial, visit:
www.igi-global.com/eresources

IGI GLOBAL
DISSEMINATOR OF KNOWLEDGE
www.igi-global.com

IGI Global
Proudly Partners with
eContent ✏ Pro

eContent Pro specializes in the following areas:

Academic Copy Editing
Our expert copy editors will conduct a full copy editing procedure on your manuscript and will also address your preferred reference style to make sure your paper meets the standards of the style of your choice.

Expert Translation
Our expert translators will work to ensure a clear cut and accurate translation of your document, ensuring that your research is flawlessly communicated to your audience.

Professional Proofreading
Our editors will conduct a comprehensive assessment of your content and address all shortcomings of the paper in terms of grammar, language structures, spelling, and formatting.

IGI Global Authors, Save 10% on eContent Pro's Services!

Scan the QR Code to Receive Your 10% Discount

The 10% discount is applied directly to your eContent Pro shopping cart when placing an order through IGI Global's referral link. Use the QR code to access this referral link. eContent Pro has the right to end or modify any promotion at any time.

Email: customerservice@econtentpro.com   econtentpro.com

Information Resources Management Association

Become an IRMA Member

Members of the **Information Resources Management Association (IRMA)** understand the importance of community within their field of study. The Information Resources Management Association is an ideal venue through which professionals, students, and academicians can convene and share the latest industry innovations and scholarly research that is changing the field of information science and technology. Become a member today and enjoy the benefits of membership as well as the opportunity to collaborate and network with fellow experts in the field.

IRMA Membership Benefits:

- **One FREE Journal Subscription**
- **30% Off Additional Journal Subscriptions**
- **20% Off Book Purchases**
- Updates on the latest events and research on Information Resources Management through the IRMA-L listserv.
- Updates on new open access and downloadable content added to Research IRM.
- A copy of the Information Technology Management Newsletter twice a year.
- A certificate of membership.

IRMA Membership $195

Scan code or visit **irma-international.org** and begin by selecting your free journal subscription.

Membership is good for one full year.

www.irma-international.org

Encyclopedia of Information Science and Technology, Third Edition (10 Vols.)

Mehdi Khosrow-Pour, D.B.A. (Information Resources Management Association, USA)
ISBN: 978-1-4666-5888-2; **EISBN:** 978-1-4666-5889-9; © 2015; 10,384 pages.

The **Encyclopedia of Information Science and Technology, Third Edition** is a 10-volume compilation of authoritative, previously unpublished research-based articles contributed by thousands of researchers and experts from all over the world. This discipline-defining encyclopedia will serve research needs in numerous fields that are affected by the rapid pace and substantial impact of technological change. With an emphasis on modern issues and the presentation of potential opportunities, prospective solutions, and future directions in the field, it is a relevant and essential addition to any academic library's reference collection.

Take An Extra 30% Off[1]

[1] 30% discount offer cannot be combined with any other discount and is only valid on purchases made directly through IGI Global's Online Bookstore (www.igi-global.com/books), not intended for use by distributors or wholesalers. Offer expires December 31, 2016.

Free Lifetime E-Access with Print Purchase

Take 30% Off Retail Price:

Hardcover with Free E-Access:[2] $2,765
List Price: $3,950

E-Access with Free Hardcover:[2] $2,765
List Price: $3,950

Recommend this Title to Your Institution's Library: www.igi-global.com/books

[2] IGI Global now offers the exclusive opportunity to receive free lifetime e-access with the purchase of the publication in print, or purchase any e-access publication and receive a free print copy of the publication. You choose the format that best suits your needs. This offer is only valid on purchases made directly through IGI Global's Online Bookstore and not intended for use by book distributors or wholesalers. Shipping fees will be applied for hardcover purchases during checkout if this option is selected.

The lifetime of a publication refers to its status as the current edition. Should a new edition of any given publication become available, access will not be extended on the new edition and will only be available for the purchased publication. If a new edition becomes available, you will not lose access, but you would no longer receive new content for that publication (i.e. updates). Free Lifetime E-Access is only available to single institutions that purchase printed publications through IGI Global. Sharing the Free Lifetime E-Access is prohibited and will result in the termination of e-access.

CPSIA information can be obtained
at www.ICGtesting.com
Printed in the USA
BVOW04*1832090417
480360BV00020B/35/P